THE LAW OF DAMAGES

Looseleaf Edition

S.M. WADDAMS

M.A., LL.B., LL.M., S.J.D.

Of the Ontario Bar
Professor of Law, University of Toronto

Canada Law Book
A Division of The Cartwright Group Ltd.

TORONTO

www.canadalawbook.ca

November 2008

Canada Law Book
A Division of The Cartwright Group Ltd.
240 Edward Street, Aurora, Ontario, L4G 3S9
www.canadalawbook.ca

Canadian Cataloguing in Publication Data
Waddams, S. M., 1942-
The law of damages

Looseleaf ed.
Includes tables of cases and statutes.
Includes bibliographical references and index.
ISBN 0-88804-124-1

1. Damages — Canada. I. Title

KE484.D3W34 1996 347.71077 C96-932540-1
KF446.W3 1996

PREFACE

The first edition of this work was published in 1983, and the second in 1991, simultaneously in bound and looseleaf form. In 1997 a third edition was published in bound form. The looseleaf edition continues and will be updated annually as before.

I am grateful to many readers for helpful suggestions, and also to Michael Gelblum, Alex Kurke, Bernice Fan, Ken Jepson, Elizabeth Evans, Marie Irvine, Mark Crow, Stephanie Chong, Sybil Johnson-Abbott, Gregory Sullivan, Chantal Beaupré, Michael Yang, Trevor Guy, Melanie Crouch, Ryan Treleaven, Shane Todd and Brendan Donovan who have given me valuable assistance in the preparation of the second edition and the annual supplements.

Toronto

S.M. Waddams
October, 2008

PREFACE TO THE FIRST EDITION

Where compensation in money has to be made for a wrong, a set of principles is needed to govern the assessment of the proper money sum. These principles constitute the law of damages.

Until recently, comparatively little attention has been paid to this area of the law, but the impact of inflation, combined with the greater tendency of courts to analyze, explain and justify their awards, has made the area one of great theoretical and practical importance. Sound theory and good practice go together. It is not less important in this area of the law than in others that the decisions of judges should be governed by rational and consistent considerations. It is hoped that this book will make a contribution. There is, moreover, in my view, a particular need for a Canadian book on damages at a time when the law in Canadian jurisdictions has diverged quite markedly from English law in several important respects.

The principal aim of the book is to give an accurate account of the present law in Canadian common law jurisdictions, with reference to English, Commonwealth, and American cases where appropriate. Recent developments and current trends are analyzed with a view to understanding not only the rules of law but the underlying reasons for them. In my view the two tasks are inseparable. Where, as is often the case, there is a conflict of underlying principles, a resolution is suggested.

Books on damages have conventionally divided the subject according to areas of substantive law, dealing with contracts separately from torts, while collecting together all kinds of damage claims arising out of the same area of law. However, from the point of view of compensation, it is the interest protected that is the logical connecting factor, not the source of the legal obligation. For this reason I have here approached the law of damages according to the interest for which the money award is a substitute, so that all claims for loss of property, for example, are dealt with together, whether the loss is caused by conversion, destruction of the property, or non-delivery by a seller. In all cases the plaintiff's complaint is that, if the wrong had not been done, he would now have property that in fact he does not have. The problems that arise in translating the plaintiff's claim into a money sum are identical, or at least very closely analogous.

In consequence, the reader will find no single chapter on sale of goods: the discussion of a buyer's damages for non-delivery appears in the context of compensation for loss of property; the discussion of a buyer's damages for delivery of defective goods is found with other cases on compensation for defects in property; the buyer's damages for personal injury are dealt with in the chapter on compensation for personal injuries; the discussion of a seller's damages for non-acceptance is to be found, with other cases of loss of sales and rents, under the heading of compensation for damage to economic interests. It is hoped that any inconvenience to the reader caused by this dispersal will be offset by the advantages of considering together cases that, though springing from diverse sources of legal obligation, raise analogous problems from the point of view of compensation.

Another innovation that has been attempted is the creation of a link between money remedies and specific relief. One hundred years after the Judicature Act, it is surely time to look at legal and equitable remedies as a whole. To this end, I have worked in close collaboration with Professor R. J. Sharpe, whose book on Injunctions and Specific Performance is published simultaneously with this work as a companion volume. Cross-references are made in both books.

I am most grateful to Professor Sharpe for his many helpful criticisms and suggestions. I wish to express my thanks also to the University of Toronto, to the Social Sciences and Humanities Research Council of Canada, to Jesus College Oxford, and to the Bodleian Library, which all contributed to enabling me to spend a very satisfying year in Oxford, during which the bulk of the work was done.

S.M.W.

Toronto
August 1983

TABLE OF CONTENTS

PART I COMPENSATORY DAMAGES

CHAPTER 2. LOSS OF SERVICES

CHAPTER 3. PERSONAL INJURIES

CHAPTER 4. LOSS OF REPUTATION

CHAPTER 5. DAMAGE TO ECONOMIC INTERESTS

CHAPTER 6. WRONGFUL DEATH

CHAPTER 7. LOSS OF MONEY

PART II NON-COMPENSATORY DAMAGES

CHAPTER 8. LIQUIDATED DAMAGES

CHAPTER 9. AWARDS MEASURED BY THE DEFENDANT'S BENEFIT

CHAPTER 10. NOMINAL AND SYMBOLIC DAMAGES

CHAPTER 11. PUNITIVE DAMAGES

CHAPTER 15. MITIGATION

CONTENTS CHECKLIST

The following is a list of the pages to allow subscribers to check that their volumes are complete and up to date.

Page	Date
Title page	Nov. 2008
iii	Nov. 2008
iv	blank
v/vi	no pages
vii and viii	Aug. 1991
C-1/2	Nov. 2008
C-3/4	Nov. 2008
C-5/6	Nov. 2008
C-7/8	Nov. 2008
CL-1/2	Nov. 2008
CL-3	Nov. 2008
Tab - Table of Cases	
TC-1 to TC-147	Nov. 2008
Tab - Table of Statutes	
TS-1/2	Oct. 2007
TS-3/4	Oct. 2007
TS-5/6	Nov. 2008
TS-7/8	Nov. 2008
TS-9/10	Nov. 2008
TS-11/12	Nov. 2008
TS-13	Nov. 2008
Tab - Compensatory Damages	
PT-I	Dec. 1992
1-1/2	Nov. 2008
1-3/4	Dec. 2002
1-5/6	Aug. 1991
1-7/8	Nov. 2008
1-9/10	Oct. 2004
1-11/12	Oct. 2004
1-13/14	Oct. 2004
1-15/16	Nov. 2008
1-17/18	Nov. 2008
1-19/20	Nov. 2008
1-21/22	Nov. 2008
1-23/24	Nov. 2008
1-25/26	Nov. 2008
1-27/28	Nov. 2008
1-29/30	Nov. 2008
1-31/32	Nov. 2008
1-33/34	Oct. 2007
1-35/36	Oct. 2007
1-37/38	Oct. 2007
1-39/40	Oct. 2007
1-41/42	Nov. 2008
1-43/44	Nov. 2008
1-45/46	Nov. 2008
1-47/48	Nov. 2008
1-49/50	Nov. 2008
1-51/52	Dec. 2002
1-53/54	Dec. 2000
1-55/56	Dec. 2000
1-56.1	Dec. 2000
1-57/58	Dec. 1999
1-59/60	Dec. 1998
1-61/62	Oct. 2007
1-63/64	Aug. 1991
1-65/66	Aug. 1991
1-67/68	Aug. 1991
1-69/70	Oct. 2004
1-71/72	Dec. 2003
1-73/74	Oct. 2007
1-75/76	Dec. 1996
1-76.1	Dec. 1992
1-77/78	Aug. 1991
1-79/80	Aug. 1991
1-81/82	Dec. 1999
1-83/84	Nov. 2008
1-85/86	Dec. 2000
1-86.1	Dec. 1992
1-87/88	Aug. 1991
1-89/90	Dec. 1997
1-91/92	Dec. 1997
1-93/94	Dec. 2002
1-95/96	Nov. 2008
1-97/98	Dec. 1996
1-99/100	Dec. 2000
1-100.1	Dec. 2000
1-101/102	Oct. 2004
1-103/104	Oct. 2004
1-105/106	Oct. 2004
1-107/108	Oct. 2004
1-109/110	Nov. 2008
1-111/112	Dec. 1999
1-113/114	Dec. 1995
1-115/116	Dec. 1997
1-117/118	Oct. 2004
1-119/120	Nov. 2008
1-120.1	Nov. 2008
1-121/122	Dec. 1999
1-123/124	Dec. 2002
1-125/126	Dec. 1998
1-127/128	Dec. 2002
1-129/130	Nov. 2008
1-130.1	Nov. 2008
1-131/132	Oct. 2007
1-133/134	Aug. 1991
1-135/136	Dec. 1994
1-137/138	Nov. 2008
1-139	Nov. 2008
2-1/2	Aug. 1991
2-3/4	Dec. 1999
2-5/6	Dec. 1999
2-7/8	Dec. 1996
2-9/10	Dec. 2006
2-11/12	Dec. 1999
2-13/14	Dec. 1999
2-15/16	Dec. 1996
2-17/18	Dec. 1999
2-19	Dec. 1999
3-1/2	Dec. 2000
3-3/4	Dec. 2003
3-5/6	Dec. 2000
3-6.1	Dec. 2000
3-7/8	Dec. 1997
3-9/10	Dec. 2006
3-11/12	Dec. 2006
3-13/14	Dec. 2006
3-15/16	Nov. 2008
3-17/18	Nov. 2008
3-19/20	Nov. 2008
3-21/22	Dec. 2002
3-23/24	Dec. 2002
3-25/26	Dec. 2006
3-27/28	Dec. 2006
3-29/30	Nov. 2008
3-31/32	Nov. 2008
3-32.1	Nov. 2008
3-33/34	Oct. 2007
3-35/36	Oct. 2007
3-37/38	Oct. 2007
3-39/40	Nov. 2008
3-40.1	Nov. 2008
3-41/42	Dec. 2006
3-43/44	Dec. 2006
3-45/46	Dec. 2006
3-47/48	Dec. 2006
3-49/50	Dec. 2006

Page	Date
3-50.1/50.2	Dec. 2006
3-51/52	Dec. 1996
3-53/54	Dec. 1998
3-55/56	Oct. 2007
3-57/58	Dec. 2000
3-59/60	Nov. 2008
3-60.1	Nov. 2008
3-61/62	Dec. 2006
3-63/64	Dec. 2006
3-65/66	Dec. 2006
3-67/68	Nov. 2008
3-69/70	Nov. 2008
3-71/72	Nov. 2008
3-73/74	Nov. 2008
3-75/76	Nov. 2008
3-77/78	Nov. 2008
3-79/80	Nov. 2008
3-81/82	Nov. 2008
3-83/84	Nov. 2008
3-85/86	Nov. 2008
3-87/88	Nov. 2008
3-89/90	Nov. 2008
3-91/92	Nov. 2008
3-93/94	Nov. 2008
3-95/96	Nov. 2008
4-1/2	Nov. 2008
4-3/4	Nov. 2008
4-5/6	Nov. 2008
4-7/8	Nov. 2008
4-9/10	Nov. 2008
4-11/12	Nov. 2008
4-13/14	Nov. 2008
4-15/16	Nov. 2008
5-1/2	Nov. 2008
5-3/4	Oct. 2005
5-5/6	Dec. 1999
5-7/8	Dec. 1999
5-9/10	Dec. 1999
5-11/12	Nov. 2008
5-12.1	Nov. 2008
5-13/14	Oct. 2005
5-15/16	Oct. 2005
5-17/18	Oct. 2005
5-19/20	Nov. 2008
5-20.1	Nov. 2008
5-21/22	Dec. 2006
5-23/24	Dec. 2006
5-25/26	Dec. 2006
5-27/28	Oct. 2007
5-29/30	Oct. 2007
5-31/32	Oct. 2007
5-33/34	Oct. 2007
5-35/36	Nov. 2008
5-37/38	Nov. 2008
5-39/40	Nov. 2008
5-41/42	Nov. 2008
5-43/44	Nov. 2008
5-45/46	Nov. 2008
5-47/48	Nov. 2008
5-49/50	Nov. 2008
5-51/52	Nov. 2008
5-53/54	Nov. 2008
5-55/56	Nov. 2008
5-57/58	Dec. 2006
5-59/60	Oct. 2005
5-61/62	Oct. 2005
5-62.1	Oct. 2005
5-63/64	Dec. 2002
5-65/66	Dec. 1992
5-67/68	Oct. 2004
5-69/70	Nov. 2008
6-1/2	Dec. 2002
6-3/4	Oct. 2005
6-5/6	Oct. 2007
6-6.1	Oct. 2007
6-7/8	Dec. 1996
6-9/10	Dec. 2001
6-11/12	Dec. 1998
6-13/14	Dec. 2002
6-15/16	Dec. 2001
6-17/18	Nov. 2008
6-19/20	Nov. 2008
6-21/22	Nov. 2008
6-22.1	Nov. 2008
6-23/24	Aug. 1991
6-25/26	Dec. 2000
6-27/28	Dec. 2002
6-29/30	Dec. 2001
6-31/32	Dec. 2001
6-33/34	Dec. 2006
6-34.1	Dec. 2006
6-35/36	Dec. 2003
6-37/38	Dec. 2001
6-38.1	Dec. 1996
6-39/40	Dec. 2002
6-41/42	Dec. 2002
6-43/44	Dec. 1996
6-45/46	Aug. 1991
6-47/48	Dec. 1999
6-49/50	Dec. 2000
6-51/52	Dec. 1996
6-53/54	Dec. 2002
6-55	Dec. 1999
7-1/2	Oct. 2005
7-3/4	Dec. 1992
7-5/6	Dec. 1995
7-6.1	Dec. 1995
7-7/8	Dec. 1992
7-9/10	Aug. 1991
7-11/12	Aug. 1991
7-13/14	Dec. 2001
7-15/16	Dec. 2001
7-17/18	Dec. 1999
7-19/20	Oct. 2007
7-21/22	Oct. 2007
7-22.1	Oct. 2007
7-23/24	Dec. 2001
7-25/26	Dec. 1999
7-27/28	Nov. 2008
7-29/30	Nov. 2008
7-31/32	Dec. 2002
7-33/34	Dec. 2006
7-35/36	Dec. 1999
7-36.1	Dec. 1999
7-37/38	Dec. 1996
7-39/40	Dec. 2003
7-41/42	Dec. 1997
7-43/44	Oct. 2007
7-45/46	Oct. 2007
7-47/48	Oct. 2007
Tab - Non-compensatory Damages	
PT-II	Dec. 1992
8-1/2	Oct. 2005
8-3/4	Dec. 2006
8-4.1	Dec. 2006
8-5/6	Oct. 2005
8-7/8	Nov. 2008
8-9/10	Nov. 2008
8-11/12	Nov. 2008
8-13/14	Dec. 1999
8-15/16	Dec. 1996
8-17/18	Dec. 2006
8-19	Dec. 2006
9-1/2	Oct. 2007
9-3/4	Nov. 2008
9-5/6	Nov. 2008
9-7/8	Nov. 2008
9-9/10	Nov. 2008
9-11/12	Nov. 2008
9-13	Nov. 2008
10-1/2	Nov. 2008
10-3/4	Nov. 2008
10-5/6	Nov. 2008
11-1/2	Nov. 2008
11-3/4	Nov. 2008
11-5/6	Nov. 2008
11-7/8	Nov. 2008

CONTENTS CHECKLIST

Page	Date	Page	Date	Page	Date
11-9/10	Nov. 2008	13-19/20	Oct. 2007	15-11/12	Nov. 2008
11-11/12	Nov. 2008	13-21/22	Oct. 2007	15-12.1	Nov. 2008
11-13/14	Nov. 2008	13-23/24	Oct. 2007	15-13/14	Dec. 2006
11-15/16	Nov. 2008	13-25/26	Oct. 2007	15-15/16	Oct. 2005
11-17/18	Nov. 2008	13-27/28	Oct. 2007	15-16.1	Oct. 2005
11-19/20	Nov. 2008	13-29/30	Oct. 2007	15-17/18	Oct. 2004
11-21/22	Nov. 2008	13-31/32	Oct. 2007	15-19/20	Nov. 2008
11-23/24	Nov. 2008	13-33/34	Oct. 2007	15-20.1	Nov. 2008
11-25/26	Nov. 2008	13-35	Oct. 2007	15-21/22	Dec. 1999
11-27/28	Nov. 2008	14-1/2	Nov. 2008	15-23/24	Aug. 1991
11-29/30	Nov. 2008	14-3/4	Nov. 2008	15-25/26	Oct. 2007
11-31/32	Nov. 2008	14-5/6	Nov. 2008	15-27/28	Dec. 1999
11-33/34	Nov. 2008	14-7/8	Nov. 2008	15-29/30	Dec. 1999
12-1/2	Dec. 2002	14-9/10	Nov. 2008	15-31/32	Dec. 2001
12-3/4	Dec. 2002	14-11/12	Nov. 2008	15-32.1	Dec. 2000
12-5/6	Dec. 2003	14-13/14	Nov. 2008	15-33/34	Nov. 2008
12-7/8	Oct. 2007	14-15/16	Nov. 2008	15-34.1	Nov. 2008
12-9/10	Oct. 2004	14-17/18	Nov. 2008	15-35/36	Oct. 2005
12-11/12	Dec. 2002	14-19/20	Nov. 2008	15-37/38	Oct. 2007
12-13	Dec. 2002	14-21/22	Nov. 2008	15-39/40	Oct. 2007
		14-23/24	Dec. 1998	15-41/42	Oct. 2007
Tab - Limiting		14-25/26	Oct. 2004		
Principles		14-26.1	Dec. 2000	**Tab - Index**	
PT-III	Dec. 1992	14-27/28	Dec. 1999	IN-1/2	Dec. 2006
13-1/2	Nov. 2008	14-29/30	Oct. 2007	IN-3/4	Dec. 2006
13-3/4	Nov. 2008	14-31/32	Oct. 2007	IN-5/6	Dec. 2006
13-4.1	Nov. 2008	14-33/34	Nov. 2008	IN-7/8	Dec. 2006
13-5/6	Oct. 2005	14-35/36	Nov. 2008	IN-9/10	Dec. 2006
13-7/8	Dec. 1999	14-37/38	Nov. 2008	IN-11/12	Dec. 2006
13-9/10	Dec. 2003	14-39	Nov. 2008	IN-13/14	Dec. 2006
13-11/12	Dec. 2002	15-1/2	Oct. 2007	IN-15/16	Dec. 2006
13-13/14	Oct. 2004	15-3/4	Nov. 2008	IN-17/18	Dec. 2006
13-15/16	Oct. 2005	15-5/6	Nov. 2008	IN-19/20	Dec. 2006
13-17/18	Nov. 2008	15-7/8	Nov. 2008	IN-21	Dec. 2006
13-18.1	Nov. 2008	15-9/10	Nov. 2008		

TABLE OF CASES

Order Copies of Original Decisions

Find case law dating back to 1892 in BestCase. This web-based research service contains Canada Law Book's leading law reports and summary services, as well as a comprehensive collection of unreported decisions. Images of reported decisions (as they appear in our law reports) and original judgments are available as PDF files.

Copies of original Canadian judicial decisions since 1977 can also be purchased online at **www.caseimage.ca** or by calling **905-841-6472** or toll free **1-800-263-2037** or **1-800-263-3269**.

NOTE: This Table of Cases incorporates new cases in Release No. 17 (highlighted in **boldface**).

PARA.

PARA.

PARA.

PARA.

TABLE OF STATUTES

CANADA

PARA.

Carriage by Air Act, R.S.C. 1985, c. C-26 .... 6.450
    Sch. I, art. 17 .... 6.10
Competition Act, R.S.C. 1985, c. C-34, s. 61(1) (am. 1990, c. 37, s. 30) 8.100
Copyright Act, R.S.C. 1985, c. C-42 .... 1.390, 5.800
    s. 35 (rep. & sub. 1997, c. 24, s. 20(1)) 5.800, 5.880
    s. 38.1 (en. 1997, c. 24, s. 20(1)) 5.800
Criminal Code, R.S.C. 1985, c. C-46 —
    s. 9 (am. 1985, c. 27 (1st Supp.), s. 6; 1995, c. 22, s. 10) 11.40
    s. 194 (rep. & sub. 1993, c. 40, s. 13) 11.100
Currency Act, R.S.C. 1985, c. C-52, s. 12 .... 7.120, 7.150
Employment Insurance Act, S.C. 1996, c. 23, s. 45 .... 3.1720, 15.860
Federal Courts Act, R.S.C. 1985, c. F-7 —
    s. 36 (rep. & sub. 1990, c. 8, s. 9; am. 2002, c. 8, s. 36) 7.380
    s. 36(4)(*a*) (rep. & sub. 1990, c. 8, s. 9) 7.980
    s. 36(4)(*b*) (rep. & sub. 1990, c. 8, s. 9) 7.950
    s. 36(4)(*d*) (rep. & sub. 2002, c. 8, s. 36(1)) 7.640
    s. 36(4)(*e*) (rep. & sub. 1990, c. 8, s. 9) 7.970
    s. 36(4)(*f*) (rep. & sub. 1990, c. 8, s. 9) 7.780
Gold Clauses Act, R.S.C. 1970, c. G-4, s. 7 .... 7.50
Income Tax Act, R.S.C. 1985, c. 1 (5th Supp.) —
    s. 56(1)(*a*)(ii) 5.1280
    s. 248(1), definition "retiring allowance" 5.1280
Interest Act, R.S.C. 1985, c. I-15 —
    s. 3 .... 7.460
    s. 12 (repealed 1992, c. 1, s. 146) 7.460, 7.1000
Marine Liability Act, S.C. 2001, c. 6 —
    ss. 1 to 4 .... 6.10
    s. 5 (am. 2002, c. 8, s. 182) 6.10
    ss. 6 to 14 .... 6.10
Supreme Court Act, R.S.C. 1985, c. S-26, s. 50 .... 7.920, 7.940

ALBERTA

Defamation Act, R.S.A. 2000, c. D-7 —
    s. 4 .... 4.170
    s. 15 .... 4.170
    s. 15(2) 4.220
    s. 16(1) 4.170

PARA.

PARA.

NOVA SCOTIA — *Continued*

Fatal Injuries Act — *Continued*

s. 5(2)(d) 6.330
s. 5(3) 6.450, 6.470, 6.480
s. 5(4) 6.240
s. 7 .... 6.750
s. 10 .... 6.750

Interest on Judgments Act, R.S.N.S. 1989, c. 233 .... 7.1000

Judicature Act, S.N.S. 1972, c. 2, s. 38(11)(c) (en. 1980, c. 55, s. 1; repealed 1981, c. 54, s. 1) 7.800

Judicature Act, R.S.N.S. 1989, c. 240 —

s. 41 .... 7.450
s. 41(j) 7.740
s. 41(k)(ii) 7.780
s. 41(k)(iii) 7.940

Residential Tenancies Act, R.S.N.S. 1989, c. 401, s. 9(1), stat. con. 6 .... 15.570

Sale of Goods Act, R.S.N.S. 1989, c. 408 —

s. 21 .... 1.1040
s. 51 .... 5.1370
s. 52(3) 1.50, 1.730
s. 54 .... 13.210
s. 54(2) 1.2550
s. 54(3) 1.2550
s. 55 .... 1.2550

Survival of Actions Act, R.S.N.S. 1989, c. 453 —

s. 2(1) 12.10
s. 2(2)(a) 12.20
s. 2(2)(b) 12.20
s. 4 .... 12.30
s. 4(a) 12.150
s. 4(b) 12.130
s. 4(c) 12.140

Workers' Compensation Act, S.N.S. 1994-95, c. 10, s. 30 (rep. & sub. 1999, c. 1, s. 3(1)) 3.1730

ONTARIO

An Act respecting Trustees and Executors and the Administration of Estates, R.S.O. 1877, c. 107, s. 8 (rep. & sub. 1886, c. 16, s. 23) 6.790, 12.10

Compensation for Victims of Crime Act, R.S.O. 1990, c. C.24, s. 17(1) 15.60

Consumer Protection Act, 2002, S.O. 2002, c. 30, Sch. A 5.670, 5.690

s. 18(1) 5.690
s. 18(2) (am. 2004, c. 19, s. 7(6)) 5.690
s. 18(11) 3.1410, 5.690

Courts of Justice Act, R.S.O. 1990, c. C.43 .... 7.70

s. 66(2)(v) 3.1180
s. 99 .... 1.860, 1.930, 5.650
s. 116 (am. 1996, c. 25, s. 1(20)) 3.260, 3.1180
s. 118 .... 3.550

PARA.

ONTARIO — *Continued*

SASKATCHEWAN

PARA.

UNITED KINGDOM — *Continued*

PART I

COMPENSATORY DAMAGES

CHAPTER 1

LOSS OF PROPERTY

I. INTRODUCTION

Many kinds of legal wrongs cause a loss of property to the plaintiff. The commonest cases are negligence, destruction of goods, conversion, non-delivery by a seller, and loss by a carrier or bailee. Classified as legal wrongs, these instances seem to have little in common, crossing the borderlines between contract and tort, negligence and trespass, and sale and service contracts. However, from the point of view of compensation, they all raise a single issue: how to provide in money a substitute for property that the plaintiff does not have, but would have had but for the defendant's wrong. **1.10**

It is common in such cases that the plaintiff complains not only of the loss of property but also of the loss of its use. Had the wrong not been done, the plaintiff would have had, at the time of the complaint, not only capital wealth represented by the property, but an accretion to wealth represented by profitable use of the property. It is often difficult, as the subsequent discussion will show, to draw a clear line between these two claims, for the capital value of property reflects the value of its anticipated use. Thus, if instant reparation could be made for the plaintiff's loss, and a perfect substitute instantly acquired, there would never be a claim for loss of use. But reparation for legal wrongs is never made instantly, and substitutes are rarely perfect. Consequently, compensation may be usefully regarded as containing two elements: a substitute for loss of the value of the property and a substitute for the loss of the opportunity to use it. **1.20**

II. COMPENSATION FOR LOSS OF PROPERTY

1. The Meaning of Loss

Actions against sellers for non-delivery of goods are commonly regarded from the perspective of the buyer who has to purchase a substitute. The disappointed buyer puts herself into the position she would have occupied if the contract had been fulfilled by procuring a substitute.[1] An alternative and simpler theory of compensation is that the buyer would have been wealthier if **1.30**

[1] See *Barrow v. Arnaud* (1846), 8 Q.B. 595 at pp. 609-10, 115 E.R. 1000. Where property has passed to the buyer, proprietary remedies will also be available: see 1.1010-1.1090, 1.1740-1.1780, *infra*.

the seller had delivered, and it is plain that in some cases this is the dominant theory. Where, for example, the buyer does not in fact procure a substitute[2] or procures one on favourable terms, he is still entitled to damages measured by the value the property would have had to him if delivered. Thus, in *Sheik Mohammad Habib Ullah v. Bird & Co.*,[3] where the plaintiff was able to supply sub-buyers by using existing stock, the defaulting seller argued that he had consequently suffered no loss. The Privy Council held the buyer entitled to recover on the basis of the value of the goods promised. Lord Dunedin said: "In the present case had the appellant supplied the timber the respondents would have made their profit and would still have had the other timber to sell upon which they were entitled to make such profit as they could."[4]

1.40 Similarly, if the buyer obtains substitute goods at a favourable price, or by way of gift, she is still entitled to recover the value promised to her.[4a] The existing law has been criticized on the ground that it puts the buyer in a better position than would have been occupied on performance by the seller, and it has been proposed that a buyer should be restricted to recovery of "actual loss".[5] It is submitted that the criticism of the existing law is misplaced. Light is shed on the question by considering it outside the context of sale of goods. In a case where the plaintiff complains of negligent destruction of property, or conversion, for example, it seems plain that he should recover the value of the property lost to him, even if he should purchase a similar article the next day at a favourable price, or if he should receive a gift of a similar article from a friend or relative. In all such cases the plaintiff is the poorer because of the defendant's wrong, by the value of the property lost. The same applies, it is submitted, to a case of non-delivery by a seller. It is most undesirable to set up different measures of damages for non-delivery and conversion, for often an action against a defaulting seller can be framed in either form. It would not therefore be conceded by the supporters of the present law that it does in fact allow a recovery greater than the plaintiff's "actual loss".

2. The Meaning of Value

1.50 Few would dispute the proposition that a person wrongfully deprived of property should recover its value. It is more difficult to find agreement on the means of ascertaining the value of property. Sometimes the value

2 See *Boehner v. Smith* (1916), 26 D.L.R. 511 (N.S.S.C.A.D.); *Tainter v. McKinnon* (1918), 39 D.L.R. 483 (Alta. S.C. App. Div.). The point seems obvious where the buyer has paid in advance.

3 (1921), 37 T.L.R. 405 (P.C.), applying the *Indian Contract Act*.

4 *Supra*, at p. 407.

4a *Skyward Resources Ltd. v. Cessna Aircraft Co.* (2007), 212 Man. R. (2d) 130 (C.A.).

5 Ontario Law Reform Commission, *Report on Sale of Goods* (Ministry of Attorney-General, 1979), p. 499; Draft Bill, s. 9.16(4). The Uniform Act (s. 9.18(5)(*c*)) excludes the *prima facie* measure of damages when the buyer has "bought substitutional goods as provided [in an earlier clause]". See Proceedings of The Uniform Law Conference of Canada, 1981. See also 1.1430, 1.1940, *infra*.

of a thing is called its market value, but the extra word adds little meaning. Nothing has an "inherent" value except the currency in which an award is to be calculated. Attribution to a thing of value depends on a real or assumed contractual transaction. "The value of all things", Hobbes said, "is measured by the appetite of the contractors."[6] But the question is: what contractors? In some cases, there may be evidence of an actual transaction in which the property to be valued has been bought or sold. The plaintiff may have bought it the day before the defendant destroyed it. Or the defendant may have converted it by selling it to a third person. The sale price in such transactions is evidential of value but cannot be conclusive, for people make good bargains and bad bargains, and an individual transaction may undervalue or overvalue the property.[7] This appears most clearly where the wrong for which compensation is to be given is the failure of a seller of property to deliver it. In litigated cases, the value is commonly found to exceed the contract price, the buyer's damages being measured by the difference between the two.[8]

1.60 Since actual transactions cannot be conclusive, it is to hypothetical transactions that courts must turn. Where similar property is regularly bought and sold and the market price can be readily ascertained, this is usually the best measure of the value of property. In *The "Clyde"*[9] Dr. Lushington said: "It is the market price which the Court looks to, and nothing else, as the value of the property. It is an old saying, 'The worth of a thing is the price it will bring.' "[10]

1.70 Even where there is a regular market in property, in all material respects identical to that valued, the question may arise whether the market price is always, as Dr. Lushington tends to suggest, conclusive evidence of value. Subsequent events might lead to disclosure of facts tending to show that an earlier market price was excessive or inadequate, and stockbrokers commonly speak of stock being overvalued or undervalued by the market. In *Peek v. Derry*,[11] the question was of the liability of directors of a tramway company for misrepresentation in the prospectus that induced the plaintiff to take shares. The House of Lords ultimately

6 Hobbes, *Leviathan*, ch. 15, Everyman, ed. (London, J. M. Dent & Sons, 1973), p. 78.

7 *Gardiner v. Metcalf*, [1994] 2 N.Z.L.R. 8 (C.A.). In *Crayden's Pharmacy Ltd. v. Standard Paving Co.* (1973), 37 D.L.R. (3d) 167, [1973] 3 O.R. 435 (C.A.), dealings between the plaintiff and its insurer were excluded as evidence of the value of damaged goods.

8 See *Sale of Goods Act* (Alta.), s. 50(3); B.C., s. 54(3); Man., s. 52(3); N.B., s. 48(3); Nfld. & Lab., s. 51(3); N.W.T., s. 58; N.S., s. 52(3); Ont., s. 49(3); P.E.I., s. 51(3); Sask., s. 50(3); Yukon, s. 48(3).

9 (1856), Swab. 23, 166 E.R. 998.

10 *Supra*, at p. 25. Many of the cases on value are admiralty cases, but as Scrutton L.J. said in *The "Canadian Transport"* (1932), 43 Ll. L.R. 409 (C.A.), at p. 410, "there are repeated statements by judges of high authority that the rule of law in damage cases is the same at common law as in Admiralty". A similar statement appears in *Darbishire v. Warran*, [1963] 1 W.L.R. 1067 (C.A.), at p. 1071, *per* Harman L.J. approved in *T. Donovan & Sons Ltd. v. Baker* (1966), 53 M.P.R. 113 (N.B.S.C. App. Div.), at p. 115.

11 (1887), 37 Ch. D. 541 (C.A.), revd on other grounds 14 App. Cas. 337 (H.L.).

held the directors not liable, in the absence of an intention to deceive. But in the Court of Appeal, where liability was imposed, the question arose of the measure of damages. At the time the plaintiff had subscribed, the shares were bought and sold generally at the price he paid. Later, the company collapsed. The defendants argued that the damages were to be measured by the difference between contract price and market price at the date of the allotment of the shares. The court, after separate argument on the point, rejected this argument, holding that the plaintiff was entitled to recover the difference between the contract price and the "real value" of the shares, which, though to be taken on the date of the allotment, might be shown by subsequent events to differ from the market price on that date. Any other conclusion would mean that while a defendant who deceived the plaintiff alone would be liable in damages, a defendant whose fraud operated on a grand scale so as to deceive the whole world would escape liability. Cotton L.J. said:

> Now, it must not be taken that the value of the shares must be what they would have sold for in the market, because that might not shew the real value at all . . . the market might have been affected by the representations which were made by the Defendants, which induced the Plaintiff to act, and which might have induced others to act.[12]

1.80 *Peek v. Derry*, however, was not a case in which the plaintiff was complaining of having been deprived of the shares — on the contrary, he was complaining of having been deprived of his money, and it was the defendant who sought to argue that the shares received in exchange were of a high value. Suppose that Peek had agreed to purchase from a private seller the identical shares involved in the case (400 shares of the Plymouth, Devonport and District Tramways Company for £4,000) and his complaint was of non-delivery. If the market price of the shares at the date fixed for delivery had exceeded the contract price, Peek would have been entitled to damages, and it would not lie in the seller's mouth to say that subsequent disclosures had now proved the shares to be worthless. The plaintiff would be entitled to assert that he had been deprived by the defendant's wrong of the opportunity of reselling the shares in the market.[13]

---

12 *Supra*, at pp. 591-2. See also *Western Oil Consultants Ltd. v. Bankeno Resources Ltd.*, [1995] 6 W.W.R. 475, 168 A.R. 81 (Q.B.). The opposite case, where later events show the true value of property to be higher than market price, was discussed in *Prudential Ass'ce Co. Ltd. v. Newman Industries Ltd.*, [1981] Ch. 257 at pp. 299-300.

13 See 1.660, 1.1360-1.1430, *infra*.

1.90 Another problem in valuation according to market price arises where, as occurs in certain markets, there is a distinct margin between the selling price and the buying price. It is commonly said in discussing cases of a seller's non-delivery that the buyer is entitled to the difference between contract price and market price (assuming the contract price is unpaid) on the theory that he should receive sufficient money to enable him to go into the market and buy a substitute.[14] This theory would suggest that in a market where there is a distinct margin between buying price and selling price, the buying price should be taken as the value of the goods. However, the more basic principle of damage assessment is that the party complaining should be put in as good a position as would have been occupied if the wrong had not been done,[15] and, it is submitted, the answer to the question of whether the buying price or the selling price is to be taken must depend on the purpose and intention of the plaintiff. Thus, a buyer of goods for use is plainly entitled to a sufficient award to permit purchase of a replacement. On the other hand, a buyer for resale should, it is submitted, be entitled only to the selling price, that is, the price at which the goods would have been resold had they been delivered, for it is the amount of the selling price that will put the buyer in the position that would have been occupied had the contract been performed. Similarly, in cases of destruction or conversion of goods, or loss by a carrier, although the plaintiff will often make out a case for an award sufficient to purchase a replacement, he should not automatically be entitled to such an award, and on proof that he would, in the absence of the wrong, have sold the goods, his recovery should be limited to the price he would have received from such a sale.

1.100 The same considerations apply to an action against a defendant for money due in a foreign currency.[16] In such cases, the plaintiff is in effect a buyer of the foreign currency. If the foreign currency is required for business or personal use, the plaintiff should recover a sufficient sum in dollars to enable her to purchase the amount of foreign currency wrongfully withheld (that is, the bank selling price). But if, as is common, the plaintiff's accounts are kept in dollars — if he "feels his loss"[17] in dollars — he ought only to recover the lesser sum in dollars that he would have been able to obtain with the sum of foreign currency had it been duly paid (that is, the bank buying price, which is always a lower price in

---

14 *Barrow v. Arnaud* (1846), 8 Q.B. 595 at pp. 609-10, 115 E.R. 1000; *Diamond Cutting Works Federation Ltd. v. Triefus & Co. Ltd.*, [1956] 1 Lloyd's Rep. 216 at p. 227; *Casswell v. Mathew Moody & Sons Co.*, [1926] 1 W.W.R. 113 (Sask. C.A.), at pp. 115-16.

15 See *Livingstone v. Rawyards Coal Co.* (1880), 5 App. Cas. 25 (H.L.), at p. 39, *per* Lord Blackburn; *J. & E. Hall v. Barclay*, [1937] 3 All E.R. 620 (C.A.), at p. 623, *per* Greer L.J.

16 See 7.80-7.320, *infra*.

17 See 7.230-7.320, *infra*.

dollars per unit of foreign currency). If the plaintiff would not have purchased replacement foreign currency, there is, it is suggested, no justification for awarding a sum of money sufficient to do so, for this would be to put the plaintiff in a better position than would have been occupied if the wrong had not been done.

1.110 In the large majority of cases where valuation is disputed, the property in question has no perfect substitute and no market exists that can exactly determine the value. The concept of value always implies a transaction of purchase and sale, and in the absence of any market in which such transactions are actually occurring, the court is compelled to construct a hypothetical transaction.

1.120 The outcome of such a hypothetical process will largely depend on the assumptions used in constructing it. If it is imagined that the plaintiff, in the absence of the wrong complained of, would have attempted to sell the property for the best price immediately obtainable, it is obvious that a low valuation will result. Forced sales are not recommended as a means of realizing maximum prices, and certain goods like used clothing, or used furniture, have a low sale value. If, on the other hand, it is supposed that the plaintiff had been approached by a hypothetical buyer anxious to buy the property and willing to pay whatever the plaintiff should demand, a very high valuation will emerge, for the plaintiff might in fact have an irrational attachment to the property and have been unwilling to sell except for fabulous wealth. Even supposing a rational plaintiff willing to sell at a price that would fully compensate, the sum demanded would be sufficient to enable the plaintiff to purchase a substitute considered by him to be adequate (with an additional sum in case no such substitute exists, to compensate for the difference), together with a sum to compensate for the inconvenience of effecting a substitution, and a sum to allow for the risk of error in valuation.

1.130 Assessments made by the courts fall between these two extremes, but approximate more closely to the higher measure, justifiably, it is submitted, in that it is the defendant's wrong that has deprived the plaintiff unwillingly of the property. It is desirable for the law, in principle, to afford as full a compensation to the plaintiff as is practicable and also to require the defendant to pay a sum equivalent to what the latter would have had to pay to purchase the plaintiff's property.

1.140 The concept of value is important in another area of the law, that is, expropriation of land by public authorities. Under statutes requiring payment of "compensation", the English and Canadian courts developed a test of "value to the owner" said by Rand J. in *Irving Oil Co. Ltd. v. The King*[18] to "represent the sum which as a prudent man he

---

18 [1946] S.C.R. 551, [1946] 4 D.L.R. 625.

would be prepared to pay rather than to fail to obtain or retain his property".[19]

1.150 This test permits compensation to take account of the particular circumstances of the owner that make the land of special value to him.[20] If this is the appropriate test when expropriation is lawful, it would seem that a test at least as generous to the owner should be applied when compensation is to be assessed for unlawful interference with property.[21]

1.160 On the other hand, the test of value used in the expropriation cases supposes an owner deprived of the property and asks what sum that person would pay to obtain it.

1.170 Although, in theory, it might be supposed that a rational person would be willing to pay for property that she did not have, the same sum that she would demand to give up similar property that she had, some commentators have suggested that the latter test would usually yield a larger sum.[22] The difference can perhaps be accounted for by the risk of error in alteration of the status quo; an owner who is to be dispossessed of familiar property he would prefer to retain will tend to demand a high price to give it up. Where it is supposed that the owner must pay in order to retain his property, he must, by hypothesis, already have lost the absolute rights of ownership. The status quo is, then, that the hypothetical valuer is no longer an owner, but must pay to acquire rights of ownership. It is understandable that, in estimating the amount of existing wealth to be given up, the valuer will tend towards a lower figure. In the case of wrongful interference with property, the conclusion would be that the basic test of value should be the sum that the plaintiff would rationally have demanded to give up the property.

1.180 In valuing corporate shares, it has been held that account must be taken of the value of a controlling interest. Thus, shares constituting part of a controlling block may have a higher value than the same shares would have as a minority holding.[23]

---

19 *Supra*, at p. 562 S.C.R., p. 634 D.L.R. See *Canada (Attorney General) v. Envoy Relocation Services*, [2008] 1 F.C.R. 291 (C.A.).

20 See also *Diggon-Hibben v. The King*, [1949] S.C.R. 712, [1949] 4 D.L.R. 785; *City of Montreal v. ILGWU Centre Inc.*, [1974] S.C.R. 59, 24 D.L.R. (3d) 694; *Arpro Developments Ltd. v. British Columbia* (1977), 5 B.C.L.R. 184 (C.A.), affd [1978] 2 S.C.R. 718*n*; and Todd, *The Law of Expropriation and Compensation in Canada*, 2nd ed. (Toronto, Carswell Co., 1992), pp. 109-30.

21 The compensation cases were relied on in a case of damages for trespass to land in *Jalbert v. The King*, [1937] S.C.R. at p. 59, [1937] 2 D.L.R. 296; *Kopf v. Superior Oils Ltd.*, [1952] 2 D.L.R. 572 (Alta. S.C.); and *Jordan v. Thomas*, [1948] 1 D.L.R. 782 (N.B.S.C. App. Div.), a case of sale under an invalid execution. See also *Chappel v. Barati* (1982), 30 C.C.L.T. 137 (Ont. H.C.J.).

22 Knetsch and Borcherding, "Expropriation of Private Property and the Basis for Compensation", 29 U.T. L.J. 237 (1979), at pp. 251-2. But in *Jordan v. Thomas, supra*, footnote 21, both formulations were used indiscriminately.

23 *Widrig v. Strazer*, [1964] S.C.R. 376, 44 D.L.R. (2d) 1; *Pelling v. Pelling* (1982), 130 D.L.R. (3d) 761 (B.C.S.C.).

1.190 The basic principle here is compensatory. In some contexts, such as breach of contract, there may be no objection to the defendant's profiting by the wrong,[24] but even in those cases, before the defendant begins to profit it would be generally agreed that he should make full compensation to the plaintiff for the loss, and this approach suggests that there is every reason to measure the compensation by the fullest practicable measure, that is, the sum a rational person in the plaintiff's position would have demanded to sell the property of which the defendant's wrong has deprived him.

1.200 By hypothesis when damage assessment is in question, it is too late to protect the plaintiff's actual interest in the specific property. This could only be done by a decree of specific performance against a defaulting seller, or by a mandatory injunction or an order of specific restitution against a converter. The plaintiff's own evidence, therefore, of what price would have been demanded cannot be conclusive, not only because of the unreliability of such evidence in view of the plaintiff's self-interest, but also because the plaintiff's formerly absolute right to refuse to sell except on his own terms cannot now be protected. It may be proved as an uncontrovertible fact that the plaintiff would only have sold the property for fabulous wealth but this cannot determine the measure of damages. It must be supposed that the plaintiff is ready to sell for a sum that a rational person would accept as full compensation. Such a calculation need not, however, exclude compensation for inconvenience, or the imperfection of available substitutes, or for the possibility of error in valuation, for all these considerations would affect a rational seller.

1.210 It is common in cases of destruction of used goods that the property can only be replaced with a superior article. The plaintiff is not, however, entitled to charge the defendant with the full cost of new goods. It was said in *African Steamship Co. v. Swanzy*[25] that the claimant is not entitled to have the value of a new ship awarded to him when he was the owner of only an old one. A rational seller of a used ship would be willing to sell it for less than the cost of a new ship recognizing the greater value of the replacement. In *The "Clyde"* it was argued before Dr. Lushington that this rule was inconsistent with the

[24] See 9.200 - 9.210, *infra*.

[25] (1856), 2 K. & J. 660, 69 E.R. 947; *G. H. Ingham & Co. Ltd. v. Fedesove* (1956), 5 D.L.R. (2d) 640 (B.C.S.C.); *Yukon Southern Air Transport Ltd. v. The King*, [1942] Ex. C.R. 181, [1943] 1 D.L.R. 305; *Walter v. Muise* (1964), 48 D.L.R. (2d) 734 (N.S.S.C.T.D.) (used clothing); *Wertman v. Fox* (1923), 24 O.W.N. 401 (S.C.), affd 25 O.W.N. 129 (Div. Ct.); *Nason v. Aubin* (1958), 16 D.L.R. (2d) 309 (N.B.S.C. App. Div.) (used car); *City of Guelph Board of Light & Heat Com'rs v. United Dairy & Poultry Co-operative Ltd.* (1966), 57 D.L.R. (2d) 385, [1966] 2 O.R. 467 (Co. Ct.), affd D.L.R. *loc. cit.* p. 387*n*, O.R. *loc. cit.* p. 469*n* (C.A.); *McKinnon v. Acadian Lines Ltd.* (1977), 81 D.L.R. (3d) 480 (N.S.S.C. App. Div.); *A-1 Rentals Sales & Services Ltd. v. Alberta Arches & Beams Ltd.* (1966), 60 D.L.R. (2d) 4 (Alta. S.C. App. Div.); *Preload Co. of Canada v. City of Regina* (1958), 13 D.L.R. (2d) 305 (Sask. C.A.), affd [1959] S.C.R. 801, 20 D.L.R. (2d) 586; *Union Carbide Canada Ltd. v. Scott-Foster Ltd.* (1965), 53 D.L.R. (2d) 407 (B.C.C.A.) (increased value of substitute offset against loss of profits); *Tepper v. Valley Equipment Ltd.* (1997), 186 N.B.R. (2d) 365 (C.A.). In *Rousseau v. Lynch & Fournier*, [1931] 4 D.L.R. 595 (N.B.S.C. App. Div.), replacement value was held to be admissible as a guide to actual value.

rule laid down by Dr. Lushington himself in *The "Gazelle"*[26] to the effect that the owner of a damaged ship was entitled to a full cost of repair regardless of the improvement to the former state of the ship effected by incorporating new materials. Dr. Lushington admitted that the owner of a damaged ship was treated better than the owner of one destroyed, but said:

> . . . it does not affect the principle. In case of partial damage, the party claiming to be restored *in integrum* gains the advantage of having sound timber put into the vessel, instead of that which had been deteriorated by wear and tear. That arises from the necessity of the case. You could not select timber of the same kind as that which was in the vessel before the collision; you could not ascertain what degree of deterioration had taken place, nor could you put the vessel precisely in the situation in which she was before.[27]

It does not seem obvious why the same argument, if sound, would not justify an award measured by replacement cost (*i.e.*, of a new ship) in the case of total destruction of an old one. However, it is submitted below that the argument in *The "Gazelle"* is unsound; that is, a repair leading to a net improvement in the plaintiff's position ought to reduce damages,[28] the net improvement to the plaintiff's wealth, if any, being taken into account.

1.220 Dr. Lushington's reference in *The "Clyde"* to the old saying that the value of a thing is the price it will bring suggests that the price to be considered is the price at which the plaintiff could actually have sold the property. However, it is clear that when damages are calculated on this basis, favourable conditions of sale will be supposed.[29] In *Piper v. Darling*[30] where the plaintiff's yacht was accidentally destroyed by an air force torpedo, it was found that the late summer of 1938 (the time of the accident) was not a propitious time for the sale of a pleasure yacht and the summer of 1939 less so, and the court went so far as to say that in August, 1940 (the date of judgment), there was no market at all. Langton J. said:

> A yacht is not like a work of art, a matter which is perhaps nothing to one person but is of almost incalculable value to another, but it is undoubtedly one in which the element of sentiment and predilection enters more fully, and, in considering the commercial value of a yacht, that is a matter that has to be borne in mind, more particularly when you may have to wait for your buyer.[31]

---

26 (1844), 2 W. Rob. 279, 166 E.R. 759 (Adm.).

27 *The "Clyde"* (1856), Swab. 23 at p. 24, 166 E.R. 998.

28 See 1.2210, 1.2730 - 1.2800, *infra*.

29 In *G.H. Ingham & Co. Ltd. v. Fedesove*, *supra*, footnote 25, it was held that the plaintiff was not obliged to accept valuation at the sum realizable at a public auction of the property.

30 (1940), 67 Ll. L.R. 419 (Adm. Div.).

31 *Supra*, at p. 423. See also *Dominion Lumber Co. v. Halifax Power Co.* (1915), 23 D.L.R. 187 (N.S.S.C.A.D.) (value of trees includes value to owner of keeping them until maturity).

Consequently a value was fixed on the basis of a hypothetical sale at the beginning of a season in peace-time conditions.

1.230 Evidence of original cost has been held in a number of cases to be of evidential value, though of inferior weight to a knowledgeable estimate of value at the time of accident.[32] If original cost is used as a base, allowance must be made for depreciation.[33] More significantly, in times of inflation, an increase must be made for the decline of the purchasing power of money. One way of doing this is to take replacement cost as the base (equivalent to the current value of the original cost) and to deduct depreciation from that figure.[34]

1.240 The amount for which property is insured has also been said to be of inferior weight, though admitted to be relevant as an indication of value.[35] It is well known that property may be overinsured or underinsured for a variety of reasons and therefore the insured value cannot be conclusive. The profit-earning capacity of property is also a relevant consideration[36] and would normally be reflected in a knowledgeable estimate of value.

1.250 The decisions of Dr. Lushington, some of which have been referred to, led to what came to be regarded as a rule of practice in the Admiralty Court that damages for the loss of a ship can never exceed her market value plus interest.[37] Dicta to this effect appear chiefly in cases of damages for lost profits, which will be discussed below in considering compensation for loss of use of property.[38] If value is to be interpreted, as the earlier discussion suggests it should be, as the price the plaintiff would have demanded to give up the property, little objection could be taken from the plaintiff's point of view to restricting compensation to "value". Some of the admiralty cases

---

32 *The "Iron-Master"* (1859), Swab. 441, 166 E.R. 1206; *The "Harmonides"* [1903] P. 1, followed in *Steamship "Giovanni Amendola" v. Powell River Co. Ltd.* [1959] Ex. C.R. 1; *Leonard v. Whitwill*, 19 F. 547 (1884, N.Y. Dist. Ct.).

33 *Reidy v. Fisher* (1953), 9 W.W.R. (N.S.) 226 (Sask. Q.B.). In *Buchanan v. Cook* (1958), 11 D.L.R. (2d) 638 (Sask. C.A.), replacement value, second-hand sale price, and depreciation since new were taken as "guides" to the value of a rug. In *Yukon Southern Air Transport Ltd. v. The King*, [1942] Ex. C.R. 181, [1943] 1 D.L.R. 305, value was based on the purchase price plus the value of repairs and improvements.

34 *Reidy v. Fisher*, *supra*, footnote 33; *Nason v. Aubin* (1958), 16 D.L.R. (2d) 309 (N.B.S.C. App. Div.); *R. v. City Gas & Electric Corp. Ltd.*, [1959] Ex. C.R. 335. In *Goodine v. Maritime Lightning Rod Co. Ltd.* (1976), 15 N.B.R. (2d) 27 (S.C.), replacement cost of livestock was allowed, there being, presumably, no depreciation. Replacement cost was allowed in *Magna Electric & Computers Ltd. v. Speedway Express Ltd.* (1978), 91 D.L.R. (3d) 310 (N.S.S.C.T.D.); *Robertson v. Stang* (1997), 38 C.C.L.T. (2d) 62 (B.C.S.C.).

35 *The "Iron-Master"*, *supra*, footnote 32.

36 *The "Harmonides"*, *supra*, footnote 32.

37 *The "Columbus"* (1849), 3 W. Rob. 158, 166 E.R. 922. See *Liesbosch, Dredger (Owners of) v. Owners of S.S. Edison*, [1933] A.C. 449 (H.L.), at p. 462, where Lord Wright rejected this as an "arbitrary" rule. If the plaintiff recovers the full value of property, he cannot in addition recover the premium paid to insure it, nor even (it has been held) a portion of the premium in respect of a period after the loss: *Ship "Perene" v. "Maid of Scotland"* [1925] S.C.R. 1, [1925] 1 D.L.R. 574 *sub nom.* S.S. Perene v. Warren. It would seem, however, that property insured for a future period has a greater current value than uninsured property and that the plaintiff ought to receive compensation for that greater value.

38 See 1.1830 - 1.1850, *infra*.

strongly suggested, however, that a less generous interpretation was being given to the concept in practice. However this may be, the House of Lords asserted in *Admiralty Com'rs v. S.S. Chekiang*[39] and *Liesbosch v. Edison*[40] that no rule of practice or "rule of thumb" can override the basic duty of the court which is to give full compensation: "... the dominant rule of law is the principle of restitutio in integrum, and subsidiary rules can only be justified if they give effect to that rule".[41]

1.260 In the *Liesbosch* case, the defendant destroyed a dredger that was under contract to perform dredging work in Patras Harbour. The plaintiff, being threatened with penalties on contractual default, hired a substitute dredger at considerable cost in order to fulfill its contract. The case is chiefly known, oddly enough, as enunciating a restriction on the plaintiff's rights in holding that the extra cost incurred by reason of the plaintiff's lack of financial resources was too remote. The case is discussed elsewhere from this point of view.[42] But in the present context it is important as establishing in the plaintiff's favour that the damages may far exceed the market selling price or the "intrinsic value" of the ship. In the particular case, the House of Lords allowed a capital sum made up of the cost of a replacement dredger, plus the cost of adapting and transporting it to Patras, plus compensation for losses incurred in carrying out the particular dredging contract at Patras, together with interest on that capital sum. Lord Wright said the measure of damages in such cases is the value of the ship to the owner as a going concern.[43] "The figure of damages is to represent the capitalized value of the vessel as a profit-earning machine, not in the abstract but in view of the actual circumstances."[44] Lord Wright went on to warn against reliance on fixed rules even in the limited world of shipping:

> Many, varied and complex are the types of vessels and the modes of employment in which their owners will use them. Hence the difficulties constantly felt in defining rules as to the measure of damages. I think it impossible to lay down any universal formula. A ship of war, a supply ship, a lightship, a dredger employed by a public authority, a passenger liner, a trawler, a cable ship, a tug boat (to take a few instances), all may raise quite different questions before their true value can be ascertained.[45]

39 [1926] A.C. 637 (H.L.), at p. 643.

40 *Supra*, footnote 37.

41 *Liesbosch*, *supra*, at p. 463.

42 Overruled on this point in *Lagden v. O'Connor*, [2004] 1 All E.R. 277 (H.L.); see 15.330 - 15.390, *infra*.

43 The phrase was used in *The "Harmonides"* [1903] P. 1. *Liesbosch v. Edison* was followed by the Exchequer Court of Canada in *Steamship "Giovanni Amendola" v. Powell River Co. Ltd.*, [1959] Ex. C.R. 1, allowing the cost of hiring a substitute vessel as an element in assessing the value of a lost ship, and in *Hislop Estates Ltd. v. Western Oil Services Ltd.*, [1978] 2 W.W.R. 632 (B.C.S.C.) (present value allowed of lost future rents of building), and *Delorme v. Metcalfe Realty Co. Ltd.* (1967), 65 D.L.R. (2d) 564, [1968] 1 O.R. 124 (H.C.J.) ("real value of [damaged] premises to the owner as part of his working plant"). In *Ralston Purina of Canada Ltd. v. Whittaker* (1973), 6 N.B.R. (2d) 443 (S.C. App. Div.), the plaintiff's proposed use for property (livestock) was considered in assessing its value.

44 *Liesbosch v. Edison*, *supra*, footnote 37, at p. 464.

1.270 It is clear from these statements, and from the result in the *Liesbosch* case itself, that the plaintiff's individual circumstances are to be considered in assessing the value to the plaintiff of the lost vessel. The test used by Lord Wright appears to come close to allowing the sum the plaintiff would have demanded to sell the vessel to the defendant. Care must be taken in applying such a test, as Lord Wright recognized, to avoid overlap with compensation for loss of use, for if the plaintiff is supposed to foresee and accurately assess all the profits to be made from the use of the vessel, all the lost profits would be automatically included in the sum the plaintiff would demand to give up the vessel. Lord Wright made the point as follows:

> In assessing that value [to the owner as a going concern] regard must naturally be had to her pending engagements, either profitable or the reverse. The rule, however, obviously requires some care in its application; the figure of damage is to represent the capitalized value of the vessel as a profit-earning machine, not in the abstract but in view of the actual circumstances. The value of prospective freights cannot simply be added to the market value but ought to be taken into account in order to ascertain the total value for purpose of assessing the damage, since if it is merely added to the market value of a free ship, the owner will be getting pro tanto his damages twice over. The vessel cannot be earning in the open market, while fulfilling the pending charter or charters.[46]

At a later point in approving a case (*The "Pacuare"*[47]) that as Lord Wright described it, had awarded, in addition to the value of a sunken lightship, the cost of a substituted vessel for 366 days, Lord Wright said: "I should prefer to state that such extra cost was an element in assessing the loss of value to the owners of the lightship, though it may be no different result would follow from the difference in statement."[48] The context shows that Lord Wright approved the award on the assumption that the year's cost of a substituted vessel could be considered to be part of the value of the ship to the owner as a going concern. One can readily accept the proposition that the value of property to a person includes the costs involved in foregoing its use, but it is odd that Lord Wright should have chosen to bring this obscurely reported case into prominence to illustrate the proposition. First, the report of the case in the *Shipping Gazette*[49] shows that the plaintiff did not in fact incur the cost of a substituted ship, having a stand-by on hand which it put into use. This complicates the matter by raising the question of whether use of a stand-by vessel that would otherwise be idle can be considered a "cost" to the plaintiff. The question is discussed below in the context of loss of use of property,

45 *Liesbosch, supra*, at pp. 464-5.

46 *Liesbosch, supra*, at p. 464.

47 *Shipping Gazette*, December 6, 1912.

48 *Liesbosch v. Edison, supra*, footnote 37, at p. 467. This passage, with the reference to *The "Pacuare"* was quoted with approval in *"Giovanni Amendola" v. Powell River Co. Ltd., supra*, footnote 43.

49 The point also emerges from the account of the case in Roscoe, *The Measure of Damages in Actions of Maritime Collisions*, 3rd ed. (London, Stevens & Sons Ltd., 1929), pp. 42-3, which was evidently Lord Wright's source.

where it is concluded that putting property out of use can, in some circumstances, be reckoned as a cost to the owner.[50] It may be accepted then, that a rational lightship owner, even if it owned a stand-by ship, will include as part of the value of the lightship the cost of a substitute for the time it would take to obtain a replacement.

1.280 If the owner considered it necessary to incur the continuing expense of maintaining a stand-by ship at all times, it would presumably insist (if selling the lightship) on a price which would enable it to continue to maintain a perpetual stand-by. However, it seems plain that the limit of recovery on this basis must be the time during which a replacement ship could be secured, for it would be absurd for the owner to recover both the capital value of the ship (with interest from the date of destruction) and also the rental value of a replacement in perpetuity.[51] Thus, the 366-day period apparently allowed in *The "Pacuare"* has a distinctly odd appearance, for one supposes it to be longer than the period necessary to secure a replacement ship. The report in the *Shipping Gazette* indicates, however, that the sum allowed was much less than the cost of hire for the full year (the £1,537.4*s*. claimed on this account being reduced to a round sum of £500). The court, in upholding the award of £500, said merely that the registrar was right in giving "something as damages to represent the loss and expense they incurred" and that "such damages must be at large" and that a jury award of £500 would not have been set aside. The case is hardly authority therefore for allowing a full year's cost of hire in addition to the capital value. It would seem that Lord Wright's approval of the case when read in its context amounts to no more than approval of the proposition that the value of goods to an owner includes the cost of foregoing their use during the time necessary to secure a replacement. Other cases support this view.[52]

1.290 Where anticipated profits are included in the assessment of value they must be discounted for advance payment, for a rational owner would take this factor into account. Otherwise, if interest is awarded on the full value from the date of the wrong, there would be a double compensation.[53]

1.300 The price that an owner would demand to give up property will normally be related to the cost of securing an acceptable substitute. As stated earlier, damages may fall short of the cost of the replacement where the replacement exceeds the original property in value or where a cheaper substitute is available.[54] Where a satisfactory substitute is not available, damages will

50 See 1.2030 - 1.2140, *infra*.

51 See *Nason v. Aubin* (1958), 16 D.L.R. (2d) 309 (N.B.S.C. App. Div.).

52 See *"Giovanni Amendola" v. Powell River Co. Ltd., supra*, footnote 43; *Clyde Navigation Trustees v. Bowring Steamship Co.* (1929), 34 Ll. L.R. 319 (Ct. of Sess.).

53 *Lister (Ronald Elwyn) Ltd. v. Dayton Tire Canada Ltd.* (1985), 52 O.R. (2d) 88 (C.A.), at p. 127, citing this passage. See *Bouchard v. Registrar, North Alberta Land Registration District* (1959), 27 W.W.R. 433 (Alta. S.C.), where the value of minerals was assessed by taking the present value of future royalty payments. On the award of interest, see 7.330 - 7.1000, *infra*.

54 *Ucktos v. Mazzaretta*, [1956] 1 Lloyd's Rep. 209.

include the cost of adapting the closest obtainable approximation. Thus in *A-1 Rentals Sales & Service Ltd. v. Alberta Arches & Beams Ltd.*[55] the cost of reconditioning a replacement was allowed, and in *Clyde Navigation Trustees v. Bowring Steamship Co.*[56] where the defendant destroyed a vessel of the plaintiff's described as a hopper digger barge, the measure of damages was said to be the "price which the pursuers would have had to pay for a barge and the cost which they would have had to incur in making it suitable for use as a hopper digger barge."[57] This measure is again consistent with the test of value suggested earlier, that is, the sum which a rational plaintiff would have demanded to give up the property.

1.310 The *Liesbosch* case illustrates that the value of property to an owner may exceed its intrinsic value. Another illustration of this principle is supplied by the Ontario case of *Thiele & Wesmar Ltd. v. Rod Service (Ottawa) Ltd.*[58] where a mail carrier lost a parcel containing accounting records. The plaintiff incurred fees of $1,200 to replace the records, and this sum was held to be recoverable, although the lost papers had been insured for $25, and presumably had no commercial value at all. The Ontario Court of Appeal said: "It is common knowledge that a very wide variety, indeed, of articles are the subject-matter of carriage by registered mail and that the damages arising from the loss of many of such articles in a reasonably foreseeable manner may far exceed the intrinsic value of the actual article insured."[59] It is possible to explain the result of this case either as a recognition that the value of the goods to the plaintiff exceeded their market value, or as a case of compensation for loss of use of property (the expense being incurred by way of mitigation of the larger loss that would presumably have been incurred by failing to replace the records). On either basis it is submitted the case is rightly decided. The decision of the court, that the loss claimed was not too remote, is consistent with the usual view that the full value of an article lost or destroyed is recoverable even though the defendant had no reason to know how valuable the article was. In *City of Guelph Board of Light & Heat Com'rs v. United Dairy & Poultry Co-operative Ltd.*[60] where the defendant destroyed the plaintiff's hydro-electricity poles, the damages included not only the intrinsic value of the poles destroyed, but also an allowance for the cost of installation. The question of the measurement of such costs is discussed below.[61]

---

55 (1966), 60 D.L.R. (2d) 4 (Alta. S.C. App. Div.).

56 *Supra*, footnote 52; *Casswell v. Mathew Moody & Sons Co.*, [1926] 1 W.W.R. 113 (Sask. C.A.).

57 *Supra*, footnote 52, at p. 320. See *Nicholais v. Dominion Express Co.* (1914), 18 D.L.R. 464 (B.C.C.A.) (cost of replacing architect's plans not allowed; the plans were no longer needed for use as plans).

58 (1962), 45 D.L.R. (2d) 503, [1964] 2 O.R. 347 (C.A.).

59 *Supra*, at p. 505 D.L.R.

60 (1966), 57 D.L.R. (2d) 385, [1966] 2 O.R. 467 (Co. Ct.), affd D.L.R. *loc. cit.* p. 387*n*, O.R. *loc. cit.* p. 469*n* (C.A.).

61 See 1.2330, *infra*.

1.320 Another case of value to the plaintiff exceeding market value is *Tremear v. Park Town Motor Hotels Ltd.*,[62] where the defendant caused the loss of keys. The plaintiff was allowed the cost of replacing the locks and cutting new keys. The court cited the *Liesbosch* case and relied also on *Buchanan v. Cooke*,[63] where the Saskatchewan Court of Appeal had said that where an award of market value would not afford due compensation, an owner could recover "the value of the property to himself", though not "a fanciful price which he may for special reasons place upon it".[64]

1.330 Similar considerations apply to the cost of transport where a substitute is available only at a place removed from the place where the property would have been if the wrong had not been done. An allowance for transport was made in *The "Liesbosch"*[65] and in *O'Hanlan v. Great Western Ry. Co.*[66] It was held that the allowance for cost of transport should include an element of profit to the importer, for as Blackburn J. said, "the importer's profit... is an element in the market price of goods".[67] The cost to a person of procuring a substitute may consist of expenditure of time as well as of money. Thus in *Lesters Leather & Skin Co., Ltd. v. Home & Overseas Brokers, Ltd.*,[68] a disappointed buyer of snakeskins was entitled to measure their value by the price at which he would have sold them in England, not by the price at which they could have been bought in India. The court expressly made reference to the cost to the buyer of searching: "I cannot say that the buyers are bound to go hunting the globe to find out where they can get skins".[69]

1.340 Where the plaintiff's intention, had the wrong not occurred, was to sell the property, the cost of procuring a substitute will not always be the appropriate measure. Thus, if the defendant destroys property that the plaintiff intends to sell for $1,000 at a market 100 miles away (the cost of transport being $1 a mile), it would be wrong to add the cost of transport to the market price, for this would over-compensate the plaintiff by $200.[70] Had the wrong not been done, the plaintiff would have realized only $900 from his property. She

---

[62] [1982] 4 W.W.R. 444 (Sask. Q.B.). See also *Chappel v. Barati* (1982), 30 C.C.L.T. 137 (Ont. H.C.J.) (loss of trees); *Cancer Control Agency of British Columbia v. Fisher Scientific* (1989), 14 A.C.W.S. (3d) 282 (B.C.S.C); *Mackenzie v. Baker* (2001), 56 O.R. (3d) 716 (S.C.J.), affd 65 O.R. (3d) 319 (C.A.) (research materials).

[63] (1958), 11 D.L.R. (2d) 638 (Sask. C.A.).

[64] *Supra*, at p. 640, quoting 17 Corp. Jur., p. 907, para. 197.

[65] [1933] A.C. 449 (H.L.).

[66] (1865), 6 B. & S. 484, 122 E.R. 1274. See also *Ewbank v. Nutting* (1849), 7 C.B. 797, 137 E.R. 316; *Hasell v. Bagot, Shakes & Lewis, Ltd.* (1911), 13 C.L.R. 374; *McCain Foods Ltd. v. Grand Falls Industries Ltd.* (1991), 80 D.L.R. (4th) 252, 116 N.B.R. (2d) 22 (C.A.).

[67] *O'Hanlan v. Great Western, supra*, footnote 66, at p. 492. A similar allowance was made in *Ship "Perene" v. "Maid of Scotland"* [1925] S.C.R. 1, [1925] 1 D.L.R. 574 *sub nom.* S.S. Perene v. Warren, where the insurance premium was included as part of the true value of the goods at their destination.

[68] (1948), 64 T.L.R. 569 (C.A.).

[69] *Supra*.

[70] See *Wertheim v. Chicoutimi Pulp Co.*, [1911] A.C. 301 (P.C.), at p. 316; *Montreal Cotton & Wool Waste Co. v. Canada Steamship Lines* (1920), 60 S.C.R. 442, 55 D.L.R. 634; *B. Shragge Iron & Metal Co. v. Western Hide & Junk Co.*, [1923] 3 D.L.R. 1 (Alta. S.C. App. Div.).

would, acting rationally, have accepted $900 to give it up. On the other hand, if the plaintiff intended to use the property, $1,100 is the appropriate measure, for that is what the plaintiff would have to pay for a replacement.[71] The difference is analogous to that between buying price and selling price discussed above, where it was also suggested that an owner of property for use should be entitled to a higher measure of damages than an owner of property for sale.[72]

1.350 Where events occur between the date of the plaintiff's acquisition of the property and its destruction that alter the value of the property, it naturally follows from the attempt to assess the value at the time of the destruction, that the events will be taken into account. Inflation is an obvious instance of increase in value (in terms of money) and in an asessment of current values based upon the plaintiff's acquisition cost, inflation must be taken into account.[73] Again, if a change in the law alters the value of property after the plaintiff's acquisition, it is the later value, whether higher or lower than the acquisition cost, that is relevant. Thus, in *Martin v. London County Council*[74] where purchase tax had been imposed on jewellery since the plaintiff's acquisition of it, it was held that it was the value after imposition of tax that was relevant, since this was the measure of the cost to the plaintiff of acquiring a replacement.

1.360 There is little authority on the problem of what is called "sentimental value". It may be that the plaintiff would not have sold his pet dog or his mother's locket at any price, but this does not entitle him to infinite damages. References to market value in the older cases suggest that a value entirely idiosyncratic to the plaintiff would be ignored, and it cannot be satisfactory to measure damages by the price the plaintiff would in fact have demanded for the property, not only because of the unreliability of the testimony on such an issue, but also because of the apparent inequity of compensating persons who have lost similar property at different rates according to the strength of their sentiments. In *Mason v. Westside Cemeteries*,[74a] nominal damages only were awarded for the value of parents' cremated ashes.

1.370 In *Clarke v. Fullerton*,[75] the defendant had converted a telescope that had been given the plaintiff's father by the British government. The defendant's act of conversion consisted of selling the instrument for $35. The jury

[71] See McCormick, *Handbook on the Law of Damages* (St. Paul, West Publishing Co., 1935), p. 182, citing *Watt v. Nevada Central Ry. Co.*, 44 P. 423, vard 46 P. 52, 23 Nev. 154 (1896, S.C. Nevada), petition for rehearing denied 46 P. 726; *Chicago G.W. Ry. Co. v. Gitchell*, 95 Ill. App. 1 (1901); *McGilvra v. Minneapolis, St. Paul & Sault Ste. Marie Ry. Co.*, 159 N.W. 854, 35 N.D. 275 (1916, North Dakota S.C.).

[72] See 1.90, *supra*.

[73] See footnote 34, *supra*.

[74] [1947] K.B. 628.

[74a] (1996), 135 D.L.R. (4th) 361, 29 C.C.L.T. (2d) 125 (Ont. Ct. (Gen. Div.)).

[75] (1871), 8 N.S.R. 348 (S.C. App. Div.). In *McNair v. Collins* (1912), 6 D.L.R. 510, 27 O.L.R. 44 (Div. Ct.), $125 was awarded for the loss of a mongrel dog to which the plaintiff was said to be attached. The court stressed also the usefulness of the dog as a farm and watch dog.

awarded damages of $350. The Nova Scotia Appeal Division held that the damages were excessive. Wilkins J. said: "The mere *pretium affectionis*, or ideal estimate of the plaintiff or of her father, having relation to the circumstance which induced the gift of the instrument to the latter by the British Government, is too vague and uncertain to form our measure of value."[76] On the other hand, the court rejected the $35 and the (presumably similar) appraised value that had been made for probate purposes: "We cannot accept as a standard of value what it brought at the private sale, and the appraisement returned in to the Probate office is very far from a satisfactory test when applied to such an instrument as this."[77] The figure thought to be proper lay between the two figures, approximating, it would seem, a generous estimation of replacement value:

> If the instrument called at the trial, and described in the pleadings as a telescope was, what it probably was, a portable ship's spy-glass of the most expensive kind, still I should not be satisfied to let the defendant remain subject to the damages found, for, in the case supposed, I cannot conceive that £20 sterling would not equal the true value. On the whole, I am of opinion that in the exercise of our control over the verdict, we should suggest a reduction in damages from the sum found so that the amount should stand at $100; and that a new trial on the ground of excessive damages alone should be ordered, if the suggestion be declined by the plaintiff.[78]

Since the plaintiff was not a mariner, and would be unlikely to purchase an actual replacement, the decision could be said to go some limited way towards compensating the plaintiff's sentimental loss. In *Jennings v. Wolfe*,[79] no sentimental damages were allowed for loss of a bear-skin, the court distinguishing *Clarke v. Fullerton* as a case involving deliberate wrongdoing.

1.380 The court's caution in openly recognizing the plaintiff's claim to sentimental damages is, it is submitted, soundly based. Compensation has been awarded for injured feelings caused by breach of contract[80] and in some cases this would offer a means of protecting sentimental value.[81] But here too caution against large awards seems desirable, for the cost of expected liability

---

[76] *Clarke v. Fullerton*, *supra*, footnote 75, at p. 358.

[77] *Clarke v. Fullerton*, *supra*, at pp. 357-8.

[78] *Clarke v. Fullerton*, *supra*, at p. 358. See also *Raymond v. United States Fire Ins. Co.*, [1973] S.C.R. 522, 27 D.L.R. (3d) 53 (insurer liable to pay insured value of unique article); *Maritime Aircraft Overhaul & Repair Ltd. v. Savoie* (1980), 30 N.B.R. (2d) 451 (Q.B.T.D.) ($1,000 allowed for plaintiff's sense of loss at damaged car); *Scobie v. Wing*, [1992] 2 W.W.R. 514, 63 B.C.L.R. (2d) 76 (C.A.). Sentimental value is excluded in expropriation cases: *Raja Vyricherla Narayana Gajapatiraju v. Revenue Divisional Officer, Vizagapatam*, [1939] A.C. 302 (P.C.), at p. 312; *Diggon-Hibben, Ltd. v. The King*, [1949] S.C.R. 712 at p. 714, [1949] 4 D.L.R. 785 at p. 786.

[79] [1950] 3 D.L.R. 442 (Alta. S.C.). But see *Chappel v. Barati* (1982), 30 C.C.L.T. 137 (Ont. H.C.J.), and *Rawson v. Maher* (1982), 15 Man. R. (2d) 6 (C.A.) (value to owner of car exceeding market value).

[80] See 3.1310 - 3.1470, *infra*.

[81] See *Newell v. Canadian Pacific Airlines, Ltd.* (1976), 74 D.L.R. (3d) 574, 14 O.R. (2d) 752 (Co. Ct.); *Ferguson v. Birchmount Boarding Kennels Ltd.* (2006), 79 O.R. (3d) 681 (S.C.J. (Div. Ct.)).

will in the long run be reflected in the contract price of the goods or services sold. Where the wrongdoing is deliberate, there may be a case for punitive or aggravated damages.[82]

3. Value Added to Property by Defendant

1.390 Where a wrongdoer adds value to the plaintiff's property, the plaintiff would be put in a better position than he was originally in if he were entitled to recover damages equal to the improved value. If a great artist converts a piece of scrap canvas and paints on it a masterpiece, the owner of the canvas would surely be over-compensated if he were to recover the value of the painting.[83] In the commercial context where the defendant puts the plaintiff's goods into saleable condition, the goods may be worth far more after the defendant's dealing with them than they were worth in the plaintiff's hands originally.

1.400 Problems of this sort have arisen in mining cases where the defendant wrongfully takes coal from the plaintiff's land. The value of the coal when severed and raised and collected in saleable form is always very much more than the value of the coal in the ground. If the plaintiff were to recover the value of the coal at the pit-head, he would seem to be over-compensated, for he would have had his coal extracted at the defendant's expense.

1.410 In a number of early cases culminating in *Martin v. Porter*,[84] it was held that the trespasser was liable to pay the full value of the severed coal with no allowance for severing. This conclusion was based on the principle, later called by Lord Blackburn "a technical rule",[85] that since the coal becomes a chattel only at the time of severance, an action for trespass to goods can come into existence only at that time, so that at the earliest point at which the plaintiff can complain of appropriation of "his goods" they already have acquired the value of severed coal.

1.420 This strict view had the effect of over-compensating the plaintiff by giving him the benefit of the defendant's work. Where the trespass is deliberate, it might be possible to support such a result as a kind of punishment. It is well recognized that one of the reasons for which punitive damages may be assessed is to deprive the defendant of a profit from wrongdoing.[86] However, even on such a basis, the technical rule laid down in *Martin v. Porter* might

[82] See 11.10 - 11.480, *infra*. And see *Mason v. Westside Cemeteries Ltd.* (1996), 135 D.L.R. (4th) 361 (Ont. Ct. (Gen. Div.)).

[83] On the measure of damages under the remedial provisions of the *Copyright Act*, see 5.800, *infra*.

[84] (1839), 5 M. & W. 351, 151 E.R. 149. The strict rule was applied to a case where the defendant was merely negligent in *Last Chance Mining Co. v. American Boy Mining Co.* (1904), 2 M.M.C. 150 (B.C.S.C.), and in *Shewish v. MacMillan Bloedel Ltd* (1990), 74 D.L.R. (4th) 345, [1991] 1 W.W.R. 27 (B.C.C.A.) (highly culpable negligence). The rule was applied to deliberate cutting of timber in *Union Bank of Canada v. Rideau Lumber Co.* (1902), 4 O.L.R. 721 (C.A.); *Laursen v. McKinnon* (1912), 4 D.L.R. 718 (B.C.S.C.), and *Faulkner v. Greer* (1907), 16 O.L.R. 123 (C.A.), affd 40 S.C.R. 399.

[85] *Livingstone v. Rawyards Coal Co.* (1880), 5 App. Cas. 25 (H.L.), at p. 39.

[86] See 11.120, 11.280, 11.290, *infra*.

be excessive, for in calculating the profit made by a wrongdoer his actual costs are taken into account, whereas the rule in *Martin v. Porter* has the effect of depriving the defendant of more than the profit, namely, the full value of the severed coal.

1.430 Where the trespass is inadvertent, the rule in *Martin v. Porter* seems even harder to justify and subsequent 19th century cases confined the application of the rule to the case of deliberate trespass. Thus, in *Jegon v. Vivian*,[87] it was said that the plaintiff ought to recover the fair value of the unmined coal. Later cases have awarded the value of the severed coal minus the costs of severance.[88] McGregor has pointed out that the fair value of unmined coal, that is, the price that a reasonable miner would pay, would not include the miner's profit, whereas the value of the severed coal minus the cost of severance appears to include the profit.[89] McGregor supports the higher measure on the ground that the plaintiff and not the defendant ought to be entitled to the profit. Whether there is a difference of principle between the two approaches, however, appears to depend on what elements are to be included in calculating the costs of severance. In calculating the costs to a miner of mining a few hundred tons of the plaintiff's coal, a fair allocation must be made of a portion of the general overhead costs of operating the mining enterprise, including some element representing a return on capital investment.[90] It is common to include in the definition of costs the value of a forgone opportunity, and certainly any attempt to calculate what it would have cost the plaintiff to mine the coal would have to take account of the cost of capital investment, including the forgone return on capital from alternative investments. On this basis, therefore, the cost of severing the plaintiff's coal will properly include an element of compensation to the defendant for the use of plant and equipment.

1.440 This analysis suggests that there may, after all, be no difference in principle between measuring the damages by the fair value of the unmined coal and measuring damages by the defendant's net profit. The plaintiff's damages would be measured by the highest price that a rational person in the defendant's position would have paid for the right to take the plaintiff's coal.

1.450 Whenever the defendant has misappropriated the plaintiff's property, the plaintiff has, in effect, been deprived of an opportunity to sell the property. If specific remedies are excluded, the most the law can do after the fact is to compensate in money. In measuring the appropriate amount of money it is

[87] (1871), L.R. 6 Ch. App. 742. See also *Wood v. Morewood* (1841), 3 Q.B. 440*n*, 114 E.R. 575; *Hilton v. Woods* (1867), L.R. 4 Eq. 432; *Townend v. Askern Coal Co.*, [1934] 1 Ch. 463; *Adams Powell River Co. v. Canadian Puget Sound Co.* (1914), 17 D.L.R. 591 (B.C.S.C.) (defendant credited with cost of severance, but not cost of transport); *Chew Lumber Co. v. Howe Sound Co.* (1913), 13 D.L.R. 735 (B.C.C.A.).

[88] *Ashton v. Stock* (1877), 6 Ch. D. 719 (H.C.J.); *Re United Merthyr Collieries* (1872), L.R. 15 Eq. 46.

[89] *McGregor on Damages*, 16th ed. (London, Sweet & Maxwell, 1997), §1409.

[90] In *Re United Merthyr Collieries, supra*, footnote 88, Bacon V.C. held that profit was to be excluded, but the case turned on the interpretation of the words "actual cost" in a prior order.

suggested that it is not unreasonable to take the highest price that the defendant would rationally have paid. This question is discussed in a later chapter.[91] There, several kinds of cases are collected that proceed upon the basis that the defendant ought not to be better off by committing a tort than she would have been by buying the right to act as she has done. The principle is compensatory, not punitive, but assumes in the plaintiff's favour that the highest price payable by a rational defendant would have been agreed upon — a reasonable assumption, it is submitted, in view of the fact that it is the defendant's wrong that has prevented certain knowledge of just what bargain would have been struck.

1.460 Waiver of tort must also be considered in this context, for it would be undesirable for the plaintiff's recovery to vary according to the form of the action. The principle of waiver of tort permits a plaintiff to require the defendant to account for the profit made from tortious conduct on the fictitious supposition that the tort has been retrospectively authorized by the plaintiff and the defendant called upon to account as an authorized agent. If the argument made earlier is accepted, to the effect that in the calculations of the defendant's cost of earning the profit it is proper to include an element representing a fair return on the defendant's capital investment, the proper measure of recovery will in principle be the same whether based on "fair value" of the plaintiff's asset in its original form, the value in the defendant's hands minus the defendant's costs, or on the defendant's "profits" (the plaintiff waiving the tort). This seems a convenient solution and one that does justice to both parties.

1.470 In *Livingstone v. Rawyards Coal Co.*,[92] the plaintiff owned only a small piece of land that could not practicably be separately mined. The defendant, an adjacent landowner, tortiously mined the plaintiff's coal. The House of Lords found the value of the coal at pit-head, minus the costs of severing and raising it, to be £500. However, only £171 was awarded, on the theory that this was the reasonable price of a royalty authorizing the taking of the coal. Lord Blackburn stressed that the principle was one of compensation for the fair value of the unmined coal, and that the reasonable royalty was taken as evidence of that value. No indication is given as to the calculation of the cost of severing and raising the coal, but it seems unlikely that any element of return on the defendant's capital was included. Allowance for this element might, therefore, reduce the defendant's net profit to the sum awarded. If, even after allowance for this element, the defendant's net profit were £500, it is submitted that the plaintiff should recover this sum.

1.480 It may be objected that if local royalty rates amounted to only £171, the plaintiff would be over-compensated by recovering the larger sum; he might indeed consider himself lucky to have got anything, for his interest was as a

[91] See 9.70 - 9.130, *infra*.

[92] *Supra*, footnote 85, followed in *Townend v. Askern Coal Co., supra*, footnote 87, and *Montreal Trust Co. v. Williston Wildcatters Corp.* (2004), 243 D.L.R. (4th) 317 (Sask. C.A.); *Freyberg v. Fletcher Challenge Oil and Gas Inc.*, [2007] 10 W.W.R. 133 (Alta. Q.B.).

practical matter only saleable to the adjacent landowner who might have refused to buy it. We do not know on what evidence the court concluded that reasonable royalties amounted to only £171. It is suggested, however, that rates payable by mine owners before establishing their mines ought not to be conclusive of the question of what rate a reasonable miner would pay for mining rights in land immediately adjacent to land already being worked. The presence of equipment and facilities on the spot must reduce the extra cost of mining the land in question. It has been suggested above that a reasonable mine owner would pay up to the full amount of the net profit (including in the calculation of net profit an allowance for the use of capital). The argument that the plaintiff should consider himself fortunate to recover anything lies ill in the mouth of a trespasser. Since it is the defendant's wrong that prevents certain knowledge of what bargain would have been made, it does not seem unjust to assume in the plaintiff's favour that he would have made the best bargain to which a rational defendant would have agreed, that is, that the defendant would have paid such a price as would have yielded a marginal net benefit after taking account of all costs (including a fair return on investment).

1.490 In the New South Wales case of *Bilambil-Terranora Pty. Ltd. v. Tweed Shire Council*,[93] where the defendant municipality had wrongfully taken the plaintiff's gravel for a period of two years, it was held that the plaintiff was entitled to recover the value of the gravel taken (measured by its value after severance minus the costs of severing), despite the fact that the plaintiff would not, and could not without a licence, have extracted the gravel itself. Mahoney J.A. said: " . . . the fact that the owner of property does not desire to use it, or to use it to the best economic advantage, has not meant that its value is less than it would be in the hands of one who regarded it differently."[94] On the question of the licence requirement Reynolds J.A. said, by way of example, that if cutting timber were illegal, a tortfeasor would still have to pay the value of the wood, even though the owner could not have profited.[95]

1.500 Mahoney J.A. added that it would be absurd if a defendant should benefit by reason of his act being illegal as well as wrong vis-á-vis the plaintiff. The defendant had argued, relying on the *Livingstone* case, that the plaintiff should recover only a royalty fee of less than the defendant's profit. The court, in awarding the full value of the gravel (with, as has been noted, an allowance for the cost of extraction), distinguished this aspect of the *Livingstone* case as depending on the special fact that there the coal was, as a practical matter, only saleable to the defendant. As has been suggested, there seems no reason why, even in such a case, the wrongdoer should not pay the full value of what he has taken.

1.510 The technical rule that formerly prevented the defendant from deducting

93 [1980] 1 N.S.W.L.R. 465 (C.A.).
94 *Supra*, at p. 494.
95 *Supra*, at p. 479.

the costs of severing coal was never applied to other costs that added to its value, such as raising the coal or transporting it to a place where it could be sold.[96] Here again it would seem that the appropriate deduction should be all of the defendant's costs including return on capital and this, it is suggested, is the method of calculation best reconcilable with the principle of compensation for fair value at the point of conversion, and with the calculation of what a rational person in the defendant's position would have paid for the goods before performing the acts that added to their value.[96a]

1.520 In *O'Hanlan v. Great Western Ry. Co.*,[97] the court had to calculate the value of goods that had been lost at a place where there was no market. It was held that the value was more than the sum of the market price at a place where the goods could be obtained and the cost of transportation. An element was to be added to represent the carrier's reasonable profit. Similarly, where a deduction falls to be made from a known value at the point of destination in order to determine the actual value at the place of departure, as where the defendant transports goods to a place where they can be sold,[98] an element falls to be deducted, in calculating the cost of shipment, to represent the shipper's reasonable return on capital.

1.530 In an early Canadian case, *Morton v. McDowell*,[99] the defendant had converted the plaintiff's logs and sawn them into lumber. It was held that the plaintiff was entitled to the value of only the unsawn logs. This was not a case in which the court was troubled with the technical rule applicable in the mining cases, since the logs were already chattels at the time the defendant took possession of them. In *Blazicevic v. B.C. Lumber Industries Ltd.*,[100] the British Columbia Supreme Court allowed only the plaintiff's actual loss on the inadvertent cutting of his timber. However, in *Wasson v. California Standard Co.*,[101] damages for cutting down trees were measured by the value of the timber as sawn fence posts. There were strong overtones of the punitive in the judgment, and exemplary damages were also awarded. It is submitted that the primary measure of damages adopted by the court can only be supported as a form of exemplary damages. Allowance for improvements made to a car by a wrongdoer was made in *Munro v. Willmott*.[102] On the other hand, there are contrary suggestions in some Canadian cases.[103] Some of these may be explained as assuming that no net benefit was conferred on the plaintiff,[104] or as involving goods for personal use where it was

---

[96] See *Morgan v. Powell* (1842), 3 Q.B. 278, 114 E.R. 513.

[96a] This paragraph was cited with approval in *Montreal Trust Co. v. Williston Wildcatters Corp.*, [2004] 3 W.W.R. 574 (Q.B.), at para. 51, affd 243 D.L.R. (4th) 317 (Sask. C.A.).

[97] (1865), 6 B. & S. 484, 122 E.R. 1274.

[98] See *Peruvian Guano v. Dreyfus Bros.*, [1892] A.C. 166 (H.L.).

[99] (1850), 7 U.C.Q.B. 338 (C.A.). See also *Scott v. McAlpine* (1857), 6 U.C.C.P. 302; *Wournell v. Rowlings*, [1965-69] 5 N.S.R. 398 (S.C.T.D.); *Grenn v. Brampton Poultry Co.* (1959), 18 D.L.R. (2d) 9 (Ont. C.A.) (wholesale price only allowed of goods converted).

[100] (1955), 15 W.W.R. 317 (B.C.S.C.).

[101] (1964), 47 D.L.R. (2d) 71 (Alta. S.C. App. Div.).

[102] [1949] 1 K.B. 295.

unreasonable to require the plaintiff to pay for unrequested inprovements.[105] In the absence of such reasons it is submitted that an allowance for improvements should be made.

1.540 The cases discussed in the preceding paragraphs, making an allowance to the wrongdoer for the cost to the wrongdoer of adding value to the plaintiff's property, are not easy to reconcile with the general rule that an owner cannot be made to pay for unrequested benefits.[106] There is some indication of a tendency in the law of restitution to take a view more favourable to the person who improves another's property, particularly when the person acts under a mistake as to title.[107]

1.550 It is very desirable for the two branches of the law to be consistent, for it would be anomalous for an owner to obtain a substantially better remedy by resorting to self-help or by suing in detinue for specific delivery[108] than she would obtain by an action for damages. In those cases, therefore, where an allowance is properly made for the defendant's improvements in calculating damages, it is suggested that the law of restitution should allow the improver to recover if the plaintiff regains possession of the goods. It does not necessarily follow that every improvement must in all circumstances be compensated. Where the owner is in possession of goods for personal use, it will usually not be just to compel her to pay for unrequested benefits. Commercial benefits, however, ought usually to be paid for, since they represent a pecuniary gain to the recipient, and it is no imposition upon her to compel repayment of the equivalent money value. Saw logs represent, to their owner, a certain money sum. In *Morton v. McDowell*[109] it was found to be

103 *Gallagher v. Ketchum & Co.* (1912), 2 D.L.R. 871, 21 O.W.R. 696 (Div. Ct.) (but the conversion took place after the improvement); *Faulkner v. Greer* (1907), 16 O.L.R. 123 (C.A.), affd 40 S.C.R. 399, though relied on in *Gallagher v. Ketchum*, is equivocal, as it concerned entitlement to a fund representing the property, and not damages as such, counsel arguing that the law as to trover trespass and conversion was beside the point (see 16 O.L.R. at p. 126). There are difficulties where goods are converted after improvement by the improver or a third person. The measure of damages is admittedly usually the value of the goods at the time of conversion, but it is suggested that, by the more general principle of damage assessment, the plaintiff should only recover such a sum as would put him in the position he would have occupied had he sought to sue the improver immediately, for this would have been his position if the wrong had not been done.

104 In *Faulkner v. Greer, supra*, footnote 103, at p. 130, Meredith J.A. said: "It may be hard upon the defendants that they should lose the cost of transportation... It would be harder still upon an owner if it were a case in which he would be obliged to bring his goods back again at his own expense."

105 *Gallagher v. Ketchum & Co., supra*, footnote 103 (automobile). The court said, at p. 874, that a person making unrequested improvements should not improve his legal position by subsequently converting the property. See 1.550, *infra*.

106 *Falcke v. Scottish Imperial Insurance Co.* (1866), 34 Ch. D. 234 at p. 248.

107 See Maddaugh and McCamus, *The Law of Restitution* (Aurora, Canada Law Book, 1990), pp. 281-306.

108 In *Glenwood Lumber Co. Ltd. v. Phillips*, [1904] A.C. 405 (P.C.), no allowance was made for improvements. Contrary suggestions, however, appear in *Peruvian Guano Co. v. Dreyfus Bros. & Co.*, [1892] A.C. 166 (H.L.), at p. 176, and *Greenwood v. Bennett*, [1973] Q.B. 195 (C.A.), at pp. 201 and 203.

109 (1850), 7 U.C.Q.B. 338 (C.A.).

£18. If they are sawn into lumber that is worth £30, the plaintiff cannot complain if he recovers damages of £18, or, having gained possession of the sawn lumber, if he were required to pay £12 to the converter. It would be altogether different if the wrongdoer cut down and sawed up a favourite tree that shaded its owner's garden. Even though the sawn lumber had a greater commercial value than the original tree, it would be unreasonable to expect the owner to pay for it. These problems are addressed by the law of restitution in terms of whether the improver has acted "officiously" and whether a "benefit" has been conferred on the owner.[110] Further discussion of them is beyond the scope of the present work.

4. Value Added by the Plaintiff

1.560 Where the plaintiff manufactures at a cost of one dollar goods that can be sold for ten dollars or where the plaintiff buys for one dollar goods that can be resold for ten dollars, the question arises of the proper measure of damages where the goods are lost or destroyed through the defendant's wrong. The question is not answered by saying that the plaintiff recovers the value of the goods, without a consideration of how value is to be determined.

1.570 The basic principle of damage assessment, that the plaintiff should be put in as good a position as would have been occupied if the wrong had not be done, appears to suggest measurement of damages in the examples given by the cost to the plaintiff of replacement. Suppose the case of a retailer who buys china vases for one dollar and sells them for ten dollars. If a customer carelessly knocks a vase off the shelf and destroys it, the retailer appears to be fully compensated by damages of one dollar plus any associated costs of ordering and replacement.[111] Assuming that there was sufficient stock to meet customers' demands,[112] the retailer has not lost a sale. The customer has not promised to buy the vase, and it seems consequently that the retailer would be over-compensated by the award of ten dollars.[113]

1.580 Some cases have, however, awarded damages based on the selling price of the property.[114] The question was discussed by the Ontario Court of Appeal in *Dor-Al's Specialty Shoppe Ltd. v. Town of Kapuskasing*[115] where stock-

[110] See Goff and Jones, *The Law of Restitution*, 6th ed. (London, Sweet & Maxwell, 2002), pp. 229-40; and Maddaugh and McCamus, *op. cit.*, footnote 107, at p. 741 *et seq.*

[111] *Mulholland & Tedd, Ltd. v. Baker*, [1939] 3 All E.R. 253 (K.B.); *Jackson v. Spector* (1951), 4 W.W.R. (N.S.) 286 (Sask. C.A.); *Furness v. Adrium Industries Pty. Ltd.*, [1996] 1 V.R. 668 (S.C. Vict.), citing this passage at pp. 681-2.

[112] If demand exceeds supply so that the plaintiff loses a sale because of the defendant's wrong, the higher figure would be appropriate.

[113] In *Lister (Ronald Elwyn) Ltd. v. Dayton Tire Canada Ltd.* (1985), 52 O.R. (2d) 88 (C.A.), the Ontario Court of Appeal held that acquisition cost to the retailer was, in principle, the proper measure.

[114] *Kullberg's Furniture Ltd. v. Flin Flon Hotel Co. Ltd.* (1958), 16 D.L.R. (2d) 270 (Man. C.A.) (but the court expressly said that loss of profit was not necessarily to be allowed, and stressed the cost to the plaintiff of disposing of the damaged goods); *Randall's Paints Ltd. v. Tanner* (1969), 4 D.L.R. (3d) 652, [1969] 2 O.R. 169 (H.C.J.); *Sony Computer Entertainment UK Ltd. v. Cinram Logistics UK Ltd.*, [2008] EWCA Civ. 955 (burden of proof that sale not lost on wrongdoer).

in-trade had been damaged by fire. The trial judge based his award on the "tagged price" but reduced it by forty per cent to allow for the possibility of clearance sales at reduced value and for what he called "obsolescence". This brought the amount allowed to a figure only about seven per cent more than the actual cash cost of the goods to the plaintiff, a difference that could be accounted for by reordering costs and costs of disposing of the damaged stock.[116] Further, Howland J.A., by referring to the fact that the stock was fast moving and that it could not be immediately replaced,[117] implied that the plaintiff might have suffered some loss of sales at normal retail prices. It is submitted, therefore, that the case is not inconsistent with the view expressed in the preceding paragraph.

1.590 In *Banco de Portugal v. Waterlow & Sons*,[118] the following dictum of Lord Atkin appears: "If [a man] manufactures for 1*d.* articles which can sell for 6*d.*, the measure of damages against the wrongdoer is 6*d.*, not 1*d.*"[119] The dictum must, however, be read in its context, where the wrong being considered is not destruction of the plaintiff's goods, but such a wrong as does deprive the plaintiff of a sale. Thus, Lord Atkin continues: "So if he was by fraud induced to promise to deliver 500 of the 6*d.* articles so that the contract could be enforced by an innocent holder of the contract, it appears to me that on well established authority the damages would be 12*l.* 10*s.*, not 2*l.* 1*s.* 8*d.*"[120] Measuring damages by the selling price of the goods is justified, it is suggested, only where the plaintiff can show that in the absence of the wrong there would have been a sale at the selling price.

1.600 A striking instance of a difference between manufacturing cost and sale value is supplied by the case, that was before the court in *Banco de Portugal v. Waterlow*, of paper money. The cost of manufacture is small but the face value may be enormous. In the case the defendant, an English printer, had contracted with the plaintiff, a Portuguese issuing bank, to print paper money. In breach of contract, the defendant allowed unauthorized persons to gain possession of Portuguese banknotes. The defendant argued that the plaintiff's loss was to be measured by the cost of the paper, ink, and labour involved in reprinting the notes. The majority of the House of Lords held, over a vigorous dissent, that damages were to be measured by the face value of the notes subject to the plaintiff's mitigating its loss by what steps were reasonable to prevent fraudulent persons from negotiating the notes. Thus, the plaintiff recalled the notes and issued a new series and recovered damages for the face value of the recalled notes that were presented by innocent or apparently

[115] (1976), 72 D.L.R. (3d) 212, 13 O.R. (2d) 710 (C.A.).

[116] See *Kullberg's Furniture Ltd. v. Flin Flon Hotel Co. Ltd., supra*, footnote 114. This would be allowable as a cost incurred to mitigate loss.

[117] *Supra*, footnote 115, at p. 218. American cases relying on *Sedgwick on Damages*, 9th ed. (New York, Baker, Voorhis, 1912), §248a, to the effect that recovery should be based on the wholesale value, were distinguished, and not disapproved.

[118] [1932] A.C. 452 (H.L.).

[119] *Supra*, at p. 490.

[120] *Supra*.

innocent holders. The result seems correct, for an issuing bank cannot afford to dishonour its own currency, nor can it reasonably be expected to "mitigate" a loss by simply issuing more current notes as, in effect, the dissenting lords asked it to do, for this must ultimately affect the value of the whole currency. On this basis an issuing bank could never recover damages for any sort of wrong, even physical damage to its premises, for it could be said that it only had to issue its own currency to repair its losses.

1.610 Similar considerations apply to tokens other than currency, for example, tickets or tokens entitling persons to transport or other benefits. In *Building & Civil Engineering Holidays Scheme Management v. Post Office*,[121] the plaintiff printed and issued tokens called "holiday stamps" designed to ensure entitlement of short-term employees to an annual vacation. Employers would purchase the stamps and issue them to their employees who then surrendered them to other employers for reimbursement from the plaintiff. The plaintiff was thus obliged to honour stamps that were put into circulation, and though trading in the stamps was illegal, it was proved to be widespread. The defendant negligently caused the loss of some stamps, and argued that the loss was to be measured only by the cost of printing new stamps. The English Court of Appeal held that the plaintiff's loss was to be measured by the face value of the stamps, reduced by the possibility of some not being presented. The *Banco de Portugal* case, though cited in argument, was not discussed in the judgments but the result seems to follow the same line of reasoning.

1.620 Similar considerations apply, it is suggested, to cases where the plaintiff is a producer of unique works, such as paintings or other copyright work. If the defendant causes the loss of the work in circumstances that make it probable that the plaintiff has been deprived of a sale, the selling price seems to be the appropriate measure. On the other hand if the defendant destroys the work, the plaintiff's replacement cost will afford full compensation.

1.630 The distinction between destruction and loss was developed in *Banco de Portugal v. Waterlow* where it was accepted by the majority that if the defendant had caused a fire and destroyed the banknotes the measure of damages would be replacement cost only.[122] The same point was made in the "holiday stamps" case. Lord Denning said:

> [The defendant's] argument would be legitimate if the books of stamps had been destroyed by fire in transit: and could never be represented. But these books were not destroyed. They were stolen in transit. And, . . . there was a good chance that they would be sold in the thieves' market and be presented for payment: and paid at face value. Every stolen stamp that was so presented and paid, meant a loss to the plaintiffs of the money paid.[123]

1.640 Where the defendant is a converter of the plaintiff's goods, the same conclusion can be supported by a slightly different line of argument, namely,

---

[121] [1966] 1 Q.B. 247 (C.A.).
[122] *Supra*, footnote 118, at p. 478, *per* Viscount Sankey, and at p. 490, *per* Lord Atkin.
[123] *Supra*, footnote 121, at pp. 262-3.

that the defendant should not by wrongful conduct be allowed to attain a better position than if there had been a bargain and subsequent sale. Thus, in the hypothetical case of a vase bought for a dollar and sold for ten dollars, a customer who converts the vase would not be permitted to argue that the loss to the plaintiff was only a dollar. Again it is suggested that the underlying justification for the higher measure of damages is usually[124] a presumption that the defendant would otherwise have bought the goods. If the defendant asserts a right to retain possession of the plaintiff's goods, she cannot be allowed to do so on terms more favourable than would have been reached by agreement. The question is further discussed in a later chapter.[125]

5. Date for Assessment of Damages

1.650 Considerable difference of legal opinion has been caused by the question of the proper date for assessment of damages. A sum of money must be assessed as a substitute for property that the plaintiff would have had if the wrong had not been done. Varying dates for assessment have been selected in different contexts with the consequence that anomalies and conflicts become apparent to one attempting to survey the law of damages as a whole. Discussion of the problems dealt with here has, in the past, been generally controlled by the form of action adopted by the plaintiff. Modern courts are rightly uncomfortable with an appearance of variation of substantive rights according to forms of action, and in several cases strenuous efforts have been made to avoid such a variation. These efforts have not always been successful, for it is never possible for the common law to discard entirely the legacy of its past. However, the task of the writer of a law book is to discover the rights actually available to a person on a given set of facts under current law, no matter what labels may have been attached to them by courts and, secondly, to suggest rational criteria by which any anomalies or conflicts may be satisfactorily resolved.

1.660 The choice of date for damage assessment becomes important in the present context, where the property of which the plaintiff has been deprived changes in value between the date of the wrong and the date of the judgment. Where the value of the property declines during this period, it is to the plaintiff's advantage to have damages assessed at the date of the wrong, and it is almost invariably held that the plaintiff is entitled to an assessment at that date.[125a] The plaintiff can assert that he was, by the defendant's wrong, deprived of the value of the property at the date of the wrong and is, therefore, entitled to have that value made good. It must be recognized that

---

124 But see *Smith Kline & French Laboratories Ltd. v. Long*, [1989] 1 W.L.R. 1 (C.A.) (property obtained by deceit, where plaintiff would not have sold if the truth had been known).

125 See 9.110 - 9.130, *infra*. See also 1.450 -1.480, *supra*.

125a *R.F. Fry & Associates (Pacific) Ltd. v. Reimer*, [1993] 8 W.W.R. 663, 83 B.C.L.R. (2d) 199 (C.A.). See *Williams v. Copperfields Hotels Ltd.* (1992), 6 O.R. (3d) 557 at pp. 562-3 (Gen. Div.), affd 62 A.C.W.S. (3d) 790 (C.A.), and *Treaty Group Inc. v. Drake International Inc.* (2007), 86 O.R. (3d) 366 (C.A.), both citing this passage.

this will often put the plaintiff in a better position than if the wrong had not been done. For, if the property had been transferred as agreed, or if it had not been taken, as the case may be, it might be shown beyond a doubt that the plaintiff would have retained the property and would have suffered a loss caused by its decline in value. Nevertheless the plaintiff will be entitled to recover the value at the date of the wrong.[125b] In *Solloway v. McLaughlin*,[126] where shares were converted and subsequently replaced on a falling market in circumstances where the plaintiff would not have sought to deal with the shares in the interim, the defendant argued that the plaintiff had suffered no loss. It was (counsel argued) as though goods in a safe had been wrongfully taken and replaced before their owner wanted them. However, the Privy Council held that the plaintiff was entitled to damages: "[He] had vested in him a right to damages for conversion which would be measured by the value of the shares at the date of the conversion."[127] Damages were reduced by the value of the replaced shares, but only by their (lower) value at the date of replacement. The result in the particular case might be supported on the narrow ground that the defendant was in a fiduciary position, but Lord Atkin's explanation applies generally: "If the shares had been converted and not returned, there can be no question that the [plaintiff] would have been entitled to receive the proceeds of the conversion though he himself had planned to hold and thought he had succeeded in holding the shares until a time when the value was nothing."[128] This dramatic example shows that a plaintiff may be enormously better off by the recovery of damages than if the wrong had not been done. In effect, the occurrence of a wrong in such a case is a stroke of luck to the plaintiff and (some would say) enables the plaintiff to gather a windfall. However, it is submitted that the result is justified, and that the justification rests on the impracticability of any alternative rule. The law of damages constantly sets a course between the one extreme of inflexible rules of thumb for damage assessment and the other extreme of excessive expenditure of time and energy in a search for the elusive goal of perfect compensation. The rule considered here represents, it is submitted, a wise refusal to pursue the latter goal too far. Human events are so uncertain that it would do greater harm than good to inquire into what the plaintiff would have done with the property if the defendant had delivered it, or had refrained from taking or destroying it.[128a] A creditor might be shown to be a

[125b] This paragraph was cited with approval in *Dumont v. Northwest Veterinary Services Ltd.* (2003), 242 Sask. R. 294 (Q.B.), at paras. 15-17.

[126] [1938] A.C. 247, [1937] 4 D.L.R. 593 (P.C.); *BBMB Finance (Hong Kong) Ltd. v. EDA Holdings Ltd.*, [1990] 1 W.L.R. 409 (P.C.); both followed in *Trailways Transport Ltd. v. Thomas*, [1996] 2 N.Z.L.R. 443 (H.C.).

[127] *Supra*, at pp. 257-8 A.C., p. 596 D.L.R.

[128] *Supra*, at p. 259 A.C., p. 597 D.L.R. See also *Aronson v. Mologa Holzindustrie A/G Leningrad* (1927), 32 Com. Cas. 276 (C.A.); *Cuff-Waldron Manufacturing Co. v. Heald*, [1930] 3 D.L.R. 901 (Sask. C.A.).

[128a] See *Clarke v. Montreal Trust Co. of Canada* (2001), 106 A.C.W.S. (3d) 561 (Ont. S.C.J.), at para. 84 of judgment, citing this passage.

spendthrift who would have wasted the amount of the debt had it been paid (who would perhaps, in that case, have suffered in health by spending the money on riotous living), but a defence along those lines to an action on the debt cannot be permitted, even though the creditor (by now reformed) is better off as a result than if there had been timely payment. One object of the rules of damage assessment must be to minimize the cost of litigation to both parties; this is in the public interest, for all members of the community are potential plaintiffs and potential defendants. The cost of inquiry into how the plaintiff would have used the property had the defendant not deprived the plaintiff of it outweighs the cost of over-compensation in the kind of case considered here. The problem is analogous to that of underuse by the plaintiff, considered below.[129]

1.670 It is the converse case, where the value of the property increases between the date of wrong and the date of judgment, that has given rise to most legal controversy.[130] Considerations of convenience again support an early "crystallization"[131] of the damages, as do considerations of symmetry: if the plaintiff is to have the advantage of assessment at the date of the wrong when it benefits her, she ought to bear the risk of that measurement when it does not. Where the plaintiff is permitted to recover judgment date value if the value rises or, at her option, date of wrong value if the value falls, she is permitted to speculate at the defendant's expense, reaping the benefit of an increase in value without bearing the risk of the loss.

1.680 This argument seems particularly strong in the case of speculative property, such as some corporate shares. If shares promised by a seller are not delivered, the buyer ought to decide immediately whether or not to speculate in those shares. If, on the seller's breach, the buyer chooses not to buy shares of the same company, but the shares of some other company, she will be entitled to keep any profit on the substitute investment and ought not to recover from the seller the profit on an investment she chose not to make. The failure of the buyer to profit by the increase in value between the date of the wrong and the date of judgment is due not to the seller's wrong but the buyer's choosing to invest the money elsewhere. If the law permitted the buyer to recover the increase in value of the shares promised when and only when they were not replaced, there would be an incentive to the buyer, if a rise in value were anticipated, not to replace the shares, even though they were the best possible investment, but rather to choose another, less profitable, investment, knowing that failure to replace the shares would increase the defendant's ultimate liability. The argument for an early crystallization of damages is that it leaves the litigants as free as possible to

---

[129] See 1.1360 - 1.1430, *infra*.

[130] This problem is discussed at greater length in Waddams, "Date for Assessment of Damages", 97 L.Q.R. 445 (1981).

[131] The word is used in this context by the Supreme Court of Canada in *Asamera Oil Corp. Ltd. v. Sea Oil & General Corp.*, [1979] 1 S.C.R. 633 at p. 674, 89 D.L.R. (3d) 1 at p. 31, and by Oliver J. in *Radford v. De Froberville*, [1977] 1 W.L.R. 1262 (Ch. D.), at p. 1287.

conduct their affairs as they would otherwise think best, thereby minimizing the total cost of prolonging the dispute.

1.690 Another argument tending in the same direction is that if damage assessment is postponed, the plaintiff will have an incentive to delay and to prolong litigation on a rising market. In the case of appeals final assessment will be further postponed. The logic of postponement would lead to the view that a search for perfect compensation requires assessment at the very latest practicable moment, that is, at the date the damages are actually paid, and that in case of a delay after judgment, evidence should be heard of any further increases in value before the judgment is actually satisfied. Few would take the argument to these lengths.[132] However, any postponement of final assessment is costly and the costs of litigation ought not to be unnecessarily increased.

1.700 It was early held that a disappointed buyer, at least when the price had not been prepaid, was entitled only to the value of the goods or shares at the date of the breach. Emphasis was placed in the early cases on the fact that the plaintiff had not prepaid, and so had had the use of the purchase money. In *Gainsford v. Carroll*,[133] the court said: "Here the plaintiff had his money in his possession and he might have purchased other bacon of the like quality the very day after the contract was broken, and if he has sustained any loss, by neglecting to do so, it is his own fault."[134] The case was followed, and its reasoning adopted, in a case of non-delivery of shares, *Shaw v. Holland*.[135]

1.710 These cases were concerned to distinguish earlier cases on non-replacement of stock in which, on a rising market, the plaintiff had been held entitled to damages assessed at the date of the trial.[136] It is natural that the court in *Gainsford v. Carroll*, in rejecting this measure, would seize on an apparent distinction between the cases, that is, that since the price had not been prepaid, the plaintiff was in a better position to purchase substitute goods in the market. But the actual decision in *Gainsford v. Carroll* denies judgment date assessment. It can hardly be said, therefore, that *Gainsford v. Carroll* is distinct authority for the proposition that where the price is prepaid, the buyer is entitled to judgment date value.

1.720 In *Startup v. Cortazzi*,[137] the case arose where a part of the price had been

---

[132] But in other fields events occurring after judgment have been taken into account, and, where a debt is payable in a foreign currency, the creditor has been given the benefit of conversion at the date of actual payment. See 7.80 - 7.320, *infra*. In *Hechter v. Thurston* (1977), 80 D.L.R. (3d) 685 (Man. Q.B.), revd 98 D.L.R. (3d) 329 (C.A.), restd [1980] 2 S.C.R. 254, 120 D.L.R. (3d) 576*n*, the relevant date for assessment of damages in a land sale case was held to be the date of judgment, not final assessment.

[133] (1824), 2 B. & C. 624, 107 E.R. 516.

[134] *Supra*, at p. 625.

[135] (1846), 15 L.J. Ex. 87. The date of breach was also taken in *Dawson v. Helicopter Exploration Co. Ltd.* (1958), 12 D.L.R. (2d) 1 (S.C.C.).

[136] *Shepherd v. Johnson* (1802), 2 East 210, 102 E.R. 349; *McArthur v. Seaforth* (1810), 2 Taunt. 257, 127 E.R. 1076.

[137] (1835), 2 C.M. & R. 165, 150 E.R. 71. The opposite view was taken, however, in *Elliot v. Hughes* (1863), 3 F. & F. 387, 176 E.R. 173.

paid in advance. It was held that the plaintiff was entitled to the return of the money with interest (this had been paid into court) and to damages based on the value of the goods at the time of breach, but not to the value of the goods at the time of trial. Counsel for the plaintiff argued that prepayment of the price entitled the plaintiff to the high measure. "If they had their money, they might have applied it in the purchase of other merchandize, by which they might have obtained a profit equivalent to the amount of damages now claimed."[138] The court, in upholding a jury verdict for the defendant, rejected this argument. Lord Abinger said: "It was not proved that the plaintiffs could have made more than 5 per cent on that money, or that they had not credit at their bankers to that extent, and thereby had sustained any peculiar inconvenience."[139] Alderson B. said:

> The more correct criterion is the price at the time when the cargo would have arrived in due course according to the contract; when, if it had been delivered, the plaintiffs would have been enabled to resell it. Another criterion is, to consider the loss of the gain which the party would have made, if the contract had been complied with. In the present case, the loss which the plaintiffs have sustained arises from their having been kept out of their money. That is a matter to be calculated by the interest of the money up to the time when, by the course of practice, the money could have been obtained out of Court.[140]

1.730 The *Sale of Goods Act*, in adopting the value of the goods at the date of breach as the basis for the *prima facie* measure of damages,[141] tends in the same direction as *Startup v. Cortazzi*, though it was held in one case[142] that the court can depart from what is a *prima facie* measure only; the rule in *Startup v. Cortazzi* has indeed been criticized on the ground that it undercompensates.[143] However, it is submitted that the rule gives fair compensation and, moreover, is by far the most practical working rule. Prepayment of the price to a defaulting seller results in the seller's wrongfully having use of the buyer's money for a period of time. This wrongful use of money can be compensated, as Alderson B. said, by an award of interest. In inflationary times, interest rates reflect the decline in the value of money which will offset a rise in the value of the goods attributable to inflation. The buyer would be doubly compensated by recovery of full interest rates (reflecting inflation) and damages based on increased value of the goods

---

[138] *Startup v. Cortazzi, supra*, footnote 137, at p. 167.

[139] *Startup v. Cortazzi, supra*, at p. 168.

[140] *Startup v. Cortazzi, supra*, at p. 169.

[141] *Sale of Goods Act* (Ont.), s. 49(3). See also *Sale of Goods Act* (Alta.), s. 50(3); B.C., s. 54(3); Man., s. 52(3); N.B., s. 48(3); Nfld. & Lab., s. 51(3); N.W.T., s. 58; N.S., s. 52(3); P.E.I., s. 51(3); Sask., s. 50(3); Yukon, s. 48(3).

[142] *Peebles v. Pfeifer*, [1918] 2 W.W.R. 877 (Sask. K.B.). But this view was rejected in *Asamera Oil Corp. Ltd. v. Sea Oil & General Corp.*, [1979] 1 S.C.R. 633, 89 D.L.R. (3d) 1.

[143] See *McGregor on Damages*, 16th ed. (London, Sweet & Maxwell, 1997), §312. In *Aronson v. Mologa Holzindustrie A/G Leningrad* (1927), 32 Com. Cas. 276 (C.A.), Atkin L.J., quoting Sedgwick (also relied on in *Peebles v. Pfeifer, supra*, footnote 142), suggested, *obiter*, that judgment date value should be allowed (pp. 289-90).

promised (also reflecting inflation). The award of interest at rates that are readily determinable is the most practical way of securing adequate but not excessive compensation.

1.740 In *The "Volturno"*,[144] Lord Wrenbury explained the rule of early crystallization in memorable terms. He was speaking in the context of a

[*The next page is* 1-33]

[144] *S.S. Celia v. S.S. Volturno*, [1921] 2 A.C. 544 (H.L.).

tortious claim, but his view is equally persuasive, it is submitted, in contract cases, provided the buyer has no claim for specific performance. Lord Wrenbury said:

> If the plaintiff had been damaged by the defendant tortiously depriving him of three cows the judgment would be: Declare that on January 1 the plaintiff suffered by the defendant's tort a loss of three cows. Declare that on January 1 the plaintiff would have been entitled to go into the market and buy three similar cows and charge the defendant with the price. Declare that the cost would have been 150*l*. Adjudge that the plaintiff recover from the defendant 150*l*. It would be nihil ad rem to say that in July similar cows would have cost in the market 300*l*. The defendant is not bound to supply the plaintiff with cows . . . The defendant is liable to pay the plaintiff damages, that is to say, money to some amount for the loss of the cows: the only question is, how much? The answer is, such sum as represents the market value at the date of the tort of the goods of which the plaintiff was tortiously deprived.[145]

With the minor modification that "the date of the tort" should be taken to mean "the earliest date at which, acting reasonably, the plaintiff could have replaced the goods",[146] it is submitted that this passage remains persuasive and, subject to certain exceptions discussed in this chapter and elsewhere,[147] represents the modern position in both contract and tort.

1.750 The argument in sale cases, that if the seller has had possession of the buyer's money the buyer is precluded from purchasing a substitute, can very rarely be substantiated as a matter of fact. The fact that the seller has the buyer's money makes the buyer less wealthy than he would otherwise be, but in the ordinary commercial case, it does not inhibit the buyer from making what investments seem to him best, possibly by borrowing money. A rule based on the principle that the buyer can postpone the date of assessment unless she has every penny in her pocket required to make a substitute purchase, would justify the postponement even in the case where the price has not been prepaid and the market price has risen by a trifling amount at the date of breach, for the buyer could argue that until the seller paid what he owed (the difference between the price and value at the date of breach) she had not the full amount of money required to purchase substitute goods. But no one has taken the argument to this length. Again, if the right to postpone assessment should depend on prepayment, problems would arise in case of prepayment of part of the price. *Startup v. Cortazzi* was itself a case where part only of the price had been prepaid. It seems most unsatisfactory for dramatic differences in damage assessment to turn on whether or not a small part payment has been made by the buyer.

---

[145] *Supra*, at p. 563.

[146] See 1.790, 1.860, *infra*. This test was applied, and this passage cited with approval, in *Beiser v. A Law Firm*, [1984] 4 W.W.R. 551, 53 B.C.L.R. 305 (S.C.), at p. 555 and in *Dumont v. Northwest Veterinary Services Ltd.* (2003), 242 Sask. R. 294 (Q.B.), at paras. 15-17. See also *Scobie v. Wing*, [1992] 2 W.W.R. 514, 63 B.C.L.R. (2d) 76 (C.A.); *Kaine v. Osterreichische*, [1993] 2 Lloyd's Rep. 1 (C.A.).

[147] See 1.820 - 1.910, *infra*.

1.760 There is another point. If judgment date assessment is supported on the theory that the buyer has been deprived of the opportunity of owning goods at present (that is, at the date of judgment), and of receiving the increase in their value, insuperable difficulties arise where the buyer has in fact purchased a substitute on the seller's default, and holds it at the date of judgment. If the buyer is still to be entitled to the judgment date value of the goods promised, he will receive twice over the rise in value between the two dates, and the theory just mentioned[148] does not support such double compensation.[149] If on the other hand he is to be deprived of judgment date assessment on the ground that he has in fact mitigated his loss, distinctions will have to be drawn between cases where he has bought identical goods to those promised, and cases where he has simply made a successful investment of money. It will also become relevant to discover whether the plaintiff would or could have purchased such goods even if the defendant had not defaulted. Intractable problems will arise where the buyer has bought goods similar but not identical to those promised. Gains to the innocent party that she could have made whether the wrong occurred or not are generally treated as collateral gains that do not reduce damages.[150] This approach also suggests the undesirability of establishing a rule which requires substitute purchases to be brought into account.

1.770 In *Asamera Oil Corp. Ltd. v. Sea Oil & General Corp.*,[151] the Supreme Court of Canada held that on failure by a bailee to return shares, the owner was not entitled to recover damages based on the value of the shares after a date at which he could reasonably have replaced them in the market. *Startup v. Cortazzi* and the other cases mentioned here were discussed, the court making it clear that the result ought not to vary according to prepayment of the price by a buyer.[152] The general rule was reaffirmed by the House of Lords in *Johnson v. Agnew*:[153]

> The general principle for the assessment of damages is compensatory, i.e.,

[148] *I.e.*, that recovery of the judgment date value is needed to put the plaintiff in the position that would have been occupied if the contract had been performed: see *Weber v. R.G. Steeves Construction Co. Ltd.* (1981), 32 B.C.L.R. 31 (S.C.), where profit made on a purchase and resale of a condominium was brought into account on an assessment of damages postponed for nine months after it became apparent that specific performance was unavailable. It is submitted that the preferable rule is early crystallization with profits on such a purchase treated as collateral.

[149] This point was made to support early crystallization in *Kaunas v. Smyth* (1976), 75 D.L.R. (3d) 368 at p. 377, 15 O.R. (2d) 237 (H.C.J.).

[150] See 15.670 - 15.880, *infra*.

[151] [1979] 1 S.C.R. 633, 89 D.L.R. (3d) 1, followed in *Claiborne Industries v. National Bank of Canada* (1989), 59 D.L.R. (4th) 533, 69 O.R. (2d) 65 (C.A.); *Hongkong Bank of Canada v. Richardson Greenshields of Canada Ltd.* (1990), 72 D.L.R. (4th) 161, [1990] 6 W.W.R. 1 (B.C.C.A.); *Hunt v. TD Securities Inc.* (2003), 229 D.L.R. (4th) 609 (Ont. C.A.); *Hillspring Farms Ltd. v. Leland Walton & Sons Ltd.* (2007), 312 N.B.R. (2d) 109 (C.A.). The earlier case of *Toronto-Dominion Bank v. Uhren* (1960), 24 D.L.R. (2d) 203 (Sask. C.A.) seems inconsistent.

[152] See *Asamera Oil Corp., supra*, footnote 151, at pp. 657-8 S.C.R., pp. 18-19 D.L.R.

[153] [1980] A.C. 367 (H.L.).

> that the innocent party is to be placed, so far as money can do so, in the same position as if the contract had been performed. Where the contract is one of sale, this principle normally leads to assessment of damages as at the date of the breach — a principle recognised and embodied in section 51 of the Sale of Goods Act 1893.[154]

1.780 The Supreme Court of Canada in the *Asamera* case, supported its conclusion on principles of mitigation, concluding that the buyer in the case under discussion could reasonably have avoided the loss claimed by buying a substitute in the market on the seller's default. The conclusion seems amply justified for the reasons mentioned. However, it may be questioned whether it is fully supported by the principle of mitigation. This is usually expressed as a rule that the innocent party must act reasonably, or more properly, that damages are not recoverable for a loss that could reasonably have been avoided.[155] It does not seem right, however, to say that a disappointed buyer acts "unreasonably" in failing to purchase a substitute. A reasonable person can rarely predict changes in market prices, because the current price at any time generally reflects predictions about the future. Thus, to fail to predict a rise in prices is rarely unreasonable and it seems unwise to rest the principle of breach date assessment on the basis that the buyer acts unreasonably in failure to purchase a substitute. The actual decision in *Asamera* indicates, it is submitted, that the Supreme Court of Canada was not, in reality, applying a test of reasonable conduct, for there was no proof that the plaintiff ever had acted unreasonably in failing to anticipate what turned out to be a rise in share prices of over 1,500 per cent. The rule seems rather that, to use Estey J.'s word, damages should "crystallize"[156] at a certain point (in the *Asamera* case it was some time after the date of the wrong), and that from then the defendant's obligation to the plaintiff is only to pay a certain money sum (the sum that would have been assessed had a tribunal determined the matter at that date), and that subsequent delay in payment of that sum is to be compensated by the award of interest.[157] This approach, it is submitted, is fully consistent with justice to the plaintiff and as argued above has a very great advantage of convenience.

1.790 The theory of crystallization depends on the assumption that the plaintiff on the defendant's default had the opportunity of replacing the goods promised to him in the market-place. In some cases, however, there is no such reasonable opportunity. The property promised by the defendant may be unique;[158] the plaintiff may be impecunious;[159] the defendant may actually

---

[154] *Supra*, at pp. 400-1. See also *MacIver v. American Motors (Canada) Ltd.* (1976), 70 D.L.R. (3d) 473 (Man. C.A.), at p. 489; *Kinbauri Gold Corp. v. IAMGOLD International African Mining Gold Corp.* (2004), 246 D.L.R. (4th) 595 (Ont. C.A.).

[155] See 15.70, *infra*.

[156] See *Asamera Oil Corp., supra*, footnote 151, at p. 674 S.C.R., p. 31 D.L.R.

[157] On the award of interest see 7.330 - 7.1000, *infra*.

[158] In that case the plaintiff will often have a reasonable claim to specific performance, or specific restitution.

[159] See 15.330 - 15.390, *infra*.

deter the plaintiff from making a substitute purchase by giving continuous assurances of performance;[160] or for other good reasons the plaintiff may think that use of the property in question will ultimately be recovered. In such cases it has been held that the plaintiff may be entitled to a greater recovery than the value of the property at the date of breach.[160a]

1.800 Where property sold to the plaintiff is unique, there is often a case to be made for specific enforcement. The effect of a decree of specific performance is to require compliance at the date of the decree, so its effect, in the case of property increasing in value, is to give to the plaintiff the benefit of the increase up to the date of judgment, and indeed beyond it to the date of actual compliance with the decree. This result is justified where the property is unique, for that very finding implies that no adequate substitute for it is available.[161] Thus, where the plaintiff is buying a unique house for personal occupation, entitlement to specific performance carries with it the implication that it is not reasonable to expect the plaintiff to purchase a substitute on the vendor's default and that on a rising market, justice to the purchaser requires the award of the benefit of the increased value of the property. This approach to specific performance suggests, however, that the remedy should not be freely available to a speculative purchaser who is quite capable of purchasing or who indeed actually has purchased a substitute property on the vendor's default.[162]

1.810 A modern approach to remedial questions requires a broad perspective; the question of the availability of a specific remedy, equitable or legal, cannot nowadays be isolated from its effect on the rules governing the assessment of damages.

1.820 A case often cited to support a judgment date assessment of damages is *Bwllfa & Merthyr Dare Steam Collieries (1891), Ltd. v. Pontypridd Waterworks Co.*[163] The following striking passage occurred in Lord Macnaghten's speech: "Why should he [the arbitrator] listen to conjecture on a matter which has become an accomplished fact? Why should he guess when he can calculate? With the light before him why should he shut his eyes and grope in the dark?"[164] It appears at first sight that this dictum would support judgment date assessment in all cases. It could be argued that in an ordinary case of non-delivery by a seller a rise in market value is always the

[160] In the *Asamera* case the defendant had urged the plaintiff not to press its claim.

[160a] See *Begusic v. Clark Wilson & Co.* (1991), 82 D.L.R. (4th) 667, [1991] 6 W.W.R. 513 (B.C.C.A.), supplementary reasons 90 D.L.R. (4th) 319, [1992] 4 W.W.R. 347 (C.A.).

[161] This seems to be the basis of the decision in *Robertson v. Dumaresq* (1864), 2 Moo P.C. 66, where damages for failure to make a government land allocation were assessed at the date of judgment.

[162] *Semelhago v. Paramedevan*, [1996] 2 S.C.R. 415, 136 D.L.R. (4th) 1. See Sharpe, *Injunctions and Specific Performance*, looseleaf ed. (Toronto, Canada Law Book, 1999), 8.10-8.90.

[163] [1903] A.C. 426 (H.L.).

[164] *Supra*, at p. 431, cited with approval in *Huntting Merritt Shingle Co. Ltd. v. Minister of National Revenue*, [1951] Ex. C.R. 148 at p. 150; *Golden Strait Corp. v. Nippon Yusen Kubishika Kaisha*, [2007] 2 W.L.R. 691 (H.L.), at paras. 36, 65, 78.

best evidence of the buyer's present loss. The inconvenience of such a rule of assessment has been alluded to earlier. It is now suggested that the *Bwllfa* case, when the actual decision is considered in the light of its facts, also supports a general rule of breach date assessment. A statute had empowered an operator of waterworks to prevent a landowner from working mines on his land where this might interfere with the waterworks, and the statute included a provision that "full compensation" was to be paid to the miner. The evidence in the case showed that after the issue of the notice inhibiting mining, but within the time that would have been required to extract the coal, the price of coal rose dramatically. The task of the court was to apply the phrase "full compensation". The case was therefore not, strictly speaking, a damages case at all though the analogy is obviously close. The decision of the House of Lords was that the higher price was to be used as the basis of compensation. But the court went to extraordinary lengths to distinguish the case from an ordinary case of sale. Lord Robertson said: "The true inquiry here is not what is the value of the coalfield or of the coal, but what would the colliery company, if they had not been prohibited, have made out of the coal during the time it would have taken them to get it."[165] Lord Halsbury said: "It was not a purchase of the coal, nor is it analogous to a purchase of the coal."[166] So anxious was he to make the distinction that he committed himself to this cryptic but vigorous dictum: "It is what it is, and it appears to me that considering what it is I think the question propounded is solved by the statement of what it is."[167] The case, then, so far from establishing a general rule of judgment date assessment, rather tends to reaffirm a general rule of breach date assessment from which the decision was thought to constitute a very special departure. However, in *Golden Strait Corp. v. Nippon Yusen Kubishika Kaisha*,[167a] the majority of the House of Lords applied the *Bwllfa* principle to a case of assessment of damages for breach of a charterparty.

1.830 The reason for the departure from the general rule in the *Bwllfa* case is, it is suggested, that no market existed in which the plaintiff could reasonably have been expected to replace the interest that the defendant had taken. The general rule in sale cases rests on the assumption that on the seller's breach the buyer can go into the market to purchase a substitute. No such possibility existed for the coal-miner. It would be a rarity indeed if the latter could find for sale in the market-place mining rights in a few acres of coal-bearing land adjacent to the already operating coal-mine.

1.840 This basis of the general rule was stressed by Oliver J. in *Radford v. De Froberville*.[168] "In contracts for the sale of goods, for instance, where there is

[165] *Bwllfa & Merthyr Dare Steam Collieries, supra*, footnote 163, at p. 433, quoting the trial judge in [1901] 2 K.B. 798 at p. 805.
[166] *Bwllfa & Merthyr Dare Steam Collieries, supra*, footnote 163, at p. 428.
[167] *Supra.*
[167a] *Supra*, footnote 164.
[168] [1977] 1 W.L.R. 1262 (Ch. D.).

an available market, the date of non-delivery is generally the appropriate date because it is open to the plaintiff to mitigate by going into the market immediately. Where there is no readily available market, a later date may be appropriate."[169] In the earlier case of *J. & E. Hall v. Barclay*,[170] Greer L.J. said: "Where you are dealing with goods which can be readily bought in the market, a man whose rights have been interfered with is never entitled to more than what he would have to pay to buy a similar article in the market."[171] The court went on to award a higher measure of damages for conversion of the plaintiff's chattels just because there was no market in which the plaintiff could purchase a substitute.

1.850 The link with specific enforcement now becomes apparent,[172] for it is in just those cases where the market cannot afford a substitute that the courts have been willing to decree specific enforcement. The advantage that this gives to the plaintiff on a rising market can be justified on the same basis as was adopted in the cases just mentioned; the reason the plaintiff is not held to the value of the property at the date of the wrong is that there was no reasonable opportunity of purchasing a substitute on that date.

1.860 Other established departures from the rule of assessment at the date of the wrong may be explained on the same basis. Rarely is a substitute instantly available. The appropriate time for crystallization would seem to be, therefore, the time of the earliest reasonable opportunity to replace the property. In *Ogle v. Vane*[173] and in *Wilson v. London & Globe Finance Corp., Ltd.*,[174] it was held that the buyer was entitled to wait, even on a rising market, until it became clear that the seller really was not going to deliver. The same was held by the Supreme Court of Canada in *Samuel v. Black Lake Asbestos & Chrome Co.*[175] Thus, if the defendant offers assurances of eventual performance, it will be reasonable for the buyer to postpone the purchase of a substitute, and not unjust to hold the defendant to the higher market price obtaining at a later date. In *Asamera Oil Corp. Ltd. v. Sea Oil & General Corp.*,[176] the owner of shares, in an action for non-return by a bailee, was held to be entitled to wait six years before purchasing substitute shares on a rising market. The long period is probably to be explained by the particular facts of the case including the fact that the defendant had urged the plaintiff to postpone litigation, thereby (it may be deduced) in effect promising eventually to return the shares. It may be confidently stated that

[169] *Supra*, at p. 1285.
[170] [1937] 3 All E.R. 620 (C.A.).
[171] *Supra*, at p. 623.
[172] See *Dawson v. Helicopter Exploration Co. Ltd.* (1958), 12 D.L.R. (2d) 1 (S.C.C.), at p. 11 (absence of specific performance given as reason for early assessment date).
[173] (1867), L.R. 2 Q.B. 275, affd 3 Q.B. 272 (Ex. Ch.); *Barnett v. Javeri & Co.*, [1916] 2 K.B. 390. *Ogle v. Vane* was distinguished in *Re Voss* (1873), L.R. 16 Eq. 155.
[174] (1897), 14 T.L.R. 15 (C.A.), followed in *Snagproof Ltd. v. Brody* (1922), 69 D.L.R. 271 (Alta. S.C. App. Div.).
[175] (1921), 62 S.C.R. 472, 63 D.L.R. 617.
[176] [1979] 1 S.C.R. 633, 89 D.L.R. (3d) 1. See also the discussion at 1.1060 - 1.1090, *infra*.

this principle survives the *Sale of Goods Act, 1893*, for the difference between contract and market price at the date of breach is stated in the Act to be only a *prima facie* measure, and *Ogle v. Vane* was expressly cited with approval by Lord Wilberforce in *Johnson v. Agnew*. Lord Wilberforce said of the rule in the *Sale of Goods Act, 1983*: "But this is not an absolute rule: if to follow it would give rise to injustice, the court has power to fix such other date as may be appropriate in the circumstances."[177] Since *Lord Cairns' Act* in 1858,[178] Courts of Equity, wherever they have jurisdiction to entertain an application for an injunction or for specific performance, have jurisdiction to award damages in substitution for a specific order. This power has survived in the *Courts of Justice Act*[179] and has recently assumed importance in the context of assessment of damages. In *Wroth v. Tyler*,[180] the vendor of a residential house was unable to make a good title on account of the registration by his wife of a charge giving her a right of occupation. The purchasers sued for specific performance and had reason to suppose, as did the trial judge,[181] up to the very last moment, that the wife would withdraw her charge and permit the contract to be performed. However, she could not be ordered to do so, and Megarry J. assessed damages in substitution for a decree of specific performance. The value of the house, along with other house prices in England, had risen dramatically between the date due for

[177] [1980] A.C. 367 (H.L.), at p. 401, applied in *Beiser v. A Law Firm*, [1984] 4 W.W.R. 551, 53 B.C.L.R. 305 (S.C.), where the plaintiff did not know of the wrong. See also *Roppo v. Avvro Developments Inc.* (2006), 51 R.P.R. (4th) 45 (Ont. C.A.), at para. 8 ("Although a departure from the norm, it is open to the court to depart from the date of breach when fixing the date for calculation of damages, provided always that it is reasonable to do so."); *Red Back Mining Inc. v. Geyser Ltd.*, [2007] 1 W.W.R. 568 (B.C.S.C.).

[178] *Chancery Amendment Act, 1858*. See Sharpe, *Injunctions and Specific Performance*, looseleaf ed. (Toronto, Canada Law Book, 1999), 1.190-1.220, 4.30.

[179] See *Courts of Justice Act* (Ont.), s. 99, and footnote 195, *infra*. In England the Act was repealed, but held to survive in effect in *Leeds Industrial Co-operative Society, Ltd. v. Slack*, [1924] A.C. 851 (H.L.).

[180] [1974] Ch. 30, followed in *Hechter v. Thurston* (1977), 80 D.L.R. (3d) 685 (Man. Q.B.), revd 98 D.L.R. (3d) 329 (C.A.), restd [1980] 2 S.C.R. 254, 120 D.L.R. (3d) 576*n*; *Metropolitan Trust Co. of Canada v. Pressure Concrete Services Ltd.* (1973), 37 D.L.R. (3d) 649, [1973] 3 O.R. 629 (H.C.J.), affd 60 D.L.R. (3d) 431, 9 O.R. (2d) 375 (C.A.); *306793 Ontario Ltd. v. Rimes* (1979), 100 D.L.R. (3d) 350, 25 O.R. (2d) 79 (C.A.); *Calgary Hardwood v. C.N.R.* (1977), 74 D.L.R. (3d) 284 (Alta. S.C.T.D.), affd 100 D.L.R. (3d) 302 (S.C. App. Div.); *E.J.H. Holdings Ltd. v. Bougie* (1977), 7 A.R. 213 (Dist. Ct.); *Western Oil Consultants v. Great Northern Oils Ltd.* (1981), 121 D.L.R. (3d) 724 (Alta. Q.B.); *Kopec v. Pyret* (1987), 36 D.L.R. (4th) 1, [1987] 3 W.W.R. 449 (Sask. C.A.); *Semelhago v. Paramedevan*, [1996] 2 S.C.R. 415, 136 D.L.R. (4th) 1. However, judgment date assessment was refused, on grounds of mitigation, in *Chand v. Sabo Bros. Realty Ltd.* (1977), 81 D.L.R. (3d) 382 (Alta. S.C.T.D.), vard 96 D.L.R. (3d) 445 (S.C. App. Div.), where the purchaser's deposit had been promptly returned after default. The same view was taken in *Kaunas v. Smyth* (1976), 75 D.L.R. (3d) 368, 15 O.R. (2d) 237 (H.C.J.). In the *Asamera* case, *supra*, footnote 176, at p. 652 S.C.R., p. 14 D.L.R., Estey J. suggested that "judgment date," for purposes of assessing value, should be taken as at the end of the trial. In *Metropolitan Trust Co. of Canada v. Pressure Concrete Services Ltd., supra*, R. E. Holland, J., directed assessment to the date of delivery of reserved judgment. In *Hechter v. Thurston, supra*, at p. 690, Nitikman J. held that assessment should be at the date of hearing, not the later date of final assessment.

[181] See *Wroth v. Tyler, supra*, footnote 180, at p. 63.

completion and the date of the trial. Megarry J. held that although common law damages might be limited to the difference between contract and market price at the date of breach (he left this point open),[182] nevertheless, damages in lieu of specific performance were to be measured at the date of judgment. The result seems to follow from an application of *Lord Cairns' Act*, for it would be odd if damages in substitution for specific performance should be assessed on a basis that would give purchasers less value than they would have received by an actual decree of specific performance.

1.870 The result of the case was thus to give to the purchasers the benefit of the increase in the value of the house between the date of breach and the date of judgment. This result had attractions in *Wroth v. Tyler* itself where the plaintiffs had invested their life savings in the purchase and might, if damages had been otherwise assessed, have lost forever their chance to own a house. The result seems less attractive, however, where the plaintiff is a corporation purchasing vacant land for speculation.[183] There seems no good reason why such a buyer, especially if the deposit is low, should not buy a substitute within a reasonable time after the vendor's default and no injustice, therefore, in estimating damages at the date of the breach. The further conclusion may eventually be accepted as some recent cases have held that such a purchaser should not be entitled to an actual decree of specific performance even where that is possible.[184]

1.880 Some of the earlier-mentioned objections to postponing the date of assessment become real in this context. The plaintiff will have an incentive to delay the final assessment as long as possible. In *Malhotra v. Choudhury*,[185] the English Court of Appeal was faced with a claim for damages in substitution for specific performance where the value of the

[*The next page is* 1-41]

[182] *Wroth v. Tyler*, *supra*, at p. 57.

[183] As in *306793 Ontario Ltd. v. Rimes* (1979), 100 D.L.R. (3d) 350, 25 O.R. (2d) 79 (C.A.).

[184] *Semelhago v. Paramedevan*, *supra*, footnote 180. See Sharpe, *Injunctions and Specific Performance*, looseleaf ed. (Toronto, Canada Law Book, 1999), 8.30.

[185] [1980] Ch. 52 (C.A.).

property had been steadily rising during protracted litigation. The defendant argued that the plaintiff should not be entitled to enhance his damages through "dragging his heels through the law courts".[186] The court reduced the damages on the ground that the plaintiff "did not sufficiently mitigate his damage by proceeding with greater celerity".[187] It is quite common in Canadian jurisdictions, even where the plaintiff is eager, for a trial to occur after a much longer delay than the two years involved in *Malhotra v. Choudhury*.[188] If it is objectionable for the plaintiff to profit by a delay of two years in *Malhotra v. Choudhury*, it seems also objectionable for the plaintiff to profit by a delay of two years occurring for any reason.[189] If possible, a rule should be chosen that makes the parties indifferent to delay. At the very least, it seems undesirable to set up a rule that gives the plaintiff an incentive to prolong litigation. Even though, as in *Malhotra v. Choudhury*, the plaintiff's conduct can be controlled in extreme cases, there will be many cases in which the plaintiff's conduct, while less than eager, will fall short of what the court would be willing to castigate.

1.890 In the case of an appeal, final assessment will be further postponed as illustrated by *Domb v. Isoz*[190] where the purchaser of a house, having sued for specific performance and having lost at the trial, appealed successfully, abandoning his claim for specific performance at the appeal hearing. The English Court of Appeal held that the plaintiff was entitled to damages based on the value of the house at the date of the appeal hearing. In the case of a further appeal, assessment could well be delayed for many years. That the result may be harsh to the defendant is illustrated by the fact of *Domb v. Isoz* where the plaintiff had bought a substitute house soon after the date of the defendant's breach. In a period of inflation, the result will be that the plaintiff is given the benefit of the increase in value of two houses, whereas if the wrong had not been done this benefit would have been received only once. The defendant, though having had a perfectly respectable defence (for he won at trial, and the case can be supposed where he also wins in the Court of Appeal but loses in the highest court), might well be ruined by such a judgment. In many cases, in order to satisfy the judgment the defendant will have to sell the house that he had (not unreasonably) considered to be his own house and his only protection against inflation.

1.900 In *Domb v. Isoz* where the plaintiff lost at trial, he could hardly be faulted for appealing, but it becomes clear from these considerations that a plaintiff, even when successful at trial, would have an incentive to appeal on a rising market in order to keep the date of final assessment open. It is perhaps

---

[186] *Supra*, at p. 81.

[187] *Supra*.

[188] On delay as a defence to specific performance, see Sharpe, *op. cit.*, footnote 184, 1.820-1.980.

[189] In *370866 Ontario Ltd. v. Chizy* (1987), 34 D.L.R. (4th) 404, 57 O.R. (2d) 587 (H.C.J.), specific performance and the benefit of judgment date assessment of damages were denied to a purchaser of land on account of an unexplained delay of four years.

[190] [1980] Ch. 548 (C.A.).

unlikely that a plaintiff, having successfully recovered full judgment date value at trial, would be able to appeal solely on the ground that a further rise in value was anticipated before the Court of Appeal should hear her case, but where the plaintiff has any legitimate ground for an appeal against the amount of her judgment, there will be an added incentive to appeal in the prospect of postponement of final assessment.

1.910 The facts of *Domb v. Isoz*, where the plaintiff had bought a substitute house soon after the defendant's default, illustrate the difficult problem earlier alluded to of whether, and if so when, the loss of the kind in question here can be said to have been avoided. The ordinary person would be inclined to say that the plaintiff in *Domb v. Isoz* had protected himself, by buying a substitute house, from the effect of subsequent increases in house prices. If so, he had mitigated his loss and the decision of the court is over-compensatory. But such a principle, as suggested earlier, is exceedingly difficult to apply, for it is impossible to set up a criterion that will easily distinguish between investments that are to be categorized as avoidance of loss and those to be categorized as collateral gains. It seems wrong for the plaintiff to be over-compensated, but it seems wrong to set up a rule that will encourage the plaintiff not to purchase a substitute, if the plaintiff would otherwise choose to do so, for fear of suffering a reduction of damages. There seems to be no solution to this dilemma so long as the law permits postponement of damage assessment in these circumstances, and postponement seems inevitable so long as the plaintiff is entitled to and is reasonably pursuing an actual decree of specific performance. The point was clearly put by Macdonald C.J. in *Horsnail v. Shute*:[191]

> But where the plaintiff is pursuing his remedy for enforcement of the contract that doctrine [*i.e.*, the doctrine of mitigation] can have no application. The plaintiff was within his rights in persisting in his claim for specific performance until the impossibility of success was disclosed. It was upon discovery of that fact, wrongly concealed from him by defendant, and then only, that he was thrown back upon his claim for damages.[192]

1.920 Another difficulty concerns the question of advance payment. If the plaintiff had paid the whole of the purchase price in advance, support might be lent to the view that the defendant's default prevented the purchase of a substitute, particularly in the case of a very substantial transaction like the purchase of a house. In most house purchase cases, the purchaser will have paid a deposit, usually a small proportion of the total price. It may still be argued that in the case of a purchaser of limited means intending to borrow a large part of the price, payment of the deposit (which will usually be held by a real estate agent during the litigation) effectively inhibits the making of a substitute purchase. Megarry J. evidently assumed that this was so in *Wroth v. Tyler*,[193] but it is not clear that proof of that fact was an essential part of

[191] (1921), 62 D.L.R. 199 (B.C.C.A.).
[192] *Supra*, at p. 203.

the plaintiff's case. A question not answered is whether the result would have been the same if the purchaser had in fact sufficient means to procure a substitute. Again, what would be the position if the plaintiff had paid only a trifling deposit or no deposit at all? It is, to say the least, inconvenient for the date of damage assessment to vary according to the plaintiff's particular financial circumstances or the amount of the deposit in particular transactions.

1.930 The postponement of the date for assessment of damages in *Wroth v. Tyler* depended on the application of *Lord Cairns' Act*. Megarry J. was at least unsure whether the same result could have been achieved at common law.[194] If Megarry J.'s doubts were justified it would become essential to discover when the court has jurisdiction to award damages in substitution for specific performance. *Lord Cairns' Act* reads as follows:

> 2. In all cases in which the Court of Chancery has jurisdiction to entertain an application for an injunction against a breach of any covenant, contract, or agreement, or against the commission or continuance of any wrongful act, or for the specific performance of any covenant, contract or agreement, it shall be lawful for the same Court, if it shall think fit, to award damages to the party injured, either in addition to or in substitution for such injunction or specific performance, and such damages may be assessed in such manner as the Court shall direct.[195]

The power given by this provision is thus available in all cases in which the court has jurisdiction to entertain an application for specific performance. But what does this mean? It can well be said that the court always has jurisdiction to entertain an application, though for many good reasons it may, after entertaining it, refuse it.[195a] On this interpretation there would be no restriction on the power to award damages under the Act. On the other hand, if it is said that the court does not have jurisdiction to entertain an application for specific performance if specific performance would for good reason be refused, then the power to award damages in substitution for specific performance has no scope at all, for where a substitution is in question it must be supposed that specific performance has been refused, presumably for good reason. Intermediate positions are not easy to define. In *Price v. Strange*,[196] Buckley L.J. said:

> There are, of course, classes of contracts of which the court acting on accepted principles will not in any circumstances decree specific performance. Contracts for the sale and purchase of any commodity readily

193 [1974] Ch. 30 at p. 57.

194 *Supra.*

195 Modern Judicature Act provisions are in similar terms. See *Courts of Justice Act* (Ont.), s. 99; *Judicature Act*, Alta., s. 19; Yukon, s. 27; N.W.T., s. 42; *Court of Queen's Bench Act* (Man.), s. 36; *Queen's Bench Act, 1998* (Sask.), s. 66; *Supreme Court Act* (P.E.I.), s. 32.

195a See *Jaggard v. Sawyer*, [1995] 1 W.L.R. 269 (C.A.), at p. 285; *Marcic v. Thames Water Utilities Ltd. (No. 2)*, [2002] Q.B. 929 (CA), revd on other grounds [2003] 3 W.L.R. 1603 (H.L.).

196 [1978] Ch. 337 (C.A.).

> available upon the market at an ascertainable market price and contracts for personal services are examples. In the case of any such contract it would, I think, be correct to say that the court has no jurisdiction to entertain an application for the specific performance of the contract.[197]

The court went on to hold however that where specific performance was possible but was refused as a matter of discretion, the court still had jurisdiction to entertain the application, so damages could be awarded in substitution therefor. This is a difficult distinction. Even though the refusal of specific performance can be reliably predicted on the basis of a well-established discretion, it appears that in Buckley L.J.'s view the jurisdiction to entertain the application remains. But in that case why can it not be said that in the ordinary sale of goods case, which he cites as one in which the Act does not apply, the court equally has discretion to entertain the application, for it is surely through the exercise of the court's discretion that specific performance is generally refused in such cases. The consequence of this line of thinking would be that the court always has power to award damages in substitution for specific performance and if so a well-advised plaintiff ought always to cast the claim in the form of a claim to specific performance or damages in substitution. This would have startling results. A disappointed buyer of gold bars, for example, would be encouraged to frame the action for non-delivery as a claim for specific performance (even knowing that it would inevitably be refused) in order to obtain the benefit of judgment date assessment on a rising market. Such a circumvention of the ordinary rules for damage assessment would be most unwelcome.

1.940 No doubt it was in part a consideration of these prospects that induced the House of Lords in *Johnson v. Agnew*[198] to hold categorically that *Lord Cairns' Act* does not warrant the assessment of damages on any basis other than at common law. Of *Wroth v. Tyler* Lord Wilberforce said:

> If this establishes a different basis from that applicable at common law, I could not agree with it, but in [a later case] Magarry J. went so far as to indicate his view that there is no inflexible rule that common law damages must be assessed as at the date of the breach. Furthermore, in *Malhotra v. Choudhury* [1980] Ch. 52 the Court of Appeal expressly decided that, in a case where damages are given in substitution for an order for specific performance, both equity and the common law would award damages on the same basis — in that case as on the date of judgment. On the balance of these authorities and also on principle, I find in the Act no warrant for the court awarding damages differently from common law damages, but the question is left open on what date such damages, however awarded, ought to be assessed.[199]

1.950 The meaning of this is that the result in *Wroth v. Tyler* is approved but only on the basis that the same measure of damages would have been

[197] *Supra*, at p. 369.
[198] [1980] A.C. 367 (H.L.).

awarded at common law. Lord Wilberforce made it clear that the general rule is that damages are assessed at the date of breach:

> The general principle for the assessment of damages is compensatory, i.e., that the innocent party is to be placed, so far as money can do so, in the same position as if the contract had been performed. Where the contract is one of sale, this principle normally leads to assessment of damages as at the date of breach — a principle recognised and embodied in section 51 of the Sale of Goods Act 1893.[200]

He adds that departure from this principle is possible but must be justified: "But this is not an absolute rule: if to follow it would give rise to injustice, the court has power to fix such other date as may be appropriate in the circumstances."[201] Lord Wilberforce then gives examples of cases where justice requires postponement. These are *Ogle v. Vane*[202] where the defendant after breach gave assurances of performance, *Hickman v. Haynes*[203] where performance was postponed at the defendant's request, and *Radford v. De Froberville*[204] where the defendant had contracted to build a wall on land adjacent to the plaintiff's and so purchase of substitute performance was impossible.

1.960 The language used by Lord Wilberforce and the examples he chose show that he considered that if the date for assessment of damages was to be postponed it had to be for reasons that would appeal to a modern court of justice assessing damages on general compensatory principles.[205] It is submitted that any other view, besides being inconvenient as argued above, perpetuates an anachronistic distinction between the equity and common law sides of the modern court.

1.970 The remaining question is what is left of the decision in *Wroth v. Tyler*. It seems plain from the passage quoted above that Lord Wilberforce thought the result acceptable, assuming that it could be justified on general compensatory principles. Megarry J. clearly thought that full compensation to the plaintiffs required the result he reached. He said, having referred to the general

199 *Supra*, at p. 400. This passage was endorsed by the Ontario Court of Appeal in *306793 Ontario Ltd. v. Rimes* (1979), 100 D.L.R. (3d) 350 at p. 354, 25 O.R. (2d) 79. See also *Ansdell v. Crowther* (1984), 11 D.L.R. (4th) 614, 55 B.C.L.R. 216 (C.A.); *Mavretic v. Bowman*, [1993] 4 W.W.R. 329, 76 B.C.L.R. (2d) 61 (C.A.); *Buchanan v. Fisher* (1993), 30 R.P.R. (2d) 317 (B.C.S.C.). To the same general effect is *Elsley v. J.G. Collins Ins. Agencies Ltd.*, [1978] 2 S.C.R. 916 at p. 934, 83 D.L.R. (3d) 1 at p. 13.

200 *Johnson v. Agnew, supra*, footnote 198, at pp. 400-1.

201 *Johnson v. Agnew, supra*, at p. 401. See also *Douse v. Mascioli* (1997), 10 R.P.R. (3d) 205 (Ont. Ct. (Gen. Div.)); *Aspen Wapiti Ltd. v. Jensen*, [2001] 7 W.W.R. 625 (Sask. C.A.), at p. 632, citing this work.

202 (1867), L.R. 2 Q.B. 275, affd 3 Q.B. 272 (Ex. Ch.), followed in *Glenn v. Schaffer* (1911), 18 W.L.R. 671 (Sask. S.C.); *Samuel v. Black Lake Asbestos & Chrome Co.* (1921), 62 S.C.R. 472, 63 D.L.R. 617.

203 (1875), L.R. 10 C.P. 598.

204 [1977] 1 W.L.R. 1262 (Ch.).

205 This passage was cited with approval in *Bitton v. Jakovljevic* (1990), 75 O.R. (2d) 143 at p. 159, 13 R.P.R. (2d) 48 (H.C.J.).

principle that an award of damages should put the party complaining so far as money can do it in the same situation as if the contract had been performed:

> In the ordinary case of a buyer of goods which the seller fails to deliver, the buyer can at once spend his money in purchasing equivalent goods from another, as was pointed out in *Gainsford v. Carroll* (1824) 2 B. & C. 624, and so the rule works well enough; but that is a very different case. It therefore seems to me that on the facts of this case there are strong reasons for applying the principle [of full compensation] rather than the rule [of breach date assessment].[206]

At a later point he said: "if the plaintiffs obtain neither a decree of specific performance nor £5,500 by way of damages [the judgment date assessment], theirs also is a dismal prospect. Having made a binding contract to purchase for £6,000 a bungalow now worth £11,500, they would recover neither the bungalow nor damages that would enable them to purchase anything like its equivalent."[207] It is evident therefore that Megarry J. was not proposing a departure from the general rule of breach date assessment in the ordinary sale of goods case, but that he considered that reasons of justice required departure from the general rule in the particular case before him. The reason may lie in the following passage:

> I am satisfied on the evidence that the plaintiffs had no financial resources of any substance beyond the £6,000 that they could have put together for the purchase of the defendant's bungalow, and that the defendant knew this when the contract was made. The plaintiffs were therefore, to the defendant's knowledge, unable at the time of the breach to raise a further £1,500 in order to purchase an equivalent house forthwith, and so, as events have turned out, mitigate their loss.[208]

This passage may be important for it is one of the reasons given for a departure from the general rule, and since *Johnson v. Agnew*, a reason other than the existence of *Lord Cairns' Act* is needed to justify the result. On this basis the case could be limited to a purchaser who is without the means of mitigating loss by the purchase of a substitute on the defendant's breach. In a case (like *Wroth v. Tyler* itself) where a couple have put up their life savings as a deposit on a first house, it is readily understandable that the means to purchase a substitute will be lacking. Thus, the result in *Wroth v. Tyler* would be justifiable on its facts. But in any case where the purchaser has the means, or access to the means, to buy substitute property, assessment of damages would, on this view, be at the date when such a purchase could reasonably have been made. On this interpretation, practically all commercial purchasers would be excluded from the benefit of postponed assessment, for rarely is the loss of the use of the deposit critical to such purchasers, and so would be a substantial number of individual purchasers who will have the capacity to borrow to finance a substitute purchase.[208a]

---

[206] *Wroth v. Tyler*, [1974] Ch. 30 at p. 57.
[207] *Supra*, at p. 62.
[208] *Supra*, at p. 57.

1.980 The question of the proper measure of damages is intimately related to the question of the availability of specific performance.[209] If the purchaser has the right to an actual decree of specific performance, where this is possible, protection against a rise in value can be procured by obtaining a decree. It seems anomalous for an award of damages instead of a decree to give substantially less than the financial equivalent of specific performance itself.[209a] The implication of holding the plaintiff to an early date for assessment of damages on the assumption that the property can be replaced in the market is that the plaintiff loses any specific proprietary interest in the actual property agreed to be sold and becomes entitled instead to a crystallized sum of money (with interest until payment). This, however, cannot be the result in any case where the plaintiff has a right to specific enforcement. But the Supreme Court of Canada held in 1996 that a purchaser of land no longer had an automatic right to specific performance.[209b] The position therefore appears to be that only a plaintiff who is properly pursuing a decree of specific performance is entitled to postpone the date for assessment,[209c] and only then until it becomes clear that actual performance will not be forthcoming (as, for example, when it is learned that performance will be impossible), but further increases beyond that date (when the contract is "lost" to use the word of Lord Wilberforce)[210] will not be chargeable to the defendant. This explanation leaves the result in *Wroth v. Tyler* intact for it was a feature of the case that the plaintiff (and indeed the judge)[211] had reason to expect right up to the last moment that the defendant's wife would remove her charge and that actual performance would be forthcoming.

1.990 Where the value of property drops after breach, postponement of the date for assessment of damages may be sought by the vendor. The British Columbia Court of Appeal held in *Ansdell v. Crowther*[212] that only in an exceptional case would a vendor be entitled to a postponed assessment. Normally, the court said, damages would be assessed at the date when, acting

---

208a See *A.V.G. Management Science Ltd. v. Barwell Developments Ltd.* (1976), 69 D.L.R. (3d) 741, [1976] 6 W.W.R. 289 (B.C.S.C.), affd 83 D.L.R. (3d) 702, [1978] 1 W.W.R. 730 (C.A.), affd on this point [1979] 2 S.C.R. 43, 92 D.L.R. (3d) 289; *Domowicz v. Orsa Investments Ltd.* (1994), 20 O.R. (3d) 722 (Gen. Div.), vard 40 O.R. (4th) 256 (C.A.).

209 See Sharpe, *Injunctions and Specific Performance*, looseleaf ed. (Toronto, Canada Law Book, 1999), 8.20-8.90.

209a *Semelhago v. Paramedevan*, [1996] 2 S.C.R. 415, 136 D.L.R. (4th) 1.

209b *Supra.*

209c *Pyne (In Trust) v. Footman* (2007), 31 B.L.R. (4th) 239 (Ont. S.C.J.) at para. 71, revd on other grounds 42 B.L.R. (4th) 224 (Ont. C.A.).

210 *Johnson v. Agnew*, [1980] A.C. 367 (H.L.), at p. 401. See also *Gaspari v. Creighton Holdings Ltd.* (1984), 13 D.L.R. (4th) 570 (B.C.S.C.); *Suleman v. Shahsavari*, [1988] 1 W.L.R. 1181 (Ch.D.); *Pepper v. Lecoure* (1990), 11 R.P.R. (2d) 235 (Ont. Dist. Ct.); *Eastwalsh Homes Ltd. v. Anatal Developments Ltd.* (1990), 68 D.L.R. (4th) 246 at p. 267, 72 O.R. (2d) 661 (H.C.J.), revd on other grounds 100 D.L.R. (4th) 469, 12 O.R. (3d) 675 (C.A.). Postponement of assessment to this point was approved in *Horsnail v. Shute* (1921), 62 D.L.R. 199 (B.C.C.A.) (see passage quoted in 1. 910, *supra*); *Schweickardt v. Thorne*, [1976] 4 W.W.R. 249 (B.C.S.C.).

211 See *Wroth v. Tyler, supra*, footnote 206, at p. 63.

reasonably, the vendor could have resold the property in the market. The court also stressed that, following the opinion of Lord Wilberforce in *Johnson v. Agnew*,[213] nothing should turn on the applicability of *Lord Cairns' Act* (or its modern equivalent) nor on the distinction between equitable and common law damages. The decision must throw doubt on the rule giving a vendor of land an automatic right to specific performance, and lend support to writers who have argued against such a right where the vendor is in the better position to mitigate by reselling the property in the market.[214]

1.1000 In cases of destruction or conversion of goods the *prima facie* measure of damages is their value at the time and place of the loss.[215] If, however, the plaintiff does not learn of the loss for a period of time during which the value rises, it would seem that she is entitled to the higher value.[216] This would be consistent with the general rule of sales cases. Justice is done to the plaintiff if a sufficient sum of money is awarded to enable her to replace the goods at the time of their loss, or at the earliest time thereafter that she could reasonably be expected to purchase a substitute. Interest should be added to this sum until payment.[217] The plaintiff, once she knows the property has been destroyed or irretrievably lost, cannot have a reasonable expectation of receiving the specific goods. Consequently, if she chooses not to replace them she is of course free to do so — in effect deciding not to invest in ownership of such goods — but she cannot hold the defendant liable for the profit she might have made from an investment she chose to forgo.[217a]

1.1010 In cases where the plaintiff can assert a proprietary interest in specific goods, there is a close analogy to cases where the plaintiff is entitled to specific performance. Thus, if the plaintiff brings an action in detinue, the court has jurisdiction to order specific delivery of the chattel claimed. Such an order has the effect of giving the plaintiff the benefit of any increase in the value of the chattel between the date of the wrong and the date of judgment. Just as in the case of damages in lieu of specific performance, it seems to follow that on refusal of specific delivery the plaintiff must be entitled to

---

[212] (1984), 11 D.L.R. (4th) 614. See 5.1440-1460, *infra.* See also *Mavretic v. Bowman*, [1993] 4 W.W.R. 329, 76 B.C.L.R. (2d) 61 (C.A.); *Garbens v. Khayami* (1994), 17 O.R. (3d) 162, 36 R.P.R. (2d) 244 (Gen. Div.) *642947 Ontario Ltd. v. Fleischer* (2001), 209 D.L.R. (4th) 182 (Ont. C.A.); *Talisman Homes Ltd. v. Endicott*, [2003] 1 W.W.R. 300 (Alta. Q.B.). See paras 5.1440-60, *infra.*

[213] [1980] A.C. 367 (H.L.).

[214] See Sharpe, *op. cit.*, footnote 209, 8.100-8.220.

[215] *Roynat Ltd. v. Northern Meat Packers* (1986), 29 D.L.R. (4th) 139 at p. 144, 71 N.B.R. (2d) 212 (C.A.), citing this passage. See *Scobie v. Wing*, [1992] 2 W.W.R. 514, 63 B.C.L.R. (2d) 76 (C.A.).

[216] See *The Queen in right of Alberta v. Arnold*, [1971] S.C.R. 209, 14 D.L.R. (3d) 574, followed in *Dominion Securities Ltd. v. Glazerman* (1984), 29 C.C.L.T. 194 (Man. C.A.). See also *Rose v. Mitton* (1994), 111 D.L.R. (4th) 217, 128 N.S.R. (2d) 99 (C.A.).

[217] On the award of interest, see 7.330 - 7.1000, *infra.*

[217a] *Tridont Leasing (Canada) Ltd. v. Saskatoon Market Mall Ltd.*, [1995] 6 W.W.R. 641 at pp. 654-5, 131 Sask. R. 169 (C.A.), citing this passage.

damages representing the value of the chattel at the date of judgment. The analogy was drawn in *Malhotra v. Choudhury*:[218]

> The equitable remedy of specific performance has features markedly different from damages at common law for breach of contract. But there is an analogy at common law to the equitable remedy of specific performance. This is to be found in the action in detinue... the action in detinue partakes of the nature of an action in rem in which the plaintiff seeks specific restitution of his chattel. In this action where an order for a writ of specific delivery can be made, the plaintiff has always been entitled instead to claim its value in money assessed at date of judgment.[219]

1.1020 An action in conversion, on the other hand, looks primarily to the date of the wrong, apparently giving the plaintiff a substantially inferior remedy on a rising market.[220] It is always awkward for results to vary according to forms of action, and in *Sachs v. Miklos*,[221] Lord Goddard C.J. made strenuous efforts to demonstrate that conversion in the circumstances here considered was as generous to the plaintiff as detinue. The case involved furniture sold during the war without authority by a bailee. The plaintiff did not discover the facts until after the war when the value of the furniture had risen tenfold. Lord Goddard, giving the judgment of the Court of Appeal, held that the measure of damages in detinue and conversion should be the same, with the increase in value to be added to the *prima facie* measure of damages for conversion as consequential damages. The entitlement of the plaintiff to recover the higher measure of damages depended, however, on his not having knowledge of the conversion, a point on which no finding of fact had been made: "If he did have that knowledge, then, it seems to me, this great rise in value which has taken place since is not damage which he can recover as flowing from the wrongful act."[222]

1.1030 Lord Goddard's assertion that the measure of damages was the same in detinue and conversion was castigated in *Malhotra v. Choudhury* as unnecessary, too wide, and based on a misleading headnote.[223] However, it is submitted that, in substance, Lord Goddard's approach was sound. So long as the plaintiff has reason to expect that the defendant will restore the specific goods, it is not reasonable to expect him to procure substitute furniture. When the plaintiff learns that the goods have been sold, he must make his own

[218] [1980] Ch. 52 (C.A.).

[219] *Supra*, at pp. 78-9, *per* Cumming-Bruce L.J. See also *Steiman v. Steiman* (1983), 143 D.L.R. (3d) 396 at p. 407, 18 Man.R. (2d) 203 (C.A.).

[220] The primary measure of damages is usually said to be the value of the goods at the time of the conversion. See *Mackenzie v. Blindman Valley Co-operative Ass'n*, [1947] 4 D.L.R. 687 (Alta. S.C.).

[221] [1948] 2 K.B. 23 (C.A.), applied in *Aitken v. Gardiner* (1956), 4 D.L.R. (2d) 119, [1956] O.R. 589 (H.C.J.), to a case of detinue for shares, and *Steiman v. Steiman* (1981), 11 Man. R. (2d) 376, 18 C.C.L.T. 133 (Q.B.), vard 143 D.L.R. (3d) 396, 18 Man. R. (2d) 203 (C.A.), a case of conversion of jewellery.

[222] *Sachs v. Miklos, supra*, footnote 221, at p. 40. See *Club 7 Ltd. v. E.P.K. Holdings Ltd.* (1993), 115 Nfld. & P.E.I.R. 271 (Nfld. S.C.), at pp. 308-9, citing this passage.

[223] *Malhotra v. Choudhury, supra*, footnote 218, at p. 79. See also *Steiman v. Steiman, supra*, footnote 219, at pp. 407-9.

decision on replacement (notionally as Lord Goddard said the measure of damages assessed at that date will be sufficient to replace the furniture)[224] and cannot hold the defendant to subsequent increases in value. It will be seen that this approach closely matches Lord Wilberforce's speech in *Johnson v. Agnew* where it was held that assessment of damages in a case where specific performance might be sought should take place at the date the contract is "lost", that is, at the date when it becomes clear that actual performance will not be forthcoming.[225] In the earlier case of *Rosenthal v. Alderton & Sons, Ltd.*,[226] also concerning the wrongful sale of second-hand furniture by a bailee, it was held that the owner could sue in detinue so as to recover the judgment date value. It was held that the bailor could elect to sue in detinue but the court added the significant words "at any rate where he was not aware of the conversion at the time".[227] These words indicate that the result in the case is not inconsistent with the rule supported here, namely, that the assessment of damages should take place at the earliest date on which the plaintiff, acting reasonably, could have replaced the goods. So long as there is a prospect of receiving the specific restitution, as there is so long as the defendant has the power to restore the goods, the plaintiff acts reasonably in not replacing them. Even though the defendant refuses absolutely to restore the goods to the plaintiff (whose ultimate legal success is of course to be assumed), the plaintiff may reasonably expect that the defendant will change his mind after taking legal advice or upon being subjected to an adverse judgment. Indeed the plaintiff, whether suing in conversion or detinue, is constantly open to the possi-

[*The next page is* 1-51]

224 *Sachs v. Miklos, supra*, footnote 221, at p. 40.
225 See 1.910, *supra*.
226 [1946] K.B. 374 (C.A.).
227 *Supra*, at p. 379.

bility of the defendant's offering to restore the goods, in which case it was early established that the plaintiff's action would be stayed on refusal to accept redelivery.[228]

1.1040 In the sale of specific goods, the property in the goods generally passes to the buyer when the contract is made.[229] In a case of non-delivery, the buyer is entitled, therefore, to sue the seller in detinue or conversion. The buyer would also be entitled to use self-help and possibly the legal remedy of replevin to gain actual possession of the goods. It appears in such cases that the buyer can reasonably refrain from replacing the goods so long as it remains in the seller's power to deliver them. It was established in *Cohen v. Roche*[230] that the buyer would not be entitled to an order of specific delivery in detinue unless the goods were of such a kind as to justify an order of specific performance. Nevertheless, so long as by the law of sale the property is vested in the buyer, it appears difficult to avoid the conclusion that the buyer is entitled to call for actual delivery, and on a rising market should be entitled to postpone the date for damage assessment to the date when it finally becomes apparent that delivery will not be forthcoming, which may be as late as the date of judgment.

1.1050 Replevin and self-help are available in all cases where the plaintiff can assert ownership of specific property. It seems to follow that so long as these remedies are available the date of the assessment of damages is postponed. If the law affords the plaintiff a remedy that if exercised would give him possession of specific property, it must in administering the alternative remedy of damages award to the plaintiff a money sum equal to the value of the property at the time the plaintiff could lawfully have repossessed it. The logic is the same as that applied in *Wroth v. Tyler*.[231] If damages were reduced to the value of the property at the date of the wrong, logic and convenience would require the elimination of the plaintiff's right to exercise proprietary remedies, but this would be to permit the defendant in effect to deprive the plaintiff of his property rights simply by making a wrongful assertion.

1.1060 Many of these difficult questions arose in the Supreme Court of Canada case of *Asamera Oil Corp. Ltd. v. Sea Oil & General Corp.*[232] This was an action for failure by a bailee to return shares. The value of the shares at the date of the wrong was 29¢; they subsequently rose to a value of $46.50, dropping back by the date of the trial (nine years after the wrong) to $22. As the dispute involved 125,000 shares it will be

228 *Fisher v. Prince* (1762), 3 Burr. 1363, 97 E.R. 876; *Earle v. Holderness* (1828), 4 Bing. 462, 130 E.R. 845.

229 *Sale of Goods Act*, Alta., s. 20(2); B.C., s. 24; Man., s. 22; N.B., s. 19; Nfld. & Lab., s. 19; N.W.T., s. 22; N.S., s. 21; Ont., s. 19; P.E.I., s. 20; Sask., s. 20; Yukon, s. 19.

230 [1927] 1 K.B. 169. To the same effect is *Chychaluk v. Protheroe* (1951), 2 W.W.R. 513 (Man. K.B.), affd 6 W.W.R. (N.S.) 48 (C.A.).

231 See 1.860, *supra*.

232 [1979] 1 S.C.R. 633, 89 D.L.R. (3d) 1. For a fuller discussion see Waddams, "Damages for Failure to Return Shares", 3 C.B.L.J. 398 (1979).

appreciated that millions of dollars turned on the choice of date of assessment of damages. Though in the lower courts the action had proceeded as one in detinue, the Supreme Court of Canada held that "the action in substance is a simple case of breach of contract".[233] Unfortunately the judgment does not explain why the plaintiff could not exercise proprietary remedies, but presumably the reason must be that the plaintiff lacked a specific interest in the particular shares or in a particular certificate, the particular shares loaned having been sold by the defendant in 1958. The defendant's obligation was evidently therefore treated as an obligation to replace rather than to restore specific shares. At least when the plaintiff came to know of the sale, it no longer had reason to assert a proprietary interest.

1.1070 The decision of the Supreme Court of Canada was that, like a buyer of goods, the plaintiff was not entitled to hold the defendant to any increase in the value of the shares after the date at which, acting reasonably in all the circumstances, it could have purchased replacement shares. The conclusion was based on the duty to act reasonably to mitigate loss. As has been suggested earlier,[234] it does not seem entirely satisfactory for the result to rest on the duty of the plaintiff to act reasonably, for it could not be shown that it was unreasonable for the plaintiff not to anticipate the rise in market value of the shares and it seems plain that the court's conclusion did not rest on any such finding. It is suggested therefore that the slightly wider formulation used here actually represents the decision of the court. The point at which damages are assessed is the point at which the plaintiff ought to say to itself that "its shares" are now lost to it and that it has to make a fresh decision whether or not to invest in similar shares.

1.1080 The Supreme Court of Canada held that a six-year period should be allowed to the plaintiff during which, in fact, the shares had risen to about $7. This seems, at first sight, a rather generous allotment of time but certain facts in the case appear to have made it reasonable for the plaintiff to postpone any decision to replace the shares. These are, first, that an injunction was obtained restraining the defendant from disposing of the shares. The injunction was interpreted not to affect any specific identifiable shares, simply requiring the defendant to retain any 125,000 shares of the company. However, the existence of the injunction may well have led the plaintiff to consider that it had a reasonable prospect of actually obtaining a block of shares from the defendant. Not until some years after the date of the wrong did the plaintiff learn that the specific shares loaned had been sold by the defendant before the date due for their replacement. This fact did not emerge incontrover-

233 *Asamera Oil Corp., supra,* at p. 644 S.C.R., p. 8 D.L.R.
234 See 1.780, *supra.*

tibly until the defendant admitted it on discovery in 1968. Thus, the plaintiff might plausibly say that for a number of years after 1960 it had reason to expect actual restitution from the defendant. The second important fact was that the defendant had strenuously urged the plaintiff not to press its action, and this too might reasonably be taken as an assurance that the plaintiff's legal rights to the shares would be observed.

1.1090 The decision may be taken to establish, then, that damages will be measured at the date when the plaintiff, acting reasonably in all the circumstances, could have made a substitute purchase.[235] Where the plaintiff maintains a proprietary interest in goods or shares, as also in the case where he was reasonably pursuing a specific remedy, he cannot be expected to consider replacing the property for, by hypothesis, he reasonably expects the defendant eventually to produce it. But where it becomes clear that the specific property is definitely lost to the plaintiff she must make her own investment decision and cannot hold the defendant to further increases in value.

1.1100 In *Westward Farms Ltd. v. Cadieux*,[236] the Manitoba Court of Queen's Bench held that damages for breach of a contract to give the plaintiff an option to buy land were to be assessed at the date when a reasonable person might have purchased a substitute. A period of six months following the breach was allowed as a reasonable time within which to acquire a substitute.

1.1110 The discussion has so far proceeded on the assumption of a steadily rising value of the property. The question now arises as to fluctuation between date of wrong and date of judgment. The *Asamera* case illustrates the possibility of a rise after the date of the wrong, followed by a fall at date of judgment to an intermediate point. Many of the cases concern the wrongful sale of shares by a broker. There is some support for a rule permitting the plaintiff to claim the highest value reached by the shares between the date of the wrong and the date of trial on the argument that he has been deprived of an opportunity to sell the shares at that price. This rule was adopted in a 19th century English case,[237]

---

235 The same view was taken in *Samuel & Escombe v. Rowe* (1892), 8 T.L.R. 488 (Q.B.); in *Steiman v. Steinman* (1983), 143 D.L.R. (3d) 396 (Man. C.A.), and in *Dominion Securities Ltd. v. Glazerman* (1984), 29 C.C.L.T. 194 (Man. C.A.).

236 [1981] 3 W.W.R. 673 (Man. Q.B.), revd on other grounds 138 D.L.R. (3d) 137 (C.A.), leave to appeal to S.C.C. refused 18 Man. R. (2d) 269*n*. See also *Cull v. Heritage Mills Developments Ltd.* (1974), 49 D.L.R. (3d) 521, 5 O.R. (2d) 102 (H.C.J.) (acceptance of anticipatory breach).

237 *Archer v. Williams* (1846), 2 Car. & K. 26, 175 E.R. 11. See also *McNeil v. Fultz* (1906), 38 S.C.R. 198 at p. 205; *Toronto General Trusts Corp. v. Roman* (1962), 37 D.L.R. (2d) 16, [1963] 1 O.R. 312 (C.A.), affd [1963] S.C.R. vi, 41 D.L.R. (2d) 290*n*, and *Brady v. Morgan* (1967), 65 D.L.R. (2d) 101, [1967] 2 O.R. 680 (C.A.), which must now be read in the light of the *Asamera* case. See also *Siscoe Gold Mines Ltd. v. Bijakowski*, [1935] S.C.R. 193, [1935] 1 D.L.R. 513.

though rejected in others,[238] and prevails in some American jurisdictions.[239] It was originally adopted in New York, but later abandoned in favour of a rule allowing the plaintiff to recover the highest value between the date of the conversion and the end of a reasonable period for the plaintiff to effect a replacement.[240] This latter rule was approved by the Supreme Court of Canada in *Asamera* and is consistent with the view put forward above. After the plaintiff learns that the shares have been sold, there is no reasonable expectation of recovering them and the plaintiff must make a new investment choice. If he could recover the highest value between conversion and trial, perhaps many years later, he would be permitted to speculate at the defendant's expense. In a case where the plaintiff's property is wrongfully detained by the defendant down to the trial, the situation is different, for there the plaintiff can assert proprietary remedies and ought, as has been suggested above, to be entitled to recover the value of the property at the date of judgment. It does not follow, however, that in case of fluctuations he should be entitled to a higher intermediate value. In the absence of evidence that the plaintiff would in fact have sold the property at its highest value, he would be over-compensated if he were awarded damages on that basis. As McCormick said, such a rule as an estimate of probabilities would be absurd: "it is in the highest degree improbable that the plaintiff with uncanny prescience would have waited until the market had reached its summit and would have sold at that moment."[241] The rule earlier discussed[242] permits the plaintiff to claim the value of the property at the date of the wrong even it it subsequently would have declined; the possibility of an action in detinue permits the plaintiff, where a proprietary claim can be asserted, to recover the value of the property at the date of judgment if this is to his advantage. If the defendant has sold the plaintiff's property he may be compelled to account for the proceeds.[243] If the plaintiff can produce evidence that he actually would have sold the property at a higher price he can recover the higher price as consequential damages for loss of the use of the property.[244] The combined effect of these rules, it is submitted, gives sufficient protection to the

---

238 *McArthur v. Seaforth* (1810), 2 Taunt. 257, 127 E.R. 1076. See also *Ames & Co. v. Sutherland* (1905), 9 O.L.R. 631 (Div. Ct.), affd 11 O.L.R. 417 (C.A.), affd 37 S.C.R. 694.

239 See McCormick, *Handbook on the Law of Damages* (St. Paul, West Publishing Co., 1935), p. 187.

240 *Op. cit.*, at pp. 187-9.

241 *Ibid.*, at p. 187. To the same effect see Estey J. in the *Asamera* case, *supra*, footnote 232, at p. 16. In *Hardie v. Trans-Canada Resources Ltd.* (1976), 71 D.L.R. (3d) 668 (Alta. S.C. App. Div.), damages for failure to give an option to purchase shares were based on the average share price during the period the option would have been open. See also *New Horizon Investments Ltd. v. Montroyal Estates Ltd.* (1982), 26 R.P.R. 268 (B.C.S.C.).

242 See 1.660, *supra*.

243 See 9.40, 9.50, *infra*.

244 See 1.1230 - 1.1350, *infra*.

plaintiff. The addition of an automatic presumption in his favour that he would have sold at the top of the market has the appearance of going beyond a genuine attempt to assess the plaintiff's probable loss.[245]

6. Allowance for Interest on Unpaid Purchase Price

1.1120 Where a buyer of property obtains an award of damages based on an increased value at the date of judgment, the question arises of whether the buyer should give credit for interest on the unpaid purchase money.[246]

1.1130 In *Wroth v. Tyler*,[247] where land values had appreciated rapidly between the date of breach and the date of judgment, the purchasers of land were held entitled to damages based on the judgment date value of the land, no allowance apparently being made for the interest on the unpaid purchase price. The reasoning was that had the contract been performed the purchasers would have had the land itself at the date of judgment. This is true, but in order to put themselves in that position the purchasers would have had to pay the purchase price on the date agreed for closing. If no allowance is made for this factor, the purchasers will be over-compensated.

1.1140 The possible over-compensation can be illustrated by considering a simple example of a contract to purchase land for $500,000. The landowner defaults, the purchaser seeks a decree, and obtains damages in lieu of specific performance based on the value of the land at the date of judgment three years after the date of breach. The land has appreciated at fifteen per cent per annum and is now worth $760,000. Current interest rates, let us suppose, are at eighteen per cent per annum.

1.1150 If the purchaser has kept the $500,000 purchase price in Bank of Canada bills under a mattress, the award of $260,000 (following the reasoning in *Wroth v. Tyler*) will put the plaintiff in the same position as though the contract had been fulfilled, with total assets worth $760,000, the current value of the land. However, in the ordinary case it is unreasonable to suppose that the purchaser derives no benefit from the postponement of payment of the purchase price.

1.1160 It might be argued that since the vendor has had free use of the land between breach date and judgment date, the purchaser should be allowed

245 See *Simmons v. London Joint Stock Bank*, [1891] 1 Ch. 270 (C.A.), at p. 284, affd *loc. cit.* p. 287 (C.A.), revd on other grounds [1892] A.C. 201 (H.L.); *Michael v. Hart & Co.*, [1902] 1 K.B. 482 (C.A.). The question was left open in *Mansell v. British Linen Co. Bank*, [1892] 3 Ch. 159. In *Ames & Co. v. Sutherland, supra*, footnote 238, the claimant admitted that he would, in the absence of the wrong, have held the shares until trial. The court held that this evidence was "very material upon the question of damages": 9 O.L.R. at p. 638. In *Goodall v. Clarke* (1910), 21 O.L.R. 614 (Div. Ct.) (see especially Clute J., at p. 620), and in *Nelson v. Baird* (1915), 22 D.L.R. 132 (Man. K.B.) (claims to highest intermediate value were rejected).

246 For a fuller discussion, see Waddams, "Inflation and Mitigation of Damages", 1 Ox. J.L.S. 134 (1981).

247 [1974] Ch. 30.

free use of the price for the same period.[248] This argument, however, ignores the fact that the value of holding the land during a period of capital appreciation is reflected in part (and in some cases in whole) in the enhanced capital value. On the other hand, high interest rates in a period of inflation reflect not only the value of the use of money but in large part the declining value of the money itself.[249] Consequently the purchaser is, in effect, protected twice over from inflation if he keeps the benefit of high interest rates and captures the capital appreciation of the land that was to be purchased with the money. Old cases on specific performance permitted the purchaser to claim the profits derived from land between breach and closing but only on payment of interest on the purchase price during the same period.[250] The effect of allowing the purchaser to claim damages based on the appreciated value of the land without paying interest on the unpaid price is to permit the purchaser to acquire the profits of holding the land during the period in question without accounting for the profits of holding the price.

1.1170 It may be assumed that usually the postponement of payment of the purchase price benefits the purchaser in one of three ways. First, she may invest the price in an interest-bearing account, which in the example just mentioned of a price of $500,000 at an interest of eighteen per cent would (ignoring income tax considerations) increase the purchaser's wealth by the date of judgment (at compound interest with annual rests) to $820,000. Secondly, she may invest the purchase money in other property that resists inflation, for example, gold, other land, or stable foreign currency. An investment could be supposed that would exactly match the appreciation of the value of the land in dispute. Thirdly, it is commonly the case that the purchaser does not have the purchase price in cash at the date agreed for closing but intends to borrow it. The effect is then equally that the purchaser benefits by the postponement of the payment, in this case by being relieved of the necessity of paying the interest on the borrowed purchase price between the date of breach and the date of judgment.

1.1180 In all these cases it is suggested that account must be taken of the benefit to the purchaser. It would not be practicable or desirable to attempt to trace particular investments allegedly made with the purchase

---

[248] This consideration evidently caused defendant's counsel to abandon a claim to interest in *306793 Ontario Ltd. v. Rimes* (1979), 100 D.L.R. (3d) 350, 25 O.R. (2d) 79 (C.A.). See p. 357 D.L.R.

[249] See 7.350, *infra*.

[250] *Esdaile v. Stephenson* (1822), 1 Sim. & St. 122, 57 E.R. 49. See *Jones v. Mudd* (1827), 4 Russ. 118, 38 E.R. 749; *Fry on Specific Performance of Contracts*, 6th ed. by Northcote (London, Stevens, 1921), §§1402-4; Sharpe, *Injunctions and Specific Performance*, looseleaf ed. (Toronto, Canada Law Book, 1999), 11.340-11.360. See also *Ribic v. Weinstein* (1982), 140 D.L.R. (3d) 258, 26 R.P.R. 247 (H.C.J.), affd 10 D.L.R. (4th) 717, 47 O.R. (2d) 126, *sub. nom. Weinstein v. A.E. LePage (Ontario) Ltd.*; *Harvela Investments Ltd. v. Royal Trust Company of Canada (C.I.) Ltd.*, [1986] A.C. 207 (H.L.) (purchaser not entitled to profits on shares unless paying interest on unpaid price).

money. A workable *prima facie* rule that is suggested is that where the purchaser claims the benefit of an appreciated land value, credit should

[*The next page is* 1–57]

be given for interest at current rates on the unpaid purchase price.[251] It would then be for the purchaser to show, if he could, because of the incidence of income tax or for other unavoidable factors, that he had not in fact benefited by the full extent of current interest rates. The same principle would seem to be applicable to the actual award of a decree of specific performance as to assessment of damages in substitution for specific performance.

1.1190 Another way of putting the vendor's argument is that, in inflationary times, the real value of the sum agreed as the price diminishes between breach and trial. Unless an allowance is made for interest, the purchaser will be enabled to enforce a substantially better bargain than was actually made.

1.1200 The decision of the House of Lords in *Johnson v. Agnew*[252] does not deal directly with this question, but in holding that there are no special damage rules applicable to damages in lieu of specific performance,[253] the House of Lords impliedly holds that ordinary principles of damage assessment apply; in particular, that the plaintiff is to be put in as good a position as, but not in a better position than, would have been occupied if the contract had been performed.

1.1210 The question came more directly before the Ontario Court of Appeal in *306793 Ontario Ltd. v. Rimes*[254] where, in awarding damages in substitution for specific performance, the court rejected any allowance for interest saved by the purchaser by postponement of payment of the purchase price. One ground for the decision was the court's apparent view that unless the purchaser had the money in hand, it derived no benefit from postponement. But as was suggested above, it seems hard to resist the argument that the purchaser is saved the cost it would otherwise have incurred by borrowing the money.

1.1220 Unfortunately, the question was obscured because the vendor expressly abandoned any claim to interest on the purchase money and argued the matter in terms of a possible reduction in damages in respect of the "carrying charges", *i.e.*, the cost to the vendor of holding the land between the date of breach and the date of judgment. To effect such a reduction in damages MacKinnon A.C.J.O. said:

> . . . would impose on the purchaser, who was not in default, the notional carrying charges and offset them against any increase in the value of the

---

251 The case is analogous to that where the purchaser claimed rental income from the land between date of breach and date of closing, in which case the purchaser was required to pay interest on the purchase money. The only difference is that the profit from the land takes the form of capital appreciation instead of rent. See also *Vanmeld Ltd. v. Cussen* (1994), 121 A.L.R. 619 (F.C.).

252 [1980] A.C. 367 (H.L.).

253 *Supra*, at p. 400, endorsed by the Ontario Court of Appeal in *306793 Ontario Ltd. v. Rimes* (1979), 100 D.L.R. (3d) 350, 25 O.R. (2d) 79.

254 *306793 Ontario, supra*. See Swan, "Damages, Specific Performance, Inflation and Interest", 10 R.P.R. 267 (1980); *Tanu v. Ray* (1981), 20 R.P.R. 22 (B.C.S.C.).

> land. Notwithstanding a superficial attractiveness to this approach, it has the effect of removing from the vendor any risk in assuming the carrying charges as well as holding the property, because he recovers those charges from the purchaser by the reduction of the damages in an amount equal to those charges, even though the new date of closing is the date of trial.[255]

He expands this thought as follows:

> . . . the illogicality of the result can, it seems to me, be illustrated by two different approaches. By electing for damages, the plaintiff has, in effect, paid the carrying charges by a reduction in his damages equivalent to those estimated charges. The defendant (vendor) for his part is still in possession of the land and able to sell it at the new valuation, recouping his carrying charges plus the profit. The defendant is in precisely the same position as if the deal had been closed on the date fixed in the agreement but has had the land for that extra period and for as much longer as he might wish to hold it. To view the other side of the coin: if the plaintiff had opted for specific performance, the adjustments would have been calculated as of the closing, *i.e.*, the date of trial.[256]

MacKinnon A.C.J.O. makes two points: first, that the vendor has in fact had possession of the land between breach and trial, and so should bear the incidental costs; secondly, that damages in lieu of specific performance must be equivalent to the economic effect of the decree itself, which MacKinnon A.C.J.O. assumed not to require any allowance in respect of postponement of payment of the price. To take the second point first, it may be conceded that specific performance and damages in lieu of specific performance ought to have a like economic effect. MacKinnon A.C.J.O.'s assumption, however, that a decree would make no allowance for postponement is open to dispute. If it is sound (as is here argued) to reduce damages in lieu of specific performance to make allowance for postponement of the payment of price, it must be right also to make a similar allowance as a condition of a decree.[257]

1.1230 MacKinnon A.C.J.O.'s first point, standing alone, does not, with respect, seem persuasive. He says that the vendor has had the benefit of possession of the land between breach and trial and so (it is implied) has received the due return on the costs associated with holding the land. But the very effect of awarding damages in lieu of specific performance is to take away from the vendor the whole of the profit (*i.e.*, the capital appreciation in the land) of holding the land in the period in question, and to give it to the purchaser. And the purchaser is given that profit

---

255 *306793 Ontario, supra*, at p. 353 D.L.R.

256 *306793 Ontario, supra*, at pp. 354-5 D.L.R.

257 See *Harvela Investments Ltd. v. Royal Trust Company of Canada (C.I.) Ltd., supra*, footnote 250, and Sharpe, *op. cit.*, footnote 250, 11.360.

without having to pay the cost of earning it (*i.e.*, of borrowing the purchase price) that it would inevitably have incurred if the contract had been duly performed. It is unfortunate that the whole question was discussed in terms of the vendor's "carrying charges" and not in what seem to be the clearer terms of benefit to the purchaser of postponed payment of the price. In view of the framework in which the case was argued, especially the express abandonment of the vendor's claim to interest on the purchase money, it seems unlikely that *Rimes* will be considered a conclusive authority against making a due allowance for the benefit to the purchaser of postponed payment of the price.[257a] In a subsequent case, the Ontario Court of Appeal made such an allowance; the point was left open in the Supreme Court of Canada.[257b]

7. Loss of Profit on Sales to Third Parties

1.1240 In many cases property has a particular value to its owner because another person has agreed to buy it. Depriving the owner of the property will deprive the owner also of the anticipated benefit of the sale. Cases of this sort are usually considered in the context of non-delivery by sellers causing loss of a resale contract. However, the problem cannot be confined to that context.

1.1250 First, an owner whose property is destroyed or lost by a defendant with whom the owner has no contract may suffer an additional loss if a third party had agreed to buy it at a price higher than the market value. Secondly, actions against defaulting sellers can often be cast into the form of an action for conversion, and it does not seem satisfactory for results to vary according to the form in which the plaintiff brings the action.

1.1260 If the test of value suggested earlier[258] were applied, that is, the sum the plaintiff would rationally demand to give up the property, the loss of the favourable contract with a third party would plainly be taken into account. *Liesbosch, Dredger v. S.S. Edison*[259] makes it clear that the plaintiff's individual circumstances can be considered in assessing value. On the other hand, if all losses of third party contracts were to be compensated, wrongdoers having no reason to know of the plaintiff's dealings would often be held liable for wholly unexpected and exceptional losses. The commitment of the law to compensation is not absolute, and the rule that damages that are too remote are not recoverable is one of the most important limits on the principle of perfect compensation.[260] Difficulties arise in attempting to fit together the principles of remoteness and the

257a See *Semelhago v. Paramadevan* (1994), 19 O.R. (3d) 479, 39 R.P.R. (2d) 215 (C.A.), affd [1996] 2 S.C.R. 415, 136 D.L.R. (4th) 1.

257b *Supra.*

258 See 1.130 - 1.320, *supra.*

259 [1933] A.C. 449 (H.L.).

260 See 14.20 - 14.740, *infra.*

principle that the plaintiff can recover the value of property wrongfully taken. The problem is that property does not have an intrinsic value. All valuation depends on finding real or hypothetical buyers. Yet if all the plaintiff's actual transactions were taken into account the defendant's liability would extend to exceptional and unanticipated losses that would ordinarily be considered too remote.

1.1270 The difficulty of the problem is illustrated by comparison of two English Court of Appeal cases, both actions in conversion brought against sellers who failed to deliver. In both cases the buyer had made an agreement with a third party to sell the goods at a favourable price. In both cases the third party contract was lost because of the seller's default. In *France v. Gaudet*,[261] the court held that the goods had an "actual value . . . fixed by circumstances at the time"[262] that is, a value equal to the resale price, which the wrongdoer was accordingly bound to make good. On the other hand, in *The "Arpad"*[263] recovery of the resale price was held by a majority of the Court of Appeal to be too remote. The buyer was held to be entitled only to the value of the goods, which was held not to be determined by the price at which the buyer had resold them several months earlier. As Maugham L.J. expressly said, the value "to him" was not allowed.[264] The contrary argument was put by Scrutton L.J., dissenting, who pointed out that a person who runs down a shabby-looking millionaire or who injures a horse that turns out to be the Derby favourite must pay the full amount of the plaintiff's loss even without notice of the exceptional circumstances.[265] The majority of the court would have agreed with Scrutton L.J.'s conclusion on these hypothetical cases and indeed the passage is often cited as illustrating the present law. So too if the defendant negligently or deliberately smashes an undistinguished-looking vase on the plaintiff's mantelpiece, he will be liable for its full value even if (quite unexpectedly to the defendant) it turns out to be of great value.[266]

1.1280 The *Liesbosch* case discussed above established that circumstances peculiar to the plaintiff, including his contractual arrangements with third parties, were relevant to the assessment of damages and could be taken into account to enhance the actual value of the plaintiff's property. This might be taken, therefore, to support Scrutton L.J.'s view in *The "Arpad"*. On the other hand, the *Liesbosch* case certainly cannot be taken to decide that principles of remoteness are irrelevant. In fact, the point for which *The "Liesbosch"* is best known is the conclusion that the plaintiff's lack of financial resources cannot be taken into account to

---

261 (1871), L.R. 6 Q.B. 199.

262 *Supra*, at p. 205, *per* Mellor J. In *Gerco Services Co. Ltd. v. Aston* (1981), 48 N.S.R. (2d) 541 (S.C.T.D.), loss of profits was allowed as consequential damages for conversion.

263 [1934] P. 189 (C.A.).

264 *Supra*, at p. 228.

265 *Supra*, at pp. 202-3.

266 See 14.550, *infra*.

enhance his damages even when he suffers actual loss, because such loss is too remote. The merits and scope of this conclusion are discussed in a later chapter.[267] Its significance in the present context is that all compensatory rules of damage measurement are restricted by considerations of remoteness.

1.1290 Scrutton L.J.'s view in *The "Arpad"*, like the reasoning in *France v. Gaudet*, if taken to its ultimate conclusion, would eliminate altogether the restrictions on recovery represented by considerations of remoteness, for with perfect foresight the plaintiff would always value the right that the defendant has infringed at an amount equal to the actual loss in all the circumstances. Thus, one could say that the millshaft in *Hadley v. Baxendale*[268] had an actual value to the miller equal to the profits lost by its absence. Since this line of reasoning would eliminate the law of remoteness it must be taken to be unsound. It is concluded, therefore, that whether the plaintiff's action is brought in contract or in tort against a defaulting seller, or against a negligent actor, recovery of loss caused by the plaintiff's arrangements with third parties is subject to considerations of remoteness.[268a]

1.1300 However, the application of these considerations to cases where a buyer claims loss of profit on a resale is by no means self-evident. Several legal principles are involved. In the case of non-delivery, the damages are normally measured by the difference between the contract price and the market price at the time of breach.[269] A resale contract above market price will not normally enhance the damages, the principle being that the buyer can mitigate the loss by going into the market at the date of breach and purchasing other goods to fill the resale contract.[270] If the resale contract is below the market price, damages are not reduced for normally the buyer will be obliged again to go into the market to purchase goods to fill the resale contract, or pay damages for not doing so.

1.1310 It often happens that particular circumstances will alter these results. Thus it may be that a buyer cannot go into the market to purchase a substitute because there is no market in the particular goods, or because he has agreed on a "string" contract to resell the particular goods to be delivered by the original seller and no others are acceptable to the sub-buyer. In these cases the focus shifts from mitigation to remoteness. The buyer has suffered a real loss (the goods having an exceptionally high value to her); the loss could not in fact be mitigated. The legal question is whether the occurrence of these events is so unusual as to excuse the seller from liability. Here the buyer has incurred a real loss, but one that arguably could not ordinarily have been anticipated.

1.1320 A quite different problem arises where the seller seeks to show that the

---

[267] See 15.330 - 15.390, *infra*.
[268] (1854), 9 Ex. 341, 156 E.R. 145.
[268a] See *Seven Seas Ltd. v. Al-Essa*, [1993] 1 W.L.R. 1083 (Ch. D.).
[269] *Sale of Goods Act* (Ont.), s. 49(3). See footnote 8, *supra*. See also *Mahinder Singh v. Acme Sawmills Ltd.* (1958), 14 D.L.R. (2d) 361 (B.C.C.A.), affd November 3, 1959 (S.C.C.).
[270] *Peterson v. Ayre* (1853), 13 C.B. 353 at p. 365, 138 E.R. 1235, *per* Maule J., *arguendo*.

goods had an exceptionally low value to the buyer. This occurs where a buyer has resold goods below market price, but is not in fact called upon to deliver them. The legal question here is a different one, namely, whether the defaulting seller is entitled to benefit from the circumstance that the buyer would not have realized the full value of the goods, had they been delivered. This problem, considered in the following section,[271] is not necessarily to be solved in the same terms as that of profit lost on a resale. It is not satisfactory, therefore, to assert that resales are always irrelevant or always relevant in the law of damages. Their relevance depends on the question in issue.

1.1330 Loss of profit on a buyer's resale, though disallowed in many cases as too remote,[272] was allowed in *Re R. & H. Hall Ltd. and W. H. Pim (Junior) & Co.'s Arbitration*[273] where the buyer had agreed to resell a specific cargo of grain at a profit. The market fell shortly before the date for delivery. On the seller's failure to deliver, the buyer was unable to fulfil the resale contract and could not mitigate by going into the market because the sub-buyer was bound to take only the specific cargo, which, of course, the first buyer could not deliver. The House of Lords treated the case as an ordinary application of the rule in *Hadley v. Baxendale*, relying chiefly on *Hammond v. Bussey*,[274] where damages for breach of warranty were held to include the cost of unsuccessfully defending an action by a sub-buyer. *Hall and Pim* does not seem to have been regarded at the time as an exceptional decision, and was not even selected for reporting in the law reports. Later cases, however, have had much difficulty with the decision, said by counsel in one case to have "astonished the Temple and surprised St. Mary Axe".[275] In *James Finlay & Co. Ltd. v. N.V. Kwik Hoo Tong Handel Maatschappij*,[276] great difficulty was found in reconciling the decision with *Williams Brothers v. Ed. T. Agius Ltd.*, a case of resale at an

[*The next page is* 1-63]

[271] See 1.1360 - 1.1430, *infra*.

[272] *Williams v. Reynolds* (1865), 6 B. & S. 495, 122 E.R. 1278; *Aryeh v. Lawrence Kostoris & Son Ltd.*, [1967] 1 Lloyd's Rep. 63 (C.A.); *Diamond v. Campbell-Jones*, [1961] Ch. 22 (land redevelopment); *Burgoyne v. Murphy*, [1951] 2 D.L.R. 556 (N.B.S.C. App. Div.). See *Castle Constructions Pty Ltd. v. Fekala Pty Ltd.*, [2006] 65 N.S.W.L.R. 648 (C.A.).

[273] [1928] All E.R. Rep. 763 (H.L.); *Patrick v. Russo-British Grain Export Co.*, [1927] 2 K.B. 535; *Rockland Industries Inc. v. Amerada Minerals Corp. of Canada Ltd.*, [1978] 2 W.W.R. 44 (S.C.T.D.), revd 95 D.L.R. (3d) 64 (S.C. App. Div.), restd [1980] 2 S.C.R. 2, 108 D.L.R. (3d) 513; *Gaklis v. Wells* (1979), 37 N.S.R. (2d) 451 (S.C. App. Div.); *Joseph & Co. Pty. Ltd. v. Harvest Grain Co. Pty. Ltd.* (1996), 39 N.S.W.L.R. 722 (Dist. Ct.).

[274] (1888), 20 Q.B.D. 79 (C.A.).

[275] See *James Finlay & Co. v. N.V. Kwik Hoo Tong Handel Maatschappij*, [1929] 1 K.B. 400 (C.A.), *per* Sankey L.J., at p. 417.

[276] *Supra*.

undervalue.[277] However, as suggested above, the problem of underuse by the plaintiff is separable. *Hall and Pim* was explained in the *Finlay* case as depending upon an implied assumption of risk by the defendant, a common technique for limiting a contract breaker's liability. In *Kwei Tek Chao v. British Traders & Shippers Ltd.*,[278] Devlin J. explained *Hall and Pim* as depending upon the seller's contemplation that the *specific* goods would be resold in circumstances that would preclude mitigation by going into the market. The case would not apply, therefore, to every case of sale to a trader. As Devlin J. said:

> . . . everybody who sells to a merchant knows that he has bought for re-sale, and it does not, as I understand it, make any difference to the ordinary measure of damage where there is a market. What is contemplated is that the merchant buys for re-sale, but if the goods are not delivered to him he will go out into the market and buy similar goods and honour his contract in that way. If the market has fallen he has suffered no damage; if the market has risen the measure of damage is the difference in the market price. There are, of course, cases where that prima facie measure of damage is not applicable because something different is contemplated [Devlin J. here gives an example of goods specially manufactured]. Similarly, it may very well be that in the case of string contracts, if the seller knows that the merchant is not buying merely for re-sale generally, but upon a string contract where he will re-sell those specific goods and where he could only honour his contract by delivering those goods and no others, the measure of loss of profit on re-sale is the right measure.[279]

1.1340 The House of Lords in *Heron II*[280] discussed *Hall and Pim* and approved it in so far as it decided that a consequence need not be contemplated as more probable than not in order to justify making the contract breaker liable for it. This proposition does not, however, determine what consequence it is that is supposed to be contemplated.[281] According to Devlin J.'s explanation of *Hall and Pim*, the defendant would not be liable unless he ought reasonably to have contemplated not just that the plaintiff was liable to resell, but that the plaintiff was liable to resell the specific goods on a contract that would permit of no substitution if the specific goods should not be available. *Heron II* is authority for the proposition that a fifty-fifty chance of the relevant occurrence suffices to impose liability; it says nothing about the definition of the occurrence that is to be contemplated, and, therefore, it is suggested, is not inconsistent with Devlin J.'s explanation of *Hall and Pim*.

1.1350 The subsale price has been taken in some cases as evidence of the market price[282] or, in the absence of a market, as the best available

277 [1914] A.C. 510 (H.L.), discussed at 1.1380, 1.1390, *infra*.
278 [1954] 2 Q.B. 459.
279 *Supra*, at pp. 489-90.
280 *Koufos v. Czarnikow Ltd.*, [1969] 1 A.C. 350 (H.L.).
281 See 14.260, *infra*.
282 See *Hong Guan & Co. Ltd. v. R. Jumabhoy & Sons Ltd.*, [1960] A.C. 684 (P.C.), at

evidence of the value of the goods.[283] Even where this is done, however, the defendant will not be liable for more than the profit that could reasonably have been anticipated.[284]

8. Underuse of Property by the Plaintiff

1.1360 A quite different problem arises where the plaintiff has agreed to sell property to a third party at less than what would otherwise have been reckoned its value. This arises where a buyer of goods agrees before delivery to resell at a price that turns out to be below the market price on the date fixed for delivery. Commonly in such cases, on non-delivery by the seller, the buyer will be compelled to go into the market to purchase equivalent goods so as to fulfil the buyer's obligation to the sub-buyer or else to pay damages to the latter. In either case the standard measure of damages, that is, the difference between contract price and market price, seems plainly appropriate.

1.1370 Even if the plaintiff is able to fill the subcontract from goods held in stock, the same loss is suffered, for the value of the goods in stock is their current market value. The point was made by Osler J. in *Ballantyne v. Watson*,[285] a case involving failure to deliver cheese:

> The damages consist of the difference between the contract price, six cents, and the market price which . . . was ten cents per lb.
>
> The ground on which the reduction is asked is that the plaintiff sold the cheese in question at eight cents, and therefore, if it had been delivered to him, his profit would not have been more than two cents per lb. But this is not the way to look at it. The defendant has nothing to do with the profit the plaintiff might have made. Assuming that the plaintiff sold this cheese, he was not able to deliver it, for he had not got it from the defendant. If the sub-sale went off for that reason, the plaintiff was not thereby disentitled from going into the market and purchasing the same quality at the market price, which was ten cents per lb. Or it is, perhaps, not assuming too much to infer that he filled the sub-contract by the delivery of other cheese, which he would have had to purchase in the market at the increased price, or to supply from his own stock, which was then worth to him ten cents per lb. In either case he would sustain a loss of four cents per lb. There seems, therefore, no reason to reduce the damages.[286]

---

p. 703 (settlement taken as evidence of market price); *Farantos Development Ltd. v. Canada Permanent Trust Co.* (1975), 56 D.L.R. (3d) 481, 7 O.R. (2d) 721 (H.C.J.).

283 *J. Leavey & Co. Ltd. v. George H. Hirst & Co., Ltd.*, [1944] K.B. 24 (C.A.); *Frank Mott & Co. Ltd. v. Wm. H. Muller & Co. (London) Ltd.* (1922), 13 Ll. L.R. 492; *Grébert-Borgnis v. Nugent* (1885), 15 Q.B.D. 85 (C.A.); *Richmond Wineries Western Ltd. v. Simpson*, [1940] S.C.R. 1, [1940] 2 D.L.R. 481. See also *Mondor v. Willets*, [1923] S.C.R. 433, [1923] 2 D.L.R. 964; *Boehner v. Smith* (1916), 26 D.L.R. 511 (N.S.S.C.A.D.) (lost profit allowed on non-delivery of logs).

284 *Household Machines Ltd. v. Cosmos Exporters Ltd.*, [1947] K.B. 217.

285 (1880), 30 U.C.C.P. 529, followed (though reluctantly) in *Yeast v. Knight & Watson*, [1919] 2 W.W.R. 467 (Alta. S.C.).

286 *Ballantyne v. Watson, supra*, footnote 285, at p. 541.

1.1380 It sometimes occurs, however, that the plaintiff escapes any obligation on the subcontract perhaps because the subsale is conditional upon the performance of the defendant's obligation (as in *Rodoconachi, Sons & Co. v. Milburn Bros.*,[287] a case of goods sold "to arrive") or where the sub-buyer is bound for some reason not to claim against the plaintiff (as in *Williams Bros. v. Ed. T. Agius, Ltd.*,[288] where the sub-buyer ceded rights to the defendant). In these cases it was held by the English Court of Appeal and by the House of Lords, respectively, that the plaintiff is nevertheless entitled to damages measured by the difference between market price and contract price at the date when the goods ought to have been delivered. The cases were expressly followed and approved by the Supreme Court of Canada in *Bainton v. John Hallam Ltd.*[289]

1.1390 Some critics have asserted that these results lead to over-compensation. The argument is that if the wrong had not been done, that is, if the goods had been duly delivered, the plaintiff would have resold them at the subcontract price and therefore would never have realized the higher market price, and is over-compensated if it is recovered. It is submitted, however, that *Rodoconachi v. Milburn* and *Williams v. Agius* and *Bainton v. John Hallam Ltd.* are rightly decided, though not all the explanations given in these cases are fully persuasive. In *Rodoconachi v. Milburn*, the subcontract was described as "accidental" as between plaintiff and defendant; Lindley L.J. obviously did not regard this as a fully satisfactory explanation for he went on to say that the "rules as to damages can in the nature of things only be approximately just".[290] Both cases laid stress on the assumed rule that the buyer could not have recovered more than the market price if he had had an exceptionally profitable subcontract. As has been seen, this rule is not absolute and does not in any case seem to demand the result reached.[291] In *Williams v. Agius*, Lord Dunedin explained the result as follows: "The buyer . . . is entitled to be put in the position in which he would have stood if he had got [the goods] at the due date. That position is the position of a man who has goods at the market price of the day."[292]

1.1400 This, it is submitted, is in substance a sound view. The defendant's argument in these cases is that the plaintiff would not have realized the full value of the goods had they been delivered and therefore (the opposite of the argument considered in the preceding section) that the value

287 (1886), 18 Q.B.D. 67 (C.A.).
288 [1914] A.C. 510 (H.L.).
289 (1920), 60 S.C.R. 325, 54 D.L.R. 537.
290 *Rodoconachi v. Milburn, supra*, footnote 287, at p. 78.
291 See 1.1240 - 1.1350, *supra*.
292 *Supra*, footnote 288, at p. 522.

to the plaintiff of the goods is exceptionally low. The same argument could be made in the case of a tort, such as negligent damage to goods or conversion, but it appears very weak in that context. A defendant who converts the plaintiff's property cannot be heard to say that the plaintiff would not in any case have put the property to good use. Neither would proof that the plaintiff had intended or had covenanted to sell the property at an undervalue or to give it away reduce the damages, although in a sense the plaintiff will in such a case be better off on receipt of damages than she would have been had the wrong not been done. As Lord Moulton said in *Williams v. Agius*: "it is immaterial what the buyer is intending to do with the purchased goods. He is entitled to recover the expense of putting himself into the position of having those goods".[293]

1.1410 A clear instance of compensation in a case where the plaintiff would not, in the absence of the wrong, have realized the value of the property is the case where realization of the value is illegal. In the New South Wales case of *Bilambil-Terranorra Pty. Ltd. v. Tweed Shire Council*,[294] the defendant municipality trespassed on the plaintiff's land and extracted its gravel. The defendant argued that since extraction of gravel by the plaintiff was unlawful under a zoning regulation the defendant had caused no loss. This argument was rejected partly because the plaintiff might have obtained a licence to extract, but also on principle. Reynolds J.A. said, by way of hypothetical example, that if cutting timber were illegal, a tortfeasor still would have to pay the value of the wood, even though the owner could not have profited.[295] It would indeed be odd, as Mahoney J.A. said, if a wrongdoer could benefit by showing that what he did was not only a civil wrong but also illegal. Mahoney J.A. added, on the more general point of underuse by a plaintiff: ". . . the fact that the owner of the property does not desire to use it or to use it to the best economic advantage, has not meant that its value is less than it would be in the hands of one who regarded it differently."[296] This conclusion is, surely, sound. It would be impractical to inquire in each case into the use likely to be made of property by the particular plaintiff.

1.1420 The problem of the plaintiff who (if the wrong had not been done) would have sold the property at an undervalue arises in the not uncommon case where the plaintiff is a non-profit-making institution owning or buying property for the benefit of members of some club or association. A club buying or owning wine is surely entitled, on non-delivery by a seller, or on conversion or negligent destruction by a tort-

---

293 *Supra*, at pp. 530-1. See also *The "London Corporation"* [1935] P. 70 (C.A.), at p. 78, *per* Greer L.J.

294 [1980] 1 N.S.W.L.R. 465 (C.A.).

295 *Supra*, at p. 479.

296 *Supra*, at p. 494.

feasor, to recover the value of the wine even upon proof that it would have been resold at below market value to club members. In *Diamond Cutting Works Federation Ltd. v. Triefus & Co. Ltd.*,[297] such a situation arose, the plaintiff buyer being a non-profit-making organization supplying industrial diamonds to its members at cost price plus a commission. In an action against the defaulting seller, the market price of diamonds having risen, defendant argued that the plaintiff had suffered no loss and would actually earn a larger commission by buying in the market at the current higher price and supplying its members at that price. Not surprisingly this argument was rejected, Barry J. remarking:

> . . . merely because an individual or company does not propose to make a profit out of goods which he purchases, it cannot, I think, be said that they are not involved in a loss if they have to pay more for goods which they intend either to give away or pass on at cost price to others. I refuse to accede to this argument and I think that here the true measure of damage is the one stated to be the *prima facie* measure, namely, the difference between the contract and market price of these goods.[298]

In *Brading v. McNeill & Co. Ltd.*,[299] the purchaser of a factory had covenanted with a third party to assign it on conveyance. The purchaser was held to be entitled to substantial damages on the vendor's default. Though Evershed J. admitted to being not entirely happy "in my mind,"[300] it is submitted that the decision is sound.

1.1430 A very similar problem arose in the New Zealand case of *Mouat v. Betts Motors Ltd.*,[301] where the buyer of a car had agreed not to sell it on the open market for a certain period but to offer it back to the dealer at a stipulated price. This arrangement was part of a country-wide scheme to control car prices during a period of shortage. Naturally the restriction on price increases caused a long waiting period and produced people willing to pay higher prices for immediate delivery of cars. In breach of his agreement, the buyer resold the car to such a person for the higher price and sought to argue that since the dealer, had the buyer fulfilled his agreement, would have resold the car for a modest profit only, the dealer would be over-compensated if it recovered the much higher price that the car commanded on what might be called the open market or a black market. The Privy Council on Appeal from New Zealand, following an earlier English case, rejected this argument. Lord Denning said: "It does not lie in Mouat's mouth to say that, if he had fulfilled his covenant, the dealers could only resell the car [at the official price]. That was a matter peculiar to the dealers which was no

297 [1956] 1 Lloyd's Rep. 216.
298 *Supra*, at p. 227.
299 [1946] Ch. 145.
300 *Supra*, at p. 152.
301 [1959] A.C. 71 (P.C.).

concern of his. The dealers were entitled in law to be put into as good a position as if he had fulfilled his covenant: and to do this they were entitled to go into the market and buy a similar car at the market price."[302] Again, it must be conceded that, in a sense, the plaintiff is in a better position on receipt of the judgment than it would have been in on performance by the defendant of his covenant. Danckwerts J., in *British Motor Trade Ass'n v. Gilbert*,[303] described the rule in *Williams v. Agius* as "anomalous" and referred to Evershed J.'s doubts in *Brading*, adding that the rule (which he felt bound to apply) appeared to over-compensate. However, it is submitted that these doubts are misplaced and that the decisions reached in all the cases discussed here are fully justifiable.

1.1440 The Ontario Law Reform Commission proposed in 1979 that damages in case of non-delivery should be limited to the buyer's "actual loss".[304] The Commission's evident intention was to reverse the result reached in *Rodoconachi v. Milburn*,[305] but it is submitted that the words of the draft bill were not apt to achieve that result for, as is argued here, *Rodoconachi v. Milburn* and *Williams v. Agius* can be defended on the ground that where the plaintiff is deprived of goods, there is an "actual loss" equal to their value, whatever use of the goods had been intended.

9. Acquisition from Third Parties of Substitutes on Favourable Terms

1.1450 It often happens that a person whose property is wrongfully destroyed or to whom goods promised are not delivered is able to obtain a substitute at less than its full value. The question then arises whether the wrongdoer is entitled to take advantage of the plaintiff's good fortune or skill. Where the defendant destroys the plaintiff's goods and the plaintiff receives a substitute as a gift from a sympathetic relative, for example, it is plain that damages are not reduced on account of the gift. Similarly in the case of a favourable purchase, the usual rule is that the plaintiff's right to full damages is unimpaired.[306] On the other hand, in some cases where beneficial acquisition is so closely associated with the circumstances of the defendant's wrong that it could not have occurred otherwise, the damages have been reduced. The principle is one of mitigation and the cases are discussed in the chapter on that topic.[307] The Ontario Law Reform Commission recom-

---

302 *Supra*, at p. 82.

303 [1951] 2 All E.R. 641 (Ch.).

304 *Report on Sale of Goods* (Ontario Law Reform Commission, 1979), p. 499; Draft Bill, s. 9.16(4). See 1.40, *supra*.

305 *Op. cit.*, pp. 499-502.

306 *Dominion Radiator Co. v. Steel Co. of Canada* (1918), 44 D.L.R. 72, 43 O.L.R. 356 (S.C. App. Div.), affd 48 D.L.R. 350 (P.C.).

307 See 15.670 - 15.880, *infra*. The analogous problem of the seller who resells goods, on the buyer's default, at more than market price, is discussed at 5.1480 - 5.1510, *infra*.

mended in its *Report on Sale of Goods* that wherever the buyer "covered" he should be restricted to recovery of the cover price.[308] This proposal raises difficulties, for often it will be impossible to say whether acquisition of goods similar to those promised amounts to a "cover" or not. It would seem absurd for the seller to be relieved of liability if the buyer happens to receive a gift from a friend, receives a part gift, or makes a favourable purchase. In all these cases, it would seem that the plaintiff does suffer an actual loss by the defendant's wrong.

10. Expenses Saved

1.1460 Where the defendant's wrong results in a saving of expense, this must be brought into account. In *Rodoconachi, Sons & Co. v. Milburn Bros.*,[309] goods were lost by a carrier's negligence. In assessing the plaintiff's damages, it was held that the freight that would have been payable to the defendant if the goods had been safely delivered ought to be deducted from the value that the goods would have had at their destination. The principle is that the plaintiff is only to be put in as good a position as would have been occupied if the goods had been delivered, and in that case, the plaintiff would have received the goods only on payment of the freight charges. The same principle was applied in *Beaver Specialty Ltd. v. Donald H. Bain Ltd.*[310] This result might seem to be open to the criticism that it entitles a carrier to recover the freight charges even though the contract is not performed, and in *Acatos v. Burns*,[311] a carrier wrongfully sold the plaintiff's goods in course of transit and was held on this ground not to be entitled to any part of the freight. It is not clear, however, from the report of the case, whether the value of the goods (upon which the parties had agreed) included the cost of shipment. The question turns on whether the value of the goods is taken at their destination, in which case, as Blackburn J. said in *O'Hanlan v. Great Western Ry. Co.*,[312] the cost of importing is an element in the market price, or whether the value is taken at the place of shipment, in which case the shipping costs will not be included. It is submitted that *Rodoconachi v. Milburn* rightly decides that if the value is taken at the place of destination, freight charges saved because of the wrong ought to be deducted. In *Pitcher v. Shoebottom*,[313] damages for failure to convey land were reduced by the cost of a survey not required because of the defendant's breach.

1.1470 Storage charges that would have been payable to the defendant, as, for example, to a bailee who loses goods, appear to stand on the same footing. However, storage charges that would have been incurred after receipt of the

---

[308] *Op. cit.*, footnote 304, at p. 499. But again the Draft Bill merely limits the buyer to his "actual loss". The *Uniform Act* is differently worded. See 1.40, *supra*.

[309] (1886), 18 Q.B.D. 67 (C.A.).

[310] [1974] S.C.R. 903, 39 D.L.R. (3d) 574, restoring the judgment of King J. in 70 D.L.R. (2d) 562, [1968] 2 O.R. 764 (H.C.J.).

[311] (1878), 3 Ex. D. 282 (C.A.).

[312] (1865), 6 B. & S. 484 at p. 492, 122 E.R. 1274. See 1.330, *supra*.

[313] (1970), 14 D.L.R. (3d) 522, [1971] 1 O.R. 106 (H.C.J.).

goods by the plaintiff are in a different category. If, on learning of the defendant's wrong, the plaintiff goes instantly into the market and purchases a substitute which is then stored in a warehouse, the plaintiff is entitled to recover the value of the property, plus interest, but not storage charges, because these would have been incurred even if the wrong had not been done. Conversely, if, on learning of the defendant's wrong, the plaintiff chooses not to purchase a substitute, but to invest the sum of money that might have been used for that purpose in another enterprise, or to leave it to earn interest at the bank, the plaintiff is again entitled to the full value of the property, plus interest, that he would have had if his rights had been observed. No deduction can be appropriate in respect of what the plaintiff would have done with the property after receiving it, for this depends on the plaintiff's investment choices. Expenses of storing goods after receipt are incurred in the hope of profit, that is, a greater ultimate benefit to the owner than would be realized by immediate sale. If the plaintiff is deprived of the opportunity to store the goods by the loss of the goods themselves, she ought not to receive less in compensation than the value of the goods to her at the time and place the goods ought to have been received. Whether the cost of storing the goods subsequently would have proved ultimately profitable or the reverse, no deduction falls to be made, for the plaintiff has been deprived of the property and must be entitled to its value, plus interest, whether the property subsequently would have been used wisely or unwisely.

11. Non-delivery in Sale Cases

1.1480 The buyer's complaint in case of non-delivery is analogous to that of one complaining of tortious destruction or conversion of goods or loss by a bailee. If the wrong had not been done, the plaintiff would have had the goods.

1.1490 Where the contract price has been paid in advance, the buyer is entitled to recover the value of the goods promised. Where, as is usual, the price has not been paid, the measure of damages is the difference between price and value. The *Sale of Goods Act* provides as follows:

> 49(1) Where the seller wrongfully neglects or refuses to deliver the goods to the buyer, the buyer may maintain an action against the seller for damages for non-delivery.
>
> (2) The measure of damages is the estimated loss directly and naturally resulting in the ordinary course of events from the seller's breach of contract.
>
> (3) Where there is an available market for the goods in question, the measure of damages is, in the absence of evidence to the contrary, to be ascertained by the difference between the contract price and the market or current price of the goods at the time or times when they ought to havebeen delivered, or, if no time was fixed, then at the time of the refusal to deliver.[314]

The first two subsections have the effect of confirming the right of the buyer

314 *Sale of Goods Act* (Ont.), s. 49, and see footnote 8, *supra*.

to recover the value of the goods (this being the loss that follows upon non-delivery) subject to rules of remoteness. Often the value will be measured by the reasonable cost of replacement, but this is not the proper measure where it is unreasonable to replace the goods, and the buyer is unlikely in fact to do so.[314a]

1.1500 Subsection (3) is evidently intended to be a subsidiary rule. It has been held that the use of the phrase "in the absence of evidence to the contrary" or its equivalent shows that it is not intended to override subsec. (2), but to provide a means of measuring the buyer's loss that will work conveniently in most cases.[315] There have been difficulties in applying subsec. (3),[316] but these have not compelled results considered unjust because it is always open to the tribunal to abandon the *prima facie* test and revert to the more general test embodied in subsec. (2).

1.1510 Where property has a special use to the buyer, it was shown in the earlier discussion of *The "Liesbosch"* that the value of the property can justly be said to be enhanced, in some cases far beyond the intrinsic value of the property.[317] Since the *Sale of Goods Act* specifies the "market or current price" as the *prima facie* increase of value, the special value of goods to a buyer, based on the use proposed for them, has been dealt with by the courts in terms of "special damages" under s. 52 of the Act, and in terms of remoteness. The cases on loss of profit on resales and on loss of use, discussed elsewhere, are illustrative.[318]

1.1520 The phrase "available market" is not self-explanatory. In a pre-Act case (*Dunkirk Colliery Co. v. Lever*),[319] it was the view of one judge that a market implied some particular place where regular business was transacted. In *W.L. Thompson Ltd. v. Robinson (Gunmakers) Ltd.*,[320] Upjohn J. considered himself bound by this view, though himself preferring a wider interpretation. It is odd that Upjohn J. should have considered the views of a single judge, not expressly assented to by the rest of the court and not essential for the decision, to be binding authority on the interpretation of a different phrase (available market) in a statute not enacted until fifteen years later. It seems doubtful that the draftsman of the *Sale of Goods Act* intended "available market" to be restricted to a physical place for transacting business. The view preferred by Upjohn J. was that all that is meant is that the goods in question in all the circumstances can be freely sold. This was in the

314a *The "Alecos M"*, [1991] 1 Lloyd's Rep. 120 (C.A.).
315 See *W.L. Thompson Ltd. v. Robinson (Gunmakers) Ltd.*, [1955] Ch. 177.
316 See 1.1520 - 1.1620, *infra*.
317 See 1.260 - 1.330, *supra*.
318 See 1.1240 -1.1350, *supra*, and 1.2150 - 1.2170, *infra*.
319 (1878), 9 Ch. D. 20 (C.A.), at p. 25. In *A.B.D. (Metals & Waste) Ltd. v. Anglo Chemical & Ore Co., Ltd.*, [1955] 2 Lloyd's Rep. 456 at p. 466, Sellers J. said: "It is not necessary to establish a market that it should have a fixed place or building, but there must be sufficient traders who are in touch with each other to evidence a market." See *Amicale Yarns Inc. v. Canadian Worsted Manufacturing Ltd.* (1968), 68 D.L.R. (2d) 131 at p. 136, [1968] 2 O.R. 59 (H.C.J.).
320 *Supra*, footnote 315.

context of breach by a buyer. In the case of non-delivery by a seller, the appropriate test may in some cases be whether a substitute could be freely bought. Probably Upjohn J.'s apparent deference to authority is to be explained by the fact that he considered the measure prescribed by subsec. (3) liable to lead to injustice in the particular case before him. Exclusion of subsec. (3), therefore, gave an added reason in support of his decision.

1.1530 In any event, it appears that nothing turns on the question, for if the court finds that there is no available market, it can reach the same conclusion by application of subsec. (2) as it would otherwise have reached under subsec. (3). Even if the court finds that there is an available market, it can still reject the measure in subsec. (3) if it seems inconsistent with subsec. (2) (that is, in effect, with the court's sense of justice), because subsec. (3) is only a *prima facie* measure. Upjohn J. in *Thompson v. Robinson*, after referring to the dictum of Jenkins L.J. in *Dunkirk Colliery Co. v. Lever*, and having held himself bound to find that there was no available market, said: "However, the point seems to me of somewhat academic interest in this case because if the word "market' is given an extended meaning, in my view on the facts I have to consider a precisely similar result is reached."[321] Upjohn J. went on to say: "I have to remember that subsection 3 provides only a prima facie rule, and if on investigation of the facts one finds that it is unjust to apply that rule, in the light of the general principles mentioned above, then it is not to be applied".[322]

1.1540 Other questions commonly raised in relation to the phrase, such as the time and place at which market price is to be taken and whether a market includes an illicit or surreptitious market, have been discussed earlier in considering valuation of property.[323]

1.1550 Where a lessor wrongfully fails to execute a lease, the court is required to estimate two uncertain sums, that is, the value of the tenancy at the date of the wrong and the value at that date of the future stream of rent payments. The measure of damages is the difference between the two sums.[324]

12. Anticipatory Repudiation

1.1560 Where the seller announces before the date of promised delivery that he will not perform, the buyer can treat the seller's conduct as an immediate wrong and can bring an action for damages.[325] He is not, however,

[*The next page is* 1-73]

321 *Thompson v. Robinson, supra*, at p. 187.
322 *Thompson v. Robinson, supra*, at pp. 187-8.
323 See 1.330, 1.1430, *supra*.
324 *Procopia v. D'Abbandanza* (1975), 58 D.L.R. (3d) 368, 8 O.R. (2d) 496 (C.A.).
325 *Hochster v. De La Tour* (1853), 2 El. & Bl. 678, 118 E.R. 922.

obliged to sue immediately and may, if he wishes, continue to call for the promised performance.[326] Whether in that case he is entitled to recover a loss that could have reasonably been avoided is a controverted question which is discussed in a wider context in a later chapter.[327] Where non-delivery of goods is in question, the usual problem is to choose between alternative dates; when the market price changes between the date of repudiation and the date of promised delivery, there is an added problem. Even if the argument made elsewhere is accepted to the effect that the innocent party is bound to act reasonably in the case of anticipatory breach,[328] it is by no means clear to what result this principle would lead in the case of an anticipatory repudiation by a seller of goods and a rise in market price between repudiation and date of due delivery. Although, in retrospect, it may have become apparent that the market was steadily rising, this is seldom obvious in advance because the current market price at any time itself represents predictions about the future. Thus, one can rarely say "the market is sure to rise" and similarly, it is submitted, it can rarely be unreasonable to fail to predict market changes.[329] Where the price rises after the repudiation, the cases have generally held that the buyer can recover damages based on the higher price at the date of promised delivery.[330] Though the analytical foundations may be open to attack, there is, it is submitted, considerable practical sense in the rule that a buyer can ignore a repudiation and recover the difference between contract and market price at date of due delivery, even if this is higher than the market price at the date of repudiation. Thus, the acceptance of a principle in contract law generally that on anticipatory repudiation the innocent party is bound to act reasonably, need not entail any change in the present position of the buyer who ought, it is suggested, unless a substitute forward contract is available,[331] not to be held to act unreasonably in awaiting the date of promised delivery.

1.1570 Setting aside the case of the buyer who refuses to accept the seller's repudiation, the case next to be considered is that of the buyer who accepts the repudiation, that is, treats it as an immediate wrong. Here the courts have held that the buyer is entitled to recover the difference between contract price and market price at the date of due performance, subject to a duty to

326 *Leigh v. Paterson* (1818), 8 Taunt. 540, 129 E.R. 493.

327 See 15.400 - 15.650, *infra*. See also the discussion of the cases of an anticipatory breach by the buyer, at 5.1420, *infra*.

328 See 15.620, *infra*.

329 See 1.780, 1.1070, *supra*.

330 *Leigh v. Paterson*, *supra*, footnote 326. *Brown v. Muller* (1872), L.R. 7 Ex. 319 (instalment contract; price taken at date of due delivery of each instalment); *St. Helen's Smelting Co., Ltd. v. Dominion Antimony Co., Ltd.* (1908), 42 N.S.R. 385 (S.C.A.D.); *Rockland Industries Inc. v. Amerada Minerals Corp. of Canada Ltd.*, [1978] 2 W.W.R. 44 (Alta. S.C.T.D.), revd 95 D.L.R. (3d) 64 (S.C. App. Div.), restd [1980] S.C.R. 2, 108 D.L.R. (3d) 513; *Canbra Foods Ltd. v. Overwater* (1977), 84 D.L.R. (3d) 350 (Alta. S.C. App. Div.). See *Phillpotts v. Evans* (1839), 5 M. & W. 475, 151 E.R. 200 (anticipatory breach by buyer); *Morrow Cereal Co. v. Ogilvie Flour Mills Co.* (1918), 57 S.C.R. 403 at pp. 414-15, 44 D.L.R. 557 at p. 565, *per* Anglin J. *Contra*, *Campbell v. Mahler* (1918), 43 O.L.R. 395 (S.C.), affd 47 D.L.R. 722, 45 O.L.R. 44 (App. Div.).

331 See 15.620, *infra*.

mitigate.[332] The duty to mitigate may involve entering into a substitute contract for forward delivery[333] or making a spot purchase of goods for immediate delivery, in which case the buyer will be entitled to add storage charges up to the date of promised performance.[334] One case dealing with a seller's duty to mitigate after anticipatory repudiation by a buyer held the seller bound to foresee a fall in the market.[335] This, it has been suggested above, cannot be justified on the principle of mitigation but may be explained as a case where the damages were held to "crystallize" on acceptance of the repudiation.[336]

1.1580 An aspect of the duty to mitigate favourable to the buyer is that if the buyer actually does make a substitute purchase, she will be entitled to recover the price from the seller, even if the market price subsequently falls, for, in accordance with general principles of mitigation, the cost of reasonable but unsuccessful attempts to avoid loss is recoverable from a wrongdoer.[337]

1.1590 If the market price falls after the date of the repudiation and the buyer does not make a substitute purchase, it follows that the buyer is entitled only to damages measured by the market price at the date of due delivery. If this is equal to or less than the contract price, there will be no damages. Consideration of this possibility has been prominent in the minds of the judges who have framed the present rules.[338] Fear of over-compensation is an important consideration, for if the buyer could wait on a falling market, buying in perhaps at less than the contract price on the date of due delivery, and recover damages based on a higher price at the date of repudiation, the buyer would appear to gather a windfall, for the market price at the date of repudiation is irrelevant. It is neither the date of promised performance nor the date of

[*The next page is* 1-75]

[332] *Melachrino v. Nickoll and Knight*, [1920] 1 K.B. 693; *Roper v. Johnson* (1873), L.R. 8 C.P. 167; *Garnac Grain Co. Inc. v. H.M.F. Faure & Fairclough Ltd.*, [1968] A.C. 1130 (H.L.); *Hillspring Farms Ltd. v. Leland Walton & Sons Ltd.* (2007), 312 N.B.R. (2d) 109 (C.A.).

[333] *Millett v. Van Heek & Co.*, [1920] 3 K.B. 535, affd [1921] 2 K.B. 369 (C.A.).

[334] *C. Sharpe & Co., Ltd. v. Nosawa & Co.*, [1917] 2 K.B. 814 at p. 820, *per* Atkin J.

[335] *Roth v. Taysen, Townsend* (1896), 12 T.L.R. 211 (C.A.). See also *Gebruder Metelmann GmbH & Co. K.G. v. NBR (London) Ltd.*, [1984] 1 Lloyd's Rep. 614 (C.A.).

[336] See 1.780, *supra*. Whereas a buyer, who has contracted for forward delivery, may find it inconvenient to buy substitute goods before he needs them, it is rarely an imposition on the seller, if he is in possession of the goods, to sell them at a date earlier than originally agreed.

[337] See 15.290 - 15.320, *infra*.

[338] See *Tai Hing Cotton Mill Ltd. v. Kamsing Knitting Factory*, [1979] A.C. 91 (P.C.), at p. 104.

any actual purchase. The Privy Council has said that such a result would be an important inroad on a fundamental principle of damage assessment.[339]

1.1600 In some commodity markets, there is an established market of forward contracts. In such cases, therefore, a perfect substitute for what the seller has promised is available. Strictly speaking, an anticipatory repudiation deprives the buyer not of tangible property in actual possession, but of an expectation of receiving property in the future. Where the buyer is a speculator in commodity futures, for example, the proper measure of damages would appear to be the difference between the contract price and the market price of a contract for future delivery of the goods promised by the seller. In *Millett v. Van Heek & Co.*,[340] Bray J. considered that entering into a forward contract might in some cases be the reasonable course to be pursued, and if (after acceptance of the repudiation) such a course would have reduced the loss, the buyer's damages should be reduced accordingly. In the case of a buyer of a property for use, it will rarely be reasonable to seek to enter the highly specialized futures market, and it was held in *Brown v. Muller*[341] that there is no general obligation to enter into a forward contract on the seller's anticipatory repudiation.

1.1610 In framing these rules, the courts have had to grapple with an odd clause in s. 49 of the *Sale of Goods Act*:

> 49(3) Where there is an available market for the goods in question the measure of damages is, in the absence of evidence to the contrary, to be ascertained by the difference between the contract price and the market or current price of the goods at the time or times when they ought to have been delivered, or, if no time was fixed, then at the time of the refusal to deliver.[342]

The concluding words seem to require, in the case of anticipatory repudiation of a contract where there is no fixed date for delivery, whether or not the buyer accepts the repudiation, that damages should be measured at the date of repudiation, this plainly, it seems, being the time of the refusal to deliver. Ordinary techniques of construction are of little help here. Indeed, it is difficult to see what possible scope the words have except to apply to anticipatory repudiation, for in cases of actual wrong or non-delivery there will always be a time "at which the goods ought to have been delivered". The solution has been the one of refusal to apply the words. In *Tai Hing Cotton Mill Ltd. v. Kamsing Knitting Factory*,[343] the Privy Council said, pointing out that it was difficult to give content to the words: "It may well be, however, that the enactment was introduced into the subsection without consideration in

339 *Supra*.
340 *Supra*, footnote 333, at p. 543.
341 (1872), L.R. 7 Ex. 319.
342 *Sale of Goods Act* (Ont.), s. 49(3).
343 *Supra*, footnote 338.

depth of the juristic position, and that on analysis it proves, exceptionally, to have no content whatever."[344] In construing codifying statutes, conclusions of this sort are, it is submitted, justified, for it is highly unlikely that Parliament or the draftsman of the Act intended to affect the case of anticipatory repudiation, and a literal construction would be likely to lead to many years of injustice.

1.1620 The position reached by the cases, despite the genuine analytical difficulties of anticipatory breach and the intractable problems of the construction of s. 49(3), make good commercial and practical sense. A buyer who has contracted for forward delivery of goods has in effect contracted that the seller shall bear the risk of price increases until the date of delivery.

1.1630 It was earlier argued that damages, in cases of non-delivery, should "crystallize" at the time when the buyer, acting reasonably, could have made a substitute purchase.[345] In the case of an anticipatory repudiation, the buyer cannot, except when there is a well-established futures market, readily make a substitute contract for forward delivery. Postponement of assessment to the date of promised delivery is not, therefore, it is submitted, inconsistent with the principles earlier discussed. Nor, it is suggested, is it inconsistent with the general principles of mitigation, for usually the buyer does not act unreasonably by awaiting the date of promised performance.[346] If the buyer does buy in the market and the price later falls, the buyer is protected against actual loss by the rule that compensates loss caused by reasonable but unsuccessful attempts to mitigate.[347] The third case is that of the buyer who fails to make a substitute purchase on a falling market. The present rule, basing compensation on the market price at the date of due delivery, again seems quite satisfactory, for the choice of the price at the date of repudiation would over-compensate.[348]

13. Justifiable Rejection

1.1640 Where the buyer rejects goods tendered on grounds that are justifiable, the situation is equivalent, from the point of view of damage assessment, to non-delivery. It has been held that a buyer is not bound to mitigate loss by accepting goods that (by sales law) she has a right to reject, because such a duty would in effect deprive the buyer of the right to reject.[349]

---

344 *Tai Hing Cotton Mill*, *supra*, at p. 104.
345 See 1.650 - 1.1110, *supra*.
346 See 15.620, *infra*.
347 See 15.290 - 15.320, *infra*.
348 See *Tai Hing Cotton Mill*, *supra*, footnote 338.
349 See 15.220, *infra*.

14. Non-return of Goods by Bailee

1.1650 A bailee who wrongfully fails to return goods to their owner is *prima facie* liable to pay the value of the goods at the time and place of due

[*The next page is* 1-77]

delivery whether the reason for non-return is loss, destruction, conversion or mis-delivery of the goods and whether the bailment is by contract or not.[350] Cases of non-delivery of goods by a carrier may be regarded as closely analogous. In all these cases, the plaintiff's complaint is that he has been deprived of property that he would have had if the wrong had not been done. The problems of valuation discussed earlier arise commonly in bailment cases. Indeed many of the leading cases on valuation are in fact cases of bailment[351] or non-delivery by carrier.[352]

1.1660 Where a hirer, under a chattel lease contract under which the hirer has an option to purchase, fails to re-deliver the goods, account must be taken of the option to purchase. If, as is common, the hirer has an option to purchase at a price less than the value of the goods (usually the price is a nominal sum), the owner would plainly be over-compensated if on the destruction of the goods just before the option came due, the owner recovered the full value, for, if the instalments of hire represent the true price, the owner would be paid twice over on recovery of, in addition to the full price of the goods, damages representing their value. Thus, in *Wickham Holdings Ltd. v. Brooke House Motors*,[353] where a hirer of a car had paid three-quarters of the instalments and the car was wrongfully (though without dishonesty) sold to a third party, it was held by the English Court of Appeal that the owner was only entitled to the balance of the hire instalments, not the full value of the car, which was about 60% higher. The hirer, on paying the instalments, would have been entitled to buy the car for a nominal sum. The hire instalments were in reality the agreed price of the car. The owner's position, therefore, if the wrong had not been done, would almost certainly have been that it would not have received the car or its value. The case may be regarded as an instance of the principle that where the wrongdoer has an option, it is assumed that she would have exercised it to her own advantage.[354] Another way of putting the matter is to say that the plaintiff had only a limited interest in the goods, in effect an unpaid seller's security interest, and that recovery of the full price is its only legitimate interest. Lord Denning put it thus:

> The finance company is only entitled to what it has lost by the wrongful act of the defendants. I am well aware, of course, that prima facie in

[350] In *Scott Maritimes Pulp Ltd. v. B.F. Goodrich Canada Ltd.* (1977), 72 D.L.R. (3d) 680 at p. 696, the Nova Scotia Court of Appeal said that the general rule was that a bailee was liable for the value of the goods only.

[351] *Asamera Oil Corp. v. Sea Oil & General Corp.*, [1979] 1 S.C.R. 633, 89 D.L.R. (3d) 1.

[352] *Rodoconachi Sons & Co. v. Milburn Bros.* (1886), 18 Q.B.D. 67 (C.A.).

[353] [1967] 1 W.L.R. 295 (C.A.). *Cf. Chubb Cash Ltd. v. John Crilley & Son*, [1983] 1 W.L.R. 599 (C.A.).

[354] See 13.390, *infra*.

> conversion the measure of damages is the value of the goods at the date of the conversion. But that does not apply where the plaintiff, immediately prior to the conversion, has only a limited interest in the goods: . . . Take this case. The hirer had a most valuable interest in the car. He had paid already £614 10s. towards the purchase price and had the right to buy it outright on paying another £274 10s. The interest of the finance company was limited correspondingly. Its interest was limited to securing the payment of the outstanding £274 10s. It is entitled to be compensated for the loss of that interest, and no more. . . . It would be most unjust that they should recover twice as much as they have lost.[355]

This case involved damages payable by a third party, but the same reasoning would apply to limit damages payable by the hirer had the hirer been sued directly.

15. Plaintiff with Limited Interest in Goods

1.1670 In *Swire v. Leach*,[356] applied and extended in *The "Winkfield"*,[357] it was held that a bailee was entitled to sue a wrongdoer for the full value of goods destroyed, it not being "open to the defendant, being a wrongdoer, to inquire into the nature or limitation of the possessor's right".[358] The analogy was drawn with the case of a finder who, it had long been established, was entitled to recover from a converter the full value of the goods.[359] In the bailment cases it was not contemplated that the plaintiff was to be put in any better position than he was in before the wrong was done, for the plaintiff would be liable to account to the bailor for any excess over his own interest in the goods: "As between bailor and bailee the real interests of each must be inquired into, and, as the bailee has to account for the thing bailed, so he must account for that which has become its equivalent and now represents it. What he has received above his own interest he has received to the use of his bailor."[360] Furthermore, the wrongdoer would not be called upon to pay

---

355 *Wickham Holdings, supra*, footnote 353, at pp. 299-300.

356 (1865), 18 C.B. (N.S.) 479, 144 E.R. 531.

357 [1902] P. 42 (C.A.), followed in *Glenwood Lumber Co. v. Phillips*, [1904] A.C. 405 (P.C.); *Donald v. Skibstead* (1954), 12 W.W.R. (N.S.) 657 (Alta. Dist. Ct.); *Tanenbaum v. W. J. Bell Paper Co. Ltd.* (1956), 4 D.L.R. (2d) 177, [1956] O.R. 278 (H.C.J.); *Chabbra Corpn. Pte. Ltd. v. Jag Shakti (Owners)*, [1986] A.C. 337 (P.C.). *The "Winkfield"* and *Glenwood Lumber Co. v. Phillips* were distinguished in *Eastern Construction Co. v. National Trust Co.*, [1914] A.C. 197, 15 D.L.R. 755 (P.C.), where the wrongdoer subsequently acquired title.

358 *The "Winkfield", supra*, at p. 55, *per* Collins, M.R. The matter is now governed in the United Kingdom by the *Torts (Interference with Goods) Act 1977*.

359 *Armory v. Delamirie* (1722), 1 Strange 505, 93 E.R. 664. See also *Schiffahrt & Kohlen G.m.b.H. v. Chelsea Maritime Ltd.*, [1982] 2 W.L.R. 422 (Q.B.) (c.i.f. buyer entitled to sue for negligent damage to goods by third party).

360 *The "Winkfield", supra*, footnote 357, at p. 60. The same point was made in *Eastern Construction Co. v. National Trust Co., supra*, footnote 357.

twice: "The wrongdoer, having once paid full damages to the bailee, has an answer to any action by the bailor".[361]

1.1680 Before *The "Winkfield"* it had been thought that this rule depended on the bailee's liability to the bailor for the loss of the goods, but in *The "Winkfield"*, where the bailee was the Post Office claiming in respect of lost mail for the loss of which it would not have been liable to the owners, full recovery was allowed. It had been argued that, the bailee being liable to account to the bailor for the proceeds of the action, the bailee's right to recover must rest on the latter's liability to the bailor. But the court said that the rule entitling the bailee to recover in full was not based on the bailee's liability to the bailor, but rather, because the bailee could recover, therefore the bailee was bound to account to the bailor for the proceeds. The same principle has been applied to cases where the plaintiff is in possession otherwise than as bailee.[362]

1.1690 It is commonly stated in these cases that the defendant may not rely on the right of a third person (*jus tertii*). The rule so stated is not self-justifying, but it may often be supported on grounds of procedural convenience. In the case of a finder, where the true owner is unidentified, the finder suffers an obvious loss on being deprived of the goods, and it would be most unjust for the wrongdoer to be left in possession of the fruits of the wrong pending the (probably indefinitely postponed) appearance of the true owner. In the bailment cases too there is, it is suggested, sound reason to avoid inquiry into the contractual relationship between bailor and bailee. If no dispute is anticipated between them, it is unnecessary for the court to determine their respective rights, and it is inconvenient to do so in proceedings to which the bailor is not a party. In *The "Winkfield"*, assuming the Post Office is bound to account to the owners for the proceeds of the judgment, the result saves the necessity of perhaps hundreds of separate actions for small amounts. Even if the bailee were not bound to account to the bailor for the proceeds of the action, it could be argued that this would be because, on the true construction of the contract between bailor and bailee, the latter had bought, and presumably paid for, the right to retain the proceeds of a judgment in such circumstances.

1.1700 In *Courtenay v. Knutson*,[363] the defendant, who had damaged a barge, settled with the owner, but was held liable to pay compensation to a bailee in possession of the barge at the time of the damage for the latter's lost profits. *The "Winkfield"* was cited with approval, the court reasoning that, since the bailee could have sued for the full amount of the damage, including his lost profits, he ought not to lose the right to

---

361 *The "Winkfield"*, *supra*, footnote 357, at p. 61.

362 See *Richard v. Nowland* (1959), 19 D.L.R. (2d) 229 (N.B.S.C. App. Div.).

363 (1957), 26 D.L.R. (2d) 768 (B.C.S.C.).

recover by reason of a settlement to which he was not a party. The reasoning seems persuasive. If the case was one in which an owner-operator would have recovered the lost profits, it would seem that the defendant's liability should be the same where the barge is operated by a bailee. The case indicates the desirability, from the defendant's point of view, of making the bailee a party to any settlement, or, at least, of allocating an identified part of the settlement to loss of profits, which the bailor would, in respect of the period of the bailment, then presumably hold for the benefit of the bailee. The principle was taken a step further in *Donna Rae Ltd. v. Seaboard G.M. Diesel Ltd.*,[364] where it was held that the master of a damaged ship could sue on behalf of the crew and recover the latter's financial loss. This amounts to giving to the crew members an action for their financial loss, an area of substantive tort law that is at present in a state of uncertainty.

1.1710 In *Steiner v. Laurentide Financial Corp. Ltd.*,[365] a mortgagee in possession of chattels was held to be entitled, as against another creditor of the mortgagor, to damages measured only by the plaintiff's limited interest. In somewhat similar circumstances in *Wickham Holdings Ltd. v. Brooke House Motors*,[366] it was held that where a hirer under a chattel lease agreement wrongfully sold the goods to a third party, the owner of the goods (*i.e.*, the finance company) was entitled to recover only the value of its interest in the goods, Lord Denning saying that the cases allowing full recovery did not apply where the plaintiff had only a limited interest in the goods. This dictum might be taken to be inconsistent with the bailment cases. However, a distinction may be suggested. In the bailment cases it is usually clear that the defendant has done a wrong to the bailor and the bailee and that he ought to pay them jointly the full value of the goods. When only one of them is a party, it is not unjust to order the wrongdoer to make payment in full; the latter is no worse off than if sued by both, and the rule allowing full recovery is a convenient way of compensating both parties injured. In a case like *Wickham Holdings*, however, the wrongdoer has done no wrong at all to the hirer (who had sold the goods) and considerations of procedural convenience point in the opposite direction, for if the finance company recovered in full, a dispute would be certain to arise between the defendant and the hirer (an action for breach of warranty of title) and between the hirer and the finance company (unjust enrichment, liability to account, or unconscionable forfeiture).

1.1720 In *Wilson v. Lombank Ltd.*,[367] the defendant wrongfully took a car

---

364 (1978), 29 N.S.R. (2d) 413 (S.C. App. Div.).

365 (1967), 61 D.L.R. (2d) 280 (B.C.C.A.). But see *Insurance & Discount Corp. Ltd. v. Motorville Car Sales*, [1953] 1 D.L.R. 560, [1953] O.R. 16 (H.C.J.), affd [1953] 4 D.L.R. 576, [1953] O.W.N. 828 (C.A.).

366 *Supra*, footnote 353.

367 [1963] 1 W.L.R. 1294 (Assizes).

from the plaintiff's possession. The car was in fact owned by a third party to whom the defendant subsequently delivered it. It was held that the plaintiff could recover the full value of the car. This result seems over-compensatory, for in the circumstances the plaintiff would almost certainly have had to give up the car to its true owner at an early date, even if the defendant had not taken it. The case is, therefore, unlike that of a finder of an article that is unlikely ever to be claimed. It is submitted that the damages payable by the defendant ought to be reduced according to the probability of the plaintiff's losing possession of the goods in the absence of the wrong.

1.1730 The cases where the plaintiff and defendant share full ownership of the goods might be expected, if procedural convenience is the test, to restrict recovery to the plaintiff's actual interest in the goods, for with both interested parties before the court, their respective rights can conveniently be determined. Most cases have followed this pattern.[368] Some 19th century English cases have held that where a creditor has wrongfully dealt with property that is a security for debt or has seized property in which the creditor had in fact no security interest, the debtor is entitled to recover the full value of the property, leaving the creditor to sue separately for the debt.[369] These cases can only be supported, it would seem, on the consideration that if the defendant were entitled to set off the amount of the debt, the court would be sanctioning the wrongful act by enabling the defendant, in effect, to realize his security. It is submitted that this is not sufficient reason, under modern procedure, to disallow a set-off, and that the deterrence and punishment of wrongful appropriation of goods should be left to the criminal law, amended if thought necessary and desirable, or to an award of exemplary damages. If the plaintiff has a strong case for immediate redelivery, the plaintiff may be able to obtain interim equitable relief requiring the defendant to restore the *status quo ante*.[370]

16. Conversion and Detinue

1.1740 Actions for wrongfully depriving the plaintiff of goods may often be brought alternatively in conversion or detinue. The possible distinction

[368] *Chinery v. Viall* (1860), 29 L.J. Ex. 180, 5 H. & N. 288, 157 E.R. 1192; *Prete v. Lauzon*, [1923] 3 D.L.R. 1152, 52 O.L.R. 334 (S.C. App. Div.); *Mellis v. Blair* (1916), 27 D.L.R. 165 (B.C.C.A.); *Buchan v. Newell* (1913), 15 D.L.R. 437, 29 O.L.R. 508 (S.C. App. Div.). See also *Donald v. Suckling* (1866), L.R. 1 Q.B. 585; *Halliday v. Holgate* (1868), L.R. 3 Ex. 299; *Ames & Co. v. Sutherland* (1905), 9 O.L.R. 631 (Div. Ct.), at p. 635, affd 11 O.L.R. 417 (C.A.), affd 37 S.C.R. 694.

[369] *Gillard v. Brittan* (1841), 8 M. & W. 575, 151 E.R. 1168; *Keen v. Priest* (1859), 4 H. & N. 236, 157 E.R. 829; *Attack v. Bramwell* (1863), 3 B. & S. 520, 122 E.R. 196. See also *MacLellan v. Melanson* (1967), 62 D.L.R. (2d) 40 (N.S.S.C. App. Div.).

[370] See Sharpe, *Injunctions and Specific Performance*, looseleaf ed. (Toronto, Canada Law Book, 1999), 2.10-2.1300. Sutton, "Damages for Conversion of Goods Sold," 43 Aust. L.J. 95 (1969), points out that, in the case of the debtor's insolvency, the creditor should not be allowed to obtain a preference by wrongful seizure of property. It would seem that this problem ought to be dealt with in the context of fraudulent preferences in insolvency.

between conversion and detinue in respect of the date for the assessment for damages has been discussed.[371]

1.1750 An offer of redelivery of the goods to the plaintiff will affect the measure of damages and, in some circumstances, will remove the right to maintain the action. When the plaintiff refuses to accept the redelivery, her action for the value of the goods will be stayed provided the court is convinced that the same goods in the same condition as they were in at the time of conversion have been tendered, and that it is not for any other reason unreasonable to expect the plaintiff to accept redelivery.[372] Damages for loss of use of the goods may still be claimed.[373] Similarly an action in detinue when the gist of the complaint is that the goods are wrongfully detained cannot proceed after a tender of the goods except in respect of damages for loss of use of the goods during the period of wrongful detention.[374]

1.1760 Where the plaintiff accepts the goods the action for detinue similarly disappears except in respect of damages for temporary loss of use. The action in conversion, however, does not disappear. First, the plaintiff will be entitled to nominal damages.[375] Secondly, where the goods have fallen in value, the plaintiff's *prima facie* action is for the value at the time of the conversion,[376] but the plaintiff is obliged to bring into account in reduction of damages only the lesser value of the goods at the time of redelivery.[377]

1.1770 Where the defendant, having converted the plaintiff's property, uses the proceeds to repay the plaintiff's debt to a third party, the question arises of whether the benefit conferred by repayment of the debt should be taken into account in assessing damages for the conversion. Had the wrong not been done, the plaintiff would have had the property, but would have owed the debt. This suggests that, in seeking to put the plaintiff in the position that would have been occupied if the wrong had

---

371 See 1.1010 - 1.1040, *supra*. Detinue has been abolished in the United Kingdom by *Torts (Interference with Goods) Act 1977*, s. 2(1).

372 *Fisher v. Prince* (1762), 3 Burr. 1363, 97 E.R. 876 (but stay refused as goods found to be of altered value); *Earle v. Holderness* (1828), 4 Bing. 462, 130 E.R. 845; *Duryea v. Kaufman* (1912), 2 D.L.R. 468, 21 O.W.R. 141 (H.C.J.); *Vancouver Machinery Co. v. Vancouver Timber & Trading Co.* (1914), 18 D.L.R. 491 (B.C.C.A.). See Culshaw, "Re-delivery of Converted Property," 6 Aust. L.J. 329 (1933). In *Harbour Equipment Ltd. v. C.N.R. Co.* (1976), 25 N.S.R. (2d) 166 (S.C.T.D.), the Nova Scotia Supreme Court discussed this principle but refused to stay the action on the grounds of delay in tendering redelivery and the absence of proof that the goods were undamaged.

373 See *Hillesden Securities Ltd. v. Ryjack Ltd.*, [1983] 1 W.L.R. 959 (Q.B.). In *Fisher v. Prince, supra*, footnote 372, at p. 1364, Lord Mansfield and Wilmot J. spoke of "any tort accompanying it that may enhance the damages above the real value of the thing".

374 *Crossfield v. Such* (1852), 8 Ex. 159, 155 E.R. 1301. See pp. 163 and 164, *per* Parke B.

375 See 10.10 - 10.40, *infra*, on nominal damages.

376 See *General Securities Ltd. v. Parsons* (1955), 14 W.W.R. 424 (B.C.C.A.).

377 *Solloway v. McLaughlin*, [1938] A.C. 247, [1937] 4 D.L.R. 593 (P.C.); *Campbell v. McMillan* (1915), 22 D.L.R. 608 (Alta. S.C.); *Trailways Transport Ltd. v. Thomas*, [1996] 2 N.Z.L.R. 443 (H.C.).

not been done, the benefit conferred by repayment of the debt should be taken into account. On the other hand, this conclusion would enable the defendant to recover for an unrequested and perhaps unwanted benefit, a result not ordinarily countenanced by the law of restitution.[378] The preferable view, therefore, seems to be not to reduce recovery, on account of repayment of the debt, in any case in which the defendant could not, in an independent action, obtain restitution for the benefit conferred upon the plaintiff by repayment of the debt.

17. Trespass

1.1780 Complaint of deprivation of goods may sometimes be brought in trespass, either where the goods are misappropriated or where they are destroyed.[379] The problems of valuation do not, it seems, differ from those already discussed.

1.1785 In *Epstein v. Cressey Development Corp.*,[379a] the defendant, by secretly encroaching on the plaintiff's land, built closer to the plaintiff's property line than would otherwise have been possible. Damages were awarded to compensate the plaintiff for the greater value the plaintiff's property would have had if the defendant had not trespassed and had built further from the property line.

18. Non-delivery of Shares

1.1790 The assessment of damages for failure to deliver or to replace shares depends on the same general principles that govern this chapter: the plaintiff is entitled to a sum of money representing the value of the shares that ought to have been delivered. As mentioned earlier, this may reflect the value of a controlling interest.[380] Assessment has often been complicated by fluctuations in value to which shares are subject. This question has been discussed earlier where it was suggested that postponement of the date for assessment beyond the date when the plaintiff could reasonably replace the shares is appropriate only when the plaintiff has a proprietary interest in the shares such as would justify initiating a suit for specific performance or a proprietary remedy at law.[381] If this view is accepted, it becomes important to know when the plaintiff has a proprietary remedy. The right to specific performance will depend upon the equitable considerations discussed in the companion volume to this work.[382] The right to assert legal proprietary

[378] See Maddaugh and McCamus, *The Law of Restitution* (Aurora, Canada Law Book, 1990), pp. 681-773.

[379] See Fleming, *The Law of Torts*, 9th ed. (Sydney, Law Book Co., 1998), pp. 58-60. Cases of damage to property are discussed below at 1.2310 - 1.2800.

[379a] (1992), 89 D.L.R. (4th) 32, [1992] 3 W.W.R. 566 (B.C.C.A.). See also *Costello v. Calgary (City)* (1997), 152 D.L.R. (4th) 453, [1998] 1 W.W.R. 222 (Alta. C.A.), leave to appeal to S.C.C. refused 154 D.L.R. (4th) ix, 227 N.R. 149*n* (wrongful expropriation).

[380] See 1.180, *supra*.

[381] See 1.910 - 1.1010, *supra*.

[382] See Sharpe, *Injunctions and Specific Performance*, looseleaf ed. (Toronto, Canada Law Book, 1999), 8.520-8.560.

remedies would seem to depend on the plaintiff's having a property interest in identifiable shares or share certificates. This question depends on the relationship between the parties. Where a specific share certificate is lent, for example, to a broker as security, on the understanding that the certificate itself will be restored, it would appear that the lender retains a proprietary interest not only in the shares represented by the certificate but in the tangible certificate itself.[383] In many cases, however, the relationship between the parties is more akin to that of debtor and creditor than bailee and bailor, the defendant's obligation being not to deliver or restore any particular identifiable shares but to deliver a certain number of shares of a particular description.[384] These cases, it is suggested, should be treated, so far as assessment of damages is concerned, like sales of unascertained goods, that is, damages should be assessed within a sufficient time of the plaintiff's learning of the wrong to permit purchase of a substitute unless there are circumstances (as in the *Asamera*[385] case) that make it reasonable for the plaintiff to wait longer. Actions in conversion and detinue have been allowed, however, even where it appears that the defendant's only obligation was to tender unascertained shares of a certain description.[386] It may be that these cases will have to be reconsidered in the light of the *Asamera* case.[387]

19. Non-conveyance of Land: The Rule in *Bain v. Fothergill*

1.1800 The general rule, that the plaintiff is entitled, so far as money can do it, to be put into as good a position as would have been occupied if the plaintiff's rights had been observed, entitles the buyer of land that is not conveyed to recover its value. As the earlier discussion indicates, so long as the buyer is reasonably pursuing a decree of specific performance, the buyer will be entitled to postpone the date for the assessment of damages, for entitlement to specific performance carries with it the implication that the buyer cannot reasonably be expected to make do with a substitute.[388]

[*The next page is* 1-85]

383 See *Whitehead v. Bridger, Hevenor & Co.*, [1936] 3 D.L.R. 408 (Ont. C.A.); *Aitken v. Gardiner* (1956), 4 D.L.R. (2d) 119, [1956] O.R. 589 (H.C.J.); Cooper and Cridlan, *Law and Procedure of the Stock Exchange* (London, Butterworths, 1971), p. 157.

384 This was the view taken by the Supreme Court of Canada in the case of a bailment of shares in *Asamera Oil Corp. v. Sea Oil & General Corp.*, [1979] 1 S.C.R. 633, 89 D.L.R. (3d) 1.

385 *Supra*, footnote 384.

386 *Aitken v. Gardiner, supra*, footnote 383.

387 See 1.770, 1.780, *supra*, and Waddams, "Damages for Failure to Return Shares", 3 C.B.L.J. 398 (1979).

388 See 1.980, *supra*.

1.1810 Where the reason for non-conveyance is the vendor's innocent failure to make a good title, there was a rule that the purchaser could rescind the contract and recover the deposit and the expenses of investigating title, but had no claim for the value of the land. This is called the rule in *Flureau v. Thornhill*[389] where it was first laid down, or the rule in *Bain v. Fothergill*,[390] where it was affirmed by the House of Lords. Viewed from the point of view of damages, the rule is bound to seem anomalous, and it has been generally,[391] though not universally,[392] criticized by writers on damages. The rule seems to be an unjustified departure from the general principle of putting the plaintiff into as good a position as if her rights had been observed. However, the original, and, it is submitted, the only modern justification for the rule rests not on any point of the law of damages, but on the construction of the contract to sell land, *i.e.*, that the vendor of land, in the ordinary case, does not warrant title but simply agrees that a showing of good title shall be a condition of the purchaser's obligation to buy, so that on innocent failure to make title, the contract is off and the deposit is returnable, but the vendor is not otherwise liable. All would agree that where this is expressly stated in the agreement, as it very commonly is, the vendor is not liable except as agreed. All that the rule in *Flureau v. Thornhill* states is that such a provision is to be implied in the ordinary land sale agreement, even when not expressly stated. It is therefore entirely a rule relating to the substantive law of sale of land and has, it is submitted, no real connection with the law of damages at all. That this was the court's view of the matter in *Flureau v. Thornhill* itself appears from Blackstone J.'s judgment: "These contracts are merely upon condition, frequently expressed, but always implied, that the vendor has a good title. If he has not, the return of the deposit, with interest and costs, is all that can be expected."[393]

1.1820 In *A.V.G. Management Science Ltd. v. Barwell Developments Ltd.*,[394] the Supreme Court of Canada expressed the opinion that the rule in *Bain v. Fothergill* was anomalous and was to be strictly limited in scope. In that case the court held that the rule did not apply, but went on to hold that the rationale of the rule had disappeared in jurisdictions having a Torrens system of land registration, and that if it were necessary to the decision, its view would be that the rule should no longer be followed in such jurisdictions. The court said that, even in other jurisdictions, the utility of

389 (1776), 2 Black. W. 1078, 96 E.R. 635.

390 (1874), L.R. 7 H.L. 158, disapproved in *A.V.G. Management Science*, [1979] 2 S.C.R. 43, 92 D.L.R. (3d) 289.

391 *McGregor on Damages*, 15th ed. (London, Sweet & Maxwell, 1988), §881; *Sedgwick on Damages*, 8th ed. (New York, Baker, Voorhis & Co., 1891), §1012; *Corbin on Contracts* (St. Paul, West Publishing Co., 1950), §1098.

392 See McCormick, *Handbook on the Law of Damages* (St. Paul, West Publishing Co., 1935), pp. 692-3.

393 *Supra*, footnote 379, at pp. 1078-9.

394 [1979] 2 S.C.R. 43, 92 D.L.R. (3d) 289.

the rule was doubtful. In a subsequent case, the Ontario Court of Appeal (Ontario having a mixed land registration system) said, *obiter*, but expressly, that the rule was no longer a part of the law of Canada,[395] and a similar view has been taken by the Saskatchewan Court of Appeal.[396] Detailed discussion of its application is therefore omitted from this edition.

III. COMPENSATION FOR LOSS OF USE OF PROPERTY

1. Introduction

1.1830 In many different kinds of cases complaint is made by the plaintiff that a wrongdoer has prevented the plaintiff from using personal property during a period of time. As mentioned earlier in the discussion of value, the capital value of property itself reflects the value of future anticipated use, so that if complete compensation could be given to the plaintiff for the full value of the property there would be no room for any additional claim.[397] For convenience, it is common for the courts to divide a claim for the value of property from a claim for the loss of use. But as Lord Wright said in *Liesbosch v. Edison*,[398] care is required to avoid double compensation. The value of a ship reflects the income-earning capacity for the full expected life of the ship. It would be wrong to add to the full value, so calculated, compensation for loss of power to earn income during any period of time after the loss. Lord Wright said: "The value of prospective freights cannot simply be added to the market value but ought to be taken into account in order to ascertain the total value for purpose of assessing the damage, since if it is merely added to the market value of a free ship, the owner will be getting *pro tanto* his damages twice over. The vessel cannot be earning in the open market, while fulfilling the pending charter or charters."[399]

---

395 *Brown v. Waterloo Regional Board of Com'rs of Police* (1983), 150 D.L.R. (3d) 729 at p. 734, 43 O.R. (2d) 113 (C.A.).

396 *Kopec v. Pyret* (1987), 36 D.L.R. (4th) 1, [1987] 3 W.W.R. 449 (C.A.). The rule has been abolished by statute in British Columbia (*Property Law Act*, s. 37), and in the United Kingdom: *Law of Property (Miscellaneous Provisions) Act 1989*, s. 3.

397 See 1.20, 1.270, *supra*.

398 [1933] A.C. 449 (H.L.). See also *Ticketnet Corp. v. Air Canada* (1997), 154 D.L.R. (4th) 271, 105 O.A.C. 87 (C.A.), leave to appeal to S.C.C. refused 161 D.L.R. (4th) vii.

399 *Supra*, at p. 464. In some cases compensation has been given for loss of profits under current engagements in addition to the value of the lost ship, but it is clear that where this is done the value taken is the value at the end of the engagement, not the value of a free ship at the beginning of the engagement. See *The "Kate"* [1899] P. 165; *The "Racine"* [1906] P. 273 (C.A.); *The "Philadelphia"* [1917] P. 101 (C.A.), at p. 111, *per* Swinfen Eady L.J.; *The "Llanover"* [1947] P. 80; *The "Fortunity"* [1961] 1 W.L.R. 351. (P.D.A.). Alternatively, the value could be taken, at the date of the loss, of a ship that had been demised for a non-profitable use for the period of the

1.1840 The test of value suggested earlier, namely, the sum that the owner acting rationally would have accepted to give up the property,[400] could always be applied so as to include compensation for loss of use, for the rational owner would take this into account in setting the price.[401] But it

[*The next page is* 1-87]

engagement. This approach would be more convenient if interest runs from the date of the loss. See 1.1870, 1.1890, *infra*.

400 See 1.120 - 1.1380, *supra*.

401 Many cases have commented that the earning power of property is one means of assessing its value: *Samula v. Robertson* (1959), 67 Man. R. 30 (Q.B.); *Monte Video Gas & Dry Dock Co. Ltd. v. Clan Line Steamers, Ltd.* (1921), 37 T.L.R. 866 (C.A.). See also *Steele v. Maurer* (1977), 79 D.L.R. (3d) 764, where the Saskatchewan Court of Appeal disallowed, as duplicative, recovery of the loss of value of calves and recovery of the profits to be obtained by using the calves for breeding purposes. In *Hutscal v. I.A.C. Ltd.* (1974), 48 D.L.R. (3d) 638 (Yukon Terr. C.A.), damages for loss of use were held to be duplicative of an award based on the value of property converted.

is convenient in many cases to separate the claim for the value of property that is lost to the plaintiff from the claim for compensation for loss of its use pending replacement, and the separation does no harm provided double compensation is avoided. A claim for loss of use arises in many cases where the property is eventually restored to the plaintiff, as in the case of delayed delivery in sales or wrongful temporary interference with property. In these cases the plaintiff will have no claim for the full value of the property, and compensation for loss of use must be assessed separately. Dr. Lushington in *The "Columbus"*[402] stated that, in cases of total loss, the full value of the vessel only was to be allowed, whereas in cases of damage an allowance could be made for demurrage or loss of profits. Though this distinction has been criticized, it is suggested that it is in substance sound provided that in cases of total destruction the particular circumstances of the plaintiff are taken into account in assessing the value of the vessel, as was done in the *Liesbosch*.[403] It is common, even in cases of destruction, to divide the elements of capital value and loss of use.[404] The distinction is that in cases of destruction it is possible and may be convenient to include compensation for loss of use in the calculation of the capital value. In the case of damage it is not possible, because the plaintiff has no claim to the full capital value.

1.1850 Where damages are awarded for the full value of the plaintiff's property as in the cases of destruction or non-delivery, and damages for loss of use are separately calculated, the latter can only be justified for the period during which the plaintiff is necessarily deprived of the use of the property, that is, the time it will take to secure a replacement.[405] Damages for loss of use cannot extend perpetually, or rather it would be more accurate to say, that if an attempt were made to calculate the present value of the use of the property for the whole of its expected life this would be equivalent to assessing its present capital value. The plaintiff cannot be entitled to this value twice over.

2. Interest on the Value of the Property

1.1860 One way of measuring the value of the use of property is by allowing interest on the capital value. In *British Columbia Saw-Mill Co. v. Nettleship*,[406] Bovill C.J. said that compensation for delay in obtaining

---

402 (1849), 3 W. Rob. 158, 166 E.R. 922 (Adm.). See also *Darling v. Collins* (1958), 25 W.W.R. 522 (B.C.S.C.).

403 See 1.260 - 1.310, *supra*.

404 See footnote 399, *supra*.

405 See 1.280, *supra*, and *Nason v. Aubin* (1958), 16 D.L.R. (2d) 309 (N.B.S.C. App. Div.); *Vanda Compania Limitada of Costa Rica v. Société Maritime Nationale of Paris*, [1974] 2 Lloyd's Rep. 502; *McKinnon v. Acadian Lines Ltd.* (1977), 81 D.L.R. (3d) 480 (N.S.S.C. App. Div.); *Armstrong Cartage Co. v. County of Peel* (1913), 10 D.L.R. 169, 24 O.W.R. 372 (S.C.).

406 (1868), L.R. 3 C.P. 499. See also *Fletcher v. Tayleur* (1855), 17 C.B. 21 at p. 29, 139 E.R. 973, *per* Willes J.

the use of goods might take the form of "interest on the value of the goods".[407] This suggestion has been implemented in Canadian cases. In *Prime Potash Corp. v. Bison Petroleum & Minerals Ltd.*,[408] where the defendant had caused a delay in the plaintiff's obtaining a potash mining interest, the court considered that the primary measure of damages would be the decline in the market value of the interest, but in the absence of evidence of the value on the date the interest was finally transferred, interest was awarded on the earlier value for the period of the delay. Johnson J. said:

> The fact is that the defendant's breach of contract has delayed the plaintiff for two and one-half years from obtaining a very valuable asset valued at $2,148,000, which it might have developed, sold or used. In my view the plaintiff is entitled to compensation for this loss of use: ". . . where there has been non-delivery or delayed delivery of land under a contract of sale or lease, the value of the loss of use or loss of profits has been awarded as damages in some cases". See *Mayne and McGregor on Damages*, 12 ed., para. 283 . . . Also see *British Columbia Saw Mill Co. v. Nettleship* . . . where Bovill, C.J., regarded the value of the use of lost goods as interest. Because of the lack of evidence as to the rate of return on invested funds since 1966, I allow interest at the rate of 5%.[409]

In *Scott Maritimes Pulp Ltd. v. B.F. Goodrich Canada Ltd.*[410] interest was similarly allowed.

1.1870 Several points arise. First, in cases of total loss where the plaintiff is awarded the full value of the property and interest on it from the date of the loss, there can be no additional claim for interest to compensate for loss of use, or indeed for any compensation for loss of use. If the wrong had not been done, the plaintiff might have sold the property and invested the proceeds at interest, or she might have put the property to use and made profits. She could not have done both, for these are alternative ways of putting capital to work.[411]

1.1880 Secondly, as is argued below,[412] a plaintiff who claims that he has suffered a loss through deprivation of the use of property ought to show that he has in fact suffered such a loss, that is, that he would, if the wrong had not been done, have made a profitable use of the property. Interest on the value of the property is an appropriate measure where, as in the *Prime Potash* case, the plaintiff shows that he has suffered a loss, but insufficient evidence is available to quantify it. The same can

---

407 *British Columbia Saw-Mill Co., supra*, at p. 507.

408 (1968), 1 D.L.R. (3d) 362 (Sask. Q.B.). See also *Saint John Motor Line, Ltd. v. Canadian National Ry. Co.* (1929), 2 M.P.R. 55 (N.B.S.C. App. Div.), revd on other grounds [1930] S.C.R. 482, [1930] 3 D.L.R. 732.

409 *Prime Potash Corp., supra*, at p. 378.

410 (1977), 72 D.L.R. (3d) 680 (N.S.S.C. App. Div.).

411 See 7.330 - 7.440, *infra*. See also *Lister (Ronald Elwyn) Ltd. v. Dayton Tire Canada Ltd.* (1985), 52 O.R. (2d) 88 (C.A.), at p. 127, citing this passage.

412 See 1.1970, *infra*.

be said of the cases discussed below of loss of use of non-profit-making chattels.[413] But an award of interest would not be appropriate in a case where the chattels were intended for the purpose of making profits but the plaintiff fails to prove the loss of any.

1.1890 Thirdly, if compensation is made by other means for loss of use of property, interest on the capital value should not be awarded in addition. Thus, an award of lost profits would exclude an award of interest in respect of the same period of time. However, where compensation is based on the theory that the plaintiff, if the wrong had not been done, could have sold the goods to a third party, interest should, it is submitted, be awarded on the full price that the plaintiff could have obtained. For, had the wrong not been done, the plaintiff could have realized the price and invested it at interest. The statutes governing pre-judgment interest, discussed in a later chapter,[414] generally permit interest on the amount of the award only, which will, in the case of delayed delivery, for example, represent only the difference between the value at the date of due delivery and the value at the date of actual delivery. Compensation for loss of use, however, measured by interest on the value can be included in the award, on the principles, here discussed, not as interest on the award but as part of the award itself. There is authority for this distinction in Canadian personal injury cases.[415]

3. Decline in the Value of Property

1.1900 There has been much controversy over the question whether a person wrongfully deprived of property during a period in which its value declines is by that fact alone entitled to claim the amount of the decline. Where the plaintiff had intended to sell the property on its delivery, she is entitled to compensation for loss of that opportunity and the proper measure of the compensation will generally be the difference between the value at the date of due delivery and the value at the date of actual delivery. Several decisions have held that this is the normal measure.[416]

1.1910 Where, however, the plaintiff was not intending to sell the property, it is by no means clear that compensation should be according to that measure. In *Brandeis Goldschmidt & Co. Ltd. v. Western Transport*

413 See 1.2030 - 1.2140, *infra*. In *The "Hebridean Coast"* [1961] A.C. 545 (H.L.), interest was allowed. It is submitted that the decision is justified only on proof of loss by the plaintiff.

414 See 7.450, *infra*.

415 See 7.1000, *infra*.

416 See *Prime Potash Corp. v. Bison Petroleum & Minerals Ltd., supra*, footnote 408; *Barrow v. Arnaud* (1846), 8 Q.B. 595, 115 E.R. 1000; *Williams v. Archer* (1847), 5 C.B. 318, 136 E.R. 899; *Dunn v. CIMA Resources Ltd.* (1982), 17 B.L.R. 162 (B.C.S.C.), affd 20 A.C.W.S. (2d) 179 (C.A.); *Toronto General Trusts Corp. v. Roman* (1962), 37 D.L.R. (2d) 16, [1963] 1 O.R. 312 (C.A.), affd [1963] S.C.R. vi, 41 D.L.R. (2d) 290*n*; *Tanenbaum v. W. J. Bell Paper Co. Ltd.* (1956), 4 D.L.R. (2d) 177, [1956] O.R. 278 (H.C.J.). See also *Lundy v. Powell* (1921), 60 D.L.R. 607 (Sask. K.B.), at p. 611 (wrongful filing of caveat).

Ltd.,[417] the English Court of Appeal held that a purchaser of copper for use in a manufacturing process was not entitled to recover compensation for decline in the market value of copper during a period of wrongful detention. The plaintiff was unable to show that it had bought any other copper to replace the copper detained or that it would have sold the copper had it been duly delivered. In these circumstances the court held that the plaintiff had failed to prove any loss, earlier cases being distinguished on the ground that the plaintiffs there were presumably buying for immediate sale.[418] Brandon L.J. said:

> Looking at the matter from the point of view of principle first, I cannot see why there should be any universally applicable rule for assessing damages for wrongful detention of goods, whether it be the rule contended for by the plaintiffs or any other rule. Damages in tort are awarded by way of monetary compensation for a loss or losses which a plaintiff has actually sustained, and the measure of damages awarded on this basis may vary infinitely according to the circumstances of any particular case.
>
> It is for the plaintiffs to prove what loss, if any, they have suffered by reason of a tort.[419]

Brandon L.J. quoted a dictum in *Williams v. Peel River Land & Mineral Co.*[420] to the same effect in even stronger terms:

> You do not give damages in an action for detention in poenam; it is not a paternal correction inflicted by the court, but simply compensation for the loss. Now [counsel] was inclined . . . to argue the question as if there were some legal crystallised rule as to damages for the detention of stock of this sort — that the law created a kind of definition which we must adhere to, whether there was a loss or not. I cannot think that the law would really lay down anything so ridiculous as that a man should be compensated whether he suffered damages or not.[421]

The *Williams* case was followed by the Ontario Court of Appeal in *Picavet v. Bache & Co. Inc.*[422]

1.1920 The same line of reasoning underlies the decision of the Privy Council in the Canadian case of *Wertheim v. Chicoutimi Pulp Co.*[423] The plaintiff had purchased pulpwood from the defendant and the action was for delayed delivery. At the date when the pulpwood should have been delivered the market price was 70*s.* per ton. At the date when it was actually delivered the price had dropped to 42*s.* 6*d.* per ton. The plaintiff claimed the difference. It was shown, however, that he had in fact resold

417 [1981] Q.B. 864 (C.A.).

418 See the passage from *Williams v. Peel River Land & Mineral Co.* (1886), 55 L.T. 689 (C.A.), at pp. 692-3, quoted in *Brandeis Goldschmidt & Co., supra*, footnote 417, at p. 872.

419 *Brandeis Goldschmidt & Co., supra*, at p. 870.

420 *Supra*, footnote 418.

421 *Brandeis Goldschmidt & Co., supra*, footnote 417, at p. 872.

422 (1972), 30 D.L.R. (3d) 136, [1973] 1 O.R. 8 (C.A.).

423 [1911] A.C. 301 (P.C.).

the wood under a number of contracts made before and after the contract sued on, for 65*s.* and that these contracts were filled, just as expected, despite the delay. The Privy Council held that the plaintiff was not entitled to more than the 5*s.* per ton which the Canadian courts had awarded. It appears that if the plaintiff's contention had prevailed he would be much better off as a result of the judgment than he would have been if the wrong had not been done. As it was he had actually resold the pulp at a handsome profit, shown by the evidence to amount to 27*s.* per ton (65*s.* minus 38*s.*, composed of the purchase price of 25*s.* and transport costs of 13*s.*). If his contention had succeeded he would add to that damages of 27*s.* 6*d.* per ton, more than doubling his profit to a total of 54*s.* 6*d.* It is not surprising that the court sought to avoid this result, and Lord Atkinson used strong terms about the injustice of over-compensation saying that it would be "against all justice" for the plaintiff to "be permitted to make a profit by the breach of contract, be compensated for a loss he never suffered and be put, so far as money can do it, not in the same position in which he would have been if the contract had been performed, but in a much better position".[424]

1.1930 The case has been very much criticized. The argument against the result is in substance that if the pulp had been delivered on time, the plaintiff could have sold it on the market for 70*s.* per ton making a profit of 32*s.* (70 minus 38), waited until the market dropped to 42*s.* 6*d.* and then bought other wood at that price to fill his subcontracts, thereby making an additional profit of 22*s.* 6*d.* per ton (65 minus 42*s.* 6*d.*) for a total profit of 54*s.* 6*d.* A comparison with cases of non-delivery and of delivery of defective goods has often been made for the purpose of showing that *Wertheim v. Chicoutimi Pulp Co.* must be wrongly decided. However, it is submitted that the problems are distinguishable. In the case of non-delivery, as of destruction of goods, the plaintiff is entitled to their value at the time of the loss notwithstanding that she would have failed to realize the value if the goods had been duly delivered.[425] Again, in the case of delivery of defective goods, as of damage to goods, the plaintiff is entitled to the diminution in the value of the goods even though he succeeds in selling them to a third party at a price appropriate to sound goods.[426] These are cases where the plaintiff can realistically assert that a capital loss is suffered at the date of the wrong and is entitled to have it made good. What would have been done with the goods later or what actually is done with the defective goods can justifiably be excluded as irrelevant. As suggested earlier,[427] there are strong arguments of simplicity for excluding such considerations. These arguments, however, are not so easily applicable to the case of delay. There the substance of the plaintiff's

424 *Supra*, at p. 308.
425 See 1.1360 - 1.1430, *supra*.
426 See 1.2570, 1.2580, *infra*.
427 See 1.650, 1.660, *supra*.

complaint is not that a capital loss has been suffered. He does not demand a sum of money that will stand instead of the property he ought to have had. A sum of money to compensate for temporary deprivation of the property is demanded, and the plaintiff ought to show therefore that, had the wrong not been done, some profitable use of the property would have been made.[428] Thus, in *Wertheim v. Chicoutimi Pulp*, if the plaintiff could have shown that in fact he would have resold the goods (at 70*s.*) on timely arrival, accurately anticipating the extraordinary drop in the market (to 42*s.* 6*d.*) that would enable him a profit separately on the subcontracts (reselling at 65*s.*), his claim would be entitled to succeed. In the absence of such proof, it is submitted that the Privy Council was on sound ground in denying the claim. Indeed it would seem to follow from the board's reasoning that even the claim to 5*s.* per ton should fail for, had the wood been delivered on time, it would have been resold (as in fact it was) for 65*s.*, not 70*s.* Thus, the plaintiff was in precisely the same position as if the wrong had not been done. Lord Atkinson, in fact, said not that 5*s.* was the proper rate but that "the damages seem to have been fixed by the lower courts at 5*s.* per ton" and "the rate per ton so fixed is, in their Lordships' opinion, the *highest* rate at which it could properly be fixed, since it *covers* the loss actually sustained"[429] [Emphasis added.]. This language appears to leave open the possibility that a cross-appeal to reduce the damages to nominal damages, had it been made, would have succeeded.

1.1940 No doubt was cast by the decision on the cases allowing recovery of full value on non-delivery. *Rodoconachi, Sons & Co. v. Milburn Bros.*[430] was cited with approval and distinguished in *Wertheim v. Chicoutimi Pulp*, and the distinction was later approved by the House of Lords in *Williams Bros. v. Ed. T. Agius, Ltd.*[431] It is submitted that, despite academic and judicial doubts, the distinction is sound for the reasons just given, and that *Rodoconachi v. Milburn, Wertheim v. Chichoutimi Pulp, Williams v. Agius*, and *Slater v. Hoyle & Smith*,[432] despite criticisms,[433] are all rightly decided.

---

428 This distinction was made by Lord Dunedin in *Williams Bros. v. Ed. T. Agius, Ltd.*, [1914] A.C. 510 (H.L.), at p. 522, followed in *W. C. Pitfield & Co. Ltd. v. Jomac Gold Syndicate Ltd.*, [1938] 3 D.L.R. 158, [1938] O.R. 427 (C.A.) and *BBMB Finance (Hong Kong) Ltd. v. EDA Holdings Ltd.*, [1990] 1 W.L.R. 409 (P.C.), at p. 413.

429 *Wertheim v. Chicoutimi Pulp Co., supra*, footnote 423, at p. 307.

430 (1886), 18 Q.B.D. 67 (C.A.).

431 *Supra*, footnote 428.

432 [1920] 2 K.B. 11 (C.A.). See 1.2570, *infra*.

433 *Report on Sale of Goods* (Ontario Law Reform Commission, 1979), pp. 501-2.

4. Loss of Profits from Use

1.1950 Where the defendant's wrong causes a profit-making chattel to be withheld from the owner's use for a period of time, the latter is entitled to be compensated for lost profits.[434] It was early established in admiralty cases that such a claim, known as demurrage, could be made in respect of ships and many of the principles were more thoroughly worked out in the admiralty cases than in the common law courts, partly, no doubt, because of the absence of a jury in the admiralty court and partly because of the large sums of money usually involved. The law of damages, as has been seen elsewhere, is often torn between the convenience of adopting a comparatively simple rule for damage assessment and the claim of one or other of the parties to investigate the precise circumstances of the case and to estimate precisely what position the plaintiff would have occupied if the wrong had not been done. This dilemma can perhaps never be fully resolved, and in the area of present discussion there can be no completely satisfactory explanation that will apply universally. Sometimes the courts measure compensation for loss of use by rather rough and ready criteria ignoring the plaintiff's argument that in fact a greater loss has been incurred or the defendant's argument that in fact the loss is less. At other times a quite thorough investigation of the particular circumstances has been pursued. The bar of remoteness of damages very often plays an important role in this context.[435] Willingness in principle to permit a claim for the plaintiff's full actual loss may turn out to be defeated by holding that the loss claimed is too remote.

1.1960 As stated above, a distinction is drawn between claims for loss of value and claims for loss of use. In the former kind of case the full value is allowable even if the plaintiff would not in fact have put it to profitable use.[436] In the latter kind of case the starting point is different, for it is usually said that the plaintiff claiming a loss of profits must prove the loss. Thus, in *The "Clarence"*[437] Dr. Lushington held that the claim for

---

434 See *Pacific Elevators Ltd. v. Canadian Pacific Ry. Co.*, [1974] S.C.R. 803, 41 D.L.R. (3d) 608; *Brown v. Hope* (1912), 2 D.L.R. 615 (B.C.C.A.); *Marson v. Grand Trunk Pacific Ry. Co.* (1912), 1 D.L.R. 850 (Alta. C.A.); *Silver v. Co-operators General Insurance Co.* (1998), 169 N.S.R. (2d) 303 at p. 308 (C.A.), leave to appeal to S.C.C. refused 169 N.S.R. (2d) 303, citing this paragraph; *Kuwait Airways Corp. v. Iraqi Airways Corp. (Nos. 4 and 5)*, [2002] 2 W.L.R. 1353 (H.L.).

435 See 14.20 - 14.740, *infra*.

436 See 1.1360 - 1.1430, *supra*.

437 (1850), 3 W. Rob. 283, 166 E.R. 968 (Adm.). Loss of profits was required to be proven in *A-1 Rentals Sales & Service v. Alberta Arches & Beams Ltd.* (1966), 60 D.L.R. (2d) 4 (Alta. S.C. App. Div.), and *Vassallo v. Trans Canada Air Lines* (1963), 38 D.L.R. (2d) 383, [1963] 2 O.R. 55 (H.C.J.). See also *Vancouver Ice & Storage Co. v. British Columbia Electric Ry. Co.*, [1927] 1 W.W.R. 631 (B.C.C.A.); *Exclusive Ambulance Ltd. v. Ball* (1952), 7 W.W.R. (N.S.) 335 (B.C.C.A.); *The "City of Peking"* (1890), 15 App. Cas. 438 (P.C.); *The King v. Saint John Tug Boat Co., Ltd.*, [1946] S.C.R. 466, [1946] 3 D.L.R. 225; *Canadian Pacific Ry. Co. v. Canadian Freightways Ltd.* (1962), 39 W.W.R. 191 (B.C.C.A.); *Smith v. McConnell Brothers* (1954), 11 W.W.R. (N.S.) 600 (Man. Q.B.); *Mortimer v. Shaw* (1922), 66 D.L.R. 311 (Sask. C.A.). In *The "Hebridean Coast"* [1961] A.C. 545 (H.L.), interest on the value of the ship was allowed. Lord Reid (p. 578)

demurrage in the case of damage to a ship must be distinctly proved and that it was not sufficient for the plaintiff to claim a moderate rate of hire for the period during which the ship was disabled. In *The "Black Prince"*[438] the plaintiff's individual circumstances were investigated to see exactly how his position in fact differed from the position he would have occupied if the wrong had not been done.

1.1970 Even after it was held in a series of cases (discussed below) that an owner of non-profit-making property was entitled to damages for loss of use,[439] the old rule was reaffirmed that when the plaintiff was using the property for the purpose of making profits there could be no recovery in this respect of more than had actually been lost. Thus, in *Admiralty Com'rs v. S.S. Valeria*[440] where the plaintiff had hired a vessel from its owners at £342 per day but was only making a net income from its use of £142 per day, it was held by the House of Lords that the plaintiff was only entitled to £142 per day demurrage, the basis of compensation being not the daily value of the ship (which might have been £342) but what the plaintiff, but for the accident, would have earned from the use of the ship. This conclusion seems anomalous at first sight in comparison with the cases where the plaintiff recovers for loss of use of non-profit-making property.[441] If the plaintiff owns goods for a non-profit-making purpose, the plaintiff recovers for loss of use, but if the goods are owned for a profit-making purpose, loss must be proven. It seems odd that the plaintiff should be better off if there is no profit than if there is a small profit. But the distinction does not rest on what profit the plaintiff in fact makes but on the purpose in owning the property. If the plaintiff owns the property to make a profit but in fact makes none she has not lost anything by being deprived of the use; indeed, if she operates at a loss, she may have gained.[442] But where the plaintiff's purpose in owning the property is to fulfil a public duty or to give pleasure to himself or to confer a benefit on a member of his family, he does suffer a real loss by being deprived of the use of the property. As a practical matter this loss can only be measured by some rough rule,

---

was evidently troubled at awarding compensation for a loss that he thought had not been proven, and it is submitted that the plaintiff ought to prove a loss.

438 (1862), Lush. Adm. 568.

439 See 1.2030 - 1.2140, *infra*.

440 [1922] 2 A.C. 242 (H.L.), and see *Exclusive Ambulance Ltd. v. Ball, supra*, footnote 437, where *The "Mediana"*, [1900] A.C. 113 (H.L.), had been relied on by the trial judge, and *Kleysen Transport Ltd. v. Northern Industrial Carriers Ltd.* (1981), 32 A.R. 541 (Q.B.), where *The "Greta Holme"* was cited, but proof of loss was required; also *Canadian Freightways Ltd. v. C.P.R. Co.* (1961), 29 D.L.R. (2d) 771 (B.C.S.C.), affd 39 W.W.R. 191 (C.A.); *Advance Rumely Thresher Co. v. Whaley* (1920), 52 D.L.R. 169 (Sask. C.A.). But see *Acadian Lines Ltd. v. Hannah*, [1965-69] 4 N.S.R. 159 (S.C. App. Div.); *New Brunswick Telephone Co. v. Wright* (1982), 140 D.L.R. (3d) 188 (N.B.Q.B.).

441 See 1.2030 - 1.2140, *infra*.

442 As in *The "Bodlewell"*, [1907] P. 286.

such as rental value or the cost of ownership. Lord Dunedin gave this illustration in *The "Valeria"*:

> Supposing a man had a house at a certain rent [*i.e.*, paying a certain rent for it] and sub-let it at a smaller rent, if that [*i.e.*, the house] were taken from him he would not get more, I take it, than the smaller rent which he had received; but if he had shown that he had let it to some member of his family at a fanciful [*i.e.*, nominal] rent, then there would have been inquiry as to what rent he could have got in the open market.[443]

1.1980 Where a particular profitable engagement is lost because of delay for which the defendant was responsible, the plaintiff is entitled to compensation for it subject to considerations of remoteness. In *The "Argentino"*[444] where a future charterparty was lost because of the delay, the defendant was held liable for the loss. Where damages are calculated on that basis, a deduction falls to be made for the earnings of the ship from other sources, and so compensation is in effect given for the loss of exceptional profit — the particular charterparty — a loss that in many circumstances might be expected to be excluded as too remote.

1.1990 Very commonly damages have been given in respect of such profits as might normally have been expected to be earned, while excluding, as too remote, compensation for loss of exceptionally lucrative uses.[445] In *Jonasson v. Dobinak*,[446] the question arose of illegal use of fishing nets; it was held that the estimated profits were to be based on the maximum legal use. This is consistent with cases holding that the value of property wrongfully damaged is recoverable, even if the property is being put to illegal use.[447] The value will be based on a legal use of the property.

1.2000 Difficulties have arisen in respect of charter parties delayed but not lost. If the defendant's wrong causes a ship to be out of service for ten days and in consequence to complete the current engagement ten days late, it is not obvious how the loss of use is to be valued. In the absence of the wrong the ship would, at the date of completion of the current engagement, have earned for ten days more than in fact the ship did earn. If the rate of daily earnings under the current engagement differs from the rate available on completion of the engagement, it would seem that, in principle, the rate to be taken is that prevailing after completion of the engagement for, had the wrong not been done, the ship would have fulfilled the current engagement ten days earlier and would have earned for ten extra days at the then prevailing rate. This argument was accepted in principle by the English Court of Appeal in *The "Soya"*[448] where the contention was rejected that there was a fixed rule requiring assessment according to the rate under an existing charter. However, it was held that in the particular case where the plaintiff claimed loss at the higher rate prevailing at the end of the current charter, the plaintiff had failed to prove its loss as a question of fact with sufficient certainty and

[443] *Supra*, footnote 440, at p. 248.
[444] (1888), 13 P.D. 191 (C.A.).

that it was in any event too remote. Lord Evershed M.R. pointed out that the plaintiff would surely be over-compensated if it were compensated at a rate based on an exceptionally profitable current charterparty — it would be receiving damages for a loss that had not been suffered, for in the cases under discussion the current charterparty is merely postponed, not lost. This situation arose in *The "Naxos"*[449] where it was held, rightly, it is submitted, that compensation for loss of use was not to be based on an exceptionally high rate under the current agreement. Brandon J. took the rates prevailing before and afterwards in order to fix an average earning capacity at the time of the delay. It is submitted that, strictly speaking, the relevant consideration is the earning capacity of the vessel during the period at the end of the current engagement when the vessel will in fact be detained under that engagement but in the absence of the wrong would have been free to earn from other sources.

1.2010 Difficult problems of causation arise here, as in other areas of law, where property is damaged by two independent causes. If a ship already

[445] *Cory v. Thames Ironworks Co.* (1868), L.R. 3 Q.B. 181; *Canada Foundry Co. v. Edmonton Portland Cement Co.* (1918), 43 D.L.R. 583 (P.C.); *Victoria Laundry (Windsor) Ltd. v. Newman Industries Ltd.*, [1949] 2 K.B. 528 (C.A.); *Re Trent and Humber Co.* (1868), L.R. 4 Ch. App. 112; *F. Leonard & Son. v. Kremer* (1912), 7 D.L.R. 244 (Alta. S.C.), affd, but damages reduced by divided court 48 S.C.R. 518, 11 D.L.R. 491; *Armstrong Cartage Co. v. Peel* (1913), 10 D.L.R. 169, 24 O.W.R. 372 (S.C.); *Fletcher v. Tayleur* (1855), 17 C.B. 21, 139 E.R. 973; *The "Kingsway"* [1918] P. 344 (C.A.); *Brown v. Hope* (1912), 2 D.L.R. 615 (B.C.C.A.) ("net earning power" allowed, but not loss of particular lucrative contract); *Parta Industries Ltd. v. Canadian Pacific Ltd.* (1974), 48 D.L.R. (3d) 463 (B.C.S.C.) (loss of business profits refused, but wasted overhead expenses allowed); *Regent Tailors Ltd. v. McArthur*, [1931] 1 D.L.R. 492, 66 O.L.R. 169 (S.C.) (loss of profits for wrongful eviction of tenant); *Mah Chong Lun v. Main Hotel Ltd.* (1956), 4 D.L.R. (2d) 359 (B.C.C.A.) (loss of profits allowed for wrongful eviction of lessor from rooming-house); *Lipinton v. Korsch* (1951), 4 W.W.R. (N.S.) 46 (B.C.S.C.) (loss of profits allowed for exclusion from rooming-house); *Budnitsky v. Gorstein*, [1947] 3 D.L.R. 905 (Man. K.B.). But see *Re Schulte–United Ltd.*, [1934] 4 D.L.R. 51, [1934] O.R. 453 (C.A.), leave to appeal to S.C.C. refused D.L.R. *loc. cit.* p. 252, and *Greenberg v. Stein* (1957), 10 D.L.R. (2d) 155 (B.C.S.C.), where damages for loss of a rooming-house business were not based on lost profits. In *Greenberg* it was pointed out that the plaintiff retained the value of his personal services, which he could use to make a profit from a substitute business. In *Karas v. Rowlett*, [1944] S.C.R. 1, 1 D.L.R. 241, *Re Schulte–United Ltd.* was explained as a case where the plaintiff had lost only the site of a business, not the business itself. In some cases the courts have simply allowed "general damages" for loss of use: *Workmen's Compensation Board v. Hoyt* (1972), 6 N.B.R. (2d) 859 (S.C.). In *Watson v. Gray* (1900), 16 T.L.R. 308, damages for increased costs of construction were allowed, on non-delivery of materials, but not for loss of business. In *Simmons & McBride Ltd. v. Kirkpatrick*, [1945] 4 D.L.R. 134 (B.C.S.C.), where the plaintiff intended originally to convert a car to use as a hearse in his funeral business, the defaulting seller was held not liable for loss of profits from use of the car as a limousine, on the ground that he had no knowledge of the proposed use. But it would seem that use as a limousine would be naturally expected without special notice. In *Walton v. Ferguson* (1914), 19 D.L.R. 816 (Alta. S.C.), crop loss from the unavailability of an engine was held to be too remote.

[446] [1928] 3 D.L.R. 501 (Man. C.A.).

[447] *Goodfellow v. O'Brien* (1921), 57 D.L.R. 432 (N.B.S.C.).

[448] [1956] 1 W.L.R. 714 (C.A.), leave to appeal to H.L. refused [1956] 2 All E.R. at p. 403*n*.

[449] [1972] 1 Lloyd's Rep. 149 (Q.B.).

in need of repair is further damaged by a wrongdoer and both sets of damage are repaired simultaneously, it would appear that the wrongdoer, though liable for the extra cost of repairing the damage caused, has not in fact caused any loss of use of the ship. This was the conclusion of the English Court of Appeal in *The "Haversham Grange"*,[450] and in *Carslogie S.S. Co. v. Royal Norwegian Government*[451] the House of Lords held that the same result was appropriate where the sequence of events was reversed, the damage by the independent cause following that of the wrongdoer. The question, as Viscount Jowitt said, was not whether the defendant caused the ship's detention but did the defendant cause the plaintiff to suffer loss as a result of the detention.[452] Since the ship would have been detained in any event, the answer was in the negative. In *The "Haversham Grange"* the Court of Appeal had held that a distinction could be drawn between liability for dock dues and liability for loss of use, but this holding was overruled in the *Carslogie* case for, as was pointed out there, the causation problem is identical in both cases. The reason for the conclusion was that, in the light of what was now known about the subsequent damage, the wrongdoer could not be held in fact to have caused either a loss of profits or a liability for dock dues. By similar reasoning it has been held that where a ship is damaged by the defendant but destroyed by another cause before repairs are carried out, the defendant is relieved of liability for loss of use.[453]

1.2015 Some uncertainty has been introduced on these questions by the decision of the Supreme Court of Canada in *Sunrise Co. v. The "Lake Winnipeg"*.[453a] Here, as in *The Carslogie*, the damage for which the defendant was responsible was followed by an incident for which no one was responsible. The Supreme Court of Canada, while saying that it proposed to follow the *Carslogie* case, nevertheless held the defendant liable in full on the ground that the second incident did not cause the loss. The difficulty with this reasoning is that the same could equally be said of the first incident, as shown by the *Carslogie* case itself.

1.2020 In the *Carslogie* and *Lake Winnipeg* cases, the independent event was one for which no one was responsible. A logical difficulty arises where successive damage is done by independent wrongdoers. In the well-known case of *Baker v. Willoughby*,[454] the plaintiff's foot was injured by the defendant and subsequently his leg was caused to be amputated by a second wrongdoer. On a strictly logical application of the principles

---

450 [1905] P.307 (C.A.). See also *The "York"*, [1929] P.178 (C.A.).

451 [1952] A.C. 292 (H.L). But see now *Sunrise Co. v. The "Lake Winnipeg"*, [1991] 1 S.C.R. 3, 77 D.L.R. (4th) 701 (wrongdoer liable in full).

452 *Supra*, at p. 301. The question of repair costs in such a case is discussed at 1.2520 - 1.2540, *infra*.

453 *The "Glenfinlas"*, [1918] P. 363*n*. See also *The "York"*, *supra*, footnote 450; *Beoco Ltd. v. Alfa Laval Co. Ltd.*, [1995] Q.B. 137.

453a [1991] 1 S.C.R. 3, 77 D.L.R. (4th) 701.

454 [1970] A.C. 467 (H.L.).

developed in the *Carslogie* case it seems that neither wrongdoer could be made liable for loss of earnings caused by the injury. The former wrongdoer could say that the plaintiff (as it turned out) was bound in any case to suffer the loss, and the second wrongdoer could say that he had injured a person who already lacked the earning capacity in issue. Since this result seems intolerable and the second wrongdoer's logic unassailable, the House of Lords adopted the only conclusion possible, namely, that the former wrongdoer was liable in full. In *Jobling v. Associated Dairies Ltd.*[455] the House of Lords, in distinguishing a case where the second injury was not tortious, expressed doubt as to the soundness of their earlier decision. It is submitted, however, that a distinction between tortious and non-tortious subsequent events is justifiable in order to avoid the inconvenience and unjust result of allowing a defence to both of two independent wrongdoers.[456] The distinction between *Carslogie* and *Jobling* on the one hand and *Baker v. Willoughby* on the other hand is to be found, therefore, it is submitted, in the fact that in the latter case, but not in the former cases, the subsequent event was wrongful.[457]

5. Loss of Use of Non-profit-making Chattels

1.2030 Where no direct monetary loss can be shown to arise from the loss of use, it might be thought that the plaintiff, suffering no harm, is entitled to no compensation for loss of use, and this was the view of the law taken in admiralty cases before 1897. In that year, however, the House of Lords held in *The "Greta Holme"*[458] that a harbour authority was entitled to recover for loss of the use of a dredger wrongfully damaged by the defendant, even though no expense was incurred to hire a replacement and no loss of profit was involved. Subsequent cases have confirmed the rule[459] stated by Lord Phillimore to be that damages are recoverable for the

455 [1982] A.C. 794 (H.L.).

456 Another explanation of *Baker v. Willoughby* is that the first wrongdoer deprives the plaintiff of the opportunity of recovering damages from the second wrongdoer. See P. Rosenthal, "The Effect of Subsequent Pre-assessment Wrongs on Damages for Personal Injury," 41 U.T. L.J. (1991).

457 These cases are discussed more fully below at 13.550 - 13.610.

458 [1897] A.C. 596 (H.L.).

459 *The "Mediana"* [1900] A.C. 113 (H.L.); *The "Marpessa"* [1907] A.C. 241 (H.L.); *Admiralty Com'rs v. S.S. Susquehanna*, [1926] A.C. 655 (H.L.); *The "West Wales"* (1932), 43 Lloyd's L.R. 504; *The "Luimneach"* (1936), 54 Lloyd's L.R. 5 (C.A.); *Basted v. Grafton*, [1948] 1 W.W.R. 614 (B.C. Co. Ct.); *Nason v. Aubin* (1958), 16 D.L.R. (2d) 309 (N.B.S.C. App. Div.); *Matthews v. Heintzman & Co.* (1914), 16 D.L.R. 522 (Sask. S.C.) (cost of renting piano allowed, even though not incurred).

detention of ships while under repair "although no gain which could be measured in money accrues . . . by the use of their ships or is lost by reason of their being put out of action".[460]

1.2040 Most of the cases have concerned ships owned by public or quasi-public bodies, but the same principle has been applied in an American case, *The "Vanadis"*,[461] to a privately owned pleasure yacht; in *Nason v. Aubin*[462] to a private automobile; and in *Acadian Lines Ltd. v. Hannah*[463] to a bus. It does not seem that the principle can logically be confined to ships or to public ownership; in *Admiralty Com'rs v. S.S. Susquehanna*,[464] Lord Dunedin specifically stated that admiralty law was the same in this respect as the common law. It has been held, however, that the principle does not apply to profit-making chattels,[465] and in *Gartland Steamship Co. v. The Queen*[466] the Supreme Court of Canada refused to apply it to damage to a bridge.

1.2050 The wide variety of arguments put forward in support of the award of damages in such cases indicates some uncertainty about the basis of recovery reflected, not surprisingly, in uncertainty about the appropriate method of calculation of damages.

1.2060 First, it is said that the defendant should not gain by the chance that the damaged ship is not being used for profit or by the fact that the plaintiff has been sufficiently far-sighted to maintain a stand-by ship.[467] If an award were refused, it is said, public authorities would be the losers, to the gain of wrongdoers. These arguments, however, do not seem fully to meet the point that if the plaintiff has not in fact suffered any loss, no principle of compensation can compel the defendant to pay damages. Wrongdoers profit every day by the chance that their wrong causes no harm and from the precautions taken by their victims.

1.2070 Secondly, an analogy has been drawn with conversion. Lord Halsbury said in *The "Mediana"*:[468] "Supposing a person took away a chair out of my room and kept it for twelve months, could anybody say you had a right to diminish the damages by shewing that I did not usually sit in that chair".[469] It may be objected, however, that this analogy is not fully

---

460 *Admiralty Com'rs v. S.S. Chekiang*, [1926] A.C. 637 (H.L.), at p. 650.

461 250 F. 1010 (1918, N.Y. Dist. Ct.).

462 *Supra*, footnote 459. But damages were said to be "nominal" or "very small". See also *Basted v. Grafton, supra*, footnote 459.

463 [1965-69] 4 N.S.R. 159 (S.C. App. Div.), followed in *New Brunswick Telephone Co. Ltd. v. Wright* (1982), 140 D.L.R. (3d) 188 (N.B.Q.B.). See also *Birmingham v. Sowsbery*, [1970] R.T.R. 84; *Toronto Transit Commission v. Orfanios* (1983), 27 C.C.L.T. 132 (Ont. H.C.J.).

464 *Supra*, footnote 459, at p. 661.

465 *B. Sunley & Co., Ltd. v. Cunard White Star Ltd.*, [1940] 1 K.B. 740 (C.A.), though wasted expenses may be allowed. See 1.1970, *supra*, and 1.2260, *infra*.

466 [1960] S.C.R. 315, 22 D.L.R. (2d) 385.

467 As in *The "Mediana"* [1900] A.C. 113 (H.L.).

468 *Supra*.

469 *Supra*, at p. 117.

persuasive in a case of negligent damage since the result in a conversion case might be explained on the principle of depriving the wrongdoer of a presumed gain or of depriving the plaintiff of an opportunity to charge the wrongdoer a fee.[470]

1.2080 A third argument is that maintenance of a ship is costly, and the plaintiff ought to be entitled to recover at least the cost of maintenance of the damaged ship (or of a stand-by if a stand-by is used) during the period of repairs. Lord Herschell in *The "Greta Holme"*[471] drew the analogy with a case where the plaintiff obtained the damaged ship on a long-term hire arrangement. In that case, he thought, the plaintiff would plainly have been entitled to the higher costs that could be said to have been wasted during the period of the repairs. He continued: "How can they the less be entitled to damages because, instead of hiring a dredger, they invested their money in its purchase? The money so invested was out of their pockets, and they were deprived of the use of the dredger, to obtain which they had sacrificed the interest on the money spent on its purchase. A sum equivalent to this, at least, they must surely be entitled to."[472] Lord Loreburn expanded the point in *The "Marpessa"*:[473]

> . . . the plaintiffs were entitled to put their case in another way. They might say: The cost to us of maintaining and working this dredger, while it is working, amounts to so much per day, and its depreciation daily amounts to so much more. We take the total daily sum which it costs us as a fair measure of the value of its daily services to us. Those services are at least worth what we are habitually paying for them year after year, including what we sacrifice in depreciation.[474]

1.2090 A fourth theory of recovery is that the plaintiff should be entitled to the potential rental value of the ship during the period of time for which she was laid up. This theory is supported by McCormick[475] and by Learned Hand J. in *The "Vanadis"*,[476] but was expressly rejected by the House of Lords in *Admiralty Com'rs v. S.S. Susquehanna*.[477] The objection seems to be that the award of full commercial rates of hire may over-compensate the plaintiff in a case where no market exists for hire of the kind of ship damaged for the period of time in question. It might be said that this objection appears to go to the difficulty of calculating the lost rental value, rather than to the theoretical basis of the argument. The argument supports the view that the plaintiff suffers a real loss, *i.e.*, the loss of the right to rent the ship. The objection that the

---

470 See 9.70, 9.130, *infra*.

471 [1897] A.C. 596 (H.L.).

472 *Supra*, at p. 605.

473 [1907] A.C. 241 (H.L.).

474 *Supra*, at pp. 244-5.

475 McCormick, *Handbook on the Law of Damages* (St. Paul, Minn., West Publishing Co., 1935), pp. 472-7.

476 250 F. 1010 (1918, N.Y. Dist. Ct.).

477 [1926] A.C. 655 (H.L.).

plaintiff would probably not have done so is answered by McCormick who says: "The owner is entitled to compensation for the most advantageous use of his property which was open to him, regardless of whether he intended so to use it or whether he intended to waste it or give it away."[478] In cases of total destruction or conversion, it is well established that the plaintiff is entitled to recover the full value of the chattel

[*The next page is* 1–101]

478 *Op. cit.*, footnote 475, at p. 477.

destroyed or converted, even if the plaintiff had no intention of putting the property to any productive use or had intended to give it away.[478a] An analogy may be drawn here with the case of personal injury. It has been argued elsewhere that an injured person should be entitled to compensation for loss of earning capacity even though there was no intention to work for monetary remuneration. However, as shown above, assessment of damages for loss of use of property has usually required proof that the plaintiff is actually worse off as a result of the wrong. A more satisfactory defence of allowing the rental value, might be, therefore, that the foregone rents represent the cost to the plaintiff of ownership, and, therefore, a measure of the value to the plaintiff of the lost use.

1.2100 As to calculation of damages in the case where there is no market for short term rentals, it may be conceded that care should be taken not to over-compensate the plaintiff, and the method of calculation described below (interest on the capital value plus depreciation and fixed maintenance costs) may be acceptable as the closest practicable approximation to the rental value of the damaged chattel.

1.2110 A fifth argument is closely related to that just discussed but expresses the plaintiff's loss in terms of a capital loss. In *The "Luimneach"*[479] Scott L.J. said:

> . . . if the ship had been a total loss there would have been no question but that the capital value of the vessel at the time of the loss would have been the measure of compensation. So if a vessel is lost for a period of time, but not totally lost, you must get such a figure for that period of time as is comparable to the capital value of the vessel at that time.[480]

This argument, like the argument of lost rental value, supports the conclusion that the plaintiff does suffer a real loss. If the plaintiff owns a depreciating chattel with a useful life of two years, a present value of $200, and an expected value in a year's time of $100, it is plain that if the defendant destroys the chattel the plaintiff is entitled to an award of $200. If the defendant wrongfully puts the chattel out of use for a year, it can be argued that the plaintiff equally suffers an immediate capital loss, because a rational purchaser would pay (assuming interest rates of ten per cent per annum) only $90.90 the moment after the occurrence of the damage, instead of the $200 former value.

1.2120 This line of argument offers theoretical support for an award of damages and might justify the method approved by the House of Lords in several cases of allowing interest on the actual capital value of the ship the moment before the collision plus depreciation during the period of detention and the fixed costs of maintenance.[481] This is the calculation that a rational purchaser would make in calculating the present value of a future (depreciated) value of

478a *Cancer Control Agency of British Columbia v. Fisher Scientific* (1989), 14 A.C.W.S. (3d) 282, [1989] B.C.J. No. 213 (Q.L.) (S.C.), citing this passage.

479 (1936), 54 Ll. L.R. 5 (C.A.).

480 *Supra*, at pp. 11-12.

goods out of service for a period of time. However, it is again inconsistent with the usual approach of the courts for damages for loss of use of property.

1.2130 If the basis used is loss of opportunity to rent, care must be taken not to over-compensate, and as McCormick points out "if the plaintiff is not in the rental business, deduction from the rentals customarily charged should be made for the fact that such charges include overhead expense, and, in any event, a similar deduction must be made because rentals include depreciation and wear and tear."[482] If these costs, including the value of the plaintiff's time that would have to be expended in arranging a rental for the exact period in question, are fully taken into account, it seems probable that the damages would in many cases approximate those calculated on the "interest on capital" method described above. In the absence of proof of factors necessary to calculate the lost rental value, therefore, the "interest on capital" method seems acceptable as the best available measure of the value of the loss of use.

1.2140 It must be conceded that these explanations of the cases are somewhat hypothetical and are not easy to reconcile with the general approach of the courts to claims for loss of use of property, where recovery is not allowed on the basis of a diminution of capital value unless the plaintiff can show that she is in fact worse off as a result of the wrong.[483] The cases on non-profit-making chattels are ultimately to be justified, it is suggested, on the basis of convenience of assessment. The owner of property who is using it to perform a public duty, or for her pleasure, or to confer a benefit on a friend or relative, does suffer a loss if the property is put out of use. The interest on the capital value of the property is a minimum measure of what the owner forgoes by not selling it and investing the money, and this (with the addition of depreciation and maintenance costs) represents a measure of the cost to the plaintiff of owning the property and therefore one acceptable measure, in the absence of better evidence, of the value of its use.

6. Loss of Profit on Sales

1.2150 Very commonly the particular profitable use which the plaintiff has in mind for the property is to sell it. A delay in delivery or a wrongful detention of the property may cause the plaintiff to lose a profitable sale either because the market generally declines or because a profitable individual contract is lost.

1.2160 Where the plaintiff has been permanently deprived of property by the defendant's wrong, the question arises whether compensation is available for loss of a sale to a third party. The principal cases have been discussed above.[484]

1.2170 Temporary deprivation, such as late delivery by a seller or by a bailee or

481 *The "Marpessa"* [1907] A.C. 241 (H.L.); *Admiralty Com'rs v. S.S. Chekiang*, [1926] A.C. 637 (H.L.); *Admiralty Com'rs v. S.S. Susquehanna*, [1926] A.C. 655 (H.L.).

482 *Op. cit.*, footnote 475, at p. 473.

483 See 1.1950 - 1.1970, *supra*.

484 See 1.1240 - 1.1350, *supra*.

temporary misappropriation, may also have the effect of depriving the plaintiff of the opportunity to sell the goods or a finished product of which the goods are to form a part. As in the cases of deprivation of property, it is clear that the plaintiff can, in principle, recover such losses subject to the rules of remoteness. In *Die Elbinger A.G. fur Fabrication von Eisenbahn Materiel v. Armstrong*,[485] the defendants delayed in the delivery of axles required by the plaintiff for the manufacture of wagons. In consequence of the defendants' default, the plaintiff was put in breach of a contract to sell the completed wagons and had to pay penalties to its buyer. It was held that a verdict for the plaintiff could be supported on the ground that the plaintiff was entitled to recover reasonable compensation for the loss of use of the property and that the principle was the same whether it was the plaintiff's own use that was interfered with or whether it was a sale to a third party that was lost. Blackburn J. put it thus:

> . . . it is equally obvious that both parties contemplated that the wheels and axles were to be put into immediate use. Under such circumstances, the natural and almost inevitable consequence of a delay in delivering a set of wheels would be that the plaintiffs, if they meant the waggon for their own use, or their customers, if the waggon was bespoke, would be deprived of the use of the waggon for a period equal to that for which the set of wheels was delayed.
>
> At all events the plaintiffs were entitled to recover at a rate per day equal to whatever the jury should find to be reasonable compensation for the loss of the use of the waggons.[486]

The case itself concerned liability for the penalties, but the reasoning indicates that loss of an opportunity to sell goods to a third party can be regarded as a loss of use of the goods.

7. Liability to Third Parties

1.2180 Frequently the deprivation of the use of goods involves the plaintiff in liability to third parties such as sub-buyers, buyers of chattels into which the goods are to be incorporated, or persons to whom the plaintiff has promised to render services for which the goods in question are needed. As the *Elbinger* case discussed above[487] indicates, liability of this sort may be regarded simply as a species of damages for loss of use of goods. In *Grébert-Borgnis v. J. & W. Nugent*,[488] recovery was allowed in respect of damages paid by the plaintiff to a foreign sub-buyer, and in *Johnstone Fabrications Ltd. v. Canadian Credit Men's Trust Ass'n Ltd.*,[489] a defendant who sold a

485 (1874), L.R. 9 Q.B. 473. See also *Nigerian National Shipping Lines Ltd. v. Mutual Ltd.*, [1998] 2 Lloyd's Rep. 664 (Q.B.), where the court awarded damages, *inter alia*, for loss of sale.

486 *Supra*, at p. 477.

487 See footnote 485, *supra*.

488 (1885), 15 Q.B.D. 85 (C.A.).

489 (1964), 47 W.W.R. 513 (B.C.S.C.). See also *Household Machines v. Cosmos Exporters*, [1947] 1 K.B. 217; *Gaklis v. Wells* (1979), 37 N.S.R. (2d) 451 (S.C. App. Div.).

crane without authority was held liable for a forfeiture payable by the plaintiff to a sublessee, though not for lost profits.

8. Expenses

1.2190 Expenses caused to the plaintiff by being deprived of the use of property are of many different types. In theory they are recoverable, subject to the rules of remoteness and mitigation. Often such expenses represent the cost of mitigating a larger loss that would otherwise be caused by the absence of the property.[490] An illustration is supplied by the Ontario case of *Thiele & Wesmar Ltd. v. Rod Service (Ottawa) Ltd.*,[491] discussed above in the context of value.[492] The defendant was responsible for the loss of accounting records, and the plaintiff recovered the cost of paying accountants to replace the records. As suggested in the earlier discussion, this case could be explained as allowing recovery of the full value to the plaintiff of the records or as compensation for the loss of use. The expense of replacing the records can be explained as a cost of mitigating what presumably would have been the larger loss of doing without the records altogether. If compensation reflecting the cost of replacement is given on the basis of awarding the full value of the property to the plaintiff, the cost of replacement cannot be awarded a second time as an expense.

1.2200 In the case of a wrongful filing of a caveat against land, damages have been held to include the cost of carrying the land while it is wrongfully tied up and the cost of removing the cloud on the title.[493]

1.2210 Frequently it is not possible for the plaintiff to procure an exact substitute for the property lost. In that case a valuation based on inferior property ought to include an allowance for the lesser value of the latter as compared with what the plaintiff ought to have had. Where valuation is based on superior property difficulties have arisen. In several cases where buyers have, on non-delivery of goods, purchased superior goods at a higher price, it has been held that in the absence of close equivalents they are entitled to damages based on the price paid for the superior substitutes.[494] Support for these cases is to be found in the consideration that it is not for the wrongdoer to complain of the cost of making good the loss caused and that the plaintiff may be mitigating a larger loss by prompt procurement of the substitute for use or for resale, as the case may be. On the other hand, a rule cannot be defended that leaves the plaintiff in a better position on receipt of damages than would have been

490 Cost of renting substitute so explained by Grant J. in *Air Equipment v. Cape Construction* (1979), 37 N.S.R. (2d) 217 (S.C.T.D.), revd 42 N.S.R. (2d) 564 (S.C. App. Div.).

491 (1962), 45 D.L.R. (2d) 503, [1964] 2 O.R. 347 (C.A.).

492 See 1.310, *supra*.

493 *Lundy v. Powell* (1921), 60 D.L.R. 607 (Sask. K.B.).

494 *Hinde v. Liddell* (1875), L.R. 10 Q.B. 265; *Blackburn Bobbin Co., Ltd. v. T.W. Allen & Sons, Ltd.*, [1918] 1 K.B. 540, affd [1918] 2 K.B. 467 (C.A.). See also *Petersen v. Fehr* (1988), 53 Man. R. (2d) 210 (Q.B.); *McCain Foods Ltd. v. Grand Falls Industries Ltd.* (1991), 80 D.L.R. (4th) 252, 116 N.B.R. (2d) 22 (C.A.), leave to appeal to S.C.C. refused 85 D.L.R. (4th) viii, 121 N.B.R. (2d) 180.

occupied if the wrong had not been done, and it is submitted elsewhere that where the plaintiff effects a net improvement in position by procuring the substitute (for example, where an old roof damaged by the defendant is replaced with a new roof), the value of the improvement should be brought into account.[495] Where, however, the plaintiff requires the property for immediate use or resale to a third party, it will usually be reasonable to purchase a substitute property, even if superior, in order to avoid a larger loss. In such a case the plaintiff is not left with a net benefit at the end of the day, for the plaintiff will (it is assumed) have put the superior property to the same use planned for the inferior and will have received only the same net return. In such a case, damages based on the cost of the substitute are, it is submitted, rightly allowed. The distinction was made by Field J. in *Hinde v. Liddell*: "If [the plaintiff] had derived any benefit from the advance in price, I should hesitate before I said he could recover the whole of the difference; but he derived no benefit whatever beyond being able to complete his contract with his vendee on the original terms upon which he had contracted."[496] In *Preload Co. of Canada Ltd. v. City of Regina*,[497] the Saskatchewan Court of Appeal held that any pecuniary advantage to the plaintiff in such a case must be brought into account.

1.2220 Where the defendant's wrong makes essential an expense that would otherwise have been optional, a somewhat similar analysis is applicable. In *The "Inflexible"*,[498] the defendant's damage to the plaintiff's ship made employment of a tug essential. There was evidence that prudent owners of undamaged ships often used tugs and the plaintiff might have used one in any event. Dr. Lushington held that the plaintiff was entitled to compensation, saying that a probable but discretionary expense cannot be deducted from a charge made indispensable by the collision. Against this it may be said that, if the plaintiff would certainly have employed a tug in any event, the defendant's wrong cannot be said to have caused that expense, and the plaintiff would be over-compensated if the defendant were compelled to pay it. Where the expense would very probably (but not certainly) have been incurred in the absence of the wrong it seems again, on the usual rules of proof, that the defendant will have shown on the balance of probabilities that the wrong has not caused the expense. It is submitted, therefore, that the plaintiff should only be entitled to recover expenses caused by the wrong, but that in cases of this sort it is not unjust to place upon the defendant the onus of proving that the expense would have been incurred in any event.[499]

1.2230 Where the wrongdoer prevents the plaintiff from purchasing a substitute, as by giving continual assurances of delivery, the wrongdoer may be liable

495 See 1.2730 - 1.2800, *infra*.
496 *Supra*, footnote 494, at p. 270.
497 (1958), 13 D.L.R. (2d) 305 (Sask. C.A.), affd [1959] S.C.R. 801, 20 D.L.R. (2d) 586.
498 (1857), Swab. 200, 166 E.R. 1094.
499 See 13.170 -13.250, *infra*, for a discussion of presumptions operating in the plaintiff's favour.

for expenses that in other circumstances would be held irrecoverable. Thus, in *Smeed v. Foord*[500] where the defendant, having defaulted in delivering a threshing machine "led the plaintiff on with assurances of delivery", the defendant was held liable for the expense of storing the unthreshed grain and drying some of it that had been damaged by rain, and for damage to the grain itself.

1.2240 In cases of temporary deprivation, such as delay in delivery by a seller or bailee, the plaintiff is entitled, subject again to considerations of remoteness and mitigation, to the cost of hiring substitute property. In land sale cases a purchaser has been held entitled to the cost of renting accommodation pending a successful action of specific performance.[501] Moving expenses have been recovered in cases of wrongful eviction and destruction of a house.[502] In the case of goods, the cost of hiring a substitute has been allowed.[503] This kind of loss can occur in cases of permanent as well as of temporary deprivation as is illustrated by *Moore v. DER Ltd.*[504] where the defendant wrongfully destroyed the plaintiff's car. The plaintiff was held entitled to recover the cost of hiring a car of the same (expensive) make for the period of eighteen weeks it took him to obtain a replacement of a new car. It was held that he was not bound to mitigate the loss by buying or hiring a cheaper car as he had defensible business reasons for owning an expensive and reliable car. In *Athabaska Airway Ltd. v. Saskatchewan Government Airways*,[505] the cost of maintenance that the plaintiff saved from hiring a substitute aircraft was deducted from his claim for the cost of hire.

1.2250 Where the deprivation of property causes the plaintiff to be liable to a third party, the defendant, as indicated above, is liable for the plaintiff's loss, including the cost of defending the action if the defence is reasonable in the circumstances.[506] The cost of defence, if reasonable, can be regarded as a means of mitigating the larger loss that would presumably have been incurred if the action had been allowed to go undefended.

---

500 (1859), 28 L.J.Q.B. 178, followed by a divided court in *Walker v. Sharpe* (1921), 56 D.L.R. 668 (Sask. C.A.), leave to appeal to S.C.C. refused 58 D.L.R. 384.

501 *Holmes v. Alexson* (1974), 54 D.L.R. (3d) 175, 7 O.R. (2d) 11 (H.C.J.), affd 69 D.L.R. (3d) 223, 12 O.R. (2d) 431 (C.A.); *Raineri v. Miles*, [1979] 3 All E.R. 763 (C.A.); *Hawryluk v. Korsakoff* (1956), 6 D.L.R. (2d) 524 (Man. C.A.). See also *Calabar Properties Ltd. v. Stitcher*, [1984] 1 W.L.R. 287 (C.A.) (premises rendered uninhabitable by landlord's breach of repair covenant); *Patel v. Hooper & Jackson*, [1999] 1 W.L.R. 1792 (C.A.) (damages for alternative accommodation against negligent surveyor).

502 *Wood v. Williams* (1980), 40 N.S.R. (2d) 63 (S.C.T.D.); *Murphy v. Atlantic Speedy Propane Ltd.* (1979), 103 D.L.R. (3d) 545 (S.C.T.D.) (loss of wages during move).

503 *The "Yorkshireman"* (1827), 2 Hagg. 30*n*, 166 E.R. 155 (Adm.). See *Dimond v. Lovell*, [2002] 1 A.C. 384 (H.L.); *Lagden v. O'Connor*, [2004] 1 All E.R. 277 (H.L.).

504 [1971] 1 W.L.R. 1476 (C.A.), followed in *Penman v. Saint John Toyota Ltd.* (1972), 30 D.L.R. (3d) 88 (S.C. App. Div.); *Leblanc v. Malcolm* (1975), 10 N.B.R. (2d) 610 (S.C.); *A. R. Menzies & Sons Ltd. v. Bartlett* (1979), 29 N.B.R. (2d) 14 (Q.B.T.D.). See also *Shulhan v. Peterson, Howell & Heather (Canada) Ltd.* (1966), 57 D.L.R. (2d) 491 (Sask. Q.B.); *Reid v. Yhard* (1975), 12 N.S.R. (2d) 506 (Co. Ct.). In *Watson Norie Ltd. v. Shaw* (1967), 111 Sol. Jo. 117 (C.A.), the cost of what was found to be an excessively expensive replacement was disallowed.

505 (1958), 14 D.L.R. (2d) 66 (Sask. C.A.).

1.2260 Expenses rendered futile by the defendant's wrong are also in principle recoverable but, as in other areas of damage law involving wasted expenses, care is needed to avoid double compensation.[507] Where the plaintiff recovers the full value of property with interest from the date of the wrong, the plaintiff is put in the same position as though the property had been replaced instantly. If the plaintiff does actually replace the property immediately with an adequate substitute, it is obvious that the expenses incurred in anticipation of the use of the original property are not "wasted". If the use of the property turns out to be unprofitable, that is because of the plaintiff's bad luck or bad management not because of the defendant's wrong. The same analysis applies if the plaintiff, though able to replace, chooses not to do so. The plaintiff is fully compensated by an award of value and interest. Choosing not to replace the property may be a wise choice or an unwise one, but in either event the defendant is not liable for expense incurred in anticipation of the use of the property.

1.2270 Where the plaintiff cannot replace the property, either because no substitute exists or because the deprivation is only temporary, more difficulty arises. If the plaintiff is allowed the cost of hiring a substitute as in *Moore v. DER*, expenses incurred in anticipation of the use of the property cannot be allowed for the same reason as given above. Having been allowed the value of the substitute the plaintiff is put in as good a position vis–vis the expense as though the wrong had not been done.

1.2280 Where no substitute is acquired the plaintiff has a stronger case, but here again care is necessary to avoid double counting. If the plaintiff recovers full compensation for loss of the use of the property (that is, a sum that puts the plaintiff in all respects in as good a position as actually having the property for use), the plaintiff cannot in addition recover the expenses incurred in anticipation of that use for they would have been incurred in any event in order to obtain the benefits of using the property, and the plaintiff has been given a money sum that is the equivalent of those benefits. Often, however, the plaintiff does not claim or cannot prove the full value of the benefit of using the property, and in those cases it is reasonable for the plaintiff to claim instead the cost incurred in anticipation of use, just as in contract claims generally it is permissible for the plaintiff to claim on the basis of reliance rather than expectation.[508] However, in the contract cases it has been held, rightly it is submitted, that if the defendant positively proves that the plaintiff would not, had the contract been performed, have recovered the expenses, the

506 *Agius v. Great Western Colliery Co.*, [1899] 1 Q.B. 413 (C.A.); *Crispin & Co. v. Evans* (1922), 68 D.L.R. 623 (B.C.S.C.), affd [1923] 3 D.L.R. 1190. In *Portman v. Middleton* (1858), 4 C.B. (N.S.) 322, 140 E.R. 1108, compensation paid to a third party was disallowed; it appeared from counsel's argument that the plaintiff could have avoided the loss by procuring a substitute.

507 See 1.2660 -1.2710, *infra*.

508 See 5.150 - 5.250, *infra*. In *Tower Equipment Rental Ltd. v. Joint Venture Equipment Sales* (1975), 60 D.L.R. (3d) 621, 9 O.R. (2d) 453 (H.C.J.), a buyer recovered the cost of storing defective goods justifiably rejected.

defendant is not liable for the irrecoverable portion of the expenses, for this would have been lost even if the wrong had not been done. So also, it is submitted, where the plaintiff is deprived of the use of property, whether tortiously or by breach of contract, the expenses ought not to be recovered unless, in the absence of the wrong, they would have been recouped by some sort of profitable use, for the expenses cannot be said to have been "wasted" by the defendant's wrong unless they would have recouped in the absence of the wrong.

1.2290 Where the plaintiff intended to use the property for a non-profit-making purpose (for example, to fulfil a public duty, for pleasure, or to confer a benefit on a friend or relative), it has been submitted earlier that the plaintiff ought to be able to recover for loss of use.[509] The measure adopted by the House of Lords allows recovery of interest on capital value together with expenses. This amounts to a rough measure of the costs of ownership to the plaintiff and is defensible as a measure of the normal assumed value to the plaintiff of the use of the property. In the context of chattels intended to be profit-making, the general principle, as has been shown, is that the plaintiff must prove the loss claimed to have been suffered by deprivation of its use.[510] In the absence of evidence to the contrary it may be assumed in the plaintiff's favour that she ordinarily recoups the cost of owning property, but it should be open to the defendant, it is submitted, to prove if possible that the plaintiff would not have recouped the expenses and in that case the defendant's wrong cannot be said to have caused the loss of that part of the expenses that would not have been recouped in the absence of the wrong. The other view allows the plaintiff to be put in a better position than she would have been if her rights had been observed.

1.2300 A number of cases have allowed recovery of expenses rendered futile by the defendant's wrong, such as the cost of paying a ship's crew while the ship was being repaired.[511] Many of these can be defended on the principle proposed above, being cases of non-profit-making use or cases where it could be assumed that the plaintiff would have recouped the expenses. In *Edmund Handcock (1929) Ltd. v. The "Ernesto" (Owners)*,[512] however, expenses of maintaining a damaged tug were allowed despite evidence that no work would have been available for the tug in the period of inactivity. It is submitted that the plaintiff was over-compensated as a result. It is not sufficient for the plaintiff to prove that it was reasonable to incur the expenses. The point is that in the absence of the defendant's wrong the plaintiff would still have incurred the expenses and would not have recouped

509 See 1.2030 - 1.2140, *supra*.

510 See 1.1950 - 1.1970, *supra*, and *B. Sunley & Co. Ltd. v. Cunard White Star Ltd.*, [1940] 1 K.B. 740 (C.A.).

511 *The "Inflexible"* (1857), Swab. 200 at p. 204, 166 E.R. 1094. See *Birmingham Corp. v. Sowsbery* (1969), 113 Sol. Jo. 877 (Q.B.D.); *The "City of Peking"* (1890), 15 App. Cas. 438 (P.C.), at p. 449; *B. Sunley & Co. v. Cunard White Star Ltd.*, *supra*.

512 [1952] 1 Lloyd's Rep. 467 (C.A.).

them during the period of inactivity caused by the wrong. The expenses might have been recouped in the long run by later use — indeed, if the plaintiff's business was profitable it must be so — but the later use has not been impeded by the defendant, and whatever ultimate rewards the plaintiff was expecting from later use will still be there to take.

IV. DEFECTS IN PROPERTY

1. Cost of Restoration, or Diminution in Value

1.2310 Compensation for deficiencies in property falls to be made in a wide variety of circumstances. The substantive legal categories are vastly different but the problems of assessment of compensation have a common theme. The cases now for consideration are those in which the complaint is that, but for the defendant's wrong, the plaintiff would have been in possession of property superior to that which the plaintiff in fact has. This is the substance of the buyer's complaint in case of breach by the seller of warranty of quality, the lessor's complaint when a lessee fails to repair or restore property, the complaint of the landowner whose land is not improved or accommodated as agreed, and the complaint of the owner whose property is negligently damaged.[513] A question commonly arising in all these kinds of cases is whether the plaintiff's loss should be measured by the cost of restoring the property or by the diminution of its capital value.

1.2320 Where the cost of restoration is equal to or less than the diminution of capital value the cost is always recoverable,[514] even if the plaintiff does not actually incur the cost.[515] This has been often described as a way of measuring the capital diminution,[516] and indeed it is arguable that wherever the cost of restoration appears to be less than the diminution of capital value,

---

513 The normal measure was said in *J. Clark & Son Ltd. v. Finnamore* (1973), 6 N.B.R. (2d) 837 (S.C. App. Div.), to be the diminution in value. An analogous problem can also occur in cases of non-delivery of goods: see *The "Alecos M"*, [1991] 1 Lloyd's Rep. 120 (C.A.).

514 *McGarry v. Richards, Akroyd & Gall Ltd.*, [1954] 2 D.L.R. 367 (B.C.S.C.), at p. 389, *per* Darcy J.

515 *The "London Corporation"* [1935] P. 70 (C.A.); *Fitzner v. MacNeil* (1966), 58 D.L.R. (2d) 651 (N.S.C.A.); *Dawson v. Sawatzky*, [1946] 1 D.L.R. 476 (Sask. C.A.); *The King v. Hochelaga Shipping Co.*, [1940] S.C.R. 153, [1940] 1 D.L.R. 369 (ship damaged by defendant subsequently sunk).

516 *The "London Corporation"*, *supra*, footnote 515 ("*prima facie*, the value of a damaged vessel is less by the cost of repairs than the value it would have if undamaged", *per* Greer L.J., at p. 77); *DeGaust v. Lacey* (1979), 34 N.S.R. (2d) 522 (S.C.T.D.); *Robertson v. Wright* (1958), 16 D.L.R. (2d) 364 (Sask. C.A.); *Jordan v. Pelletier* (1970), 72 W.W.R. 641 (Alta. Dist. Ct.) (cost of repair recoverable even though property surrendered to finance company); *Regnier v. Nelson* (1956), 19 W.W.R. 36 (Man. Q.B.); *Lloy v. Town of Dartmouth* (1897), 30 N.S.R. 208 (S.C.), at p. 211, *per* Meagher J.; *Horne v. New Glasgow*, [1954] 1 D.L.R. 832 (N.S.S.C.). In *GUS Property Management Ltd. v. Littlewoods Mail Order Stores Ltd.* (1982), The Times, June 21, 1982, the House of Lords held that, where the damaged property had been transferred to a third party before being repaired, damages (measured by the cost of repair if appropriate) were recoverable by the original owner. See also 1.2520 - 1.2540, *infra*.

the two are, on analysis, properly considered to be equal, for a rational purchaser, knowing that perfect restoration can be achieved for a certain sum, will deduct just that sum and no more from the price she would have been willing to pay for the undamaged property.[517] The cost of replacement will not be allowed if the owner could have repaired at a lesser cost.[518] Where the property, after undergoing repair, would still be of less value than it was originally, the owner will be entitled to the cost of repair and to an additional sum to compensate for the residual deficiency.[518a] In *Moss v. Christchurch Rural District Council*,[519] Salter J. gave this example: "Suppose irreparable damage has been done to some historic building. No one would suggest that the mere cost of putting new bricks in place of the old would be full measure of damage or would fairly represent the actual loss. The true measure of damage is the difference between the money value of [the plaintiff's] interest before the fire and the money value of her interest after the fire."[520] In *Payton v. Brooks*[521] this principle was approved by the English Court of Appeal in respect of damage to a

[*The next page is* 1-111]

[517] In *McGarry v. Richards, Akroyd & Gall Ltd.*, [1954] 2 D.L.R. 367 (B.C.S.C.), at p. 389, Davey J. put the point in terms of "the plaintiff's duty to take any reasonable steps to mitigate his damage by doing what is required". In *Illsley v. Baltzer* (1960), 22 D.L.R. (2d) 537 (N.S.S.C.), it was held that the trade-in allowance for a damaged car was not a reliable guide to its value.

[518] *Pacific Blasting Ltd. v. D. J. Byrne Construction Co. Ltd.*, [1977] 2 W.W.R. 505 (B.C.S.C.); *Khalon v. Done Fair Janitorial Services Inc.* (2007), 155 A.C.W.S. (3d) 1111 (Alta. C.A.), at para. 30, citing this passage (onus of proof on wrongdoer).

[518a] See *Tridan Developments Ltd. v. Shell Canada Products Ltd.* (2002), 57 O.R. (3d) 503 (C.A.) (cost of expensive reparation of contaminated land allowable in order to eliminate residual "stigma"); *Strachan v. Ship "Constant Craving" (The)* (2003), 227 F.T.R. 300 (F.C.T.D.).

[519] [1925] 2 K.B. 750.

[520] *Supra*, at p. 752.

[521] [1974] R.T.R. 169 (C.A.).

car. Though the plaintiff failed, on the facts, to prove any residual loss after repair, the court accepted that he would, on appropriate facts, be entitled to recover. Roskill L.J. said:

> There are many cases which arise, whether in the field of contract law or of tort, where the cost of repairs is a prima facie method of ascertaining the diminution in value. It is not, however, the only method of measuring the loss. In a case where the evidence justifies a finding that there has been, on top of the cost of repairs, some diminution in market value — or, to put the point another way, justifies the conclusion that the loss to the plaintiff has not been fully compensated by the receipt of the cost of complete and adequate repairs, because of a resultant diminution in market value — I can see no reason why the plaintiff should be deprived of recovery under that head of damage also.[522]

The same rule has been applied in Canadian cases.[523] Prospective damage likely to be caused by the wrong is reflected in a diminution of the current value.[524]

1.2330 Where the plaintiff personally carries out the repairs, the plaintiff is entitled to include a reasonable sum for overhead costs,[525] though not for profits.[526]

1.2340 The difficulties arise when the cost of restoration exceeds the diminution in capital value. This problem was much discussed in the case of a lessee's promise to repair. Often on the termination of the lease, the lessee being in breach of the covenant to repair, the lessor would not in fact carry out the repairs. The latter might, for example, be intending to demolish the premises and in fact demolish them the day the lease falls in. The question is whether it can be right in those circumstances for the lessor to recover the cost of repairs that will never be carried out. For

---

522 *Supra*, at p. 176.

523 *Chotem v. Porteous* (1920), 51 D.L.R. 507 (Sask. C.A.); *Walter v. Seibel*, [1927] 2 D.L.R. 1005 (Sask. C.A.); *Nesbitt v. Carney*, [1931] 1 D.L.R. 106 (Sask. C.A.); *Green v. White* (1975), 10 N.B.R. (2d) 299 (S.C.); *Burthwick v. Lucas*, [1940] 4 D.L.R. 288 (Sask. C.A.) (proof of depreciation required).

524 *Ridley Ice Ltd. v. City of Vancouver* (1969), 68 W.W.R. 764 (B.C.S.C.); *Rombough v. Crestbrook Timber Ltd.* (1966), 57 D.L.R. (2d) 49 (B.C.C.A.) (nuisance), and see the cases on damages in lieu of injunctions discussed in Sharpe, *Injunctions and Specific Performance*, looseleaf ed. (Toronto, Canada Law Book, 1999), 4.40.

525 *Associated Quarries & Construction Ltd. v. Township of Etobicoke*, [1953] O.W.N. 204 (H.C.J.); *Hydro-Electric Power Com'n of Ontario v. Mather*, [1954] O.W.N. 382 (C.A.); *Canadian Pacific Ry. Co. v. Canadian Freightways Ltd.* (1962), 39 W.W.R. 191 (B.C.C.A.) (principle accepted, but proof of actual overhead required); *Bell Telephone Co. of Canada v. Montreal Dual Mixed Concrete Ltd.* (1959), 23 D.L.R. (2d) 346 (Que. Q.B. Appeal Side); *C.P.R. Co. v. Fumagalli* (1962), 38 D.L.R. (2d) 110 (B.C.C.A.); *Acadian Lines Ltd. v. Hannah*, [1965-69] 4 N.S.R. 159 (S.C. App. Div.); *British Columbia Hydro and Power Authority v. Marathon Realty Co.* (1992), 89 D.L.R. (4th) 419, 1 C.L.R. (2d) 270 (B.C.C.A.); *Miller Dredging Ltd. v. The "Dorothy MacKenzie"* (1994), 119 D.L.R. (4th) 63, [1995] 1 W.W.R. 270 (B.C.C.A.); *Canadian National Railway Co. v. Norsk Pacific Steamship Co.*, [1994] 2 F.C. 318, 71 F.T.R. 47 (T.D.).

526 *Moore's Taxi (1961) Ltd. v. Shore* (1968), 73 W.W.R. 558 (Man. Co. Ct.). See *Drew v. MacNeil* (1985), 17 D.L.R. (4th) 488 (B.C.C.A.).

the lessor it was said that the lessee ought not to profit by a breach, that the obligation to repair was part of the price of the lease, and that simplicity requires a rule that the lessee is always liable. None of these points fully meets the argument that the lessor will be in a far better position upon receipt of the full cost of repair than would have been occupied if the covenant had been observed. Another argument that has more substance is that the lessor's intentions and arrangements with third parties must in principle be irrelevant to the lessee's liability which cannot vary according to whether or not the lessor makes a favourable contract to sell the property or chooses to demolish it. This argument may be accepted, however, without adopting a rule that the lessee is always liable for the cost of repairs. A proper position seems to be that the lessee should be liable for the amount by which the value of the premises falls short of the value they would have had if the covenant had been observed. If a rational owner would carry out the repairs, the diminution in value will be measured by their cost. In that case the lessee should be liable for that cost irrespective of what arrangements the lessor happens to make with others (there may be a lucky sale), and irrespective of the lessor's actual intentions (the lessor may very wastefully pull down a property that should have been repaired). But if no rational person would carry out the repairs, then the lessee's liability is limited to the diminution in capital value, if any, caused by the breach of covenant. This position was persuasively expressed by Wright J. in *Joyner v. Weeks*[527] but, unfortunately, he was reversed by the Court of Appeal which held that the lessee was always to be liable for the full cost, apparently on the ground that Wright J.'s formulation was too complex. However, a United Kingdom Act in effect restored the position favoured by Wright J.[528] *Joyner v. Weeks* was followed by the British Columbia Court of Appeal in *Buscombe v. Stark*[529] and by the Exchequer Court in *National Trust Company v. The King*.[530] However, in *Miles v. Marshall*,[531] Weatherston J. preferred the view of Wright J., saying: "I am unable to find that in this Province there has been an inveterate practice such as Lord

527 [1891] 2 Q.B. 31 (C.A.).

528 *Landlord and Tenant Act, 1927*, s. 18(1). See *Smiley v. Townshend*, [1950] 2 K.B. 311 (C.A.), at p. 323, *per* Denning L.J. ("the real question is: what is the injury to the reversion"); *Miles v. Marshall* (1975), 55 D.L.R. (3d) 644 at p. 673, 7 O.R. (2d) 544 (H.C.J.).

529 (1916), 30 D.L.R. 736 (B.C.C.A.), followed in *Church of Scientology of B.C. v. Ahmed* (1983), 146 D.L.R. (3d) 219, 44 B.C.L.R. 297 (S.C.). But in both cases damages were reduced to allow for the dilapidated condition of the premises before the tenant's occupancy.

530 [1949] 2 D.L.R. 472 (Ex. Ct.). See also *Royal Trust Co. v. The King*, [1924] Ex. C.R. 121, where it was held that the lessor's right to recover is not extinguished by a sale of the property; this is not inconsistent with the view of Wright J. in *Joyner v. Weeks*, *supra*, footnote 527. And see *Maori Trustee v. Rogross Farms Ltd.*, [1994] 3 N.Z.L.R. 410 (C.A.) (*Joyner v. Weeks* a *prima facie* rule).

531 (1975), 55 D.L.R. (3d) 664, 7 O.R. (2d) 544 (H.C.J.).

Esher [in *Joyner v. Weeks*] said existed in England, and I see no reason to depart from the general rule that damages are limited to the actual loss sustained by an injured party. . . . I propose, therefore, to assess damages at the diminution of the value of the property by reason of the non-repair."[532] It is submitted that, for the reasons given earlier, this is a sound view and should be followed in future Canadian cases.

1.2350 In the case of failure by a lessee to repair during a long lease, with damages to be assessed while the lease is still running, it was early settled that the cost of repair is the wrong measure where this exceeds the diminution in value of the reversion for "when the damages are awarded to the landlord, he is not bound to expend them in repairs, neither can he do so without the tenant's permission to enter on the premises."[533] In the case of a short lease or one nearing completion, the damages may well approximate the cost of repairs; in the case of a lease with many years to run, they are likely to fall far short of it.[534]

1.2360 Some well-known American cases have discussed the problem of damage measurement where the lessee fails to restore land. In *Groves Co. v. John Wunder Co.*,[535] the lessee of a gravel pit convenanted to grade the land at the end of a lease but failed to do so. The cost of grading was $60,000, but it was proved that the land after grading would only be worth $15,000. The Minnesota Supreme Court held, by a majority, that the plaintiff was entitled to the larger sum. It is hard to avoid the conclusion that the plaintiff was over-compensated. The interest in the land was purely commercial and the plaintiff certainly could not be expected, as a rational person, to expend the proceeds of the judgment on levelling the land. That the breach was wilful and that the defendant profited by the breach seem irrelevant to an assessment of damages on a compensatory theory. In an earlier American case, Cardozo J. had given the example of a house agreed to be built on foundations of stone to be quarried in Vermont. After construction it is discovered that the foundations are of stone of equal quality but quarried in New Hampshire. The measure of damages, he said, is not the cost of reconstruction.[536] A later case,[537] involving failure to restore a strip mining site, declined to follow *Groves v. John Wunder Co.*, and in *Tito v. Waddell (No. 2)*[538] Megarry V.-C. held that the proper measure of damages for failure to restore an island after phosphate mining was, in

532 *Supra*, at p. 673 D.L.R.

533 *Doe d. Trustees of Schools and Almshouses of City of Worcester v. Rowlands* (1841), 9 Car. & P. 734 at p. 739, 173 E.R. 1030, *per* Coleridge, J.

534 See *Conquest v. Ebbetts*, [1896] A.C. 490 (H.L.), at pp. 493-4, *per* Lord Herschell.

535 205 Minn. 163, 286 N.W. 235 (1939).

536 *Jacob & Youngs Inc. v. Kent*, 230 N.Y. 239, 129 N.E. 889 (1921). See *Bellgrove v. Eldridge* (1954), 90 C.L.R. 613.

537 *Peevyhouse v. Garland Coal & Mining Co.*, 382 P.2d 109 (Okla. S.C. 1962), *cert. denied* 375 U.S. 906 (1963).

538 [1977] Ch. 106 at p. 335.

the absence of evidence that the plaintiffs would actually restore it, the diminution in value, not the cost of restoration.

1.2370 In *Wigsell v. School for the Indigent Blind*,[539] a purchaser of land covenanted to build a wall to enclose the premises purchased. On breach of the covenant, the plaintiff was not awarded the cost of building. Field J., after pointing out that in a suitable case a decree of specific performance might be possible, added: "[The plaintiffs] will be under no obligation whatever to expend the amount recovered in erecting the wall, and most probably would never think for a moment of any such expenditure, which to us, at least, would seem a simple waste of money."[540] In *James v. Hutton*,[541] where a lessee had covenanted to reinstate a shop front but no diminution in value was caused by breach of the contract, the lessor was held entitled only to nominal damages, *Joyner v. Weeks*[542] being distinguished on the rather unconvincing ground that there some damage had occured, whereas in *James v. Hutton* no damage at all had been caused by breach of the covenant. In *James v. Hutton*, the court indicated that it was open to the plaintiff to prove an actual intention to reinstate the premises, and in *Radford v. De Froberville*,[543] damages were allowed for construction of a wall, even though uneconomic, on proof that the plaintiff was likely actually to effect the work.

1.2380 Several Canadian cases have discussed the proper measure of damages for failure to drill oil wells. Often the very reason for the failure to drill is that oil is unlikely to be found, and so the expenditure is, on the latest evidence, uneconomic. In *Cunningham v. Insinger*,[544] the Supreme Court of Canada allowed the cost of drilling, but only upon the assumption that the work would actually be done. Anglin J. said: "it is a fair inference not only that [the plaintiff] regards the work as essential but that it is work which he will have done".[545] He added:

> It is probably necessary to reach that conclusion in order to justify the departure made by the trial Judge from the ordinary rule that the measure of damages for breach by a defendant of a contract to perform work on the plaintiff's land is the actual pecuniary loss sustained by the plaintiff as a result of such breach, *i.e.*, the difference between what would have been the value of the premises had the work contracted for been done and their value with it unperformed.[546]

539 (1882), 8 Q.B.D. 357.
540 *Supra*, at p. 364.
541 [1950] 1 K.B. 9 (C.A.).
542 [1891] 2 Q.B. 31 (C.A.).
543 [1977] 1 W.L.R. 1262 (Ch.D.). Oliver J. said, at p. 1270, that the plaintiff must be "seeking compensation for a genuine loss and not merely using a technical breach to secure an uncovenanted profit". See also *Dean v. Ainley*, [1987] 1 W.L.R. 1729 (C.A.).
544 [1924] S.C.R. 8, [1924] 2 D.L.R. 433.
545 *Supra*, at p. 16 S.C.R., p. 439 D.L.R.
546 *Supra*.

In *Carson v. Willitts*,[547] the Ontario Appellate Division held that the measure of damages was the diminution in value and not the cost of drilling. Masten J.A. said:

> In my opinion, what the plaintiff lost by the refusal of the defendant to bore two more wells was a sporting or gambling chance that valuable oil or gas would be found when the two further wells were bored. If the wells had been bored and no oil or gas of value had been found, the effect would be that the plaintiff had lost nothing by the refusal of the defendant to go on boring. On the other hand, if valuable oil or gas had been discovered, by the boring of these two wells, he had lost substantially. It may not be easy to compute what that chance was worth to the plaintiff, but the difficulty in estimating the quantum is no reason for refusing to award any damages.[548]

In *Cotter v. General Petroleums Ltd.*,[549] Kerwin J. (with whom Rinfret C.J.C. agreed) said: "The proper measure is not the cost of performance to the respondents but the value of performance to the appellant".[550] However, Cartwright J. (with whom Fauteux J. agreed) said: "the proper measure of his damages . . . is the difference between the value to [the plaintiff] of the consideration for which the respondents agreed to drill the well and the value to him of the consideration which, acting reasonably, he should find it necessary to give to have the well drilled by others."[551] This implies that the full cost of drilling might be allowed, though Cartwright J. concurred with Kerwin J. in the result, on the ground that there was no evidence of the terms on which a substitute contract for drilling could be arranged by the plaintiff.

1.2390 In *Sunshine Exploration Ltd. v. Dolly Varden Mines Ltd. (N.P.L.)*,[552] the Supreme Court of Canada allowed the full cost of drilling in a case where the prospects were good and the plaintiff had actually entered into an alternative contract to have the drilling done. *Wigsell v. School for the Indigent Blind* and *James v. Hutton* were distinguished on the ground that there the work was not likely to be performed by the plaintiff. The Supreme Court of Canada in the *Dolly Varden* case said that the consideration for the obligation to drill had been "received in full",[553] evidently considering the case to be equivalent to one in which the plaintiff had paid in advance

547 [1930] 4 D.L.R. 977, 65 O.L.R. 456 (S.C. App. Div.).

548 *Supra*, at p. 980 D.L.R., p. 458 O.L.R.

549 [1951] S.C.R. 154, [1950] 4 D.L.R. 609.

550 *Supra*, at p. 160 S.C.R., p. 615 D.L.R. This was followed in *Albrecht v. Imperial Oil Ltd.* (1957), 21 W.W.R. 560 (Alta. S.C.).

551 *Cotter v. General Petroleums, supra*, footnote 549, at p. 175 S.C.R., p. 629 D.L.R. These cases were held in *McGarry v. Richards, Akroyd & Gall Ltd.*, [1954] 2 D.L.R. 367 (B.C.S.C.), at p. 389, to "establish that the primary measure of damages for non-performance of a contract to build on another's land is the diminution in value resulting from such default". See also *Prudential Trust Co. Ltd. v. Wagner Oils Ltd.* (1954), 11 W.W.R. (N.S.) 371 (Alta. S.C.).

552 [1970] S.C.R. 2, 8 D.L.R. (3d) 441.

553 *Supra*, at pp. 15 and 21 S.C.R., pp. 450 and 455 D.L.R.

in cash for the work.[554] This finding is a little puzzling, because it appears from the facts reported that the consideration for the drilling was to have been a share in the potential output, and upon the driller's default it would seem that the owner recovered his unrestricted rights in the land. If so, the case would appear to be analogous to one where a cash price had *not* been paid in advance. In that case the damages would be, even if the basic measure were the cost of effecting the work, not the full cost of drilling, but the difference between the price and the cost of effecting substitute drilling. However, accepting the court's finding that the price had been paid, the case is, it is submitted, rightly decided, bearing in mind the other finding of the court that undertaking the drilling was, on the facts, an economic proposition. The fact that the court distinguished the *Wigsell* and *James* cases without disapproving them[555] suggests that, had the work not been economic, the cost of performing it would not have been awarded.

1.2400 In cases involving breach of building contracts, it has been held that the plaintiff is not entitled to the cost of restoration or reinstatement if the expenditure would be unreasonable or oppressive,[556] but in judging the reasonableness of the expenditure, the court will lean in favour of the plaintiff as the innocent party.[557]

1.2410 In *Attica Sea Carriers Corp. v. Ferrostaal Poseidon Bulk Reederei G.m.b.H.*,[558] the charterer of a ship by demise covenanted to repair the ship before returning her to the owner. The charterer sought to return the ship without doing so and it was proved that the cost of repair was $2,000,000 but the value of the ship after repairs would have been only $1,000,000. The case turned on whether the shipowner could ignore the charterer's attempt to return the ship and sue for the accruing hire. The Court of Appeal held that it could not do so, for this would compel the charterer to make an uneconomic expenditure. For the same reason the owner could not get specific performance. The court did not expressly state what the

554 *Supra*, at p. 22 S.C.R., p. 456 D.L.R.

555 See *Sunshine Exploration, supra*, footnote 552, at p. 21 S.C.R., p. 454 D.L.R.

556 *Ruxley Electronics and Construction Ltd. v. Forsyth*, [1996] 1 A.C. 344 (H.L.); *McGarry v. Richards, Akroyd & Gall Ltd., supra*, footnote 551; followed in *Strata Corp. NW 1714 v. Winkler* (1987), 45 D.L.R. (4th) 741, 20 B.C.L.R. (2d) 116 (C.A.); *G. & J. Parking Lot Maintenance Ltd. v. Oland Construction Co. Ltd.* (1978), 16 A.R. 293 (S.C.T.D.). In *Worrall v. Northwestern Mutual Ins. Co.* (1962), 36 D.L.R. (2d) 752 (B.C.S.C.), on failure of an insurer to make proper restoration of a damaged house, the measure of damages for work improperly done was said to be the difference in value, not the cost of reconstruction. See also 1.2440, *infra*.

557 *Nu-West Homes Ltd. v. Thunderbird Petroleums Ltd.* (1975), 59 D.L.R. (3d) 292 (Alta. S.C. App. Div.). See footnote 576, *infra*. In *Wood v. Stringer* (1890), 20 O.R. 148 (H.C.J.), the cost of replacing defective church pews was allowed, and in *Mack v. Stuike* (1963), 43 D.L.R. (2d) 763 (Sask. Q.B.), damages for failure to construct a basement of proper materials were based on the cost of moving the house and reconstructing the basement. See also *Bellingham v. Greentree Homes Ltd.* (1987), 47 Man.R. (2d) 238 (C.A.); *Vogt v. Saskatchewan Housing Corp.* (1985), 17 C.L.R. 52 (Sask. Q.B.); *Chappel v. Barati* (1982), 30 C.C.L.T. 137 (Ont. H.C.J.).

558 [1976] 1 Lloyd's Rep. 250 (C.A.).

measure of damages would be, but it is obvious from the tenor of the judgment that it would not be $2,000,000, but would be based on the diminished value (if any) of the ship.

1.2420 The likelihood of the plaintiff actually performing the restoration is an important factor.[559] A hypothetical but often cited example is a contract to build a monumental fountain so ugly that it would reduce the value of the owner's land, followed by a breach of the contract to build.[560] No one doubts that the owner is entitled to the cost of completion, as in case of wrongful damage to the completed fountain, the owner would, if genuinely intending to rebuild, usually be entitled to the cost of restoration. The reason is that the plaintiff is entitled to indulge a specific taste in monumental fountains and is likely to expend the damage award on actual restoration. A plaintiff is bound to act reasonably to mitigate loss, but a court will not say that it is unreasonable for the plaintiff to build the particular fountain wanted, for the court will not substitute its judgment for the plaintiff's on an aesthetic matter. In *Radford v. De Froberville*,[561] the plaintiff was held to be entitled to recover the cost of building a wall on her land even though the cost exceeded the diminution in value to the land caused by the defendant's breach of covenant, and even though the plaintiff's purpose was not personal use, for the land was rented, but to benefit her tenants. The court evidently took the view that it was not unreasonable for a landowner to make the same sort of improvements for the benefit of tenants as would be made for the owner's own benefit.

1.2430 Similar problems have arisen in cases of damage to chattels. In many cases it has been held that the plaintiff is not entitled to the cost of repair, where this is uneconomic.[562] This conclusion rests on the assumption that a replacement is reasonably available in the market; where this is not so,

559 See *McGarry v. Richards, Akroyd & Gall Ltd.*, *supra*, footnote 551, at p. 391; *Strata Corp. NW 1714 v. Winkler*, *supra*, footnote 556; *Sampson v. Boudreau* (1975), 13 N.S.R. (2d) 645 (S.C.T.D.); *Strachan v. Barton* (1993), 10 C.L.R. (2d) 142 (B.C.S.C.), at p. 177; *Hospitality Investments Ltd. v. Everett Lord Building Construction Ltd.* (1993), 143 N.B.R. (2d) 258 at p. 303 (Q.B.), affd 166 N.B.R. (2d) 241 (C.A.). But see *Bellgrove v. Eldridge* (1954), 90 C.L.R. 613; *De Cesare v. Deluxe Motors Pty. Ltd.* (1996), 67 S.A.S.R. 28 (S.C.). In *Eldon Weiss Home Construction Ltd. v. Clark* (1982), 39 O.R. (2d) 129 (Co. Ct.), at p. 133, and in *Chase v. deGroot*, [1994] 1 N.Z.L.R. 613 (H.C.), where the plaintiff had sold the property before trial, cost of reinstatement was refused. The court indicated that the cost would have been allowed if the plaintiffs "had demonstrated a genuine interest in having such work done".

560 The example was taken from the American Law Institute's *Restatement of the Law of Contracts* (St. Paul, West Publishing Co., 1932), 1, §346, and was discussed in *Groves Co. v. John Wunder Co.*, 205 Minn. 163, 286 N.W. 235 (1939), at p. 244. See also *Ruxley Electronics and Construction Ltd. v. Forsyth*, *supra*, footnote 556, at pp. 370-71, *per* Lord Lloyd.

561 [1977] 1 W.L.R. 1262 (Ch.).

562 *Dewees v. Morrow*, [1932] 2 D.L.R. 800 (B.C.C.A.), leave to appeal to S.C.C. refused 45 B.C.R. at p. 158; *Peet v. Stonehouse* (1954), 34 M.P.R. 269 (Nfld. S.C.); *Darbishire v. Warran*, [1963] 1 W.L.R. 1067 (C.A.); *Morin v. Brunswick Construction Ltd.* (1979), 25 N.B.R. (2d) 505 (Co. Ct.); *Lengert v. Gladstone* (1970), 11 D.L.R. (3d) 726 (B.C.C.A.); *Comeau v. Ross Estate* (1991), 118 N.B.R. (2d) 217 (Q.B.).

repairing the damaged chattel may be reasonable, and in some such cases the cost of repair has been allowed.[563] Plainly, there must be limits on the plaintiff's right to recover the cost of repairs even if the plaintiff will certainly[563a] or has actually spent money on having them done. The cost of actually restoring a seriously damaged automobile might be astronomical. The plaintiff who claims the cost of repair must show that she has not acted (or would not act) unreasonably in actually effecting the repairs. The possibility of actually carrying them out (or actually having carried them out) is evidential but not conclusive that the repairs are reasonable. It may be added that in the case of property for personal use, such as an automobile or residential land, it is probable the courts will be sympathetic to the plaintiff whose personal preferences, though not conclusive, are worthy of some protection.[564] In *Golko v. Clarke Simpkins Ltd.*,[565] the purchaser of a car supplied, in breach of contract, without tinted glass was allowed only the difference in value, and not the cost of installing tinted glass. The court evidently assumed that the result would have been different if the defendant, instead of being a seller had been an installer who had actually contracted to install tinted glass in the plaintiff's car. It is submitted that the test should be whether the plaintiff reasonably intends actually to effect the installation. If he has made a contract specifically for the installation of tinted glass in a car he already owns, that is strong evidence of a genuine intention actually to carry out the work, and of a personal preference for tinted glass that the court will not hold to be unreasonable.

1.2440 Analogous problems arise on damage to land or buildings. In one case, a building was burnt to the ground by the defendant's negligence.[566] The land was not being put to its most economic use before the fire, and the plaintiff had intended to demolish the building and redevelop the land. In fact, it was found that the fire had actually increased the value of the land by the cost of pulling down the building. The plaintiff (or its insurer by subrogation)[567] claimed the cost of reconstruction, but the defendant was held not to be liable for it. The result is supported by the analogous cases discussed here and is, it is submitted, sound, the plaintiff's interest being purely commercial. The opposite conclusion was reached in *Evans v. Balog*[568] where the building had been the plaintiffs' personal residence which they intended to rebuild. The New South Wales Court of Appeal there held that the proper test is the

563 *Reliance Lumber Co. v. Dyck* (1951), 3 W.W.R. (N.S.) 332 (Dist. Ct.); *O'Grady v. Westminster Scaffolding Ltd.*, [1962] 2 Lloyd's Rep. 238 (Q.B.), explained in *Darbishire v. Warran, supra*, footnote 562, as a case where the damaged car was "unique". See also *Mackenzie v. Baker* (2001), 56 O.R. (3d) 716 (S.C.J.), affd 65 O.R. (3d) 319 (C.A.).

563a In *Ruxley Electronics and Construction Ltd v. Forsyth*, [1996] 1 A.C. 344 (H.L.), an undertaking was offered by the plaintiff, but nevertheless the cost of reinstatement was refused. The plaintiff's offer of an undertaking cannot be conclusive, because if it were the plaintiff would be in a position to bargain for a settlement based on the cost to the defendant of performing the work.

564 See footnote 557, *supra*.

565 (1957), 23 W.W.R. 88 (B.C.C.A.).

reasonableness of the plaintiffs' desire to reinstate the property. The fact that it was their personal residence was rightly, it is submitted, considered important: "They had, in effect, lost their family home. That is the nature of their damage, and not some diminution in value of their land."[569] The action had been brought in nuisance, negligence and breach of contract (the

[566] *C.R. Taylor (Wholesale) Ltd. v. Hepworths Ltd.*, [1977] 1 W.L.R. 659 (Q.B.). Similar results were reached in *Witwicki v. Yadlowski* (1978), 91 D.L.R. (3d) 340 (Alta. Dist. Ct.); *Moss v. Christchurch Rural District Council*, [1925] 2 K.B. 750; *Simon v. Gastonguay*, [1931] 2 D.L.R. 75 (N.S.S.C.); *Barrette v. Franki Compressed Pile Co. of Canada Ltd.*, [1955] 2 D.L.R. 665, [1955] O.R. 413 (H.C.J.); *Montreal Trust Co. v. Hercules Sales Ltd.* (1968), 3 D.L.R. (3d) 504, [1969] 1 O.R. 661 (C.A.); *Gendron v. Town of Dalhousie* (1977), 18 N.B.R. (2d) 61 (S.C.); *Veitch v. Town of Mount Pearl (No. 2)* (1980), 25 Nfld. & P.E.I.R. 307 (Nfld. S.C.T.D.); *Grant v. MacKay Construction Ltd.* (1972), 3 Nfld. & P.E.I.R. 458 (P.E.I.S.C.); *Waterloo Warehousing & Storage Ltd. v. Swenco Manufacturing Ltd.* (1975), 58 D.L.R. (3d) 180, 8 O.R. (2d) 404 (H.C.J.); *Hole & Sons (Savers Common) Ltd. v. Harrisons of Thurnscoe Ltd.*, [1973] 1 Ll. L.R. 345 (Q.B.); *Lloy v. Town of Dartmouth* (1897), 30 N.S.R. 208 (S.C.); *Nor-Video Services Ltd. v. Ontario Hydro* (1978), 84 D.L.R. (3d) 221, 19 O.R. (2d) 107 (H.C.J.), affd (unreported, March 12, 1979, C.A.) (interference with television reception); *Bridges Bros. Ltd. v. Beth-Canada Mining Co.* (1983), 50 N.B.R. (2d) 42 (C.A.); *Bishop's Falls (Town) v. Abitibi-Price Inc.* (1987), 64 Nfld. & P.E.I.R. 100 (Nfld. S.C.T.D.); *Ziehlke v. Amisk Drilling Co.* (1993), 110 D.L.R. (4th) 172, [1994] 2 W.W.R. 107 (Man. C.A.); *Boudreau v. Leblanc* (1988), 91 N.B.R. (2d) 330 (C.A.); *Duff v. Dutkiewicz* (1993), 137 N.B.R. (2d) 266 (Q.B.); *Ouellette v. Fleck* (1995), 158 N.B.R. (2d) 141 (Q.B.); *Taylor v. King*, [1993] 8 W.W.R. 92, 82 B.C.L.R. (2d) 108 (C.A.); *Buckingham v. Graham* (1996), 174 N.B.R. (2d) 330 (Q.B.); *Smith v. Johnson* (2006), 287 Sask. R. 45 (Q.B.). See *Redland Bricks Ltd. v. Morris*, [1970] A.C. 652 (H.L.); *Hislop Estates v. Western Oil Ltd.*, [1978] 2 W.W.R. 632 (B.C.S.C.); *Stevens v. Abbotsford Lumber, Mining & Development Co.*, [1924] 1 D.L.R. 1163 (B.C.C.A.); *Kerlenmar Holdings Ltd. v. Matsqui (District)* (1991), 81 D.L.R. (4th) 334, [1991] 5 W.W.R. 481 (B.C.C.A.); *Cousins v. McColl-Frontenac Inc.* (2007), 322 N.B.R. (2d) 159 (C.A.), leave to appeal to S.C.C. granted *per* S.C.C. Bulletin 4/4/08, p. 525. In *Jones v. Gooday* (1841), 8 M. & W. 146, 151 E.R. 985, where the defendant had removed some of the plaintiff's soil, the cost of restoration was refused, Alderson B. saying, at p. 147, that it would be absurd to hold liable one, who let the sea in on land worth £20, for the cost of expensive engineering operations to exclude it.

[567] The insurer had been held liable for the full cost of reconstruction, but the court said that this result turned on the construction of the insurance policy and was irrelevant to the plaintiff's rights against the defendant. In *Cyrand Investments Ltd. v. Aetna Ins. Co.* (1979), 8 R.P.R. 107 (Ont. C.A.), leave to appeal to S.C.C. refused October 3, 1979, an insurer was similarly held liable for the cost of reconstruction of a burned building despite the insured's intent to demolish it. See also *Ardill v. Citizens' Ins. Co.* (1893), 20 O.A.R. 605; *Leger v. Royal Ins. Co.* (1968), 70 D.L.R. (2d) 344 (N.B.S.C. App. Div.); *Jakimowich v. Halifax Ins. Co.* (1966), 57 D.L.R. (2d) 542 (Man. Q.B.), affd 60 D.L.R. (2d) 191 (C.A.). On the other hand, in *Colonsay Hotel v. Canadian National Fire Ins. Co.*, [1923] S.C.R. 688, [1923] 3 D.L.R. 1001; *Vanderburgh v. Oneida Ins. Co.*, [1935] 1 D.L.R. 257, [1935] O.R. 67 (C.A.); *Scott v. Canadian Mercantile Ins. Co.* (1965), 49 D.L.R. (2d) 601, [1965] 2 O.R. 66 (H.C.J.); and *Zigby v. Laurentienne Générale Cie d'Assurance* (1994), 118 D.L.R. (4th) 390, [1994] R.J.Q. 1868 (C.A.), the insured failed to recover the cost of reinstatement. These cases were followed in *Falcon v. State Ins. General Manager*, [1975] 1 N.Z.L.R. 520 (S.C.). The insurance cases, though sometimes cited, are not, it is submitted, necessarily determinative in damages cases. Even if it is properly held, on the construction of an insurance policy, that the insured has bargained for reinstatement cost, this is no reason to impose an excessive burden on a wrongdoer who has made no such bargain. The distinction was made by Dr. Lushington in *The "Gazelle"* (1844), 2 W.Rob. 279, pp. 280-1.

[568] [1976] 1 N.S.W.L.R. 36 (C.A.).

defendant having undertaken to rebuild). The court held that the measure of damages was the same under each cause of action.

1.2450 In *Hollebone v. Midhurst & Fernhurst Builders*,[570] the cost of reinstatement of a house was allowed, the court saying that: "By reason of its size its position, its features, its seclusion and the area in which it is located, the property is properly termed unique or of a nature that comparable properties are few and far between."[571] It seems unlikely that the cost of reinstatement would be refused unless wholly unreasonable, where the property in question is the plaintiff's home and the court is satisfied that reinstatement will actually be effected.[572] In *Lodge Holes Colliery Co. v. Wednesbury Corp.*,[573] where the defendant had caused a subsidence in a highway vested in the plaintiff, which the plaintiff restored to its former state at a cost of £400, the House of Lords refused to allow the full cost of reinstatement on proof that a less expensive restoration (costing about £65) would have produced an equally commodious road.[574] The case indicates that actual expenditure of money by the plaintiff, though undoubtedly evidential, cannot be conclusive on the question of reasonableness.[575] In *Lodge Holes Colliery Co.*, it was admitted that the plaintiff had acted in good faith and on expert advice. The court stressed too that the onus was on the wrongdoer to show that the expenditure was unreasonable: "a court should be very indulgent and always bear in mind who was to blame".[576] Nevertheless the cost was not allowed, Lord Loreburn L.C. saying:

[569] *Supra*, at p. 40. See also *Carr-Harris v. Schacter* (1956), 6 D.L.R. (2d) 225, [1956] O.R. 994 (H.C.J.); *Hutchison v. Davidson*, [1945] S.C. 395; *Peters v. Diamond* (1963), 41 D.L.R. (2d) 311, [1964] 1 O.R. 139 (Co. Ct.) (cost of replanting trees allowed); *Tridan Developments Ltd. v. Shell Canada Products Ltd.* (2000), 57 O.R. (3d) 503 (Ont. C.A.) (cost of restoring contaminated land); *Fondrick v. Gross*, [2004] 6 W.W.R. 367 (Sask. Q.B.) (trees and shrubs); *Young v. Arnyek* (2007), 298 Sask. R. 251 (Q.B.).

[570] [1968] 1 Lloyd's Rep. 38.

[571] *Supra*, at p. 39.

[572] In *Jens v. Mannix Co. Ltd.* (1978), 89 D.L.R. (3d) 351 at p. 358 (B.C.S.C.), vard 30 D.L.R. (4th) 260, [1986] 5 W.W.R. 563 (C.A.), the cost of rebuilding was allowed, the court saying, however, "I would feel more secure ... if [the plaintiffs] had actually built a new house by now." See also *Eldon Weiss Home Construction Ltd. v. Clark* (1982), 39 O.R. (2d) 129 (Co. Ct.), at p. 133; *Ward v. Cannock Chase District Council*, [1986] Ch. 546; *Ziehlke v. Amisk Drilling Co.*, *supra*, footnote 566.

[573] [1908] A.C. 323 (H.L.), followed in *Dewees v. Morrow*, [1932] 2 D.L.R. 800 (B.C.C.A.), leave to appeal to S.C.C. refused 45 B.C.R. at p. 158.

[574] See also *Town of Radisson v. Amson* (1919), 49 D.L.R. 517 (Sask. C.A.) (injurious affection: measure of compensation diminished value, not cost of altering claimant's premises).

[575] In *Darbishire v. Warran*, [1963] 1 W.L.R. 1067 (C.A.) also, the repairs had been effected.

[576] [1908] A.C. 323 (H.L.), at p. 325. See also footnote 557, *supra*.

The point of law which was advanced by the plaintiffs, namely, that they were entitled to raise the road to the old level, cost what it might and whether it was more commodious to the public or not, will not, in my opinion, bear investigation. Such a rule might lead to a ruinous and wholly unnecessary outlay. There is no authority for it . . . Even those who have been wronged must act reasonably, however wide the latitude of discretion that is allowed to them within the bounds of reason.[577]

[*The next page is* 1-121]

[577] *Lodge Holes Colliery Co.*, *supra*, at p. 326. See also *Sinkewicz v. Schmidt*, [1994] 4 W.W.R. 569, 118 Sask. R. 112 (Q.B.); *Goebel v. Koenig*, [1998] 6 W.W.R. 56, 162 Sask. R. 81 (Q.B.); *Jordan v. Norfolk County Council*, [1994] 1 W.L.R. 1353 (Ch. Div.).

On the other hand, this case suggests that the plaintiff could not be compelled to "make do" with a substantially inferior road in order to save the defendant money. In the case of publicly owned land, "diminution in value" is rarely an appropriate measure because the public authority is usually bound to maintain the land for public use and cannot mitigate its loss by selling it and buying other land for its purpose.[578]

1.2460 Where the wrong consists of a breach of contract, the relationship between the measure of damages and the plaintiff's right to specific enforcement must be considered. If the plaintiff is entitled to a decree of specific enforcement of the defendant's obligation, damages, if awarded in substitution for such a decree, will naturally be measured by the actual cost of reinstatement.[579] Thus, in *Radford v. De Froberville*[580] where the defendant had covenanted to build a wall to enclose the plaintiff's land, the court considered that the case would, in principle, be one for specific performance though this was impossible in the particular case as the defendant had sold the land on which the wall was to be built. Thus, if justice would support a specific order against the defendant requiring actual reinstatement there can be no injustice in an award of damages measured by the reasonable cost of effecting that reinstatement. On the other hand equity would not lightly make a specific order in such a case, being conscious of the probable outcome where performance is uneconomic, that is, that the plaintiff with decree in hand would settle for a sum of money approaching the cost to the defendant of performance.[581] The plaintiff might thus recover far more than compensation for the diminution in value of his property, and the court of equity will be reluctant to deliver the defendant "bound hand and foot"[582] to submit to such a negotiation. In *Attica Sea Carriers Corp. v. Ferrostaal Poseidon Bulk Reederei G.m.b.H.*,[583] involving uneconomic repairs to a ship, the English Court of Appeal stated very clearly that no decree of specific performance would be made, since damages were an adequate remedy. It must follow that the measure of those damages would be the diminution in value, not the cost of actual repair. Thus, it seems that the cost of reinstatement should only be awarded in the sort of case in which a court of equity would, in principle, award a decree of specific enforcement if such a decree were otherwise possible and appropriate.

578 *Prince Rupert (City) v. Pederson*, [1995] 1 W.W.R. 421, 98 B.C.L.R. (2d) 84 (C.A.). But see *Bishop's Falls v. Abitibi-Price Inc.* (1987), 64 Nfld. & P.E.I.R. 100 (Nfld. S.C.T.D.).

579 See Sharpe, *Injunctions and Specific Performance*, looseleaf ed. (Toronto, Canada Law Book, 1999), 7.130-7.180.

580 [1977] 1 W.L.R. 1262 (Ch. D.).

581 See Sharpe, *op. cit.*, footnote 579, 1.150-1.180, 7.110.

582 *Isenberg v. East India House Estate Co., Ltd.* (1863), 3 De G.J. & S. 263, at p. 273, 46 E.R. 637.

583 [1976] 1 Lloyd's Rep. 250 (C.A.).

1.2470 Another point often raised in discussion of the contractual cases is whether it is objectionable for the defendant to profit from the breach of contract, as the defendant may appear to do if the higher measure of damages is refused. There is some ambiguity in the notion of "profit from breach". If what is meant is that the defendant will be better off than if the contract had actually been performed, all these cases, wherever the higher measure is refused, enable the defendant to profit from breach. But this kind of profit is not, it is submitted, objectionable. The object of a civil remedy for breach of contract is to give fair compensation to the plaintiff, not to punish the defendant, or even (except where the plaintiff is entitled to an order of specific enforcement) to compel performance. Where the defendant finds it advantageous to break a contract and pay damages, the defendant profits from breach, but this is not usually considered objectionable.[584] It is often argued that performance of the defendant's covenant (to repair or restore property) is part of the price of the benefits received under the contract and that therefore the defendant ought to pay it. It may be conceded that all contractual promises are, in a sense, the price of what is given or promised in return, but it does not follow from this that the plaintiff is entitled to the actual cost of performance. Unless the plaintiff is entitled to specific performance or to recover a debt[585] (and an action on a debt is a kind of specific performance), the plaintiff has no right to compel the defendant to perform; the plaintiff's right is to be put, so far as money can do it, in the same position that would have been occupied if performance had been rendered. In many of the cases under consideration this is effected by an award of damages measured by diminution in value of the property. It should be noted also that the salient feature of an action for the price of goods or land is that it is an action for the recovery of a debt, not an action for damages. Thus, it begs the question of the appropriate measure of damages to say that the defendant's obligation is part of the "price".

1.2480 These arguments, in suggesting that the defendant profits from breach, do not depend on any overall assessment of the value of the contract to the defendant. Even if it were a losing contract for the defendant it can still be argued that the defendant profits from breach in the sense that even more would be lost by actually rendering the agreed performance. Another meaning of the phrase "profit from breach" might be that the defendant by breaking the contract can make a net profit at the plaintiff's expense, and situations can be imagined where this is objectionable, as, for example, where the plaintiff pays a sum of money in advance for the performance of an uneconomic repair. Certainly the defendant cannot be allowed to keep the payment in case of failure to render performance,

---

584 See 9.200 - 9.210, *infra*.

585 Julius J., Olsen J. dissenting, in *Groves Co. v. John Wunder Co.*, 205 Minn. 163, 286 N.W. 235 at p. 244 (1939), pointed out that it was always open to the plaintiff to stipulate for liquidated damages to be payable on breach.

and in these cases the plaintiff may be entitled to restitution of the benefits conferred on the defendant. This entitlement will depend, among other things, on whether the defendant's breach is substantial in relation to the whole contract. Thus, if the defendant's entire contractual obligation consists of the promise to repair, restitution will be more readily available than where the main purpose of the contract is a lease, the covenant to repair being incidental. Again, if the parties have set off a specific sum of money against the defendant's obligation so that the repair covenant can be regarded as a severable contract with an ascertainable price actually paid to the defendant, there will be a strong case for restitution of the sum so allocated. The question of restitution as a remedy for breach of contract is discussed in a later chapter.[586]

2. Date for Assessment

1.2490 Assuming that the cost of reinstatement is to be allowed, the question sometimes arises of the date for its assessment. In *Dodd Properties Ltd. v. Canterbury City Council*,[587] where the defendant had damaged the plaintiff's building, it was held that the plaintiff was entitled to the cost of repair prevailing at the date of the trial nine years after the date of the wrong though this was much higher than the cost at the earlier date. Earlier in this chapter it was submitted that there is good reason for an early crystallization of damages,[588] and these reasons apply with equal force to the case of repair costs. Postponement of the date for assessment enables the plaintiff to speculate at the defendant's expense and actually encourages the plaintiff, if a dramatic rise in building costs is foreseen, to make an inferior investment, knowing that the defendant will have to pay for the increased cost of building if (but only if) repairs are postponed. The defendant has an important interest in having the repairs effected early but no power to carry them out. It was said by the Court of Appeal in the *Dodd Properties* case that it was reasonable for the plaintiff to await the outcome of litigation before repairing, but if the damage to the property was worth repairing at all it would still have been worth repairing even if the plaintiff had lost its case. If it was not, as a commercial proposition, worth repairing, it is hard to see why the establishment of the defendant's liability should make any difference. The plaintiff is not usually bound to use the proceeds of its judgment to effect repairs and presumably will not do so if they are uneconomic. It was early settled in sale cases that a buyer's

586 See 9.220 - 9.250, *infra*.

587 [1980] 1 W.L.R. 433 (C.A.), followed in *Alcoa Minerals of Jamaica Inc. v. Broderick*, [2002] 1 A.C. 371 (P.C.). A similar conclusion was reached in *Cormier Enterprises Ltd. v. Costello* (1979), 108 D.L.R. (3d) 472 (N.B.S.C. App. Div.) (breach of warranty by builder), and *Karod v. Lingstrom* (1983), 30 R.P.R. 1 (B.C.S.C.) (breach of warranty by builder).

588 See 1.650 - 1.1110, *supra*. For a fuller discussion see Waddams, "The Date for the Assessment of Damages", 97 L.Q.R. 445 (1981). For a contrary view, see Wallace, "Inflation and Assessment of Construction Cost", 98 L.Q.R. 406 (1982).

damages for non-delivery were to be assessed on the date of the seller's breach even if the buyer had paid the price in advance.[589] The buyer was not permitted to say that he was awaiting the return of his money before deciding to make a substitute purchase. Only if the effect on Dodd's total wealth of success in the litigation was such as to affect the economic soundness of its carrying out the repairs would it be rational for Dodd to await the outcome to litigation before repairing.[590] Cantley J. had found the plaintiff was "very short of ready cash" but "not impecunious". It could "probably have raised the money".[591] Moreover, the effect of the plaintiff's evidence was, in the words of Megaw L.J., that, "If there had been no money problem . . . he would still not have spent money on the building before he was sure of recovering the cost from the defendants. It would not have made commercial sense to spend this money on a property which would not produce correspondingly additional income."[592] In that case it is hard to see why establishing the defendant's liability would change the calculus. All it does is to make the plaintiff more wealthy; it does not affect the profitability of carrying out the repairs.

1.2500 The argument that the defendant has had the use of the plaintiff's money should be met, it is suggested, by the award of interest at market rates from the date of the wrong.[593] An award so measured also meets the plaintiff's claim that the plaintiff has been kept out of the money during that time.

1.2510 It may be argued that the defendant is the wrongdoer and that the prospects of heavier damages will encourage the defendant to concede liability or to compensate the plaintiff for the burden of litigation.[594] But this argument would justify penal consequences for an unsuccessful defence. It is not contrary to the public interest for actions (even ultimately successful actions) to be defended. Unmeritorious defences can be discouraged by the rules relating to costs and interest. The rules of damage

---

589 See 1.720 - 1.730, *supra*.

590 This may be the case with an individual plaintiff. See *Perry v. Sidney Phillips & Son*, [1982] 1 W.L.R. 1297 (C.A.); *Alcoa Minerals of Jamaica Ltd. v. Broderick, supra*, footnote 587. See also *London Congregational Union Inc. v. Harriss & Harriss*, [1985] 1 All E.R. 335 (Q.B.), vard [1988] 1 All E.R. 15.

591 *Dodd Properties, supra*, footnote 587, at p. 442.

592 *Dodd Properties, supra*, at pp. 451-2.

593 See 7.330 - 7.1000, *infra*, and see *Perry v. Sidney Phillips & Son, supra*, footnote 590, at p. 1302. The result in the *Dodd* case may be explained by the inability of the English courts to award interest. Megaw L.J. said, at p. 452, that "the plaintiffs . . . could not claim interest on the amount of their compensation starting to run before the date when the money was expended on repairs".

594 The "scales should move heavily in the favour of the innocent party as against the wrongdoer", *per* Megaw L.J., in *Dodd Properties Ltd. v. Canterbury City Council, supra*, footnote 587, at p. 452. In *Groves Co. v. John Wunder Co., supra*, footnote 585, stress was laid on the wilful nature of the defendant's breach of contract.

assessment should attempt to minimize the total costs to both parties of litigation. Increased pressure on the defendant will not necessarily facilitate settlements, for the plaintiff will be encouraged to hold out for more than she might otherwise have been willing to accept knowing that she can well afford to delay. It is submitted, therefore, that by analogy with the cases of non-delivery and non-conveyance of property, damages for diminution in value of property should be assessed at the earliest date when, acting reasonably, the plaintiff could have effected a reinstatement.[595] A further consideration is that if the plaintiff sells the property before judgment, or before appeal, without carrying out the repairs, the judgment date cost of repairs is admittedly irrelevant and the court is thrown back onto a breach date assessment.[596] It is anomalous and inconvenient for the plaintiff's entitlement to vary according to subsequent conduct.

3. Damage by Successive Incidents

1.2520 Where property is damaged by successive incidents, difficult causation problems arise. Where the defendant damaged a fender on the plaintiff's car that had already been damaged by another person so as to require a respraying of part of the car, it was held that the defendant was not liable for the cost of respraying for he had not caused the necessity for it.[597] Similarly, where the defendant causes greater damage to property that has already been damaged, liability is only for the difference between the cost of restoring the property in its prior state and the cost of restoring it after the damage for which the defendant is responsible.[598] The first of two wrongdoers would, on the principles discussed elsewhere,[599] be liable for the full cost of the damage caused by the wrong notwithstanding that the loss would have occurred in any event due to the second wrong. Where, after the defendant's wrong, the property is damaged or destroyed by a non-tortious incident, it might be supposed that, following the personal injury and loss of use of property cases, the defendant would not be liable on the ground that, as events now reveal, the loss would have occurred in any event. However, it has been held in such cases that the defendant

595 This measure is supported by *Van den Hurk v. R. Martens & Co. Ltd.*, [1920] 1 K.B. 850; *East Ham Corp. v. Bernard Sunley & Sons Ltd.*, [1966] A.C. 406 (H.L.); *Biranda v. Anderson* (1978), 16 A.R. 330 (Dist. Ct.); *Green v. White* (1975), 10 N.B.R. (2d) 299 (S.C.); *Mertens v. Home Freeholds Co.*, [1921] 2 K.B. 526 (C.A.) (see passage quoted at 2.270, *infra*); *Reyno v. G.M.N. Construction Co. Ltd.* (1975), 16 N.S.R. (2d) 149 (S.C.T.D.); *Farah v. Craig* (1978), 31 N.S.R. (2d) 238 (S.C.T.D.); *Lumsden v. MacLean* (1972), 8 N.S.R. (2d) 33 (S.C.T.D.); *Jens v. Mannix Co. Ltd.* (1979), 30 D.L.R. (4th) 260, [1986] 5 W.W.R. 563 (C.A.).

596 See *Perry v. Sidney Phillips & Son*, *supra*, footnote 590 (sale by plaintiff between trial and appeal); *Clancy v. Shanahan* (1997), 150 Nfld. & P.E.I.R. 340, 9 R.P.R. (3d) 55 (Nfld. S.C.).

597 *Performance Cars Ltd. v. Abraham*, [1962] 1 Q.B. 33 (C.A.).

598 *Pound v. National Cartage Co.*, [1946] 1 W.W.R. 353 (Sask. C.A.).

599 See 1.2010 - 1.2020, *supra*, and 13.550 - 13.610, *infra*.

remains liable.[600] The argument in favour of this result can be defended on the ground that the wrongdoer causes an immediate diminution of the value of the property at the time of the wrong and that the plaintiff's cause of action crystallizes then. The cases of loss of earnings from personal injuries and damages for loss of use of property can be distinguished on this ground, for it is more difficult in those cases to frame the plaintiff's claim in terms of immediate capital loss.

1.2530 The argument for the plaintiff thus rests on the same kind of considerations as justify recovery of the full value of property destroyed or converted by the defendant even though the plaintiff would not have put the property to profitable use had it been preserved. Thus, if the defendant steals the plaintiff's watch, the defendant could not, it is submitted, argue that there should be no payment of damages on the ground that the watch, if not stolen, would have been destroyed a few hours later by an accidental fire.[601] Similarly, if the defendant damages the watch, the defendant should pay the diminution in its value (usually measured by the cost of repairs), even if it subsequently turns out that the watch is accidentally destroyed. The argument for the defendant here is that the substance of the plaintiff's complaint is that the plaintiff has lost an opportunity to sell the property, and that by analogy with the cases where damages for loss of use are claimed,[602] the plaintiff ought to prove, on the balance of probabilities, that there would in fact have been a sale between the time of the wrong and the time of its subsequent destruction. The arguments appear fairly even.

1.2540 On balance, it is submitted that the plaintiff's arguments are the more persuasive. In the case of complete loss of property, the plaintiff recovers its value; proof is not necessary that the value would in fact have been realized.[603] Similarly, in the case of a partial loss, the plaintiff should recover the diminution in value, usually measured by the cost of repair.

4. Damages for Breach of Warranty of Quality

1.2550 The *Sale of Goods Act* provides:

> 51(2) The measure of damages for breach of warranty is the estimated loss directly and naturally resulting in the ordinary course of events from the breach of warranty.

---

600 *The "Glenfinlas"* [1918] P. 363*n*. See *The "York"* [1929] P. 178 (C.A.); *The "London Corporation"* [1935] P. 70 (C.A.), at p. 79.

601 If the plaintiff had fire insurance, he would not recover the value of the watch from the insurer; if the watch had been damaged by the defendant before the fire, the plaintiff would only recover the value of a damaged watch from the insurer. Hence, it appears that the plaintiff does suffer a real loss by the defendant's wrong. But a contrary view of this question is taken by Williams, "Causation in the Law," [1961] Camb. L.J. 62 at p. 78.

602 See 1.1950 - 1.1970, *supra*.

603 See 1.1360, 1.1430, *supra*.

> (3) In the case of breach of warranty of quality, such loss is, in the absence of evidence to the contrary, the difference between the value of the goods at the time of delivery to the buyer and the value they would have had if they had answered to the warranty.
>
> . . . . .
>
> 52. Nothing in this Act affects the right of the buyer . . . to recover . . . special damages in a case where by law . . . special damages may be recoverable . . .[604]

The *prima facie* measure thus depends on the value the goods would have had if they answered to the warranty. This is very often taken to be equal to the contract price,[605] though it is clear that the price is only evidential. If the buyer can prove that the warranted value was higher than the price, the buyer is entitled to recover more, and if the seller can show, perhaps because the market has fallen, that the warranted value was less than the price, damages would be reduced.[606] The other figure necessary for the calculation is the value the goods actually had at the time of delivery. This is often difficult to establish. Where the plaintiff has resold, the resale price will often be taken as evidence of the value.[607] A series of Canadian cases has held that the burden of proof is on the seller to show what value the goods had.[608] The courts have often spoken of "residual value" with reference to the value of the goods at the date of the hearing.[609] In principle, the residual value is only evidential of the actual value of the goods at the time of delivery, but if the goods have deteriorated after delivery because of a defect for which the seller is responsible, the buyer would be permitted to recover compensation for the deterioration as consequential damages. The use of the residual value may, therefore, be justified as a compendious way of allowing the buyer the damages specified by s. 51(3), and compensation for further depreciation. The latter head of compensation would, however, not be appropriate if the decline in value since the date of delivery were caused by some factor for which the defendant was not responsible, such as misuse of the goods by the plaintiff or fall in market prices after a point where the plaintiff, acting reasonably, could have sold the goods.

1.2560 Where goods are warranted to be fit for a particular purpose, it has been held that the buyer is entitled to the cost of procuring a suitable

604 *Sale of Goods Act* (Ont.), ss. 51(2), (3), 52; Alta., ss. 52(2), (3), 53(a); B.C., ss. 56(2), (3), 57; Man., ss. 54(2), (3), 55; N.B., ss. 50(2), (3), 51; Nfld. & Lab., ss. 54(2), (3), 55; N.W.T., ss. 62(1), (2), 63; N.S., ss. 54(2), (3), 54; P.E.I., ss. 53(2), (3), 54; Sask., ss. 52(2), (3), 53; Yukon, ss. 50(2), (3), 51.

605 See *Dingle v. Hare* (1859), 29 L.J.C.P. 143, where, as McGregor points out (*McGregor on Damages*, 16th ed. (London, Sweet & Maxwell, 1997), §876), one report speaks of contract price and the other of market value.

606 *Loder v. Kekule* (1857), 3 C.B. (N.S.) 128, 140 E.R. 687.

607 See *Graham v. Bigelow* (1912), 3 D.L.R. 404 (N.S.S.C.), affd 48 S.C.R. 512, 15 D.L.R. 294.

608 See 13.200 - 13.210, *infra*.

609 *Ibid.*

substitute for unfit goods. Thus, in *Sealand of the Pacific v. Robert C. McHaffie Ltd.*,[610] where the seller of a type of concrete had warranted that it would enable the plaintiff's aquarium to float, the plaintiff recovered the cost of replacement of the concrete (which was not fit for the purpose) with styrofoam, minus the unpaid price of the defective concrete. On the last point the court commented that, though the concrete was worthless, the plaintiff would have had to pay the agreed price in order to obtain a suitable product, and so ought to deduct the price from the cost of a suitable product installed at the defendant's expense.

(1) Resale by buyer

1.2570 The price at which the buyer sells defective goods may be evidential of their actual value. In *Biggin v. Permanite*,[611] Devlin J. said: "If the actual damaged goods are sold with all faults, good evidence can be obtained of the difference in value."[612] The resale price, however, cannot be conclusive. This is illustrated by *Slater v. Hoyle & Smith*,[613] where the buyer resold defective goods at the same price that would have been paid for sound goods. The English Court of Appeal held that the buyer was, nevertheless, entitled to recover the difference between the value of the goods and the value they would have had if answering to the warranty. It might seem that the buyer is over-compensated in such a case, and certainly is, in fact, in a better position than would have been occupied if the contract had been performed, but the result may be defended on the ground that the buyer suffers an immediate capital loss on the delivery of defective goods and that the seller is liable for that loss, whether the buyer gives the goods away or whether they are sold for less or for more than their true value. Scrutton L.J. put the point as follows: "If the buyer is lucky enough, for reasons with which the seller has nothing to do, to get his goods through on the sub-contract without a claim against him, this on principle cannot affect his claim against the seller."[614] But in *Bence Graphics International Ltd. v. Fasson U.K. Ltd.*,[614a] where defective goods had been incorporated into a different product and resold, the supplier was held liable not for the difference in value of the goods at the time of delivery, but only for the (lesser) amount of the buyer's liability to the end users.

1.2580 Similarly, it is submitted, if the buyer of defective goods gives them away as a present or sells them at a low price by way of part gift,

610 (1974), 51 D.L.R. (3d) 702 (B.C.C.A.).

611 [1951] 1 K.B. 422, revd on other grounds [1951] 2 K.B. 314 (C.A.).

612 *Supra*, at p. 438, doubted in *Bence Graphics International Ltd. v. Fasson U.K. Ltd.*, [1998] Q.B. 87 (C.A.).

613 [1920] 2 K.B. 11 (C.A.).

614 *Supra*, at p. 23. See also *A.-G. Can. v. Corrie* (1951), 3 W.W.R. 207 (Man. K.B.); *Schrader Mitchell & Weir v. Robson Leather Co.* (1912), 3 D.L.R. 838, 3 O.W.N. 962 (H.C.J.); *Hussey v. Eels*, [1990] Q.B. 227 (C.A.).

614a *Supra*, footnote 612.

whether before or after discovering the defect, the buyer would be entitled to recover damages from the seller even though, financially, the former will be better off as a result than if the wrong had not been done.[615]

(2) Physical damage caused by defective goods

1.2590 Where defective goods cause damage to the buyer's personal property, the *prima facie* measure of damages becomes must less important than the general measure in s. 51(2). Recovery for personal injury and property damage is always stated to be subject to the principle of remoteness, and the language of s. 51(2) is directly derived from *Hadley v. Baxendale*, the leading case on remoteness. However, the principle of remoteness has not prevented the buyer of defective goods from regularly recovering compensation for personal injury and property damage. The test is whether such loss would be anticipated as a natural consequence by one knowing in advance of the particular debt. It is often very easy to foresee that defects in products will cause injury.[616]

(3) Loss of use of defective goods

1.2600 Much difficulty has arisen from claims for lost profit due to defective goods. In principle, the problem is the same as that discussed earlier in the case of complete deprivation of property. The plaintiff is entitled, ordinarily, to the value of the property. Compensation for loss of use, if separately calculated, can only be justified for the period during which the plaintiff is necessarily deprived of its use, that is, for the time that it would take, acting reasonably, to secure a replacement.[617] For to give compensation representing anticipated profits for the whole of the expected life of the goods would be to assess the full present value of the goods, and the plaintiff cannot be entitled to this twice over.[618]

1.2610 The same principle applies in the case of defective goods. If the plaintiff recovers a sum sufficient to make up the full value of the goods as warranted (and interest upon it), the plaintiff cannot also be entitled to lost profits for the full expected life of the goods. The plaintiff may, however, be entitled to profits lost during the period it would have taken, acting reasonably, to secure

---

615 The justification is that the buyer suffers an actual loss when the defective goods are delivered. For parallel cases see 1.1360-1.1430, *supra*. If the rule were otherwise, no action would lie against a seller when defective goods were bought as a gift for a third person if they were given before the defects were discovered. This would seem most unjust. In *Dipple v. Wylie* (1916), 30 D.L.R. 59 (Man. K.B.), damages were reduced, as the wrongdoer was able to show that he had caused a delay which had actually benefited the claimant, as prices had risen in the interim. In *Eldon Weiss Home Construction Ltd. v. Clark* (1982), 39 O.R. (2d) 129 (Co. Ct.), at p. 133, the resale price was taken as evidence that the defendant's breach had caused no diminution in value.

616 See 14.320, *infra*.

617 *Freedhoff v. Pomalift Industries Ltd.* (1971), 19 D.L.R. (3d) 153, [1971] 2 O.R. 733 (C.A.); *Harbour Equipment Ltd. v. C.N.R. Co.* (1976), 25 N.S.R. (2d) 166 (S.C.T.D.).

618 See 1.1830, *supra*.

a replacement. This period may be extended by the seller's assurances that the defects can be remedied or by the buyer's reasonable attempt to remedy the defects.[619]

1.2620 In *Cullinane v. British "Rema" Manufacturing Co.*,[620] a buyer claimed damages for breach of warranty in respect of a defective clay pulverizing plant. He claimed, first, the difference between the price paid and the value of the defective equipment and, second, the loss of profits that would have been earned with a sound machine for a three-year period up to the date of the trial. It was held that the two claims could not be combined. Lord Evershed M.R. said:

> It seems to me, as a matter of principle, that the full claim of damages in the form in which it is pleaded was not sustainable, in so far as the plaintiff sought to recover both the whole of his original capital loss and also the whole of the profit which he would have made. I think that that is really a self-evident proposition, because a claim for loss of profits could only be founded upon the footing that the capital expenditure had been incurred.[621]

Jenkins L.J. said:

> ... while no doubt the plaintiff can at his option claim damages based on the difference between the value to him of the article as actually supplied and the contract price of the article, he cannot claim both that amount, representing his capital expenditure thrown away by reason of the breach, and also the full amount of the profit which he can show that he would have made in the event of the article answering the warranty.[622]

The basis of the decision is that the plaintiff ought not to have double compensation. That is, it is submitted, a sound principle. The court holds that the plaintiff must elect between compensation for the capital value and compensation for loss of profits. But the point not emphasized in the *Cullinane* case is that in most cases the plaintiff will be able to replace the machine and will not be able to recover profit lost after a date when, acting reasonably, a substitute could have been purchased. The court was rightly concerned to prevent the plaintiff from claiming the value of a sound machine and, in addition, profits for its full anticipated life (ten years). But there is no duplication in a claim for the value of a sound machine and profits lost up to the point at which the plaintiff, acting reasonably, could have acquired a substitute.[623]

[619] In *R. G. McLean Ltd. v. Canadian Vickers Ltd.* (1970), 15 D.L.R. (3d) 15, [1971] 1 O.R. 207 (C.A.), the plaintiff's claim for lost profits was allowed, subject to a duty to act reasonably to mitigate loss. The argument that the plaintiff should have abandoned efforts to work the machine as soon as the defects appeared was dismissed as "a counsel of perfection", *per* Arnup J.A., at p. 23 D.L.R.

[620] [1954] 1 Q.B. 292 (C.A.), followed in *R. G. McLean Ltd., supra*, footnote 619, but doubted by the Alberta Supreme Court Appellate Division in *Sunnyside Greenhouses Ltd. v. Golden West Seeds Ltd.* (1972), 27 D.L.R. (3d) 434, affd [1973] S.C.R. v, 33 D.L.R. (3d) 384*n*.

[621] *Cullinane, supra*, footnote 620, at p. 302.

[622] *Cullinane, supra*, at p. 308.

[623] *R. G. McLean Ltd., supra*, footnote 619. See the equivalent cases on loss of property, 1.2850, *supra*.

1.2630 In *R. G. McLean Ltd. v. Canadian Vickers Ltd.*,[624] the Canadian Court of Appeal purported to follow *Cullinane*. The breach of warranty was in respect of a colour printing machine, and the buyer claimed, as damages, the work time and materials wasted to make the machine function properly and, in addition, profits it would have made had the machine worked. At the time of trial, the buyer had paid about one-fifth of the purchase price, and the trial judge, in allowing the buyer's claim for damages, dismissed the seller's counterclaim for the balance of the price on the ground that the salvage value

[*The next page is* 1-131]

[624] *Supra*, footnote 619.

of the machine was equal to approximately the portion of the price paid by the buyer. The Ontario Court of Appeal reduced the award of damages on the ground that the seller ought to be credited with the balance of the price. Arnup J.A. said:

> If the contract had been performed, and profits earned by use of the machine, the plaintiff would have had to pay the purchase price. In any calculation of damages, on a basis as if the contract had been performed, the purchase price must stand as a debit against the plaintiff; any damages awarded in its favour can be used to extinguish the purchase price, but only the excess can then be allowed to the plaintiff by way of further damages.[625]

But the court also limited the claim for lost profits to the period until it was reasonable for the plaintiff to purchase a replacement machine (ten months). This, it is submitted, is a critical point of distinction from the *Cullinane* case. In the result, it would appear that the rule adopted in the *McLean* case is unfair to the plaintiff, unless the period for which profits are allowed is equal to the full expected life of the machine. In *McLean*, if the machine had answered to the warranty, the plaintiff would have had both its profits for the ten-month period and a working (ten-month-old) machine with (presumably) a considerable useful life ahead of it. It is submitted that the buyer, in such a case, should be entitled to recover the difference between the actual value of the machine and the value it would have had if it had answered to the warranty, and loss of profits until the buyer, acting reasonably, could have replaced the machine. However, as was submitted in the parallel case of deprivation of property, the buyer should not be entitled to interest on the amount of diminished value during the period for which lost profits are allowed, because the buyer could not have earned profit from use of the machine at the same time as earning interest on its capital value.[626]

1.2640 In the case of breach of warranty of quality of seeds for planting, there is a very great discrepancy between the loss based on the value of the seed at the date of breach and the loss based on the value of the anticipated crop. It has been held in a number of cases that the plaintiff is entitled to the value of the lost crop.[627] The same principle was applied by the Saskatchewan Court of Appeal in *Steele v. Maurer*[628] to a sale of bull's semen, where damages were awarded based on the difference in the value between the calves produced with the semen supplied and that of the calves that would have been produced had the semen answered to the warranty. Recovery of lost profits is always stated to be subject to the principle of remoteness, but the principle of

[625] *Supra*, at p. 22.

[626] See 1.1870 - 1.1890, *supra*.

[627] *Wagstaff v. Shorthorn Dairy Co.* (1884), Cab. & El. 324; *Uhle v. Kroeker*, [1928] 1 D.L.R. 97 (Man. C.A.); *Carlstadt Development Co. v. Alberta Pacific Elevator Co.* (1912), 7 D.L.R. 200 (Alta. S.C.); *Caners v. Eli Lilly Canada Inc.* (1996), 134 D.L.R. (4th) 730, [1996] 5 W.W.R. 381 (Man. C.A.) (breach of warranty of herbicide).

[628] (1977), 79 D.L.R. (3d) 764 (Sask. C.A.). See also *Hartman v. The Queen in right of Ontario* (1973), 42 D.L.R. (3d) 488, 2 O.R. (2d) 244 (C.A.) (defective raspberry cane stock).

remoteness in case of defective goods has been generously interpreted in favour of the buyer.[629]

(4) Depreciation

1.2650 If the period for which lost profits are allowed amounts to a substantial portion of the expected useful life of the goods, it will be necessary to take into account depreciation.[630] If the contract had been performed, the plaintiff would have had, in the *McLean* case, at the end of the ten-month period for which lost profits were allowed, profits for those ten months and also a sound ten-month-old machine. If the expected life of the machine were, say, a year, the plaintiff would plainly be over-compensated if it recovered the full value of the new machine in addition to profits that it would almost have to wear out the machine to earn. As Biger and Rosen have shown, in an article written from an accounting perspective,[631] an exact cash flow comparison of the plaintiff's position in fact with the position it would have occupied if the wrong had not been done will take account of the fact that, at the end of the useful life of the goods, their value in the plaintiff's hands would

[*The next page is* 1-133]

[629] See 14.320, *infra*.

[630] In *Cullinane v. British "Rema" Manufacturing Co. Ltd.*, *supra*, footnote 620, at p. 303, Lord Evershed M.R. said that where the plaintiff claims on the basis of lost profit "depreciation has nothing whatever to do with it". This comment was explained by the Australian High Court in *T.C. Industrial Plant Pty. Ltd. v. Robert's Queensland Pty. Ltd.*, [1964] A.L.R. 1083 (Full Court), at pp. 1090-1, as meaning that if the purchase price of the machine is deducted in calculating the profits, it should not be deducted again by way of depreciation.

[631] Biger and Rosen, "A Framework for the Assessment of Business Damages for Breach of Contract", 5 C.B.L.J. 302 (1981).

have been nil, even if they had been sound in the first place. If, as the authors recommend, an exact comparison on a cash flow basis can be made, depreciation can be ignored for it will be automatically taken into account by the residual value assigned to the asset at the end of the accounting period selected. However, it would appear that in applying the *prima facie* measure of damages in s. 51(3) of the *Sale of Goods Act*, courts, if giving lost profits in addition, ought to make an allowance for depreciation.[632] Alternatively, it would be possible in a suitable case where the necessary evidence was available, to depart altogether from s. 51(3), which is only a *prima facie* measure, and to calculate the cash flow anticipated and the cash flow actually received, and to award the plaintiff the difference, making due allowance for interest. Considerations of convenience very commonly affect the rules of damage assessment. In most cases the *prima facie* rule in the *Sale of Goods Act*, together with lost profits subject to mitigation, will be the most convenient measure. In particular cases, however, where one party or the other can show by detailed comparison of cash flows that the *prima facie* measure is inaccurate, the more detailed measure may be applied.

(5) Wasted expenses

1.2660 Elsewhere in this book the problem has been discussed of a claim for wasted expenses.[633] It is evident that the plaintiff would be doubly compensated by recovery of compensation based on the gross revenue that would have been earned if the wrong had not been done, and also the expenses that would have been incurred to earn that revenue. The word "profit" can be misleading. If it means net profit (that is, revenue minus expenses), the plaintiff, to be put into the position that would have been occupied if the wrong had not been done, ought to recover the amount of the net profit and, in addition, any expenses that could not be saved by acting reasonably after the wrong; on the other hand, if profit means gross revenue (with no deduction for expenses), the plaintiff cannot recover both the revenue and the expenses that would have been necessary to earn it.

1.2670 In *Sunnyside Greenhouses Ltd. v. Golden West Seeds Ltd.*,[634] the defendant, in breach of warranty, supplied greenhouse panels that had a considerably shorter life than they should have had. The plaintiff claimed, in addition to damages based on the value of the panels, the cost of initial installation and the cost of the removal of the defective panels and loss of profits. The court allowed the installation costs saying: "This was an expense that was unavoidable in order to make the intended use of the panels, and as the panels had to be replaced

632 See footnote 630, *supra*.

633 See 1.2190 - 1.2300, *supra*.

634 (1972), 27 D.L.R. (3d) 434 (Alta. S.C. App. Div.), affd [1973] S.C.R. v, 33 D.L.R. (3d) 384*n*.

(including those of which the replacement was postponed), the expense was wasted by reason of the breaches."[635] On the other hand, the cost of removal was not allowed in full:

> . . . it was in contemplation by both parties that the panels would in any event have to be replaced after a period of time; and that if the matter were to be taken into account at all it should only be on the footing that the replacement was at an earlier date than contemplated and the proper compensation in that state of affairs is interest on the expenditures actually made in advance of the time at which they would otherwise be made. I am of opinion that this is the correct view.[636]

In addition, the court allowed a loss of profit based on the amount by which the gross sales for 1979 fell short of the average over a five-year period.

1.2680 The evidence revealed that the panels, if sound, would have had an expected life of seven years. In the event, those installed on the south side of the greenhouse had a useful life of three years and those on the north side, five years. The court allowed the full cost of installation for both sides.

1.2690 It is difficult to avoid the conclusion that this allowance was over-compensatory when added to full compensation for the lost revenue. In order to earn the revenue, had the panels been sound, the plaintiff would have had to incur the installation costs. However, the plaintiff does suffer a loss by reason of having to repeat the installation expenses to replace the panels after three years and five years (in respect of each half) instead of after seven years as anticipated. To put it another way, the installation costs have not been wholly wasted, because (after the court's award) the plaintiff will have earned (about) four years of profits from them, but they are partially wasted in that they yield only four-sevenths of the expected return. It is submitted, therefore, that three-sevenths only of the installation expenses should have been allowed.[637]

1.2700 The court's approach to the cost of removing the defective panels was that, since the replacement would have been necessary after seven years in any event, the plaintiff had lost only the interest on the money between the two dates. It would seem, however, that an allowance for early expenditure will not fully compensate the plaintiff, because the

---

635 *Supra*, at p. 439.

636 *Supra*, at pp. 439-40.

637 In *City of Guelph Board of Light and Heat Com'rs v. United Dairy & Poultry Co-operative Ltd.* (1966), 57 D.L.R. (2d) 385, [1966] 2 O.R. 467 (Co. Ct.), affd D.L.R. *loc. cit.* p. 387*n*, O.R. *loc. cit.* p. 469*n* (C.A.), full installation costs were allowed of poles to replace poles damaged by the defendant. It is submitted that in consequence the plaintiff was better off than it would have been if the wrong had not been done, for, after the judgment, the plaintiff could look forward to an extra period of useful life of the poles beyond what had originally been anticipated, without the need to incur installation costs in respect of that period.

expenditure will not have yielded its full seven years' expected return. That is, the expenditure will perpetually recur four and two years earlier than anticipated, for all future roofs will require earlier replacement. Had the plaintiff received a sound roof it would have had to incur installation expenses in year one and dismantling expenses in year seven. In the event it receives a roof that lasts only four years and has to incur the dismantling expenses in year four, receiving only four-sevenths of the anticipated benefit from the expenses. It is submitted that the plaintiff's loss is three-sevenths of the expenses, plus an allowance for the advance expenditure of the dismantling costs.

1.2710 In many cases the court will be justified in ignoring these complexities, for the period of time during which lost profits are awarded will often (in view of the plaintiff's obligation to mitigate loss) be an insignificant proportion of the expected useful life of sound goods. Thus, where defective goods with a twenty-year life expectancy are installed by the plaintiff and replaced a week later because of a defect, the plaintiff will be able to support a claim for the full amount of the installation and dismantling costs, for these can be said to have been, in effect, wholly wasted.

(6) Liability to third parties

1.2720 The supply of defective goods often involves the plaintiff in liability to sub-buyers, and it has been frequently held that the plaintiff is entitled to recover compensation for such losses, and for the costs of reasonably defending legal proceedings.[638] It has also been held that criminal penalties incurred by the buyer can be recovered from the supplier.[639]

5. Improvements by Repairs (the "Betterment" Question)

1.2730 It commonly occurs that a plaintiff, in making good damage to property, will not be able to restore herself to her pre-loss position without improving it. If the plaintiff's ten-year-old roof is damaged, she will not be able to purchase a replacement ten-year-old roof. The only reasonable course will be to replace with a new roof. If roofs have a life of twenty years, and the defendant is compelled to pay the full cost of the replacement, the plaintiff will be in a better position after satisfaction of the judgment than if the damage had not occurred in the first place. It would seem, therefore, that the damages should be reduced by the value

638 *Mowbray v. Merryweather*, [1895] 2 Q.B. 640 (C.A.); *Vogan v. Oulton* (1899), 81 L.T. 435 (C.A.); *Burrard Drydock Co. v. Canadian Union Line Ltd.*, [1954] S.C.R. 307, [1954] 3 D.L.R. 561 (defective workmanship); *Biggin & Co. Ltd. v. Permanite Ltd.*, [1951] 1 K.B. 422, revd on other grounds [1951] 2 K.B. 314 (C.A.).

639 *Cointat v. Myham & Son*, [1913] 2 K.B. 220, revd on other grounds 30 T.L.R. 282; *Stephenson v. Sanitaris Ltd.* (1913), 16 D.L.R. 695, 30 O.L.R. 60 (S.C. App. Div.).

of the improvement of the plaintiff's position.[640] The contrary argument is that it is the defendant's wrong that has caused the need for replacement, and that the plaintiff should not be compelled to invest money in a replacement that the plaintiff might not have chosen to make. These arguments, however, do not appear to be conclusive. The fact that the defendant is a wrongdoer is not sufficient reason for over-compensation. The argument that the plaintiff is forced to make an unwanted investment can be met by conceding the point and increasing the damages by any loss suffered by the plaintiff's making such an investment.[641]

1.2740 The English cases, however, have held, though not at the highest level, that a plaintiff is entitled to recover the full cost of restoration, irrespective of the improvement to his position. In *The "Gazelle"*,[642] Dr. Lushington said: "if that party [the plaintiff] derives incidentally a greater benefit than mere indemnification, it arises only from the impossibility of otherwise effecting such indemnification without exposing him to some loss or burden, which the law will not place upon him".[643] Dr. Lushington's view has been followed in some Canadian cases.[644] It was applied by the English Court of Appeal in *Harbutt's "Plasticine" v. Wayne Tank & Pump Co.*[645] a case of loss of a factory building by fire, where Lord Denning said: "True it is that they got new for old; but I do not think the wrongdoer can diminish the claim on that account.[646]

1.2750 This view has been followed in *Bacon v. Cooper (Metals) Ltd.*[647] where the defendant damaged a metal fragmenting machine that included an expensive part called a rotor. Because of the nature of the machine, the rotor, new, had an expected life of only seven years; the one damaged by the defendant had been used for almost half that time. The question was whether an allowance should be made for the benefit to the plaintiff by acquiring a new rotor. Cantley J. found the defendant's argument on this

---

640 See Brown, "Developments in the Law of Damages for Breach of Contract" in *Special Lectures of the Law Society of Upper Canada on Current Problems in the Law of Contracts* (1975), p. 1; Berryman, "Betterment Before Canadian Common Law Courts", 72 Can. Bar Rev. 54 (1993).

641 *North York (City) v. Kert Chemical Industries Inc.* (1985), 33 C.C.L.T. 184 at p. 206 (Ont. H.C.J.) and *James Street Hardware & Furniture Co. v. Spizziri* (1987), 62 O.R. (2d) 385 at pp. 403-4, 43 C.C.L.T. 9 (C.A.), citing this paragraph.

642 (1844), 2 W. Rob. 279, 166 E.R. 759.

643 *Supra*, at p. 281.

644 *National Theatres Ltd. v. Macdonald Consolidated Ltd.*, [1940] 1 W.W.R. 168 (Alta. Dist. Ct.); *The King v. Toronto Transportation Com'n*, [1946] Ex. C.R. 604, [1947] 1 D.L.R. 657, revd on other grounds [1949] S.C.R. 510, [1949] 3 D.L.R. 161; *T. Donovan & Sons Ltd. v. Baker* (1966), 53 M.P.R. 113 (N.B.S.C. App. Div.); *Busenius v. Pott* (1988), 87 A.R. 270 (Q.B.); *Sullivan v. Weis* (1989), 99 A.R. 233 (Q.B.).

645 [1970] 1 Q.B. 447, followed in *The Ship "Dumurra" v. Maritime Telegraph & Telephone Co. Ltd.* (1977), 75 D.L.R. (3d) 766 (Fed. C.A.), leave to appeal to S.C.C. refused June 20, 1977.

646 *Harbutt's "Plasticine", supra*, footnote 645, at p. 468.

647 [1982] 1 All E.R. 397 (Q.B.). In *Nan v. Black Pine Manufacturing Ltd.* (1991), 80 D.L.R. (4th) 153, [1991] 5 W.W.R. 172 (B.C.C.A.), the court allowed the cost of rebuilding a house without deduction on account of "betterment".

point "attractive"[648] and admitted that it would be an "absurd result"[649] to allow the full cost of replacing a rotor that had only a few days of useful life left. Nevertheless he felt bound to allow the full cost of a new rotor unless the result seemed absurd on the particular facts. He also made the point that the plaintiff might not receive the full benefit from the new rotor, because there might well be design changes that could make the machine obsolete within seven years.[650]

1.2760 On the other hand, McCormick states as an uncontroversial proposition that the proper measure of damages is the reasonable cost of repair "less any enhancement, if the repaired article is more valuable than before the accident."[651] Several Canadian cases support this view.[652] In *Wertman v. Fox*,[653] Lennox J. said that the plaintiff (whose car had been damaged) was not to be allowed "to convert his dilapidated vehicle into a new car at the defendant's expense".[654]

1.2770 The latter view seems in principle to be the better one. In the case of destruction of a nineteen-year-old roof (roofs lasting for twenty years), it is hard to resist the conclusion that the plaintiff would be over-compensated if he recovered the full cost of a new roof.[654a] *The "Gazelle"* might be distinguished on the ground that replacing damaged timbers in a ship rarely adds appreciably to the expected life of the ship or, in a practical sense, to her value and therefore that it is of no real benefit to the plaintiff, just as patching

---

648 *Supra*, at p. 400.

649 *Supra*.

650 *Supra*, at pp. 400-401.

651 McCormick, *Handbook on the Law of Damages* (St. Paul, Minn., West Publishing Co., 1935), p. 471.

652 *Reliance Lumber Co. v. Dyck* (1951), 3 W.W.R. (N.S.) 332 (Dist. Ct.); *Dominion Chain Co. Ltd. v. Eastern Construction Co. Ltd.* (1974), 46 D.L.R. (3d) 28 at p. 57, 3 O.R. (2d) 481 (H.C.J.), vard 68 D.L.R. (3d) 385, 12 O.R. (2d) 201 (C.A.), affd [1978] 2 S.C.R. 1346, 84 D.L.R. (3d) 344; *Regnier v. Nelson* (1956), 19 W.W.R. 36 (Man. Q.B.); *Parallel Productions Ltd. v. Goss Contracting Co. Ltd.* (1968), 69 D.L.R. (2d) 609 (B.C.S.C.); *McAlinden v. Lohnes* (1979), 25 N.B.R. (2d) 58 (Q.B.); *Kinnaird v. C. L. Martin & Co. Ltd.* (1969), 7 D.L.R. (3d) 139, [1969] 2 O.R. 817 (C.A.); *Johnston v. Mills* (1917), 37 D.L.R. 767 (Alta. S.C. App. Div.). See also *National Trust Co. Ltd. v. The King*, [1949] 2 D.L.R. 472 (Exch. Ct.); *Church of Scientology of B.C. v. Ahmed* (1983), 146 D.L.R. (3d) 219, 44 B.C.L.R. 297 (S.C.); *Mueller v. Tait* (1993), 33 R.P.R. (2d) 157 (B.C.S.C.); *Upper Lakes Shipping Ltd. v. St. Lawrence Cement Inc.* (1992), 89 D.L.R. (4th) 722 (Ont. C.A.); *Canada (Attorney General) v. Clorey* (1996), 144 Nfld. & P.E.I.R. 132 (P.E.I.S.C.); *Domokos v. Phillips* (1996), 5 R.P.R. (3d) 33 (N.B.Q.B.); *Bookman v. U-Haul Co. (Canada) Ltd.* (2007), 229 O.A.C. 194 (S.C.J. (Div. Ct.)), at paras. 20-21, citing this passage. See *Graham v. Owen* (1987), 25 O.A.C. 280 (Div. Ct.), at p. 281, citing this passage. See also footnote 641, *supra*.

653 (1923), 24 O.W.N. 401 (S.C.), affd 25 O.W.N. 129 (C.A.).

654 *Supra*. See also *Eldridge v. Jellison* (1997), 192 N.B.R. (2d) 337 (Q.B.) (cost of repairing truck based on used not new parts); *Lamont Health Care Centre v. Delnor Construction Ltd.* (2003), 29 Alta. L.R. (4th) 113 (Q.B.) (destruction of building previously scheduled for replacement).

654a *Dartmouth (City) v. Acres Consulting Ltd.* (1995), 138 N.S.R. (2d) 81, 19 C.L.R. (2d) 247 (S.C.). See *Sheds Manor Holdings Ltd. v. Dale Mann Ltd.* (1995), 25 C.L.R. (2d) 290 (Ont. Ct. (Gen. Div.)) (betterment factor offset by other losses).

a coat with new cloth adds nothing to its value. This point has been made in connection with repair of houses.[655]

1.2780 The question cannot be considered in isolation from the cases on mitigation of loss. The general rule is that benefits accruing from making good a loss, if they could not otherwise have been gained by the plaintiff, are to be taken into account to reduce damages. In *British Westinghouse Electric & Manufacturing Co. Ltd. v. Underground Electric Rys. Co. of London, Ltd.,*[656] where a buyer, upon the seller's breach of warranty on the sale of machinery for the buyer's use, purchased substitute machinery that was superior to that originally promised by the seller, the profit derived from the superior machinery was taken into account in reduction of the buyer's damages. Again, in *Erie County Natural Gas & Fuel Co., Ltd. v. Carroll,*[657] the Privy Council held on appeal from the Ontario Court of Appeal that a plaintiff who acquired gas leases to secure a supply of gas in substitution for a supply wrongfully withheld by the defendant was obliged to bring into account profit made on the ultimate disposition of the leases. Otherwise, said Lord Atkinson, the plaintiff would make "a profit by the defendant's breach of their obligation of about $128,965.22, a somewhat grotesque result".[658]

1.2790 These cases seem inconsistent with a rule that improvements to the plaintiff's position by effecting repairs are to be ignored. The increase in the plaintiff's wealth is one that could not have occurred in the absence of the wrong. It is suggested, therefore, that an anticipated benefit accruing to the plaintiff on repairing damaged property ought to be taken into account to reduce damages, with compensation however for the cost to the plaintiff of the unexpected expenditure required.[659]

1.2800 A comparison with the cases on destruction of property supports the same conclusion. If property is wholly destroyed, it is well established that the plaintiff can only recover the value of the property.[660] It would

---

[655] *Barrette v. Franki Compressed Pile Co. of Canada Ltd.*, [1955] 2 D.L.R. 665, [1955] O.R. 413 (H.C.J.); *Jens v. Mannix Co. Ltd.* (1978), 89 D.L.R. (3d) 351 (B.C.S.C.), vard 30 D.L.R. (4th) 250, [1986] 5 W.W.R. 563 (C.A.); *Nan v. Black Pine Manufacturing Ltd.*, *supra*, footnote 647.

[656] [1912] A.C. 673 (H.L.).

[657] [1911] A.C. 105 (P.C.).

[658] *Supra*, at p. 115.

[659] *Lamont Health Care Centre v. Delnor Construction Ltd.* (2003), 29 Alta. L.R. (4th) 113 (Q.B.). See *Bacon v. Cooper (Metals) Ltd.*, [1982] 1 All E.R. 397 (Q.B.), where the result might be justified on the basis that the plaintiff would not (in the light of probable design changes) derive the full benefit from the replacement part. See also the comment on *The "Gazelle"* at 1.2770, *supra*. Non-delivery cases where the buyer is permitted to purchase a more expensive substitute may also be supported on the ground that, whether the purchase is for use or for fulfilling a subcontract, the buyer will rarely acquire any realizable benefit from the superiority of the substitute: *Hinde v. Liddell* (1875), L.R. 10 Q.B. 265; *Blackburn Bobbin Co., Ltd. v. T.W. Allen & Sons, Ltd.*, [1918] 1 K.B. 540. Some leniency may be expected to be exercised in favour of the plaintiff on these questions (see footnote 576, *supra*, and 13.170 - 13.250, *infra*), though not (as suggested in §287 of the first edition of this work) an actual reversal of the onus of proof.

[660] See 1.210, *supra*.

be anomalous if, by categorizing his case as one for repair rather than replacement,[661] the plaintiff were able to put himself in a better position than he would have occupied in the absence of the wrong.

[661] In *Canadian National Railway Co. v. Canadian Steamship Lines Ltd.*, [1949] O.W.N. 583 (H.C.J.), the court took account of depreciation in valuing buildings destroyed by fire. There was no suggestion that the plaintiff could avoid this result by claiming the full cost of repair. The case was approved in *City of Guelph Board of Light & Heat Com'rs v. United Dairy & Poultry Co-operative Ltd.* (1966), 57 D.L.R. (2d) 385 at p. 387, [1966] 2 O.R. 467 (Co. Ct.), affd D.L.R. *loc. cit*, O.R. *loc. cit.* (C.A.).

CHAPTER 2

LOSS OF SERVICES

1. Contracts of Employment and Contracts for Services

2.10 Where an employee fails to render services promised to an employer, damages would, on the general principle of putting the employer in as good a position as would have been occupied if the contract had been performed, be measured by the value of the promised services minus the remuneration due to the employee (assuming this to be unpaid).[1] The same principle applies whether the contract is technically an employment contract or some other form of contract of services. The difference between a contract of service and a contract for services is often of legal importance but from the point of view of compensation there is a close similarity. In either case the complaint of the innocent party is of deprivation of the value of services that should have been rendered.

2.20 The usual measure of the value of services will be the cost of purchasing a substitute if the plaintiff actually procures substitute services.[2] The measure of damages will be the difference between the value and the price. In the previous chapter the problem was discussed of the proper measure of damages in cases where the defendant had failed in breach of contract to repair or replace property.[3] These cases may all be regarded, from the compensatory point of view, as contracts for services. Although the *prima facie* measure of damages is the cost of remedying the deficiency, that measure will not always be used where the cost is out of all proportion to the value to be attained by doing the work. The same conclusion seems appropriate where no improvement to property is in question. Thus, the plaintiff would not be entitled to damages measured by the cost of hiring substitute services if circumstances had occurred that made the employment of those services useless. As in the property cases, however, if the plaintiff has a legitimate non-pecuniary interest in actually procuring the services and is likely to do so, the cost of the substitute will be allowed. The case might

---

1 This is most clearly established in building contracts: *e.g.*, *Armstrong v. Roslyn Park Land Co.* (1951), 4 W.W.R. (N.S.) 270 (B.C.S.C.). See *Cotter v. General Petroleums Ltd.*, [1951] S.C.R. 154 at p. 175, [1950] 4 D.L.R. 609 at p. 628, *per* Cartwright J.

2 *Richards v. Hayward* (1841), 2 Man. & G. 574, 133 E.R. 875 (substitute ship's surgeon employed for higher allowance against fare than agreed with defendant); *Detroit Football Co. v. Dublinski* (1957), 7 D.L.R. (2d) 9, [1957] O.R. 58 (C.A.).

3 See 1.2310-1.2480, *supra*.

be supposed of the hire of persons to stand in the plaintiff's garden wearing 18th century dress. If the purpose were to make a movie that had subsequently been cancelled, the plaintiff would not be entitled to hire substitutes at the defendant's expense, or to obtain damages measured by the cost of doing so. But if the purpose were to entertain the plaintiff's guests at a fancy dress party, the plaintiff would, it is submitted, be entitled to recover from the defendant the reasonable expense of hiring substitutes assuming this had actually been done or was likely to be done.

2.30 An alternative measure of the value of services is the benefit that the plaintiff would have derived. Profits lost by reason of the defendant's failure to provide services, although in principle recoverable, are in practice difficult to establish. The plaintiff's claim, even if problems of factual causation are overcome, is very vulnerable to the rules of remoteness and mitigation. This is illustrated by *Anglia Television Ltd. v. Reed*,[4] where the defendant wrongfully repudiated his promise to play the leading role in a television film to be made by the plaintiff. The plaintiff on the defendant's default cancelled the film altogether and claimed to recover its expenses. The primary reason why no claim was made for lost profits is probably that the plaintiff could not have established as a matter of fact that the film would have been successful if the defendant had performed his contract. Lord Denning said: "Anglia Television do not claim their profit. They cannot say what their profit would have been on this contract if Mr. Reed had come here and performed it."[5] And indeed the description of the plot does not sound very promising: "Anglia Television Ltd., the plaintiffs, were minded in 1968 to make a film of a play for television entitled 'The Man in the Wood.' It portrayed an American man married to an English woman. The American has an adventure in an English wood. The film was to last for 90 minutes."[6] But even supposing that a probable profit could have been established in fact that was not too remote, as a matter of law, the plaintiff would ordinarily be expected to mitigate the loss by hiring a substitute actor rather than abandoning so successful a movie altogether. The two points are connected. If the enterprise is profitable, it will usually be feasible to replace the defendant's services; if the project is abandoned on the defendant's default, the probability is that it cannot have been very profitable in the first place.

2.40 A third possible measure of damages is wasted expense. In *Anglia Television v. Reed* the plaintiff claimed, instead of anticipated profits,

---

4 [1972] 1 Q.B. 60 (C.A.).

5 *Supra*, at p. 63.

6 *Supra*, at p. 62.

its expenses, and succeeded in recovering expenses incurred both before and after the contract was made on the ground that these were "wasted" by the defendant's breach.[7] A critic wrote that the result put the plaintiff in a better position than it was in before the contract was made (for a portion of the expenses held to be recoverable had already been incurred before the defendant agreed to appear),[8] and also in a better position than if the contract had been performed (for it was never established that the film would have been profitable).[9] A further ground of criticism is that the plaintiff had not in fact established that its expenses had been "wasted", for the use of the word implies that they would have been saved if the defendant had not broken his contract. But this would only have been so if the film would have been profitable or at least would have broken even, the very thing that the plaintiff failed to prove. The result may perhaps be defended, however, on the basis of a presumption that (unless the defendant proves the contrary) the film would at least have broken even, and this approach would justify recovery of the pre-contract as well as the post-contract expenses. On this basis the plaintiff's recovery is not a recovery of expenses incurred in reliance on the contract (for these would not include the pre-contract expenses) but of a limited measure of the plaintiff's "expectation interest", assumed (until the defendant proves the contrary[10]) to amount to a sufficient sum to cover the total expenses. In a subsequent British Columbia case, *Bowlay Logging Ltd. v. Domtar Ltd.*,[11] it was held that reliance expenses could only be recovered to the extent that they would have been covered by profits in the absence of the defendant's breach, for otherwise the plaintiff would be in a better position by recovery of damages than he would have been in on performance of the contract.[12]

2. Action for Loss of Employee's Services

2.50 The action for loss of services (*actio per quod servitium amisit*), often simply called the action *per quod*, is an action available to an employer, husband, or parent for the loss of services of an employee, wife, or child where this is caused by wrongful injury. The action is widely regarded as antiquated and anomalous, resting, as it does, on the theory of the plaintiff's proprietary interest in the services of the injured person.[13] As

---

7 *Supra*, at p. 64.

8 Pre-contract expenses were disallowed in *Hodges v. Earl of Litchfield* (1835), 1 Bing. (N.C.) 492, 131 E.R. 1207, but allowed in *Lloyd v. Stanbury*, [1971] 2 All E.R. 267 (Ch. Div.).

9 Ogus, Note, "Damages for Pre-Contract Expenditure", 35 Mod. L.R. 423 (1972).

10 The onus of proof of this issue was placed on the defendant in *Bowlay Logging Ltd. v. Domtar Ltd.* (1982), 135 D.L.R. (3d) 179, [1982] 6 W.W.R. 528 (B.C.C.A.), and *CCC Films (London) Ltd. v. Impact Quadrant Films Ltd.*, [1985] Q.B. 16.

11 (1978), 87 D.L.R. (3d) 325 (B.C.S.C.), affd 135 D.L.R. (3d) 179 (C.A.).

12 See 5.200-5.250, *infra*.

13 See Fleming, *The Law of Torts*, 9th ed. (Sydney, Law Book Co., 1998), pp. 723, 751-2.

has often been pointed out, this theory is barely compatible with the general view of employment. Still less is the notion of the husband's proprietary interest in his wife's services easily compatible with modern views of family relationships.[14]

2.60 In *Inland Revenue Com'rs v. Hambrook*,[15] the English Court of Appeal very drastically reduced the scope of an employer's action by holding that it was available only in cases of injury to domestic servants. Some Canadian cases have followed *Hambrook*,[16] but the weight of authority appears to be against acceptance of this restriction.[17] Some uncertainty remains, however, about whether high level employees are included within the principle.[18]

2.70 It might be thought that wrongfully killing an employee would be the clearest possible case of depriving the employer of the employee's services, but in fact the action *per quod* is not available in case of wrongful death,[19] nor is there any equivalent common law action.[20] The only available action for the death of a person (except by the estate) is

---

14 See Hansen and Mullan, "Private Corporations in Canada, Principles of Recovery for the Tortious Disablement of Shareholder/Employees" in *Studies in Canadian Tort Law*, ed. Klar (Toronto, Butterworths, 1977), p. 215, at p. 242: "It is rare to find a judgment, even when the *per quod* action is recognized, where the court does not condemn the action as anomalous, state that it should be confined within narrow limits, and even go as far as recommending legislative abolition." The action has been abolished in the United Kingdom (*Administration of Justice Act 1982*), in British Columbia (*Law and Equity Act*, s. 63) and in New Brunswick (*Law Reform Act* of 1993, s. 1(1)). The Ontario Law Reform Commission has recommended abolition (*Report on Compensation for Personal Injuries and Death* (1987), pp. 66-9).

15 [1956] 2 Q.B. 641 (C.A.).

16 *Pagan v. Leifer* (1969), 6 D.L.R. (3d) 714 (Man. Q.B.); *Swift Canadian Co. Ltd. v. Bolduc* (1961), 29 D.L.R. (2d) 651 (N.S.S.C.); *Flakstad v. Wright*, [1971] 5 W.W.R. 697 (B.C.S.C.); *Schwartz v. Hotel Corp. of America (Manitoba) Ltd.* (1970), 15 D.L.R. (3d) 764 (Man. Q.B.), affd on other grounds 20 D.L.R. (3d) 759 (C.A.).

17 *The King v. Richardson*, [1948] S.C.R. 57, [1948] 2 D.L.R. 305; *The King ex rel. A.-G. Can. v. Canadian Pacific Ry.*, [1947] S.C.R. 185, [1947] 2 D.L.R. 1; *Nykorak v. A.-G. Can.*, [1962] S.C.R. 331, 33 D.L.R. (2d) 373; *Genereux v. Peterson Howell & Heather (Canada) Ltd.* (1972), 34 D.L.R. (3d) 614, [1973] 2 O.R. 558 (C.A.); *Ward v. Jaques*, [1976] 3 W.W.R. 400 (Alta. S.C.T.D.); *Nugent v. Board of Rosetown School Unit No. 43 of Saskatchewan* (1975), 60 D.L.R. (3d) 357 (Sask. Q.B.), affd 79 D.L.R. (3d) 394, [1977] 5 W.W.R. 224 (C.A.); *Kneeshaw and Latendorff* (1965), 54 D.L.R. (2d) 84 (Alta. S.C.); *Bursey v. Avis Transport of Canada Ltd.* (1970), 1 Nfld. & P.E.I.R. 131 (Nfld. S.C.T.D.); *Chambers v. Miles*, [1978] 3 W.W.R. 188 (B.C.S.C.); *LeBlanc v. Fougere* (1977), 24 N.S.R. (2d) 675 (S.C.T.D.); *Davidson v. Pun* (1982), 137 D.L.R. (3d) 181 (B.C.S.C.), revd on other grounds 57 B.C.L.R. 240, 30 C.C.L.T. 316 (C.A.); *R. v. Buchinsky*, [1983] 1 S.C.R. 481, 145 D.L.R. (3d) 1; *Canada (Attorney General) v. Lavery* (1989), 64 D.L.R. 420 (4th) (B.C.S.C.), vard 76 D.L.R. (4th) 97, 52 B.C.L.R. (2d) 273 (C.A.), leave to appeal to S.C.C. refused 83 D.L.R. (4th) vii, 136 N.R. 416*n*; *Canada (Attorney General) v. Szaniszlo* (1985), 25 D.L.R. (4th) 606, 69 B.C.L.R. 96 (S.C.).

18 See Hansen and Mullan, *op. cit.*, footnote 14, at p. 222. There seems, however, no persuasive reason for excluding high level employees, whose injury may cause the greater loss to the employer.

19 Hansen and Mullan, *op. cit.*, footnote 14, at pp. 235-6.

20 See 6.10, *infra*.

under *Lord Campbell's Act* by the relations named in that Act.[21] This adds to the anomalous nature of the action *per quod*.

2.80 The action is derivative in the sense that the defendant's conduct must be wrongful vis-à-vis the employee.[22] There has been a difference of judicial opinion on the question of contributory negligence. It has been held in England,[23] Nova Scotia,[24] Australia,[25] and New Zealand[26] that contributory negligence of a wife is no defence to a husband's action for loss of consortium since the husband's action is not derivative but independent. On the other hand, a number of Canadian decisions and dicta, many dealing with a parent's action for injury to a child, have gone the other way[27] and in *Enridge v. Copp*,[28] Aikins J. said that the "mainstream of Canadian authority"[29] was that the action was derivative and so affected by the contributory negligence of the wife. On balance this seems the preferable view. It is suggested below that the action *per quod* in all its forms should be replaced by a personal action by the injured person.[30] This assimilation will be impeded if larger damages are recoverable by the husband than by the wife. To hold the husband unaffected by the wife's contributory negligence indeed accentuates the proprietary nature of the action, by treating the injury to a husband's rights as independent of the injury to the wife.

2.90 Other legal questions may turn on the derivative nature of the action. There is uncertainty on the question of limitation periods.[31] On the question of double recovery it has been assumed that recovery or settlement by the employee for the full value of his services would extinguish the employer's action,[32] and that recovery by the employer would extinguish the employee's action.[33]

---

21 See 6.10-6.1090, *infra*.

22 *A.-G. Can. v. Jackson*, [1946] S.C.R. 489, [1946] 2 D.L.R. 481; *Scott v. Marshall* (1965), 55 D.L.R. (2d) 58 (B.C.S.C.).

23 *Mallett v. Dunn*, [1949] 2 K.B. 180.

24 *MacDonald v. McNeil*, [1953] 1 D.L.R. 755 and [1953] 2 D.L.R. 248 (N.S.S.C.).

25 *Curran v. Young* (1965), 112 C.L.R. 99.

26 *Cook v. Wright*, [1967] N.Z.L.R. 1034 (S.C.), at p. 1037.

27 *McKittrick v. Byers*, [1926] 1 D.L.R. 342, 58 O.L.R. 158 (S.C. App. Div.); *Dority v. Ottawa Roman Catholic Separate Schools Trustees*, [1930] 3 D.L.R. 633, 65 O.L.R. 360 (S.C. App. Div.); *Graham v. Toronto Transportation Com'n*, [1945] O.W.N. 904 (H.C.J.), affd [1946] O.W.N. 274 (C.A.); *Trapp v. Hnatuk* (1976), 71 D.L.R. (3d) 63 (Fed. C.A.); *McLaughlin v. Long*, [1927] S.C.R. 303 at p. 311, [1927] 2 D.L.R. 186 at p. 191; *Oliver Blais Co. Ltd. v. Yachuk*, [1946] S.C.R. 1 at p. 17, [1946] 1 D.L.R. 5 at pp. 18-19, revd on other grounds [1949] A.C. 386, [1949] 3 D.L.R. 1 (P.C.). In *Whitehouse v. Fearnley* (1964), 47 D.L.R. (2d) 472 (B.C.S.C.), contributory negligence was not pleaded against the parent.

28 (1966), 57 D.L.R. (2d) 239 (B.C.S.C.).

29 *Supra*, at p. 253.

30 See 2.130, 3.760-3.830, *infra*.

31 See Hansen and Mullan, "Private Corporations in Canada, Principles of Recovery for the Tortious Disablement of Shareholder Employees" in *Studies in Canadian Tort Law*, ed. Klar (Toronto, Butterworths, 1977), p. 241. *The King v. Richardson*, [1948] S.C.R. 57, [1948] 2 D.L.R. 305.

32 See Hansen and Mullan, *op. cit.*, footnote 31, at p. 232.

33 See *Lee v. Sheard*, [1956] 1 Q.B. 192 (C.A.), at p. 195, *per* Denning L.J., quoted in

2.100 The action being one for loss of services, the basic measure of damages would be expected to be the value of the services to the plaintiff. As appeared in the earlier discussion of actions by employers against employees, there are various ways in which the value of services can be measured. One measure is cost of replacement; another is the loss of profit ensuing on the loss of the services; a third measure is the expense, such as continuing wages, that can be said to have been wasted by the employee's disability during the period of their payment. Each of these measures offers a theoretical equivalent to the value of the employee's services. Each aims at putting the employer in the position that would have been occupied if the wrong had not been done. They are therefore, logically, alternative and not cumulative.

2.110 In *Genereux v. Peterson Howell & Heather (Canada) Ltd.*[34] where the plaintiff was a solicitor and the injured employee was his wife who worked for no pay, the court permitted recovery of the cost of hiring a substitute during the wife's disability, but disallowed the further sum claimed for loss of profits. Kelly J.A. said: "Save in exceptional circumstances, the damages recoverable by the master are the same as those which in a proper case would be recovered by the servant."[35] This view paves the way to the eventual replacement of the action *per quod* by a right of recovery in the injured person. If the injured person recovers the full value of the lost earning capacity, there seems no justification for any further recovery by the employer, for the complaint of the employer is that a contractual relationship has been interfered with, and negligent interference with contract is not generally actionable.[36] It seems, however, that Kelly J.A. did not intend to lay down an absolute rule on the matter, for he evidently considered that the injured employee would not have recovered the value of her services in her own right.[37] He added, also, as a reason for denying recovery of lost profit that it was too remote.[38] The wages paid to an employee are often a fair measure of the value of the services; if the wages are continued during the employee's disability, it can be fairly said that the employer has lost the amount of the wages.[39] If the wages are not

---

Sullivan v. Riverside Rentals Ltd. (1973), 47 D.L.R. (3d) 293 (N.S.S.C. App. Div.), at p. 309, *per* Coffin J.A.

34 (1972), 34 D.L.R. (3d) 614, [1973] 2 O.R. 558 (C.A.). See also *Kneeshaw v. Latendorff* (1965), 54 D.L.R. (2d) 84 (Alta. S.C.).

35 *Genereux, supra*, footnote 34, at p. 626 D.L.R. See *Vaccaro v. Giruzzi* (1992), 93 D.L.R. (4th) 180 (Ont. Ct. (Gen. Div.)).

36 See Fleming, *The Law of Torts*, 9th ed. (Sydney, Law Book Co., 1998), pp. 761-2.

37 *Genereux, supra*, footnote 34, at p. 626 D.L.R., describing the case as "unusual" and implying a departure from the principle quoted at footnote 35, *supra*. But see 3.760-3.830, *infra*, on the measure of damages for loss of earning capacity of non-earners.

38 *Genereux, supra*, at p. 627 D.L.R. It was this point that was relied on in *Ward v. Jaques*, [1976] 3 W.W.R. 400 (Alta. S.C.T.D.), and *Racicot v. Saunders* (1979), 103 D.L.R. (3d) 567, 27 O.R. (2d) 15 (H.C.J.).

39 *Racicot v. Saunders, supra*, footnote 36; *Nugent v. Board of Rosetown School Unit No. 43 of Saskatchewan* (1977), 79 D.L.R. (3d) 394 (Sask. C.A.). But in *Davidson v. Pun* (1984), 57 B.C.L.R. 240, 30 C.C.L.T. 136 (C.A.), it was held that statutory sick pay was payment in the nature of insurance and not recoverable by an employer from a tortfeasor.

continued, wages saved will affect the value of the services lost. If the basis of recovery is the value of lost services, proof that the value of the employee's services was less than the amount of his wages ought, theoretically, to reduce damages, but the defendant would face a heavy onus of proof in seeking to show that the employee was not worthy of hire. Where the employee is underpaid, as in *Genereux v. Peterson Howell & Heather* where the injured person worked for nothing, the court will award the cost of hiring a substitute. Loss of profits, although refused in *Genereux* partly on the ground of remoteness, has been allowed in some cases.[40] It seems that a claim for lost profits, although in principle a possible measure of the value of the injured person's services, is, in practice, as in the employment contract cases,[41] vulnerable to difficulties of proof and to the rules of remoteness and mitigation. The defendant will often be able to argue that if great profits were available to be made from the services, their loss should have been avoided by employment of a substitute, the cost of which represents the limit of the defendant's liability. Where the services of the injured person are so specialised that no substitute is available that can avoid the loss of profits, the defendant will often be able to support an argument that the loss is too remote as in the *Genereux* case itself.

2.120 Medical expenses paid by an employer on behalf of an employee or by a husband or father on behalf of his wife or children, raise rather different considerations. Here, the claim is not for the value of services lost, but for an expense caused to one person by an injury to another. The claim will be discussed below in that context.[42] It is worth saying here, however, that logic and simplicity strongly favour permitting the injured person to recover such expense in that person's own right, for the need for medical treatment is surely a loss suffered by the injured person alone and the cost of meeting that need, therefore, is a cost that falls upon the injured person, whether or not it is subsequently made good by a third party.[43]

2.130 The action *per quod* in all its forms is usually agreed to be anomalous.[44] The only arguments for supporting its continued existence run along the lines that a tortfeasor who has impaired a person's earning capacity ought to pay damages to someone for the loss.[45] The action *per quod* can be supported, therefore, if the law is that the injured person cannot recover. But surely a much better solution would be for the injured person to

40 *Mankin v. Scala Theodrome Co. Ltd.*, [1947] 1 K.B. 257; *Bursey v. Avis Transport of Canada Ltd.* (1970), 1 Nfld. & P.E.I.R. 131 (Nfld. S.C.T.D.); *Gibson v. Dool* (1969), 12 D.L.R. (3d) 325, [1970] 3 O.R. 60 (Dist. Ct.); *Bermann v. Occhipinti*, [1954] 1 D.L.R. 560, [1953] O.R. 1035 (H.C.J.).

41 See 2.30, *supra*.

42 See 5.1300-5.1340, *infra*.

43 See 3.430, *infra*.

44 See footnote 14, *supra*.

45 See Parsons, Note, "Loss of Consortium", 18 Mod. L.R. 514 (1955).

recover in her own right for loss of earning capacity. It will be seen that discussion of the usefulness of the action is intimately connected with the measure of damages in the injured person's own action against the wrongdoer. If the injured person can recover in full for the loss of earning capacity, as it is argued later that she should, whether or not she works for money remuneration and whether or not the loss is made good by continuation of wages, gifts, insurance or social welfare,[46] it follows that the wrongdoer will always be bound to make full compensation to the injured person. In that case, the only substantial argument for retaining the action *per quod* disappears. If it is objected that recovery by the employee for loss that has been made good will over-compensate, the answer is that giving to the employee the initial right to recover from the wrongdoer does not determine the ultimate disposition of the proceeds of recovery. A number of devices, including subrogation, creation of a trust, and requiring an undertaking by the plaintiff to pay over the damages to a third party, can be employed to prevent double recovery,[47] and the appropriateness of such devices, if disputed, is more conveniently determined in a framework where the wrongdoer has to pay in full (and so a fund exists to which rival claims can be made), than in a framework where the wrongdoer can only be made to pay at all upon the bringing of an action of very doubtful status and scope, not applicable to all relevant cases, everywhere regarded as anomalous and obsolete, and abolished in some of its forms in various jurisdictions.

3. Action for Loss of Spouse's Services

2.140 A husband was entitled at common law to recover damages for loss of his wife's services consequent on injury to her.[48] Damages were usually measured, where the wife was resident in the home, by the reasonable cost of securing a substitute housekeeper.[49] The action was available to a husband only,[50] and its survival is undoubtedly out of keeping with the modern view of family relationships.[51] The appropriate solution, as elsewhere, appears to be to permit the injured person to recover in full in her own right for lost earning capacity,[52] with the consequence that the

46 See 3.760-3.830, 3.1610-3.1640, *infra*.

47 See 3.1540, 3.1630-3.1640, *infra*.

48 *Lawrence v. Biddle*, [1966] 2 Q.B. 504; *Cutts v. Chumley*, [1967] 1 W.L.R. 742 (Q.B.); *Toohey v. Hollier* (1955), 92 C.L.R. 618; *Kerr v. T. Eaton Co. Ltd.* (1958), 14 D.L.R. (2d) 464 (Sask. C.A.); *Corkill v. Vancouver Recreational Parks Ltd.*, [1933] 1 W.W.R. 413 (B.C.S.C.); *Goldberg v. McInnis* (1959), 19 D.L.R. (2d) 306 (Sask. Q.B.); *Fostey v. Moore's Taxi (1961) Ltd.*, [1973] 1 W.W.R. 673 (Man. Q.B.). See 2.160-2.180, *infra*.

49 See *Cutts v. Chumley*, *supra*, footnote 48.

50 *Best v. Samuel Fox Ltd.*, [1952] A.C. 716 (H.L.); *Dvorkin v. Stuart*, [1971] 2 W.W.R. 70 (Alta. S.C.); *Hynes v. Coffill* (1978), 30 N.S.R. (2d) 204 (S.C.T.D.). See 2.160, *infra*.

51 Abolition was recommended by the Ontario Law Reform Commission, *Report on Family Law*, 1969, Part 1, p. 101, but the *Dower and Miscellaneous Abolition Act* (Ont.), s. 69(3), speaks only of "consortium" not "servitium". See also 5.1340, *infra*.

52 See 3.760-3.830, *infra*.

husband's action will become obsolete. It will be open, it is submitted, to a court, even where the action has not been abolished by legislation, to hold that nominal damages only are available to the husband, on the ground that the injured wife would recover full compensation for the loss of her earning capacity, which presumably will be available for the purchase of any substitute housekeeping services.

4. Loss of Consortium

2.150 Closely linked with the husband's action for loss of services is the action for loss of consortium (*per quod consortium amisit*). Again the action is based on proprietary notions and, at common law, is available to the husband only.[53] The action has often been called anomalous, and in *Montreal Tramways Co. v. Deeks*,[54] the Supreme Court of Canada said that it was not to be extended. Some Canadian courts have accordingly held that no action lies for partial loss of consortium;[55] others have held that an action does lie for partial loss,[56] while usually insisting that the amounts to be awarded should be moderate.[57] The Supreme Court of Canada, in summing up the position at common law, has given its support to the latter view:

> It is fair ... to say that a review of the authorities on the common law action leads to the conclusion that judicial opinion in this country has been, on balance, that the remedy is open to husbands only (though there are cases to the contrary);[58] that the remedy is anomalous in today's world and

53 *Best v. Samuel Fox Ltd., supra*, footnote 50. See Popescul, "Action per Quod Consortium Amisit", 43 Sask. Law Rev. 27 (1979). The unequal treatment of the sexes was criticized by Addy J. in *Canestraro v. Larade* (1972), 28 D.L.R. (3d) 290 at p. 296, [1972] 3 O.R. 382 (H.C.J.). In *Power v. Moss* (1986), 61 Nfld. & P.E.I.R. 5, 38 C.C.L.T. 31 (Nfld. S.C.T.D.), the action was extended to both spouses. In *Shkwarchuk v. Hansen* (1984), 34 Sask. R. 211, 30 C.C.L.T. 121 (Q.B.); *Blotnicky v. Oliver* (1988), 84 N.S.R. (2d) 14 (S.C.); *Baker v. Pleasant* (1989), 89 N.S.R. (2d) 301 (S.C.); it was held to be available to neither spouse.

54 [1953] 2 S.C.R. 404, [1954] 1 D.L.R. 583.

55 *Schendel v. Peggie* (1955), 16 W.W.R. 499 (Man. C.A.); *Forstner v. Midgley*, [1958] O.W.N. 100 (H.C.J.); *Bates v. Fraser* (1963), 38 D.L.R. (2d) 30, [1963] 1 O.R. 539 (H.C.J.); *V v. C* (1972), 26 D.L.R. (3d) 527, [1972] 2 O.R. 723 (H.C.J.); *Canestraro v. Larade, supra*, footnote 53; *Szmerski v. Robinson* (1961), 36 W.W.R. 46 (Man. Q.B.); *Martens v. Briliz* (1964), 44 D.L.R. (2d) 13 (Alta. S.C.), taking the same view of the Alberta *Domestic Relations Act*, s. 46(1), is now impliedly overruled by *Woelk v. Halvorson, infra*, footnote 59.

56 *Honsey v. Sykes* (1963), 37 D.L.R. (2d) 225 (Sask. C.A.); *Finney v. Callender* (1971), 20 D.L.R. (3d) 301 (B.C.C.A.), affd [1971] S.C.R. v, 21 D.L.R. (3d) 640*n*; *Hambrook v. Gamble*, [1972] 5 W.W.R. 271 (Alta. S.C.T.D.); *Dietelbach v. Public Trustee* (1973), 37 D.L.R. (3d) 621 (B.C.S.C.); *MacKinnon v. Coldwell* (1973), 36 D.L.R. (3d) 709 (N.S.S.C.T.D.); *Urbanski v. Patel* (1978), 84 D.L.R. (3d) 650 (Man. Q.B.) (award described as "solatium"); *Gardner v. McCarthy* (1960), 26 D.L.R. (2d) 603 (B.C.S.C.); *Guimont v. Williston* (1980), 30 N.B.R. (2d) 178 (C.A.), leave to appeal to S.C.C. refused 34 N.R. 356*n*; *Armstrong's Estate v. Dionne* (1978), 23 N.B.R. (2d) 420 (S.C.); *Aynsley v. Toronto General Hospital* (1967), 66 D.L.R. (2d) 575, [1968] 1 O.R. 425 (H.C.J.), vard 7 D.L.R. (3d) 193, [1969] 2 O.R. 829 (C.A.), affd [1972] S.C.R. 435 *sub nom.* Toronto General Hospital v. Matthews, 25 D.L.R. (3d) 241.

57 See *Dallas v. Hinton*, [1937] 4 D.L.R. 260 at p. 272 (B.C.C.A.), affd [1938] S.C.R. 244, [1938] 2 D.L.R. 673, *sub nom. Dallas and Hinton v. Home Oil Distributors Ltd.* (single sum for loss of consortium and servitium), followed in *Hamilton v. Hayes* (1962), 36 D.L.R. (2d) 687 (B.C.S.C.).

should not be extended; when applied, damage awards, except in exceptional cases, should be modest; and that an impairment, as distinct from a destruction of the *consortium*, should suffice to found the action.[59]

2.160 The action has been abolished in several Canadian jurisdictions.[60] But in Alberta,[61] the *Domestic Relations Act* has, in effect, codified and extended the action by giving a cause of action to either spouse for deprivation of the "society and comfort" of the other. In *Woelk v. Halvorson*,[62] the Supreme Court of Canada restored a trial judgment of $10,000 to a wife whose husband had undergone a personality change as the result of an injury. The court said that the action, in its statutory form, applied to impairment as well as destruction of consortium, was not to be regarded as anomalous, and not to be restricted by the award of insignificant levels of damages.

2.170 This leaves the position in other jurisdictions a little uncertain. It is submitted that the preferable rule is that an injured person should be able to recover, in his own right, the full loss caused by the injury. If an injured person of either sex, whether or not resident in the home, is able to recover in full for lost earning capacity, as is recommended elsewhere,[63] it is submitted that there is little justification for a separate action by the uninjured spouse. Even if the common law action were extended to both sexes, there would be difficulties, in the light of modern family relationships, in restricting recovery to spouses in the strict sense. It is suggested, therefore, that the most satisfactory solution, in jurisdictions where the common law action survives, would be to award only nominal damages, on the ground that full compensation can be made to the injured person in her own right, out of which she can make financial provision for her spouse as she sees fit.

[*The next page is* 2-11]

58 Examples appear to be scarce. In *Drewry v. Towns* (1951), 2 W.W.R. (N.S.) 217 (Man. K.B.), a wife's action for loss of consortium was dismissed without reference to any rule excluding such actions altogether.

59 *Woelk v. Halvorson*, [1980] 2 S.C.R. 430 at p. 438, 114 D.L.R. (3d) 385 at p. 391. This was accepted in *Stein v. Sobczak* (1981), 9 Man. R. (2d) 49 (C.A.), as impliedly overruling *Schendel v. Peggie, supra*, footnote 55.

60 *Dower and Miscellaneous Abolition Act* (Ont.), s. 69(3); *Family Relations Act* (B.C.), s. 75(1); *Equality of Status Act* (Man.), s. 1(1)(c); *Equality of Status of Married Persons Act* (Sask.), s. 6. In Ontario, however, a new action was substituted. See 5.1330-5.1340, 6.330-6.7000, *infra*.

61 *Domestic Relations Act*, s. 46(1).

62 *Supra*, footnote 59. See also *McDonald v. Nguyen* (1991), 3 Alta. L.R. (3d) 27, 138 A.R. 81 (Q.B.); *Benstead v. Murphy* (1994), 23 Alta. L.R. (3d) 251, 157 A.R. 198 (C.A.) (loss of housekeeping capacity); *Joyce v. Canadian Pacific Hotels Corp.* (1994), 26 Alta. L.R. (3d) 72, 161 A.R. 53 (Q.B.); *Phillips v. Rost* (1996), 185 A.R. 241, 40 Alta. L.R. (3d) 246 (Q.B.). See also *Herman v. Alberta (Public Trustee)* (2005), 46 Alta. L.R. (4th) 330 (Q.B.).

63 See 3.760-3.830, *infra*.

2.180 In Ontario, the *Family Law Reform Act, 1978*, in abolishing the action for loss of consortium, introduced an action for the benefit of all the relatives eligible to claim in case of wrongful death for pecuniary loss caused by non-fatal injuries to other persons, including an amount to compensate for loss of guidance care and companionship. In *Zik v. High*,[64] $1,500 was awarded to a husband, and $1,000 to each of two children, for loss of companionship of a wife and mother; her injuries did not, it seems, prevent her from being physically present with her family, but they prevented her from performing some services and imposed a "strain on the relationship". J. Holland J. commented that:

> . . . s. 60 of the *Family Law Reform Act, 1978* cries out for the exercise of judicial restraint in the general interest of the public in the assessment of damages consequent upon an injury to another as in this case. I say this because uncontrolled by such restraint the ceiling under the heading of loss of guidance, care and companionship for an award could be unlimited.[65]

The operation and scope of this provision is further discussed below, in the context of fatal accident claims.[66]

5. Enticement, Seduction and Harbouring

2.190 These torts are also generally regarded as obsolete and have been abolished in some jurisdictions insofar as they affect family relationships.[67] So far as employees are concerned, the actions have in effect been superseded by the tort of inducing breach of contract, discussed below.[68] The gist of the plaintiff's complaint is for loss of services and the appropriate measure of damages, therefore, would seem to be, as in the case of the action for loss of services, the cost of replacement. In *Judge v. Smith*,[69] it was held that compensatory damages only were to be awarded, although $6,500 was allowed despite the absence of proof of substantial financial loss.

6. Loss of Child's Services

2.200 The action *per quod servitium amisit* is available at common law to a parent, in the case of injury to a child, for loss of services.[70] It was held in *Hall v. Hollander*[71] that the relationship of the plaintiff to the injured

64 (1981), 35 O.R. (2d) 226 (H.C.J.).
65 *Supra*, at p. 237.
66 See 6.330-6.390, *infra*.
67 *Dower and Miscellaneous Abolition Act* (Ont.), s. 69(2); *Family Relations Act* (B.C.), s. 123(2)(a), (b); *Administration of Justice Act 1982* (U.K.); *Equity of Status Act* (Man.), s. 1(1)(b).
68 See 5.260-5.300, *infra*.
69 (1961), 30 D.L.R. (2d) 521 (B.C.S.C.).
70 The action is abolished in Ontario (*Dower and Miscellaneous Abolition Act* (Ont.), s. 69(4)) and in England (*Administration of Justice Act 1982*).
71 (1825), 4 B. & C. 660, 107 E.R. 1206.

child was not enough; loss of services must actually be proved. As in the other cases discussed above, the preferable solution appears to be to permit the child to recover in the child's own right the whole lost earning capacity, including the full value of such services as might be rendered gratuitously by a child to parents. The effect would then be that nominal damages only would be recoverable by the parent.

7. Inducing Breach of Contract

2.210 The old action for harbouring and enticing servants has now been effectively replaced by the tort of inducing breach of contract. Damages have been said to be at large.[72] The aspect of the claim considered here is the claim for loss of services (including employment contracts and other contracts for the supply of services), and, it is suggested, the same principles are applicable as have been earlier discussed. Thus, if a substitute is available, the measure of damages will be the cost of securing it. As an alternative, wasted expenses should in principle be allowable, as, for example, wages paid to an employee in advance, or expenses incurred in preparation for an enterprise to which the services are essential. Loss of profits, as was earlier argued, is a third possible measure of the value of an employee's services.[73] Whereas in actions against employees and negligent injurers, loss of profits will be difficult to establish, it is otherwise in actions for inducing breach of contract. The very fact that the defendant has deliberately induced the breach usually means that the employee's services are unique (often the case will be one for specific relief against the supplier of the services),[74] and the defendant's motive is commonly to divert profits that would, if the employee's contract had been observed, have enured to the plaintiff. Furthermore, the fact that the plaintiff chooses to sue the defendant for inducing breach rather than relying on his action against the contracting party for breach of contract usually indicates that important interests are at stake.

2.220 Thus, it is not unusual, in the cases of inducing breach of contract, to find damages measured by the profits lost to the plaintiff.[75] One way of measuring such profits, as of measuring the value of property rights that the defendant has taken, would be to ask what sum the plaintiff would rationally have accepted to release the employee from the contract.[76] Any expenses saved by the plaintiff, such as remuneration not paid to the employee, must be deducted in calculating the loss.

---

72 *Exchange Telegraph Co. v. Gregory*, [1896] 1 Q.B. 147 (C.A.), at p. 153.

73 See 2.30, *supra*.

74 See Sharpe, *Injunctions and Specific Performance*, looseleaf ed. (Toronto, Canada Law Book, 1999), 7.540-7.630.

75 *Exchange Telegraph Co. v. Gregory*, *supra*, footnote 72; *Goldsoll v. Goldman*, [1914] 2 Ch. 603.

76 See 9.70-9.130, *infra*.

8. Building Contracts

2.230 Breaches of building contracts involve damage to various kinds of interest. The aspect considered in this chapter is compensation for failure by the contractor to supply the agreed services.

2.240 Building contracts usually involve material as well as services and may be regarded as contracts to effect an improvement in property (that is, the plaintiff's land). The excess cost of procuring substitute services and materials over the contract price is the normal measure of damages.[77] The problems arising where the cost of actually carrying out the building exceeds the value of the improvement to the land (that is, the contract is uneconomic from the plaintiff's point of view) have been discussed in an earlier chapter.[78]

2.250 In *Mertens v. Home Freeholds Co.*,[79] the defendant failed to proceed expeditiously with the building of a house in 1916, with the consequence that building was prohibited under wartime regulations, and the plaintiff was only able to complete in 1919 when the cost of building had risen. The English Court of Appeal held that the proper measure of damages was to be based on the cost of building in 1919 to the point that the defendant would have reached in 1916 if he had acted with dispatch. The court reversed the decision of the Divisional Court which had based damages on the value of the work that would have been completed by the date of the prohibition if the defendant had proceeded with dispatch. The Court of Appeal restored the order of a referee, who had calculated damages by deducting from what it would have cost "to complete the house" the unpaid part of the price, and the value of the work that had been done.

2.260 It would seem that the referee must, by cost "to complete", have meant the total cost of construction, from the beginning to the point that the builder ought to have reached. A builder is entitled to credit for work done. If sound foundations are in place, the builder cannot be made to pay for the plaintiff to build them again. Accordingly the plaintiff's basic entitlement, the cost of providing substitute services, is the price a reasonable builder would charge for finishing the work that the defendant has abandoned. From this should be deducted only the unpaid part of the price. But if, as a starting point, the whole cost of construction is taken, the value must also be deducted of work done by the defendant, that is,

---

77 See *Allen v. Pierce* (1895), 3 Terr. L.R. 319 (S.C.); *Wood v. Stringer* (1890), 20 O.R. 148 (H.C.J.); *Mertens v. Home Freeholds Co.*, [1921] 2 K.B. 526 (C.A.); *Acme Investments Ltd. v. York Structural Steel Ltd.* (1974), 9 N.B.R. (2d) 699 (S.C. App. Div.); *Pitcher v. Alcan Design Homes Ltd.* (1973), 13 N.S.R. (2d) 546 (S.C.T.D.); *City of Moncton v. Aprile Contracting Ltd.* (1980), 29 N.B.R. (2d) 631 (S.C. App. Div.); *Pearson-Burleigh Ltd. v. Pioneer Grain Co.*, [1933] 1 D.L.R. 714 (Man. C.A.); *Spence v. Sunshine Enterprises Ltd.* (1988), 87 N.S.R. (2d) 253, 31 C.L.R. 231 (C.A.).

78 See 1.2310-1.2480, *supra*.

79 *Supra*, footnote 77, followed in *Worrall v. Northwestern Mutual Ins. Co.* (1962), 36 D.L.R. (2d) 752 (B.C.S.C.), as to work left unperformed. For defective work see 1.2310-1.2480, *supra*.

the amount by which the cost of completion is less than the full cost of construction on account of the defendant's work. It should be noted that this is not always the same as calculating the earned portion of the contract price. If the defendant agrees to construct a building for $8,000, making a bad bargain, the reasonable value of the work being $10,000, and defaults having built half, the plaintiff's damages (if half the price has been paid to the defendant) will be $1,000 — enough, when put together with the $4,000 unpaid part of the price, to pay for completion of the building. It would be wrong to value the completed portion of the building at $4,000 (that is, half the contract price) and allow the plaintiff $2,000 in damages, for this would be to give the benefit of the bargain twice over. McGregor criticizes the calculation made in the *Mertens* case on the grounds that the market value of the work already done ought not to be deducted from the cost of completion.[80] If by completion is meant finishing the work, the plaintiff should recover the full cost of its excess over the price. It must be admitted that the word "completion" is ambiguous, but it would seem that the referee must have meant the total cost of construction starting from the beginning and, in that case, it is submitted that deduction of the value of the work done was correct.

2.270 The *Mertens* case also had to deal with the proper date for assessment of the damages. It has been submitted in Chapter 1 that there is merit in fixing an early date for the assessment of damages[81] and the arguments developed there apply equally to building contracts. The *Mertens* case gives support to the general proposition that damages should be assessed at the earliest date at which the reinstatement could reasonably have been carried out. Lord Sterndale M.R. said:

> But the building owner must set to work to build his house at a reasonable time and in a reasonable manner, and is not entitled to delay for several years and then, if prices have gone up, charge the defaulting builder with the increased price. I quite agree . . . that a man is not entitled to gamble on the chance of getting the work done cheaper, and then when it proves to be dearer turn round and charge the defaulter with the enhanced price.[82]

Warrington L.J. said:

> . . . the plaintiff being entitled to what it would have cost him . . . the defendant is entitled to say that the plaintiff must proceed with all reasonable diligence . . .; that he must not wait in the hope that the cost of building materials will go down and then when he finds that they have

80 *McGregor on Damages*, 16th ed. (London, Sweet & Maxwell, 1997), §1142.

81 See 1.650-1.1110, 1.2490-1.2510, *supra*; *Armstrong v. Roslyn Park Land Co.* (1951), 4 W.W.R. (N.S.) 270 (B.C.S.C.).

82 *Mertens, supra*, footnote 77, at pp. 535-6.

> not gone down but have gone up, claim against the defendant the cost of doing the work at that higher price.
>
> That, of course, is right.[83]

The court allowed the higher cost in 1919 only because the plaintiff could not reasonably (or indeed lawfully) have completed the house earlier.

9. Carriage Contracts

2.280 Breach of contracts to carry goods can cause damage to many different interests.[84] The aspect discussed in this chapter is compensation for failure to supply the service.

2.290 In the case of failure to carry goods, the natural measure of damages, on analogy with other cases of loss of services, would be the cost of procuring substitute transport, and this has been usually allowed.[85] Where substitute carriage is not available, another way of valuing the services must be found, and the analogy with other cases of loss of services suggests that one acceptable method of valuation is the profit that the plaintiff would have made if the service had been rendered as agreed. As in the other cases, such a claim will be vulnerable to rules of mitigation and remoteness. Usually the plaintiff can be expected to save the profits by engaging a substitute carrier; if the circumstances are such that a substitute carrier cannot be obtained, the resulting loss will often be too remote.

2.300 Lost profits have been allowed in several cases, calculated, in the case of carriage of goods, by the value the goods would have had at the time and place of due delivery,[86] minus the value of the goods left on the plaintiff's hands and any costs saved by the defendant's breach, such as insurance and freight.[87] By analogy with other loss of service cases, it would seem that, in an appropriate case, another acceptable measure of the value of the service to the plaintiff would be expenses that are wasted on the defendant's failure to perform, provided the defendant cannot prove that these would have been wasted in any event.[88]

2.310 The plaintiff is bound to act reasonably and, as in the cases of damage to property, cannot, it is submitted, claim the cost of substitute carriage

---

83 *Mertens, supra*, at p. 539.

84 See Chapter 1, *supra*, for loss of or damage to property.

85 See *Monarch Steamship Co. Ltd. v. Karlshamns Oljefabriker (A/B)*, [1949] A.C. 196 (H.L.), at p. 220, *per* Lord Wright.

86 This will be the buying price if the goods are for use, and the selling price if the goods are for resale. See 1.90, *supra*.

87 See *Stroms Bruks Aktie Bolag v. Hutchison*, [1905] A.C. 515 (H.L.); *Nissho Co., Ltd. v. Livanos* (1941), 69 Ll.L. Rep. 125 (K.B.); *Koufos v. C. Czarnikow Ltd.*, [1969] 1 A.C. 350 (H.L.) (fall in market price at place of delivery). In *Featherston v. Wilkinson* (1873), L.R. 8 Exch. 122, the plaintiff recovered loss caused by a rise in the price of the goods at the place of shipment.

88 See 2.40, *supra*, and 5.200-5.250, *infra*.

when this serves no useful purpose and where the cost is out of all proportion to the value to the plaintiff. In *Hinde v. Liddell*,[89] Blackburn J. said that, in the case of a carrier failing to carry a passenger, the latter is "entitled to take the best substitute in the shape of a conveyance he can get, no matter that it costs much more than the fare".[90] He does not say "no matter what it costs", and the assumption is, it is suggested, that the plaintiff has a legitimate interest (which may be a non-economic interest) in actually incurring the higher cost. As in the cases of improvement to property, the fact that the plaintiff has actually incurred the cost is relevant, for it usually shows that the plaintiff considers it a reasonable expenditure.[91] But it cannot be conclusive, and if a case should occur where the litigation takes place in advance of the time of the alternative travel, it would become relevant whether the plaintiff was actually likely to make substitute arrangements. If, for example, the defendant contracted to carry a journalist to the South Pole to observe a scientific expedition and the expedition was subsequently cancelled, the plaintiff, having no reason to go to the South Pole and being unlikely ever to do so, would not, surely, be entitled to recover the cost of alternative transport.

10. Defective Services

2.320 Defective services frequently cause damage to, or loss of, property, or damage to other interests and these cases are discussed in other chapters.[92] The date for the assessment of damages is generally the date of the loss.[92a]

2.330 Where the defendant is an agent who has wrongfully failed to effect a beneficial contract on the plaintiff's behalf, the damages will include the anticipated benefit of the contract. This is by application of the ordinary principle that, had the wrong not been done, the contract would have been made and the plaintiff would have benefitted.[93]

2.340 Where, however, the defendant gives bad advice to the plaintiff, as for example, where an engineer fails to detect structural defects in a house, or where a solicitor fails to detect defects in title, and the plaintiff buys the property, the measure of damages is not the plaintiff's expected gain. Some have doubted this conclusion, and some cases and dicta suggest that damages should be measured by the difference between the value of

---

89 (1875), L.R. 10 Q.B. 265.

90 *Supra*, at p. 268.

91 See 1.2430, *supra*.

92 See Chapter 1, on loss of and damage to property, and Chapter 5, on damage to economic interests.

92a *Rose v. Mitton* (1994), 111 D.L.R. (4th) 217, 128 N.S.R. (2d) 99 (C.A.), leave to appeal to S.C.C. refused 115 D.L.R. (4th) vii, 178 N.R. 392*n*.

93 *Neilson v. James* (1882), 9 Q.B. 546 (C.A.); *Keppel v. Wheeler*, [1927] 1 K.B. 577 (C.A.); *Kienzle v. Stringer* (1981), 130 D.L.R. (3d) 272, 35 O.R. (2d) 85 (C.A.), leave to appeal to S.C.C. refused D.L.R. *loc. cit.*, 38 O.R. (2d) 159*n*; *New Yorker Boiler Co. Ltd. v. Elliott Ins. Ltd.* (1980), 30 N.B.R. (2d) 564 (Q.B.T.D.).

the property with defects and its value without defects, or by the cost of making good the defects.[94] It is submitted, however, that these cases and dicta cannot be supported, although they may often be explained as assuming that there was no difference between the price paid by the plaintiff for the property and the value of sound property.[95] The argument in favour of the contractual measure of damages is that the defendant certifies the soundness of the structure, or, where the defendant is a solicitor, "certifies" title, from which it is sought to deduce that the defendant should make good the client's expectations if the certificate proves false. The defendant, however, in these cases is selling services, not land. In no sense can it be said that had the defendant performed the duty, the plaintiff would have had a sound building, or a sound title. The effect would have been that the plaintiff would have been warned of the defect in time not to buy the land at all. As Arnup J.A. said in *Messineo v. Beale*:[96]

> . . . it is obvious that the defendant's breach of duty was not the cause of the plaintiffs getting no title to Murch's Point [the land in issue in the case]. The vendor had no title to Murch's Point, and could give none. Nothing the defendant could have done would have changed the situation.[97]

The Ontario Court of Appeal in this case gave full consideration to the proper measure of damages in the case of a negligent solicitor. Arnup J.A. said: "The measure of damages is the difference in money between the amount paid by the client to the vendor, and the market value of the land to which the client received a good title".[98] There is one instance, referred to by the court, in which the measure of damages may be higher; this is where the plaintiff has been deprived by the defendant's wrong of obtaining an abatement of the purchase price. Thus, if the plaintiff buys 100 acres of land for $100,000 from a vendor having title only to ninety acres, the plaintiff would in many cases be entitled to a decree against the

94 *Pilkington v. Wood*, [1953] 1 Ch. 770; *Philips v. Ward*, [1956] 1 W.L.R. 471 (C.A.); *Cantwell v. Petersen* (1982), 139 D.L.R. (3d) 466 (B.C.S.C.); *McKay v. Livspac Ltd.* (1996), 174 N.B.R. (2d) 213, 28 C.L.R. (2d) 184 (Q.B.).

95 See *Ford v. White & Co.*, [1964] 1 W.L.R. 885 (Ch.), at pp. 890-1, so explaining *Pilkington v. Wood, supra*, footnote 92, and *Philips v. Ward, supra*, footnote 92; *Ford v. White* was approved in *McMorran's Cordova Bay Ltd. v. Harman & Co.* (1979), 106 D.L.R. (3d) 495 (B.C.C.A.), where the plaintiff was a vendor. This explanation was approved in *Messineo v. Beale* (1978), 86 D.L.R. (3d) 713 at p. 717, 20 O.R. (2d) 49 at p. 53 (C.A.).

96 *Supra*, footnote 95, followed in *Clarke v. Milford* (1987), 38 D.L.R. (4th) 139, 78 N.S.R. (2d) 337 (C.A.). See also *Spencer v. King* (1992), 131 N.B.R. (2d) 243 (C.A.).

97 *Messineo v. Beale, supra*, footnote 95, at p. 716 D.L.R.

98 *Messineo v. Beale, supra*; *Perry v. Sidney Phillips & Son*, [1982] 1 W.L.R. 1297 (C.A.); *Watts v. Morrow*, [1991] 1 W.L.R. 1421 (C.A.); *Canada Trust Co. v. Sorkos* (1996), 135 D.L.R. (4th) 383, 3 R.P.R. (3d) 262 (Ont. C.A.); *Gardner v. Marsh & Parsons*, [1997] 1 W.L.R. 489 (C.A.). See *Toronto Industrial Leaseholds Ltd. v. Posesorski* (1994), 119 D.L.R. (4th) 193 at p. 214, supplementary reasons 121 D.L.R. (4th) 766 (C.A.), citing this paragraph.

vendor of specific performance with an abatement of the purchase price. If, due to the defendant's solicitor's negligence, the defect is not discovered in time, and the plaintiff pays the full price, it would seem that the plaintiff ought to be entitled to damages from the solicitor of $10,000, even if the land to which good title is received is worth $100,000 or more. The basis of such an award is not that the solicitor is supposed to have warranted the title but that, had the wrong not been done, the plaintiff would probably have obtained the land for $10,000 less than was actually paid.[99]

2.350 The principle of *Messineo v. Beale* does not apply to the case where there is no defect in title but the solicitor fails to effect the conveyance properly. In this case, had the wrong not been done, the plaintiff would have had a clear title. In *Kienzle v. Stringer*,[100] the Ontario Court of Appeal held that such a case was to be distinguished from *Messineo v. Beale*, Zuber J.A. said:

> It would have been far different if the vendor had owned [the land] and the solicitor had omitted the property from the deed or in some other way had caused the plaintiff to lose the property. In that case, the plaintiff's damage would have been the value of the missing property despite the fact that the value of what he received was greater than the purchase price.[101]

2.360 Where the defendant's defective performance involves the plaintiff in a liability to a third party, the defendant is liable if the damage is not too remote. In *Burrard Drydock Co. Ltd. v. Canadian Union Line Ltd.*,[102] the defendant failed to secure properly some valves on the deck of a ship, with the consequence that the plaintiff was held liable to a cargo owner for water damage to the cargo. The plaintiff's liability was based on want of due diligence creating a condition of unseaworthiness. The defendant argued that this want of diligence was the cause of the liability. The Supreme Court of Canada held, however, that the defendant's failure to perform was the effective cause of the loss. It is submitted that the decision is correct. The defendant's argument amounted to saying that the plaintiff should not have relied on the defendant's performing the very thing that it had promised to do, that is, to see that the valves were secure.

2.370 In *William R. Barnes Co. Ltd. v. MacKenzie*,[103] an employee who had made secret profits and caused losses to his employer by trading on his own account, was held liable to pay compensation for the losses, but not for the return of his salary. The Ontario Court of Appeal pointed out that it

---

99 In *Messineo v. Beale, supra*, footnote 95, at p. 716 D.L.R., Arnup J.A. commented that the case was not one for specific performance with abatement. See Sharpe, *Injunctions and Specific Performance*, looseleaf ed. (Toronto, Canada Law Book, 1999), 11.20-11.190.

100 *Supra*, footnote 93.

101 *Kienzle v. Stringer, supra*, at p. 275 D.L.R.

102 [1954] S.C.R. 307, [1954] 3 D.L.R. 561.

103 (1974), 44 D.L.R. (3d) 9, 2 O.R. (2d) 659 (C.A.).

would be duplicative for the employer to recover both the salary and the profits it would have made if faithful service had been rendered, for it would have had to pay the salary to obtain the service.

2.380 In *Globe & Rutgers Fire Ins. Co. v. Wetmore Ltd.*,[104] an insurance agent had committed the plaintiff to a risk at a lower premium than the plaintiff had authorized. A loss occurred, and the agent was held liable to pay the plaintiff the full amount of the loss. As the facts showed that the plaintiff was prepared to accept the risk at the higher premium, it is submitted that the difference between the premiums would be adequate compensation, for, had the wrong not been done, the insurer would have accepted the risk at the higher premium.

104 (1915), 23 D.L.R. 33 (N.S.S.C.).

CHAPTER 3

PERSONAL INJURIES

1. Form of Damages

3.10 Compensation for personal injuries involves, to a large extent, compensation for losses that will not yet have occurred at the time of trial. The common law system of assessing damages has always been as a single, once-and-for-all lump sum,[1] and it was affirmed by the Privy Council in 1927 that no other form of damages was permissible.[2] Other countries, however, have systems of periodic payments[3] and from time to

---

1 *Fitter v. Veal* (1701), 12 Mod. 542, 88 E.R. 1506; *Hodsoll v. Stallebrass* (1840), 11 Ad. & E. 301, 113 E.R. 429; *Darley Main Colliery Co. v. Mitchell* (1886), 11 App. Cas. 127 (H.L.), at p. 132. In *Brunsden v. Humphrey* (1884), 14 Q.B.D. 141 (C.A.), at p. 147, Bowen L.J. said: "It is a well settled rule of law that damages resulting from one and the same cause of action must be assessed and recovered once for all." In *Conquer v. Boot*, [1928] 2 K.B. 336 at p. 340, Sankey L.J. said: "with regard to the personal injuries, it would have been impossible . . . to sue one day for the loss of a leg and another day for the loss of another leg and later to sue because he lost his fingers". The Supreme Court of Canada's disapproval of *Brunsden v. Humphrey* in *Cahoon v. Franks*, [1967] S.C.R. 455, 63 D.L.R. (3d) 274, does not detract from these statements but rather reinforces them by holding that even in respect of property damage there is no separate claim from a claim for damages for personal injuries.

2 *Fournier v. Canadian National Ry. Co.*, [1927] A.C. 167 (P.C.). See also *Waldron v. Rur. Mun. of Elfros* (1922), 70 D.L.R. 726 (Sask. K.B.), affd [1923] 4 D.L.R. 1209 (C.A.). The rule was accepted by the Supreme Court of Canada in *Andrews v. Grand & Toy Alberta Ltd.*, [1978] 2 S.C.R. 229 at pp. 236-7, 83 D.L.R. (3d) 452 at p. 458, and reaffirmed in *Watkins v. Olafson*, [1989] 2 S.C.R. 750, 61 D.L.R. (4th) 577. See also *Fedorowicz v. Fedorowicz* (1951), 3 W.W.R. (N.S.) 230 (Man. K.B.) (agreement to support plaintiff for life). But see *Deeny v. Gooda Walker Ltd.*, [1995] 1 W.L.R. 1206, where a claim for recovery of future uncertain losses was deferred.

3 See McGregor, *International Encyclopedia of Comparative Law*, Vol. XI, ch. 9, §§48-63. Western Australia permits reviewable periodic payments for claims arising out of motor vehicle accidents, *Motor Vehicle (Third Party Insurance) Act*, s. 16(4). South Australia gives a general power to the court to order periodic payments, *Supreme Court Act*, s. 30c. See Luntz, *Assessment of Damages for Personal Injury and Death*, 3rd ed. (Chatswood, N.S.W., Butterworth Pty. Ltd., 1990), pp. 29-34. Several American States have adopted periodic payment provisions, mainly in medical malpractice cases, but almost all exclude subsequent review. See Elligett, "The Periodic Payment of Judgments", 46 Ins. Counsel J. 130 (1979), and *Watkins v. Olafson*, *supra*, footnote 2, at p. 581 D.L.R. Many of these provisions were enacted hastily to deal with the perceived "medical malpractice crisis" and their constitutionality is in doubt. See *American Bank & Trust Co. v. Community Hospital of Los Gatos — Saratoga*, 163 Cal. Rptr. 513 (Cal. C.A. 1980); *Carson v. Maurer*, 424 A. 2d 825 (N.H.S.C. 1980).

time, academic writers and judges have suggested that such a system should be introduced into the common law.[4] A strong argument for such a change was put by Dickson J. in *Andrews v. Grand & Toy Alberta Ltd.*:[5]

> . . . it is highly irrational to be tied to a lump-sum system and a once-and-for-all award.
>
> The lump-sum award presents problems of great importance. It is subject to inflation, it is subject to fluctuation on investment, income from it is subject to tax. After judgment new needs of the plaintiff arise and present needs are extinguished; yet our law of damages knows nothing of periodic payment. The difficulties are greatest where there is a continuing need for intensive and expensive care and a long-term loss of earning capacity. It should be possible to devise some system whereby payments would be subject to periodic review and variation in the light of the continuing needs of the injured person and the cost of meeting those needs.[6]

3.20 The strongest argument in favour of a change from the present system is increased accuracy of assessment. This point seems to have weighed most heavily with Dickson J. as he said: "After judgment new needs of the plaintiff arise and present needs are extinguished." The lump-sum system therefore may undercompensate (*e.g.*, where unforeseen medical complications occur) or over-compensate (*e.g.*, where the plaintiff makes a speedy recovery or dies shortly after judgment and the estate succeeds to the proceeds). Where there is a chance of the occurrence of an identifiable future event, an award discounted by the probability of occurrence is certain to be either too high or too low in the individual case.[7] Another aspect of the same matter, also apparent in Dickson J.'s words, is the dissatisfaction felt by judges in facing the impossible task of estimating accurately the plaintiff's future needs. Additional support for periodic payments is found in the argument that the claimant does not really suffer any loss until it is actually incurred. Perfect compensation, therefore, would be compensation of the plaintiff's actual losses as they accrued.

3.30 Comparison with social security programmes tends to support these considerations. Welfare, unemployment insurance and workers' compensation programmes have adopted periodic payments as the standard medium of compensation. As the tort system comes to be seen more and

---

4 See Fleming, "Damages: Capital or Rent?", 19 U.T.L.J. 295 (1969).

5 [1978] 2 S.C.R. 229, 83 D.L.R. (3d) 452.

6 *Supra*, at p. 236 S.C.R., p. 458 D.L.R.

7 In *Lim Poh Choo v. Camden and Islington Area Health Authority*, [1980] A.C. 174 (H.L.), at p. 183, Lord Scarman, while rejecting Lord Denning M.R.'s attempts in the court below to introduce a system of interim awards under the existing Rules of Court, said: "Knowledge of the future being denied to mankind, so much of the award as is to be attributed to future loss and suffering — in many cases the major part of the award — will almost surely be wrong. There is really only one certainty: the future will prove the award to be either too high or too low."

more as a kind of accident compensation scheme funded by liability insurance,[8] the comparison with social security schemes gains cogency.

3.40 A further argument for a scheme of periodic payments is that the present system compels the plaintiff to delay trial as long as possible in order to gather the best possible evidence of the long-term effects of the injury. If the plaintiff knew that the assessment could be re-opened if unexpected complications ensued, the plaintiff would have less incentive to delay: prompt trials would be in the interests of both parties and of the courts. Against this argument, however, must be set the costs of review procedures under any periodic payment system permitting adjustments subsequent to judgment.

3.50 Another argument is that the present system delays the plaintiff's rehabilitation by inducing the plaintiff to postpone serious attempts at rehabilitation until after the assessment of damages. Against this argument, however, must be set the consideration that with a system of periodic payments liable to be reduced if the plaintiff regained health, the plaintiff would have an indefinite incentive against rehabilitation.

3.60 Related arguments against the present system are that the delay caused by the once-and-for-all system means that the plaintiff must do without compensation for the months, and probably years, immediately following the accident, the time at which there is the greatest need for speedy rehabilitation.[9] Another point is that a system of adjustable periodic payments would eliminate or reduce the anxiety, and hence the deleterious effect on the plaintiff's mental health, of the whole future support depending on a single proceeding. A related point is that the long delay before trial, depriving the plaintiff of compensation when needed most, will put undue pressure on the plaintiff to settle on terms favourable to the defendant.

3.70 Dickson J. in the passage quoted above[10] mentioned the problem of income tax payable by the plaintiff on the interest derived from the investment of any lump-sum award. In order to achieve perfect compensation, the courts are obliged to make complex calculations[11] which would be eliminated if periodic payments could be ordered, leaving it to Parliament to determine the incidence of taxation, if any. A different point is the potential tax advantage to the claimant of tax-free periodic payments as opposed to a lump sum to be invested to produce (taxable) income. Voluntarily agreed schemes of periodic payments known as "structured settlements" have an important income tax advantage in that the Canadian taxing authorities have been willing to treat receipts under such settlements as tax-free in the plaintiff's hands,[12] whereas if the plaintiff accepted a lump sum and

8 See P. Cane, *Atiyah's Accidents, Compensation and the Law*, 6th ed. (London, Butterworths, 1999), pp. 191-212.

9 This effect is alleviated to some extent by no-fault automobile insurance payments available in most provinces.

10 *Andrews v. Grand & Toy, supra,* footnote 5, at p. 236 S.C.R., p. 458 D.L.R.

11 See 3.1180, *infra.*

purchased an annuity, tax would be payable on the interest element in the annuity payments. In times of high interest rates, the difference in tax treatment is very substantial and the benefit can, in effect, be divided between the parties in settlement negotiations.

3.80 It has been claimed as an advantage of periodic payments that they would avoid the distasteful necessity of assessing the claimant's prospect of remarriage in fatal accident cases,[13] the argument being that periodic payments would simply cease if the claimant later remarried.[14] Such a scheme, however, is open to the serious objection that it sets up the even more distasteful prospect of providing an economic disincentive to remarriage. Any scheme whereby periodic payments ceased on *de facto* remarriage would be open to the hardly less serious objection of encouraging "snooping" into the plaintiff's private life.[15]

3.90 An argument commonly made in favour of a change from the present system is that plaintiffs tend to squander the proceeds of their judgments and that a scheme of periodic payments would restrain dissipation of the proceeds of awards.[16] The point raises the question of whose money is the award. If it really is the plaintiff's money and the plaintiff is of full age and understanding,[17] it is difficult to object to the plaintiff doing what she likes with it. However, as the tort system comes to be seen more and more as an accident compensation scheme funded indirectly by the public through liability insurance premiums (now compulsory for motorists in many jurisdictions) it becomes clear that dissipation of judgment proceeds is a matter of public concern, especially as the plaintiff, if he leaves himself destitute, will be thrown upon the public purse for support by the social welfare system.[18]

3.100 Some advocates of periodic payments suggest that they provide a better protection than lump-sum awards against inflation.[19] This depends on what system of cost-of-living indexing is employed for a periodic

12 See report of Ontario Committee on Tort Compensation (1980), reprinted in *Report on Compensation for Personal Injuries and Death* (Ontario Law Reform Commission, 1987), pp. 259-275. See also *Yepremian v. Scarborough General Hospital (No. 2)* (1981), 120 D.L.R. (3d) 341, 31 O.R. (2d) 384 (H.C.J.).

13 See 6.520-6.650, *infra*.

14 Luntz, *Assessment of Damages for Personal Injury and Death*, 3rd ed. (Chatswood, N.S.W., Butterworth Pty. Ltd., 1990) §1.2.15.

15 As Fleming commented, this would amount to "including a "dum casta et sola' clause in every award": *op. cit.*, footnote 4, at p. 312.

16 *Royal Commission on Civil Liability and Compensation for Personal Injury* (London, H.M.S.O., 1978), §565 (Pearson Commission Report); Luntz, *op. cit.*, footnote 14, §1.2.16.

17 The Ontario Committee on Tort Compensation, 1980, *supra*, footnote 12, recommended a power in the court to order payment of damages to the Public Trustee, to deal with cases where the plaintiff was not fully competent.

18 See Pearson Commission Report, *supra*, footnote 16, §565, "a form of double compensation paid for by taxpayers".

19 Pearson Commission Report, *supra*, footnote 16, §568.

payment system.[20] If periodic payments are inadequately indexed, the plaintiff would be better off with a lump sum that could, at least in theory, be invested to give protection against the decline in value of money. A periodic payment system fully indexed against inflation would certainly offer an attractive alternative to the present system, but, would almost certainly require state participation.[21] This might appear too costly, and it might be difficult to justify a state guarantee against inflation for the benefit of a very select class of citizens.[22]

3.110 The arguments against a change to a system of periodic payments depend generally on the interest in finality.[23] Any system of periodic payments adjustable in the light of changing circumstances will involve the direct costs of the review process. The burden on the court of hearing applications to vary awards and appeals from variations could be expected to be considerable. The costs to the parties of legal representation and of assembling and presenting the necessary evidence must also be taken into account. Expert witnesses would almost always be required on both sides whenever a change in medical condition was alleged.[24]

3.120 Applications for variation could be expected in respect of changes in the value of money, changes in costs not reflected in the change in value of money, and changes in the claimant's actual needs. A formula could be envisaged that would automatically vary the claimant's award according to some predetermined measure of the change in the value of money.[25] Such a change would, however, almost never exactly match the claimant's actual costs. In principle, therefore, a search for perfect compensation would require a hearing to determine the amount of each loss as it accrued.[26] Changes in the claimant's needs would require similar treatment.

3.130 The burden of rehearings might be reduced by setting some threshold requirement, for example, that only substantial changes in costs or in needs would be considered. Such a proposal raises considerable difficulties, however, in finding a satisfactory definition of "substantial changes". If the phrase is undefined, litigation will be required in each case to determine if a matter can be reopened. If defined, for example, in dollar

---

20 See Fleming, "Damages: Capital or Rent?", 19 U.T.L.J. 295 (1969), at p. 315.

21 See Pearson Commission Report, *supra*, footnote 16, §§601, 606.

22 This was the conclusion of the Ontario Committee on Tort Compensation, 1980, *op. cit.*, footnote 12, at p. 24.

23 See *Watkins v. Olafson*, [1989] 2 S.C.R. 750, 61 D.L.R. (4th) 577 at pp. 584-6, *per* McLachlin J.

24 The dissenting Pearson commissioners said that periodic payments would lead to "an undesirable continuation of the adversarial process and relationship which is not in the plaintiff's best interests". *Op. cit.*, footnote 16, §621.

25 The Pearson Commission favoured annual revision in line with the movement of average earnings, *op. cit.*, footnote 16, §600.

26 The Pearson Commission proposal was limited to review of changes in the plaintiff's medical condition, rejecting a comprehensive review as "too complicated, at least initially", *op. cit.*, footnote 16, §590.

or percentage figures, it will give rise to anomalies and injustice in depriving claimants of a variation where the change falls short of the specified figure and a tendency to inflate claims in order to cross the threshold.

3.140 One possibility is to make the variation dependent on the occurrence of a specified event foreseen as a possibility at trial.[27] Such a scheme (as compared with a scheme of periodic payments) reduces the burden of continual reassessment but gives rise to its own anomalies. Everything depends on the exact words used by the trial judge in defining the circumstances that would permit review: "The plaintiff may apply for a reassessment if he develops epilepsy" would not cover the case if the plaintiff developed a brain tumor. One could foresee a tendency on the part of trial judges to define very broadly the circumstances that would permit review. Such a tendency would lead to the difficulties mentioned above and would make more anomalous those cases where review was denied.[27a]

3.150 The burden of review would be reduced by a provision that applications could be made only once, or only once in a long period of time, or only within a certain period of time following judgment, but such systems would have most of the deficiences of the present one.

3.160 Another point made against variable systems of periodic payments is that if it paid the claimant to remain disabled, some claimants would have an incentive to remain disabled, whereas with compensation settled, they might achieve more rapid rehabilitation. Supporters of a change from the present system generally concede this point, but consider it to be offset by the ill-effects on the plaintiff's health of the present system.[28] It can be pointed out that malingering or its psychological equivalent has not proven an insuperable obstacle to periodic payments in social security schemes such as workers' compensation, or in schemes of disability insurance.

3.170 Another point is that the defendant or the defendant's insurer will be encouraged to snoop into the plaintiff's private life in order to prove health is better than admitted or that earnings are greater. This aspect would be particularly distasteful in fatal accident claim cases if the claim for lost support were to be diminished by the claimant's obtaining support from other sources.[29]

---

27 Recommended by the Law Commission, *Report on Personal Injury Litigation — Assessment of Damages* (Law Com. No. 56, 1973), §239, and implemented by the *Administration of Justice Act 1982* (U.K.), s. 6. See *Hurditch v. Sheffield Health Authority*, [1989] Q.B. 562 (C.A.). See *Willson v. Ministry of Defence*, [1991] 1 All E.R. 638 (Q.B.D.).

27a See Lewis, *Structured Settlements: The Law and Practice* (London, Sweet & Maxwell, 1993), pp. 3-05 to 3-07.

28 See *Royal Commission on Civil Liability and Compensation for Personal Injury* (London, H.M.S.O., 1978), §571 (Pearson Commission Report).

29 See footnote 15, *supra*.

3.180 Another basic argument against periodic payments is that a compulsory scheme of periodic payments deprives the plaintiff of the preferred

[*The next page is* 3–7]

result.[30] The plaintiff can always purchase an annuity if desired with the proceeds of a lump-sum judgment or can invest the award in a business. Moreover, the plaintiff can agree on a structured settlement, and this is being done with increasing frequency.[31] It has been argued that there is no justification for compelling the plaintiff to accept periodic payments, and that the net effect will be to lower the plaintiff's bargaining power in settlement negotiations, leaving the plaintiff who prefers a lump sum simply with a smaller lump-sum settlement than would be obtained under the present system. Experience of foreign systems seems to indicate that plaintiffs, when given a choice, strongly prefer lump-sum settlements.[32]

3.190 It is also argued that under the present system of private insurance and individual responsibility an open-ended system of periodic payments, especially if inflation-proofed, will put an intolerable burden on insurers. Against this argument it may be said that insurers, better than anyone else, should be able to estimate the value of uncertain future events. Where the uncertainty is the length of the claimant's life, it must surely be conceded that there can be no actuarial difficulty. Where the uncertainty is the future state of the claimant's health, it can be argued that cases where health improves unexpectedly will balance those where it deteriorates. The force of this argument depends on the weight to be given to the point made earlier about the claimant's tendency to malinger (deliberately or sub-consciously) — a problem from the insurance point of view of "moral hazard". In respect of inflation, the burden on the insurer could be made predictable by limiting cost of living increases to

---

30 See Pearson Commission Report, *supra*, footnote 28, §628.

31 See *Yepremian v. Scarborough General Hospital (No. 2)* (1981), 120 D.L.R. (3d) 341, 31 O.R. (2d) 384 (H.C.J.); *Kenyeres (Litigation Guardian of) v. Cullimore* (1992), 13 C.P.C. (3d) 385 (Ont. Ct. (Gen. Div.)), appeal dismissed as settled 46 A.C.W.S. (3d) 438 (C.A.). See also Lewis, *op. cit.*, footnote 27a.

32 McGregor writes:

> In France and Switzerland, in both of which the court has complete control of the form of the award, the proportion of personal injury and wrongful death claims which end up with capital awards is put as high as over 99 per cent. And what is even more arresting is in Germany, with its express code provision that only . . . "a serious reason" will entitle the court to make a capital award . . . the claimants who obtain capital sums are also said to number over 99 per cent. How then does the German practice square with the dictates of the Civil Code? The answer is to be found in the strong predilection of both plaintiff and defendant for a capital sum . . . A court . . . can resort to the technique of "suggesting" to the parties that they should come to an agreement between themselves — and the "suggestion" can hint at a figure . . . There are no restrictions on the form of settlements; it is up to the parties as to how they settle, and the parties generally settle for a capital sum.

McGregor, *International Encyclopedia of Comparative Law*, Vol. XI, ch. 9, §§60-1. The point about the adverse effect of a compulsory scheme of periodic payments on the plaintiff's bargaining power was made by Rea, "Lump-Sum versus Periodic Damage Awards," 10 J. Leg. Stud. 131 (1981), and relied on by the Ontario Special Committee on Tort Compensation (1980), reprinted in *Report on Compensation for Personal Injuries and Death* (Ontario Law Reform Commission, 1987), pp. 269-70.

some standard measure of interest rates, such as the government treasury bill rate,[33] or by a state-run insurance scheme of some sort.[34]

3.200 A further argument against periodic payments is that the plaintiff who loses earning capacity is deprived of a capital asset[35] and ought to have the option of receiving a capital sum in compensation, so that it could, for example, be invested in a business to replace the lost income stream. If the plaintiff's loss is a capital loss, there seems to be no ground for depriving the plaintiff of capital compensation.[36] A substantial portion of the cost of future care, the other major component of future pecuniary loss, is already subject to subrogation in favour of the provincial health plan, and the plaintiff receives no lump sum in respect of this loss. This leaves only the cost of future care not covered by a provincial insurance scheme that could legitimately be made the subject of periodic payments. A major change in the present system hardly seems needed in respect of that element alone.

3.210 Another line of argument against periodic payments is that they would put an undue burden on the uninsured or the underinsured defendant. The defendant would be constantly liable to an unpredictable continuing burden. As the dissenting Pension Commissioners commented, "To convert a plaintiff into a pensioner of the defendant throughout the period of disability is an innovation which cannot be desirable even if practicable."[37] An award of a relatively modest annual sum would rise to astronomical heights after fifteen or twenty years if fully indexed against inflation. A related point is that a scheme of indexed periodic payments is incompatible with the current North American practice of liability insurance with fixed dollar limits. Supporters of periodic payments reply to these points by saying that insurance practices would have to change so that liability of the insured for periodic payments would be fully covered by the insurer if the capitalized value of the award was within the policy limits.[38]

3.220 An important objection to the argument that periodic payments prevent the squandering of the award is that any scheme of periodic payments could be evaded by a lump-sum settlement unless the court were willing

33 This is proposed in the *American Draft Model Periodic Payment of Judgments Act* (National Conference of Commissioners on Uniform State Laws, 1980). Such a link will not always guarantee rises in line with the actual rate of inflation.

34 The Pearson Commission accepted that state participation would be necessary. See Pearson Commission Report, *supra*, footnote 28, §§601, 605.

35 The Supreme Court of Canada and the House of Lords have held that loss of earning capacity is to be treated as a capital loss: *The Queen in right of Ontario v. Jennings*, [1966] S.C.R. 532, 57 D.L.R. (2d) 644; *Andrews v. Grand & Toy Alberta Ltd.*, [1978] S.C.R. 229, 83 D.L.R. (3d) 452; *Pickett v. British Rail Engineering Ltd.*, [1980] A.C. 136 (H.L.).

36 See footnote 30, *supra*.

37 See footnote 24, *supra*. It is true that matrimonial support obligations impose such a burden, but even there there is a move towards the "clean break".

38 See the provisions of the American Uniform Model Act, *supra*, footnote 33. Unlimited liability insurance might be required for automobile drivers, but is hardly practicable universally.

to undertake the control of all settlement negotiations.[39] So long as voluntary settlements for lump sums are permitted, it seems difficult to justify a compulsory scheme of judicially awarded periodic payments and, as pointed out previously,[40] the net effect would often simply be that plaintiffs settled for smaller lump sums than at present.

3.230 A number of subsidiary points have been raised by critics of a periodic payment scheme, which have the status more of practical problems associated with implementation than fundamental objections to the concept of periodic payments itself. These are that a scheme would have to be devised to see that the statutory beneficiaries under the fatal accidents legislation would be entitled to claim an appropriate amount if the plaintiff died as a result of the defendant's wrong before receiving all the periodic payments[41] and a scheme would have to be devised to see that an appropriate portion of the unpaid periodic payments was available to the plaintiff's estate whether or not death was caused by the defendant's wrong.[42] Arrangements would have to be made for adequate security to be provided by the defendant; restrictions might be appropriate on the plaintiff's ability to assign rights to periodic payments, and exemptions from claims of creditors might be appropriate in some circumstances. Procedural changes would be required to compel trial courts to make specific findings of the precise components of periodic payment awards for purposes of capitalizing the award or the remaining part of it or the lost earnings portion of it in the event of a failure of the defendant's security or of the plaintiff's death or of the commutation of the award to a lump sum for other good reason if that were permitted and for rational calculations of adjustments to portions of the award in the light of changing circumstances.[43]

3.240 One possible solution that has been suggested to some of the objections

---

[39] The Pearson Commission proposed to allow lump sum settlements but recommended that "the plaintiff's professional adviser should be under a duty to point out the advantages of periodic payments and the normal court practice in such cases": see *Royal Commission on Civil Liability and Compensation for Personal Injury* (London, H.M.S.O., 1978), §578 (Pearson Commission Report). In view of the evidence of the strong preference of plaintiffs for lump sum payments it is doubtful whether this proposal would effectively restrain a plaintiff who was likely to squander the proceeds of his award.

[40] *Supra*, 3.180.

[41] The Pearson Commission recommended that the dependants should be able to bring a separate action, *op. cit.*, footnote 39, §594. As the dissenting Commissioners point out (§629), this might be unfair to the defendant. An alternative would be to give the dependants a right to the capitalized value of the periodic payments ordered for the remaining period of the deceased's pre-accident life expectancy. See the provisions of the American Model Act, *supra*, footnote 32.

[42] It has been held that a claim for lost future earning capacity survives to the estate of a deceased person: *Gammell v. Wilson*, [1982] A.C. 27 (H.L.). Consequently the estate suffers a loss in case of death. Where the death is caused by a non-culpable cause, it may be said that the estate ought not to recover prospective future earnings on the ground that events have now shown the initial estimate of life expectancy to have been erroneous. On the other hand, if death is caused by the defendant's wrong (as in *Gammell v. Wilson*) or by another culpable cause (as to which, see 13.550-13.610), the estate ought to recover.

[43] Provisions on these matters appear in the American Model Act, *supra*, footnote 33.

involves the creation of a fund to which the defendant would pay a lump sum and from which the plaintiff would draw periodic payments.[44] This proposal would involve the creation of some sort of board or tribunal, or a branch of the court, to administer the fund. The solvency of the fund would require state insurance, though in theory the gains and losses would even out in the long term. This proposal would in effect create a state-run insurance agency, operating in one small field of personal injury compensation, and it seems difficult to justify confining such a scheme to those accident victims who have succeeded in finding a solvent defendant who is legally responsible for their injuries.[45]

3.250 In conclusion, therefore, it seems difficult to graft a system of periodic payments onto the present system of fault-based individual responsibility. It may very well be, however, that the future of personal injury compensation will lie with a state-run compensation fund, as in New Zealand[47] and, in that case, periodic payments would be the most natural medium of compensation.

3.260 In 1989 the Supreme Court of Canada reaffirmed that, unless the law is changed by legislation, the plaintiff remains entitled to a lump-sum award.[48] Legislation has been enacted in several jurisdictions.[48a] In Ontario the court has been empowered by legislation to order periodic payments where all affected parties consent or where "the plaintiff requests that an amount be included in the award to offset any liability for income tax on income from the investment of the award".[49] In the latter case, the award is only to be made if in the "best interest" of the plaintiff. The court is also to consider whether a scheme of periodic payments is "practicable having regard to all the circumstances of the case". The court has power to order that the award be subject to future review on such terms as it considers just. These provisions, though permitting periodic payments in some circumstances, leave it to the courts to develop guide-lines as to when they are appropriate, and what steps, if any, will be taken to meet the difficulties that will necessarily arise. It is probable that the considerations discussed in the preceding paragraphs will be taken into account in deciding when the new

---

44 Feldthusen and McNair, "General Damages in Personal Injury Suits: The Supreme Court's Trilogy", 28 U.T.L.J. 381 (1978), at p. 425.

45 This argument was made by the Ontario Committee on Tort Compensation, 1980, reprinted in *Report on Compensation For Personal Injuries and Death* (Ontario Law Reform Commission, 1987).

46 [Footnote deleted.]

47 *Accident Rehabilitation and Compensation Insurance Act, 1992* (N.Z.), No. 13, and successor legislation.

48 *Watkins v. Olafson*, [1989] 2 S.C.R. 750, 61 D.L.R. (4th) 577; *Correa v. Dow Jones Markets Canada Inc.* (1997), 35 O.R. (3d) 126, 30 C.C.E.L. (2d) 248 (Gen. Div.).

48a See, *e.g.*, *Court of Queen's Bench Act*, S.M. 1988-89, c. 4, ss. 88.1-88.9. See *Webster v. Chapman*, [1996] 9 W.W.R. 652 at pp. 688-92, 114 Man. R. (2d) 1 (Q.B.), revd 155 D.L.R. (4th) 82, [1998] 4 W.W.R. 335 (C.A.), leave to appeal to S.C.C. refused 159 D.L.R. (4th) vii; *Lusignan (Litigation Guardian of) v. Concordia Hospital*, [1997] 6 W.W.R. 185, 117 Man. R. (2d) 241, supplementary reasons [1999] 1 W.W.R. 733, 130 Man. R. (2d) 73 (Q.B.).

49 *Courts of Justice Act*, s. 116. See 3.1180, *infra*.

provisions are to be used and with what safeguards for the interests of both parties.

2. General Purpose of Award

3.270 In one sense it is obviously impossible to give perfect compensation in money for personal injuries. When it was the practice, as in the past, to award damages in the form of a "global" sum, not differentiated as between compensation for pecuniary and non-pecuniary loss, it could fairly be said that perfect compensation was impossible and could not be the purpose of an award.[50] Now, however, that damage awards must distinguish between compensation for pecuniary and non-pecuniary loss, perfect compensation is in theory obtainable in respect of the pecuniary loss. Both the Supreme Court of Canada[51] and the House of Lords[52] have held that in respect of pecuniary losses the plaintiff can in principle recover full compensation. The acceptance of this principle does not remove the practical difficulties of assessment, and because of these difficulties it can be said that compensation can never in practice be "complete" or "perfect".[53] One kind of difficulty, not markedly different from that facing the court in many cases, arises from the need to estimate the probability of uncertain future events. Future changes in the plaintiff's medical condition, the effect of the accident on the plaintiff's expectation of life, the cost of future care, and the salary the plaintiff would have earned if not injured, are all matters that the court must estimate, and in so far as estimates prove inaccurate, compensation will be imperfect.

3.280 There is another kind of practical difficulty in assessment that is peculiar to personal injury cases. This is the necessity for determining what living conditions a seriously injured plaintiff can be expected to adopt. Since no amount of money will enable the plaintiff to live exactly as before the injury, "perfect" compensation is, for this reason again, impossible. The claims of the injured party must be "legitimate and justifiable".[54] There is a duty on the plaintiff's part to be reasonable,[55] and fair compensation for pecuniary loss is not to be augmented by considerations of sympathy or retribution.[56] On the other hand, the plaintiff has no duty to mitigate in the sense of being forced to accept less than compensation for real loss.[57] In *Andrews v. Grand & Toy Alberta Ltd.*, the question arose whether a quadraplegic could claim damages

---

[50] See, for example, *Ficko v. Thibault* (1967), 59 W.W.R. 500 (Sask. C.A.); *Joynt v. Topp (No. 3)* (1963), 42 W.W.R. 689 (Sask. C.A.); *Taylor v. University of Saskatchewan*, [1955] 4 D.L.R. 146 (Sask. C.A.) (fatal accident case).

[51] *Andrews v. Grand & Toy Alberta Ltd.*, [1978] 2 S.C.R. 229 at p. 241, 83 D.L.R. (3d) 452 at p. 462.

[52] *Pickett v. British Rail Engineering Ltd.*, [1980] A.C. 136 (H.L.), at p. 168, *per* Lord Scarman.

[53] *Per* Dickson J., in *Andrews v. Grand & Toy Alberta Ltd.*, *supra*, footnote 51, at p. 242 S.C.R., p. 462 D.L.R.

[54] *Andrews v. Grand & Toy*, *supra*, at pp. 242-3 S.C.R., p. 463 D.L.R.

[55] *Andrews v. Grand & Toy*, *supra*, at p. 242 S.C.R., p. 462 D.L.R.

[56] *Andrews v. Grand & Toy*, *supra*.

[57] *Andrews v. Grand & Toy*, *supra*.

on the basis of a future life in his own home where special adaptations and nursing care would be needed. The defendant had argued, and the Alberta Appellate Division had held,[58] that the plaintiff should receive damages on the more economical basis of a future life to be spent in a hospital. The Supreme Court of Canada disagreed:

> The standard to be applied to Andrews is not merely "provision", but "compensation", *i.e.*, what is the proper compensation for a person who would have been able to care for himself and live in a home environment if he had not been injured? The answer must surely be home care. If there were severe mental impairment, or in the case of an immobile quadriplegic, the results might well be different; but, where the victim is mobile and still in full control of his mental faculties, as Andrews is, it cannot be said that institutionalization in an auxiliary hospital represents proper compensation for his loss. Justice requires something better.[59]

3.290 Compensation for non-pecuniary loss stands on a different basis. Here, the difficulties of achieving perfect compensation are not merely practical difficulties of assessment but are inherent in the nature of the loss itself. As the Supreme Court of Canada said in *Andrews v. Grand & Toy:*

> But the problem here is qualitatively different from that of pecuniary losses. There is no medium of exchange for happiness. There is no market for expectation of life. The monetary evaluation of non-pecuniary losses is a philosophical and policy exercise more than a legal or logical one. The award must be fair and reasonable, fairness being gauged by earlier decisions; but the award must also of necessity be arbitrary or conventional. No money can provide true restitution.[60]

3. Itemization of Damages

3.300 It was formerly the practice of the courts to award an unexplained and undifferentiated "global" sum in respect of all future loss.[61] A number of factors have led the courts to attempt a more exact explanation of their calculations. One factor has been the practice, and in most jurisdictions now the requirement, that interest be awarded on damages.[62] Different considerations in respect of interest may often apply to different portions of the award. Probably more significant has been the generally increased concern that the principles governing damage awards should be consistent, fair, and rational.[63] In *Andrews v. Grand & Toy*, this factor was given as the predominant reason

[58] (1975), 64 D.L.R. (3d) 663, [1976] 2 W.W.R. 385 (Alta. S.C. App. Div.).

[59] *Andrews v. Grand & Toy (Alberta) Ltd.*, [1978] 2 S.C.R. 229 at p. 246, 83 D.L.R. (3d) 452 at p. 465. See also 3.1160, *infra*.

[60] *Supra*, at p. 261 S.C.R., pp. 475-6 D.L.R.

[61] See *Veinot v. Veinot* (1977), 81 D.L.R. (3d) 549 (N.S.S.C. App. Div.); *Doxtator v. Burch* (1971), 23 D.L.R. (3d) 52, [1972] 1 O.R. 321 (H.C.J.), affd 29 D.L.R. (3d) 542, [1972] 3 O.R. 806 (C.A.); cases cited by Kirby J. in *Andrews v. Grand & Toy Alberta Ltd.* (1974), 54 D.L.R. (3d) 85 (Alta. S.C.T.D.), at pp. 92-3.

[62] See 7.500-7.580, *infra*; *Jefford v. Gee*, [1970] 2 Q.B. 130 (C.A.).

[63] *George v. Pinnock*, [1973] 1 W.L.R. 118 (C.A.), at p. 126, *per* Sachs L.J. See also *Lai Wee Liam v. Singapore Bus Service (1978) Ltd.*, [1984] A.C. 729 (P.C.); *C.S.R. Readymix (Australia) Pty. Ltd. v. Payne*, [1998] 2 V.R. 505 (C.A.).

for the Supreme Court of Canada's requirement of itemized awards. Dickson J. said:

> The method of assessing general damages in separate amounts, as has been done in this case, in my opinion, is a sound one. It is the only way in which any meaningful review of the award is possible on appeal and the only way of affording reasonable guidance in future cases. Equally important, it discloses to the litigants and their advisers the components of the overall award, assuring them thereby that each of the various heads of damage going to make up the claim has been given thoughtful consideration.[64]

3.310 A fourfold division was approved by the Supreme Court of Canada as follows: pecuniary loss occurring before trial, non-pecuniary loss, loss of earning capacity, and cost of future care.

3.320 It was formerly the practice to review the total award, the judge exercising a residual discretion to adjust it if it seemed out of keeping with other awards in similar cases. In *Andrews v. Grand & Toy*, Dickson J. appeared to disapprove of this practice. In a paragraph headed "Total Award", he said:

> This is largely a matter of arithmetic. Of course, in addition, it is customary for the Court to make an overall assessment of the total sum. This, however, seems to me to be a hangover from the days of global sums for all general damages. It is more appropriate to make an overall assessment of the total under each head of future care, prospective earnings, and non-pecuniary loss, in each case in light of general considerations such as the awards of other Courts in similar cases and an assessment of the reasonableness of the award.[65]

However, in *Keizer v. Hanna*,[66] a fatal accident case decided contemporaneously, Dickson J. said: "At the end of the day the only question of importance is whether, in all the circumstances, the final award is fair and adequate."[67] In *Lewis v. Todd*,[68] the same judge said:

> ... the award of damages is not simply an exercise in mathematics which a Judge indulges in, leading to a "correct" global figure. The evidence of actuaries and economists is of value in arriving at a fair and just result ... If the Courts are to apply basic principles of the law of damages and seek to achieve a reasonable approximation to pecuniary *restitutio in integrum* expert assistance is vital. But the trial Judge, who is required to make the decision, must be accorded a large measure of freedom in dealing with the evidence presented by the experts. If the figures lead to an award which in all the circumstances seems to the Judge to be inordinately high it is his duty, as I conceive it, to adjust those figures downward; and in like manner

64 *Supra*, footnote 59, at pp. 235-6 S.C.R., pp. 457-8 D.L.R., followed on this point in *Reibl v. Hughes* (1978), 89 D.L.R. (3d) 112, 21 O.R. (2d) 14 (C.A.), revd on other grounds [1980] 2 S.C.R. 880, 114 D.L.R. (3d) 1. See *Marky v. Arnold* (1995), 15 B.C.L.R. (3d) 294, 108 W.A.C. 209 (C.A.).

65 *Supra*, footnote 59, at p. 265 S.C.R., pp. 478-9 D.L.R.

66 [1978] 2 S.C.R. 342, 82 D.L.R. (3d) 449.

67 *Supra*, at p. 351 S.C.R., p. 461 D.L.R. See also *Giang v. Clayton*, [2005] 7 W.W.R. 468 (B.C.C.A.).

68 [1980] 2 S.C.R. 694, 115 D.L.R. (3d) 257.

> to adjust them upward if they lead to what seems to be an unusually low award.[69]

These last two passages were cited with approval by the British Columbia Court of Appeal in *Killeen v. Kline*[70] where a fifty per cent deduction for contingencies was approved as a rough and ready device for reducing an excessive award.

3.330 It is submitted that intuitive adjustments to awards are inconsistent with the principles, laid down in *Andrews v. Grand & Toy*, of facilitating appellate review, increasing predictability, and assuring litigants that their claims have received detailed consideration. On the other hand, as Dickson J. indicated in *Lewis v. Todd*, it can never be right for a judge to defer entirely to expert evidence. The principles just mentioned require that a judge should understand and be able to explain in language that satisfies the judge, the reasons that support an award. The solution, it is suggested, is for the judge to indicate in respect of each item of loss claimed the tenor of the expert evidence and the amount at which the loss is assessed, with reasons satisfactory to a non-expert.

4. Pecuniary Losses Occurring before Trial

3.340 Loss of earnings and expenses for care incurred before trial, often called "special damages",[71] have long been separately claimed and calculated. Theoretically, it would be possible to calculate the amount that would have been payable by the defendant had instant reparation been made at the moment of the injury, but this calculation would involve the artificial exercise of the court's supposing that it had been able to make the fictional assessment at the moment of injury. It seems more in accordance with reality to award damages for losses actually proved to have been incurred at the date of trial. In a 1903 case, Lord Macnaghten said:

> In order to enable him [an arbitrator] to come to a just and true conclusion it is his duty ... to avail himself of all information at hand at the time of

---

69 *Supra*, at pp. 708-9 S.C.R., pp. 267-8 D.L.R.

70 [1982] 3 W.W.R. 289 (B.C.C.A.).

71 The term "special damages" has different meanings in other contexts. See 4.10-4.40, 7.510, *infra*. In *Stroms Bruks Aktie Bolag v. Hutchison*, [1905] A.C. 515 (H.L.), at pp. 525-6, special damages were said to be unusual damages requiring special pleading. In *Ratcliffe v. Evans*, [1892] 2 Q.B. 524 (C.A.), at p. 529, Bowen L.J. said of "special damage": "In this judgment we shall endeavour to avoid a term which, intelligible enough in particular contexts, tends, when successively employed in more than one context and with regard to different subject-matter, to encourage confusion in thought." See also *Darling v. Collins* (1958), 25 W.W.R. 522 (B.C.S.C.) (term used "loosely"). But the use of the term is unlikely to disappear in the present context. It was used by the Supreme Court of Canada in *Andrews v. Grand & Toy Alberta Ltd.*, [1978] 2 S.C.R. 229 at p. 266, 83 D.L.R. (3d) 452 at p. 479, and in *Thornton v. Prince George School Board*, [1978] 2 S.C.R. 267, at p. 285, 83 D.L.R. (3d) 480 at p. 491, and in *Arnold v. Teno*, [1978] 2 S.C.R. 287 at p. 320, 83 D.L.R. (3d) 609 at p. 630. The term also appears in the statute governing pre-judgment interest in British Columbia: 7.500-7.580, *infra*. See *Baart v. Kumar* (1985), 22 D.L.R. (4th) 354 at pp. 368-9, [1986] 1 W.W.R. 100 (B.C.C.A.), and *Ryan v. Sun Life Assurance Co. of Canada* (2005), 249 D.L.R. (4th) 628 (N.S.C.A.), at p. 637, both citing this passage.

making his award which may be laid before him. Why should he listen to conjecture on a matter which has become an accomplished fact? Why should he guess when he can calculate? With the light before him, why should he shut his eyes and grope in the dark?[72]

3.350 For purposes of awarding interest, the English Court of Appeal held in *Jefford v. Gee*,[73] that pre-trial pecuniary loss must be separately calculated, and in *Cookson v. Knowles*[74] and *Wieser v. Pearson*,[75] the principle was extended to fatal accident cases. In some provinces the statutory provisions governing the award of interest on damages make particular reference to "special damages",[76] and in *Andrews v. Grand & Toy*,[77] *Thornton v. Prince George School District*,[78] and *Arnold v. Teno*[79] (the 1978 "trilogy"), the Supreme Court of Canada approved the separate assessment of pre-trial pecuniary loss by listing it separately in each case, though the question did not arise for discussion on the appeals.

(1) Loss of pre-trial earning capacity

3.360 A plaintiff's claim for loss of earnings before trial, being separately calculated, is sometimes regarded as fundamentally distinct from the calculation of lost future earning capacity. The term "special damages" applied to pre-trial loss tends to suggest that exact proof of particular money losses is required.[80] However, it should be recalled that in Canada it is well established that compensation as to the future is not for lost earnings as such, but for loss of earning capacity. There can be no justification for applying a different principle to losses occurring before trial.[80a] The only difference is that knowledge of events occuring before trial takes the place of prediction.[80b] Thus if the plaintiff is entitled to recover compensation for future lost earning capacity, the plaintiff should be entitled to the compensation on the same principle in respect of the period before the trial.

[72] *Bwllfa & Merthyr Dare Steam Collieries (1891), Ltd. v. Pontypridd Waterworks Co.*, [1903] A.C. 426 (H.L.), at p. 431. See 1.820, *supra*.
[73] [1970] 2 Q.B. 130 (C.A.).
[74] [1979] A.C. 556 (H.L.).
[75] (1981), 126 D.L.R. (3d) 237 (B.C.C.A.).
[76] See 7.500-7.580, *infra*.
[77] [1978] 2 S.C.R. 229, 83 D.L.R. (3d) 452.
[78] *Supra*, footnote 71.
[79] *Supra*, footnote 71.
[80] See *Dojczman v. Ste. Marie* (1969), 6 D.L.R. (3d) 649, [1969] 2 O.R. 745 (C.A.); *Hansen v. Saskatchewan Power Corp.* (1961), 31 D.L.R. (2d) 189 (Sask. C.A.); *Staats v. C.P.R. Co.* (1914), 17 D.L.R. 309 (Sask. S.C. en banc); *Michaud v. J. Clark & Sons Ltd.* (1980), 31 N.B.R. (2d) 98 (Q.B.T.D.), vard 36 N.B.R. (2d) 420 (C.A.) (specific pleading required). In *Zalameda v. Pigozzo* (1976), 74 D.L.R. (3d) 522 at p. 526, 14 O.R. (2d) 716 at p. 721 (H.C.J.), Lerner J. said: "The burden is on the plaintiff to prove his special damages, such as loss of income, with accuracy." See also *Sales v. Clarke* (1998), 165 D.L.R. (4th) 241 (B.C.C.A.); and Cooper-Stephenson, *Personal Injury Damages in Canada*, 2nd ed. (Toronto, Carswell, 1996), pp. 129-38.
[80a] *Jacques v. Passey* (2000), 73 Alta.L.R. (3d) 392 (C.A.), citing this passage at p. 396.
[80b] *G. (B.M.) v. Nova Scotia (Attorney General)* (2007), 288 D.L.R. (4th) 88 (N.S.C.A.), at para. 175, citing this passage.

In the Australian case of *Arthur Robinson (Grafton) Pty. Ltd. v. Carter*,[81] Barwick C.J. pointed out that the use of the term "special damages" was apt to be misleading:

> But though this is I think the recognized position in Australia, [i.e. that compensation is for loss of earning capacity and not loss of earnings] the wages which would have been earned between the receipt of the injury and the date of the trial are somewhat illogically, as I think, calculated and treated as special damages. In my opinion, it would be better that they should not be so treated for amongst other things, such treatment tends to plant in the mind the idea that it is the loss of the earnings which is to be compensated. On the other hand, not to so treat them would help to emphasize that it is the loss of the earning capacity which is the subject of the damages.[82]

3.370 It is unlikely, as indicated previously, that the term "special damages" will disappear in this context,[83] but it is important in cases where the difference between recovery for earnings and for earning capacity becomes crucial, to ensure that the plaintiff is not deprived of compensation in the period before trial.[84] Thus it is argued below that an unpaid teacher should be allowed to recover the loss of earning capacity despite the absence of anticipated money payment.[85] If this argument is sound, there can be no justification for withholding compensation for the lost capacity during the period before the trial even though no precise proof of monetary loss can be made.[86]

3.380 On the same principle, recovery is allowed of losses other than of wages such as loss of professional practice,[87] damage to the plaintiff's interest in a

[81] (1968), 122 C.L.R. 649 (Aust. H.C.).

[82] *Supra*, at p. 658, quoted in *Rowe v. Bobell Express Ltd.* (2005), 251 D.L.R. (4th) 290 (B.C.C.A.), at p. 300.

[83] Some cases have held that pre-trial loss of earnings is to be treated as general damages: *Trache v. C.N.R.*, [1929] 2 D.L.R. 321 (Sask. C.A.); *Taylor v. Addems*, [1932] 1 W.W.R. 505 (Sask. C.A.); *Tubb v. Lief*, [1932] 3 W.W.R. 245 (Sask. C.A.); *MacLeod v. Gallant* (1975), 9 Nfld. & P.E.I.R. 254 (P.E.I.S.C.); *Noonan v. Heaney* (1979), 23 Nfld. & P.E.I.R. 1 (P.E.I.S.C.); *Knapp v. Steele* (1955), 2 D.L.R. (2d) 21 (N.S.S.C.); *McLeod v. Boultbee*, [1931] 4 D.L.R. 912 (B.C.S.C.); *MacIvor v. The King*, [1948] 3 D.L.R. 509 (Ex. Ct.). *Contra: Wersch v. Wersch*, [1945] 2 D.L.R. 572 (Man. C.A.); *Stevens v. Biddington*, [1943] 4 D.L.R. 341 (N.B.S.C. App. Div.). The question was expressly left open in *Hunter v. Ballingall* (1962), 37 W.W.R. 703 (Man. C.A.). The use of the term by the Supreme Court of Canada in the 1978 "trilogy" establishes that special damages is, at the least, an acceptable usage to describe pre-trial loss of earning capacity. But important consequences should not, it is submitted, turn on verbal usage alone. Whether it is "correct" to categorize pre-trial losses as "special damages" depends, as in all legal questions, on the purpose for which the categorization is sought to be made.

[84] See 3.340, *supra*. But see *Gryden v. McLean* (1971), 24 D.L.R. (3d) 404, [1972] 1 O.R. 860 (C.A.), where delay in obtaining qualifications was held to be general damages because not capable of exact computation.

[85] *Semeniuk v. Cox*, [2000] 4 W.W.R. 310 (Alta. Q.B.). See 3.800-3.830, *infra*.

[86] See *Dobbin v. Alexander Enterprises Ltd.* (1987), 63 Nfld. & P.E.I.R. 1 (Nfld. C.A.); *McCallum v. Ritter* (1990), 72 D.L.R. (4th) 49, [1990] 5 W.W.R. 660 (Sask. C.A.); *Knoblauch v. Biwer Estate; Biwer v. Sopatyk; Besteman v. Biwer*, [1992] 5 W.W.R. 725, 104 Sask. R. 31 (Q.B.); *Reid v. Joy* (1999), 181 Nfld. & P.E.I.R. 246 (Nfld. C.A.); *Kielley v. General Hospital Corp.* (2000), 183 Nfld. & P.E.I.R. 1 (Nfld. C.A.).

[87] *Phillips v. London & Southwestern Ry.* (1879), 5 Q.B.D. 78 (C.A.).

business for which the plaintiff works,[88] or other financial opportunities.[89] General increases in rates of pay between injury and trial for the plaintiff's work will be known at the time of trial and these are taken into account.[90] In the case of a long delay before trial, the plaintiff may also be able to show that there would have been a chance of promotion in the interval or an individual merit pay increase.[91]

3.390 It has been held that income tax is not to be deducted in calculating compensation for pre-trial lost earnings.[92] The same rule has thus applied to pre-trial as to future losses. The merits of the rule are discussed later in relation to future losses.[93] It must be conceded that one of the chief arguments in favour of ignoring tax in compensation for future loss (namely, that the plaintiff will have to invest the proceeds of the award and pay tax on the future income from it that replaces the lost earnings) does not apply to pre-trial loss. However, it is submitted that the other arguments are applicable to pre-trial losses and that there are reasons of convenience for having the same principle applicable to pre-trial as to post-trial loss. It could not be considered unjust if the income tax rules were to be altered or interpreted[94] to impose income tax on damages representing compensation for past lost earnings. But the clear implication of *The Queen in right of Ontario v. Jennings* is that any such interpretation is for "proceedings in which the Minister of National Revenue is a party"[95] and any change in tax law is for Parliament. In any event the defendant should not benefit from generous tax treatment afforded to the plaintiff.[96]

---

88 *Duce v. Rourke* (1951), 1 W.W.R. (N.S.) 305 (Alta. S.C.); *Korenicky v. Arrow Leasing Ltd.* (1972), 28 D.L.R. (3d) 59, [1972] 3 O.R. 281 (Co. Ct.); *Dyler v. Benoche* (1963), 41 W.W.R. 431 (Alta. S.C.); *Lee v. Sheard,* [1956] 1 Q.B. 192 (C.A.); *Jason v. Batten (1930) Ltd.*, [1969] 1 Lloyd's Rep. 281. But see *Hardwick v. Hudson*, [1999] 3 All E.R. 426 (C.A.) (plaintiff not entitled to recover damages in respect of gratuitous services performed for his business). In several cases claims have failed for lack of proof: *Ashcroft v. Curtin*, [1971] 1 W.L.R. 1731 (C.A.); *Kummen v. Alfonso*, [1953] 1 D.L.R. 637 (Man. C.A.); *Johnstone v. Melina*, [1975] 3 W.W.R. 655 (B.C.S.C.); *Alexandroff v. The Queen in right of Ontario* (1968), 70 D.L.R. (2d) 162, vard but affd on this point [1970] S.C.R. 753, 14 D.L.R. (3d) 66; *Mercantile Mutual Ins. Co. Ltd. v. Argent Pty. Ltd.* (1972), 46 A.L.J.R. 432 (H.C.). On the question of the company's claim for loss of services, see 2.50-2.130, *supra.*

89 *The Queen in right of Ontario v. Jennings*, [1966] S.C.R. 532, 57 D.L.R. (2d) 644 (loss of stock option).

90 See *Yepremian v. Scarborough General Hospital* (1978), 88 D.L.R. (3d) 161 at pp. 187-8, 20 O.R. (2d) 510 (H.C.J.), vard 110 D.L.R. (3d) 513, 28 O.R. (2d) 494 (C.A.).

91 See 3.720, *infra.*; *Hunt (Litigation Guardian of) v. Sutton Group Incentive Realty Inc.* (2001), 196 D.L.R. (4th) 738 (Ont. S.C.J.), revd on other grounds 215 D.L.R. (4th) 193 (C.A.).

92 *Armstrong v. Stewart* (1978), 7 C.C.L.T. 164 (Ont. H.C.J.); *Wightman v. Coley* (1979), 100 D.L.R. (3d) 689, 25 O.R. (2d) 269 (H.C.J.), where Lerner J. referred to *Price v. Milawski* (1977), 82 D.L.R. (3d) 130 at p. 144, 18 O.R. (2d) 113, where the Ontario Court of Appeal had deducted income tax from pre-trial lost earnings, but without comment.

93 See 3.950-3.980, *infra.*

94 In *The Queen in right of Ontario v. Jennings*, [1966] S.C.R. 532 at p. 544, 57 D.L.R. (2d) 644 at p. 655, Judson J. said: "To the extent that an award includes an identifiable sum for loss of earnings up to the date of judgment the result might well be different." (*i.e.*, income tax might be payable by the plaintiff).

95 *Supra*, at p. 544 S.C.R., p. 655 D.L.R.

3.395 The question has sometimes arisen concerning the relevance of the claimant's income tax returns. A number of cases have held that a plaintiff is precluded, on policy grounds, from claiming a loss of earnings greater than that declared in previous years to the tax authorities.[96a] Others have held, however, that income tax returns are evidential, but not conclusive[96b] and this seems to be the preferable view. Removing the plaintiff's right to recover a proven loss from a wrongdoer is not a satisfactory method of punishing the making of false income tax returns.

3.400 Negative contingencies have often been ignored in calculating pre-trial losses[97] and this may be justifiable where the delay before trial is comparatively short and there is no evidence of particular events likely to interrupt the plaintiff's earnings. But, in principle, a reduction falls to be made. Often this will be less than is appropriate in calculating loss of future earnings because some matters, uncertain as to the future, will be known. Thus it will be known at the time of trial that the plaintiff has not suffered a disabling illness unrelated to the injury. It will also generally be known whether or not a recession in the plaintiff's kind of employment would have caused a layoff in the absence of the injury. There remain the possibilities that the plaintiff might have been injured by a different accident from that for which the defendant is responsible or that the plaintiff might have lost the job for reasons other than a general recession.[98] In *Holian v. United Grain Growers Ltd.*,[99] there was evidence of ill health prior to the accident which might in any event have prevented the plaintiff from working. Morse J. considered that this evidence justified a deduction of twenty per cent, and the Manitoba Court of Appeal, while upholding this figure, indicated that it "would have made a deduction in the range of 30% to 35%" adding: "There

---

96 *Supra*, footnote 94, at p. 546 S.C.R., p. 656 D.L.R.

96a *Frenette v. Audet* (1988), 89 N.B.R. (2d) 306 (C.A.), leave to appeal to S.C.C. refused [1989] 1 S.C.R. viii, 91 N.B.R. (2d) 43*n*; *Grivicic v. Doyle*, [1991] 4 W.W.R. 661, 121 A.R. 137 (Q.B.); *Poirier v. Bourque* (1992), 128 N.B.R. (2d) 296 (Q.B.), at p. 323; *LeBreton v. Patriacca* (1992), 128 N.B.R. (2d) 190 (Q.B.); *Kinsella v. Logan* (1995), 163 N.B.R. (2d) 1 (Q.B.), vard 179 N.B.R. (2d) 161 (C.A.).

96b *Bush v. Air Canada* (1992), 87 D.L.R. (4th) 248, 109 N.S.R. (2d) 91 (C.A.); *Squires v. Lang* (1992), 94 Nfld. & P.E.I.R. 108 (Nfld. S.C.); *Iannone v. Hoogenraad* (1992), 66 B.C.L.R. (2d) 106 (C.A.), leave to appeal to S.C.C. refused 154 N.R. 399*n*, 53 W.A.C. 79*n*; *Colliar v. Tolksdorff* (1992), 74 B.C.L.R. (2d) 145, 29 W.A.C. 308 (C.A.); *Milton-Coates v. Wolfe* (1992), 132 A.R. 241 (Q.B.); *Rustecki v. Da Silva* (1993), 10 O.R. (3d) 637, 11 C.P.C. (3d) 52 (Gen. Div.); *Slaney v. Ellis* (1993), 108 Nfld. & P.E.I.R. 181 (Nfld. S.C.); *English v. Locke* (1993), 125 N.S.R. (2d) 250 (S.C.); *Sivret v. Kenny* (1993), 142 N.B.R. (2d) 161 (Q.B.).

97 In *Holian v. United Grain Growers Ltd.*, *infra*, footnote 99, deduction was said to have been "novel".

98 Short absences from work will often be covered by disability insurance or sick pay. It would seem that the plaintiff can properly argue that the defendant has caused a loss if, in the absence of the accident, the plaintiff would have been off work but in receipt of sick pay. See *Hspahic v. Fernandez* (1987), 47 Man. R. (2d) 306 (C.A.); *L. (H.) v. Canada (Attorney General)*, [2005] 1 S.C.R. 401, 251 D.L.R. (4th) 604 (no compensation for loss of earnings during imprisonment); *Zastowny v. MacDougall*, [2008] 1 S.C.R. 27, 290 D.L.R. (4th) 219.

99 (1980), 114 D.L.R. (3d) 449 (Man. C.A.), leave to appeal to S.C.C. refused D.L.R. *loc. cit.*

are too many 'ifs and buts', when one attempts to compensate fully and at the same time, attempts to be fair both to the plaintiff and to the defendant, as the defendant should not be called to build up an estate for the plaintiff's heirs."[100] This last comment appears very odd in its context, for the future life expectancy of the plaintiff and the disposition of the plaintiff's assets on death are surely irrelevant to the calculation of damages for pre-trial losses. There are other passages in the judgment plainly indicating that the court considered the compensation excessive,[101] chiefly because of the rule requiring the plaintiff's pension benefits to be ignored.[102] It appears therefore that the court may have supported a large deduction for contingencies in order to offset the benefit to the plaintiff of the pension receipts. If so, it need hardly be said that this is a most unsatisfactory approach. If the collateral benefit rule is to be attacked, it should be dealt with directly.[103] The mention of a figure as high as thirty-five per cent may well lead to excessive deductions in future cases where there is no pension benefit. It is suggested that the *Holian* case can only be justified on the basis of the specific evidence there of serious illness prior to the accident. Rarely, it is suggested, will a large deduction for adverse contingencies be supported by the evidence, particularly when offset against the possibility of favourable contingencies such as promotion or salary increase.

(2) Cost of pre-trial care

3.410 Relationship of the cost of pre-trial care to the cost of future care is analogous to that of pre-trial earning capacity to future earning capacity. All expenses that would be allowable[104] in calculating the cost of future care should be allowed if they have been incurred before trial.

3.420 In *Shearman v. Folland*[105] the plaintiff had, before the accident, lived in hotels. The defendant argued that his liability for the cost of nursing home care necessitated by the accident should be reduced by the saving of hotel bills. The English Court of Appeal held that damages should be reduced by the portion of the nursing home fees that represented the cost of board and lodging, though not by amounts that the plaintiff had been accustomed to spend in excess of supplying necessaries.[106] This conclusion seems sound. In

---

[100] *Supra*, at p. 454.

[101] *Supra*, at p. 450 ("extremely large"); at p. 456 ("exceedingly high"). Costs were awarded to the defendant despite the plaintiff's substantial success (at p. 457).

[102] See 3.1590, 3.1600, *infra*.

[103] See 3.1490-3.1810, *infra*.

[104] Reasonable expenses only will be recoverable. See *Pollard v. Makarchuk* (1958), 16 D.L.R. (2d) 225 (Alta. S.C.). A reduction may be required for overlap if the medical services include food and shelter: *Wong v. Stefura* (1961), 36 W.W.R. 478 (Man. Q.B.). See 3.1050-3.1100, *infra*.

[105] [1950] 2 K.B. 43 (C.A.).

[106] Otherwise, as Asquith L.J. observed, a millionaire accustomed to living in a palatial hotel where the expenses exceeded that of the nursing home could recover nothing by way of special damages.

most cases, however, the plaintiff will have to maintain a home during any pre-trial period of hospitalization, and, in such a case, there will be no substantial saving of living costs. This point was made in *Land v. Canada Permanent Toronto General Trust Co.*,[107] when it was held that the onus was on the defendant to establish a net saving. The problem is analogous to that of overlap between the cost of future care and lost earning capacity, discussed later.[108]

3.430 In *Oliversen v. Mills*,[109] the British Columbia Supreme Court, following older English and Canadian cases, held that a married woman could not recover her medical expenses caused by the injury on the ground that only her husband was liable for the expenses. The same view was taken in *Gage v. The King*.[110] This view was rejected by the Ontario High Court of Justice in *Lang v. Gambareri*.[111] Haines J. pointed out that a married woman was capable of incurring debts on her own behalf and so should be entitled to recover compensation, even if her debts were in fact discharged by her husband. In *Andrews v. Arnot*,[112] Kirke Smith J. reaffirmed that the presumption was that only the husband was liable, though he held it to be rebutted in that case. Similarly in *Gagnon v. Ryland*,[113] the British Columbia Supreme Court permitted a married woman to recover, distinguishing *Oliversen v. Mills*, on the ground that the plaintiff in the *Gagnon* case earned an independent income and had actually paid some of the expenses for herself. It is submitted that a married woman should be able to recover in full the cost of her treatment whether or not she earns an independent income, whether or not her husband actually pays the expenses, and whether or not the husband is under any legal obligation to the provider of the services. It would be most anomalous in the light of modern family relationships to perpetuate a disability on the part of married women to contract in their own right, and since most medical expenses are paid by provincial health insurance plans, it would be anomalous for the wrongdoer's liability to vary according to whether the husband of an injured woman was joined as a party to the action. Furthermore, recovery by the husband can only rest (apart from statutory provision)[114] on the action for the loss of a wife's services or consortium generally agreed to be obsolete and abolished in several jurisdictions.[115] Failure to allow the wife to recover in her own right might in those jurisdictions mean that neither spouse could recover the expenses.

---

[107] (1964), 47 D.L.R. (2d) 448 (B.C.S.C.).
[108] See 3.1050-3.1100, *supra*.
[109] (1964), 50 D.L.R. (2d) 768 (B.C.S.C.).
[110] [1961] 1 Q.B. 188, followed in *Miller v. Charron* (1962), 39 W.W.R. 526 (B.C.S.C.).
[111] (1968), 70 D.L.R. (2d) 464, [1968] 2 O.R. 736 (H.C.J.).
[112] (1972), 27 D.L.R. (3d) 49 (B.C.S.C.).
[113] (1972), 28 D.L.R. (3d) 504 (B.C.S.C.).
[114] As in Ontario. See 3.1120, 5.1330, 5.1340, *infra*.
[115] See 3.1120, 3.1130, *infra*.

3.440 An injured person receives benefits in the shape of services, commonly[116] from close relatives, for which payment is not required. It appears at first sight that the injured person in such a case suffers no pecuniary loss, and until quite recently this was the position taken by the courts.[117] This position, however, gives rise to difficulties. First it is inconsistent with the general view taken by the courts on collateral benefits.[118] If the plaintiff receives a money gift, the plaintiff is not required to account to the wrongdoer for it; it seems anomalous that the rule should be otherwise in the case of services. If the plaintiff actually pays[119] or undertakes to pay[120] for the services, the plaintiff can be said to have shown a pecuniary loss. It was held, too, in several English cases that if there was a moral obligation to pay, the plaintiff could recover from the wrongdoer.[121] Once it is accepted that a contract to pay (even though it would probably never be enforced)[122] is sufficient to support recovery, the general rule denying recovery is difficult to sustain. Most of the cases involve services provided by close relatives. It seems anomalous to favour the plaintiff who was far-sighted enough to record an agreement to pay and "repulsive" as Megaw L.J. said in *Donnelly v. Joyce*[123] to favour the provider who stipulates for repayment. Further, the rule becomes unpredictable, for an implied contract will suffice or even, according to some cases,[124] a moral obligation

116 But not always, see *Carroll v. Baer*, [1924] 2 D.L.R. 452 (Sask. C.A.).

117 *Carroll v. Baer, supra*, footnote 116; *Greenaway v. C.P.R.*, [1925] 1 D.L.R. 992 (Alta. S.C. App. Div.); *Stewart v. Lepage's Inc.*, [1955] O.R. 937 (H.C.J.); *Taylor v. Turner*, [1925] 3 D.L.R. 574 (Alta. S.C.); *Hamilton v. Hayes* (1962), 36 D.L.R. (2d) 687 (B.C.S.C.); *Fabiszewski v. Hutchings* (1969), 4 D.L.R. (3d) 187 (B.C.S.C.), affd 28 D.L.R. (3d) 219 (C.A.); *Lamb v. Toronto and York Ry. Co.* (1921), 64 D.L.R. 527 (Ont. S.C. App. Div.); *Hagger v. De Placido*, [1972] 1 W.W.R. 716 (Crown Ct.); *Donovan v. Sterling* (1986), 72 N.B.R. (2d) 104 (Q.B.). Recovery was allowed however in *Sunston v. Russell* (1921), 21 O.W.N. 160 (H.C.); *Roach v. Yates*, [1938] 1 K.B. 256 (C.A.); *Liffen v. Watson*, [1940] 1 K.B. 556 (C.A.); *Povey v. Governors of Rydal School*, [1970] 1 All E.R. 841. See also *Fujiwara v. Affleck* (1962), 36 D.L.R. (2d) 284 (B.C.C.A.) (compensation for loss of future care not reduced by reason of expected free nursing).

118 See 3.1490-3.1810, *infra.*

119 *Einarson v. Keith* (1961), 36 W.W.R. 215 (Man. Q.B.).

120 *Haggar v. De Placido*, [1972] 1 W.L.R. 716 (Crown Ct.); *Swejda v. Martin* (1968), 3 D.L.R. (3d) 426 (Sask. Q.B.); *Sauve v. Provost* (1990), 66 D.L.R. (4th) 338 at p. 345, 71 O.R. (2d) 774 (H.C.J.), citing this passage. See *Mortimer v. Cameron* (1994), 111 D.L.R. (4th) 428, 17 O.R. (3d) 1 (C.A.) leave to appeal to S.C.C. refused 114 D.L.R. (4th) vii, 178 N.R. 146*n*.

121 *Roach v. Yates*, [1938] 1 K.B. 256 (C.A.); *Liffen v. Watson*, [1940] 1 K.B. 556 (C.A.); *Wattson v. Port of London Authority*, [1969] 1 Lloyd's Rep. 95. See Carr, "Measuring the Pecuniary Loss in Damages for Personal Injuries", 37 Mod. L.R. 341 (1974).

122 In *Wattson v. Port of London Authority, supra*, footnote 121, at p. 102 Megaw L.J. said that it would be "a blot on the law" if there were a financial disadvantage where the provider of the service behaved "like an ordinary decent human being". See, for the correct version of this passage, *Donnelly v. Joyce*, [1974] Q.B. 454 (C.A.), at p. 466.

123 [1974] Q.B. 454, at p. 463.

124 *Supra*, footnote 121. Where liability to repay is contingent on recovery of damages, there is a logical difficulty in making the award. See Luntz, *Assessment of Damages for Personal Injury and Death*, 3rd ed. (Chatswood, N.S.W., Butterworth Pty. Ltd., 1990), §4.3.1-4.3.4.

to repay. There will be no principle to prevent a court finding such a contract or obligation wherever it seems reasonable that payment should be made.

3.450 In two cases decided in 1973, *Cunningham v. Harrison*[125] and *Donnelly v. Joyce*,[126] the English Court of Appeal held that an injured person who had in each case been nursed by a close relative could recover the value of the services even though there was no legal obligation to reimburse the provider. In *Donnelly v. Joyce*, Megaw L.J. said: "the question whether or not the plaintiff is or is not under a legal or moral liability to repay, [is] so far as the defendant and his liability [is] concerned, . . . irrelevant".[127] The basis for the decision was that the plaintiff does suffer a loss even if it is made good by receipt of free services:

> His loss is the existence of the need for . . . nursing services, the value of which for purposes of damages — for the purpose of the ascertainment of the amount of his loss — is the proper and reasonable cost of supplying those needs . . . So far as the defendant is concerned, the loss is not someone else's loss. It is the plaintiff's loss.[128]

These cases have been followed in England[129] and in Canada,[130] and were applied by the Supreme Court of Canada in *Thornton v. Prince George School Board*.[131] The conclusion is much to be welcomed in that it avoids

125 [1973] Q.B. 942 (C.A.).

126 *Supra*, footnote 123. The cases were argued and decided together.

127 *Supra*, at p. 462.

128 *Supra*. This passage was doubted in *Hunt v. Severs*, [1994] 2 A.C. 350 (H.L.), at pp. 360-61, and *Dimond v. Lovell*, [2002] 1 A.C. 384 (H.L.), at p. 399.

129 *Davis v. Borough of Tenby*, [1974] 2 Lloyd's Rep. 469 (C.A.); *Taylor v. Bristol Omnibus Co.*, [1975] 1 W.L.R. 1054 (C.A.); *Housecroft v. Burnett*, [1986] 1 All E.R. 332 (C.A.).

130 See *Teno v. Arnold* (1974), 55 D.L.R. (3d) 57, 7 O.R. (2d) 276 (H.C.J.), vard 67 D.L.R. (3d) 9, 11 O.R. (2d) 585 (C.A.), vard [1978] 2 S.C.R. 287, 83 D.L.R. (3d) 609; *Veldhuizen v. Blokzyl*, [1977] 1 W.W.R. 526 (B.C.S.C.); *Hasson v. Hamel* (1977), 78 D.L.R. (3d) 573, 16 O.R. (2d) 517 (Co. Ct.); *De Marco v. Toronto Transit Com'n* (1978), 86 D.L.R. (3d) 451, 19 O.R. (2d) 691 (Co. Ct.); *Cavanaugh v. MacQuarrie* (1979), 35 N.S.R. (2d) 687 (S.C.T.D.); *Morey v. Kawaja* (1977), 18 Nfld. & P.E.I.R. 57 (Nfld. S.C. T.D.); *Lunnon v. Reagh* (1978), 25 N.S.R. (2d) 196 (S.C. App. Div.); *Grover v. Lowther* (1982), 52 N.S.R. (2d) 22 (S.C.T.D.); *Thomson v. MacLean* (1983), 57 N.S.R. (2d) 436 (S.C.T.D.); *Crane v. Worwood*, [1992] 3 W.W.R. 638, 65 B.C.L.R. (2d) 16 (S.C.); *Wenden v. Trikha* (1992), 116 A.R. 81 (Q.B.); *Turnbull v. Hsieh* (1990), 108 N.B.R. (2d) 33 (C.A.); *Rayner v. Knickle* (1991), 88 Nfld. & P.E.I.R. 214, supplementary reasons 32 A.C.W.S. (3d) 702 (P.E.I.C.A.); *Benstead v. Murphy* (1994), 23 Alta. L.R. (3d) 251, 157 A.R. 198 (C.A.); *Jacobsen v. Nike Canada Ltd.* (1996), 133 D.L.R. (4th) 377, [1996] 6 W.W.R. 488 (B.C.S.C.). In *Foucault v. Paradis* (1973), 8 N.B.R. (2d) 555 (Q.B.), and *Levesque v. Grondin* (1972), 7 N.B.R. (2d) 98 (S.C.), travel expenses were allowed even though transport was provided by a relative free of charge. See also *Montgomery v. Regional Administrative School Unit No. 2* (1995), 127 Nfld. & P.E.I.R. 91 (P.E.I.S.C.). But see *Michols v. McWilliams* (1980), 24 A.R. 102 (Q.B.), refusing to follow *Cunningham* and *Donnelly*, and *Wipfli v. Britten* (1984), 13 D.L.R. (4th) 169 at p. 191, [1984] 5 W.W.R. 385 (B.C.C.A.).

131 [1978] 2 S.C.R. 267, 83 D.L.R. (3d) 480; *Yepremian v. Scarborough General Hospital* (1978), 88 D.L.R. (3d) 161, 20 O.R. (2d) 510 (H.C.J.), revd on other grounds 110 D.L.R. (3d) 513, 28 O.R. (2d) 494 (C.A.); *Redden v. Hector* (1980), 42 N.S.R. (2d) 96 (S.C.T.D.); *Shaw's Estate v. Roemer* (1981), 46 N.S.R. (2d) 629 (S.C.T.D.), affd 134 D.L.R. (3d) 590 (S.C. App. Div.), leave to appeal to S.C.C. refused December 6, 1982.

the anomalies mentioned earlier and brings the law into line with the approach to collateral benefits.

3.460 As in the case of collateral benefits, the right of the plaintiff to recover against the defendant does not preclude the possibility of the plaintiff's ultimately being bound to account to the provider of the services.[132] In several of the cases the plaintiff recovered the money in trust for the provider.[133] In *Coderre v. Ethier*,[134] the plaintiff gave an undertaking to pay the money over, which would, it seems, have the same effect in most cases as a trust. The propriety of such a trust will depend on the justice of the case as between the plaintiff and the provider. Very often, as in the case of collateral benefits, it will be just for the damages to be held on trust. In this way the wrongdoer does not benefit from the provision of the services, and the plaintiff is not enriched by a double compensation.[135] Cases silent on the question are not inconsistent with this view for, if there is no dispute, there is no need for the court to determine the matter. The House of Lords has held that the underlying rationale of recovery is to enable the voluntary provider of care to receive proper compensation.[135a] The implications of this approach are that the damages should generally be held in trust for the provider and that where (as in the case before the House of Lords) care is provided by the defendant personally, the plaintiff is not entitled to recover. But in an Australian case where the care was provided by the defendant personally, the High Court held that the plaintiff's claim did not abate.[135b] It is to be observed, in favour of the Australian view, that where the defendant is a close relative it is not to be assumed that a benefit conferred on the plaintiff is intended as part satisfaction of a legal claim, particularly where there is insurance.[135c]

132 See 3.1490-3.1810, *infra*.

133 See *per* Lord Denning M.R., in *Cunningham v. Harrison, supra*, footnote 125, at p. 952; *Lunnon v. Reagh, supra*, footnote 130; *Thomson v. MacLean, supra*, footnote 130; *Grover v. Lowther, supra*, footnote 130; *Montgomery v. Regional Administrative School Unit No. 2, supra*, footnote 130. In *Thornton v. Prince George School Board, supra*, footnote 131, the money was ordered to be held on trust. In *Rawson v. Kasman* (1956), 3 D.L.R. (2d) 376 (Ont. C.A.), payment over to the provider was directed. See also *Turnbull v. Hsieh, supra*, footnote 130; *Rayner v. Knickle, supra*, footnote 130; *Matheson v. Bartlett* (1993), 121 N.S.R. (2d) 373 (S.C.); *West v. Cotton* (1995), 10 B.C.L.R. (3d) 73, 104 W.A.C. 53 (C.A.); *Jacobsen v. Nike Canada Ltd., supra*, footnote 130; *McCloskey v. Lymn* (1996), 26 B.C.L.R. (3d) 118, supplementary reasons 38 C.C.L.I. (2d) 279 (S.C.).

134 (1978), 85 D.L.R. (3d) 621, 19 O.R. (2d) 503 (H.C.J.) (here money had been paid out by the third party for the services); *Schneider v. Eisovitch*, [1960] 2 Q.B. 430. See *Dennis v. London Passenger Transport Board*, [1948] 1 All E.R. 779 (K.B.). On the other hand in *Wattson v. Port of London Authority, supra*, footnote 121, Megaw L.J. said that it did not matter that no firm undertaking had been given, and in *Liffen v. Watson*, [1940] 1 K.B. 556 (C.A.), at p. 558, in a passage approved in *Donnelly v. Joyce*, Goddard L.J. said that what the plaintiff does with the compensation received "is a matter for her and nobody else". See also *Housecroft v. Burnett, supra*, footnote 129, at p. 343. Many of the recent cases do not refer to the question.

135 See 3.1490-3.1810, *infra*.

135a *Hunt v. Severs, supra*, footnote 128.

135b *Kars v. Kars* (1997), 141 A.L.R. 37 (H.C.).

135c These points and others are made by Luntz in "Note", 113 L.Q.R. 201 (1997).

3.470 The measure of recovery was said in *Donnelly v. Joyce* to be the reasonable cost of supplying the plaintiff's needs.[136] In that case the recovery was measured by the wages given up by the provider of the service.[137] But this cannot be conclusive, for recovery is based on the injured person's own loss not that of anyone else.[137a] Moreover, recovery will be available even if the provider has not suffered any loss of income at all. If the provider's foregone income exceeds the value of the services, it would seem that the value should set a limit on recovery for, as Megaw L.J. pointed out in *Donnelly v. Joyce*,[138] the ordinary principles of mitigation would generally require the plaintiff in that case to purchase services at the market rate unless perhaps there were special reasons to justify nursing by a close relative.

3.480 The Ontario *Family Law Act* gives rights to certain relatives to recover pecuniary loss caused by injury, including "where, as a result of the injury, the claimant provides nursing, housekeeping or other services . . . a reasonable allowance for loss of income or the value of the services".[139] The action is available only to certain relatives[140] and is subject to special procedural restrictions.[141] It is not therefore a complete substitute for the common law action. The relationship of the statutory right to the common law right raises difficult problems, which are discussed later in the context of claims for lost earning capacity.[142] It is there submitted that the Act should be construed to provide a cause of action in the relative only in respect of losses not recoverable by the injured person himself. It may be argued that this interpretation would leave s. 61(2)(d) devoid of content. It is submitted, however, that there is nothing absurd in supposing that the Legislature, being uncertain as to the extent of the injured person's own common law right, created a right of action in the relative, in order to fill any gap that might be left by the common law. The legislative purpose is not therefore frustrated if there turns out to be no gap in the light of common law development. An alternative line of argument, supporting the same conclusion, is that the Act enables the provider of the service to recover only the pecuniary loss caused by the injury; if the injured person recovers compensation for

---

136 [1974] Q.B. 454 at p. 462.

137 As also in *Theriault v. Day & Ross Ltd.* (1977), 18 N.B.R. (2d) 112 (S.C.), affd 21 N.B.R. (2d) 120 (S.C. App. Div.).

137a *Van Gervan v. Fenton* (1992), 175 C.L.R. 327 (Aust. H.C.); *Newman v. Nugent* (1992), 12 W.A.R. 119 (S.C.).

138 *Supra*, footnote 136. See also *Housecroft v. Burnett, supra*, footnote 129, at p. 343; *Crane v. Worwood*, [1992] 3 W.W.R. 638, 65 B.C.L.R. (2d) 16 (S.C.).

139 Section 61(2)(d).

140 Those entitled to claim for wrongful death. See 3.1120, *infra*.

141 As in actions for wrongful death. See 6.1050, *infra*.

142 See 3.1120-3.1140, *infra*. In *Dziver v. Smith* (1983), 146 D.L.R. (3d) 314, 41 O.R. (2d) 385 (C.A.), it was held that the *Family Law Reform Act* did not preclude recovery by the injured person.

which that person is obliged to account to the provider, the latter suffers no pecuniary loss.

3.490 The approach taken by the Supreme Court of Canada in the 1978 trilogy to non-pecuniary loss is that its purpose is to enable the plaintiff to purchase a solace for disabilities. No reference was made in this connection to pre-trial losses, but it would seem that any money reasonably expended before trial on such a solace should be recoverable under the head of pre-trial losses. By its reference to solace, the court indicated that expenses beyond ordinary medical care may be justifiable in the case of a seriously injured person.[143]

(3) Other pre-trial expenses

3.500 In *Wellington v. Odlum*,[144] an injured person recovered expenses incurred by his brother in looking after the plaintiff's property. Recovery can be supported in such a case by analogy with the cases discussed previously of medical care supplied gratuitously to the plaintiff. In *Rose v. Gay*,[145] the plaintiff, who failed a year in law school because of his injuries, recovered the wasted cost of tuition, books, and supplies. This seems an acceptable alternative to attempting to measure the impairment of earning capacity by future lost income; the plaintiff is entitled to a presumption that at least the value of the wasted expenses has been lost.

5. Non-pecuniary Losses

3.510 As indicated earlier, damages for non-pecuniary losses stand on a different basis. As Spence J. said in *Arnold v. Teno*: "There is simply no equation between paralyzed limbs and/or injured brain and dollars. The award is not reparative: there can be no restoration of the lost function."[146]

3.520 There is no doubt that English and Canadian courts have been concerned that damage awards in personal injury cases should be held within reasonable limits. In the typical cases of personal injury claims, the defendant is either a large government or private organization, or is insured and whether the claim is against a motorist, a physician, a hospital, a manufacturer of products, a large corporation as occupier of land, or a government agency, the cost of liability will be borne ultimately by a wide section of the public. However seriously injured the plaintiff, it cannot be in the public interest to overcompensate at the defendant's expense. Spence J. said in *Arnold v. Teno:*

---

[143] See *Hayes v. Nanaimo Shipyard Ltd.*, [1972] 5 W.W.R. 337 (B.C.C.A.) (special equipment for injured yachtsman).

[144] (1971), 7 N.S.R. (2d) 1 (S.C.T.D.).

[145] (1976), 16 N.B.R. (2d) 84 (S.C.).

[146] [1978] 2 S.C.R. 287 at p. 332, 83 D.L.R. (3d) 609 at p. 638. For a collection of sums awarded for specific injuries, see *Goldsmith's Damages for Personal Injury and Death in Canada, 2002/2003-2005*, M. Reinhart, ed. (Toronto, Carswell, 1999), and D. Kemp and A. Macnab, eds., *Damages for Personal Injury and Death*, 7th ed. (London, Sweet & Maxwell, 1999).

> There can be no doubt that awards for non-pecuniary damages in the immediate past have been increasing apace. In the case of many verdicts in the United States, it may well be said that they have been soaring. The reasons probably are many. Firstly, I have pointed out the impossibility of accurate assessment. Then there must be many cases of what really are expressions of deep sympathy for the terribly injured plaintiff and a mistaken feeling that his or her sore loss of the amenities of life may be assuaged by the feeling of satisfaction from a pocket-full of money. There may even be some element of punishment for the wrongdoer or, the most irrelevant of considerations, a measuring of the depth of the defendant's purse. Certainly, such awards, which one may well characterize as exorbitant, fail to accord with the requirement of reasonableness, a proper gauge for all damages.
>
> [Once full compensation for pecuniary losses is accomplished] one may and should have regard for the social impact of very large and, as I have said, non-compensatory awards for non-pecuniary damages. The very real and serious social burden of these exorbitant awards has been illustrated graphically in the United States in cases concerning medical malpractice. We have a right to fear a situation where none but the very wealthy could own or drive automobiles because none but the very wealthy could afford to pay the enormous insurance premiums which would be required by insurers to meet such exorbitant awards.[147]

Although Spence J. disavowed the intention of awarding an "arbitrary conventional sum",[148] in *Andrews v. Grand & Toy*[149] and *Thornton v. Prince George School Board*[150] Dickson J. several times used the terms "arbitrary or conventional" and "conventional". The same phrase appears in *Lindal v. Lindal.*[151] Since the sum is not based on probable actual expenses, no reduction is appropriate for contingencies.[151a]

3.530 The theoretical basis of compensation for non-pecuniary losses has been much disputed. In an article written in 1972, Professor Ogus suggested three approaches, namely, the conceptual approach (putting an objective valuation on each facility lost), the personal approach (valuing the loss of happiness to the individual plaintiff) and the "functional" approach (measuring the amount needed to provide reasonable solace to the plaintiff after the injury).[152] Dickson J. in *Andrews v. Grand & Toy* having referred to Professor Ogus' article said:

> The third, or "functional" approach, accepts the personal premise of the second, but rather than attempting to set a value on lost happiness, it

[147] *Supra*, at pp. 332-3 S.C.R., pp. 638-9 D.L.R. See also the comments of the Alberta Appellate Division in *Prather v. Hamel* (1976), 66 D.L.R. (3d) 109.

[148] *Supra*, at p. 333 S.C.R., p. 639 D.L.R.

[149] [1978] 2 S.C.R. 229 at p. 261, 83 D.L.R. (3d) 452 at p. 475 ("arbitrary or conventional"), at p. 262 S.C.R., p. 477 D.L.R. ("largely arbitrary or conventional").

[150] [1978] 2 S.C.R. 267 at p. 270, 83 D.L.R. (3d) 480 at p. 490 ("Canadian conventional award").

[151] [1981] 2 S.C.R. 629, 129 D.L.R. (3d) 263.

[151a] *Graham v. Rourke* (1990), 74 D.L.R. (4th) 1, 75 O.R. (2d) 622 (C.A.); *York v. Johnston* (1997), 148 D.L.R. (4th) 225, [1997] 9 W.W.R. 739 (B.C.C.A.).

[152] Ogus, "Damages for Lost Amenities: For a Foot, a Feeling or a Function?", 35 Mod. L. Rev. 1 (1972).

> attempts to assess the compensation required to provide the injured person "with reasonable solace for his misfortune". "Solace" in this sense is taken to mean physical arrangements which can make his life more endurable rather than "solace" in the sense of sympathy. To my mind, this last approach has much to commend it, as it provides a rationale as to why money is considered compensation for non-pecuniary losses such as loss of amenities, pain and suffering, and loss of expectation of life. Money is awarded because it will serve a useful function in making up for what has been lost in the only way possible, accepting that what has been lost is inacapable of being replaced in any direct way.[153]

It is very clear that the court was concerned to find a principle that would justify moderation in awards. Dickson J. said:

> The sheer fact is that there is no objective yardstick for translating non-pecuniary losses, such as pain and suffering and loss of amenities, into monetary terms. This area is open to widely extravagant claims. It is in this area that awards in the United States have soared to dramatically high levels in recent years. Statistically, it is the area where the danger of excessive burden of expense is greatest.[154]

The express reference here and by Spence J. in the passage quoted earlier,[155] to the United States makes it clear that the court was anxious to establish a sharp distinction between American and Canadian common law on this question.

3.540 The theme of moderation appears, too, in the following comments:

> The award must be fair and reasonable, fairness being gauged by earlier decisions; but the award must also of necessity be arbitrary or conventional. No money can provide true restitution. Money can provide for proper care: this is the reason that I think the paramount concern of the Courts when awarding damages for personal injuries should be to assure that there will be adequate future care.[156]

Dickson J. adopted as the theoretical basis of the award the provision to the plaintiff "[of] reasonable solace for his misfortune".[157] The "functional" approach rests on reparation of loss suffered by the plaintiff and accordingly is not distinct in purpose from the award of damages for pecuniary losses, especially as the calculation of the latter may often include psychological considerations in the determination of what provision is reasonable for the plaintiff's future welfare. The compensation for non-pecuniary loss appears to be seen by the court as a further sum to make good the plaintiff's psychological losses not earmarked for expenditure on any particular item.

3.550 An important feature of the trilogy is the deliberate intention of the Supreme Court of Canada to establish national uniformity. Dickson J. said:

---

153 *Supra*, footnote 149, at pp. 261-2 S.C.R., p. 476 D.L.R.

154 *Supra*, at p. 261 S.C.R., p. 476 D.L.R.

155 *Arnold v. Teno, supra*, footnote 146, at pp. 332-3 S.C.R., pp. 638-9 D.L.R.

156 *Supra*, footnote 149, at p. 261 S.C.R., pp. 475-6 D.L.R.

157 *Supra*, at p. 262 S.C.R., p. 476 D.L.R.

> The amounts of such awards should not vary greatly from one part of the country to another. Everyone in Canada, wherever he may reside, is entitled to a more or less equal measure of compensation for similar non-pecuniary loss. Variation should be made for what a particular individual has lost in the way of amenities and enjoyment of life, and for what will function to make up for this loss, but variation should not be made merely for the Province in which he happens to live.[158]

And in *Thornton v. Prince George School Board*, he spoke of a "Canadian conventional award".[159] Thus, the Supreme Court of Canada seems plainly to have closed the door on any tendency there may have been in Canada to follow American patterns of extravagant awards by civil juries. Dickson J.'s emphasis on uniformity seems inconsistent with any possibility of higher awards in those provinces where jury trial is common.[160]

3.560 The figure fixed by the Supreme Court of Canada in each of the cases of the 1978 trilogy was $100,000. Although Spence J. in *Arnold v. Teno* spoke of flexibility to meet each differing individual case[161] it seems plain that $100,000 was intended by the court to be the general ceiling. All three cases involved very severe disabilities, and Dickson J. said of the plaintiff in *Andrews v. Grand & Toy:* "It is difficult to conceive of a person of his age losing more than Andrews has lost",[162] though he added: "Of course, the figures must be viewed flexibly in future cases in recognition of the inevitable differences in injuries, the situation of the victim, and changing economic conditions."[163]

3.570 The reference to "differences in injuries" and the "situation of the victim" appears to allow for the possibility of higher awards in particular cases, and there have been several cases subsequent to 1978 where higher awards have been made. In *Lindal v. Lindal*,[164] the British Columbia Supreme Court concluded, after discussion, that: "The door is . . . open to make a higher award".[165] The trial court awarded $135,000. The British Columbia Court of Appeal reduced the award to $100,000, finding that the physical injuries suffered by the plaintiff were less than those suffered by Andrews and Thornton, and that the mental disability suffered by Teno was "at least as

---

158 *Supra*, at pp. 263-4 S.C.R., p. 477 D.L.R.

159 *Supra*, footnote 150, at p. 270 S.C.R., p. 490 D.L.R.

160 In *ter Neuzen v. Korn*, [1995] 3 S.C.R. 674 at para. 112, 127 D.L.R. (4th) 577, it was held that "the trial judge should instruct the jury as to an upper limit, if . . . he or she is of the opinion that the damages by reason of the type of injury sustained might very well be assessed in the range of or exceeding the upper limit". See comments in *Dilello v. Montgomery* (2005), 250 D.L.R. (4th) 83 (B.C.C.A.) at paras. 29 and 40-45, and *Stapley v. Hejslet* (2006), 263 D.L.R. (4th) 19 (B.C.C.A.) at para. 41 (deference to jury must be balanced against need for predictability). The Ontario *Courts of Justice Act*, s. 118, provides that the court may give guidance to the jury on the amount of damages. See *Padfield v. Martin* (2003), 227 D.L.R. (4th) 670 (Ont. C.A.), and 13.460, *infra*.

161 *Arnold v. Teno*, [1978] 2 S.C.R. 287 at p. 334, 83 D.L.R. (3d) 609 at p. 640.

162 *Andrews v. Grand & Toy*, [1978] 2 S.C.R. 229 at p. 263, 83 D.L.R. (3d) 452 at p. 477.

163 *Supra*.

164 [1978] 4 W.W.R. 592 (B.C.S.C.), revd in part 115 D.L.R. (3d) 745 (C.A.), affd [1981] 2 S.C.R. 629, 129 D.L.R. (3d) 263.

165 [1978] 4 W.W.R. 592 at p. 602.

severe and probably more severe" than that sustained by Lindal. Consequently, the court considered that the $100,000 limit should prevail.[166] In the Supreme Court of Canada, Dickson J., in dismissing the appeal, said that a higher award would be "rare indeed".[167] In *ter Neuzen v. Korn*,[168] Sopinka J. quoted these words with approval but added that "the trilogy has imposed as a rule of law a *legal limit* to non-pecuniary damages", and that a larger award would be "as a matter of law" excessive. It would seem from this that the maximum figure cannot be exceeded even in rare cases.[169]

3.590 The reference to "changing economic conditions"[174] seems plainly to contemplate the adjustment of the conventional limit in accordance with the declining value of money. Otherwise, in an inflationary period, the court would have ordered not a fixed conventional limit, but in real terms, a perpetually declining limit. The English Court of Appeal has held that the figures used in that country for compensation for non-pecuniary loss are to rise with inflation,[175] and other conventional figures have been similarly treated.[176] In *Lim Poh Choo v. Camden and Islington Area Health Authority*, Lord Scarman said: "Like awards for loss of expectation of life, there will be a tendency in times of inflation for awards to increase, if only to prevent the conventional becoming the contemptible."[177] It is clear that the $100,000 figure is to be regarded as measured in 1978 dollars and is to be adjusted accordingly. This was expressly stated by the Supreme Court of Canada in *ter Neuzen v. Korn*.[178] Lower awards than the maximum are also to be adjusted.[179]

3.600 In *Hatton v. Henderson*,[180] the British Columbia Court of Appeal held that the conventional limits should be annually adjusted for inflation from January 1978, the date of the judgment of the Supreme Court of Canada. The trial judge had taken the trial date in *Andrews v. Grand & Toy* (1974) as the base, but the majority of the British Columbia Court of Appeal held that 1978 was the appropriate date, on the ground that the Supreme Court of Canada

[166] (1980), 115 D.L.R. (3d) 745 at p. 753.

[167] [1981] 2 S.C.R. 629 at p. 643, 129 D.L.R. (3d) 263 at p. 274.

[168] *Supra*, footnote 160, at para. 114 [Emphasis added].

[169] *Lee v. Dawson* (2006), 267 D.L.R. (4th) 138 (B.C.C.A.), leave to appeal to S.C.C. refused [2006] 2 S.C.R. ix, 269 D.L.R. (4th) vii (limit binding on lower courts and not contrary to Charter).

[170] [Footnotes 170-173 omitted.]

[174] *Andrews v. Grand & Toy*, [1978] 2 S.C.R. 229 at p. 263, 83 D.L.R. (3d) 452 at p. 477.

[175] *Walker v. John McLean & Sons Ltd.*, [1979] 1 W.L.R. 760 (C.A.).

[176] For example, damages for loss of expectation of life. See *McGregor on Damages*, 16th ed. (London, Sweet & Maxwell, 1997), §697. But see *Braun Estate v. Vaughan*, [2000] 3 W.W.R. 465 (Man. C.A.) (award for death of mother).

[177] *Lin Poh Choo v. Camden and Islington Area Health Authority*, [1980] A.C. 174 (H.L.), at p. 189.

[178] [1995] 3 S.C.R. 674 at para. 104, 127 D.L.R. (4th) 577 ($240,000 in respect of trial in 1991).

[179] *Montaron v. Wagner* (1989), 100 A.R. 194, 70 Alta. L.R. (2d) 86 (C.A.); *Bunce v. Flick*, [1991] 5 W.W.R. 623, 93 Sask. R. 53 (C.A.), leave to appeal to S.C.C. refused 137 N.R. 395*n*; *Dhugga v. Sodhi* (2004), 25 B.C.L.R. (4th) 160 (S.C.).

[180] (1981), 126 D.L.R. (3d) 50 (B.C.C.A.), followed in *MacDonald v. Alderson*, [1982] 3 W.W.R. 385 (Man. C.A.).

was, in the 1978 trilogy, not correcting errors on the part of the courts below but announcing a new rule to have effect from the date of its announcement. Nemetz C.J.B.C. dissented, on the ground that this was to attribute legislative functions to the court.

3.610 It is submitted that the view of the majority is sound. The result depends on an interpretation of the court's meaning and by far the more natural interpretation is that the court was speaking in terms of 1978 dollars. This is not to attribute legislative functions to the court; it is implicit that the proper conventional sum to have been awarded at trial in *Andrews v. Grand & Toy* in 1974 would have been a sum of about $80,000 (allowing for the inflation between 1974 and 1978). An appellate court will often admit new evidence to assess other aspects of personal injury awards in the light of the true facts, including evidence of prices higher than at the date of trial because of inflation.[181] The same should apply to an appellate court's assessment of a conventional sum for non-pecuniary loss. Relationship of these considerations to interest on the award is considered in a later chapter.[182]

3.620 A question that is not expressly dealt with in the 1978 trilogy is whether compensation for lesser injuries than those suffered by the plaintiffs in those cases is to be calculated on a sliding scale, so that $50,000 would be the appropriate award for a plaintiff suffering half the loss suffered by the 1978 plaintiffs, and so on, assuming that proportionate losses could be estimated. Some cases have adopted such a scale.[183] Others seem to have regarded $100,000 as a rough upper limit but have not treated it as imposing a proportionate limit on less serious injuries.[184] It would seem that some sort of scale ought to be adopted. Conventional though the $100,000 figure is, justice must still be done between plaintiff and plaintiff, and if $100,000 is the proper figure for injuries approaching the most serious imaginable, smaller

[181] See 13.620-13.650, *infra*. In *Lindal v. Lindal* (1980), 115 D.L.R. (3d) 745, an adjustment for inflation was disallowed by the British Columbia Court of Appeal for lack of evidence, the court saying, at p. 754, "There was no application before us to introduce new evidence." In *Hatton v. Henderson, supra*, footnote 180, at p. 56, Taggart J.A. stressed that in *Lindal v. Lindal* no application had been made to introduce the material evidence. Craig J.A. said that "the fact that there is not any specific evidence does not preclude a trial Judge from giving some recognition to the fact that there is inflation" referring to the duty of judges to take judicial notice of facts which are known to intelligent persons generally. In *Lindal v. Lindal* in the Supreme Court of Canada, Dickson J. held that a court could take judicial notice of inflation but not of the "precise rate" ([1981] 2 S.C.R. 629 at p. 641, 129 D.L.R. (3d) 263 at p. 273). See also *MacDonald v. Alderson, supra*, footnote 180, *Somers v. Fournier* (2002), 214 D.L.R. (4th) 611 (Ont. C.A.).

[182] See 7.660-7.720, *infra*.

[183] See *McLeod v. Palardy* (1981), 124 D.L.R. (3d) 506, 10 Man. R. (2d) 181 (C.A.); *Senft v. MacGregor* (1979), 99 D.L.R. (3d) 766 (B.C.C.A.); *Robson v. Official Administrator, County of Cariboo – Prince George* (1979), 101 D.L.R. (3d) 306 (B.C.C.A.); *Halliday v. Sanrud* (1979), 15 B.C.L.R. 4 (C.A.); *Bond v. Loutit*, [1979] 2 W.W.R. 154 (Man. Q.B.); *Keating v. Lenihan* (1978), 32 N.S.R. (2d) 111 (S.C.T.D.); *Epstein v. Wyle* (1980), 25 B.C.L.R. 341 (C.A.); *Schulz v. Leeside Developments Ltd.* (1978), 90 D.L.R. (3d) 98 (B.C.C.A.); *Letourneau v. McCoy* (1980), 21 B.C.L.R. 21 (C.A.); *Hodgson v. Walsh* (1999), 44 O.R. (3d) 598, 121 O.A.C. 255 (C.A.); *Reeves v. Arsenault* (1998), 168 Nfld. & P.E.I.R. 251 (P.E.I.C.A.), leave to appeal to S.C.C. refused 256 N.R. 193*n*.

figures must surely be appropriate for less serious cases.[185] Whenever an appellate court increases an award on the ground of inadequacy or reduces one on the ground of excess, it makes a comparison, implicit or explicit, with other similar cases.[185a]

3.630 In *Lindal v. Lindal*,[186] Dickson J. for the Supreme Court of Canada in confirming the "functional" approach to assessment said:

> Thus the amount of an award for non-pecuniary damage should not depend alone upon the seriousness of the injury but upon its ability to ameliorate the condition of the victim considering his or her particular situation. It therefore will not follow that in considering what part of the maximum should be awarded the gravity of the injury alone will be determinative. An appreciation of the individual's loss is the key and the "need for solace will not necessarily correlate with the seriousness of the injury" . . . In dealing with an award of this nature it will be impossible to develop a "tariff". An award will vary in each case "to meet the specific circumstances of the individual case".[187]

---

[184] *Savard v. Richard* (1979), 25 N.B.R. (2d) 45 (S.C. App. Div.); *Godin v. Bourque* (1980), 28 N.B.R. (2d) 643 (Q.B.T.D.), vard 32 N.B.R. (2d) 45 (C.A.); *Richards v. B & B Moving & Storage Ltd.*, [1978] 3 A.C.W.S. 113 (Ont. C.A.), referred to in *Savard v. Richard, supra; Noonan v. Heaney* (1979), 23 Nfld. & P.E.I.R. 1 (P.E.I.S.C.); *Howes v. Crosby* (1984), 6 D.L.R. (4th) 698, 45 O.R. (2d) 449 (C.A.); *Bracchi v. Horsland* (1983), 147 D.L.R. (3d) 182, 44 B.C.L.R. 100 (C.A.); *Leischner v. West Kootenay Power & Light Co. Ltd.* (1986), 24 D.L.R. (4th) 641, [1986] 3 W.W.R. 97 (B.C.C.A.); *Pendergras v. McGrath* (1988), 60 Alta. L.R. (2d) 276, 86 A.R. 291 (C.A.), leave to appeal to S.C.C. refused 97 N.R. 396*n*, 92 A.R. 320*n*; *Boyd v. Harris* (2004), 237 D.L.R. (4th) 193 (B.C.C.A.); *Dilello v. Montgomery* (2005), 250 D.L.R. (4th) 83 (B.C.C.A.); *Stapley v. Hejslet* (2006), 263 D.L.R. (4th) 19 (B.C.C.A.); *Sharpe v. Abbott* (2007), 276 D.L.R. (4th) 80 (N.S.C.A.). See *Koukounakis v. Stainrod* (1995), 23 O.R. (3d) 299, 12 M.V.R. (3d) 78 (C.A.) (upper limit relevant but only a "very rough" guide in less serious cases).

[185] In *Woelk v. Halvorson*, [1980] 2 S.C.R. 430, 114 D.L.R. (3d) 385, an award at trial of $30,000 had been reduced by the Alberta Court of Appeal as excessive in relation to the $100,000 limit. The award was restored by the Supreme Court of Canada, MacIntyre J. calling it "generous" but not "wholly erroneous". See p. 437 S.C.R., p. 390 D.L.R. See also *Hohol v. Pickering*, [1984] 3 W.W.R. 673, 51 A.R. 321 (C.A.); *Vieczorek v. Piersma* (1987), 36 D.L.R. (4th) 136, 58 O.R. (2d) 583 (C.A.) (jury award set aside); *Kamis v. Oaks*, [1988] 3 W.W.R. 428, 57 Alta. L.R. (2d) 307 (C.A.) (award reduced). On the question of jury instruction, see 3.550, *supra*.

[185a] *Peecock v. Altrogge* (1995), 131 Sask. R. 241, 95 W.A.C. 241 (C.A.); *Cody v. Leonard*, [1996] 4 W.W.R. 96, 15 B.C.L.R. 117 (C.A.); *Baas v. Jellema* (1998), 158 D.L.R. (4th) 633, 48 B.C.L.R. (3d) 310 (C.A.), leave to appeal to S.C.C. refused 163 D.L.R. (4th) vii, 232 N.R. 199*n*; *Tomer v. Wood* (1997) 188 N.B.R. (2d) 380 (C.A.); *Stubbert v. Smith* (1992), 117 N.S.R. (2d) 118 (C.A.); *White v. Slawter* (1996), 149 N.S.R. (2d) 321 (C.A.), leave to appeal to S.C.C. refused 208 N.R. 78*n*; *Rombough (Litigation Guardian of) v. Madonick Estate*, [1998] 9 W.W.R. 489 (Sask. C.A.). See also *Marky v. Arnold* (1995), 15 B.C.L.R. (3d) 294, 108 W.A.C. 209 (C.A.); *Taylor v. Hogan* (1998), 160 Nfld. & P.E.I.R. 93 (Nfld. C.A.), at p. 117, citing this paragraph; *Reid v. Joy* (1999), 181 Nfld. & P.E.I.R. 246 (Nfld. C.A.); *LeClerc v. Westfair Foods Ltd.*, [2000] 8 W.W.R. 592 (Man. C.A); *Unger v. Singh* (2000), 72 B.C.L.R. (3d) 353 (C.A.); *Vaillancourt v. Molnar Estate* (2002), 8 B.C.L.R. (4th) 260 (C.A.); *White v. Gait* (2004), 244 D.L.R. (4th) 347 (B.C.C.A.); *Courdin v. Meyers* (2005), 250 D.L.R. (4th) 213 (B.C.C.A.). In Alberta compensation for minor injuries in automobile accidents is limited by statute: *Insurance Act*, R.S.A. 2000, c. I-3; *Minor Injury Regulation*, Alta. Reg. 123/2004.

[186] [1981] 2 S.C.R. 629, 129 D.L.R. (3d) 263.

[187] *Supra*, at p. 637 S.C.R., p. 270 D.L.R.

The Ontario Court of Appeal in *Katsiroumbas v. Dasilva*[188] interpreted this passage to support the view that no "scaling down" was necessary for injuries less than the most serious. However, the passage would not seem to support this view. The point made by Dickson J. is that awards will vary with the plaintiff's need for solace. Although this will not necessarily increase with the gravity of the injury Dickson J. may well have had in mind the case of an unconscious plaintiff or one so seriously injured that he cannot enjoy anything that money can buy. The implication is that usually a grievous injury will justify a higher award than a less serious one.

3.640 In the later case of *Mulroy v. Aqua Scene*,[189] the same court, having referred to *Katsiroumbas v. Dasilva*, added:

> Large differences in awards to individuals who do not differ greatly in their age, sex or personal characteristics and reactions should not be encouraged. I do not accept the principle, hinted at during argument, that trial judges now have an unlimited scope to award what general damages they will, in disregard of principle and evidence, free from appellate correction and supervision.[190]

The court reduced an award of $25,000 for facial scarring to $10,000. It would seem from these comments that the court though disavowing the expressions "scale or tariff" is requiring, rightly it is submitted, that justice should be done as between plaintiff and plaintiff and as between defendant and defendant. This requires that similar injuries should, *prima facie*, receive similar compensation. These points were accepted by the Ontario Court of Appeal in 1999, when the court expressly spoke of a "scaling down" effect:

> The value of the trilogy limitation and the scaling down effect in cases below the upper limit that it is now recognized that it has ... is that it removes the lottery approach to the assessment of non-pecuniary damages and tends to facilitate reasonable predictability and uniformity in awards for these kinds of damages.[190a]

On the other hand, in *Boyd v. Harris*[190b] the British Columbia Court of

[188] (1982), 132 D.L.R. (3d) 696 (Ont. C.A.).

[189] (1982), 36 O.R. (2d) 653 (C.A.).

[190] *Supra*, at pp. 657-8. See also *Dhalla v. Jodrey* (1985), 16 D.L.R. (4th) 732, 66 N.S.R. (2d) 245 (C.A.) (award of $200,000 for injury to breasts reduced to $40,000); *Bisheimer v. Bryce*, [1991] 2 W.W.R. 738, 89 Sask. R. 302 (C.A.), leave to appeal to S.C.C. refused 136 N.R. 420*n*, 97 Sask. R. 239*n*; *Bunce v. Flick*, [1991] 5 W.W.R. 623, 93 Sask. R. 53 (C.A.), leave to appeal to S.C.C. refused 137 N.R. 395*n*. See *Kelloway v. Landry* (1995), 162 N.B.R. (2d) 348 (C.A.), at p. 352, where the New Brunswick Court of Appeal stated: "slavish reliance on ranges of compensation place the usefulness of the idea in danger of succumbing to an undesirable rigidity. Each plaintiff is entitled to have his or her case decided, not on the basis that the case falls by default within a range, but according to the evidence adduced."

[190a] *Hodgson v. Walsh* (1999), 121 O.A.C. 255 (C.A.), at p. 263, See also *Padfield v. Martin*, *supra*, note 160, *Bob v. Bellerose* (2003), 227 D.L.R. (4th) 602 (B.C.C.A.).

[190b] (2004), 237 D.L.R. (4th) 193 (B.C.C.A.); *Dilello v. Montgomery* (2005), 250 D.L.R. (4th) 83 (B.C.C.A.); *Sharpe v. Abbott* (2007), 276 D.L.R. (4th) 80 (N.S.C.A.); *Rizzi v. Marvos* (2008), 165 A.C.W.S. (3d) 1042 (Ont. C.A.); *Sandhu (Litigation Guardian of) v. Wellington Place Apartments* (2008), 291 D.L.R. (4th) 220 (Ont. C.A.), at para. 25. But see *White v. Gait* (2004), 244 D.L.R. (4th) 347 (B.C.C.A.).

Appeal took the opposite view. In *G. (B.M.) v. Nova Scotia (Attorney General)*,[190c] the Nova Scotia Court of Appeal considered the appropriate range of awards for sexual battery. Cromwell J.A. said that the functions of the award were to "provide solace for the victim's pain and suffering and loss of enjoyment of life, to vindicate the victim's dignity and personal autonomy and to recognize the humiliating and degrading nature of the wrongful acts".[190d] He added that "an acceptable range of damages must be identified. Recognizing that any figure will of necessity be 'arbitrary or conventional', it must also be 'fair and reasonable, fairness being gauged by earlier decisions'."[190e] The court held that the proper range was "between $125,000 and $250,000".[190f]

[*The next page is* 3-33]

[190c] (2007), 288 D.L.R. (4th) 88 (N.S.C.A.).
[190d] *Supra*, at para. 132.
[190e] *Supra*, at para. 136.
[190f] *Supra*, at para. 140.

3.650 Former cases had treated damages for non-pecuniary losses under several heads: pain and suffering, loss of amenities of life and loss of expectation of life. Some cases had spoken of "disfigurement".[191] Psychological injuries, such as neuroses, had also been held to be compensable.[192] The Supreme Court of Canada in *Andrews v. Grand & Toy* disapproved of the itemization of damages. Dickson J. said:

> It is customary to set only one figure for all non-pecuniary loss, including such factors as pain and suffering, loss of amenities, and loss of expectation of life. This is a sound practice. Although these elements are analytically distinct, they overlap and merge at the edges and in practice. To suffer pain is surely to lose an amenity of a happy life at that time. To lose years of one's expectation of life is to lose all amenities for the lost period, and to cause mental pain and suffering in the contemplation of this prospect. These problems, as well as the fact that these losses have the common trait of irreplaceability, favour a composite award for all non-pecuniary losses.[193]

There has been a difference of judicial opinion on whether aggravated

[191] *Jackson v. Millar* (1972), 31 D.L.R. (3d) 263 at p. 273, [1973] 1 O.R. 399 at p. 409 (C.A.), revd on other grounds [1976] 1 S.C.R. 225, 59 D.L.R. (3d) 246; *Charters v. Brunette* (1973), 39 D.L.R. (3d) 499, 1 O.R. (2d) 131 (C.A.); *Gagnon v. Beaulieu*, [1977] 1 W.W.R. 702 (B.C.S.C.); *Walton v. Todoruk* (1967), 66 D.L.R. (2d) 556 (B.C.S.C.). See *Strong v. Laughlin*, [1973] 1 W.W.R. 289 (B.C.S.C.); *Mulroy v. Aqua Scene, supra*, footnote 189; *Duff v. Westfair Foods Ltd.*, [1997] 9 W.W.R. 537, 156 Sask. R. 157 (Q.B.). In *Parlee v. Sun Oil Co.* (1977), 3 C.C.L.T. 159 (Ont. C.A.), the trial judge instructed the jury to consider how far money could buy pleasures that would "compensate for the misery of having scars on your face". Although the Court of Appeal disapproved of this approach, it can be said to have been vindicated by the 1978 Supreme Court of Canada decisions. Although in the past women have been more generously compensated than men in this respect (see *Munson v. Poirier* (1954), 12 W.W.R. (N.S.) 193 (Alta. S.C. App. Div.); *Baldwin v. Lyons* (1961), 29 D.L.R. (2d) 290, [1961] O.R. 687 (C.A.), affd [1962] S.C.R. vii, 36 D.L.R. (2d) 244; Kemp & Kemp, *The Quantum of Damages in Personal Injury and Fatal Accident Claims*, 4th ed. (London, Sweet & Maxwell, 1975), §3-651), it is submitted that in the light of modern views of equality of the sexes no such difference is justified.

[192] *Stein v. Sinclair* (1967), 61 W.W.R. 23 (Man. Q.B.); *Regush v. Inglis (No. 2)* (1962), 38 W.W.R. 245 (B.C.S.C.); *Shane v. Loiselle* (1961), 35 W.W.R. 190 (Man. Q.B.); *Canning v. McFarland*, [1954] O.W.N. 467 (H.C.J.), at p. 471, *per* Schroeder J.; *Diederichs v. Metropolitan Stores Ltd.* (1956), 6 D.L.R. (2d) 751 (Sask. Q.B.). But in *Enge v. Trerise* (1960), 26 D.L.R. (2d) 529 (B.C.C.A.), schizophrenia caused by a scar was held to be too remote. In *Montgomery v. Murphy* (1982), 136 D.L.R. (3d) 525, 37 O.R. (2d) 631 (H.C.J.), damages were awarded for depression caused by injuries to the plaintiff, though not for grief and sorrow at the death of his wife. In *Fobel v. Dean* (1991), 83 D.L.R. (4th) 385, [1991] 6 W.W.R. 408 (Sask. C.A.), leave to appeal to S.C.C. refused 87 D.L.R. (4th) vii, 97 Sask. R. 240*n*, non-pecuniary loss was held to include an award for pre-trial loss of housekeeping capacity. See also *Mann v. Jugdeo*, [1993] 4 W.W.R. 760, 108 Sask. R. 20 (Q.B.); *Hunter v. Manning*, [1993] 5 W.W.R. 738, 108 Sask. R. 26 (award to male plaintiff); *Marcotte v. Martin* (2004), 234 Nfld. & P.E.I.R. 208 (Nfld. & Lab. S.C.T.D.); *Beam v. Pittman* (1994), 147 Nfld. & P.E.I.R. 166 (Nfld. & Lab. C.A.).

[193] [1978] 2 S.C.R. 229 at p. 264, 83 D.L.R. (3d) 452 at p. 478. It would seem that impotence caused by the defendant should be compensated. *Meglio v. Kaufman Lumber Ltd.* (1977), 79 D.L.R. (3d) 104, 16 O.R. (2d) 678 (H.C.J.), refusing to follow *V v. C* (1972), 26 D.L.R. (3d) 527, [1972] 2 O.R. 723 (H.C.J.). Inability to bear children was treated as a loss of amenity in *Briody v. St. Helens and Knowsley Area Health Authority*, [2002] 2 W.L.R. 394 (C.A.), and pre-trial loss of capacity to perform household services in *Lyne v. McClarty*, [2003] 5 W.W.R. 598 (Man. C.A.).

damages are to be included.[193a] The analogy with defamation might suggest that they should not be subject to the trilogy limit, but this conclusion would open the door to unlimited awards in every case where there was an element of deliberate wrongdoing. In *McIntyre v. Grigg*,[193b] the Ontario Court of Appeal held that aggravated damages were "part of the general non-pecuniary award and subject to the upper limit for personal injury set by the Trilogy".

3.660 The "functional" approach adopted in 1978 by the Supreme Court of Canada invites a new look at the problem of the unconscious plaintiff. The majority of the House of Lords held in *H. West & Son Ltd. v. Shephard*,[194] over a vigorous dissent,[195] that a plaintiff, even if permanently unconscious and incapable of suffering, was entitled to compensation for loss of amenities of life. This decision was followed without debate by the Supreme Court of Canada in *The Queen in right of Ontario v. Jennings*,[196] but rejected by the Australian High Court in *Skelton v. Collins*.[197] More recently in *Lim Poh Choo v. Camden and Islington Area Health Authority*,[198] also a case of an unconscious plaintiff, the House of Lords required the drawing of "a clear distinction" between damages for pain and suffering and damages for loss of amenities, holding that an unconscious plaintiff, though not aware of her loss and incapable of suffering, was entitled to an award of £20,000 for loss of amenities of life. It may be persuasively argued that, in the light of the Supreme Court of Canada's stated general purpose of damages for non-pecuniary loss (to give solace to the plaintiff for his loss and to make his life more tolerable), there is no case for non-pecuniary damages at all where the plaintiff is unconscious; indeed, Lord Scarman in *Lim Poh Choo* recognized the force of such an argument, though considering that any change should be legislatively implemented.[199] However, *The Queen in right of Ontario v. Jennings*[200] was followed by the Supreme Court of Canada in the 1978 cases on another point, with no reference to a possible revision of the law with

193a *Brandner v. Brandner* (1991), 71 Man. R. (2d) 265 (Q.B.); *L. (H.) v. Canada (Attorney General)* (2002), 227 Sask. R. 165 (C.A.), at p. 219, varied [2005] 1 S.C.R. 401, 251 D.L.R. (4th) 604; *Y. (S.) v. C. (F. G.)*, [1997] 1 W.W.R. 229 (B.C.C.A.); *A. (T.W.N.) v. Clarke* (2003), 235 D.L.R. (4th) 13 (B.C.C.A.) (aggravated damages not a separate head). The question was left open in *Bob v. Bellerose* (2003), 227 D.L.R. (4th) 602 (B.C.C.A.), *supra*, note 190a. See also *Young v. Bella*, [2006] 1 S.C.R. 108, 261 D.L.R. (4th) 516.

193b (2006), 274 D.L.R. (4th) 28 (Ont. C.A.), at para. 48.

194 [1964] A.C. 326 (H.L.), following *Wise v. Kaye*, [1962] 1 Q.B. 638 (C.A.). See also *Andrews v. Freeborough*, [1966] 2 All E.R. 721 (C.A.).

195 Supported by *McGregor on Damages*, 16th ed. (London, Sweet & Maxwell, 1997), §1709.

196 [1966] S.C.R. 532, 57 D.L.R. (3d) 644. The decision was also followed in *Laird v. Costain* (1978), 24 N.B.R. (2d) 510 (S.C.), and *Krujelis v. Esdale* (1971), 25 D.L.R. (3d) 557 (B.C.S.C.). No allowance is made for pain and suffering while the plaintiff is unconscious: *Drewry v. Towns* (1951), 2 W.W.R. (N.S.) 217 (Man. K.B.).

197 (1966), 115 C.L.R. 94 (Aust. H.C.).

198 [1980] A.C. 174 (H.L.), at p. 188. In the Court of Appeal, Lord Denning (dissenting) had suggested that compensation for loss of earnings should also be withheld from an unconscious plaintiff, a suggestion supported by McLachlin, "What Price Disability?", 59 Can. Bar Rev. 1 (1981), at pp. 11 and 42, on the ground that the plaintiff cannot enjoy the use of the money.

respect to the unconscious plaintiff. On the other hand, *Skelton v. Collins*,[201] a decision diametrically opposed to *Jennings* was also cited with approval and for the very point (the functional approach) that had led the Australian court to reject *West v. Shephard*.[202] Consequently, it appears that the question of the unconscious plaintiff remains to be resolved in a future case.[203] *Lindal v. Lindal*[204] stressed the importance of the individual's need for the award and suggested that damages would be refused in the case of unconsciousness. This conclusion was reached by the majority of the British Columbia Court of Appeal in *Knutson v. Farr*,[205] though an award was supported in that case on the basis of evidence showing a slight possibility of the plaintiff reaching a level of awareness where some solace could be afforded. Impairment of, and reduction of life expectancy have been treated as reasons for reducing awards, since the solace that money can buy in those circumstances is reduced.[205a]

3.670 Damages for loss of expectation of life, that is for the shortening of the plaintiff's life, are also to be treated as indistinguishable from damages for pain and suffering, and for loss of amenities. Dickson J. clearly implies that it is the mental pain and suffering caused by the plaintiff's contemplation of the prospect of shortened life that justifies compensation.[206] Consequently, it would seem that for the reasons discussed previously, damages for loss of expectation of life ought not to be awarded to an unconscious plaintiff or to a plaintiff killed instantly by a defendant's wrong. Survival legislation provides in most Canadian jurisdictions that damages for loss of expectation of life do not survive to the estate.[207] It would seem that even in the other jurisdictions damages for loss of expectation of life could not, on the principle applied in the 1978 trilogy, be extensive where the plaintiff dies shortly after the accident. If the underlying basis of such damage is compensation for mental suffering, presumably, the shorter the plaintiff's life, the less the suffering. Previous decisions,[208] including a decision of the Supreme Court of Canada,[209] had held that moderate damages were recoverable for loss of

---

199 *Supra*, at p. 189. In *Housecroft v. Burnett*, [1986] 1 All E.R. 332 (C.A.), the English Court of Appeal identified lack of awareness as one of the factors operating to reduce awards for non-pecuniary loss.

200 *Supra*, footnote 196.

201 *Supra*, footnote 197.

202 *Supra*, footnote 194. See *Andrews*, *supra*, footnote 193, at p. 262 S.C.R., p. 476 D.L.R.

203 In *Laird v. Costain*, *supra*, footnote 196, $25,000 was awarded for loss of amenities to a permanently unconscious plaintiff, Cormier C.J.Q.B.D. referring to *Wise v. Kaye* and *West v. Shephard*, *supra*, footnote 194, but not to the Supreme Court of Canada cases which were presumably not drawn to his attention.

204 [1981] 2 S.C.R. 629, 129 D.L.R. (3d) 263.

205 (1984), 12 D.L.R. (4th) 658, [1984] 5 W.W.R. 315 (B.C.C.A.), leave to appeal to S.C.C. refused 58 N.R. 78*n*.

205a *McGlone (Guardian ad litem of) v. Kelly* (2002), 5 B.C.L.R. (4th) 134 (S.C.).

206 "To lose years of one's expectation of life is to lose all amenities for the lost period, and to cause mental pain and suffering in the contemplation of this prospect": *Andrews v. Grand & Toy*, [1978] 2 S.C.R. 229 at p. 264, 83 D.L.R. (3d) 452 at p. 478.

207 See 12.130, *infra*.

expectation of life, even where the plaintiff was killed instantly. Since these cases were not referred to in the 1978 trilogy, this question also remains to be resolved in a future case.[210]

3.680 The quality of the plaintiff's particular life and the particular prospects lost by the injury were not referred to by Dickson J. In *Rodzinski v. Modern Dairies*,[211] damages for loss of expectation of life were reduced because the plaintiff had led a life of crime and laziness (albeit a happy life as the judge was prepared to assume). It would seem that under the "functional" approach the quality of the life lost is not the primary factor to be considered. However, it would be arguable that the plaintiff's need for solace will be greater where a useful and productive life has been shortened than in the contrary case. The point remains to be resolved.

3.690 A point not explained by Dickson J. is the basis of compensation for pain and suffering (including mental suffering) occurring before trial. Suppose it to be established that the pain and suffering is over by the time of trial, because the plaintiff has made a complete recovery or for the opposite reason because the plaintiff has died or lapsed into a permanent coma. It would seem that little or no damages would be awarded on a strict application of the principle adopted by Dickson J. of making the plaintiff's life more endurable or of offering a solace for loss. As Fleming pointed out in 1973,[212] the justification for damages for past pain and suffering has not always been accepted as obvious. Fleming quotes Chief Baron Pollock as saying in 1854: "In my personal judgment, it is an unmanly thing to make such a claim",[213] and Lord Halsbury in 1900 said: "What manly mind cares about pain and suffering that is past?"[214] Nevertheless, it has been generally accepted that pain and suffering, even that occurring before trial, is an injury deserving of compensation. The justification is presumably that though money cannot make perfect reparation, it is the only medium of compensation available. It might be possible, also, to describe the award as a "solace" for past suffering.[215] It is difficult to believe, therefore, that the Supreme Court of Canada intended in 1978 to overrule the many cases that have given

---

208 *Anderson v. Chasney*, [1949] 4 D.L.R. 71 (Man. C.A.), affd [1950] 4 D.L.R. 223 (S.C.C.); *Rodzinski v. Modern Dairies Ltd.*, [1949] 4 D.L.R. 438 (Man. K.B.); *Gayhart v. Registrar of Motor Vehicles* (1956), 6 D.L.R. (2d) 474 (Man. C.A.); *Pollock v. Milbury* (1975), 65 D.L.R. (3d) 472 (Man. C.A.) ($6,500). In England it was held in *Benham v. Gambling*, [1941] A.C. 157 (H.L.) (£200), and in *Yorkshire Electricity Board v. Naylor*, [1968] A.C. 529 (H.L.) (£500), that conventional awards adjusted for inflation were to be made. By the *Administration of Justice Act 1982* (U.K.), damages for loss of expectation of life are abolished except in so far as suffering is increased.

209 *Crosby v. O'Reilly*, [1975] 2 S.C.R. 381, 51 D.L.R. (3d) 555 ($10,000). See 12.130, *infra*.

210 In *Farnham Estate v. Glass* (1978), 15 A.R. 176 (S.C.T.D.), Kirby J. awarded $12,000 allowing for inflation since *Crosby v. O'Reilly*. The Supreme Court of Canada 1978 cases were not referred to.

211 [1949] 4 D.L.R. 438 (Man. K.B.).

212 Fleming, "Damages for Non-Material Losses" in *Law Society of Upper Canada Special Lectures on Assessment of Damages for Personal Injuries*, 1973, 1, at pp. 1-6.

213 *Theobald v. Ry. Passengers Ass'ce Co.* (1854), 18 Jur. 583 at p. 586, *arguendo*.

214 *The "Mediana"*, [1900] A.C. 113 (H.L.), at p. 117.

compensation for pain and suffering before trial, and in fact the summaries of the damages at the end of Dickson J.'s judgments in *Andrews*[216] and *Thornton*[217] use the phrase "pain and suffering endured and to be endured". In *Fenn v. City of Peterborough*,[218] the Ontario Court of Appeal gave as a reason for increasing the award for non-pecuniary loss to $125,000 that the plaintiff "has suffered substantially more pain than any of the plaintiffs in *Teno, Andrews and Thornton*."[219] It would certainly be anomalous if the damages were to be greatly reduced on account of a delay of the trial until the worst of the plaintiff's pain was past.[220]

3.700 The English Court of Appeal in 2001 reviewed the level of awards in that jurisdiction, mentioning a figure of £200,000 in respect of the most serious injuries.[221]

6. Loss of Earning Capacity and Related Losses

(1) Capital value of loss

3.710 The loss to a disabled plaintiff of potential future earnings can be looked at either as a series of future losses or as a present loss. The Supreme Court of Canada held in *The Queen in right of Ontario v. Jennings*[223] that the latter view was the correct one in relation to considerations of income tax,[224] and this position was reaffirmed in *Andrews v. Grand & Toy Alberta Ltd.*[225] The House of Lords has also held in *Pickett v. British Rail Engineering*

---

[215] Though this is not the sense in which Dickson J. used the word in *Andrews v. Grand & Toy*. See passage quoted at footnote 153, *supra*. Windeyer J. said in *Skelton v. Collins* (1966), 115 C.L.R. 94 (Aust. H.C.), at p. 132, "It may be that giving damages for physical pain that is wholly past ... is simply an anomaly, for there can be no solace for past pain."

[216] *Supra*, footnote 206, at pp. 265-6 S.C.R., p. 479 D.L.R.

[217] [1978] 2 S.C.R. 267 at p. 285, 83 D.L.R. (3d) 480 at p. 491.

[218] (1979), 104 D.L.R. (3d) 174, 25 O.R. (2d) 399 (C.A.), affd [1981] 2 S.C.R. 613, 129 D.L.R. (3d) 507.

[219] *Supra*, at p. 226 D.L.R., p. 452 O.R.

[220] This point is made by Cooper-Stephenson, *Personal Injury Damages in Canada*, 2nd ed. (Toronto, Carswell, 1996), p. 518.

[221] *Heil v. Rankin*, [2001] Q.B. 272 (C.A.).

[222] [Text deleted.]

[223] [1966] S.C.R. 532, 57 D.L.R. (2d) 644. "The plaintiff has been deprived of his capacity to earn income. It is the value of that capital asset which has to be assessed", *per* Judson J., at p. 546 S.C.R., p. 656 D.L.R.

[224] See 3.950-3.980, *infra*.

[225] [1978] 2 S.C.R. 229 at p. 251, 83 D.L.R. (3d) 452 at p. 469, *per* Dickson J. ("not loss of earnings but, rather, loss of earning capacity ... A capital asset has been lost"). See also *Embleton v. Wiseman* (1981), 128 D.L.R. (3d) 183 (B.C.C.A.), at p. 186; *Bunce v. Flick*, [1991] 5 W.W.R. 623, 93 Sask. R. 53 (C.A.), leave to appeal to S.C.C. refused 137 N.R. 395*n*; *Dillon v. LeRoux*, [1994] 6 W.W.R. 280, 89 B.C.L.R. (2d) 376 (C.A.); *Pallos v. Insurance Corp. of British Columbia*, [1995] 3 W.W.R. 728, 100 B.C.L.R. (2d) 260, supplementary reasons 7 B.C.L.R. (3d) 211, 41 C.P.C. (3d) 39 (C.A.); *Graff v. Bennett*, [1995] 9 W.W.R. 609, 134 Sask. R. 161 (C.A.); *Lee v. Swan*, [1996] 6 W.W.R. 665, 19 B.C.L.R. (3d) 21 (C.A.); *Morris v. Rose Estate* (1996), 23 B.C.L.R. (3d) 256, 123 W.A.C. 263 (C.A.); *Reed v. Steele* (1997), 148 D.L.R. (4th) 695, 36 B.C.L.R. (3d) 90 (C.A.); *Friesen v. Pretorius Estate* (1997), 37 B.C.L.R. (3d) 255, 40 C.C.L.T. (2d) 72 (C.A.); *Exide Electronics Ltd. v. Webb* (1999), 177 N.S.R. (2d) 147 (C.A.); *Ryan v. Sun Life Assurance Co. of Canada* (2005), 249 D.L.R. (4th) 628 (N.S.C.A.), at p. 638, citing this paragraph.

Ltd.[226] and in *Gammell v. Wilson*[227] that the loss is to be regarded as a present capital loss of earning capacity. Australian cases have taken the same view.[228] This is the prevailing view also in the United States.[229] The categorization has important implications in calculating the appropriate measure of compensation, as will appear from the following paragraphs.

(2) Calculation of annual loss

3.720 Since a person's earning capacity does not have a market value, the usual way of determining its value is to estimate the plaintiff's probable annual lost earnings,[229a] the number of years during which the loss extends, and to multiply the one figure by the other.[230] When the plaintiff is an established member of the work-force, the salary at the time of injury provides an obvious starting point. If the plaintiff's earning capacity is only partially destroyed, recovery will be based on the difference between prospective earnings before and after the injury.[231] The possibility of promotion should be taken into account.[232] In *Andrews v. Grand & Toy*,[233] the annual level of earnings was fixed at a point between Andrew's level of earnings at the time of the accident, and the maximum level obtainable in his type of work. This figure was taken as his average annual expected income. More difficulties arise where the plaintiff has not entered the work-force. In the case of an adult who has a definite expectation of entering a particular trade or profession, average earnings in that trade or profession will provide a guide.[234] In the case of children at school the court takes account of the

[226] [1980] A.C. 136 (H.L.).

[227] [1982] A.C. 27 (H.L.).

[228] *Skelton v. Collins* (1966), 115 C.L.R. 94 (Aust. H.C.). See Luntz, *Assessment of Damages for Personal Injury and Death*, 3rd ed. (Chatswood, N.S.W., Butterworth Pty. Ltd., 1990), §5.1.3, suggesting little practical significance.

[229] See McCormick, *Handbook on the Law of Damages* (St. Paul, West Publishing Co., 1935), pp. 299-309; Dobbs, *Handbook on the Law of Remedies: Damages-Equity-Restitution* (St. Paul, West Publishing Co., 1973), p. 540; *McLaughlin v. Chicago, Milwaukee, St. Paul & Pacific Ry. Co.*, 143 N.W. 2d 32 (Wis. S.C. 1966).

[229a] Probabilities less than 50 per cent are to be taken into account: *Anderson v. James* (1992), 87 D.L.R. (4th) 419, 63 B.C.L.R. (2d) 176 (C.A.); *Norris v. Blake (by his Tutor Porter) (No. 2)* (1997), 41 N.S.W.L.R. 49 (C.A.).

[230] See 3.990-3.1040, 3.940, *infra*, for discounting to present value, and adjustments for contingencies.

[231] *Floyd v. Bowers* (1978), 89 D.L.R. (3d) 559, 21 O.R. (2d) 204 (H.C.J.), vard 106 D.L.R. (3d) 702, 27 O.R. (2d) 487 (C.A.); *Conklin v. Smith*, [1978] 2 S.C.R. 1107, 88 D.L.R. (3d) 317; *Joyce v. Yeomans*, [1981] 2 All E.R. 21 (C.A.); *Webber v. Lowrie* (1979), 15 B.C.L.R. 289 (S.C.). See *Kwei v. Boisclair* (1991), 60 B.C.L.R. (2d) 393, 13 W.A.C. 314 (C.A.); *Dillon v. LeRoux*, *supra*, footnote 225; *Hall v. Zhou* (1996), 21 B.C.L.R. (3d) 355, 119 W.A.C. 148 (C.A.) (plaintiff not entitled to insist on outdoor work); *Parypa v. Wickware* (1999), 169 D.L.R. (4th) 661 (B.C.C.A.); *Hay v. Hofmann* (1999), 61 B.C.L.R. (3d) 275 (C.A.).

[232] *Schroth v. Innes* (1976), 71 D.L.R. (3d) 647 (B.C.C.A.); *Fair v. London & North West Ry.* (1869), 21 L.T. 326; *Bisson v. District of Powell River* (1967), 66 D.L.R. (2d) 226 (B.C.C.A.), affd 68 D.L.R. (2d) 765*n* (S.C.C.); *Bilde v. Cooke*, [1974] 4 W.W.R. 89 (B.C.S.C.); *Wynn v. NSW Insurance Ministerial Corporation* (1995), 184 C.L.R. 485 (Aust. H.C.).

[233] *Supra*, footnote 225.

plaintiff's success in school work.[235] In the case of younger children, the problem is more difficult still.[236] The English Court of Appeal in *Joyce v. Yeomans*[237] declined to estimate an annual loss, choosing instead a lump sum. But in *Arnold v. Teno*,[238] where the plaintiff was a four-year-old child, the Supreme Court of Canada assessed her annual probable level of earnings at $7,500, a figure apparently reached by halving the difference between the poverty level and her mother's annual income.[239] The approach of the Supreme Court of Canada in basing its award on an estimated annual income is, it is submitted, to be welcomed for otherwise there is a danger of undercompensation.[240] It seems doubtful, however, whether the figures chosen can be shown to be a reliable guide to predicting a child's future income. An alternative approach would be, in the absence of better evidence, to base the award on the average annual wage.[241] In *McLeod v. Palardy*,[242] the Manitoba Court of Appeal upheld an award for loss of earning capacity of a thirty-one-year-old woman, despite the fact that she had worked only sporadically before the accident. The court based the award on a figure slightly above the minimum wage, but discounted the total by forty per cent to allow for uncertainty of employment.[243]

3.730 The value of fringe benefits should, in principle, be added to the money income.[244] However, care is needed to avoid duplication of damages, where

---

[234] In *Conklin v. Smith, supra*, footnote 231, account was taken of the plaintiff's former intention to become a commercial air pilot, and in *McKay v. Board of Govan School Unit No. 29 of Saskatchewan*, [1968] S.C.R. 589, 68 D.L.R. (2d) 519, of the plaintiff's ambition to become an architect. See also *Daigle v. Theo Couturier Ltd.* (1973), 43 D.L.R. (3d) 151 (N.B.S.C. App. Div.) (loss of opportunity to become professional hockey player); *Hearndon v. Rondeau* (1984), 54 B.C.L.R. 145, 29 C.C.L.T. 149 (C.A.); *Freitag v. Davis*, [1984] 6 W.W.R. 188 (B.C.C.A.); *Herring v. Ministry of Defence*, [2004] 1 All E.R. 44 (C.A.) (loss of opportunity to become a police officer); *Kern v. Steele* (2003), 220 N.S.R (2d) 51 (C.A.) (loss of opportunity to become a press woman); *Haile v. Johns* (2005), 50 B.C.L.R. (4th) 241 (B.C.C.A.) (loss of opportunity to return to work as a glazier).

[235] *Bogusinski v. Rashidagich*, [1974] 5 W.W.R. 53 (B.C.S.C.); *Floyd v. Bowers, supra*, footnote 231; *Rudd v. Hamiota Feedlot Ltd.* (2006), 200 Man. R. (2d) 26 (Q.B.).

[236] See *Jones v. Lawrence*, [1969] 3 All E.R. 267; *S. v. Distillers Co. (Biochemicals)*, [1970] 1 W.L.R. 114 (Q.B.); *Taylor v. Bristol Omnibus Co. Ltd.*, [1975] 1 W.L.R. 1054 (C.A.). Some cases have omitted any award to a child for lost earning capacity: *Loney v. Voll*, [1974] 3 W.W.R. 193 (Alta. S.C.T.D.). Other cases have included it as a factor in an undifferentiated global sum: *Oman v. Public Trustee*, [1973] 2 W.W.R. 577 (Alta. S.C.); *Lillico v. Glimps*, [1971] 1 W.W.R. 750 (Alta. S.C.), affd [1971] S.C.R. v; *McKay v. Board of Govan School Unit No. 29 of Saskatchewan*, [1968] S.C.R. 589, 68 D.L.R. (2d) 519. These cases, it is submitted, are superseded by the 1978 "trilogy".

[237] [1981] 2 All E.R. 21 (C.A.). See also *Taylor v. Bristol Omnibus Co.*, [1975] 1 W.L.R. 1054 (C.A.).

[238] [1978] 2 S.C.R. 287, 83 D.L.R. (3d) 609.

[239] *Supra*, at pp. 328-31 S.C.R., pp. 636-8 D.L.R.

[240] Even on the basis mentioned and a further reduction for contingencies Teno recovered $54,000. Awards based on a rounded sum tend to be low. See *Connolly v. Camden and Islington Area Health Authority*, [1981] 3 All E.R. 250 (Q.B.) (£7,500). In *Croke v. Wiseman*, [1981] 3 All E.R. 852, where the English Court of Appeal approved an award based on the national average annual wage, the plaintiff recovered £25,000. In *Webster v. Chapman*, [1996] 9 W.W.R. 652, 114 Man. R. (2d) 1 (Q.B.), revd 155 D.L.R. (4th) 82, [1998] 4 W.W.R. 335 (C.A.), leave to appeal to S.C.C. refused 159 D.L.R. (4th) vii, the court considered the education of the child's parents and socio-economic factors.

the fringe benefits constitute insurance against a risk that is obviated by the damage award itself.[244a] Thus if the plaintiff is awarded the full value of a lost income stream, the plaintiff ought not, in addition, recover the value of the employer's contribution to a disability insurance plan; indeed the plaintiff's own contribution should be deducted from the estimate of the annual loss. But in that case the sum awarded for loss of income ought not to be reduced for the contingency of disability. For, had the wrong not been done, the plaintiff would have (on payment of her portion of the disability insurance premiums) been protected against that particular contingency.[245]

3.740 Delay caused by the injury in obtaining qualifications is compensable.[246] Sometimes this may form part of the pre-trial loss. Often, however, the effect of the accident will be to delay the future commencement of the plaintiff's stream of earnings, and this delay represents a compensable loss.[247]

3.750 Loss of financial benefits other than salary is also compensable. Cases have awarded compensation in respect of the loss of the value of the shares in a closely held corporation for which the plaintiff had expected to work.[248] Compensation has been awarded for the loss of opportunity of winning prizes at sport[249] and for the loss of unconventional business opportunities.[249a] There must however be a dependable basis for assessment.[249b]

---

[241] As in *Croke v. Wiseman, supra,* footnote 240, at p. 862 ("national average wage for a young man"); *Wipfli v. Britten* (1984), 13 D.L.R. (4th) 169, [1984] 5 W.W.R. 385 (B.C.C.A.) (figure somewhat below average wage for young men). The courts have assumed in the past that women have a restricted earning capacity, on account of the prospects of marriage. See *per* Clement J.A., in *Prather v. Hamel* (1976), 66 D.L.R. (3d) 109 (Alta. S.C. App. Div.), at p. 114. However no such suggestion appears in *Arnold v. Teno.* See *Hughes v. McKeown,* [1985] 1 W.L.R. 963 (Q.B.). The minimum wage was used as a basis in *Cromwell v. Dave Buck Ford Lease Ltd.* (1980), 109 D.L.R. (3d) 82 (B.C.S.C.). And see *Tucker (Guardian Ad Litem) v. Asleson* (1993), 102 D.L.R. (4th) 518, [1993] 6 W.W.R. 45 (B.C.C.A.) (female plaintiff; average male earnings used), not followed in *MacCabe v. Westlock Roman Catholic Separate School District No. 110,* [2002] 1 W.W.R. 610 (Alta. C.A.). In *Walker v. Ritchie* (2005), 25 C.C.L.I. (4th) 60 (Ont. C.A.), vard on another point [2006] 2 S.C.R. 428, 273 D.L.R. (4th) 240, figures for graduates in the entire population were used. This last question was left open by the Supreme Court of Canada in *Toneguzzo-Norvell (Guardian ad Litem of) v. Burnaby Hospital,* [1994] 1 S.C.R. 114, 110 D.L.R. (4th) 289. See also *Rudd v. Hamiota Feedlot Ltd.* (2006), 200 Man. R. (2d) 26 (Q.B.).

[242] (1981), 124 D.L.R. (3d) 506 (Man. C.A.).

[243] [Footnote deleted.]

[244] *Liffen v. Watson,* [1940] 1 K.B. 556 (C.A.) (board and lodging for domestic servant); *Loomis v. Rohan* (1974), 46 D.L.R. (3d) 423 (B.C.S.C.) (welfare benefits); *The Queen in right of Ontario v. Jennings,* [1966] S.C.R. 532, 57 D.L.R. (2d) 644 (stock option). See *May v. Municipality of Metropolitan Toronto* (1968), 2 D.L.R. (3d) 659, [1969] 1 O.R. 419 (H.C.J.) (value of car taken into account in fatal accident case); *Lan v. Wu,* [1981] 1 W.W.R. 64 (B.C.C.A.), leave to appeal to S.C.C. refused 33 N.R. 583*n*.

[244a] *Mortimer v. Cameron* (1994), 111 D.L.R. (4th) 428 at p. 445, 17 O.R. (3d) 1 at pp. 19-20 (C.A.), leave to appeal to S.C.C. refused 114 D.L.R. (4th) vii, 178 N.R. 146*n*.

[245] See 3.940, *infra.* In *Lan v. Wu, supra,* footnote 244, the Court of Appeal corrected a duplication of recovery of holiday pay.

[246] *Gruden v. McLean* (1971), 24 D.L.R. (3d) 404, [1972] 1 O.R. 860 (C.A.).

[247] *Deziel v. Deziel,* [1953] 1 D.L.R. 651 (Ont. H.C.J.); *Albert v. Pelletier* (1983), 54 N.B.R. (2d) 188 (Q.B.); *Treberg v. Jarvis* (2007), 268 Nfld. & P.E.I.R. 42 (Nfld. & Lab. S.C.T.D.); *Oates v. Morgan* (2007), 268 Nfld. & P.E.I.R. 1 (Nfld. & Lab. C.A.).

[248] See 3.380, *supra.*

3.760 Where the plaintiff is a partner in a business enterprise and on account of the injury is unable to render services to the partnership, difficulties arise, for it can be argued that the plaintiff's loss is only the loss to the interest in the

[*The next page is* 3-41]

[249] *Leis v. Gardner*, [1965] Qd. R. 181 (Full Ct.); *Mulvaine v. Joseph* (1968), 112 S.J. 927 (M.C.).

[249a] *Anderson v. James* (1992), 87 D.L.R. (4th) 419, 63 B.C.L.R. (2d) 176 (C.A.).

[249b] *Franklin v. Aviscar Inc.*, [1997] 3 W.W.R. 521, 27 B.C.L.R. (3d) 181 (C.A.).

partnership. In *Lee v. Sheard*,[250] Denning L.J. said: "So, too, a partner in a partnership would be entitled to recover his own real loss and no more."[251] The same argument could be made if the plaintiff owned only a fifty per cent share or some other share less than 100 per cent in a business corporation.[252] But the conclusion suggested by Denning L.J. is, it is submitted, inconsistent with the view now prevailing in most common law jurisdictions that compensation is for loss of earning capacity.[253] In a later case, it was said: "The issue . . . can be encapsulated in the question: 'what was [the plaintiff's] real loss of earnings and/or earning capacity?'".[253a] A person who is disabled loses earning capacity whether intending to work for a salary or for a corporation or partnership in which the person had an interest. The plaintiff's recovery ought not to vary according to the particular way in which the plaintiff proposed to gain remuneration for services. Several cases have held that, where sufficient proof is made of the corporation's loss, the injured person can recover it in the person's own right.[254] In *Engel v. Salyn*,[254a] where the plaintiff owned a half-share in a family business, the Supreme Court of Canada held that the appropriate method of calculation depended on the circumstances of the case. The court approved a method based on one-half of the cost of replacement staff, describing it as "reasonable in the circumstances" and "even ... somewhat conservative".[254b] In *D'Amato v. Bodger*,[254c] the plaintiff owned a half-share in the corporation that employed him. The Supreme Court of Canada held the plaintiff entitled, in his own right, to full compensation for his lost earning capacity. The court upheld, in addition, an award to the plaintiff of one-half of the corporation's loss, adding

[250] [1956] 1 Q.B. 192 (C.A.).

[251] *Supra*, at p. 196.

[252] These were the facts in *Lee v. Sheard, supra*, footnote 250. See also *Seymour v. Gough* (1994), 1 Qd. R. 89 (C.A.).

[253] See *D'Amato v. Badger*, [1996] 2 S.C.R. 1071, 137 D.L.R. (4th) 129; *Husher v. Husher* (1999), 197 C.L.R. 138 (Aust. H.C.); *Madge v. Meyer*, [2000] 5 W.W.R. 38 (Alta. Q.B.), affd [2001] 7 W.W.R. 635 (C.A.). See also 3.710, *supra*.

[253a] *Ward v. Newalls Insulation Co. Ltd.*, [1998] 1 W.L.R. 1722 (C.A.).

[254] In *Craig Bros. v. Sisters of Charity*, [1940] 4 D.L.R. 561 (Sask. C.A.), Taylor J., at pp. 564-5, spoke of the plaintiff's "actual earning power". See also *Haley v. Morris*, [1981] 4 W.W.R. 488 (B.C. Co. Ct.); *Everett v. King*, [1982] 1 W.W.R. 561 (B.C.S.C.), affd 53 B.C.L.R. 144 (C.A.); *Korenicky v. Arrow Leasing Ltd.* (1972), 28 D.L.R. (3d) 59, [1972] 3 O.R. 281 (Co. Ct.); *Cabral v. Gupta* (1991), 77 Man. R. (2d) 98 (Q.B.), vard [1993] 1 W.W.R. 648, 83 Man. R. (2d) 2 (C.A.); *Kummen v. Alfonso*, [1953] 1 D.L.R. 637 (Man. C.A.) (insufficient proof of loss); *Dyler v. Benoche* (1963), 41 W.W.R. 431 (Alta. S.C.T.D.); *Ashcroft v. Curtin*, [1971] 3 All E.R. 1208 (C.A.); *Desroches v. Mazerolle* (1978), 23 N.B.R. (2d) 361 (Q.B.) (insufficient proof of loss); *Johnstone v. Melina*, [1975] 3 W.W.R. 655 (B.C.S.C.) (insufficient proof of loss); *Sandilands v. Edwards* (1993), 11 Alta. L.R. (3d) 22, 140 A.R. 161, supplementary reasons Alta. L.R. *loc. cit.* p. 59, 146 A.R. 1 (Q.B.). See Luntz, *Assessment of Damages for Personal Injury and Death*, 3rd ed. (Chatswood, N.S.W., Butterworth Pty. Ltd., 1990), §§5.5.9-5.5.11, citing Australian cases.

[254a] [1993] 1 S.C.R. 306, 99 D.L.R. (4th) 401.

[254b] *Supra*, at p. 313.

[254c] *Supra*, footnote 253. See also *Rowe v. Bobell Express Ltd.* (2005), 251 D.L.R. (4th) 290 (B.C.C.A.); *Cuppen v. Queen Charlotte Lodge Ltd.* (2005), 32 C.C.L.T. (3d) 103 (B.C.S.C.), affd 2006 BCCA 443.

however that this aspect of the award had not been argued and might be reconsidered in a future case. It is suggested that the additional award is duplicative: full compensation to the injured person for lost earning capacity is sufficient.

3.770 A somewhat analogous point arose in a case where the plaintiff's lost earning capacity was made good by extra work gratuitously performed by his wife, who was jointly employed with the plaintiff. It was held that the husband was entitled to compensation for the lost earning capacity.[255]

3.780 Precise proof of probable future loss is not required. For example, in several cases the plaintiff has continued in her pre-accident employment at the same or an increased salary, but nevertheless has been able to demonstrate that she has suffered a reduced earning capacity on account of the injuries that will hold her back in the future from the level of earnings that could have been achieved in the absence of the accident. In such cases, the courts have estimated the reduction and awarded damages on that basis.[256]

3.790 If the plaintiff held two jobs before the accident and is disabled by the injury from retaining either, in principle the plaintiff is entitled to compensation for the loss from both sources, for the full measure of earning capacity requires account to be taken of both sources. Thus, remunerative spare time activities should be taken into account also.[257] However, there is a limit to the amount of time the ordinary person can reasonably spend on remunerative activities and, beyond this limit, loss of leisure time should not, it is submitted, be compensated under this head. Some leisure time is needed by everyone, and it would be over-compensatory to measure lost earning capacity on the basis that the plaintiff would have devoted every waking minute to earning. Loss of enjoyment of leisure activities can be compensated under the head of non-pecuniary loss.[258]

---

[255] *Hall v. Miller* (1989), 64 D.L.R. (4th) 369, 41 B.C.L.R. (2d) 46 (C.A.); *Randall v. Dul* (1994), 13 W.A.R. 205 (S.C.). See also *Johnson v. Shelest* (1988), 22 B.C.L.R. (2d) 230 (C.A.).

[256] *Roche v. Newfoundland* (1996), 136 Nfld. & P.E.I.R. 285 (Nfld. C.A.), citing this paragraph at p. 293; *McIntyre v. Woodward Stores Ltd.* (1957), 21 W.W.R. 380 (B.C.S.C.); *Toronto Board of Education v. Monarch Brass Manufacturing Co.* (1923), 24 O.W.N. 490 (H.C.), affd 25 O.W.N. 705 (S.C. App. Div.); *Puchach v. Bozek* (1963), 43 W.W.R. 58 (Man. C.A.); *Cochrane v. O'Brien* (2000), 190 Nfld. & P.E.I.R. 8 (Nfld. S.C.), at p. 119, citing this passage. See also *Boyko v. Penstone* (1995), 6 B.C.L.R. (3d) 248, 98 W.A.C. 87 (C.A.); *Isert v. Santos* (1999), 65 B.C.L.R. (3d) 104 (C.A.), leave to appeal to S.C.C. refused 253 N.R. 196*n*; *Cochrane v. O'Brien* (2002), 225 Nfld. & P.E.I.R. 285 (Nfld. & Lab. C.A.).

[257] *Kovach v. Smith*, [1972] 4 W.W.R. 677 (B.C.S.C.); *Gehrmann v. Lavoie*, [1976] 2 S.C.R. 561, 59 D.L.R. (3d) 634 (spare time electrical business to be taken into account in fatal accident case); *Boyles v. Landry* (1980), 30 N.B.R. (2d) 1 (Q.B.T.D.), vard 34 N.B.R. (2d) 466 (C.A.) (loss of ability to paint house); *Urbanski v. Patel* (1978), 84 D.L.R. (3d) 650 (Man. Q.B.) (loss of value of vegetable garden and keeping chickens). In *Benson v. Tucker*, 252 Mich. 385, 233 N.W. 354 (1930), a seventy-nine-year-old man recovered for lost earning capacity. Similarly, in *Hyrnchuk v. Fetterly*, [1995] 5 W.W.R. 48, 101 Man. R. (2d) 51 (Q.B.), a plaintiff who maintained the same income but as a result of the injury had to work longer hours recovered for lost earning capacity.

(3) Plaintiff working at under-capacity

3.800 Where the plaintiff was not working or working at less than full capacity by choice, it would seem that the plaintiff should be entitled to compensation on the basis of what could have been earned if the plaintiff had chosen to work full time. A carpenter who spends time playing amateur golf presumably does so because he values the pleasure derived from golf more highly than the income that could have been earned by practising his trade. If he loses an arm, so that he can practise neither golf nor carpentry, it would seem that he should be compensated according to the earnings that he could have made as a carpenter.[259] Similar considerations apply to persons who render services gratuitously, such as a member of a religious order who teaches at a college without pay,[260] or one who provides voluntary care to a disabled person.[260a] A comparison may be made with the case of damage to non-profit earning chattels where recovery is allowed for loss of use despite the fact that, in the absence of the damage, no remunerative use would be made of the chattels.[261] In *Skelton v. Collins*, Menzies J. said: "The general damages awarded as compensation for lost capacity have the same character, whether or not the capacity which has been lost would have been used to earn money".[262]

[258] See 3.510-3.700, *supra*. In *Watson v. Grant* (1970), 72 W.W.R. 665 (B.C.S.C.), the cost of completing a hobby project was allowed, but the case was doubted in *Trim v. Patrick* (1980), 22 A.R. 196 (Q.B.).

[259] In *Skelton v. Collins* (1966), 115 C.L.R. 94 (Aust. H.C.), at p. 127, Menzies J. said, "if a great cricketer were to be rendered permanently unconscious by the negligence of another, the injured man would be entitled to substantial damages for lost capacity to play cricket, whether or not he happened to be an amateur or a professional." It might be argued that if the golfer values amateur golf more highly than his forgone earnings, he should recover even more. But the excess pleasure can, it is submitted, be compensated only under the head of non-pecuniary loss. In *Varkonyi v. Canadian Pacific Ry. Co. Ltd.* (1980), 26 A.R. 422 (Q.B.), where the plaintiff was working by choice at less than full capacity, the court, though not allowing recovery for full lost earning capacity, increased the damages for non-pecuniary loss. In *Zapf v. Muckalt* (1996), 142 D.L.R. (4th) 438 at p. 454, [1997] 1 W.W.R. 617 (B.C.C.A.), leave to appeal to S.C.C. refused 147 D.L.R. (4th) vii, 223 N.R. 73*n*, the Court of Appeal, citing this passage on opportunity costs, held this was "not an appropriate case to bring the opportunity cost concept into the law of [the] Province".

[260] *Turenne v. Chung* (1962), 40 W.W.R. 508 (Man. C.A.); *McLaughlin v. Chicago, Milwaukee, St. Paul and Pacific Railway Co.*, 143 N.W. 2d 32 (Wis. S.C. 1966). It can surely make no difference whether the plaintiff received a notional salary that he notionally returned or whether he simply waived the salary.

[260a] *Lowe v. Guise*, [2002] Q.B. 1369 (C.A.).

[261] The comparison was made in *Forsberg v. Maslin*, [1968] S.A.S.R. 432 (S.C.), at pp. 435-6, where Bray C.J. quoted from *The "Mediana"* [1900] A.C. 113. See 1.2030-1.2140, *supra*.

[262] *Supra*, footnote 259. To the same effect is a statement of Waller J. in *Keating v. Elvan Reinforced Concrete Co.*, [1967] 3 All E.R. 611 (Q.B.), at p. 613, affd [1968] 1 W.L.R. 722 (C.A.). But see *Price v. Stoley* (1984), 59 A.R. 1, 34 Alta. L.R. (2d) 356 (Q.B.), *Vincent v. Abu-Bakare* (2003), 259 N.B.R. (2d) 66 (C.A.).

(4) Loss of capacity to perform household work

3.810 Difficulties arise in valuing the claim of a plaintiff prevented by injury from performing household work. It is generally accepted that such an injury causes a loss to the plaintiff personally,[262a] but it is not obvious how the loss should be valued. Some cases have awarded a global sum;[262b] others have measured the loss by the increased burden falling on other family members.[262c] A number of recent cases have adopted a "replacement cost" approach, awarding damages on the basis of the cost of hiring persons to perform the various services that the plaintiff can no longer perform personally.[263] The principle has been applied to part-time as well as full-time household work.[264]

3.820 Some cases have added an income tax supplement ("gross-up").[265] This is appropriate if the replacement costs are conceived of as actual expenses that the plaintiff will probably incur, analogous to the costs of future care,[266] but not if they are conceived of as a way of measuring a capital loss, analogous, or perhaps equivalent, to loss of earning capacity.[267]

3.830 Alternative approaches to valuation of this head of compensation include compensation for loss of earning capacity,[268] for loss of working capacity[269]

[262a] See *Lowe v. Guise*, [2002] 3 W.L.R. 562 (C.A.) (loss of ability to provide care to injured brother).

[262b] *Hildebrandt v. W.F. Botkin Construction Ltd.*, [1998] 7 W.W.R. 418, 162 Sask. R. 92 (Q.B.); *Miller v. Folkertsma Farms Ltd.* (2001), 197 N.S.R. (2d) 282 (C.A.); *Lyne v. McClarty*, *supra*, note 193; *Banga v. Takhar* (2003), 22 B.C.L.R. (4th) 372 (S.C.); *Byron v. Larson*, [2005] 3 W.W.R. 337 (Alta. C.A.).

[262c] *Landry v. McCormick Estate* (1997), 161 N.S.R. (2d) 197 (C.A.).

[263] *Daly v. General Steam Navigation Co.*, [1981] 1 W.L.R. 120 (C.A.); *Fobel v. Dean* (1991), 83 D.L.R. (4th) 385, [1991] 6 W.W.R. 408 (Sask. C.A.), leave to appeal to S.C.C. refused 87 D.L.R. (4th) vii, 97 Sask. R. 240*n*; *McCallum v. Ritter* (1990), 72 D.L.R. (4th) 49, [1990] 5 W.W.R. 660 (Sask. C.A.); *Cairns v. Harris* (1994), 117 Nfld. & P.E.I.R. 216 (P.E.I.C.A.); *Kroeker v. Jansen* (1995), 123 D.L.R. (4th) 652, [1995] 6 W.W.R. 5 (B.C.C.A.), leave to appeal to S.C.C. refused 127 D.L.R. (4th) vii, 197 N.R. 320*n*; *Johnston v. Murchison* (1993), 112 Nfld. & P.E.I.R. 181 (P.E.I.S.C.), vard 127 Nfld. & P.E.I.R. 1 (P.E.I.C.A.); *Rombough (Litigation Guardian of) v. Madonick Estate*, [1997] 7 W.W.R. 464, 154 Sask. R. 91 (Q.B.), vard 168 Sask. R. 12, 173 W.A.C. 12 (C.A.); *Carter v. Anderson* (1998), 160 D.L.R. (4th) 464 (N.S.C.A.); *Gilchrist v. Oatway* (1997), 209 A.R. 225, 56 Alta. L.R. (3d) 64 (C.A.); *Barton v. Gulliver* (1998), 161 Nfld. & P.E.I.R. 279 (Nfld. S.C.); *Lawrence v. Bateman* (1997), 162 N.S.R. (2d) 257 (S.C.); *Taylor v. Hogan* (1998), 160 Nfld. & P.E.I.R. 93 (Nfld. C.A.), at p. 111, citing this work; *McLaren v. Schwalbe*, [1994] 4 W.W.R. 532, 148 A.R. 1 (Q.B.); *Brouwer v. Grewal* (1995), 168 A.R. 342, 30 Alta. L.R. (3d) 244 (Q.B.); *Regnier v. Molnar*, [1996] 6 W.W.R. 538, 145 Sask. R. 16 (Q.B.); *McTavish v. MacGillivray* (2000), 74 B.C.L.R. (3d) 281 (C.A.); *Ross v. Welsh* (2003), 18 C.C.L.T. (3d) 107 (Ont. S.C.J.); *Pelletier v. Oullette* (2003), 258 N.B.R. (2d) 218 (Q.B.); *French v. Hodge* (2005), 231 N.S.R. (2d) 95 (S.C.); *Davis v. Leblanc* (2005), 288 N.B.R. (2d) 316 (Q.B.). A different view is taken in Australia: *CSR Ltd. v. Eddy* (2006), 222 A.L.R. 1 (Aust. H.C.).

[264] *Hoffman v. Sofaer*, [1982] 1 W.L.R. 1350 (Q.B.); *Fobel v. Dean*, *supra*, footnote 263; *Knipple v. Buliziuk* (1995), 129 Sask. R. 116 (Q.B.); *Vykysaly v. Jablowski* (1992), 8 O.R. (3d) 181, supplementary reasons 8 O.R. (3d) 199 (Gen. Div.).

[265] *Fobel v. Dean*, *supra*, footnote 263; *Gilchrist v. Oatway*, *supra*, footnote 263; *Regnier v. Molnar*, *supra*, footnote 263; *Carter v. Anderson*, *supra*, footnote 263.

[266] See 3.1180, *infra*.

[267] See 3.950, *infra*.

[268] See former editions of this work.

and for opportunity lost.[270] Each of these approaches has advantages and disadvantages. They do not invite proof of the particular work likely to have been done by the individual plaintiff and so might be said to be, in a sense, less precise than the replacement cost method but (partly for this reason) they have the merits of easier calculability, and greater consistency and predictability.

(5) Illegal earnings

3.880 Where the plaintiff's source of income was illegal, obvious difficulties arise in giving compensation. In *Burns v. Edman*,[277] a fatal accident case, a widow failed to recover damages when it was proved that her deceased husband's income was derived from theft. Crichton J. said that: "the deceased man would not have been able, in my view at any rate, to maintain an action against the defendant for loss of earnings".[278] The problem is eased, however, when it is recognized that compensation is not for loss of earnings, as such, but for loss of earning capacity. A person who is wholly disabled loses a capacity to earn an honest living and, it is submitted, is entitled to full compensation for that loss. No principle entitles the court to deprive a person of compensation for a real loss on the ground that the court disapproves of past conduct. Nor should the court assume that the plaintiff would necessarily have continued a life of crime in the absence of the injury. Even if this probability were proved it would not, it is submitted, justify a forfeiture of compensation for loss of earning capacity.

3.890 The measure of the lost earning capacity is a different matter and it should, it is submitted, correspond with what the plaintiff could have earned lawfully, for it is only for loss of capacity to earn lawfully that the plaintiff can legitimately complain.[279] Thus, if the plaintiff had no skill except as a thief, the plaintiff ought to recover compensation based on unskilled wage rates. Even so, the illegal activity might be relevant to indicate a lawful earning capacity: a skilled forger might have a legitimate career as a commercial artist. In *Foster v. Kerr*,[280] Ewing J. said: "The fact that his earnings . . . came from an illegal source would not necessarily prevent these earnings from being some measure of his earning power."[281] Ewing J. went on to say that

---

[269] See Réaume, "Rethinking Personal Injury Damages: Compensation for Lost Capacities", 67 Can. Bar Rev. (1989).

[270] See Komesar, "Towards a General Theory of Personal Injury Loss", 3 J. Leg. Stud. 457 (1974); Pottick, "Tort Damages for the Injured Homemaker: Opportunity Cost or Replacement Cost?", 50 U. Col. L.R. 59 (1978).

[271-6] [Text deleted.]

[277] [1970] 2 Q.B. 541.

[278] *Supra*, at p. 545. See also *Adams v. Forbes*, [1944] O.W.N. 231 (H.C.J.).

[279] See *Union Gas Co. of Canada Ltd. v. Brown* (1968), 67 D.L.R. (2d) 44, [1968] 1 O.R. 524 (H.C.J.), revd on other grounds 9 D.L.R. (3d) 337, [1970] 1 O.R. 715 (C.A.) (Sunday work excluded from calculation).

[280] [1939] 4 D.L.R. 745, [1939] 3 W.W.R. 428 (Alta. S.C.), vard [1940] 2 D.L.R. 47 (S.C. App. Div.).

[281] *Supra*, at p. 432 W.W.R.

his lawful earnings would probably be less than his illegal earnings because the plaintiff had chosen the illegal course and because there was a risk of the law being enforced and the earnings cut off.[282] This approach, it is submitted, is fully justifiable and, for the reasons given above, involves no conflict with public policy, even if the illegality is a serious one.[283] Where the illegality is trivial it may well be that the court will simply ignore it, and this approach can be justified on the basis that the plaintiff's lawful earning capacity can be assumed to be equivalent to his unlawful earning capacity.[284]

(6) Length of earning life

3.900 Commonly courts calculate the number of years of life expectancy to retirement age and base the value of the loss of earning capacity on that figure. Where, as is usual, the plaintiff would have expected to retire on a pension funded in whole or in part by employer contributions, the value of the pension ought, it would seem, to be included.[285] This could be done either by augmenting the plaintiff's annual wage before retirement age by the value of the employer's contributions or alternatively, by calculating the wages up to retirement age net of employees' and employers' pension contributions,[286] but then adding to the award the value of annual pension benefits during the plaintiff's life expectancy after retirement. Few cases have expressly dealt with the point, but in *Lim Poh Choo v. Camden and Islington Area Health Authority*,[287] the House of Lords approved an award in respect of lost pension.

(7) Pre-accident life expectancy

3.910 The English Court of Appeal had held in 1962 in *Oliver v. Ashman*,[288] that the plaintiff was only to be compensated for loss of earnings during actual life expectancy, and if that had been reduced by accident, recovery would correspondingly be reduced. The reason for this result was that the plaintiff could not realistically be said to suffer a loss of earnings during a period when the plaintiff would not be living. This reasoning was liable to produce strikingly unfair results where the plaintiff's life was very drastically

---

[282] This point was made in *Lepine v. Demeule* (1972), 30 D.L.R. (3d) 49 (N.W.T. Terr. Ct.), affd 36 D.L.R. (3d) 388 (C.A.).

[283] See also Cooper-Stephenson, *Personal Injury Damages in Canada*, 2nd ed. (Toronto, Carswell, 1996), pp. 246-9.

[284] *Mills v. Baitis*, [1968] V.R. 583 (S.C.) (business carried on in breach of zoning regulation).

[285] *Boyles v. Landry* (1981), 34 N.B.R. (2d) 466 (C.A.); *Kiddell v. Kulczycki*, [1977] 3 W.W.R. 216 (Man. Q.B.); *Embleton v. Wiseman* (1981), 128 D.L.R. (3d) 183 (B.C.C.A.); *Smith v. Canadian Pacific Ry. Co.* (1963), 41 D.L.R. (2d) 249 (Sask. Q.B.); *Myshrall v. Vu* (1994), 156 N.B.R. (2d) 241 (Q.B.).

[286] See *Holian v. United Grain Growers Ltd.* (1980), 114 D.L.R. (3d) 449 (Man. C.A.), leave to appeal to S.C.C. refused D.L.R. *loc. cit.*, where the plaintiff's contributions were deducted, and *Dews v. National Coal Board*, [1988] A.C. 1 (H.L.).

[287] [1980] A.C. 174 (H.L.).

[288] [1962] 2 Q.B. 210 (C.A.).

shortened but where the plaintiff lived long enough to obtain a judgment or settlement from the defendant. Since judgment or settlement obtained by the injured party precludes an action by survivors under fatal accident legislation, the result was that the dependants were left without adequate compensation for their loss of support. The Supreme Court of Canada indicated in 1978 in *Andrews v. Grand & Toy*[289] that *Oliver v. Ashman* would not be followed in Canada and shortly thereafter *Oliver v. Ashman* was actually overruled by the House of Lords in *Pickett v. British Rail Engineering Ltd.*[290] where there were dependants who would otherwise be left without remedy. The legal reason for the result reached in the *Pickett* case was that the plaintiff whose life expectancy was reduced had suffered a present loss of earning capacity. The social reason was to see that the dependants were compensated.[291] The House of Lords held in *Pickett* and again in *Gammell v. Wilson*[292] that the recovery during the "lost years" was to be limited to the excess of income over personal living expenses for the plaintiff can, by hypothesis, have no living expenses during those years. This has been held to be the law in Canada also.[292a]

3.920 "Personal living expenses" are to be deducted from gross income in calculating the amount recoverable in respect of the lost years. But the phrase leaves some room for doubt. In a sense all expenditures are part of the "cost of living" — a cost which, therefore, will not be incurred during the "lost years". The costs of food, clothing, housing, and everything the plaintiff would have spent on pleasure ought to be deducted. So should costs of earning income, such as transport to work, or tools, or work clothes, for these will not have to be incurred. A strong argument can be made for the deduction of taxation, municipal, provincial and national, on the ground that this represents an expense of living that will not be incurred. This leaves, in effect, only savings, and the amount that would have been spent on dependants. If only these items are recoverable, the net result in a case where the plaintiff dies soon after judgment will often approximate the result that would have been reached if the plaintiff had been killed instantly: the dependants as heirs to the estate will recover much the same as they would have recovered under the *Fatal Accidents Act*. This equivalence is highly desirable.[293]

3.930 Where it is clear that the plaintiff will not have dependants, for example because life expectancy is very short indeed or because of permanent

[289] [1978] 2 S.C.R. 229, 83 D.L.R. (3d) 452.

[290] [1980] A.C. 136 (H.L.).

[291] See [1980] A.C. at p. 146 (Lord Wilberforce); p. 152 (Lord Salmon); and p. 170 (Lord Scarman).

[292] [1981] 2 W.L.R. 248 (H.L.).

[292a] *Toneguzzo-Norvell (Guardian ad Litem of) v. Burnaby Hospital*, [1994] 1 S.C.R. 114, 110 D.L.R. (4th) 289. See *Semenoff v. Kokan* (1991), 84 D.L.R. (4th) 76 at p. 79, 59 B.C.L.R. (2d) 195 (C.A.), citing this paragraph. And see *Duncan Estate v. Baddeley* (1997), 145 D.L.R. (4th) 708, 196 A.R. 161 (C.A.), leave to appeal to S.C.C. refused 151 D.L.R. (4th) vii, 168 W.A.C. 397*n*.

unconsciousness, the proper approach would seem to be to calculate what the plaintiff would probably have spent on personal needs had the plaintiff lived out pre-accident life expectancy as a single person.[293a] In that case the portion of income available for dependants would go to increase personal living expenses and savings, mostly the former. Only the probable savings will therefore be recoverable. It will be seen that this approach will lead to very moderate awards where a person without dependants, such as a child, is deprived of the expectation of life.[294] This approach also offers an acceptable solution to the problem of survival to the estate of an action for lost earnings of a person killed. Where there are dependants, the estate will succeed to a substantial sum, and the dependants can claim from the estate. Where there are no dependants, the recovery by the estate will be quite modest and unlikely to appear to anyone as an immoderate windfall.[295]

(8) Contingencies

3.940 Dickson J. said in *Andrews v. Grand & Toy*:[296] "The figure used to take account of contingencies which might have affected future earnings,[297] such as unemployment,[298] illness,[299] accidents[300] and business depression, is obviously an arbitrary one." As Dickson J. went on to point out, not all

---

[293] But in *Harris v. Empress Motors Ltd.*, [1984] 1 W.L.R. 212 (C.A.), the English Court of Appeal concluded that greater deductions should be made in valuing the "lost years" than would be made under the *Fatal Accident Act*. The result is to restore in part the anomaly of *Oliver v. Ashman*, that dependants will be better off in case of death before judgment. In *Toneguzzo-Norvell (Guardian ad Litem of) v. Burnaby Hospital, supra*, the deduction was 50%. See also *Pittman Estate v. Bain* (1994), 112 D.L.R. (4th) 482 (Ont. Ct. (Gen. Div.)) (40%); *Duncan Estate v. Baddeley, supra* (50-70%); *Brown (Next friend of) v. University of Alberta Hospital* (1997), 145 D.L.R. (4th) 63, [1997] 4 W.W.R. 645 (Alta. Q.B.) (33% deduction).

[293a] But see *Semenoff v. Kokan, supra*, note 292a, at p. 80, when it was assumed that the plaintiff would have had two children.

[294] See *Gammell v. Wilson, supra*, footnote 292.

[295] In some jurisdictions, including, since 1982, England, damages for lost future earning capacity do not survive to the estate. See 12.170-12.230, *infra*.

[296] *Supra*, footnote 289, at p. 232 S.C.R., p. 470 D.L.R.

[297] The same principle applies to pre-trial earnings. See 3.360-3.400, *supra*.

[298] The probability of unemployment is diminished by seniority rights. See *Hellens v. Pederson*, [1977] 3 W.W.R. 372 (B.C.S.C.).

[299] *Kamis v. Oaks*, [1988] 3 W.W.R. 428, 84 A.R. 55 (C.A.). In *Corrie v. Gilbert*, [1965] S.C.R. 457, 52 D.L.R. (2d) 1, it was held that damages were not to be reduced on account of a pre-existing disability that made a future illness more probable than in the average person. However, the reason given (that the defendant must take the plaintiff as he finds him) does not seem to support the conclusion, for if the defendant finds the plaintiff already weakened, he finds him with an earning capacity that is already of less value than that of a healthy person. See *Cutler v. Vauxhall Motors Ltd.*, [1971] 1 Q.B. 418 (C.A.); *Barnaby v. O'Leary* (1956), 5 D.L.R. (2d) 41 (N.S.S.C.); *Smith v. Maximovitch* (1968), 68 D.L.R. (2d) 244 (Sask. Q.B.). See 14.570, *infra*, and the analogous property damage cases: 1.2010, 1.2020, 1.2520, *supra*.

[300] *Graham v. Rourke* (1990), 74 D.L.R. (4th) 1, 75 O.R. (2d) 622 (C.A.). In respect of accidents caused tortiously it seems that no deduction should be made, for the subsequent occurrence of a tortious injury does not relieve the original wrongdoer. See *Faulkner v. Keffalinos* (1970), 45 A.L.J.R. 80 (H.C.), and 13.550-13.610, *infra*.

contingencies are adverse.[301] The possibility of promotion should be taken into account, either, as in the *Andrews* case, by increasing the annual loss above the plaintiff's pre-accident salary or by including it as a favourable contingency. Further, the real rate of growth in wages or productivity has been in the order of two per cent annually, and this the Supreme Court of Canada has affirmed should be included in the plaintiff's favour.[302] Dickson J. approved a deduction of twenty per cent in *Andrews* while indicating dissatisfaction with the lack of evidence.[303] In *Thornton* he approved a deduction of ten per cent, saying that the appropriate deduction depended on the facts of each case, and that the court below could not be said to have erred.[304] Plainly, there is an invitation to the parties here to adduce statistical evidence of the actual probable incidence of contingencies on employment income.[305] It seems likely that these would reveal a chance of interruption of income very much lower than the figures used by the courts in the past. In view of the explicit policy of the Supreme Court of Canada to require full compensation for pecuniary loss, the burden of proof (which lies generally on the plaintiff) should not be made too difficult to discharge on this issue.[306] Care must be taken to avoid double account of contingencies. Thus, if contingencies are taken into account in the initial calculation of loss, no further deduction is warranted.[307] Again, insurance premiums paid out of salary to protect the earner against contingencies, such as disability or unemployment, ought not to be deducted from the initial calculation of the

[301] A remark repeated in *Lewis v. Todd*, [1980] 2 S.C.R. 694 at p. 714, 115 D.L.R. (3d) 257 at p. 271. See also *Bilde v. Cooke*, [1974] 4 W.W.R. 89 (B.C.S.C.), citing *Bresatz v. Przibilla* (1962), 108 C.L.R. 541 (H.C.).

[302] *Lewis v. Todd, supra*, footnote 301, at pp. 711-12 S.C.R., p. 270 D.L.R. (two per cent). See also *Malat v. Bjornson (No. 2)*, [1979] 4 W.W.R. 673 (B.C.S.C.) (one and one-half per cent), and *Davies v. Robertson* (1984), 5 O.A.C. 393 (C.A.). In *Julian v. Northern & Central Gas Corp. Ltd.* (1979), 118 D.L.R. (3d) 458, 31 O.R. (2d) 388 (C.A.), leave to appeal to S.C.C. refused D.L.R. *loc. cit.*, O.R. *loc. cit.*, and *Ligate v. Abick* (1996), 134 D.L.R. (4th) 538, 28 O.R. (3d) 1 (C.A.), this factor was set against the discount rate but this method is not convenient where a single discount rate is applied to future lost income and to the cost of future care. In British Columbia, B.C. Reg. 352/81 provides a reduced discount rate for this purpose.

[303] [1978] 2 S.C.R. 229 at p. 231, 83 D.L.R. (3d) 452 at p. 468. See *Benallick v. Sakukhan* (1993), 86 B.C.L.R. (2d) 368, 57 W.A.C. 206 (C.A.) (20%).

[304] [1978] 2 S.C.R. 267 at p. 270, 83 D.L.R. (3d) 480 at p. 489.

[305] The invitation was made more explicit in *Lewis v. Todd, supra*, footnote 301, at p. 714 S.C.R., p. 272 D.L.R., where Dickson J. said that contingencies were susceptible to more exact calculation than is usually appreciated. See *Wynn v. N.S.W. Insurance Ministerial Corp.* (1995), 133 A.L.R. 154 (H.C.); Cooper-Stephenson, *Personal Injury Damages in Canada*, 2nd ed. (Toronto, Carswell, 1996), pp. 382-3.

[306] See 13.70-13.160, *infra*. In *Weare v. Anthony* (1981), 47 N.S.R. (2d) 411 (S.C. App. Div.), a jury award with no contingency deduction was approved. In *Dugdale v. Boissneau* (1983), 41 O.R. (2d) 152 (C.A.), leave to appeal to S.C.C. refused May 16, 1983, the court reversed the trial judge's deduction of 30.6% for contingencies on the ground that the plaintiff had been well protected, by job security and fringe benefits, from adverse contingencies. See *Tronrud v. French* (1991), 84 D.L.R. (4th) 275, 75 Man. R. (2d) 1 (C.A.), leave to appeal to S.C.C. refused 87 D.L.R. (4th) vii, 138 N.R. 407*n* (no deduction); *Bisheimer v. Bryce*, [1991] 2 W.W.R. 738 (Sask. C.A.) (4%).

[307] See *McLeod v. Palardy* (1981), 124 D.L.R. (3d) 506 (Man. C.A.), at pp. 527-8.

plaintiff's annual loss if a separate reduction is made for the actual occurrence of the contingency in respect of which the premiums were paid.

(9) Incidence of taxation

3.950 The Supreme Court of Canada in *The Queen in right of Ontario v. Jennings*[308] had held in 1966 that income tax that would have been payable by the plaintiff on future earnings was not to be deducted in calculating the damages. The Supreme Court of Canada thereby rejected the view taken by the majority of the House of Lords in *British Transport Commission v. Gourley*,[309] and the Canadian position was reaffirmed in the 1978 trilogy,[310] in *Guy v. Trizec Equities Ltd.*[311] a year later, and again in 1994.[311a] The argument for deducting tax is that the plaintiff could not have been said to have lost more than net after-tax income, that being all that would have been received if the wrong had not been done. The contrary argument is that the incidence of taxation is a matter between the plaintiff and the revenue. If the rules relating to taxation of damage awards are overgenerous, let Parliament amend them.[312] The wrongdoer should pay the full amount of the actual loss, whether or not the plaintiff is subsequently required to account to the revenue. It may be objected that exclusion of tax considerations will over-compensate the plaintiff, who could only have expected to enjoy the residue of income after tax. But to this it may be said that, regarded as a loss of earning capacity, the plaintiff's loss of future income is of a capital nature and can realistically be valued as a capital asset.[313] A defendant who wrongfully deprives the plaintiff of an annuity yielding $10,000 a year for twenty years would be bound to pay the full capital value of the annuity, whether or not the income from it would have been taxable in the plaintiff's hands. The Canadian position can gather support from the consideration that it is presumably contemplated that the plaintiff will use the damage award to replace the lost income stream, and that whether an annuity or a business is purchased, the income will be taxable. If income tax were to be deducted in

[308] [1966] S.C.R. 532.

[309] [1956] A.C. 185 (H.L.).

[310] *Supra*, footnote 71. See 5.1280, 5.1290, *infra*, for a discussion of income tax in the context of wrongful dismissal.

[311] [1979] 2 S.C.R. 756 at p. 766, 99 D.L.R. (3d) 243 at p. 250 ("no room for debate as to the law in this country"). *Gourley* is also rejected in New Zealand in the context of wrongful dismissal: *N. Island Wholesale Groceries v. Hewin*, [1982] 2 N.Z.L.R. 176 (C.A.); *Horsburgh v. New Zealand Meat Processing Industrial Union of Workers*, [1988] 1 N.Z.L.R. 698 (C.A.), at p. 704.

[311a] *Cunningham v. Wheeler; Cooper v. Miller; Shanks v. McNee*, [1994] 1 S.C.R. 359 at pp. 417-18, 113 D.L.R. (4th) 1 at p. 23.

[312] The point was made by Lord Keith, dissenting in *Gourley*, *supra*, footnote 309, at p. 218. A summary of the arguments against the *Gourley* case appears in *Soltys v. Middup Moving & Storage Ltd.* (1963), 41 D.L.R. (2d) 576 (Man. Q.B.), *per* Nitikman J., quoting Stewart J., "What a Judge Looks for When Assessing Damages" in *Law Society of Upper Canada Special Lectures on Assessment of Damages for Personal Injury*, Part I, 1958, p. 120.

[313] See 3.710, *supra*.

the initial calculation of the award, therefore, the resulting sum ought to be "grossed up" as in fatal accident cases, so as to provide the plaintiff with a sufficient sum to provide an after-tax income equivalent to the lost earnings.[314] If this process were carefully undertaken, it might sometimes lead to a larger award than would be reached by attempting to compensate the capital loss.[315] A case could be made for compensating the plaintiff for this extra loss, but this was certainly not the argument of the majority in *Gourley* who sought to reduce the plaintiff's recovery, not to increase it.[316] A consequence of this process would be that if two persons, each earning an identical income at the same job were disabled, the recovery of each might vary according to their independent income.[317]

3.960 As the Pearson Commission demonstrated, very large sums indeed would be required to compensate a high income earner over a long period of time.[318] Four Commissioners dissented for this reason, pointing out that with the top slice of investment income taxed in England at ninety-eight per cent, £10,000 gross income is required in order to yield £200 of net income.[319] A conscientious attempt to calculate on such a basis would result in enormous awards to the wealthy that would not only seem anomalous in relation to the awards to less wealthy plaintiffs but might well be over-compensatory, for the wealthy are likely to have access to better investments than those that will subject the full amount to income tax at the highest rates.

3.970 The Australian High Court, having rejected *Gourley* in *Atlas Tiles Ltd. v. Briers*,[320] changed its mind and restored *Gourley* in *Cullen v. Trappell*[321] making it clear, however, that allowance ought to be made for the notional tax payable on income from investment of the award.[322] The complexities

---

314 It seems plain from *Andrews v. Grand & Toy Alberta Ltd.*, [1978] 2 S.C.R. 229 at p. 259, 83 D.L.R. (3d) 452 at p. 474, that this process is not required where the Canadian rule is followed, and damages are based on the gross earnings, for the plaintiff would be over-compensated if a sufficient capital sum to replace gross earnings after payment of tax on the proceeds of investment were recovered. See also *Leischner v. West Kootenay Power & Light Co.* (1986), 24 D.L.R. (4th) 641, [1986] 3 W.W.R. 97 (C.A.). But see 3.820, *supra*.

315 See Rea, "Inflation, Taxation and Damage Assessment", 58 Can. Bar Rev. 280 (1980).

316 The award was reduced by a factor of six from £37,720 to £6,695. No mention is made of "grossing up" to allow for income tax on a notional investment of the proceeds of the award.

317 Lord Keith, dissenting in *Gourley*, made such a comparison but assumed that the rule adopted by the majority would benefit the less wealthy plaintiff. See footnotes 315, 316, *supra*.

318 "The Actions for Loss of Services and Loss of Consortium" in *Royal Commission on Civil Liability and Compensation for Personal Injury* (Pearson Commission Report, London, H.M.S.O., 1978), Cmnd. 7054-1, §686. A single man earning £240 per week ought, on the majority view, to recover about three and one-half times the sum awarded under the existing system. At higher income levels presumably the sum required would be larger.

319 *Ibid.*, at §713. At §722 the minority said: "A very high earner would receive an extravagant award. There might exceptionally be an award of as much as £§ million (at present values). We feel that such an award would be excessive and unreasonable. Also there would be an excessive disproportion between the lump-sum awards to low earners and the lump-sum awards to high earners."

320 (1978), 52 A.L.J.R. 707 (H.C.) (3:2 majority).

321 (1980), 54 A.L.J.R. 295 (H.C.) (Full bench: 4:3 majority).

322 *Supra*, at pp. 298-300. See also *Taylor v. O'Connor*, [1971] A.C. 115 (H.L.).

and uncertainties of this process are illustrated by *Paul v. Rendell*,[323] a Privy Council appeal from South Australia. Lord Diplock said, after describing the complexity of the calculation:

> Their Lordships have thus being presented with a selection of detailed calculations of capital sums from which to choose as representing the true value at the date of trial of the future economic loss sustained by the plaintiff as a result of his injuries. They range from as little as $46,000 to as much as $103,000.[324]

[*The next page is* 3-51]

[323] (1981), 55 A.L.J.R. 371 (P.C.).
[324] *Supra*, at p. 376.

Lord Diplock went on to say:

> . . . quite apart from the unreliability in varying degrees of each and every factor in the formulae on which are based the detailed calculations . . . for arriving at that component of the total award which represents the court's assessment of the capital sum that will fairly compensate the plaintiff for future economic loss, those calculations bear no relation to what the plaintiff will in fact do with the whole or any part of the capital sum . . . He will be free to do whatever he likes with it . . .
>
> To undertake detailed mathematical calculations in which nearly every factor is so speculative or unreliable in order to assess the capital sum to represent what is only one of several components in a total award of compensation for personal injuries, is, in their lordships' view, not only not worth while but, worse than this, it has a tendency to mislead . . .
>
> The reality is that as a result of the judgment the plaintiff will have at his disposal a single capital sum to compensate him for all the loss, economic and non-economic, past and future, that he has sustained or will sustain. This is the figure that matters to the plaintiff.[325]

Lord Diplock's apparent suggestion that courts should revert to awarding an unexplained global sum has been authoritatively rejected in the Canadian context, and has, in any event, it is submitted, little to recommend it.[326] But the complexities of the calculations required by taking account of notional tax on a notional investment of the award lends support to the rejection of *Gourley*. It is submitted that the Australian difficulties demonstrate that there is very good sense in the Canadian rule ignoring both the income tax that the plaintiff would have paid on earnings and the income tax that might be paid on a future investment of the damage award.

3.980 An argument sometimes made is that the position of the Supreme Court of Canada on taxation of damage awards in personal injury cases is inconsistent with its position in fatal accident cases.[327] However, it is submitted that the court is on sound ground in distinguishing the two kinds of cases. In personal injury cases the plaintiff has a *prima facie* entitlement to his gross earnings; income tax is owed to the revenue by the plaintiff out of gross earnings; payroll deduction is simply a convenient method of collection. On the other hand in a fatal accident case the claimant never had nor would have had a right to the deceased's gross earnings.[328] The claimant's only interest is in what would have been provided by the deceased after necessary outgoings (including income tax) had been paid.

325 *Supra*, at pp. 376-7. Lord Diplock described the complex calculation used in *Tracey v. Churchill*, [1980] 1 N.S.W.L.R. 442 (C.A.), as piling "unreality upon unreality".

326 See 3.300-3.330, *supra*.

327 See Rea, *op. cit.*, footnote 315, at p. 298. See 6.180-6.200, *infra*.

328 *Keizer v. Hanna*, [1978] 2 S.C.R. 342, 82 D.L.R. (3d) 449. In *Lewis v. Todd*, [1980] 2 S.C.R. 694, 115 D.L.R. (3d) 257, in the absence of evidence of the necessary "grossing up" element the Supreme Court of Canada disregarded the tax impact on both the dependency and the notional investment.

The necessary starting point here is the disposable income of the deceased, because the claimant's interest depends on a disposition (that would have been made in the absence of the wrong) by the deceased to the claimant, not on the disposition by the deceased's employer to the deceased. The Canadian rule of ignoring income tax is, therefore, it is submitted, justified as a short-cut to the complex and uncertain process of deducting first the tax that the plaintiff would have had to pay on the income, and then adding back the tax the plaintiff will presumably have to pay on the income from the investment of the award. As on many damages questions, the search for perfect compensation in the individual case must be balanced against the need for rules that are fair, regular, workable, and reasonably inexpensive to apply.

(10) Discounting to present value

3.990 A plaintiff with a life expectancy of twenty years and an annual loss of $20,000 is not entitled to an award of $400,000.[329] Account must be taken of the fact that the money is to be paid in advance, presumably immediately following the court's judgment, and will earn interest. It would not be correct to award a sufficient capital sum to replace the lost income entirely out of interest, because the plaintiff could then make the losses good and have a capital sum left over at the end. A proper award must be a sum sufficient to replace the lost income out of blended payments of interest and capital, leaving nothing at the end (a "self-extinguishing" fund).[330] Mention of these factors is equivalent simply to saying that a sum must be awarded equal to the present value of the lost income stream. The English courts have chosen to effect this calculation by what has been called the rough-and-ready method[331] of reducing the "multiplier", *i.e.*, the figure of twenty in the example just given. Lord Scarman explained this method in the context of the cost of future care in *Lim Poh Choo v. Camden and Islington Area Health Authority*,[332] where the plaintiff's life expectancy was thirty-seven years. He said:

> In the present case I attach major importance to the following elements of discount: the accelerated payment, the contingency that Dr. Lim may not live out her full expectation of life,[333] and the availability of capital as

329 See, however, *Julian v. Northern & Central Gas Corp. Ltd.* (1979), 118 D.L.R. (3d) 458, 31 O.R. (2d) 388 (C.A.), where the discount rate was offset by an allowance for productivity. And see 3.940, *supra*.

330 See *Lim Poh Choo v. Camden and Islington Area Health Authority*, [1980] A.C. 174 (H.L.), at pp. 192-3, *per* Lord Scarman (in the context of cost of future care).

331 See P. Cane, *Atiyah's Accidents, Compensation and the Law*, 4th ed. (Weidenfeld & Nicolson, London, 1987), p. 176.

332 *Supra*, footnote 330.

333 Presumably Lord Scarman is here referring to a reduction in life expectancy caused by the accident and not already taken account of in reaching the figure of thirty-seven years. It would not, of course, be right to reduce an award on the ground that a plaintiff might not live out his post-accident life expectancy; that possibility is already included in the notion of life "expectancy". Further, this consideration is relevant only to cost of future care, not to earning capacity. See 3.910-3.930, *supra*.

> well as income to meet the cost of care . . . A fair multiplier would, in my judgment, be 12 years' purchase . . .[334]

Since Lord Scarman referred to "the very helpful evidence" of an accountant,[335] it is apparent that the multiplier chosen will be based on the use of "present value" tables, in common use among accountants and actuaries.

3.1000 In *Mallett v. McMonagle*,[336] Lord Diplock pointed out that a multiplier of sixteen "represents the capital value of an annuity certain for a period of 26 years at interest rates of 4 per cent, 29 years at interest rates of 4½ per cent or 33 years at interest rates of 5 per cent".[337] It is plain that the English judges are not pulling these figures out of their heads. Although reduction of the multiplier has been called "a rough-and-ready" approach, it is capable of complete mathematical accuracy so far as reducing to present value is concerned, if based on sound arithmetical calculations. Once the proper discount rate is fixed, reduction to present value is an exact mathematical procedure not a guess.[338] There is, of course, an inevitable "rough-and-ready" element in making reductions for estimated contingencies. But it makes no difference whether a reduction of, say, twenty per cent, is applied to the "multiplier", the "multiplicand" (*i.e.*, the estimated annual loss), or to the product of the two figures. All three methods are mathematically identical, and each is just as "rough-and-ready" as the initial choice of the twenty per cent figure.

3.1010 Though the terminology of "multiplier" and "multiplicand" has been used in some Canadian cases,[339] the more common practice has been for the courts to refer to present value tables proved, if necessary, by expert evidence, and in *Andrews v. Grand & Toy*,[340] Dickson J. referred to actuarial evidence as "a sharper tool than the 'multiplier-multiplicand' approach".[341] It seems that the two methods do not actually differ in substance, for the choice of the correct multiplier must, as mentioned previously,[342] be based on the same mathematical principles as used by the drafter of present value tables which usually are drawn to show the present

---

334 *Supra*, footnote 330, at p. 196. The effective maximum is eighteen; see Pearson Commission Report (London, H.M.S.O., 1978), §648.

335 *Lim Poh Choo, supra*, footnote 330, at p. 196.

336 [1970] A.C. 166 (H.L.).

337 *Supra*, at p. 177.

338 See *per* Bull J.A., in *Schroth v. Innes* (1976), 71 D.L.R. (3d) 647 (B.C.C.A.), at p. 658: "The actuarial calculation is nothing mysterious. It is the result of the application of simple mathematics. In fact, it is purely mechanical or 'computerized'".

339 *Kwong v. The Queen in right of Alberta* (1978), 96 D.L.R. (3d) 214 (Alta. S.C. App. Div.), affd [1979] 2 S.C.R. 1010*n*, 105 D.L.R. (3d) 576*n*; *Meeks v. White* (1972), 27 D.L.R. (3d) 681 (N.S.S.C.T.D.), affd 39 D.L.R. (3d) 126 (S.C. App. Div.); *Janke v. Chamber's Estate* (1981), 29 A.R. 68 (C.A.), revd on other grounds [1982] 1 S.C.R. 281; *Coco v. Nicholls* (1981), 31 A.R. 386 (C.A.).

340 [1978] 2 S.C.R. 229, 83 D.L.R. (3d) 452.

341 *Supra*, at p. 236 S.C.R., p. 458 D.L.R.

342 See footnote 338, *supra*.

value of a dollar a year paid monthly for a given number of years at various assumed interest rates, and therefore yield no more nor less than a "multiplier" to be applied to the annual loss expressed in dollars. The only real point of difference between the two methods seems to be whether the courts' resort to tables should be openly acknowledged. Since standard present value tables are readily available, the Canadian approach of referring to them directly seems the more desirable, and better adapted than the English approach to a clear explanation of the reasons for the conclusion reached.[343]

(11) Allowance for inflation

3.1020 The discussion of the method of discounting future damages to present value has so far ignored the impact of inflation. In times of stable currency, the long-term rate of interest is said by economists to be about two and one-half per cent per annum,[344] and in the absence of inflation, therefore, the method of discounting described above calculated at a two and one-half per cent discount rate would produce the appropriate sum. It appears at first sight as though a substantial increase ought to be allowed for the prospect of inflation, but analysis has shown this appearance to be false. In *Mallett v. McMonagle*,[345] Lord Diplock said that courts ought to ignore both inflation and "high interest rates which reflect the fear of it".[346] Although this solution seems simplistic, and was indeed castigated by Dickson J. in *Andrews v. Grand & Toy* as having "an air of unreality",[347] it would appear that it is mathematically sound.

3.1030 Current interest rates are composed of two elements (leaving aside risk of default), a payment by the borrower for the use of money and a payment for the anticipated depreciation in the value of money. A mathematician, asked to adjust present value tables assuming a rate of inflation properly reflected in current interest rates, would reply that no adjustment fell to be made. The present value of one hundred dollars a year from now at an assumed interest rate of two and one-half per cent with no inflation is $97.56. Assuming inflation of ten per cent and an

---

343 In *Lai Wee Liam v. Singapore Bus Service (1978) Ltd.*, [1984] A.C. 729 (P.C.), the trial judge had improperly combined the two methods, selecting a multiplier on the basis of English precedent, and then applying it to tables that incorporated an element of discount for advance payment, resulting in a double deduction for advance payment.

344 See Rea, "Inflation, Taxation and Damage Assessment", 58 Can. Bar Rev. 280 (1980), at pp. 282-3, 285; Posner, *Economic Analysis of Law*, 5th ed. (New York, Aspen Law & Business Publishers, 1998), p. 213 (2%); Manitoba Law Reform Commission, *Report on Prejudgment Compensation on Money Awards: Alternatives to Interest* (1982), p. 37 (3%).

345 *Supra*, footnote 336, followed in *Haley v. Richardson* (1975), 60 D.L.R. (3d) 480 (N.B.S.C. App. Div.); *Babineau v. MacDonald (No. 2)* (1975), 59 D.L.R. (3d) 671 (N.B.S.C. App. Div.).

346 *Supra*, footnote 336, at p. 176. See also *Mitchell v. Mulholland (No. 2)*, [1972] 1 Q.B. 65 (C.A.).

347 *Supra*, footnote 340, at p. 254 S.C.R., p. 471 D.L.R.

interest rate of twelve and one-half per cent the present value is exactly the same.[348] Of course, current interest rates might not accurately predict future inflation, but the court is unlikely to find a more reliable predictor. Accordingly, all that is required of the court is to fix a discount rate that represents the long-term value of the use of money in times of currency stability. Unfortunately, in the 1978 trilogy of personal injury cases, together with *Keizer v. Hanna*,[349] a fatal accident case decided at the same time, the Supreme Court of Canada arrived at the figure of seven per cent as a proper discount rate, reached by deducting the figure of three per cent as an (unreliably based)[350] estimate of future inflation from the current interest rates of ten per cent. Subsequent cases have not, however, treated the seven per cent figure as a binding rule of law. In *Fenn v. City of Peterborough*,[351] the Ontario Court of Appeal said:

> In this case, the uncontradicted evidence, accepted by the trial Judge, was that the long-term probable differential between investment return and inflation was not greater than 3% and this figure should be used as the discount rate.[352]

3.1040 In *Lewis v. Todd*,[353] the Supreme Court of Canada confirmed that there was no rule fixing the rate at seven per cent and that the appropriate figure depended upon the evidence in each case. This approach yields a much more satisfactory result than the seven per cent discount figure used in the 1978 trilogy[354] but requires proof in each case of the proper discount rate.[355] In several provinces the further sensible step has been taken of eliminating the need for expert evidence on the point by fixing the discount rate by statute or regulation.[356] The appropriate figure is generally agreed by economists to be between two and three per cent.[356a]

(12) Avoidance of overlap with other heads of damage

3.1050 A totally disabled plaintiff who will require residential care for life ought not to be compensated twice over for the cost of necessaries of life such as

[348] See Rea, *loc. cit.*, footnote 344, at p. 283.
[349] [1978] 2 S.C.R. 342, 82 D.L.R. (3d) 449.
[350] See Rea, *op. cit.*, footnote 344, at pp. 284-5.
[351] (1979), 104 D.L.R. (3d) 174, 25 O.R. (2d) 399 (C.A.), affd [1981] 2 S.C.R. 613, 129 D.L.R. (3d) 507. See also *Cattapan v. Mitchell* (1978), 105 D.L.R. (3d) 508, 27 O.R. (2d) 87 (H.C.J.); *McLeod v. Palardy* (1980), 4 Man. R. (2d) 218 (Q.B.), vard 124 D.L.R. (3d) 506 (C.A.) (3-4%); *MacDonald v. Alderson*, [1982] 3 W.W.R. 385 (C.A.) (3%); *Yepremian v. Scarborough General Hospital* (1978), 88 D.L.R. (3d) 161 at p. 189, 20 O.R. (2d) 510 at p. 539 (H.C.J.) (3%), vard 110 D.L.R. (3d) 513, 28 O.R. (2d) 494 (C.A.).
[352] *Fenn v. City of Peterborough, supra*, footnote 351, at p. 227 D.L.R., p. 453 O.R.
[353] [1980] 2 S.C.R. 694, 115 D.L.R. (3d) 257.
[354] Rea calls it a "crucial error", *op. cit.*, footnote 344, at p. 284.
[355] See *Lewis v. Todd*, [1980] 2 S.C.R. 694, 115 D.L.R. (3d) 257, at pp. 710-11 S.C.R., p. 269 D.L.R.; *McLeod v. Palardy, supra*, footnote 351, at p. 525 D.L.R., "The present state of the law is far from satisfactory. Inconsistent decisions as to the magnitude of the net discount rate are inevitable . . .The parties will be put to the expense of retaining the services of economists and actuaries to support their respective positions", *per* Huband, J.A. See *Jeselon v. Waters*, [1981] 3 W.W.R. 715 (B.C.S.C.) (2½%); *Young v. Wells* (2007), 264 Nfld. & P.E.I.R. 217 (Nfld. & Lab. C.A.).

food, lodging and clothing. Thus, either the portion of the award for future care ought to exclude this "domestic element" or the award for loss of earning capacity should exclude what the plaintiff would have expended on necessaries. In *Andrews v. Grand & Toy*[357] Dickson J. outlined the two possible methods:

> When calculating the damage award, however, there are two possible methods of proceeding. One method is to give the injured party an award for future care which makes no deduction in respect of the basic necessities for which he would have had to pay in any event. A deduction must then be made for the cost of such basic necessities when computing the award for loss of prospective earnings, *i.e.*, the award is on the basis of net earnings and not gross earnings. The alternative method is the reverse, *i.e.*, to deduct the cost of basic necessities when computing the award for future care and then to compute the earnings award on the basis of gross earnings.[358]

Dickson J. then went on to prefer the first approach:

> In my opinion, the approach of the trial Judge [i.e., the first approach] is to be preferred. This is in accordance with the principle which I believe should underline the whole consideration of damages for personal injuries: that proper future care is the paramount goal of such damages. To determine accurately the needs and costs in respect of future care, basic living expenses should be included. The costs of necessaries when in an infirm state may well be different from those when in a state of health. Thus, while the types of expenses would have been incurred in any event, the level of expenses for the victim may be seen as attributable to the accident. In my opinion, the projected costs of necessities should, therefore, be included in calculating the cost of future care, and a percentage attributable to the necessities of a person in a normal state should be reduced from the award for future earnings.[359]

---

[356] Ontario Rules of Civil Procedure, r. 53.09 (held to be mandatory in *Giannone v. Weinberg* (1989), 68 O.R. (2d) 767, 33 O.A.C. 11 (C.A.), leave to appeal to S.C.C. refused 105 N.R. 239*n*, 71 O.R. (2d) x). See also Nova Scotia Civil Procedure Rules, r. 31.10(2); New Brunswick Rules of Court, r. 54.10(2); Saskatchewan Queen's Bench Rules, r. 284B(1)(b); *Judicature Act* (N.W.T.), s. 57(1); *Court of Queen's Bench Act* (Man.), s. 83(2); *Law and Equity Act* (B.C.), s. 56; B.C. Reg. 352/81. And in Nova Scotia see *Corkum v. Sawatsky* (1993), 126 N.S.R. (2d) 317 (C.A.). In *Mountain v. Hickox* (1981), 34 Nfld. & P.E.I.R. 473 (P.E.I.S.C.), the 2§% rate was said to be a matter of "local precedent". In *Lewis v. Todd*, [1980] 2 S.C.R. 694, 115 D.L.R. (3d) 257, Dickson J. said, at pp. 710-11 S.C.R., p. 269 D.L.R., "I know of no authority by which this Court, if so minded, could legislate a fixed discount rate, applicable for all cases ... The principle remains that, absent legislation ... which directs the manner of calculating discount rate ... the discount rate will vary according to the expert testimony led at trial." But, it is submitted, it cannot be beyond the power of the Supreme Court of Canada to lay down as a principle, as Lord Diplock did in *Mallett v. McMonagle*, [1970] A.C. 166 (H.L.), that both inflation and high interest rates are to be ignored. Expert evidence would then only be required on the "real" interest rate. See McLachlin, "What Price Disability?", 59 Can. Bar Rev. 1 (1981), at p. 26.

[356a] In *Wells v. Wells*, [1999] 1 A.C. 345 (H.L.), the House of Lords adopted a figure of 3%, the then-current discount rate for index-linked government securities. In 2001 the rate of 2.5% was prescribed by the Lord Chancellor. See *Warriner v. Warriner*, [2002] 1 W.L.R. 1703 (C.A.); *Cooke v. United Bristol Healthcare NHS Trust*, [2004] 1 W.L.R. 251 (C.A.).

[357] [1978] 2 S.C.R. 229, 83 D.L.R. (3d) 452.

[358] *Supra*, at p. 250 S.C.R., p. 468 D.L.R.

[359] *Supra*.

This last percentage Dickson J. fixed at fifty-three per cent. This method was also applied in *Thornton*[360] with a reduction of fifty-two per cent. On the other hand, in *Arnold v. Teno*[361] decided by the Supreme Court of Canada at the same time as *Andrews* and *Thornton*, Spence J., in whose judgment Dickson J. concurred, evidently took the opposite approach. He said, "It must be remembered that the allowance for future care provides only for the cost of attendants and that like everyone else the infant plaintiff has to eat, clothe herself and shelter herself."[362] **3.1060**

In *Lim Poh Choo v. Camden and Islington Area Health Authority*[363] also, the House of Lords preferred deduction of the cost of necessaries from the award for future care, Lord Scarman saying: **3.1070**

> In the present case . . . it is perfectly possible to estimate the domestic element in Dr. Lim's cost of care. The estimated figure must, therefore, be deducted in the assessment of her damages for the cost of her care. In the result, Dr. Lim will recover in respect of her future loss a capital sum which, after all the proper discounts, will represent her loss of earnings, net after allowing for working expenses, and her cost of care, net after deducting the domestic element.[364]

In *Fenn v. City of Peterborough*,[365] the Ontario Court of Appeal, having noted the different approaches in the 1978 Supreme Court of Canada cases, considered that an award based on a loss of $6,000 per annum could be justified either as part of the cost of future care, or as lost earning capacity.

It seems that although both methods were used in the 1978 trilogy, the Supreme Court of Canada can fairly be said to have favoured a full award for the cost of future care and an appropriate deduction from the award for lost earning capacity.[366] Dickson J. gave specific reasons for favouring this approach, whereas Spence J. in *Arnold v. Teno* adopted the alternative approach without any specific reasons. Moreover, the approach of Dickson J. appears to have some advantages of convenience. First, omitting necessaries from the cost of future care may tend to the under-evaluation of the cost of necessaries. As Dickson J. pointed out,[367] the costs to a disabled person of necessaries may well exceed the cost to a plaintiff **3.1080**

---

360 [1978] 2 S.C.R. 267, 83 D.L.R. (3d) 480. *MacDonald v. Alderson, supra*, footnote 351, deducted ninety per cent, but this seems excessive on the theory, approved by the Supreme Court of Canada, that pecuniary losses are to be compensated in full.

361 [1978] 2 S.C.R. 287, 83 D.L.R. (3d) 609.

362 *Supra*, at p. 329 S.C.R., p. 637 D.L.R. See also *Semenoff v. Kokan* (1991), 84 D.L.R. (4th) 76, 59 B.C.L.R. (2d) 195 (C.A.).

363 [1980] A.C. 174 (H.L.).

364 *Supra*, at pp. 191-2.

365 (1979), 104 D.L.R. (3d) 174, 25 O.R. (2d) 399 (C.A.), affd [1981] 2 S.C.R. 613, 129 D.L.R. (3d) 507.

366 This was the method used also in *McLeod v. Palardy* (1981), 124 D.L.R. (3d) 506 (Man. C.A.), and in *Wipfli v. Britten* (1984), 13 D.L.R. (4th) 169, [1984] 5 W.W.R. 385 (B.C.C.A.).

367 *Supra*, footnote 357, at pp. 250-1 S.C.R., p. 468 D.L.R.

leading a healthy life, and the excess cost is a legitimate part of the plaintiff's compensation. Second, the failure to deduct necessaries from the compensation for lost earning capacity may lead to underevaluation of the latter. The Ontario Court of Appeal in *Fenn v. City of Peterborough*,[368] in awarding the plaintiff in compensation for lost earning capacity only the estimated cost of necessaries ($6,000 a year), appears to have assumed that her earning capacity was only equal to the provision of necessaries. In the particular case, the evidence might have justified that conclusion, but the court seemed a little uneasy with it[369] and had it been clear that the cost of necessaries was to be deducted from the compensation for lost earning capacity, the court might well have tended to value the plaintiff's earning capacity somewhat higher, for example, as suggested earlier as an appropriate measure in the absence of better evidence, at an average wage.[370]

3.1090 Another potential overlap has been suggested between loss of earning capacity and damages for non-pecuniary loss. It was suggested in the English case of *Fletcher v. Autocar & Transporters Ltd.*[371] that a disabled person who is compensated for loss of amenities of life ought to deduct, from an award for loss of earning capacity, the cost that would have been incurred to purchase those amenities.[372] The argument is that a disabled golfer can be said to be compensated by the award for loss of amenities for the lost enjoyment of golfing, and therefore can be said to have been "saved" the cost of the green fees that would have been incurred had there been no injury. This argument, however, seems fallacious for, as Salmon L.J. pointed out in his dissenting judgment, the disabled golfer will not be fully compensated for the lost enjoyment of playing golf by the conventional award for loss of amenities of life.[373] As Professor Luntz puts it, the "saving" of the green fees cannot be greater than the value to the plaintiff of the enjoyment of golf, since the plaintiff by hypothesis thought it worthwhile so to expend the fees.[374] In *Lindal v. Lindal*[375] the availability of full compensation for loss of earning capacity was adduced as a reason for moderation in assessing damages for non-pecuniary loss. There is no reason why the plaintiff who spent all her discretionary income on enjoyment should recover less than the plaintiff who saved all her income,[376] and the Canadian restrictions on recovery of non-pecuniary

368 *Supra*, footnote 365.

369 See 1.2220, *supra*.

370 [Footnote deleted.]

371 [1968] 2 Q.B. 322 (C.A.).

372 *Supra*, at p. 337, *per* Lord Denning, and p. 342 *per* Diplock L.J.

373 *Supra*, at p. 364. Salmon L.J. pointed out that the majority approach might leave the defendant with a credit balance, see pp. 359 and 364-5.

374 Luntz, *Assessment of Damages for Personal Injury and Death*, 3rd ed. (Chatswood, N.S.W., Butterworth Pty. Ltd., 1990), §1.5.17.

375 [1981] 2 S.C.R. 629, 129 D.L.R. (3d) 263.

376 See *per* Salmon L.J. dissenting, in *Fletcher v. Autocar & Transporters Ltd., supra*, footnote 371, at p. 361.

losses[377] make it all the more important to insure full compensation for pecuniary loss.[378] In *Lim Poh Choo v. Camden and Islington Area Health Authority*,[379] Lord Scarman said on this point:

> Upon the point of principle whether damages for non-pecuniary loss can properly be reduced to avoid an overlap with damages for pecuniary loss I express no final opinion. I confess, however, that I doubt the possibility of overlap: and I note that the Pearson Commission[380] considers it wrong in principle to reduce the one by reason of the size of the other.[381]

3.1100 The argument of overlap was carried by Lord Denning (dissenting) in the Court of Appeal in *Lim Poh Choo*[382] to its logical conclusion, when he suggested that in cases of catastrophic injury there should be no award at all for loss of earning capacity, since the only value of earnings was to purchase the necessaries and amenities of life, and since the loss of these was compensated under other heads, there was no place for compensation for lost earnings. This argument was summarily rejected by the House of Lords and is inconsistent with the view that compensation is for loss of earning capacity as a capital loss.[383] It may be concluded, therefore, that the courts both in England and Canada are unlikely to accept the possibility of any overlap between non-pecuniary loss and lost earning capacity.

(13) Management fees

3.1110 The assumption on which damages for future financial loss are calculated is that the plaintiff will invest the award in order to replace the lost income stream and in order to meet the recurring costs of future care. If this is to be done effectively, some plaintiffs will require expert financial advice, and the courts have recognized this fact by allowing a reasonable management fee as part of the damages.[384] In a number of cases, awards have been refused in the absence of evidence that the plaintiff is likely actually to incur a fee,[384a] but

---

377 See 3.510-3.700, *supra*.

378 See *per* Dickson J., in *Andrews v. Grand & Toy Alberta Ltd.*, [1978] 2 S.C.R. 229 at p. 263, 83 D.L.R. (3d) 452 at p. 477, and in *Lewis v. Todd*, [1980] 2 S.C.R. 694 at p. 708, 115 D.L.R. (3d) 257 at p. 267.

379 [1980] A.C. 174 (H.L.).

380 Pearson Commission Report (London, H.M.S.O., 1978), §759.

381 *Supra*, footnote 379, at p. 192.

382 [1979] Q.B. 196 at p. 216.

383 See 3.710, *supra*. The House of Lords affirmed the view of loss of earning capacity as a capital loss in *Pickett v. British Rail Engineering Ltd.*, [1980] A.C. 136, cited by Lord Scarman in *Lim, supra*, footnote 379, at p. 190.

384 *Arnold v. Teno*, [1978] 2 S.C.R. 287, 53 D.L.R. (4th) 606; *Mandzuk v. Vieira*, [1988] 2 S.C.R. 650, 53 D.L.R. (4th) 606; *Watkins v. Olafson*, [1989] 2 S.C.R. 750, 61 D.L.R. (4th) 577; *Semenoff v. Kokan* (1991), 84 D.L.R. (4th) 76, 59 B.C.L.R. (2d) 195 (C.A.); *Unruh (Guardian ad Litem of) v. Webber* (1994), 112 D.L.R. (4th) 83, [1994] 5 W.W.R. 270 (B.C.C.A.), leave to appeal to S.C.C. refused 115 D.L.R. (4th) viii, 178 N.R. 397*n*; *Maloney v. Phoenix Enterprises Ltd.*, [1993] 4 W.W.R. 693, 84 Man. R. (2d) 294 (Q.B.), affd 92 Man. R. (2d) 250, 61 W.A.C. 250 (C.A.); *Scott v. Pettigrew* (1994), 132 N.S.R. (2d) 60 (S.C.). But see *Nominal Defendant v. Gaudikitis* (1996), 136 A.L.R. 1 (H.C.) (award only where incapacity to manage is caused by the wrong).

in *Townsend v. Kroppmanns* this consideration was held to be irrelevant.[384b] It has been held that a management fee is not appropriate in respect of non-pecuniary losses.[384c]

(14) Independent action by relatives

3.1120 The Ontario *Family Law Act* provides that certain relatives have an independent action for pecuniary loss resulting from injury. Section 61 provides:

> 61(1) If a person is injured or killed by the fault or neglect of another under circumstances where the person is entitled to recover damages, or would have been entitled if not killed, the spouse, as defined in Part III (Support Obligations), children, grandchildren, parents, grandparents, brothers and sisters of the person are entitled to recover their pecuniary loss resulting from the injury or death from the person from whom the person injured or killed is entitled to recover or would have been entitled if not killed, and to maintain an action for the purpose in a court of competent jurisdiction.
>
> (2) The damages recoverable in a claim under subsection (1) may include,
>
> (a) actual expenses reasonably incurred for the benefit of the person injured or killed;
>
> (b) actual funeral expenses reasonably incurred;
>
> (c) a reasonable allowance for travel expenses actually incurred in visiting the person during his or her treatment or recovery;
>
> (d) where, as a result of the injury, the claimant provides nursing, housekeeping or other services for the person, a reasonable allowance for loss of income or the value of the services; and
>
> (e) an amount to compensate for the loss of guidance, care and companionship that the claimant might reasonably have expected to receive from the person if the injury or death had not occurred.
>
> (3) In an action under subsection (1), the right to damages is subject to any apportionment of damages due to contributory fault or neglect of the person who was injured or killed.

3.1130 This provision appears at first sight to entitle the named relatives to bring an action, analogous to that long familiar to our system in the case of death, for the portion of the lost future earnings of the injured person that would have probably benefited the claimants. It is not at all clear, however, how this new right of action fits in with the injured person's rights to recover the whole of lost future earnings. The Act says nothing of the rights of injured persons and presumably is not to be construed to diminish those rights.[385]

[384a] *Wilson v. Martinello* (1995), 125 D.L.R. (4th) 240, 23 O.R. (3d) 417 (C.A.); *Kielley v. General Hospital Corp.* (1996), 136 Nfld. & P.E.I.R. 189 (Nfld. S.C.), vard 183 Nfld. & P.E.I.R. 1 (C.A.); *O'Neill v. Campbell* (1995), 161 N.B.R. (2d) 1, supplementary reasons 161 N.B.R. (2d) 57 (Q.B.); *Terris v. Crossman* (1995), 129 Nfld. & P.E.I.R. 181 (P.E.I.S.C.), affd 139 Nfld. & P.E.I.R. 87 (C.A.), leave to appeal to S.C.C. refused 206 N.R. 160*n*, 148 Nfld. & P.E.I.R. 360*n*; *Brown (Next friend of) v. University of Alberta Hospital* (1997), 145 D.L.R. (4th) 63, [1997] 4 W.W.R. 645 (Alta. Q.B.).

[384b] [2004] 1 S.C.R. 315, 235 D.L.R. (4th) 577.

[384c] *Bystedt (Guardian ad Litem of) v. Bagdan* (2007), 66 B.C.L.R. (4th) 16 (C.A.).

This suggests that the relatives' rights are additional to the injured person's rights. On the other hand it is difficult to suppose that the legislature intended

[*The next page is* 3-61]

[385] So held in *Dziver v. Smith* (1983), 146 D.L.R. (3d) 314, 41 O.R. (2d) 385 (C.A.).

the wrongdoer to pay twice over in respect of future lost earnings.[385a] It appears from the Law Reform Commission Report that preceded the Act[386] that the legislature had no intention of making a fundamental change in the law on this matter, the main intention apparently being to provide a modern equivalent to the old actions for loss of consortium and servitium which were abolished by s. 69 of the *Family Law Reform Act, 1978*. It is perhaps possible therefore to restrict s. 61(1) to such loss as is not recoverable by the injured person. Admittedly, this requires reading into the Act a restriction that is not expressed but in the light of s. 69 (abolishing the action for loss of consortium) this seems the most probable intention of the legislature.

3.1140 In *Hartwick v. MacIntyre*,[387] it was held that a claim under the Act could not be asserted by the injured person. The court did not say, however, that the common law rights of the injured person had been reduced. Insofar, therefore, as there is a claim at common law by the injured person for any loss it is submitted that it remains unimpaired. It has been suggested that the legislation could be construed to create in the relatives a right of action only for such loss as is not recoverable by the injured person.[388] With the tendency of the courts to extend the rights of injured persons to recover,[389] s. 61(1) of the *Family Law Act* may turn out to have a rather narrow scope in cases where the injured person survives. However, this does not mean that it is useless for it will be available to fill any gap left in the injured person's own rights.

(15) Opportunity to Form Interdependent Relationship

3.1145 It has been held that compensation may be given for the pecuniary consequences of loss of opportunity to form a permanent interdependent relationship (such as marriage).[389a] This claim is closely interconnected with the claim for loss of earning capacity, and a single figure may cover both.[389b] Cogent evidence is required in support of the claim.[389c]

[385a] See *Fera (Litigation Guardian of) v. Gailitis* (1994), 21 O.R. (3d) 630 (Gen. Div.), at p. 634, citing this paragraph.

[386] *Report on Family Law* (Ontario Law Reform Commission, Part I, Torts, 1969), pp. 106-10, especially at p. 106.

[387] (1980), 113 D.L.R. (3d) 253, 29 O.R. (2d) 417 (H.C.J.), affd 131 D.L.R. (3d) 333, 35 O.R. (2d) 119 (C.A.).

[388] See also 3.480, *supra*.

[389] *Ibid.*

[389a] *Reekie v. Messervey* (1989), 59 DLR (4th) 481 (B.C.C.A.), leave to appeal to S.C.C. refused in part 62 D.L.R. (4th) viii, granted in part [1990] 1 S.C.R. 219, 66 D.L.R. (4th) 765, *Walker v. Ritchie*, *supra*, note 241.

[389b] *Reekie v. Messervey*, *supra*, at p. 487.

[389c] *Belyea v. Hammond* (2000), 193 D.L.R. (4th) 476 (N.B.C.A.), at p. 486.

7. Cost of Future Care

(1) Introduction

3.1150 The second major head of pecuniary loss is the cost of future care of a totally or partially disabled plaintiff. Difficulties have arisen in a number of cases, particularly in England and Australia, where the plaintiff has an expectation of receiving free medical treatment from public or private sources.[390] The Canadian position is that although there is a universal health insurance scheme, the provincial health plans are entitled to be subrogated to any claim of an insured person against a wrongdoer.[391] Consequently, the expectation that the plaintiff's medical expenses will be met by provincial health insurance does not reduce the damages payable by the wrongdoer. The question of gifts of services from private sources is dealt with later.[392] Again, the usual rule is that neither the receipt nor the expectation of gifts from third parties affects the assessment of damages against the wrongdoer.

(2) Standard of reasonableness

3.1160 As mentioned previously,[393] the Supreme Court of Canada has approved the view that the plaintiff is entitled to a level of care that is appropriate to the plaintiff's needs without regard to the cost to the defendant. This includes actual medical and other reasonably necessary treatment,[394] the cost of special clothing and equipment,[395] costs of personal travel,[396] costs of travel

[390] See *McGregor on Damages*, 16th ed. (London, Sweet & Maxwell, 1997), §1686. Section 2(4) of the *Law Reform (Personal Injuries) Act 1948* provides that, in estimating whether expenses are reasonable, the possibility of avoiding or reducing them by resort to the National Health Service shall be disregarded, but in *Harris v. Brights Asphalt Contractors Ltd.*, [1953] 1 Q.B. 617 at p. 635, Slade J. said that this did not entitle the plaintiff "to recover expenses which in fact he will never incur", and this dictum was approved by the Court of Appeal in *Cunningham v. Harrison*, [1973] Q.B. 942 at p. 957, and by the House of Lords in *Lim Poh Choo v. Camden and Islington Area Health Authority*, [1980] A.C. 174 at p. 188. See also *Eagle v. Chambers (No. 2)*, [2004] 1 W.L.R. 3081 (C.A.). On the Australian position, see Luntz, *Assessment of Damages for Personal Injury and Death*, 3rd ed. (Chatswood, N.S.W., Butterworth Pty. Ltd., 1990) §§4.2.3-4.2.4, 4.4.1-4.4.8.

[391] See 3.1740-3.1760, *infra*.

[392] See 3.1550-3.1580, *infra*.

[393] See 3.280, *supra*.

[394] *Andrews v. Grand & Toy Alberta Ltd.*, [1978] 2 S.C.R. 229, 83 D.L.R. (3d) 452; *French v. Hodge* (2005), 231 N.S.R. (2d) 95 (S.C.).

[395] *Thornton v. Prince George School District*, [1978] 2 S.C.R. 267, 83 D.L.R. (3d) 480; *DeChamplain v. Etobicoke General Hospital* (1985), 34 C.C.L.T. 89 (Ont. H.C.J.); *Giannone v. Weinberg* (1989), 68 O.R. (2d) 767, 33 O.A.C. 11 (C.A.), leave to appeal to S.C.C. refused 105 N.R. 239*n*, 71 O.R. (2d) x; *French v. Hodge* (2005), 231 N.S.R. (2d) 95 (S.C.); *Campbell-MacIsaac v. Deveaux* (2004), 224 N.S.R. (2d) 315 (C.A.).

[396] *Bishop v. Arts & Letters Club of Toronto* (1978), 83 D.L.R. (3d) 107, 18 O.R. (2d) 471 (H.C.J.); *Cropp v. Potashville School Unit No. 25* (1977), 81 D.L.R. (3d) 115 (Sask. Q.B.) ("best available" treatment allowed even though involving expensive treatment abroad); *Bendel v. Danylchuk* (1952), 6 W.W.R. (N.S.) 625 (Sask. Q.B.); *Martin v. Cantafio* (1971), 20 D.L.R. (3d) 725 (Man. C.A.) (cost of treatment in Switzerland allowed); *Anderson v. James* (1992), 87 D.L.R. (4th) 419, 63 B.C.L.R. (2d) 176 (C.A.); *Williams v. Brocker* (2004), 188 Man. R. (2d) 61 (Q.B.); *Lynne v. Taylor* (2004), 39 Alta. L.R. (4th) 82 (Q.B.), revd on other grounds 53 Alta. L.R. (4th) 1 (C.A.).

for relatives,[397] the cost of purchasing or adapting suitable accommodation,[398] nursing or attendants' service costs.[399] Plainly there are some financial limits and the plaintiff will not be entitled to compensation on the basis of a level of care that is extravagant or totally unreasonable,[400] or to compensation for expenses that have only a small probability of success.[400a] However, the tenor of Dickson J.'s judgment in *Andrews v. Grand & Toy*[401] makes it clear that the court will lean in favour of the plaintiff in judging the reasonableness of the claim. The court made it plain that the restraint imposed on damages for non-pecuniary losses was an added reason for insuring the adequacy of pecuniary compensation.[402]

(3) Discounting to present value

3.1170 The considerations here are the same as those discussed previously in respect of loss of earning capacity,[403] with the proviso that the incidence of future costs of care will often be more sporadic than lost earnings.

(4) Income tax supplement ("gross-up")

3.1180 The question arises whether an award for future care should be supplemented, or "grossed up", to allow for the incidence of taxation on the income from investment of the award. In many cases the bulk of the award will consist of medical expenses to which the provincial health insurance plans will be subrogated. This will not be the plaintiff's to invest. Furthermore, medical expenses in excess of three per cent of a taxpayer's income are deductible under present Canadian tax law. However, the definition of deductible medical expenses may not always correspond exactly with the costs of future care constituting the award of damages. In *Andrews v. Grand & Toy*[404] and in *Arnold v. Teno*,[405] an allowance for this factor was

---

[397] *Wilson v. McLeay* (1961), 106 C.L.R. 523 (H.C.).

[398] *Thornton v. Prince George School District, supra*, footnote 395; *McLeod v. Palardy* (1981), 124 D.L.R. (3d) 506 (Man. C.A.); *Joubert v. Rosetown (Town)* (1987), 60 Sask. R. 200 (C.A.); *Watkins v. Olafson*, [1989] 2 S.C.R. 750, 61 D.L.R. (4th) 577; *Roberts v. Johnstone*, [1989] Q.B. 878 (C.A.); *York v. Johnston* (1997), 148 D.L.R. (4th) 225, [1997] 9 W.W.R. 739 (B.C.C.A.).

[399] *Andrews v. Grand & Toy Alberta Ltd., supra*, footnote 394; *Watkins v. Olafson, supra*, footnote 398; *McErlean v. Sarel* (1987), 42 D.L.R. (4th) 577, 61 O.R. (2d) 396 (C.A.), leave to appeal to S.C.C. refused [1988] 1 S.C.R. xi, 46 D.L.R. (4th) vi.

[400] *Thornton v. Prince George School District, supra*, footnote 395, at pp. 280-1; *Andrews v. Grand & Toy Alberta Ltd., supra*, footnote 394, at pp. 240-1. See *Q. (A.) v. Canada (Attorney General)* (1998), 169 Sask. R. 1 (Q.B.).

[400a] *Briody v. St. Helens and Knowsley Area Health Authority*, [2002] 2 W.L.R. 394 (C.A.) (cost of proposed surrogacy arrangement).

[401] *Supra*, footnote 394. See 3.280, *supra*. See also *Wallace v. Taylor Estate* (1992), 73 B.C.L.R. (2d) 296, 34 W.A.C. 123 (C.A.).

[402] *Supra*, at pp. 262-3 S.C.R., p. 477 D.L.R.

[403] See 3.990-3.1040, *supra*. The Supreme Court of Canada in *Andrews v. Grand & Toy Alberta Ltd., supra*, footnote 394, treated it as a consideration relevant to both heads of pecuniary loss, at p. 232 S.C.R., p. 471 D.L.R.

[404] *Supra*, footnote 394.

denied but, after several years of uncertainty on the question, the Supreme Court of Canada held in 1989 that an allowance for income tax was to be included.[406] The court anticipated the development of "a computer model which would yield an estimate of the gross-up on the basis of the factors relevant to the particular case".[406a] There are, however, some difficulties here. Computer programs produce substantially different results according to the assumptions that are used in designing them. The question of the proper assumptions must ultimately be a matter of law, not of arithmetic. The principal matters on which assumptions are necessary in this context are the rate of future inflation,[407] the future impact of income taxation,[407a] the nature of investments to be made with the capital sum,[408] the rate of withdrawal from the fund[408a] and the amount of the plaintiff's other income.[409] Following a recommendation of the Ontario Law Reform Commission, power is now given in Ontario to the Rules Committee to make rules governing the method of calculation.[410] Statute also provides, in Ontario, that where the plaintiff requests that an amount be included in the award to offset any liability for income tax on income from the investment of the award, the court is to order periodic payment of all or part of the award unless contrary to the best interest of the plaintiff.[411] These provisions represent a compromise among conflicting proposals on this topic from various interests, and are not easy to interpret. The proper procedure is for the court to calculate damages on the ordinary basis including gross-up, and for the defendant

[405] See *Arnold v. Teno*, [1978] 2 S.C.R. 287, 83 D.L.R. (3d) 609.

[406] *Watkins v. Olafson*, [1989] 2 S.C.R. 750, 61 D.L.R. (4th) 577; *Scarff v. Wilson*, [1989] 2 S.C.R. 776, 61 D.L.R. (4th) 749; *Oleschak Estate v. Wilganowski* (1991), 70 Man. R. (2d) 149 (C.A.) (calculation before reduction for contributory negligence); *Tronrud v. French* (1991), 84 D.L.R. (4th) 275, 75 Man. R. (2d) 1 (C.A.), leave to appeal to S.C.C. refused 87 D.L.R. (4th) vii, 138 N.R. 407*n*. But see *Martin v. Listowel Memorial Hospital* (1999), 31 C.P.C. (4th) 242 (Ont. Ct. (Gen. Div.)), vard 192 D.L.R. (4th) 250 (C.A.) (no gross-up in respect of non-pecuniary loss).

[406a] *Watkins v. Olafson, supra*, at p. 589 D.L.R.

[407] Rule 53.09(2)(b) of the Ontario *Rules of Civil Procedure*, R.R.O. 1990, Reg. 194, supplies a formula for future inflation based on Government of Canada bonds.

[407a] *Tucker (Guardian Ad Litem) v. Asleson* (1992), 86 D.L.R. (4th) 73, 62 B.C.L.R. (2d) 78 (S.C.), vard on another point 102 D.L.R. (4th) 518, [1993] 6 W.W.R. 45 (C.A.) (indexing assumed at 2 per cent).

[408] See *Scarff v. Wilson* (1990), 66 D.L.R. (4th) 52, 42 B.C.L.R. (2d) 273 (S.C.); *Unruh (Guardian ad Litem of) v. Webber* (1994), 112 D.L.R. (4th) 83, [1994] 5 W.W.R. 270 (B.C.C.A.), leave to appeal to S.C.C. refused 115 D.L.R. (4th) viii, 178 N.R. 397*n*. Ontario rule 53.09(2)(a) provides that it is to be assumed that the entire amount will be invested in fixed income securities.

[408a] *Tucker (Guardian Ad Litem) v. Asleson, supra*, footnote 407a (one-third assumed spent in first ten years); *Unruh (Guardian ad Litem of) v. Webber, supra* (probability of future house purchase).

[409] *Scarff v. Wilson, supra*, footnote 408 (other parts of award to be taken into account); *Tucker (Guardian Ad Litem) v. Asleson, supra*, footnote 407a; *Cherry (Guardian ad Litem of) v. Borsman* (1992), 94 D.L.R. (4th) 487, 70 B.C.L.R. 273 (C.A.), leave to appeal to S.C.C. refused 99 D.L.R. (4th) vii, 152 N.R. 240*n*. See *Report on Compensation for Personal Injuries and Death* (Ontario Law Reform Commission, 1987), pp. 131-8.

[410] *Courts of Justice Act*, s. 66(2)(v).

[411] *Ibid.*, s. 116.

either to accept the calculation, or to propose an alternative scheme of periodic payments. It is then for the plaintiff to establish that the scheme would not be in the plaintiff's best interests. In one case, the plaintiff succeeded in obtaining a lump sum, including gross-up, by asserting an intention to invest in a franchise. The evidence was not very specific, but the court said that "the court is not required to scrutinize too critically the investment plans of the plaintiff".[411a] This appears to suggest that a competent adult plaintiff will usually in practice be able to secure a full lump sum award by asserting an intention to make an investment. On the other hand, in *Roberts v. Morana*[411b] the Ontario Court of Appeal, in holding that a plaintiff was entitled to a structured award equal to the full present value of the cost of future care (not including "gross-up"), added: "The [defendants] have been relieved of the obligation to pay approximately $4 million by way of gross-up for income tax. That is the benefit intended by s. 116." This suggests that the legislation embodies a positive intention to confer a benefit on the defendant, in which case it may be argued that a plaintiff should not be entitled to reject a structured award solely in order to insist on receiving the "gross-up" as a lump sum.

(5) Overlap with loss of earning capacity

3.1190 The question of overlap was discussed previously[412] where it was suggested that the preferable solution was that favoured by Dickson J. in *Andrews*, that is to award the cost of future care in full, including the cost of necessaries, and to reduce the award for loss of earning capacity by the amount that the plaintiff would spend on necessaries.

(6) Overlap with non-pecuniary loss

3.1200 As mentioned previously the approach now adopted by the Supreme Court of Canada to non-pecuniary losses is that they are an allowance for "solace" to the plaintiff for the lost amenities of life.[413] It was suggested that this amounts to treating the damages as the same kind as damages for the cost of future care, that is, a sum to make good the plaintiff's psychological loss not earmarked for expenditure on any particular items. It becomes apparent, therefore, that a possibility of overlap exists. If a plaintiff calls expert witnesses to prove, for example, that expensive holidays are recommended as psychiatric treatment, there might be a double recovery.

3.1205 In *Tronrud v. French*,[413a] the costs of adapting and using a recreational

[411a] *Wilson v. Martinello* (1995), 125 D.L.R. (4th) 240 at p. 253, 23 O.R. (3d) 417 (C.A.); *Chesher v. Monaghan* (2000), 186 D.L.R. (4th) 595 (Ont C.A.), leave to appeal to S.C.C. refused 195 D.L.R. (4th) vii. See also *Bishop v. Pinto* (2002), 21 CPC (5th) 286 (Ont. S.C.J.).

[411b] (2000), 187 D.L.R. (4th) 577 (Ont. C.A.), at p. 580.

[412] See 3.1050-3.1110, *supra*.

[413] See 3.510-3.700, *supra*.

cabin were disallowed. The trial judge, in a passage approved by the Court of Appeal said " 'the claim for pecuniary damages tends to overlap and to merge with the claim for nonpecuniary general damages.' "[413b]

(7) Management fees

3.1210 The considerations mentioned previously in relation to compensation for lost earning capacity are also relevant to awards for future care. It should be noted, however, that in many cases the bulk of the award for future care will not be at the plaintiff's disposal, for the provincial health insurance schemes will be subrogated to the plaintiff's rights. In respect of such amounts the plaintiff will have no management to do, and so no management fee is appropriate.[414] On the other hand, a "care management fee" has been allowed to enable a brain-injured plaintiff to secure advice on expenditures.[414a]

(8) Deduction for contingencies

3.1220 In estimating the appropriate award for the cost of future care, a reduction is appropriate for the possibility that the need for care might be reduced or might cease at an earlier date than predicted in the initial calculations, and amelioration of the plaintiff's condition might reduce future costs, as might also a deterioration necessitating, for example, (cheaper) institutional care, instead of the otherwise more desirable but more expensive home care.[415] An award calculated by a period of years based on the plaintiff's pre-accident expectation of life may be legitimately reduced if evidence shows that the plaintiff's post-accident expectation of life is reduced, but of course if the initial calculation was based on the plaintiff's post-accident life expectancy, no further reduction is appropriate.[416] In *Andrews* and *Thornton* a reduction of twenty per cent was approved, Dickson J. stating that the question was "fraught with difficulty".[417]

3.1230 In *Fenn v. City of Peterborough*,[418] the Ontario Court of Appeal made no reduction at all for contingencies on the ground that: "Those possibilities which may tend to increase the financial burden on [the plaintiff] are at the least the equal to those possibilities which may tend to diminish the sums

---

[413a] (1991), 84 D.L.R. (4th) 275, 75 Man. R. (2d) 1 (C.A.), leave to appeal to S.C.C. refused 87 D.L.R. (4th) vii, 138 N.R. 407*n*.

[413b] *Supra*, at p. 280.

[414] See 3.1110, *supra*.

[414a] *Anderson v. James* (1992), 87 D.L.R. (4th) 419, 63 B.C.L.R. (2d) 176 (C.A.). See also *Bracey (Public Trustee for) v. Jahnke* (1997), 147 D.L.R. (4th) 632, [1997] 7 W.W.R. 237, supplementary reasons 149 D.L.R. (4th) 461, 154 W.A.C. 119 (B.C.C.A.) (fees of public trustee); *Wood v. Boutilier* (1998), 171 N.S.R. (2d) 18 (S.C.).

[415] *Andrews v. Grand & Toy Alberta Ltd.*, [1978] 2 S.C.R. 229, 83 D.L.R. (3d) 452. See also *Graham v. Rourke* (1990), 74 D.L.R. (4th) 1, 75 O.R. (2d) 622 (C.A.).

[416] See 3.990, *supra*.

[417] *Andrews v. Grand & Toy Alberta Ltd., supra*, footnote 415, at p. 231 S.C.R., p. 468 D.L.R.

[418] (1979), 104 D.L.R. (3d) 174, 25 O.R. (2d) 399 (C.A.), affd [1981] 2 S.C.R. 613, 129 D.L.R. (3d) 507.

awarded."[419] It should be noted that the plaintiff's life expectancy had already been reduced to post-accident level, and that one of the contingencies causing greater expense mentioned by the court was the possibility of tax liability.[420] The result may be explained therefore as an allowance for tax considered to be offset by a reduction for contingencies. The question will depend on the evidence in each case, but where there is evidence of a substantial possibility of a reduction of expenses (for example, because of a compelled substitution of institutional for home care) or of an increase, an adjustment should be made.[421]

3.1240 The question of voluntary substitution of less expensive treatment raises difficulties. The argument for reducing recovery in such a case is that compensation for the cost of future care is compensation for a pecuniary loss composed of anticipated expenses, and if it is not in fact anticipated that an expense will be incurred, it cannot be counted as a loss.[422] The contrary argument is that once the plaintiff establishes that it would be reasonable to incur the cost, the plaintiff is entitled to recover damages measured by that cost, and that what the plaintiff chooses to actually do with the proceeds of the award is irrelevant. This view is supported by two decisions of the Manitoba Queen's Bench[423] and by *Andrews v. Grand & Toy Alberta Ltd.*,[424] where Dickson J., with specific reference to the argument that the plaintiff might not in fact use his award for the treatment supposed, said:

> It is not for the Court to conjecture upon how a plaintiff will spend the amount awarded to him. There is always the possibility that the victim will not invest his award wisely but will dissipate it. That is not something which ought to be allowed to affect a consideration of the proper basis of compensation within a fault-based system. The plaintiff is free to do with that sum of money as he likes.[425]

This approach was reaffirmed in *Townsend v. Kroppmanns.*[425a]

This view is also supported by the cases permitting recovery of the cost of services provided gratuitously, which rest on the proposition that the plaintiff's loss is the need for services not the actual cost of procuring

---

[419] *Supra*, at p. 233 D.L.R. The court rejected a "ritualistic" reduction for contingencies.

[420] *Fenn, supra*, at p. 232 D.L.R. See 3.1180, *supra*.

[421] See *Pickering v. Deakin*, [1985] 1 W.W.R. 289, 58 B.C.L.R. 145 (C.A.); *Wipfli v. Britten* (1984), 13 D.L.R. (4th) 169, [1984] 5 W.W.R. 385 (B.C.C.A.).

[422] See the dictum of Slade J., and *Harris v. Brights Asphalt Contractors Ltd.*, approved by the House of Lords in *Lim Poh Choo v. Camden and Islington Area Health Authority*, [1980] A.C. 174.

[423] *Kuales v. Svenson* (1957), 24 W.W.R. 24 (Man. Q.B.), where Williams, C.J.Q.B., speaking of cosmetic surgery, said at p. 26: "The plaintiffs should be put in the position to have their injuries so treated if they desire and the possibility that they may elect not to have such treatment and may prefer to have the cash should not enter into the assessment of damages." The case was followed in *Meade v. Ohirko* (1963), 39 D.L.R. (2d) 707 (Man. Q.B.).

[424] *Supra*, footnote 415.

[425] *Supra*, at pp. 246-7 S.C.R., pp. 465-6 D.L.R. As is pointed out by Cooper-Stephenson, *Personal Injury Damages in Canada*, 2nd ed. (Toronto, Carswell, 1996), p. 416, there is an element of circularity here because the amount of the award is the very question at issue.

[425a] [2004] 1 S.C.R. 315, 235 DLR (4th) 577.

them.[426] In the light of Dickson J.'s comments, it can be said that the weight of authority in Canada is on the side of allowing full recovery,[427] especially in the light of the restrictions now imposed on recovery for non-pecuniary losses. It would, however, be open to the defendant to show that the plaintiff who definitely intended not to incur a particular expense has, in fact, no need of it, for it is the plaintiff's own reasonable needs that form the basis of the award.[428] This would be a rare case, for it would usually be open to the plaintiff to demand compensation based on reasonable needs, and to say (if asked about future intentions) that the right was reserved to reconsider the actual disposition of the award.[428a]

8. Intangible Injuries

(1) Tort

3.1250 The law of torts has been understandably reluctant to establish a cause of action for negligent injury to feelings and mental distress standing alone, but it seems to be moving in the direction of enlarging liability.[429] Deliberate infliction of mental distress is actionable.[430] In the leading case compensation was said to be for the physical harm.[431] It is submitted that in light of recent cases allowing compensation for mental distress caused by breach of contract,[432] mental distress caused tortiously ought also to be compensable even if it cannot be said to have caused physical harm.[433] It is a question for the substantive law of torts whether the defendant's conduct is initially actionable.[434]

3.1260 In defamation cases it is well established that injury to feelings may be compensated. In *McCarey v. Associated Newspapers Ltd. (No. 2)*,[435] Pearson L.J. said:

> Compensatory damages ... may include not only actual pecuniary loss and anticipated pecuniary loss or any social disadvantages which result, or may be thought likely to result from the wrong which has been done. They may

[426] See 3.440-3.490, *supra*.

[427] This conclusion is also supported by *McLeod v. Palardy* (1981), 124 D.L.R. (3d) 506 (Man. C.A.), where damages based on the cost of a new house were upheld even though the court accepted that, since the damages were reduced for the plaintiff's contributory negligence, the plaintiff would not have enough in fact to make such a purchase.

[428] This point is made by Cooper-Stephenson, *op. cit.*, footnote 425, pp. 415, 418-19.

[428a] See *Townsend v. Kroppmanns* (2002), 2 B.C.L.R. (4th) 10 (C.A.).

[429] See Fleming, *The Law of Torts*, 9th ed. (Sydney, Law Book Co., 1998), pp. 173-81; *Aubry v. ditions Vice-Versa Inc.*, [1998] 1 S.C.R. 591, 157 D.L.R. (4th) 577; *Anderson v. Wilson* (1999), 175 D.L.R. (4th) 409 (C.A.), leave to appeal to S.C.C. refused 185 D.L.R. (4th) vii; *W. v. Essex County Council*, [2000] 2 All E.R. 237 (H.L.). In *Tooman v. Veley* (1974), 48 D.L.R. (3d) 767 (Man. C.A.), damages for inconvenience were disallowed.

[430] See Fleming, *ibid.*, at pp. 37-40. See also *Prinzo v. Baycrest Centre for Geriatric Care* (2002), 215 D.L.R. (4th) 31 (Ont. C.A.).

[431] *Wilkinson v. Downton*, [1897] 2 Q.B. 57 at p. 59, *per* Wright J. In *Purdy v. Woznesensky*, [1937] 2 W.W.R. 116 (Sask. C.A.) and in *Bielitzki v. Obadiak* (1921), 61 D.L.R. 494 (C.A.), affd 65 D.L.R. 627 (C.A.), emphasis was also laid on the physical symptoms of the plaintiff's distress.

[432] See 3.1310-3.1450, *infra*.

also include the natural injury to his feelings — the natural grief and distress which he may have felt at having been spoken of in defamatory terms, and if there has been any kind of high-handed, oppressive, insulting or contumelious behaviour by the defendant which increases the mental pain and suffering caused by the defamation and may constitute injury to the plaintiff's pride and self-confidence, those are proper elements to be taken into account ...[436]

3.1270 Mental distress caused by serious personal injury is compensated under the heads of non-pecuniary loss, which includes pain and suffering, loss of amenities of life and loss of expectation of life.[437] Assault, false imprisonment and malicious prosecution amount to interferences with the person which may not however result in serious physical injury. Damages have been given in these cases for mental and emotional distress,[438] and also in cases of

[433] See *Young v. Bella*, [2006] 1 S.C.R. 108, 261 D.L.R. (4th) 516; *Phillip (Next Friend of) v. Whitecourt General Hospital*, [2004] 7 W.W.R. 228 (Alta. Q.B.), citing this passage at para. 276, and again in *Phillip (Next Friend of) v. Whitecourt General Hospital*, [2005] 7 W.W.R. 269 (Alta. Q.B.) at para. 389. See *Mason v. Westside Cemeteries Ltd.* (1996), 135 D.L.R. (4th) 361 (Ont. Ct. (Gen. Div.)); *Peters-Brown v. Regina District Health Board*, [1997] 1 W.W.R. 638, 148 Sask. R. 248 (C.A.) (invasion of privacy); *Butler v. Newfoundland (Workers' Compensation Commission)* (1998), 165 Nfld. & P.E.I.R. 84, 38 C.C.E.L. (2d) 91 (Nfld. S.C.). It is often impossible to draw a clear line between mental stress and physical harm. In *Pratt v. British Medical Ass'n*, [1919] 1 K.B. 244, damages were awarded for "humiliation and menace" caused by the defendant's wrongful interference with the plaintiff's practice of his profession, referred to with approval but distinguished in *Jones v. Fabbi* (1973), 37 D.L.R. (3d) 27 (B.C.S.C.), at p. 34. In *McLoughlin v. O'Brian*, [1982] 2 All E.R. 298 (H.L.), damages were given for nervous shock suffered by the plaintiff on the injury of relatives elsewhere. In *Page v. Smith*, [1996] 1 A.C. 155 (H.L.), the plaintiff recovered damages for nervous shock even though other physical injury did not occur; see also *Kean v. Sobey's Inc.* (1997), 155 Nfld. & P.E.I.R. 27 (Nfld. S.C.). In *Archer v. Brown*, [1985] Q.B. 401, aggravated damages were awarded to compensate for mental distress caused by fraud.

[434] See *Mustapha v. Culligan of Canada Ltd.* (2008), 293 D.L.R. (4th) 29 (S.C.C.). As in other questions of remoteness, it is impossible to distinguish clearly between questions of liability and damages. See 14.420, *infra*.

[435] [1965] 2 Q.B. 86 (C.A.). See also *Uren v. Fairfax (John) & Sons Pty. Ltd.* (1966), 117 C.L.R. 118, at p. 150, *per* Windeyer J., affd [1969] 1 A.C. 590 *sub nom.* Australian Consolidated Press Ltd. v. Uren (P.C.); *Hubert v. DeCamillis* (1963), 41 D.L.R. (2d) 495 (B.C.S.C.); *Khodaparast v. Shad*, [2000] 1 W.L.R. 618 (C.A.) (malicious falsehood).

[436] *McCarey v. Associated Newspapers Ltd. (No. 2)*, *supra*, footnote 435, at pp. 104-5.

[437] See 3.510-3.700, *supra*.

[438] See *Edmonds v. Armstrong Funeral Home*, [1931] 1 D.L.R. 676 (Alta. S.C. App. Div.), *per* Harvey C.J.A.; *Markey v. Sloat* (1912), 6 D.L.R. 827 (N.B.S.C. App. Div.) ("mental suffering and indignity", *per* Barry J., at p. 842, citing *Sedgwick on Damages*, 8th ed. (New York, Baker, Voorhis & Co., 1891), §§461-463 and 49); *Wood v. Kennedy* (1998), 165 D.L.R. (4th) 542 (Ont. Ct. (Gen. Div.)). See also *Stewart v. Stonehouse*, [1926] 2 D.L.R. 683 (Sask. C.A.); *Whitehouse v. Reimer* (1979), 107 D.L.R. (3d) 283 (Alta. Q.B.), revd on other grounds 116 D.L.R. (3d) 594 (C.A.); *Perry v. Fried* (1972), 32 D.L.R. (3d) 589 (N.S.S.C.T.D.); *Carr v. Gauthier* (1992), 97 D.L.R. (4th) 651, [1993] 2 W.W.R. 111 (Q.B.); *B.(P.) v. B.(W.)* (1992), 11 O.R. (3d) 161, supplementary reasons November 27, 1992 (Gen. Div.); *G.(E.D.) v. D.(S.)* (1993), 101 D.L.R. (4th) 101, 77 B.C.L.R. (2d) 106 (C.A.) (sexual assault); *A. (D.A.) v. B. (D.K.)* (1995), 27 C.C.L.T. (2d) 256 (Ont. Ct. (Gen. Div.)) (sexual assault); *Thompson v. Commissioner of Police of the Metropolis*, [1998] Q.B. 498 (C.A.) (aggravated damages); *Jane Doe v. Metropolitan Toronto (Municipality) Commissioners of Police* (1998), 160 D.L.R. (4th) 697 (Ont. Ct. (Gen. Div.)) ($175,000 to rape victim for non-pecuniary loss).

enticement and related torts,[439] and in cases of breach of fiduciary duty.[439a] In *Young v. Bella*,[439b] a jury award of $430,000 for non-pecuniary loss caused by a false report of suspicion of child abuse was upheld by the Supreme Court of Canada.

3.1280 In *Bone v. Seale*[440] a nuisance case, damages were given for distress caused by a noxious odour even though the value of the plaintiff's property was found not to have been affected. The trial judge had awarded over £6,000 for twelve and one-half years. This referred to past damage only, since the award was coupled with an injunction. The English Court of Appeal, in reducing the award to £1,000, expressly made a comparison with personal injury cases. Stephenson L.J. said:

> The nearest analogy would seem to be the damages which are awarded almost daily for loss of amenity in personal injury cases; it does seem to me that there is perhaps a closer analogy than at first sight appears between losing the enjoyment of your property as a result of some interference by smell or by noise caused by a next door neighbour, and losing an amenity as a result of a personal injury. Is it possible to equate loss of sense of smell as a result of the negligence of a defendant motor driver with having to put up with positive smells as a result of a nuisance created by a negligent neighbour? There is, as it seems to me, some parallel between the loss of amenity which is caused by personal injury and the loss of amenity which is caused by a nuisance of this kind. If a parallel is drawn between those two losses, it is at once confirmed that this figure [£6,000] is much too high. It is the kind of figure that would be given for a serious and permanent loss of amenity as the result of a very serious injury, perhaps in the case of a young person.[441]

Scarman L.J. said: "It is not, I think, possible to say that we must adopt, or seek to adopt, any rigid standard of comparison between a nuisance case and personal injury litigation. Nevertheless overall, the law ought to remain consistent when it is dealing with analogous situations."[442] Stephenson L.J.'s comparison between the infliction upon the plaintiff of noxious smells and loss of the sense of smell altogether may seem bizarre at first sight. However if one could imagine a personal injury that had the effect of causing the sensation of a noxious smell (as some injuries may cause ringing in the ears), the comparison seems very apt. Though the legal causes of action in nuisance and negligence are quite different, there is good reason, as Scarman L.J. suggested, for consistency in measurement of damages.

[439] *D. v. Hilligenn* (1955), 15 W.W.R. 287 (B.C.S.C.) (seduction); *Stephen v. Stephen*, [1931] 2 D.L.R. 892 (Sask. C.A.); *Kenny v. Semchuk* (1958), 15 D.L.R. (2d) 301 (Sask. C.A.) (criminal conversation); *Powell v. Billington* (1958), 27 W.W.R. 24 (B.C.S.C.) (criminal conversation).

[439a] *Norberg v. Wynrib*, [1992] 2 S.C.R. 226, 92 D.L.R. (4th) 449; *Taylor v. McGillivray* (1993), 110 D.L.R. (4th) 64, 143 N.B.R. (2d) 241 (Q.B.); *R. (J.) v. White* (2001), 52 O.R. (3d) 353 *sub nom.* R. (J.) v. W. (E.S.) (S.C.J.).

[439b] [2006] 1 S.C.R. 108, 261 D.L.R. (4th) 516.

[440] [1975] 1 W.L.R. 797 (C.A.).

[441] *Supra*, at pp. 803-4.

[442] *Supra*, at p. 805.

3.1290 In *Edmonds v. Armstrong Funeral Home*,[443] the Alberta Appellate Division held that damages were recoverable for mental distress caused to a wife by an unauthorized autopsy of her husband's body. Harvey C.J.A. said:

> If mental suffering can be properly considered in assessing damages in such actions as assault, defamation, malicious prosecution, seduction etc., as it properly can, there seems no good reason why it should not be so considered in such a case of misconduct as this is alleged to be when it is a natural and certain consequence of the defendants' acts.[444]

Trespass to goods may also, in certain circumstances, cause mental distress, as where a creditor wrongfully seizes goods.[445] Trespass to land may cause loss of enjoyment of the land.[445a] In *Williams v. Settle*,[446] damages were given to compensate the plaintiff for invasion of privacy by the misuse of a wedding photograph. Damages have also been given for inconvenience and discomfort arising out of professional negligence[447] and for negligent misrepresentation.[447a] Many of the cases in this area involve deliberate wrong-doing by the defendant and the awards are frequently explained as exemplary, vindictive, or punitive.[448] In *Rookes v. Barnard*,[449] where the House of Lords restricted the power of English courts to award exemplary damages, Lord Devlin indicated that many of the cases were to be explained as compensatory in character, that is, cases of aggravated damages.[450] In Canada it is possible that substantial damages for injury to feelings in such cases will continue to be given in the form of exemplary damages.[451] A distinction between compensatory and exemplary damages is, however,

---

443 *Supra*, footnote 438.

444 *Supra*, at p. 681. But see *McNeil v. Forest Lawn Memorial Services Ltd.* (1976), 72 D.L.R. (3d) 556 (B.C.S.C.) (no damages for cremation of body depriving plaintiff of opportunity to view it).

445 But in *Dixon v. Calcraft*, [1892] 1 Q.B. 458 (C.A.), Lord Esher M.R. said, at p. 464: "[Compensation] could not be given by way of aggravation of damages in respect of wounded feelings. Such a thing was never heard of." (Seizure of ship on ground of safety). See 11.230, *infra*. In *Smith v. Enright* (1893), 63 L.J.Q.B. 220, damages for wrongful distress included an allowance for "annoyance" and injury to the plaintiff's credit and reputation. In *Murray v. Quigg* (1980), 32 N.B.R. (2d) 631 (Q.B.T.D.), revd on other grounds 36 N.B.R. (2d) 458 (C.A.), damages for trouble, harassment, and worry were awarded.

445a *Ouellette v. Fleck* (1995) 158 N.B.R. (2d) 141 (Q.B.); *Craig v. North Shore Heli Logging Ltd.* (1997), 34 B.C.L.R. (3d) 330, 34 B.L.R. (2d) 119 (S.C.).

446 [1960] 1 W.L.R. 1072 (C.A.).

447 *Jenkins v. Leclaire* (1976), 15 N.S.R. (2d) 473 (S.C. App. Div.) (architect); *Caldwell v. Fitzgerald* (1977), 26 N.S.R. (2d) 140 (S.C.T.D.) (solicitor); *Stoddard v. Atwil Enterprises Ltd.* (1991), 105 N.S.R. (2d) 315 (S.C.T.D.), supplementary reasons 109 N.S.R. (2d) 254 (S.C.T.D.) (builder).

447a *Queen v. Cognos Inc.* (1987), 63 O.R. (2d) 389, 18 C.C.E.L. 146 (H.C.J.), revd 69 D.L.R. (4th) 288, 74 O.R. (2d) 176 (C.A.), restd [1993] 1 S.C.R. 87, 99 D.L.R. (4th) 626.

448 *E.g.*, *Williams v. Settle*, *supra*, footnote 446 ("exemplary"); *Owen and Smith v. Reo Motors (Britain), Ltd.* (1934), 151 L.T. 274 (C.A.) ("exemplary").

449 [1964] A.C. 1129 (H.L.).

450 *Supra*, at p. 1230 ("Aggravated damages in this type of case can do most, if not all, of the work that could be done by exemplary damages."). See 11.10, *infra*.

451 See 11.190, 11.200, *infra*.

useful, because in some cases great distress may be caused to the plaintiff without the elements of arbitrary and high-handed misconduct that justify an award of exemplary damages. Thus, a wrongful arrest made in good faith might cause distress and humiliation to the plaintiff for which moderate compensation could, it is submitted, properly be given, even though no case were made out for exemplary damage or for aggravated damages.[451a] The recent cases on mental distress caused by breach of contract[452] show that there is no necessary connection between the blameworthiness of the defendant's conduct and the distress caused to the plaintiff.

3.1300 Damages for inconvenience caused by deceit have been allowed in a case where the plaintiff was tricked into giving up a valuable tenancy.[453] Damages for inconvenience and lost time have been awarded in a case of destruction of goods.[453a] In two Canadian cases substantial general damages were awarded to compensate plaintiffs who had been induced to go through a ceremony of marriage by the defendant's false claim to single status.[454] But in *Karas v. Rowlett*,[455] the Supreme Court of Canada disallowed an award for worry and distress caused by a fraud leading to the loss of a business lease.

(2) Breach of contract

3.1310 Breaches of contract often cause mental distress, both in the shape of disappointment for the loss of anticipated enjoyment of the promised performance and of anger, frustration and, in some cases, humiliation caused by the very occurrence of the breach. A corporation cannot suffer mental distress and cannot recover aggravated damages.[455a]

3.1320 One case in which such intangible injuries have always been recognized is that of breach of promise of marriage, now abolished in several jurisdictions.[456] A passage from Sedgwick's work on damages, cited with approval in England[457] and Canada,[458] summarizes the position:

[451a] *Spautz v. Butterworth* (1996), 41 N.S.W.L.R. 1 (C.A.), at p. 18; *Dulude v. Canada* (2000), 192 D.L.R. (4th) 714 (F.C.A.).

[452] See 3.1310-3.1450, *infra.*

[453] *Mafo v. Adams*, [1970] 1 Q.B. 548 (C.A.). See also *Archer v. Brown*, [1985] Q.B. 401.

[453a] *Yoon v. Singh* (2000), 272 A.R. 332 (Prov. Ct.).

[454] *Graham v. Saville*, [1945] 2 D.L.R. 489, [1945] O.R. 301 (C.A.); *Beoulne v. Ricketts* (1979), 96 D.L.R. (3d) 550 (Alta. S.C.T.D.), but see *Baran v. Wilensky* (1959), 20 D.L.R. (2d) 440 (Ont. H.C.J.) ("nominal" damages only, but in amount of $500 for misrepresentation inducing cohabitation).

[455] [1944] S.C.R. 1, [1944] 1 D.L.R. 241.

[455a] *Walker v. CFTO Ltd.* (1987), 37 D.L.R. (4th) 224 (Ont. C.A.); *Thomas Management Ltd. v. Alberta (Minister of Environmental Protection)* (2006), 276 D.L.R. (4th) 430 (Alta. C.A.).

[456] *Law Reform (Miscellaneous Provisions) Act 1970* (U.K.), s. 1; *Marriage Act* (Ont.), s. 32(1); *Equality of Status Act* (Man.), s. 4; *Marriage Act 1961* (Cth of Aust.), s. 111a. The British Columbia Law Reform Commission proposed abolition: *Breach of Promise of Marriage* (Working Paper No. 39, 1983). See also *Dupuis v. Austin* (1998), 168 D.L.R. (4th) 483 (N.B.Q.B).

[457] *Smith v. Woodfine* (1857), 1 C.B. (N.S.) 660, 140 E.R. 272 (*per* Willes J., at p. 669); *Finlay v. Chirney* (1888), 20 Q.B.D. 494 (C.A.) (*per* Bowen L.J., at p. 506).

> The action for breach of promise of marriage . . . though nominally an action founded on the breach of an agreement, presents a striking exception to the general rules which govern contracts. This action is given as an indemnity to the injured party for the loss she has sustained, and has always been held to embrace the injury to the feelings, affections, and wounded pride, as well as the loss of marriage . . . From the nature of the case, it has been found impossible to fix the amount of compensation by any precise rule; and, as in tort, the measure of damage is a question for the sound discretion of the jury in each particular instance . . .[459]

Apart from this well-recognized exception, it was constantly asserted for many years that no damages could be awarded for breach of contract causing mere mental distress or disappointment,[460] though damages could be given for actual physical inconvenience[461] or physical illness, if foreseeable.[462] The case usually cited for this proposition was *Addis v. Gramophone Company*[463] where the House of Lords rejected an award of damages to an employee for wrongful dismissal: "in respect of the harsh and humiliating way in which he was dismissed, including, presumably, the pain he experienced by reason, it is alleged, of the imputation upon him conveyed by the manner of his dismissal."[464]

3.1330 In *Cook v. Swinfen*,[465] an action by a client against a solicitor, Lord Denning M.R. said: "It can be foreseen that there will be injured feelings;

458 *D. v. B.* (1917), 38 D.L.R. 243 (Ont. S.C. App. Div.), at p. 249. See also *Lafayette v. Vignon*, [1928] 3 D.L.R. 613 (Sask. C.A.) ("wounded feelings and affections and wounded pride", *per* MacKenzie J.A., at pp. 619-20); *Croll v. Edgley* (1963), 41 W.W.R. 439 (B.C.S.C.); *Tschcheidse v. Tschcheidse* (1963), 41 D.L.R. (2d) 138 (Sask. Q.B.); *Baxter v. Lear* (1975), 23 R.F.L. 342 (Man. Q.B.). See also *Thomson v. McEwen*, [1953] 1 D.L.R. 151 (N.B.S.C. App. Div.); *Chizek v. Tripp* (1912), 4 D.L.R. 369 (Sask. S.C.).

459 *Sedgwick on Damages*, 8th ed. (New York, Baker, Voorhis & Co., 1891), §637.

460 See *Peso Silver Mines Ltd. (N.P.L.) v. Cropper*, [1966] S.C.R. 673 at p. 684, 58 D.L.R. (2d) 1 at p. 10: "the claim being founded on breach of contract the damages cannot be increased by reason of ... wounded feelings"; *Kristinacki v. Bongard* (1970), 12 D.L.R. (3d) 254 (Alta. S.C.T.D.); *Neville v. Page* (1977), 5 A.R. 8 (S.C.T.D.); *Johnson v. Gore Wood & Co.*, [2002] 2 A.C. 1 (H.L.). *McGregor on Damages*, 13th ed. (London, Sweet & Maxwell, 1972), §67, though arguing in favour of exceptions in proper cases, §68.

461 *Hobbs v. London & South Western Ry. Co.* (1875), L.R. 10 Q.B. 111; *Bailey v. Bullock*, [1950] 2 All E.R. 1167 (K.B.); *Watts v. Morrow*, [1991] 1 W.L.R. 1421 (C.A.); *Stoddard v. Atwil Enterprises Ltd.* (1991), 105 N.S.R. (2d) 315 (S.C.T.D.), supplementary reasons 109 N.S.R. (2d) 254 (S.C.T.D.). See also *Spatz v. Metropolitan Trust Co.* (1972), 4 N.S.R. (2d) 803 (S.C. App. Div.); *Nurmi v. Michauel Pump Sales & Service Ltd.* (1975), 16 N.S.R. (2d) 161 (S.C.T.D.); *Reyno v. G.M.N. Construction Co. Ltd.* (1975), 16 N.S.R. (2d) 149 (S.C.T.D.); *Duemler v. Air Canada* (1980), 109 D.L.R. (3d) 402 (Alta. Q.B.); *Greenberg v. Stein* (1957), 10 D.L.R. (2d) 155 (B.C.S.C.). In *Thode Construction Ltd. v. Ross Brothers Cartage Ltd.* (1959), 20 D.L.R. (2d) 227 (Sask. C.A.), an award of damages for "trouble and other expenses" was set aside in the absence of proof of particular loss. A similar conclusion was reached in *Hawryluk v. Korsakoff* (1956), 6 D.L.R. (2d) 524 (Man. C.A.).

462 See *Kolan v. Solicitor* (1969), 7 D.L.R. (3d) 481, [1970] 1 O.R. 41 (H.C.J.), affd 11 D.L.R. (3d) 672, [1970] 2 O.R. 686 (C.A.) (physical illness held too remote).

463 [1909] A.C. 488 (H.L.), overruled on another point in *Mahmud v. Bank of Credit and Commerce Int. S.A.*, [1998] A.C. 20 (H.L.).

464 *Supra*, at p. 493.

465 [1967] 1 W.L.R. 457 (C.A.).

mental distress; anger; and annoyance; but for none of these can damages be recovered."[466] Six years later, however in *Jarvis v. Swans Tours Ltd.*[467] the English Court of Appeal, reversing the trial court, awarded damages against a travel agent both for loss of expected enjoyment of the holiday promised by the defendant, and for the mental distress and disappointment caused by the breach of contract. Lord Denning M.R. said, referring to what had been regarded as a rule denying such damages: "I think that those limitations are out of date. In a proper case damages for mental distress can be recovered in contract, just as damages for shock can be recovered in tort."[468]

3.1340 In *Jarvis v. Swan Tours Ltd.*, a contract to provide a holiday was held to be such a proper case, and this conclusion was reaffirmed in *Jackson v. Horizon Holidays*,[469] where Lord Denning said, referring to the *Jarvis* case, that it had been: "held by this court that damages for the loss of a holiday may include not only the difference in value between what was promised and what was obtained, but also damages for mental distress, inconvenience, upset, disappointment and frustration caused by the loss of the holiday."[470]

3.1350 The measurement of damages poses an obvious difficulty. This, however, did not deter the court. In *Jarvis v. Swans Tours* Lord Denning said: "I know that it is difficult to assess in terms of money, but it is no more difficult than the assessment which the courts have to make every day in personal injury cases for loss of amenities."[471] The price paid for the holiday had been £63. Lord Denning assessed the damages as follows: "Looking at the matter quite broadly, I think the damages in this case should be the sum of £125."[472] As one commentator said, it seems generous to allow the plaintiff, who had received the tangible benefits of transport and accommodation, 100 per cent profit on his disappointment.[473] In the *Jackson*[474] case, where the award included compensation for the distress and disappointment of the plaintiff's family, Lord Denning M.R. said:

> . . . I think that the figure of £1,100 was about right. It would, I think, have been excessive if it had been awarded only for the damage suffered by Mr. Jackson himself. But when extended to his wife and children, I do not think it is excessive. People look forward to a holiday. They expect the promises to be fulfilled. When it fails they are greatly disappointed and upset. It is difficult to assess in terms of money; but it is the task of the judges to do the best they can.[475]

3.1360 It was thought by some that the new doctrine might be confined to cases

[466] *Supra*, at p. 461.
[467] [1973] Q.B. 233 (C.A.).
[468] *Supra*, at pp. 237-8.
[469] [1975] 1 W.L.R. 1468 (C.A.). See also *Baltic Shipping Co. v. Dillon* (1993), 176 C.L.R. 344 (Aust. H.C.).
[470] *Supra*, at p. 1472.
[471] *Supra*, footnote 467, at p. 238.
[472] *Supra*.
[473] Yates, "Damages for Non-Pecuniary Loss", 36 Mod. L. Rev. 535 (1973), at p. 540.
[474] *Supra*, footnote 469.
[475] *Supra*, at p. 1473.

such as holidays, where peace of mind might be said to be the very thing bargained for. But in *Heywood v. Wellers*,[476] the English Court of Appeal extended the doctrine to the case of a solicitor who failed in breach of contract to secure protection for a client against molestation. Lord Denning's own decision in *Cook v. Swinfen*[477] was cited together with an earlier case[478] also denying damages for mental distress against a solicitor. Lord Denning said of these cases: "But those cases may have to be reconsidered."[479]

3.1370 It would still be arguable that a case like *Heywood v. Wellers* is distinguishable from the ordinary case of a solicitor's services, in that peace of mind was obviously the client's main concern in seeking to restrain molestation, and mental distress was plainly to be contemplated as liable to occur if the molestation continued.[480] However, in view of Lord Denning's remarks that the earlier cases may have to be reconsidered, it remains unclear how far damages will be awarded for breach of contracts of professional service. It is well known that litigation causes mental stress, and it could well be held to be within the contemplation of a reasonable solicitor that, on failure to conduct litigation properly, the client would be liable to suffer unnecessary mental distress.[480a]

3.1380 Some English and Commonwealth cases have suggested that damages of this kind are only recoverable when the subject-matter of the contract is to provide peace of mind,[480b] but not all the Canadian cases fall into this category. Damages have been awarded in Canada for breaches of contract by a travel agent,[481] by an airline,[481a] by the supplier of a vacation motor

[476] [1976] Q.B. 446 (C.A.).

[477] *Supra*, footnote 465.

[478] *Groom v. Crocker*, [1939] 1 K.B. 194 (C.A.). See also *Kolan v. Solicitor* (1969), 7 D.L.R. (3d) 481, [1970] 1 O.R. 41 (H.C.J.), affd 11 D.L.R. (3d) 672, [1970] 2 O.R. 686 (C.A.).

[479] *Supra*, footnote 476, at p. 459.

[480] *Supra*, *per* Bridge L.J., at pp. 463-4.

[480a] See *Boudreau v. Benaiah* (1999), 182 D.L.R. (4th) 569 (Ont. C.A.) (negligence in criminal case).

[480b] *Hayes v. Dodd*, [1990] 2 All E.R. 815 (C.A.); *Watts v. Morrow*, [1991] 1 W.L.R. 1421 (C.A.); *Johnson v. Gore Wood & Co.*, [2002] 2 A.C. 1 (H.L.); *Baltic Shipping Co. v. Dillon* (1993), 176 C.L.R. 344 (Aust. H.C.); *Musumeci v. Winadell Ltd.* (1994), 34 N.S.W.L.R. 723 (Equity Div.); *Crump v. Wala*, [1994] 2 N.Z.L.R. 331 (H.C.); *Anderson v. Davies*, [1997] 1 N.Z.L.R 616 (H.C.), doubting *Rowlands v. Collow*, [1992] 1 N.Z.L.R. 178 (H.C.). In *Ruxley Electronics and Construction Ltd. v. Forsyth*, [1996] 1 A.C. 344 (H.L.), damages were awarded for loss of amenity for failure to construct a swimming pool to the specified depth, and in *Patel v. Hooper & Jackson*, [1999] 1 W.L.R. 1792 (C.A.), and *Farley v. Skinner*, [2001] 3 W.L.R. 899 (H.L.), against a negligent surveyor. In *Hamilton Jones v. David & Snape (a firm)*, [2004] 1 W.L.R. 924 (Ch.) damages were awarded against a solicitor for lost custody of children. See also *Warrington v. Great-West Life Assurance Co.* (1996), 139 D.L.R. (4th) 18, [1996] 10 W.W.R. 691 (B.C.C.A.); *McIsaac v. Sun Life Assurance Co. of Canada* (1999), 173 D.L.R. (4th) 649 (B.C.C.A.), leave to appeal to S.C.C. refused 179 D.L.R. (4th) vii (contract for disability insurance is for peace of mind).

[481] *Keks v. Esquire Pleasure Tours Ltd.*, [1974] 3 W.W.R. 406 (Man. Co. Ct.); *Fuller v. Healey Transportation Ltd.* (1978), 92 D.L.R. (3d) 277, 22 O.R. (2d) 118 (Co. Ct.); *Pitzel v. Saskatchewan Motor Club Travel Agency Ltd.* (1983), 149 D.L.R. (3d) 122, 26 Sask. R. 96 (Q.B.); *Fenton v. Sand and Sea Travel Ltd.* (1992), 4 Alta. L.R. (3d) 86, 134 A.R. 317 (Prov. Ct.).

[481a] *Loder v. Triton Airlines Inc.* (1994), 127 Nfld. & P.E.I.R. 129 (Nfld. Prov. Ct.).

home,[482] by the lessor of a vacation cottage,[482a] by the owner of a kennel for failing to ensure the plaintiff's dog was properly secured,[482b] by one who failed to provide entertainment at a wedding,[483] by a wedding photographer,[484] by an air carrier which caused the death of the plaintiff's pet dog,[485] by a surgeon who failed to improve the shape of the plaintiff's nose,[486] in a case of breach of warranty of title to goods,[487] for breach of warranty of quality,[487a] for the diversion of funds paid for the construction of a new home,[487b] and for failure by an insurer to make prompt payment.[488] In a Nova Scotia case, damages were awarded by a trial court against a solicitor for mental distress caused to a client by failure to incorporate a company.[489] The Appeal Division, in allowing the appeal on procedural grounds, made no criticism of the principle of such an award.[490] Damages have been awarded for breach by either party of land sale contracts[491] and for negligent advice in a criminal case.[492] On the other hand, in *Turczinski v. Dupont Heating & Air Conditioning Ltd.*,[492a] the Ontario Court of Appeal said that "generally before damages for mental distress can be awarded for breach of contract, the contract must be one where peace of mind is contracted for, such as a contract

---

[482] *Elder v. Koppe* (1974), 53 D.L.R. (3d) 705 (N.S.S.C.T.D.).

[482a] *Clancy v. Harvey* (2006), 203 Man. R. (2d) 204 (Q.B.).

[482b] *Ferguson v. Birchmount Boarding Kennels Ltd.* (2006), 79 O.R. (3d) 681 (S.C.J. (Div. Ct.)).

[483] *Dunn v. Disc Jockey Unlimited Co. Ltd.* (1978), 87 D.L.R. (3d) 408, 20 O.R. (2d) 309 (Sm. Cl. Ct.).

[484] *Wilson v. Sooter Studios Ltd.* (1988), 55 D.L.R. (4th) 303, [1989] 3 W.W.R. 166 (B.C.C.A.).

[485] *Newell v. Canadian Pacific Airlines, Ltd.* (1976), 74 D.L.R. (3d) 574, 14 O.R. (2d) 752 (Co. Ct.). See also *Weinberg v. Connors* (1994), 21 O.R. (3d) 62 (Gen. Div.); *Ferguson v. Birchmount Boarding Kennels Ltd.* (2006), 79 O.R. (3d) 681 (S.C.J. (Div. Ct.)).

[486] *LaFleur v. Cornelis* (1979), 28 N.B.R. (2d) 569 (Q.B.).

[487] *Zuker v. Paul* (1982), 135 D.L.R. (3d) 481, 37 O.R. (2d) 161 (Div. Ct.).

[487a] See *Wharton v. Tom Harris Chevrolet Oldsmobile Cadillac Ltd.*, [2002] 3 W.W.R. 629 (B.C.C.A.).

[487b] *Shillingford v. Dalbridge Group Inc.*, [1997] 3 W.W.R. 645, 197 A.R. 56 (Q.B.).

[488] *Thompson v. Zurich Insurance Co.* (1984), 7 D.L.R. (4th) 664, 45 O.R. (2d) 744 (H.C.J.); *Warrington v. Great-West Life Assurance Co., supra,* footnote 480b; *McIsaac v. Sun Life Assurance Co. of Canada, supra,* footnote 480b; *Evans v. Crown Life Insurance Co.* (1996), 25 B.C.L.R. (3d) 234, 37 C.C.L.I. (2d) 6 (S.C.); *Goodman v. Royal Insurance Co. of Canada*, [1996] 6 W.W.R. 744, 109 Man. R. (2d) 308 (Q.B.), revd on other grounds 118 Man. R. (2d) 20, 149 W.A.C. 20 (C.A.), leave to appeal to S.C.C. refused 225 N.R. 231*n*, 126 Man. R. (2d) 153*n*; *Eddie v. Unum Life Insurance Co. of America* (1999), 177 D.L.R. (4th) 738 (B.C.C.A.); *Lumsden v. Manitoba* (2007), 219 Man. R. (2d) 97 (Q.B.). Damages were denied in *Blouin v. Maritime Life Assurance Co.* (1988), 88 N.S.R. (2d) 23, 37 C.C.L.I. 128 (S.C.); *Beaird v. Westinghouse Canada Inc.* (1999), 171 D.L.R. (4th) 279 (Ont. C.A.).

[489] *Allen v. P. A. Wournell Contracting Ltd.* (1979), 100 D.L.R. (3d) 62 (N.S.S.C.T.D.).

[490] 108 D.L.R. (3d) 723 (N.S.S.C. App. Div.).

[491] *Taylor v. Gill*, [1991] 3 W.W.R. 727, 78 Alta. L.R. (2d) 349 (Q.B.); *Gourlay v. Osmond* (1991), 104 N.S.R. (2d) 155, 19 R.P.R. (2d) 59 (S.C.T.D.); *Kempling v. Hearthstone Manor Corp.* (1996), 137 D.L.R. (4th) 12, [1996] 8 W.W.R. 735 (Alta. C.A.); *Shillingford v. Dalbridge Group Inc., supra,* footnote 487b; *Vivian v. Pye* (1996), 146 Nfld. & P.E.I.R. 1, 7 R.P.R. (3d) 184 (Nfld. S.C.).

[492] *Boudreau v. Benaiah* (2000), 182 D.L.R. (4th) 569 (Ont. C.A.).

[492a] (2004), 246 D.L.R. (4th) 95 (Ont. C.A.), leave to appeal to S.C.C. refused 252 D.L.R. (4th) vi.

for a holiday . . . or for insurance"[492b] adding that "there are persuasive reasons to confine within narrow limits the circumstances when damages will be awarded for exacerbation of mental illness for breach of a consumer contract."[492c] Plainly the court was concerned in this case with the possibility of open-ended damage awards disproportionate to the contract price (in the *Turczinski* case damages of $35,000 had been awarded at trial for breach of a small home-renovation contract of which the price was $11,000). The difficulty with "peace of mind" as an excluding criterion is that almost all contracts can, in a sense, be said to offer peace of mind to one or both of the parties. In *Fidler v. Sun Life Assurance Co. of Canada*,[492d] the Supreme Court of Canada reviewed the question at some length. The court stated that damages for mental distress were in principle recoverable for breach of contract subject to the rule of remoteness in *Hadley v. Baxendale*.[492e] But the court added that "in normal commercial contracts" damages for mental distress would not ordinarily be within the reasonable contemplation of the parties: "[i]t is not unusual that a breach of contract will leave the wronged party feeling frustrated and angry. The law does not award damages for such incidental frustration."[492f] But, the court continued, "[t]he matter is otherwise . . . when the parties enter into a contract, an object of which is to secure a particular psychological benefit".[492g] In such a case damages for mental distress, if within the parties' reasonable contemplation, could be awarded. In the *Fidler* case an award of $20,000 was upheld for breach by an insurer of a disability insurance contract. In the later case of *Mustapha v. Culligan of Canada Ltd.*,[492h] the court held that damages for mental distress caused by seeing a dead fly in a bottle of water were not recoverable because it was not within the reasonable contemplation of the parties.

3.1390 Damages for mental distress have been awarded for breach of employment contracts.[493] In an Ontario High Court case, *Pilon v. Peugeot Canada Ltd.*,[494] a long-term employee was wrongfully dismissed. The employee had served the company loyally for many years, and the company had led him to expect permanent security of employment. Because the plaintiff had mitigated his loss quite successfully, he was held to be entitled only to damages of about $1,000 in respect of the period for which he ought to have been given notice. Nevertheless, the Ontario High Court awarded damages for mental distress of $7,500.

3.1400 The case is interesting and significant both in its application to employment contracts and in its departure from the comparatively modest level of

[492b] *Supra*, footnote 492a, at p. 104.
[492c] *Supra*, footnote 492a, at pp. 106-7.
[492d] [2006] 8 W.W.R. 1 (S.C.C.).
[492e] (1854), 9 Exch. 341, 156 E.R. 145.
[492f] *Supra*, footnote 492d, at para. 45. But see *Kelly v. Aliant Telecom/Island Tel* (2008), 273 Nfld. & P.E.I.R. 177 (P.E.I.S.C.) (damages awarded for interruption of telephone service).
[492g] *Supra*, footnote 492d, at para. 45.
[492h] (2008), 293 D.L.R. (4th) 29 (S.C.C.).

damage awards manifested by previous cases on mental distress. It has been suggested that punitive considerations are entering the calculation of damages in these cases.[495] Another possible explanation of the *Pilon* case is that the court intended to give compensation for the employee's expectation of permanent employment, even though unwilling to find an enforceable contract to that effect.[496] Later cases have, however, held that damages are recoverable only for the distress caused by the actual breach of contract, *i.e.*, the failure to give proper notice, and not for distress caused by the fact of the dismissal itself or by its manner and circumstances.[497] In *Vorvis v. Insurance Corp. of British Columbia*,[498] a refusal to award damages for mental distress was upheld by the Supreme Court of Canada on

[493] *Pilon v. Peugeot Canada Ltd.* (1980), 114 D.L.R. (3d) 378, 29 O.R. (2d) 711 (H.C.J.); *Ribeiro v. Canadian Imperial Bank of Commerce* (1993), 13 O.R. (3d) 278, 44 C.C.E.L. 165 (C.A.), leave to appeal to S.C.C. refused 157 N.R. 500*n*, 65 O.A.C. 79*n*. See *Delmotte v. John Labatt Ltd.* (1978), 92 D.L.R. (3d) 259, 22 O.R. (2d) 90 (H.C.J.); *Speck v. Greater Niagara General Hospital* (1983), 2 D.L.R. (4th) 84, 43 O.R. (2d) 611 (H.C.J.), affd 19 D.L.R. (4th) 576*n*, 51 O.R. (2d) 192*n* (C.A.) (damages for manner of dismissal); *Pilato v. Hamilton Place Convention Centre* (1984), 7 D.L.R. (4th) 342, 45 O.R. (2d) 652 (H.C.J.); *Johnson v. Famous Players Inc.* (1992), 77 Man. R. (2d) 25 (Q.B.); *Swain v. Northern Fortress Ltd.* (1993), 131 N.B.R. (2d) 342 (Q.B.). Damages were, however, refused in *Cringle v. Northern Union Ins. Co. Ltd.* (1981), 124 D.L.R. (3d) 22 (B.C.S.C.); *Vorvis v. Insurance Corp. of British Columbia* (1982), 134 D.L.R. (3d) 727, 17 B.C.L.R. 150 (S.C.), vard 9 D.L.R. (4th) 40, 53 B.C.L.R. 63 (C.A.), affd [1989] 1 S.C.R. 1085, 58 D.L.R. (4th) 193; *Dobson v. T. Eaton Co. Ltd.* (1982), 141 D.L.R. (3d) 362 (Alta. Q.B.) (no damages for insult); *Hiltz v. Saskatchewan Property Management Corp.* (1993), 112 Sask. R. 297, 93 C.L.L.C. 12,394 (Q.B.), affd 128 Sask. R. 316, 85 W.A.C. 316 (C.A.); *Russell v. Nova Scotia Power Inc.* (1996), 150 N.S.R. (2d) 271, 22 C.C.E.L. (2d) 208 (S.C.); *Deildal v. Tod Mountain Development Ltd.*, [1997] 6 W.W.R. 239, 33 B.C.L.R. (3d) 25 (C.A.), leave to appeal to S.C.C. refused 225 N.R. 398*n*, 166 W.A.C. 239*n*. See also *Levi v. Chartersoft Canada Inc.*, [1995] 2 W.W.R. 279, 99 Man. R. (2d) 241 (Q.B.); *Blackmore v. Cablenet Ltd.*, [1995] 3 W.W.R. 305, 26 Alta. L.R. (3d) 108 (Q.B.); *Trask v. Terra Nova Motors Ltd.* (1995), 127 Nfld. & P.E.I.R. 310, 9 C.C.E.L. (2d) 157 (Nfld. C.A.); *Gerber v. Telus Corp.*, [2004] 6 W.W.R. 201 (Alta. C.A.).

[494] *Supra*, footnote 493.

[495] Veitch, "Sentimental Damages in Contract", 16 U.W.O.L. Rev. 227 (1977). See also *Brown v. Waterloo Regional Board of Com'rs of Police* (1982), 150 D.L.R. (3d) 729 at p. 735, 43 O.R. (2d) 113 (C.A.); *Smith v. Fearon* (1984), 87 N.S.R. (2d) 119 (S.C.); *Blouin v. Maritime Life Assurance Co., supra*, footnote 488; *Pearl v. Pacific Evercon Inc.* (1985), 19 D.L.R. (4th) 392, 7 C.C.E.L. 252 (B.C.C.A.); *Lockhart v. Chrysler Canada Ltd.* (1984), 16 D.L.R. (4th) 392, 7 C.C.E.L. 43 (B.C.C.A.); *Rahemtulla v. Vanfed Credit Union*, [1984] 3 W.W.R. 296, 51 B.C.L.R. 200 (S.C.); *Zarnett v. Adler* (1988), 30 C.L.R. 133 (Ont. H.C.J.); *Russello v. Jannock Ltd.* (1987), 37 D.L.R. (4th) 372 (Ont. Div. Ct.).

[496] In *Pilon, supra*, footnote 493, Galligan J. said, at p. 382 D.L.R.: "Long-term employees in positions of responsibility, such as Mr. Pilon, were paid less than the going rate in the industry for comparable jobs and in return were told that they have lifetime security. Pilon accepted that assurance and relied upon it."

[497] *Brown v. Waterloo Board, supra*, footnote 495; *Bohemier v. Storwal International Inc.* (1982), 142 D.L.R. (3d) 8, 40 O.R. (2d) 264 (H.C.J.), vard 4 D.L.R. (4th) 383*n*, 44 O.R. (2d) 361*n* (C.A.), leave to appeal to S.C.C. refused 54 N.R. 319*n*, 3 C.C.E.L. 79*n*; *Fitzgibbons v. Westpres Publications Ltd.* (1983), 3 D.L.R. (4th) 366, 50 B.C.L.R. 219 (S.C.); *McHugh v. City Motors (Nfld.) Ltd.* (1989), 58 D.L.R. (4th) 753, 74 Nfld. & P.E.I.R. 263 (Nfld. C.A.); *Loder v. Newfoundland (Minister of Municipal and Provincial Affairs)* (1995), 132 Nfld. & P.E.I.R. 286, 13 C.C.E.L. (2d) 81 (Nfld. S.C.); *Killorn v. Healthvision Corp.* (1997), 143 D.L.R. (4th) 477, 156 N.S.R. (2d) 1, supplementary reasons 158 N.S.R. (2d) 357 (C.A.).

the ground that what the majority of the court called "aggravated damages"[498a] were not available where the conduct complained of preceded the dismissal. There was evidence of harsh and distressing treatment by the employer before dismissal, and the British Columbia Court of Appeal had indicated that if this were the wrong complained of, damages might be awarded for breach of an implied term in the contract, a possibility not excluded by the reasons of the Supreme Court of Canada and accepted by the New Zealand Court of Appeal[498b] but rejected by the High Court of Australia.[498c] In *Keays v. Honda Canada Inc.*,[498d] the Supreme Court of Canada held that damages for mental distress were available, if not too remote, on the same principles as other damages. The court departed from an earlier decision, *Wallace v. United Grain Growers Ltd.*,[498e] in which it had held that such damages should be reflected in a lengthened period of notice. Decisions applying the *Wallace* case, however, remain relevant as indicative of the circumstances in which damages for mental distress may be appropriate.[498f] Another possibility is an award of damages for intentional infliction of mental distress, and such an award was made by the Ontario Court of Appeal in 2002 in a wrongful dismissal case.[498g]

3.1410 This area of the law has developed rapidly since 1972. Several writers have put forward interesting suggestions as to the underlying principles. The suggestion referred to earlier, that punitive considerations are appearing, cannot be lightly dismissed. Professor Veitch has written:

> These awards for mental distress arising from breach of contract look very much like the punitive and exemplary awards which are regular features of intentional tort actions in Canada . . . In contract situations we have seen the unscrupulous vacation operator, the too busy law firm, the callous employer, the greedy investment broker, the impersonal conglomerate and the vindictive trade union held liable in damages for the intangible injuries

---

498 [1989] 1 S.C.R. 1085, 58 D.L.R. (4th) 193. See also *Wurster v. Universal Environmental Services Inc.* (1998), 167 D.L.R. (4th) 166 (Ont. C.A.); *McKinley v. BC Tel*, [2001] 2 S.C.R. 161, 200 D.L.R. (4th) 385.

498a But this usage was disapproved in *Fidler v. Sun Life Assurance Co. of Canada*, [2006] 2 S.C.R. 3, 271 D.L.R. (4th) 1, at para. 53. The court also indicated that it is not necessary for the plaintiff to establish "an independent actionable wrong" (at para. 42).

498b *Stuart v. Armourguard Security Ltd.*, [1996] 1 N.Z.L.R. 484 (C.A.). See *Deildal v. Tod Mountain Development Ltd.*, *supra*, footnote 493.

498c *Byrne v. Australian Airlines Ltd.* (1995), 185 C.L.R. 410 (Aust. H.C.). See *Johnson v. Unisys Ltd.*, [2001] 2 W.L.R. 1076 (H.L.) (no common law duty in light of English statutory scheme).

498d (2008), 294 D.L.R. (4th) 577 (S.C.C.).

498e [1997] 3 S.C.R. 701, 152 D.L.R. (4th) 1, explained in *Fidler v. Sun Life Assurance Co. of Canada*, *supra*, footnote 498a, as an instance of compensation for mental distress within the parties reasonable contemplation. See also *Cassady v. Wyeth-Ayerst Canada Inc.* (1998), 163 D.L.R. (4th) 1 (B.C.C.A.).

498f *Keays v. Honda Canada Inc.*, *supra*, footnote 498d, at para. 59. See *Benko v. Scott* (2007), 295 Sask. R. 202 (Q.B.); *Therrien v. True North Properties Ltd.*, [2007] 8 W.W.R. 739 (Alta. Q.B.); *Schwindt v. Sulkers (Jann and Neil) Ltd.* (2007), 295 Sask. R. 226 (Q.B.).

498g *Prinzo v. Baycrest Centre for Geriatric Care* (2002), 215 D.L.R. (4th) 31 (Ont. C.A.).

caused by their proven lack of concern for the interests and expectations of the ordinary individual.[499]

Professor Veitch welcomes the award of exemplary damages in such cases, deriving support for his thesis from the statutory provisions in several jurisdictions expressly allowing exemplary damages for unfair business practices.[500] Another point is that some of the cases have involved injury to reputation which, as the defamation cases show, is notoriously hard to dissociate from punitive considerations.[501]

3.1420 There are, however, some difficulties in seeking to explain and justify these awards as punitive. First, there is no general rule that breach of contract ought always to be deterred. It is not generally improper for a promisor deliberately to break a contract in order to make a greater profit elsewhere, for the prevailing view is that if full compensation is tendered to the plaintiff, the contract breaker does the plaintiff no wrong. This general position is defended elsewhere in this book.[502] Consequently, the present writer would not accept that a mere breach of contract justifies exemplary damages. The case of a breach of a statutory code of fair business practice can be distinguished as a case that involves more than a mere breach of contract, and therefore is of public concern. The other side of the coin is that if the awards of damages were to be rested on punitive considerations, no award could be made where the defendant had acted innocently or even negligently (in the absence of some element of recklessness).[503] But the distress and disappointment suffered by Mr. Jarvis would have been the same whether or not the conduct of Swans Tours or any of its particular employees was considered worthy of punishment. In *Fidler v. Sun Life Assurance Co. of Canada*,[503a] the Supreme Court of Canada rejected an award of punitive damages precisely because the defendant insurer had acted in good faith, but upheld an award of damages for mental distress.

3.1430 Discussion of the cases from an economic point of view has taken two quite different approaches. In an article in the Law Quarterly Review in 1979, it was suggested that *Jarvis v. Swans Tours* and the cases that followed it were in effect giving compensation for the "consumer surplus", that is, the particular value to the plaintiff of goods or services in excess of their market value.[504] The decisions were welcomed as recognizing and compensating a real loss.

3.1440 On the other hand, another economic analysis took quite a different line.

[499] *Supra*, footnote 495, at p. 238.

[500] *Consumer Protection Act, 2002* (Ont.), s. 18(11).

[501] See 4.180, *infra*.

[502] See 9.200-9.250, 11.250, 11.260, *infra*.

[503] See 11.210, 11.220, *infra*. See also *McIsaac v. Sun Life Assurance Co. of Canada* (1999), 173 D.L.R. (4th) 649 (B.C.C.A.), leave to appeal to S.C.C. refused 179 D.L.R. (4th) vii (motive immaterial).

[503a] [2006] 2 S.C.R. 3, 271 D.L.R. (4th) 1.

[504] Harris, Ogus and Phillips, "Contract Remedies and the Consumer Surplus", 95 L.Q.R. 581 (1979).

Professor Rea's conclusion in a paper published in 1982[505] was that an attempt to give full compensation for non-pecuniary losses might be economically inefficient. The reason seems to be that a rational person would not choose fully to insure against mental distress caused by breach of contract because the cost of the insurance would be too high. Since the risk of paying damages must be passed on to customers as a cost of doing business, the effect of the *Jarvis* case is to compel all travellers to purchase unwanted insurance along with agents' services. It might be more efficient for travellers to be able to buy the services and to insure themselves if they wish to do so, separately, against mental distress.

3.1450 There appears to be some force in this argument, and indeed it can plausibly be argued that similar considerations lie behind the exclusion in *Hadley v. Baxendale*[506] itself of damages for extraordinary losses. However, this seems more an argument for restraint in measuring compensation than an argument for the exclusion of damages for mental distress as such. There is an argument to be made in favour of a known range of damage awards for the sake of predictability both at the stage of contracting and to facilitate settlements after disputes have arisen, and for the sake of ensuring like treatment of like cases.[506a] There is an analogy with compensation for non-pecuniary losses in personal injury cases where similar reasons for a predictable range apply. Moreover there is reason for assuring some compatibility between the different kinds of case: a rational system of law could not support an award for mental distress caused by a spoiled vacation that exceeded the award to a quadriplegic for a lifetime of suffering.[506b] In *Young v. Bella*,[506c] the Supreme Court of Canada left open the question of extending the rough upper limit in personal injury cases to an award for non-pecuniary loss caused by negligently reporting unfounded suspicions of child abuse.

(3) Mental distress caused by injury to third person

3.1460 No damages were allowed by the common law or under the *Fatal Accidents Act* for grief caused to survivors by the wrongful death of a person.[507] Scots law, in contrast, permits the court to award a sum of money as a solatium,[508] and limited provisions to the same effect have been introduced by statute in common law jurisdictions.[509] In case of injury to a

[505] Rea, "Non-pecuniary Loss and Breach of Contract", 11 J. Leg. Stud. 35 (1982).

[506] (1854), 9 Ex. 341, 156 E.R. 145. See 14.20-14.410, *infra*.

[506a] See *Vento v. Chief Constable of West Yorkshire Police*, [2002] EWCA Civ. 1871.

[506b] *Nagy v. Canada* (2005), 41 Alta. L.R. (4th) 61 (Q.B.) at para. 132, affd 272 D.L.R. (4th) 601.

[506c] [2006] 1 S.C.R. 108, 261 D.L.R. (4th) 516 at para. 66. See also *Westlake v. Granby Steel Tanks* (2006), 156 A.C.W.S. (3d) 607 (Ont. C.A.).

[507] See *Clerk & Lindsell on Torts*, 14th ed. (London, Sweet & Maxwell, 1975), §426. See also 6.310, *infra*.

[508] See Walker, *The Law of Civil Remedies in Scotland* (Edinburgh, W. Green & Son Ltd., 1974), pp. 941-6; Veitch, "Solatium – A Debt Repaid?", 7 Ir. Jur. (N.S.) 77 (1972).

third party, not causing death, damages for simple grief are not allowed, although some cases have, within cautiously set limits, allowed damages for nervous shock. A discussion of these cases is to be found in the books on tort law.[510]

3.1470 Under the Ontario *Family Law Act*, an action lies, in the case of death or injury to a close relative, for pecuniary loss including "an amount to compensate for the loss of guidance, care and companionship".[511] In *Ordon Estate v. Grail*,[511a] the Supreme Court of Canada held that such an action lies even where the legislature is silent. The provisions of this section are discussed elsewhere in the context of claims for wrongful death.[512] In the present context, the statute and its judicially developed equivalents should be noted as a means of giving some element of compensation for intangible losses caused by injury to third parties, as, for example, where a close relative is rendered unconscious, but not killed. The restriction imposed by the limitation of compensation to "pecuniary" loss is also discussed in the context of wrongful death.[513]

3.1480 In Alberta, the *Domestic Relations Act* provides that a person is entitled to damages if "deprived of the society and comfort" of a spouse.[514] It was held in *Woelk v. Halvorson*[515] that this applied to a case of injury to the plaintiff's husband causing a change in the husband's personality which in turn caused distress to the plaintiff. The Supreme Court of Canada held that "deprivation" included "impairment", and further that a substantial award was proper, restoring the $10,000 award that had been reversed by the Alberta Court of Appeal.[516] It should be noted that the husband also recovered a substantial sum ($30,000) in his own right largely for the loss caused to him by the personality change.[517]

9. Collateral Benefits

(1) Introduction

3.1490 Commonly, a plaintiff receives benefits, in money and services, designed to make good in whole or in part the loss for which the defendant is responsible. The courts have had considerable difficulty with the problem of when, if ever, these benefits should be taken into account in assessing the damages payable by the defendant. If credit is given to the defendant it seems

[509] See 6.320-6.390, *infra*.
[510] See Linden, *Canadian Tort Law*, 6th ed. (Toronto, Butterworths, 1997), pp. 385-403.
[511] Section 61(2)(e).
[511a] [1998] 3 S.C.R. 437, 166 D.L.R. (4th) 193.
[512] See 6.320-6.390, *infra*.
[513] See 6.310-6.390, *infra*.
[514] Section 46(1).
[515] [1980] 2 S.C.R. 430, 114 D.L.R. (3d) 385.
[516] (1978), 92 D.L.R. (3d) 150 (Alta. S.C.T.D.), vard 106 D.L.R. (3d) 726 (C.A.), revd [1980] 2 S.C.R. 430, 114 D.L.R. (3d) 385.
[517] The award was described by the Supreme Court of Canada as "generous" but not "wholly erroneous". See *Woelk, supra*, footnote 515, at p. 390.

that the wrongdoer reaps an undeserved benefit. If no credit is given, it appears that the plaintiff is compensated twice over.

3.1500 The question is sometimes posed in terms of the philosophy of tort law. If the purpose of tort law is purely compensatory, it is said, over-compensation of plaintiffs is always inexcusable.[518] Full compensation is, by definition, adequate. If it is said that damage awards never do compensate fully, the remedy is to increase the measure of damages, not to double the "inadequate" compensation in a few cases. On the other hand, tort law is often said to perform a deterrent function by assigning to the wrongdoer, or at least to the activity in which the wrongdoer is engaged, the full cost of the wrongful act. On that basis, collateral benefits received by the victim should never be counted in relief of the tortfeasor. So long as someone is bearing a cost because of the defendant's wrong, the defendant should pay it.[519]

3.1510 This philosophical dichotomy does not provide an entirely adequate framework for discussion of the problem. First, the problem is not confined to tort law but arises equally in calculating damages for breach of contract. Secondly, an acceptance of a deterrent function in tort law does not necessarily justify compelling the defendant to pay more than the actual loss. The more basic question is the amount of the plaintiff's loss. Thirdly, even if the purpose of the law of damages is seen as entirely compensatory, the problem is not solved, because it is arguable that the plaintiff suffers a loss when the wrong is done. The receipt of a collateral benefit does not remove the loss; it simply causes the financial consequences to be shared by a third party. It is argued in a later chapter that such a sharing of financial consequences ought not to reduce a wrongdoer's liability.[520] This conclusion is assisted in the personal injury field by categorizing the plaintiff's claim as one for "loss of earning capacity"[521] or as "a need for nursing services"[522] rather than as a claim for loss of earnings or for the cost of services.

3.1520 The notion that the wrongdoer should bear the full cost of wrongdoing is very much weakened as a practical explanation of the existing system by the widespread use of liability insurance.[523] The cost of negligent driving, for example, is generally spread among all drivers; the cost of injuries caused by defective products is spread among millions of product users. The Pearson Commission, in recommending that damages should be reduced by the full value of social security benefits received by the plaintiff, seems to have accepted that the defendant's costs were, in effect, society's costs. The reason for the Commission's recommendation was that the elimination of overlap would bring about a "substantial saving in costs".[524]

[518] See *Royal Commission on Civil Liability and Compensation for Personal Injury* (London, H.M.S.O., 1978), §§277-9.

[519] See Posner, *Economic Analysis of Law*, 5th ed. (New York, Aspen Law & Business Publishers, 1998), p. 219.

[520] See 15.870, 15.880, *infra.*

[521] See 3.710-3.980, *supra.*

[522] See 3.450-3.470, *supra.*

[523] See *Lincoln v. Hayman*, [1982] 1 W.L.R. 488 (C.A.), at p. 492.

3.1530 Nevertheless, the deterrence argument may perhaps be defended in a weakened form. The allocation to a manufacturer of products of the full cost of damage caused by defects will tend, in the long run, to encourage cost-justified safety measures. If a substantial part of the medical expenses, for example, of persons injured by defective products, were borne by the community at large, the community would, in effect, be subsidizing the production of dangerous products. Manufacturers would be discouraged from producing a much safer product at a somewhat higher price; if the more dangerous product bore its full costs, consumers might be encouraged to buy safer products of a competing manufacturer or perhaps to do without the dangerous type of product altogether. Again, there is an argument for compelling automobile drivers to bear the full costs of accidents. The consequent level of insurance premiums may well induce some persons to alter their behaviour, as, for example, by refraining from buying a car or a second car, or refraining from making it available to teenage children, or refraining from using the car to drive to work.

3.1540 As Fleming pointed out many years ago,[525] the dichotomy between compensation and deterrence tends to distract attention from the possible solution to the problem that would be consistent with both objectives. This is to compel the defendant to pay the full cost of wrongdoing and to reimburse the collateral source. In this way the wrongdoer pays the full cost of the wrong, and double compensation to the plaintiff is avoided. There is a variety of techniques for securing this result. The best known is subrogation: the provider of the benefit is subrogated to the plaintiff's right to recover from the defendant in respect of the same loss.[526] It is also possible for the court to order that a portion of the award is to be held on trust for a third party or to require an undertaking from the plaintiff to make over a portion of the award to a third party.[527] These latter techniques, while avoiding double compensation, would not necessarily give the provider of the benefits an independent right of action against the wrongdoer. Yet another approach would be to allow the provider an independent right of action for the pecuniary loss caused by the wrong.[528]

(2) Gifts

3.1550 All cases agree that private, charitable, or benevolent gifts are not to be

[524] *Supra*, footnote 518, §541.

[525] Fleming, "The Collateral Source, Role and Loss Allocation in Tort Law", 54 Cal. L.R. 1478 (1966).

[526] This is the usual solution in cases of private indemnity insurance. See *Glynn v. Scottish Union & National Ins. Co. Ltd.* (1963), 40 D.L.R. (2d) 929, [1963] 2 O.R. 705 (C.A.); *Fortin v. Li* (1992), 96 D.L.R. (4th) 574, [1993] 1 W.W.R. 709 (B.C. S.C.).

[527] See 3.460, *supra*.

[528] See 3.510, 3.1120-3.1140, *supra*. On recovery of economic loss in tort, see *Canadian National Railway Co. v. Norsk Pacific Steamship Co.*, [1992] 1 S.C.R. 1021, 91 D.L.R. (4th) 289; *Winnipeg Condominium Corp. No. 36 v. Bird Construction Co.*, [1995] 1 S.C.R. 85, 121 D.L.R. (4th) 193.

brought into account.[529] In *Redpath v. Belfast and County Down Railway*,[530] Sir James Andrews L.C.J. said, quoting a submission of counsel in the case:

> . . . that it would be startling to the subscribers to that fund if they were to be told that their contributions were really made in ease and for the benefit of the negligent Railway Company. To this last submission I would only add that if the proposition contended for by the defendants is sound the inevitable consequence in the face of future disasters of a similar character would be that the springs of private charity would be found to be largely, if not entirely, dried up.[531]

Lord Reid, in *Parry v. Cleaver*:[532]

> It would be revolting to the ordinary man's sense of justice, and therefore contrary to public policy, that the sufferer should have his damages reduced so that he would gain nothing from the benevolence of his friends or relations or of the public at large, and that the only gainer would be the wrongdoer. We do not have to decide in this case whether these considerations also apply to public benevolence in the shape of various uncovenanted benefits from the welfare state, but it may be thought that Parliament did not intend them to be for the benefit of the wrongdoer.[533]

The force of Lord Reid's comments is overwhelming. It is not, however, to disagree with him to point out that to deny the wrongdoer the benefit of the donor's contributions is not to settle the question as between the donor and donee of whether the benefit should be restored or paid for by the plaintiff. Ultimately, this question must depend on the terms of the gifts, but if no express provision had been made for the possibility of the donee's recovering damages from a wrongdoer, the court will have to imply reasonable terms. It is suggested that it is not unreasonable to suppose that in most cases where money or services are rendered to relieve a need caused by a legal wrong, the donor's reasonable expectation would be to be repaid — or at least to be offered repayment — out of any compensation that should subsequently become available from a wrongdoer. The donor can, of course, always choose subsequently to forego this right of repayment.

3.1560 In a number of English and Canadian cases, recovery has been allowed of the value of nursing services rendered gratuitously to the plaintiff by third parties.[534] In *Cunningham v. Harrison*,[535] Lord Denning said that the money

[529] A possible exception is where payment is made by the wrongdoer. See 3.460, *supra*, and 6.510, 15.910, *infra*.

[530] [1947] N.I. 167. See also *Dawson v. Sawatzky*, [1946] 1 D.L.R. 476 (Sask. C.A.), at p. 479, *per* Gordon J.A.; *Bowers v. Hollinger*, [1946] 4 D.L.R. 186, [1946] O.R. 526 (H.C.J.); *Herbert v. Misuga* (1994), 111 D.L.R. (4th) 193, [1994] 3 W.W.R. 457 (Sask. C.A.); *Clement v. Backo & Suncorp. Metway Insurance Ltd.*, [2007] QCA 81, 2 Qd. R. Pt. 1 (Queensland S.C.).

[531] (1947) N.I. 167, at p. 170.

[532] [1970] A.C. 1 (H.L.).

[533] *Supra*, at p. 14.

[534] See 3.450-3.470, *supra*.

[535] [1973] Q.B. 942 (C.A.).

so recovered was to be held on trust for the provider, and this was expressly followed in *Thornton v. Prince George School Board.*[536] It is submitted that Lord Denning's view is soundly based, though if the plaintiff objects, an opportunity should be provided for the determination of the entitlement to the money between the injured person and the provider of the services. In *Rawson v. Kasman,*[537] the plaintiff recovered medical expenses that had been paid by her son, with a direction to pay over the amount to the son.

3.1570 The Ontario *Family Law Act* provides that an action for pecuniary loss caused by injury may be brought independently by a person within the classes of relationship established for fatal accident claims. The existence of an independent action raises several complications. The Act does not refer to the injured person's own right of action, and presumably is not to be construed to diminish it. But it seems unlikely that the Legislature intended the defendant to pay twice over. It has been submitted elsewhere that the easiest solution is to construe the legislation to allow an action only for losses not recoverable by the injured person.[538] The classes of relatives listed in the statute are not, of course, exhaustive of persons who may render gratuitous services, and in the case of services rendered by a person not related to the injured person, recovery can only be by the route of an action by the injured person. The question of "pecuniary loss" will also raise difficulties when, for example, a wife provides nursing services to an injured husband but does not give up an alternative source of income. "Pecuniary loss" is plainly relevant to claims by relatives in the case of death, but less clearly relevant to claims by persons rendering gratuitous services to the injured. Presumably in case of doubt as to the provider's independent action under the *Family Law Act*, the injured person will include a claim for the value of services received. If the proceeds are then held on trust for the provider, this will go to extinguish or reduce the latter's independent claim under the *Family Law Act*. This would seem to produce a satisfactory relationship between the two causes of action, and is, it is suggested, an added reason for imposing a trust in favour of the provider of gratuitous services on the portion of damages attributable to those services. Those advising defendants in settling claims ought either to secure a release from the providers of the services or to secure that a proportion of the settlement is to be held on trust for the providers in order to reduce or extinguish their independent claims.

3.1580 It is not clear how the Act applies to claims for future expenses or the value of future services. It seems inconvenient, and probably unjust to the injured person, to award to a third party the cost of future nursing and housekeeping services, for no absolute assurance can be possible that the services will in fact be rendered. It seems preferable therefore to construe the

---

[536] [1978] 2 S.C.R. 267, 83 D.L.R. (3d) 480.
[537] (1956), 3 D.L.R. (2d) 376 (Ont. C.A.).
[538] See 3.480, *supra*.

Act to leave in the injured person alone the right to recover the cost of future care.

(3) Insurance benefits

3.1590 A similar unanimity to that found in connection with gifts pervades the cases dealing with private insurance benefits.[539] An explanation commonly given for this result is that the defendant ought not to have the benefit of the plaintiff's providence and expenditure of premiums. But this is not fully convincing because there is no doubt that the defendant can and should derive a benefit from a precaution that actually prevents a loss from arising. Causation theories are also unconvincing,[540] for it is clear that, in fact, the wrong does cause the receipt of the benefit.[541] The better explanation, it is submitted, is that insurance does not prevent the loss; it is simply an arrangement for the sharing of its financial consequences.[542] In *Bradburn v. Great Western Railway*,[543] insurance benefits were excluded from the calculations. In *Guy v. Trizec Equities Ltd.*,[544] the Supreme Court of Canada held that a pension payable on the plaintiff's early retirement was to be similarly treated. Accepting that the plaintiff must have the benefit of what has been paid for, the exact measure of what the plaintiff has paid for will depend on the insurance agreement. It may be that the plaintiff has paid only for an indemnity, in which case the insurer will be subrogated to the claim against any wrongdoer.[545] On the other hand, on the construction of the insurance policy, the plaintiff may have paid for a sum of money payable over and above any recovery from other sources. In the case of social welfare benefits, it must depend on the terms of the legislation whether or not there is a right of subrogation. As Dubin J.A. said in *Boarelli v. Flannigan*:[546]

539 *Bradburn v. Great Western Ry. Co.* (1874), 10 Ex. 1; *Stead v. Elliott* (1963), 39 D.L.R. (2d) 170 (N.S.S.C.T.D.); *Douglas v. Isenor*, [1952] 2 D.L.R. 286 (N.S.S.C. in banco) (employer's contributory plan); *Sheasgreen v. Morgan*, [1952] 1 D.L.R. 48 (B.C.S.C.); *Ratych v. Bloomer*, [1990] 1 S.C.R. 940 at pp. 971-3, 69 D.L.R. (4th) 25 at pp. 46-7. See *Cunningham v. Wheeler; Cooper v. Miller; Shanks v. McNee*, [1994] 1 S.C.R. 359, 113 D.L.R. (4th) 1; *Fortus v. Allegretti*, [1994] 10 W.W.R. 194, 22 Alta L.R. (3d) 221 (Q.B.). But see *Taylor v. Turner*, [1925] 3 D.L.R. 574 (Alta. S.C.) (agreement with physician to render what services the plaintiff should need for an agreed prepayment). Statutory provisions in some jurisdictions provide for deduction of insurance benefits from compensation for injuries suffered in automobile accidents: see, *e.g.*, *Insurance Act* (Ont.), s. 267.

540 See Cooper-Stephenson, *Personal Injury Damages in Canada*, 2nd ed. (Toronto, Carswell, 1996), p. 579.

541 See Ganz, "Mitigation of Damages by Benefits Received", 25 Mod. L. Rev. 559 (1962), at pp. 561-2.

542 See 15.870, 15.880, *infra*.

543 (1874), 10 Ex. 1, followed in *Wagar v. Newton* (1977), 3 A.R. 29 (S.C. App. Div.). See also *State of New South Wales v. Davies* (1998), 43 N.S.W.L.R. 182 (C.A.), at p. 187.

544 [1979] 2 S.C.R. 756, 99 D.L.R. (3d) 243; *Smoker v. London Fire and Civil Defence Authority*, [1991] 2 A.C. 502 (H.L.).

545 See *Glynn v. Scottish Union & National Insurance Co.* (1963), 40 D.L.R. (2d) 929, [1963] 2 O.R. 705 (C.A.); *Orion Ins. Co. Ltd. v. Hicks* (1972), 32 D.L.R. (3d) 256 (Man. Q.B.).

546 (1973), 36 D.L.R. (3d) 4, [1973] 3 O.R. 69 (C.A.).

> I cannot conclude that there is any equitable principle which should permit a tortfeasor to obtain the advantage of benefits earned by the person who has been injured. It is for the contracting parties to determine whether such benefits are to be subrogated and it is of no concern of the party otherwise liable in damages.[547]

3.1600 In fatal accident claims it is provided in every jurisdiction that insurance payments are to be left out of account,[548] and in *Canadian Pacific Ltd. v. Gill*,[549] the Supreme Court of Canada held that pension benefits fell within the scope of the exclusion.

(4) Employment benefits

3.1610 More difficulty has arisen in respect of benefits received from the plaintiff's employer. In *Browning v. War Office*,[550] the English Court of Appeal held that veterans' benefits received from the plaintiff's employer were to be taken into account to reduce damages payable by the defendant. However, in 1969, this case was overruled by the House of Lords in *Parry v. Cleaver*,[551] where it was held that a pension payable by the plaintiff's employer was not to be taken into account. The House of Lords pointed out that disability pension benefits, like other forms of disability insurance, are in fact paid for by the employee; even if no cash contribution is required, the employee does, in a real sense, pay for the benefits by forgoing a reward for labours in another form. The House of Lords accepted that gifts were not to be taken into account. If gifts are excluded,[552] and all benefits are excluded that the employee has in any sense paid for, there would seem to be no kind of residual category. Yet the House of Lords took the view that a continuation of the employee's wages, in the form of sick pay, for example, would prevent any claim for loss of wages accruing, and this view was adopted by the Supreme Court of Canada in *Ratych v. Bloomer*.[553] This approach led to difficult distinctions, and was modified[554] by the Supreme Court of Canada in *Cunningham v. Wheeler*.[555]

[547] *Supra*, at p. 14 D.L.R. Similarly *Bourgeois v. Tzrop* (1957), 9 D.L.R. (2d) 214 (N.B.S.C. App. Div.) (unemployment insurance); *Dambrowsky v. Olson* (1953), 8 W.W.R. (N.S.) 716 (Alta. S.C. App. Div.) (municipal hospital scheme).

[548] See 6.450-6.500, *infra*.

[549] [1973] S.C.R. 654, 37 D.L.R. (3d) 229. See *Dall Estate v. Adams* (1994), 116 D.L.R. (4th) 189, 19 O.R. (3d) 93 (C.A.); *Briffett v. Gander and District Hospital Board* (1996), 29 C.C.L.T. (2d) 251 (Nfld. C.A.); *Cugliari v. White* (1998), 159 D.L.R. (4th) 254 (C.A.), leave to appeal to S.C.C. refused 165 D.L.R. (4th) vii.

[550] [1963] 1 Q.B. 750 (C.A.).

[551] [1970] A.C. 1 (H.L.). See also *Longden v. British Coal Corporation*, [1998] A.C. 653 (H.L.).

[552] The case of gratuitous payments was expressly left open in *Ratych v. Bloomer*, [1990] 1 S.C.R. 940, 69 D.L.R. (4th) 25 at p. 47, but in *Bloom v. Klein* (1992), 63 B.C.L.R. (2d) 130 (S.C.), gratuitous payments were taken into account.

[553] *Supra*. Loss of the value of accumulated sick leave, however, is recoverable (see *Lavigne v. Doucet* (1976), 14 N.B.R. (2d) 700 (S.C. App. Div.), approved in *Ratych v. Bloomer*, 69 D.L.R. (4th) 25 at p. 46).

[554] See discussion in 3.1635, *infra*.

3.1620 In *Ratych v. Bloomer*, the Supreme Court of Canada accepted that benefits payable under a private insurance policy were not deductible, and said that "where the employee can demonstrate a loss or a contribution equivalent to payment of an insurance premium,"[556] recovery of full damages "might be entirely appropriate". It would seem, therefore, that if evidence is adduced that the employee has contributed the equivalent of an insurance premium in exchange for the benefit, full compensation will be available.[557] Such evidence will often — perhaps usually — be forthcoming, because the cost of employment benefits is often expressly calculated in collective bargaining, and the employee, in a real sense, pays for the benefits, whether funded by the employer itself or, as is common, through an insurer. Moreover, the court said that if there were a legal or moral obligation on the employee to repay the employer out of the damages, the employee would be entitled to full recovery, subject to a trust in favour of the employer. Evidence will not infrequently be forthcoming that an employee recognizes a moral obligation of this sort.[558]

3.1630 The House of Lords in *Parry v. Cleaver* was plainly concerned with the argument that it would be absurd to allow a claim for loss of retirement pension by a plaintiff whose retirement pension continued in full. Similarly, it was argued that an employee whose salary continued could not claim for loss of salary. Lord Reid seems to have accepted the analogy, conceding that in both cases recovery ought to be reduced, but distinguishing the problem in *Parry v. Cleaver* itself (a disability pension) on the basis that like was not being compared with like (*i.e.*, pension and salary).[559] However, a sounder distinction would appear to be that in the case of the retirement pension, the recipient does not lose any pension-earning capacity (ability to work not being a requirement of earning retirement pensions), whereas the employee who is disabled does suffer a loss of earning capacity during the period of his disability. The employee suffers the loss even though it may subsequently be made good in her hands by some sort of benevolence (which may include an employer's benevolence) or through some sort of insurance (which may include an employer's contractual obligation to pay wages during disability). Moreover, if the suggestion made below is accepted, that, in the absence of a

[555] *Cunningham v. Wheeler; Cooper v. Miller; Shanks v. McNee*, [1994] 1 S.C.R. 359, 113 D.L.R. (4th) 1.

[556] *Ratych v. Bloomer, supra*, footnote 552, at p. 47 D.L.R.

[557] *Smoker v. London Fire and Civil Defence Authority*, [1991] 2 A.C. 502 (H.L.); *Cunningham v. Wheeler, supra*, footnote 552; *McNamara v. Alexander Centre Industries Ltd.* (2001), 199 D.L.R. (4th) 717 (Ont. C.A.) (wrongful dismissal).

[558] See *Harris v. Manchester* (1974), 50 D.L.R. (3d) 90 (Man. Q.B.); *Willox v. Wagner* (1992), 106 Sask. R. 243 (Q.B.); *Kask v. Tam*, [1996] 7 W.W.R. 494, 21 B.C.L.R. (3d) 11, supplementary reasons [1996] 7 W.W.R. 503, 21 B.C.L.R. (3d) 21 (C.A.); *Frers v. De Moulin* (2002), 1 B.C.L.R. (4th) 131 (S.C.), at 179. See also *Fortin v. Li* (1992), 96 D.L.R. (4th) 574, [1993] 1 W.W.R. 709 (B.C.S.C.) (no right of subrogation). But in *Courtney v. Neville* (1995), 141 N.S.R. (2d) 241 (S.C.), *ex gratia* payments from the plaintiff's employer were deducted.

[559] *Supra*, footnote 551, at pp. 20-21.

contrary intention, the employer ought to receive the ultimate benefit of the portion of the damages attributable to wages, it can be said that the employer is the party really interested in the defendant's being made to pay, and the employer certainly suffers a loss by reason of the defendant's wrong. The tenor of this argument is to suggest that *Ratych v. Bloomer* is likely to give rise to more difficulties than it resolves.

3.1635 In *Cunningham v. Wheeler*,[559a] the Supreme Court of Canada modified the effect of *Ratych v. Bloomer*[559b] by holding that employment benefits were not deductible if paid for by the employee directly or indirectly, and that evidence that the benefits formed part of the collective bargaining process was sufficient to establish indirect payment by the employee. As such evidence will usually be forthcoming,[559c] it may be said that *Ratych v. Bloomer*, though not technically overruled, is very substantially limited in effect.

3.1640 As mentioned previously, it is open to the court, in allowing full recovery, to require an undertaking from the plaintiff to repay the employer or to hold the relevant part of the damages on trust for the employer.[560] The Supreme Court of Canada, in *Ratych v. Bloomer*, accepted that this was a proper disposition when "the judge is satisfied that this is both necessary and appropriate in the interests of justice",[561] as, for example, where the employee has a legal or moral obligation to repay the employer. It is suggested that this solution will often be appropriate, and that it generally does conform to the interests of justice: it ensures that the wrongdoer bears the full cost of the wrong and the plaintiff is not overcompensated. The benevolent employer who still wishes to benefit an employee can always decline to enforce the trust, or to enforce the employee's undertaking.

(5) Welfare benefits

3.1650 Welfare benefits, formerly treated by Canadian courts as non-deductible, were held by the Supreme Court of Canada in *B (M) v. British Columbia*[562] to be deductible. The court rejected the analogy with gifts, and rejected also any policy ground for not deducting the benefits from the award. It remains

[559a] *Supra, footnote 555.*

[559b] *Supra, footnote 552.*

[559c] But see *Kozak v. Funk*, [1996] 1 W.W.R. 79, 135 Sask. R. 81 (Q.B.), affd on this point [1998] 5 W.W.R. 232, 158 Sask. R. 283 (C.A.).

[560] See *Dennis v. London Passenger Transport Board*, [1948] 1 All E.R. 779 (K.B.); *Rawson v. Kasman* (1956), 3 D.L.R. (2d) 376 (Ont. C.A.); *Sullivan v. Riverside Rentals Ltd.* (1973), 47 D.L.R. (3d) 293 (N.S.S.C. App. Div.); *Myers v. Hoffman* (1955), 1 D.L.R. (2d) 272 (Ont. H.C.J.), and 3.460, 3.1560, *supra*. In *Terry v. Lotocky* (1961), 28 D.L.R. (2d) 640, 35 W.W.R. 335 (B.C.S.C.), and *MacKinnon v. Coldwell* (1973), 36 D.L.R. (3d) 709, 8 N.S.R. 651 (S.C.T.D.), the employee undertook to repay. A direction to pay over was, however, refused in *Smith v. Toms* (1963), 44 W.W.R. 592 (B.C.S.C.) and *Gilliss v. Breau* (1971), 19 D.L.R. (3d) 615, 3 N.B.R. (2d) 397 (S.C. App. Div.).

[561] *Ratych v. Bloomer, supra*, footnote 552, at p. 54 D.L.R.

[562] [2003] 2 S.C.R. 477, 230 D.L.R. (4th) 567, followed in *L. (H.) v. Canada (Attorney General)*, [2005] 1 S.C.R. 401 at para 148, 251 D.L.R. (4th) 604.

open to the legislatures to provide, if thought desirable, by subrogation, assignment, trust, undertaking, or equivalent device, for repayment to the government where a wrongdoer is liable. In that way neither would the wrongdoer gain by the claimant's receipt of welfare benefits, nor would the claimant be over-compensated. The same effect may be achieved, it would seem, by an administrative requirement that the welfare recipient acknowledge an obligation to repay.[563] The English Court of Appeal commented in *Crofton v. National Health Service Litigation Authority*,[564] that there was "no good policy reason why damages which are about to be awarded specifically for the provision of care to the claimant, needed only as a result of the tort, should be reduced, thereby shifting the burden from the tortfeasor to the public purse".

(6) Benefits in kind

3.1670 Where benefits take the form of the free or subsidized provision of services, difficult problems arise. The argument in favour of recovery is that the plaintiff suffers an immediate loss measured by the reasonable cost of future care, and whether the care is purchased or provided by the state or some private benefactor is irrelevant.

3.1690 On the other hand it can be argued that in assessing the cost of any article or service account must be taken of the actual price prevailing in the community, for things do not have an inherent value. If nursing services in Manitoba are cheap, it can be argued that the cost to an injured person of incurring a need for such services is low. It seems to follow that if they are free, the cost is nothing. On balance this seems a persuasive argument, and it was accepted by the British Columbia Court of Appeal in *Wipfli v. Britten*[568] and by the Manitoba Court of Appeal in *Tronrud v. French*.[569] Where, however, there is evidence that the plaintiff might cease to be eligible for free services, or might move to another jurisdiction where benefits were less generous, these possibilities should be taken into account.[569a]

3.1700 An important consideration is that publicly funded welfare payments are very vulnerable to government cost-cutting measures, the possible extent of

[563] See *Jones v. Trudel* (2000), 185 D.L.R. (4th) 193 (B.C.C.A.).

[564] [2007] 1 W.L.R. 923 (C.A.), at para. 89.

[565] [Text of para. 3.1660 and footnotes 565 to 567f deleted.]

[568] (1984), 13 D.L.R. (4th) 169, [1984] 5 W.W.R. 385 (B.C.C.A.).

[569] (1991), 84 D.L.R. (4th) 275, 75 Man. R. (2d) 1 (C.A.), leave to appeal to S.C.C. refused 87 D.L.R. (4th) vii, 138 N.R. 407*n*.

[569a] See *McLeod v. Palardy* (1981), 124 D.L.R. (3d) 506, 10 Man. R. (2d) 181 (C.A.); *Krangle (Guardian ad Litem of) v. Brisco*, [2002] 1 S.C.R. 205, 208 D.L.R. (4th) 193; *Jones (Guardian ad Litem of) v. Rostvig* (2003), 17 C.C.L.T. (3d) 253 (B.C.S.C.); *Zhang v. Kan* (2003), 15 C.C.L.T. (3d) 1 (B.C.S.C.); *Lurtz v. Duchesne* (2005), 136 A.C.W.S. (3d) 1055 (Ont. C.A.), at para. 25; *Gerelus v. Lim* (2006), 206 Man. R. (2d) 241 (Q.B.), affd 57 C.C.L.T. (3d) 157 (Man. C.A.); *Fullerton (Guardian ad Litem of) v. Delair*, [2006] 9 W.W.R. 205 (B.C.C.A.) (public benefits found to be contingent on plaintiff not recovering tort award). See also *Crofton v. National Health Service Litigation Authority*, [2007] 1 W.L.R. 923 (C.A.).

which can rarely be foreseen at the time of the trial. This was a point taken into account by the Ontario Court of Appeal in *Stein v. Sandwich West (Township)*.[570]

(7) Employment insurance

3.1720 The cases, both in contract and tort, were formerly divided on the question of employment insurance benefits. Some cases have made a deduction,[572] but it is now established by the Supreme Court of Canada that no deduction is to be made.[573] The *Employment Insurance Act* provides that if a claimant, having received benefits, subsequently receives earnings for the same period from a person liable to pay them, the benefits are to be repaid.[574] Damages for wrongful dismissal are included,[575] but there is no express reference to damages for personal injury.

(8) Workers' compensation

3.1730 Provincial workers' compensation legislation generally provides a right of subrogation in favour of the compensation board.[576]

(9) Health insurance

3.1740 The provincial health insurance Acts have very widely varying provisions on subrogation.[577] Rendall has written that "most of the statutes reinforce the common law rule that [a tortfeasor] could not defend by pointing to [a victim's] insurer".[578] A number of cases have held that, in the absence of

570 (1995), 25 M.P.L.R. (2d) 170, 77 O.A.C. 40 (C.A.). See also *Jacobsen v. Nike Canada Ltd.* (1996), 133 D.L.R. (4th) 377 at p. 415, [1996] 6 W.W.R. 488 (B.C.S.C.).

571 [Footnote deleted.]

572 *Nabi v. British Leyland (U.K.) Ltd.*, [1980] 1 W.L.R. 529 (C.A.); *David v. Eastend Union Hospital Board* (1979), 99 D.L.R. (3d) 73 (Sask. Q.B.); *Baker v. United Grain Growers Ltd.*, [1978] 5 W.W.R. 370 (Alta. S.C.T.D.).

573 *Jorgenson v. Jack Cewe Ltd.*, [1980] 1 S.C.R. 812, 111 D.L.R. (3d) 577. See 15.860, *infra.* See also *Mitchell v. Day* (1981), 44 N.S.R. (2d) 541 (S.C.T.D.); *Drisdelle v. Barton* (1984), 56 N.B.R. (2d) 401 (C.A.). The principle has been held to survive *Ratych v. Bloomer*: *Regehr v. Nagle* (1993), 8 Alta. L.R. (3d) 116, 138 A.R. 229 (Q.B.). But see *Boertien v. Carter* (1995), 135 Nfld. & P.E.I.R. 91 (P.E.I.S.C.).

574 Section 45.

575 See 15.860, *infra.*

576 See, *e.g.*, *Workers Compensation Act* (B.C.), s. 10(6); Man., s. 9(5); *Workers' Compensation Act* (Alta.), s. 22(1); N.B., s. 10(10); N.S., s. 30; P.E.I., s. 11(3); Sask., s. 40; N.W.T., s. 64; Nfld. & Lab., *Workplace Health, Safety and Compensation Act*, s. 45(8); Ont., *Workplace Safety and Insurance Act*, s. 30(10), (11). But see *White v. F.W. Woolworth Co.* (1993), 109 Nfld. & P.E.I.R. 187 (Nfld. S.C.), affd 139 Nfld. & P.E.I.R. 324, 22 C.C.E.L. (2d) 110 (C.A.), leave to appeal to S.C.C. refused 222 N.R. 80*n*, 161 Nfld. & P.E.I.R. 90*n*.

577 See Rendall, "Subrogation in Medical and Hospital Insurance Schemes: Judicial Philosophy Versus Legislative Pragmatism", 6 Ottawa L. Rev. 291 (1974).

578 *Ibid.*, at p. 309. See *Grant v. Stewart* (1964), 48 D.L.R. (2d) 650 (N.S.S.C.); *Doucette v. McInnis* (1964), 43 D.L.R. (2d) 90 (P.E.I.S.C.).

statutory provisions, the plaintiff's recovery should be reduced.[580] In *White v. Ashfield*,[581] Stevenson J. held that there was no right of action against a wrongdoer for future medical expenses covered by provincial health insurance, since the New Brunswick Act made a provision for subrogation to claims for future expenses. The case was affirmed by the Court of Appeal, and later expressly approved by the same court.[582] One of the reasons given by Stevenson J. however, that "the Court will not attribute a specified portion of a general damage award to the element of future hospital and medical costs"[583] is now obsolete after the requirement, introduced by the Supreme Court of Canada in 1978, of itemized awards.[584] In principle, it is submitted that insurance, public or private, ought not to reduce a wrongdoer's liability.[585] Over-compensation can be avoided by a statutory right of subrogation. It is submitted that this approach is consistent with recent decisions of the Supreme Court of Canada on insurance benefits,[586] has the merit of attributing to the defendant the full cost of his tortious activity, and ought to be followed unless the statute expressly provides otherwise.[586a] In a number of cases, however, damages have been reduced.[587]

3.1750 The Ontario *Health Insurance Act* provides a right of subrogation for past and future medical expenses, and requires an injured person to include in the claim a claim on behalf of the Health Insurance Plan.[588] In some cases defendants have requested that the portion of the damages attributable to future medical costs be held on trust with the balance repayable to the defendant if the plaintiff's medical needs fall short of what is expected. The order has, however, been refused in the absence of consent of the Health Insurance Plan.[589] Indeed, it would seem more consistent with principle for the plaintiff rather than the defendant to be entitled to any excess, though the

579 [Footnote deleted.]

580 *Schaeffer v. Mish*, [1950] 4 D.L.R. 648 (Sask. C.A.); *Flaherty v. Hughes*, [1952] 4 D.L.R. 43 (B.C.C.A.); *Vermett v. Winning* (1960), 26 D.L.R. (2d) 765 (Man. Q.B.); *Hebson v. Sutherland* (1952), 7 W.W.R. (N.S.) 382 (B.C.S.C.); *Schiffner v. Canadian Pacific Ry. Co.*, [1951] 4 D.L.R. 172 (Sask. C.A.); *Moore v. Day* (1958), 16 D.L.R. (2d) 371 (Nfld. S.C.T.D.); *Curtis v. Mayne* (1960), 24 D.L.R. (2d) 506 (Nfld. S.C.T.D.). See *Fortus v. Allegretti*, [1994] 10 W.W.R. 194, 22 Alta. L.R. (3d) 221 (Q.B.). In *Gaskell v. Moshagen* (1958), 13 D.L.R. (2d) 60 (B.C.S.C.), and *Thomas v. Gram* (1958), 12 D.L.R. (2d) 621 (Ont. H.C.J.), legal liability to pay, even though it might not have been enforced by the Department of Veterans' Affairs, was held sufficient to support recovery.

581 (1974), 8 N.B.R. (2d) 546 (S.C.Q.B. Div.), affd *loc. cit.* p. 541 (S.C. App. Div.).

582 *Godin v. Bourque* (1980), 32 N.B.R. (2d) 45 (C.A.).

583 (1974), 8 N.B.R. (2d) 546 at p. 553.

584 See 3.300-3.330, *supra*.

585 See 3.1590, 3.1600, *supra;* 15.870, 15.880, *infra*.

586 See *Canadian Pacific Ltd. v. Gill*, [1973] S.C.R. 654, 37 D.L.R. (3d) 229; *Guy v. Trizec Equities Ltd.*, [1979] 2 S.C.R. 756, 99 D.L.R. (3d) 243; *Jorgenson v. Jack Cewe Ltd.*, [1980] 1 S.C.R. 812, 111 D.L.R. (3d) 577. But see 3.1610-3.1640, *supra*.

586a *Stein v. Sandwich (Township)* (1995), 25 M.P.L.R. (2d) 170, 77 O.A.C. 40 (C.A.).

587 See 3.1690, *supra*.

588 *Health Insurance Act*, s. 30.

589 *Holmes v. Board of Hospital Trustees of City of London* (1977), 81 D.L.R. (3d) 67, 17 O.R. (2d) 626 (H.C.J.). See *Bishop v. Arts & Letters Club of Toronto* (1978), 83 D.L.R. (3d) 107 at pp. 115-16, 18 O.R. (2d) 471 (H.C.J.).

point does not seem to have been argued in the cases just mentioned. In principle, the damages are the plaintiff's, and the Health Insurance Plan can only be entitled in so far as it can claim reimbursement for services rendered. Against this it can be argued that since the Health Insurance Plan will bear the risk of undercompensation where the plaintiff's needs exceed what is anticipated, so it should be entitled to retain the benefits of over-compensation. This latter argument appears sensible from an insurance standpoint, and there would seem to be a case for implementing it by legislation. It is not easy to see how, in the absence of such legislation, a court could avoid the argument that any excess in the award belongs to the plaintiff or the plaintiff's estate.

3.1760 Another problem concerns the case where the defendant has insufficient assets to satisfy both the subrogated claim of the health plan and the plaintiff's claim for other damages. It was at first held that the claims ranked *pari passu* but the effect was to require the plaintiff to pay out of the damage award for the cost of insured health services.[590] Because of this consideration, the Supreme Court of Canada established in *Ledingham v. Ontario Hospital Services Commission*[591] that the plaintiff's claim was to be given priority over the health plan's subrogated claim.

(10) Automobile insurance benefits

3.1770 Several provinces provide compulsory first party insurance benefits to persons injured in automobile accidents. The legislation generally provides that benefits paid or payable go to reduce the recipient's damages against a tortfeasor.[592] This disposition is contrary to the trend of common law developments described earlier and contrary to most social security legislation in Canada. However, the result may be justified by the observation that the same insurers carry both the first party accident insurance and the third party liability insurance.[593] Thus, subrogation by the accident insurer to the claim against the tortfeasor would in most cases simply shift the loss from one automobile insurer to another. Reduction of liability, rather than subrogation, may be regarded as having been accepted by the legislature as an economical method of resolving disputes within the insurance industry. In either case the defendant's activity (automobile driving) still bears the full cost of accidents.[593a]

3.1780 A further complication arose in *Cattapan v. Mitchell*,[594] where the

[590] *Re Ledingham v. Di Natale* (1972), 31 D.L.R. (3d) 18, [1973] 1 O.R. 291 (C.A.), revd [1975] 1 S.C.R. 332, 46 D.L.R. (3d) 699.

[591] [1975] 1 S.C.R. 332, 46 D.L.R. (3d) 699, followed in *Baldelli v. Wellington Fire Ins. Co.* (1976), 66 D.L.R. (3d) 577, 11 O.R. (2d) 513 (H.C.J.). To the same effect in *MacDonald v. Parrish* (1971), 24 D.L.R. (3d) 467 (N.S.S.C.T.D.).

[592] See, *e.g., Insurance Act* (Ont.), s. 267(1)(a). Future benefits must be discounted to present value: *Malat v. Bjornson*, [1981] 2 W.W.R. 59 (B.C.S.C.).

[593] But the statutory release may apply to an uninsured defendant. See *Milne v. Dargie* (1975), 63 D.L.R. (3d) 619, 10 O.R. (2d) 507 (Co. Ct.); *Van Beurden v. Brackett* (1977), 79 D.L.R. (3d) 127, 16 O.R. (2d) 707 (H.C.J.).

plaintiff had settled with the no-fault insurer releasing it from obligations in respect of future benefits. The Ontario High Court of Justice held that such a release could not be allowed to prejudice the position of the defendant and accordingly ordered that a portion of the damage award was to be paid into court so as to generate sufficient income to pay to the defendant the value of the no-fault benefits to which the plaintiff should turn out to be entitled. Again, this is a situation in which the plaintiff has commuted the claim to future benefits to a lump sum, and the effect of the court's disposition is that the plaintiff bears the risk of having underestimated the value of his future benefits. It does not appear whether, if the sum paid into court should prove insufficient, the defendant would have a further claim against the plaintiff. The rather odd result is that after such a judgment, it will be in the plaintiff's interest to prove that the plaintiff has ceased to be entitled to benefits, because in that event the defendant's claim on the fund in court will cease, and it will be paid out to the plaintiff.

3.1790 A simpler alternative might be to presume that the amount of the compromise represented the true value of the plaintiff's entitlement to future benefits and to deduct a larger sum only on proof by the defendant that the settlement was unreasonably low. Since, if the plaintiff makes a favourable compromise, he will suffer full deduction (since the amount of settlement will be a "payment made") the plaintiff should, in the absence of proof of unreasonableness, recover the full capitalized loss from the two sources combined (usually two automobile insurers).

3.1800 The interpretation and application of insurance Act provisions give rise to a number of other difficulties. First, can a claimant who fails to make an appropriate claim be said to be "entitled" to benefits? In *Madill v. Chu*,[595] the Supreme Court of Canada held that a person was "entitled" to receive the benefits of a workers' compensation plan, if that person could successfully have claimed the benefits whether or not the person actually did so. Where a claim is made and rejected by the insurer, it was held by the Ontario Court of Appeal in *Brown v. Bouwkamp*,[596] that the claimant was not "entitled to" benefits, even though it appeared subsequently that the plaintiff might successfully have disputed the insurer's disallowance of the claim. The Ontario Court of Appeal relied on its own decision in *Madill v. Chu*[597] which was subsequently reversed by the Supreme Court of Canada. The status of *Brown v. Bouwkamp* is therefore in some doubt, and it might be argued that just as a person who fails to claim is "entitled", so is one whose claim is wrongly rejected. However, it is possible to distinguish the cases, in that a

593a *Fulton v. Eastcoast Oilfield Services Ltd.* (1991), 108 N.S.R. (2d) 18, 33 M.V.R. (2d) 42 (C.A.), citing this paragraph.

594 (1978), 105 D.L.R. (3d) 508, 27 O.R. (2d) 87 (H.C.J.).

595 [1977] 2 S.C.R. 400, 71 D.L.R. (3d) 295.

596 (1975), 58 D.L.R. (3d) 59, 8 O.R. (2d) 363 (H.C.J.), affd 67 D.L.R. (3d) 620, 12 O.R. (2d) 33 (C.A.).

597 (1974), 51 D.L.R. (3d) 481, 5 O.R. (2d) 729 (C.A.), revd [1977] 2 S.C.R. 400, 71 D.L.R. (3d) 295.

person whose claim is actually rejected is not, as a practical matter, "entitled" to the benefits or, alternatively, that the benefits are not "available" to the claimant. It would seem intolerably harsh to demand that the claimant litigate the dispute with a no-fault insurer, perhaps to the highest court possible, on pain of risking the loss of compensation from the defendant. In *Stante v. Boudreau*,[598] *Madill v. Chu* was distinguished on this basis.

3.1810 In *Cox v. Carter*[599] the question arose of future no-fault benefits to be paid after the date of judgment. One obvious method of dealing with this problem would be to estimate the amount of a plaintiff's future entitlement, and deduct it from the damage award. However, this would involve a risk of error in estimating the plaintiff's future entitlement, and for this reason the court rejected it, ordering instead that the defendant pay damages in full but that future no-fault benefits were to be held on trust by the plaintiff for the defendant and paid over as received. The effect is to enable the plaintiff to convert a periodic payment into a lump sum.

598 (1980), 112 D.L.R. (3d) 172, 29 O.R. (2d) 1 (C.A.).

599 (1976), 13 O.R. (2d) 717 (H.C.J.). See also *Whittle v. Ontario (Minister of Transportation and Communications* (1995), 24 O.R. (3d) 394, 16 M.V.R. (3d) 226, supplementary reasons 31 O.R. (3d) 16 (Gen. Div.), vard 31 O.R. (3d) 573*n* (C.A.). *Cox v. Carter* was approved by the Ontario Court of Appeal in *Chrappa v. Ohm* (1998), 159 D.L.R. (4th) 215, 38 O.R. (3d) 651 (C.A.); *Bannon v. McNeely* (1998), 159 D.L.R. (4th) 223, 38 O.R. (3d) 659 (C.A.); *Cugliari v. White* (1998), 159 D.L.R. (4th) 254, 38 O.R. (3d) 641 (C.A.), leave to appeal to S.C.C. refused 165 D.L.R. (4th) vii, 236 N.R. 388*n*. See also *Wilson v. Campbell (Litigation Administrator of)* (2003), 267 N.B.R. 334 (Q.B.).

CHAPTER 4

LOSS OF REPUTATION

1. Defamation

(1) Special damage in slander

4.10 Liability for slander is limited by a rule at common law[1] that, with certain exceptions, spoken words are actionable only on proof of special damage. The scope of the exceptions (four in number) in which a slander is said to be actionable *per se*[2] falls outside a discussion of the law of damages.

4.20 Special damage means actual financial or material loss.[3] It is not sufficient for the plaintiff to establish that reputation has been damaged, for that would open the door to general damages for slander. It has been held that loss of friends is not enough,[4] though loss of hospitality of friends is sufficient if the particular loss is specifically proved.[5] Loss of business profits is sufficient.[6] Loss or postponement of a marriage has been held to be special damage.[7] Loss of social relationships is not,[8] but in *Chamberlain v. Boyd*,[9] Bowen L.J. suggested that loss of a club membership "may be a matter of temporal advantage, and the deprivation of it may be an injury or damage of which the law will take cognisance".[10]

4.30 A limit is placed on liability for slander not only by the requirement of the type of damage that must be proved but by strict application of the rule of remoteness. A slander is not actionable unless the plaintiff shows special damage and that the damage is the natural and probable consequence of the slander complained of.[11] The most important aspect of this rule is that damage caused by unauthorized repetition of the words has often been held to

---

1 Reversed by statute in several jurisdictions: see Brown, *The Law of Defamation in Canada*, 2nd ed. (Toronto, Carswell, 1994), para. 8.4.

2 See *Gatley on Libel and Slander*, 10th ed. (London, Sweet & Maxwell, 2004), c. 4; Brown, *ibid.*, at para. 8.5.

3 See Gatley, *ibid.*, c. 5.

4 *Ashford v. Choate* (1870), 20 U.C.C.P. 471; *Palmer v. Solmes* (1880), 30 U.C.C.P. 481, 45 U.C.Q.B. 15.

5 *Palmer v. Solmes, supra.*

6 *Shore v. Britski*, [1942] 3 D.L.R. 285 (Sask. C.A.); *Ratcliffe v. Evans*, [1892] 2 Q.B. 524 (C.A.) (loss may be inferred from circumstances: see 13.80, *infra*). See *Allman v. Kensel* (1862), 3 P.R. (Ont.) 110 (insufficient proof of loss); *Glo-Klen Distributors Ltd. v. B.C. Chemicals Ltd.* (1959), 19 D.L.R. (2d) 635 (B.C.C.A.) (insufficient proof of loss).

7 *Bordeaux v. Jobs* (1913), 14 D.L.R. 451 (Alta. S.C.).

8 See *Palmer v. Solmes, supra*, footnote 4.

9 (1883), 11 Q.B.D. 407 (C.A.).

10 *Supra*, at p. 415.

be too remote,[12] even though nothing is more foreseeable than that slander will be repeated. This rule, though affirmed by the House of Lords in *Weld-Blundell v. Stephens*,[13] is criticized by Fleming who argues for liability wherever the defendant had reason to anticipate repetition of the slander.[14] The question is one of policy for, as Fleming also points out in another context,[15] the interest of the plaintiff must be balanced against the general interest in free speech. Damage caused by other wrongful acts of third parties, such as breach of contract, is not too remote if it occurs as a natural and probable consequence of the slander.[16]

4.40 When special damage has been shown, the question arises of whether the plaintiff is limited to recovery of special damage or whether the door is open to a claim for general damages. There is little authority on the question which again raises the broad policy issue of the general interest in free speech.[16a] Fleming favours liability for general damages: "There is no justification for pushing the policy of discouraging actions for slander beyond the point where the potentiality for mischief of the particular slander has been demonstrated by proof of actual damage."[17] There is considerable force in this argument. The argument is that, when once the slander has been shown to be actionable, it should be treated like a libel. On the other hand, this position would introduce the anomaly, always present when parasitic damages are concerned, of the plaintiff's recovery of a large sum of general damages depending on proof of an unrelated trivial item of special damages. It would seem that if the requirement of proof of special damage for slander is sound, the less anomalous view is that recoverable damages should be similarly restricted.

(2) General damages

(a) Amount

4.50 General damages in a defamation case are at large[17a] and the amount of them has been said, in *Davis v. Shepstone*[18] and elsewhere,[19] to be

[11] *Lynch v. Knight* (1861), 9 H.L.C. 577, 11 E.R. 854; *Chamberlain v. Boyd, supra*, footnote 9; *Ludlow v. Batson* (1903), 5 O.L.R. 309 (Div. Ct.); *Stewart v. Sterling* (1918), 42 D.L.R. 728, 42 O.L.R. 477 (S.C. App. Div.); *Merkoff v. Pawluk*, [1931] 1 W.W.R. 669 (Alta. S.C.).

[12] *Weld-Blundell v. Stephens*, [1920] A.C. 956 (H.L.); *Merkoff v. Pawluk, supra*, footnote 11; *Stewart v. Sterling, supra*, footnote 11.

[13] *Supra*, footnote 12.

[14] Fleming, *The Law of Torts*, 9th ed. (Sydney, Law Book Co., 1998), at p. 609.

[15] *Ibid.*, at p. 580.

[16] See *Lynch v. Knight, supra*, footnote 11, at pp. 600-1; *Bowen v. Hall* (1881), 6 Q.B.D. 333 (C.A.), at p. 338, *per* Brett, L.J.

[16a] *Chakravarti v. Advertiser Newspapers Ltd.* (1998), 154 A.L.R. 294 (H.C.), at p. 324, citing this passage.

[17] Fleming, *op. cit.*, footnote 14, at p. 608.

[17a] See *John v. Kim* (2007), 52 C.C.L.T. (3d) 123 (B.C.S.C.), at para. 94.

[18] (1886), 11 App. Cas. 187 (P.C.).

[19] *Cassell & Co. Ltd. v. Broome*, [1972] A.C. 1027 (H.L.), at p. 1065, *per* Lord Hailsham; *Hill v. Church of Scientology of Toronto*, [1995] 2 S.C.R. 1130, 126 D.L.R. (4th) 129.

"peculiarly the province of the jury". An appellate court will only interfere with a jury award if convinced that it is wholly erroneous.[20] In practice, awards are rarely set aside as too low, as there is usually some ground that would justify a low award, and the court can seldom say with certainty that greater loss has been caused.[21] In *Kelly v. Sherlock*,[22] a verdict of one farthing damages was upheld even though the libels were, in the words of Blackburn J.:

> . . . of a gross and offensive character, and if the question had been one of punishing the defendant, no one could have doubted that the verdict ought to have been heavy. But the question was not what fine ought to be imposed on the defendant, but what compensation ought the plaintiff to have for his injured feelings for it is to be observed that there was no actual pecuniary damage; and that no one, who in these unhappy controversies was not already prejudiced against the plaintiff, would think worse of him in consequence of the vulgar abuse of the defendant.[23]

In *Dennison v. Sanderson*[24] an award of one cent was upheld for similar reasons.

4.60 More frequently excessive awards have been set aside, as in *Ross v. Lamport*[25] where an award of $40,000 to a taxi driver who had been defamed by the mayor of Toronto was set aside. In *McCarey v. Associated Newspapers (No. 2)*,[26] an award of £9,000 to a physician who had suffered no pecuniary or social disadvantage was set aside. Pearson L.J. described the sum as "excessive and extravagant and exorbitant".[27] In *Allan v. Bushnell T.V. Co. Ltd.*,[28] an award of $58,000 ($6,000 exemplary damages) was set aside as extravagant. In *Walker v. CFTO Ltd.*,[29] an award of $883,000 was set aside as extravagant and based on an irrational criterion.

4.70 A comparison is often made with awards for intangible losses in personal injury cases. Fleming has written that "reputation [seems] to be considered of much greater value than life or limb, dishonour an infinitely greater injury than agonizing and protracted physical suffering".[30] In *McCarey v. Associated Newspapers*,[31] Diplock L.J. said:

> I am convinced that it is not just (and I do not think that it is the law, as Mr. Eastham has contended it is) that in equating incommensurables when

[20] See 13.420-13.480, *infra*.

[21] But see *Safeway Stores Ltd. v. Harris*, [1948] 4 D.L.R. 187 (Man. C.A.) (damages increased from $3,000 to $20,000); *Holt v. Sun Publishing Co.* (1979), 100 D.L.R. (3d) 447 (B.C.C.A.) ($2,000 increased to $5,000). See also *Pamplin v. Express Newspapers Ltd.*, [1988] 1 W.L.R. 116 (C.A.).

[22] (1866), L.R. 1 Q.B. 686.

[23] *Supra*, at p. 698.

[24] [1946] 4 D.L.R. 314, [1946] O.R. 601 (C.A.).

[25] [1956] S.C.R. 366, 2 D.L.R. (2d) 225.

[26] [1965] 2 Q.B. 86 (C.A.).

[27] *Supra*, at p. 106.

[28] (1969), 4 D.L.R. (3d) 212, [1969] 2 O.R. 6 (C.A.).

[29] (1987), 37 D.L.R. (4th) 224, 59 O.R. (2d) 104 (C.A.).

[30] Fleming, *The Law of Torts*, 9th ed. (Sydney, Law Book Co., 1998), p. 657.

[31] *Supra*, footnote 26.

> a man's reputation has been injured the scale of values to be applied bears no relation whatever to the scale of values to be applied when equating those other incommensurables, money and physical injuries. I do not believe that the law today is more jealous of a man's reputation than of his life or limb. That is the scale of values of the duel. Of course, the injuries in the two kinds of case are very different, but each has as its main consequences pain or grief, annoyance or unhappiness, to the plaintiff.[32]

Diplock L.J. went on to refer to a recent unreported case in which Court of Appeal had refused to disturb a jury award of £2,000 to a thirty-year-old woman for the loss of a leg. He thought the award of £9,000 in the McCarey case plainly excessive by comparison.[33]

4.80 The comments must, however, be read in the light of *Cassell & Co. Ltd. v. Broome*[34] where the House of Lords declined to interfere with an award of £40,000 (of which £25,000 was exemplary damages) in respect of an allegation of wartime incompetence and misconduct. Other high awards by English and Canadian courts have been upheld.[35]

4.90 The reason for such high awards is primarily that the notion of compensation for loss of reputation includes so many intangible considerations that it is very difficult for an appellate court to fix with confidence on a money sum. Secondly, in Canada, as often still in England, it is proper for the tribunal to include in its award a punitive element that again cannot be easily measured by an appellate court.[36]

4.100 Even a strictly compensatory approach allows the inclusion of many intangible factors. In *McCarey v. Associated Newspapers (No. 2)*,[37] Pearson L.J. said, having referred to the clear distinction required by English law since *Rookes v. Barnard* between exemplary and compensatory damages:

> Compensatory damages, in a case in which they are at large, may include several different kinds of compensation to the injured plaintiff. They may include not only actual pecuniary loss and anticipated pecuniary loss or any

32 *McCarey v. Associated Newspapers, supra*, at p. 109. But see *Sutcliffe v. Pressdram Ltd.*, [1990] 2 W.L.R. 271 (C.A.), at pp. 286-7.

33 *McCarey v. Associated Newspapers, supra*. See also *Carson v. John Fairfax & Sons Ltd.* (1993), 178 C.L.R. 44 (Aust. H.C.); *John v. MGN Ltd.*, [1997] Q.B. 586 (C.A.) (English Court of Appeal reduced damages to well-known singer from £350,000 to £75,000); *Kiam v. MGN Ltd.*, [2002] 2 All E.R. 219 (C.A.) (£105,000 upheld).

34 [1972] A.C. 1027 (H.L.).

35 *Bremner v. Odhams Newspapers*, The Times, February 4, 1982; *Hill v. Church of Scientology of Toronto*, [1995] 2 S.C.R. 1130, 126 D.L.R. (4th) 129; *Botiuk v. Toronto Free Press Publications Ltd.*, [1995] 3 S.C.R. 3, 126 D.L.R. (4th) 609; *Leenen v. Canadian Broadcasting Corp.* (2001), 54 O.R. (3d) 612 (C.A.), leave to appeal to S.C.C. refused 289 N.R. 200*n*. See Mears, "The Libel Law: Life After Sutcliffe and Aldington", [1990] N.L.J. 176.

36 See *Mack v. North Hill News Ltd.* (1964), 44 D.L.R. (2d) 147 (Alta. S.C.); *Hubert v. DeCamillis* (1963), 41 D.L.R. (2d) 495 (B.C.S.C.); *McCain Foods Ltd. v. Agricultural Publishing Co. Ltd.* (1978), 22 N.B.R. (2d) 30 (Q.B.); *Morgenstern v. Oakville Record Star* (1962), 33 D.L.R. (2d) 354, [1962] O.R. 638 (H.C.J.); *St. Michael's Extended Care Centre Society v. Frost*, [1994] 6 W.W.R. 718, 18 Alta. L.R. (3d) 65 (Q.B.).

37 [1965] 2 Q.B. 86 (C.A.).

> social disadvantages which result, or may be thought likely to result, from the wrong which has been done. They may also include the natural injury to his feelings — the natural grief and distress which he may have felt at having been spoken of in defamatory terms, and if there has been any kind of high-handed, oppressive, insulting or contumelious behaviour by the defendant which increases the mental pain and suffering caused by the defamation and may constitute injury to the plaintiff's pride and self-confidence, those are proper elements to be taken into account in a case where the damages are at large. But there is a sharp distinction between damages of that kind and truly punitive or exemplary damages... The object of the award of damages in tort nowadays is not to punish the wrongdoer but to compensate the person to whom the wrong has been done.[38]

The comments on the exclusion of exemplary damages must, in Canada, be read in the light of the general Canadian rejection of the limits laid down in *Rookes v. Barnard*.[39] But the description of what elements may be included in a purely compensatory award is of importance, and was, in fact, followed by the Nova Scotia Appeal Division in *Barltrop v. Canadian Broadcasting Corp.*[40]

4.110 The awards in Canadian defamation cases were, until 1995, modest amounts. *Ross v. Lamport*[41] is an example. There an award of $40,000 was set aside, but after a second trial, an award of $25,000 was upheld.[42] In *Platt v. Time International of Canada*,[43] an award of $35,000 was made by McRuer J. and upheld by the Ontario Court of Appeal in respect of an allegation of opium smuggling. In *Barltrop v. Canadian Broadcasting Corp.*,[44] an award of $20,000 was made by the Appeal Division of the Nova Scotia Supreme Court in respect of an allegation that a physician had not given an honest opinion on a matter of public interest. These cases are significant guides because in both the latter cases the awards were made by judges not by juries. Further in *Barltrop*, MacKeigan C.J.N.S. specifically said that the case was not one for exemplary damages (though he considered that the court had power to award such damages in an appropriate case). He said: "Serious damage to reputation requires heavy compensation, even if no specific loss is or can be shown. Here, a man of international reputation is vilified in the eyes of his professional confreres. He thus suffers greatly, though he may not lose a single dollar."[45]

4.120 In *Vogel v. Canadian Broadcasting Corp.*,[46] the British Columbia

---

38 *Supra*, at pp. 104-5. See also *Ross v. Holley* (2004), 28 C.C.L.T. (3d) 83 (Ont. S.C.J.) at para. 9.

39 [1964] A.C. 1129 (H.L.). See 11.190, 11.200, *infra*.

40 (1978), 86 D.L.R. (3d) 61 (N.S.S.C. App. Div.).

41 [1956] S.C.R. 366, 2 D.L.R. (2d) 225.

42 *Ross v. Lamport* (1957), 9 D.L.R. (2d) 585, [1957] O.R. 402 (C.A.).

43 (1964), 44 D.L.R. (2d) 17, [1964] 2 O.R. 21 (H.C.J.), affd 48 D.L.R. (2d) 508*n*, [1965] 1 O.R. 510*n* (C.A.).

44 *Supra*, footnote 40.

45 *Barltrop, supra*, footnote 40, at p. 79.

46 [1982] 3 W.W.R. 97 (B.C.S.C.).

Supreme Court, having commented that awards in Canada had tended to be modest,[47] awarded $100,000 general damages and $25,000 exemplary damages to the Deputy Attorney General in respect of an allegation that he had improperly influenced the course of justice. On the other hand, in *Hill v. Church of Scientology of Toronto*[47a] the Supreme Court of Canada upheld an award of $1.6 million, including $800,000 exemplary damages, in respect of a somewhat similar allegation. Subsequently, however, in reducing an award of damages for slander from $450,000 to $160,000, the British Columbia Court of Appeal remarked of the *Hill* case that it "is not a benchmark in ordinary cases of defamation. One does not start with the awards in *Hill v. Church of Scientology*, and work oneself down."[47b] The British Columbia Court emphasized that in the *Hill* case the defendant persisted until a late stage in a plea of justification.

4.130 In *Rook v. Fairrie*,[48] it was suggested that damages assessed by a judge alone should be reduced below what a jury would award, because of the judge's opportunity to express views on the defendant's behaviour and so vindicate the plaintiff by what is said. This suggestion was, however, disapproved by the House of Lords,[49] and has been rejected also in Canada.[50]

4.140 In the light of the limits set by the Supreme Court of Canada on compensation for intangible losses in personal injury cases ($100,000 in 1978),[51] it has been suggested that there should be a similar conventional limit in defamation cases, but this suggestion was rejected by the Supreme Court of Canada in *Hill v. Church of Scientology of Toronto*.[52] One difficulty with the suggestion is that it is common for exemplary damages to be included with general compensatory damages as part of a single award, and it would seem that, so long as exemplary damages are accepted as a legitimate part of tort law, as they are in Canada, there can be no

---

47 See *Snyder v. Montreal Gazette* (1978), 87 D.L.R. (3d) 5 (Que. S.C.), revd 5 D.L.R. (3d) 206 (C.A.), restd [1988] 1 S.C.R. 494, 49 D.L.R. (4th) 17, where $135,000 was referred to as the largest award, with the comment that exemplary damages are not available in Quebec, as such. The award was reduced on appeal to $13,500 but restored by the Supreme Court of Canada. See also *Derrickson v. Tomat* (1992), 88 D.L.R. (4th) 401, [1992] 2 W.W.R. 724, supplementary reasons 94 D.L.R. (4th) 453, 44 C.P.R. (3d) 210 (B.C.C.A.), leave to appeal to S.C.C. refused 93 D.L.R. (4th) vii, 146 N.R. 159*n* (award of $400,000 set aside).

47a [1995] 2 S.C.R. 1130, 126 D.L.R. (4th) 129. See also *Hiltz and Seamone Co. v. Nova Scotia (Attorney General)* (1998), 164 N.S.R. (2d) 161 (S.C.), vard 172 D.L.R. (4th) 488 (C.A.) ($200,000 general damages and $100,000 punitive damages).

47b *Brown v. Cole* (1998), 186 W.A.C. 73 at p. 90 (B.C.C.A.), leave to appeal to S.C.C. refused 243 N.R. 400*n*. See also *Hodgson v. Canadian Newspapers Co.* (2000), 189 D.L.R. (4th) 241 (Ont. C.A.), leave to appeal to S.C.C. refused 197 D.L.R. (4th) vii.

48 [1941] 1 K.B. 507 (C.A.).

49 *Associated Newspapers v. Dingle*, [1964] A.C. 371 (H.L.).

50 *Hubert v. DeCamillis* (1963), 41 D.L.R. (2d) 495 (B.C.S.C.); *Safeway Stores Ltd. v. Harris*, [1948] 4 D.L.R. 187 (Man. C.A.).

51 See 3.510-3.700, *supra*.

52 *Supra*, footnote 47a. See also *Botiuk v. Toronto Free Press Publications Ltd.*, [1995] 3 S.C.R. 3, 126 D.L.R. (4th) 609; *Crampton v. Nugawela* (1996), 41 N.S.W.L.R. 176 (C.A.); *Dinyer-Fraser v. Laurentian Bank* (2005), 40 B.C.L.R. (4th) 39 (S.C.) at para. 238; *Young v. Bella*, [2006] 1 S.C.R. 108, 261 D.L.R. (4th) 516.

conventional limit on that part of the award.[53] It has also been pointed out that an award of general damages in defamation (unlike the non-pecuniary portion of a personal injuries award) includes compensation for pecuniary loss, and that it is not easy to apply the "functional approach", adopted by the Supreme Court of Canada in personal injury cases, to damages for defamation.[54] The plaintiff is not expected to purchase a solace for lost reputation. Nevertheless, the comparison is necessary[54a].

4.145 Another important aspect of the matter concerns free speech. In *Derrickson v. Tomat*,[54b] the British Columbia Court of Appeal, in setting aside an award of $350,000 general and $50,000 exemplary damages, remarked that in case of politically motivated comment, particularly by private individuals on the public conduct of officials, damages should be restricted to a sum sufficient to indicate that the comment was unwarranted. Exemplary damages would rarely be appropriate. In this way, public interest in free speech can be balanced against the plaintiff's interest in reasonable protection of reputation. The English Court of Appeal in *Rantzen v. Mirror Group Newspapers (1986) Ltd.*[54c] commented that an unfettered power in a jury to award damages was inconsistent with Britain's obligations in respect of freedom of expression under the European Convention for the Protection of Human Rights and such a conclusion was subsequently reached in respect of English law by the European Court of Human Rights.[54d] Similarly, it has been argued that the parallel freedoms recognized in the *Canadian Charter of Rights and Freedoms*, whether applied to the common law of defamation directly or by analogy, require the courts to place some restrictions on the power of juries to award damages for defamation. But in *Hill v. Church of Scientology of Toronto*,[54e] an argument along these lines was rejected by the Supreme Court of Canada, which upheld an award of $1.6 million. The court commented, however, that awards of punitive damages must serve a rational purpose. The Ontario Court of Appeal, quoting the English Court of Appeal, has recognized the danger of "jury awards in sums wildly disproportionate to any damage conceivably suffered by the plaintiff".[54f]

(b) Defendant's conduct and circumstances

4.150 The mode and extent of publication is always an important factor in

[53] See 11.10-11.480, *infra*.
[54] Irvine, annotation to *Munro v. Toronto Sun* (1982), 21 C.C.L.T. 261 (H.C.J.), at p. 264.
[54a] See para. 3-1450, *supra*.
[54b] *Derrickson v. Tomat*, *supra*, footnote 47.
[54c] [1994] Q.B. 670 (C.A.).
[54d] *Miloslavsky v. U.K.* (1995), 20 E.H.R.R. 442.
[54e] [1995] 2 S.C.R. 1130, 126 D.L.R. (4th) 129. See also *Quinn v. Television New Zealand Ltd.*, [1995] 3 N.Z.L.R. 216 (H.C.); *Pressler v. Lethbridge* (1997), 153 D.L.R. (4th) 537, [1998] 5 W.W.R. 215 (B.C.S.C.).
[54f] *Hodgson v. Canadian Newspapers Co.* (2000), 189 D.L.R. (4th) 241 at p. 267 (Ont. C.A.), leave to appeal to S.C.C. refused 197 D.L.R. (4th) vii, quoting Lord Bingham M.R. in *John v. MGN Ltd.*, [1997] Q.B. 586 (C.A.).

defamation cases,[54g] as is also the credibility of the defendant.[54h] If the defendant is a newspaper with a large circulation or a broadcasting corporation that gives an aura of authenticity to the libel, damages will be enhanced. In *Barltrop v. Canadian Broadcasting Corp.*,[55] MacKeigan C.J.N.S. said: "The prestige and apparent authority with which the defendant's programme falsely condemned the plaintiff, and its wide dissemination, without apology or explanation, throughout the northern half of North America greatly magnified the derogatory impact on Dr. Barltrop's reputation and pride."[56] On the other hand in *McElroy v. Cowper-Smith*,[57] the fact that the defendant lacked credibility, being a person considered mentally unstable, justified the reduction of damages.

4.160 Apology by the defendant is also relevant. A prompt apology will reduce damages.[58] On the other hand, if the defendant persists in attempting to justify[59] or, as in *Ross v. Lamport*,[60] attempts an apology only in counsel's closing speech to the jury, damages will be enhanced.

4.170 A variety of statutory provisions deal with apologies. Most of the statutes have three separate relevant provisions.[61] For example, by s. 20 of the Ontario *Libel and Slander Act*, the defendant may, where the plaintiff has not sought to justify in defence, prove in mitigation of damages the offer of a written apology. In actions against newspapers or broadcasters, by s. 9, the defendant may prove good faith and a prompt apology in mitigation of damages,[62] and by s. 5 it is provided that the plaintiff, in an action against a newspaper or broadcaster, shall in certain specified circumstances recover

---

[54g] See *Barrick Gold Corp. v. Lopehandia* (2004), 239 D.L.R. (4th) 577 (Ont. C.A.); *Ross v. Holley* (2004), 28 C.C.L.T. (3d) 83 (Ont. S.C.J.) at para. 11, for a discussion of electronic media.

[54h] *Kerr v. Conologue*, [1992] 4 W.W.R. 258, 65 B.C.L.R. (2d) 70 (S.C.); *Benko v. Scott* (2007), 295 Sask. R. 202 (Q.B.).

[55] (1978), 86 D.L.R. (3d) 61 (N.S.S.C. App. Div.).

[56] *Supra*, at pp. 78-9. See also *Leenen v. Canadian Broadcasting Corp.* (2000), 48 O.R. (3d) 656 (S.C.J.), affd 54 O.R. (3d) 612 (C.A.), leave to appeal to S.C.C. refused 289 N.R. 200*n*; *Barrick Gold Corp. v. Lopehandia* (2004), 239 D.L.R. (4th) 577 (Ont. C.A.).

[57] [1967] S.C.R. 425, 62 D.L.R. (2d) 65.

[58] The statutory provisions are discussed below. In *Grabarevic v. Northwest Publications Ltd.* (1968), 67 D.L.R. (2d) 748 (B.C.C.A.), it was held that the plaintiff has no obligation to give the defendant an opportunity to apologize. See also *Stieb v. Vernon News*, [1947] 4 D.L.R. 397 (B.C.S.C.) (apology need not be abject).

[59] *Stopforth v. Goyer* (1978), 87 D.L.R. (3d) 373, 20 O.R. (2d) 262 (H.C.J.), revd on other grounds 97 D.L.R. (3d) 369, 23 O.R. (2d) 696 (C.A.); *Nagy v. Webb*, [1930] 2 D.L.R. 234 (Sask. C.A.); *Wagner v. Lim* (1994), 22 Alta. L.R. (3d) 169, 158 A.R. 241 (Q.B.); *Clark v. Ainsworth* (1996), 40 N.S.W.L.R. 463 (C.A.); *Leenen* v. *Canadian Broadcasting Corp.*, *supra*, footnote 56; *Fiola v. LeBrun*, [2003] 2 W.W.R. 700 (Man. Q.B.). See also *Hill v. Church of Scientology of Toronto*, [1995] 2 S.C.R. 1130, 126 D.L.R. (4th) 129.

[60] (1957), 9 D.L.R. (2d) 585, [1957] O.R. 402 (C.A.). See also *Farrell v. Canadian Broadcasting Corporation* (1987), 43 D.L.R. (4th) 667, 66 Nfld. & P.E.I.R. 145 (C.A.) (delayed apology).

[61] *Libel and Slander Act* (Ont.), ss. 5, 9, 20; *Defamation Act* (Alta.), ss. 4, 15, 16(1); *Libel and Slander Act* (B.C.), ss. 6, 7, 10; *Defamation Act* (Man.), ss. 4, 16(1), 17(1); *Defamation Act* (N.B.), ss. 4, 16(1), 17(1); *Defamation Act* (N.W.T.), ss. 4, 18, 19; *Defamation Act* (N.S.), ss. 5, 21(1), 22(1); *Libel and Slander Act* (Sask.), ss. 4, 7, 8(1).

"only actual damages" if, among other things, the newspaper has published a full and fair retraction. The term "actual damages" is not defined, but it seems likely that it is intended to have the same meaning as special damages in slander, that is, financial or material loss. In the majority of Canadian jurisdictions, the equivalent section, in fact, uses the term "special damages".[63]

4.180 As has been stated, exemplary damages are considered proper in Canada in defamation cases. Often, however, it is difficult to separate the element of exemplary damage from that of aggravated damages,[64] and in England after *Rookes v. Barnard*,[65] the tendency has been to classify as aggravated damages much of what formerly went under the name of exemplary or punitive damages. Lord Devlin himself in *Rookes v. Barnard* was anxious to save as much as he could of the pre-existing law and said: "Aggravated damages in this type of case can do most, if not all, of the work that could be done by exemplary damages."[66] Lord Devlin explained *Ley v. Hamilton*,[67] a defamation case, where the House of Lords in upholding a jury award had referred to a punitive element, as a case where the damages were in reality based on compensatory principles, with the conduct of the defendant taken into account in so far as it affected the insult and pain suffered by the plaintiff.[68] It will be seen that a sharp dividing line here is rather artificial, for measurement of compensation for insult and mental pain is so vague an undertaking that it is difficult to exclude elements of the punitive.[69] In *Barltrop v. Canadian Broadcasting Corp.*,[70] MacKeigan C.J.N.S., though holding that the circumstances "do not quite call for exemplary or punitive damages", went on to say: "The very factors which, if more pronounced, might have warranted punitive damages may, however, aggravate and increase the general damages which should be awarded to compensate the plaintiff for the injury to his reputation and feelings."[71] A distinction between

62 It was held in *Munro v. Toronto Sun* (1982), 39 O.R. (2d) 100 (H.C.J.), that the defendant could plead the apology even though it could not satisfy the requirement of showing good faith ("without actual malice and without gross negligence"). See also *Tait v. New Westminster Radio Ltd.* (1984), 15 D.L.R. (4th) 115, [1985] 1 W.W.R. 451 (B.C.C.A.).

63 The term "actual damages" occurs in British Columbia (s. 7) and Saskatchewan (s. 8(1)); "special damages", in Alberta (s. 16(1)), Manitoba (s. 17(1)), New Brunswick (s. 17(1)), Nova Scotia (s. 22(1)) and Northwest Territories (s. 19).

64 See 11.10, *infra*.

65 [1964] A.C. 1129 (H.L.).

66 *Supra*, at p. 1230.

67 (1935), 153 L.T. 384 (H.L.).

68 *Rookes v. Barnard, supra*, footnote 65, at pp. 1230-1.

69 See 3.1410, 3.1420, *supra*.

70 (1978), 86 D.L.R. (3d) 61 (N.S.S.C. App. Div.).

71 *Supra*, at p. 78. But see *Laufer v. Bucklaschuk* (1999), 181 D.L.R. (4th) 83 (Man. C.A.), leave to appeal to S.C.C. refused 189 D.L.R. (4th) vii (deterrence irrelevant to compensatory damages); *Rogacki v. Belz* (2004), 243 D.L.R. (4th) 585 (Ont. C.A.), leave to appeal to S.C.C. refused 249 D.L.R. (4th) vi (post-publication conduct). It was held in *Ager v. Canjex Publishing Ltd.* (2005), 259 D.L.R. (4th) 727 (B.C.C.A.), that an award of aggravated damages requires a finding of actual malice.

aggravated and exemplary damages is essential, however, where the plaintiff is a corporation.[72]

(c) Plaintiff's circumstances

4.190 The plaintiff's position, status, and prior reputation are relevant to assessing the amount of injury. In *Kelly v. Sherlock*,[73] Blackburn J. said: "the jury might fairly consider the plaintiff's conduct and the degree of respect which the plaintiff himself had shewn for the feelings of others".[74] This was not, as Blackburn J. expressly said, because any kind of set-off was allowed of one libel or misconduct against another;[75] the relevance of the plaintiff's conduct is, it is suggested, that a person who becomes known as one who voluntarily engages in a vulgar slanging match is not greatly damaged by the return shots of opponents. In the case the plaintiff, a clergyman, had involved himself in unseemly disputes with almost everyone with whom he came in contact. He described the defendant's paper as "the dregs of provincial journalism" and had preached from the pulpit suggesting that his opponents were guilty of subornation of perjury and would, as he charitably hoped, repent on their deathbeds and confess their guilt. The trial judge had said to the jury:

> It certainly is a most unfortunate thing that a gentleman who tells you that he is a minister of religion, and of love, and charity, should have managed to have embroiled himself with so many different people, and about such trash, that he should have been the plaintiff at these assizes in four actions . . . he has brought an action against the churchwarden of his church; he has managed to quarrel with the corporation and with the organist, and has had a scuffle with somebody else, according to the conviction for assault against him ... If you think the defendant is guilty, then the plaintiff is entitled to something; but that something rests with you, and rests with you entirely, upon a review of all the circumstances of the case.[76]

The jury's verdict of one farthing damages was upheld on appeal.

4.200 The plaintiff's prior bad reputation is relevant and is said to go "in mitigation of damages".[77] Similarly a defence of justification, though it fails as a complete defence, may succeed in eliciting facts that justify a reduction of damages on the ground that, had the truth been said, the plaintiff's reputation would have been so low that it would not have been significantly reduced by the untrue part of the defendant's statement.[78] Limits, however,

---

72 In *Walker v. CFTO Ltd.* (1987), 37 D.L.R. (4th) 224, 59 O.R. (2d) 104 (C.A.), it was held that aggravated damages based on personal humiliation and distress could not be claimed by a corporation. See also *Thomas Management Ltd. v. Alberta (Minister of Environmental Protection)* (2006), 276 D.L.R. (4th) 430 (Alta. C.A.).

73 (1866), L.R. 1 Q.B. 686. See also *Neeld v. Western Broadcasting Co. Ltd.* (1976), 65 D.L.R. (3d) 574 (B.C.S.C.).

74 *Supra*, at p. 698.

75 *Kelly v. Sherlock*, *supra*, footnote 73.

76 *Kelly v. Sherlock*, *supra*, footnote 73, at p. 691.

77 See *Plato Films Ltd. v. Speidel*, [1961] A.C. 1090 (H.L.); *Hobbs v. C.T. Tinling & Co. Ltd.*, [1929] 2 K.B. 1 (C.A.); *Kelly v. Ross* (1909), 14 O.W.R. 1078 (Master in Chambers).

have been placed on the defendant's ability to attack the plaintiff's character. Evidence of general bad reputation is admissible but it must be confined to the sector of the plaintiff's character relevant to the defamation. In *Plato Films Ltd. v. Speidel,*[79] Lord Denning said: "Thus, if the libel imputes theft the relevant sector is his character for honesty, not his character as a motorist."[80] Further, it has been held that mere rumours are not admissible.[81] Nor can specific acts of misconduct be adduced except in order to show the plaintiff's reputation in fact. Gatley summed up the position as follows:

> It is thus the plaintiff's reputation in fact, and not his reputation in merit, or, to put it another way, his reputation and not his character, which is considered in assessing damages. It follows that if the defendant is sued for saying that the plaintiff stole B's watch, he cannot prove in mitigation of damages that the plaintiff stole C's, D's and E's watches, nor can he give evidence that there were rumours that B's watch had also fallen to him. But he may call a detective to say that the plaintiff is a notorious pickpocket, or prove that the plaintiff has been convicted on a number of occasions for theft.[82]

In many jurisdictions, notice must be given of the introduction of such evidence if the defendant does not justify in the defence.[83]

4.210 Mental distress suffered by the plaintiff is compensable.[84] This element, as has been said, is difficult to separate entirely from punitive damages. It is also difficult to separate it entirely from questions of the plaintiff's status and prior reputation, for it is when these are substantially infringed that the plaintiff can be expected to suffer substantial distress. In *Barltrop v. Canadian Broadcasting Corp.*,[85] MacKeigan C.J.N.S. spoke of injury to the plaintiff's "feelings" and "pride" as a matter worthy of compensation.[86]

4.220 Receipt or likely receipt of compensation from another source in respect of the same libel was inadmissible in mitigation of damages at common law.[87] However, statute in most jurisdictions now provides the contrary in certain cases. The Ontario *Libel and Slander Act* for example provides:

> 10. In an action for a libel in a newspaper or in a broadcast, the defendant may prove in mitigation of damages that the plaintiff has already brought action for, or has recovered damages, or has received or agreed to receive

[78] *Supra*, footnote 77; *Grobbelaar v. News Group Newspapers Ltd. and Another*, [2002] 1 W.L.R. 3024 (H.L.); *Makow v. Winnipeg Sun*, [2004] 6 W.W.R. 45 (Man. C.A.); *G. (H.R.) v. L. (M.S.)*, [2008] 5 W.W.R. 529 (B.C.S.C.).

[79] *Supra.*

[80] *Plato Films, supra*, at p. 1140. See also *Moore v. Mitchell* (1886), 11 O.R. 21 (Q.B.).

[81] "Rumour is a lying jade, begotten by gossip out of hearsay, and is not fit to be admitted to audience in a court of law", *per* Lord Denning, in *Plato Films Ltd. v. Speidel, supra*, footnote 77, at p. 1136.

[82] *Gatley on Libel and Slander*, 8th ed. (London, Sweet & Maxwell, 1981), §1423.

[83] Supreme Court Practice, 1991 (U.K.), O. 82, r. 7; *Libel and Slander Act* (Ont.), s. 21; Rules of Practice and Procedure (Sask.), R. 276.

[84] See 3.1250, *supra.*

[85] (1978), 86 D.L.R. (3d) 61 (N.S.S.C. App. Div.).

[86] *Supra*, at pp. 78 and 79.

[87] *Gatley on Libel and Slander*, 9th ed. (London, Sweet & Maxwell, 1998), §33.52.

compensation in respect of a libel or libels to the same purport or effect as that for which such action is brought.[88]

In *Allan v. Bushnell Television,*[89] it was held that this section permitted proof of a settlement actually reached with another party. Where there are concurrent actions, Lord Reid for the majority of the House of Lords in *Rubber Improvement Ltd. v. Daily Telegraph*[90] said:

> I do not think it is sufficient merely to tell each jury to make such allowance as they may think fit. They ought, in my view, to be directed that in considering the evidence submitted to them they should consider how far the damage suffered by the plaintiffs can reasonably be attributed solely to the libel with which they are concerned and how far it ought to be regarded as the joint result of the two libels. If they think that some part of the damage is the joint result of the two libels they should bear in mind that the plaintiffs ought not to be compensated twice for the same loss. They can only deal with this matter on very broad lines and they must take it that the other jury will be given a similar direction. They must do the best they can to ensure that the sum which they award will fully compensate the plaintiffs for the damage caused by the libel with which they are concerned, but will not take into account that part of the total damage suffered by the plaintiffs which ought to enter into the other jury's assessment.[91]

It would seem that unless the juries in the two actions retire simultaneously, it will always be possible to tell a second jury what the other has awarded. It was held by the Ontario Court of Appeal in *Allan v. Bushnell T.V.*[92] that it was proper for the defendant to tell the jury the amount of the settlement made by another party; presumably, therefore, there would be no objection to telling the jury the amount of a prior award.

2. Torts Other than Defamation

4.230 Damage to reputation can be caused by other torts besides defamation. Damages for malicious prosecution[92a] and wrongful imprisonment may include an element of compensation for injury to reputation, though it is often difficult to distinguish such compensation from compensation for the affront and insult to the plaintiff.[93] Business reputation is specifically protected by the economic torts of trade libel and passing off.[94]

4.240 In actions for trespass to goods, injury to reputation was held to be

[88] *Libel and Slander Act* (Ont.), s. 10. Similar provisions appear in *Defamation Act* (Alta.), s. 15(2); Man., s. 16(2); N.B., s. 16(2); N.S., ss. 6, 21(2); N.W.T., s. 18(2); *Libel and Slander Act* (B.C.), s. 11; Sask., s. 17.

[89] (1969), 4 D.L.R. (3d) 212, [1969] 2 O.R. 6 (C.A.).

[90] [1964] A.C. 234 (H.L.).

[91] *Supra*, at p. 261.

[92] *Supra*, footnote 89.

[92a] *Wood v. Kennedy* (1998), 165 D.L.R. (4th) 542 (Ont. Ct. (Gen. Div.)).

[93] *Whitehouse v. Reimer* (1979), 107 D.L.R. (3d) 283 (Alta. Q.B.), revd on other grounds 116 D.L.R. (3d) 594 (C.A.); *Savile v. Roberts* (1698), 1 Ld. Raym. 374 at p. 378, 91 E.R. 1147, *per* Lord Holt; *Walter v. Alltools Ltd.* (1944), 61 T.L.R. 39 (C.A.), at p. 40, *per* Lawrence L.J. See *Wilson v. City of Winnipeg* (1887), 4 Man. L.R. 193 (Q.B.), *per* Killam J., at p. 197 (damages reduced because "very little if any damage to his reputation can have been sustained by the plaintiff").

compensable in *Thurston v. Charles*[95] where a private letter, the property of the plaintiff, had been published by the defendant, and in *Brewer v. Dew*[96] where damages were given for the imputation of insolvency caused by the wrongful seizure of goods. However, in *Dixon v. Calcraft*[97] the English Court of Appeal in construing a statutory right to "compensation for any loss or damage" held, though without referring to the earlier cases, that loss of reputation caused by wrongful detention of a ship by the government was not compensable. Lord Esher said categorically:

> The damage alleged is that, by seizing the ship on a suspicion of being unsafe, an imputation was cast on the character of the plaintiffs as shipowners. No such claim for damages was ever yet sustained in an action for seizing a chattel. If compensation were given for such an injury, it would be a kind of compensation unknown to the English law. It seems to me clear that this damage could not be recovered in an action for such a detention of a chattel, if wrongful. It could not be given by way of aggravation of damages in respect of wounded feelings. Such a thing was never heard of. Nor could it be given for injury to character, because that would really be giving damages as for libel or slander, though the matter complained of is not anything written or spoken.[98]

Lopes L.J. said: "No such damage [as loss of reputation] is known to the law in the case of a trespass to goods."[99] It may be suggested that, as in the analogous cases of breach of contract discussed later,[100] there is no fundamental objection to compensating the injury to the plaintiff's reputation in a legal action other than defamation, provided that a fair opportunity is allowed to the defendant to raise the same kind of defences as could have been raised in an action of defamation. On this view, the question is at base one of procedural convenience.[101] In *Young v. Bella*,[101a] the Supreme Court of Canada upheld a large award of damages for negligence that caused a false suspicion of child abuse.

3. Breach of Contract

4.250 In *Addis v. Gramophone Co. Ltd.*,[102] an action for wrongful dismissal, the House of Lords held that the plaintiff could not recover damages for injury to his reputation. Lord Atkinson said:

---

94 This paragraph was cited with approval in *Clark v. Scotiabank* (2004), 25 C.C.L.T. (3d) 109 (S.C.J.), at pp. 116-17. See 5.750-5.1040, *infra*.

95 (1905), 21 T.L.R. 659 (K.B.).

96 (1843), 11 M. & W. 625, 152 E.R. 955.

97 [1892] 1 Q.B. 458 (C.A.).

98 *Supra*, at p. 464.

99 *Supra*, at p. 466.

100 See 4.250-4.310, *infra*.

101 See also *B.P.I. Resources Ltd. v. Merrill Lynch Canada Inc.* (1989), 95 A.R. 211, 67 Alta. L.R. (2d) 97 (C.A.) (negligence); *Apple Bee Shirts Ltd. v. Lax* (1988), 27 C.P.C. (2d) 226 (Ont. H.C.J.) (conspiracy and breach of fiduciary duty).

101a [2006] 1 S.C.R. 108, 261 D.L.R. (4th) 516.

102 [1909] A.C. 488 (H.L.), followed in *Malik v. Bank of Credit and Commerce International S.A.*, [1995] 3 All E.R. 545 (C.A.).

> I can conceive nothing more objectionable and embarrassing in litigation than trying in effect an action of libel or slander as a matter of aggravation in an action for illegal dismissal, the defendant being permitted, as he must in justice be permitted, to traverse the defamatory sense, rely on privilege, or raise every point which he could raise in an independent action brought for the alleged libel or slander itself.[103]

This conclusion has been followed in a number of Canadian cases.[104] In *Tippett v. International Typographical Union*,[105] however, the British Columbia Supreme Court awarded damages against a union for injury to reputation caused to a member by wrongful expulsion. It would seem that Lord Atkinson's objection is purely procedural: a separate claim for defamation is not excluded.[106] A number of Canadian cases have permitted the inclusion, in wrongful dismissal cases, of claims for loss of reputation, or have permitted the joinder of actions for wrongful dismissal and for defamation,[107] and in 1997 *Addis* was overruled on this point.[107a]

4.260 A well-established line of cases has awarded damages against banks for failure to honour business customers' cheques.[108] Lord Atkinson said that in such a case where the plaintiff had become bankrupt:

> It would appear to me that injury to the credit and reputation of a trader is

---

[103] *Supra*, at p. 496. In *Maw v. Jones* (1890), 25 Q.B.D. 107, it was said that damages for wrongful dismissal might take into account the increased difficulty in finding new employment because of the dismissal. This seems a sound application of the principles of mitigation, but the case was doubted by Lord Loreburn in *Addis v. Gramaphone Co. Ltd.*, at p. 491.

[104] In *Peso Silver Mines (N.P.L.) v. Cropper*, [1966] S.C.R. 673 at p. 684, 58 D.L.R. (2d) 1 at p. 10, Cartwright J. said: "the claim being founded on breach of contract the damages cannot be increased by reason of the circumstances of dismissal whether in respect of the respondent's wounded feelings or the prejudicial effects upon his reputation and chances of finding other employment." See also *McMinn v. Town of Oakville* (1978), 85 D.L.R. (3d) 131, 19 O.R. (2d) 366 (H.C.J.); *Abouna v. Foothills Provincial General Hospital Board* (1978), 83 D.L.R. (3d) 333 (Alta. S.C. App. Div.), leave to appeal to S.C.C. refused 10 A.R. 269*n*; *Neville v. Page* (1977), 5 A.R. 8 (S.C.T.D.); *Desloges v. Radio-Television Representatives Ltd.* (1987), 62 O.R. (2d) 633, 18 C.C.E.L. 1 (H.C.J.); *Hiltz v. Saskatchewan Property Management Corp.* (1993), 112 Sask. R. 297, 93 C.L.L.C. 12,394 (Q.B.), affd 128 Sask. R. 316, 85 W.A.C. 316 (C.A.).

[105] (1976), 71 D.L.R. (3d) 146 (B.C.S.C.). In *McMinn v. Town of Oakville*, *supra*, footnote 104, this case was distinguished as involving "more than a commercial contract" whereas the contract of employment in *McMinn* was said to be "clearly a commercial contract". It would seem, however, that a contract of employment could well be held to be more than a commercial contract. See *Pilon v. Peugeot Canada Ltd.* (1980), 114 D.L.R. (3d) 378, 29 O.R. (2d) 711 (H.C.J.), discussed at 3.1390, *supra*. The *McMinn* case was disapproved in *Cleary v. Cabletronics Inc.* (1982), 140 D.L.R. (3d) 110, 39 O.R. (2d) 456 (H.C.J.), and in *Johnston v. Muskoka Lakes Golf and Country Club Ltd.* (1983), 40 O.R. (2d) 762, 33 C.P.C. 239 (H.C.J.).

[106] See *Jerome v. Anderson*, [1964] S.C.R. 291, 44 D.L.R. (2d) 516.

[107] *Bilbrough v. Board of Education of Toronto*, [1934] O.W.N. 44 (H.C.J.); *Cleary v. Cabletronics Inc.*, *supra*, footnote 105; *Johnston v. Muskoka Lakes Golf and Country Club Ltd.*, *supra*, footnote 105; *Foley v. Signtech Inc.* (1988), 55 D.L.R. (4th) 152, 66 O.R. (2d) 79 (H.C.J.). In *Ribeiro v. Canadian Imperial Bank of Commerce* (1992), 13 O.R. (3d) 278, 44 C.C.E.L. 165 (C.A.), leave to appeal to S.C.C. refused 157 N.R. 400*n*, 65 O.A.C. 79*n*, the question was left open.

[107a] *Mahmud v. Bank of Credit and Commerce Int. S.A.*, [1998] A.C. 20 (H.L.).

> not only a natural and reasonable result of his being made a bankrupt, i.e., such a consequence as would, in the ordinary course of things, flow from it, but must, in the present case, have been in the contemplation of the parties when they entered into the contract as the result which would probably follow from the breach of it.[109]

4.270 In *Aerial Advertising v. Batchelors Peas,*[110] compensation was allowed for the damage to the reputation of an advertiser caused by the exhibition of an aerial advertisement during the two-minute silence on Armistice Day. In *Foaminol Laboratories Ltd. v. British Artid Plastics, Ltd.,*[111] it was held that damages for loss of reputation might properly be included in a claim for non-delivery of goods. Hallett J. said: "I think that, if pecuniary loss can be established, the mere fact that the pecuniary loss is brought about by the loss of reputation caused by a breach of contract is not sufficient to preclude the plaintiffs from recovering in respect of that pecuniary loss."[112]

4.280 In *Dunk v. George Waller Ltd.,*[113] the plaintiff was held to be entitled, for breach of an apprenticeship agreement, to damages for the injury to his future earning prospects. Lord Denning M.R. said:

> We were also referred to *Addis v. Gramophone Co. Ltd.* [1909] A.C. 488, 491, when it was said that an employee cannot get compensation "for the loss he may sustain from the fact that his having been dismissed of itself makes it more difficult for him to obtain fresh employment". I do not think that applies in the case of an apprenticeship. The very object of an apprenticeship agreement is to enable the apprentice to fit himself to get better employment.[114]

4.290 Damages for loss of reputation are an established part of the action for breach of promise of marriage, and although the action has been abolished in many jurisdictions, it stands as an illustration of the practicability of combining a claim for loss of reputation with a contractual action.[115]

4.300 An established line of cases has awarded damages to actors for loss of promised publicity on the ground that the publicity is, in reality, an important part of the remuneration promised to the actor.[116] In *Clayton & Waller Ltd. v. Oliver,*[117] Lord Buckmaster said:

---

[108] See *Addis v. Gramophone Co. Ltd., supra,* footnote 102, at p. 495; *Wilson v. United Counties Bank,* [1920] A.C. 102 (H.L.); *Smith v. Commonwealth Trust Co.* (1969), 10 D.L.R. (3d) 181 (B.C.S.C.) (solicitor); *Rolin v. Steward* (1854), 23 L.J.C.P. 148. Nominal damages only were awarded to a non-business customer in *Gibbons v. Westminster Bank, Ltd.,* [1939] 2 K.B. 882.

[109] *Wilson v. United Counties Bank, supra,* footnote 108, at p. 132.

[110] [1938] 2 All E.R. 788 (K.B.).

[111] [1941] 2 All E.R. 393 (K.B.). These cases were followed in *Wyman v. Vancouver Real Estate Board (No. 6)* (1962), 39 W.W.R. 698 (B.C.S.C.) (wrongful expulsion of real estate board member).

[112] *Foaminol Laboratories, supra,* footnote 111, at p. 400. See also *Canlin Ltd. v. Thiokol Fibres Canada Ltd.* (1983), 142 D.L.R. (3d) 450, 40 O.R. (2d) 687 (C.A.); *J.R. Klady Agencies (1971) Ltd. v. Noma Inc.* (1986), 9 C.P.C. (2d) 29 (Ont. H.C.J.).

[113] [1970] 2 Q.B. 163 (C.A.).

[114] *Supra,* at p. 168.

[115] See 3.1320, *supra.*

> Here both parties knew that as flowing from the contract the plaintiff would be billed and advertised as appearing at the Hippodrome, and in the theatrical profession this is a valuable right.
>
> In assessing the damages, therefore, it was competent for the jury to consider that the plaintiff was entitled to compensation because he did not appear at the Hippodrome, as by his contract he was entitled to do, and in assessing those damages they may consider the loss he suffered (1.) because the Hippodrome is an important place of public entertainment and (2.) that in the ordinary course he would have been "billed" and otherwise advertised as appearing at the Hippodrome. The learned judge put the matter as a loss of reputation, which I do not think is the exact expression, but he explained that as the equivalent of loss of publicity and that summarizes what I have stated as my view of the true situation.[118]

In *Withers v. General Theatre*,[119] it was held by the English Court of Appeal that damage to existing reputation could not be included, but the case was overruled on this point in 1997.[119a]

4.310 It would seem from these cases that there is no cogent reason why damages should not be given for loss of reputation in a contract case,[119b] and it seems probable that the limitation expressed by Lord Atkinson in *Addis v. Gramophone Co. Ltd.*[120] will continue to attract exceptions.[121] The reason given by Lord Atkinson for excluding such damages was the possible procedural inconvenience of trying what would be in effect an action for defamation along with an action for breach of contract. There may in some cases be cogent procedural reasons for separating the actions, but it appears from the cases considered previously that these will not always be present, and that there is no inherent impossibility in combining the claims.

---

[116] *Clayton & Waller, Ltd. v. Oliver*, [1930] A.C. 209 (H.L.); *Withers v. General Theatre Corp.*, [1933] 2 K.B. 536 (C.A.); *Marbé v. George Edwardes (Daly's Theatre) Ltd.*, [1928] 1 K.B. 269 (C.A.), referred to with approval by the Alberta Appellate Division in *Abouna v. Foothills Provincial General Hospital Board* (1978), 83 D.L.R. (3d) 333 (Alta. S.C. App. Div.), leave to appeal to S.C.C. refused 10 A.R. 269*n*, and by the Ontario High Court in *Magee v. Channel Seventynine Ltd.* (1976), 75 D.L.R. (3d) 201, 15 O.R. (2d) 185. In *Burmeister v. Regina Multicultural Council* (1985), 40 Sask. R. 183, 8 C.C.E.L. 144 (C.A.), the Saskatchewan Court of Appeal refused to extend the principle to the director of a multicultural program.

[117] *Supra*, footnote 116.

[118] *Clayton v. Oliver, supra*, footnote 116, at p. 220.

[119] *Supra*, footnote 116.

[119a] *Mahmud v. Bank of Credit and Commerce Int. S.A.*, [1998] A.C. 20 (H.L.).

[119b] See *Summertime Holdings v. Environmental Defender's Office* (1998), 45 N.S.W.L.R. 291 (Eq. Div.), where the plaintiffs were entitled to damages not for the original defamation but for the failure to have an apology published as promised.

[120] [1909] A.C. 488 (H.L.).

[121] See *Bilbrough v. Board of Education of Toronto*, [1934] O.W.N. 44 (H.C.J.); *Cleary v. Cabletronics Inc.* (1982), 140 D.L.R. (3d) 110, 39 O.R. (2d) 456 (H.C.J.); *Johnston v. Muskoka Lakes Golf and Country Club Ltd.* (1983), 40 O.R. (2d) 762, 33 C.P.C. 239 (H.C.J.); *Foley v. Signtech Inc.* (1988), 55 D.L.R. (4th) 152, 66 O.R. (2d) 79 (H.C.J.). In *Ribeiro v. Canadian Imperial Bank of Commerce* (1992), 13 O.R. (3d) 278, 44 C.C.E.L. 165 (C.A.), leave to appeal to S.C.C. refused 157 N.R. 400*n*, 65 O.A.C. 79*n*, the question was left open.

CHAPTER 5

DAMAGE TO ECONOMIC INTERESTS

1. Contractual Benefits

5.10 One of the most significant of all economic interests is the benefit of a favourable contract. A person who has made a good bargain is treated by the law for many purposes as one who has a present right, the value of which is measured by the value of the promised performance. The primary manifestation of this approach is reflected in the measure of damages for breach of contract; the contract breaker is bound to make good the loss caused by the breach, a loss measured by the value of the performance promised. The notion of an enforceable contract as a present valuable right affects many other branches of the law where the measure of damages naturally reflects the primary measure for breach of contract.[1] Thus, assignments of contractual rights are common and the measure of damages for wrongful failure to assign would be based upon the value of the contractual right. Actions for breach of warranty of authority and for inducing breach of contract also lead to damages measured by the value of the contract lost to the plaintiff.

5.20 It is commonly said that the measure of damages for breach of contract differs from that in tort in that contract damages, but not tort damages, give to the plaintiff the benefit of the bargain.[1a] The most generally accepted formulations of compensatory principles, however, are wide enough to embrace both contract and tort. Thus, it is usually said that the object of compensatory damages is to put the party complaining in the position that would have been occupied "if the wrong had not been done"[2] or "if his rights had been observed".[3] It will be seen that these formulations are quite capable of supporting a rule of contract damages that gives to the promisee the benefit of the bargain, for if the wrong had not been done the contract would have been performed and the promisee would have received the benefit of performance.

5.30 It may be objected that there is an element of circularity in this. No wrong would have been done to the plaintiff if no contract had been made in the first

[1] *Agricultural Research Institute of Ontario v. Campbell-High* (2002), 58 O.R. (3d) 321 (C.A.).

[1a] See *McGregor on Damages*, 16th ed. (London, Sweet & Maxwell, 1997), §810.

[2] *Livingstone v. Rawyards Coal Co.* (1880), 5 App. Cas. 25 (H.L.), at p. 39.

[3] *Victoria Laundry (Windsor) Ltd. v. Newman Industries Ltd.*, [1949] 2 K.B. 528 (C.A.), at p. 539, *per* Asquith L.J.; *Paziuk v. Rural Municipality of Ethelbert* (1963), 44 D.L.R. (2d) 165 (Man. Q.B.), at p. 173.

place. To describe the wrong as the breaking of the contract rather than as the making of a contract that is not kept is to beg the question. Independent justification is still needed for a rule measuring compensation by the value of the contractual benefit. Several writers have indeed questioned the necessity and the desirability of maintaining the present rule, and the arguments will be discussed in the following paragraphs.[4] So far as the courts are concerned, the general rule continues to be asserted as the normal rule of contract damages that the promisee is entitled to the full value of the promised performance. In *Robinson v. Harman*,[5] Parke B. said: "The rule of the common law is, that where a party sustains a loss by reason of a breach of contract, he is, so far as money can do it, to be placed in the same situation, with respect to damages, as if the contract had been performed."[6] A very similar statement, from a Canadian Privy Council case frequently cited in Canadian courts, appears in *Wertheim v. Chicoutimi Pulp Co*:

> And it is the general intention of the law that, in giving damages for breach of contract, the party complaining should, so far as it can be done by money, be placed in the same position as he would have been in if the contract had been performed ... That is a ruling principle. It is a just principle.[7]

5.40 From time to time writers have asked whether this rule is indeed a just rule. It may be argued that the main social purpose of the law of contracts is to protect reliance, and that thought should be given to changing the present rule, at least in cases where it is clear that the plaintiff has not altered position in reliance on the defendant's promise. Answers can be given to the various arguments that have been adduced in support of enforcement. First the argument that reasonable expectations ought to be protected is met by pointing out its circularity and its tendency to prove too much by being theoretically applicable beyond the realm of promises.[8] Professor Atiyah has written:

> To raise an expectation and then to decline to fulfil it is, in some measure, to worsen the position of the promisee, certainly an individual promisee. Prima facie this is something that should be avoided, other things being equal. But I am bound to say that it does appear to me to be a very weak ground for the enforcement of executory contracts, and one that could

[4] See 5.50-5.140, *infra*.

[5] (1848), 1 Ex 850, 154 E.R. 363.

[6] *Supra*, at p. 855.

[7] [1911] A.C. 301 (P.C.), at p. 307. *Haack v. Martin*, [1927] S.C.R. 413 at p. 416, [1927] 3 D.L.R. 19 at p. 21; *Norquay v. G.T.P. Town & Dev. Co.* (1915), 25 D.L.R. 59 (Alta. C.A.), at pp. 64-5; *Ascent Financial Services Ltd. v. Blythman*, [2008] 5 W.W.R. 638 (Sask. C.A.).

[8] Atiyah, "Contracts, Promises and the Law of Obligations", 94 L.Q.R. 193 (1978), at pp. 214-15.

> very easily be counterbalanced by proof that other things are not equal ... it might well be thought by most people that the inconvenience to the promisor of being held to his contract would be enough to outweigh the prima facie desirability of not disappointing the promisee.[9]

5.50 A second argument, that enforcing all promises as a matter of principle even where there has been no reliance will better protect reliance when reliance occurs, can be met by proposing a change in the onus of proof. If the reason for enforcement is reliance, it can be argued that the promisee's position is sufficiently protected by a requirement that the promisor is bound unless reliance is disproved.[10]

5.60 The argument that contracts are deliberate allocations of risk can be met by pointing out that not all contracts can be so categorized.[11] The moral argument for enforceability can be met by pointing out that, from a moral point of view, no distinction can be drawn between purely gratuitous promises and executory promises that have not been relied on.[12]

5.70 In his later book, *The Rise and Fall of Freedom of Contract*,[13] Professor Atiyah returns to the same theme. He writes:

> Nevertheless, it remains true in current law, generally speaking, that expectations are the basis of the damages which will be awarded for breach of contract where such liability does exist. Even where there has been some element of reliance, or some benefit rendered, and where it might have been thought that the damages would be confined to the element of reliance or the value of the benefit, this is not generally the case. Doubtless, there are arguments for maintaining the traditional principle here (see Fuller and Perdue "The Reliance Interest in Contract Damages") though it might be better to recognize them frankly for what they are. Frequently, the best justification for awarding such expectation damages is not that the plaintiff's expectations in fact deserve such handsome protection, but that proof of the losses flowing from reliance would be too difficult or costly, and that if the damages are excessive by way of compensation, then this is a deserved penalty on the defendant anyhow. But in view of the declining belief in the idea that the law should actually deter parties from breaking their contracts, it would not be surprising if future developments tend to show a still further whittling down of expectation damages.[14]

Professor Atiyah concludes his book with this comment: "So too, the role of expectations, their relationship to promises, and their importance even where they arise without promises, must be reexamined ... The task is one to which I hope to return."[15]

5.80 A change in the present rule would, however, raise a number of difficulties. First, if specific performance[16] is available to enforce some

9 *Ibid.*, at pp. 215-16.

10 *Ibid.*, at p. 216.

11 *Ibid.*, at p. 217.

12 *Ibid.*, at pp. 218-20.

13 (Oxford, Clarendon Press, 1979).

14 *Ibid.*, at pp. 763-4.

15 *Ibid.*, at p. 779. In *Promises, Morals, and Law* (Oxford, Clarendon Press, 1981), Atiyah explores the philosophical bases for enforcement of promises.

contracts without a need for reliance, it seems difficult to contemplate a measure of damages that is not in principle of equivalent value. If the *prima facie* measure of damages ceased to be the value of the promised performance, there would be increased incentive to claim specific performance, an argument that damages were never "adequate" compensation and an anomalous discrepancy in economic result between cases where specific performance was awarded and cases where damages were given. A change in the basic measure of damages, therefore, would require a corresponding narrowing of the circumstances in which specific enforcement is available.

5.90 Secondly, in the case of a formal contract, for example a gift promise under seal, it has generally been accepted that the appropriate measure of enforcement is the value of the promise.[17] It would be anomalous if formal contracts were fully enforceable but informal contracts only to the extent of reliance.

5.100 Thirdly, it must surely be conceded that completed exchanges, after execution, are final. The result of exchanges is often to confer a benefit on one of the parties. It is difficult to contemplate a rule permitting the rescission of executed transactions on the ground that one party has benefited to a greater extent than his reliance. If this is a sound position, it is hard to see why, in principle, parties should not agree in respect to a future planned exchange that the legal relationship between the two shall now be as though the exchange were actually effected. If this can be done expressly if can surely be done by implication, and arguably such an implication is a fair one in the case of the usual exchange transaction. If the parties do not intend to commit themselves to the full extent of the exchange they can always, under present law, make express provision. If the law normally only protected reliance, a new class of contracts would surely emerge where the promisor fully guaranteed performance. Following normal rules of contract construction such a guarantee could be implicit, as well as express, and this would bring us back to the present position. In other words, the argument is that the normal measure of contract damages simply reflects the usual implications of a contractual transaction.

5.110 This point is strengthened, it is submitted, by the existence of the doctrine of consideration as the normal test of contract enforcement. One of the reasons for allowing the promisee to recover the value of the promised performance is that the promisee has "bought" the right to it.

16 See Sharpe, *Injunctions and Specific Performance*, looseleaf ed. (Toronto, Canada Law Book, 1999).

17 See Waddams, *The Law of Contracts*, 5th ed. (Toronto, Canada Law Book, 2005), pp. 127-31. In *Promises, Morals and Law*, *supra*, footnote 15, at p. 212, Atiyah suggests that the theoretical case for enforcement of gratuitous promises is weak.

The doctrine of consideration is, in essence, a test of when a promise has been "bought". It is widely acknowledged that some measure of enforcement should be and has been given to promises that have not been bought (*i.e.*, where there is no consideration), but it is in just those cases that, as has been argued elsewhere,[18] the measure of damages ought to be restricted to the protection of reliance. When the promisee has not bought the right to performance, there is much less reason to allow recovery of its value.

5.120 Fourthly, it would generally be conceded that risk allocation contracts ought to be enforced.[19] It does not seem that a ready means is available to distinguish "risk allocation" contracts from other contracts. Every agreed exchange can be said to allocate risks of error in assessing the comparative value of the properties to be exchanged. One of the simplest explanations of the theoretical basis of contract law is that it enables persons to make their future less uncertain; this explanation also provides a strong support for a remedial scheme that protects the promisee's expectations, for uncertainty about the future is only removed if the promisee can count on a legal remedy that will give the anticipated benefit of performance.

5.130 Lastly, Fuller and Perdue's argument that only a measure of expectation damages can adequately protect reliance does not seem fully to be met by putting the onus of proof upon the promisor to disprove reliance. A promisee who had made a beneficial bargain would know that reliance on performance of the promise was not safe until losses (not disprovable) or expenses equivalent to the contractual advantage had been incurred. Similarly, it would be profitable for the promisor to break a promise as long as the promisor calculated that it could be shown that such losses had not been incurred. These considerations would inhibit reliance and encourage the manufacture of otherwise unnecessary evidence of reliance for purposes of possible litigation. Furthermore, there is almost always reliance in the shape of foregone alternative opportunities that is very hard to measure. If a reversal of the onus of proof combined with consideration of the possibility that the promisee might have foregone other opportunities to contract will make it practically impossible for the promisor to disprove reliance, the present position will remain in substance unchanged in which case the present rule might as well be preserved. If, on the other hand, it is envisaged that reliance can be readily disproved on a showing that the promisee would probably not have found another opportunity to make a similar contract, it may be objected that reliance, in the form of a possibility (up to a probability of .49) of the promisee's making an alternative contract, will be left unprotected.

---

18 Waddams, *ibid.*, at pp. 130-31.

19 See Atiyah, "Contracts, Promises and the Law of Obligations", 94 L.Q.R. 193 (1978), at p. 217.

5.140 For these reasons there seems to be insufficient reason to advocate the judicial or legislative change of the present rule.

2. Third Party Beneficiary Contracts

5.150 Where one person makes a promise to another for the benefit of a third, the promise is enforceable at the suit of the promisee but not generally, according to current law, at the suit of the beneficiary. Ultimately, it seems desirable and likely that the law of contracts will be altered to permit an action to be brought by the beneficiary.[19a] The precise form of such a change raises complex questions and falls outside the scope of this work. The only question addressed here is the proper scope of the promisee's remedy.

5.160 It has been recognized since the decision in *Beswick v. Beswick*[20] in 1968 that the promisee may sue for specific performance of the contractual obligation. However the view was then expressed, by four of the five law lords, that in an action for damages the promisee would recover only nominal damages.[21] If the beneficiary has no remedy and the promisee can recover only nominal damages, it is no exaggeration to describe the result, as Lord Reid did, as "grossly unjust".[22]

5.170 The injustice was avoided in *Beswick v. Beswick* by granting a decree of specific performance, chiefly because damages were inadequate. There is an oddity in the reasoning here. If nominal damages are appropriate because the plaintiff really has suffered no loss, it follows that no compensation is deserved. Damages in that case are not "inadequate": they fully meet the justice of the plaintiff's claim. On the other hand if, as the court held, the promisee is entitled to specific performance, that must be because the promisee has bought the benefit of the promised performance and is therefore entitled to compel a performance that has been paid for. It seems odd, in those circumstances, to say that the promisee suffers no loss if the performance is not rendered.

5.180 There are arguments, however, that substantial damages are appropriate in such a case. One argument is that the promisee will lose the satisfaction of benefiting the third party, a satisfaction that is presumably worth to the promisee what otherwise could have been asked of

---

19a See *London Drugs Ltd. v. Kuehne & Nagel International Ltd.*, [1992] 3 S.C.R. 299, 97 D.L.R. (4th) 261.

20 [1968] A.C. 58 (H.L.).

21 *Supra*, at p. 72 (Lord Reid), p. 80 (Lord Hodson), p. 83 (Lord Guest, agreeing with Lord Reid), pp. 101-2 (Lord Upjohn). *Contra*, Lord Pearce at p. 88. To the same effect is Megarry V.-C., in *Ross v. Caunters*, [1979] 3 All E.R. 580 (Ch.), at p. 583, where he said of a case where a solicitor fails to effect an intended gift to a third party: "the only person who has a valid contractual claim (*i.e.*, the client or the client's estate) has suffered no loss". But see Briggs, "Privity Problems in Damages for Breach of Contract", 131 New L.J. 343 (1981).

22 *Beswick v. Beswick*, *supra*, footnote 20, at p. 73.

the promisor.[23] Another argument is that the promisee's right to have performance rendered in accordance with the promise is a valuable right that could be compromised for a cash payment; a rational promisor would pay up to the full cost of performance for release from the obligation. If the promisor breaks the promise and specific enforcement is not decreed, there would seem to be a case for an award of damages in lieu of specific enforcement, and there is ample reason for measuring such damages by the price that a rational promisor would have paid for release from the obligation.[24] It is suggested in a later chapter[25] that this measure of damages is defensible on compensatory principles, for the promisor, by breaking the promise in such circumstances as to preclude an actual decree of specific performance, deprives the promisee of a valuable right, namely the right to bargain with the promisor for release. Against this argument can be made the accusation of circularity. It is only where a contract is specifically enforceable that damages in lieu of specific performance can properly be measured by the defendant's gain from breach, but the third party beneficiary contract is said to be specifically enforceable only because damages are nominal, and therefore, inadequate. So if a persuasive case is made for substantial damages the case for specific enforcement disappears. A possible answer to this point is that an injunction restraining breach could be granted to the promisee even though damages were considered to be adequate, inadequacy of damages not being a requirement for an injunction.[26] Substantial damages could then be defended on the basis of an award in lieu of an injunction.

5.190 These complexities indicate, it is submitted, that the only ultimately satisfactory solution will be the recognition of a right of action in the third party, either directly or by some such device as trust. In the absence of such recognition, however, it is not alien to the traditions of the common law to use such devices as are available to achieve just results.

3. Damages Measured by Reliance

5.200 By the normal rule of contract damages the party complaining is entitled to be put in as good a position, so far as money can do it, as

23 This being the opportunity foregone, and so the cost to the promisee of benefiting the third party. See Briggs, *op. cit.*, footnote 21. In *Woodar Investment Development Ltd. v. Wimpey Construction U.K. Ltd.*, [1980] 1 W.L.R. 277 (H.L.), at p. 297, Lord Keith suggested that where a person contracted for a holiday for himself and his family, damage caused to the family members for non-performance might properly be recoverable by the person as part of his own damages on the basis of expenses incurred by him to replace the benefits of which the family had been deprived, or as mitigation of the consequences of the deprivation. Lord Wilberforce, at p. 283, also suggested that such a result might be supported "as a broad decision on the measure of damages". See also *Linden Gardens Trust Ltd. v. Lenesta Sludge Disposals Ltd.*, [1994] 1 A.C. 85 (H.L.); *Darlington Borough Council v. Wiltshier Northern Ltd.*, [1994] 1 W.L.R. 68 (C.A.).

24 See 9.70-9.130, *infra*.

25 *Ibid.*

26 See Sharpe, *op. cit.*, footnote 16, at 9.10-9.20.

though the contract had been performed.[27] Where the plaintiff can show that a profitable contract was made, therefore, the normal rule will afford full compensation. The plaintiff will not be entitled, in addition, to recover expenses incurred in reliance on the contract because such expenses would have had to be incurred in any event in order to earn the promised performance.[28]

5.210 If, on the other hand, the contract was an unprofitable one to the plaintiff, the expenses may exceed the value of the defendant's expected performance. In such a case it is not clear that the plaintiff ought to recover the full amount of the expenses. In a sense, the defendant's breach confers a benefit on the plaintiff, the benefit of releasing the latter from a losing bargain. If the plaintiff is to be put by the award of damages only into as good a position as would have been occupied had the contract been performed, this benefit ought to be taken into account.

5.220 These questions arose in the English Court of Appeal in *Anglia Television Ltd. v. Reed*.[29] The defendant, an actor, agreed to play a leading part in a television film to be produced by the plaintiff. The plaintiff had incurred expenses in preparation for production, some before the agreement with the defendant and some afterwards. On the defendant's repudiation of the contract, the plaintiff cancelled the production and abandoned the enterprise altogether. Application of the normal rule for measurement of contract damages would have required an assessment of the profits likely to have been made from the film had it not been cancelled. It was clearly, at best, a highly speculative matter. Further, there are facts that suggest that the film probably would not have been profitable. If the enterprise had been likely to succeed, one would have expected the plaintiff to have procured a substitute actor rather than to have abandoned the enterprise altogether. Nor does Lord Denning's bald summary of the plot suggest the prospect of a great artistic achievement: "Anglia Television Ltd., the plaintiffs, were minded in 1968 to make a film of a play for television entitled 'The Man in the Wood'. It portrayed an American man married to an English woman. The American has an adventure in an English wood. The film was to last for 90 minutes."[30] The English Court of Appeal held that the plaintiff was entitled to elect to recover the expenses, including the pre-contract expenses, as an alternative to the normal measure of contract damages. One way of explaining the election would be to say that the plaintiff is entitled, if the plaintiff so wishes, to be put in as good a position as was occupied before the contract was made. But this rationale would not explain recovery of the pre-contract expenses,

27 See 5.30, *supra*.

28 See *Pitcher v. Shoebottom* (1970), 14 D.L.R. (3d) 522, [1971] 1 O.R. 106 (H.C.J.).

29 [1972] 1 Q.B. 60 (C.A.). Reliance expenses were also allowed in *Bell v. Robutka* (1964), 48 D.L.R. (2d) 755 (Alta. Dist. Ct.), affd 55 D.L.R. (2d) 436 (S.C. App. Div.).

30 *Anglia Television Ltd. v. Reed*, *supra*, footnote 29, at p. 62.

which the plaintiff had already incurred before the defendant had undertaken any obligation at all.[31] Lord Denning justified the recovery of the pre-contract expenses as follows: "He [the defendant] must have contemplated — or, at any rate, it is reasonably to be imputed to him — that if he broke his contract, all that expenditure would be wasted, whether or not it was incurred before or after the contract. He must pay damages for all the expenditure so wasted and thrown away."[32] This, however, does not seem fully convincing, for the conclusion that the pre-contract expense was "wasted" by the defendant's breach implies a supposition that had the defendant not broken his contract the expense would not have been "wasted". In other words, the presumption is that, had the defendant performed his contract, the expenses including the pre-contract expenses would have been recovered in profits, the very thing that the plaintiff failed to prove.

5.230 Nevertheless, the result of the case may be supported on the basis that, in the absence of proof one way or the other of the profitability of the movie, it is to be assumed against the wrongdoer that the enterprise would at least have broken even, that is, that the expenses would at least have been covered by revenue. It is suggested that it is not unjust to make such a presumption against the defendant who is the party in breach of contract. It would still be open, on this approach, for the defendant to prove, if possible, that the expenses would not have been recovered from revenues, and on proof of that fact, the defendant ought not to be liable to pay for the expenses.[32a]

5.240 This view of the law is supported by the decision of the British Columbia Court of Appeal in *Bowlay Logging Ltd. v. Domtar Ltd.*,[33] where a logging contract was terminated by the timber owner's breach. It was held that in principle the logger could elect to claim its expenses, but that if the owner could show that the logger would have incurred a loss on completion of the contract, nominal damages only should be awarded. Berger J., at first instance, said clearly that the plaintiff was not to be put in a better position than it would have occupied on full performance and that the onus of showing the contract to be unprofitable was on the defendant. He said:

---

31 The question of pre-contract expenses is discussed at 2.40, *supra*.

32 *Anglia Television Ltd. v. Reed, supra*, footnote 29, at p. 64.

32a *Health Care Developers Inc. v. Newfoundland* (1996), 136 D.L.R. (4th) 609 (Nfld. C.A.), at pp. 640-41, citing this paragraph.

33 (1978), 87 D.L.R. (3d) 325 (B.C.S.C.), affd 135 D.L.R. (3d) 179 (C.A.), followed in *C. & P. Haulage v. Middleton*, [1983] 1 W.L.R. 1461 (C.A.); *CCC Films (London) Ltd. v. Impact Quadrant Films Ltd.*, [1985] Q.B. 16; *Sunshine Vacation Villas Ltd. v. Hudson's Bay Co.* (1984), 13 D.L.R. (4th) 93, 58 B.C.L.R. 33 (C.A.), citing this passage; *DSI Management Inc. v. A.T.S. Electro-lube Ltd.* (1989), 24 C.P.R. (3d) 193 (B.C.S.C.); *Accord Holdings Ltd. v. Excelsior Life Insurance* (1985), 62 A.R. 234 (C.A.).

> If the law of contract were to move from compensating for the consequences of breach to compensating for the consequences of entering into contracts, the law would run contrary to the normal expectations of the world of commerce. The burden of risk would be shifted from the plaintiff to the defendant. The defendant would become the insurer of the plaintiff's enterprise. Moreover the amount of the damages would increase not in relation to the gravity or consequences of the breach but in relation to the inefficiency with which the plaintiff carried out the contract. The greater his expenses owing to inefficiency, the greater the damages.
>
> The fundamental principle upon which damages are measured under the law of contract is *restitutio in integrum*. The principle contended for here by the plaintiff would entail the award of damages not to compensate the plaintiff but to punish the defendant. So it has been argued that a defendant ought to be able to insist that the plaintiff's damages should not include any losses that would have been incurred if the contract had been fully performed. According to Treitel, *Law of Contract*, 3rd ed. (1970), at p. 798:
>
> > "It is uncertain whether the plaintiff can recover his entire expenses if those exceed the benefit which he would have derived from the contract, had there been no breach."
>
> Ogus, in *The Law of Damages* (1973), has said at p. 347 that, "it is not yet clear whether English law imposes this limitation".
>
> The tendency in American law is to impose such a limitation. And I think Canadian law ought to impose it too.
>
> The onus is on the defendant.[34]

Berger J. went on to hold that the onus had been met, and that the plaintiff was therefore entitled only to nominal damages.

5.250 In the British Columbia Court of Appeal, the decision and the reasoning were affirmed. Seaton J.A. made it clear that the damages recoverable, in the case of an unprofitable enterprise, will be the amount (if any) by which the plaintiff's loss is greater than it would have been if there had been no breach, approving a passage to this effect from Corbin:

> If, on the other hand, it is proved that full performance would have resulted in a net loss to the plaintiff, the recoverable damages should not include the amount of this loss. If the amount of his expenditure at the date of breach is less than the expected net loss, he should be given judgment for nominal damages only. If these expenditures exceed this loss, he should be given judgment for the excess.[35]

4. Wrongful Interference with Contracts

5.260 Several kinds of action may lie against one who induces another to break a contract with the plaintiff. These include the tort of inducing

34 *Supra*, at p. 335. See also *Commonwealth of Australia v. Amann Aviation Pty. Ltd.* (1991), 174 C.L.R. 64 (Aust. H.C.).

35 *Corbin on Contracts*, Vol. 5A (St. Paul, West Publishing Co., 1964), §1033, quoted in *Bowlay Logging Ltd. v. Domtar Ltd.* (1982), 135 D.L.R. (3d) 179 (C.A.), at p. 181.

breach of contract,[36] conspiracy,[37] intimidation[38] and causing harm by wrongful means.[39] The gist of the plaintiff's complaint is that the plaintiff has been deprived of the benefit of a contract and the *prima facie* measure of damages will be the amount that could have been recovered in a judgment against the contracting party for breach of contract. A primary reason for the development of the action against the person inducing breach was that the contracting party might be unable to pay: "The servant or contractor may be utterly unable to pay anything like the amount of the damage sustained entirely from the wrongful act of the defendant; and it would seem unjust, and contrary to the general principles of law, if such wrongdoer were not responsible for the damage caused by his wrongful and malicious act."[40]

5.270 However, the plaintiff is not entitled to recover damages twice over for the same loss, and it was accepted in *Jones v. Fabbi*[41] that judgment could be given against both the contract breaker and the inducer on the understanding that satisfaction of the judgment by the inducer would reduce the liability of the contract breaker.

5.280 The inducer's liability, however, is not necessarily restricted to that of the contract breaker. In *Lumley v. Gye*,[42] it was stressed that the actions were different actions for different wrongs and might lead to different damages: "the action on the contract and the action against the malicious wrong-doer may be for a different matter; and the damages occasioned by such malicious injury might be calculated on a very different principle from the amount of the debt which might be the only sum recoverable on the contract".[43] Erle J. gave the following examples:

> The remedy on the contract may be inadequate, as where the measure of damages is restricted; or in the case of non-payment of a debt where the damage may be bankruptcy to the creditor who is disappointed, but the measure of damages against the debtor is interest only; or, in the case of the non-delivery of the goods, the disappointment may lead to a heavy forfeiture under a contract to complete a work within a time, but the measure of damages against the vendor of the goods for non-delivery may be only the difference between the contract price and the market value of the goods in question at the time of the breach. In such cases, he who procures the damage maliciously might justly be made responsible beyond the liability of the contractor.[44]

[36] *Lumley v. Gye* (1853), 2 El. & Bl. 216, 118 E.R. 749 (Q.B.). See *OBG Ltd. v. Allan*, [2008] 1 A.C. 1, where the House of Lords held that liability for inducing breach of contract was a form of accessory liability.
[37] *Quinn v. Leathem*, [1901] A.C. 495 (H.L.).
[38] *Rookes v. Barnard*, [1964] A.C. 1129 (H.L.); *Morgan v. Fry*, [1968] 1 Q.B. 521, revd on other grounds [1968] 2 Q.B. 710 (C.A.).
[39] See *Pratt v. British Medical Ass'n*, [1919] 1 K.B. 244.
[40] *Lumley v. Gye*, *supra*, footnote 36, at pp. 230-1, *per* Crompton J.
[41] (1973), 37 D.L.R. (3d) 27 (B.C.S.C.), at p. 28, *per* Hinkson J.
[42] *Supra*, footnote 36.
[43] *Lumley v. Gye*, *supra*, footnote 36 at pp. 229-30, *per* Crompton J.
[44] *Lumley v. Gye*, *supra*, at p. 234. Another possibility is that an award might be based on the profit made by the wrongdoer. See chapter 9, *infra*.

5.290 It has been held that the inducer may be liable not only for the loss of the contract breach which was induced but also subject to rules of remoteness, for other losses such as the loss of another contract which the loss of the broken contract made inevitable,[45] for expenses incurred in preparing a case against the defendant,[46] and where some pecuniary loss is shown, for intangible losses.[47] It is clear too that when renewal of the contract was probable, damages may be given against the tortfeasor that exceed those recoverable from the contracting party for breach of contract. The principle is subject to remoteness, and in *Jones v. Fabbi*[48] a claim based on probable renewal of the contract in question was held to be too speculative, but in *Morgan v. Fry*[49] where the defendant wrongfully caused the plaintiff to be dismissed from his employment, damages were allowed on the basis that the plaintiff would probably have retained his employment for five years. The judge found on the evidence that the plaintiff would probably not have retained his job until retirement age, but it would seem that if he probably would have done so, damages would be calculated on that basis with an appropriate discount for contingencies[50] even though the employer would presumably if sued be liable only for the period of reasonable notice he ought to have given. Even where the contract is technically unenforceable, damages may be given for inducing breach if the contract probably would have been performed.[51] In *Vale v. Int'l Longshoremen's and Warehousemen's Union, Local 508*,[52] the defendant union had wrongfully procured the plaintiff's dismissal from his employment. The plaintiff had already recovered damages from his employer but was held to be entitled to recover from the defendant any additional loss that he could establish.

5.300 Damages for inducing breach of contract are said to be at large[53] by which is meant that in a case where damage would be expected to ensue damage will be inferred even though it cannot be specifically proved.[54] Many cases of

---

45 *Jones v. Fabbi, supra*, footnote 41; *Polar Ice Express Inc. v. Arctic Glacier Inc.* (2007), 83 Alta. L.R. (4th) 299 (Q.B.), at para. 117.

46 *British Motor Trade Ass'n v. Salvadori*, [1949] Ch. 556.

47 *Pratt v. British Medical Ass'n, supra*, footnote 39. See 3.1250-3.1430, *supra*.

48 *Supra*, footnote 41.

49 [1968] 1 Q.B. 521, revd on other grounds [1968] Q.B. 710 (C.A.).

50 See *Edwards v. Society of Graphical & Allied Trades*, discussed at 5.1270, *infra*.

51 *Unident Ltd. v. DeLong* (1981), 131 D.L.R. (3d) 225 (N.S.S.C.T.D.). But see *OBG Ltd. v. Allan*, [2008] 1 A.C. 1, where liability for inducing breach of contract was said to be "accessory".

52 [1979] 5 W.W.R. 231 (B.C.C.A.).

53 *Goldsoll v. Goldman*, [1914] 2 Ch. 603; *L.M. Rosen Realty Ltd. v. D'Amore* (1982), 132 D.L.R. (3d) 648 (H.C.J.), vard 7 D.L.R. (4th) 285, 45 O.R. (2d) 405 (C.A.). See also *Ernst & Young v. Stuart* (1997), 144 D.L.R. (4th) 328, [1997] 5 W.W.R. 253 (B.C.C.A.); *Polar Ice Express Inc. v. Arctic Glacier Inc.* (2007), 83 Alta. L.R. (4th) 299 (Q.B.); *Drouillard v. Cogeco Cable Inc.* (2007), 282 D.L.R. (4th) 644 (C.A.), at para. 42. And see 13.80, *infra*.

54 "[T]he damage may be inferred, that is to say, that if the breach which has been procurred by the defendant has been such as must in the ordinary course of business inflict damage upon the plaintiff, then the plaintiff may succeed without proof of any particular damage which has been occasioned him", *per* Neville J., in *Goldsoll v. Goldman, supra*, footnote 53, at p. 615.

inducing breach of contracts lend themselves to assessment of damages on the basis of what reasonable fee the plaintiff might have demanded to release the contractor from the engagement.[55] Even where the plaintiff cannot prove any other specific loss, the plaintiff can often realistically claim to have lost the opportunity to bargain with the defendant for such a release.[55a]

[*The next page is* 5-13]

[55] See 1.450-1.480, *supra*, and 9.70-9.130, *infra*.

[55a] See *Delphinium Ltée v. 512842 N.B. Inc.* (2006), 307 N.B.R. (2d) 284 (Q.B.), at para. 224, vard 2008 NBCA 56, citing this and the preceding paragraphs.

5. Breach of Warranty of Authority

5.310 The imposition of liability on an agent for breach of warranty of authority is on the borderline between contract and tort and has sometimes been said to be an instance of strict liability for innocent misrepresentation.[56] But if the juridicial basis of the action were tortious, one would expect damages to be measured by the loss to the plaintiff, if any, rather than by the gain that would have been made if the agent really had had authority. It is the latter measure that has been generally adopted,[57] indicating that for the purposes of damage assessment at least, the action is regarded as more closely akin to contract than tort. The difficulty with a contractual analysis is that it seems that the plaintiff gives no consideration to the agent in exchange for the latter's warranty. The only contract envisaged (besides the agency contract between the principal and agent) is usually one between the plaintiff and the principal. However, it is possible, as in analogous situations[58] to construct a collateral contract[59] whereby the agent warrants authority and in return the plaintiff enters into the transaction proposed, thereby changing position and incurring a detriment, and also often conferring some sort of benefit on the agent (for example, enabling the agent to earn a commission).

5.320 Liability can be imposed on an agent for breach of warranty of authority even where the agent has not purported to enter into a contract. In *Starkey v. Bank of England*,[60] the rule was stated to extend "to every transaction of business into which a third party is induced to enter by a representation that the person with whom he is doing business has the authority of some other person".[61]

5.330 A warranty of authority however is not necessarily a guarantee of the success of the transaction. The defendant warrants that the defendant has authority not that the principal will perform,[62] or even that the principal will be liable.[62a] Thus, where the principal would not have been liable even if the

56 Williston, "Liability for Honest Misrepresentation", 24 Harv. L.R. 415 (1911), at pp. 422-3. See *Firbank's Executors v. Humphreys* (1886), 18 Q.B.D. 54 (C.A.), at p. 62, *per* Lindley L.J.; *Austin v. Real Estate Exchange* (1912), 2 D.L.R. 324 (B.C.C.A.), at p. 325, *per* Irving J.; *Alberta Pacific Grain Co. v. Merchants Cartage Co.* (1914), 18 D.L.R. 584 (B.C.C.A.), at p. 585, *per* Irving J.

57 *Godwin v. Francis* (1870), L.R. 5 C.P. 295 at p. 308; *Re National Coffee Palace Co.; Ex p. Panmure* (1883), 24 Ch. D. 367 (C.A.), at p. 371, *per* Brett M.R.; *Simons v. Patchett* (1857), 7 El. & Bl. 568 at p. 574, 119 E.R. 1357, *per* Crompton J.; *V/O Rasnoimport v. Guthrie & Co.*, [1966] 1 Lloyd's Rep. 1; *Austin v. Real Estate Exchange*, *supra*, footnote 56; *Bank of Nova Scotia v. Hatfield* (1921), 58 D.L.R. 136 (N.B.K.B.), at p. 144, *per* Chandler J. In *Still Creek Terminals Ltd. v. Karlsruher-Sanatorium A.G.* (1983), 49 B.C.L.R. 245 (C.A.), out of pocket loss was awarded in a case where loss of bargain damages were not available.

58 See Waddams, *The Law of Contracts*, 5th ed. (Toronto, Canada Law Book, 2005), pp. 307-8.

59 This was the basis of *Collen v. Wright* (1857), 8 El. & Bl. 647 at pp. 657-8, 120 E.R. 241, *per* Willes J.

60 [1903] A.C. 114 (H.L.).

61 *Supra*, at p. 119, *per* Lord Davey. This case was followed in *British Russian Gazette & Trade Outlook, Ltd. v. Associated Newspapers, Ltd.*, [1933] 2 K.B. 616 (C.A.); *Heskell v. Continental Express Ltd.*, [1950] 1 All E.R. 1033 (K.B.); *Austin v. Real Estate Exchange*, *supra*, footnote 56.

defendant had the authority claimed, the latter will not be liable either for loss of the bargain[63], though the defendant may be liable for out-of-pocket loss.[64] In *Heskell v. Continental Express*,[65] a broker had signed a bill of lading on behalf of the shipowners although the goods had not been shipped and there was in fact no contract of carriage. Devlin J. held that the broker was not liable because the shipowner would not in these circumstances have been liable even if the broker had had authority or indeed, even if the shipowner had signed the bill personally:

> The right way of testing the matter is, I think, to treat the bill of lading as if it had been signed personally by the owner and issued personally by him.
> On that supposition how does the matter stand? In considering this, it seems to me of the first importance to remember that the bill of lading is not itself a contract of carriage and that it is not contended that any contract of carriage was ever made ... The whole truth of this matter is that, in the absence of a contract of carriage, the bill of lading is a nullity, and it would have been none the less so even if it had been issued at a board meeting of [the shipowners] or passed by a resolution of the company in a general meeting. The fact that it was issued without authority robbed it of no virtue ... Accordingly, [the plaintiff] would have no claim against the shipowner, and so can recover no damages against the broker.[66]

5.340 A number of cases concerning the issue of securities appear to contradict this approach. These are cases where the defendant, purporting to act on behalf of a corporate body of some sort, issues securities to the plaintiff that turn out to be beyond the powers of the corporate body to issue. An example is *Richardson v. Williamson*[67] where the plaintiff lent £70 to a building society and received from the defendant directors a receipt with the society's promise to repay. It turned out that the society had no power to borrow. It would appear that on the principle applied in *Heskell v. Continental Express*,[68] the defendants should not have been liable for even if they had had the authority they claimed, the society itself would not have been liable,

---

62 The measure of damages was said in *Re National Coffee Palace, supra*, footnote 57, at p. 372, *per* Brett M.R., to be "what the plaintiff would have gained by the contract which the defendant warranted should be made". Where the principal is insolvent, no damages will be recoverable against the agent; *Spedding v. Nevell* (1869), L.R. 4 C.P. 212 at p. 226; *Simons v. Patchett, supra*, footnote 57, at p. 574, *per* Crompton J.; *Godwin v. Francis, supra*, footnote 57, at p. 308, *per* Montague Smith J.; *Delta Construction Co. Ltd. v. Lidstone* (1979), 96 D.L.R. (3d) 457 (Nfld. S.C.T.D.).

62a See *Siculiana Holdings Inc. v. J. Gioia Holdings Inc.* (1994), 42 R.P.R. (2d) 143 (Ont. Ct. (Gen. Div.)), at p. 154, citing this passage.

63 *Pow v. Davis* (1861), 1 B. & S. 220, 121 E.R. 697 (insufficient documents for effective lease); *Duncan v. Beck* (1914), 20 D.L.R. 682 (Sask. S.C.), at pp. 683-4, *per* Lamont J.; *Kortzman v. O'Brien* (1932), 41 O.W.N. 344 (H.C.J.), affd [1933] O.W.N. 215 (C.A.); *Burt v. Woodward*, [1942] 2 W.W.R. 464 (B.C.C.A.). But see *Still Creek Terminals Ltd. v. Karlsruher-Sanatorium A.G., supra*, footnote 57.

64 *Still Creek Terminals Ltd. v. Karlsruher-Sanatorium A.G., supra*, footnote 57.

65 [1950] 1 All E.R. 1033 (K.B.).

66 *Supra*, at pp. 1043-5.

67 (1871), L.R. 6 Q.B. 276.

68 *Supra*, footnote 65.

and so the plaintiff lost nothing by breach of warranty of authority. Nevertheless, the plaintiff recovered and the same result has been reached in several other similar cases.[69] The explanation, it is submitted, is that the warranty is construed to be not only a warranty of authority, but a warranty of validity of the securities. That this is so appears from statements in the cases:

> ... I think upon the facts the inference is, that the defendants do represent upon this instrument that they are authorized on behalf of the society to borrow money, and that the society *will be liable* on this contract of loan.[70]
> ... the defendants, in effect, representing that they had authority on behalf of the society to give ... a *binding* certificate of indebtedness.[71]
> If the [defendant's] assertion had been true he [the plaintiff] would have had *valid* debenture stock.[72]

5.350 These cases are to be explained, it is submitted, as cases where there was a warranty of validity of the security and are not authority for departure from the general rule in cases of simple warranty of authority.

5.360 The damages against the purported agent are measured by what the plaintiff would in fact have gained had the defendant actually had authority.[73] It has often been stressed that this is not always the same as the damages that would have been recovered in an action against the alleged principal.[74] Thus, the question is not necessarily answered by determining that the principal would in that case have been legally liable. Not every debtor pays debts and it has often been stated that if the principal were insolvent, the plaintiff would not be entitled to any substantial damages from the defendant, for it could not be shown in that case that the plaintiff would have been better off even if the defendant had had the authority claimed and the alleged principal had been legally bound.[75]

5.370 There may be other circumstances than insolvency that make it improbable that a debtor will actually pay. An example is the case of a foreign debtor with no assets in the jurisdiction, who has refused to pay. In *Meek v. Wendt*,[76] the plaintiff had obtained a judgment in England against an American insurance company for £1,000 but the defendant had refused to pay. The defendant purported to settle the insurer's liability for £300 and issued certificates on their face entitling the plaintiff to payment at a bank in London. The settlement was repudiated by the insurance company on the ground that the defendant had no authority, and the certificates were dishonoured. It was held that the plaintiff was entitled to recover £300 from

69 *Weeks v. Propert* (1873), L.R. 8 C.P. 427; *Firbank's Executors v. Humphreys* (1886), 18 Q.B.D. 54 (C.A.).
70 *Richardson v. Williamson*, *supra*, footnote 67, at p. 279, *per* Cockburn C.J. [emphasis added].
71 *Richardson v. Williamson*, *supra*, at p. 280, *per* Hannen J. [emphasis added].
72 *Firbank's Executors v. Humphreys* (1886), 18 Q.B.D. 54 (C.A.), *per* Lord Esher M.R. [emphasis added].
73 *Austin v. Real Estate Exchange* (1912), 2 D.L.R. 324 (B.C.C.A.).
74 *Simons v. Patchett* (1857), 7 El. & Bl. 568 at p. 574, 119 E.R. 1357, *per* Crompton J.
75 See footnote 62, *supra*.
76 (1888), 21 Q.B.D. 126.

the defendant. At first sight this appears to put the plaintiff in a better position than would have been occupied if the defendant had had authority: after all, the plaintiff already had a judgment against the insurance company for £1,000; there seems no reason to suppose that a contractual promise to pay £300 (even a binding one) is of any greater value. But the court evidently took the view that had the bank certificates been issued with authority they would in fact have been honoured. The court plainly did not intend to depart from the general rule that the measure of damages was what the plaintiff would have gained had the defendant had authority. Having quoted a rule to this effect from *Re National Coffee Palace Co.*,[77] Charles J. continued: "Applying this rule to the present case the plaintiff by losing the particular contract which was to have been made has primƒ facie lost the expenses thrown away, and the sum of 300*l*., which I have no doubt he would have obtained without delay or difficulty in London from the Anglo-Californian Bank within three days after sight of the approved certificates."[78]

5.380 The result of the case can be defended, it is submitted, but only on the basis of a finding of fact that the certificates, if duly authorized, would probably have been honoured. There may perhaps have been a loss of commercial reputation involved in the dishonour of bank certificates that would not have attended the mere failure to pay a judgment debt.

5.390 Another case which raises the question of a different measure of recovery against the defendant from that against the alleged principal is *Chitholie v. Nash & Co.*[79] There the defendant wrongly purported to have authority to sell land to the plaintiff. When it became clear that the defendant had no authority and so the owner of the land was not bound, the plaintiff sued the defendant. The value of the land had risen by the time the action came to trial and the plaintiff claimed damages based on the judgment date value of the land arguing that he would have recovered that measure from the owner on the basis of the then recent case of *Wroth v. Tyler*.[80] Talbot J. rejected this argument saying that:

> . . . he thought himself bound to remember . . . that he was dealing with an action for damages for breach of warranty of authority. He was not, as against these defendants, awarding damages in substitution for an order of specific performance. He was bound, as he saw it, to follow the normal common law rule as to the measure of damages for breach of contract for sale of land. In his view, to depart from that normal rule would be to place upon the shoulders of the defendants the burden of a higher award of damages due not to their breach but to events which had occurred after the breach and over which they had no control.[81]

5.400 Against this result it might be argued that, had the defendant had authority,

77 (1883), 24 Ch. D. 367 (C.A.).

78 *Meek v. Wendt*, *supra*, footnote 76, at p. 129.

79 (1973), 229 E.G. 787 (Q.B.).

80 [1974] Ch. 30.

81 *Supra*, footnote 79.

the plaintiff could have sued the owner and recovered, and therefore should recover the same measure of damages from the defendant. Further, it has since been held in *Johnson v. Agnew*[82] that the calculation of damages should not vary according to whether or not the claim was made under *Lord Cairns' Act*. However, it is submitted that the result reached by Talbot J. is sound. It was argued in an earlier chapter that there is merit in a rule that crystallizes the buyer's damages in such cases at the earliest date when the plaintiff acting reasonably could have made a substitute purchase.[83] In an action against the owner, supposing the defendant to have had authority, it would usually be reasonable for the plaintiff to refrain from making a substitute purchase because the plaintiff would reasonably expect to obtain a decree of specific performance. But in an action against the agent, as soon as it appears that there was no authority, the plaintiff knows that possession of the land will never be recovered, and the plaintiff ought, therefore, to make a decision at that point on whether to purchase a substitute. *Johnson v. Agnew*, as has earlier been argued,[84] is authority for early crystallization of damages as soon as, to use Lord Wilberforce's words, the contract is "lost" to the plaintiff. In the *Chitholie* case, this was when the plaintiff learned of the defendant's lack of authority.[85]

5.410 The plaintiff will be entitled to expenses incurred that would not have been incurred if the defendant had been duly authorized, subject to the rules of remoteness and mitigation. Such expenses include costs of litigation with the alleged principal where the proceedings are naturally, reasonably, and *bona fide* instituted in consequence of the warranty.[86] In *Spedding v. Nevell*,[87] where the defendant had purported to give a lease and the plaintiff had assigned the lease to a third party, the plaintiff was involved in two sets of litigation. He recovered the costs of the litigation with the alleged principal but not the costs of the dispute with the assignee, for this was held to be too remote. As an alternative[88] to damages for the loss of the bargain with the alleged principal, the plaintiff can recover expenses incurred in reliance on the contract.[89]

82 [1980] A.C. 367 (H.L.).

83 See 1.650-1.1100, *supra*.

84 See 1.1020, *supra*.

85 In *Suleman v. Shahsavari*, [1988] 1 W.L.R. 1181 (Ch. D.) where the plaintiff did not know until the judgment of the lack of the defendant's authority, damages based on the judgment date value were awarded. Similarly, in *Habton Farms v. Nimmo*, [2003] 3 W.L.R. 633 (C.A.), where the contract was for the sale of a horse that later died, the full contract price was held to be recoverable because the postponement of a new sale was caused by the defendant's warranty of authority.

86 *Hughes v. Graeme* (1864), 33 L.J.Q.B. 335; *Cunliffe v. Planta* (1920), 54 D.L.R. 196 (B.C.C.A.).

87 (1869), L.R. 4 C.P. 212.

88 See 5.200-5.250, *supra*.

89 *Collen v. Wright* (1857), 7 El. & Bl. 301, 119 E.R. 1259, affd 8 El. & Bl. 647, 120 E.R. 241; *Pow v. Davis* (1861), 1 B. & S. 220, 121 E.R. 697; *Kortzman v. O'Brien* (1932), 41 O.W.N. 344 (H.C.J.), affd [1933] O.W.N. 215 (C.A.).

6. Misrepresentation[90]

(1) Introduction

5.420 Liability for misrepresentation is an area of law that crosses the boundaries between contract, tort, and restitution. A false statement is made that induces the plaintiff to buy goods from the defendant. If the statement is treated as a promise, the plaintiff will be entitled to the value the goods would have had if the statement had been true. If the misrepresentation is treated as a tort, the plaintiff will be entitled to be put back in the position occupied before the statement was made. From the restitution point of view, it is unjust that the defendant should in making a false statement be enriched at the plaintiff's expense. In the following paragraphs the measure of damages in each of these circumstances is discussed. In several jurisdictions statutory provisions are applicable, and these are also discussed. It has been held that damages for other wrongful conduct inducing a transaction, such as breach of fiduciary duty, are to be assessed on the same basis as damages for fraud.[91]

(2) Contractual terms

5.430 The question of when statements are to be treated as promises is outside the scope of a work on damages,[92] but it is important to note that the test for determining when statements made to induce contracts are themselves contractual is a very elusive one — so elusive indeed that some commentators have concluded that there is no practical distinction at all. Lord Denning on one occasion went so far as to say: "Whenever . . . the man ought to pay damages, I find that the statement is a warranty."[93]

5.440 This being the state of the law, it can hardly be doubted that the perceived justice of the contractual measure of damages will in many cases determine the initial classification of the statement as contractual. The application of the contractual measure of damages may have quite startling consequences. Thus, suppose that a private seller honestly and carefully describes a painting as a Constable and agrees to sell it to a dealer for $1,000. In fact it is a copy with an actual value, let it be supposed, of $800, but the value of a genuine Constable would have been $50,000. It seems a very harsh result to hold the seller liable for damages of $49,200. That measure of damages is only justified if the seller can be taken to have promised to deliver a genuine Constable, and the injustice of awarding contractual damages is a natural and,

---

90 See McLauchlan, "Assessment of Damages for Misrepresentation Inducing Contract", 6 Otago L.R. 370 (1986).

91 *Jacks v. Davis*, [1980] 6 W.W.R. 11 and 112 D.L.R. (3d) 223 (B.C.S.C.), affd 141 D.L.R. (3d) 355 (C.A.); *Canson Enterprises Ltd. v. Boughton & Co.*, [1996] 1 W.W.R. 412, 11 B.C.L.R. (3d) 262 (C.A.), leave to appeal to S.C.C. refused 203 N.R. 78*n*, 48 C.P.C. (3d) 384*n*.

92 See Waddams, *The Law of Contracts*, 5th ed. (Toronto, Canada Law Book, 2005), pp. 289-93.

93 See 41 Aust. L.J. (1967), at p. 293.

it is submitted, perfectly respectable reason for the court's declining to categorize the seller's statement as a warranty in the first place.

5.450 Even more startling consequences would ensue if an innocent private seller were liable for consequential damages such as personal injuries caused by reliance on an innocent and careful statement of roadworthiness of an automobile. Again, it is probable that these results will in practice be avoided by the court's failing to categorize such a statement as contractual though this solution is not available where statutory definitions sweep in under the definition of warranty all statements calculated to induce a sale.[94]

(3) Fraudulent misrepresentation

5.460 Where the defendant makes a statement knowing it to be false or makes a statement not caring whether it is true or false, the defendant commits a tort known as deceit or fraud and is liable to pay damages to the person who relies on the statement.[95] Where, as is common, the statement induces the plaintiff to enter into a contract with the defendant, the question arises whether the contractual or the tortious measure of damages is appropriate. The English and Canadian cases have consistently held that the proper measure is the tortious measure, that is the amount of money required to put the plaintiff in the position that would have been occupied not if the statement had been true but if the statement had not been made.[95a] The point was made clearly in *McConnel v. Wright*:[96]

> It is not an action for breach of contract, and, therefore, no damages in respect of prospective gains which the person contracting was entitled by his contract to expect come in, but it is an action of tort — it is an action for a wrong done whereby the plaintiff was tricked out of certain money in his pocket; and therefore, prima facie, the highest limit of his damages is the whole extent of his loss, and that loss is measured by the money which was in his pocket and is now in the pocket of the company. That is the ultimate, final, highest standard of his loss.[97]

5.470 This view has been followed in Canada.[98] If, however, the plaintiff is deprived by the fraud of a contractual right, the plaintiff will recover the value of that right, for in that case the plaintiff would have enjoyed that value if the wrong had not been done.[99] The American jurisdictions are divided, the majority favouring the contractual measure of damages on the ground that the tortious measure provides insufficient deterrence to fraud. McCormick wrote:

---

[94] See 5.680, *infra*.

[95] See Fleming, *The Law of Torts*, 9th ed. (Sydney, Law Book Co., 1998), pp. 694-703.

[95a] This passage was cited with approval in *Chang v. Martin* (2004), 128 A.C.W.S. (3d) 1022, [2004] B.C.J. No. 258 (Q.L.) (B.C.S.C.), at para. 11; *Xerex Exploration Ltd. v. Petro-Canada* (2005), 256 D.L.R. (4th) 218 (Alta. C.A.) at para. 95; *Esfahani v. Kaboodani* (2007), 54 C.C.L.T. (3d) 1 (B.C.S.C.), at para. 9, citing this passage.

[96] [1903] 1 Ch. 546 (C.A.). See *Doyle v. Olby (Ironmongers) Ltd.*, [1969] 2 Q.B. 158 (C.A.).

[97] *McConnel v. Wright*, *supra*, footnote 96, at pp. 554-5, *per* Collins M.R.; *Yeoman's Row Management Ltd. v. Cobbe*, 2008 UKHL 55, at paras. 4 and 38.

> . . . If the defendant by willful falsehood has cozened the plaintiff into risking his property upon a bargain which, upon the information given by the defendant, would have been profitable, a remedy which merely seeks to place the plaintiff back in the position he was in before seems hardly adequate. The plaintiff might well be given the value of the expected bargain. A willful fraud should cost as much as a broken promise. If the cheat can anticipate that the worst that can happen is that he shall be called upon to pay back his profit upon the trade, he may be encouraged to defraud. The force of this last argument, however, is somewhat weakened by the fact that, in most states, exemplary damages may be given by the jury in cases of deliberate or wanton fraud, and it may be argued that this furnishes an adequate deterrent.[100]

It would seem that a more forceful argument against this is the existence of the criminal law. Attempts to obtain benefits by fraud are almost always punishable in criminal courts, and, it is submitted, it is there that a deterrent should be sought.

---

[98] *Parna v. G. & S. Properties Ltd.*, [1971] S.C.R. 306, 15 D.L.R. (3d) 336; *Gosse-Millerd Ltd. v. Devine*, [1928] S.C.R. 101, [1928] 2 D.L.R. 869; *Lamont v. Wenger* (1909), 22 O.L.R. 642 (H.C.J.); *Blanke v. New Good Eats Cafe Ltd.*, [1947] 2 D.L.R. 431 (B.C.S.C.); *Levas v. Litras*, [1947] 3 D.L.R. 927 (B.C.C.A.); *C.R.F. Holdings Ltd. v. Fundy Chemical International Ltd.* (1980), 21 B.C.L.R. 345, 14 C.C.L.T. 87 (S.C.), vard [1982] 2 W.W.R. 385, 33 B.C.L.R. 291 (C.A.), leave to appeal to S.C.C. refused 42 N.R. 357*n*, 42 N.R. 358*n*; *Steele v. Pritchard* (1907), 7 W.L.R. 108 (Man. C.A.); *Rosen v. Lindsay* (1907), 7 W.L.R. 115 (Man. C.A.); *Hathaway v. McIntyre* (1951), 1 W.W.R. (N.S.) 460 (B.C.C.A.); *Tree Island Steel Co. Ltd. v. Treeter* (1978), 15 A.R. 266 (S.C.T.D.); *Hepting v. Schaaf*, [1964] S.C.R. 100, 43 D.L.R. (2d) 168; *Enns v. Panju*,, [1978] 5 W.W.R. 244 (B.C.S.C.); *Ferguson v. Stright* (1979), 37 N.S.R. (2d) 41 (S.C.T.D.); *McDonald v. Palanio* (1960), 31 W.W.R. 43 (B.C.S.C.); *Carveth v. Mosiman*, [1923] 2 D.L.R. 725 (S.C.C.); *Noonan v. Roe* (1971), 21 D.L.R. (3d) 102 (B.C.S.C.); *Sorensen v. Kaye Holdings Ltd.*, [1979] 6 W.W.R. 193 (B.C.C.A.), leave to appeal to S.C.C. refused 31 N.R. 445*n*; *Zorzi v. Barker* (1957), 8 D.L.R. (2d) 164 (B.C.C.A.); *Northern & Central Gas Corp. Ltd. v. Hillcrest Collieries Ltd.* (1975), 59 D.L.R. (3d) 533 (Alta. S.C.T.D.); *Hjort v. Wilson*, [1954] 2 D.L.R. 705 (B.C.C.A.); *Bango v. Holt* (1971), 21 D.L.R. (3d) 66 (B.C.S.C.); *Chua v. Van Pelt* (1977), 74 D.L.R. (3d) 244 (B.C.S.C.); *B.G. Preeco I (Pacific Coast) Ltd. v. Bon Street Development Ltd.* (1989), 60 D.L.R. (4th) 30, 37 B.C.L.R. (2d) 258 (C.A.); *Sugar v. Peat Marwick Ltd.* (1988), 55 D.L.R. (4th) 230, 66 O.R. (2d) 766 (H.C.J.); *Burns v. Kelly Peters & Associates Ltd.* (1987), 41 D.L.R. (4th) 577, [1987] 6 W.W.R. 1 (B.C.C.A.); *Goldstar Management Ltd. v. Varvis* (1995), 175 A.R. 321, 34 Alta. L.R. (3d) 74 (Q.B.). See *Opron Construction Co. v. Alberta* (1994), 151 A.R. 241 at p. 381, 14 C.L.R. (2d) 97 (Q.B.), citing this paragraph. *Thompson v. Aiken* (1977), 2 B.C.L.R. 23 (S.C.), allowing the cost of remedying the defect, seems inconsistent, as does *Goulet v. Clarkson*, [1949] 1 D.L.R. 847 (B.C.S.C.). There may, however, be a *prima facie* presumption that the price is equal to the value the property would have had if answering to its description: see *Hepting v. Schaaf, Northern & Central Gas Corp., supra*. Australia follows the same basic rule: *Potts v. Miller* (1940), 64 C.L.R. 282; *Toteff v. Antonas* (1952), 87 C.L.R. 647 (Aust. H.C.). In *Thomas v. Penner* (1958), 25 W.W.R. 173 (B.C.C.A.), the defendant was held to be bound by the agreed valuation of property exchanged by the plaintiff, even though excessive; this seems punitive. In *Ruptash v. Goyan*, [1971] S.C.R. 553, 16 D.L.R. (3d) 1, actual value, not agreed value, was used. *Gusella v. Lewellan*, [1938] 3 D.L.R. 800 (Alta. S.C.), where a tenant farmer recovered the value the crop would have had if as represented, may be explained as a case giving compensation for the plaintiff's wasted labour. See footnote 133, *infra*.

[99] *Karas v. Rowlett*, [1944] S.C.R. 1, [1944] 1 D.L.R. 241.

[100] McCormick, *Handbook on the Law of Damages* (St. Paul, West Publishing Co., 1935), pp. 453-4.

5.480 Some further points may be added in support of the Anglo-Canadian position. Whenever there is a strong case for holding a defendant liable for

[*The next page is* 5-21]

the plaintiff's expectation, there will be an argument that the defendant's statement should be treated as contractual: the law of contract formation has been criticized as uncertain but it has at least the merit of flexibility. To say there is a strong case for compelling the defendant to satisfy the plaintiff's expectation is to say that there is a strong case for finding a contract.[101]

5.490 The American majority rule is not consistently followed, for it does not apply, it seems, to a case where the defendant's statement induces some transaction other than a contract with the defendant. Thus, if a plaintiff is induced to spend money for someone else's benefit, the measure of damages will be the plaintiff's loss not the benefit the plaintiff would have acquired from the third party had the statement been true.[102]

5.500 The American position also must allow for cases where it would not be to the plaintiff's benefit to sue on a contractual basis. One example of such a case is where the defendant is the buyer of property which the plaintiff is induced to sell by the defendant's fraudulent statement that the property is of low value.[103] Another case is where the plaintiff has made a bad bargain even on the basis that the defendant's statement was true. Thus, if the defendant sells to the plaintiff goods in fact worth $800, inducing the plaintiff to buy them for $1,500 by fraudulently asserting a fact that would if true have made their value $1,000, the contractual measure (supposing the contract to have been executed) would give the plaintiff $200: the difference between the value of the goods and the value they would have had if they had answered to the description. But it is surely plain that the plaintiff ought to be entitled to rescind or to recover damages of $700 — the economic equivalent of rescission — thereby putting the plaintiff in the position that would have been occupied if the fraud had not been committed.

5.510 For these reasons, the Second Restatement, adopting what it calls the compromise position,[104] makes the loss of bargain measure of damages subsidiary to the main rule of out-of-pocket loss, giving the plaintiff an option to recover loss of bargain damages, but only in the case of "a misrepresentation in a business transaction" and specifically requiring proof of damages claimed on this basis "with reasonable certainty".[105] In the writer's view, the Anglo-Canadian position gives sufficient protection to the plaintiff. The "admonitory function of the law", as the Restatement calls it,[106] is sufficiently performed by the criminal law, with the aid possibly of

[101] See Waddams, *The Law of Contracts*, 5th ed. (Toronto, Canada Law Book, 2005), pp. 18-19.

[102] See American Law Institute, *Restatement of the Law, Second: Torts 2d* (St. Paul, American Law Institute Publishers, 1977), §549, comment *g* on subsec. (2), p. 114; Prosser, *Handbook of the Law of Torts*, 4th ed. (St. Paul, West Publishing Co., 1971), §110.

[103] See *Restatement of the Law*, *ibid.*, at p. 115.

[104] *Supra*, comment *h* on subsec. (2), p. 115.

[105] *Supra*, §549(2). Although comment *h* states that recovery is to be "in accordance with the usual rules of certainty in damages", the express inclusion of the reference in the text suggests some uneasiness with the rule.

[106] *Supra*, comment *i* on subsec. (2), p. 115.

exemplary damages.[107] If the plaintiff seeks protection for expectations, it is to the law of contracts that the plaintiff ought to turn.[108] If the plaintiff cannot meet the tests of contract formation, a case for compelling the defendant to make good the expectations has not been established. If one were to ask what position in fact the plaintiff would have occupied in these cases, if the defendant's statement had been true and the property really had had the virtues ascribed to it, the answer will be not that the plaintiff would have enjoyed the benefit of the bargain but that the transaction would never have taken place; for cynical though it may seem to say so, the facts will almost always show that the fraudulent defendant would not have sold property that really had the merits claimed for it at the price agreed.

5.520 Difficulties sometimes arise in assessing the value of the property transferred to the plaintiff particularly in the case of shares where value is apt to fluctuate rapidly. The time at which the value is to be taken is usually said to be the time of the transfer.[109] Thus, if the plaintiff is fraudulently induced to purchase for $1,000 shares that are worth $800 at the time of transfer, the damages will be $200 even though the shares subsequently decline further. The loss suffered beyond the $200 is caused not by the defendant's wrong but by the plaintiff's unwise investment decision. Cotton L.J. in *Peek v. Derry*[110] put it thus:

> The damage to be recovered by the Plaintiff is the loss which he sustained by acting on the representations of the Defendants. That action was taking the shares. Before he was induced to buy the shares, he had the £4000 in his pocket. The day when the shares were allotted to him, which was the consequence of his action, he paid over the £4000, and he got the shares; and the loss sustained by him in consequence of his acting on the representations of the Defendants was having the shares, instead of having in his pocket the £4000. The loss, therefore, must be the difference between the £4000 and the then value of the shares ... If the company at the time was a good company and the shares had an intrinsic value, then no fact which subsequently occurred ... ought to add to the damages to be paid by the Defendants.[111]

5.530 In *Waddell v. Blockey*[112] where a person was induced to buy Indian debt securities on the fraudulent misrepresentation that they were being sold to him by a third party, whereas in fact they were the defendant's own, the court again held that the defendant was not liable for a subsequent diminution in value. Bramwell L.J. said: "It was for the [buyer] to consider whether he would sell it or retain it. The retention of it was his own voluntary act. If he

---

[107] See 11.10-11.480, *infra*.
[108] See footnote 101, *supra*.
[109] *Waddell v. Blockey* (1879), 4 Q.B.D. 678 (C.A.); *Peek v. Derry* (1887), 37 Ch. D. 541 (C.A.), revd on other grounds 14 App. Cas. 337 (H.L.). In *Allan v. McLennan* (1916), 31 D.L.R. 617 (B.C.C.A.), the court spoke of value at the time of discovery of the deceit. See 5.570, *infra*.
[110] *Supra*, footnote 109.
[111] *Peek v. Derry*, *supra*, footnote 109, at pp. 591-2.
[112] *Supra*, footnote 109.

elected to remain owner after the rupee paper began to fall in price, his loss was not owing simply to his having purchased it but to his having purchased it and retained it."[113] In this case, as Thesiger L.J. pointed out, there was in no sense any defect in the securities themselves.[114] The defendant's fraud went solely to the question of prior ownership. *Waddell v. Blockey* was, however, disapproved by the Supreme Court of Canada in *Hodgkinson v. Simms*,[114a] where La Forest J. said that a plaintiff "should not suffer from the fact that he did not discover the breach until such time as the market had already taken its toll on his investments". In *Smith New Court Securities Ltd. v. Scrimgeour Vickers (Asset Management) Ltd.*,[114b] the House of Lords held that the rule stated in *Waddell v. Blockey* was generally "practical and just" but the rule was not inflexible, and should yield to the "overriding compensatory rule"[114c] and would not apply when the plaintiff was "locked into the transaction by reason of the fraud".[114d]

5.540 The value of the property at a later date than the date of transfer may be relevant evidence of its value at the date of transfer itself. In *Peek v. Derry*,[115] Cotton L.J. went on to say:

> Although the value of the shares is not to be ascertained at the subsequent period so as to take into account for the benefit of the Plaintiff events subsequent which depreciated their value, yet those events, if they shewed that the company was originally, with the capital which it had got, a company which was worthless, may, in my opinion, be taken into account as evidence of what was the value of the shares immediately after they were allotted to the Plaintiff. So that it may be that, useful as this discussion has been in order to elucidate what ought to be the proper time for ascertaining the value it may ultimately produce no good result to the defendants.[116]

5.550 The evidential effect of a later value is particularly important where the plaintiff seeks to show that the true value of the shares at the date of transfer was less than their market value at that date. It might be supposed that since value has no meaning apart from exchange value, it would be a contradiction in terms to assert a difference between true value and market value. If the plaintiff pays $1,000 and receives property that is saleable for $1,000, it might seem that there is no loss. This approach, however, as was pointed out

---

113 *Waddell v. Blockey, supra*, footnote 109, at p. 681.

114 *Supra*, at p. 683: "the thing purchased had at the time of purchase no inherent defect". See also *Banque Bruxelles Lambert S.A. v. Eagle Star Insurance Co. Ltd.*, [1997] A.C. 191 (H.L.).

114a [1994] 3 S.C.R. 377, 117 D.L.R. (4th) 161.

114b [1997] A.C. 254 (H.L.).

114c *Supra*, at p. 1076.

114d *Supra*, at p. 1078.

115 *Supra*, footnote 109.

116 *Peek v. Derry, supra*, footnote 109, at p. 592. In *Whittaker v. Taylor* (1911), 1 W.W.R. 259 (Alta. S.C.), where the plaintiff had been fraudulently induced to convey land to the defendant, the value was taken at the time of the action, on the ground that the plaintiff was entitled to a reconveyance of the land and in default to its current value. See *Xerex Exploration Ltd. v. Petro-Canada* (2005), 256 D.L.R. (4th) 218 (Alta. C.A.), where recovery was not restricted by market values as known at the date of the transaction.

in the discussion of value in an earlier chapter,[117] would have the effect of excusing the fraudulent defendant from liability where the fraud was successful enough to deceive not only the plaintiff but the whole marketplace. This point was also dealt with in *Peek v. Derry*, the Court of Appeal holding that the plaintiff was entitled to the difference between the price he had paid and the value the shares would have had if the true facts had been known:

> Now, it must not be taken that the value of the shares must be what they would have sold for in the market, because that might not shew the real value at all. I do not know whether there was any market in this case, but the market might have been affected by the representations which were made by the Defendants, which induced the Plaintiffs to act, and which might have induced others to act.[118]

As it was put in the earlier case of *Twycross v. Grant*:[119]

> There is no evidence whatever that the shares ever had any value except that which resulted from the wrongful acts of the defendants; and it would be contrary to all principle to allow them to take advantage of their own wrong, and claim credit for the market-price of the shares, when but for their own [wrongful acts] there is no reason to suppose that the shares would have had any market value at all.[120]

5.560 One difficulty with this approach is that if the plaintiff having been fraudulently induced to buy shares for $1,000, promptly resells them for the same price (or more) before the defendant's fraud is discovered, it would seem that the plaintiff could claim to have suffered a loss of $1,000 if the shares are subsequently shown in the light of the true facts to be worthless. It was specifically stated, however, both in *Peek v. Derry*[121] and *Twycross v. Grant*,[122] that if the plaintiff does in fact resell, the proceeds must be brought into account. This result is, it is suggested, consistent with the usual rules as to mitigation for the resale is intimately connected with the defendant's wrong and the profit could not have been made otherwise.[123] Indeed, the resale on the facts supposed can only be called profitable when it appears that the plaintiff has been defrauded and the shares are worthless.

5.570 Another question is whether the damages crystallize at the point where the

117 See 1.70, 1.80, *supra*.

118 *Peek v. Derry*, *supra*, footnote 109, at pp. 591-2. The opposite case where subsequent events show the shares to be of higher value than market price was discussed in *Prudential Ass'ce Co. Ltd. v. Newman Industries Ltd.*, [1981] C.L.R. 257 at pp. 299-300, and in *Uncle Ben's Tartan Holdings Ltd. v. Northwest Sports Enterprises* (1974), 46 D.L.R. (3d) 280 (B.C.S.C.).

119 (1877), 2 C.P.D. 469 (C.A.).

120 *Supra*, at pp. 489-90, followed in *Burke v. Cory* (1959), 19 D.L.R. (2d) 252, [1959] O.W.N. 129 (C.A.).

121 (1887), 37 Ch. D. 541 (C.A.), at p. 593, revd on other grounds 14 App. Cas. 337 (H.L.), *per* Cotton L.J. ("Of course if he sells and does not sell unreasonably, whatever he gets he must bring into account").

122 *Supra*, footnote 119, at p. 489, *per* Lord Coleridge, C.J. ("although, of course, if the plaintiff has sold his shares, he must have credited the defendants with whatever he might have realized by the sale").

123 See 15.670-15.880, *infra*.

plaintiff discovers the truth about the defendant's wrongful conduct. In *Burke v. Cory*,[124] the Ontario Court of Appeal held that the plaintiff could not recover loss caused by a further decline in the value of shares after he knew of the falsity of the defendant's representation. In *Allan v. McLennan*,[125] Macdonald C.J. said:

> It is the difference between the value of the shares at the time respondents discovered the fraud and what they paid for them with interest, which is the true measure of damages, not "the difference between the amount of money paid by each plaintiff plus interest at 5% from the date of such payment *and the present value of the shares*".[126]

In *Central B.C. Planers Ltd. v. Hocker*,[127] however, the plaintiff was held entitled to recover compensation in respect of a later decline in value, on the ground that he had acted reasonably in holding onto the shares. It is submitted that the preferable view is that damages crystallize at the time the plaintiff discovers the truth. If the plaintiff chooses to hold the property after that date, freed from the influence of the defendant's representations, the plaintiff speculates for profit and, it is submitted, should assume the risk. The test of reasonableness and mitigation is not entirely satisfactory for it is rarely unreasonable to fail to predict market changes. But it cannot be right for the plaintiff to be entitled to speculate indefinitely at the defendant's expense. In *Hodgkinson v. Simms*,[127a] La Forest J. spoke of the time of discovery of the breach as crucial.

5.580 It would follow from this view that when the value of the property rises after the facts come to light, the plaintiff's recovery ought not to be diminished, but this view was rejected in *Uncle Ben's Tartan Holdings Ltd. v. Northwest Sports Enterprises*,[128] where the value of shares was less than the purchase price when the true facts came to light, but later rose above the purchase price. The court said that the plaintiff was entitled only to the actual loss and not to "some fictional loss measured at the time the fraud is ascertained".[129] It is submitted, however, that there is a stronger argument for the plaintiff than is here recognized. Had the shares been sold on discovery of the fraud, the plaintiff would have recovered the difference between the purchase price and the selling price. The plaintiff ought not to lose that right by choosing to retain the shares.[130] In *C.R.F. Holdings Ltd. v. Fundy Chemical Int'l Ltd.*,[131] this view prevailed at trial where Taylor J. pointed out

124 *Supra*, footnote 120.

125 (1916), 31 D.L.R. 617 (B.C.C.A.), cited with approval in *Hodgkinson v. Simms*, [1994] 3 S.C.R. 377, 117 D.L.R. (4th) 161.

126 *Supra*, at p. 619, as the trial judge had held.

127 (1970), 10 D.L.R. (3d) 689 (B.C.C.A.), affd [1971] S.C.R. v, 16 D.L.R. (3d) 368*n* and 21 D.L.R. (3d) 639*n*.

127a [1994] 3 S.C.R. 377, 117 D.L.R. (4th) 161.

128 *Supra*, footnote 118.

129 *Uncle Ben's Tartan Holdings Ltd. v. Northwest Sports Enterprises* (1974), 46 D.L.R. (3d) 280 (B.C.S.C.), at p. 285.

130 See also 6.900-6.1000, *infra*.

that an inflationary increase after the date of the wrong did not represent any real gain to the plaintiff. The B.C. Court of Appeal affirmed the principle that the proper date for assessment was the date of conveyance, but allowed the appeal on the ground that there was no evidence of its value at that date.

5.590 Although, as has been shown, a plaintiff complaining of fraud is not entitled to recover a contractual measure of damages, it has been held that the plaintiff is entitled to consequential damages caused by the fraud.[132] If the plaintiff can prove that she would probably, in the absence of the wrong, have negotiated better terms with the defendant, compensation may be given for the loss of that opportunity.[132a] In *Doyle v. Olby (Ironmongers) Ltd.*[133] the plaintiff had been fraudulently induced to purchase a business. At trial the plaintiff recovered £1,500 apparently representing the diminished capital value of the business at the time of the transfer. The English Court of Appeal increased the damages to £5,500 to compensate the plaintiff for further losses incurred in attempting to run the business profitably. The rules of mitigation and remoteness were, as against a fraudulent defendant, to be construed generously to the plaintiff: Lord Denning M.R. said:

> The defendant is bound to make reparation for all the actual damages directly flowing from the fraudulent inducement. The person who has been defrauded is entitled to say:
>
> > "I would not have entered into this bargain at all but for your representation. Owing to your fraud, I have not only lost all the money I paid you, but what is more, I have been put to a large amount of extra expense as well and suffered this or that extra damages."
>
> All such damages can be recovered: and it does not lie in the mouth of the fraudulent person to say that they could not reasonably have been foreseen. For instance, in this very case Mr. Doyle has not only lost the money which he paid for the business, which he would never have done if there had been no fraud: he put all that money in and lost it; but also he has been put to expense and loss in trying to run a business which turned out to be a disaster for him. He is entitled to damages for all his loss, subject, of course to giving credit for any benefit that he has received. There is nothing to be

[131] [1982] 2 W.W.R. 385, 33 B.C.L.R. 291 (C.A.), leave to appeal to S.C.C. refused 42 N.R. 357*n*, 42 N.R. 358*n*.

[132] *Barron v. Kelly* (1918), 56 S.C.R. 455, 41 D.L.R. 590; *Carrique v. Catts* (1914), 20 D.L.R. 737, 32 O.L.R. 548 (S.C. App. Div.); *Anderson v. Fuller* (1915), 22 D.L.R. 66 (B.C.S.C.), revd on other grounds 21 B.C.R. 509 (C.A.).

[132a] *Clef Aquitaine SARL v. Laporte Materials (Barrow) Ltd.*, [2001] Q.B. 448 (C.A.). Damages will be discounted according to the improbability of success.

[133] [1969] 2 Q.B. 158 (C.A.), approved in *Smith New Court Securities Ltd. v. Scrimgeour Vickers (Asset Management) Ltd.*, [1997] A.C. 254 (H.L.), and followed in *Siametis v. Trojan Horse (Burlington) Inc.* (1979), 104 D.L.R. (3d) 556, 25 O.R. (2d) 120 (H.C.J.), affd 123 D.L.R. (3d) 767*n*, 32 O.R. (2d) 782*n* (C.A.); *C.R.F. Holdings Ltd. v. Fundy Chemical Int'l Ltd., supra*, footnote 131; *Shull v. Clauson* (1969), 7 D.L.R. (3d) 410, [1970] 1 O.R. 31 (H.C.J.).; *Archer v. Brown*, [1985] Q.B. 401; *Canson Enterprises Ltd. v. Boughton & Co.* (1989), 61 D.L.R. (4th) 732, [1990] 1 W.W.R. 375 (B.C.C.A.); *Sevidal v. Chopra* (1987), 64 O.R. (2d) 169 (H.C.J.); *Goldstar Management Ltd. v. Varvis* (1995), 175 A.R. 321, 34 Alta. L.R. (3d) 74 (Q.B.).

taken off in mitigation; for there is nothing more that he could have done to reduce his loss. He did all that he could reasonably be expected to do.[134]

5.600 Lord Denning's comments on remoteness are not to be construed, it would seem, as always excluding remoteness in cases of fraud, for Winn L.J. added:

> . . . no element in the consequential position can be regarded as attributable loss and damage if it be too remote a consequence: it will be too remote not necessarily because it was not contemplated by the representor, but in any case where the person deceived has not himself behaved with reasonable prudence, reasonable common sense, or can in any true sense be said to have been the author of his own misfortune.[135]

The position seems to be not that the rules of remoteness and mitigation are entirely excluded, but that the defendant will not be permitted to claim as too remote or to say that the plaintiff should have avoided loss arising from reasonable attempts (even if unsuccessful) to salvage something out of the financial difficulties the defendant has caused.[136] In *Smith New Court Securities Ltd. v. Scrimgeour Vickers (Asset Management) Ltd.*,[136a] the House of Lords said that there must be a "sufficient causal link" between the fraud and the loss, and quoted an old example that a person fraudulently induced to buy a horse could not recover its full value if it subsequently caught a disease and died.[136b]

(4) Negligent misrepresentation

5.610 Since the decision of the House of Lords in 1963 in *Hedley Byrne Ltd. v. Heller & Partners Ltd.*,[137] it has been established that an action lies for negligent misrepresentation causing economic loss. It naturally follows from acceptance of out-of-pocket loss rather than the contractual measure as the basic measure of damages for fraud, that the same basic measure applies to negligent misrepresentation.[138]

5.620 In *Esso Petroleum Co. v. Mardon*,[139] the plaintiff had induced the defendant to take a lease of a gasoline filling station by overestimating the expected annual volume of business. This had been estimated at 200,000 gallons of fuel on the basis that as originally planned, the filling station would be accessible from the main street. When the plans for access were changed, the plaintiff carelessly omitted to revise the estimate. It was held by the English Court of Appeal that the defendant had a cause of action either for

---

[134] *Doyle v. Olby (Ironmongers) Ltd.*, *supra*, footnote 133, at p. 167.

[135] *Doyle v. Olby (Ironmongers) Ltd.*, *supra*, at p. 168. See *Royscot Trust Ltd. v. Rogerson*, [1991] 2 Q.B. 297 (C.A.).

[136] *Sugar v. Peat Marwick Ltd.* (1988), 55 D.L.R. (4th) 230, 66 O.R. (2d) 766 (H.C.J.). See *Wynne v. William M. Mercer Ltd.* (1995), 131 D.L.R. (4th) 256, [1996] 4 W.W.R. 418 (B.C.C.A.); and 15.290-15.320, *infra*.

[136a] [1997] A.C. 254 (H.L.).

[136b] *Supra*, at pp. 281 and 285, *per* Lord Steyn.

[137] [1964] A.C. 465 (H.L.), approved and followed in Canada; see *Haig v. Bamford*, [1977] 1 S.C.R. 466, 72 D.L.R. (3d) 68; Linden, *Canadian Tort Law*, 5th ed. (Toronto, Butterworths, 1993), pp. 399-432.

breach of warranty or in negligence. It might be supposed that a different measure of damages would be applicable, but the court avoided such a difference by construing the warranty not as a guarantee that the business would amount to 200,000 gallons but as a guarantee that the estimate had been carefully made. Thus, the scope of the warranty as construed was identical with the defendant's duty in tort. Damages, as in *Doyle v. Olby*,[140] extended to loss suffered by the plaintiff in attempting to make a success of the business:

> Just as in *Doyle v. Olby (Ironmongers) Ltd.* ... he can say: "... I would not have entered into this contract at all but for your representation. Owing to it, I have lost all the capital I put into it. I also incurred a large overdraft. I have spent four years of my life in wasted endeavour without reward: and it will take me some time to re-establish myself."
>
> For all such loss he is entitled to recover damages.[141]

It appears from this passage that damages will include the loss of opportunity to earn from other sources, just as though the plaintiff had suffered a loss of earning capacity through injury. Indeed, Lord Denning made the analogy:

> [The loss] is to be measured in a similar way as the loss due to a personal injury. You should look into the future so as to forecast what would have been likely to happen if he had never entered into this contract: and contrast it with his position as it is now as a result of entering into it. The future is necessarily problematical and can only be a rough-and-ready estimate. But it must be done in assessing the loss.[142]

---

[138] *Bango v. Holt* (1971), 21 D.L.R. (3d) 66 (B.C.S.C.); *Wooldridge v. H.B. Nickerson & Sons Ltd.* (1979), 39 N.S.R. (2d) 45 (S.C.T.D.), vard 115 D.L.R. (3d) 97, 40 N.S.R. (2d) 388 (S.C. App. Div.); *West Coast Finance Ltd. v. Gunderson, Stokes Walton & Co.* (1975), 56 D.L.R. (3d) 460 (B.C.C.A.); *Rainbow Industrial Caterers Ltd. v. Canadian National Railway Co.*, [1991] 3 S.C.R. 3, 84 D.L.R. (4th) 291; *Queen v. Cognos Inc.*, [1993] 1 S.C.R. 87, 99 D.L.R. (4th) 626; *Unryn v. Melcor Developments Ltd.* (1994), 22 Alta. L.R. (3d) 355, 159 A.R. 336 (Q.B.); *1874000 Nova Scotia Ltd. v. Adams* (1997), 146 D.L.R. (4th) 466, 159 N.S.R. (2d) 260 (C.A.); *Lakefield (Village) v. Black* (1998), 166 D.L.R. (4th) 96 (Ont. C.A.); *Chang v. Martin* (2004), 128 A.C.W.S. (3d) 1022, [2004] B.C.J. No. 258 (Q.L.) (S.C.), citing this passage, at para. 12. Again, if the plaintiff seeks protection for expectations it is submitted that the plaintiff should turn to the law of contracts: see 5.510, *supra*. Often there will be concurrent liability in contract and tort: see *BG Checo International Ltd. v. British Columbia Hydro and Power Authority*, [1993] 1 S.C.R. 12, 99 D.L.R. (4th) 577; *BG Checo International Ltd. v. British Columbia Hydro and Power Authority* (1994), 109 D.L.R. (4th) 1 (B.C.S.C.), affd 126 D.L.R. (4th) 127, 9 B.C.L.R. (3d) 338 (C.A.); *Conex Services Inc. v. Bogner Developments Ltd.* (1999), 70 B.C.L.R. (3d) 1, supplementary reasons 94 A.C.W.S. (3d) 362 (C.A.), leave to appeal to S.C.C. refused 262 N.R. 392*n*; *Dol v. Marlene Musclow Insurance Agency Ltd.* (2006), 45 R.P.R. (4th) 297 (Ont. S.C.J.).

[139] [1976] Q.B. 801 (C.A.).

[140] *Supra*, footnote 133.

[141] *Esso Petroleum Co.v. Mardon, supra*, footnote 139, at pp. 820-1; *System Contractors Ltd. v. 2349893 Manitoba Ltd.*, [1994] 4 W.W.R. 488, 91 Man. R. (2d) 125 (Q.B.). Principles of causation suggest that damages are not recoverable for losses that would have occurred in any event, but the onus of proof is on the defendant: *Rainbow Industrial Caterers v. Canadian National Railway Co., supra*, footnote 138. The plaintiff must mitigate the loss. See *Haida Inn Partnership v. Touche Ross & Co.* (1989), 64 D.L.R. (4th) 305, 42 B.C.L.R. (2d) 151 (S.C.); *Downs v. Chappell*, [1997] 1 W.L.R. 426 (C.A.).

5.630 In *Lowenburg, Harris & Co. v. Wolley*[143] where the defendant negligently overvalued land, inducing the plaintiff to lend money on inadequate security, the Supreme Court of Canada held that the damages should not include loss caused by depreciation of the land after the date of the loan. The same view was taken by the House of Lords in *Banque Bruxelles Lambert S.A. v. Eagle Star Ins. Co. Ltd.*[144] but rejected by the Australian Federal Court in *Kenny & Good Pty. Ltd. v. MGICA (1992) Ltd.*[144a] The position taken in the *Banque Bruxelles* case is, in the writer's opinion, to be preferred: the valuer cannot reasonably be supposed to take the risk of loss caused by subsequent depreciation insofar as it exceeds the security margin anticipated by the lender; the valuer usually has no control over the degree of risk that the lender chooses to take nor over the interest rate agreed to by the borrower. Where, as is common in such cases, the defaulting borrower had promised an exceptionally high rate of interest, some cases have allowed compensation for the loss of the interest.[145] It is suggested, however, that this measure is usually overcompensatory for, had the valuation been accurate, the plaintiff would probably not have had the opportunity of investing money so profitably.[146]

(5) Innocent misrepresentation

5.640 A misrepresentation that is neither fraudulent nor negligent is not actionable as a tort. If it is not a term of a contract, it is not actionable as a breach of contract. But this does not mean that the plaintiff is necessarily without recourse. Where the defendant by a false statement induces the plaintiff to enter into a transaction whereby the defendant profits at the plaintiff's expense, there is a strong case for requiring the defendant to restore the profit even if the statement is entirely innocent.[147]

142 *Esso Petroleum Co. v. Mardon, supra*, at p. 821. See *Avco Financial Services v. Holstein* (1980), 109 D.L.R. (3d) 128 (Sask. Q.B.); *De Groot v. St. Boniface Hospital*, [1994] 6 W.W.R. 541, 3 C.C.E.L. (2d) 280 (Man. C.A.) (loss must be proved). On this basis, recovery for loss of profits was allowed in *V.K. Mason Construction Ltd. v. Bank of Nova Scotia*, [1985] 1 S.C.R. 271, 16 D.L.R. (4th) 598, and in *East v. Maurer*, [1991] 1 W.L.R. 461 (C.A.). But see *Vita Health Co. (1985) Ltd. v. Toronto-Dominion Bank* (1994), 118 D.L.R. (4th) 289, 57 C.P.R. (3d) 449 (Man. C.A.), leave to appeal to S.C.C. refused 122 D.L.R. (4th) vii, 60 C.P.R. (3d) vi (no loss of profit-making opportunity).

143 (1895), 25 S.C.R. 51, distinguished in *Avco Financial Services v. Holstein, supra*. See also *Indian Head Credit Union Ltd. v. A. Hosie & Co.*, [1994] 4 W.W.R. 674, 120 Sask. R. 73 (C.A.).

144 [1997] A.C. 191 (H.L.). See also *Platform Home Loans Ltd. v. Oyston Shipways Ltd.*, [2000] 2 A.C. 190 (H.L.).

144a (1997), 147 A.L.R. 568 (F.C. (Full Ct.)), affd (unreported, June 17, 1999, H.C.). And see *Hodgkinson v. Simms*, [1994] 3 S.C.R. 377, 117 D.L.R. (4th) 161.

145 *Baxter v. Gapp (F.W.) & Co. Ltd.*, [1939] K.B. 271 (C.A.).

146 See *Swingcastle v. Alastair Gibson (a firm)*, [1991] 2 A.C. 223 (H.L.); *Seeway Mortgage Investment Corp. v. First Citizens Financial Corp.* (1983), 45 B.C.L.R. 87 (S.C.), at p. 101. And see 2.350, *supra*.

147 See Waddams, *The Law of Contracts*, 4th ed. (Toronto, Canada Law Book, 1999), pp. 301-2.

5.650 The courts of equity evolved a remedy that had this result, namely, rescission.[148] The effect of rescission of the contract was to prevent the defendant from profiting at the plaintiff's expense as would be the case if the contract were enforced. The courts of equity were willing also upon ordering rescission to assess and award a money sum in order to effect complete rescission and make perfect restoration of the status quo ante.[149] The difficulty was that when the contract had been executed or partly performed, there were often bars to an actual order of rescission, and unfortunately the Court of Equity seems usually to have declined to award a money sum in lieu of rescission.[150] It has been submitted elsewhere that almost all the difficulties in this area of law would have been very much alleviated if the court had developed such a power.[151] *Lord Cairns' Act*[152] gives jurisdiction to the courts of equity to award damages in lieu of an injunction and of specific performance but does not refer to damages in lieu of rescission.

5.660 However, it is surely not impossible for the modern court to develop such a power, even in the absence of a specific statutory provision. The modern court has all the powers of the old Court of Equity, which was often willing to award money sums where the circumstances required it.[153] It cannot be beyond the capacity of the modern court of justice to award the monetary equivalent of rescission. This, it is submitted, is the proper remedy where the plaintiff would in principle be entitled to rescind a contract for misrepresentation but where rescission itself is impracticable. Thus if the plaintiff is induced to buy a picture for $1,000 by the defendant's innocent misrepresentation that it is a Constable, and its true value is $800, the plaintiff would, before execution of the contract, be entitled to rescission. If rescission for some adequate reason proves impossible, the plaintiff ought surely to be entitled instead to recover a money sum of $200. Practical impossibility of rescission can rationally be held to relieve the defendant from an actual order of rescission. There is no reason why it should relieve the defendant from

[148] *Redgrave v. Hurd* (1881), 20 Ch. D. 1 (C.A.); *MacKenzie v. Royal Bank of Canada*, [1934] A.C. 468, [1934] 4 D.L.R. 1 (P.C.); *Sanitary Refuse Collectors Inc. v. City of Ottawa* (1971), 23 D.L.R. (3d) 27, [1972] 1 O.R. 296 (H.C.J.); *Guest v. Beecroft* (1957), 10 D.L.R. (2d) 657 (B.C.S.C.); *Comeller v. Billinkoff* (1953), 11 W.W.R. (N.S.) 279 (Man. Q.B.); *Eisenschiml v. Western Drilling Co. Ltd.*, [1943] 1 W.W.R. 605 (Alta. S.C. App. Div.).

[149] *Newbigging v. Adam* (1886), 34 Ch. D. 582 (C.A.); *Whittington v. Seale-Hayne* (1900), 82 L.T. 49.

[150] See *Waxman v. Yeandle*, [1953] 2 D.L.R. 475, [1953] O.R. 367 (C.A.); *Hjort v. Wilson*, [1954] 2 D.L.R. 705 (B.C.C.A.); *Guest v. Beecroft* (1957), 10 D.L.R. (2d) 657 (B.C.S.C.). But in *Fleischhaker v. Fort Garry Agencies Ltd.* (1957), 11 D.L.R. (2d) 599 (Man. C.A.), it was held that damages could be given in lieu of rescission. *Fleischhaker* was applied in *Bank of Montreal v. Murphy*, [1986] 6 W.W.R. 610, 6 B.C.L.R. (2d) 169 (C.A.). See also *Dusik v. Newton* (1985), 62 B.C.L.R. 1 (C.A.).

[151] Waddams, *op. cit.* footnote 147, at pp. 306-7.

[152] *Chancery Amendment Act, 1858*; *Courts of Justice Act* (Ont.), s. 99; *Judicature Act* (Alta.), s. 19; Yukon, s. 27; N.W.T., s. 42; *Court of Queen's Bench Act* (Man.), s. 36; *Queen's Bench Act, 1998* (Sask.), s. 66.

[153] Examples are accounting, specific performance in favour of a vendor, and indemnities on rescission of contracts.

liability to pay the financial equivalent. The Court of Equity undoubtedly had good reason before the *Judicature Act* for its reluctance to award damages alone, for this would have had the appearance of trespassing on the jurisdiction of the common law courts. But no such reason can justify the refusal of the modern court to make use of the most appropriate money remedy.[154] In *Fleischhaker v. Fort Garry Agencies Ltd.*[155] the Manitoba Court of Appeal, in awarding rescission of a sale of defective radios, said that damages should, if awarded instead, have the same effect: "But in any event the result to defendant must be precisely the same whether it be reached by the road of rescission or damages. Under the judgment plaintiff is to receive back from defendant $25,402.60 with interest and to return the radios to defendant. Were damages to be allowed they would clearly be the same sum and interest *less* the value of the radios."[156]

(6) Statutory provisions

5.670 Statutory provisions now impose liability for misrepresentation in several common law jurisdictions.[157] The measure of damages is rarely stated expressly and it will turn therefore on the presumed intention of the Legislature, to be gathered from the statutory language and framework.

5.680 The New Zealand *Contractual Remedies Act*[158] specifically provides that the contractual measure of damages shall apply. Where, as in the Saskatchewan *Consumer Protection Act*[159] and the New Brunswick *Consumer Product Warranty and Liability Act*[160] misrepresentations are expressly included within the definitions of warranties, the contractual measure of damages seems inevitably to be applicable. Consequential damages, including damages for personal injuries, as well as exemplary damages, are also expressly provided for in the Saskatchewan Act.[161]

5.690 The Ontario *Consumer Protection Act, 2002* provides that "any agreement . . . entered into by a consumer after or while a person has engaged in an unfair practice may be rescinded by the consumer and the consumer is entitled to any remedy that is available in law, including damages". If rescission is impossible, the consumer "is entitled to recover the amount by which the consumer's payment under the agreement exceeds the value that

[154] *Dusik v. Newton, supra*, footnote 150, at p. 47, citing this passage.
[155] *Supra*, footnote 150.
[156] *Fleischhaker, supra*, footnote 150, at p. 605, *per* Tritschler J.A.
[157] *Fair Trading Act* (Alta.); *Business Practices and Consumer Protection Act* (B.C.); *Consumer Product Warranty and Liability Act* (N.B.); *Consumer Protection Act, 2002* (Ont.); *Consumer Protection Act* (Sask.); *Trade Practices Act 1974* (Aust.); *Contractual Remedies Act* (N.Z.); *Misrepresentation Act 1967* (U.K.).
[158] Section 6(1)(a). See McLauchlan, "Assessment of Damages for Misrepresentation Inducing Contract", 6 Otago L.R. 370 (1986), at p. 375.
[159] Section 45(1).
[160] Section 4(1).
[161] *Consumer Protection Act*, ss. 64, 65. See *Prebushewski v. Dodge City Auto (1984) Ltd.*, [2005] 1 S.C.R. 649, 253 D.L.R. (4th) 209.

the goods or services have to the consumer or to recover damages, or both".[162]

Provision is also made for exemplary or punitive damages.[163] This appears to give the court complete flexibility to award whatever damages would be appropriate at common law, and express mention of the restitutionary measure of damages makes it clear that it may in some cases be the proper measure. The Alberta *Fair Trading Act* giving power to "award damages for damage or loss suffered",[164] and the British Columbia *Business Practices and Consumer Protection Act* giving power to award damages "if a person has suffered damage or loss"[165] should, it is submitted, be construed to allow a similar flexibility. The Alberta statute allows for punitive damages.[166]

5.700 Much controversy has arisen on the measure of damages to be applied under the United Kingdom *Misrepresentation Act 1967*.[167] The Act provides in s. 2(2) for "damages in lieu of rescission". This presumably is the restitutionary measure. But s. 2(1) provides that:

> 2(1) Where a person has entered into a contract after a misrepresentation has been made to him by another party thereto and as a result thereof he has suffered loss, then, if the person making the misrepresentation would be liable to damages in respect thereof had the misrepresentation been made fraudulently, that person shall be so liable notwithstanding that the misrepresentation was not made fraudulently, unless he proves that he had reasonable ground to believe and did believe up to the time the contract was made that the facts represented were true.

This convoluted provision does not make it clear whether the measure of damages is contractual or tortious. It has been held in one English case[168] that the contractual measure applies and there are a number of dicta to the same effect,[169] but these are vigorously criticized by McGregor in his book on damages.[170] It is submitted that McGregor's criticism is persuasive. In view of the rule, well established in the English cases,[171] that the proper measure of damages for a fraudulent misrepresentation is out-of-pocket loss only, it would be odd to suppose that the Legislature intended to apply the contractual measure not only to fraudulent misrepresentation under the Act, but as well to negligent statements and even to statements that the defendant cannot prove to be non-negligent. The Canadian statutes should, it is

---

162 *Consumer Protection Act, 2002*, s. 18(1) and (2).

163 *Consumer Protection Act, 2002*, s. 18(11).

164 Section 13(2)(b).

165 Section 171(1).

166 *Fair Trading Act* (Alta.), s. 13(2)(c).

167 See Atiyah and Treitel, "Misrepresentation Act 1967", 30 Mod. L.R. 369 (1967); *McGregor on Damages*, 16th ed. (London, Sweet & Maxwell, 1997), §§2000-2002.

168 *Watts v. Spence*, [1976] Ch. 165.

169 *Jarvis v. Swans Tours Ltd.*, [1973] Q.B. 233 (C.A.), at p. 237; *Davis & Co. (Wines) Ltd. v. Afa-Minerva (E.M.I.) Ltd.*, [1974] 2 Lloyd's Rep. 27.

170 *McGregor on Damages*, 15th ed., *supra*, footnote 167, §§1746-49.

171 See *McConnel v. Wright*, [1903] 1 Ch. 546 (C.A.); *Doyle v. Olby (Ironmongers) Ltd.*, [1969] 2 Q.B. 158 (C.A.).

submitted, when the wording allows it, also be construed to exclude the contractual measure.

7. Breach of Promise of Marriage

5.710 The action for breach of promise of marriage is now widely regarded as obsolete and has been abolished in many jurisdictions.[172] The action constitutes an exception to the general principle governing damages for breach of contract, in that damages have always been allowed for the plaintiff's injured feelings and loss of reputation, and aggravated and exemplary damages are allowed where the defendant has behaved badly.[173]

5.720 The main theory of the action, however, is that the plaintiff (usually, although not necessarily,[174] the woman) has been deprived of the economic benefit and social status that would have been enjoyed if the marriage had taken place.[175] The assumptions underlying the action, justifiable in the 19th century, were that a woman owed her social status to her marriage, that she obtained a valuable benefit from what was regarded as a "good" marriage, and that her prospects of marriage were damaged by a broken engagement, particularly where the defendant was responsible for a seduction and the birth of an illegitimate child.[176] It is no reproach to the law that it attempted to give substantial compensation for losses that were, in the social circumstances of the time, substantial losses.

5.730 A strictly compensatory approach might be thought to lead to reduced damages in the case of bad behaviour by the defendant for, as Lord Buckmaster said in *Clayton & Waller, Ltd. v. Oliver*:[177] "strictly assessed, the loss to a woman as a husband of a man who declines with insult to marry her might be assumed to be nil".[178] But this would be to allow the defendant to take advantage of his own bad behaviour and Lord Buckmaster added: "but that is not the way such damages are determined".[179]

---

172 See 3.1320, *supra*.

173 See 3.1320, 4.290, *supra*, and 11.250, *infra*.

174 See *Harrison v. Cage* (1698), Carth. 467, 90 E.R. 870; *Cherry v. Thompson* (1872), L.R. 7 Q.B. 573; *Brownlee v. Partridge*, [1947] 2 W.W.R. 805 (B.C.S.C.) (action dismissed on other grounds).

175 In *Dickie v. Curtis* (1920), 17 O.W.N. 494 (H.C.), Lennox J. said: "The pecuniary measure of the plaintiff's loss was, of course, to be gauged by the financial standing and aptitude of the defendant." See also *Naujokat v. Bratushesky*, [1942] 2 D.L.R. 721 (Sask. C.A.); *Henderson v. Muncey*, [1943] 3 D.L.R. 515 (B.C.S.C.), affd [1943] 4 D.L.R. 758 (C.A.); *Collard v. Armstrong* (1913), 12 D.L.R. 368 (Alta. S.C.) (fair proportion of defendant's wealth may be given to plaintiff); *Tuttle v. Swanson* (1972), 9 R.F.L. 59 (B.C.S.C.); *Shaw v. Shaw*, [1954] 2 Q.B. 429 (C.A.) (supposed marriage proving invalid); *Pavao v. Vieira* (1978), 8 R.F.L. (2d) 173 (Man. Q.B.) (one dollar only awarded where plaintiff remarried before trial). Reliance expenses have also been compensated; *Baxter v. Lear* (1975), 23 R.F.L. 342 (Man. Q.B.) (travel expenses and lost income); *Thomson v. McEwen*, [1953] 1 D.L.R. 151 (N.S.S.C. App. Div.) (trousseau).

176 *Berry v. Da Costa* (1866), 35 L.J.C.P. 191; *Ewart v. Tetzloff* (1959), 18 D.L.R. (2d) 539 (B.C.S.C.); *Thomson v. McEwen*, [1953] 1 D.L.R. 151 (N.B.S.C. App. Div.).

177 [1930] A.C. 209 (H.L.).

178 *Supra*, at p. 220.

179 *Supra*.

5.740 In jurisdictions where the action has not been abolished, the courts are bound to take account of changing social conditions. A modern case illustrating the effect of changing social conditions of the measure of damages is *Stuwe v. Baron*,[180] where an independent businesswoman of fifty-seven, twice divorced, sued a sixty-nine-year-old man whose only income was his old age pension. It was held by the British Columbia Supreme Court that in the light of modern views of marriage, the plaintiff had suffered no loss, and indeed that the defendant had acted "perhaps sensibly" in concluding that the marriage would be unlikely to succeed. The plaintiff had suffered no financial loss. In respect of injured feelings, Taylor J. said: "I cannot believe the plaintiff's feelings would have been less injured had the marriage taken place. She would then have been faced both with the misery of a third marriage breakdown and also a three-year wait to regain her freedom."[181] Taylor J. refused to award even nominal damages, saying: "The claim could, perhaps, be allowed, with nominal damages. But that, I think, might appear a rather insulting and insensitive response to the unhappy human consequences of what was, in truth, a well-intentioned, if ill-advised, attempt of two lonely people to find companionship. I think it more appropriate that the claim be dismissed."[182] This is a departure from the general rule that nominal damages are awarded whenever a breach of contract is established.[183] These comments must, however, be read in the light of Taylor J.'s earlier comments to the effect that the action itself had become anomalous in the context of modern matrimonial law.[184]

8. Business Losses

(1) Introduction

5.750 In many kinds of cases, the plaintiff's complaint is of damage to a business interest. Damage of this sort arises from a wide variety of legal wrongs, crossing the boundaries between contract and tort, between law and equity, and between the law of obligations and the law of property. The cases include trade libel, passing off, breach of confidence, infringement of patents, copyrights, trademarks and designs, breach of covenants against competition, interference with contractual relations, wrongful termination of a franchise, and loss caused to business interests by supply of defective goods. In many of these cases the defendant is in competition with the plaintiff and makes a profit from the wrong. In these cases, problems arise, familiar in other areas of the law, of the relationship between the just measure of compensation to the plaintiff, and the profit made by the defendant from the wrong.[185] The scope of the present work excludes a discussion of the substantive law in

[180] (1981), 121 D.L.R. (3d) 199 (B.C.S.C.).
[181] *Supra*, at p. 200.
[182] *Supra*, at p. 203.
[183] See 10.10-10.30, *infra*.
[184] *Stuwe v. Baron*, *supra*, footnote 180, at p. 200.
[185] See 1.450-1.480, *supra*, and 5.990, 9.70-9.130, *infra*.

these various areas. It is assumed throughout that the plaintiff has established a legal wrong; the only questions addressed here are those of relevance to the measurement of compensation.

(2) Injunctions and damages in substitution for injunctions

5.760 Where the plaintiff secures an injunction to restrain the defendant's wrong, as is often possible if the plaintiff acts in time,[186] the plaintiff will be enabled to bargain with the defendant and to exact whatever the latter is willing to pay for the right to compete, or to use the plaintiff's property, as the case may be. Where the defendant has made a large investment that would be wasted by enforcement of the injunction, the plaintiff will be in a position to demand a larger amount than could have been demanded before the defendant's investment was made. If the defendant has acted in good faith, this will often be a ground for refusing an injunction and awarding damages in substitution.[187]

5.770 The measure of damages in substitution for specific relief has been held by the House of Lords in *Johnson v. Agnew*[188] not to differ from the measure of damages at common law. From this it may be deduced that damages awarded in lieu of an injunction must always be justifiable on the same principles that would justify damages at common law, though the effect of the case may be to widen the scope of common law damages rather than to restrict equitable damages.[189] It is suggested elsewhere, however, that this does not mean that the profit made by the defendant is irrelevant, for the profitability of the defendant's actions affect the amount that she would have been willing to pay for the right to compete.[190] It is by no means a departure from the compensatory principle to assert that the plaintiff has been deprived of the opportunities to sell to the defendant the right to compete or to use the plaintiff's property.

(3) Accounting

5.780 In cases of wrongful competition, including breach of covenant and infringement of industrial property rights, the plaintiff is frequently entitled to recover the defendant's net profits, and the procedure for this is the equitable remedy of account.[191] This remedy is usually sharply distinguished from damages as being an equitable remedy measured by the defendant's gain rather than by the plaintiff's loss. However, it is suggested that the relationship between account and damages cannot in modern times be ignored. First, one of the purposes of equity, if not the sole purpose, was to

186 See Sharpe, *Injunctions and Specific Performance*, looseleaf ed. (Toronto, Canada Law Book, 1999).
187 *Ibid.*, 1.590-1.620.
188 [1980] A.C. 367 (H.L.).
189 See 1.940-1.970, *supra*.
190 See 5.990, 9.70-9.130, *infra*.

secure more perfect compensation to the plaintiff than the common law allowed. Wigram V.-C. said in *Colburn v. Simms*:[192] "The jurisdiction as to the account is founded upon this, that it is impossible in damages to measure the injury done by an infringement of the copyright; the Court therefore takes from the wrongdoer all his profits, and gives them to the person who is wronged".[193] Though the primary purpose may have been compensatory, however, the effect was that the recovery might exceed what the plaintiff could show to have been lost, for Wigram V.-C. continued: "though the Court in so doing may give a party more than he is entitled to, for *non constat* that a single copy more would have been sold by the plaintiff, if the injury had not been committed".[194]

5.790 It might seem from this that the remedy of account would be a very attractive one to the plaintiff. However, it seems not to have been widely used.[195] No doubt the explanation lies in the fact that the court will only allow the plaintiff to recover net profits actually shown to have been made by the defendant from the wrongful act, and a conscientious inquiry into these questions may be difficult and expensive.[196]

5.800 Under the Canadian *Copyright Act* the plaintiff's burden is eased. Section 35 provides:

> 35(1) Where a person infringes copyright, the person is liable to pay such

---

[191] *Peter Pan Manufacturing Corp. v. Corsets Silhouette, Ltd.*, [1963] 3 All E.R. 402 (Ch.); *Weingarten Bros. v. Charles Bayer Ltd.* (1905), 22 R.P.C. 341 (H.L.); *Lubrizol Corp. v. Imperial Oil Ltd.* (1992), 98 D.L.R. (4th) 1, 45 C.P.R. (3d) 449 (F.C.A.), leave to appeal to S.C.C. refused 104 D.L.R. (4th) vii, 50 C.P.R. (3d) v; *J.M. Voith GmbH v. Beloit Corp.*, [1997] 3 F.C. 497, 73 C.P.R. (3d) 321 *sub nom.* Beloit Canada Ltd. v. Valmet-Dominion Inc (C.A.) (remedy under *Patent Act* discretionary); *Merck & Co. v. Apotex Inc.* (2006), 276 D.L.R. (4th) 686 (F.C.A.) (remedy is discretionary).

[192] (1843), 12 L.J. Ch. 388.

[193] *Supra*, at p. 392.

[194] *Supra.*

[195] See Blanco White, *Patents for Inventions and the Protection of Industrial Designs*, 4th ed. (London, Stevens, 1974), §12-129: "An account of profits ... commonly turns out to be less advantageous to the patentee than might prima facie be expected: it is also difficult and expensive to take."; Fox, *Canadian Patent Law and Practice*, 4th ed. (Toronto, Carswell Co. Ltd., 1969), pp. 503-4: "It has been said that an account of profits is extremely difficult to work out and should rarely be chosen ... To determine that profit is not only a matter of difficulty but is also, very often, a scant return to the plaintiff for the loss he may have sustained"; Laddie, Prescott and Vitoria, *The Modern Law of Copyright* (London, Butterworths, 1980), §12.28: "Since the taking of an account is usually complicated and expensive, this is a form of relief which is rarely sought in copyright actions."

[196] *Supra*, footnote 195. See *Monsanto Canada Inc. v. Schmeiser*, [2004] 1 S.C.R. 902, 239 D.L.R. (4th) 271 (causation must be established). See also the comments of Lindley L.J. in *Siddell v. Vickers* (1892), 9 R.P.C. 152 (C.A.), at pp. 162-3, cited in *Dubiner v. Cheerio Toys & Games Ltd.*, [1966] Ex. C.R. 801 at pp. 825-42, where the registrar's report occupied seventeen small print pages. In *Jostens Canada Ltd. v. Gibsons Studio Ltd.* (1999), 174 D.L.R. (4th) 351 (B.C.C.A.), and in *Community Credit Union Ltd. v. Ast* (2007), 82 Alta. L.R. (4th) 173 (Q.B.), it was held that the plaintiff could claim revenues wrongfully received by the defendant without making any allowance for expenses, but this approach might lead to extravagant results and go beyond compensation or restitution of unjust enrichment. Even if punishment were thought appropriate, this measure might bear no relation to the appropriate penalty.

damages to the owner of the copyright as the owner has suffered due to the infringement and, in addition to those damages, such part of the profits that the infringer has made from the infringement and that were not taken into account in calculating the damages as the court considers just.

(2) In proving profits,

(a) the plaintiff shall be required to prove only receipts or revenues derived from the infringement; and

(b) the defendant shall be required to prove every element of cost that the defendant claims.

In addition, s. 38 provides that the copyright owner may recover possession of infringing copies, subject to a power in the court to order the copies to be destroyed, or to make any other order that it considers appropriate, provided that nothing in the Act "entitles the copyright owner to damages in respect of the possession or conversion of the infringing copies or plates". Formerly, s. 38 provided that infringing copies were deemed to be the property of the copyright owner, who was entitled to damages for conversion, a provision that might have permitted double compensation.[197-207] The Act also provides for "statutory damages", to a maximum figure, as an alternative to damages under s. 35.[207a]

5.840 The plaintiff is entitled to net profit only and this means that all the defendant's expenses properly incurred in exploiting the right in question will fall to be deducted.[208] These include not only direct expenses, such as advertising and the cost of materials and machinery,[209] but also a fair proportion of overhead expenses.[210] A defendant should also be entitled, in an appropriate case, to a fair return on capital investment, for, as has been argued in the analogous context of improvements to the plaintiff's property effected by a wrongdoer, the opportunity foregone of securing a return on capital from other sources can fairly be claimed as a cost of the defendant's enterprise.[211] Plainly if the defendant borrows $1,000 to market the plaintiff's invention, the cost of borrowing the money is a cost of the enterprise.

---

[197] For footnotes 197-207 see discussion in third edition of this work (*The Law of Damages*, 3rd ed. (Toronto, Canada Law Book, 1997), 5.800-5.830).

[207a] *Copyright Act* (Can.), s. 38.1. See *Wing v. Van Velthuizen* (2000), 9 C.P.R. (4th) 449 (F.C.T.D.); *Telewizja Polsat S.A. v. Radiopol Inc.*, [2007] 1 F.C.R. 444; *Video Box Enterprises Inc. v. Lam* (2006), 52 C.P.R. (4th) 265 (F.C.).

[208] See *Caxton Publishing Co. v. Sutherland Publishing Co.*, [1939] A.C. 176 (H.L.), at pp. 204-5, where Lord Porter also said, dealing with damages for conversion, that the onus of proof lay upon the wrongdoer, a position expressly adopted by s. 35 of the *Canadian Copyright Act*. See also *Teledyne Industries Inc. v. Lido Industrial Products Ltd.* (1982), 31 C.P.C. 285, 68 C.P.R. (2d) 56 (F.C.T.D.); *Dart Industries Inc. v. Decor Corp. Pty. Ltd.* (1993), 179 C.L.R. 101 (Aust. H.C.); *Microsoft Corporation v. Auschina Polaris Pty Ltd.* (1996), 142 A.L.R. 111 (F.C. (Gen. Div.)); *Hertzog v. Highwire Information Inc.*, [1997] 3 F.C. D-32 (T.D.).

[209] *Roy Export Co. Establishment v. Gauthier* (1973), 10 C.P.R. (2d) 11 (Fed. Ct. T.D.), at p. 18; *Dubiner v. Cheerio Toys & Games Ltd.*, [1966] Ex. C.R. 801, 55 D.L.R. (2d) 420.

[210] *Roy Export Co., supra* (overhead expense attributed to the defendant's use of own time); *Dubiner v. Cheerio Toys & Games Ltd., supra*; *Dart Industries Inc. v. Decor Corp. Pty. Ltd., supra*, footnote 208.

[211] See 1.460-1.480, *supra*. In *Dubiner v. Cheerio Toys & Games Ltd., supra*, depreciation was allowed on capital assets.

Similarly if the defendant invests $1,000 or uses $1,000 worth of equipment, the defendant foregoes at the very least the interest that could have been earned by putting the money in the bank or by selling the equipment and investing the proceeds.

5.850 In *Dubiner v. Cheerio Toys & Games Ltd.*,[212] the question arose of the proper time period for the accounting. It was held that the profits should be assessed up to the time of the assessment by the registrar, but that the plaintiff was entitled to exclude the period between the judgment and assessment during which there had been a net loss. In principle, it is submitted that the plaintiff should not be entitled to pick out the profitable periods only; the notion is inconsistent with recovery of net profits; it would be absurd, for example, to allow the plaintiff to include days, or parts of days, during which revenues were received, excluding other days when expenses were incurred. However, the registrar's report in the *Dubiner* cases stressed that the loss after judgment was largely caused by expenses of litigation, which would not be allowable as a deduction in calculating the net profits derived from the infringement. Consequently, the result of the case may be supported on this ground.

5.860 Another aspect of the matter is that the plaintiff is only entitled to profit actually made from the defendant's wrongful act, not to profit that the defendant could have made without infringing the plaintiff's rights. Lord Watson said in *United Horse-Shoe & Nail Co. Ltd. v. Stewart & Co.*:[213]

> When a patentee elects to claim the profits made by the unauthorized use of his machinery, it becomes material to ascertain how much of his invention was actually appropriated, in order to determine what proportion of the net profits realized by the infringer was attributable to its use. It would be unreasonable to give the patentee profits which were not earned by the use of his invention.[214]

It is evident that difficult problems of causation will arise in a case where, as in the *United Horse-Shoe* case, the defendant has manufactured ordinary articles using a machine incorporating one minor feature that infringes the plaintiff's patent. The plaintiff must show how much the defendant has saved by the infringing feature. In some cases, as Blanco White comments, "such a calculation might be almost impossible".[215]

5.870 It may be noted that in the *United Horse-Shoe* case, the intermediate Appeal Court had calculated the defendant's profit at £50. The House of Lords restored the trial judge's assessment, based on the (at first sight) less generous measure of the plaintiff's loss: £530 — more than ten times as

---

212 *Supra.*

213 (1888), 13 App. Cas. 401 (H.L.).

214 *Supra*, at pp. 412-13. See also *Dubiner v. Cheerio Toys & Games Ltd., supra*, footnote 209.

215 Blanco White, *Patents for Inventions and the Protection of Industrial Designs*, 4th ed. (London, Stevens, 1974), §12-129; *Reading & Bates Construction Co. v. Baker Energy Resources Corp.*, [1995] 1 F.C. 483, 58 C.P.R. (3d) 359 (C.A.), leave to appeal to S.C.C. refused 191 N.R. 238*n*, 60 C.P.R. (3d) vi; *Stenner v. ScotiaMcLeod* (2007), 62 C.P.R. (4th) 1 (B.C.S.C.), at para. 183.

much. The possibility of this sort of result goes far to explain the unpopularity with plaintiffs of the remedy of account.[216]

5.880 Another restrictive feature of the remedy is that it has been held in several cases that the plaintiff must elect between an account and damages.[217] It has been argued, persuasively it is submitted, that the only necessary and legitimate rule is that the plaintiff may not be compensated twice over for the same loss.[218] Thus, if the plaintiff recovers the defendant's profits, the plaintiff ought not to be entitled as well to the profit that might have been made by selling products to the same customers, for they would not presumably have bought both from the plaintiff and the defendant. But often the plaintiff may legitimately claim an account of profits for a certain period of time and in addition residual damage to the plaintiff's interest, and some cases have permitted such claims to be combined. The ground for demanding an election was said in *Neilson v. Betts*[219] to be that "if you take an account of profits you condone the infringement".[220] But as Street points out,[221] this is a fictional condonation — as fictional as the "waiver" in waiver of tort which was held by the House of Lords in *United Australia, Ltd. v. Barclays Bank Ltd.*[222] not to constitute a binding election. It would seem therefore that a modern Canadian court should permit the plaintiff to combine a claim for accounting and for damages whenever there is no double compensation. Further, there seems no reason why a plaintiff who has initially claimed an

---

[216] See Blanco White, *Patents for Inventions and the Protection of Industrial Designs*, 4th ed. (London, Stevens, 1974), §12-129: "An account of profits ... commonly turns out to be less advantageous to the patentee than might prima facie be expected: it is also difficult and expensive to take."; Fox, *Canadian Patent Law and Practice*, 4th ed. (Toronto, Carswell Co. Ltd., 1969), pp. 503-4: "It has been said that an account of profits is extremely difficult to work out and should rarely be chosen ... To determine that profit is not only a matter of difficulty but is also, very often, a scant return to the plaintiff for the loss he may have sustained"; Laddie, Prescott and Vitoria, *The Modern Law of Copyright* (London, Butterworths, 1980), §12.28: "Since the taking of an account is usually complicated and expensive, this is a form of relief which is rarely sought in copyright actions."

[217] *Neilson v. Betts* (1871), L.R. 5 H.L. 1; *United Horse-Shoe & Nail Co. Ltd. v. Stewart & Co., supra*, footnote 213, at p. 412; *De Vitre v. Betts* (1873), L.R. 6 H.L. 319; *Caxton Publishing Co. Ltd. v. Sutherland Publishing Co., supra*, footnote 208, at p. 199. The remedies were permitted to be combined, however, in *Llynvi v. Brogden* (1870), L.R. 11 Eq. 188; *Jegon v. Vivian* (1871), 6 Ch. App. 742; *Ashover Fluor Spar Mines, Ltd. v. Jackson*, [1911] 2 Ch. 355. See also *Island Records Ltd. v. Tring International plc*, [1995] 3 All E.R. 444 (Ch. D.); *Dr. Martens Australia Pty Ltd. v. Bata Shoe Company of Australia Pty Ltd.* (1997), 145 A.L.R. 233 (F.C. (Gen. Div.)) (election may be postponed); *Tang Man Sit (decd) (personal representative) v. Capacious Investments Ltd.*, [1996] 1 All E.R. 193 (P.C.) (receipt of part of profit does not constitute election); *3925928 Manitoba Ltd. v. 101029530 Saskatchewan Ltd.* (2005), 44 C.P.R. (4th) 161 (F.C.). By s. 35(1) of the Canadian *Copyright Act* the court may award, in addition to damages, "such part of the profits ... as the court may decide to be just and proper".

[218] See Street, *Principles of the Law of Damages* (London, Sweet & Maxwell, 1962), pp. 263-6, and Vaver, "Civil Liability for Taking or Using Trade Secrets in Canada", 5 C.B.L.J. 253 (1981), at p. 299.

[219] *Supra*, footnote 217.

[220] *Neilson v. Betts, supra*, at p. 22.

[221] *Op. cit.*, footnote 218, at pp. 265-6.

[222] [1941] A.C. 1 (H.L.).

accounting, should not, on payment of the defendant's costs if appropriate, amend the claim at a later stage in the proceedings to claim loss of profits instead. In *Watson Laidlaw & Co. Ltd. v. Pott, Cassels & Williamson*[223] Lord Shaw said: "although it be true that a patentee cannot have other remedies at the same time, namely, the damage to his own business and the profits of the infringer's business, still this is true simply because it is in that way that overlapping is prevented".[224]

(4) Loss to plaintiff

5.890 The commonest claim for business losses is loss of profits, that is, the profit that the plaintiff would have made if the wrong had not been done. As Lord Watson said in the *United Horse-Shoe*[225] case: "That must always be more or less matter of estimate, because it is impossible to ascertain, with arithmetical precision, what in the ordinary course of business would have been the amount of the [plaintiffs'] sales and profits."[226] He went on to say that it was not to be presumed against the defendant that all the defendant's customers would have been the plaintiffs' customers if the wrong had not been done.[227] In the *United Horse-Shoe* case, the defendant manufactured horseshoe nails using a machine that incorporated a minor feature which infringed the plaintiff's patent. It would be expected that the defendant could successfully have competed to some extent even without infringing, and to ignore that fact "would be tantamount to giving the respondents not compensation merely, but profits which they would never have earned if the appellants had not infringed".[228]

5.900 On the other hand, Lord Watson added, that it was not to be presumed in favour of the infringers that they would certainly have competed with equal success had they acted lawfully.[229] On this point Lord MacNaughten said:

> I think it would be going too far to say that if the respondents had not been in the field the appellants would have sold an additional quantity, equal to the amount sold by the respondents. But ... I think it is a fair inference that if the appellants had been left undisturbed the natural increase of their

[223] (1914), 31 R.P.C. 104 (H.L.).

[224] *Supra*, at p. 119.

[225] (1888), 13 App. Cas. 401 (H.L.).

[226] *Supra*, at p. 413, followed in *Colonial Fastener Co. v. Lightning Fastener Co.*, [1937] S.C.R. 36, [1937] 1 D.L.R. 21; *Cons. Wafer Co. Ltd. v. Int'l Cone Co., Ltd.*, [1926] 4 D.L.R. 74, 59 O.L.R. 205 (S.C.). See *Toronto Type Foundry Ltd. v. Miehle-Goss-Dexter Inc.* (1968), 5 D.L.R. (3d) 578, [1969] 2 O.R. 431 (H.C.J.) (loss of profits on termination of franchise); *AlliedSignal Inc. v. Du Pont Canada Inc.* (1998), 78 C.P.R. (3d) 129, 142 F.T.R. 241 (T.D.), affd 86 C.P.R. (3d) 324, 235 N.R. 185 (C.A.); *Ben-Israel v. Vitacare Medical Products Inc.* (1999), 87 C.P.R. (3d) 518 (C.A.), at p. 521, citing this passage; *Cadbury Schweppes Inc. v. FBI Foods Ltd.*, [1999] 1 S.C.R. 142, 167 D.L.R. (4th) 577.

[227] *United Horse-Shoe, supra*, footnote 225, at p. 414, followed in *Colonial Fastener Co. v. Lightning Fastener Co., supra*, footnote 226.

[228] *United Horse-Shoe, supra*, footnote 225. A similar point was made in *Tasco Telephone Answering Exchange Ltd. v. Ellerbeck* (1966), 57 D.L.R. (2d) 500 (B.C.S.C.) (wrongful competition).

[229] *United Horse-Shoe, supra*, footnote 225.

business would have come near the aggregate of the quantity sold by the appellants and respondents together.[230]

In *Colonial Fastener Co. v. Lightning Fastener Co.*,[231] where the feature infringed was an integral part of the finished product, the Supreme Court of Canada pointed out that the plaintiff had lost sales of the finished product not of components.

5.910 In *Draper v. Trist*,[232] it was held that in an action for passing off, substantial damages could be inferred from proof that deceptive goods had been put into circulation by the defendant. If the wrong causes the plaintiff to lose an opportunity that would not have been profitable, no loss is proven.[233] If the defendant's wrongful competition causes the plaintiff to lower the price of her product, the defendant will be liable for the loss,[234] but again the plaintiff must show that legitimate competition would not have forced lower prices. In the *United Horse-Shoe* case, Lord Watson inferred that on account of legitimate competition, the pursuers' sales level "could not have been maintained without a reduction of price".[235]

5.920 In *W.Y. McCarter, Burr Co. Ltd. v. Harris*,[236] the Alberta Appellate Division stressed that, in estimating lost profits, the uncertainties of business must be taken into account and the plaintiff's optimistic estimate cannot be accepted at face value. Stuart J.A. said, in commenting on an award of $12,000 at trial for loss of profits for breach of a patent medicine agency contract:

> ... if the choice had been given of accepting half that sum in ready cash or of going on and of taking all the uncertain chances of the popularity of a patent medicine continuing, of going on with business expenses in the way of persistent and costly advertising and of seeking and filling orders and of paying salaries to its officers, I feel sure that it, the plaintiff, would have hesitated long before refusing it and would, in its consideration of the offer, not have felt so much certainty about its future business as its officers seemed at the trial to entertain.
>
> Of course, this is not strictly the correct basis upon which to estimate damages for loss of profits. The plaintiff is not to be made to take merely what its contract would bring if put on the market for sale, nor is the defendant entitled to buy the contract back at what the Court may think a fair price by deliberately breaking it. The plaintiff was entitled to its chance

230 *United Horse-Shoe*, *supra*, at p. 417.
231 *Supra*, footnote 226.
232 (1939), 56 R.P.C. 429 (C.A.). See *Edward Chapman Ladies' Shop Ltd. v. Edward Chapman Ltd.* (2006), 49 C.P.R. (4th) 39 (B.C.S.C.), affd 60 C.P.R. (4th) 1 (B.C.C.A.).
233 *Findlay v. Howard* (1919), 58 S.C.R. 516, 47 D.L.R. 441; *Sommerfeldt v. Petrovitch*, [1949] 4 D.L.R. 825 (Sask. C.A.).
234 *Meters, Ltd. v. Metropolitan Gas Meters, Ltd.* (1911) 104 L.T. 113 (C.A.), at p. 118, *per* Cozens-Hardy, M.R., at p. 120, *per* Buckley L.J.; *Colonial Fastener Co. v. Lightning Fastener Co.*, *supra*, footnote 220.
235 *United Horse-Shoe*, *supra*, footnote 219, at p. 414; *Colonial Fastener Co. v. Lightning Fastener Co.*, *supra*, footnote 220.
236 (1922), 70 D.L.R. 420 (Alta. S.C. App. Div.). See also *Nathu v. Imbrook Properties Ltd.* (1992), 89 D.L.R. (4th) 751, 41 C.P.R. (3d) 458, supplementary reasons 96 D.L.R. (4th) 223, 45 C.P.R. (3d) 419 (Alta. C.A.).

of profits and to have the Court estimate its probable profits. But I cannot avoid the conviction that the plaintiff will be very much better off with $12,000 in cash now than with a continuance of the contract.[237]

5.930 The probable loss of future business profits, though difficult to estimate,[238] has been awarded in a wide variety of circumstances.[239] In assessing the loss, any advantages accruing to the plaintiff because of the wrong will be taken into account to reduce damages. Thus in one case of wrongful competition, the plaintiff received a subsidy from its supplier to assist in meeting the defendant's competition. It was held that damages were to be reduced accordingly.[240]

5.940 Damage to a business interest is sometimes estimated as a capital sum. In principle, as has been argued in relation to damage to property,[241] a diminution in capital value of an income producing asset is simply an alternative measure of the potential loss of income. Thus, care is needed to avoid a double compensation.[242] Full compensation for the diminution in capital value of the plaintiff's business interest is equivalent to full compensation for the estimated loss of profit. The plaintiff therefore cannot have both.[242a] Choice of method is a matter of convenience.[242b] It is common for the plaintiff to claim a loss of goodwill as a capital sum, estimated by the lesser amount that a rational purchaser would pay for the plaintiff's business in view of the defendant's wrong.[242c] An estimate of this sort is often made in cases of trade libel,[243] and in *Caron Ltée v. U.S. Dungaree Seafarers Ltd.*[244]

---

[237] *Supra*, at p. 430.

[238] On problems of uncertainty, see 13.10-13.60, *infra*.

[239] *Lister (Ronald Elwyn) Ltd. v. Dunlop Canada Ltd.*, [1982] 1 S.C.R. 726, 135 D.L.R. (3d) 1 (wrongful seizure of stock causing cessation of business); *Barnes (William R.) Co. Ltd. v. MacKenzie* (1974), 44 D.L.R. (3d) 9, 2 O.R. (2d) 659 (C.A.) (losses caused by employee trading on account: salary not recoverable in addition); *Nathu v. Imbrook Properties Ltd.*, *supra*, footnote 236; *D.J. Lowe (1980) Ltd. v. Nova Scotia (Attorney General)* (1993), 121 N.S.R. (2d) 361, 9 C.L.R. (2d) 181 (S.C.); *Ticketnet Corp. v. Air Canada* (1997), 154 D.L.R. (4th) 271, 105 O.A.C. 87 (C.A.), leave to appeal to S.C.C. refused 161 D.L.R. (4th) vii; *Roe, McNeill & Co. v. McNeill*, [1998] 7 W.W.R. 175 (B.C.C.A.); *Cadbury Schweppes Inc. v. FBI Foods Ltd.*, [1999] 1 S.C.R. 142, 167 D.L.R. (4th) 577; *3317447 Manitoba Ltd. v. Beaver Lumber Inc.* (2006), 286 Sask. R. 290 (Q.B.). See also the cases on breach of warranty, 14.320, *infra*.

[240] *White Oaks Welding Supplies v. Tapp* (1983), 149 D.L.R. (3d) 159, 42 O.R. (2d) 445 (H.C.J.). But see the Australian case of *Masters Dairy Ltd. v. Nagy* (1998), 156 A.L.R. 262 (F.C.A.), where the court held that statutory payments and damages exist independent of each other.

[241] See 1.1830, 1.1840, *supra*.

[242] *Lister (Ronald Elwyn) Ltd. v. Dayton Tire Canada Ltd.* (1985), 52 O.R. (2d) 88 (C.A.), at p. 112, citing this passage.

[242a] *Duhigh Holdings Ltd. v. 24 Hour Entertainment Group Ltd.* (2004), 25 R.P.R. (4th) 185 (B.C.S.C.).

[242b] *Silver v. Co-operators General Insurance Co.* (1998), 169 N.S.R. (2d) 303 (C.A.), at p. 308 citing this paragraph, leave to appeal to S.C.C. refused 169 N.S.R. (2d) 303.

[242c] *Air Canada v. WestJet Airlines Ltd.* (2004), 72 O.R. (3d) 669 (Ont. S.C.J.), at p. 676, citing this passage. See also *Ascent Financial Services Ltd. v. Blythman* (2006), 276 Sask. R. 23 (Q.B.), affd [2008] 5 W.W.R. 638 (Sask. C.A.).

[243] *Worsley v. Cooper*, [1939] 1 All E.R. 290 (Ch.).

[244] [1978] 4 W.W.R. 681 (B.C.S.C.).

damages for passing off were measured in this way. Cases of copyright infringement are also dealt with by estimating the residual value of the copyright in the plaintiff's hands after infringement, or as Lord Wright put it in *Sutherland Publishing Co. v. Caxton Publishing Co.*,[245] "the depreciation caused by the infringement to the value of the copyright as a chose in action".[246] In *Campbell, Imrie & Shankland v. Park*[247] the defendant, in breach of a covenant against competition, caused the loss of one third of the plaintiff's accounting practice. The court based damages on evidence that an accounting practice was commonly valued, for sale purposes, at one year's gross fees, but increased the basic award to allow for the fact that such a large proportion of the practice had been lost.

5.950 The method is convenient where evidence is available to estimate the capital value of the plaintiff's asset before and after infringement. A capital sum has also been awarded to represent the damage caused to the plaintiff by a competitor's obtaining a "head start", or "springboard", by the misuse of confidential information.[248]

5.960 In *Talbot v. General Television Corp.*,[249] an Australian court used similar methods to compensate the plaintiff for misuse in breach of confidence of the plaintiff's idea for a television game show. The court held that no single method of assessing damages could be laid down for such cases, but that a fair method in the particular case was to estimate the depreciation in market value of the plaintiff's idea by the defendant's infringement. A sum of $15,000 was awarded.

(5) Reasonable licence fee or royalty rate

5.970 In a number of cases damages have been awarded representing the reasonable fee or royalty rate that the plaintiff might have charged to license the defendant's actions.[250] It is clear that this may go beyond what the plaintiff could recover as lost profits, for the defendant might have had a profitable use for the plaintiff's property that would not have been available to the plaintiff. Consequently, a reasonable fee from the defendant's point of view might far exceed any profit the plaintiff could have made.

245 [1936] Ch. 323 (C.A.), affd [1939] A.C. 178 (H.L.).

246 *Supra*, at p. 336.

247 [1954] 2 D.L.R. 170 (B.C.S.C.).

248 *Ascent Financial Services Ltd. v. Blythman* (2006), 276 Sask. R. 23 (Q.B.), affd [2008] 5 W.W.R. 638 (Sask. C.A.), at para. 46, citing this and the two preceding paragraphs; *Schauenburg Industries Ltd. v. Borowski* (1979), 101 D.L.R. (3d) 701, 25 O.R. (2d) 737 (H.C.J.); *Terrapin Ltd. v. Builders Supply Co. (Hayes) Ltd.*, [1960] R.P.C. 128 (C.A.).

249 [1980] V.R. 224 (S.C.).

250 *Stovin-Bradford v. Volpoint*, [1971] Ch. 1007 (C.A.); *Seager v. Copydex Ltd. (No. 2)*, [1969] 1 W.L.R. 809 (C.A.); *Chabot v. Davies*, [1936] 3 All E.R. 221 (Ch.); *Meikle v. Maufe*, [1941] 3 All E.R. 144 (Ch.); *Watson Laidlaw & Co. Ltd. v. Pott, Cassels & Williamson* (1914), 31 R.P.C. 104 (H.L.); *Hager v. ECW Press Ltd.*, [1999] 2 F.C. 287 (T.D.); *2 For 1 Subs Ltd. v. Ventresca* (2006), 48 C.P.R. (4th) 311 (Ont. S.C.J.); *Jay-Lor International Inc. v. Penta Farm Systems Ltd.* (2007), 313 F.T.R. 1 (F.C.); *Freyberg v. Fletcher Challenge Oil and Gas Inc.*, [2007] 10 W.W.R. 133 (Alta. Q.B.).

5.980 In *Watson Laidlaw & Co. Ltd. v. Pott, Cassels & Williamson*[251] this point was discussed at length by Lord Shaw, who held that a patentee was entitled to a reasonable licence fee for an infringement even though the plaintiff could not have exploited the market exploited by the infringer. He said:

> ... in such cases it appears to me that he correct and full measure is only reached by adding that a patentee is also entitled, on the principle of price or hire, to a royalty for the unauthorised sale or use of every one of the infringing machines in a market which the [patentee] if left to himself, might not have reached. Otherwise, that property which consists in the monopoly of the patented articles granted to the patentee has been invaded, and indeed abstracted, and the law, when appealed to, would be standing by and allowing the invader or abstractor to go free. In such cases a royalty is an excellent key to unlock the difficulty ...[252]

5.990 It has been objected that this approach blurs the line between a restitutionary theory of recovery (represented in this field by account) and a compensatory theory. But it has been argued elsewhere that the blurring of this line is not objectionable, indeed, that it is desirable for on a compensatory theory the plaintiff is entitled to damages for loss of the opportunity to license the infringement, and the fee that the defendant would have paid is directly related to the profitability of the right in the plaintiff's hands.[253] Lord Shaw was indeed aware of the relationship of account and damages for he said:

> In the first place, it is clear to my mind, that suppose the Respondents had chosen to ask for an account of profits made by the infringers upon the infringing machines, they would have been entitled to obtain it and a decree for the amount, and it would have been no answer to say: "The account shall be given, but there shall be excluded from it places which we shall establish your trade would never have reached." In the second place ... it appears to me that, although it be true that a patentee cannot have both remedies at the same time, namely, the damages to his own business and the profits of the infringers' business, still this is true simply because it is in that way that overlapping is prevented. But in the instances of which the present is an excellent type there is no overlapping whatsoever. If with regard to the general trade which was done, or would have been done by the Respondents within their ordinary range of trade, damages be assessed, these ought, of course, to enter the account and to stand. But in addition there remains that class of business which the respondents would not have done ...[254]

Lord Shaw plainly considered that a reasonable royalty could be regarded as an alternative to an account and that the profits made by the wrongdoer were relevant to its assessment.

5.1000 In *Stovin Bradford v. Volpoint*,[255] an architect's plans prepared for

[251] *Supra.*

[252] *Watson Laidlaw, supra*, at p. 120, applied in *Colonial Fastener Co. v. Lightning Fastener Co.*, [1937] S.C.R. 36, [1937] 1 D.L.R. 21.

[253] See 9.70-9.130, *infra*, and Sharpe and Waddams, "Damages for Lost Opportunity to Bargain", 2 Ox. J.L.S. 290 (1982).

[254] *Watson Laidlaw, supra*, footnote 250, at pp. 119-20.

purposes of obtaining planning permission were used in breach of copyright in the actual construction of the building. The plaintiff was awarded £500, that being the sum that he might reasonably have demanded for a licence to use the drawings. An earlier case[256] was followed in which the court had laid down the following question as a test: "What is the remuneration which the plaintiff would fairly have got for his plan if the defendant had applied for his leave and licence to use it?"[257] Though the plaintiff appears in these cases to suffer no loss, the plaintiff does lose the right to license the defendant and, it is submitted, compensation for that loss is fully in accord with the general principles of damage assessment.

5.1010 In *Seager v. Copydex Ltd. (No. 2)*,[258] a similar measure was applied to a misuse of confidential information. The Court of Appeal drew a distinction between the case where the information might easily be obtained from a consultant in which case the proper measure would be a reasonable fee, and a case where the information involved a "truly inventive step" in which case the plaintiff should be awarded the capitalized value of a reasonable royalty payment. This distinction corresponds to that found in property cases between cases where there is an available market substitute for what the defendant has taken, in which case its reasonable value is the limit of the defendant's liability, and cases where the plaintiff is the only supplier of the property, in which case damages are based on what the defendant would reasonably have paid.[259]

5.1020 The amount of the reasonable fee in such cases is never easy to calculate, but it is submitted that the profitability to the defendant of the right to use the plaintiff's property must be a most relevant consideration. It has been suggested in the context of the property cases that it is not unfair to presume that the defendant would have paid up to an amount equal to the net advantage of the use of the right.[260] In *General Tire & Rubber Co. v. Firestone Tyre & Rubber Co. Ltd.*,[261] Lord Wilberforce held that the proper measure in a case of patent infringement was what the defendant would have paid not "what the infringer ought fairly to have paid".[262] But there was, in that case, very definite evidence ("strong and concrete evidence of actual bargains")[263] of the licence fee in fact regularly accepted by the plaintiff.

255 *Supra*, applied in *Interfirm Comparison (Australia) Pty. Ltd. v. Law Society of New South Wales*, [1975] 2 N.S.W.L.R. 104.
256 *Chabot v. Davies, supra*, footnote 250.
257 *Chabot v. Davies, supra*, at p. 228.
258 *Supra*, footnote 250. The result then is that the defendant, having paid its full value, acquires the right to use the information. *Seager* was applied in *Lake Mechanical Systems Corp. v. Crandell Mechanical Systems Inc.* (1985), 31 B.L.R. 113, 9 C.C.E.L. 52 (B.C.S.C.), and distinguished in *Dowson & Mason Ltd. v. Potter*, [1986] 1 W.L.R. 1419 (C.A.) (loss of profits the primary measure of damages). See also *Cadbury Schweppes Inc. v. FBI Food Ltd.*, [1999] 1 S.C.R. 142, 167 D.L.R. (4th) 577.
259 See 9.70-9.130, *infra*, and Sharpe and Waddams, *op. cit.*, footnote 253, at p. 296.
260 See 9.70-9.130, *infra*, and Sharpe and Waddams, *op. cit.*, footnote 253.
261 [1975] 1 W.L.R. 819 (H.L.).
262 *Supra*, at p. 833.

Where, as is usual, it is uncertain what fee the plaintiff would have charged, Lord Wilberforce's speech is not inconsistent, it is suggested, with an estimate of the reasonable fee at the highest amount that a rational person in the defendant's position would have paid. Indeed, Lord Wilberforce himself said in the same case that it was an essential principle of assessment of damages that: "the defendants being wrongdoers, damages should be liberally assessed but that the object is to compensate the plaintiffs and not punish the defendants".[264]

5.1030 As has been submitted earlier, taking account of the profitability of infringement to the defendant does not seem to be inconsistent with the compensatory objective, considering that a liberal assessment is justifiable against a wrongdoer.

5.1040 Further support is lent to this approach by another decision of the House of Lords, *Caxton Publishing Co. v. Sutherland Publishing Co.*,[265] where the court had to interpret provisions of the *Copyright Act* by which copies of works that infringed the plaintiff's rights were deemed to be the plaintiff's property. The defendant had incorporated some material, in which the plaintiff had copyright, in a larger work. It was held that the plaintiff was entitled to damages for conversion measured by a just proportion of the value of the sales by the defendant of the entire work. This was held to be one shilling per copy. Thus, in effect, the plaintiff was given a share in the defendant's profits. Lord Porter pointed out that the plaintiff would have been entitled, before the sheets were bound up as a book, to demand the excision and delivery up of the portions containing the infringing material. The plaintiff could presumably have obtained an injunction to restrain binding and, Lord Porter added, the defendant would presumably have paid a substantial sum for the right to use the material — he thought up to one shilling per volume. Admittedly Lord Porter described this as an artificial way of considering the problem,[267] but it seems plain by the fact that he thought it relevant to mention it, that it supported in his mind the justice of the conclusion reached by the court, which amounted by the route of the statutory fiction of the proprietary interest in the actual copies of the infringing material to an award of the profits derived by the defendant from the infringement. The case is not an ordinary one of conversion for the plaintiff was not deprived of any tangible property that had formerly been his. His property in the paper sheets came into existence when the defendant printed certain words on them. The statutory provision as to property is primarily intended to give the plaintiff a remedy for breach of copyright and the conclusion reached in the case is, it is submitted, a sound one consistent

---

263 *Supra*, at p. 832.
264 *Supra*, at p. 824.
265 [1939] A.C. 178 (H.L.).
266 [Footnote deleted.]
267 *Caxton Publishing Co. v. Sutherland Publishing Co.*, *supra*, footnote 265, at p. 204.

on the basis here suggested, with the remedy that the court might have given even in the absence of the statutory fiction.

9. Costs of Investigating the Wrong

5.1050 Litigation costs are not generally considered to be part of the law of damages and are not discussed in this book. However, some cases have permitted recovery, not as costs but as damages, of the expense of investigating the defendant's wrong. Such recovery has been allowed in cases of breach of contract[268] and of inducing breach of contract,[269] and nuisance,[270] and there seems no reason why recovery should not be supported wherever investigatory costs can be anticipated as a natural and probable consequence of the defendant's wrong.

10. Loss of Earnings

5.1060 This section is concerned with compensation for loss by the plaintiff of the opportunity to earn money by supplying services. Most of the cases are those of breach of contract by employers. Some of the cases, however, involve wrongful interference by third parties with a person's opportunity to render services. The discussion is not limited to employment contracts in the strict sense, but deals also with contracts for services, including building contracts and contracts of carriage.

5.1070 In wrongful dismissal cases, the first question is usually the extent of the employer's obligation. If the parties have expressly agreed to a particular term of employment, this will be the extent of the employer's obligation. Where the employer can terminate the employment on notice, the period of notice, either as expressly agreed or as determined by the court to be reasonable, will measure the extent of the employer's liability. When the employee enjoys security of tenure or has the right of actual reinstatement, damages will be more extensive.[271] Against a third party, the employee may be entitled to compensation for loss of the chance of future renewals of the employment contract.[272] The length of proper notice is a question of substantive law not of damages.[273]

5.1080 An employee wrongfully dismissed is entitled to compensation not only for loss of wages and salary but also for other forms of remuneration, such as commissions,[274] gratuities[275] and other benefits[276] insofar as the plaintiff

---

268 *Acme Investments Ltd. v. York Structural Steel Ltd.* (1974), 9 N.B.R. (2d) 699 (S.C. App. Div.)

269 *British Motor Trade Ass'n v. Salvadori*, [1949] Ch. 556.

270 *Nor-Video Services Ltd. v. Ontario Hydro* (1978), 84 D.L.R. (3d) 221, 19 O.R. (2d) 107 (H.C.J.), affd (unreported, March 12, 1979, C.A.).

271 See *Rankin v. National Harbours Board* (1979), 99 D.L.R. (3d) 631 (B.C.S.C.), vard 127 D.L.R. (3d) 714 (C.A.); *Cohnstaedt v. University of Regina*, [1995] 3 S.C.R. 451, 131 D.L.R. (4th) 605.

272 See *Hornak v. Paterson* (1967), 62 D.L.R. (2d) 289 (B.C.S.C.). See also 5.300, *supra*.

273 The leading Canadian case is *Bardal v. Globe & Mail Ltd.* (1960), 24 D.L.R. (2d) 140, [1960] O.W.N. 253 (H.C.J.). The law is discussed in Christie, England and Cotter, *Employment Law in Canada*, 2nd ed. (Toronto, Butterworths, 1993), pp. 598-627.

suffers actual loss.[277] Pension payments received during the notice period are not deductible from compensation for loss of salary, but they are to be taken into account in determining loss of pension.[277a] Costs of moving in search of alternative employment have been allowed in some cases,[278] but, it would seem, these can only be justified if they are expenses reasonably incurred in an attempt to mitigate the loss caused by the employer's breach, for the

---

[274] *Addis v. Gramophone Co.*, [1909] A.C. 488 (H.L.); *Trollope v. Martyn*, [1934] 2 K.B. 436 (C.A.); *Laishley v. Goold Bicycle Co.* (1903), 6 O.L.R. 319 (C.A.), leave to appeal to S.C.C. refused 35 S.C.R. 184; *Bishop v. Vachon Inc.* (1979), 22 Nfld. & P.E.I.R. 148 (Nfld. S.C.T.D.); *Lingelbach v. James Tire Centres Ltd.* (1994), 120 D.L.R. (4th) 456, [1995] 2 W.W.R. 330 (Sask. C.A.). But commission is only recoverable if the defendant is in breach of an obligation in respect of it. See *Robertson v. Equivest Securities Ltd.* (1980), 19 B.C.L.R. 274 (S.C.), where the employer ceased business and was held not to have guaranteed any particular level of sales.

[275] *Manubens v. Leon*, [1919] 1 K.B. 208.

[276] *Hardie v. Trans-Canada Resources Ltd.* (1976), 71 D.L.R. (3d) 668 (S.C. App. Div.); *Manning v. Surrey Memorial Hospital Society* (1975), 54 D.L.R. (3d) 312 (B.C.S.C.); *Gillespie v. Bulkley Valley Forest Industries Ltd.* (1973), 39 D.L.R. (3d) 586 (B.C.S.C.), affd 50 D.L.R. (3d) 316 (C.A.); *Bursey v. Acadia Motors* (1980), 35 N.B.R. (2d) 587 (C.A.); *Bagby v. Gustavson Int'l Drilling Co.* (1979), 20 A.R. 244 (S.C.), affd 24 A.R. 181 (C.A.); *Paziuk v. Rural Municipality of Ethelbert* (1963), 44 D.L.R. (2d) 165 (Man. Q.B.); *Carey v. F. Drexel Co.*, [1974] 4 W.W.R. 492 (B.C.S.C.); *Rooney v. Reed Ltd.* (1978), 88 D.L.R. (3d) 414, 20 O.R. (2d) 665 (H.C.J.); *Smith v. Worldwide Church of God* (1980), 39 N.S.R. (2d) 430 (S.C.T.D.); *Rahmath v. Louisiana Land & Exploration Co.* (1989), 59 D.L.R. (4th) 606, 97 A.R. 246, supplementary reasons 65 D.L.R. (4th) 150, 104 A.R. 391 (C.A.); *Wiebe v. Central Transport Refrigeration (Man.) Ltd.* (1993), 84 Man. R. (2d) 273, 45 C.C.E.L. 1 (Q.B.), vard [1994] 6 W.W.R. 305, 3 C.C.E.L. (2d) 1 (C.A.); *Knox v. Interprovincial Engineering Ltd.* (1993), 120 N.S.R. (2d) 288 (S.C.) (bonus, even though discretionary (see 5.1240, *infra*)); *Corbin v. Standard Life Assurance Co.* (1995), 167 N.B.R. (2d) 355, 15 C.C.E.L. (2d) 71 (C.A.).

[277] *Sorel v. Tomenson Saunders Whitehead Ltd.* (1987), 39 D.L.R. (4th) 460, 15 B.C.L.R. (2d) 38 (C.A.); *Cronk v. Canadian General Insurance Co.* (1995), 128 D.L.R. (4th) 147, 25 O.R. (3d) 505 (C.A.); *Swinamer v. Unitel Communications Inc.* (1996), 147 N.S.R. (2d) 249, 17 C.C.E.L. (2d) 59 (S.C.). This passage was cited with approval in *Mandavia v. Central West Health Care Institutions Board* (2004), 236 Nfld. & P.E.I.R. 45 (Nfld. & Lab. S.C.T.D.), at para. 5, vard 245 Nfld. & P.E.I.R. 107 (Nfld. & Lab. C.A.); *Unrau v. Calm Air International Ltd.* (1995), 103 Man. R. (2d) 220, 12 C.C.E.L. (2d) 235 (Q.B.) (free travel passes); *Scott v. Lillooet School District No. 29* (1991), 60 B.C.L.R. (2d) 273, 11 W.A.C. 254 (C.A.) (not vacation pay); *Fitzgerald v. Waterford Hospital Board* (1997), 146 D.L.R. (4th) 60, 148 Nfld. & P.E.I.R. 271 (Nfld. C.A.) (not vacation pay); *Bergmann v. CPT Canada Power Technology Ltd.*, [1998] 1 W.W.R. 319, 207 A.R. 212 (Q.B.) (not car allowance); *Sherrard v. Moncton Chrysler Dodge (1980) Ltd.* (1991), 113 N.B.R. (2d) 355, 33 C.C.E.L. 72 (C.A.) (not use of company car); *Peddle v. Rowan Companies, Inc.* (1993), 123 N.S.R. (2d) 409, 47 C.C.E.L. 48 (S.C.); *Regiec v. Breezy Bend Country Club* (1999), 137 Man. R. (2d) 237, supplementary reasons 141 Man. R. (2d) 316 (Q.B.) (not medical benefits if no actual claims). But the Ontario Court of Appeal has allowed the value of medical benefits even though the plaintiff suffered no actual loss: *Davidson v. Allelix Inc.* (1991), 86 D.L.R. (4th) 54 (C.A.).

[277a] *Peet v. Babcock & Wilcox Industries Ltd.* (2001), 197 D.L.R. (4th) 633 (Ont. C.A.).

[278] *Logan v. Board of Trustees District 14* (1974), 8 N.B.R. (2d) 274 (S.C.Q.B.), revd on other grounds *loc. cit.*, p. 269 (S.C. App. Div.); *Vos v. Security Trust Co. Ltd.* (1969), 68 W.W.R. 310 (Alta. S.C.); *Erlund v. Quality Communication Products Ltd.* (1972), 29 D.L.R. (3d) 476 (Man. Q.B.); *O'Grady v. Ins. Corp. of British Columbia* (1975), 63 D.L.R. (3d) 370 (B.C.S.C.); *Vautour v. Miramichi Air Services Ltd.* (1978), 26 N.B.R. (2d) 391 (Co. Ct.); *Husain v. Portage La Prairie School District No. 24* (1981), 121 D.L.R. (3d) 758 (Man. C.A.), leave to appeal to S.C.C. refused 38 N.R. 540*n*.

plaintiff might have had to move even if proper notice had been given.[279] Similarly, damages have been awarded for business losses incurred in a reasonable attempt to mitigate.[279a] An employee may be entitled to severance pay in addition to reasonable notice of termination.[279b]

5.1090 It appears to be firmly established in Canada that, on wrongful dismissal, the employee's action is for damages; the employee cannot, normally, ignore the repudiation and sue for the remuneration promised.[280] In *Vine v. National Dock Labour Board*,[281] Viscount Kilmuir L.C. said in a passage approved in *Michaels v. Red Deer College*:[282] "if the master wrongfully dismisses the servant, either summarily or by giving insufficient notice, the employment is effectively terminated, albeit in breach of contract".[283] In *Canadian Ice Machine Co. Ltd. v. Sinclair*,[284] Kellock J. said "The law is clearly settled that the remedy of a person [wrongfully dismissed] is to sue for damages. He is not entitled to wait until the termination of the period for which he was engaged and sue for the whole amount of the wages which have fallen due in the interim."[285]

5.1100 Similarly, in *Cemco Electrical Manufacturing Co. Ltd. v. Van Snellenberg*[286] Kerwin J. said for the majority of the Supreme Court of Canada: "The Company having broken the contract, the plaintiff was not entitled to consider it as still subsisting."[287] Though this is the normal rule, there are

---

[279] See *Rooney v. Reed Ltd.* (1978), 88 D.L.R. (3d) 414 at p. 418, 20 O.R. (2d) 665 (H.C.J.), *per* Southey J.; *Emery v. Royal Oak Mines Inc.* (1995), 24 O.R. (3d) 302, 11 C.C.E.L. (2d) 149 (Gen. Div.); *McNamara v. Price Wilson Ltd.* (1979), 12 B.C.L.R. 300 (S.C.) (moving expenses taken into account in fixing period of reasonable notice); *Schmidt v. Saskatchewan Oil and Gas Corp.* (1993), 107 Sask. R. 114 (Q.B.).

[279a] *Graceffo v. Alitalia*, [1995] 2 W.W.R. 351, 99 Man. R. (2d) 81 (Q.B.).

[279b] *Fitzgerald v. Waterford Hospital Board*, *supra*, footnote 277.

[280] *Prozak v. Bell Telephone Co. of Canada* (1984), 10 D.L.R. (4th) 382 at p. 399, 46 O.R. 385 (C.A.), citing this passage; *Philp v. Expo 86 Corp.* (1987), 45 D.L.R. (4th) 449, 19 B.C.L.R. (2d) 88 (C.A.); *Neilson v. Vancouver Hockey Club Ltd.* (1988), 51 D.L.R. (4th) 40, [1988] 4 W.W.R. 410 (B.C.C.A.), leave to appeal to S.C.C. refused 92 N.R. 240*n*. But see *Smart v. South Saskatchewan Hospital Centre* (1989), 60 D.L.R. (4th) 8, [1989] 5 W.W.R. 289 (Sask. C.A.), where the Saskatchewan Court of Appeal held otherwise in order to avoid the effect of a short limitation period.

[281] [1957] A.C. 488 (H.L.).

[282] (1974), 44 D.L.R. (3d) 447 at p. 456 (Alta. S.C. App. Div.), affd [1976] 2 S.C.R. 324, 57 D.L.R. (3d) 386.

[283] *Vine v. National Dock Labour Board*, *supra*, footnote 281, at p. 500.

[284] [1955] S.C.R. 777, [1955] 5 D.L.R. 1.

[285] *Supra*, at p. 781 S.C.R., p. 4 D.L.R., Cartwright J. concurred with Kellock J. The other judges did not expressly deal with the general rule, but Kerwin C.J. and Estey J. spoke of an obligation to mitigate (at p. 778 S.C.R., p. 2 D.L.R.), which seems inconsistent with a theory of recovery of the salary promised as a debt. Kellock J.'s formulation was expressly approved in *Forest Products Consulting Co. Ltd. v. Newfoundland Hardwoods Ltd.* (1956), 38 M.P.R. 374 (Nfld. S.C.), and in *Michaels v. Red Deer College*, *supra*, footnote 282. See also *Drayton v. W.C.W. Western Water Enterprises Inc.* (1989), 63 D.L.R. (4th) 71, 28 C.C.E.L. 134 (B.C.S.C.).

[286] [1947] S.C.R. 121, [1946] 4 D.L.R. 305.

[287] *Supra*, at p. 127 S.C.R., p. 309 D.L.R., cited with approval in *Red Deer College v. Michaels*, [1976] 2 S.C.R. 324 at p. 329, 57 D.L.R. (3d) 386 at p. 389. See also *Emms v. The Queen*, [1979] 2 S.C.R. 1148, 102 D.L.R. (3d) 193, where a declaration of continued employment was refused.

exceptions. The question is further discussed in the context of mitigation,[288] where it is suggested that, in cases where (but only where) the plaintiff has such an interest in continuing the employment status as the courts would recognize by a decree of specific enforcement, the plaintiff should be entitled to ignore the wrongful dismissal and to recover the agreed remuneration.

5.1110 A consequence of the principle that the employee is entitled only to damages is that the damages are to be assessed on the basis of the period of reasonable notice to which the employee was entitled. Thus, in *Prozak v. Bell Telephone Co. of Canada*,[289] the plaintiffs' terms of employment were, in breach of contract, altered so as to reduce their rights to commission. The Ontario Court of Appeal held that, in assessing damages, only commissions that would probably have been earned during the period of reasonable notice were to be taken into account. The decision is, it is submitted, justifiable on the principle that the defendant could, without any wrong, have given the employees due notice of termination.[290] The employees' position, where lengthy efforts are required to earn commissions, can be protected, as in the *Prozak* case, by the selection of a suitably lengthened period for reasonable notice of dismissal.[291]

5.1120 Loss of earnings caused by personal injuries is dealt with in the chapter on personal injuries.[292] There are reasons of convenience for this approach. First, the assessment of compensation for loss of earnings in personal injury cases involves questions of overlap with other heads of compensation and is constantly discussed in relation to them. Secondly, compensation in personal injury cases is, in the view of the Supreme Court of Canada and the House of Lords, properly based not on loss of earnings as such but on loss of earning capacity as an immediate loss caused by the injury.

5.1130 Where the plaintiff has rendered services that, by the terms of the relevant contract entitle the plaintiff to recover the agreed price for them, a loss of earnings has not been suffered. It is a question of the substantive law governing the particular contract whether on the facts sufficient performance has been rendered to entitle the plaintiff to recover the agreed price. The action in that case will be for a debt for wages, for an agreed commission, or for an agreed price for the service that has been rendered. In most jurisdictions statutory procedures facilitate the recovery of unpaid wages.[293]

5.1140 Another possible remedy for breach of a service contract that has been partly performed is a restitutionary action for the value of the services rendered. This is an important possibility where the plaintiff has made an unprofitable contract and in consequence the value of the services is greater

---

288 See 15.630, *infra*.

289 *Supra*, footnote 280.

290 See 13.390, *infra*; *Evans v. Teamsters Local Union No. 31* (2008), 292 D.L.R. (4th) 577 (S.C.C.), at para. 29.

291 Eighteen months.

292 See 3.710-3.1140, *supra*.

293 See, Christie, England and Cotter, *Employment Law in Canada* (Toronto, Butterworths, 1993), pp. 809-34.

than the compensation for them that would have been earned under the contract. Restitutionary remedies are discussed in a later chapter.[294]

5.1150 The basic principle of compensation is that the plaintiff is entitled to be put, so far as money can do it, in the position that would have been occupied if the wrong had not been done.[295] This principle in a case where the plaintiff is deprived of opportunities to render services and earn a reward suggests as a starting point the amount of the reward (wages, commission or price) that would have been earned. From this, however, must be deducted, as Anglin J. said in a building case: "the time, labour and expense which the plaintiffs have been saved through being relieved of their obligation to carry out the contract under which they would have earned it."[296] Thus, out-of-pocket expenses that have been saved, such as the cost to a builder of materials, must be deducted. This is merely to say that the plaintiff is entitled to the expected net profit not to gross revenues.[296a] Allowance must also be made for trouble and risk avoided by the breach.[297] In cases where part performance has been rendered, that profit may be calculated either by deducting the cost of completion from the contract price, or by deducting the total cost of performance from the contract price, adding back the cost of the performance rendered. As McCormick has shown, the methods yield identical results where the contract is profitable, and the choice depends on whether it is easier to prove the cost of the work already performed or the cost of the work remaining to be done.[298] A third possible measure also yields the same result and is possibly more convenient in some cases. This is the proportion of the contract price that the cost of the work done bears to the total cost plus, for the work remaining, the profit that would have been made on it.[299]

5.1160 Some difficulty has arisen with respect to overhead costs. If a builder is

[294] See 9.10-9.250, *infra*.

[295] See 5.20, *supra*. The principle was applied to an employment contract in *Cockburn v. Trusts & Guarantee Co.* (1917), 33 D.L.R. 159 at p. 164, 38 O.L.R. 396 at pp. 401-2 (S.C. App. Div.), affd 55 S.C.R. 264, 37 D.L.R. 701.

[296] *Jones v. Lyttle, Ltd. v. Mackie*, [1918] 2 W.W.R. 82 (S.C.C.), at p. 97. See *D.H. Howden & Co. Ltd. v. Sparling*, [1970] S.C.R. 883 at p. 893, 11 D.L.R. (3d) 746 at p. 753 (costs of earning not deducted, but only because basic award too small). See also *Karas v. Rowlett*, [1944] S.C.R. 1 at p. 8, [1944] 1 D.L.R. 241 at pp. 252-3: "by the default or wrong there is released a capacity to work or to earn. That capacity becomes an asset in the hands of the injured party, and he is held to a reasonable employment of it in the course of events flowing from the breach", *per* Rand J., cited with approval in *Asamera Oil Corp. v. Sea Oil & General Corp.*, [1979] 1 S.C.R. 633 at p. 656, 89 D.L.R. (2d) 1 at p. 17; *Brainer v. Hedges*, [1947] 2 D.L.R. 49 (Man. K.B.).

[296a] See *George C. Sweet Agencies Ltd. v. Sklar-Peppler Furniture Corp.* (1995), 138 N.S.R. (2d) 101 at p. 104, 10 C.C.E.L. (2d) 43 (C.A.), and *Novelty Holdings Ltd. v. FMF Construction & Trading Ltd.* (2008), 71 C.L.R. (3d) 86 (B.C.S.C.), at para. 149, both citing this passage.

[297] *Connors & Rutledge v. McGregor*, [1924] 2 D.L.R. 86 (Alta. S.C. App. Div.). See also *Ontario Lantern Co. v. Hamilton Brass Manufacturing Co.* (1900), 27 O.A.R. 346.

[298] McCormick, *Handbook on the Law of Damages* (St. Paul, West Publishing Co., 1935), at pp. 640-2. In *Whitehead v. R.B. Cameron Ltd.* (1967), 63 D.L.R. (2d) 180 (N.S.S.C. App. Div.), a claim for a builder's lost profit was allowed.

[299] McCormick, *ibid.*

awarded the amount of the contract price minus what it would have cost in actual variable costs to earn it, the builder is not entitled, in addition, to overhead costs, for these would have had to be incurred even if the contract had been performed and the price earned.[300] A claim for wasted expenses is, in principle, alternative to a claim for the contract price.[301] On the other hand, where the builder is complaining of delay, the situation is different. In *Shore & Horwitz Construction Co. Ltd. v. Franki of Canada Ltd.*,[302] the defendant had wrongfully caused a five-month delay in the plaintiff's completion of a construction contract with a third party. The Supreme Court of Canada held that the plaintiff was entitled to overhead expenses during this period. Spence J. said: "the overhead costs were continuing to run but [the plaintiff] was obtaining no revenue from which to defray the overhead costs".[303]

5.1170 The implied assumption is that had the delay not occurred, the plaintiff would have made a profitable use of its equipment and of the employees' time during the five months following completion of the project. It is suggested that, in the absence of proof to the contrary, it is not unreasonable to make such an assumption, and the decision may be supported on that ground. However, if the defendant could prove that the plaintiff would have had no other business for five months after timely completion of its current project, it is submitted that no overhead expenses should be recovered. An analogy may be drawn with cases on loss of use of property discussed in an earlier chapter.[304]

5.1180 Where the complaint is of impeding the plaintiff's work so as to make it more difficult and expensive, the plaintiff is entitled to the extra costs attributable to the impediment. It was held by the Supreme Court of Canada in *Penvidic Contracting Co. Ltd. v. Int'l Nickel Co. of Canada Ltd.*[305] that an acceptable way of measuring the extra cost was to estimate the higher price at which the plaintiff would reasonably have tendered on the entire project had the plaintiff known of the impediment in advance. The measures are in principle the same for a rational tenderer would increase the tender by precisely the amount of the additional costs. In a case where, as in *Penvidic* itself, proof of the actual additional cost caused by the defendant's breach is difficult, convenience may well favour the alternative approved by the court.

5.1190 More difficulty arises in making an allowance for the value of the plaintiff's time. On repudiation by an employer of a contract for personal

[300] In *Eastland Construction Ltd. v. Village of Gondola Point* (1979), 25 N.B.R. (2d) 129 (S.C.), affd 26 N.B.R. (2d) 604 (S.C. App. Div.), a claim for overhead costs was disallowed in the absence of proof of loss.

[301] See 5.200-5.250, *supra*.

[302] [1964] S.C.R. 589.

[303] *Supra*, at p. 592. The case was applied in *Parta Industries Ltd. v. Canadian Pacific Ltd.* (1974), 48 D.L.R. (3d) 463 (B.C.S.C.), to a case of damage to goods causing failure of a business to open.

[304] See 1.2190-1.2300, *supra*.

[305] [1976] 1 S.C.R. 267, 53 D.L.R. (3d) 748.

services, the plaintiff will have the use of time that would otherwise have been occupied. A strict analogy with sale contracts might suggest that the plaintiff will not be entitled to any damages unless it can be shown that the contract price for the services exceeded their value.[306] This would put a burden on the plaintiff of proving that the services were of lower value than the remuneration that was to be paid for them. It is plain that the analogy with sale contracts is imperfect, for personal services are not instantly saleable in the market at a readily ascertainable price. Consequently the rule in employment contracts has always been that it is for the employer, in case of wrongful discharge, to show that the employee has earned or could, acting reasonably, earn money in mitigation of the loss.[307] In contracts for services, the onus is also, in practice, upon the employer to show that the plaintiff has secured or could have secured substitute earnings; this will usually be a difficult burden to discharge, for unlike an employee who is normally expected only to hold one full-time job at a time, an independent contractor can often undertake simultaneous tasks.[308] Thus, if an artist is commissioned to paint a picture and the contract is repudiated by the employer, the latter will not be able to avoid liability by showing that the artist has plenty of other commissions, unless it can positively be shown that other commissions would have had to be abandoned if the defendant's had been performed. The artist can often show in such cases that had the contract been performed, there would have been one more commission than in fact there was. On the other hand, circumstances can be imagined in which the plaintiff has undertaken work that is inconsistent with the performance of the defendant's contract, and in that case damages ought to be reduced by the amount of the remuneration from the alternative sources. There is an analogy with the "lost volume" problem in sales.[309]

5.1200 If the plaintiff in a case of wrongful dismissal actually undertakes alternative employment, damages will be reduced whether the employment was similar or not to that promised by the defendant.[310] On the other hand if the plaintiff remains unemployed, it will not be held against her if she has reasonably refused employment in a different field from her former

306 See 1.1490, *supra*.

307 *Red Deer College v. Michaels*, [1976] 2 S.C.R. 324, 57 D.L.R. (3d) 386; *Peidl v. Bonas*, [1931] 2 D.L.R. 362 (Sask. C.A.); *Sydney Land & Loan Co. v. Rountree* (1907), 42 N.S.R. 49 (S.C.), affd 39 S.C.R. 614; *Evans v. Teamsters Local Union No. 31*, *supra*, footnote 290, at para. 30.

308 See McCormick, *op. cit.*, footnote 298, at p. 150, and *Canadian Ice Machine Co. Ltd. v. Sinclair*, [1955] S.C.R. 777, [1955] 5 D.L.R. 1.

309 See 5.1380-5.1400, *infra*.

310 *Ellis v. Whitepass Transportation Ltd.* (1983), 42 B.C.L.R. 351 (C.A.). It is assumed in many cases that actual earnings go to reduce damages, without reference to the similarity of employment. See, *e.g.*, *Pilon v. Peugeot Canada Ltd.* (1980), 114 D.L.R. (3d) 378, 29 O.R. (2d) 711 (H.C.J.); *Bishop v. Vachon Inc.* (1979), 22 Nfld. & P.E.I.R. 148 (Nfld. S.C.T.D.); *Donovan v. New Brunswick Publishing Co.* (1996), 174 N.B.R. (2d) 23, 17 C.C.E.L. (2d) 51 (Q.B.), affd 184 N.B.R. (2d) 40 (C.A.). On deductibility of unemployment insurance benefits, see 15.860, *infra*.

employment or at an inferior level.[311] This is, it is suggested, not a departure from the general rules of mitigation but an application of them, for though it may save money in the short run, it is usually unwise in the long run for an employee to accept an inferior position.[311a] The defendant has no right to expect the plaintiff to jeopardize long term prospects in order to reduce the damages. On this basis, however, the plaintiff could not expect to remain unemployed indefinitely if comparable employment seemed indefinitely unobtainable. Thus, an employee seeking damages for breach of a long term contract who found herself without any prospects of comparable employment, might well be restricted to damages assessed on the assumption that, after a reasonable interval, she would settle for the next best alternative. This would be the plaintiff's only reasonable course of action in the circumstances. However, in *Edwards v. Society of Graphical and Allied Trades*,[312] Buckley J. held that a skilled tradesman permanently excluded from employment by the defendant's wrong was not bound to mitigate damages by seeking employment as a labourer.

5.1210 Several cases have dealt with offers by the defendant to reinstate the plaintiff. As stated previously, it is generally held that it would not be reasonable for the plaintiff to accept a substantial demotion.[313] However, where equivalent employment is offered, the employee may be bound to accept it. In *Brace v. Calder*[314] where the reconstitution of a partnership operated as a technical wrongful dismissal, damages were refused because the plaintiff rejected an offer by the remaining partners to stay on under the same terms. If a personal relationship has broken down, it will generally not be reasonable for the plaintiff to accept an offer of reinstatement even on the same terms as formerly. An example given in *Payzu v. Saunders*[315] (itself involving a commercial sale of goods) illustrates the point:

> There may be cases where as matter of fact it would be unreasonable to expect a plaintiff to consider any offer made in view of the treatment he has received from the defendant. If he had been rendering personal services and had been dismissed after being accused in presence of others of being a thief, and if after that his employer had offered to take him back into service, most persons would think he was justified in refusing the offer, and

---

[311] *Yetton v. Eastwoods Froy*, [1967] 1 W.L.R. 104 (Q.B.); *Abbott v. Longshoremen's Protective Union, Local 1953* (1977), 18 Nfld. & P.E.I.R. 335 (Nfld. S.C.T.D.). In *Gallant v. L'Huillier* (1975), 12 N.B.R. (2d) 327 (S.C. App. Div.), and *Gould v. Hermes Electronics Ltd.* (1978), 34 N.S.R. (2d) 321 (S.C.T.D.), employees were bound to accept reasonable offers, even outside their preferred fields.

[311a] *Nevin v. British Columbia Hazardous Waste Management Corp.* (1995), 129 D.L.R. (4th) 569, [1996] 3 W.W.R. 237 (B.C.C.A.).

[312] [1970] 1 W.L.R. 379 (Ch.).

[313] See *Washer v. British Columbia Toll Highways & Bridges Authority* (1965), 53 D.L.R. (2d) 620 (B.C.C.A.); *Walerius v. McDiarmid Lumber Ltd.*, [1999] 12 W.W.R. 757 (Man. Q.B.), affd 191 D.L.R. (4th) 742 (C.A.).

[314] [1895] 2 Q.B. 253 (C.A.). The same view was taken in *Lloy v. Billman* (1906), 1 E.L.R. 351 (N.S.S.C.). See also *Constantinoff v. Racine* (2000), 191 Sask. R. 60 (Q.B.), and 15.200, *infra*.

[315] [1919] 2 K.B. 581 (C.A.).

> that it would be unreasonable to ask him in this way to mitigate the damages in an action of wrongful dismissal. But that is not to state a principle of law, but a conclusion of fact to be arrived at on a consideration of all the circumstances of the case.[316]

In *Evans v. Teamsters Local Union No. 31*, it was held that an employee had failed to act reasonably in refusing an offer or re-employment by the defendant. Bastarache J. said, "Although the fears expressed by Mr. Evans may have been subjectively justified, there was no evidence of acrimony . . . it was not objectively unreasonable for him to return to work to mitigate his damages.[316a]

5.1220 Earnings from alternative sources ought not, as suggested earlier, to be taken into account if the plaintiff could have combined them with performance of the contract in question, for then, in the absence of the wrong, the plaintiff would have had both the remuneration under the contract and the additional earnings. It is often a matter of difficulty to determine what earnings are to be treated as collateral and which are to be taken into account to reduce damages.[317] In *Lavarack v. Woods of Colchester Ltd.*,[318] the plaintiff, having been wrongfully dismissed by the defendant, took employment with another company at a lower salary, making profitable purchases of shares in his new employer and also in a third company. The English Court of Appeal held that he was bound to bring into account the profit made in the shares of his new employer, for this was held to be a form of remuneration for his services. But the investment in the third company was to be treated as collateral, even though the terms of his employment with the defendant had precluded investment in that particular company. The distinction is, it is submitted, sound. The profits from the third company were a return on capital not remuneration for time. As Lord Denning said: "he might have invested his money in any other company and made similar profits".[319] On the other hand, in *Cockburn v. Trusts & Guarantee Co.*,[320] the Supreme Court of Canada held that damages for wrongful dismissal were to be reduced by a profitable purchase made by the plaintiff on the liquidation of the employer's assets. The decision is justifiable on its facts, it is submitted, for the liquidation of the company was the cause of the plaintiff's dismissal, and he

[316] *Supra*, at pp. 588-9. However, in *Mifsud v. MacMillan Bathurst Inc.* (1989), 63 D.L.R. (4th) 714, 70 O.R. (2d) 701 (C.A.), leave to appeal to S.C.C. refused 68 D.L.R. (4th) vii, 39 O.A.C. 153*n*, the Ontario Court of Appeal held that an employee who had been demoted failed to act reasonably in rejecting the employer's terms. See also *Greaves v. Ontario Municipal Employees Retirement Board* (1995), 129 D.L.R. (4th) 347, 15 C.C.E.L. (2d) 94 (Ont. Ct. (Gen. Div.)); *Rodger v. Falcon Machinery (1965) Ltd.*, [2007] 1 W.W.R. 714 (Man. Q.B.) (offer of re-employment unclear). See 15.140, *infra*.

[316a] (2008), 292 D.L.R. (4th) 577, at para. 50.

[317] See 15.670-15.880, *infra*.

[318] [1967] 1 Q.B. 278 (C.A.). In *McCuaig v. Leydon* (1955), 1 D.L.R. (2d) 657, 17 W.W.R. 369 (Sask. C.A.), an employee recovered damages from a third party for loss of earning capacity during a paid vacation period. It was held that the employer remained liable to pay the full agreed salary.

[319] *Supra*, at p. 290.

[320] (1917), 55 S.C.R. 264, 37 D.L.R. 701. See 15.800, *infra*.

would never have made the profit if the event had not occurred. It was not therefore a case in which "he might have invested his money" in the absence of the dismissal "and made similar profits".

5.1230 Where the form or amount of remuneration were uncertain, the plaintiff is entitled only to the estimated value of the chance of having earned it.[321] This applies to commission and gratuities probably payable

[*The next page is* 5-57]

[321] *Addis v. Gramophone Co.*, [1909] A.C. 488 (H.L.); *Trollope v. Caplan*, [1936] 2 K.B. 382 (C.A.). See also 13.260-13.370, *infra*.

by third parties. Where payment of the remuneration depended on an option exercisable by the defendant, the usual rule is that the plaintiff is not entitled to damages in respect of it, on the principle that a defaulting party is presumed to have acted in the way most beneficial to him.[322] However, this approach may lead to undercompensation in a case where an employment benefit though technically optional, is almost certain to have been paid in the absence of the wrong.

5.1240 A number of Canadian cases have dealt with bonuses. In *Bardal v. Globe & Mail Ltd.*,[323] McRuer C.J. said, in refusing compensation for loss of an expected bonus: "The Christmas bonus was a purely voluntary gift distributed among the employees as a matter of good will between employer and employee."[324] On the other hand, in more recent cases compensation has been allowed.[325] In *Ditmars v. Ross Drug Co. Ltd.*,[326] Dickson J. spoke of a bonus as: "such an integral part of [the] wage structure that its payment must be considered virtually a matter of right".[327] In an Alberta case a bonus was said to have "acquired many attributes of salary entitlement".[328]

5.1250 In *Brown v. Waterloo Regional Board of Com'rs of Police*,[329] the dismissal of a chief of police was subsequently, after considerable litigation, quashed by the court. The Board of Commissioners conceded liability to pay salary during the period after the dismissal but disputed the employee's claim to annual increases and fringe benefits. Linden J. held that the plaintiff had a contractual right to reasonable annual increases and to reasonable fringe benefits. Quantification was based on the benefits received by the plaintiff's successor as chief of police.

5.1260 It is submitted that similar reasoning will often justify the award of compensation where an employment benefit, though technically optional,

---

322 *Lavarack v. Woods of Colchester Ltd., supra*, footnote 318; *Beach v. Reed Corrugated Cases Ltd.*, [1956] 1 W.L.R. 807 (Q.B.); *Rooney v. Reed Ltd.* (1978), 88 D.L.R. (3d) 414, 20 O.R. (2d) 665 (H.C.J.). See 13.390-13.410, *infra*.

323 (1960), 24 D.L.R. (2d) 140, [1960] O.W.N. 253 (H.C.J.), followed in *Rogerson v. A.E. MacLennan Ltd.* (1976), 12 Nfld. & P.E.I.R. 48 (P.E.I.S.C.).

324 *Bardal, supra*, at p. 146 D.L.R., p. 255 O.W.N. See also *Carignan v. Nu Salt Corp.* (2000), 197 Sask. R. 108 (Q.B.).

325 *Hunt v. Cimco Ltd.* (1976), 2 A.R. 514 (S.C.T.D.); *Hermann v. Manalta Coal Ltd.* (1978), 16 A.R. 322 (S.C.T.D.); *Ditmars v. Ross Drug Co. Ltd.* (1970), 3 N.B.R. (2d) 139 (S.C.); *Bagby v. Gustavson Int'l Drilling Co.* (1979), 20 A.R. 244 (S.C.), affd 24 A.R. 181 (C.A.); *Walsh v. Alberta and Southern Gas Co.* (1992), 121 A.R. 341, 84 Alta. L.R. (2d) 75 (Q.B.); *Henderson v. Bristol-Myers Squibb Canada Inc.*, [1996] 8 W.W.R. 415, 146 Sask. R. 127 (Q.B.); *Lloyd v. Imperial Parking Ltd.*, [1997] 3 W.W.R. 697, 192 A.R. 190 (Q.B.); *White v. F.W. Woolworth Co.* (1996), 139 Nfld. & P.E.I.R. 324, 22 C.C.E.L. (2d) 110 (Nfld. C.A.), leave to appeal to S.C.C. refused 222 N.R. 80*n*, 161 Nfld. & P.E.I.R. 90*n*; *Sampson v. Melanson's Waste Management Inc.* (2005), 277 N.B.R. (2d) 76 (Q.B.), affd 297 N.B.R. (2d) 13 (C.A.).

326 *Supra*, footnote 325.

327 *Ditmars v. Ross Drug Co. Ltd., supra*, at p. 146.

328 *Hermann v. Manalta Coal Co. Ltd., supra*, footnote 325, at p. 324, *per* McClung J. See also *Bagby v. Gustavson Int'l Drilling Co., supra*, footnote 325, at p. 257 ("integral part of wage structure").

329 (1982), 136 D.L.R. (3d) 49, 37 O.R. (2d) 277 (H.C.J.), affd on this point 150 D.L.R. (3d) 729, 43 O.R. (2d) 113 (C.A.).

could not in fact be effectively withheld on an individual basis. The result may be supported in some cases on the basis that, as an implied term of the contract, the employer undertakes to treat the plaintiff fairly vis-á-vis his fellow employees. The employer, therefore, would not have an option to discriminate unfairly against the plaintiff.[330]

5.1270 In the case of long term contracts, the same kinds of consideration will be relevant as in the case of personal injury. The plaintiff's lost future stream of income will have to be discounted to present value and adjusted for contingencies, including the possibilities of the plaintiff's death, incapacity, or resignation before the end of the contract term. There are few illustrations in the reports, for breach of long-term employment contracts is infrequent. In *Edwards v. Society of Graphical and Allied Trades*,[331] however, where the defendant's wrongful exclusion from a trade union resulted in the permanent loss of employment, Buckley J. drew the analogy with personal injury cases, and awarded a sum comparable to what the plaintiff would have recovered if he had been disabled by injury. It was submitted earlier that it will be a rare case in which it is reasonable for a plaintiff who is not physically disabled to ask the court to assume lifetime unemployment because of the defendant's wrong. In most cases, the basis for calculating the plaintiff's annual loss will not be the full salary anticipated before the wrong was done, but the difference between that and the lesser salary that, acting reasonably, could have been earned from other sources. Subject to these comments, however, the *Edwards* case[332] indicates what seems to be a sound method of calculating long term losses.

5.1280 It has been held in England[333] that income tax is to be deducted in calculating the plaintiff's earnings for the purpose of compensating loss of earnings caused by personal injury. This position was rejected by the Supreme Court of Canada in the field of personal injuries in *The Queen in right of Ontario v. Jennings*,[334] and has also been rejected in wrongful dismissal cases.[335] The Canadian position seems preferable, especially as damages for wrongful dismissal are now taxable by Canadian law in the plaintiff's hands.[336] Even if such damages are not taxable, it is submitted that

[330] *Bold v. Brough Nicholson & Hall Ltd.*, [1964] 1 W.L.R. 201 (Q.B.) (pension benefits). In *Ditmars v. Ross Drug Co. Ltd., supra*, footnote 325, at p. 147, Dickson J. said that "arbitrary exclusion" of the plaintiff from the bonus scheme would have been improper. *Lavarack v. Woods of Colchester Ltd.*, [1967] 1 Q.B. 278 (C.A.), where the plaintiff was denied compensation for loss of a bonus, may be distinguished as a case where the plaintiff's remuneration was individually negotiated and could be altered without affecting other employees.

[331] [1971] Ch. 354. Damages were reduced by the Court of Appeal because the defendant union reinstated the plaintiff after the trial.

[332] See 5.300, *supra*. In *Cooke v. CKOY Ltd.* (1963), 39 D.L.R. (2d) 209, [1963] 2 O.R. 257 (H.C.J.), damages for loss of permanent employment were estimated at about 14% of the full capitalized value of the remuneration, the court stressing the impact of contingencies.

[333] *British Transport Com'n v. Gourley*, [1956] A.C. 185 (H.L.), distinguished in *Deeny v. Gooda Walker Ltd. (No 2.)*, [1996] 1 All E.R. 933 (H.L.), where the damages were taxable.

[334] [1966] S.C.R. 532, 57 D.L.R. (2d) 644. See 3.950-3.980, *supra*.

the argument for following the English rule is weak. There seems no reason why in a case of wrongful dismissal, the employer should benefit by the defendant's tax obligations. If it is thought that the plaintiff is over-compensated by recovery of full remuneration, the remedy is to amend the tax law and to tax awards of compensation for lost earnings, making due allowance for the effect of the accelerated receipt by the plaintiff. In that way the Revenue and not the wrongdoer would benefit. This is surely the appropriate result on general considerations, for where an employer wrongfully refuses to pay remuneration to an employee, the employer causes a loss to the employee and to the Revenue jointly. Whatever the proper disposition as between the employee and the Revenue, there seems no justification for permitting the wrongdoing employer to retain the Revenue's share of what should have been paid.

5.1290 An analogy may be drawn with the case of an employee who covenants to pay over one-third of future salary to a charity. It can hardly be doubted that damages for wrongful dismissal recoverable from the employer are to be assessed on the basis of the full salary due. It may be that the covenant does not apply to damages paid in lieu of salary; that is a question that will depend on the terms of the covenant, and, if it is to be disputed, must be disputed between the employee and the charity. But even if it were clear that the covenant did not affect the proceeds of a judgment, the employer would be obliged to pay in full. It is true that in such a case the employee would be better off financially than if the wrong had not been done. But that is because the employee happens to have made a particular covenant the terms of which apply to salary but not to damages. The employer cannot be permitted to take advantage of these circumstances. This is not the only instance in which the law wisely refuses to pursue to its logical end the comparison between the plaintiff's present position and the position that would have been occupied if the wrong had not been done.[337]

11. Economic Loss Caused by Injury to Others

5.1300 The action for loss of services (*per quod servitium amisit*), where still in

---

335 *Harte v. Amfab Products Ltd.* (1970), 73 W.W.R. 561 (B.C.S.C.); *Ofstedahl v. Cam-set Mechanical Contractors Ltd.* (1973), 42 D.L.R. (3d) 116 (Alta. S.C. App. Div.); *Bower v. J.M. Schneider Inc.* (1986), 34 D.L.R. (4th) 77, 9 B.C.L.R. (2d) 145 (C.A.). In England the *Gourley* case has been applied to compensation for wrongful dismissal. See *Parsons v. B.N.M. Laboratories Ltd.*, [1964] 1 Q.B. 95 (C.A.), and the same view was adopted in some Canadian cases, but these must now be read in the light of *The Queen in right of Ontario v. Jennings, supra*, footnote 334. See *Posluns v. Toronto Stock Exchange* (1964), 46 D.L.R. (2d) 210, [1964] 2 O.R. 547 (H.C.J.), affd 53 D.L.R. (2d) 193, [1966] 1 O.R. 285 (C.A.), affd [1968] S.C.R. 330, 67 D.L.R. (2d) 165; *Walker v. Copp Clark Publishing Co. Ltd.* (1962), 33 D.L.R. (2d) 338, [1962] O.R. 622 (H.C.J.); *Power v. Stoyles* (1958), 17 D.L.R. (2d) 239 (Nfld. S.C.); *Widrig v. Strazer & Gardiner* (1963), 37 D.L.R. (2d) 629 (Alta. S.C. App. Div.), vard [1964] S.C.R. 376, 44 D.L.R. (2d) 1.

336 *Income Tax Act*, ss. 56(1)(*a*)(ii), 248(1), definition "retiring allowance". See *McWilliam v. Nestlé Enterprises Ltd.* (1992), 129 N.B.R. (2d) 277 (Q.B.), leave to appeal to C.A. refused 133 N.B.R. (2d) 269.

337 See 1.660, 1.1360-1.1430, *supra*.

force, permits an employer, husband, or parent to recover medical expenses paid on behalf of an injured servant, wife, or child. In *Best v. Fox*,[338] Lord Porter explained this recovery as resting on the plaintiff's obligation to pay the expenses:

> Today the damages which a husband receives for injury to his wife are commonly measured by his expenses, whether for medical treatment of the wife or in payment for household services which her injuries prevent her from performing ... The expenses so recovered by the husband fall upon *him* whereas his wife does not incur any similar liability and therefore it is natural that he should recover and she should not.[339]

This approach has led some courts to conclude that a married woman cannot recover in her own right the costs of medical treatment.[340] It was suggested in the earlier discussion of these cases that medical expenses should always be recoverable by an injured woman in her own right.[341] It has also been suggested that an injured housekeeper of either sex should always be able to recover for his or her own lost earning capacity.[342] If these suggestions are adopted, there will be no need for the action for loss of services or consortium. The abolition of these actions in some jurisdictions[343] lends force to the argument in support of the injured person's right to recover in full. In *Dean v. Law*,[344] a mother recovered medical expenses incurred on behalf of her child. Again, it is submitted, the better solution is recovery by the child in its own right.

5.1310 Recovery by the injured person does not necessarily mean that the plaintiff should retain the proceeds, as against the person who has actually paid the expenses. This question will depend on the terms, as between payer and injured person, on which payment was made. The matter is discussed elsewhere.[345]

5.1320 In *The King v. C.P.R.*,[346] it was held that the Crown could not, apart from an action *per quod servitium amisit*, recover money paid to compensate an employee injured by the defendant. As damages such loss was held to be too remote. Similarly, travel expenses and earnings foregone by friends and relatives in order to visit an injured person have been held in a number of cases not to be recoverable.[347] A significant number of cases, however, have allowed such claims, either directly by the person incurring the loss[348] or

338 [1952] A.C. 716 (H.L.).

339 *Supra*, at p. 728. In *Stead v. Elliott* (1963), 39 D.L.R. (2d) 170 (N.S.S.C.), a father's right to recover medical expenses for his injured son was rested on the action for loss of services.

340 See 3.430, *supra*.

341 *Ibid.*

342 See 3.810-3.830, *supra*.

343 See 2.160, *supra*.

344 (1964), 50 D.L.R. (2d) 770 (B.C.S.C.). See also *Clouston v. Sunburst Motor Coaches Ltd.*, [1939] 1 D.L.R. 795 (Alta. S.C.).

345 See 3.1490-3.1540, *supra*.

346 [1947] S.C.R. 185, [1947] 2 D.L.R. 1. See also *Lamb v. Toronto & York Ry. Co.* (1921), 64 D.L.R. 527, 50 O.L.R. 481 (S.C. App. Div.) (no recovery by daughter of expense of caring for injured mother).

indirectly as part of the injured person's claim.[349] In the case of visits by close relatives, particularly to an injured child, a case can often be made that the visits are a necessary part of the care and treatment of the injured person. *Donnelly v. Joyce*,[350] discussed in an earlier chapter, allowed recovery, as part of the injured person's claim, not only of the value of nursing services rendered to an injured child by his mother but also of the parents' travelling expenses. As in the analogous cases discussed elsewhere,[351] it would seem appropriate for the proceeds of the recovery to be held on trust by the injured person for the person actually incurring the expenses. Alternatively, in the light of the expansion of substantive tort law in some areas of economic loss, there seems no overriding objection to permitting the person incurring the expenses to recover.

5.1330 The Ontario *Family Law Reform Act*, while abolishing the husband's action for loss of consortium and the parent's action for loss of a child's services,[352] established an independent right of action in all the persons eligible to claim in case of death, to pecuniary loss caused by injury.[353] The scope of this new action is potentially wide enough to eat very substantially

347 *Weagle v. Brown*, [1965-69] 1 N.S.R. 565 (S.C.); *Shaw's Estate v. Roemer* (1981), 46 N.S.R. (2d) 629 (S.C.T.D.), affd 134 D.L.R. (3d) 590 (S.C. App. Div.), leave to appeal to S.C.C. refused December 6, 1982; *Mitchell v. Canadian National Ry. Co.* (1974), 17 N.S.R. (2d) 697 (S.C.T.D.). In *Behrens v. Bertram Mills Circus*, [1957] 2 Q.B. 1; *Kirkham v. Boughey*, [1958] 2 Q.B. 338; *Blythe v. Seed* (1962), 35 D.L.R. (2d) 280 (B.C.S.C.), and *McNeill v. Johnstone*, [1958] 1 W.L.R. 888 (Q.B.), it was suggested that caring for or visiting an injured wife might be a means of mitigating loss of consortium. This route, however, is artificial and will not be available in jurisdictions where the action for loss of consortium has been abolished.

348 *Sheasgreen v. Morgan*, [1952] 1 D.L.R. 48 (B.C.S.C.); *Young v. Burgoyne* (1981), 122 D.L.R. (3d) 330 (S.C.T.D.); *Lelarge v. Blakney* (1978), 21 N.B.R. (2d) 100 (Q.B.), revd on other grounds 92 D.L.R. (3d) 440 (N.B.S.C. App. Div.); *McArdle v. St. Pierre* (1976), 16 N.B.R. (2d) 292 (Q.B.); *Levesque v. Lurette* (1978), 20 N.B.R. (2d) 587 (Q.B.); *Roos v. Myers Motors Co. Ltd.* (1968), 68 D.L.R. (2d) 488, [1968] 2 O.R. 189 (H.C.J.); *Stevens v. Kachman* (1978), 10 A.R. 192 (S.C.T.D.); *Mazepa v. Ewaskiw* (1953), 10 W.W.R. (N.S.) 565 (Alta. S.C.); *Green v. Hibbs* (1978), 84 D.L.R. (3d) 80 (Nfld. S.C.T.D.); *Page v. Solicitor* (1971), 20 D.L.R. (3d) 532 (N.B.S.C. App. Div.), affd [1972] S.C.R. vi *sub nom. Pelletier v. Page*, 29 D.L.R. (3d) 386*n* (expenses allowed only in so far as beneficial to injured person). But see *Canada (Attorney General) v. Lavery* (1991), 76 D.L.R. (4th) 97, 53 B.C.L.R. (2d) 273 (C.A.), leave to appeal to S.C.C. refused 83 D.L.R. (4th) vii, 136 N.R. 416*n* (value of medical treatment given to employee by plaintiff not recoverable).

349 *Cavanaugh v. MacQuarrie* (1979), 35 N.S.R. (2d) 687 (S.C.T.D.); *Foster v. Pawsey* (1980), 28 N.B.R. (2d) 334 (Q.B.T.D.). Recovery was refused in *Lewis v. Leighside Holdings Ltd.* (1970), 15 D.L.R. (3d) 770 (S.C. App. Div.), on the ground that the injured person had undertaken no obligation to repay the person incurring the expenses. This requirement raises difficulties discussed in an earlier chapter (see 3.450-3.470, *supra*), and would probably not be insisted upon in the light of subsequent cases discussed there.

350 [1974] Q.B. 454 (C.A.). See 3.450-3.470, *supra*.

351 See 3.1490-3.1540, *supra*.

352 *Family Law Reform Act*, Ont., s. 69(3) and (4), preserved by s. 71 of the *Family Law Act*, 1986 and renamed *Dower and Miscellaneous Abolition Act*. Section 69(3) speaks only of "loss of the consortium" but presumably it is intended to abolish the husband's action for loss of servitium also. See *Report on Family Law* (Ontario Law Reform Commission, 1969) Part I, p. 101, and *Chapman v. Verstraete*, [1977] 4 W.W.R. 214 (B.C.S.C.), where the B.C. *Family Relations Act* was so interpreted.

353 See now *Family Law Act* (Ont.), s. 61.

into the ordinary claim of an injured person. On the face of it the statute now vests in the named relatives of a disabled wage earner exactly the same rights they would have if the earner had been killed. In the case of an injured spouse, it would seem that the uninjured spouse could recover for loss of the value of housekeeping services or lost income. It seems unlikely, however, that the Legislature intended to detract from the right of the injured person to recover compensation for lost earning capacity,[354] and it seems unlikely, too, that it was intended that the wrongdoer should pay twice over for the same loss. Probably, therefore, the statutes will be construed to operate only in respect of losses that the injured person cannot claim in his own right. As the courts expand the rights of injured persons to recover, the scope of the relatives' independent right will be correspondingly reduced. Still, the amendment serves as a useful purpose, on this construction, in ensuring that, if the courts hesitate to hold the injured person entitled to recover in full, it will be clear that the relatives can recover in their own right.[355]

5.1340 Admittedly, this gives rather a narrow construction to the section, but it seems the only way of avoiding a possible double recovery or a diminution of the injured person's own rights. A narrow construction of the section may be defended on the basis that the presumed intention of the Legislature was not radically to alter the rules governing damages for personal injury, but simply to ensure that no gap was created by the repeal of the old action for loss of service and consortium, and to make it clear that a wife was now equally entitled to any remedy formerly available to husbands only. Subparagraphs (c) and (e) will still be of importance, on this view, for it is at least doubtful whether an injured person can recover for travelling expenses of visitors[356] and for loss of the care, companionship, and guidance afforded by the injured person to relatives.[357]

12. Loss of Sales and Rents

5.1350 The cases now for consideration are those where the plaintiff has been deprived of the benefit of a contract to sell property or to sell the right to use property. The cases to be considered are those in which, had the wrong not been done, the plaintiff would have earned a price or a rent. As was pointed out in respect of earnings for services in an earlier section,[358] if the plaintiff is, according to the substantive law governing the transaction in question, entitled to recover the price from the buyer or the rent from a lessee, the plaintiff has not lost an opportunity to earn it. Though not entitled to damages in such a case, the plaintiff has an action for the agreed sum. The question of whether or not the agreed sum has fallen due depends on the terms of the

354 See *Dziver v. Smith* (1983), 146 D.L.R. (3d) 314, 41 O.R. (2d) 385 (C.A.).

355 See 3.480, 3.1120-3.1140, *supra*.

356 See 5.1320, *supra*.

357 The injured person could only, presumably, recover for (non-pecuniary) loss in being unable to provide the companionship. It might, however, be arguable that this loss includes the cost of purchasing for the family what substitutes money can buy.

358 See 5.1130, *supra*.

contract and is, in general, one of concern to the relevant substantive law. The action by a seller of land for the price, however, usually takes the form of an action for specific performance and consequently, unlike the seller's action for the price of goods, is always considered to be a remedial question and is fully discussed from this point of view in the companion volume to this work.[359]

5.1360 The typical case in which losses of the kind considered here are caused to a seller is non-acceptance by the buyer, but the same loss occurs in case of any breach of contract by the buyer that justifies termination (*i.e.*, a course of conduct by the buyer that will lead to the

[*The next page is* 5-63]

359 Sharpe, *Injunctions and Specific Performance*, looseleaf ed. (Toronto, Canada Law Book, 1999), 8.100-8.220.

seller's not earning the price), such as anticipatory repudiation, or failing to give security for payment. The same loss may also occur in cases of wrongful interference by a third party with a contractual relationship, or failure of an agent to effect a sale.[360]

5.1370 The *Sale of Goods Act* provides as follows:

> 48(1) Where the buyer wrongfully neglects or refuses to accept and pay for the goods, the seller may maintain an action against the buyer for damages for non-acceptance.
>
> (2) The measure of damages is the estimated loss directly and naturally resulting in the ordinary course of events from the buyer's breach of contract.
>
> (3) Where there is an available market for the goods in question, the measure of damages is, in the absence of evidence to the contrary, to be ascertained by the difference between the contract price and the market or current price at the time or times when the goods ought to have been accepted, or, if no time was fixed, for acceptance, then at the time of the refusal to accept.[361]

The meaning of the phrase "available market" has been discussed in an earlier chapter where it was suggested that a wide interpretation seemed appropriate.[362] However, the question is academic because if there is no available market the result thought to be appropriate on general principles can always be achieved under the broad test of subsec. (2) and if there is an available market subsec. (2) still can be made to prevail over subsec. (3) because the latter lays down only a *prima facie* test.

5.1380 The effect of this is illustrated by the cases where the seller's loss is not based on the price of particular goods but on the loss of profit on a transaction. This kind of loss arises on breach by a buyer of a contract to buy a standard item in which the seller deals. If the market price does not differ from (or is higher than) the contract price, it seems at first that by the application of subsec. (3) the seller suffers no loss. But in *W.L. Thompson Ltd. v. Robinson (Gunmakers) Ltd.*,[363] it was held in such a case that the seller does suffer a loss of business (sometimes called lost volume)[364] for even if the seller resells the particular item that the defendant

360 *Kristinacki v. Bongard* (1970), 12 D.L.R. (3d) 254 (Alta. S.C.) (plaintiff recovered difference between price that should have been received, and price actually received).

361 *Sale of Goods Act* (Ont.), s. 48; Alta. s. 49; B.C., s. 54; Man., s. 51; N.B., s. 47; Nfld. & Lab., s. 50; N.W.T., s. 57; N.S., s. 51; P.E.I., s. 50; Sask., s. 49; Yukon, s. 47; U.K., s. 50.

362 See 1.1520, *supra*.

363 [1955] Ch. 177, followed in *Victory Motors Ltd. v. Bayda*, [1973] 3 W.W.R. 747 (Sask. Dist. Ct.); *Canadian Union College v. Camsteel Industries Ltd.* (1979), 17 A.R. 98 (Dist. Ct.). See also *Re Vic Mill, Ltd.*, [1913] 1 Ch. 465 (C.A.); *Hill & Sons v. Edwin Showell & Sons, Ltd.* (1918), 87 L.J.K.B. 1106 (H.L.); *Cameron v. Campbell & Worthington, Ltd.*, [1930] S.A.S.R. 402; *Mason & Risch Ltd. v. Christner* (1920), 54 D.L.R. 653, 48 O.L.R. 8 (S.C. App. Div.); *Brown v. Buck*, [1934] 4 D.L.R. 446 (Man. C.A.); *Kay-Son Steel Fabricators & Erectors Ltd. v. Atkinson-Harvey Corp.* (1979), 12 B.C.L.R. 222 (S.C.).

364 See Note, "A Theoretical Postcript: Microeconomics and the Lost-volume Seller", 24 Case W. Res. L. Rev. 712 (1973).

would have bought, the seller has, at the end of the day, made one less sale than would otherwise have been made and so has lost the profit on one transaction. Upjohn J. thought that this was a loss plainly recoverable under subsec. (2). As for subsec. (3) he considered that there was no available market, but that even if there were an available market subsec. (3) being only a *prima facie* measure would yield to the broader terms of subsec. (2).[365] The same result had been earlier reached in Canadian cases, without reference to the *Sale of Goods Act*.[366] A similar conclusion was reached also in *Interoffice Telephones v. Robert Freeman Co.*,[367] a case of breach by a hirer of an equipment rental agreement. The *Sale of Goods Act* did not apply, but the general problem of assessment of damages was identical and the same conclusion was reached, namely, that the owner, even though it had rented the particular equipment that the hirer would have taken to another user at the same price, had suffered a loss of profit on one rental transaction.

5.1390 A further refinement was introduced in *Charter v. Sullivan*[368] where the plaintiff (a seller of automobiles) did not have a sufficient supply of cars to meet the demands of buyers. It was held that there the seller had not suffered a loss of profit because the buyer's default in fact made no difference to the total number of sales, that number being limited, not by the number of buyers, but by the number of cars supplied. *Thompson v. Robinson* has also been distinguished in the case of sale of a specific second-hand car, *Lazenby Garages v. Wright*.[369] When this was resold on the buyer's default at above the contract price it was held, rightly it is submitted, that the seller had suffered no loss, for each second-hand car is different from all others and there was no guarantee that the second buyer would have bought any car at all from the plaintiff if the defendant had performed the contract. Lord Denning M.R. having referred to *Thompson v. Robinson*, said:

> But it is entirely different in the case of a secondhand car. Each second-hand car is different from the next, even though it is the same make . . . The buyer in this case could not have contemplated that the dealer would sell one car less. At most he would contemplate that, if they resold this very car at a lower price, they would suffer by reason of that lower price

365 *W.L. Thompson Ltd., supra*, footnote 363, at pp. 187-8.

366 *Manery v. Kampe*, [1941] 4 D.L.R. 493 (B.C.C.A.); *Mason & Risch Ltd. v. Christner, supra*, footnote 363.

367 [1958] 1 Q.B. 190 (C.A.), cited with approval in *Rockland Industries Inc. v. Amerada Minerals Corp. of Canada Ltd.*, [1978] 2 W.W.R. 44 (S.C.T.D.), at p. 58, *per* Brennan, J., revd 95 D.L.R. (3d) 64 (S.C. App. Div.), but restd [1980] 2 S.C.R. 2, 108 D.L.R. (3d) 513.

368 [1957] 2 Q.B. 117 (C.A.).

369 [1976] 1 W.L.R. 459 (C.A.).

and should recover the difference. But if they resold this very car at a higher price, they would suffer no loss.[370]

5.1400 Another situation in which loss of profit was successfully claimed despite the absence of any loss under subsec. (3) arose in *Trans Trust S.P.R.L. v. Danubian Trading Co.*[371] Here the defendant agreed to buy steel that the plaintiff was to obtain from a Belgian supplier, the defendant undertaking to procure a banker's credit in favour of the supplier. As the defendant knew, the plaintiff did not expect itself to put up the money to purchase the steel. On the defendant's failure to procure the credit, it was argued that the plaintiff had suffered no loss because the market price of steel had risen, and exceeded the contract price. If the plaintiff had had the steel in its possession, this would have been a compelling argument, for the plaintiff, like the used car dealer in *Lazenby Garages v. Wright*, could have resold the goods without loss. But as was known to the defendant from the outset the plaintiff never had intended to finance the purchase. Consequently the defendant's breach of contract had caused the plaintiff to lose its anticipated profit on the transaction which was held by the English Court of Appeal to be recoverable.

5.1410 Where the buyer is in breach of a contract to buy goods to be specially manufactured, the plaintiff will be entitled to the actual loss on the transaction. Such a case arose in *Consolidated Plate Glass Co. v. McKinnon Dash Co.*[372] where the defendant repudiated an agreement to buy automobile windshields to be manufactured by the plaintiff. Middleton J. commented that it would have been "absolutely suicidal"[373] for the plaintiff to manufacture the windshields for which the defendant now had no use. The damages were based on the profit that the plaintiff would have made, together with expense incurred in extricating itself from a contract with its own supplier.

5.1420 Section 48(3) of the *Sale of Goods Act* provides, as the time of assessing damages, "the time or times when the goods ought to have been accepted, or, if no time is fixed, for acceptance, then at the time of the refusal to accept". These words give rise to the same difficulties of interpretation as the corresponding words in s. 49 discussed in an earlier chapter.[374] In the case of anticipatory breach by the buyer it has been held that the seller is entitled to await the date of due acceptance and to recover damages based on the market value at that date.[375] Alterna-

370 *Supra*, at p. 462.
371 [1952] 2 Q.B. 297 (C.A.).
372 (1917), 40 D.L.R. 47, 41 O.L.R. 188 (S.C.).
373 *Supra*, at p. 48 D.L.R.
374 See 1.1610, 1.1620, *supra*.
375 *Tredegar Iron & Coal Co. Ltd. v. Hawthorn Bros. & Co.* (1902), 18 T.L.R. 716 (C.A.); *Phillpotts v. Evans* (1839), 5 M. & W. 475, 151 E.R. 200 (but it was not at that date established that an action lay for anticipatory repudiation; see *per* Parke B. at p. 477). The corresponding cases on anticipatory breach by a seller are discussed at 1.1560-1.1630, *supra*. See also 15.400-15.650, *infra*.

tively, the seller may accept the repudiation in which case it has been held that damages are assessed at that date.[376] In *Roth & Co. v. Taysen Townsend & Co.*[377] the seller accepted the buyer's anticipatory repudiation but failed to resell the goods on a falling market. The seller's damages were limited to the difference between the contract price and the market price at the date of acceptance of the repudiation, and the result was justified on the ground that the seller should have mitigated loss by selling. As has been argued in an earlier chapter,[378] it seems that seldom can a failure to anticipate market trends be properly held to be unreasonable and if the result in the case is to be defended it must be on the ground that damages crystallized the time of acceptance of the repudiation.[379] It is suggested that the result is defensible on this basis. The seller who "accepts" an anticipatory repudiation thereby indicates that the goods for the buyer's account are no longer being held. From that point the buyer can no longer call for delivery. The goods are the seller's own; the seller could, acting reasonably, dispose of them at that time. Of course the seller is not compelled to do so; if the seller thinks it a wise investment, the goods can be held, and it is desirable for the seller to make the decision as to their disposition at the seller's own risk and for the seller's own profit. Thus, if the seller were to retain the goods on a rising market the seller ought, it is submitted, to be entitled to keep any profit made on resale, for the goods are held after acceptance of the buyer's repudiation entirely at the seller's own risk. If the rule were otherwise it would profit the seller, if the market were likely to rise, to sell the goods intended for delivery to the buyer and immediately to repurchase the same quantity of similar goods, and the law ought not unnecessarily to encourage such artificial transactions.

5.1430 Where the defaulting party requests an extension of time by giving assurances of performance, the date for assessment, as in the corresponding case of a seller's default, was held in *Hickman v. Haynes*[380] to be extended. This is in keeping with the view that the proper time to measure damages is the time at which the plaintiff, acting reasonably, could have disposed of the goods in the market.[381] Though *Hickman v.*

---

376 *Sudan Import & Export Co. (Khartoum) Ltd. v. Société Général de Compensation*, [1957] 2 Lloyd's Rep. 528 (Q.B.).

377 (1896), 12 T.L.R. 211 (C.A.). See also *York Glass Co. Ltd. v. Jubb* (1926), 134 L.T. 36 (C.A.). *Roth v. Taysen, supra*, was cited with approval by the Supreme Court of Canada in *Morrow Cereal Co. v. Ogilvie Flour Mills Co.* (1918), 57 S.C.R. 403, 44 D.L.R. 557, in a case of repudiation by a seller.

378 See 1.780, *supra*.

379 *Ibid.* Another difficulty with the mitigation approach is that if the market subsequently rises and the plaintiff resells at a profit, it would seem that (on a mitigation theory) the profit should be taken into account. But see 5.1480, *infra*.

380 (1875), L.R. 10 C.P. 598.

381 See *Hongkong Bank of Canada v. Richardson Greenshields of Canada Ltd.* (1990), 72 D.L.R. (4th) 161, [1990] 6 W.W.R. 1 (B.C.C.A.).

Haynes is a pre-Act case it seems clear that the rule is the same under the Act, and the case was cited with approval by the House of Lords in *Johnson v. Agnew*.[382]

5.1440 In *Ansdell v. Crowther*,[383] the British Columbia Court of Appeal held that a vendor of real property, who held the property after the purchaser's default on a falling market, was entitled only to damages assessed at the date at which, acting reasonably, the vendor could have resold. It was held that the vendor could not increase the damages by claiming specific performance. This decision must cast doubt on the general right of a vendor of land to specific performance, for it seems inconsistent to say at the same time that the vendor has a right to specific performance and a duty to mitigate loss by reselling.

5.1450 The time at which the plaintiff, acting reasonably, will be able to dispose of property depends very much on the nature of the property. This point was made by the Ontario Court of Appeal in *100 Main Street Ltd. v. W.B. Sullivan*,[384] where it was pointed out that a large apartment building cannot be disposed of instantly on the market like shares listed on a stock exchange. Morden J.A. said:

> The damages should have been calculated on the basis of a finding of the highest price obtainable within a reasonable time after the contractual date for completion following the making of reasonable efforts to sell the property commencing on that date. What is reasonable, in each instance, of course, is a question of fact to be decided on the basis of all relevant market circumstances.[385]

Morden J.A. also indicated that the same general principles applied to the sale of land contracts as to sale of goods.[386]

5.1460 Where there has been an actual resale of the property before trial, the resale price is relevant but not conclusive evidence of the market value, that is, the price at which the plaintiff, acting reasonably, could have disposed of the property. Often where the plaintiff seeks to recover the difference between the contract price and the actual price obtained, the court will quite naturally assume in the plaintiff's favour that the price obtained is the best that could reasonably have been obtained, for the plaintiff is the innocent party and usually has every incentive to obtain the best price. But some cases have refused recovery.[387] In *100 Main Street Ltd. v. W.B. Sullivan Ltd.*[388]

---

382 [1980] A.C. 367 (H.L.), at p. 387.

383 (1984), 11 D.L.R. (4th) 614, 55 B.C.L.R. 216 (C.A.). See 1.990, *supra*. See also *Alta-West Group Investments Ltd. v. Femco Financial Corp. Ltd.* (1984), 57 A.R. 33, 34 A.R. 33 (Q.B.); *LeMesurier v. Andrus* (1986), 25 D.L.R. (4th) 424 at p. 431, 54 O.R. (2d) 1 (C.A.), leave to appeal to S.C.C. refused 74 N.R. 239*n*, 63 O.R. (2d) x; *642947 Ontario Ltd. v. Fleischer* (2001), 209 D.L.R. (4th) 18 (Ont. C.A.).

384 (1978), 88 D.L.R. (3d) 1, 20 O.R. (2d) 401 (C.A.), leave to appeal to S.C.C. refused D.L.R. *loc. cit.*, O.R. *loc. cit.*

385 *Supra*, at p. 21 D.L.R. See also *Keck v. Faber* (1916), 60 Sol. Jo. 253; *Woodford Estates Ltd. v. Pollack* (1978), 93 D.L.R. (3d) 350, 22 O.R. (2d) 340 (H.C.J.) (damages assessed at date of breach).

386 *100 Main Street Ltd.*, *supra*, footnote 384, at p. 16 D.L.R.

where the purchaser of an apartment building repudiated and the repudiation was accepted by the vendor, the trial judge had held that the vendor was entitled to recover the full contract price unless the purchaser showed that the loss could have been reduced.[389] The Ontario Court of Appeal held that this was a mistaken view. The onus was on the vendor to prove a difference between contract price and market value:

> The basic principle is that the onus is on the plaintiff to prove its damages on a reasonable preponderance of credible evidence. Its damages are that sum of money which would put it in the same position as if the defendant had performed. The well-established method for determining this is to give the difference between the contract price and the market value. It is basic that the plaintiff cannot have the contract price and the land. Thus, I do not think that the plaintiff has proven its case by merely proving the contract price and then the defendant's breach, in the expectation that he will recover the full price unless the defendant proves that "the property could be sold to someone else without loss to the plaintiff".[390]

This does not necessarily mean that the onus will be difficult to discharge, and two Supreme Court of Canada cases[391] referred to by the court, as well as other cases, indicate that the plaintiff if reselling at a loss will often be able to recover the full amount of that loss.

387 *Tozer v. Berry*, [1955] O.W.N. 399 (C.A.); *Macklin v. Newbury Sanitary Laundry* (1919), 63 Sol. Jo. 337 (sale at half the contract price of property as "in dispute" and without warranty held no proof of true value). In "Remedies with Respect to Contracts of Purchase and Sale" in *Law Society of Upper Canada Special Lectures*, 1960, p. 427 at pp. 432-3, Weir advises a vendor to inform the defaulting purchaser of the proposed price before reselling.

388 *Supra*, footnote 384.

389 A similar rule was applied in *Pankhurst v. Gairdner & Co. Ltd.* (1960), 25 D.L.R. (2d) 515 (Alta. S.C. App. Div.), to a case where the defendant stockbroker had failed to sell shares as instructed. It is submitted that this approach can only be supported on the basis of a trade custom incorporated in the parties' agreement.

390 *100 Main Street Ltd.*, *supra*, footnote 384, at pp. 22-3 D.L.R. In *Laird v. Pim* (1841), 7 M. & W. 474 at p. 478, 151 E.R. 852, Parke B. said: "It is clear that [the vendor] cannot have the land and its value too." See also *Crestvalley Homes Ltd. v. Krklinski* (1996), 50 R.P.R. (2d) 283 (Ont. Ct. (Gen. Div.)), affd 79 A.C.W.S. (3d) 413 (C.A.), leave to appeal to S.C.C. refused 235 N.R. 200*n*; *Agricultural Research Institute of Ontario v. Campbell-High* (2002), 58 O.R. (3d) 321 (C.A.).

391 *Dobson v. Winton & Robbins Ltd.*, [1959] S.C.R. 775, 20 D.L.R. (2d) 164; *Hickey v. Paletta* (1973), 14 N.R. 3 (Ont. C.A.), affd [1974] 1 S.C.R. vi. See also *Davies v. Russell* (1971), 19 D.L.R. (3d) 23, [1971] 2 O.R. 699 (H.C.J.); *Bradley v. Bailey*, [1923] 2 D.L.R. 504, 52 O.L.R. 439 (S.C. App. Div.). In *Hal H. Paradise Ltd. v. Apostolic Trustees of Friars Minor* (1966), 55 D.L.R. (2d) 671 (Sask. Q.B.), the seller recovered the loss caused on returning goods to its suppliers.

As part of the calculation for net loss, the plaintiff is entitled to the cost of effecting the substitute transaction[392] and, in case of delay, to interest.[393]

5.1470 The same principle applies to a claim for damages for loss of rents as for loss of sales. The plaintiff is entitled to recover as damages the difference between what that would have been received from the lessee and the amount actually received, or that could, acting reasonably, have been received by renting the property to another person.[394] In *Cox Towing Line v. Dunfield & Co.*,[395] this principle was applied to a charterparty, broken by the charterer, the court pointing out that no additional compensation could, consistently with this principle, be given for demurrage.

5.1480 Where the plaintiff resells at a higher price than the market price a different question arises, namely, whether the defendant is entitled to take advantage of the plaintiff's profitable transaction. It may seem at first sight that if the plaintiff, on the buyer's default, retains the property that would otherwise have been delivered and later resells it at the contract price or above, the plaintiff suffers no loss. But in *Jamal v. Moolla Dawood, Sons & Co.*,[396] a share sale case, the Privy Council held in such a case that the seller was entitled to retain the profit: "If the seller retains the shares after the breach, the speculation as to the way the market will subsequently go is the speculation of the seller, not of the buyer; the seller cannot recover from the buyer the loss below the market price at the date of the breach if the market falls, nor is he liable to the purchaser for the profit if the market rises."[397] This reasoning is, it is submitted, sound; the case has been cited with approval by Canadian courts.[398] The seller on the buyer's default knows that no one is now bound to take the shares. The seller can choose to keep them or not. If the seller decides to hold them and they decline in value, the seller will stand the loss. The seller ought, it is submitted, to retain the profit if they rise in value.[399]

5.1490 This argument seems even more forceful in respect to purely inflationary

---

392 *Triple Five Corp. Ltd. v. Crown Zellerbach Stores Ltd.* (1981), 33 A.R. 513, 12 Alta. L.R. (2d) 178 (Q.B.), affd 25 Alta. L.R. (2d) 116 (C.A.); *Dobson v. Winton & Robbins Ltd., supra*; *Chapman v. Larin* (1879), 4 S.C.R. 349; *Davis v. Russell, supra*, footnote 391 (taxes incurred while holding property for resale); *Thurlow Logging Co. v. National Pole Co.*, [1923] 3 D.L.R. 958 (B.C.C.A.), affd [1923] 4 D.L.R. 655 (S.C.C.).

393 *Dobson v. Winton & Robbins Ltd., supra*, footnote 391; *Davies v. Russell, supra*, footnote 391; *E. & B. Mortgages Ltd. v. Skrivanos* (1980), 118 D.L.R. (3d) 139, 18 R.P.R. 215 (B.C.S.C.).

394 See also 15.560-15.570, *infra*, on mitigation.

395 (1922), 68 D.L.R. 133 (N.B.S.C. App. Div.).

396 [1916] 1 A.C. 175 (P.C.).

397 *Supra*, at p. 179.

398 *Bradley v. Bailey Tobacco Co.* (1921), 62 D.L.R. 397 (S.C.C.); *Burke v. Cory* (1959), 19 D.L.R. (2d) 252; *100 Main Street Ltd. v. W.B. Sullivan* (1978), 88 D.L.R. (3d) 1, 20 O.R. (2d) 401 (C.A.), leave to appeal to S.C.C. refused D.L.R. *loc. cit.*, O.R. *loc. cit.*; *Hongkong Bank of Canada v. Richardson Greenshields of Canada Ltd.* (1990), 72 D.L.R. (4th) 161, [1990] 6 W.W.R. 1 (B.C.C.A.). See also *Boxer v. Reesor* (1984), 55 B.C.L.R. 385 (S.C.), at p. 389, citing this passage.

399 See Waddams, "The Date for the Assessment of Damages", 97 L.Q.R. 445 (1981).

increases in value. Suppose that a purchaser agrees to buy property for $100,000 and defaults at a time when it is proved that the property is worth $80,000. No question of specific performance is in issue. By the time of the trial two years later the value of the property has risen to $100,000 for which sum the plaintiff sells it. It is submitted that the plaintiff should recover $20,000 plus interest, for had the contract been performed the plaintiff would have had $100,000 to invest at the date of breach and could have been protected against inflation by purchasing other property with that sum. The seller ought not to lose this protection simply because of a choice, on the buyer's default, to retain the original property rather than sell it for $80,000 and invest that sum in other property.

5.1500 In *Campbell Mostyn v. Barnett*,[400] the conclusion reach in *Jamal v. Moolla Dawood* was applied to a sale of goods case where the seller retained goods that rose in value after the buyer's default. In *Mavretic v. Bowman*,[401] it was applied to a sale of land.

5.1510 The Ontario Law Reform Commission in its report on sale of goods, though making no reference to these cases, appeared to consider them unsound, describing the result as an "unjustifiable windfall".[402] The Commission asserted that the seller "where he has actually resold the goods for a price higher than market ... should be bound by the results of the resale".[403] This proposal would necessitate inquiry into the seller's business arrangements to discover whether goods had been "appropriated" to the contract; if so, profitable sales would be for the buyer's benefit; if not, presumably the buyer would not benefit. This would be a difficult and, it is submitted, undesirable inquiry and would encourage the seller who wished to retain goods to effect an artificial transaction, selling goods allegedly appropriated to the buyer's contract in order to crystallize damages and then repurchasing similar goods for investment. However, the Commission's draft bill proposed that the seller should recover "actual loss".[404] The result in the cases discussed above can be defended on the basis that the seller does suffer an actual loss on the buyer's default equal to the difference between the price the buyer agreed to pay and the price at which the property could reasonably be sold on the market at a reasonable time after breach.[405]

[400] [1954] 1 Lloyd's Rep. 65.
[401] [1993] 4 W.W.R. 329, 76 B.C.L.R. (2d) 61 (C.A.).
[402] Ontario Law Reform Commission, *Report on Sale of Goods* (Dept. of Attorney-General, 1979), p. 410.
[403] *Ibid.*, at p. 422.
[404] Draft Bill, clause 9.10(4)(a).
[405] See also 1.40, 1.360-1.1430, 1.2570, 1.2590, *supra*.

CHAPTER 6

WRONGFUL DEATH

1. Losses Compensable

(1) Introduction

6.10 At common law no action in tort lay for loss caused to a person by another's responsibility for the death of a third person.[1] In the case of death caused by breach of a contract between the plaintiff and defendant as, for example, when a defective product is purchased by the plaintiff, damages may include medical and funeral expenses and damages for loss of the deceased's services.[2] In the case of tortious conduct causing death, however, the defendant was under no liability. By a statute of 1846, known as *Lord Campbell's Act*,[3] a new cause of action was created in favour of certain categories of relatives separate from any action that the deceased might have had. Though the actions are separate, they are not unrelated because the statute provides[4] that the claimant's action lies only if the deceased if not killed would have been entitled to maintain an action in respect of the injuries. This Act has been introduced into every Canadian jurisdiction, where it is most commonly called the *Fatal Accidents Act*.[5]

1 *Baker v. Bolton* (1808), 1 Camp. 493, 170 E.R. 1033; *Osborn v. Gillett* (1873), L.R. 8 Ex. 88; *Admiralty Com'rs v. S.S. Amerika*, [1917] A.C. 38 (H.L.); *Monaghan v. Horn* (1882), 7 S.C.R. 409; *Good v. Husband Transport Ltd.* (1977), 83 D.L.R. (3d) 127, 18 O.R. (2d) 497 (Co. Ct.); *Pilfold v. Skog Estate* (1989), 64 D.L.R. (4th) 186, 40 B.C.L.R. (2d) 122 (C.A.), leave to appeal to S.C.C. refused 65 D.L.R. (4th) viii, 105 N.R. 240*n*.

2 *Jackson v. Watson & Sons*, [1909] 2 K.B. 193 (C.A.). Where the death is caused by breach of contract with the deceased, as where the deceased personally buys defective goods, it has been held that recovery is available to relatives under the *Fatal Accidents Act: Woolworth, Ltd. v. Crotty* (1942), 66 C.L.R. 603; *Grein v. Imperial Airways*, [1937] 1 K.B. 50 (C.A.), at p. 70, *per* Greer L.J. The *Family Law Reform Act, 1978* (Ont.), s. 60(1), by substituting "fault or neglect" for the original formula "wrongful act, neglect, or default" may have altered this result. The *Fatal Accidents Act* (P.E.I.), s. 1(n), which speaks of "failure to exercise reasonable skill or care", may have the same effect, and may even exclude the murderer. The question of entitlement to claim is beyond the scope of this book.

3 *An Act for Compensating the Families of Persons Killed by Accidents, 1846*, now replaced by the *Fatal Accidents Act 1976* (U.K.).

4 Except in P.E.I.: *Fatal Accidents Act*, s. 2(2)(a).

5 *Fatal Accidents Act* (Alta., Man., N.B., Nfld. & Lab., N.W.T., P.E.I., Sask., Yukon); *Fatal Injuries Act* (N.S.); *Family Compensation Act* (B.C.); *Family Law Act* (Ont.), ss. 61-63. See also *Carriage by Air Act* (Can.), Sch. I, art. 17; *Marine Liability Act*, S.C. 2001, c. 6, ss. 1-14; *Ordon Estate v. Grail* (1996), 140 D.L.R. (4th) 52, 30 O.R. (3d)

6.20 The damages recoverable under the statute, though not originally restricted by the statutory wording, were early held to extend to "pecuniary" losses only,[6] and several Canadian statutes now expressly provide that recovery shall be for pecuniary loss.[7] However, the meaning of the restriction is not at all apparent. Specific relief being out of the question in the context of a fatal accident claim, all losses must be compensated, if at all, in money. If "pecuniary" refers to the medium of compensation, it imposes no restriction at all on recovery. On the other hand, if "pecuniary" losses means losses consisting of deprivations of actual cash, it would be far too restrictive, for it has long been settled that loss of services is a proper subject of compensation under the statute,[8] and it is not to be reasonably supposed that modern legislation intended to alter the law in this respect by making specific reference to "pecuniary losses". In *Vana v. Tosta*,[9] the Supreme Court of Canada held that a child's loss of a mother's care and guidance was a loss of a pecuniary character. It is not easy to see, therefore, precisely what losses are intended to be excluded by the expression "pecuniary loss". In *Ordon Estate v. Grail*,[9a] the Supreme Court of Canada held that, even where the legislature is silent, damages may be claimed for loss of guidance, care and companionship, in cases of both fatal and non-fatal accidents. The question will be discussed further later.[10]

6.30 The claimants are often called "dependants" by judges and writers, and the value of the claim is often called "lost dependency" or "lost support". These phrases, however, are not always apt as a claim may be made by a relative named in the statute for losses incurred by death that could not, without straining the language, be described as lost dependence or lost support.[11] In a time of radically changing ideas about family relationships, it can be expected often in the future that a claim will be made for a loss of family income by a person, of either sex, who could not

---

643 (C.A.), affd [1998] 3 S.C.R. 437, 166 D.L.R. (4th) 193 (provincial statutes may be applied in a maritime law context).

6 *Blake v. Midland Ry.* (1852), 18 Q.B. 93; *St. Lawrence & Ottawa Ry. v. Lett* (1885), 11 S.C.R. 422; *Grand Trunk Ry. v. Jennings* (1888), 13 App. Cas. 800 (P.C.); *Sakaluk v. Lepage*, [1981] 2 W.W.R. 597 (Sask. C.A.); *Stokes v. Levesque*, [1995] 9 W.W.R. 61, [1996] N.W.T.R. 182 (S.C.). The reasonable expectation of future pecuniary loss is sufficient: *Pym v. Great Northern Ry. Co.* (1863), 4 B. & S. 396, 122 E.R. 508; *Franklin v. South Eastern Ry. Co.* (1858), 3 H. & N. 211, 157 E.R. 448; *Proctor v. Dyck*, [1953] 1 S.C.R. 244, [1953] 2 D.L.R. 257.

7 *Fatal Accidents Act* (Man.), s. 3(2); N.B., s. 3(2); P.E.I., s. 6(2); *Family Law Act* (Ont.), s. 61(1).

8 See 6.280 - 6.300, *infra*.

9 [1968] S.C.R. 71, 66 D.L.R. (2d) 97.

9a [1998] 3 S.C.R. 437, 166 D.L.R. (4th) 193.

10 See 6.300 - 6.330, *infra*. See also *Reeves Estate v. Croken* (1991), 84 Nfld. & P.E.I.R. 298 (P.E.I.S.C.), leave to appeal to S.C.C. refused 130 N.R. 154*n*, 91 Nfld. & P.E.I.R. 270*n*.

11 See *Proctor v. Dyck*, *supra*, footnote 6; *Taff Vale Ry. Co. v. Jenkins*, [1913] A.C. 1 (H.L.); *Cox v. Hockenhull*, [2000] 1 W.L.R. 750 (C.A.) (state benefits).

reasonably be described as dependent upon or supported by the deceased. Curiously enough, the sidenote to s. 61 of the Ontario *Family Law Act*,[12] which replaces the *Fatal Accidents Act*, reads "Right of dependants to sue in tort" and the title to Part V of the Act is "Dependants' Claim For Damages", no such limitation being implied by the former *Fatal Accidents Act*. However, the words of s. 61 itself do not include any provision limiting claims to "dependants" and it seems improbable that the Legislature intended to restrict the scope of the former statute. Modern legislation in some jurisdictions[13] actually uses the word "dependant" but again it seems unlikely that a restriction is intended on the scope of recovery.

6.40 Although dependency is not a requirement of recovery, it has been held that the loss claimed must be a loss of a benefit attributable to the family relationship. In *Burgess v. Florence Nightingale Hospital for Gentlewomen*,[14] a husband and wife formed a professional dancing partnership. It was held that no compensation could be paid to the husband under the *Fatal Accidents Act* for loss of income caused by the death of the wife. Devlin J. said:

> I have ... come to the conclusion that there were here no services that were rendered by the wife to the husband, and there was no benefit arising in the dancing partnership, that can properly be attributed to the relationship of the husband and wife. If this claim were to be allowed, then any partner whose prospects were similarly affected by the death of the other, whatever their relationship was, ought logically to be compensated, too.[15]

It is submitted that this reasoning is not persuasive, for the mere fact that the *Fatal Accidents Act* does not apply to unrelated persons is no reason for restricting the recovery of those who are included. Furthermore, the conclusion is inconvenient in the light of the present tendency to view the relationship between spouses as one of partnership rather than of dependency. It would be wrong, it is submitted, where husband and wife contributed their services jointly to running a farm or other family business to deny the husband a claim for the pecuniary loss suffered by the loss of his wife's services. The question whether the value of the services can "properly be attributed to the relationship of the husband and wife" is unanswerable in such a case.[16]

6.50 In *Danchuk v. Murray*,[17] a claim by a mother for loss of the expectation of repayment by her deceased son of money that she had been compelled to pay under a guarantee of his debts was disallowed. Fawcus J. said that no authority had been cited to support recovery of a debt. However, it is

12 See footnote 5, *supra*.

13 *Fatal Accidents Act 1976* (U.K.); *Fatal Accidents Act* (P.E.I.).

14 [1955] 1 Q.B. 349, followed in *Katz v. Little* (1963), 38 D.L.R. (2d) 515 (Man. Q.B.).

15 *Burgess v. Nightingale Hospital, supra*, footnote 14, at p. 361.

16 This point is made by Cooper-Stephenson, *Personal Injury Damages in Canada*, 2nd ed. (Toronto, Carswell, 1996), p. 645.

17 (1979), 14 B.C.L.R. 270 (S.C.), followed in *Smith v. Cook* (1981), 125 D.L.R. (3d) 457, 33 O.R. (2d) 567 (H.C.J.).

submitted that the claim was, in effect, for loss of an anticipated benefit that the mother expected to receive from her son's earning capacity — a capacity destroyed by the defendant. If she had said, "I intended to make no legal claim but I anticipated that my son would pay me the amount that he owed me as a gift," she would have had, it seems, an unanswerable claim.[18]

6.60 In a number of cases *Burgess v. Florence Nightingale Hospital* has been distinguished. Thus, in *Malyon v. Plummer*,[19] where the claimant received a generous salary from her husband's one-man corporation, she recovered the difference between the value of her services and the amount of the salary. In *Saikaley v. Pelletier*,[20] where the deceased had performed valuable housekeeping services for her son for a low remuneration, his loss was held to be recoverable as the contract was not "such a one as strangers might enter into" but one "heavily weighted in favour of one party to the contract by reason of the familial relationship between the parties".[21]

6.70 In *Klassen v. Soloway*,[22] the loss to a father of the benefit of his son's services to a corporation owned by the father was allowed. In *Dueck v. Mensink*,[23] however, the British Columbia Court of Appeal disallowed recovery by parents owning a private corporation for loss caused by the death of their son who had worked for the corporation for low wages. The Court of Appeal reversed an award in favour of the claimant on the ground that the trial judge had apparently assumed that the corporation's loss was the same as the claimant's loss. McFarlane J.A. said: "In my opinion, that was an error on the facts of this case, because the evidence does not show that a sum of anything like $28,000 was suffered by the parents as a consequence of the death of their son."[24] The case, therefore, appears to turn on a question of evidence. If the claimants could show that they had suffered the loss, it is submitted that they should be entitled to recover it, and in a subsequent case the British Columbia Court of Appeal took this view.[24a] The intervention of a corporation, either as provider of the benefit, as in *Malyon v. Plummer*,[25] or as recipient of it, as in the British Columbia cases, should not in itself preclude recovery.

18 See 6.230, *infra*.

19 [1964] 1 Q.B. 330 (C.A.).

20 (1966), 57 D.L.R. (2d) 394, [1966] 2 O.R. 476 (H.C.J.), followed in *Swejda v. Martin* (1968), 3 D.L.R. (3d) 426 (Sask. Q.B.).

21 *Saikaley v. Pelletier*, *supra*, footnote 20, at p. 398 D.L.R., p. 480 O.R.

22 (1978), 7 B.C.L.R. 85 (S.C.).

23 [1981] 5 W.W.R. 136 (B.C.C.A.), leave to appeal to S.C.C. refused 38 N.R. 443*n*.

24 *Supra*, at p. 138.

24a *Takacs v. Gallo* (1998), 157 D.L.R. (4th) 623 at p. 629 (B.C.C.A.), leave to appeal to S.C.C. refused 163 D.L.R. (4th) vii.

25 *Supra*, footnote 19.

In *Macartney v. Warner*,[25a] the shock and distress caused by the death of a child prevented the parents from earning income. The majority of the Ontario Court of Appeal held that this was a "pecuniary loss resulting from the death" within the meaning of the *Family Law Act*. This is a significant extension of the scope of the legislation in that the compensation was not given in respect of anything that, even loosely speaking, would have been supplied by the deceased had he lived. The expression "pecuniary loss" however has been held not to include exemplary damages.[25b] **6.75**

(2) Loss of monetary contributions of deceased

(a) Introduction

The typical subject of a fatal accident claim is the loss of the periodic contributions that the deceased would have made to the income of the family had there been no death. A claim under the statute lies only in respect of the claimant's actual loss. Consequently, the total income of the deceased is not by any means the same as the claimant's recovery.[25c] The claim under the statute is only for that portion of the deceased's income that could fairly be said to have been likely to accrue to the claimant's benefit. The starting point, therefore, is the deceased's disposable income, not the gross income.[26] It has been held, however, that income tax returns are not conclusive evidence of the value of the disposable income, for benefits other than cash can be taken into account.[27] Illegally earned income is excluded.[27a] **6.80**

The usual method of calculation is to start with the deceased's total annual income and deduct from it all expenditures that the deceased would have made for purposes other than the claimant's benefit, including what would have been spent on the deceased's support, for the deceased's own pleasure,[28] and for other purposes.[29] The remaining sum is the claimant's loss or, in the case of several claimants, such as a spouse and children, the total loss of the group. But the concept of expenditure by the deceased for the deceased's own purposes is not self-explanatory. Expenditures on family assets are presumably made for the joint benefit of the deceased and the family, **6.90**

[25a] (2000), 183 D.L.R. (4th) 345 (Ont C.A.).

[25b] *Lord (Litigation Guardian of) v. Downer* (1999), 179 D.L.R. (4th) 430 (Ont. C.A.), leave to appeal to S.C.C. refused 183 D.L.R. (4th) vii.

[25c] *Holloway Estate v. Giles* (2004), 233 Nfld. & P.E.I.R. 229 (Nfld. & Lab. C.A.), citing this passage.

[26] *Keizer v. Hanna*, [1978] 2 S.C.R. 342, 82 D.L.R. (3d) 449; *May v. Municipality of Metropolitan Toronto* (1968), 2 D.L.R. (3d) 659, [1969] 1 O.R. 419 (H.C.J.).

[27] *Mallory v. Soo Security Motorways Ltd.* (1961), 38 W.W.R. 48 (Sask. Q.B.).

[27a] *Beljanski (Guardian ad Litem of) v. Smithwick* (2006), 275 D.L.R. (4th) 116 (B.C.C.A.).

[28] *Nance v. British Columbia Electric Ry. Co.*, [1951] A.C. 601 (P.C.); *Heatley v. Steel Co. of Wales*, [1953] 1 W.L.R. 405 (C.A.); *Mallet v. McMonagle*, [1970] A.C. 166 (H.L.); *Bishop v. Cunard White Star, Ltd.*, [1950] 2 P. 240 (H.C.J.).

[29] Charitable contributions were deducted in *Krause v. Davey* (1971), 18 D.L.R. (3d) 674, [1971] 2 O.R. 670 (H.C.J.); *Willey v. Cambridge Leaseholds Ltd.* (1975), 57 D.L.R. (3d) 550 (P.E.I.S.C.).

though the claimant's loss may be greater than a proportionate share, in that persons can live more cheaply together than separately.[30] In *Lamont v. Pederson*,[31] the Saskatchewan Court of Appeal accepted that a wife, resident in the home, could reasonably expect to receive for her own benefit 70% of her husband's net income, and a figure in this range is commonly accepted in cases of low and middle income earners.[32]

6.100 The calculation has much in common with that used for lost earnings in personal injury cases.[33] Thus, allowance is made for future increases in income due to promotion or increased productivity.[34] Deductions are made for contingencies and a method is required of capitalization. However, since the starting point is the claimant's loss and not the earner's loss, all expenses that would have reduced the earner's disposable income must be deducted, including income tax.[35] Fringe benefits should only be added insofar as they would have benefited the claimant.[36] Premiums that would have been paid by the deceased for insurance for the latter's own benefit should be deducted, but, insofar as the contribution would have been for the benefit of the claimants, as it is submitted below is the case for life insurance premiums, no deduction should be made.[37]

6.110 The period of the future loss of a spouse is normally based on the joint life expectancy of the claimant and the deceased.[38] Where the claimant would have enjoyed the benefit of a pension payable to the deceased after retirement, compensation is appropriate for this loss,[39] though usually at a reduced rate. The division of future loss into at least two periods will, therefore, usually be required.[40]

---

[30] See *Hay v. Hughes*, [1975] Q.B. 790 (C.A.), at p. 812, where Buckley L.J. pointed out that the claimant "lived in a whole house, not in one-sixth of a house". In *Meeks v. White* (1972), 27 D.L.R. (3d) 681 (N.S.S.C.T.D.), affd 39 D.L.R. (3d) 126 (S.C. App. Div.), no deduction was made for mortgage payments.

[31] [1981] 2 W.W.R. 24 (Sask. C.A.).

[32] See *Young v. Percival*, [1975] 1 W.L.R. 17 (C.A.) (75%); *Cookson v. Knowles*, [1979] A.C. 556 (H.L.) (66% of combined earnings); *Lewis v. Todd*, [1980] 2 S.C.R. 694 at p. 702, 115 D.L.R. (3d) 257 at p. 262 (60%); *Braun v. Roy* (1957), 22 W.W.R. 609 (Man. Q.B.), vard 12 D.L.R. (2d) 390 (C.A.) (66%); *Harris v. Empress Motors Ltd.*, [1984] 1 W.L.R. 212 (C.A.) (66% if children; 75% if no children); *Nielsen v. Kaufmann* (1986), 26 D.L.R. (4th) 21, 54 O.R. (2d) 188 (C.A.) (60% for surviving husband and 4% for each child in two income family); *Davies v. Robertson* (1984), 5 O.A.C. 393 (C.A.) (70% for the spouse and 4% for each of two children); *Millott Estate v. Reinhard*, [2002] 2 W.W.R. 678 (Alta. Q.B.). See also *MacNeil Estate v. Gillis* (1995), 138 N.S.R. (2d) 1, 10 M.V.R. (3d) 8 (C.A.) (smaller percentage in case of lower income in two-income family); *Hechavarria v. Reale* (2000), 51 O.R. (3d) 364 (Ont. S.C.J.).

[33] See 3.710-3.1140, *supra*.

[34] *Lewis v. Todd*, *supra*, footnote 32, at p. 711 S.C.R., p. 270 D.L.R., *per* Dickson J.; *Uhryn v. British Columbia Telephone Co. Ltd.*, [1974] 4 W.W.R. 609 (B.C.S.C.).

[35] *Keizer v. Hanna*, *supra*, footnote 26.

[36] *May v. Municipality of Metropolitan Toronto* (1968), 2 D.L.R. (3d) 659, [1969] 1 O.R. 419 (H.C.J.).

[37] See 6.490, *infra*; *Meeks v. White* (1972), 27 D.L.R. (3d) 681 (N.S.S.C.T.D.), affd 39 D.L.R. (3d) 126 (S.C. App. Div.).

[38] *Lewis v. Todd*, *supra*, footnote 32, at p. 702 S.C.R., p. 262 D.L.R.

[39] See 6.210, *infra*.

6.120 In the case of a child claimant, the period of loss will *prima facie* extend until the majority of the child.[41] However, the period can vary with the particular facts, and in *Trudel v. Canamerican Auto Lease & Rental Ltd.*,[42] the period of loss was extended to age twenty-four.

(b) Savings

6.130 Amounts that the deceased would have saved out of income would not have been available for the claimant's immediate use. However, in many cases, the claimant might reasonably have expected to derive eventual enjoyment from the proceeds of saving by the purchase of assets for the benefit of the household or by inheritance upon the deceased's eventual death.[43] On the other hand, it would not necessarily

[*The next page is* 6-7]

40 See *Kernested v. Desorcy*, [1978] 3 W.W.R. 623 (Man. Q.B.), at p. 638, affd [1979] 1 W.W.R. 512 (C.A.), leave to appeal to S.C.C. refused January 23, 1979.

41 *Lewis v. Todd, supra*, footnote 32, at p. 702 S.C.R., p. 262 D.L.R.; *Krause v. Davey* (1971), 18 D.L.R. (3d) 674, [1971] 2 O.R. 670 (H.C.J.). In *McLean v. Lutz*, [1952] 1 D.L.R. 770 (B.C.S.C.), the age of nineteen was selected.

42 (1975), 59 D.L.R. (3d) 344, 9 O.R. (2d) 18 (H.C.J.).

43 Often this will be set off against the allowance for acceleration of enjoyment of the estate. See 6.410, *infra*. In some cases, however, separate calculations have been made: *Jung v. Krimmer* (1990), 47 B.C.L.R. (2d) 145 (C.A.); *Clement v. Leslies Storage Ltd.* (1979), 97 D.L.R. (3d) 667 (Man. C.A.); *Kwong v. The Queen in right of Alberta* (1978), 96 D.L.R. (3d) 214 (Alta. S.C. App. Div.), at pp. 265-6, *per* Moir J.A., affd [1979] 2 S.C.R. 1010*n*, 105 D.L.R. (3d) 576*n*. See *Royal Trust Co. v. Canadian Pacific Ry. Co.* (1922), 67 D.L.R. 518 (P.C.), at p. 520 (benefit from "probable savings").

be expected that the savings would be spent entirely on the claimant to the exclusion of the deceased. In accordance with this argument, it was held in *Gavin v. Wilmot Breeden Ltd.*[44] that only part of the deceased's savings could be expected to benefit the claimants (in that case a wife and child). The court allowed the claimants £7 as their expected benefit out of estimated weekly savings of £10.

(c) Method of capitalization

6.140 As in the case of calculation of awards for future losses caused by personal injuries,[45] a method is required of converting estimated future losses into a lump sum. Mortality tables are available to estimate the pre-accident life expectancy of the deceased, life expectancy to retirement age, and the life expectancy of the claimant. Where the claimant is a spouse and the deceased was expected to provide benefits for life, the total loss will be based on the joint life expectancy of the claimant and the deceased. Since damages are awarded as a lump sum, however, there must be a discount for the benefit of advance payment. The considerations are the same as those in personal injury cases, discussed in an earlier chapter.[46] In *Keizer v. Hanna*,[47] the Supreme Court of Canada indicated that the same method was to be used for discounting future pecuniary losses in both kinds of case.

(d) Division between pre-trial and future loss

6.150 The former practice in fatal accident cases was not to distinguish between pre-trial and future loss,[48] but the appearance of rapid inflation has made a distinction necessary. For purposes of awarding interest, pre-trial loss must be separately assessed.[49] Moreover, if there is a delay between the death and the trial, the figures on which the annual loss is calculated may have changed significantly. The income that the deceased would have earned between the death and trial can be assessed with some degree of certainty; it is natural to take advantage of what is known at the time of trial and to estimate past loss on the basis of what is now known about wage rates,[50] and future loss on the basis of what the deceased would

---

44 [1973] 1 W.L.R. 1117 (C.A.).

45 See 3.990 - 3.1040, *supra*.

46 *Ibid.*

47 [1978] 2 S.C.R. 342, 82 D.L.R. (3d) 449.

48 See, for example, *Keizer v. Hanna, supra*, footnote 47. See *Jefford v. Gee*, [1970] 2 Q.B. 130 (C.A.), at p. 148.

49 *Wieser v. Pearson* (1981), 126 D.L.R. (3d) 237 (B.C.C.A.); *Cookson v. Knowles*, [1979] A.C. 556 (H.L.); *MacNeil Estate v. Gillis* (1995), 138 N.S.R. (2d) 1 at p. 43, 10 M.V.R. (3d) 8 (C.A.); *Julian v. Northern & Central Gas Corp.* (1980), 118 D.L.R. (3d) 458, 31 O.R. (2d) 388 (C.A.), leave to appeal to S.C.C. refused D.L.R. *loc. cit.*, O.R. *loc. cit.* It was held in *Miller v. Riches* (1984), 5 D.L.R. (4th) 1, 50 A.R. 92 (C.A.), followed in *Hatlen's Estates v. Kaps Transport Ltd.* (1985), 66 A.R. 162 (C.A.), that no adjustment for inflation should be made except by way of prejudgment interest.

50 *The "Swynfleet"* (1947), 81 Ll. L.R. 116.

have been earning at the date of the trial, not on the basis of what the deceased would have been earning at the date of death.[51]

6.160 Failure to make the division results in very great complexity, as is illustrated by *Julian v. Northern & Central Gas Corp.*,[52] where the trial judge had used figures based on the deceased's income at the date of his death three and one-half years before the trial, and had discounted the award as though it were paid at the date of death. The Ontario Court of Appeal held that, if this method were adopted, a sum had to be included to compensate the plaintiff for the delay between the date of death and the date of trial. Following *Fenn v. City of Peterborough*,[53] the court held that interest could be included, not as interest on the award, but as part of the award itself. But Morden J.A. added that the preferable method was to divide the claim:

> With respect, this process was more artificial than it needed to have been. In this regard the approach approved by the House of Lords in *Cookson v. Knowles*, [1978] 2 W.L.R. 978, has much to commend it. This approach involves splitting the damages into two parts: (1) the pecuniary loss which it is estimated the dependants have already sustained between the date of death and the date of trial; and (2), the loss which it was estimated they would suffer from the trial onward. If this approach had been followed in the present case there would have been no need to reach back to the date of death to see to it that the fund contemplated in the evidence is actually established. There are other obvious advantages in approaching the assessment in this realistic and logical way.[54]

6.170 The British Columbia Court of Appeal in *Wieser v. Pearson*[55] has also held that a division is necessary for the purpose of applying the provisions of the *Court Order Interest Act*, which preclude interest in respect of future losses.[56] In the *Julian* case, the plaintiff withdrew her claim for prejudgment interest. If she had not done so, the court would presumably have refused interest in the exercise of its discretion. But difficulties would arise in jurisdictions, like British Columbia, where the award of interest is mandatory.[57]

(e) Income tax

6.180 Since the statutory claim is only for loss actually suffered by the claimant, the relevant sum, as has been mentioned, is that part of the deceased's income estimated to have been available to benefit the

51 See 3.340, *supra*.

52 *Supra*, footnote 49.

53 (1979), 104 D.L.R. (3d) 174, 25 O.R. (2d) 399 (C.A.), affd [1981] 2 S.C.R. 613, 129 D.L.R. (3d) 507, approved on this point in *Lewis v. Todd*, [1980] 2 S.C.R. 694 at pp. 716-17, 115 D.L.R. (3d) 257 at pp. 273-4. See 7.1000, *infra*.

54 *Julian v. Northern Gas, supra*, footnote 49, at p. 482 D.L.R.

55 *Supra*, footnote 49.

56 See 7.600 - 7.640, *infra*.

57 See 7.640, *infra*.

claimant after meeting all expenses. These expenses include income tax payable by the deceased, and the Supreme Court of Canada held in *Keizer v. Hanna*[58] departing from an earlier decision,[59] that, in contrast to a claim for loss of income by a living plaintiff, income tax must be deducted in calculating the loss in a fatal accident claim.[60] However, since the object of the award is to put the claimant in as good a position financially as though the wrong had not been done, allowance must be made for tax payable by the claimant on the invested proceeds of the award.[61] The award, then, having been reduced by making allowance for the tax payable, must be "grossed up" so as to provide, when prudently invested, a sufficient sum to replace the claimant's annual losses after tax paid on the investment income.[61a] Commonly, however, the two rates of tax will differ.

6.190 In calculating the claimant's future tax liability in *Keizer v. Hanna*, the court does not seem to have considered the detailed effect of particular tax rates. Dickson J. said simply:

> On the other hand, in order to yield the sum required net of taxes a greater sum would obviously be called for [greater than $95,000]. The resulting amount would not reach the figure of $120,000 which the trial judge chose. The sum of $100,000, the amount claimed, can be justified, however, with reasonable allowance made for income tax impact and contingency deduction.[62]

6.200 Calculations of tax liability are potentially quite complex,[63] since it must be supposed that the plaintiff so invests the money as to encroach on capital each year to such an extent as to produce a sufficient income which,

---

58 [1978] 2 S.C.R. 342, 82 D.L.R. (3d) 449.

59 *Gehrmann v. Lavoie*, [1976] 2 S.C.R. 561, 59 D.L.R. (3d) 634.

60 See 3.950-3.980 and 5.1280-5.1290, *supra*. The *Fatal Accidents Act* (P.E.I.) (s. 7(1)(i)) provides that "there shall not be taken into account any annual income tax liability of the deceased except such portion of the annual income tax liability of the deceased as is reasonably referable to that portion of the income of the deceased retained or used for his own benefit". It is not easy to see the precise meaning or rationale of this provision.

61 See also *Taylor v. O'Connor*, [1971] A.C. 115 (H.L.); *Malat v. Bjornson* (1980), 110 D.L.R. (3d) 6 (B.C.S.C.); *Lewis v. Todd, supra*, footnote 53. *Julian v. Northern & Central Gas Corp.* (1978), 5 C.C.L.T. 148 (Ont. H.C.J.), affd 118 D.L.R. (3d) 458, 31 O.R. (2d) 388 (C.A.), leave to appeal to S.C.C. refused D.L.R. *loc. cit.*, O.R. *loc. cit.*; *Kwong v. The Queen in right of Alberta* (1978), 96 D.L.R. (3d) 214 (Alta. S.C. App. Div.), affd [1972] 2 S.C.R. 1010*n*, 105 D.L.R. (3d) 576*n*; *Comeau v. Marsman* (1981), 47 N.S.R. (2d) 550 (S.C.T.D); *Haley v. Richardson* (1975), 60 D.L.R. (3d) 480 (N.B.S.C. App. Div.); *McNichol v. Mardell*, [1984] 5 W.W.R. 177, 55 A.R. 161 (C.A.), leave to appeal to S.C.C. refused 56 N.R. 239*n*, 58 A.R. 38*n*; *Spurr v. Naugler* (1974), 50 D.L.R. (3d) 105 (N.S.S.C.T.D.), reducing the initial deduction of tax to take account of this factor is superseded by *Keizer v. Hanna, supra*, footnote 58.

61a See 3.1180, *supra*.

62 *Supra*, footnote 58, at p. 353 S.C.R., pp. 462-3 D.L.R. In *Julian v. Northern & Central Gas Corp., supra*, footnote 61, a 25% "gross up" was approved based on actuarial evidence.

63 See *Nielsen v. Kaufmann* (1986), 26 D.L.R. (4th) 21, 54 O.R. (2d) 188 (C.A.) (uniformity not attainable except by legislation).

after tax, added to the annual capital encroachments, will produce the estimated annual costs, extinguishing the fund at the end of the estimated period of the loss. A further point is that the claimant's other income will affect the rates of income tax. In *Taylor v. O'Connor*,[64] Lord Reid and Viscount Dilhorne stated that the possibility of a rise in the claimant's tax rate due to other income should be ignored, apparently on the ground that another rule would benefit the rich but not the poor. As Professor Luntz points out,[65] there does not seem to be any justification, in principle, for ignoring the claimant's probable actual rate of income tax. It is true that to take the probable actual rate into account would involve giving a larger recovery to the wealthy claimant than to the impoverished claimant, but this is required by the principle of the statute, which is to compensate actual losses not to relieve poverty. If a wealthy claimant needs more to compensate actual loss, the claimant should recover the necessary sum.[66] In *Malat v. Bjornson*,[67] the British Columbia Supreme Court drew a distinction between income derived from sources available to the claimant before the death and income derived from wealth inherited because of the death. The latter was excluded from the calculation. The result would appear to undercompensate the claimant, assuming a deduction for the benefit derived from inheritance is made in accordance with the principles discussed below.[68]

(f) Pension income of deceased

6.210 Commonly a wage-earner expects to work until retirement age and then to receive a pension until death. A claimant under the fatal accidents legislation could often expect, therefore, to enjoy pecuniary benefits from the deceased's income even after the latter's retirement, though usually at a reduced rate. Some pension plans also include survivorship benefits payable to a spouse after the pensioner's death. These too are valuable assets of which the claimant can be said to have been deprived by the deceased's death, and several cases have included the loss in calculating the claimant's damage.[69] If these losses are included, it would seem that the premiums expected to be paid by the deceased ought to be

---

64 *Supra*, footnote 61, at p. 129, *per* Lord Reid, and p. 139, *per* Viscount Dilhorne, followed in *Kwong v. The Queen, supra*, footnote 61, at p. 261; *Janke v. Chamber's Estate* (1981), 29 A.R. 68 (C.A.), revd on other grounds [1982] 1 S.C.R. 281.

65 *Assessment of Damages for Personal Injury and Death*, 3rd ed. (Chatswood, N.S.W., Butterworth Pty. Ltd., 1990), §6.3.4.

66 *Nielsen v. Kaufmann, supra*, footnote 63, at p. 38 D.L.R., citing this passage.

67 *Supra*, footnote 61.

68 See 6.400, *infra*. In *Malat v. Bjornson, supra*, footnote 61, at p. 12, Ruttan J. stressed that no deduction had been made from the award in respect of the inheritance from the deceased's estate.

69 *Lamont v. Pederson*, [1981] 2 W.W.R. 24 (Sask. C.A.); *Lewis v. Todd*, [1980] 2 S.C.R. 694, 115 D.L.R. (3d) 257 (retirement benefit); *Keddy v. Minshull* (1969), 5 D.L.R. (3d) 156 (N.S.S.C.); *Julian v. Northern & Central Gas Corp., supra*, footnote 61, at p. 161 C.C.L.T.; *Smith v. Canadian Pacific Ry.* (1963), 41 D.L.R. (2d) 249 (Sask. Q.B.).

excluded in calculating the claimant's annual expected benefit during the deceased's working life. The claimant would be doubly compensated on receipt of the benefit of the premiums and, in addition, the value of the pension that would have been purchased with those premiums.[70]

(g) Death of children

6.220 Recovery has been allowed for the anticipated benefit that a parent could have expected from a deceased child.[71] In some cases, awards have been made without proof of any definite expectation of financial benefit.[72] Other cases have insisted, in the absence of such proof, that there should be no award.[73] With reference to the death of young children, it was said in one case that the claim will usually be "pressed to extinction by the weight of multiplied contingencies",[74] but several Canadian cases have made awards.[75] Courts have been capable of estimating the loss of future

---

70 See *Kernested v. Desorcy*, [1978] 3 W.W.R. 623 (Man. Q.B.), at pp. 632-3, affd [1979] 1 W.W.R. 512 (C.A.), leave to appeal to S.C.C. refused January 23, 1979.

71 *Mock v. Regina Trading Co.* (1922), 68 D.L.R. 159 (Sask. C.A.) ($3,500 for twelve-year-old); *Marsden Kooler Transport Ltd. v. Pollock*, [1953] 1 S.C.R. 66, [1953] 1 D.L.R. 1 ($6,000 for seventeen-year-old); *Franklin v. South Eastern Ry. Co.* (1858), 3 H. & N. 211, 157 E.R. 448; *Taff Vale Ry. Co. v. Jenkins*, [1913] A.C. 1 (H.L.) (sixteen-year-old daughter); *Bianco v. Fromow* (1998), 161 D.L.R. (4th) 765 (B.C.C.A.) ($53,000 for thirty-year old); *Guitard v. MacDonald* (1970), 14 D.L.R. (3d) 252 (N.B.S.C. App. Div.) (eight-year-old son); *McKeown v. Toronto Ry. Co.* (1908), 19 O.L.R. 361 (C.A.) (four-year-old child); *Courtemanche v. McElwain* (1962), 37 D.L.R. (2d) 595, [1963] 1 O.R. 472 (C.A.) (seven-year-old); *Lai v. Gill*, [1980] 1 S.C.R. 431 ($25,000 for death of fourteen-year-old); *Landry v. Lamothe* (1975), 14 N.B.R. (2d) (Q.B.); *Stewart v. Sheldrake* (1976), 22 N.S.R. (2d) 279 (S.C.T.D.); *Chapman v. Coates* (1975), 21 N.S.R. (2d) 477 (S.C.T.D.) ($5,000 for sixteen-year-old); *Neville v. Brace* (1978), 28 N.S.R. (2d) 387 (S.C.T.D.) ($3,000 for twenty-one-year old); *Moddejonge v. Huron County Board of Education* (1972), 25 D.L.R. (3d) 661, [1972] 2 O.R. 437 (H.C.J.); *French v. Blake* (1971), 19 D.L.R. (3d) 244 (B.C.C.A.) ($4,000 for fifteen-year-old); *McGee v. Smith* (1964), 48 D.L.R. (2d) 476 (N.B.S.C. App. Div.) ($1,200 for twelve-year-old); *Biggar v. Green*, [1949] 1 D.L.R. 407 (P.E.I.S.C.) ($1,697.60 for seventeen-year-old); *Cox v. Fleming* (1995), 15 B.C.L.R. (3d) 201, 108 W.A.C. 220 (C.A.) ($20,000 for loss of eighteen-year old); *Lian v. Money*, [1996] 4 W.W.R. 263, 15 B.C.L.R. (3d) 1 (C.A.) (support from other children to be taken into account).

72 *Power's Estate v. Roussell Estate* (1978), 23 N.B.R. (2d) 298 (Q.B.); *Deslaurier v. Carmichael* (1978), 23 N.B.R. (2d) 30 (Q.B.).

73 *Gorrill v. Ross* (1980), 22 B.C.L.R. 140 (S.C.); *Leopold v. Knight* (1980), 116 D.L.R. (3d) 260 (N.S.S.C.T.D.); *Vale v. R. J. Yohn Construction Co. Ltd.* (1970), 12 D.L.R. (3d) 465, [1970] 3 O.R. 137 (C.A.); *Paruk v. Nygren* (1972), 25 D.L.R. (3d) 377 (B.C.C.A.); *Mogck v. Woldum* (1965), 52 D.L.R. (2d) 322 (Alta. S.C.); *Cashin v. Mackenzie*, [1951] 3 D.L.R. 495 (N.S.S.C.); *Craig v. Canadian Northern Pacific Ry. Co.*, [1934] 1 D.L.R. 484 (B.C.S.C.); *Piper v. Hill*, [1923] 4 D.L.R. 1175, 53 O.L.R. 233 (S.C. App. Div.); *Pedlar v. Toronto Power Co.* (1913), 15 D.L.R. 684, 29 O.L.R. 527 (H.C.), affd 19 D.L.R. 441, 30 O.L.R. 581 (S.C. App. Div.); *Stokes v. Levesque*, [1995] 9 W.W.R. 61, [1996] N.W.T.R. 182 (S.C.); *Fraser v. Leblanc* (1996), 22 B.C.L.R. (3d) 133 (S.C.).

74 *Barnett v. Cohen*, [1921] 2 K.B. 461 at p. 472; *Chudleigh v. Ross*, [1955] 4 D.L.R. 437 (B.C.S.C.); *West v. Werseen* (1958), 26 W.W.R. 707 (B.C.S.C.); *Nickerson v. Forbes* (1955), 1 D.L.R. (2d) 463 (N.S.S.C. in banco); *Alaffe v. Kennedy* (1973), 40 D.L.R. (3d) 429 (N.S.S.C.T.D.).

75 See footnote 71, *supra*.

income in cases of disabling injury of very young children.[76] In the case of a fatal accident claim, however, the cost of raising the child must be set off against any anticipated benefit[77] and there are the added contingencies of the parents not surviving until the child's earning years, or not, in fact, claiming or receiving any portion of the child's income perhaps due to competing claimants, such as the child's own spouse and children.[78] In *Mason v. Peters*,[79] where the claim was by a mother for the death of an eleven-year-old boy, the court said that it would be necessary to consider the attitude and disposition of the boy towards his mother, the circumstances of the mother, and the likelihood of the child, on attaining his majority, of contributing to his mother's care and comfort. The court awarded $45,000 to the mother, but an alternative ground for the award was compensation for loss of care and companionship under the *Family Law Act, 1986*.[80]

(3) Loss of expectation of gifts

6.230 Though the usual claim is based on the support or maintenance expected more or less continuously from the deceased by a spouse or children, there is no requirement that the deceased should have been under a legal obligation to provide the benefits the loss of which is claimed,[81] nor any requirement that the benefits should have been expected periodically. If children could reasonably have expected parental support past the age of majority, the expectation will be compensable even though the legal obligation of support may, in fact, run from the child to the parent.[82] The value of anticipated future gifts can properly be included, as can an expectation of an increased inheritance on the deceased's eventual death.[83] If the expected benefit to the claimants of the deceased's savings has been fully included in the calculation of their annual loss, however, no additional allowance can logically be made for an increased estate that might result from those savings, or from gifts that might have been made out of those savings.[84]

---

76 See 3.720, *supra*.

77 *Fenn v. City of Peterborough* (1979), 104 D.L.R. (3d) 174, 25 O.R. (2d) 399 (C.A.), affd [1981] 2 S.C.R. 613, 129 D.L.R. (3d) 507.

78 *Eisan v. Bonang* (1958), 14 D.L.R. (2d) 750 (N.S.S.C.).

79 (1980), 117 D.L.R. (3d) 417, 30 O.R. (2d) 409 (H.C.J.), affd 139 D.L.R. (3d) 104, 39 O.R. (2d) 27 (C.A.), leave to appeal to S.C.C. refused 46 N.R. 538*n*.

80 See 6.330-6.390, *infra*.

81 See *Proctor v. Dyck*, [1953] 1 S.C.R. 244, [1953] 2 D.L.R. 257; *Taff Vale Ry. Co. v. Jenkins*, [1913] A.C. 1 (H.L.).

82 *Trudel v. Canamerican Auto Lease & Rental Ltd.* (1975), 59 D.L.R. (3d) 344, 9 O.R. (2d) 18 (H.C.J.).

83 *Nance v. British Columbia Electric Ry. Co.*, [1951] A.C. 601 (P.C.), at p. 614; *Proctor v. Dyck*, *supra*, footnote 81, at pp. 250-51 S.C.R., pp. 262-3 D.L.R. But in *Miller Estate v. Bowness* (1988), 55 D.L.R. (4th) 286, 66 O.R. (2d) 750 (C.A.), the possibility that the deceased, had she not been killed, would have inherited under a will was excluded.

84 See 6.130, *supra*.

(4) Funeral, medical and other expenses

6.240 It was held by the English Court of Appeal in *Clark v. London General Omnibus Co.*,[85] followed by the Supreme Court of Canada in *Toronto Ry. Co. v. Mulvaney*,[86] that funeral expenses are not recoverable under *Lord Campbell's Act*. The legislation in all Canadian jurisdictions now, however, specifically provides that funeral expenses are recoverable.[87] Reasonable expenses only are recoverable; this has been taken to include a grave marker[88] or headstone[89] but not a (presumably more elaborate) memorial.[90] The cost of holding a funeral in Germany was disallowed in one case[91] though the cost of travel (by train, not by air) from Saskatchewan to Newfoundland was allowed[92] as was the cost of a funeral banquet.[92a]

6.250 Survival legislation in some jurisdictions also provides for recovery by the estate of funeral expenses.[93] The relationship between the two sets of remedies is unclear. Presumably, the defendant cannot be made to pay twice over and if actions are brought both under the fatal accidents legislation and under the survival legislation and recovery has been allowed in one action, it would seem that it ought to be disallowed in the other.[94] Even where the claimant under the fatal accidents legislation is the sole beneficiary of the estate, it may make a difference under which statute the claim is made, as was shown by *Mulholland v. McCrea*,[95] where the claimant's contributory negligence was held by the Northern Ireland Court

85 [1906] 2 K.B. 648 (C.A.).

86 (1907), 38 S.C.R. 327; *West v. Werseen* (1958), 26 W.W.R. 707 (B.C.S.C.); *Mogck v. Woldum* (1965), 52 D.L.R. (2d) 322 (Alta. S.C.); *Beahan v. Nevin* (1913), 11 D.L.R. 679, 4 O.W.N. 1399 (H.C.). But in *Chudleigh v. Ross*, [1955] 4 D.L.R. 437 (B.C.S.C.) and *Mogck v. Woldum, supra*, funeral expenses were held to be recoverable at common law.

87 *Fatal Accidents Act* (Alta.), s. 7; Man., s. 3(3); N.B., s. 3(3); Nfld. & Lab., s. 9; N.W.T., s. 4(1)(b); P.E.I., s. 6(3)(a); Sask., s. 4(2)(b); Yukon, s. 3(3); *Fatal Injuries Act*, N.S., s. 5(4); *Family Compensation Act*, B.C., s. 3(9)(b); *Family Law Act* (Ont.), s. 61(2)(b).

88 *Stanton v. Youldon*, [1960] 1 W.L.R. 543 (Q.B.); *Power's Estate v. Roussel Estate* (1978), 23 N.B.R. (2d) 298 (Q.B.); *Flaherty's Estate v. Flynn* (1976), 10 Nfld. & P.E.I.R. 72 (Nfld. S.C.) (survival action).

89 *Sorensen v. Beach*, [1971] 5 W.W.R. 488 (B.C.S.C.). But in *Hamilton v. White* (1971), 7 N.S.R. (2d) 47 (S.C.T.D.), the cost of a tombstone was disallowed and in *Lombard v. Phillips* (1964), 46 D.L.R. (2d) 347 (N.S.S.C.), vard [1965-69] 5 N.S.R. 482 (S.C. in banco), and *Walter v. Muise* (1964), 48 D.L.R. (2d) 734 (N.S.S.C.), the cost of a "monument", presumably meaning a tombstone, was disallowed.

90 *Stanton v. Youldon, supra*, footnote 88; *Keddy v. Minshull* (1969), 5 D.L.R. (3d) 156 (N.S.S.C.); *Eisan v. Bonang* (1958), 14 D.L.R. (2d) 750 (N.S.S.C.) (under wording of Nova Scotia Act at the time, cost must actually *have been* incurred).

91 *Sorensen v. Beach*, [1971] 5 W.W.R. 488 (B.C.S.C.).

92 *Hickey v. Laatsch* (1957), 11 D.L.R. (2d) 210 (Sask. Q.B.). See also 12.250, *infra*.

92a *Sum Estate v. Kan* (1997), 44 B.C.L.R. (3d) 250, 163 W.A.C. 17 (C.A.).

93 See, *e.g.*, *Trustee Act* (Man.), s. 53(1); *Survival of Actions Act* (Alta.), s. 6; N.B., s. 6; P.E.I., s. 6(a).

94 *Clement v. Leslies Storage Ltd.* (1977), 82 D.L.R. (3d) 469 (Man. Q.B.), at p. 477, affd 97 D.L.R. (3d) 667 (C.A.). Double compensation is excluded by statute in Manitoba (s. 3(3)) and P.E.I. (s. 6).

95 [1961] N.I. 135.

of Appeal to reduce his claim under the fatal accidents legislation but not to affect the claim by the estate.

6.260 Medical expenses incurred on behalf of the deceased before death are not losses caused by the death.[96] However, in some jurisdictions it is specifically provided that, in an action under the Act, damages may be awarded in respect of medical expenses that would have been recoverable by the injured person if death had not ensued.[97] It was argued in an earlier chapter that the cost of medical services should be recoverable by the injured person, whether or not paid by another person. Where, as in most jurisdictions,[98] this right survives to the estate, there will be no place for an additional action by the relatives. Recovery by the estate offers, it is submitted, a more rational basis, for it will not be limited, as is the legislation mentioned here, to expenses that happen to be borne by a relative eligible to claim under the fatal accidents legislation.

6.270 The Prince Edward Island statute provides for the recovery of up to $500 "toward the expenses of taking out administration of the estate".[99] Again, this is not, in the absence of legislation, a loss caused by the defendant's wrong.[100] Two provinces permit recovery of out-of-pocket expenses incurred for the benefit of an injured person, an allowance for travel expenses incurred in visiting an injured person and for lost income in caring for the person.[101] It would seem that these claims could be combined with a claim for loss caused by death, in the event of subsequent death.[102] In *D'Ascenzo v. Biro*,[103] travelling and telephone expenses were allowed under the Ontario Act. Management fees may be allowed where the plaintiff is likely to need professional help with investing the proceeds of an award.[103a]

---

96 *Mayer v. Prince Albert*, [1926] 4 D.L.R. 1072 (Sask. C.A.); *Duggan v. Harnish*, [1955] 3 D.L.R. 860 (N.S.S.C. in banco).

97 *Family Compensation Act*, B.C., s. 3(9)(a); *Fatal Accidents Act*, Sask., s. 4(2)(a); *Fatal Accidents Act* (N.W.T.), s. 4(1). The Ontario Act provides for recovery for such expenses even if death does not occur. See 5.1330-5.1340, *supra*.

98 [Footnote deleted.]

99 *Fatal Accidents Act*, P.E.I., s. 6(3)(b).

100 *Ferguson v. Underwood* (1972), 7 N.S.R. (2d) 459 (S.C.T.D.); *Constable v. Ulan* (1969), 7 D.L.R. (3d) 377 (Alta. S.C. App. Div.).

101 *Family Law Act* (Ont.), s. 61(2); *Fatal Injuries Act* (N.S.), s. 5(2).

102 See *Fread v. Chislett* (1981), 123 D.L.R. (3d) 181, 32 O.R. (2d) 733 (H.C.J.). See also *Mason v. Peters* (1982), 139 D.L.R. (3d) 104, 39 O.R. (2d) 27 (C.A.), leave to appeal to S.C.C. refused 46 N.R. 538*n*, overruling *Chitale v. Sandford* (1980), 1 A.C.W.S. (2d) 309 (Ont. H.C.J.), affd 1 F.L.R.A.C. 614 (C.A.); *Fulcher v. Near* (1981), 131 D.L.R. (3d) 338, 35 O.R. (2d) 184 (H.C.J.), affd (unreported, March, 1983, C.A.) (recovery by grandchildren); *Thornborrow v. MacKinnon* (1981), 123 D.L.R. (3d) 124, 32 O.R. (2d) 740 (H.C.J.).

103 (1980), 1 F.L.R.A.C. 627 (Ont. H.C.J.).

103a See *Wilson v. Martinello* (1995), 125 D.L.R. (4th) 240 at p. 254, 23 OR (3d) 417 at p. 432 (C.A.), where the plaintiff was found to be capable of managing his own investments.

(5) Loss of services

6.280 Compensation has long been held to include loss of services as, for example, household services of a spouse[104], a child[105], or a parent.[106] It is universally accepted that the cost of hiring reasonable services on a commercial basis to replace lost domestic services is an allowable claim.[107] In some cases, income forgone by the claimant has been allowed as a measure of the value of the lost services.[108]

6.290 Attempts have been made to justify a higher level of compensation on the basis of the value of the deceased's lost housekeeping capacity, or of the deceased's forgone earning capacity where this is higher.[109] The problems of valuation of housekeeping services have given rise to difficulties in personal injury claims also. In the latter context it may be argued that an injured housekeeper ought to be entitled to the full value of lost earning capacity, for it can truly be said that the defendant's wrong has deprived the injured housekeeper of the highest value to which the earning capacity could have been put.[110] However, so long as fatal accident compensation rests on the theory of loss to the claimant, it is difficult to justify recovery of the deceased's lost earning capacity. Suppose a household where the wife is a physician who chooses to forgo high earnings in order to keep house. Even if one accepts that the loss to her of disablement is the loss of a physician's income, it seems difficult to

---

104 *St. Lawrence & Ottawa Electric Ry. Co. v. Lett* (1885), 11 S.C.R. 422; *Tarasoff v. Zielinsky* (1921), 59 D.L.R. 177 (Sask. C.A.); *Berry v. Humm & Co.*, [1915] 1 K.B. 627; *Feay v. Barnwell*, [1938] 1 All E.R. 31 (K.B.); *Franco v. Woolfe* (1976), 69 D.L.R. (3d) 501, 12 O.R. (2d) 549 (C.A.); *Vana v. Tosta*, [1968] S.C.R. 71, 66 D.L.R. (2d) 97; *Griffiths v. Canadian Pacific Rys.* (1978), 6 B.C.L.R. 115 (C.A.); *Wallis v. Lichty*, [1952] O.W.N. 116 (H.C.J.); *Coco v. Nicholls* (1981), 31 A.R. 386 (C.A.); *McNichol v. Mardell*, [1984] 5 W.W.R. 177, 55 A.R. 161 (C.A.), leave to appeal to S.C.C. refused 56 N.R. 239*n*, 58 A.R. 38*n*; *Taguchi v. Stuparyk* (1995), 29 Alta. L.R. (3d) 175 (C.A.), leave to appeal to S.C.C. refused 181 A.R. 79*n*, 116 W.A.C. 79*n*; *Parsons Estate v. Guymer* (1998), 162 D.L.R. (4th) 390 (Ont. C.A.), leave to appeal to S.C.C. refused 178 D.L.R. (4th) vii.

105 *Fenn v. City of Peterborough* (1979), 104 D.L.R. (3d) 174, 25 O.R. (2d) 399 (C.A.), affd [1981] 2 S.C.R. 613, 129 D.L.R. (3d) 507; *French v. Blake* (1971), 19 D.L.R. (3d) 244 (B.C.C.A.); *Cahoose v. Insurance Corp. of British Columbia* (1999), 201 W.A.C. 301 (B.C.C.A.). See *Lapointe v. Godin* (1972), 32 D.L.R. (3d) 100 (N.B.S.C. App. Div.) (commercial services).

106 *Grant v. Jackson* (1985), 24 D.L.R. (4th) 598, [1986] 2 W.W.R. 413 (C.A.); *Manning (Guardian ad Litem of) v. British Columbia (Minister of Transportation and Highways)* (1993), 77 B.C.L.R. (2d) 189 (S.C.).

107 See *Franco v. Woolfe*, *supra*, footnote 104; *Griffiths v. Canadian Pacific Rys.*, *supra*, footnote 104; *Nielsen v. Kaufmann* (1986), 26 D.L.R. (4th) 21 at p. 30, 54 O.R. (2d) 188 (C.A.), citing this passage but pointing out that joint responsibility of spouses for household management is to be presumed.

108 *Mehmet v. Perry*, [1977] 2 All E.R. 529 (Q.B.). But this measure was refused in *Luethi v. Hague* (1977), 5 A.R. 225 (S.C.T.D.).

109 See Komesar, "Toward a General Theory of Personal Injury Loss", 3 J. Leg. Stud. 457 (1974); Pottick, "Tort Damages for the Injured Homemaker: Opportunity Cost or Replacement Cost?", 50 U. Colo. L. Rev. 59 (1978).

110 See 3.800, *supra*.

conclude that the husband suffers the same loss on her death. The question of the economic relationship between spouses is one of the most controversial issues of the day. It is by no means clear whether the forgone income of the housewife-physician (admitting it to be a loss to her if she is disabled) can be said to be a loss to the "household unit" or to her spouse if she is killed.[111] In *Franco v. Woolfe*,[112] the Ontario Court of Appeal excluded economic evidence designed to show the general value of household services, while allowing evidence of the actual probable cost to the claimants of replacing the deceased's services. The court is, it is suggested, on sound ground in insisting on proof of loss to the claimant, so long as the problem is addressed within the framework of the fatal accidents legislation. These considerations, however, may suggest that there is at least the merit of simplicity in choosing the alternative route of recovery by the deceased's estate, where damages are measured by the loss to the deceased.[113]

6.300 More difficulty arises in respect of valuing services of a spouse or parent that cannot be replaced. Intangible losses of this sort have been compensated in many Canadian cases. In *Vana v. Tosta*,[114] the Supreme Court of Canada approved a passage of Ruttan J. in the B.C. Supreme Court:

> The guiding principle as contained in the judgment of Chief Justice Ritchie in the Supreme Court decision of *Lett v. St. Lawrence and Ottawa Elec. Ry.*[115] keeps re-appearing in extensive quotation in many of the cases that have been decided in the succeeding 70 years. Pecuniary loss is the loss of some benefit or advantage which is capable of being estimated in terms of money, as distinct from mere sentimental loss. Here we must value the loss of the services of a young wife to a young husband, their respective ages being 30 and 32 at the time of the accident; and the loss of a mother of two small children, aged three and five years.[116]

It appears that the court may be opening the door here to some compensation for loss of affection and companionship. It is apparently

---

111 In *Grant v. Jackson*, *supra*, footnote 106, children were held entitled to recover in their own right for the loss of housekeeping services of their mother (who had sole custody).

112 *Supra*, footnote 104, cited with apparent approval in *Griffins v. Canadian Pacific Rys.* (1978), 6 B.C.L.R. 115 (C.A.), where it was pointed out that if the deceased's services are valued at commercial rates, the cost to the claimant of maintaining the deceased should be deducted. See *Nielsen v. Kaufmann*, *supra*, footnote 107 (housekeeping costs not to be added to compensation for lost income from anticipated full-time employment).

113 See 6.760-6.1090, *infra*.

114 *Supra*, footnote 104, at p. 87 S.C.R., p. 106 D.L.R., and see p. 77 S.C.R., p. 115 D.L.R.

115 *Supra*, footnote 104.

116 *DeBrincat v. Mitchell* (1958), 26 W.W.R. 634 (B.C.S.C.), at p. 635. Similar awards were made in *Farish v. Papp* (1957), 23 W.W.R. 690 (Alta. S.C.); *Walter v. Muise* (1964), 48 D.L.R. (2d) 734 (N.S.S.C.), and *Griffiths v. Canadian Pacific Rys.*, (1978), 6 B.C.L.R. 115 (C.A.); *Kovats v. Ogilvie* (1970), 17 D.L.R. (3d) 343 (B.C.C.A.); *Trudel v. Canamerican Auto Lease & Rental Ltd.* (1975), 59 D.L.R. (3d) 344, 9 O.R. (2d) 18 (H.C.J.); *Lewis v. Todd* (1978), 5 C.C.L.T. 167 (Ont. C.A.), affd [1980] 2 S.C.R. 694, 115 D.L.R. (3d) 257; *Coco v. Nicholls* (1981), 31 A.R. 386 (C.A.). See also *Franco v. Woolfe*, *supra*, footnote 104, at pp. 502-3 D.L.R., pp. 550-1 O.R.

only "mere sentimental loss" that is to be excluded. The Supreme Court of Canada, in upholding awards to children of $2,000 and $1,000 for loss of their mother's "care and training", expressly departed from the position taken in a New Zealand case[117] and in a Canadian Privy Council case of 1888.[118]

(6) Intangible losses

6.310 As has been mentioned above, claims under the fatal accidents legislation were early held to be restricted to "pecuniary losses", a phrase not in the original statute but now embodied in the legislation of some provinces.[119] Thus claims for grief at the defendant's death or for solatium were disallowed,[120] but the Supreme Court of Canada in *Vana v. Tosta*[121] allowed a claim for loss of a parent's care and guidance. This was followed in *Julian v. Northern & Central Gas Corp.*, where bereaved children were awarded $5,000 each for loss of a father's "guidance, training and encouragement".[122] The British Columbia Court of Appeal has held no damages are allowable for loss of love, affection or companionship.[122a]

6.320 In Alberta and Saskatchewan the statutes provide for the award of fixed sums to a spouse, parents or children for grief and loss of guidance, care and

[117] *Marsh v. Absolum*, [1940] N.Z.L.R. 448 (C.A.).

[118] *Grand Trunk Ry. Co. of Canada v. Jennings* (1888), 13 App. Cas. 800 (P.C.). English cases appear to be moving in the same direction: *Regan v. Williamson*, [1976] 1 W.L.R. 305 (Q.B.); *Mehmet v. Perry*, [1977] 2 All E.R. 529 (Q.B.). In *Preston v. Hunting Air Transport*, [1956] 1 Q.B. 454, compensation for loss of a mother's care was allowed under the Warsaw Convention, which Ormerod J. held not to be limited to "financial loss".

[119] See 6.20, *supra*.

[120] Ritchie C.J., in *St. Lawrence & Ottawa Ry. Co. v. Lett* (1885), 11 S.C.R. 422, said that damages must not be a "mere solatium". See *Pym v. Great Northern Ry. Co.* (1863), 4 B. & S. 396 at p. 401, 122 E.R. 508; *Blake v. Midland Ry. Co.* (1852), 18 Q.B. 93; *Hinz v. Berry*, [1970] 2 Q.B. 40 (C.A.) (personal action at common law for nervous shock); *Vale v. R.J. Yohn Construction Co. Ltd.* (1970), 12 D.L.R. (3d) 465, [1970] 3 O.R. 137 (C.A.); *Royal Trust Co. v. C.P.R. Co.* (1922), 67 D.L.R. 518 (P.C.); *MacDonald v. Deson* (1970), 13 D.L.R. (3d) 722 (B.C.C.A.); *Lord (Litigation Guardian of) v. Downer* (1999), 179 D.L.R. (4th) 430 (Ont. C.A.), leave to appeal to S.C.C. refused 183 D.L.R. (4th) vii (aggravated damages disallowed). See 6.75, *supra*.

[121] [1968] S.C.R. 71, 66 D.L.R. (2d) 97, approved in *Ordon Estate v. Grail*, [1998] 3 S.C.R. 437, 166 D.L.R. (4th) 193.

[122] (1978), 5 C.C.L.T. 148 (Ont. H.C.J.), affd 118 D.L.R. (3d) 458 31 O.R. (2d) 388 (C.A.), leave to appeal to S.C.C. refused D.L.R. *loc. cit.*, O.R. *loc. cit.*; *Chapman v. Verstraete*, [1977] 4 W.W.R. 214 (B.C.S.C.); *Jeselon v. Waters*, [1981] 3 W.W.R. 715 (B.C.S.C.); *Furi v. Ryall*, [1976] 3 W.W.R. 680 (Sask. Q.B.); *Trowsdale v. McDonald* (1980), 20 B.C.L.R. 1 (S.C.); *Shaw's Estate v. Roemer* (1981), 46 N.S.R. (2d) 629 (S.C.T.D.), affd 134 D.L.R. (3d) 590 (S.C. App. Div.), leave to appeal to S.C.C. refused December 6, 1982; *Gregorie v. Spencer* (1991), 119 N.B.R. (2d) 1 (Q.B.): (damages for loss of mother's "care and moral training"); *Naeth Estate v. Warburton* (1992), 103 Sask. R. 130 (Q.B.), vard 116 Sask. R. 11, 59 W.A.C. 11 (C.A.) ($11,700 to infant whose mother died in childbirth); *Redlick-Lynn (Next Friend of) v. Halfe* (1994), 21 Alta. L.R. (3d) 195, 156 A.R. 210, supplementary reasons 24 Alta. L.R. (3d) 415, 161 A.R. 134 (Q.B.), affd 37, 181 A.R. 157, Alta. L.R. (3d) 355, 116 W.A.C. 157 (C.A.) ($24,000 for loss of mother's care, education, training, guidance, example and encouragement); *Sickel Estate v. Gordy*, 2008 SCKA 100.

[122a] *Bianco v. Fromow* (1998), 161 D.L.R. (4th) 765 (B.C.C.A.); *Zeleniski Estate v. Fairway* (1998), 60 B.C.L.R. (3d) 76 (C.A.).

companionship,[123] and a similar provision with respect to guidance, care and companionship is in force in Manitoba.[123a]

6.330 The Ontario legislation provides:

> 61(1) If a person is injured or killed by the fault or neglect of another under circumstances where the person is entitled to recover damages, or would have been entitled if not killed, the spouse, as defined in Part III (Support Obligations), children, grandchildren, parents, grandparents, brothers and sisters of the person are entitled to recover their pecuniary loss resulting from the injury or death from the person from whom the person injured or killed is entitled to recover or would have been entitled if not killed, and to maintain an action for the purpose in a court of competent jurisdiction.
>
> (2) The damages recoverable in a claim under subsection (1) may include,
>
> (a) actual expenses reasonably incurred for the benefit of the person injured or killed;
>
> (b) actual funeral expenses reasonably incurred;
>
> (c) a reasonable allowance for travel expenses actually incurred in visiting the injured person during his or her treatment or recovery;
>
> (d) where, as a result of the injury, the claimant provides nursing, housekeeping or other services for the person, a reasonable allowance for loss of income or the value of the services; and
>
> (e) an amount to compensate for the loss of guidance, care and companionship that the claimant might reasonably have expected to receive from the person if the injury or death had not occurred.[124]

The effect of these provisions on recovery for intangible losses is somewhat unclear but the section has been held to apply to such losses in several cases affirmed by the Ontario Court of Appeal.[125] It seems probable that the Legislature, in introducing the phrase "pecuniary loss" in s. 61(1) did not intend to restrict recovery but simply intended to affirm the current

[123] *Fatal Accidents Act* (Alta.), s. 8(2); *Fatal Accidents Act*, R.S.S. 1978, c. F-11, s. 4.1. In *Ferraiuolo Estate v. Olson* (2004), 246 D.L.R. (4th) 225 (Alta. C.A.), age and marital status restrictions relating to children were struck down as contrary to the *Canadian Charter of Rights and Freedoms*. A fixed figure is also provided in the United Kingdom by the *Administration of Justice Act 1982*.

[123a] *Fatal Accidents Act* (Man), s. 3.1(2).

[124] *Family Law Act*, s. 61. The Nova Scotia and Prince Edward Island statutes also provide compensation for "loss of guidance, care and companionship": *Fatal Injuries Act* (N.S.), s. 5(2)(d); *Fatal Accidents Act* (P.E.I.), s. 6(3)(c), extended to Admiralty law in *Ordon Estate v. Grail* (1996), 140 D.L.R. (4th) 52, 30 O.R. (3d) 643 (C.A.), affd [1998] 3 S.C.R. 437, 166 D.L.R. (4th) 193. The *Fatal Accidents Act* (N.B.), s. 3(4) provides for compensation to parents for loss of companionship and grief. See *Seede v. Camco Inc.* (1985), 50 O.R. (2d) 218, 50 C.P.C. 78 (H.C.J.), affd 55 O.R. (2d) 352*n* (unborn child not included).

[125] *Mason v. Peters* (1982), 139 D.L.R. (3d) 104, 39 O.R. (2d) 27 (C.A.), leave to appeal to S.C.C. refused 46 N.R. 538*n*, overruling *Chitale v. Sandford* (1980), 1 A.C.W.S. (2d) 309 (Ont. H.C.J.), affd 1 F.L.R.A.C. 614 (C.A.). See also *Fulcher v. Near* (1981), 131 D.L.R. (3d) 338, 35 O.R. (2d) 184 (H.C.J.), affd (unreported, March, 1983, C.A.) (recovery by grandchildren); *Thornborrow v. MacKinnon* (1981), 123 D.L.R. (3d) 124, 32 O.R. (2d) 740 (H.C.J.); *Fread v. Chislett* (1981), 123 D.L.R. (3d) 181, 32 O.R. (2d) 733 (H.C.J.); *Macartney v. Warner* (2000), 183 D.L.R. (4th) 345 (Ont. C.A.) (claim allowable for loss of income from nervous shock).

interpretation of the courts in fatal cases, adding subsec. (2)(e) to increase allowable compensation in certain cases.

6.340 It should be noted that in *Vana v. Tosta*[126] the Supreme Court of Canada did not say that a claimant could recover for non-pecuniary losses. The court said that loss of a parent's care and guidance was a loss of a pecuniary character. Quoting from *St. Lawrence & Ottawa Ry. Co. v. Lett*,[127] the court held that it had power to award "such damages as will afford a reasonable ... compensation for the substantial loss sustained".[128] Evidently this test is intended to exclude damages awarded as a solatium,[129] but it seems difficult to draw a clear line. Money can purchase education, training and baby-sitting services, but surely it can in no sense purchase a substitute for maternal care and guidance, the item allowed in *Vana v. Tosta*, any more than money awarded as a solatium could purchase substitute affection or companionship. Damages for mental distress and shock at witnessing or hearing of the death of a close relative have been allowed in several cases in a direct action for personal injuries,[130] and intangible injuries have been held to be proper subjects of compensation in other parts of the law.[131] It has been held, however, that damages are not available to a parent for the loss of the companionship of a child in the absence of an express statutory provision.[132]

6.350 The arrangement of s. 61 of the Ontario Act leaves it uncertain whether the legislature regarded an amount to compensate for loss of guidance, care and companionship as a pecuniary loss or a non-pecuniary loss. The basic provision of s. 61 restricts recovery to "pecuniary loss" which, it is then said, "may include" an amount to compensate for loss of guidance, care, and companionship. It might seem that the Legislature regarded this latter amount as a species of pecuniary loss. However, in *Thornborrow v. MacKinnon*,[133] Linden J. said:

> From now on, the damages awarded for injury to a child or for the loss of the life of a child include not only pecuniary losses, but also the non-pecuniary elements of guidance, care and companionship that parents and other relatives receive from a child . . . Thus, when a member of the family is injured or killed the Courts are now required to compensate the other

[126] *Supra*, footnote 121.

[127] *Supra*, footnote 120.

[128] *Vana v. Tosta, supra*, footnote 121, at p. 90 S.C.R., p. 109 D.L.R.

[129] See footnote 120, *supra*.

[130] *Hinz v. Berry*, [1970] 2 Q.B. 40 (C.A.); *Cox v. Fleming* (1995), 15 B.C.L.R. (3d) 201, 108 W.A.C. 220 (C.A.).

[131] See 3.1250, *supra*.

[132] See *Reeves Estate v. Croken* (1991), 84 Nfld. & P.E.I.R. 298 (P.E.I.C.A.) (not referring to earlier contrary decision in *Reeves v. Croken* (1986), 22 D.L.R. (4th) 272); *Stokes v. Levesque*, [1995] 9 W.W.R. 61, [1996] N.W.T.R. 182 (S.C.). But in *Lian v. Money*, [1996] 4 W.W.R. 263, 15 B.C.L.R. (3d) 1 (C.A.), which was distinguished in *Bianco v. Fromow* (1998), 161 D.L.R. (4th) 765 (B.C.C.A.), the British Columbia Court of Appeal upheld an award for loss of "love, guidance and companionship" of a child. See also *Ordon Estate v. Grail*, [1998] 3 S.C.R. 437, 166 D.L.R. (4th) 193.

[133] *Supra*, footnote 125.

members of the family for certain losses they may suffer as a result, both economic and non-economic.[134]

6.360 The decision of the Supreme Court of Canada in *Vana v. Tosta* indicates that "pecuniary" loss need not be a narrow category. One possible interpretation of the Ontario legislation is that s. 61(2)(e) shows that the Legislature intended a very wide meaning for the term "pecuniary loss".[135] Alternatively, s. 61(2)(e) could be read as meaning that the losses described there are deemed to be pecuniary losses, *i.e.*, are meant to be recoverable, notwithstanding that they are non-pecuniary losses.[136] The latter view was accepted by the Ontario Court of Appeal in *Mason v. Peters*.[137] Subsequent decisions under the statute have allowed recovery of losses suffered by grandchildren on the death of a grandparent[138] and parents on the death of a child.[139] It would seem that all the eligible relatives are entitled to an award on this basis for loss of companionship. Linden J. considered in *Thornborrow v. MacKinnon* that guidance and care might also be given by a child to parents or older relatives. Though not required to fix a figure, Linden J. indicated that his award (for the death of a child) would have been substantial, though somewhat less than the figures of $45,000 and $25,000 awarded in other recent cases.[140] The prospect is thus opened up of very large awards in cases where the deceased has many eligible relatives. Claims by twenty or more relatives would not be out of the question.

6.370 In interpreting the legislation, it is legitimate and indeed necessary, to take into account the general trends in the legal approach to similar questions. Linden J. evidently considered that the express intention of the legislation was to reverse the restrictions of the former law and to invite generous compensation of intangible losses. On the other hand, the insertion of the express limitation of recovery to "pecuniary" losses in s. 61(1) seems to point in the opposite direction. There would seem little point in that restriction if s. 61(2)(e) is to be so widely interpreted as to embrace almost all cases of intangible loss. The decisions of the Supreme Court of Canada in the 1978 "trilogy" may be cited in favour of moderation.[141] High awards must be paid for indirectly by large sections of the public; it is, therefore, not in the public

[134] *Thornborrow v. MacKinnon, supra,* at p. 129 D.L.R., cited with approval by Potts L.J.S.C. in *Fulcher v. Near* (1981), 131 D.L.R. (3d) 338, 35 O.R. (2d) 184 (H.C.J.), affd (unreported, March, 1983, C.A.).

[135] This seems to be the view taken by Hollingworth J. in *Mason v. Peters, supra,* footnote 125, at p. 422 D.L.R., and by Boland J. in *Fread v. Chislett, supra,* footnote 125, at p. 186 D.L.R. See also 6.75, *supra.*

[136] This was the view of Linden J. in *Thornborrow v. MacKinnon* (1981), 123 D.L.R. (3d) 124 at p. 128, 32 O.R. (2d) 740 (H.C.J.). See also *Wessell v. Kinsmen Club of Sault Ste. Marie Ontario Inc.* (1982), 137 D.L.R. (3d) 96, 37 O.R. (2d) 481 (H.C.J.).

[137] (1982), 139 D.L.R. (3d) 104, 39 O.R. (2d) 27 (C.A.), leave to appeal to S.C.C. refused 46 N.R. 538*n*.

[138] *Fulcher v. Near, supra,* footnote 134.

[139] *Thornborrow v. MacKinnon, supra,* footnote 136.

[140] *Mason v. Peters, supra,* footnote 137. *Lai v. Gill,* [1980] 1 S.C.R. 431. Presumably these awards included compensation for loss of financial support as well as for loss of intangible matters.

interest to award compensation at a level beyond that to which the reasonable person would choose to insure. However, in *Woelk v. Halvorson*,[142] the Supreme Court of Canada held that an Alberta statute, empowering the court to compensate for loss of a spouse's society, was not to be construed to require a nominal or insignificant sum. Uncertainty on such questions adds to the cost of litigation and of the insurance paid indirectly by every member of society. In each case, litigation on the actual value of the care, guidance, and companionship of the particular deceased to the particular claimant, opens up the prospect of still more costly and distasteful inquiries into the relationship of the deceased with the relatives. On balance, it is submitted that the preferable solution is for the courts to develop conventional awards at a modest level that will be reasonably predictable to defendants and their insurers. It should be remembered that the full cost of compensation is ultimately borne by a large section of the public, through liability insurance premiums or through the price of goods and services. There is no merit in rules of damage assessment that compel the members of the public to purchase life insurance for their relatives at a price that no rational person would choose to pay voluntarily. The need for consistency, that is, fairness between one claimant and another and between one defendant and another, also supports the case for developing a conventional award.[142a]

6.380 A plea for restraint was made by J. Holland J. in *Zik v. High*,[143] a non-fatal case:

> . . . s. 60 of the *Family Law Reform Act, 1978*, cries out for the exercise of judicial restraint in the general interest of the public in the assessment of damages consequent upon an injury to another as in this case. I say this because uncontrolled by such restraint the ceiling under the heading of loss of guidance, care and companionship for an award could be unlimited. Much of s. 60, as I view it, was a legislative attempt to codify the principle laid down in *St. Lawrence & Ottawa Railway Co. v. Lett* ... and enunciated once again by the Supreme Court of Canada in *Vana v. Tosta* ... that loss of care and guidance, where a mother was killed leaving children, was a measurable pecuniary loss but that the amount to be awarded under that heading should be modest, although not merely conventional.[144]

Similarly, in *Lawrence v. Good*,[145] the Manitoba Court of Appeal held that a modest sum was appropriate, reducing an award for the death of a spouse from $15,000 to $10,000.

---

[141] The comparison was made by Krever J. in *Gervais v. Richard* (1984), 12 D.L.R. (4th) 738 at p. 749, 48 O.R. (2d) 191 (H.C.J.).

[142] (1980) 2 S.C.R. 430, 114 D.L.R. (3d) 385.

[142a] See comments of Supreme Court of Canada in *Augustus v. Gosset*, [1996] 3 S.C.R. 268, 138 D.L.R. (4th) 617.

[143] (1981), 35 O.R. (2d) 226 (H.C.J.).

[144] *Supra*, at p. 237.

[145] (1985), 18 D.L.R. (4th) 734, [1985] 4 W.W.R. 652 (Man. C.A.). See also *Larney v. Friesen* (1986), 29 D.L.R. (4th) 444, [1986] 4 W.W.R. 467 (Man. C.A.); *Rose v. Belanger* (1985), 17 D.L.R. (4th) 212, [1985] 3 W.W.R. 612 (Man. C.A.).

6.385 In *Nightingale v. Mazerall*[145a] the New Brunswick Court of Appeal also stressed the need for objectivity, predictability and certainty.

6.390 However, in *Mason v. Peters,*[146] the Ontario Court of Appeal upheld awards of $45,000 to the mother, and $5,000 to the sister of an eleven-year-old boy.[147] The court held that elements of grief, sorrow and mental anguish were to be excluded,[148] but it will not be easy to separate damages for loss of companionship from damages for grief. The mother in *Mason v. Peters* was herself disabled and separated from her husband, so she was particularly dependent on her son. However, it does not seem that large awards will be limited to such circumstances. *Thornborrow v. MacKinnon* was cited with approval and the court stressed the reluctance of an appellate court to interfere with an award supported by the evidence and the court's comments on loss of companionship (as distinct from loss of care and guidance) were not linked to any reference to Mrs. Mason's particular circumstances. The court said that the deprivation:

> . . . constitutes an irreplaceable loss for which she is entitled to recovery. It is true that money cannot cure the loss, but it remains the only means available to society to recompense the wrongful destruction of the family relationship.
>
> In any given case, the amount of compensation will depend on the facts and circumstances in evidence in the case.[149]

This passage appears to suggest that an inquiry is needed, in each case, into the particular relationship of the deceased with each of his relatives and that high awards will be common. It has been suggested above that this development may lead to greater difficulties than the former denial of recovery for non-pecuniary loss.[150]

6.395 In an important 1991 decision[150a] the Ontario Court of Appeal reduced a

---

[145a] (1991), 87 D.L.R. (4th) 158, 121 N.B.R. (2d) 319 (C.A.). See also *Braun Estate v. Vaughan* (2000), 48 C.C.L.T. (2d) 142 (Man. C.A.), at p. 145. See 6.320, *supra.*

[146] *Supra,* footnote 137.

[147] See also *Howes v. Crosby* (1984), 6 D.L.R. (4th) 698, 45 O.R. (2d) 449 (C.A.).

[148] See *Nielsen v. Kaufmann* (1986), 26 D.L.R. (4th) 21, 54 O.R. (2d) 188 (C.A.); *Aerts v. Olson* (1999), 170 D.L.R. (4th) 183 (Ont. Div. Ct.).

[149] *Mason v. Peters* (1982), 139 D.L.R. (3d) 104 at p. 118, 39 O.R. (2d) 27 (C.A.), leave to appeal to S.C.C. refused 46 N.R. 538*n*. The same view was taken in *Neilsen v. Kaufmann, supra,* footnote 148 (though suggesting the eventual possibility of a conventional award (at p. 33 D.L.R.)), and *Reidy v. McLeod* (1986), 27 D.L.R. (4th) 317, 54 O.R. (2d) 661*n* (C.A.) (though saying that the assessment should be "objective and unemotional" (at p. 318 D.L.R.)). See also *Macartney v. Warner* (2000), 183 D.L.R. (4th) 374 (Ont. C.A.), at p. 380; *Robb Estate v. Canadian Red Cross Society* (2000), 1 C.C.L.T. (3d) 70 at p. 133, supplementary reasons 103 A.C.W.S. (3d) 680 (Ont. S.C.J.).

[150] See 6.370, *supra.*

[150a] *Hamilton v. Canadian National Railway Co.* (1991), 80 D.L.R. (4th) 470, 47 O.A.C. 329 (C.A.). See also *Levesque v. Lipskie* (1991), 80 D.L.R. (4th) 243, 3 O.R. (3d) 98 (C.A.), leave to appeal to S.C.C. refused 83 D.L.R. (4th) vii, 137 N.R. 156*n* (awards to elderly parents reduced from $30,000 and $20,000 to $15,000 and $10,000); *Scamolla v. Tenax Ltd.,* [1995] O.J. No. 1121 (C.A.), leave to appeal to S.C.C. refused 203 N.R. 79*n*, 93 O.A.C. 400*n* (jury award of $1,000,000 to widow reduced to $75,000); *To v. Toronto Board of Education* (2001), 204 D.L.R. (4th) 704 (Ont. C.A.).

jury award to a mother for the death of a nine-year old child from $150,000 to $50,000 and also reduced smaller awards to the deceased's brothers and sister. This decision clearly recognizes the need for a rough upper limit for high awards and for some sort of scale for ensuring consistency and fairness in smaller awards. In *Sandhu (Litigation Guardian of) v. Wellington Place Apartments*,[150b] the Ontario Court of Appeal upheld awards of $100,000 to each of the parents of a child seriously injured by the defendant's wrong. The awards were said to be "at the high end of the range for derivative awards" but not so high as to warrant interference.[150c]

2. Deductions from Claim

(1) Benefits derived from deceased's estate

6.400 The claim under the fatal accident legislation is for actual loss caused by the wrongful death and consequently, the claimant must, except in Prince Edward Island,[151] bring into account any financial benefits accruing by reason of the wrong.[152] Commonly claimants under fatal accident legislation are also beneficiaries under the will or on the intestacy of the deceased. Benefits derived from the estate, that would not have accrued except for the wrongful death, must be brought fully into account. These include damages for the death itself or for loss of expectation of life in jurisdictions where these claims survive to the estate.[153] Similarly, damages for future lost income of the deceased have been

[*The next page is* 6-23]

150b (2008), 291 D.L.R. (4th) 220 (C.A.).

150c *Supra*, at paras. 36 and 38.

151 *Fatal Accidents Act*, P.E.I., s. 7(1)(h).

152 *Davies v. Powell Duffryn Associated Collieries*, [1942] A.C. 601 (H.L.); *Maltais v. Canadian Pacific Ry.*, [1950] 2 W.W.R. 145 (Alta. S.C.); *Berg v. Northern Mountain Airlines Ltd.* (1970), 73 W.W.R. 481 (N.W.T.C.A.); *Ciniewicz v. Braiden* (1965), 52 D.L.R. (2d) 226 (Alta. S.C. App. Div.); *Lombard v. Phillips* (1964), 46 D.L.R. (2d) 347 (N.S.S.C.), vard [1965-69] 5 N.S.R. 482 (S.C. in banco); *Braun v. Roy* (1957), 22 W.W.R. 609 (Man. Q.B.), vard 12 D.L.R. (2d) 390 (C.A.); *Farish v. Papp* (1957), 23 W.W.R. 690 (Alta. S.C.); *Sarantis v. Read* (1959), 30 W.W.R. 335 (Alta. S.C.); *Constable v. Ulan* (1969), 7 D.L.R. (3d) 377 (Alta. S.C. App. Div.); *Dearing v. Hebert* (1957), 9 D.L.R. (2d) 697 (Alta. S.C. App. Div.); *Shybunka v. Kapolka* (1951), 4 W.W.R. (N.S.) 673 (Alta. S.C.); *Shaw v. Roemer* (1982), 134 D.L.R. (3d) 590 (N.S.S.C. App. Div.), leave to appeal to S.C.C. refused December 6, 1982; *Lefebvre v. Dowdall* (1964), 46 D.L.R. (2d) 426, [1965] 1 O.R. 1 (H.C.J.) (benefits from *Dependants' Relief Act*); *Dellaert v. Canadian Northern Ry. Co.*, [1939] 3 D.L.R. 50 (Man. C.A.); *Foster v. Kerr*, [1940] 2 D.L.R. 47 (Alta. S.C. App. Div.); *Joyce v. Bartlett*, [1955] 1 D.L.R. 615 (Man. Q.B.); *Dowhy v. Lamontagne*, [1945] 2 D.L.R. 515 (Man. K.B.); *Ponyicky v. Sawayama*, [1943] S.C.R. 197, [1943] 2 D.L.R. 545. *Contra*, *Yawney v. Rural Municipality of Clayton* (1955), 1 D.L.R. (2d) 65 (Sask. C.A.). No deduction was made in *Rawlinson v. Babcock & Wilcox Ltd.*, [1966] 3 All E.R. 882 (Assizes), where the claimant had inherited property only indirectly from the deceased, through the estate of another person.

153 *Bishop v. Cunard White Star, Ltd.*, [1950] P. 240 (H.C.J.); *Foster v. Kerr, supra*, footnote 152; *Ponyicky v. Sawayama, supra*, footnote 142; *Gallant v. Boklaschuk* (1978), 90 D.L.R. (3d) 370 (Man. Q.B.); *Hossack v. Hertz Drive Yourself Stations of Ontario Ltd.*, [1966] S.C.R. 28, 54 D.L.R. (2d) 148.

held to be deductible from a fatal accident claim.[154] Damages for losses incurred by the deceased before death would not appear to be deductible; since the fatal accident legislation affords compensation only in respect of the period after death, there is no overlap.[155] In respect of property owned by the deceased, where the claimants would have expected to receive the property on the natural death of the deceased, the only benefit ordinarily[156] accuring to the fatal accident claimants because of the wrong is the acceleration of receipt caused by the premature death.[157] This is the approach generally taken to assets of the deceased; the claimant could generally have expected to receive the assets eventually, even if the deceased had lived out a normal life span. It is the benefit of the acceleration, not the full capital value, that is to be deducted. Furthermore, in many cases, the benefit of the acceleration will be offset by the anticipated savings of the deceased.[158] Another aspect of the benefits received by the claimant is the certainty of receipt and the removal of contingencies that might have prevented inheritance in the absence of wrongful death. The greater the contingencies, the greater the benefit of accelerated and certain receipt in the claimant's hands.[159]

6.410 Assets in household use, such as house, car, and furniture, are treated differently, no deduction being made against a claimant who already enjoyed the use of the assets before the deceased's death. The reasoning is that the change of ownership is no real benefit to the claimant who had all the practical benefits of ownership before the deceased's death.[160]

---

154 *Pickett v. British Rail Engineering Ltd.*, [1980] A.C. 136 (H.L.); *Kandalla v. British European Airways Corp.*, [1981] Q.B. 158; *Gammell v. Wilson*, [1982] A.C. 27 (H.L.).

155 However, in *McLeod v. O'Keefe* (1963), 38 D.L.R. (2d) 45 (N.B.S.C. App. Div.), damages for pain and suffering recovered by the estate were deducted.

156 An exception would be where payments on account are made by the defendant to the deceased during his lifetime. In *Trawford v. B.C. Electric Ry. Co. (No. 2)* (1913), 9 D.L.R. 817 (B.C.C.A.), affd 49 S.C.R. 470, 18 D.L.R. 430, a payment made under an ineffective settlement was assumed to be properly taken into account.

157 *May v. Municipality of Metropolitan Toronto* (1968), 2 D.L.R. (3d) 659, [1969] 1 O.R. 419 (H.C.J.); *Clement v. Leslies Storage Ltd.* (1979), 97 D.L.R. (3d) 667 (Man. C.A.); *Carrington v. James* (1961), 34 W.W.R. 356 (Sask. Q.B.); *Hawryluk v. Hodgins* (1972), 29 D.L.R. (3d) 403, [1972] 3 O.R. 741 (C.A.); *Goodwin v. Michigan Central Ry. Co.* (1913), 14 D.L.R. 411, 29 O.L.R. 422 (S.C. App. Div.). In *Sakaluk v. Lepage*, [1981] 2 W.W.R. 597 (Sask. C.A.), the benefit of the accelerated receipt reduced the claim to nil.

158 See 6.130, *supra*; *Julian v. Northern & Central Gas Corp.* (1978), 5 C.C.L.T. 148 (Ont. H.C.J.), affd 118 D.L.R. (3d) 458, 31 O.R. (2d) 388 (C.A.), leave to appeal to S.C.C. refused D.L.R. *loc. cit.*, O.R. *loc. cit.*; *Keizer v. Hanna*, [1978] 2 S.C.R. 342, 82 D.L.R. (3d) 449; *Kassam v. Kampala Aerated Water Co. Ltd.*, [1965] 2 All E.R. 875 (P.C.); *Daniels v. Jones*, [1961] 1 W.L.R. 1103 (C.A.), at p. 1114, *per* Willmer L.J.; *Clement v. Leslies Storage Ltd.*, *supra*, footnote 157; *Goodwin v. Michigan Central Ry. Co.*, *supra*, footnote 157; *Miller v. Riches* (1984), 5 D.L.R. (4th) 1, 50 A.R. 92 (C.A.).

159 See *Daniels v. Jones*, *supra*, footnote 158.

160 *Heatley v. Steel Co. of Wales*, [1953] 1 W.L.R. 405 (C.A.); *Roberts v. Semchyshyn*

6.420 Where the fatal accidents claim precedes the claim by the estate, it has been held that the court must estimate the value of benefits likely to be received by the claimant from the estate.[161]

6.430 Funeral expenses are recoverable in some jurisdictions, both by the estate[162] and under fatal accident legislation.[163] It has been held that there is to be no duplication of damages,[164] but, as was shown in *Mulholland v. McCrea*,[165] it may make a difference under which Act the claim is made. There the claimant under the fatal accident legislation had been partly responsible for his wife's death. It was held by the Northern Ireland Court of Appeal that his claim under the fatal accident legislation was to be reduced for contributory negligence, but that the estate's claim could be asserted in full. In such a case, in jurisdictions that have abolished inter-spousal tort immunity, the claimant might presumably be called upon by the defendant to contribute to liability to the estate.

6.440 Sums payable under a contract of insurance are specifically stated by statute not to be taken into account,[166] and the statutory prohibition has been held to apply whether the claimant receives insurance money directly from the insurer or indirectly from the deceased's estate.[167] Accordingly, any portion of the estate consisting of insurance money paid or payable on the deceased's death is not to be taken into account to reduce the claim under the fatal accident legislation. In jurisdictions where estate duties are payable, it has been held that the proper procedure is notionally to divide the estate into two parts, insurance money and other assets, and to charge the estate duties only against the other assets, reducing the fatal accident claim only on the basis of the reduced other assets.[168] The basis for this conclusion is that, if duties were charged against the whole estate, the insurance money would indirectly

---

(1956), 6 D.L.R. (2d) 266 (Man. C.A.); *Daniels v. Jones*, *supra*, footnote 158, at p. 1114, *per* Willmer L.J.; *Hawryluk v. Hodgins*, *supra*, footnote 157; *Kwong v. The Queen in right of Alberta* (1978), 96 D.L.R. (3d) 214 (Alta. S.C. App. Div.), affd [1979] 2 S.C.R. 1010*n*, 105 D.L.R. (3d) 576*n*; *Spurr v. Naugler* (1974), 50 D.L.R. (3d) 105 (N.S.S.C.T.D.); *Comeau v. Marsman* (1981), 47 N.S.R. (2d) 550 (S.C.T.D.); *Bentley's Estate v. Macdonald* (1977), 27 N.S.R. (2d) 152 (S.C.T.D.); *Sexton v. Beak* (1972), 27 D.L.R. (3d) 181 (B.C.S.C.). But see *Keddy v. Minshull* (1969), 5 D.L.R. (3d) 156 (N.S.S.C.), where a deduction was made. In *Meeks v. White* (1973), 39 D.L.R. (3d) 126 (N.S.S.C. App. Div.), where the claimants were a daughter and a mother, the latter having a short life expectancy, a deduction was made.

161 *Davies v. Powell Duffryn Associated Collieries, Ltd.*, [1942] A.C. 601 (H.L.).

162 See footnote 93, *supra*.

163 See footnote 87, *supra*.

164 *Clement v. Leslies Storage Ltd.*, *supra*, footnote 157. Express provision against duplication is made in *Fatal Accidents Act*, P.E.I., ss. 6(3), 7(1)(g).

165 [1961] N.I. 135.

166 See 6.450, *infra*.

167 Or from a third person: *Malyon v. Plummer*, [1964] 1 Q.B. 330 (C.A.).

168 *Baker v. Hopkins*, [1958] 1 W.L.R. 993 (Q.B.).

go to reduce the fatal accident claim, contrary to the statutory provision. Similar reasoning has been applied to the case of creditors' claims.[169] The reasoning has been applied also to the portion of estate duties payable on the insurance moneys themselves, so that the non-insurance portion of the estate is used, in effect, to pay the estate duty on the insurance moneys.[170] It might be thought that this interpretation treats the claimant in an unduly favourable manner. The meaning of the statutory provision on insurance moneys is plainly that insurance money received by the claimant should not go to reduce the claim, but if the insurance money attracts an estate tax, the net proceeds in the claimant's hands might well be thought of as the reduced sum after tax has been paid, and the intent of the statute might seem, therefore, to be that only the reduced sum should be excluded from being brought into account in reduction of the claim. However, the statutory provision refers to sums "paid or payable under a contract of insurance" not to sums received, and it is certainly the gross sum before tax that is "paid or payable" by the insurer.

(2) Insurance benefits

6.450 The fatal accidents legislation in each jurisdiction contains a provision excluding sums payable under insurance contracts from being brought into account.[171] Early cases had interpreted the original Act to require insurance benefits to be brought into account[172] and this was widely thought to be unjust for the effect was to enable the tortfeasor to benefit by the providence of the deceased. Accordingly, the statute was amended in England in 1908 to provide that:

> 1. In assessing damages . . . there shall not be taken into account any sum paid or payable on the death of the deceased under any contract of assurance or insurance.[173]

Some of the Canadian statutes continue to refer to contracts of assurance as well as of insurance[174] but there seems to be no difference in meaning

169 *Ciniewicz v. Braiden* (1965), 52 D.L.R. (2d) 226 (Alta. S.C. App. Div.). See Kemp and Kemp, *The Quantum of Damages in Personal Injury and Fatal Accident Claims*, 4th ed. (London, Sweet & Maxwell, 1975), p. 227.

170 *Baker v. Hopkins, supra*, footnote 168. *Newman v. Clements*, [1966] W.A.R. 84 (S.C.). See Luntz, *Assessment of Damages for Personal Injury and Death*, 3rd ed. (Chatsworth, N.S.W., Butterworth Pty. Ltd., 1990), §9.5.4.

171 *Fatal Accidents Act* (Alta.), s. 6; Man., s. 6(a); N.B., s. 7(a); Nfld., s. 6(a); N.W.T., s. 4(2); P.E.I., s. 7(1)(b); Sask., s. 4(3); Yukon, s. 7(a); *Fatal Injuries Act* (N.S.), s. 5(3); *Family Compensation Act* (B.C.), s. 3(8); *Family Law Act* (Ont.), s. 63.

172 *Hicks v. Newport, Abergavenny & Hereford Ry. Co.* (1857), 4 B. & S. 403*n*, 122 E.R. 510; *Grand Trunk Ry. Co. of Canada v. Jennings* (1888), 13 App. Cas. 800 (P.C.). This position continues under the *Carriage by Air Act*. See *Frederick v. Ottawa Aero Services Ltd.* (1963), 42 D.L.R. (2d) 122, [1964] 1 O.R. 315 (H.C.J.), affd 44 D.L.R. (2d) 628*n*, [1964] 2 O.R. 248*n* (C.A.), affd [1965] S.C.R. vi, 48 D.L.R. (2d) 702*n*.

173 *Fatal Accidents (Damages) Act, 1908* (U.K.), s. 1.

174 *Fatal Accidents Act* (Man.), s. 6(a); N.B., s. 7(a); N.W.T., s. 4(2); P.E.I., s. 7(1)(b); Sask., s. 4(3); Yukon, s. 8(1)(a); *Family Compensation Act* (B.C.), s. 3(7). These provisions are not affected by *Ratych v. Bloomer*, [1990] 1 S.C.R. 940, 69 D.L.R. (4th) 25: see *Knowles Estate v. Walton Estate* (1992), 93 D.L.R. (4th) 734, 69 B.C.L.R. (2d) 139 (C.A.).

between the two words.[175] Several statutes refer simply to contracts of insurance.[176]

6.460 The statutory provisions are silent on the identity of the insured and the beneficiary.[177] Money paid to the deceased's employer by an insurer and then paid over to the claimant was held in an Australian case to be money paid under a contract of insurance, even though the claimant's right to receive the money arose under the deceased's contract of employment.[178] In *Green v. Russell*[179] the English Court of Appeal reached the same conclusion where the claimant, being a third party beneficiary, had no legal right to the money at all. However, in *Montreal Trust Co. v. A.-G. N.S.*,[180] money paid to the deceased's estate under a share purchase agreement funded by life insurance was held not to fall within the statutory words, and accordingly the claim was reduced by the amount received from the deceased's estate.

6.470 In some jurisdictions legislation has been enacted to exclude from being taken into account a variety of other benefits such as pensions, superannuations, state and private welfare benefits.[181] In other jurisdictions, it appears that the same result is reached without the assistance of specific legislation. In *Canadian Pacific Ltd. v. Gill*,[182] the Supreme Court of Canada held that benefits under the Canada Pension Plan were sums paid under a contract of insurance within the meaning of the statute. Since the payment of benefits depended upon contingencies, the court held that the Plan was an exact substitute for a privately arranged insurance policy. As for the requirement that benefits be paid under a contract of insurance, the court said:

---

175 See Luntz, *op. cit., supra*, footnote 170, §9.5.2.

176 *Family Law Act* (Ont.), s. 63; *Fatal Accidents Act* (Alta.), s. 6; *Fatal Injuries Act* (N.S.), s. 5(3) (though with reference to premiums payable under "any contract of assurance or insurance".

177 See *Green v. Russell*, [1959] 2 Q.B. 226 (C.A.), *per* Romer L.J.

178 *McPhee v. Carlsen*, [1946] V.L.R. 316.

179 *Supra*, footnote 157.

180 (1959), 21 D.L.R. (2d) 287 (N.S.S.C.).

181 See *McGregor on Damages*, 16th ed. (London, Sweet & Maxwell, 1997), §1818; Luntz, *op. cit.*, footnote 170, §§9.5.9-9.5.13. The *Fatal Accidents Act* (Man.), s. 6(c); N.B., s. 7(c); *Fatal Accidents Act*, N.S., s. 5(3); *Fatal Accidents Act 1976* (U.K.), s. 4(2) (see *Pidduck v. Eastern Scottish Omnibuses Ltd.*, [1990] 1 W.L.R. 993 (C.A.), and *Auty v. National Coal Board*, [1985] 1 W.L.R. (C.A.)) contain varying exclusions.

182 [1973] S.C.R. 654, 37 D.L.R. (3d) 229, followed, in respect of a non-contributory pension, in *Bates v. Illerburn* (1976), 70 D.L.R. (3d) 154, 12 O.R. (2d) 721 (C.A.); *Miller v. Riches* (1984), 5 D.L.R. (4th) 1, 50 A.R. 92 (C.A.) (survivor's allowance under private pension plan); *Crew v. Nicholson* (1989), 58 D.L.R. (4th) 111, 68 O.R. (2d) 232 (C.A.) (survivor's benefits payable under statute); *Muldrew v. Harris* (1988), 52 D.L.R. (4th) 455, 29 B.C.L.R. (2d) 67 (C.A.). The older case of *Western Trust Co. v. British American Oil Co. Ltd.* (1951), 2 W.W.R. (N.S.) 529 (Sask. K.B.), would seem to be inconsistent.

> There are, of course, many forms of insurance and surely one of them may be considered to be the social insurance now exemplified by the Canada Pension Plan. In so far as the word "contract" is concerned, there is, in result, a contract between the contributor to the Canada Pension Plan and the Government which, by virtue of the statute, exacts from such contributor weekly deductions from his wages.[183]

It would seem from this reasoning that any benefit payable on the death of the deceased whether by the state, the deceased's employer, or by a union or private benefit society, provided that the benefit has been directly or indirectly paid for in some way, can be said to be under a contract of insurance.[184] The existence of legislation, excluding such benefits in several jurisdictions, strongly suggests that exclusion of them is generally considered to be a socially desirable result.

6.480 Benefits paid under no-fault automobile insurance schemes generally are expressly made to constitute a release of any claim under the fatal accident legislation, and it was held in *Gorrie v. Gill*,[185] approved by the Supreme Court of Canada in *Keizer v. Hanna*,[186] that the *Insurance Act* provision took effect after the initial assessment of damages to create a subsequent credit in favour of the defendant. The effect was, therefore, that the no-fault benefits were deducted from the fatal accident claim. Legislation in several Canadian jurisdictions makes specific reference to future premiums that would have been paid under an insurance contract had the deceased survived. The Manitoba Act, for example, provides:

> 6. In assessing damages in an action brought under this Act there shall not be taken into account,
>
> . . . . .
>
> (b) any premium that would have been payable in future under any contract of insurance or assurance if the deceased had survived.[187]

The meaning of this reference to future premiums is not self-evident. If, as is the usual case, premiums are paid by the deceased from income, one interpretation, adopted in *Kernested v. Desorcy*,[188] would be that

183 *Canadian Pacific v. Gill, supra*, footnote 182, at p. 670 S.C.R., pp. 239-40 D.L.R.

184 See *Plachta v. Richardson* (1974), 49 D.L.R. (3d) 23, 4 O.R. (2d) 654 (H.C.J.), where *Hawryluk v. Hodgins* (1972), 29 D.L.R. (3d) 403, [1972] 3 O.R. 741 (C.A.), was held to have been impliedly overruled by *C.P. v. Gill, supra*, footnote 182. The same would seem to be true of *Pollington v. Air-Dale Ltd.* (1968), 67 D.L.R. (2d) 565, [1968] 1 O.R. 747 (H.C.J.) (U.S. Social Security benefits).

185 (1975), 59 D.L.R. (3d) 481, 9 O.R. (2d) 73 (C.A.); *Fong v. Bamford* (1995), 25 O.R. (3d) 147, 15 M.V.R. (3d) 254 (Gen. Div.). See also *Tucker v. Lindstrom*, [1972] 6 W.W.R. 757 (B.C.S.C.); *Plachta v. Richardson, supra*, footnote 184; see *Campbell Estate v. Varanese* (1991), 102 N.S.R. (2d) 104 (S.C. App. Div.). *Schiedel v. Rick* (1972), 25 D.L.R. (3d) 30, [1972] 2 O.R. 114 (C.A.), is now superseded.

186 [1978] 2 S.C.R. 342, 82 D.L.R. (3d) 449.

187 *Fatal Accidents Act* (Man.), s. 6(b). See also *Fatal Accidents Act* (N.B.), s. 7(b); Nfld. & Lab., s. 7(b); *Fatal Injuries Act* (N.S.), s. 5(3).

188 [1978] 3 W.W.R. 623 (Man. Q.B.), affd [1979] 1 W.W.R. 512 (C.A.), leave to appeal to S.C.C. refused January 23, 1979.

future premiums that would have been paid by the deceased are not to be included in the initial assessment of loss as benefits that the claimant has lost. The opposite interpretation, however, would also be possible, on the assumption that the deceased's expenditure on premiums is initially counted as a benefit to the claimant, and the meaning of the statute is that the *saving* of the premiums (which now are not payable) is not to be taken into account to reduce the claimant's damages.

6.490 In provinces where there is no express provision, the question must be decided on principle, rather than as a matter of statutory interpretation. The underlying principle of the exclusion of insurance benefits appears to be that the tortfeasor should not profit by the claimant's or the deceased's providence in having purchased insurance. Life insurance policies are generally taken out for the benefit of dependants, and therefore it seems fair to assume that, where premiums were to be paid by the deceased, they were to be paid out of money that otherwise would have been available to the claimant in the form of current benefits. Accordingly, it is suggested that the deceased's estimated future expenditure on life insurance premiums should be included in the claimant's initial assessment of loss, with no deduction for the saving by the fact that the premiums turn out not to be payable.[189] The defendant is thus in the same position as would have been occupied if the deceased had not taken out a policy of life insurance at all but had spent the premium money on the claimant periodically. Accident and disability insurance premiums and pension contributions[190] can be regarded, however, as a cost of securing a steady or extended stream of income. These, it is suggested, should not be treated as current benefits to the claimant but should be taken into account in the claimant's favour to reduce the impact of the contingencies that might have possibly interrupted the deceased's stream of earnings.[191]

6.500 Where life insurance premiums would have been paid by the claimant, the same result seems to be indicated as where the deceased would have paid them, that is, no deduction should be made for the claimant's savings. If a deduction were made, the tortfeasor would benefit by the claimant's having taken out the insurance, and this result appears to be contrary to the intention of the statutes.[192]

---

189 As was done, as a matter of statutory interpretation in *Fuller v. Atlantic Trust Co.* (1967), 62 D.L.R. (2d) 109 (N.S.S.C.) in respect of life insurance premiums.

190 See *Fuller v. Atlantic Trust Co.*, *supra*, footnote 189.

191 See 6.660, 6.6670, *infra*.

192 In *Grand Trunk Ry. Co. of Canada v. Jennings* (1888), 13 App. Cas. 800 at p. 805, the Privy Council, in holding that a deduction should be made for the benefit of the accelerated receipt of proceeds of a life insurance policy, approved as a method of calculating this benefit the deduction of the amount of future premiums payable by the deceased. Deduction of premiums for the full life expectancy of a young person would, in effect, amount to deducting the value of the life insurance policy and so seems contrary to the intention of the statutes that now provide that insurance proceeds shall not be taken into account. See also *Baker v. Dalgleish Steam Shipping Co.*, [1922] 1 K.B. 361 (C.A.), at pp. 371-2; *Tower v. Murphy*, [1954] 2 D.L.R. 447 (N.S.S.C.).

(3) Gifts

6.510 A number of early cases held that gifts should be taken into account if directly consequent on the death.[193] However, as was said in the context of a personal injury claim, it is obviously contrary to the intention of donors that gifts given to relieve need should inure to the benefit of the tortfeasor who has caused the need,[194] and in *Vana v. Tosta* Spence J. said that it was "trite law that a wrongdoer cannot claim the benefit of services donated to the injured party".[195] It may be concluded, then, that gifts of money or services will not be taken into account to reduce damages.[196] A possible exception arises where the tortfeasor is the donor, and it may be supposed that the gift was made with the intention of reducing the tortfeasor's obligations.[197] Such cases are comparatively rare in Canada in the absence of employers' liability for injuries to workers. As in the case of collateral benefits in personal injury claims, the refusal to allow the wrongdoer to take advantage of gifts to the claimant does not settle the question of whether, as between donor and donee, the gift may be returnable.[198]

(4) Formation of new relationships

6.520 Where a claim is made by a dependant for pecuniary loss caused by a death, the question commonly arises of what consideration is to be given to the possibility of the claimant's entering into a new relationship of dependence or the actual formation of such a relationship where this occurs before trial. The typical case has been remarriage of a widow but the theoretical scope of the question is wider. The problem can arise in relation to other claimants, for example, the widower, or children who may acquire a step-parent or adoptive parent. The question is whether benefits received by the claimant, or likely to be received, from sources other than the defendant, are to be taken into account as reducing the loss for which the defendant is responsible, or whether the claimant can

---

193 *Baker v. Dalgleish Steam Shipping Co., supra*, footnote 192; *Jenner v. Allen West & Co. Ltd.*, [1959] 1 W.L.R. 554 (C.A.); *Dalton v. Higgins* (1964), 43 D.L.R. (2d) 574 (P.E.I.S.C.). However, in *Peacock v. Amusement Equipment Co.*, [1954] 2 Q.B. 347 (C.A.), gifts made by relatives were not deducted.

194 *Redpath v. Belfast & County Down Ry.*, [1947] N.I. 167 at p. 170, *per* Andrews L.C.J.

195 [1968] S.C.R. 71 at p. 75, 66 D.L.R. (2d) 97 at p. 113. See also *Hay v. Hughes*, [1975] Q.B. 790 (C.A.) (free care from grandmother).

196 *Workmen's Compensation Bd. v. Rutherford*, [1926] 4 D.L.R. 635, 30 O.W.N. 384 (H.C.). See also *Grant v. Jackson* (1985), 24 D.L.R. (4th) 598, [1986] 2 W.W.R. 413 (B.C.C.A.); *Sheppard v. McAllister* (1987), 40 D.L.R. (4th) 233, 60 O.R. (2d) 309 (C.A.); *Harris Estate v. Roy's Midway Transport Ltd.* (1989), 60 D.L.R. (4th) 99, 97 N.B.R. (2d) 251 (C.A.); *McNichol v. Mardell*, [1984] 5 W.W.R. 177, 55 A.R. 161 (C.A.), leave to appeal to S.C.C. refused 56 N.R. 239*n*, 58 A.R. 38*n*. Gratuities and gratuitous services are specifically excluded by the *Fatal Accidents Act* (P.E.I.), s. 7(1)(e) and (f).

197 *Jenner v. Allen West & Co. Ltd., supra*, footnote 193; *Hayden v. Hayden*, [1993] 1 W.L.R. 986 (C.A.). See 15.870, *infra*.

198 See 3.1550-3.1560, *supra*.

treat these benefits as collateral advantages to be justifiably retained in addition to the compensation payable by the defendant. In essence the question is one of mitigation, though it is to be noted that no one has ever suggested that the claimant in a fatal accident action has any "duty" to look for an alternative source of benefits. It would, of course, be absurd to suggest that a desire to reduce the damages payable by the defendant should play any part in the decision of a claimant spouse to remarry. This consideration, however, does not in itself show that the actual formation of a new relationship, or the reasonable chance of its actual formation in the future, should not be taken into account.

6.540 The courts in England[199] and Canada[200] have held that the actual remarriage of a spouse before trial is to be taken into account and that the prospects of the claimant's future remarriage are also to be taken into account.[201] From time to time trial judges have objected to the task of assessing the remarriage prospects of individual claimants, and it has been sometimes suggested that the assessment is insulting to the claimant and distasteful to the judge. Phillimore J. gave support to this view in *Buckley v. John Allen & Ford (Oxford) Ltd.*,[202] where he said:

> Is a judge fitted to assess the chance or chances or wishes of a lady about whom he knows so little and whom he has only encountered for 20 minutes when she was in the witness-box, especially when no one has broached the topic with her? Judges should, I think, act on evidence rather than guesswork. It seems to me that this particular exercise is not only unattractive but is not one for which judges are equipped. Am I to label the lady to her face as attractive or unattractive? If I have the temerity to apply the label, am I likely to be right? . . . The fact is that this exercise is a mistake. If there are statistics as to the likelihood of a widow remarrying based on her age and the amount of her compensation, just as there are statistics on the expectancy of life, they might provide a yardstick for deduction in the absence of evidence of some special factor in the

---

199 *Goodburn v. Thomas Cotton Ltd.*, [1968] 1 Q.B. 845 (C.A.). Now reversed by statute. See 6.570, *infra*.

200 *Keizer v. Hanna*, [1978] 2 S.C.R. 342, 82 D.L.R. (3d) 449; *Franco v. Woolfe* (1976), 69 D.L.R. (3d) 501, 12 O.R. (2d) 549 (C.A.); *Lefebvre v. Dowdall* (1964), 46 D.L.R. (2d) 426, [1965] 1 O.R. 1 (H.C.J.); *Wallis v. Lichty*, [1952] O.W.N. 116 (H.C.J.); *Mercer v. Sijan* (1976), 72 D.L.R. (3d) 464, 14 O.R. (2d) 12 (C.A.); *Maitland v. Drozda*, [1983] 3 W.W.R. 193, 22 Sask. R. 1 (C.A.); *Ball v. Kraft* (1966), 60 D.L.R. (2d) 35 (B.C.S.C.) (onus of proof on defendant); *May v. Municipality of Metropolitan Toronto* (1968), 62 D.L.R. (3d) 659, [1969] 1 O.R. 419 (H.C.J.); *Jeselon v. Waters*, [1981] 3 W.W.R. 715 (B.C.S.C.) (only small weight given); *Chapman v. Verstraete*, [1977] 4 W.W.R. 214 (B.C.S.C.) (remarriage prospects of widower); *Twerdochlib v. Hanns*, [1935] 2 D.L.R. 363 (Alta. S.C. App. Div.); *Taguchi v. Stuparyk* (1994), 16 Alta. L.R. (3d) 72, 148 A.R. 359 (Q.B.), affd on this point 29 Alta. L.R. (3d) 175 (C.A.), leave to appeal to S.C.C. refused 181 A.R. 79*n*, 116 W.A.C. 79*n*; *MacNeil Estate v. Gillis* (1995), 138 N.S.R. (2d) 1, 10 M.V.R. (3d) 8 (C.A.); *Parsons Estate v. Guymer* (1998), 162 D.L.R. (4th) 390 (Ont. C.A.), leave to appeal to S.C.C. refused 178 D.L.R. (4th) vii. Consideration of remarriage of either spouse is excluded in the *Fatal Accidents Act* (P.E.I.), s. 7(1)(a).

201 The American position is different. See Kober, Note (1980), 15 N.E.L.R. 227.

202 [1967] 2 Q.B. 637.

individual case. In the absence of some such yardstick I question whether having decided what she has lost by the death of her husband, any judge is qualified to assess whether or when she is likely to remarry. Supposing she marries a man who is only concerned to spend her money? Is he to be treated as her new support in place of her former husband? I venture to suggest it is time judges were relieved of the need to enter into this particular guessing game. In this case I make no deduction for this lady's chances of remarrying.[203]

This passage was quoted in *Keizer v. Hanna*,[204] by Dunlap Co. Ct. J. who added unnecessarily: "On the question of the widow's prospects of remarriage my discerning eye provokes me to rate same highly . . .".[205] Following the dicta of Phillimore J. he refused to make any deduction in respect of the prospects of remarriage.

6.550 Higher courts, however, have not endorsed these views. In *Goodburn v. Thomas Cotton Ltd.*,[206] the English Court of Appeal rejected Phillimore J.'s views saying that, distasteful, difficult, and invidious though the task might be, a judge was obliged to assess the actual prospects of a claimant's remarriage. The same court, incidentally, held that detailed cross-examination as to the claimant's relationship with a named man was perfectly proper and indeed part of the duty of defence counsel. Willmer L.J., indeed, suggested that, in effect, the claimant had deliberately misled the court on examination-in-chief and remarked that "the truth was gradually dragged out of the plaintiff".[207] This kind of procedure will strike many persons as distasteful, and it ought surely to be disallowed unless essential to the administration of justice. It will be suggested later that the evidential value of such an inquiry is minimal.[207a]

6.560 In Canada these considerations are equally applicable, but judicial analysis has been less common. Dunlap Co. Ct. J.'s comment, mentioned previously, in *Keizer v. Hanna*, was impliedly disapproved by the Ontario Court of Appeal who reduced the damages to take account, *inter alia*, of prospects of the claimant's remarriage.[208] The Supreme Court of Canada restored the trial judge's assessment, excluding any allowance for the prospect of remarriage. Spence J. gave his support to Dunlap Co. Ct. J.'s view.[209] But Dickson J. for the majority supported the restoration of the trial judgment on the ground that there was no evidence on which to find that Dunlap Co. Ct. J. had not given due consideration to the claimant's remarriage prospects.[210] The position seems to be then in

203 *Supra*, at p. 645.
204 (1975), 55 D.L.R. (3d) 171, 7 O.R. (2d) 327 (Co. Ct.).
205 *Supra*, at p. 178 D.L.R., p. 334 O.R.
206 *Supra*, footnote 199.
207 *Goodburn v. Thomas Cotton*, *supra*, footnote 199, at p. 851.
207a See 6.630, *infra*.
208 *Keizer v. Hanna* (1975), 64 D.L.R. (3d) 193, 10 O.R. (2d) 597 (C.A.).
209 *Keizer v. Hanna*, [1978] 2 S.C.R. 342 at pp. 359-60, 82 D.L.R. (3d) 449 at p. 454.
210 *Supra*, at p. 349 S.C.R., p. 460 D.L.R. In *Lamb v. Brandt* (1984), 56 B.C.L.R. 74, 30 C.C.L.T. 280 (C.A.), it was held that a trial judge was not in error in failing to make a deduction.

Canada that the trial judge must give due consideration to the prospect of the claimant's remarriage but that if, having duly considered it, the judge chooses to value it at a minimal sum, an appellate court will be very reluctant to interfere.[210a]

6.570 In England, as a result of the cases referred to earlier, legislation was enacted in 1971 precluding the court from taking account of the prospects of remarriage or of the actual remarriage of a widow.[211] In Prince Edward Island marriage of any claimant is excluded.[212] This legislation leads to anomalous results in a scheme where recovery depends on proof of the claimant's own loss.[213] A young claimant, for example, whose spouse is wrongfully killed and who actually remarries a wealthier person before trial, will recover damages in respect of the late spouse's lifetime earnings and, in addition, will enjoy the support of the second spouse. An older claimant, whose need is much greater and whose prospects of remarriage are low, will recover far less. Furthermore, the U.K. statute discriminates on the basis of sex in that it applies only to widows and not to widowers. A further difficulty is that the U.K. statute does not deal with claims by dependent children so that considerations of remarriage remain relevant where a claim is made by a person with dependent children.[214] Another difficulty is that with the extension of rights of support to *de facto* spousal relationships, actual or probable formation of such relationships become relevant, and the statutes do not preclude inquiry into *de facto* relationships.[215]

6.580 The Law Commission, in its 1973 report on assessment of damages in personal injury cases, recognized these anomalies but, while admitting that the Act led to "gross over-compensation", felt itself unable to recommend repeal.[216] Evidently the Commission considered that the question was a clear one, that the merits had been fully debated in Parliament, and that it was not for the Commission to recommend repeal of a statute on a sensitive issue very recently enacted after full debate. In the event, the Law Commission actually was driven, for the sake of

210a On the other hand, appellate courts have quite frequently varied awards on the ground that too much weight has been given to prospects of remarriage: see, *e.g.*, *Parsons Estate v. Guymer* (1998), 162 D.L.R. (4th) 390 (Ont. C.A.), leave to appeal to S.C.C. refused 178 D.L.R. (4th) vii; *Brown v. Finch*, [1998] 4 W.W.R. 679, 42 B.C.L.R. (3d) 116 (C.A.).

211 *Law Reform (Miscellaneous Provisions) Act 1971* (U.K.), s. 4(1) (repealed 1976, c. 30, s. 6(2)); *Fatal Accidents Act 1976* (U.K.), s. 3(3).

212 *Supra*, footnote 196.

213 But it is suggested below that recovery by the deceased person's estate of his lost earning capacity is justifiable, and recovery on this basis will not be affected by remarriage.

214 But the P.E.I. statute excludes the effect of the probability of a claimant's marriage on any other claimant. *Supra*, footnote 196.

215 But see *Bennett v. Liddy* (1979), 25 A.L.R. 340 (S.C.N.T.), where it was held under a statute permitting *de facto* spouses to claim that formation of future *de facto* relationships fell within the meaning of "remarriage".

216 Law Commission, *Report on Personal Injury Litigation — Assessment of Damages*, No. 56 (London, H.M.S.O., 1973), §261.

consistency, to recommend the extension of what it conceded to be an unsound provision to apply to widowers and to the claims of children.[217]

The Pearson Commission, reporting in 1978, was also critical of the 1971 Act, saying that ignoring an actual remarriage led to "the manifest absurdity of awarding damages for a loss which is known to have ceased."[218] The question of the prospect of future remarriage took on a new aspect in the light of the Pearson Commission's recommendation to introduce periodic payments. The possibility of periodic payments, however, hardly makes the problem easier since the prospect of cessation of periodic payments on remarriage would act as an obvious and, it may be expected in these times, often effective disincentive to remarriage. Further, it would encourage a claimant to apply in the first place for a lump sum or to apply for a commutation of periodic payments before remarrying, both options being contemplated by the Commission as part of the proposed regime of periodic payments. The Pearson Commission was "almost equally divided" on what should be done, some commissioners favouring cessation of payments on remarriage (with a lump sum payment as a consolation), some favouring continuation of periodic payments even at the cost of over-compensation, and two commissioners favouring a formal test of the prospects of remarriage based only on the age of the claimant and not on individual prospects.[219] The commissioners agreed, however, on the desirability of removing the discriminatory aspects of the Act and extending the rules, whatever they were to be, to widowers. **6.590**

What guidance then can these considerations offer to Canadian courts? It is suggested that it is possible to develop a principle that will do justice to all parties without involving the embarrassing or distasteful kind of inquiry mentioned above into the claimant's private affairs. The starting point is to ask why remarriage should be relevant. In some jurisdictions the class of persons entitled to claim for loss caused by a fatal accident is enlarged to include what is sometimes called a *de facto* or "common law" spouse, defined in the Ontario Act as a man and woman who have lived together for three years or "in a relationship of some permanence" if they are the natural or adoptive parents of a child,[220] and also to include same-sex partners.[220a] If the claimant need not be married to the deceased in the first place, obviously "remarriage" becomes an inapplicable concept. The relevant question to ask is: Has the claimant formed, or is the claimant likely to form, a new relationship of dependence from which benefits will be derived?[221] This must surely be the relevant question also in claims by the deceased's spouse. Social **6.600**

[217] *Supra*, at 1.2440, 1.2520.

[218] *Report of the Royal Commission on Civil Liability and Compensation for Personal Injury* (Pearson Commission Report) (London, H.M.S.O., 1978), Cmnd 7054-1, §414.

[219] *Ibid.*, at §416.

[220] *Family Law Act* (Ont.), s. 29. See also *Fatal Accidents Act* (N.B.), s. 1, definition " "wife' and "husband' "; (P.E.I.), s. 1(f)(vi).

[220a] The Ontario *Family Law Act* was amended in 1999 to include same-sex partners: see s. 61(1).

customs are such that a relationship giving rise to benefits is equally probable within or outside marriage, and the law now provides, in an increasing number of jurisdictions, that a legal right to support may exist outside marriage. If it is justifiable to consider remarriage, it must be justifiable also to consider the re-formation of a relationship outside marriage carrying with it an expectation of benefits, especially if the expectation is based on legal rights.

6.610 Not every transient relationship from which the claimant might derive a pecuniary advantage can rationally be taken into account. Gifts and earnings from future employment are not taken into account,[222] the reason being, it is suggested, that these benefits could have been received even if the deceased had survived and the relationship with the claimant had continued. Generally, however, what may be called a full-time relationship can exist with only one person at a time so that it might be argued, by analogy with principles of mitigation,[223] that since the claimant would not have enjoyed both sources of income had the deceased remained alive, the second source should go to reduce the damages attributable to the loss of the deceased's financial benefit.

6.620 An added consideration is that remarriage carries no guarantee of greater financial benefit than relationships outside marriage.[223a] Under the Ontario *Family Law Act*, partners to a marriage may by agreement exclude most of their property sharing and support obligations.[224] It is uncertain how common such marriage contracts will be but it is likely that they will be far more common in cases of second and subsequent marriages than in the case of first marriages. The relevance of remarriage, as such, to the financial prospects of a wrongful death claimant, is thus further reduced. Relationships outside marriage may be financially profitable; marriage may not be.[225]

6.630 These considerations tend to the conclusion that no rule can be satisfactory that depends on marriage, as such. The only rational inquiry is so wide that it becomes impractical to pursue it on an individual basis. Possible future relationships are so many and varied and the financial consequences inside or outside marriage so uncertain that the court will, it is suggested, be justified

[221] In *Wild v. Eves* (1970), 92 W.N. (N.S.W.) 347, the New South Wales Court of Appeal held that cohabitation was not relevant to reduce damages, but the applicable statute (*Compensation to Relatives Act*) did not extend to *de facto* spouses as claimants, and the majority of the court distinguished marriage as involving "the legal obligation to the wife in relation to maintenance" and "in a class by itself". Recent developments in family law cast doubt on this distinction. Future *de facto* marriage was considered relevant in: *Comeau v. Marsman* (1981), 47 N.S.R. (2d) 550 (S.C.T.D.); *Hildebrand v. Butler* (1979), 11 B.C.L.R. 234 (S.C.); *Naeth Estate v. Warburton* (1993), 116 Sask. R. 11, 59 W.A.C. 11 (C.A.).

[222] See 6.510, *supra*, and 6.700-6.730, *infra*.

[223] See 15.800-15.880, *infra*.

[223a] See *Brown v. Finch*, [1998] 4 W.W.R. 679, 42 B.C.L.R. (3d) 116 at p. 120 (C.A.).

[224] *Family Law Act* (Ont.), ss. 51-57.

[225] See *Dormuth v. Untereiner*, [1964] S.C.R. 122, 43 D.L.R. (2d) 135; *Lyons v. Hembrough* (1964), 46 D.L.R. (2d) 769 (B.C.S.C.) (no deduction where second marriage annulled); *Mogck v. Woldum* (1965), 52 D.L.R. (2d) 322 (Alta. S.C.) (no reduction where second husband separated from claimant); *Lamb v. Brandt* (1984), 56 B.C.L.R. 74, 30 C.C.L.T. 280 (C.A.).

in disregarding almost all the claimant's individual circumstances. Inquiry into the claimant's personal attractions or actual relationships with other persons should, it is suggested, be

[*The next page is* 6-35]

ruled out on the ground that the uncertainty and instability of sexual relationships is such that this information is of marginal evidential value, and its usefulness is outweighed by the embarrassing and distasteful nature of the inquiry and by the public policy represented by the claimant's right to privacy.[225a] The court should, it is suggested, take into account only the claimant's age, on the basis that a younger claimant has a substantially greater chance than an older claimant of forming some relationship from which financial benefits will be derived. The Saskatchewan Court of Appeal took this approach in *Lamont v. Pederson*,[226] holding that an objective statistical test should be used without regard to the claimant's particular attributes.

6.640 Where a marriage has actually taken place before trial or where a relationship that shows signs of permanence has actually been formed, somewhat different considerations apply. Here the court is dealing with known facts and must give them consideration.[227] However, it is not to be assumed that marriage or any other relationship will be permanent, and the claimant's expectation of receiving benefits should not be overvalued. The suggested conclusion, then, is that so long as the theory of recovery continues to rest on the claimant's own loss,[228] the claimant's actual remarriage or formation of a relationship with equivalent expectation of benefits would be taken into account to effect a limited reduction of damages[228a] but future prospects of receipt of such benefits would be measured by a conventional factor varying only with the claimant's age.

6.650 Where the claimant is a child and the question is of taking into account benefits received from a step-parent, similar considerations apply. Actual remarriage of the child's surviving parent before trial has been taken into account in some cases,[229] particularly where the child has a legal right of support from the step-parent. In *Fawns v. Green*,[230] the adoption of a child claimant was taken into account, Gregory J. remarking that the case was even

225a See *De Sales v. Ingrilli* (2002), 193 A.L.R. 130 (Aust. H.C.).

226 [1981] 2 W.W.R. 24 (Sask. C.A.).

227 See 13.620-13.650, *infra.*

228 See 6.760-6.1090, *infra.*

228a *Naeth Estate v. Warburton* (1992), 103 Sask. R. 130 at p. 155 (Q.B.), affd 116 Sask. R. 11 (C.A.), citing this passage; *Schiewe Estate v. Skogan*, [1996] 8 W.W.R. 635, 185 A.R. 321 (Q.B.).

229 *Mead v. Clarke Chapman & Co. Ltd.*, [1956] 1 W.L.R. 76 (C.A.); *Thompson v. Price*, [1973] Q.B. 838; *Lefebvre v. Dowdall* (1964), 46 D.L.R. (2d) 426, [1965] 1 O.R. 1 (H.C.J.) (but burden of proof on defendant); *Ball v. Kraft* (1966), 60 D.L.R. (2d) 35 (B.C.S.C.); *Walter v. Muise* (1964), 48 D.L.R. (2d) 734 (N.S.S.C.); *Watson v. Willmott*, [1991] 1 Q.B. 140 (Q.B.); *Skelding (Guardian ad Litem of) v. Skelding* (1994), 118 D.L.R. (4th) 537, [1994] 9 W.W.R. 538, leave to appeal to S.C.C. refused 119 D.L.R. (4th) vii.

230 [1972] 1 W.W.R. 272 (B.C.S.C.). See also *Manning (Guardian ad Litem of) v. British Columbia (Minister of Transportation and Highways)* (1993), 77 B.C.L.R. (2d) 189 (S.C.); *Watson v. Willmott, supra.* In *Adkins v. Mintz* (1973), 54 D.L.R. (3d) 358, 7 O.R. (2d) 102 (H.C.J.), affd March 14, 1974 (C.A.); *Stewart v. Sheldrake* (1976), 22 N.S.R. (2d) 279 (S.C.T.D.); adoption was held to be relevant but not conclusive evidence of probable receipt of financial benefit by the claimant.

stronger than that of a widow who remarries for remarriage can end in divorce but adoption is permanent. Other cases, however, have declined to reduce damages on this account[231] making an analogy with cases treating benefits derived from relatives as gifts.[232] The theory of compensating the claimant's actual pecuniary loss here conflicts with the court's instinctive desire that the wrongdoer should not benefit by the generosity of relatives or adoptive parents. The only solution to this dilemma would be to base recovery on the loss to the deceased's estate.[233]

(5) Deduction for other contingencies

6.660 Deductions are to be made for contingencies that might have interrupted or extinguished the stream of benefits provided by the deceased. The possibility of premature death of the claimant or of the deceased is automatically taken into account by the use of mortality tables to calculate life expectancy.[234] The possibilities of loss of employment, declining income in future years, sickness, or accident can legitimately be taken into account especially if the deceased's employment was particularly hazardous but, as suggested above, the impact of various forms of disability insurance, private and social, must be considered and will often drastically reduce the likelihood of interruption of earnings and eliminate the possibility of their complete cessation.[235] If, for example, the deceased paid premiums for a disability insurance policy that guaranteed continuation of full income, it would be wrong to make any deduction at all for the contingency of disability, for the claimant could, if there had been no disability insurance, have expected to enjoy the current benefits of part, at least, of the premiums. It would be unfair to reduce the calculation of the claimant's benefit by the amount of the premiums and then to reduce it further by the contingency that the premiums were paid to obviate. It should be recalled, too, that not all contingencies are adverse.[236] The deceased might have lost a job and become unemployed but might also have risen brilliantly to the top of a profession.

231 *Stonehouse v. Gamble* (1982), 44 B.C.L.R. 375, 24 C.C.L.T. 133 (C.A.); *Sheppard v. McAllister* (1987), 40 D.L.R. (4th) 233, 60 O.R. (2d) 309 (C.A.); *Redlick-Lynn (Next Friend of) v. Halfe* (1994), 21 Alta. L.R. (3d) 195, 156 A.R. 210, supplementary reasons 24 Alta. L.R. (3d) 415, 161 A.R. 134 (Q.B.); *Comeau v. Saint John Regional Hospital* (2001), 244 N.B.R. (2d) 201 (N.B.C.A.).

232 See *Hay v. Hughes*, [1975] Q.B. 790 (C.A.) (care provided by grandmother); *Ratansi v. Abery* (1995), 5 B.C.L.R. (3d) 88 (S.C.) (care provided by aunt); *Vana v. Tosta*, [1968] S.C.R. 71, 66 D.L.R. (2d) 97 (gratuitous services); *Collins (Guardian ad Litem of) v. Savovich* (1996), 20 B.C.L.R. (3d) 126 (S.C.). See *H v. S*, [2002] 3 W.L.R. 1179 (C.A.).

233 See 6.960-6.1090, *infra*.

234 See *Keizer v. Hanna*, [1978] 2 S.C.R. 342 at p. 359, 82 D.L.R. (3d) 449 at p. 454. For this reason the reference in *Nance v. British Columbia Electric Ry. Co.*, [1951] A.C. 601 (P.C.), at p. 615, by Viscount Simon, to a reduction for the possibility of premature death, is puzzling.

235 See 3.720, 3.940, *supra*.

236 See 3.940, *supra*.

6.670 Account has been taken, in several cases, of the possibility of divorce or separation,[237] and relief has been denied altogether where the claimant was a spouse living apart from the deceased with no prospect of reconciliation or of receiving support.[238] Where there is a chance of reconciliation, compensation has been given for the value of the chance.[238a] In making such assessments, it should be recalled that dissolution of marriage is not always financially disadvantageous to the less wealthy party or at least that the financial disadvantages may be substantially mitigated by claims for support and for a share in the other party's property. In dealing with contingencies affecting only one of several claimants, it is important to reduce only the recovery of the claimant affected.[239]

(6) Deceased's contributory negligence

6.680 The legislation has been interpreted so that the claimant's right to damages is subject to apportionment on account of contributory fault or neglect on the part of the deceased.[240] In some jurisdictions this result is expressly provided.[241] The situation is not analogous to the ordinary case of contributory negligence because the claimant does not contribute in any way to the loss, and the claimant's action is independent of any action that the deceased or the estate might have had. The theory behind the apportionment rule seems to be one of joint responsibility for the claimant's loss, though the deceased owed no legal duty to the claimant to preserve the deceased's own life. Nevertheless, it can be said that where death is caused partly by the deceased's carelessness, the wrongdoer is only partly responsible for the claimant's loss and it would seem to be on this theory that apportionment is required.

---

237 *Julian v. Northern & Central Gas Corp.* (1978), 5 C.C.L.T. 148 (Ont. H.C.J.), affd 118 D.L.R. (3d) 458, 31 O.R. (2d) 388 (C.A.), leave to appeal to S.C.C. refused D.L.R. *loc. cit.*, O.R. *loc. cit.*; *Kwong v. The Queen in right of Alberta* (1978), 96 D.L.R. (3d) 214 (Alta. S.C. App. Div.) affd [1979] 2 S.C.R. 1010*n*, 105 D.L.R. (3d) 576*n*; *Jeselon v. Waters*, [1981] 3 W.W.R. 715 (B.C.S.C.); *Griffiths v. Canadian Pacific Rys.* (1978), 6 B.C.L.R. 115 (C.A.); *Janke v. Chamber's Estate* (1981), 29 A.R. 68 (C.A.), vard [1982] 1 S.C.R. 281. In *Davies v. Taylor*, [1974] A.C. 207 (H.L.); *McKenna v. Nolan* (1959), 21 D.L.R. (2d) 120 (Sask. C.A.), affd October 13, 1960 (S.C.C.); *Newell v. Mitchell* (1974), 19 R.F.L. 391 (B.C.S.C.); *LeBlanc v. Burcevski* (1995), 176 A.R. 373, 34 Alta. L.R. (3d) 289 (Q.B.), affd 200 A.R. 218, 51 Alta. L.R. (3d) 245 (C.A.).

238 *Lerman v. MacLean* (1978), 13 A.R. 276 (S.C.T.D.); *Brooks v. Stefura*, [1998] 9 W.W.R. 312, supplementary reasons 222 A.R. at p. 380 (Q.B.), vard 192 D.L.R. (4th) 40 (C.A.).

238a *Home v. Corbeil* (1956), 2 D.L.R. (2d) 543, [1956] O.W.N. 391 (C.A.); *Hildebrand v. Butler* (1979), 11 B.C.L.R. 234 (S.C.); *Young v. Fletcher* (1995), 161 N.B.R. (2d) 116, 12 M.V.R. (3d) 147 (C.A.).

239 See 6.690, *infra*, on the question of contributory negligence of one of several claimants.

240 *Littley v. Brooks*, [1932] S.C.R. 462, [1932] 2 D.L.R. 386; *Foster v. Kerr*, [1940] 2 D.L.R. 47 (Alta. S.C. App. Div.); *Jenner v. Allen West & Co. Ltd.*, [1959] 1 W.L.R. 554 (C.A.); *Stewart v. Ottawa Electric Ry. Co.*, [1945] O.W.N. 639 (C.A.); *Wiksech v. General News Co.*, [1948] 1 D.L.R. 753, [1948] O.R. 105 (C.A.).

241 *Fatal Accidents Act* (P.E.I.), s. 8(3); N.B., s. 4(2); Man., s. 4(2); *Family Law Act* (Ont.), s. 61(3).

(7) Claimant's contributory negligence

6.690 In *Trueman v. Hydro Electric Power Com'n of Ontario*,[242] the Ontario Court of Appeal held that the contributory negligence of the claimant defeated the claim, though not that of other claimants who had not been negligent. The theory was said by Ferguson J.A., quoting *Beven on Negligence*, to be that "the harm I bring upon myself I must bear myself". After the enactment of apportionment legislation, the proper conclusion appears to be that the claim of any person who is partly responsible for the deceased's death should be subject to apportionment, and this is expressly provided in some jurisdictions.[243] The same conclusion was reached in the Northern Ireland case of *Mulholland v. McCrea*.[244] This latter case held that a claim by the deceased's estate was not subject to apportionment on account of the claimant's negligence, but presumably, unless there were a bar, such as inter-spousal immunity, the claimant would be jointly liable with the tortfeasor to the estate and could be called upon by the tortfeasor to make appropriate contribution to damages demanded by the estate.

(8) Claimant's earning capacity

6.700 A problem that has become more difficult in the light of recent changes in family relationships is how to take account of the claimant's earning capacity. This question is relevant both to the calculation of the claimant's initial loss and to the question of deductions in respect of earnings anticipated after the death. In *Shiels v. Cruikshank*,[245] the House of Lords held that a widow's independent income, though not to be deducted from her claim as such, might be relevant to the calculation of the initial loss. In other words, if the claimant were living entirely off her own income before the deceased's death and would have been likely to continue to do so, she could show no loss resulting from the death. In the usual case, the incomes of spouses are placed in a common pool, and it is impossible to say whether household expenses are met from the income of the one spouse rather than the other. In *Lamont v. Pederson*,[246] where the claimant, a widow, was not working at the time of her husband's death but took a job shortly afterwards, the Saskatchewan Court of Appeal held that seventy per cent of her husband's income should be taken as the claimant's basic loss. The court remarked that, had the husband and wife been making equal contributions to household expenses, the appropriate figure would have been fifty per cent.

---

242 [1924] 1 D.L.R. 405 at p. 423, 53 O.L.R. 434 (S.C. App. Div.), quoting Beven, *Negligence in Law*, 3rd ed. (London, Stevens & Haynes, 1908), p. 149.

243 *Fatal Accidents Act* (Man.), s. 4(1); N.B., s. 4(1); P.E.I., s. 8(1).

244 [1968] N.I. 135.

245 [1953] 1 All E.R. 874 (H.L.).

246 [1981] 2 W.W.R. 24 (Sask. C.A.); *Isaacs v. Boldt* (1971), 25 D.L.R. (3d) 34, [1972] 2 O.R. 118 (C.A.) (earning capacity "totally irrelevant").

6.710 It is not immediately apparent why fifty per cent is selected. If husband and wife were living in separate households, earning equal incomes but supporting themselves out of their own income, it would seem that neither suffers a pecuniary loss on the other's death. Where they make equal contributions to the expenses of a single household, the survivor does suffer a loss by the other's death because two persons can be

[*The next page is* 6–39]

supported more cheaply in a single household than in separate households. The appropriate measure of damages would seem, therefore, to be the difference between the contribution made by the claimant to household expenses before the death and the full expense of maintaining the household after the death. In a case where each spouse was contributing equally to the household expenses, therefore, the amount of the claim would be something less than fifty per cent of the total household expenses. In some cases this might be approximately equal to fifty per cent of the deceased's income but, it is suggested, there is no reason why this should always be so.

6.720 In *Cookson v. Knowles*,[247] the English Court of Appeal held that a widow's earning capacity was to be taken into account, even though she could not continue with her former employment after her husband's death (she had helped him in his work). Lord Denning M.R. said: "After his death, she retained her earning capacity . . . It is true that she could no longer do her previous work as a cleaner after his death. But she could do other work, at any rate part-time work, whilst the children were at school, and full-time work later."[248] It would seem to follow from this that, even if the claimant were not working at all at the date of the death, her earning capacity should be taken into account in calculating the loss. Lord Denning conceded that former cases had suggested the contrary,[249] but implied that they might be reconsidered:

> It is very different from those cases where the widow was not working at the time of his death, so that her earnings did not come into the family pool. In those cases it may be said that she is not bound to go out to work so as to reduce the award . . . though we are not so sure about this. She may prefer to go out to work rather than sit at home grieving over the loss of her husband.[250]

It is suggested that the proper test here is whether the claimant would probably have earned an independent income had the deceased lived. If so, this is a consideration that may go to reduce the basic amount of the claimant's probable loss, and the court may properly take account of the fact that, in modern times, it is common for both spouses to use their independent earning capacities. If, however, the claimant would probably not have earned a separate income during the deceased's life, the different question arises of whether to take into account the probable earnings of the claimant after the deceased's death. The courts have been reluctant to reduce the award on this account for fear of appearing to

247 [1977] Q.B. 913 (C.A.), affd [1979] A.C. 556 (H.L.).

248 *Supra*, at p. 922.

249 See *Howitt v. Heads*, [1973] Q.B. 64 (Assizes).

250 *Supra*, footnote 247, at p. 922. In *Hildebrand v. Butler* (1979), 11 B.C.L.R. 234 (S.C.), where the spouses were already separated the claimant's earning capacity was taken into account. See also *McNicol v. P. Burns & Co., Ltd.* (1919) 49 D.L.R. 132 (Alta. S.C. App. Div.), at p. 137, affd 60 S.C.R. 648, 56 D.L.R. 695.

force claimants into employment that they would not have had to accept but for the death — and all for the benefit of the wrongdoer who has caused the death. It is submitted that this reluctance is justified, for it is hard to resist the conclusion that a person suffers a real loss if compelled to rely on that person's own earning capacity in place of the support of the deceased spouse. Lord Denning's comment that the claimant may "prefer to go out to work" does not seem to be a satisfactory answer to this point, for the loss is the same whatever the claimant's future preferences, and it seems patronizing to reduce the claim on the basis that work outside the household will be better for the claimant than grieving at home.

6.730 In *Lamont v. Pederson*,[251] the Saskatchewan Court of Appeal held that a widow's damages were not to be reduced by her own earnings, even though she had undertaken employment after the death that seemed likely to continue. The court said that she had a right to remain a housewife after her husband's death and that she should not be penalized for going to work.[252] The issue is a difficult one. Often a claimant who was formerly a housekeeper will have an earning capacity equal to or greater than that of the deceased. If this is taken into account, the claim will disappear. If it is not taken into account, the claimant appears to be over-compensated. On balance, the best solution appears to be, as suggested in *Shiels v. Cruikshank*, to reduce the initial calculation of loss by the claimant's probable earning capacity during the marriage but not to reduce the claim any further on this account by way of deduction.[253]

6.735 In *Levesque v. Lipskie*,[253a] the Ontario Court of Appeal said that the fact that a surviving spouse is capable of working is "entirely irrelevant in assessing damages in a fatal accident case".

3. Division of Damages Among Claimants

6.740 It has consistently been held by the courts that each eligible claimant has a separate individual claim and the defendant is liable to pay to each claimant all loss proved to have been caused by the death.[254] However, in the interests of protecting the defendant from a multiplicity of actions, the legislation gives to the claim some of the characteristics of a representative action. Most statutes provide that one action only is to be brought[255] and procedures are set out for insuring that the interests of

---

251 *Supra*, footnote 246.

252 *Lamont v. Pederson*, *supra*, footnote 246, at pp. 31-2.

253 This was the approach taken in *Cummings v. Halliburton Services Ltd.* (1980), 27 A.R. 181 (Q.B.).

253a (1991), 80 D.L.R. (4th) 243, 3 O.R. (3d) 98 (C.A.), leave to appeal to S.C.C. refused 83 D.L.R. (4th) vii, 137 N.R. 156*n*, citing *Isaacs v. Boldt* (1971), 25 D.L.R. (3d) 34, [1972] 2 O.R. 118 (C.A.).

254 *Pym v. Great Northern Ry.* (1863), 4 B. & S. 396, 122 E.R. 508.

255 *Fatal Accidents Act* (Alta.), s. 4; Man., s. 7(1); N.B., s. 8(1); Nfld. & Lab., s. 6(4); N.W.T., s. 6(1); P.E.I., s. 11(1); Sask., s. 6; Yukon, s. 8(1); *Fatal Injuries Act* (N.S.), s. 10; *Family Compensation Act* (B.C.), s. 6.

potential claimants are represented.[256] The defendant may pay into court a single sum without specifying the division among the claimants.[257]

6.750 In calculating the damages, also, the courts often treat the claim, for convenience, as though it were a single claim, using as the starting point the resources of the deceased estimated to have been available for support of the dependants as a class, and then dividing the loss so calculated among the claimants.[258] This, however, is only a practice of convenience; it should not be allowed to prejudice the claim of any individual claimant.[259] Where the claimants are a surviving parent and young children, it might be thought that the children suffer no loss at all, since they have a claim against the surviving parent whose resources should be sufficient after the receipt of the award to replace the benefits expected from the deceased. However, the courts have always, in such cases, awarded a portion of the damages to the children.[260] In principle, a younger child is entitled to a larger share on the ground that the period of anticipated receipt of benefits is longer,[261] but many cases have awarded equal amounts to young children of approximately equal age.[262]

4. Relationship of Fatal Accidents and Survival of Actions Legislation

6.760 A series of English cases in 1980-82 has raised, in an acute form, the problem of the relationship of the two theories underlying liability for

256 The most elaborate procedures are in the *Fatal Accidents Act* (P.E.I.), s. 13, where also the widest variety of claimants is permitted.

257 *Fatal Accidents Act* (Man.), s. 8; N.B., s. 9; Nfld., s. 6(2); N.W.T., s. 5; P.E.I., s. 14; Sask., s. 5; Yukon, s. 10; *Fatal Injuries Act* (N.S.), s. 7; *Family Compensation Act* (B.C.), s. 3(6); *Family Law Act* (Ont.), s. 62(1).

258 *Royal Trust Co. v. C.P.R. Co.* (1922), 67 D.L.R. 518 (P.C.); *McKenna v. Nolan* (1959), 21 D.L.R. (2d) 120 (Sask. C.A.); *McDonald v. Mason* (1953), 8 W.W.R. (N.S.) 553 (B.C.S.C.) (no formula governs the division).

259 See *Kovats v. Ogilvie* (1970), 17 D.L.R. (3d) 343 (B.C.C.A.), at pp. 349-50; *Norris v. Kennedy* (1970), 18 D.L.R. (3d) 352 (B.C.C.A.). See also Street, *Principles of the Law of Damages* (London, Sweet & Maxwell, 1962), pp. 149-55.

260 In *Goodburn v. Thomas Cotton Ltd.*, [1968] 1 Q.B. 845 (C.A.), at pp. 852-3, Willmer L.J. pointed out that it could not always be assumed that the adult claimant would use the proceeds of his own claim for the children's benefit. In *Hickey v. Laatsch* (1957), 11 D.L.R. (2d) 210 (Sask. Q.B.), the child's portion was ordered to be paid to the Official Guardian and in *Braun v. Roy* (1957), 22 W.W.R. 609 (Man. Q.B.), vard 12 D.L.R. (2d) 390 (C.A.), to "some recognized trustee" and in *Roberts v. Semchyshyn* (1956), 4 D.L.R. (2d) 764 (Man. Q.B.), affd 6 D.L.R. (2d) 266 (C.A.), to a trustee approved by the court. *Western Trust Co. v. British American Oil Co. Ltd.* (1951), 2 W.W.R. (N.S.) 529 (Sask. K.B.) (Official Guardian); *MacLean v. MacDougall*, [1944] 4 D.L.R. 574 (P.E.I.S.C.) (payment in court). In *MacDonell v. Maple Leaf Mills Ltd.* (1972), 26 D.L.R. (3d) 106 (Alta. S.C. App. Div.), the court awarded the bulk of the recovery to the mother, saying it was unwise to tie up a large portion in the hands of the Public Trustee. The division of the award becomes important where an award for lost future earnings is made under survival legislation. Claimants (as a group) will benefit from any discrepancy between the division under the fatal accident legislation and the division of the proceeds of the estate. See *Harris v. Empress Motors Ltd.*, [1984] 1 W.L.R. 212 (C.A.), and 6.1040, *infra*.

261 *MacLean v. MacDougall, supra*, footnote 260.

262 *Julian v. Northern & Central Gas Corp.* (1978), 5 C.C.L.T. 148 (Ont. H.C.J.), affd 118 D.L.R. (3d) 458, 31 O.R. (2d) 388 (C.A.), leave to appeal to S.C.C. refused D.L.R. *loc. cit.*, O.R. *loc. cit.*

wrongful death: loss to the survivors and loss to the estate. It has generally been assumed that loss to the survivors is the preferable theory. But it will be suggested here that there are substantial advantages to a regime where only the estate can recover for wrongful death and survivors' claims are against the estate not against the wrongdoer.

6.770 This suggestion is not original. It was made in 1846 during the Parliamentary debate[263] on *Lord Campbell's Act* by Sir Frederick Thesiger, later Baron Chelmsford L.C. The suggestion was again put forward, though without enthusiasm, in 1981 in *Gammell v. Wilson*,[264] discussed later.

6.780 The pre-1846 rule that a tortfeasor could not be made to pay damages for wrongfully causing a death rested on two separate principles. The first was that personal actions (with some exceptions) did not survive to a deceased plaintiff's estate. The second rule (the rule in *Baker v. Bolton*)[265] was that a living plaintiff could not sue a living defendant for the death of a third person even where the death caused financial loss. It is the latter rule that was modified by *Lord Campbell's Act*.[266]

6.790 The rule that personal actions did not survive to a deceased plaintiff's estate, though subjected to almost universal criticism, lasted in Ontario until 1886[267] and in England until 1934.[268] The survival of actions statutes[269] provide that (with certain exceptions) all actions survive to the estate, adding usually that the rights given by the Act are "in addition to and not in derogation of any rights conferred on the dependants of deceased persons by the Fatal Accidents Act". The courts thus have had to deal after 1886 with two separate actions against a wrongdoer for the death of a person, one by the statutory claimants under *Lord Campbell's Act*, the other by the deceased person's estate under the survival legislation. Often the claimants under *Lord Campbell's Act* were identical with the beneficiaries of the estate, and in those cases double recovery was avoided by the rule that, in calculating a claimant's loss under *Lord Campbell's Act*, credit had to be given for benefits received from the estate.[270] Where the claimants and beneficiaries were

263 (1846), 87 Hansard, col. 1365.
264 [1982] A.C. 27 (H.L.).
265 (1808), 1 Camp. 493, 170 E.R. 1033. See Malone, "The Genesis of Wrongful Death", 17 Stan. L. Rev. 1043 (1965).
266 See 6.10, *supra*.
267 *An Act respecting Trustees and Executors and the Administration of Estates*, s. 8 (rep. & sub. 1886, c. 16, s. 23).
268 *Law Reform (Miscellaneous Provisions) Act, 1934* (U.K.), ss. 1(1), 1(5).
269 See 12.10-12.260, *infra*.
270 *Davies v. Powell Duffryn Associated Collieries, Ltd.*, [1942] A.C. 601 (H.L.). See 6.400, *supra*.

different, no serious problem of overlap arose because it was held by the English Court of Appeal in 1961 in *Oliver v. Ashman*[271] that an injured plaintiff, suing on his own behalf, whose life was shortened by the defendant's tort, could not recover income lost during the period of the shortening of his life. Thus if a person's working life were reduced from forty years to two years, the person could not recover lost income in respect of the thirty-eight "lost years". It followed that if the person were killed instantly (*i.e.*, life expectancy reduced to nil), no action for lost earnings would survive to the estate. The only action was assumed to be under *Lord Campbell's Act* if there were eligible claimants.

6.800 The rule in *Oliver v. Ashman* has a certain logical attraction. Many would say instinctively that a person cannot be said to suffer a financial loss during a period when the person will not be alive to enjoy the use of any compensation that might be awarded for lost earnings. However, this view would lead also to the denial of recovery in the case of a plaintiff rendered permanently unconscious for of such a person it can also be said that the person will not be able to enjoy the use of compensation.[272] A more serious difficulty with *Oliver v. Ashman* is that it gives rise to a potential injustice when an injured person's life is shortened so that the person lives just long enough to recover judgment or to settle the claim. The plaintiff with a forty-year life expectancy tortiously reduced to two years will recover nothing in respect of the thirty-eight lost years' earning capacity. Assuming the prediction of post-accident life expectancy is accurate and death occurs two years after the accident, the person will leave the estate without any money representing the lost earning capacity. If there are dependants, they will receive nothing in this respect either from the estate or under *Lord Campbell's Act* because the action under that Act is precluded by satisfaction of the deceased's claim. This seems very harsh and highly anomalous. The dependants would have been much better off if the deceased had been killed instantly, in which case they would have benefited from an action under *Lord Campbell's Act*.

6.810 One possible approach to this problem might be to permit an action by the dependants for lost earning capacity despite settlement or judgment in the deceased's lifetime. This would raise difficult procedural problems, and in *Pickett v. British Rail Engineering Ltd.*[273] the House of Lords assumed that this route was unavailable. Consequently the House took the alternative route, overruling *Oliver v. Ashman* and allowing an award of damages for lost future earning capacity. The injured person had actually died by the time the case reached the House of Lords, so the result

---

271 [1962] 2 Q.B. 210 (C.A.).

272 This view was favoured by Lord Denning M.R. in *Lim Poh Choo v. Camden and Islington Area Health Authority*, [1979] Q.B. 196 (C.A.), and by McLachlin, "What Price Disability?" 59 Can. Bar Rev. 1 (1981), at p. 11, but rejected by the House of Lords [1980] A.C. 174.

273 [1980] A.C. 136 (H.L.).

of the decision was to increase very considerably the size of the estate that Mr. Pickett's widow inherited. The legal reason for the result was that an injured plaintiff whose earning capacity is reduced by shortening of life suffers a present immediate capital loss and is entitled to recover.[274] The real social and policy reason for the result was very plainly the sense of injustice at the prospect of Mr. Pickett's widow receiving no compensation under either statute for her husband's lost earning capacity.

6.820 The law was thus established that a person whose life was tortiously shortened was entitled to recover for lost earning capacity on the basis of pre-accident life expectancy. It was only a matter of time — as it turned out a very short time — before the question arose whether the injured person's estate succeeded to the benefit of this claim if the person died before judgment, or before instituting action, or death occurred instantly. The House of Lords in *Pickett* was aware of some of the probable difficulties ahead, but so plainly did justice seem to require some way of securing compensation for Mr. Pickett's widow that the House of Lords stated almost in so many words that it was willing to face any difficulties that should arise.[275]

6.830 Cases of immediate death were not long in arising. In *Kandalla v. British European Airways*,[276] it was held that a claim for lost earning capacity survived to the estate of persons killed in an aircraft crash. In *Gammell v. Wilson*,[277] the case arose of the immediate death of a twenty-two-year-old man, unmarried, without dependants, with good earning prospects. The House of Lords consolidated the case with another similar case to consider the current relationship between the two statutes. It was held that an action for lost future earning capacity vested in the deceased at the instant of his death and that under the 1934 Act (survival of actions) the benefit of the action passed to the estate. This decision has several far-reaching consequences. First, where the same persons are the beneficiaries of the estate and entitled to claim under *Lord Campbell's Act* (as is usual), recovery under the Act was effectively superseded, for the estate's recovery of the lost earning capacity will always equal or exceed the value of the lost dependency. A second consequence is that a tortfeasor who causes the death

---

274 See *Pickett, supra*, footnote 273, at pp. 149-50, *per* Lord Wilberforce. The same view had been earlier adopted in Canada. See *The Queen in right of Ontario v. Jennings*, [1966] S.C.R. 532, 57 D.L.R. (2d) 644, and 3.910-3.930, *supra*.

275 See *Pickett, supra*, at p. 150, *per* Lord Wilberforce, and pp. 170-1, *per* Lord Scarman.

276 [1981] Q.B. 158.

277 [1982] A.C. 27 (H.L.). The effect is now reversed by the *Administration of Justice Act 1982* (U.K.).

of an unmarried wage-earner has to pay much larger damages than formerly thought to be exigible, for the value of the lost earning capacity will be recoverable by the estate. Thirdly, if it should happen that the estate beneficiaries and the *Lord Campbell's Act* claimants are different persons, there is a real prospect of the defendant being made to pay twice over for the loss of the deceased's earning capacity.

6.840 Lord Scarman made the following comments on these features of the law:

> My Lords, there is some disquiet expressed by judges, and understandably felt by insurers, about two aspects of the law — the "double recovery" now possible in some cases, and the very great discrepancy which can arise, as happened in [one of the cases in issue], between the damages recoverable by the estate for the lost years and the damages recoverable by the dependants under the Fatal Accidents Act. Each of these possibilities may well be a mischief: certainly a law which allows the discrepancy to arise, wears the appearance of anomaly, and is unlikely to be understood or acceptable.
>
> The logical, but socially unattractive, way of reforming the law would be to repeal the Fatal Accidents Act, now that the rule "actio personalis moritur cum persona" has itself belatedly perished. This would leave recovery to the estate; and the dependants would look, as in a family where the breadwinner is not tortiously killed, to him (or her) for their support during life and on death. They would have the final safeguard of the Inheritance (Family Provision) Act 1975. But the protection of the Fatal Accidents legislation has been with us for so long, that I doubt whether its repeal would be welcomed. If, therefore, the law is anomalous (and it certainly bears hardly on insurers and ultimately the premium-paying-public), the way forward would appear to be that adopted by Parliament for Scotland. The Damages (Scotland) Act 1976 appears to work well: and the Royal Commission on Civil Liability and Compensation for Personal Injury 1978 . . . recommends its adoption in English law. The denial of damages to the estate, but not to a living plaintiff, is the denial of a right vested in the estate: but social and financial circumstances, as well as the legal situation, of which the Fatal Accidents Act is now an integral part, suggest that, though illogical, this is the reform which is needed.[278]

These remarks are a little puzzling. The comments in the first paragraph reflect a fear that recovery by the estate may lead to overcompensation. Yet the phrases "socially unattractive" and "protection that has been with us so long" seem to reflect a fear of undercompensation. It will be suggested in the following discussion that neither objection is conclusive.

6.850 The principal effect of repealing *Lord Campbell's Act* would be that the courts would have to deal with only one kind of action for wrongful death and only one kind of action for lost earning capacity. The princi-

---

278 *Supra*, at pp. 80-1.

ples applicable and the damages payable would be the same whether the injured person was disabled or killed outright and whether or not there were dependants. Some force would be removed from the old taunt that tort law makes it cheaper to kill than to maim. Destruction of a person's earning capacity would always lead to damages calculated according to a single scheme.

6.860 Some might argue that this is not a desirable result. It is cheaper to kill than to maim, it may be argued, for the good reason that the two kinds of injuries cause different losses to different persons. There is no justification, it might be added, for enriching an estate where the beneficiaries are not dependent on the deceased. Lord Scarman indeed suggests as much when he points to the discrepancy between damages recoverable by the estate and by the dependants. The implication is that the estate gathers a windfall. But, in reply, it can be said that this kind of windfall is an inevitable consequence of the survival of actions legislation. Once the old rule is abandoned and it is accepted that a personal action survives, it inevitably follows that a deceased's estate will receive what some might describe as a windfall. Indeed the real cause of the enrichment is not even the legislation but the very concept of inheritance of wealth. Suppose that a living plaintiff whose life is shortened to one year lives to recover judgment or to settle the claim and is paid in full for lost earning capacity. It can hardly be doubted that on the death of the plaintiff, the estate inherits the whole of the wealth, even if there are no dependants eligible to claim under *Lord Campbell's Act*. If the injured person dies before recovering judgment or before instituting the action, the legislation simply provides that the benefit of the claim survives to the estate. The enrichment of the estate is due to the personal entitlement in the deceased before death to recover damages together with the statutory rule of survival. The point has no necessary connection with shortening of life or wrongful death. The same enrichment inures to the estate if an injured person, totally disabled but life *not* being shortened by the defendant's tort, recovers judgment in full for lost earning capacity and is then killed by an extraneous cause.[279] The compensation for the lost earning capacity will enrich the estate, some might say unjustly, if the beneficiaries are not dependants. But if this result is to be challenged, it must be on the ground of objection to the lump sum system of accident compensation or to the general principle of inheritance of wealth.

---

279 The same point could be made in relation to death from an extraneous cause before judgment if the extraneous cause were one for which a third person could be made liable. An extraneous cause (such as death from natural causes) for which no one was responsible would lead to an elimination of damages for the lost future earning capacity because this would be seen not to have been caused by the defendant's wrong. See *Baker v. Willoughby*, [1970] A.C. 467 (H.L.); *Jobling v. Associated Dairies Ltd.*, [1981] 3 W.L.R. 155 (H.L.). See 13.550-13.650, *infra*.

6.870 If it is provided by legislation, as it is in some jurisdictions,[280] that the claim of an injured person for lost earning capacity shall not survive to the estate, new anomalies are created. An injured person who lives just long enough to recover a judgment will leave a substantial sum to the estate; if death occurs just before judgment, the estate will recover nothing for lost earning capacity. Some might say that it is the lump sum system of accident compensation that leads to the undesirable result of enriching survivors where an injured person recovers damages and then unexpectedly dies; perhaps (they will say) we have to live with that anomaly, but why tolerate its extension to the case where the injured person dies before judgment?

6.880 This is the sort of dilemma that very commonly faces courts, commentators, and legislators considering the desirability of changes in the law. Is it better to extend an anomaly to its logical limits or to restrict the anomaly even at the expense of logic? The answer depends on the preferences of the observer. If the observer sees the anomaly as intolerable, restriction at all costs will be favoured for such an observer would rather accept illogical distinctions than see the anomaly extended. If, on the other hand, the observer is fairly tolerant of the anomaly, as is the writer of the lump-sum system of compensation and of inheritance of wealth, the observer will tend to regard the sacrifice of logic as a greater evil than the extension of the anomaly. From this point of view the conclusion seems preferable that the estate of an injured person who then dies should have the same rights whether death occurs just before or just after judgment.

6.890 The opposite objection to repealing *Lord Campbell's Act* is that it may undercompensate the dependants. One can suppose three situations: the injured person dies intestate; the person leaves property away from the dependants by will; the person dies insolvent and creditors claim the assets of the estate. Also, there might be estate tax problems.

6.900 The cases of intestacy and an adverse will can be met, as Lord Scarman suggested, by succession legislation.[281] The claims of creditors and of the revenue could, if this were thought desirable on policy grounds, be subordinated to claims of relatives by specific provisions. The merits of such provisions are debatable but this question should not, it is submitted, determine the main issue of whether *Lord Campbell's Act* could satisfactorily be replaced.

6.910 The principal benefit of replacement would be the substitution of a single theory of recovery for lost earning capacity.

6.920 It is suggested that there would also be important incidental benefits. The first of these relates to the awkward problem now faced by the

280 *Damages (Scotland) Act 1976* (U.K.), s. 2(3)(b); *Estate Administration Act* (B.C.), s. 59(3)(c); *Administration of Justice Act 1982* (U.K.).

281 See *Succession Law Reform Act* (Ont.), s. 58(1); *Inheritance (Provision for Family and Dependants) Act 1975* (U.K.), s. 1(1)(e).

courts of double recovery, or more strictly, of the defendant's having to pay twice over for the loss of earning capacity. Where, as is usual, the claimants under *Lord Campbell's Act* are also beneficiaries under the estate, benefits received or expected from the estate go to reduce the claim (except in Prince Edward Island).[282] This, as *Gammell v. Wilson* shows, has the effect of eliminating the *Lord Campbell's Act* claim in most cases.[283] But if the estate is insolvent or if the deceased has left a will that leaves property away from the relatives and is immune from attack under dependants' relief legislation, there is now a real possibility of the defendant being compelled to pay twice. Several approaches have been suggested to this overlap.[284]

6.930 It is very difficult to avoid the duplication by ordinary principles of statutory construction. One solution, favoured by Lord Scarman and implemented in some jurisdictions,[285] is to provide by express legislation that damages for lost future earning capacity should not survive to the estate. Such a revision, as suggested above, creates an anomalous exception to the principle that the death of a plaintiff should not diminish a wrongdoer's liability; everything is made to turn on whether death occurs before or after judgment. Moreover, legislation in that simple form leaves dependants without any compensation from any source where a person is disabled by one wrongdoer and then killed by another. The first wrongdoer would not be liable under *Lord Campbell's Act* for the wrongdoer would not have caused the death. The second wrongdoer would not be liable either for that wrongdoer would not have caused the loss of earning capacity.[286] The only possible source of compensation is, in this case, through the estate.

6.940 A troublesome problem in calculating damages under *Lord Campbell's Act* concerns the possibility of the claimant's forming future relationships of dependency. The typical case has been remarriage of a widow, which as the earlier discussion shows has given rise to considerable difficulties.[287]

6.950 If claims were made against the estate, these problems would disappear. The loss of earning capacity would entitle the estate to recover and assuming the surviving spouse (or *de facto* spouse) were the beneficiary of the estate, there would be full recovery. Future intentions as to remarriage or actual remarriage would be quite irrelevant.

6.960 This, it is suggested, is a very desirable solution. It is because *Lord Campbell's Act* depends theoretically on proof of the claimant's own loss that these intractable problems of remarriage arise. The change of

---

282 See 6.400-6.440, *supra*.
283 But see footnote 260, *supra*.
284 See Fleming, *The Law of Torts*, 9th ed. (Sydney, Law Book Co., 1998), pp. 743-4.
285 See footnote 280, *supra*.
286 See footnote 279, *supra*.
287 See 6.520-6.650, *supra*.

theoretical basis to recovery by the estate removes these problems because the extent of the beneficiaries' loss becomes irrelevant. The actual result of the 1971 English Act, that is ignoring remarriage, can thus be justified despite the criticisms. It may be suggested that behind the feeling of distaste that prompted the legislation lay an instinctive appreciation that recovery ought not to depend on the claimant's future matrimonial prospects; this view is compatible only with a theory of recovery by the deceased's estate. Problems of adoption of child claimants would also disappear.[288]

6.970 A hardly less problematic or distasteful inquiry required by current principles of damage assessment under *Lord Campbell's Act* concerns the stability of the claimant's marriage with the deceased. It has been held that it is relevant to reduce damages to show that the claimant was separated from the deceased[289] and, therefore, it must be relevant also to show that future separation was probable. The line of investigation and cross-examination opened up to the defendant by this prospect and the difficulties presented to the court in making a judgment on the matter suggest that there is merit in an approach that will avoid the inquiry if one can be found that is otherwise consistent with justice.

6.980 This inquiry would not necessarily be eliminated in a claim by the estate, however, because the same questions might be relevant to determining the probable future living expenses of the deceased (a single person having greater personal living expenses) and, therefore, might affect the calculation of the amount to be recovered by the estate. The variation due to this factor would, however, in most cases be comparatively small and so would not often warrant an investigation by the defendant into the stability of a marriage.

6.990 Another problem is the definition of the statutory class of claimants. With the changing social view of family relationships, there is constant pressure to enlarge the class of claimants. Amendments in most jurisdictions have included illegitimate and adopted children;[290] some have included foster children,[291] *de facto* spouses[292] and same-sex relationships.[292a] But there is no persuasive reason to stop at that point. It is foreseeable that with the declining significance of the marriage relationship as such, there will be an extension of the statutory benefits to same-sex relationships and to non-sexual household arrangements. Quite a strong case can then theoretically be made for including remote dependent relatives and unrelated dependent persons especially if they are elderly or

---

288 See 6.650, *supra*.

289 See 6.670, *supra*.

290 See, for example, *Fatal Accidents Act 1976* (U.K.), s. 1(5)(b).

291 *Compensation to Relatives Act* (N.S.W.), s. 7(1).

292 See, *e.g.*, *Family Law Act* (Ont.), s. 61(1).

292a See, *e.g.*, *Family Law Act* (Ont.), s. 61(1) (amended in 1999 to include same-sex partners). See 6.600, *supra*.

handicapped. Similar problems may of course arise in dealing with claims against estates, but if the estate only could recover for the death of a person, these problems could be dealt with in a single framework. No sound principle appears to justify different treatment of such claims in the two contexts.

6.1000 It might be said that there is no great difficulty in amending the *Fatal Accidents Act* from time to time to keep pace with changing social ideas. But amendment to statutes of this sort is not always promptly secured and this route seems to lead to two separate lists of beneficiaries, one in the intestate succession legislation and one in the *Fatal Accidents Act*, the second list never quite catching up with the first. There is a more fundamental difficulty. The *Fatal Accidents Act* in most jurisdictions requires one action only to be brought;[293] it is the responsibility of the plaintiff to join all persons entitled to claim. This is easy when the statutory claimants are limited to immediate relatives but if the list is extended, difficult procedural problems will appear. First, it will be difficult to discover who all the potential claimants are; secondly, there will often be a severe conflict of interest between the various claimants that will make the conduct and settlement of a single action difficult. One needs only to think of a spouse, a former spouse and a *de facto* spouse and the children of each to see that these are claimants, adverse in interest, seeking shares in a limited pot — the precise situation to which the procedures for distribution of an estate are well adapted and a single claim under the *Fatal Accidents Act* is not. Again, the underlying assumptions of 1846 become apparent. It was then assumed that the family would have, in substance, a single interest. As the definition of family for this purpose becomes looser, the scheme of a single action becomes less convenient.

6.1010 All these considerations raise a broader issue, that is, whether the concept of dependency is really useful or appropriate in the context of modern family relationships. In fact, *Lord Campbell's Act* did not use the word "dependant"; dependency has never been a strict requirement for recovery.[294] Financial loss caused by the death is the test and from the earliest cases it has been held that an earner can recover for the loss of a spouse's household services. Yet it cannot be doubted that in the social context of 1846, the Act was seen as designed to benefit widows and children, and courts and writers have always used the words "dependants" and "dependency" in discussing the Act and calculating the amount recoverable. In modern times, however, it is often not obvious that one spouse is dependent upon the other and the decline of the concept of dependency calls into question the soundness of the concept of enabling one spouse to collect damages for the death of the other. In 1846 there was a general consensus that a wife suffered a financial loss

293 See 6.740, *supra*.
294 See 6.30, *supra*.

on the death of her husband. Today, the *Fatal Accidents Act* requires the court in calculating damages for the loss of a spouse to venture into territory where any social consensus is conspicuous by its absence. The difficulties are illustrated not only by the matters already discussed, but by the most basic calculation of all — the annual value of the dependency. This is usually calculated by deducting from the net income of the deceased money that would have been spent on the deceased, and savings. But where the claimant also has earnings, it is not clear whether the claimant's own maintenance is deemed to come first from the claimant's own earnings, enhancing the deceased's savings, or whether the claimant can claim support as a first charge on the deceased's income, allocating earnings to savings. It seems very artificial for the result to turn on the particular manner in which the claimant and the deceased during their life together chose to allocate their income to current expenses. There is also the difficult problem of how to treat the claimant's future earning capacity.[295] In short, the assumption that the loss of earning power of one spouse automatically affects the future wealth of the other is not always justified where both are earners and is likely to be less often justified in the future. A claim under *Lord Campbell's Act* may require assertion of a dependency that the claimant might vigorously have repudiated during the deceased's lifetime. Many recent family law cases have preferred the analogy of partnership to that of dependency. Yet there is a decision specifically rejecting a claim under *Lord Campbell's Act* for loss of business income to a husband and wife partnership.[296] These problems will not disappear on the repeal of *Lord Campbell's Act*, for the extent of the estate's recovery will vary in response to some of these questions. But a claim against the deceased's estate by a survivor not requiring the assertion or proof of dependency will, it is suggested, ease the task of the courts and fit better into modern family law.

6.1020 Where the person killed was resident in the home, the problem arises of valuation of household services.[297] The solution is not obvious but, it is suggested, there is merit in a single rule that will lead to the same valuation whether the housekeeper is permanently disabled or killed outright. This would have the advantage of simplicity, would avoid the difficult question of whether loss to the housekeeper is the same as loss to the spouse, and also would put the problem in the wider context of valuation of lost working capacity of non-earners.

6.1030 This approach is in keeping with the modern view that an injured person's loss is that person's own loss not anyone else's. Thus the old actions by a husband for loss of his wife's services are everywhere now regarded as obsolete.[298] Most people would say that the loss to an injured

295 See 6.700-6.730, *supra*.

296 See 6.40, *supra*.

297 See 3.800-3.830, 6.280-6.300, *supra*.

298 Repealed by, *e.g.*, *Dower and Miscellaneous Abolition Act* (Ont.), s. 69(3).

housekeeper is that person's own loss not the spouse's. It follows naturally that, if the person dies, the loss is the estate's loss and still not the spouse's. Again the assumptions of 1846 are apparent. It was then taken for granted that a husband had a right to his wife's services and that a wife had a right to her husband's support. Like the action for loss of services, these assumptions are based on a pattern of family relationships that can no longer be taken for granted.

6.1040 A number of other benefits would flow from amalgamating the claims. The special statutory provisions requiring the exclusion of insurance benefits and pension benefits and the problems of their interpretation[299] would disappear. The need to evaluate the benefits received by a fatal accidents claimant from the deceased's estate (often a complex and contentious procedure) would be eliminated.[300] The procedural rules designed to avoid a multiplicity of suits by the various claimants would be unnecessary and the problem of division of the proceeds among them would also disappear. This last question raises another thorny issue, that is, the division between adult claimant (usually a widow) and dependent children. Do the children recover in their own right for their full expected benefits or is it to be assumed that their dependency is transferred to the surviving spouse who should recover the damages representing the children's support? The one view may imply a distrust of the reliability of the adult claimant; the other may do an injustice to the children.[301]

6.1050 From the beginning, *Lord Campbell's Act* which created an independent right in the statutory claimants has included important elements that can only be explained by a theory that the claim is derived from the deceased's own rights. Thus, the action depended on the deceased's having been entitled to sue,[302] and if the deceased settled or secured a judgment before death,[303] the claimant's action was defeated, as also if the deceased lost an action or allowed it to become time barred.[304] The action

---

299 See 6.450-6.500, *supra*.

300 See 6.400-6.440, *supra*.

301 See 6.740, 6.750, *supra*.

302 See *Re Butler Trucking Co. and Brydges* (1984), 10 D.L.R. (4th) 275 at p. 278, 46 O.R. (2d) 686 (Div. Ct.) ("purely a derivative action depending on the entitlement of the deceased to personally maintain an action").

303 *Read v. Great Eastern Ry. Co.* (1868), L.R. 3 Q.B. 555; *Conrod v. The King* (1914), 49 S.C.R. 577 (release agreed before accident); *Pickett v. British Rail Engineering Ltd.*, [1980] A.C. 136 (H.L.). But in *Gray v. Cotic* (1981), 124 D.L.R. (3d) 641, 33 O.R. (2d) 356 (C.A.), affd [1983] 2 S.C.R. 2, 1 D.L.R. (4th) 187, the Ontario Court of Appeal, without citing these cases, held that the action was not barred by settlement in the deceased's lifetime. Now that it is established that recovery by the injured person is based on pre-accident life expectancy (see 3.910-3.930, *supra*), it seems that *Gray v. Cotic* potentially allows a double recovery. In *Trawford v. British Columbia Electric Ry. Co. (No. 2)* (1913), 9 D.L.R. 817, the British Columbia Court of Appeal assumed that payment under an ineffective settlement made by the defendant during the deceased's lifetime would reduce liability *pro tanto*, and the same would apply, it seems, to partial payments.

304 *Williams v. Mersey Docks & Harbour Board*, [1905] 1 K.B. 804 (C.A.). See *British Columbia Electric Ry. Co. Ltd. v. Gentile*, [1914] A.C. 1034 (P.C.), at pp. 1041-2.

had to be a single action only brought in the name of the deceased's personal representative and was liable to reduction for the deceased's contributory negligence. All these factors are inconsistent with the notion of an entirely independent action vested in the claimants personally.

6.1060 The considerations discussed here suggest that the interests of dependants can, even when they are not beneficiaries of the estate, be protected by giving them claims against the estate and that the preservation of *Lord Campbell's Act* is likely to involve the courts and the legislature in a continuing series of tendentious and inconclusive debates on highly controversial questions. Of course, where individual or social justice requires it, neither judge nor legislator should hesitate to grapple with controversial issues. But where another route lies open that promises equal justice with greater simplicity, comprehensibility, and public acceptance, it can make a strong claim to the greater social attractiveness.

6.1070 A critic might admit these advantages but argue that they can be purchased only at a cost, namely, allowing a windfall to the estate where there are no dependants, and that the cost is too high. Admittedly, defendants will have, in some cases, to pay more than formerly. But it is clear from *Gammell v. Wilson* that the sums involved will be modest. In *Gammell v. Wilson* it was held that the entire estimated future living expenses of the deceased are deducted in calculating the net annual loss. In the case of a person with no dependants, the expenses are to be estimated on the basis of a single person living alone. That is to say, only the anticipated savings out of income will form the basis of the award. This approach ensures that awards for children and young single persons will be moderate while permitting an increase in the award for the benefit of dependants or other persons eligible to claim from the estate.[305] The larger of the two awards considered in *Gammell v. Wilson* was based on a sum of £19,000 for a lifetime's lost earnings, a figure reached on the assumption of savings of one-quarter of net income. Future awards are likely to be lower,[306] for several of the law lords commented that the award was high and savings of one-quarter of net income would be higher than average. The estates of younger children will receive lower awards, discounted for contingencies and advance payment.[307] An award to the estate of a young person of, say, $20,000 does not seem astonishingly

305 See *Harris v. Empress Motors Ltd.*, [1984] 1 W.L.R. 212 (C.A.); *Toneguzzo-Norvell (Guardian ad Litem of) v. Burnaby Hospital*, [1994] 1 S.C.R. 114, 110 D.L.R. (4th) 289; *Brooks v. Stefura* (2000), 192 D.L.R. (4th) 40 (Alta. C.A.); *Duncan Estate v. Baddeley* (2000), 192 D.L.R. (4th) 53 (Alta. C.A.).

306 In *MacDonald v. Sutcliffe*, The Times, March 6, 1982, damages of £6,722 were awarded against a murderer of a young unmarried woman; £5,000 represented the lost earning capacity. See also *Adsett v. West* [1983] Q.B. 826 (15% saving assumed).

307 See *Connolly v. Camden and Islington Area Health Authority*, [1981] 3 All E.R. 250 (Q.B.), where Comyn J. held that damages were available to a young child in respect of the lost years but assessed them, on the material before him in that case, at nil.

high. It would be unlikely to seem so to the ordinary person who, it was said by the Pearson Commission, is more apt to be shocked by the absence of liability for the wrongful death of children.[308] Nor would it trouble the insurance industry, being a moderate and readily predictable figure.

6.1080 Suggestions of introducing an award for grief or loss of society ensuing on wrongful death which accompanied recent English proposals[309] to reverse *Gammell v. Wilson* show that there is public support for increased rather than diminished recovery for survivors. An open-ended award for loss of society would be very difficult to assess or to predict. A fixed conventional sum, as proposed by the Pearson Commission and adopted in some jurisdictions,[310] seems arbitrary and might even be considered insulting. Indeed the whole concept of money for loss of society seems more distasteful than the idea of survival of an action for the deceased person's own loss. *Gammell v. Wilson* did not, of course, set out to solve this problem. Nevertheless, its effect is that in the ordinary case of the wrongful death of a child, the parents succeed to a moderate sum of money. This seems, as it happens, as good a solution as is likely to be found to the problem of compensation for grief or loss of society. The provisions of the Ontario *Family Law Act*, allowing unlimited compensation to each relative eligible to claim for loss of care, guidance, and companionship, may well turn out to be more expensive to insurers and so to the premium-paying public than recovery by the estate of the deceased's lost earning capacity. It is suggested that other Canadian jurisdictions should adopt the latter course.

6.1090 *Gammell v. Wilson* has been subjected to a barrage of criticism, commencing with the apologetic speeches of the law lords themselves, and continuing in the learned journals and even in the daily press. The government's decision to introduce legislation reversing its effect was announced almost immediately. But, it is suggested, *Gammell v. Wilson* points in a direction that deserves further exploration.[311] In Canadian jurisdictions where the survival of actions legislation permits it,[312] it is submitted that *Gammell v. Wilson* should be followed. When it is seen that survivors are regularly and satisfactorily compensated by claims against the deceased's estate, the way will be open to propose the repeal of the fatal accidents legislation. In Ontario and Prince Edward Island where the fatal accidents legislation has been revised in terms that may exclude the

---

308 *Report of the Royal Commission on Civil Liability and Compensation for Personal Injury* (London, H.M.S.O., 1978), §370.

309 See government proposals in 131 New L.J. 228 (1981); *Administration of Justice Act 1982* (U.K.).

310 *Fatal Accidents Act* (Alta.), s. 8(2); *Administration of Justice Act 1982* (U.K.).

311 The Ontario Law Reform Commission proposed that an action for damages for personal injuries should survive to the injured person's estate (*Report on Compensation for Personal Injuries and Death*, 1987).

312 See 12.170-12.210, *infra*. But see *Balkos Estate v. Cook* (1990), 75 O.R. (2d) 593, 41 O.A.C. 151, 40 E.T.R. 1 (C.A.); *MacLean v. MacDonald* (2002), 211 D.L.R. (4th) 474 (N.S.C.A.), at p. 503.

case where the deceased would have had an action for breach of contract[313] (*e.g.*, a case of death caused by a defective product sold in breach of warranty), it is particularly important to preserve the possibility of an action by the deceased's estate for this will be the only means available to secure compensation to survivors for the deceased's lost earning capacity.

313 See 6.10, *supra*.

CHAPTER 7

LOSS OF MONEY

1. Debt and Damages

7.10 There is an important distinction between debt and damages; in an action on a debt the plaintiff claims money that is owed as money. The law of damages is concerned with the assessment of money compensation for legal wrongs — the translation, so to speak, of a legal wrong into a money sum. But in the case of a debt there is no translation to be done. To say that the debt is due is to say that the amount of the debt is recoverable. Difficult questions may of course arise as to whether a debt is or is not due, but these are usually considered to be of concern to the substantive law from which the debt arises rather than to the law of damages.

7.20 This distinction cannot be rigidly adhered to, however. Some kinds of debts raise questions that are closely related to matters of concern to the law of damages. Foreign currency obligations are one example. These are discussed in this chapter. Another example is liquidated damages, a topic discussed in the next chapter.[1] A third kind of problem arises in cases where a contracting party performs acts which the other party considers unreasonable in order to bring a debt into existence. This problem, though turning on the construction of the contract, is closely related to questions of mitigation and is discussed later in that context.[2] Compensation for use of money in the form of interest or otherwise also straddles the borderline between debt and damages.[3]

2. Nominalism and Inflation

7.30 The principle of nominalism epitomized in the dictum that "a dollar is a dollar", though at first sight unrealistic in an inflationary period is, as F.A. Mann has shown, citing authorities from several countries, an essential part of every stable monetary system.[4] Money does not have an intrinsic value in terms of any metal or other commodity. Dr. Mann writes: "As the unit of account e.g. the pound sterling, is not identical with a quantity of metal the obligation to pay pounds cannot be equiparated to an obligation to deliver a certain weight of metal."[5] Nor does money have an intrinsic value in terms of buying power: "Moreover the extent of monetary obligations is independent

1 See 8.10-8.340, *infra*.
2 See 15.400-15.650, *infra*.
3 See 7.330-7.1000, *infra*.
4 Mann, *The Legal Aspect of Money*, 5th ed. (Oxford, University Press, 1992).
5 *Ibid.*, at p. 87.

of any *functional* or exchange value of money, i.e. its purchasing power."[6] Scrutton L.J. said in *The "Baarn"*:[7] "A pound in England is a pound whatever its international value."[8] Denning L.J. in *Treseder-Griffin v. Co-operative Ins. Society*[9] said: "A man who stipulates for a pound must take a pound when payment is made, whatever the pound is worth at that time."[10]

7.40 It is indeed difficult to see how any other principle could operate in respect of debts, because certainly in modern times the declining value of currency is well known to the parties at the time of their transaction. If they stipulate for payment of a certain sum of money on a date five years in the future, it is obvious that the debtor gets an advantage from the decline in value of the money. But that is presumably obvious to the creditor as well and so it must be taken that the anticipated advantage has been allowed for in the terms of the contract, as by an agreed interest rate, or by index or escalation clauses, or else by stipulating for payment of a larger nominal sum five years in the future than would have been required in a period of monetary stability. If this is so, the debtor has paid for the benefit of the change in the value of money and it would be most unjust, except perhaps in the case of a complete monetary breakdown, to remove the benefit by revaluing the debtor's obligation.

7.50 Well-known and well-understood devices are available to protect creditors from the effects of nominalism. In former times gold clauses were common whereby the debtor's obligation was linked to the current value of gold bullion or gold coin.[11] In 1939 these were made illegal in Canada.[12] But equally effective devices are freely available and commonly used, such as linking payments to an agreed index like the cost of living index[13] or to the value of a named foreign currency.[14] Escalation clauses and short repayment periods for loans are other common methods. If the creditor does not stipulate for such a protection, it can legitimately be assumed that, in the absence of some vitiating factor like mistake or unconscionability, the creditor has taken the risk of a decline in the value of money, up to the date when payment falls due.

---

6 *Op. cit.*, footnote 4, at p. 87.

7 [1933] P. 251 (C.A.).

8 *Supra*, at p. 265.

9 [1956] 2 Q.B. 127 (C.A.).

10 *Supra*, at p. 144. See also his comments in *Re United Rys. of Havana and Regla Warehouses Ltd.*, [1961] A.C. 1007 (H.L.), at p. 1070.

11 See Mann, *op. cit.*, footnote 4, at pp. 143-88.

12 *Gold Clauses Act*, s. 7.

13 *Multiservice Bookbinding Ltd. v. Marden*, [1979] Ch. 84 at p. 104.

14 *Supra*.

7.60 It has been argued that there are good reasons for crystallizing a damages claim at a fixed sum at an early date.[15] In summary, the argument is that an early crystallization reduces the distorting effect of pending litigation on the plaintiff's investment decisions. Delay in payment of the crystallized sum can, it has been suggested, more conveniently be compensated by interest than by delaying the date for damage assessment.

7.70 In several recent cases, Canadian courts have been pressed to adjust damage awards to take account of inflation between the date of the wrong and the date of judgment.[16] The argument is that if the defendant causes a loss in 1980 for which the just measure of compensation would then be $100,000, the defendant ought, at the date of judgment in 1982, to pay $125,000 if that is the sum of money having the same purchasing power in 1982 as $100,000 would have had in 1980. This argument has been rejected by the British Columbia Court of Appeal in *McCaig v. Reys*[17], the Ontario Court of Appeal in *Leitch Transport Ltd. v. Neonex Int'l Ltd.*[18] and the Alberta Court of Appeal in *Miller v. Riches*.[19] The conclusion reached in these cases is, it is submitted, sound. Certainly some protection is required for the plaintiff. The question is whether an allowance for inflation is the most convenient method. It is submitted that the person entitled to damages can be adequately protected by an award of interest. Courts have power to award interest on damages at commercial rates and though interest rates do not usually exactly match inflation, they reflect inflationary expectations. It would certainly be over-compensatory for a plaintiff to recover both interest at commercial rates from the date of the wrong and, in addition, an allowance to adjust the damages for inflation.[20] The Ontario Court of Appeal in the *Leitch Transport*[21] case relied upon the difficulties of fixing and applying an acceptable measure of inflation and suggested that a reasonable business person would not have foreseen the sharp decline in the purchasing

---

15 See 1.650-1.1100, *supra*.

16 In *Hatch v. Fillmore* (1968), 1 D.L.R. (3d) 475 (N.S. Co. Ct.) and in *Stephens v. Gulf Oil Canada Ltd.* (1974), 45 D.L.R. (3d) 161, 3 O.R. (2d) 241 (H.C.J.), an allowance was made. The point was not decided on reversal by the Court of Appeal, 65 D.L.R. (3d) 193, 11 O.R. (2d) 129. An allowance was refused in *McCaig v. Reys* (1978), 90 D.L.R. (3d) 13 (B.C.C.A.); *Genessee Holdings Ltd. v. West York Motors Canada Ltd.* (1978), 6 C.P.C. 63 (Ont. C.A.); *Leitch Transport Ltd. v. Neonex Int'l Ltd.* (1976), 106 D.L.R. (3d) 315, 27 O.R. (2d) 363 (C.A.). An allowance for increased building costs was refused in *Inder Lynch Devoy & Co. v. Subritzky*, [1979] 1 N.Z.L.R. 87 (C.A.).

17 *Supra*, footnote 16.

18 *Supra*, footnote 16.

19 (1984), 5 D.L.R. (4th) 1, 50 A.R. 92 (C.A.).

20 See 7.660-7.730, *infra*. The Manitoba Law Reform Commission has proposed that damage awards be adjusted for inflation but with prejudgment interest limited to three per cent: *Prejudgment Compensation on Money Awards: Alternatives to Interest*, No. 47, 1982.

21 *Supra*, footnote 16, at pp. 324-5 D.L.R.

power of money. These reasons are not, it is submitted, very convincing. An index of inflation could quite readily be chosen and the difficulties of application could be surmounted; further, nothing is more foreseeable than continuing inflation; indeed, that point was advanced above as one of the reasons for *not* revaluing debts. Evidently the court itself was a little uncertain of the force of its arguments because it added: "Since we are bound by authority in this Province to disallow the claim for an allowance for inflation, we are not required to answer these very difficult questions."[22] This sounds like a reluctant conclusion with an invitation to the Supreme Court of Canada to consider a change in the law. However, it is submitted that the conclusion of the Ontario Court of Appeal is sound. The plaintiff's complaint is in substance that the use of the money that would have been paid if prompt recompense had been made has been lost for, had it been paid promptly, the plaintiff could have guarded against inflation by capital investment or by investment at commercial interest rates. The award of interest, with the discretion of the court, as under the Ontario *Courts of Justice Act*, to vary the rate up or down from the prime rate if appropriate, provides, it is submitted, the fairest and most convenient way of compensating the plaintiff for the loss.

3. Foreign Currency Obligations

7.80 In a period of rapidly changing international exchange rates, rules governing conversion of foreign money obligations become important. When a foreign currency obligation is enforced in Canada there must, at some point, be a conversion of foreign money into Canadian dollars. Even if judgment is actually given in a foreign currency, as is now possible in England,[23] a conversion into the domestic currency is required for purposes of levying execution.[24] Even if a foreign currency obligation should be enforced by equitable means such as receivership or sequestration, a point of time would usually come at which the receiver or sequestrator has to make conversion for the purpose of determining how many of the defendant's receipts or assets should be taken.

7.90 Possible dates for conversion include the date of the wrong, the date of the institution of the action, the date of judgment and the date of actual payment.

7.100 Before 1970 it was thought to be firmly established law in England[25] and Canada[26] that the "breach date" rule applied in such circumstances.

---

22 *Leitch Transport, supra*, footnote 16, at p. 325 D.L.R. The authority referred to is the oral judgment in *Genessee Holdings Ltd. v. West York Motors Canada Ltd., supra*, footnote 16, in which the point was discussed only very briefly.

23 *Miliangos v. George Frank (Textiles) Ltd.*, [1976] A.C. 443 (H.L.).

24 *Supra*, at pp. 468-9. See Practice Direction, [1976] 1 W.L.R. 83.

25 *Re United Rys. of Havana and Regla Warehouses Ltd.*, [1961] A.C. 1007 (H.L.).

26 *Custodian v. Blucher*, [1927] S.C.R. 420, [1927] 3 D.L.R. 40; *Gatineau Power Co. v. Crown Life Ins. Co.*, [1945] S.C.R. 655, [1945] 4 D.L.R. 1; *Presse v. Serra* (1985), 52

Not only did judgment have to be given in the domestic currency, but conversion had to take place at the date of default. The argument for this view is that the damage complained of is done to the plaintiff on the date of default; the cause of action arises at that date, and the remedy is the amount that would then have been recovered had instant justice been done. The delay between default and judgment can be fully compensated by an adequate award of interest. The creditor ought not to throw upon the debtor the risk of currency fluctuations; the creditor could have mitigated the loss in the case of a depreciating domestic currency by hedging against the change in exchange rates. Against this, it can be argued that the creditor is entitled to be made whole according to the facts as they appear at the time of judgment. It is by the debtor's default that the creditor is being compelled to bear the undesired risk of a decline in the domestic currency. Mitigation of loss by currency speculation is often impracticable and may be illegal.

7.110 In 1976 the House of Lords, reversing the former law, accepted these last arguments and held that an English court could make an award of damages expressed in foreign currency.[27] In a remarkable speech, Lord Wilberforce clearly indicated that considerations of justice and commercial convenience ought to prevail over legal precedent. He said:

> But if I am faced with the alternative of forcing commercial circles to fall in with a legal doctrine which has nothing but precedent to commend it or altering the doctrine so as to conform with what commercial experience has worked out, I know where my choice lies. The law should be responsive as well as, at times, enunciatory, and good doctrine can seldom be divorced from sound practice.[28]

At a later point in his speech he said:

> The law on this topic is judge-made: it has been built up over the years from case to case. It is entirely within this House's duty, in the course of administering justice, to give the law a new direction in a particular case where, on principle and in reason, it appears right to do so.[29]

7.120 In Canada the question is complicated by the *Currency Act*[30] which provides:

> 12. All public accounts established or maintained in Canada shall be in the currency of Canada, and any reference to money or monetary value in any indictment or other legal proceedings shall be stated in the currency of Canada.

N. & P.E.I.R. 87 (P.E.I.S.C.). But see *Smith v. Canadian Pacific Ry Co.* (1963), 41 D.L.R. (2d) 249 (Sask. Q.B.) (damages for personal injuries awarded in United States currency).

27 *Miliangos, supra*, footnote 23.

28 *Supra*, footnote 22, at p. 464.

29 *Supra*, footnote 22, at p. 469.

30 R.S.C. 1985, c. C-52, s. 12.

7.130 The Ontario *Courts of Justice Act* provides that conversion should be made at the date of payment, with power in the court to fix another date if the date of payment would be inequitable.[31]

7.140 Several Canadian cases have declined to apply the *Miliangos* approach.[32] Others, however, have followed *Miliangos* to the extent of converting the foreign currency at the date of judgment.[33] The Supreme Court of Canada has left the matter open.[34]

7.150 The weight of Canadian authority is that s. 12 of the *Currency Act* requires judgments to be given in Canadian dollars. It would seem, however, that the section does not prevent a court from giving judgment in the following form: "The defendants shall pay such a sum in Canadian dollars as shall at the date of payment be equal to [a named sum in a foreign currency]."[35] This is the approach of s. 121 of the Ontario *Courts of Justice Act* and it would be possible for other Canadian jurisdictions to make similar orders even in the absence of statutory assistance. It is true that such an order would raise certain procedural problems but these would be no more difficult than those successfully overcome in England where judgments are actually given in foreign currency. A Practice Direction[36] was issued soon after the *Miliangos* case explaining in detail how execution was to be levied on judgments in foreign currency. A similar procedure could, it would seem, be evolved by Canadian courts to enforce an order such as is here contemplated if it were clear that justice required that result.

---

31 Section 121.

32 *Am-Pac Forest Products v. Phoenix Doors Ltd.* (1979), 14 B.C.L.R. 63, 12 C.P.C. 97 (S.C.); *Farmer's National Bank v. Coles* (1981), 33 N.B.R. (2d) 248 (Q.B.); *Agrex S.A. v. Canadian Dairy Commission* (1984), 24 B.L.R. 206 (F.C.T.D.); *N.V. Bocimer S.A. v. Century Insurance Co. of Canada* (1984), 53 N.R. 383, 7 C.C.L.I. 165 (F.C.A.), revd on other grounds [1987] 1 S.C.R. 1247, 39 D.L.R. (4th) 465; *Kruger Inc. v. Baltic Shipping Co.*, [1988] 1 F.C. 262, 11 F.T.R. 80 (T.D.), affd 57 D.L.R. (4th) 498 (C.A.).

33 *Williams & Glyn's Bank Ltd. v. Belkin Packaging Ltd.* (1979), 108 D.L.R. (3d) 585, 18 B.C.L.R. 279 (S.C.), revd on other grounds 123 D.L.R. (3d) 612, 28 B.C.L.R. 96 (C.A.), affd [1983] S.C.R. 661, 147 D.L.R. (3d) 577; *Prasad v. Frandsen* (1985), 60 B.C.L.R. 343 (S.C.); *Salzburger Sparkasse v. Total Plastics Services Inc.* (1988), 50 D.L.R. (4th) 639, [1988] 6 W.W.R. 408 (B.C.S.C.); *Dino Music AG v. Quality Dino Entertainment Ltd.*, [1994] 9 W.W.R. 137, 96 Man. R. (2d) 46 (Q.B.). See also *Gross v. Marvel Office Furniture Manufacturing Ltd.* (1979), 93 D.L.R. (3d) 342, 22 O.R. (2d) 331 (H.C.J.); *Airtemp Corp. v. Chrysler Airtemp Canada Ltd.* (1980), 121 D.L.R. (3d) 236, 31 O.R. (2d) 481 (H.C.J.), affd *loc. cit.* D.L.R. p. 240, O.R. p. 484 (Div. Ct.); *National Westminister Bank v. Burston* (1980), 28 O.R. (2d) 701, 61 C.P.C. 27 (S.C.); *Clinton v. Ford* (1982), 137 D.L.R. (3d) 281, 37 O.R. (2d) 448 (C.A.).

34 *Williams & Glyn's Bank Ltd. v. Belkin Packaging Ltd., supra*, footnote 33, 108 D.L.R. (3d) 585 at p. 593; *N.V. Bocimar S.A. v. Century Insurance Co. of Canada* (1984), *supra*, footnote 32, at pp. 468-69 D.L.R.

35 The scope and constitutionality of the section are discussed by the British Columbia Law Reform Commission in Working Paper No. 33, "Foreign Money Liabilities," 1981. See also Riordan, "The Currency of Suit in Actions for Foreign Debts", 24 McGill L.J. 422 (1978).

36 [1976] 1 W.L.R. 83. See also *Courts of Justice Act* (Ont.), s. 121(5).

7.160 The question of the power to give judgments in foreign currency is not identical with the question of what date should be chosen for

[*The next page is* 7–7]

conversion of foreign obligations into Canadian currency, but the questions are closely related. If it is concluded that judgment should be given in foreign currency, the automatic effect is to postpone conversion to the date of payment or to the date of levying of execution if that proves to be necessary. On the other hand, if it is concluded that judgment should not or cannot be given in foreign currency, the question is still open whether conversion to Canadian dollars should take place at the date of the wrong or at the date of the judgment. The arguments on this question are fairly evenly balanced and analogies are close to other areas in which the choice of date for the assessment of damages has become important. As has been shown, the cases are divided on whether Canadian courts are free to depart from the rule of assessment at the date of the wrong and, in Ontario, the court has power to depart from conversion at the date of payment where the use of that date would be "inequitable".[37] An examination of the arguments on the question is therefore of importance.

7.170 It is useful to discuss first the case where the domestic currency appreciates. A creditor is owed a debt, let us suppose, of 10,000 francs. At the date when the debt should have been paid, the exchange rate is ten francs to the dollar. If at the date of judgment the Canadian dollar has appreciated to twenty francs to the dollar, the creditor will seek conversion at the date of breach, for a recovery of $1,000. The debtor's argument against this result is that the creditor receives a windfall by obtaining judgment for enough dollars to buy 20,000 francs — twice the amount owed. On the other hand, if the Canadian dollar depreciates to five francs to the dollar, the shoe is on the other foot. It is the creditor who will seek conversion at the date of judgment on the ground that $2,000 is needed to buy the 10,000 francs owed.

7.180 These are distinct problems, as is shown by the analogy with property cases. The case of the appreciation of Canadian currency is analogous to a case where the plaintiff is wrongfully deprived of property that later diminishes in value. As was shown in an earlier chapter,[38] the conclusion here is always that the plaintiff is entitled to the value of the property at the date of the wrong even though, as a result, the plaintiff may be better off than if the wrong had not been done. This rule, it has been suggested, rests on a wise refusal to pursue too far the inquiry into what would have happened if the wrong had not been done. It is sufficient for the plaintiff to show that the plaintiff was impoverished by the defendant's wrong at the date of the wrong and the damages are the amount of that impoverishment.[39] In the foreign currency case the cred-

---

37 *Courts of Justice Act*, s. 121(3).

38 See 1.660, *supra*.

39 This point is very forcefully made by *Corbin on Contracts* (St. Paul, West Publishing Co., 1964), §1005: "[The judgment date rule] results in a severe loss to the creditor and is in direct conflict with our most fundamental rule as to compensatory damages."

itor is, in effect, a buyer of foreign currency complaining of non-delivery. There is a strong argument for allowing recovery of the value of the currency when it should have been delivered. Had the currency been paid promptly the plaintiff would have invested it in some way; the plaintiff might have converted it promptly into Canadian dollars, gold, or some other asset that would have resisted the depreciation of the currency of payment. The plaintiff might have used the money to meet business expenses that would have led to profits that would have resisted the fall in the value of that currency. In *Miliangos v. George Frank (Textiles) Ltd.*,[40] Lord Simon of Glaisdale, dissenting, put a dramatic example of a foreign seller delivering valuable goods to an English buyer, which the buyer refuses to pay for until after the collapse of the foreign currency, when the latter tenders a truck-load of worthless foreign banknotes.[41] This example stresses both the potential unfairness to the creditor and the unjust enrichment of the debtor when the breach date rule is departed from in such a case. In *Re Dawson*,[42] an action against a trustee who had misappropriated trust funds in foreign currency, it was suggested (though the question did not arise for decision) that in the case of a depreciation in the foreign currency, the trust beneficiaries would be entitled to claim the amount of the funds in domestic currency measured at the date of the misappropriation.

7.190 In *Quartier v. Farah*,[43] the Ontario Appellate Division held that a French lawyer, suing for the amount of his fee after the decline of the French currency, was not entitled to damages measured by conversion at the date of breach, but was entitled only to the lesser amount converted at the date of judgment. The court stressed that the plaintiff was entitled only to the nominal sum owed to him in francs and pointed out that the defendant might have effectively tendered this amount in France or satisfied a French judgment by paying that amount.[44] However, it may be said in reply to this point that expectations of weakening currency will often give rise to rules designed to protect creditors in such circumstances, so that the foreign law in such cases might well make provision for the creditor to recover a high rate of interest and a tender might well be held to be insufficient if it did not include interest up to the date of the tender. Such are now the rules in Canada protecting domestic creditors with respect to purely domestic claims.[45] But whether or not such rules would protect the creditor in the particular foreign country cannot be determinative of the proper remedy in the Canadian court. If general considerations of justice favour recovery

40 [1976] A.C. 443 (H.L.).
41 *Supra*, at pp. 488-9.
42 [1966] 2 N.S.W.R. 211 (S.C.), at p. 220, *per* Street J.
43 (1921), 64 D.L.R. 37, 49 O.L.R. 186 (S.C. App. Div.).
44 *Supra*, at pp. 47-8 D.L.R.
45 See 7.740, 7.750, *infra*.

of the breach date sum, it cannot be an answer that the creditor would have fared worse had the creditor sued in a foreign jurisdiction.[46]

7.200 The case of *Quartier v. Farah* has been rarely cited and probably was considered to have been impliedly overruled by later Supreme Court of Canada decisions adopting the breach date rule.[47] The uncertainty introduced by the varied reactions to the *Miliangos* case now makes it arguable that *Quartier v. Farah* should be followed. It is here submitted, however, that on general principles the creditor's arguments are the stronger and that the breach date rule should be preserved in case of appreciation of Canadian currency.

7.210 It is not entirely clear whether the *Miliangos* case preserves the creditor's right in England to conversion at the date of breach where that is advantageous. The *Miliangos* case did not expressly say that the creditor was ever to be *compelled* to accept judgment in foreign currency. Indeed, Lord Wilberforce said that a creditor who wants judgment in foreign currency must specifically request it in the pleadings.[48]

7.220 On the other hand there are some indications the other way. Lord Wilberforce emphasized that the creditor's concern was with the value of the foreign currency "for good or ill".[49] Lord Simon of Glaisdale in his dissenting speech gave a dramatic example of the collapse of a foreign currency, apparently assuming that the acceptance of the majority view carried with it the implication that the creditor would be restricted to recovery in the now worthless foreign money.[50] The English Law Commission assumed in a working paper that a creditor would be compelled, in some cases at least, to accept judgment in a foreign currency.[51]

7.230 In *Ozalid Group (Export) Ltd. v. African Continental Bank Ltd.*,[52] the defendant delayed in paying a sum of United States dollars to the plaintiff. The plaintiff, by exchange control regulations, was obliged to convert all United States dollars promptly into sterling and would have done so if the money had been duly paid. Sterling appreciated against the dollar during the period of the delay, and the plaintiff claimed the loss in sterling caused by the relative decline in the value of the dollar. It was held that the plaintiff was entitled to compensation for this loss. Donaldson J. said:

---

46 This point is made by Corbin, *op. cit.* footnote 39: "It is true that this 'severe loss' is one that he would have had to suffer if he had brought his suit in the country where payment was to be made in the currency of that country . . . . But if he can and does sue for just reparation in the courts of the United States, there is nothing that requires us to adopt the remedial system of another country."

47 *Custodian v. Blucher*, [1927] S.C.R. 420, [1927] 3 D.L.R. 40; *Gatineau Power Co. v. Crown Life Ins. Co.*, [1945] S.C.R. 655, [1945] 4 D.L.R. 1.

48 *Supra*, footnote 40, at p. 468.

49 *Supra*, at p. 466.

50 *Supra*, at pp. 488-9.

51 Law Commission, *Private International Law: Foreign Money Liabilities*, Working Paper No. 80 (London, H.M.S.O., 1981).

52 [1979] 2 Lloyd's Rep. 231 (Q.B.).

> I can find no trace in the speeches [in *Miliangos*] of any intention to make a claim in this form [in foreign currency] obligatory. The overriding reason for changing the law was to provide a procedure which would enable the courts to compensate the plaintiff in full for the wrong which he had suffered. A change which *required* the plaintiff to claim in foreign currency and to accept sterling at the rate prevailing at the date of judgment could in some circumstances work as great an injustice as the old procedure requiring him to claim in sterling and to adopt the date of breach rate of exchange. (His italics.)[53]

He added, however, "but this is not to say that a plaintiff has a free choice" and he went on to say that in this case it was sterling that would "most truly express his loss and accordingly most fully and exactly compensate him for that loss."[54] He subsequently cited a case in which he said that the plaintiff would now be "required" to make the claim in francs.[55] It appears from this that, while the plaintiff does not have a "free choice", the plaintiff can seek to persuade the court that it is not the foreign currency that "would most truly express his loss and most fully and exactly compensate him", in which case the plaintiff will be allowed the benefit of breach date conversion. An alternative explanation of the case favoured by the English Law Commission in its working paper on foreign money liabilities is that the judgment should be regarded not as a judgment for a debt but as one for the compensation for loss caused by delay in payment — a loss that was, in the circumstances, within the defendant's contemplation.[56]

7.240 It is, of course, often possible to reach similar results by different legal routes. A creditor to whom an obligation is owed in foreign currency may, it seems, be protected against depreciation of the currency on several theories. The creditor might be permitted to take advantage of the breach date rate of exchange; the creditor might persuade the court that although the money of account was foreign the domestic currency "most truly expressed" the loss; the creditor might recover damages as compensation for the loss caused by the debtor's failure to make prompt payment. A fourth possibility is that the creditor might recover interest at a rate that compensated for the depreciation in value of the foreign currency.[57] Any of these theories might yield the same result though there are significant differences in onus of proof and in the operation of the rules of remoteness. It appears that the law in England after the *Miliangos* case is that the creditor, when the foreign currency depreciates, has no automatic right to elect conversion into sterling at the date of breach, but if the creditor can

---

53 *Supra*, at pp. 233-4.

54 *Supra*, at p. 234.

55 *Supra*, citing *Société des Hôtels Le Touquet Paris-Plage v. Cummings*, [1922] 1 K.B. 451 (C.A.).

56 *Supra*, footnote 51, at p. 108.

57 See 7.830-7.860, *infra*.

prove an actual loss that the defendant should have contemplated, the equivalent result may be attained under another theory.

7.250 Where Canadian currency depreciates between the date of wrong and the date of judgment, the problem is analogous to that of a purchaser of property that increases in value in the same period. The plaintiff's argument is that had the wrong not been done the plaintiff would now (that is at the date of judgment) be in possession of property more valuable than at the date of the wrong. As has been seen, the general rule in property cases is in favour of assessment at the earliest date after the wrong at which the plaintiff, acting reasonably, could have replaced the property, though there have been some recent inroads on that principle.[58] In the context of a foreign currency debt the application of the general principle would lead to a denial of the creditor's claim for judgment date conversion and, by stronger reasoning, of a claim for judgment actually expressed in foreign currency. The creditor's argument that there is undercompensation unless the creditor recovers sufficient money to pay the debt now in the foreign currency would be met by the argument that the loss flowing from the depreciation of Canadian currency is not caused by the wrong; the creditor could have prevented that loss by transferring funds from Canadian into the foreign currency.

7.260 Lord Wrenbury put the comparison with the purchase of property in vivid language:

> Assume that a judge is sitting in July to try an action for damages for a tort committed on the preceding January 1. Let me express the judgment in the form of a declaration, followed by an adjudication upon it. The judgment should, I think, be as follows: Declare that on January 1 the plaintiff suffered by reason of the defendant's tort a loss of 300,000 lire. Declare that on January 1 the equivalent sum in British currency was (say) 7500*l*. Adjudge that the plaintiff owes the defendant 7500*l*. There is no difference in principle arising from the fact that the loss is of lire as distinguished from (say) cows. If the plaintiff had been damaged by the defendant tortiously depriving him of three cows the judgment would be: declare that on January 1 the plaintiff would have been entitled to go into the market and buy 3 similar cows and charge the defendant with the price. Declare that the cost would have been 150*l*. Adjudge that the plaintiff recover from the defendant 150*l*. It would be nihil ad rem to say that in July similar cows would have cost in the market 300*l*. The defendant is not bound to supply the plaintiff with cows. He is liable to pay him damages for having, on January 1, deprived him of cows. The plaintiff may be going out of farming and may not want cows, or, when judgment is given, he may have enough already. The plaintiff is not bound to take cows and the defendant is not bound to supply them. The defendant is liable to pay the plaintiff damages, that is to say, money to some amount

58 See 1.650-1.1110, *supra*.

> for the loss of the cows: the only question is, how much? The answer is, such sum as represents the market value at the date of the tort of the goods of which the plaintiff was tortiously deprived.[59]

Lord Wrenbury went on to say that compensation for delay in payment should be given in the form of interest: "They [that is interest] would be damages not for the original tort, but for another and a subsequent wrongful act."[60]

7.270 In *Miliangos*, Lord Wilberforce made scathing reference to Lord Wrenbury's example:

> Whereas in the case of the inevitable contract to supply a foreign cow, the intending purchaser has to be treated as going into the market to buy one as of the date of breach, this doctrine cannot be applied to a foreign money obligation, for the intending creditor has nothing to buy his own currency with — except his own currency.[61]

The application of this comment will however depend very much on the particular facts. It is undeniable that some creditors — those, for example, with bank accounts in both the relevant currencies — usually have the means to guard against currency fluctuations. Secondly, Lord Wilberforce speaks of the foreign currency as the creditor's "own currency" but this will not always be the case. Both parties to the dispute may be Canadian and the foreign currency transaction might, indeed, be purely speculative. In the latter case there seems no reason to depart from the sale analogy. Moreover, the transaction needed to protect the creditor, foreign or domestic, against a decline in Canadian currency is simpler than Lord Wilberforce suggests. All that is needed is for the creditor to borrow the requisite sum of Canadian money immediately on the debtor's default and purchase foreign currency to the amount of the debt due.[62] Then, on recovering judgment in Canada for the amount of the debt converted into Canadian currency at the date of breach, together with interest at Canadian rates, the creditor will be fully compensated. This transaction though not convenient to a private individual creditor resident abroad, would be readily available to many business creditors.

7.280 One way of testing the justice of judgment date assessment (and *a fortiori* of judgment in foreign currency) is to ask whether, supposing the plaintiff to have been protected in one of the ways described against a decline in Canadian currency, justice would be done if the creditor then recovered the sum converted at judgment date (or if judgment were given in foreign currency). Suppose a debt of 10,000 francs and a

---

59 *The "Volturno"*, [1921] 2 A.C. 544 (H.L.), at pp. 562-3.

60 *Supra*, at p. 564.

61 *Miliangos v. George Frank (Textiles) Ltd.*, [1976] A.C. 443 (H.L.), at p. 468.

62 An even simpler method, where the creditor has accounts in both currencies, is for the creditor to transfer the appropriate sum from the Canadian dollar account to the foreign currency account immediately on the occurrence of the breach.

breach date exchange rate of ten francs to the dollar. The creditor, correctly anticipating a decline in Canadian currency, immediately borrows $1,000 and buys 10,000 francs or transfers $1,000 from a Canadian dollar account to a franc account. Two years later the creditor obtains judgment when the exchange rate is five francs to the dollar. Surely the creditor is adequately compensated by an award of $1,000 plus interest at Canadian rates. Most people would say that the creditor would recover a windfall if there was judgment for $2,000 (especially if interest were added).[63] If this conclusion is correct in a case where the creditor has in fact anticipated the depreciation, there is a very strong argument of convenience for adopting it as a general rule wherever the creditor was capable of self-protection in this way. For it would be inconvenient to have a rule that required examination of the plaintiff's entire financial dealings, particularly in the case of a large enterprise, in order to determine whether or not the plaintiff had profited from the alteration in the exchange rate.

7.290 In a case where specific performance is available, a plaintiff can, in a sense, profit twice over from a rise in value if the plaintiff purchases a similar property at the date of breach. But in cases where a judgment of specific performance is given, there is rarely a perfect substitute to be found; indeed it is usually because there is no readily available substitute that damages are considered to be an inadequate remedy. In the case of money, a substitute is always available. There seems no good reason therefore to allow the creditor what is the equivalent of specific performance (that is, the value of the foreign currency owed at the date of payment) or damages in substitution for specific performance (that is, the value of the foreign currency at the date of the judgment).

7.300 The conclusion from these considerations is that Canadian courts should be cautious before departing from the breach date rule of conversion and still more cautious before adopting a rule of practice of actually ordering payment in foreign currency. In Ontario, the court should be ready to use its power to depart from the date of payment rule. No doubt there are some cases in which, as a matter of fact, the creditor could not reasonably have been protected against a decline in Canadian currency. These cases can be met, it is suggested, by a *prima facie* breach date rule, with a power to depart from it where the creditor could not reasonably have secured protection.[63a] The result reached in the *Miliangos* case may well be defensible on this basis, and for this reason a power in the court to award judgment in a foreign currency is to be welcomed. But it is suggested that any such power, whether introduced by legislation or by judicial decision, should be left unfettered by any rigid verbal formula.

---

63 See 7.830-7.860, *infra*.

63a See *Promech Sorting Systems B.V. v. Bronco Rentals & Leasing Ltd.*, [1994] 4 W.W.R. 374, 93 Man. R. (2d) 36 at p. 44 (Q.B.), revd on another point 123 D.L.R. (4th) 111 (C.A.), citing this paragraph.

The discussion in the preceding paragraphs indicates that there will be a substantial number of cases in which justice requires adherence to the breach date rule of conversion. The existence of a general power to depart from that rule would not mean that the power would be exercised arbitrarily or that principles for its exercise would not develop. An analogy may be made with the power of the court to award specific performance, which indeed has a close affinity with judgment in foreign currency. The power to award specific performance is unfettered by any rigid formula, but the courts have developed rules to govern its exercise: this enables courts to develop rational principles on a case-by-case basis while maintaining the necessary flexibility to take account of new arguments and changing circumstances.[64]

7.310 In the *Miliangos* case itself the new rule was not extended beyond contract debts. Lord Wilberforce said: "In my opinion it should be open for future discussion whether the rule applying to money obligations, which can be a simple rule, should apply as regards claims for damages for breach of contract or for tort."[65] It is, however, difficult to draw a distinction on this question between damages and debt, or between contract and tort, and a series of English cases has extended *Miliangos* to those areas.[66] In cases where there is more than one foreign currency involved, as where a shipping enterprise that keeps its accounts in francs incurs repair costs in pesos, the question arises of a choice between francs and pesos. Although this question can arise whether or not judgment is given in a foreign currency,[67] it did not normally arise under the former breach date conversion rule since at that date the relationship of each of the foreign currencies to the domestic currency was normally the same as their relationship to each other. It is departure from the breach date rule that produces problems, for in the interval between the date of the wrong and the date of conversion the relationship of the currencies to each other and to Canadian money may well have altered. In *The "Despina R."*[68] the House of Lords held that the proper currency was "the currency in which his [the plaintiff's] loss is felt". Lord Wilberforce said:

> It appears to me that a plaintiff, who normally conducts his business through a particular currency, and who, when other currencies are immediately involved, uses his own currency to obtain those currencies, can reasonably say that the loss he sustains is to be measured not by the immediate currencies in which the loss first emerges but by the amount

64 See Sharpe, *Injunctions and Specific Performance*, looseleaf ed. (Toronto, Canada Law Book, 1999).

65 *Supra*, footnote 61, at p. 468.

66 *The "Despina R."* [1979] A.C. 685 (H.L.); *Services Europe Atlantique Sud v. Stockholms Rederiaktiebolag SVEA of Stockholm, ibid.* But see *Lines Bros. Ltd.*, [1983] Ch. 1 (C.A.) (liquidation of company).

67 See *The "Canadian Transport"* (1932), 43 Ll. L.R. 409 (C.A.).

68 *Supra*, footnote 66.

of his own currency, which in the normal course of operation, he uses to obtain those currencies.[69]

7.320 Assuming that a departure is to be made from conversion at the date of the wrong, Lord Wilberforce's approach seems sound. The currency must be chosen, as Lord Wilberforce expressed it in a case decided concurrently with *The "Despina R."*, "which most truly expresses the plaintiff's loss."[70] In case of doubt Lord Wilberforce made it clear that the burden of proof was on the plaintiff to show that the enterprise really was conducted in a currency other than that of the immediate loss and that the loss had been felt in that other currency.[71] It would follow from proof of these facts that the date for conversion of the currency of immediate loss into the plaintiff's operating currency would always be at the earliest time at which, acting reasonably, the plaintiff could have transferred funds from operating currency to meet the expense. Subsequent variations in the value of the currency of initial loss either against the second foreign currency or against Canadian dollars would therefore be irrelevant.

4. Interest[72]

(1) Introduction

7.330 One who fails to pay promptly money justly due to another does the other a wrong.[73] This wrong consists of delay in payment of what is owed and is entirely separate from the question of whether the sum was owed in the first place. Thus, if liability on a debt is disputed and the debtor withholds payment for four years pending litigation, the debtor can be said (assuming liability is ultimately established) to have done the creditor two wrongs, that is, by failing to pay on the due date and by withholding payment for four years. The separation between the two kinds of wrong appears most clearly in the case of damages. If the defendant destroys the plaintiff's property and then disputes liability, finally submitting to judgment after four years' litigation, the defendant has done the plaintiff two wrongs: the defendant has destroyed the plaintiff's property and has failed to make proper recompense.[74] It is not implied, of course, that the defendant always acts maliciously or even improperly in disputing liability;[75] nevertheless when it turns out that the defence, however promising it

69 *Supra*, footnote 66, at p. 697.

70 *Services Europe Atlantique Sud, supra*, footnote 66, at p. 701, adopting a phrase used by Lord Denning M.R. in the Court of Appeal, [1979] Q.B. 491 at p. 514. See also *Société Française Bunge SA v. Belcan NV*, [1985] 3 All E.R. 378 (Q.B.); *The "Texaco Melbourne"*, [1993] 1 Lloyd's Rep. 471 (C.A.).

71 *The "Despina R.", supra*, footnote 66, at p. 699.

72 See Waldron, *The Law of Interest in Canada* (Toronto, Carswell, 1992).

73 *Ontario v. OPSEU* (1986), 34 D.L.R. (4th) 101 at p. 109, 57 O.R. (2d) 641 (H.C.J.), citing this passage, and 7.350, *infra*.

74 See *The "Amalia"* (1864), 5 New Rep. 164, *per* Dr. Lushington, and passage cited at 7.420, *infra*.

75 See *Irvington Holdings Ltd. v. Black* (1987), 35 D.L.R. (4th) 641, 58 O.R. (2d) 449 (C.A.).

may have seemed, has proven unmeritorious, it can be said to have been established that if the plaintiff's rights had been observed, first, the property would not have been destroyed and, second, immediate recompense would have been made at the date of destruction. Other ways of putting this point are that the plaintiff has been kept out of the plaintiff's money[76] and that the defendant has withheld the plaintiff's money.[77]

7.340 Often in cases of debt arising out of agreements, a right to interest after maturity will be afforded by the agreement that created the debt itself. Commonly this is done by express words. When express words are not used, problems of interpretation arise. Many of the decided cases on interest concern the question of whether parties to a contract have impliedly agreed that interest shall be payable after a default.[78] These cases are not of direct concern to a writer on damages. But they are related to the law of interest as damages, because if the general rule is that no interest is recoverable as damages it will become vital for the plaintiff claiming interest to establish an implied contractual right. On the other hand if interest is regularly given as damages for delay in payment, there will be less need for the plaintiff to strive to establish an implied agreement.[79]

7.350 Interest consists of two elements: compensation for the loss of use of money and compensation for decline in its value.[80] Consequently, in times of rapid inflation interest rates tend to be high. The loss to the plaintiff who has been deprived of money and the enrichment of the defendant who has retained it pending the resolution of the dispute are correspondingly increased. With interest rates of twenty per cent and litigation lasting for four years, the loss to the plaintiff caused by the delay will actually exceed the principal amount in issue. It is not surprising, therefore, that in recent times (when interest rates and delays in litigation have exceeded the figures mentioned), there has been a strong tendency towards permitting the recovery of interest.

---

76 *Supra*, footnote 74. In *Re Westcoast Transmission Co. Ltd. and Majestic Wiley Contractors Ltd.* (1982), 139 D.L.R. (3d) 97, [1982] 6 W.W.R. 149 (B.C.C.A.), leave to appeal to S.C.C. refused 46 N.R. 87*n*, it was held that an arbitrator had power to award interest, the *Court Order Interest Act* being part of the general law according to which disputes were to be resolved. Seaton J.A. said [at p. 101 D.L.R.], "An award in a commercial case that does not take into account the cost of money will not do justice between the parties". A similar conclusion was reached in *Re Hope and Co-operators Insurance Association* (1986), 24 D.L.R. (4th) 78, 53 O.R. (2d) 208 (Div. Ct.).

77 *Di Domenicontonio v. Finnigan* (1986), 33 D.L.R. (4th) 71 at pp. 78-9, citing this paragraph (Q.B.), revd on other grounds 40 D.L.R. (4th) 175 (C.A.), leave to appeal to S.C.C. refused 50 D.L.R. (4th) vii, 86 N.R. 264*n*. See *Apotex Inc. v. Wellcome Foundation Ltd.* (2000), 195 D.L.R. (4th) 641 (C.A.), at p. 675.

78 See the cases discussed in *London, Chatham & Dover Ry. Co. v. South Eastern Ry. Co.*, [1893] A.C. 429 (H.L.).

79 See *Niagara Air Bus Inc. v. Camerman* (1991), 80 D.L.R. (4th) 611, 3 O.R. (3d) 108 (C.A.), leave to appeal to S.C.C. refused 87 D.L.R. (4th) vii, 138 N.R. 413*n*, where the interest payable before maturity was restricted by operation of the *Interest Act* (Can.), s. 4.

80 See 3.1030, *supra*, and 7.680, *infra*.

7.360 The trend of legislation in this field has been wholly in the direction of more readily allowing interest. The provinces have varying provisions, but on the whole those in which legislation has been recently revised are those most generous to the claimant.

7.370 The position at common law is also of importance because statutes never cover all cases.[81] In considering the common law position, it is to be presumed that the common law is capable of development as it is in other areas of the law of damages. Changing social conditions, in particular the appearance of rapid inflation, have provoked changes throughout the law of damages. The same flexibility should also, it is submitted, properly be found in the area of interest.

(2) Actions against the federal Crown

7.380 The *Federal Court Act* formerly provided that no interest was payable in an action against the Crown but the Act now provides that in respect of a cause of action arising in a province, the law of that province relating to prejudgment interest applies. In respect of a cause of action arising outside any province, or in more than one province, interest is to be awarded at such rate as the court considers reasonable on liquidated claims from the date the cause of action arises and, on unliquidated claims, from the date of notice in writing.[82]

(3) Interest at common law

7.390 The leading case on interest as damages is generally taken to be *London, Chatham & Dover Ry. Co. v. South Eastern Ry. Co.*[85] The issue arose out of a dispute as to amounts due from one railway to another under a joint operating agreement. The statute then in force in England was *Lord Tenterden's Act* of 1833, which empowered the jury to award interest, in certain circumstances, on "all debts or sums certain, payable . . . by virtue of some written instrument".[86] The House of Lords held that the money due under the operating agreement did not fall within these words, because the amount due depended on the state of accounts between the parties. Further, it was held that no interest was recoverable at common law. Lord Herschell, though considering that justice required the award of interest, held that the question had been settled in *Page v. Newman*,[87] though he

---

81 See 7.390-7.440, *infra*.

82 *Federal Court Act*, s. 36. See Waldron, *op. cit.*, footnote 72, pp. 160-61.

83-4 [Text deleted.]

85 *Supra*, footnote 78.

86 *Civil Procedure Act, 1833*, s. 28. See also the comments of Morden J.A. on *Lord Tenterden's Act* in *Lister (Ronald Elwyn) Ltd. v. Dayton Tire Canada Ltd.* (1985), 52 O.R. (2d) 88 (C.A.).

87 (1829), 9 B. & C. 378, 109 E.R. 140, followed in *Hawker Industries Ltd. v. H.B. Nickerson & Sons Ltd.* (1970), 16 D.L.R. (3d) 459 (N.S.S.C.). In Newfoundland, where there was no statutory provision, it was held that interest is payable only by agreement: *Pratt Representatives (Nfld.) Ltd. v. Hostess Food Products Ltd.*, (1978), 18 Nfld. & P.E.I.R. 412 (Nfld. S.C.T.D.).

expressly said that he was dissatisfied with the reasons given in that case.[88] Of the statute he said: "Speaking for myself, they [the statutory limits] seem to be too narrow for the purposes of justice."[89] Older cases had taken a more generous view but Lord Herschell concluded: "I do not think it would be possible nowadays to reopen the question, even in this House, and to hold that interest under such circumstances could be awarded."[90]

7.400 This deference to settled law was typical of the period. Subsequently a more flexible view has prevailed. In *Trans Trust S.P.R.L. v. Danubian Trading Co.*,[91] where damages were allowed for loss caused by failure to provide a commercial credit, Denning L.J. said:

> It was said that the breach here was a failure to pay money and that the law has never allowed any damages on that account. I do not think that the law has ever taken up such a rigid standpoint. It did undoubtedly refuse to award interest until the introduction of the recent statute: see *London, Chatham and Dover Railway Co. v. South Eastern Railway Co.;* but the ground was that interest was "generally presumed not to be within the contemplation of the parties" . . . That is, I think, the only real ground on which damages can be refused for non-payment of money. It is because the consequences are as a rule too remote. But when the circumstances are such that there is a special loss foreseeable at the time of the contract as the consequence of non-payment, then I think such a loss may well be recoverable.[92]

Romer L.J. in the same case said:

> I am not, as at present advised, prepared to subscribe to the view that in no case can damages be recovered for non-payment of money; I agree with Denning L.J. that in certain circumstances such damages might well be recoverable provided that the loss occasioned to the plaintiff by the defendant's default was reasonably within the contemplation of the parties when the bargain between them was made.[93]

These dicta were taken up in *Wadsworth v. Lyddall*[94] where, because of the defendant's delay in paying money, the plaintiff was compelled to borrow. It was held that, even though the 1934 statute[95] governing interest did not apply, the plaintiff could recover the interest charges incurred as damages. The *London, Chatham & Dover* case was distinguished as not

---

88 *London, Chatham & Dover Ry. Co. v. South Eastern Ry. Co.*, [1893] A.C. 429 (H.L.), at p. 440.

89 *Supra*, at pp. 440-1.

90 *Supra*, at p. 441.

91 [1952] 2 Q.B. 297 (C.A.).

92 *Supra*, at p. 306. In *Compania Financiera Soleada SA v. Hamoor Tucker Corp. Inc.*, [1981] 1 All E.R. 856 (C.A.), extravagant interest charges incurred by the plaintiff were held to be too remote.

93 *Trans Trust S.P.R.L., supra*, footnote 91, at p. 307.

94 [1981] 1 W.L.R. 598 (C.A.), approved by the House of Lords in *President of India v. La Pintada Compania Navigacion S.A.*, [1985] A.C. 104 (H.L.). See also *President of India v. Lips Maritime Corp.*, [1988] A.C. 395 (H.L.); *Armstrong v. Canada (Attorney General)*, [1998] 6 W.W.R. 537 (Man. C.A.), at p. 543, citing this work.

95 *Law Reform (Miscellaneous Provisions) Act, 1934*.

having been concerned with a claim for special damages. Brightman L.J. said:

> . . . the House of Lords was not concerned with a claim for special damages. The action was an action for an account. The House was concerned only with a claim for interest by way of general damages. If a plaintiff pleads and can prove that he has suffered special damage as a result of the defendant's failure to perform his obligation under a contract, and such damages are not too remote on the principle of *Hadley v. Baxendale* (1854), 9 Exch. 341, [156 E.R. 145], I can see no logical reason why such special damages should be unrecoverable merely because the obligation on which the defendant defaulted was an obligation to pay money and not some other type of obligation.[96]

7.410 A very similar view has been taken in Nova Scotia where, at the time, a statute based on *Lord Tenterden's Act* was still in force. In *Atlantic Salvage Ltd. v. City of Halifax*,[97] interest was allowed on a claim against a harbour authority for services rendered in cleaning spilt oil. Cooper J.A. considered that the law of Nova Scotia differed from the law of England in 1893, relying on an earlier case where compensation had been awarded for interest charges incurred by the plaintiff, when borrowing money to repair damage for which the defendant was responsible.[98] In the *Atlantic Salvage* case, it was sufficient to found the plaintiff's claim for interest that it had "throughout the relevant period [been] indebted to its bank"[99] in a sum exceeding the amount of the claim. The net effect of these cases appears to be that interest can be allowed at common law if the plaintiff can bring the claim as one of special damages. It will, it seems, be sufficient if the claimant actually incurs interest charges by borrowing money on the defendant's default or if the plaintiff owes money to anyone equal to the amount of the claim and is paying interest on it.[100]

7.420 In Admiralty, as is so often the case on damage questions, the matter was satisfactorily settled at an early date. In *The "Amalia"* Dr. Lushington said:

> Interest is not given by reason of indemnification for the loss, for the loss was the damage which had accrued, but interest was given for this reason, namely, that the loss was not paid at the proper time. If a man is kept out of his money it is a loss in the common sense of the word, but a loss of a totally different description and clearly to be distinguished from a loss which has occurred by damage done at the moment of a collision.[101]

In *The "Pacifico" v. Winslow Marine Ry. & Shipbuilding Co.*[102] in a

---

[96] *Wadsworth v. Lyddall, supra*, footnote 94, at p. 603.

[97] (1978), 94 D.L.R. (3d) 513 (N.S.S.C. App. Div.).

[98] *Leslie R. Fairn & Associates v. Colchester Developments Ltd.* (1975), 60 D.L.R. (3d) 681 (N.S.S.C. App. Div.), followed in *Municipal Spraying & Contracting Ltd. v. J. Harris & Sons Ltd.* (1979), 35 N.S.R. (2d) 237 (S.C.T.D.), and in *Champion v. Quick-Pik Transfers Ltd.* (1981), 121 D.L.R. (3d) 720 (P.E.I.S.C.), where the plaintiff owed interest to contractors who repaired the damage for which the defendant was responsible.

[99] *Atlantic Salvage Ltd., supra*, footnote 97, at p. 528.

[100] In the *Municipal Spraying* case, *supra*, footnote 98, at p. 247, the court pointed out that it was anomalous to allow interest only to a plaintiff who had an overdraft.

[101] *The "Amalia"* (1864), 5 New Rep. 164*n*.

passage later approved by the Supreme Court of Canada,[103] Maclean, J. said:

> The principle adopted by the Admiralty Court in its equitable jurisdiction ... as founded upon the civil law, is that interest was always due to the obligee when payment was delayed by the obligor, and that, whether the obligation arose *ex contractu* or *ex delicto*. It seems that the view adopted by the Admiralty Court has been, that the person liable in debt or damages, having kept the sum which ought to have been paid to the claimant, ought to be held to have received it for the person to which the principle is payable. Damages and interest under the civil law is the loss which a person has sustained, or the gain he has missed.[104]

The Supreme Court of Canada in *Canadian General Electric Co. Ltd. v. Pickford & Black Ltd.*[105] also cited with approval a statement of Lord Esher in *The "Baron Aberdare"*[106] defending the practice of the Admiralty Division as "more just than the common law rule". There would seem to be some encouragement here for the common law to follow the lead of Admiralty.[107]

7.425 In *Hungerford v. Walker*,[107a] the Australian High Court held that compensation for loss of use of money was available at common law and in *Bank of America Canada v. Mutual Trust Co.*[107b] the Supreme Court of Canada, in holding there was power at common law to award compound interest, established by implication that simple interest also would, in an appropriate case, be awarded at common law. The House of Lords came to a

---

[102] [1925] Ex. C.R. 32, [1925] 2 D.L.R. 162. See also *Canadian Brine Ltd. v. The "Scott Misener"* [1962] Ex. L.R. 441 at p. 452, *per* Wells D.J.A.

[103] *Canadian General Electric Co. Ltd. v. Pickford & Black Ltd.*, [1972] S.C.R. 52 at p. 57, 20 D.L.R. (3d) 432 at pp. 435-6.

[104] *The "Pacifico," supra*, footnote 102, at pp. 37-8 Ex. C.R., p. 167 D.L.R.

[105] *Supra*, footnote 103, at p. 60 S.C.R., p. 438 D.L.R. See also *Bell Telephone Co. of Canada — Bell Canada v. The Ship "Mar-Tirenno"* [1974] 1 F.C. 294, 52 D.L.R. (3d) 702 (T.D.), affd [1976] 1 F.C. 539, 71 D.L.R. (3d) 608*n* (C.A.); *Voest-Alpine Canada Corp. v. Pan Ocean Shipping Co.*, [1993] 7 W.W.R. 112, 79 B.C.L.R. (2d) 379 (C.A.); *Omega Salmon Group Ltd. v. "Pubnico Gemini" (The)*, [2007] 6 W.W.R. 428 (B.C.C.A.).

[106] (1888), 13 P.D. 105 (C.A.).

[107] As in other areas of the law of damages. See 1.210-1.270, 1.1830-1.2040, *supra*. However, in *Swiss Bank Corp. v. Air Canada*, [1982] 1 F.C. 756, 129 D.L.R. (3d) 85 (T.D.), affd [1988] 1 F.C. 71, 44 D.L.R. (4th) 680 (C.A.), the Federal Court held that it had no power to award interest in a non-admiralty case and, in *President of India v. La Pintada Compania Navigacion S.A.*, [1985] A.C. 104 (H.L.), the House of Lords refused to establish a general common law right to interest on the ground that the legislature, in giving a power to award interest, had subjected the power to certain restrictions and qualifications. It is submitted, however, that a partial legislative reversal of a common law rule ought not generally to be taken as manifesting an intention to prevent the courts from completing the reversal. In *Chatham Motors Ltd. v. Fidelity & Casualty Insurance Co. of New York* (1986), 53 O.R. (2d) 581 at pp. 586-87, 7 C.P.C. (2d) 251 (H.C.J.), affd 63 O.R. (2d) 205*n* (C.A.), the Ontario High Court held that prejudgment interest was recoverable, for a period before the current statute came into force, "on equitable principles". See also *Pittman v. Manufacturers Life Insurance Co.* (1990), 76 D.L.R. (4th) 320, [1991] I.L.R. 1-2708 (Nfld. C.A.).

[107a] (1989), 171 C.L.R. 125 (Aust. H.C.); *Simeone v. Pesatura General Contractors Pty. Ltd.* (1993), 60 S.A.S.R. 453 (S.C.).

[107b] [2002] 2 S.C.R. 601, 211 D.L.R. (4th) 385.

similar conclusion in *Sempra Metals Ltd. v. Her Majesty's Commissioners of Inland Revenue.*[107c]

(4) Interest as consequential damages

7.430 The Supreme Court of Canada in *General Securities Ltd. v. Don Ingram Ltd.*[108] allowed recovery of a business loss incurred by a borrower on breach of the lender's obligation to advance the money. The case was followed in *Pelletier v. Pe Ben Industries Co. Ltd.*[109] where damages were awarded for loss caused by default on a truck purchase contract due to the defendant's wrongful dismissal of the plaintiff from his employment. It must follow from these cases that if the plaintiff reasonably incurs a cost by borrowing money to avoid such a loss, the cost of borrowing will be recoverable. This will generally be the reasonable course for the plaintiff to pursue.

7.440 It has often been said that no damages beyond interest are recoverable for failure to pay a debt,[110] but in the light of the cases just mentioned it would seem that this must be taken to be because, as a general rule, consequential damages (other than interest) are too remote, not because of an absolute exclusion.

(5) Provincial legislation

7.450 Legislation in each province permits or requires the court to award interest on money judgments.[111] The statutes are similar in their general features, but there are important differences among them in substance and terminology.[112] Although in each province there is a statutory right to interest, in significant respects the discretion of the court is fettered, with provisions in some cases that interest *shall* be awarded and in other cases that interest shall *not* be awarded. In the discussion that follows, therefore, it must be borne in mind that decisions in some jurisdictions may not be capable of application in others, though it is notable that in many cases similar results have been reached by different techniques. In a jurisdiction where there is no overriding discretion, the court will often adjust the rate of interest, the period during which interest accrues, or the principal sum on which interest is payable, in order to achieve indirectly what cannot be achieved directly. The decision of

---

[107c] [2007] UKHL 34.

[108] [1940] S.C.R. 670, [1940] D.L.R. 641.

[109] [1976] 6 W.W.R. 640 (B.C.S.C.). The *General Securities* case was also applied in *Prince Rupert Sawmills Ltd. v. M.C. Logging Ltd.* (1967), 65 D.L.R. (2d) 300 (B.C.C.A.).

[110] *Fletcher v. Tayleur* (1855), 17 C.B. 21 at p. 29, 139 E.R. 973; *Hamilton v. Johnstone* (1956), 22 W.W.R. 686 (B.C.S.C.), affd *loc. cit.*, p. 691 (C.A.).

[111] *Judgment Interest Act* (Alta.); *Court Order Interest Act* (B.C.); *Court of Queen's Bench Act* (Man.); *Judicature Act* (N.B.), s. 45; *Judgment Interest Act* (Nfld. & Lab.); *Judicature Act* (N.W.T.), ss. 55, 56, 56.1, 56.2; *Judicature Act* (N.S.), s. 41; *Courts of Justice Act* (Ont.), ss. 127-8; *Supreme Court Act* (P.E.I.), ss. 49-52; *Pre-judgment Interest Act* (Sask.). See Waldron, "The Law of Interest in Canada" (Toronto, Carswell, 1992), pp. 131-59.

[112] A proposed "Uniform Judgment Interest Act" was published in 1983 (*Proceedings of the Commissioners of the Conference of Uniformity of Law in Canada, 1982*), p. 32.

the Supreme Court of Canada in *Bank of America Canada v. Mutual Trust Co.*,[112a] holding that compound interest was available at common law despite its exclusion from the Ontario legislative scheme, indicates that provincial legislation will often be capable of being supplemented, or even bypassed, by judicial development of a general common law right to interest.

(6) Rate of interest

7.460 For many years five per cent was taken to be the "legal rate of interest" and was generally the amount awarded in commercial cases.[113] The *Interest Act* provides, by s. 3, that "whenever any interest is payable by the agreement of parties or by law, and no rate is fixed by the agreement or by law, the rate of interest shall be five per cent per annum"[114] and s. 12 provided that "every judgment debt shall bear interest at the rate of five per cent per annum until it is satisfied".[115] However, the Supreme Court of Canada held in *Prince Albert Pulp Co. v. Foundation Co. of Canada*[116] that s. 3 did not apply to prejudgment interest because where a court ordered prejudgment interest to be paid, the court fixed the rate and so the rate was "fixed by law."[117] Section 12 was held to apply only after judgment.

7.470 The court is free now in all provinces to award interest at commercial rates. In the *Prince Albert* case itself, interest was based on the claimant's borrowing rate[118] which was proved to be the "minimum rate" (presumably the prime rate) plus three-quarters of one per cent. A commercial plaintiff can almost always show that had the debt in question been paid promptly, it could have reduced its outstanding indebtedness, and in all such cases it would seem that the cost to the claimant of borrowing is the appropriate rate provided that it was within the reasonable contemplation of the defendant. Where the plaintiff has not borrowed and could not have reduced an indebtedness if the money had been paid promptly, a lesser measure may be appropriate on the basis of the rate that the plaintiff would have earned, by depositing the money at the bank, a rate that may also be justified on the basis of depriving the defendant of the minimum benefit to the defendant of holding the plaintiff's money for the period between the date of the wrong and the date of the judgment. Some cases have awarded interest at lending rates.[119]

[112a] *Supra*, footnote 107b.

[113] See *Re Roberts* (1880), 14 Ch. D. 49 (C.A.).

[114] *Interest Act* (Can.), s. 3.

[115] Section 12 (repealed 1992, c. 1, s. 146). See 7.1000, *infra*.

[116] [1977] 1 S.C.R. 200, 68 D.L.R. (3d) 283.

[117] *Supra*, at p. 211 S.C.R., p. 291 D.L.R.

[118] Borrowing rates were also used in *Stevenson v. Stanek*, [1980] 4 W.W.R. 239 (Q.B.); *Nor-Min Supplies Ltd. v. Canadian National Ry. Co.* (1979), 106 D.L.R. (3d) 325, 27 O.R. (2d) 390 (C.A.); *Mitchell v. Day* (1981), 44 N.S.R. (2d) 541 (S.C.T.D.) (prime rate); *Ross Steel Fabricators & Contractors v. Loaring Construction Company Ltd.* (1986), 15 C.P.C. (2d) 27 (Ont. H.C.J.).

7.490 Some provinces specify the rate.[121] In cases where the plaintiff has had to borrow at higher rates, interest at the bank rate may undercompensate.

[*The next page is* 7-23]

---

119 *Jefford v. Gee*, [1970] 2 Q.B. 130 (C.A.) (rate on money paid into court); *Gillis v. Bates* (1979), 100 D.L.R. (3d) 682 (B.C.S.C.); *Sheehy v. Edmonton World Hockey Enterprises Ltd.* (1979), 105 D.L.R. (3d) 644 (Alta. Q.B.); *Poon v. Dickson* (1982), 134 D.L.R. (3d) 559 (Alta. C.A.). In *QCTV Ltd. v. Edmonton (City)* (1984), 16 D.L.R. (4th) 71, [1985] 2 W.W.R. 414 (Alta. C.A.), where the claimant was at times a net borrower and at times a net lender, a variable rate was used.

120 [Text deleted.]

121 *E.g., Courts of Justice Act* (Ont.), s. 127(1).

Rapid variations in the bank rate might also make the rate in the month specified too high or too low. No doubt it is for these reasons that the legislatures in several provinces have given the court a discretion to vary the rate, and it would seem that in such cases the discretion could properly be exercised.[122]

(7) Losses occurring after the date of the wrong and before trial

7.500 The purpose of awarding interest is, as Dr. Lushington said in *The "Amalia"*,[123] to compensate the plaintiff for the wrong that is done by failure to make prompt reparation. In the case of destruction of a ship, for example, all the damage is done at the date of the collision and interest on the whole amount of the judgment naturally runs from that date.[124] Where, however, the plaintiff claims in respect of expenses incurred after the date of the wrong, for example repair costs[125] or medical expenses in personal injury cases,[126] interest runs only from the date the cost is incurred, for it would normally be on that day that the defendant (if meeting obligations instantly) could have been expected to make reimbursement.

7.510 In most jurisdictions the application of these principles is discretionary,[127] but in some provinces pre-trial losses attract interest only from periods of fixed length.[128] Presumably the intention of the legislatures was to deal with cases where a large number of small expenses are incurred at different dates between the date of the wrong and the date of the judgment. The legislation provides a rough and ready but practical means of calculating interest in such cases. But the use of the term "special damages" in some jurisdictions is unfortunate. The term is undefined in the statutes and has no settled meaning in the law of damages.[129] In personal injury cases the term is commonly used to designate losses (such as medical expenses) incurred between the date of the injury and the date of the trial. In *Jefford v. Gee*,[130] Lord Denning M.R. said: "Special damages

---

122 *Borland v. Muttersbach* (1984), 23 D.L.R. (4th) 664, 53 O.R. (2d) 129 (C.A.); *Spencer v. Rosati* (1985) 50 O.R. (2d) 661, 1 C.P.C. (2d) 301 (C.A.). It was held in *Dugdale v. Boissneau* (1983), 41 O.R. (2d) 152 (C.A.), leave to appeal to S.C.C. refused May 16, 1983, and in *Pace v. Delzotto* (1996), 1 C.P.C. (4th) 310 (Ont. Ct. (Gen. Div.)), that the judge must have sound reasons for departing from the specified rate. The factors listed in the *Courts of Justice Act* (Ont.), s. 130(2), include "changes in market interest rates". See also *Cairns v. Harris* (1995), 129 Nfld. & P.E.I.R. 250 (P.E.I.S.C.).

123 (1864), 5 New Rep. 164.

124 *The "Northumbria"* (1869), L.R. 3 A. & E. 6; *The "Berwickshire"* [1950] P. 204.

125 *The "Hebe"* (1847), 2 W. Rob. 503 (Adm.); *The "Norseman"* [1957] P. 224.

126 See 7.650, *infra*. No interest is available on expenses not actually incurred: *Mortimer v. Cameron* (1994), 111 D.L.R. (4th) 428, 17 O.R. (3d) 1 (C.A.), leave to appeal to S.C.C. refused 114 D.L.R. (4th) vii.

127 See *Huber v. Monteith* (1989), 100 A.R. 161, 68 Alta. L.R. (2d) 363 (Q.B.).

128 *Court Order Interest Act* (B.C.), s. 1(2); *Courts of Justice Act* (Ont.), s. 128(3); *Prejudgment Interest Act* (Sask.), s. 6(2).

129 See 3.360, 3.370, 4.10-4.40, *supra*.

130 *Supra*, footnote 119.

mean the *actual pecuniary* loss suffered by the plaintiff, up to the date of the trial".[131]

7.520 There have been occasional cases holding that lost earnings before trial are not special damages,[132] but most of these cases were concerned with deductions for contingencies and should not, it is submitted, control the meaning of the phrase in a statute dealing with interest especially as the Supreme Court of Canada in the 1978 "trilogy" treated pre-trial lost earnings as special damages.[133] Outside the field of personal injury the meaning of the phrase is even more uncertain. In *Hope Hardware & Building Supply Co. Ltd. v. Fields Stores Ltd.*[134] the claim was for loss caused by fire. The plaintiff claimed the cost of rebuilding and cleaning up and loss of rental income. Bouck J. held that these were general damages, applying as a test of general damages whether "the law would presume [a certain loss] to be the natural or probable consequences of the act complained of".[135] The result of this reasoning is that almost all recoverable damages will be general damages; the consequence might well be over-compensatory because, as pointed out previously, if the plaintiff claims a loss based on expenditure after the date of the wrong the plaintiff ought only to be entitled to interest from the date of the expenditure. But unfortunately, the British Columbia statute gives no general discretion. Once the damages are classified as general damages it seems that the court *must* allow interest. Bouck J. realizing that there was a danger of over-compensation, managed to reach a result that accorded with his view of justice by reducing the rate of interest. He said:

> Some kind of balance must be struck which represents in a rough way the nature of the claim and the precise amount withheld by the defendant over the period involved. Here the plaintiffs did not lose all of their money on September 30, 1975 — the date of the fire. Rather they paid it out or failed to receive it from the defendant in bits and pieces from September 30, 1975 until judgment.
>
> This kind of withholding is different from those situations where a judgment debtor has failed to pay the whole of a debt on its due date and

131 *Supra*, at p. 146. In *Grincelis v. House* (2000), 201 C.L.R. 321 (Aust. H.C.), interest was awarded on damages for pre-trial care supplied voluntarily by relatives.

132 *Trache v. C.N.R.*, [1929] 2 D.L.R. 321 (Sask. C.A.), followed in *Taylor v. Addems*, [1932] 1 W.W.R. 505 (Sask. C.A.), and *Tubb v. Lief*, [1932] 3 W.W.R. 245 (Sask. C.A.), but not followed in *Wersch v. Wersch*, [1945] 2 D.L.R. 572 (Man. C.A.), and *Parisian v. Canadian Pacific Ltd.* (1983), 25 C.C.L.T. 105 (Sask. Q.B.). The question was expressly left open in *Hunter v. Ballingall* (1962), 37 W.W.R. 703 (Man. C.A.).

133 See 3.360-3.400, *supra*. Lost earnings were treated as special damages in *Baart v. Kumar* (1985), 22 D.L.R. (4th) 354 at p. 369, [1986] 1 W.W.R. 100 (B.C.C.A.), citing this passage, in *McPhillips v. British Columbia Ferry Corp.* (1996), 17 C.C.E.L. (2d) 298, 46 C.P.C. (3d) 13 (B.C.S.C.), and in *McEvoy v. Ford Motor Co.* (1989), 41 B.C.L.R. (2d) 224 (S.C.), affd 88 D.L.R. (4th) 358, 63 B.C.L.R. (2d) 362 (C.A.) (lost support under *Family Compensation Act*). In *Digby v. Doe* (1986), 32 D.L.R. (4th) 319, 15 C.P.C. (2d) 162 (B.C.S.C.), lost wages were called special damages, but the statute was interpreted to require interest from the date of the principal loss.

134 (1978), 90 D.L.R. (3d) 49 (B.C.S.C.), vard 137 D.L.R. (3d) 58 (C.A.).

135 *Supra*, at p. 63.

> the plaintiff is out all the money from that time until judgment. For these reasons the usual rate may be too high in this instance.[136]

Consequently Bouck J. reduced the rate from eight per cent to seven and one-half per cent. The case shows that judges can usually reach a just result even in the face of intractable legislation, but it is most unfortunate that the legislation requires such a convoluted process. The purpose of the provisions on special damages was presumably to simplify calculations. The result is that now a complex calculation must be made to determine how much the plaintiff would have recovered if interest at full rates had run from the date of each expense, and another calculation to determine what reduction in the rate of interest on the whole amount is necessary to give to the plaintiff the same net recovery as would have been obtained by full interest for the proper periods.

7.530 Bouck J.'s decision was reversed on this point by the British Columbia Court of Appeal. The court said that the cost of reconstruction was to be treated as a repair cost.[137] The decision was referred to in the following terms by Esson J. in *Davies v. Safeco Ins. Co. of America*.[138] "I think that decision is authority for saying that, if the nature of the damages is payments made by the plaintiff after the cause of action arises, they are special damages within the meaning of the *Court Order Interest Act*."[139] This interpretation perhaps reads more into the judgment of the Court of Appeal than appears in the published reasons. Not all losses occurring between the date of the wrong and the date of judgment can be described as repair costs. However, Esson J.'s approach is to be welcomed as, it is submitted, the best way of giving effect to the overall statutory purpose, that is, to give just interest on claims.

7.540 The arithmetical double calculation may, however, be necessary to deal with other instances of statutory rigidity. An approach similar to Bouck J.'s was approved by the British Columbia Court of Appeal in *Killeen v. Kline*[140] where Lambert J.A. said:

> Because of the wording of the Court Order Interest Act . . . it may be necessary to set a reduced rate of interest for the full period . . . even though, on the facts, the rate should be the full rate, but for only a part of the period, to reflect the fact that the income is not lost for the full period.[141]

7.550 In some other provinces, such as Ontario, the matter is less complicated because there is an overriding discretion.[142] Thus an Ontario court

136 *Supra*, at pp. 64-5.
137 (1980), 137 D.L.R. (3d) 58 (B.C.C.A.), at p. 61, followed in *Kranz v. Nelson (City)* (1996), 141 D.L.R. (4th) 301, 32 B.C.L.R. (3d) 271 (C.A.).
138 (1982), 137 D.L.R. (3d) 66 (B.C.S.C.).
139 *Supra*, at p. 68.
140 [1982] 3 W.W.R. 289 (B.C.C.A.).
141 *Supra*, at p. 316.
142 See *Courts of Justice Act*, (Ont.), s. 130.

in a case like *Hope Hardware* could classify the losses claimed as general damages and still, in its discretion, calculate interest only from the date each loss was incurred, or treat the losses like special damages by analogy. Similar difficulties to those found in British Columbia, however, will arise in Nova Scotia where the court is required to include interest and no exception is made in any form for losses arising after the date of the wrong. Several cases have indicated that the problem will be solved by the kind of calculation used by Bouck J., that is by reducing the rate of interest so as to reach the proper result.[143]

7.560 It was noted in an earlier chapter that in both England and Canada personal injury damage awards are required to be divided into pecuniary losses occurring before trial (sometimes called "special damages"), pecuniary losses occurring after trial (the cost of future medical care and loss of earnings), and non-pecuniary losses (pain and suffering, loss of amenities and expectation of life). The earlier practice of awarding an undivided "global sum" has now been disapproved.[144] The reason given by the Supreme Court of Canada for requiring specification is that appellate courts must know the reasons for each constituent part of the award, both because of considerations of fairness to the parties and in order to give rational guidance in future cases. An added reason becomes apparent in the present context. Rational application of principles governing the award of interest requires a distinction to be made among different kinds of damage.

7.570 Pecuniary losses occurring before the trial (usually medical expenses and lost earnings) will not, of course, have occurred at the date of the injury. Some will usually have been incurred shortly thereafter; some will not have been incurred until shortly before the trial date. The English Court of Appeal in *Jefford v. Gee*[145] held that the appropriate award was of interest on the accumulated total of pre-trial pecuniary losses but at half the current short-term rate of interest. The solution was approved by the House of Lords in *Cookson v. Knowles*.[146] The English Law Commission in a Report in 1973 recommended enactment of the rule as a statutory provision, while recognizing that it represented rather rough

---

143 *Whitehead v. Misner* (1981), 48 N.S.R. (2d) 416 (S.C.T.D.), var'd 51 N.S.R. (2d) 111 (S.C. App. Div.); *Mitchell v. Day* (1981), 44 N.S.R. (2d) 541 (S.C.T.D.); *Comeau v. Marsman* (1981), 47 N.S.R. (2d) 550 (S.C.T.D.).

144 See 3.300-3.330, *supra*.

145 [1970] 2 Q.B. 130 (C.A.), followed in *Schriver v. Clark* (1977), 17 N.B.R. (2d) 63 (Q.B.), aff'd 18 N.B.R. (2d) 579 (C.A.).

146 [1979] A.C. 556 (H.L.), followed on this point in *Dexter v. Courtaulds Ltd.*, [1984] 1 W.L.R. 372 (C.A.), and *Killeen v. Kline*, [1982] 3 W.W.R. 289 (B.C.C.A.), at p. 316; *Mitchell v. Day, supra*, footnote 143; *Comeau v. Marsman, supra*, footnote 143; *Guimont v. Williston* (1980), 30 N.B.R. (2d) 178 (C.A.), leave to appeal to S.C.C. refused 34 N.R. 356*n*; *Despres v. Manuel* (1980), 36 N.B.R. (2d) 257 (Q.B.T.D.); *Brideau v. Brideau* (1980), 32 N.B.R. (2d) 541 (S.C. App. Div.); *Clement v. Clement Estate* (1981), 36 N.B.R. (2d) 275 (Q.B.T.D.); *Borland v. Muttersbach* (1984), 23 D.L.R. (4th) 664, 53 O.R. (2d) 129 (C.A.).

justice and recommending a power in the court to depart from the rule in special circumstances.[147] The matter was again referred to in the Law Commission's 1978 *Report on Interest*[148] but no further recommendations were made. The Pearson Commission agreed with the Law Commission "that the half rate rule is a fair compromise" although it recognized "that it sometimes represents only rough justice".[149]

7.580 The legislation in some provinces provides that "special damages" are to be cumulated for a certain period and that interest is payable only on the cumulated total from the end of each period.[150] There is considerable uncertainty, as has been indicated, as to the meaning of "special damages", but it would seem probable that pre-trial pecuniary losses in a personal injury claim do fall within the meaning of the phrase.[151] Pre-trial losses in a fatal accident case could also, it is submitted, be similarly treated, either as an interpretation of "special damages" to include all pre-trial pecuniary losses[152] or, by analogy, where the court has a discretion. In *Killeen v. Kline*,[153] however, the British Columbia Court of Appeal approved the reduced rate technique used in *Cookson v. Knowles*. In most other jurisdictions the matter will be in the discretion of the court. In *Henrikson v. Parke*[154] the Alberta Court of Queen's Bench calculated pre-trial loss of earnings at trial date rates, in order to make a rough allowance for delay in compensation. In an age that has put an electronic calculator into everyone's pocket, there seems no overwhelming difficulty in calculating the exact amount of interest due on each item of loss claimed. It is suggested that, when convenient, an exact calculation should be made, and that the half-rate rule should be resorted to only when a precise calculation is impracticable.

7.590 There has been a division of judicial opinion in cases of wrongful dismissal. If the plaintiff recovers interest on the full award from the date of the dismissal, the plaintiff will be better off than would have been the case if the wrong had not been done for if the defendant had given proper notice, the plaintiff would have received salary in instalments not as a lump sum paid in advance. This argument was accepted by the Saskatchewan Court of Appeal,[154a] the British Columbia Court of Appeal[155] and the Alberta Court of Appeal[155a] but has been rejected by the Nova Scotia Court of Appeal[156] and the Newfoundland Supreme Court.[156a] Ontario cases are divided.[157] The

147 Law Commission, *Report on Personal Injury Litigation – Assessment of Damages*, No. 56 (London, H.M.S.O., 1973), §§281, 286.

148 Law Commission, *Law of Contract: Report on Interest*, No. 88, Cmnd. 7229 (1978).

149 *Report of the Royal Com'n on Civil Liability and Compensation for Personal Injury* (Pearson Commission Report) (London, H.M.S.O., 1978), §742.

150 See 7.510, 7.520, *supra*.

151 But see 3.370, *supra*, where it is indicated that some kinds of pre-trial loss are not readily so called. See *Baart v. Kumar* (1985), 22 D.L.R. (4th) 354, [1986] 1 W.W.R. 100 (B.C.C.A.).

152 *McEvoy v. Ford Motor Co.* (1989), 41 B.C.L.R. (2d) 224 (S.C.), affd 88 D.L.R. (4th) 358, 63 B.C.L.R. (2d) 362 (C.A.).

153 *Supra*, footnote 146.

154 (1981), 29 A.R. 431 (Q.B.). The court described this as an allowance for inflation, which forms the largest part of current interest rates.

argument for full interest is that the defendant, having wrongfully dismissed the plaintiff, had an immediate obligation to pay the full amount of the salary measured by the period of reasonable notice. However, the counter-argument is that if notice had been given, the employer's obligation to pay salary during the notice period would not have been accelerated: a salary payable monthly would continue to be payable monthly while the notice period was running. If instant justice had been done and the court sat on the day of the wrongful dismissal, a just measure of compensation would require future salary to be discounted on account of advance payment. Although it has often been assumed in the past that full damages are due on the date of termination, this assumption should (in the writer's view) yield to the more basic principle that the plaintiff should not by an award of compensatory damages be put into a better position than would have been occupied if the wrong had not been done.[157a]

(8) Loss anticipated after the date of the trial

7.600 In respect of compensation for losses not yet incurred, no interest should on principle be awarded because, viewed as an expense, the plaintiff has not yet incurred the cost.[157b] Consequently, so far from the plaintiff being entitled to recover interest, there ought to be an allowance to the defendant for advance payment and this is precisely the principle that underlies the process of discounting damages in personal injury cases to their present value.[158] The value of the future losses is capitalized at the date of judgment. If the judgment were to be instantly satisfied, no further interest calculations would be required.

7.610 If, however, the value of all losses occurring after the date of the wrong were to be capitalized at the date of the wrong, the situation would be

[154a] *Janke v. Cenalta Oilwell Servicing Ltd.* (1997), 143 D.L.R. (4th) 613 at p. 625, [1997] 3 W.W.R. 406 (Sask. C.A.), citing this passage.

[155] *Suttie v. Metro Transit Operating Co.* (1985), 28 D.L.R. (4th) 36, [1986] 3 W.W.R. 289 (B.C.C.A.); *Neilson v. Vancouver Hockey Club Ltd.* (1986), 31 D.L.R. (4th) 475, 7 B.C.L.R. (2d) 155 (S.C.), vard 51 D.L.R. (4th) 40, [1988] 4 W.W.R. 410 (C.A.).

[155a] *Christianson v. North Hill News Inc.* (1993), 106 D.L.R. (4th) 747, 13 Alta. L.R. (3d) 78 (C.A.).

[156] *George C. Sweet Agencies Ltd. v. Sklar-Peppler Furniture Corp.* (1995), 140 N.S.R. (2d) 69 (C.A.); *Rogers v. Canadian Acceptance Corp. Ltd.* (1982), 50 N.S.R. (2d) 537 (S.C.T.D.);*Connor v. Canada Life Assurance Co.* (1991), 108 N.S.R. (2d) 361, 92 C.L.L.C. 14,017 (S.C.); *Cardenas v. Clock Tower Hotel Ltd. Partnership* (1993), 120 N.S.R. (2d) 49, 47 C.C.E.L. 156 (S.C.).

[156a] *Squires v. Corner Brook Pulp and Paper Ltd.* (1996), 141 Nfld. & P.E.I.R. 150 (Nfld. S.C.).

[157] *Rushton v. Lake Ontario Steel Co. Ltd.* (1980), 112 D.L.R. (3d) 144, 29 O.R. (2d) 68 (H.C.J.); *Blackburn v. Coyle Motors Ltd.* (1983), 44 O.R. (2d) 690, 3 C.C.E.L. 1 (H.C.J.). See *Stevens v. Globe and Mail* (1996) 135 D.L.R. (4th) 240, 28 O.R. (3d) 481 (C.A.) (award of full interest upheld).

[157a] See *Peterson v. Electro Sonic Inc.* (2000), 98 A.C.W.S. (3d) 198 (Ont. S.C.J.), at paras. 2-6, citing this passage; *Weaver v. Casey's Welding Service Ltd.* (2007), 57 C.C.E.L. (3d) 47 (Ont. S.C.J.), at para. 13, citing this paragraph and awarding interest on an installment basis.

[157b] *LeClerc v. Sunbury Transport Ltd.* (1997), 184 N.B.R. (2d) 1 (C.A.).

[158] *Hines v. Englund* (1993), 124 N.S.R. (2d) 156 (S.C.). See 3.990-3.1040, *supra*.

different. Damages so calculated aim at assessing the value of what the plaintiff lost at the date of the wrong, and so the delay between that date and the date of judgment requires an award of interest on the full amount.[158a]

7.620 Lambert J.A. pointed out the distinction in *Killeen v. Kline*[159] (a fatal accident case):

> If the determination of lost future benefit is made *as of the date of trial* by a discount going back to that date and on the basis of a life expectancy running from the date of trial, and if the loss to date of trial is made the subject of a separate and less unreliable calculation, then the prejudgment interest should be awarded only on the loss to date of trial and should not be awarded on the lost benefit after the date of trial.
>
> If, on the other hand, the determination of lost future benefit is made *as of the date of death* through a discount going back to the date of death for a life expectancy measured from the date of death, then prejudgment interest should be awarded on the full amount of the discounted benefit in order to bring the benefit up to what it would have been at the date of trial.
>
> In a simple case these two approaches will produce the same result.[160]
>
> [Emphasis in original.]

Lambert J.A. went on to say[161] that the "better course" was to make separate assessments of pre-trial and post-trial losses. The same distinction was drawn, and the same preference expressed, by the Ontario Court of Appeal in *Julian v. Northern & Central Gas Corp.*[162] The English[163] and Australian[164] courts have taken the same view.

7.630 This view seems amply justified, both in principle and in view of the Ontario and British Columbia interest legislation. In principle it is easier, more accurate, and less artificial to make the assessment of pre-trial loss in the light of what is now known about events between the wrong and the trial, and of future loss in the light of the latest information at the time of trial.[165] It is important to note that the use of Lambert J.A.'s second method (*i.e.*, assessment as of the date of the wrong) would require the use of the income levels *then* prevailing and the evidence that would *then* have been given of future medical costs,[166] for the plaintiff would be over-compensated if losses were recovered, assessed at trial date values, but capitalized at the date of the

158a See *Ulmer (Guardian Ad Litem) v. Henderson* (1991), 80 D.L.R. (4th) 761, [1991] 5 W.W.R. 764 (C.A.).

159 *Supra*, footnote 146. See *Romanick (Guardian ad Litem of) v. Konrad* (1995), 121 D.L.R. (4th) 261, 1 B.C.L.R. (3d) 88 (C.A.).

160 *Supra*, at pp. 312-13.

161 *Supra*, at pp. 315-16, though saying at p. 316 that the other approach was "not an error in principle" if applied consistently. The same approach was adopted in *Wieser v. Pearson* (1980), 109 D.L.R. (3d) 63 (B.C.S.C.), affd 126 D.L.R. (3d) 237 (C.A.).

162 (1979), 118 D.L.R. (3d) 458, 31 O.R. (2d) 388 (C.A.), leave to appeal to S.C.C. refused D.L.R. *loc. cit.*, O.R. *loc. cit.*

163 *Cookson v. Knowles*, [1979] A.C. 556 (H.L.), *Jefford v. Gee*, [1970] 2 Q.B. 130 (C.A.).

164 *Thompson v. Faraonio*, [1979] 1 W.L.R. 1157 (P.C.). See also *Fire & All Risks Ins. Co. Ltd. v. Callinan* (1978), 52 A.L.J.R. 637 (Aust. H.C.); *Atlas Tiles Ltd. v. Briers* (1978), 52 A.L.J.R. 707 (Aust. H.C.); *Ruby v. Marsh* (1975), 132 C.L.R. 642 (Aust. H.C.).

165 See *per* Lord Fraser in *Thompson v. Faraonio, supra*, footnote 164, at p. 1162.

166 See *Julian v. Northern & Central Gas Corp. Ltd., supra*, footnote 162.

wrong, with full interest from the date of the wrong. This would be to mix incompatible elements of the two methods, a practice against which Lambert J.A. warned in *Killeen v. Kline*.[167]

7.640 The provisions of the Ontario and British Columbia statutes also favour the division between pre-trial and post-trial losses, for interest on awards for future loss is specifically excluded.[168] This exclusion can be conveniently applied only if a division is made between pre-trial and post-trial losses. In provinces such as Nova Scotia, however, where there is no such provision,[169] it would appear that over-compensation can be avoided only by resort to a notional capitalization at the date of the wrong. The question will be: what would the defendant have had to pay if instant justice had been done? The amount so assessed properly bears interest to the date of judgment. An alternative (but, it is submitted, more artificial) method would be to reduce the interest rate on the award measured as at the date of judgment to whatever level should be necessary to reach the same result as is reached in other jurisdictions by the exclusion of interest on future losses.[170]

(9) Personal injury

(a) Power to award interest

7.650 Before 1970 it was generally assumed in Anglo-Canadian jurisdictions that no interest was payable on an award of damages for personal injuries.[171] In that year the United Kingdom enacted legislation making the award of interest compulsory, in the absence of special circumstances,[172] and since then all Canadian provinces have enacted legislation to the effect that, generally, pecuniary judgments should bear interest.[173] In all jurisdictions, therefore, personal injury and wrongful death awards will generally carry interest.[174]

---

[167] [1982] 3 W.W.R. 289 (B.C.C.A.), at p. 314. See *Shaw v. Roemer* (1982), 134 D.L.R. (3d) 590 (N.S.S.C. App. Div.), at p. 617, leave to appeal to S.C.C. refused December 6, 1982 (interest awarded on damages assessed "as at date of death").

[168] *Courts of Justice Act* (Ont.), s. 128(4)(*d*); *Court Order Interest Act* (B.C.), s. 2(a); *Federal Court Act*, s. 36(4)(*d*). See also *Robson v. Official Administrator County of Caribou – Prince George* (1979), 101 D.L.R. (3d) 306 (B.C.C.A.).

[169] See footnote 111, *supra.*

[170] In *Shaw v. Roemer, supra*, footnote 167, interest was awarded at twelve per cent on a fatal accident award. No reference was made to the possibilities discussed in *Killeen v. Kline* of capitalization at the date of the accident.

[171] See *McGregor on Damages*, 16th ed. (London, Sweet & Maxwell, 1997), §645. See also *Kernested v. Desorcy*, [1979] 1 W.W.R. 512 (Man. C.A.), leave to appeal to S.C.C. refused January 23, 1979; *B. (K.L.) v. British Columbia* (2001), 197 D.L.R. (4th) 431 (B.C.C.A.),.

[172] *Administration of Justice Act 1969*, s. 22.

[173] See 7.450, *supra.*

[174] See *Gillis v. Bates* (1979), 100 D.L.R. (3d) 682 (B.C.S.C.); *Blair's Plumbing & Heating Ltd. v. McGraw* (1981), 34 N.B.R. (2d) 678 (Q.B.T.D.).

(b) Non-pecuniary losses

7.660 In *Jefford v. Gee*,[175] the English Court of Appeal held that interest should be awarded at the full rate on damages for non-pecuniary losses, the argument being that it was not practicable to divide these losses into pre-trial and post-trial segments, that theoretically the defendant should have made immediate payment and that consequently the plaintiff had been kept out of money until trial. In *Cookson v. Knowles*,[176] however, the English Court of Appeal in a wrongful death case suggested a reversal of this rule. The question was left open by the House of Lords in that case.[177] In *Pickett v. British Rail Engineering Ltd.*,[178] the House of Lords held that interest was allowable. Lord Wilberforce said:

> . . . interest . . . was varied by the Court of Appeal on the theory that as damages are now normally subject to increase to take account of inflation, there is no occasion to award interest as well. I find this argument, with respect, fallacious. Increase for inflation is designed to preserve the "real" value of money: interest to compensate for being kept out of that "real" value. The one has no relation to the other.[179]

7.670 The Law Commission discussed the matter in its *Report on Personal Injury Litigation-Assessment of Damages*[180] and in its *Report on Interest*.[181] The Commission favoured refusal of interest on the ground that the plaintiff would benefit from the probable higher level of assessment of non-pecuniary losses at the date of judgment as compared with assessment at the date of the loss. However, the Pearson Commission rejected this argument, saying like Lord Wilberforce in the passage quoted above, that any increase in the scale of assessment between the loss and the trial will presumably be designed to take account of inflation. Consequently, it is only in a qualified sense that the plaintiff can be said to gain from an increase in the scale. The plaintiff will receive more money in nominal terms but no real compensation for being kept out of money.[182]

7.680 Notwithstanding the views of Lord Wilberforce and of the Pearson Commission, it would seem that if the scale of damages were fully adjusted to take account of inflation, the plaintiff would be over-compensated if the full commercial interest rate from the date of the loss was received. High rates of interest are composed in large part of an

175 [1970] 2 Q.B. 130 (C.A.).

176 [1977] Q.B. 913 (C.A.), affd [1979] A.C. 556 (H.L.).

177 [1979] A.C. 556 (H.L.).

178 [1980] A.C. 136 (H.L.). Interest was allowed at full rates in *Brideau v. Brideau* (1980), 32 N.B.R. (2d) 541 (S.C. App. Div.).

179 *Pickett, supra*, footnote 178, at p. 151, followed on this point in *Daly v. General Steam Navigation Co.*, [1981] 1 W.L.R. 120 (C.A.), but explained in *Birkett v. Hayes*, [1982] 1 W.L.R. 816 (C.A.), at p. 822, *per* Eveleigh L.J., as not precluding the court from recognizing that current interest rates reflect inflation.

180 No. 56 (London, H.M.S.O., 1973).

181 No. 88, Cmnd. 7229, 1978.

182 Pearson Commission Report (London, H.M.S.O., 1978), §746.

allowance for inflation and if inflation is already taken into account by an adjustment in the principal amount of the award, the plaintiff ought to receive only, in addition, interest at a rate reduced to exclude considerations of inflation, probably a rate of about two to three per cent.[183] The rate is fixed by statute or, in some jurisdictions, by rule at a figure reflecting these considerations.[184]

7.690 In *Birkett v. Hayes*,[185] the English Court of Appeal adopted this approach, awarding interest at two per cent, and recommending that figure as a guideline for future cases. The case involved an award in 1981 for a non-pecuniary loss of £30,000, in respect of injuries sustained in 1976. Had the assessment occurred in 1976, the award would have been about £20,000. The plaintiff would be over-compensated if she received £30,000 and interest on that sum at full rates for five years, because in no sense had she been kept out of that sum for five years. Lord Denning put it this way:

> I can see no reason why that £20,000 should be any different from a contract debt. Suppose that the plaintiff was owed a debt of £20,000 due in May 1976, but judgment was only given in January 1981. The plaintiff would get interest only on £20,000 for those 4⅔ years. The interest would have been about £8,000. She would only have got £28,000 at the trial. She would not get £30,000.
>
> But the currency did not remain stable from 1976 to 1981. There was racing inflation. So that the plaintiff in 1981 received £30,000. I can see no possible justification for giving her interest on that inflated figure for the 4⅔ years — when she would not be given it on an admitted debt of £20,000 due at the date of the service of the writ. Taking Lord Herschell's words: she was not kept out of £30,000 for those 4⅔ years. She was only kept out of £20,000.[186]

7.700 In Canada, where non-pecuniary losses are compensated on a "functional basis", the theory is that the purpose of compensation is to provide solace in the future.[187] In this respect, the award is analogous to damages for future costs, and it is well established that no interest is to be awarded on damages for future losses.[188] There seems, therefore, an even stronger case in Canada for following the approach taken in *Birkett v. Hayes* and it

183 See 3.990-3.1040, *supra*. The Manitoba Law Reform Commission recommended fixing the "real" rate of interest at 3%: *Report on Prejudgment Compensation on Money Awards: Alternatives to Interest*, No. 47 (1982). This was also the recommendation of the Ontario Law Reform Commission *Report on Compensation for Personal Injuries and Wrongful Death* (1987), p. 209 (2.5%), but the rule enacted under subsequent legislation fixed the rate at 5% (Rules of Civil Procedure, r. 53.10; *Courts of Justice Act*, s. 128(2)).

184 *Judgment Interest Act* (Alta.), s. 4(1) (4%); Ontario Rules of Civil Procedure, r. 53.10.

185 [1982] 1 W.L.R. 816 (C.A.), approved by the House of Lords in *Wright v. British Railways Board*, [1983] 3 W.L.R. 211.

186 *Supra*, at pp. 820-1.

187 See 3.510-3.700, *supra*.

188 See 7.600-7.640, *supra*. But in *Chisholm v. Cameron* (1982), 49 N.S.R. (2d) 320 (S.C.T.D.), interest at full rates was awarded on non-pecuniary compensation.

has been accepted by some Canadian courts[189] though rejected by others.[190] In several jurisdictions, the rate is fixed by statute or rule.[191]

7.710 In its final conclusion the Pearson Commission agreed in the result with the Law Commission, though for a different reason, namely the conventional nature of compensation for non-pecuniary losses. The Pearson Commission Report[193] considered that it would be piling artificiality on convention to calculate interest on an essentially arbitrary sum. The Commission also pointed out that in theory interest ought only to be awarded on the portion of the damages applicable to pre-trial losses, but that a division of the damages would be a difficult and artificial exercise.

7.720 The conventional nature of a sum of damages does not seem in itself sufficient reason for depriving the plaintiff of interest when it is not paid. Conventional though the sum may be, the plaintiff was still entitled to have it paid promptly; the plaintiff suffers a loss and the defendant reaps a gain from its unjust retention. Indeed, it seems to add insult to injury to say to a plaintiff: "The law recognizes that this conventional sum is quite inadequate compensation for serious bodily injury; and for that reason you are not even entitled to interest on it if it is wrongfully withheld." It would seem therefore that an appropriate solution is to award interest on damages for non-pecuniary losses but, if the principal amount has been adjusted for inflation, the appropriate rate of interest will be two or three per cent.[193a] Suppose, for example, that the plaintiff was made a quadriplegic in 1978 at the time that the Supreme Court of Canada held that $100,000 was the appropriate conventional award for such an injury.[194] A court assessing damages in 1998 would award a sum of about $250,000. The rate of interest that would put the

[189] *Leischner v. West Kootenay Power & Light Co.* (1986), 24 D.L.R. (4th) 641, [1986] 3 W.W.R. 97 (B.C.C.A.) (awarding minimum rate of 5%); *Graham v. Grant* (1990), 46 B.C.L.R. (2d) 151 (C.A.) (minimum rate of 5%); *Braddick v. Simon* (1992), 72 B.C.L.R. (2d) 364, 12 C.P.C. (3d) 94 (S.C.) (3.5%); *Sibley v. Kanigan*, [1993] 7 W.W.R. 722, 86 Man. R. (2d) 113 (Q.B.) (3%); *Bush v. Air Canada* (1992), 87 D.L.R. (4th) 248 (N.S.C.A.) (2.5%); *Boertien v. Carter* (1995), 135 Nfld. & P.E.I.R. 91 (P.E.I.S.C.) (6.75%); *Flanagan v. Levesque* (1994), 148 N.B.R. (2d) 101 (Q.B.) (2.5%); *Wintle v. Piper*, [1994] 9 W.W.R. 390, 93 B.C.L.R. (2d) 387 (C.A.) (3.5%); *Bezanson v. Boutilier* (1994), 131 N.S.R. (2d) 386 (S.C.) (2.5%). See *MBP (SA) Pty. Ltd. v. Gogic* (1991), 98 A.L.R. 193 (H.C.) (4%).

[190] *Borland v. Muttersbach* (1984), 23 D.L.R. (4th) 664, 53 O.R. (2d) 129 (C.A.); *Graham v. Persyko* (1986), 27 D.L.R. (4th) 699, 55 O.R. (2d) 10 (C.A.), leave to appeal to S.C.C. refused 34 D.L.R. (4th) 160*n*, 74 N.R. (2d) 317*n*; *Power v. McDonald* (1992), 96 Nfld. & P.E.I.R. 181 (Nfld. S.C.); *Ismail (Guardian ad Litem of) v. Dartmouth Surplus Ltd.* (1992), 114 N.S.R. (2d) 171 (S.C.); *Mayo v. Harding* (1993), 111 Nfld. & P.E.I.R. 271 (Nfld. S.C.).

[191] *Court Order Interest Act* (B.C.), s. 2(e) (no interest); *Court of Queen's Bench Act* (Man.), s. 80(3) (no interest but allowance to be made for loss of investment opportunity); *Judgment Interest Act* (Alta.), s. 4(1) (4%): see *Herman v. Alberta (Public Trustee)* (2005), 46 Alta. L.R. (4th) 330 (Q.B.) at para. 6; *Supreme Court Act* (P.E.I.), s. 50(2) (discount rate as determined by rules); Ontario Rules of Court, rule 53.10 (5%).

[192] [Text deleted.]

[193] Pearson Commission Report, *supra*, footnote 149, at §747.

[193a] See *B. (K.L.) v. British Columbia* (1998), 163 D.L.R. (4th) 550 at p. 558 (B.C.S.C.), revd on other grounds 197 D.L.R. (4th) 431 (C.A.), citing this passage, leave to appeal to S.C.C. granted 205 D.L.R. (4th) vi.

[194] See 3.510, *supra*.

plaintiff in the same position that would have been occupied if $100,000 had been paid in 1978 is, when applied to a principal sum of $250,000, about 2.5 per cent. But if, for some reason, the court should decline to adjust the $100,000 figure for inflation, interest at full commercial rates would be justified.

7.730 Similar considerations apply to awards of aggravated damages[195] and to awards outside the field of personal injuries as, for example, an award for defamation[195a] or for non-pecuniary loss in a wrongful death case. The Ontario Court of Appeal, however, awarded full interest on an award for loss of care, companionship, and guidance under the *Family Law Reform Act* in *Mason v. Peters*,[196] and in *Botiuk v. Toronto Free Press Publications Ltd.* the Supreme Court of Canada awarded full interest in a defamation case.[196a]

(10) Payment into court

7.740 The statutes of several provinces provide that where money is paid into court by the defendant and not accepted by the plaintiff and the plaintiff subsequently recovers judgment for an amount equal to or less than the amount paid into court, interest shall be withheld after the date of payment-in.[197] Since interest actually earned by the money paid into court belongs to the defendant, the effect of this rule is that the plaintiff will suffer an interest penalty, as well as the usual cost penalty, for refusing a reasonable offer of settlement. In jurisdictions where the award of interest is entirely discretionary this factor might be taken into account, at least in cases where the plaintiff's refusal is wholly unreasonable. It has been held that unreasonably prolonging litigation is a ground for refusing interest.[198] However, the mere fact that the defendant's offer exceeds the plaintiff's ultimate recovery would not seem to be a sufficient reason for

[195] But in *Storrie v. Newman* (1982), 139 D.L.R. (3d) 482 (B.C.S.C.), interest at full rates was awarded on aggravated damages.

[195a] *Hiltz and Seamone Co. v. Nova Scotia (Attorney General)* (1999), 172 D.L.R. (4th) 488 (N.S.C.A.). And see *Laufer v. Bucklaschuk* (1998), 128 Man. R. (2d) 156 (Q.B.), revd on other grounds 181 D.L.R. (4th) 83 (Man. C.A.), leave to appeal to S.C.C. refused 189 D.L.R. (4th) vii.

[196] (1982), 139 D.L.R. (3d) 104, 39 O.R. (2d) 27 (C.A.), leave to appeal to S.C.C. refused December 6, 1982.

[196a] [1995] 3 S.C.R. 3, 126 D.L.R. (4th) 609, approving *Borland v. Muttersbach, supra*, footnote 190. But in *Hiltz and Seamone Co. v. Nova Scotia (Attorney General), supra*, footnote 195a, it was held that the law on the point in Nova Scotia remained as declared in *Bush v. Air Canada, supra*, footnote 189.

[197] *Court Order Interest Act* (B.C.), s. 4; *Judicature Act* (N.S.), s. 41(j); *Judgment Interest Act* (Alta.), s. 3. In *Re Anderson and Atlantic Enterprises* (1979), 107 D.L.R. (3d) 566 (B.C.S.C.), interest was refused where, on a compulsory acquisition of the plaintiff's shares, the plaintiff established a right only to what the defendant had originally offered. This appears to penalize the plaintiff for rejecting a reasonable offer, without any payment into court.

[198] See 7.930-7.940, *infra*.

holding the plaintiff's conduct to be unreasonable and exacting a forfeiture of interest: the cost penalty is already quite severe.

7.750 A problem of interpretation arises in a case where the defendant's offer is sufficient to cover the plaintiff's principal claim but is less than the total amount of the judgment (including interest). It would seem that the probable legislative intention was that the forfeiture of interest should operate as a penalty for the refusal of reasonable offers of settlement. A reasonable offer is one that includes interest up to the date of the offer. The desirable result on this basis would be to construe the legislation to mean that interest is forfeited where the plaintiff ultimately recovers a principal amount which, with interest from the date of the wrong up to the date of the payment-in, is equal to or less than the amount of the payment in. This is not, however, what the statutes say. The alternative interpretations appear to be to read the word "amount" as meaning "principal" or "total" amount. The former interpretation would be most unjust to the plaintiff because it would have the effect of depriving the plaintiff of interest where a payment in was made even though the payment in (not meeting the plaintiff's proper claim for interest up to that date) was inadequate. The latter interpretation therefore seems the more probable. This will have the effect of saving the plaintiff from the forfeiture in some cases, even where the plaintiff has refused a settlement that was reasonable at the time, but since the plaintiff will in any event suffer the cost penalty in such a case this may be thought to be a sufficient deterrent. Similar questions arise under rules of court that impose a cost penalty on a party refusing a reasonable offer to settle litigation. The rules have been, in several jurisdictions, construed to mean that the penalty will only be exacted where the offer includes interest up to the date of the offer.[199]

(11) Interest payable by agreement

7.760 Where interest is, on the proper construction of an agreement between the parties, payable after default, the plaintiff is not entitled to recover interest as damages.[200] Plainly, interest as damages in addition to the interest agreed would be over-compensatory. Circumstances can be envisaged in which the creditor would wish to take interest as damages instead of interest at the agreed rate. Where interest rates have risen since the date of the agreement, the rate of prejudgment interest given by the court may well exceed the rates specified in the agreement. In such a case, ironically, it will benefit the creditor to show that no interest is payable under the

---

199 *Kellner v. Greig* (1980), 103 D.L.R. (3d) 244, 15 B.C.L.R. 126 (C.A.); *Rushton v. Lake Ontario Steel Co. Ltd.* (1980), 112 D.L.R. (3d) 144, 29 O.R. (2d) 68 (H.C.J.); *Whittle v. Davies* (1987), 45 D.L.R. (4th) 331, [1988] 1 W.W.R. 444 (Alta. C.A.); *Veronneau v. Gregory* (1979), 13 B.C.L.R. 42, 13 C.P.C. (S.C.) (offer by plaintiff); *Peters v. Zanatta* (1987), 10 B.C.L.R. (2d) 395, 15 C.P.C. (2d) 229 (S.C.).

200 Express provision is made to this effect in several provinces.

agreement after default. But if the creditor fails to establish this point, the creditor will, it would seem, be restricted to the rate specified in the agreement on the principle that by contracting for the rate that was to be paid after default, the creditor took the risk that the rate might turn out to be lower than the current rates at that time; so, as the creditor would have benefited by a drop in general interest rates, the creditor must take the risk of a rise.

7.770 An express agreement that no interest should be paid after default was held not to exclude a right to interest under the Nova Scotia statute.[201] In provinces where there is a discretion, such an agreement would be a relevant consideration.[201a]

(12) Interest payable otherwise by law

7.780 Some statutes also provide for the withholding of interest where interest is payable "otherwise by law" and the Ontario provision speaks of interest "payable by a right other than under this section".[202] Plainly, in a case where interest is allowed as special damages or under another statute, it would be over-compensatory to award interest as well under the statute governing prejudgment interest. Difficulties may be encountered in provinces where interest is mandatory and there is no exception for interest otherwise allowable. It may be that the courts will have to solve this problem by the complex process of reducing the rate on the whole amount so as to reach the appropriate result.[203]

(13) Reimbursement of plaintiff by third parties

7.790 In *Harbutt's "Plasticine" Ltd. v. Wayne Tank & Pump Co. Ltd.*,[204] the English Court of Appeal held that where a plaintiff had been indemnified by its insurer, interest should run only to the date of indemnification. Lord Denning said:

> In assessing damages, we ignore, of course, the fact that the plaintiffs are insured. But, in awarding interest, it is different. An award of interest is discretionary. It seems to me that the basis of an award of interest is that the defendant has kept the plaintiff out of his money; and the defendant

---

201 *Cleveland v. Sunderland Marine Mutual Insurance Co.* (1987), 45 D.L.R. (4th) 340, 81 N.S.R. (2d) 1 (N.S.S.C.). See *Court Order Interest Act* (B.C.), s. 2(b); *Judgment Interest Act* (Alta.), s. 2(2)(h).

201a See *Niagara Air Bus Inc. v. Camerman* (1991), 80 D.L.R. (4th) 611, 30 O.R. (3d) 108 (C.A.), leave to appeal to S.C.C. refused 87 D.L.R. (4th) vii, 138 N.R. 413*n* (rate agreed to by parties before maturity held to be relevant).

202 *Judicature Act* (N.S.), 41(k)(ii); *Judgment Interest Act* (Alta.), s. 2(2)(i); *Courts of Justice Act* (Ont.), s. 128(4)(g); *Federal Court Act*, s. 36(4)(*f*).

203 See 7.520-7.540, *supra*.

204 [1970] 1 Q.B. 447 (C.A.). Approved *obiter* by the New Brunswick Court of Appeal in *John Maryon Int'l Ltd. v. N.B. Telephone Co. Ltd.* (1982), 141 D.L.R. (3d) 193 (C.A.), leave to appeal to S.C.C. refused 46 N.R. 262*n*. See also *Robustelli v. Charlottetown (City)* (1998), 166 Nfld. & P.E.I.R. 143 (P.E.I.S.C.).

> has had the use of it himself. So he ought to compensate the plaintiff accordingly.
>
> This reasoning does not apply when the plaintiff has not been kept out of his money but has in fact been indemnified by an insurance company. I do not think the plaintiff should recover interest for himself on the money when he has not been kept out of it. The receipt from the insurance company should go in relief of the defendants. The wind should be tempered to the shorn lamb.[205]

The defendant will have had the use of the money whether or not the plaintiff has been indemnified. The plaintiff's insurer will suffer a loss by being kept out of that money between the date of indemnification and the date of judgment. Lord Denning says the plaintiff should not recover

[*The next page is* 7–37]

205 *Supra*, at p. 468.

the interest "for himself", but on ordinary principles of subrogation one would expect that the plaintiff would have to account for it to the insurer.[206] It is perhaps relevant to make another point. The interest question was a minor aspect of the *Harbutt's "Plasticine"* case, the main effect of which was to deny to the defendant the benefit of a contractual clause limiting liability for an accidental loss. Many would have said that the court went too far against the defendant's legitimate interest in that case. It seems perhaps that even Lord Denning thought so and that it was for this reason that he felt the need for "temper the wind to the shorn lamb." If the defendant had not been shorn so thoroughly of the protection it thought it had contracted for, the court might not have felt the need to withhold interest.[207]

7.800 In the following year the English Court of Appeal in effect reversed the interest point in *Harbutt's "Plasticine"*. In *H. Cousins and Co. Ltd. v. D. & C. Carriers Ltd.*,[208] it was held that ordinarily an insurer would be entitled to be subrogated to the plaintiff's claim for interest after the date of indemnification and that therefore the decision on this point in *Harbutt's "Plasticine"* had proceeded on a false premise. There was no question of the plaintiff recovering interest "for himself". Only if it were established that the insurer could not claim the interest would the court be justified in exercising its discretion to withhold it.[209] Even then, it may be suggested, it is arguable that the court should not withhold interest because if, on the true construction of the insuring agreement, the insurer has given up its ordinary right to be subrogated to the claim for interest in such circumstances, the plaintiff will presumably have paid for the benefit of the right to retain the interest, in the shape of an increased premium or by other terms of the contract. In Canada therefore, in jurisdictions where interest is in the court's discretion, it is submitted that indemnification by an insurer ought to be irrelevant to the award of interest. In Nova Scotia the statute formerly provided that the court, in its discretion, might decline to award interest if the claimant has been compensated in whole or in part by insurance or other payment.[210] If the argument made above is sound, there will not be sufficient reason to withhold interest even if the plaintiff has been indemnified and will retain the interest.

7.810 Where the plaintiff is indemnified from another source than insurance, for example under an employment contract or by gifts from the third party, the usual rule in Canadian cases is that the principal amount of

---

206 See *H. Cousins & Co. Ltd. v. D. & C. Carriers Ltd.*, [1971] 2 Q.B. 230 (C.A.).

207 See Waddams, *The Law of Contracts*, 3rd ed. (Toronto, Canada Law Book, 1993), p. 321.

208 *Supra*, footnote 206.

209 *Supra*, footnote 206, at p. 240, *per* Widgery L.J.

210 See *Judicature Act*, s. 38(11)(c) (repealed 1981, c. 54, s. 1). See *Court Order Interest Act* (B.C.), s. 1(4). And see *Lehman v. Reid* (1994), 93 B.C.L.R. (2d) 84 (S.C.).

damages recoverable from the wrongdoer is not to be reduced.[211] On the same principle it would seem that interest also should be recoverable in full: it should, it is submitted, be a matter between the plaintiff and the third party whether the plaintiff is bound to account to the latter for the interest, just as it is a question between them whether the plaintiff is bound to account for the principal sum. As in the case of insurance, it would seem desirable for the court to allow interest, at any rate unless it is proved that the plaintiff would, as against the third party, be entitled to retain the interest if it were awarded.

(14) Payment on account by defendant

7.820 Where the defendant pays on account, it would not be just to award interest on the amount paid after the date of payment.[212] Indeed, such a rule would discourage the desirable practice of interim payments. In jurisdictions where interest is discretionary, no problem arises. The legislation of some provinces, however, present difficulties. If judgment is given for the whole amount of the plaintiff's entitlement (the advance payments being treated as credits to be applied subsequently), the legislation seems to require interest on the full amount. This would be unfair to the defendant. If, on the other hand, the plaintiff is treated as recovering judgment only for the balance due, no interest would be recoverable on the prepayments, but this would be unfair to the plaintiff if the prepayments were made shortly before judgment. In *Gillis v. Bates*,[213] where the defendant had made a series of prepayments, the British Columbia legislation was construed to permit interest to be calculated on the declining balance due from time to time. Taylor J. said:

> . . . in the absence of agreement to the contrary . . . a plaintiff who accepts payments on account thereby releases the defendant to the extent of the payment, both by way of reduction in the amount ultimately payable and also with respect to prejudgment interest on the amount so paid from the date of its acceptance.[214]

The just solution was thus reached by constructing an agreement between the parties to the effect that interest should be paid only on the declining balance. This solution, though artificial, seems necessary where the statute gives inadequate discretion and may prove necessary in other jurisdictions also. However, in *Ammerlaan v. Drummond*,[215] Spence J.

211 See 3.1490-3.1580, *supra*. However, in *Shaw v. New Brunswick Society for the Prevention of Cruelty to Animals* (1975), 13 N.B.R. (2d) 435 (Q.B.), interest was withheld on the ground that the plaintiff had received a subsidy. See also *Hepworth v. Zerbin*, [1993] 6 W.W.R. 119, 110 Sask. R. 53, supplementary reasons [1993] 8 W.W.R. 198, Sask. R. *loc. cit.* p. 59 (Q.B.).

212 There is now express provision on this point in Ontario: *Courts of Justice Act*, s. 128(4)(e).

213 (1979), 100 D.L.R. (3d) 682 (B.C.S.C.).

214 *Supra*, at p. 685.

215 (1982), 132 D.L.R. (3d) 375 and 136 D.L.R. (3d) 571 (B.C.S.C.).

held that the wording of the *Court Order Interest Act* by its reference to "the amount ordered to be paid" excluded power to award interest on the declining balance, despite the potential injustice to the plaintiff.[216] In *Baart v. Kumar*,[217] the British Columbia Court of Appeal held that due credit for prepayment could nevertheless be given by adjustment to the rate of interest.

(15) Foreign currency obligations

7.830 The power of the Canadian courts to award judgment in foreign currency is uncertain, as is the power to postpone conversion of the foreign currency claim to the date of judgment.[218] However, some courts have held that conversion at date of judgment is appropriate, and in Ontario statute provides for conversion at the date of payment.[219] Either possibility has important implications for the rate of interest.

7.840 Where money is owed in a foreign currency that has strengthened vis–vis the Canadian dollar, and the creditor is awarded judgment in foreign currency or permitted to take advantage of conversion at the date of judgment, the creditor is thereby protected against the comparative decline in the value of Canadian money. Generally, weak currencies attract high interest rates. These protect the creditor from the decline in value of a weak currency. It would be over-compensatory for the plaintiff to recover judgment in foreign currency (or a sum converted at judgment date) and also prejudgment interest at Canadian rates where these exceed the foreign currency rate.[220] Had the debt been paid promptly in Swiss francs, let us suppose, for which the interest rate is four per cent, the plaintiff could have invested the money at four per cent. If the plaintiff recovers a sum that is the equivalent of the debt in francs at the date of judgment, four per cent interest is sufficient compensation for the delay. Interest at Canadian rates (of, say, twelve per cent) would protect twice over from a decline in the value of the dollar.

7.850 The opposite case is where the foreign currency depreciates. If the plaintiff creditor should be compelled to take judgment for a sum of Canadian dollars converted at date of judgment (or judgment in foreign currency), the creditor should be entitled to interest at the rate appropriate

216 See 132 D.L.R. (3d) at p. 377, where the potential injustice was stressed. See also *IM Properties plc v. Cape & Dalgleish*, [1998] 3 All E.R. 203 (C.A.).

217 (1985), 22 D.L.R. (4th) 354, [1986] 1 W.W.R. 100 (B.C.C.A.). See now *Court Order Interest Act* (B.C.), s. 1(4).

218 See 7.80-7.320, *supra*.

219 See 7.130, *supra*. See also *Foreign Money Liabilities* (British Columbia Law Reform Commission, Working Paper No. 33, 1981).

220 *Swiss Bank Corp. v. State of New South Wales* (1993), 33 N.S.W.L.R. 63 (Comm. Div.). This point is made by Bowles and Whelan, "The Currency of Suit in Actions for Damages", 25 McGill L.J. 236 (1979), criticizing *Helmsing Schiffahrts G.m.b.H. v. Malta Drydocks Corp.*, [1977] 2 Lloyd's Rep. 444 (Q.B.). See *Reading and Bates Construction Co. v. Baker Energy Resources Corp.*, [1995] 1 F.C. 483 at p. 506 (C.A.), leave to appeal to S.C.C. refused 60 C.P.R. (3d) vi, citing this paragraph.

to the foreign currency, probably a higher rate than that applicable to Canadian money.

7.860 Where interest rates are in the discretion of the court, as in most jurisdictions, these factors can be taken into account. Difficulties may arise in jurisdictions where there is inadequate judicial discretion. This point may be adduced as a reason for not departing from the breach date rule.[221]

(16) Damages measured at the date of judgment

7.870 Analogous problems arise when damages are measured at the date of judgment or at any date later than the date of the wrong. If, for example, the plaintiff is a purchaser of land that appreciates in value between the date of breach and the date of judgment and the plaintiff is awarded damages based on the judgment date value of the land, the plaintiff is thereby protected from inflation between the date of the wrong and the date of judgment. Interest, in inflationary times, is largely composed of an element to protect the creditor from the declining value of money, and if interest at full rates were to be awarded in addition to the judgment date value of the land, the plaintiff would be over-compensated.[222] In no sense can it be said that the defendant should have paid the amount of the judgment at the date of the wrong; the amount payable if immediate recompense had been made would have been the lesser amount based on the value of the land at that time.

7.880 Where the court has a discretion to withhold interest on part of the sum, the matter can be dealt with in that way. Interest should only be awarded on the amount that would have been payable if immediate recompense had been made. In some jurisdictions, however, the legislation is too narrowly drafted to permit this approach. In *Schweickardt v. Thorne*[223] Meredith J., in awarding judgment date value of a piece of land, said:

> Judgment in this case will amount to $5,400. Of this amount $5,000 represents loss of bargain as at the date of breach and $400 the appreciation of the value of the property since then, less expenses. I think there may be an anomaly in granting interest to judgment on the $400 because it is in a sense an investment return. If interest is not to be awarded on interest, I would have thought it inappropriate to award

221 See 7.280-7.310, *supra*.

222 Interest was refused for this reason in *Malone v. The Queen* (1977), 79 D.L.R. (3d) 677 (F.C.T.D.), and in *Canadian Laboratory Supplies Ltd. v. Engelhard Industries of Canada Ltd.*, [1979] 2 S.C.R. 787 at pp. 807-8, 97 D.L.R. (3d) 1 at p. 16, *per* Laskin C.J.C. But see *Sutherland v. Canada (Attorney General)* (2002), 212 D.L.R. (4th) 378 (B.C.S.C.), revd 215 D.L.R. (4th) 1 (B.C.C.A.). The Manitoba Law Reform Commission has proposed that compensation for loss of value should run from the date at which damages are assessed: *Report on Prejudgment Compensation on Money Awards: Alternatives to Interest* (No. 47, 1982), pp. 42-3.

223 [1976] 4 W.W.R. 249 (B.C.S.C.).

> interest on any other return (be it capital or income) between the date the cause of action arose and judgment.[224]

It might be added that the case against interest is even stronger than Meredith J. says. To award interest on the $400 from the date of the breach is not simply to award compound interest but to award interest on a sum from a date before it fell due, for the $400 would not have been due at the date of the breach, and only half of it would have been due half-way between breach and judgment. Nevertheless, Meredith J. found himself bound to make an award: "The Act requires me to award interest on the whole judgment."[225]

7.890 The only route open seems to be that of reducing the rate on the whole judgment so as to yield the net result that would have been reached by withholding interest on the amount of the inflationary increase.[226]

7.900 The same problem arises wherever damages are assessed at a date later than the date of the wrong. In *Dodd Properties Ltd. v. Canterbury City Council*,[227] the cost of repairing a building had tripled during the nine-year period between the date of the wrong and the date of the judgment. The English Court of Appeal awarded the judgment date cost of repair. This decision has been criticized elsewhere as overgenerous to the plaintiff.[228] But the court rightly recognized that the plaintiff could not be entitled to interest as well. Megaw L.J. said:

> . . . the plaintiff's alternative ground of appeal, as to the appropriate calculation of interest, does not arise. For it is a necessary part of their submission on the first issue that, damages being referable to the deferment of repairs, interest is not payable up to the date of the hearing.[229]

It would indeed be gilding the lily to allow the plaintiff to recover the judgment date cost of repair (three times the amount that would have been required nine years earlier if the defendant had made prompt recompense) and, in addition, interest on the larger sum for nine years. In most Canadian jurisdictions the court has sufficient discretion to deal with this question satisfactorily. In some provinces there will be difficulties that, it seems, can be solved only by adjusting the rate of

---

224 *Supra*, at p. 263.

225 *Supra*. However, in *C.R.F. Holdings Ltd. v. Fundy Chemical Int'l Ltd.* (1980), 21 B.C.L.R. 345 (S.C.), at p. 361, vard [1982] 2 W.W.R. 385 (C.A.), leave to appeal to S.C.C. refused 42 N.R. 357*n*, 42 N.R. 358*n*, interest was simply withheld where damages were measured at the date of trial, and in *Gaspari v. Creighton Holding Ltd.* (1984), 13 D.L.R. (4th) 570 (B.C.S.C.), it was held that the cause of action did not arise, within the meaning of the *Court Order Interest Act*, until the defendant finally refused to comply with a decree of specific performance. See Swan, Annotation to *Weber v. R. G. Steeves Construction Co. Ltd.* (1981), 22 R.P.R. 31.

226 See 7.520-7.540, *supra*. In *Baud Corp., N.V. v. Brook (No. 2)* (1979), 97 D.L.R. (3d) 300, the Supreme Court of Canada, in reducing the interest otherwise allowable, took account of the fact that the delay had increased the plaintiff's recovery.

227 [1980] 1 W.L.R. 433 (C.A.).

228 See 1.2510-1.2520, *supra*.

229 *Supra*, footnote 227, at p. 453.

interest[230] or, alternatively, by assessing damages at the date of the wrong and giving interest at full rates from that date. The effect of the interest legislation may indeed be adduced as an additional argument for choosing the earlier date for assessment of damages.

(17) Overlap with damages for loss of use

7.910 Care is required to see that compensation for loss of use of property is not duplicated. As was indicated in the chapter on compensation for property, damages for loss of use can be expressed either as a capital sum or in the form of damages for loss of profits.[231] If full compensation for loss of use of property up to the date of judgment is given by awarding lost profit, there is no room for interest to be awarded in addition. In the case of destruction of a ship, damages measured by the market value of the ship at the date of the loss should carry interest because the plaintiff, had immediate reparation been made, could have invested the money and earned interest. But if compensation is given in the principal award for loss of use of the ship between the date of the wrong and the date of judgment, no interest should be awarded because the plaintiff could not have had the use of both the ship and the sum of money that represents the ship's value.[232] Where a capital sum is awarded representing the value of the property that includes the value of anticipated use, the latter element should be discounted for notional advance payment at the date of the loss if interest at full rates is to run from that date.[233]

7.920 In most jurisdictions there is adequate judicial discretion. In British Columbia and Nova Scotia there will be difficulties that can be solved either by reduction in the interest rate or by insuring that the principal sum awarded does not include compensation for loss of use.[233a]

(18) Delay

7.930 Where interest is in the court's discretion, it can be withheld to mark the court's disapproval of excessive delay by the plaintiff in prosecuting

230 In *Park Projects Ltd. v. Halifax Developments Ltd.* (1984), 65 N.S.R. (2d) 237 (S.C.A.D.), the rate of interest was reduced for this reason to 1%.

231 See 1.1830, 1.1840, *supra*.

232 In *The "Northumbria"* (1869), L.R. 3 A. & E. 6, where compensation had been given for lost freight, Sir Robert Phillimore, in refusing interest in respect of the same period, said at p. 12: "by giving freight you [have] really given the interest on the use of the vessel . . . to have given interest as well as freight would have been to place the sufferer in a better position than he would have been but for the collision."

233 *Lister (Ronald Elwyn) Ltd. v. Dayton Tire Canada Ltd.* (1985), 52 O.R. (2d) 88 (C.A.), at p. 127, citing this paragraph. In *Liesbosch Dredger v. S.S. Edison*, [1933] A.C. 449 (H.L.), at pp. 467-8, Lord Wright said that the plaintiffs should recover "the value of the dredger to the owners at Patras . . . as a going concern" and interest "on the true value so ascertained". It is submitted that interest can logically be awarded only on the value of the ship at the time of the loss, and in calculating that value anticipated profits should be discounted to their value at the same date.

233a But see *Canson Enterprises v. Boughton & Co.*, [1996] 1 W.W.R. 412, 11 B.C.L.R. (3d) 262 (C.A.), leave to appeal to S.C.C. refused 203 N.R. 78*n*, 48 C.P.C. (3d) 384*n*.

the claim or increased in case of excessive delay by the defendant. In *Jefford v. Gee*,[234] Lord Denning said: "In exceptional cases, such as when one party or the other has been guilty of gross delay, the court may depart from the [usual rules] by diminishing or increasing the award of interest, or altering the periods for which it is allowed."[235]

7.940 In *Baud Corp., N.V. v. Brook (No. 2)*,[236] the Supreme Court of Canada, in exercising its discretion under s. 50 of the *Supreme Court Act* (dealing with interest after the date of the trial judgment) reduced the interest that would normally have been allowable, because of the plaintiff's delay in prosecuting the litigation. A similar discretion is exercisable in most jurisdictions in respect of prejudgment interest.[237]

(19) Compound interest

7.950 Compound interest was not formerly awarded at common law[237a] and is specifically excluded in several provinces[238] following the English statute in this respect.[239] But in *Bank of America Canada v. Mutual Trust Co.*,[239a] the Supreme Court of Canada affirmed a common law power to award compound

[234] [1970] 2 Q.B. 130 (C.A.); *Somers v. Fournier* (2002), 214 D.L.R. (4th) 611 (Ont. C.A.), at para. 26, citing this paragraph.

[235] *Supra*, at p. 151. And see *Corbett v. Barking, Havering and Brentwood Health Authority*, [1991] 1 Q.B. 408 (C.A.); *Landry Estate v. Metropolitan Life Insurance Co.* (1992), 131 N.B.R. (2d) 277, 16 C.C.L.I. (2d) 55 (Q.B.); *Thomas-Canning v. Juteau* (1993), 122 N.S.R. (2d) 23 (S.C.); *Osborne v. Kelly* (1993), 61 S.A.S.R. 308 (S.C.). The discretion must be exercised judicially and is reviewable by an appellate court: *Young v. Dawe* (1998), 156 D.L.R. (4th) 626, 160 Nfld. & P.E.I.R. 233 (Nfld. C.A.); *Roynat Ltd. v. Northern Meat Packers* (1986), 29 D.L.R. (4th) 139, 71 N.B.R. (2d) 212 (C.A.), leave to appeal to S.C.C. refused 27 N.R. 158*n*, 78 N.B.R. (2d) 90*n*. See also *Derby Resources A.G. v. Blue Corinth Marine Co. Ltd. (No. 2)*, [1998] 2 Lloyd's Rep. 425 (Q.B. (Comm. Div.)), where the court reduced the rate of interest due to the plaintiffs' unjustifiable delay.

[236] *Supra*, footnote 226.

[237] See *Judicature Act* (N.S.), s. 41(k)(iii); *Courts of Justice Act* (Ont.), s. 130(2)(f). Section 130(2)(d) refers to "the circumstances of medical disclosure by the plaintiff". It was held in *Dugdale v. Boissneau* (1983), 41 O.R. (2d) 152 (C.A.), leave to appeal to S.C.C. refused May 16, 1983, that lapse of time before delivery is not in itself a reason to reduce interest. Interest was withheld or reduced in: *Moncton (City) v. Aprile Contracting Ltd.* (1980), 29 N.B.R. (2d) 631 (S.C. App. Div.); *Al-Qahtani-Shaw-Leonard Ltd. v. Crossworld Freight Ltd.* (1986), 54 D.L.R. (4th) 192*n*, 66 O.R. (2d) 256 (C.A.); *Holt v. Thomas* (1987), 38 D.L.R. (4th) 117, 71 A.R. 131 (Q.B.); *Pugsley v. Albert* (1996), 179 N.B.R. (2d) 241 (C.A.). But see *Maryon (John) International Ltd. v. N.B. Telephone Co. Ltd.* (1982), 141 D.L.R. (3d) 193, 43 N.B.R. (2d) 469 (C.A.), leave to appeal to S.C.C. refused 46 N.R. 262*n*, 43 N.B.R. (2d) 468*n* (unco-operative behaviour insufficient reason to withhold interest); *Oakville Storage and Forwarding Ltd. v. Canadian National Railway Co.* (1991), 84 D.L.R. (4th) 326, 52 O.R. (3d) 1 (C.A.), leave to appeal to S.C.C. refused 86 D.L.R. (4th) vii, 137 N.R. 238*n* (delay in production of documents); *Sawadski v. Heil* (1991), 86 D.L.R. (4th) 364, 2 C.P.C. (3d) 101 (Ont. C.A.) (delay in prosecution of action); *Hill v. Church of Scientology of Toronto* (1994), 114 D.L.R. (4th) 1, 18 O.R. (3d) 385 (C.A.), affd [1995] 2 S.C.R. 1130, 126 D.L.R. (4th) 129 (delay at plaintiff's request); *Kaip v. Bagamery* (1996), 146 Sask. R. 249 (Q.B.). See also *Greek v. Ernst* (1980), 43 N.S.R. (2d) 191 (S.C.T.D.).

[237a] *Westdeutsche Landesbank Girozentrale v. Islington London Borough Council*, [1996] A.C. 669 (H.L.).

[238] *Court Order Interest Act* (B.C.), s. 2(c); *Courts of Justice Act* (Ont.), s. 128(4)(b); *Judgment Interest Act* (Alta.), s. 2(2)(b); *Federal Court Act*, s. 36(4)(*b*).

interest, even though specifically excluded from the statutory scheme, in order to effect complete compensation and to prevent the defendant from profiting at the plaintiff's expense. The same conclusion was reached by the House of Lords in *Sempra Metals Ltd. v. Her Majesty's Commissioners of Inland Revenue*.[239b] It is understandable, in view of the slow recognition of simple interest, that compound interest has not been awarded in the past. However, there seems in principle no reason why compound interest should not be awarded. Had prompt recompense been made at the date of the wrong the plaintiff would have had a capital sum to invest; the plaintiff would have received interest on it at regular intervals and would have invested those sums also. By the same token the defendant will have had the benefit of compound interest. Awards of compound interest are regularly available where equitable damages are awarded for breach of fiduciary duty[240] and in the award of compensation for expropriation,[241] and they have been made in some other cases[242] It may well be that in jurisdictions where the court has power to do so, compound interest will be more frequently awarded in the future.[242a] Compound interest has been awarded in Admiralty.[242b] A general entitlement to compound interest has been recommended by the Ontario and British Columbia Law Reform Commissions.[243] It is true that this will add to the

[239] *Law Reform (Miscellaneous Provisions) Act*, 1934, s. 3(1)(a), now superseded by *Administration of Justice Act 1982*, c. 53, s. 15 and Sch. I.

[239a] [2002] 2 S.C.R. 601, 211 D.L.R. (4th) 385.

[239b] [2007] UKHL 34.

[240] *Harrison v. Mathieson* (1916), 30 D.L.R. 150, 36 D.L.R. 347 (S.C.A.D.); *Wallersteiner v. Moir*, [1975] Q.B. 373 (C.A.); *O'Sullivan v. Management Agency and Music Ltd.*, [1985] Q.B. 428 (C.A.); *Wotherspoon v. Canadian Pacific Ltd.* (1979), 92 D.L.R. (3d) 545 at pp. 740-1, 22 O.R. (2d) 385 (H.C.J.), vard 129 D.L.R. 1, 35 O.R. (2d) 449 (C.A.), affd [1987] 1 S.C.R. 953, 39 D.L.R. (4th) 169; *Brock v. Cole* (1983), 142 D.L.R. (3d) 461, 40 O.R. (2d) 97 (C.A.); *Claiborne Industries v. National Bank of Canada* (1989), 59 D.L.R. (4th) 533, 69 O.R. (2d) 65 (C.A.); *Calmont Leasing v. Kredl*, [1995] 8 W.W.R. 179, 165 A.R. 343 (C.A.).

[241] *British Pacific Properties Ltd. v. Minister of Highways & Public Works*, [1980] 2 S.C.R. 283, 112 D.L.R. (3d) 1; *Mannix v. The Queen* (1984), 31 L.C.R. 299 (Alta. C.A.); *Hat Development Ltd. v. Medicine Hat (City)* (1988), 39 L.C.R. 29 (Alta. Land Comp. Bd.); *Morriss v. British Columbia* (2007), 92 L.C.R. 222 (B.C.C.A.).

[242] *Cummings v. Halliburton Services Ltd.* (1980), 27 A.R. 181 (Q.B.); *Will Millar Associates Co. Ltd. v. Carr* (1978), 19 N.B.R. (2d) 561 (Q.B.), affd 21 N.B.R. (2d) 407 (S.C. App. Div.); *Roman Catholic Diocese of Calgary Assn. for Senior Citizens v. Century Insurance Co. of Canada* (1984), 8 D.L.R. (4th), 52 A.R. 295 (C.A.); *Domo Gasoline Corp. v. Shell Canada Products Ltd.* (2006), 207 Man. R. (2d) 245 (Q.B.). See *Brideau v. Brideau* (1980), 32 N.B.R. (2d) 541 (S.C. App. Div.), at p. 548; *Hungerford v. Walker* (1989), 171 C.L.R. 125 (Aust. H.C.).

[242a] See comments in *Air Canada v. Ontario (Liquor Control Board)*, [1997] 2 S.C.R. 581, 148 D.L.R. (4th) 193. Compound interest was awarded in *Clarke v. Milford* (1987), 38 D.L.R. (4th) 139, 78 N.S.R. (2d) 337 (C.A.); *Hannah v. Canadian General Insurance Co.* (1989), 92 N.S.R. (2d) 271, 41 C.C.L.I. at p. 87 (S.C.); *Mathers v. Mathers* (1992), 113 N.S.R. (2d) 284 at p. 308, supplementary reasons N.S.R. *loc. cit.* p. 310 (S.C.), revd on other grounds 123 N.S.R. (2d) 14, 16 C.P.C. (3d) 16 (C.A.); *Armstrong v. Baker* (1992), 113 N.S.R. (2d) 420 (S.C.); but was refused in *ACA Cooperative Assn. v. Associated Freezers of Canada Inc.* (1992), 93 D.L.R. (4th) 559, 113 N.S.R. (2d) 1 (C.A.).

[242b] *Monk Corp. v. Island Fertilizers Ltd.* (1989), 97 N.R. 384, 26 F.T.R. 240 (C.A.), restd [1991] 1 S.C.R. 779, 80 D.L.R. (4th) 58; *Fraser River Pile & Dredge Ltd. v. Can-Dive Services Ltd.*, [1995] 9 W.W.R. 376, 9 B.C.L.R. (3d) 260 (S.C.).

complexity of the calculation but it would be possible for the court to make the calculation on the basis of comparatively long rests, perhaps semi-annual, on the theory that many bank accounts pay interest semi-annually.[244] It has been pointed out[245] that there appears to be no economic reason for the refusal to award compound interest.

7.960 The reasoning in the *Bank of America Canada*[245a] case relied on the wording of the Ontario statute, which excluded "interest ... on interest accruing under this section", and which recognized interest payable "by a right other than under this section". Statutes in other provinces are differently worded and may not be susceptible to exactly the same reasoning. The Supreme Court of Canada also stressed that both parties in the *Bank of America Canada* case were in the business of lending money and that the defendant would profit by its breach unless compound interest were awarded. The court stated:

> An award of compound pre and post-judgment interest will generally be limited to breach of contract cases where there is evidence that the parties agreed, knew, or should have known, that the money which is the subject of the dispute would bear compound interest as damages. It may be awarded as consequential damages in other cases but there would be the usual requirement of proving that damage component.[245b]

The decision does not, therefore, amount to the establishment of a general rule of compound interest and the various theories that have supported compound interest in the past continue to be relevant. They include the award of simple interest as special damages, with an additional award of interest on those damages,[246] and the award of interest "as part of the award".[247]

(20) Consent judgments

7.970 The British Columbia Act provides that interest is not to be awarded

[243] See *Report on Court Order Interest Act* (British Columbia Law Reform Commission, 1987) and *Report on Compensation for Personal Injuries and Death* (Ontario Law Reform Commission, 1987). See also *Claiborne Industries Ltd. v. National Bank of Canada, supra*, footnote 240, at p. 576.

[244] See *Lutz v. Larocque*, [1981] 5 W.W.R. 1 (B.C.C.A.), at p. 15, where Lambert J.A. pointed out that money in court is compounded semi-annually.

[245] Bowles and Whelan, "Judgment Awards and Simple Interest Rates", 1 Int. Rev. of Law & Econ. 111 (1981); Bowles and Whelan, "The Law of Interest: Dawn of a New Era?", 64 Can. Bar Rev. 142 (1986). The Manitoba Law Reform Commission recommended compounding the real rate of interest (three per cent) but not the separate allowance for inflation: *Report on Prejudgment Compensation on Money Awards: Alternatives to Interest* (Manitoba Law Reform Commission, No. 47, 1982).

[245a] *Bank of America Canada v. Mutual Trust Co., supra*, footnote 239a.

[245b] *Supra*, at pp. 401-402.

[246] In *Brock v. Cole, supra*, footnote 240, followed in *Claiborne Industries Ltd. v. National Bank of Canada, supra*, footnote 240, the statute was construed not to prohibit compound interest against a defaulting trustee. See *Nillson Livestock v. MacDonald* (1995), 172 A.R. 81, 31 Alta. L.R. (3d) 28 (Q.B.).

[247] *Lewis v. Todd*, [1980] 2 S.C.R. 694 at p. 717, 115 D.L.R. (3d) 257 at p. 274. In *Lutz v. Larocque, supra*, footnote 244, semi-annual compounding was adopted. See 7.1000, *infra*.

"where the creditor waives in writing his right to an award of interest".[248] The Ontario Act provides that interest shall not be awarded except by consent of the judgment debtor when judgment is given on consent.[249] The question at issue here is usually one of the true construction of settlement agreements. If parties agree to settle a claim or agree to the entering of judgment for a named sum and nothing is expressly said about interest, it is probably a fair conclusion in most cases that no interest is intended to be payable. The British Columbia Act may therefore produce an unexpected result in the case of an oral settlement or consent judgment, and will give rise to difficulties of interpretation where the creditor agrees in writing to a certain sum but no express reference is made to interest.[250] The question is, as has been said, one of interpretation of the contract and wherever possible the applicable legislation should, it is submitted, be construed to give effect to the intention of the parties. This will generally be that the sum agreed to be paid in settlement satisfies the whole of the plaintiff's claim, including the claim to interest up to the date of the settlement.

(21) Exemplary damages

7.980 Some provinces expressly exclude interest on exemplary damages.[251] The argument is that, since exemplary damages are not compensatory, the plaintiff cannot claim to have been kept out of money that should have been paid. On the other hand it might be said that had the trial taken place the day after the wrong, exemplary damages might still have been thought appropriate, and in that case would have been payable immediately. The defendant, it might be added, should not benefit by the delay of litigation. In some provinces, Nova Scotia and British Columbia for example, it appears that interest on exemplary damages is required, but where the award is made by a judge the amount of exemplary damages can be reduced so as to impose what is thought to be the appropriate punishment upon the defendant after the addition of interest. In jurisdictions where the matter is in the court's discretion, it is suggested that interest should not be awarded.[251a] It cannot be said that the defendant should have paid promptly — the damages become payable only upon the decision of the court, which acts in respect of exemplary damages like a criminal court. The damages are not payable by way of recompense but as a punishment, and the punishment cannot occur

[248] *Court Order Interest Act*, s. 2(d).

[249] *Courts of Justice Act*, s. 128(4)(f); *Federal Court Act*, s. 36(4)(*e*). On mere acceptance of a payment into court, there is no "judgment" and so no statutory right to interest: *Saikeley v. Royal Ins. Co. of Canada* (1979), 98 D.L.R. (3d) 575, 24 O.R. (2d) 601 (H.C.J.).

[250] See *Gillis v. Bates* (1979), 100 D.L.R. (3d) 682 (B.C.S.C.), where an implied agreement was constructed to overcome the narrow drafting of the British Columbia Act.

[251] See, *e.g.*, *Courts of Justice Act* (Ont.), s. 128(4)(a); *Judgment Interest Act* (Alta.), s. 2(2)(c); *Federal Court Act*, s. 36(4)(*a*). See also *Levison-Viner v. Baudreau* (1984), 33 R.P.R. 34 (Ont. H.C.J.).

[251a] Interest was disallowed in *Royal Bank of Canada v. Wilton* (1991), 83 D.L.R. (4th) 568, 122 A.R. 353 (Q.B.), vard 123 D.L.R. (4th) 266 (C.A.).

until the decision of the court that imposes it. The amount assessed as exemplary damages is the amount then thought to be proper to be paid at that time. Another point concerns inflation. Exemplary damages, being assessed at the time of the hearing, will reflect the punishment thought appropriate in terms of money at that time. Had the hearing been held at the date of the wrong a smaller nominal sum would presumably have been thought appropriate, reflecting the higher value of money at that time. It would be wrong, therefore, for the defendant to have to pay exemplary damages measured in inflated dollars, together with interest at rates that themselves reflect inflation between the date of the wrong and the date of the judgment.[252]

(22) Costs

7.990 Some provinces exclude interest on costs.[253] In other jurisdictions the matter is in the court's discretion. In so far as the plaintiff has made actual out-of-pocket disbursements to meet the cost of litigation, an argument could be made that the plaintiff should receive interest from the date of the disbursements. On the other hand, party-and-party costs are not awarded as a complete recompense, and the amount due is not determined until the end of the trial. The measurement of costs on a taxation could properly, it would seem, be made on the assumption that the solicitor's account was not to be paid until the end of the trial; in theory, the amount of the reasonable fee will be greater than if advance payment had been required; thus an element of interest would be included automatically in the allowable party-and-party costs and in that case no additional interest on the costs should be allowed. However, in a case where the court awards solicitor-and-client costs with the express intention of securing to the plaintiff a complete recompense for the expense, a stronger case can be made for allowing interest on actual disbursements from the date of the disbursements.

(23) Interest on judgments

7.1000 The Canadian *Interest Act* formerly provided for Manitoba, British Columbia, Saskatchewan, Alberta, and the Territories that judgments should bear interest at five per cent.[254] A similar rate was specified by provincial legislation in some other provinces. In general, post-judgment interest falls outside a study of the law of damages.[255] However, one technique of

[252] See *Huff v. Price* (1990), 76 D.L.R. (4th) 138, 51 B.C.L.R. (2d) 282 (C.A.) (minimum permissible rate to be used); *Mustaji v. Tjin* (1996), 25 B.C.L.R. (3d) 220, 30 C.C.L.T. (2d) 53 (C.A.). See 7.660-7.700, *supra*, on the analogous question of interest on non-pecuniary damages.

[253] *Judgment Interest Act* (Alta.) s. 2(2)(d); *Court Order Interest Act* (B.C.) s. 2(c), *Courts of Justice Act* (Ont.), s. 128(4)(c); *Federal Court Act*, s. 36(4)(*c*).

[254] *Interest Act* (Can.), s. 12 (repealed 1992, c. 1, s. 146).

[255] See Waldron, *Law of Interest in Canada* (Toronto, Carswell, 1992), pp. 163-82.

[256] [Text deleted.]

avoiding low post-judgment interest rates is relevant. This technique, employed by the Ontario Court of Appeal in *Fenn v. City of Peterborough*,[257] was upheld by the Supreme Court of Canada in *Lewis v. Todd*[258] and has been applied also by courts in other jurisdictions.[259] The basis of the award is that since the capital sum must be adequate at the time of its actual payment, the trial judge could and should have included as part of the award an order for an appropriate increase of the sum payable until the date of actual payment. This increase is said to be given "not as interest on the sum awarded but as part of the sum awarded".[260] There seems in principle no reason why all money judgments should not be cast in this form whenever allowable prejudgment interest exceeds the rate of post-judgment interest, for all judgment creditors can make the argument that they are entitled to adequate compensation at the date of its actual payment. An incidental advantage to the creditor is that interest awarded by this technique is compounded.[261]

[257] (1979), 104 D.L.R. (3d) 174, 25 O.R. (2d) 399 (C.A.), affd [1981] 2 S.C.R. 613.

[258] [1980] 2 S.C.R. 694, 115 D.L.R. (3d) 257.

[259] *McLeod v. Palardy* (1981), 124 D.L.R. (3d) 506 (Man. C.A.); *Lutz v. Larocque*, [1981] 5 W.W.R. 1 (B.C.C.A.); *Comeau v. Marsman* (1981), 47 N.S.R. (2d) 550 (S.C.T.D.); *Hohol v. Pickering* (1982), 35 A.R. 181 (Q.B.), affd [1984] 3 W.W.R. 673, 51 A.R. 321 (C.A.); *Tronrud v. French* (1991), 84 D.L.R. (4th) 275, 75 Man. R. (2d) 1 (C.A.), leave to appeal to S.C.C. refused 87 D.L.R. (4th) vii, 138 N.R. 407*n*; *Skelding (Guardian ad Litem of) v. Skelding* (1992), 98 D.L.R. (4th) 219, 79 B.C.L.R. (2d) 177, supplementary reasons D.L.R. *loc. cit.* pp. 245 and 251, 15 C.P.C. (3d) 352 and 362 (S.C.), revd on other grounds 118 D.L.R. (4th) 537, [1994] 9 W.W.R. 538, leave to appeal to S.C.C. refused 119 D.L.R. (4th) vii.

[260] *Lewis v. Todd, supra*, footnote 258, at p. 716 S.C.R., p. 273 D.L.R., *per* Dickson J. See also *Joubert v. Rosetown (Town)* (1987), 60 Sask. R. 200 (C.A.).

[261] See *Lutz v. Larocque, supra*, footnote 259. In this case, five per cent under the *Interest Act* was awarded in addition, the court taking the combined effect into account. To avoid over-compensation, the period of time for interest to run under the *Interest Act* can be reduced. See *per* Lambert J.A., at p. 17. *Bank of America Canada* v. *Mutual Trust Co.* [2002] 2 S.C.R. 601, 211 D.L.R. (4th) 385, applies both to pre-judgment and to post-judgment interest.

PART II

NON-COMPENSATORY DAMAGES

CHAPTER 8

LIQUIDATED DAMAGES

1. Introduction

8.10 It is common for a party to whom a contractual performance is promised to seek to secure it by stipulating for a certain fixed sum of money to be payable on breach. The consequence of enforcing such a stipulation may have the effect of enabling the promisee to recover far more than compensation for the loss caused by the failure of performance. The effect is akin to a forfeiture. For over 300 years the courts have given relief against some provisions of this sort.[1]

8.20 The legal issues in this area are not, strictly speaking, remedial issues. Contracting parties agree that in a certain event one will pay the other $10,000. If the agreement is enforced, the $10,000 is recoverable as a debt not as damages. If the $10,000 is not recoverable, even though payment of it has been promised, the promise is unenforceable and the reasons for the result must be sought among the legal principles that determine enforceability of promises;[2] again it is not a question of damages.

8.30 Nevertheless, there are reasons of convenience, as well as historical and theoretical reasons, that require a writer on the law of damages to give attention to this area. As a practical matter, enforcement of a promise to pay an agreed sum is, in effect, a remedy for breach. The treatment of such promises in the 19th century was closely linked with damages, and though a modern writer might urge that unconscionability has always been and should be recognized as the underlying basis for relief, the fact is that the courts themselves have, until recently,[3] based relief on remedial theories. There is, in addition, a theoretical link with remedies in that the question of the enforceability of a promise to pay a stipulated sum on breach is part of the wider question of the power of the parties to control by their agreement the remedies that will be applied in case of default.[4]

8.40 Until the 19th century the desired security was commonly sought by use of a penal bond. The obligor entered into a bond whereby the obligor undertook to pay a certain sum. Then it was stated, as the condition of the bond, that it

1 Power to relieve against penalties is expressly preserved in some modern statutes; see, *e.g.*, *Law and Equity Act* (B.C.), s. 24.

2 See Waddams, *The Law of Contracts*, 5th ed. (Toronto, Canada Law Book, 2005), pp. 320-27.

3 For recent cases recognizing unconscionability as the basis of relief, see 8.150, 8.170, *infra*.

4 See Sharpe, *Injunctions and Specific Performance*, looseleaf ed. (Toronto, Canada Law Book, 1999), 7.640-7.810.

should be void if some other act were performed by a certain date. The purpose was to secure performance of the other act.[5] Alternatively, penal clauses were inserted into contracts. From the earliest times, equity relieved against enforcement of these bonds and clauses on the same principles on which it relieved against forfeitures;[6] the obligee's legitimate expectation was performance of the act and if full compensation was recovered for its non-performance, the obligee had received all that was due. The principal amount of the bond or the amount specified in the penalty clause, like mortgaged land, was intended only as a security, and resort to security ought not to make the obligee substantially richer than performance of what was, in substance, the primary obligation. In 1801 it was said that "the jurisdiction of Courts of Equity in relieving on penalties is of very high antiquity."[7] In 1880 Bramwell L.J., having referred to relief against forfeiture, described the approach of equity as follows:

> In other cases the Court of Chancery said that a penalty to secure the payment of a sum of money or the performance of an act should not be enforced; the parties were not held to their agreement; equity in truth refused to allow to be enforced what was considered to be an unconscientious bargain.[8]

8.50 Until the end of the 17th century, penal bonds and penalty clauses were theoretically enforceable at common law but equity granted relief.[9] In 1697 the equitable view was directly imposed on the common law courts by a statute providing that in an action on a penal bond, or on a penal clause in a contract, the plaintiff could have judgment for the amount due, but on payment into court by the defendant of the amount of the loss caused by breach, execution would be stayed, though the judgment remained as a security for future breaches.[10] In 1705 a similar statute was enacted dealing with late payment of debts secured by penal bonds.[11]

8.60 Though penal provisions were thus rendered entirely unenforceable, equity did not strike down every agreement to pay a sum of money on breach. If the agreement was not classified as "penal" the plaintiff was entitled to enforce it as a debt — that is, as a stipulated (or liquidated) sum payable upon breach.[12] The courts came to contrast (unenforceable) "penalty clauses" with (enforceable) "liquidated damages" clauses.

8.70 The modern position is that the courts have inherited a power, unusual

5 See *Corbin on Contracts* (St. Paul, West Publishing Co., 1964), §1056.

6 See Waddams, *op. cit.*, footnote 2, at pp. 315-20.

7 *Astley v. Weldon* (1801), 2 Bos. & Pul. 346 at p. 354, 126 E.R. 1318, *per* Chambre J.

8 *Protector Endowment Loan & Annuity Co. v. Grice* (1880), 5 Q.B.D. 592 (C.A.), at p. 596. See also *Re Dixon*, [1900] 2 Ch. 561 at p. 576, *per* Rigby L.J.

9 See *Lowe v. Peers* (1768), 4 Burr. 2225 at p. 2228, 98 E.R. 160, *per* Lord Mansfield.

10 *Administration of Justice Act, 1697*, s. 8. See *Ainslie v. Chapman* (1849), 5 U.C.Q.B. 313 at pp. 314-15.

11 *Administration of Justice Act, 1705*, ss. 12, 13.

12 In *Lowe v. Peers, supra*, footnote 9, Lord Mansfield said "where the covenant is "to pay a particular liquidated sum,' a Court of Equity can not make a new covenant for a man; nor is there any room for compensation or relief."

from the point of view of 19th century contract law, to strike down clauses in otherwise enforceable contracts. Since this power operated against the express intention of the parties, it followed that, just as in the analogous case of equitable relief from forfeiture, the form of words used by the parties could not be conclusive. Thus, it is very common for such clauses to be expressly described as "liquidated damages" and for the parties to agree that the named sum will be payable "as liquidated damages and not as a penalty". Nevertheless, the courts have not hesitated to disregard such expressions.[13] Less commonly the parties have described the stipulated sum as a penalty, and the courts have nevertheless held it to be enforceable.[14] As Lord Dunedin said in *Dunlop Pneumatic Tyre Co. Ltd. v. New Garage & Motor Co., Ltd.*,[15] the expression used by the parties is not conclusive. The court must find out whether the payment stipulated is "in truth" a penalty or liquidated damages.

8.80 The generally accepted test for determining this "truth" was thus described by Lord Dunedin: "The essence of a penalty is a payment of money stipulated as in terrorem of the offending party; the essence of liquidated damages is a genuine covenanted pre-estimate of damage".[16] Lord Dunedin then adds various tests that may be helpful or even conclusive:

> (*a*) It will be held to be penalty if the sum stipulated for is extravagant and unconscionable in amount in comparison with the greatest loss that could conceivably be proved to have followed from the breach ...
> (*b*) It will be held to be a penalty if the breach consists only in not paying a sum of money, and the sum stipulated is a sum greater than the sum which ought to have been paid ... This though one of the most ancient instances is truly a corollary to the last test ...
> (*c*) There is a presumption (but no more) that it is penalty when "a single lump sum is made payable by way of compensation, on the occurrence of one or more or all of several events, some of which may occasion serious and others but trifling damage"...
> On the other hand:

13 See, for example, *Shatilla v. Feinstein*, [1923] 3 D.L.R. 1035 (Sask. C.A.); *Craig v. Dillon* (1881), 6 O.A.R. 116 at pp. 118-19, *per* Burton J.A.; *Moose Jaw Industrialization Fund Committee Ltd. v. Chadwick*, [1943] 2 W.W.R. 219 (Sask. K.B.); *Ainslie v. Chapman*, *supra*, footnote 10. But see *Dominion Art Co. Ltd. v. Murphy* (1923), 54 O.L.R. 332 (S.C. App. Div.), where strong emphasis was put on freedom of contract, *per* Meredith C.J.C.P., at pp. 339-40; *Dezcam Industries & Dezura v. Kwak*, [1983] 5 W.W.R. 32, 44 B.C.L.R. 105 (C.A.); *Federal Business Development Bank v. Eldridge* (1986), 76 N.B.R. (2d) 399 (C.A.). See also *Edwards v. Moore* (1906), 1 E.L.R. 422 (N.B. Full Ct.).

14 *Elphinstone v. Monkland Iron & Coal Co., Ltd.* (1886), 11 App. Cas. 332 (H.L.); *Clydebank Engineering & Shipbuilding Co., Ltd. v. Don Jose Ramos Yzquierdo y Castaneda*, [1905] A.C. 6 (H.L.); *McManus v. Rothschild* (1911), 25 O.L.R. 138 (Div. Ct.); *Canada (Attorney General) v. Khimani* (1985), 50 O.R. (2d) 476 (C.A.). But see *Huffman v. Spalding* (1989), 57 D.L.R. (4th) 589, 56 Man. R. (2d) 317 (C.A.) (agreed system of fines struck down without regard to its reasonableness). Business persons commonly speak of penalty clauses to include agreements to pay liquidated damages. See *Crippen v. Hitchner* (1911), 18 W.L.R. 259 (B.C. Co. Ct.), at p. 265; *869163 Ontario Ltd. v. Torrey Springs II Associates Limited Partnership* (2005), 256 D.L.R. (4th) 490 (Ont. C.A.) at paras. 33-4.

15 [1915] A.C. 79 (H.L.).

16 *Supra*, at p. 86.

> (*d*) It is no obstacle to the sum stipulated being a genuine pre-estimate of damage, that the consequences of the breach are such as to make precise pre-estimation almost an impossibility. On the contrary, that is just the situation when it is probable that pre-estimated damage was the true bargain between the parties.[17]

In *Canadian General Electric Co. v. Canadian Rubber Co.*,[18] Fitzpatrick C.J. laid down a test in similar terms: "A penalty is the payment of a stipulated sum on breach of the contract, irrespective of the damage sustained. The essence of liquidated damages is a genuine covenanted pre-estimate of damage."[19]

8.90 Lord Dunedin's tests, perhaps because they are given in a catalogue form that seems easy to apply, have been very often cited,[20] but like all judicial opinions Lord Dunedin's speech must be read in the context of the particular case. The New Garage Company had covenanted not to resell Dunlop's products below current prices, not to supply to persons named by Dunlop, and not to exhibit or expose the products without consent. The disputed clause was a promise to pay £5 "for each and every tyre, cover or tube sold or offered in breach of this agreement, as and by way of liquidated damages and not as a penalty". The House of Lords unanimously held that the clause was enforceable.

8.100 The purpose of Dunlop's price maintenance scheme was, as explained by Lord Atkinson,[21] to protect its system of distribution, which was through agents who could not make a profit if they were liable to be undersold by Dunlop's other customers. In modern times resale price maintenance might be considered contrary to public policy as in restraint of competition,[22] but it was plainly assumed by the House of Lords that Dunlop had a legitimate and proper interest in maintaining resale prices. Given this premiss, the £5 clause was bound to seem an entirely reasonable — indeed almost the only practical — means of implementing the scheme.[23]

8.110 The speeches of Lords Atkinson, Parker, and Parmoor do not repeat Lord Dunedin's formula and do not make express reference to his speech. It would be a mistake therefore to read Lord Dunedin's tests as though they had the express approval of the House of Lords — still less as though they had anything like the force of statute. Lord Dunedin formulated his tests in order to reconcile the result in the *Dunlop* case with statements in former cases,[24]

---

17 *Supra*, at p. 87.

18 (1915), 52 S.C.R. 349, 27 D.L.R. 294.

19 *Supra*, at p. 351 S.C.R., p. 295 D.L.R.

20 *Shatilla v. Feinstein*, *supra*, footnote 13; *Waugh v. Pioneer Logging Co. Ltd.*, [1949] S.C.R. 299, [1949] 2 D.L.R. 577; *Turnbull v. Dobrovalsky*, [1946] 1 D.L.R. 200 (Sask. C.A.); *Reimer v. Rosen* (1919), 45 D.L.R. 1 (Man. C.A.); *Nordin v. Metal Fabricating & Construction Ltd.*, [1995] 2 W.W.R. 750, 126 Sask. R. 259 (Q.B.).

21 *Supra*, footnote 15, at pp. 91-3.

22 *Competition Act* (Can.), s. 61(1).

23 See also *Schrader v. Lillis* (1886), 10 O.R. 358 (H.C.J.).

24 Particularly *Elphinstone v. Monkland Iron & Coal Co. Ltd.*, *supra*, footnote 14.

but the tests are not easy to apply to the *Dunlop* case itself. The first test is said to be that the essence of a penalty is that it is stipulated "in terrorem".

[*The next page is* 8-5]

This must mean that the object is to deter breaches of contract by inducing a fear in the party tempted to commit breach of having to pay the stipulated sum. It seems plain, however, that this was exactly what was intended by the Dunlop Company, and the fact that the case was litigated to the highest court suggests that the threat was probably an effective one.

8.120 The second branch of Lord Dunedin's main test is equally difficult to apply to the result of the case: "the essence of liquidated damages is a genuine covenanted pre-estimate of damage". This must mean an attempt to estimate what actual loss would be caused by breach, but Dunlop did not prove that any single sale or offer to sell a single article below the listed price would cause any loss at all. As is clear from Lord Atkinson's speech,[25] it was not the individual sale that would cause loss but the undermining of Dunlop's agency system of marketing. Then, it is often said that where a single sum is payable on a variety of breaches, some serious and some trivial, "the strength of the chain must be taken at its weakest link",[26] that is, the clause is to be struck down if the amount stipulated is excessive in respect of the most trivial breach that would make it contractually payable.[27] But the result in the *Dunlop* case is flatly against this test, for £5 would be extravagant compensation for a single sale or for an individual offer to sell at one penny less than the listed price. Lord Dunedin reconciled the result with the test, by saying that the loss for any breach was indirect damage and so all of the same nature.[28] The other lords said that though there might be a presumption that a sum payable on a variety of breaches was a penalty, the presumption could easily be rebutted and had been rebutted in this case.[29]

8.130 Many phrases throughout the speeches indicate that what concerned the court was whether the agreement was fair and reasonable in the circumstances. Lord Dunedin said at the outset that the first question was whether the sum was extravagant and unconscionable,[30] and he explained a former case as having held the sum stipulated not "unconscionable".[31] Lord Atkinson said that the agreement contained nothing "unreasonable, uncon-

25 *Supra*, footnote 15, at pp. 90-7.

26 *Supra*, at p. 89, *per* Lord Dunedin.

27 *Dimech v. Corlett* (1858), 12 Moore 199 at p. 230, 14 E.R. 887 (P.C.); *Elphinstone v. Monkland Iron & Coal Co., Ltd.* (1886), 11 App. Cas. 332 (H.L.), at pp. 342-3; *Shatilla v. Feinstein*, *supra*, footnote 13; *Waugh v. Pioneer Logging Co. Ltd.*, [1949] S.C.R. 299, [1949] 2 D.L.R. 577; *The King v. London Guarantee & Accident Co. Ltd.* (1920), 19 Ex. C.R. 385, 51 D.L.R. 624; *Pelee Island Navigation Co. v. Doty Engine Works Co.* (1911), 23 O.L.R. 402 (Div. Ct.), at pp. 411 and 413-14; *Dezcam Industries & Dezura v. Kwak*, [1983] 5 W.W.R. 32, 44 B.C.L.R. 105 (C.A.). See *Craig v. Dillon* (1881), 6 O.A.R. 116 at pp. 118-19; *McPhee v. Wilson* (1866), 25 U.C.Q.B. 169 (small sum payable for each day of default upheld); *Corp. of Village of Brussels v. Ronald* (1885), 11 O.A.R. 605. See *Com'r of Public Works v. Hills*, [1906] A.C. 368, followed in *Lund v. Vancouver Exhibition Ass'n* (1915), 25 D.L.R. 863 (B.C.C.A.).

28 [1915] A.C. 79 at p. 88.

29 *Supra*, at p. 96, *per* Lord Atkinson; pp. 98-9, *per* Lord Parker; p. 102, *per* Lord Parmoor.

30 *Supra*, at p. 87.

31 *Elphinstone v. Monkland Iron & Coal Co. Ltd.* (1886), 11 App. Cas. 332 (H.L.). See *Dunlop Pneumatic Tyre*, *supra*, footnote 28, at p. 89.

scionable, or extravagant".[32] Lord Parker said "I can see nothing to justify the court in refusing to give effect to this bargain".[33] Lord Parmoor said the agreed sum was not "extravagant or extortionate".[34] Similar phrases appear in a Supreme Court of Canada case decided shortly afterwards.[35] Now that unconscionability or a similar principle of fairness is widely recognized as a general defence in contract law,[36] there seems strong reason to assimilate the law relating to penalty clauses. The Supreme Court of Canada has given support to this approach. In *Elsley v. J.G. Collins Ins. Agencies Ltd.*[37] Dickson J. said: "It is now evident that the power to strike down a penalty clause is a blatant interference with freedom of contract and is designed for the sole purpose of providing relief against oppression for the party having to pay the stipulated sum. It has no place where there is no oppression."[38] This dictum is itself difficult to reconcile with some of the cases, including a decision of the Supreme Court of Canada.[39] It is submitted, however, that Dickson J.'s view is sound and that open recognition of unconscionability as the basis of relief will greatly facilitate the rational development of this branch of the law.

2. Disguised Penalty Clauses

8.140 It was stated previously that the parties cannot ensure the validity of the clause by describing it as a "liquidated damages" clause.[40] Similarly, clauses aimed at producing the same effect as penalty clauses have sometimes been struck down. An example is *Graham v. Wagman*[41] where the defendant agreed to supply indoor parking spaces for the plaintiff at a monthly rent of $25 each, to be reduced to $5 until all the agreed places were provided. The effect of the reduction in agreed rent was to increase the damages calculated on the ordinary basis of the difference between contract and market price. The Ontario Court of Appeal held that the price reduction clause was

32 *Supra*, at p. 97.

33 *Supra*, at p. 99.

34 *Supra*, at p. 101.

35 *Canadian General Electric Co. v. Canadian Rubber Co.* (1915), 52 S.C.R. 349 at pp. 356, 371, 27 D.L.R. 294 at pp. 298, 308. Similar phrases appear in early Canadian cases: see *Henderson v. Nichols* (1849), 5 U.C.Q.B. 398 at p. 400, *per* Robinson C.J. (clause construed as penalty if effect of enforcing it "unjust").

36 See cases cited by Waddams, *The Law of Contracts*, 5th ed. (Toronto, Canada Law Book, 2005), pp. 313-92, and *Hunter Engineering Co. v. Syncrude Canada Ltd.*, [1989] 1 S.C.R. 426, 57 D.L.R. (4th) 321.

37 [1978] 2 S.C.R. 916, 83 D.L.R. (3d) 1. See also *Prudential Insurance Co. of America v. Cedar Hills Properties Ltd.*, [1995] 3 W.W.R. 360, 100 B.C.L.R. (2d) 312 (C.A.); *Fern Investments Ltd. v. Golden Nugget Restaurant (1987) Ltd.* (1994), 19 Alta. L.R. (3d) 442, 149 A.R. 303 (C.A.); *32262 B.C. Ltd. v. See-Rite Optical Ltd.*, [1998] 9 W.W.R. 442 (Alta. C.A.), at p. 448, citing this paragraph.

38 *Supra*, at p. 937 S.C.R., p. 15 D.L.R; *McNamara Construction Co. v. Newfoundland Transshipment Ltd.* (2002), 213 Nfld. & P.E.I.R. 1 (Nfld & Lab. S.C.T.D.) (price reduction for delayed delivery).

39 *H.F. Clarke Ltd. v. Thermidaire Corp. Ltd.*, [1976] 1 S.C.R. 319, 54 D.L.R. (3d) 385.

40 See 8.70, *supra*.

41 (1978), 89 D.L.R. (3d) 282, 21 O.R. (2d) 1 (C.A.).

unenforceable as a penalty. Another example is *Macdonald v. N.W. Biscuit Co. Ltd.*[42] where a builder agreed, in case of default, to pay a sum calculated by deducting the actual value of the incomplete work plus fifty per cent from the contract price. The fifty per cent addition was held by the Alberta Appellate Division to be penal.

8.150 It is common in leases of land or chattels to find "acceleration clauses" whereby the whole of the rent or a predetermined part of it becomes immediately payable on default. Some cases have held that such a provision is not a penalty because it simply provides for payment of an agreed price.[43] Other cases, however, have struck down such clauses where they have the effect of putting the plaintiff in a better position than would have been occupied on performance of the contract.[44] A number of Canadian cases have held that such clauses, being "penal in nature", are to be "strictly construed".[45] Several recent cases have directly stated that such clauses are enforceable if not unconscionable.[46] In England where a chattel lease with an option to purchase is used as a consumer sales credit device, clauses enabling the lessor to recover a fixed portion of the rent in addition to repossessing the goods have been struck down.[47] It may be pointed out that at times of high interest rates even the acceleration (without repossession of goods) of

[42] [1924] 1 D.L.R. 987 (Alta. S.C. App. Div.). See also *Jobson v. Johnson*, [1989] 1 W.L.R. 1026 (C.A.).

[43] *Protector Endowment Loan & Annuity Co. v. Grice* (1880), 5 Q.B.D. 592 (C.A.); *Wallingford v. Mutual Society* (1880), 5 App. Cas. 685 (H.L.); *Re Emerald Christmas Tree Co. and Boel & Sons Enterprises* (1979), 105 D.L.R. (3d) 75 (B.C.C.A.); *Alwest Neon Signs Ltd. v. Henze* (1989), 105 A.R. 343 (C.A.). In *Neonette Sign Co. v. Stankovic & Petrovic* (1961), 66 B.C.L.R. 269 (C.A.), and *Direct Leasing Ltd. v. Chu* (1976), 71 D.L.R. (3d) 303 (B.C.S.C.), an acceleration clause was upheld on the ground that the chattels leased would have had little salvage value to the lessor on repossession.

[44] *Charterhouse Leasing Corp. Ltd. v. Sanmac Holdings Ltd.* (1966), 58 D.L.R. (2d) 656 (Alta. S.C.); *Canadian Acceptance Corp. Ltd. v. Regent Park Butcher Shop Ltd.* (1969), 3 D.L.R. (3d) 304 (Man. C.A.); *Bridge v. Campbell Discount Co. Ltd.*, [1962] A.C. 600 (H.L.); *International Harvester Credit Corp. of Canada Ltd. v. Dolphin* (1978), 88 D.L.R. (3d) 326 (Alta. S.C.T.D.); *RCA Victor Co. Ltd. v. Pelletier* (1968), 68 D.L.R. (2d) 13 (N.B.S.C. App. Div.); *Neonoex International Ltd. v. Wassill*, [1974] 1 W.W.R. 587 (Sask. Dist. Ct.); *Millbrook Holdings Inc. v. Ken Nelson & Sons Trucking Ltd.*, [1978] 5 W.W.R. 107 (B.C.S.C.); *Car Leasing (Alberta) Ltd. v. Swinhoe* (1978), 15 A.R. 22 (Dist. Ct.); *Diamond Neon (Manufacturing) Ltd. v. Dufour* (1980), 18 B.C.L.R. 334 (Co. Ct.); *Unilease Inc. v. York Steel Construction Ltd.* (1978), 83 D.L.R. (3d) 275, 18 O.R. (2d) 559 (C.A.).

[45] *General Motors Acceptance Corp. of Canada Ltd. v. Hiebert*, [1955] 3 D.L.R. 857 (B.C.S.C.); *Child & Gower Piano Co. Ltd. v. Gambrel*, [1933] 2 W.W.R. 273 (Sask. C.A.); *Gill v. Yorkshire Ins. Co.* (1913), 12 D.L.R. 172 (Man. K.B.); *Mayer v. Abrams* (1965), 51 D.L.R. (2d) 128 (B.C.S.C.), affd 55 D.L.R. (2d) 194*n* (C.A.).

[46] *Claude Neon Ltd. v. KDJ Enterprises Ltd.*, [1996] 1 W.W.R. 390, 136 Sask. R. 66 (Q.B.) (agreement should be enforced *unless* highly unreasonable); *Security Leasing Co. v. Balkan Restaurant Ltd.*, [1976] 5 W.W.R. 590 (B.C. Co. Ct.); *Francis Fuels Ltd. v. Taggart* (1976), 72 D.L.R. (3d) 22, 13 O.R. (2d) 619 (Small Claims Ct.); *Tkachuk Farms Ltd. v. Le Blanc Auction Service Ltd.*, [2007] 2 W.W.R. 662 (Sask. Q.B.), para. 101, affd [2008] 6 W.W.R. 132 (Sask. C.A.) (clause not "extravagant or unconscionable"). See *Nordin v. Metal Fabricating & Construction Ltd.*, [1995] 2 W.W.R. 750, 126 Sask. R. 259 (Q.B.); *32262 B.C. Ltd. v. See-Rite Optical Ltd.*, [1998] 9 W.W.R. 442 (Alta. C.A.), at p. 448, citing this paragraph.

periodic payments will confer a marked benefit on the recipient which might, in some cases, be sufficient to invite judicial intervention.[48]

8.160 A common way of disguising a penalty clause is by way of a discount for prompt payment. Early cases held such a provision to be outside the court's control,[49] with the consequence, as Jessel M.R. pointed out, of making the results depend, irrationally, on form and not on substance.[50] It is submitted that a modern Canadian court would, in the light of the cases just mentioned, look to the substance of the matter and strike down such a clause if persuaded that it was unconscionable.

8.170 Unconscionability is, it is submitted, the only workable criterion, for a payment that seems extravagant in one context may appear quite reasonable in another. As in the case of disguised mortgages,[51] the court must look at the agreement as a whole and ask whether, in substance, the clause sought to be enforced is designed to secure the performance of another obligation. If so and if enforcement of the clause will confer a benefit on the promisee out of all proportion to the benefit that would have been received if the primary obligation had been fulfilled, the clause should be struck down as unconscionable.[52]

8.180 A severe problem with the current law of penalty clauses is that it has been held to apply only to money payable on breach of contract.[53] So a hirer who terminates a chattel lease contract in accordance with an option in the contract to do so (the contract expressly providing for termination on payment of a certain sum) has no claim to relief because there is no breach of contract. "Let no one mistake the injustice of this" Lord Denning was moved to say: "It means that equity commits itself to this absurd paradox: it will grant relief to a man who breaks his contract but will penalise the man who keeps it."[54] In *Alder v. Moore*[55] the defendant, who had received £500 from

---

47 *Cooden Engineering Co. v. Stanford*, [1953] 1 Q.B. 86 (C.A.); *Bridge v. Campbell Discount Co. Ltd.*, [1962] A.C. 600 (H.L.). It should be noted that in Canada other devices are available in most provinces to protect consumer credit buyers.

48 See *Anglo Auto Finance Co. v. James*, [1963] 1 W.L.R. 1042 (C.A.), at pp. 1046-7. In *Highway Properties Ltd. v. Kelly, Douglas & Co. Ltd.*, [1971] S.C.R. 562, 17 D.L.R. (3d) 710, an acceleration clause in a land lease was held (*obiter*) to be enforceable, but the clause was for three months' rent only and the agreement was a commercial one. Similarly in *John Burrows Ltd. v. Subsurface Surveys Ltd.*, [1968] S.C.R. 607, 68 D.L.R. (2d) 354, an acceleration clause in an agreement securing the unpaid price of a business was enforced, but the interest was separately calculated, and again, the agreement was a commercial one with no suggestion of inequality of bargaining power.

49 *Astley v. Weldon* (1801), 2 Bos. & Pul. 346 at p. 353, 126 E.R. 1318, *per* Heath J.

50 *Wallis v. Smith* (1882), 21 Ch. D. 243 (C.A.), at p. 261.

51 See Waddams, *The Law of Contracts*, 5th ed. (Toronto, Canada Law Book, 2005), pp. 328-32.

52 *Meunier v. Cloutier* (1984), 9 D.L.R. (4th) 486 at p. 492, 46 O.R. (2d) 188 (H.C.J.), citing this paragraph.

53 *Bridge v. Campbell Discount Co. Ltd.*, [1962] A.C. 600 (H.L.); *Export Credits Guarantee Department v. Universal Oil Products Co.*, [1983] 2 All E.R. at p. 222 (H.L.). See *United Dominions Trust (Commercial) Ltd. v. Ennis*, [1968] 1 Q.B. 54 (C.A.), at p. 67; *Ellis v. Frughtman* (1912), 8 D.L.R. 353 (Alta. S.C. en banc), at p. 356 (reservation of rights to terminate upon payment of agreed sum).

the plaintiff under a disability insurance policy, promised not to play professional football "and in the event of infringement of this condition I will be subject to a penalty [of £500]." It was held that the clause was enforceable, one reason given being that the contract created an option in the defendant not to play football or to pay £500. But the real reason was plainly that, as Sellers L.J. said several times,[56] the promise was in no way unreasonable or unjust or extravagant or unconscionable. If it were recognized that it was unconscionability that was at the root of the court's intervention the court could, as equity has always done with forfeitures, look at the substance of the matter and not at the form in which the obligation is cast.

8.190 In *Ellis v. Frughtman*,[57] an employment agreement provided that, on termination by either party, the sum of $500 should be paid. On a termination by the employer it was held that the sum was recoverable. Simmons J. held that the agreed sum was liquidated damages, but Walsh J. rested his decision on a right to terminate:

> This agreement specially reserves to either of the parties the right to terminate it, and the sum which is mentioned is the price agreed upon for the exercise of that right.
>
> The defendants exercised the right thus reserved to them, and they should therefore be made to pay the agreed price.[58]

8.195 In *Doman Forest Products Ltd. v. GMAC Commercial Credit Corp. - Canada*,[58a] an agreed "early termination fee" in a loan agreement was held to be enforceable.

8.200 It is submitted that a sharp distinction between sums payable on breach and sums payable on lawful termination is irrational and will create anomalies. If the agreement is objectionable, it should be set aside in whichever form it is cast; if it is fair and reasonable, it should be upheld in either form. It is suggested that unconscionability offers the only satisfactory solution to these problems. In New Brunswick, statute provides that a penalty clause or liquidated damages clause is enforceable "to the extent that it is reasonable in all of the circumstances that the clause should be enforced".[58b]

3. Time for Application of Test

8.210 The established view in Anglo-Canadian law is that the character of the disputed clause is to be assessed at the time of the contract.[59] Thus, if the

---

54 *Bridge v. Campbell Discount Co. Ltd., supra*, footnote 53, at p. 629.

55 [1961] 2 Q.B. 57 (C.A.).

56 *Supra*, at pp. 64-6.

57 *Supra*, footnote 53.

58 *Supra*, footnote 53, at p. 356.

58a (2007), 65 B.C.L.R. (4th) 1 (C.A.). See also *Hargobind Shake & Shingle Ltd. v. Golden Gate Land Co. & Associates Inc.* (2007), 66 B.C.L.R. (4th) 90 (C.A.) (cancellation fee enforced).

58b *Law Reform Act* of 1993, s. 5(1).

59 *Clydebank Engineering Co. v. Don Jose Ramos Yzquierdo y Castaneda*, [1905] A.C. 6 (H.L.); *Com'r of Public Works v. Hills*, [1906] A.C. 368 (P.C.); *Jobson v. Johnson*, [1989] 1 W.L.R. 1026 (C.A.).

clause is a genuine pre-estimate of likely damage at that time, it is valid and enforceable even though subsequent events prove that the loss actually caused by the defendant's breach is negligible. It is submitted that this is a sound approach and is consistent with the usual tests of unconscionability.[60] If the reason for refusing enforcement is that the agreement is unfair, the proper time to judge the unfairness must be the time of the agreement. The scope of the parties' agreement, however, may often have to be determined in the light of subsequent events.[61] Thus it may well be argued, if unexpected events occur that have the effect of making the breach harmless to the plaintiff, that the sum stipulated was not, as a matter of construction, payable in those circumstances. If this argument fails, the defendant will then be able to argue that the clause is not a genuine pre-estimate (or that it is unconscionable) because, as construed, it compels payment of a large sum in circumstances where there is no actual loss.[62]

4. Sum Stipulated as Limit on Recovery

8.220 Where a stipulated sum is struck down as a penalty, the plaintiff can always recover the actual loss if this is less.[63] Where the plaintiff's actual loss exceeds the sum stipulated it will often be found, judging the matter as at the time of the contract, that the stipulated sum was a genuine preestimate of loss. In that case the clause will usually be taken to operate for the benefit of either party. If the plaintiff's actual loss is less, the plaintiff will recover the sum stipulated. If the actual loss is more, the plaintiff will be limited to the same sum.[64] This conclusion rests on the intention of the parties. The plaintiff cannot recover the actual loss because (as the contract is construed) the plaintiff has agreed that the stipulated sum shall be the limit of the defendant's liability. Since the conclusion rests on the parties' intention, it can be rebutted where, on ordinary principles of construction, the parties do

---

60 The same conclusion is reached from an economic perspective, by Rea, "Efficiency Implications of Penalties and Liquidated Damages", 13 J. Leg. Stud. 147 (1984).

61 *Meunier v. Cloutier*, *supra*, footnote 52.

62 In the American case of *Massman Const. Co. v. City Council of Greenville, Miss.*, 147 F. 2d 925 (C.A., 1945), where an agreed daily sum was to be paid for late completion of a bridge, the court took into account the fact that the bridge would in any case have been unusable because the road leading to it had not been completed by state authorities. It is suggested that the technique of construction proposed here would enable a Canadian court to reach the same conclusion.

63 *Com'r of Public Works v. Hills*, *supra*, footnote 59; *Shatilla v. Feinstein*, [1923] 3 D.L.R. 1035 (Sask. C.A.); *R.C.A. Victor Co. Ltd. v. Pelletier* (1968), 68 D.L.R. (2d) 13 (N.B.S.C. App. Div.).

64 *Diestal v. Stevenson*, [1906] 2 K.B. 345; *Gisvold v. Hill* (1963), 37 D.L.R. (2d) 606 (B.C.S.C.); *Dorge v. Dumesnil* (1973), 39 D.L.R. (3d) 750 (Man. Q.B.); *Cellulose Acetate Silk Co., Ltd. v. Widnes Foundry (1925) Ltd.*, [1933] A.C. 20 (H.L.); *Empire Theatre v. Regal Films Ltd.* (1922), 22 O.W.N. 343, affd 23 O.W.N. 383 (Div. Ct.); *MacKenzie v. D.M. Bruce Agencies Ltd.* (1977), 21 N.S.R. (2d) 668 (S.C. App. Div.); *Maxwell v. Gibsons Drugs Ltd.* (1979), 103 D.L.R. (3d) 433 (B.C.S.C.); *Seeley v. Conroy* (1977), 19 N.B.R. (2d) 1 (S.C. App. Div.); *Labatt (John) Ltd. v. Financial Trustco Capital Co.* (1989), 96 A.R. 56 (Q.B.); *Erskine Building Corp. v. First College Grenville Holdings Inc.* (1993), 13 C.L.R. (2d) 51 (Ont. Ct. (Gen. Div.)).

not intend the sum to limit liability. Such a case arose in *Wall v. Rederiaktiebolaget Luggude*,[65] where a clause in a charterparty read: "Penalty for non-performance of this agreement proved damages, not exceeding estimated amount of freight." It was held that the charterers were entitled to waive the clause and to recover their actual damages, which were about three times the estimated amount of freight. An important point in Bailhache J.'s reasoning was that limitation of liability had customarily been effected in charter-parties by a very different kind of clause, and it was wholly unreasonable to suppose that a charterer would have read what was always called the "penalty" clause as a clause actually preventing it from recovering its true loss. The words "proved damages not exceeding" had been added to the older form of the clause in order to express the inability of the charterer to recover *more* than its actual loss not to restrict it to less than that loss. Bailhache J. said:

> Upon this I should like to observe that I should require the strongest arguments to induce me to hold that a clause so like the common and undoubted penalty clause has been transformed by the addition of a few words into a limitation of liability clause, to which in form it bears no resemblance. It would be unfair to the charterers in this or any similar case to do so unless the few additional words were of compelling force. Business men are familiar with the usual charterparty clauses. They do not read apparently common form clauses carefully. They know the penalty clause is of no effect, and when they see a clause beginning "Penalty for non-performance" they assume it is their familiar negligible penalty clause, and they pass on. It would never strike them that a clause beginning in that way was a limitation of liability clause, the very appearance of which is usually totally different, and is one to which they know they must pay attention or put up with the consequences.[66]

This is, it is submitted, a sound approach consistent with the ordinary principles of contract law. It was expressly approved by the House of Lords in *Watts & Co., Ltd. v. Mitsui & Co., Ltd.*[67] However there is some uncertainty about the effect of a decision of the Supreme Court of Canada in *Elsley v. J.G. Collins Ins. Agencies Ltd.*[68] where $1,000 was agreed to be paid "as and for liquidated damages" for breach of a covenant against competition. It was held that this clause had the effect of limiting the plaintiff to damages of $1,000.

8.230 The primary ground on which the court rested its conclusion appears to be that the clause, on its true construction, was intended to limit damages. Thus Dickson J. said: "if the parties have agreed on a set amount of damages at law, or a maximum amount, it would be unconscionable, in my opinion, to

---

65 [1915] 3 K.B. 66. See also *Beitel v. Sorokin* (1973), 38 D.L.R. (3d) 455 (Alta. S.C. App. Div.), affd 42 D.L.R. (3d) 319*n* (S.C.C.) (forfeiture clause may be waived); *Sleeman v. Waterous* (1873), 23 U.C.C.P. 195 (recovery of actual damages allowed in excess of penalty).

66 *Supra*, footnote 65, at pp. 74-5.

67 [1917] A.C. 227 (H.L.).

68 [1978] 2 S.C.R. 916, 83 D.L.R. (3d) 1.

allow recovery of a greater amount of damages in equity."[69] The passage quoted above, indicating that the jurisdiction to interfere with contracts "is designed for the sole purpose of providing relief against oppression",[70] also suggests that the intention of the parties should prevail (unless oppressive). On this basis the decision rests on construction of the liquidated damages clause and is fully consistent with the earlier cases.

8.240 However, Dickson J. goes on to say:

> If the actual loss turns out to exceed the penalty, the normal rule of enforcement of contract should apply to allow recovery of only the agreed sum. The party imposing the penalty should not be able to obtain the benefit of whatever intimidating force the penalty clause may have in inducing performance, and then ignore the clause when it turns out to be to his advantage to do so. A penalty clause should function as a limitation on the damages recoverable, while still being ineffective to increase damages above the actual loss sustained when such loss is less than the stipulated amount. As expressed by Lord Ellenborough in *Wilbeam v. Ashton* [(1807), 1 Camp. 78, 170 E.R. 883,] "beyond the penalty you shall not go; within it you are to give the party any compensation which he can prove himself entitled to."[71]

The earlier part of this passage, referring to the normal rule of enforcement of contracts, is consistent with the view put forward earlier. The later part might be taken to suggest that the very existence of the penalty operates (irrespective of the parties' intention) as a limitation of liability. This view is inconsistent with the decisions mentioned previously (not cited by the Supreme Court of Canada) and seems difficult to reconcile with general principle. There seems no compelling reason to deny the plaintiff compensation for the loss unless on the true

[*The next page is* 8-13]

69 *Supra,* at p. 935 S.C.R., pp. 13-14 D.L.R.
70 *Supra,* at p. 937 S.C.R., p. 15 D.L.R. See 8.130, *supra.*
71 *Supra.*

construction of the contract, the plaintiff has agreed to a limitation of liability. The mere fact that the plaintiff stipulates for a penalty cannot always be taken to amount to a promise to limit liability. It is to be hoped, therefore, that the words of Dickson J. just quoted will be read in the light of the whole judgment and the decision in the case itself, neither of which, it is submitted, is necessarily inconsistent with the view expressed here.

8.250 Further support for the view that mention of a stipulated sum is not inconsistent with recovery of larger damages is lent by the Alberta Court of Appeal case of *Lozcal Holdings Ltd. v. Brassos Developments Ltd.*[72] where, in a land sale agreement, it was provided that on the purchaser's default the deposit was to be forfeited as liquidated damages. It was held that the vendor was entitled to recover the actual damages exceeding the amount of the deposit. The court reached this conclusion on principles of construction:

> Certainly . . . the parties may, by their contract, govern the arrangements between them, and if they provide that the vendor's damages in the event of breach by the purchaser were to be limited to the deposit paid, it would have been competent for them to do so. The question here is whether they have done this by providing that the deposit shall be "forfeited as liquidated damages".
>
> In my view, if the intention were to limit the purchaser's liability, that could have been easily said, and the Court should not import into the words "as liquidated damages" (particularly when they appear in a printed form) any such intention. It seems to me that very much more express language is required.[73]

The question of the proper construction is debatable. There is, perhaps, a stronger argument than the court admitted for the view that the vendor, having stipulated for a substantial benefit if the damages should prove to be less than the deposit, should be held to the same amount where damages prove to be greater;[74] but in approaching the matter as a question of construction the court was, it is submitted, on sound ground.

72 (1980), 111 D.L.R. (3d) 598 (Alta. C.A.). But see *Labatt (John) Ltd. v. Financial Trustco Capital Co., supra*, footnote 64, and *Bains & Sarai Holdings Ltd. v. Sahota* (1985), 63 B.C.L.R. 206, 37 R.P.R. 70 (C.A.).

73 *Supra*, at p. 603. The same conclusion was reached in *Mitchell v. Paddington Homes Ltd.* (1977), 3 B.C.L.R. 330 (S.C.) ("on account of liquidated damages"), and in *Raymer v. Stratton Woods Holdings Ltd.* (1988) 51 D.L.R. (4th) 145, 65 O.R. (2d) 16 (C.A.).

74 In discussing the earlier case of *Gisvold v. Hill* (1963), 37 D.L.R. (2d) 606 (B.C.S.C.), the court emphasized that the intention of the parties should prevail and that the use of a phrase in a document (such as "liquidated damages"), while relevant, was not determinative of a genuine intention to limit recovery. See *Lozcal Holdings, supra*, footnote 72, at p. 606. In *Seeley v. Conroy* (1977), 19 N.B.R. (2d) 1 (S.C. App. Div.), a deposit of $200, to be forfeited as liquidated damages on breach, was held to limit the vendor's recovery. In *E. & B. Mortgages Ltd. v. Skrivanos* (1980), 118 D.L.R. (3d) 139, 18 R.P.R. 215 (B.C.S.C.), it was held that a purchaser guilty of an anticipatory repudiation could not rely on a similar clause to limit damages. See 12.260, *infra*. See also *Goulet & Son Ltd. v. Lalonde* (1983), 149 D.L.R. (3d) 577, 23 Man. R. (2d) 166 (C.A.), where a vendor's recovery was limited to the deposit despite the absence of any reference to "liquidated damages". The agreement was construed to exclude a right to

5. Availability of Specific Relief

8.260 The mere fact that a liquidated damages clause limits the sum payable on breach does not foreclose the possibility of specific remedies, where these are on other grounds appropriate. The exclusion of specific remedies would only be appropriate if the contract were to be interpreted as giving the defendant an option to perform or to pay the stipulated sum at choice, and this is not, according to most cases, the effect of an ordinary liquidated damages clause.[75]

8.270 If the plaintiff recovers an injunction that assures full actual performance, the plaintiff cannot then recover liquidated damages because, as Osler J.A. said in *Snider v. McKelvey*,[76] the plaintiff would then be "obtaining performance of the agreement in specie and also what he was only to be entitled to recover in the case of its non-performance."[77] In *Elsley v. J.G. Collins Ins. Agencies*,[78] the Supreme Court of Canada held that the plaintiff could obtain liquidated damages of $1,000 and, also, an injunction to restrain future breaches of a covenant against competition. Dickson J. said:

> The injunction relates to the latter part of the period in respect of which the restrictive covenant imposes restraint, the damages (not exceeding the stipulated liquidated damages) relate to the period prior to the granting of the injunction and are in substitution for injunctive relief during that period.[79]

This conclusion must, it seems, be based on a construction of the $1,000 sum agreed as applicable only to breaches occurring in the eighteen-month period before the granting of the injunction. Though artificial, this construction seems necessary, for if the $1,000 were really interpreted as the genuine pre-estimated agreed damages for a breach of the full five-year period of the restrictive covenant, it would be inconsistent, on Dickson J.'s own analysis,[80] to award that sum in addition to an injunction restraining breach for part of the period. The corollary is that if an injunction seems appropriate, the parties probably did not intend the money sum to be an agreed limitation on the defendant's liability.

---

damages on forfeiture of the deposit. See also *Leibel v. Glenway Land Corp.* (1996), 1 R.P.R. (3d) 276 (Ont. Ct. (Gen. Div.)).

75 See Sharpe, *Injunctions and Specific Performance*, looseleaf ed. (Toronto, Canada Law Book, 1999), 7.680-7.700; *Elsley v. J.G. Collins Ins. Agencies Ltd., supra*, footnote 66. But see *Bains & Sarai Holdings Ltd. v. Sahota* (1985), 63 B.C.L.R. 206, 37 R.P.R. 70 (C.A.).

76 (1900), 27 O.A.R. 339, approved in *Elsley v. J.G. Collins Ins. Agencies Ltd., supra*, footnote 66.

77 *Snider v. McKelvey, supra*, footnote 76, at p. 341.

78 [1978] 2 S.C.R. 916, 83 D.L.R. (3d) 1.

79 *Supra*, at p. 935 S.C.R., p. 14 D.L.R.

80 See especially, *supra*, at p. 932 S.C.R., pp. 11-12 D.L.R., where, referring to *Snider v. McKelvey*, he said: "The agreed liquidated damages sum is to be a complete remedy for the entire breach specified. Once this sum has been awarded, to grant an injunction for even part of the breach would be to have overlapping remedies."

6. Damages Exceeding what Court Would Award

8.280 Some difference of judicial opinion has arisen over whether a clause is valid that pre-estimates damages at a figure commensurate with the plaintiff's probable actual loss but at a figure greater than the damages that the court would award on ordinary compensatory principles. An instance arises where special circumstances would cause the plaintiff exceptional loss. If the circumstances are beyond the reasonable contemplation of the defendant, the defendant would not be liable for the loss, but if the defendant has agreed to pay a liquidated sum that turns out to be no more than the plaintiff's actual loss the question arises whether the agreed sum is payable. The answer will depend on what is taken to be the underlying basis of the jurisdiction of the court to strike down penalty clauses. If, as suggested above, the basis is unconscionability, the clause should be enforceable in those circumstances for there is nothing unconscionable about an agreement to pay the plaintiff's actual loss. In *Robophone Facilities Ltd. v. Blank*,[81] the English Court of Appeal by a majority adopted this view:

> The onus of showing that such a stipulation is a "penalty clause" lies upon the party who is sued on it . . . it may seem at first sight that the stipulated sum is extravagantly greater than any loss which is liable to result from the breach in the ordinary course of things, i.e., the damages recoverable under the so-called "first rule" in *Hadley v. Baxendale* [9 Exch. 341, 156 E.R. 145]. This would give rise to the prima facie inference that the stipulated sum was a penalty; but the plaintiff may be able to show that, owing to special circumstances outside "the ordinary course of things", a breach in those special circumstances would be liable to cause him a greater loss of which the stipulated sum does represent a genuine estimate . . . If the contract contained an express undertaking by the defendant to be responsible for all actual loss to the plaintiff occasioned by the defendant's breach, whatever that loss might turn out to be, it would not affect the defendant's liability for the loss actually sustained by the plaintiff that the defendant did not know of the special circumstances which were likely to cause any enhancement of the plaintiff's loss. So, if at the time of the contract the plaintiff informs the defendant that his loss in the event of a particular breach is likely to be £X by describing this sum as liquidated damages in the terms of his offer to contract, and the defendant expressly undertakes to pay £X to the plaintiff in the event of such breach, the clause which contains the stipulation is not a "penalty clause" unless £X is not a genuine and reasonable estimate by the plaintiff of the loss which he will in fact be likely to sustain. Such a clause is, in my view, enforceable, whether or not the defendant knows what are the special circumstances which make the loss likely to be £X rather than some lesser sum which it would be likely to be in the ordinary course of things.[82]

---

81 [1966] 1 W.L.R. 1428, [1966] 3 All E.R. 128 (C.A.).

82 *Supra*, at pp. 1447-8 W.L.R., pp. 142-3 All E.R.

8.290 On the other hand, if the view taken of the court's jurisdiction over penalty clauses is that it is designed to prevent departure from the damages that the court would assess, a different view will prevail. In *H.F. Clarke Ltd. v. Thermidaire Corp. Ltd.*,[83] Laskin C.J.C. held that a clause was to be struck down if the stipulated sum was "disproportionate and unreasonable when compared with the damages sustained or which would be recoverable through an action in the courts for breach of the covenant in question".[84] It is true that the reference to damages recoverable through an action in the court suggests that a clause, even though a reasonable pre-estimate of actual damages, would be struck down if it exceeded damages that a court would award. However, the phrase follows upon the phrase "unreasonable when compared with the damages sustained" and other references in the judgment to reasonableness[85] suggest that Laskin C.J.C. did not intend to lay down a rule that a reasonable pre-estimate could never exceed the damages that a court would award. It is submitted, therefore, that the preferable view is that a fair and reasonable agreement should be upheld even though it stipulates for payment of a sum greater than that which a court would award.

8.300 This principle would apply not only to problems of remoteness as in *Robophone v. Blank* but also to legitimate intangible interests of the plaintiff that the court might be reluctant to recognize in damages, such as the enjoyment of a view[86] or, to take an example discussed from an economic point of view in an article by Charles Goetz and Robert Scott where a strong argument is made for enforcement, enjoyment of a particular athletic event to which the defendant had promised transport.[87] The fact that the courts would be reluctant to protect such interests in damages should not, it is submitted, lead necessarily to the conclusion that a moderate sum stipulated to be paid for their violation is extravagant or unreasonable.[88] The uncertainty of the amount of probable recovery and the difficulty of estimating damages have always been treated as factors

---

83 [1976] 1 S.C.R. 319, 54 D.L.R. (3d) 385.

84 *Supra*, at p. 338 S.C.R., p. 398 D.L.R.

85 See p. 331 S.C.R., p. 392 D.L.R., where Laskin C.J.C. describes the jurisdiction over penalty clauses as "simply a manifestation of a concern for fairness and reasonableness".

86 In *Astley v. Weldon* (1801), 2 Bos. & Pul. 346 at p. 354, 126 E.R. 1318, Chambre J. said: "A man in possession of his own estate may set his own value upon the view, the timber, or other ornaments and conveniences of the estate".

87 Goetz and Scott, "Liquidated Damages, Penalties and the Just Compensation Principle: Some Notes on an Enforcement Model and a Theory of Efficient Breach," 77 Columbia L. Rev. 554 (1977). See *County of Halton v. Grand Trunk Ry. Co. of Canada* (1892), 19 O.A.R. 252 at p. 261, affd 21 S.C.R. 716 (railway company's remaining independent "a matter to which the plaintiffs attached great importance"). See also *Hall v. Cooper* (1994), 3 R.F.L. (4th) 29 (Ont. Ct. (Gen. Div.)), at pp. 36-7, citing this paragraph. Other economic analysis favours judicial control of penalty clauses on the ground that enforcement gives an incentive to the promisee to procure a breach: Clarkson, Miller and Muris, "Liquidated Damages v. Penalties: Sense or Nonsense?", [1978] Wis. L. Rev. 351.

88 The greater willingness of the court to award damages for violation of such intangible interests (see 3.1250-3.1480, *supra*) is an added reason for enforcing an agreed liquidated damages clause. See *Reimer v. Rosen* (1919), 45 D.L.R. 1 (Man. C.A.).

lending weight to arguments for enforcement of the agreed clause.[89] In *Clydebank Engineering & Shipbuilding Co. v. Don Jose Ramos Yzquierdo y Castaneda*,[90] Lord Halsbury said:

> The very reason why the parties do in fact agree to such a stipulation is that sometimes, although undoubtedly there is damage and undoubtedly damages ought to be recovered, the nature of the damage is such that proof of it is extremely complex, difficult, and expensive.[91]

The passage was applied by Cameron J.A. in *Reimer v. Rosen*.[92]

7. Relationship with Forfeiture Clauses

8.310 The topic of relief from forfeiture is outside the realm of damages but it is closely related to penalty clauses. Indeed, a penalty clause is an attempt to secure the benefits of forfeiture as security for a contractual performance without the necessity of effecting an actual transfer of money or property. The courts have, in general, been more ready to enforce forfeitures than penalties.[93] But the distinction between the two kinds of security almost disappears in a case where the defendant has promised to pay a deposit which is to be subject to forfeiture on breach but has failed to pay it. It was held in *Hinton v. Sparkes*[94] that the defendant cannot be better off by committing two breaches rather than one and that, consequently, the defendant was liable for the amount of the promised deposit, even though, had the same sum been payable on breach, it would have been struck down as a penalty. The only way to reconcile the two branches of the law, it is submitted, is to accept that all agreements should be enforceable, whether for forfeiture or for payment

---

89 See *Dunlop Pneumatic Tyre Co. Ltd. v. New Garage and Motor Co. Ltd.*, [1915] A.C. 79 (H.L.), at pp. 87-8; *McCuaig v. Kilbach*, [1945] 3 D.L.R. 117 (Sask. C.A.); *Turnbull v. Dobrovalsky*, [1946] 1 D.L.R. 200 (Sask. C.A.); *Pitman v. Pletzke*, [1949] 2 D.L.R. 219 (Sask. C.A.); *Associated Growers of B.C. Ltd. v. B.C. Fruit Land Ltd.*, [1925] 1 D.L.R. 871 (B.C.S.C.); *Bank of British North America v. Simpson* (1874), 24 U.C.C.P. 354; *Knowlton v. MacKay* (1879), 29 U.C.C.P. 601; *Pine Wyn Investments Ltd. v. Banhap Investments Ltd.* (1974), 46 D.L.R. (3d) 186, 3 O.R. (2d) 566 (H.C.J.), affd 61 D.L.R. (3d) 486*n*, 8 O.R. (2d) 647*n* (C.A.); *McManus v. Rothschild* (1911), 25 O.L.R. 138 (Div. Ct.); *Oliver Ltd. v. Belik*, [1931] 1 W.W.R. 24 (Alta. Dist. Ct.); *Canadian Fairbanks Morse v. U.S. Fidelity & Guaranty* (1915), 26 D.L.R. 12 (B.C.S.C.); *Saskatchewan Co-op, Wheat Producers, Ltd. v. Zurowski*, [1926] 3 D.L.R. 810 (Sask. C.A.); *McArdle v. Mannle* (1955), 17 W.W.R. 329 (Sask. C.A.); *St. Catharines Improvement Co. v. Rutherford* (1914), 19 D.L.R. 662, 31 O.L.R. 574 (S.C. App. Div.).

90 [1905] A.C. 6 (H.L.).

91 *Supra*, at p. 11.

92 (1919), 45 D.L.R. 1 (Man. C.A.), at p. 14.

93 See Waddams, *The Law of Contracts*, 5th ed. (Toronto, Canada Law Book, 2005), pp. 328-32. However, in *Empire Loan & Savings Co. v. McRae* (1903), 5 O.L.R. 710 (K.B.), and *Brandon Construction Co. v. Saskatoon School Board (No. 2)* (1913), 13 D.L.R. 379 (Sask. S.C. en banc), relief was granted against forfeiture as against a penalty clause. See also *Waugh v. Pioneer Logging Co. Ltd.*, [1949] S.C.R. 299, [1949] 2 D.L.R. 577 (relief against forfeiture of trust fund).

94 (1868), L.R. 3 C.P. 161. See also *Dewar v. Mintoft*, [1912] 2 K.B. 373; *Lowe v. Hope*, [1970] Ch. 94 (taking a contrary view); *Pollway Ltd. v. Abdullah*, [1974] 1 W.L.R. 493 (C.A.); Zuckerman, "Cheque Given for Deposit in the Purchase of Land," 38 Mod. L. Rev. 349 (1975).

on breach, subject to a general rule of unconscionability. The way is open to this conclusion for unconscionability has been recognized as the governing principle in the forfeiture cases and in the penalty cases. Thus, where a forfeiture, for example, of a moderate deposit on a land sale agreement would be upheld as not unconscionable, so also a clause should be upheld whereby (in the absence of any deposit) the same moderate sum was payable as a penalty upon breach. Adoption of such a principle would not alter the results of many cases, which can often be explained as, in effect, though not in words, applying a test of unconscionability. The effect would be, rather, to provide a more rational framework for the decisions on both forfeitures and penalties. The Ontario Court of Appeal has said that "courts should, whenever possible, favour analysis on the basis of equitable principles and unconscionability over the strict common law rule pertaining to penalty clauses".[94a]

8. Relationship with Exemption Clauses

8.320 Clauses excluding and limiting liability have given the courts much trouble. A full discussion is out of place in a book on damages, but again the relationship with penalty clauses is close. A liquidated damages clause generally does have the effect of limiting liability to the sum stipulated. A clause that limits or excludes liability can be just as unfair and oppressive as a penalty clause. As is well known, the courts have by a variety of devices struck down clauses limiting liability.[95] There is a strong case for finding a unifying principle that will explain both these lines of cases, and the principle of unconscionability or unfairness is the obvious choice.[96]

9. Conclusion

8.330 It is useful to remember that the jurisdiction to strike down penalty clauses represents an exception to a general principle of freedom of contract.[97] The force of the general principle should not be underestimated. There are strong arguments for enabling parties to set their own value on performance. The power to do so gives flexibility to the contracting process; it enables the promisor to offer an assurance of performance while limiting liability for consequential damages and thereby making the cost of breach predictable. It enables the promisee to avoid the cost of securing compensation by litigation and the risks of undercompensation that may be caused by the legal

---

[94a] *869163 Ontario Ltd. v. Torrey Springs II Associates Limited Partnership* (2005), 256 D.L.R. (4th) 490 (Ont. C.A.) at para. 32, citing this paragraph.

[95] See Waddams, *The Law of Contracts*, 5th ed. (Toronto, Canada Law Book, 2005), pp. 325-52.

[96] See *Hunter Engineering Co. v. Syncrude Canada Ltd.*, [1989] 1 S.C.R. 426, 57 D.L.R. (4th) 321.

[97] Such clauses are said to be enforced in civil law jurisdictions, subject to a power to relieve if the sum stipulated is "manifestly excessive". See Lowry, "Penalty Clauses and Breach of Contract", 131 New L.J. 306 (1981). The arguments in favour of enforcement were summarized by Diplock L.J. in *Robophone Facilities Ltd. v. Blank*, [1966] 1 W.L.R. 1428 (C.A.), at p. 1447.

restrictions on damages, such as remoteness, certainty of proof, mitigation, and failure to recognize intangible losses; it reduces the cost to the parties and to the state of settling a dispute after breach; it enables the promisee to purchase insurance against default from the party in the best position to provide it at the lowest cost. A further point is that the striking down of the clause may represent an injustice to the promisee for the price of performance will have been agreed in the light of all the promisor's obligations, including the promise to pay an agreed sum on breach; if that promise is struck down, the promisee does not receive what has been paid for. [97a]

8.340 These arguments suggest that it is often in the interest of both parties to make the cost of non-performance predictable. In substance, the arguments are the same as those supporting freedom of contract generally. This suggests that the arguments can be met only by a general principle of contract law that gives an excuse for non-performance. The relevant principle, it has been suggested, is unconscionability.[98] Recognition of so broad a principle might seem to undermine freedom of contract. But a study of the law of penalty clauses indicates, it is suggested, that failure to recognize the principle of unconscionability leads, ironically, to the greater undermining of freedom of contract. Without a coherent and rational basis to explain judicial control, the courts are led to strike down clauses that are perfectly fair and reasonable and that have been freely agreed and paid for by parties of equal bargaining power.

[97a] See *869163 Ontario Ltd. v. Torrey Springs II Associates Limited Partnership*, *supra*, footnote 94a, at para. 34, citing this paragraph.

[98] See Rea, "Efficiency Implications of Penalties and Liquidated Damages", 13 J. Leg. Stud. 147 (1984), where it is argued that economic considerations favour enforcement of penalty clauses, unless unreasonable at the time of contracting, in which case the doctrine can be justified as identifying cases of mistake or unconscionability.

CHAPTER 9

AWARDS MEASURED BY THE DEFENDANT'S BENEFIT

1. Introduction

9.10 The ordinary measure of damages is designed to put the party complaining, so far as money can do it, in the position that would have been occupied if the wrong had not been done.[1] This measure does not enable the plaintiff to capture a benefit derived by the defendant from the wrong. The decision of the Supreme Court of Canada in *Asamera Oil Corp. Ltd. v. Sea Oil & General Corp.*[2] established that, at least in contract, depriving the defendant of an ill-gotten gain is not to be counted as one of the normal purposes of damage assessment.

9.20 Nevertheless, decisions are known in every branch of the law that do have the effect of compelling a wrongdoer to account for an enrichment. Whether these devices form a proper or convenient part of a study of the law of damages is debatable. They are means whereby the law gives money compensation and they do constitute exceptions to the usual rule limiting money compensation to the amount of the plaintiff's loss. These considerations suggest that they should be included. On the other hand, the boundaries of legal subjects are determined by usage and convenience as much as by logic. The basic principle that governs recovery of a benefit derived from a wrong is restitution, which has been firmly established by textbook writers[3] and by decisions of the Supreme Court of Canada[4] as a fully independent source of legal obligation. The matters in issue here are treated in the leading textbooks on restitution. In the following paragraphs, therefore, the reader's attention is drawn to the devices available and to their relationship with the law of damages, but no full treatment is attempted.

2. Benefits Derived from Torts

9.30 Although the basic principle of damage assessment is compensatory, a

1 *Livingstone v. Rawyards Coal Co.* (1880), 5 App. Cas. 25 (H.L.), at p. 39; *Wertheim v. Chicoutimi Pulp Co.*, [1911] A.C. 301 (P.C.), at p. 307 – both these cases rely on the compensatory principle to deny a larger recovery.

2 [1979] 1 S.C.R. 633 at pp. 672-3, 89 D.L.R. (3d) 1 at p. 30, followed in *Hillspring Farms Ltd. v. Leland Walton & Sons Ltd.* (2007), 312 N.B.R. (2d) 109 (C.A.).

3 Goff and Jones, *The Law of Restitution*, 6th ed. (London, Sweet & Maxwell, 2002); Palmer, *The Law of Restitution* (Boston, Little, Brown & Co., 1978), c. 4; Maddaugh and McCamus, *The Law of Restitution* (Aurora, Canada Law Book, 1990).

4 *Deglman v. Guaranty Trust Co.*, [1954] S.C.R. 725, [1954] 3 D.L.R. 785; *Pettkus v. Becker*, [1980] 2 S.C.R. 834, 117 D.L.R. (3d) 257.

number of cases in a wide variety of circumstances have awarded damages measured by the benefits derived by the defendant from wrongful acts. Several techniques have been used to transfer profit from a tortfeasor to the plaintiff.[4a]

9.40 Where the defendant has deliberately calculated that a profit can be made from committing a tortious act, the courts have often assessed punitive damages in order to strip the defendant of the profit. Thus, in *Townsview Properties Ltd. v. Sun Construction & Equipment Co. Ltd.*[5] where the defendant had trespassed on the plaintiff's land in constructing a building on its own neighbouring land, the court awarded punitive damages. Even in England, where the power to award punitive damages has been severely restricted by the decision of the House of Lords in *Rookes v. Barnard,*[6] an express exception was made for the case where the defendant has deliberately set out to profit from the tort.[7]

9.50 A second technique for stripping the defendant of a profit is the device known as waiver of tort. The plaintiff can sometimes treat a tortfeasor as though the latter had been authorized to act and demand an account of the profits derived by the defendant as though these had been earned on the plaintiff's behalf and with the plaintiff's authority.[8]

9.60 These devices have drawbacks from the plaintiff's point of view and fall short of establishing a principle that a defendant must account for profit derived from tortious conduct. Punitive damages can be awarded only where the defendant has knowingly infringed the plaintiff's interests. It is not an apt device, therefore, in the quite common case of profits derived from an inadvertent trespass to land or an innocent conversion of goods. The device of waiver of tort also has drawbacks: it is misleadingly named, rests on archaic principles and depends on palpable fictions. Moreover, doubt exists on what torts can be waived. It has been assumed, for example, that trespass to land, one of the most common kinds of tort from which profit is derived, cannot be waived.[9]

9.70 Both of these difficulties were overcome in a series of mining cases dealing with unauthorized use by the defendant of passages under the plaintiff's land for the transport of coal. Despite the absence of any damage to the plaintiff's land, it was held in such cases that the plaintiff was entitled to a reasonable payment for the use of the passages

---

4a This paragraph was cited with approval in *Montreal Trust Co. v. Williston Wildcatters Corp.* (2004), 243 D.L.R. (4th) 317 (Sask. C.A.), at p. 342, leave to appeal to S.C.C. refused 249 D.L.R. (4th) vii.

5 (1974), 56 D.L.R. (3d) 330, 7 O.R. (2d) 666 (C.A.); *Epstein v. Cressey Development Corp.* (1992), 89 D.L.R. (4th) 32, [1992] 3 W.W.R. 566 (B.C.C.A.).

6 [1964] A.C. 1129 (H.L.).

7 See 11.120-11.150, *infra*.

8 See Goff and Jones, *op. cit.*, footnote 3, pp. 152-55; Maddaugh and McCamus, *op. cit.*, footnote 3, at pp. 507-529.

9 *Phillips v. Homfray* (1883), 24 Ch. D. 439 (C.A.).

(called "way-leave"), even if the trespass was inadvertent.[10] Further, the artificialities of waiver of tort were avoided. Curiously enough, the very dispute which led to the holding that trespass to land is not a tort that can be waived,[11] had also led to a decision twelve years earlier that the plaintiff was entitled to a reasonable way-leave payment to compensate for the unauthorized use by the defendant of underground passages.[12] In the later decision holding that the tort could not be waived, the issue was whether the action could be continued against the defendant's executor: it was held that it could not, but no doubt was cast on the propriety of the award of a way-leave payment in an action against a living defendant for unauthorized use of underground passages.

9.80 Subsequent cases awarding damages measured by the amount of a reasonable fee include patent infringement,[13] trespass to land by the dumping of waste,[14] refusal to return goods lent to the defendant,[15] obtaining by deception property that the plaintiff would not otherwise have sold,[16] refusal to remove goods purchased by the defendant from the plaintiff's property,[17] misuse of confidential information,[18] refusal by an overholding tenant to vacate premises,[19] wrongful ejection of a lessee by a lessor,[19a] unauthorized use of the plaintiff's sewer system,[20] and unauthorized use of a design depicting a professional sportsman.[21] In *Wrotham Park Estate Co. v. Parkside Homes,*[22] the defendant developed land in breach of a restrictive covenant. Although the value of the plaintiff's land was unaffected, damages were awarded measured by the fee reasonably payable to the plaintiff for a relaxation of the covenant. The case was followed in *Bracewell v. Appleby,*[23] where the defendant built a house accessible only over the plaintiff's land. An injunction restraining the trespass was refused because of the plaintiff's

---

10 *Martin v. Porter* (1839), 5 M. & W. 351, 151 E.R. 149; *Morgan v. Powell* (1842), 3 Q.B. 278, 114 E.R. 513; *Jegon v. Vivian* (1871), L.R. 6 Ch. 742; *Hilton v. Woods* (1867), L.R. 4 Eq. 432.

11 *Phillips v. Homfray, supra,* footnote 9.

12 *Phillips v. Homfray* (1871), L.R. 6 Ch. 770.

13 *Watson, Laidlaw & Co. Ltd. v. Pott, Cassels, & Williamson* (1914), 31 R.P.C. 104 (H.L.).

14 *Whitwham v. Westminster Brymbo Coal Co.*, [1896] 2 Ch. 538 (C.A.). See *Lawson v. Hartley-Brown* (1995), 71 P. & C.R. 242 (C.A.).

15 *Strand Electric & Engineering Co. v. Brisford Entertainments Ltd.*, [1952] 2 Q.B. 246 (C.A.); *Hillesden Securities Ltd. v. Ryjack Ltd.*, [1983] 1 W.L.R. 959 (Q.B.); *Gaba Formwork Contractors v. Turner Corp.* (1993), 32 N.S.W.L.R. 175 (Comm. Law Div.).

16 *Smith Kline & French Laboratories Ltd. v. Long*, [1989] 1 W.L.R. 1 (C.A.).

17 *Penarth Dock Engineering Co. Ltd. v. Pounds*, [1963] 1 Lloyd's Rep. 359.

18 *Seager v. Copydex Ltd. (No. 2)*, [1969] 1 W.L.R. 809 (C.A.); *ICAM Technologies Corp. v. EBCO Industries Ltd.*, [1994] 3 W.W.R. 419, 52 C.P.R. (3d) 61 (B.C.C.A.).

19 *Swordheath Properties Ltd. v. Tabet*, [1979] 1 W.L.R. 285 (C.A.); *Ministry of Defence v. Ashman* (1993), 66 P. & C.R. 195 (C.A.).

19a *Inverugie Investments Ltd. v. Hackett*, [1995] 1 W.L.R. 713 (P.C.).

20 *Daniel v. O'Leary* (1976), 14 N.B.R. (2d) 564 (S.C.).

21 *Athans v. Canadian Adventure Camps Ltd.* (1977), 80 D.L.R. (3d) 583, 17 O.R. (2d) 425 (H.C.J.).

22 [1974] 1 W.L.R. 798 (Ch. D.), approved in *Jaggard v. Sawyer*, [1995] 1 W.L.R. 269 (C.A.), and in *Attorney-General v. Blake*, [2001] 1 A.C. 268 (H.L.).

undue delay, but damages were awarded based on "a proper and fair price which would be payable for the acquisition of the right of way".[24]

9.90 The principle of the way-leave cases was said in *Whitwham v. Westminster Brymbo Coal Co.*[25] to be that, "if one person has without leave of another been using that other's land for his own purposes, he ought to pay for such user".[26] In *Watson, Laidlaw & Co. Ltd. v. Pott, Cassels & Williamson,*[27] Lord Shaw said:

> If A, being a liveryman keeps his horse standing idle in the stable, and B, against his wish or without his knowledge, rides or drives it out, it is no answer to A for B to say: "Against what loss do you want to be restored? I restore the horse. There is no loss. The horse is none the worse: it is better for the exercise."[28]

In the *Wrotham Park*[29] case Brightman J. said: "is it just that the plaintiffs should receive no compensation and that the defendants should be left in undisturbed possession of the fruits of their wrongdoing? Common sense would seem to demand a negative answer to this question."[30]

9.100 Some criticism has been directed at such cases as departing from a compensatory theory of damages.[31] It is generally conceded, however, that the results may be justified, either as restitutionary or as a non-compensatory response to wrongs. In *Experience Hendrix LLC v. PPX Enterprises Inc.*,[31a] Mance L.J. said that:

> Whether the adoption of a standard measure of damages represents a departure from a compensatory approach depends upon what one understands by compensation and whether the term is only apt in circumstances where an injured party's financial position, viewed subjectively, is being precisely restored . . . In a case such as *Wrotham Park* the law gives effect to the instinctive reaction that, whether or not the appellant would have been better off if the wrong had not been committed, the wrongdoer ought not to gain an advantage for free, and should make some reasonable recompense.

9.110 Many of the cases may be defended on another ground. It is arguable that, in most of the cases under consideration, the plaintiff has suffered an actual loss in that the defendant has deprived the plaintiff of the opportunity of

---

23 [1975] Ch. 408, but distinguished in *Surrey County Council v. Bredero Homes Ltd.*, [1993] 1 W.L.R. 1361 (C.A.), where there was no right to an injunction at the time of the action. See *WWF-World Wide Fund for Nature v. World Wrestling Federation Entertainment Inc.*, [2007] EWCA Civ. 286; Waddams, "Gains Derived from Breach of Contract" in D. Saidov and R. Cunnington, editors, *Contract Damages: Domestic and International Perspectives* (Oxford, Hart Publishing, 2008), at p. 187.

24 *Supra*, at p. 419.

25 *Supra*, footnote 14.

26 *Whitwham, supra*, footnote 14, at pp. 541-2, *per* Lindley L.J.

27 *Supra*, footnote 13.

28 *Watson, Laidlaw, supra*, at p. 119.

29 *Supra*, footnote 22.

30 *Wrotham Park, supra*, at p. 812.

31 See *McGregor on Damages*, 16th ed. (London, Sweet & Maxwell, 1997), §1421. See also *Stoke-on-Trent City Council v. W. & J. Wass Ltd.*, [1988] 1 W.L.R. 1406 (C.A.).

31a [2003] EWCA Civ. 323, at para. 26.

selling to the defendant the right appropriated by the latter.[32] It is usually certain that the defendant would have paid something for the right taken. It must have been worth something for the mine owner to have the use of the plaintiff's passages, for the lessee of lighting equipment to retain the use of the equipment, and for the tenant of residential premises to remain in occupation of them. The court cannot now be sure how much the defendant would have paid, but this is because of the defendant's wrong, and it seems not unjust to presume against the defendant that the defendant would have paid a fair value for the right to acquire the interest in question. The cases were so explained by Megarry V.-C. in *Tito v. Waddell (No. 2)*:[33]

> If the plaintiff has the right to prevent some act being done without his consent, and the defendant does the act without seeking that consent, the plaintiff has suffered a loss in that the defendant has taken without paying for it something for which the plaintiff could have required payment, namely, the right to do the act. The court therefore makes the defendant pay what he ought to have paid the plaintiff, for that is what the plaintiff has lost.[34]

This explanation would not apply to a case where it could be positively shown that the defendant would not have paid for the right to act. But it is suggested that it is not unjust to hold that the defendant is precluded from asserting that the defendant would have deliberately taken the plaintiff's property without paying for it.[35] Even when this approach cannot, standing alone, support an award based wholly or partly on the defendant's profit, it has, together with other considerations, been influential.

9.120 Where there is a market in the interest in question, as in the case of residential premises and lighting equipment or storage facilities for floating docks, the appropriate measure of the fair value will be what the defendant would have had to pay in the market-place for comparable facilities. Where the situation is one where the plaintiff is the only person from whom the right of question could be acquired, as in the case of rights of way over land or relaxation of restrictive covenants, it seems not unjust to assume that a rational person, in the position of the defendant, would have paid up to the full value of the right in question, and it seems again not unjust to assume against the wrongdoing defendant that the plaintiff would have demanded the greatest sum that the defendant would rationally have agreed to pay. In the *Wrotham Park* case the court, having said that the principle was the award of such a sum as might reasonably have been demanded by the plaintiffs, awarded only five per cent of the sum calculated to be the developer's total anticipated profit. However, Brightman J. stressed that there were peculiar

32 See Sharpe and Waddams, "Damages for Lost Opportunity to Bargain", 2 Ox. J.L.S. 290 (1982).

33 [1977] Ch. 106.

34 *Supra*, at p. 335, approved in *Jaggard v. Sawyer*, [1995] 1 W.L.R. 269 (C.A.).

35 But see Farnsworth, "Your Loss or My Gain: The Dilemma of the Disgorgement Principle in Breach of Contract", 94 Yale L.J. 1339 (1985), pp. 1365-6, arguing that compensation should be restricted to what the plaintiff might reasonably have obtained for release of rights.

factors including delay on the plaintiff's part that justified "great moderation".[36] In *Bracewell v. Appleby* the court, in estimating "a proper and fair price which would be payable for the acquisition of the right of way in question", awarded forty per cent of the defendant's profit (the difference between the overall cost of building the house and its present value). In the latter case, Graham J. said: "[The plaintiffs] must not be treated as if they were in the extremely powerful bargaining position which an interlocutory injunction would have given them if it had been obtained before the defendant started operations and incurred expense. Such is to my mind the penalty of standing by until the house is built."[37]

9.130 It may be conceded that the plaintiff should not recover what the plaintiff would have demanded; the plaintiff might have been unwilling to sell at any price or only for fabulous wealth. If an injunction is not to be granted or if the damages are in respect of a past trespass, the plaintiff's right to refuse to sell cannot now be protected. The court must, therefore, construct a hypothetical bargain, and it seems appropriate to suppose a negotiation between a plaintiff willing to sell at the highest price obtainable and a defendant willing to pay the highest price that would leave the latter with a net advantage from the transaction. It is submitted that Graham J.'s dictum is not inconsistent with this view. It was only because the plaintiffs had "stood by" until the house was built that they were deprived of the price they could have obtained before building started. The several principles adduced in support of recovery all seem to suggest that the plaintiff ought to recover the highest sum that the defendant would have willingly paid for the right. The principle that the defendant should not be better off by trespassing than by contracting seems to lead to this result. So also does the principle that the defendant should be deprived of the fruits of the wrong, for what the defendant has saved by the trespass is the price that would have had to be paid if there had been an agreement. Again, on the principle that the plaintiff has actually suffered a loss of opportunity to sell the right in question, the highest price payable by a rational defendant seems a fair measure of the loss. Thus, if it could be established in a case like *Bracewell v. Appleby,* that the defendant's unimproved land with the right of way exceeded the value of the unimproved land without the right of way by $1,000, it is submitted that $1,000 is, on any of the principles discussed here, the proper measure of damages. The result in *Bracewell v. Appleby* may well be consistent with this test. Graham J. said that the sum should not be "so high as to deter the defendant from building at all".[38] Although he awarded only forty per cent of the defendant's "profit", the profit was calculated by deducting the building costs from the improved value. It may well be that, even if the defendant had owned the right of way from the outset, his building would have added a value to the land greater

---

[36] *Wrotham Park Estate Co. v. Parkside Homes,* [1974] 1 W.L.R. 798 (Ch.), at p. 815.
[37] *Bracewell v. Appleby,* [1975] Ch. 408 at pp. 419-20.
[38] *Supra,* at p. 420.

than the cost of the building. This difference would not be a profit derived from the wrong and, it is suggested, should be excluded in calculating damages. But, it is submitted, on the principles discussed previously, where the profit derived from the wrong can be isolated (in this case, the difference between the value of the unimproved land with and without a right of way), the appropriate award is the full amount of that profit. Where the question is whether the defendant must pay to the claimant a substantial sum of money, an affirmative answer has been influenced both by the consideration that the defendant has wrongfully derived a profit from acting as it did, and also by the consideration that the claimant has lost the opportunity to demand a fee for giving permission. Often the two lines of thinking tend to converge in their result.[38a]

3. Proprietary Remedies

9.140 Whenever the plaintiff can assert an ownership interest in specific property, the effect will be to enable the plaintiff to capture any increase in value of the property in the defendant's hands. This question was discussed in Chapter 1 in connection with the date for the assessment of damages.[39] The questions of the right and the remedy, as is often the case, are intertwined. If property is wrongly taken from the plaintiff but the plaintiff is only allowed to recover its value at the date of the wrong, this amounts to saying that the plaintiff has lost proprietary interest, for if the law will not assist the plaintiff to regain possession of the property, one of the chief incidents of ownership is denied to the plaintiff. On the other hand, if the starting point is that the plaintiff remains, in the full sense, owner of the property, it follows that the plaintiff cannot be limited to compensation measured by its value at the date of the wrong, because the plaintiff will — for such are the incidents of ownership — be entitled to use self-help to recapture the property and to the legal remedies of replevin and detinue, and probably to injunctive and declaratory relief as well.[40]

9.150 Tracing is a device for following property into the hands of a wrongdoer and of third parties. It rests on proprietary principles and enables the plaintiff to assert title to specific property. The rules of tracing, particularly in equity, have enabled the plaintiff to go far beyond following specific tangible property.[41] Money has no earmark, as was said in an early case,[42] but plaintiffs have been allowed to trace property in and out of bank accounts and through purchases and sales of various kinds of property.[43] It will be seen,

---

[38a] See footnote 31a, *supra*.

[39] See 1.650-1.1110, *supra*.

[40] See Sharpe, *Injunctions and Specific Performance*, looseleaf ed. (Toronto, Canada Law Book, 1999), 4.10-4.20, 4.690.

[41] See Goff and Jones, *The Law of Restitution*, 6th ed. (London, Sweet & Maxwell, 2002), pp. 107-19; Maddaugh and McCamus, *The Law of Restitution* (Aurora, Canada Law Book, 1990), pp. 109-158.

[42] *Taylor v. Plumer* (1815), 3 M. & S. 562 at p. 575, 105 E.R. 721.

[43] See Goff and Jones, *op. cit.*, footnote 41, pp. 63-77.

therefore, that there is an element of legal fiction involved; it would be fair to say that, in a case where the plaintiff successfully traces property, the plaintiff is treated by the law as the owner of specific property. Very often, the significance of the assertion of ownership in tracing cases is to give the plaintiff a priority over the defendant's general creditors in an insolvency. A discussion of the extent and propriety of such a result is quite outside the scope of this book. Another effect, however, more closely related to the law of damages, is that if the property has increased in value since the date of the wrong, a plaintiff, by successfully tracing the property, will capture the increase in value.[44]

4. Equitable Remedies

9.160 Besides equitable tracing, a number of other equitable devices permit the plaintiff to claim profits made by a wrongdoer. Chief among these is the constructive trust, to which a wide scope has recently been given by the Supreme Court of Canada.[45] The effect of an express trust of specific property is that the *cestui que trust* owns the property and so is entitled to any accretion to its value. Now that the constructive trust is apparently recognized in Canada as a purely remedial device, always at the court's command to avoid unjust enrichment, it would seem that the device will often be available to enable a plaintiff to capture a profit made by the defendant from any sort of wrongful appropriation of the plaintiff's property.

9.170 Another equitable device is accounting. This was discussed briefly, in an earlier chapter, in the context of business losses.[46] In cases of infringement by the defendant of industrial property interests, it is open to the plaintiff to demand an accounting of profits. The remedy has, as was pointed out in Chapter 5, been of limited popularity with plaintiffs, because the defendant will be entitled to deduct all her expenses, and what looks at first like a handsome gross profit may turn out to be a net loss. However, there is no doubt that, in an appropriate case, an accounting may yield rich rewards to the plaintiff.

9.180 It has been argued earlier[47] that very often the recovery of such profits can be defended on a compensatory theory, namely, that the defendant has deprived the plaintiff of an opportunity to license the infringement. It has been argued that the court is justified in such cases in holding, against the interests of the wrongdoer, that the appropriate licence fee is equal to what has turned out to be the defendant's net profit.

---

[44] See *Re Tilley's Will Trusts*, [1967] Ch. 1179 at p. 1189; *F.L. Jones & Sons (Trustee) v. Jones*, [1997] Ch. 159 (C.A.).

[45] In *Pettkus v. Becker*, [1980] 2 S.C.R. 834, 117 D.L.R. (3d) 257. See also *R. v. Guerin*, [1984] 2 S.C.R. 335, 13 D.L.R. (4th) 321 (breach of fiduciary duty); *LAC Minerals Ltd. v. International Corona Resources Ltd.*, [1989] 2 S.C.R. 574, 61 D.L.R. (4th) 14 (breach of confidence); *Peter v. Beblow*, [1993] 1 S.C.R. 980, 101 D.L.R. (4th) 621; *Minera Aquiline Argentina SA v. IMA Exploration Inc.*, [2007] 10 W.W.R. 648 (B.C.C.A.).

[46] See 5.780-5.880, *supra*.

[47] See 9.70-9.130, *supra*.

9.190 Account must be made of any profit made by a trustee from trust property and any profit made out of a fiduciary position by a fiduciary.[48] Since the categories of fiduciary relationships cannot be precisely defined — they have been said never to be closed[49] — the effect is to put another flexible device into the hands of the court whereby certain kinds of wrongdoers can be made to account for profits. Thus, secret profits made by agents or from the misuse of confidential information must be accounted for.[50]

5. Breach of Contract

9.200 No principle exists whereby a defendant can be made to account for a profit derived from a simple breach of contract.[51] Unless the plaintiff is entitled to specific enforcement, the defendant is allowed to break the contract on payment of compensation. Economists have argued that breach in these circumstances is efficient, because the defendant gains by the breach and the plaintiff, being fully compensated, is no worse off;[51a] this theory was endorsed by the Supreme Court of Canada in *Bank of America Canada v. Mutual Trust Co.*[52] Also general opinion usually takes the view that there is nothing dishonourable, still less immoral, in a breach of contract coupled with an offer of fair compensation. A simple example is of a person who, having agreed to paint the plaintiff's house, decides to attend university instead. No moral fault can here be assigned to a breach of contract with an offer to pay compensation. The refusal of the courts to order specific performance in such cases reflects the public policy of a certain amount of freedom to break contracts and most would consider it wrong that the plaintiff should be able, by bargaining or by judicial award, to capture any share of the benefit expected by the defendant from attending university; the ordinary rules of damage assessment will sufficiently compensate by giving the plaintiff enough to enable the plaintiff to employ another painter. In 1997

---

[48] See *McNeil v. Fultz* (1906), 38 S.C.R. 198; *Guertin v. Royal Bank of Canada* (1983), 1 D.L.R. (4th) 68, 43 O.R. (2d) 363 (H.C.J.), affd 12 D.L.R. (4th) 640*n*, 47 O.R. (2d) 799*n* (C.A.); *R. v. Guerin, supra*, footnote 45; *Ho v. Yip* (1995), 22 C.L.R. (2d) 66 (B.C.S.C.); *Warman International Ltd. v. Dwyer*, [1994-95] 182 C.L.R. 544, 69 A.L.J.R. 362 (H.C.). See Goff and Jones, *The Law of Restitution*, 6th ed. (London, Sweet & Maxwell, 2002), pp. 703-48.

[49] See *Laskin v. Bache & Co. Inc.* (1971), 23 D.L.R. (3d) 385 at p. 392, [1972] 1 O.R. 465 (C.A.); *R. v. Guerin, supra,* footnote 45.

[50] See 5.780-5.880, *supra*; *Canson Enterprises Ltd. v. Boughton & Co.* (1991), 85 D.L.R. (4th) 129, [1991] 3 S.C.R. 534; *3464920 Canada Inc. v. Strother*, [2007] 2 S.C.R. 177, 281 D.L.R. (4th) 640.

[51] *Asamera Oil Corp. Ltd. v. Sea Oil & General Corp.*, [1979] 1 S.C.R. 633, 89 D.L.R. (3d) 1; *Surrey County Council v. Bredero Homes Ltd.*, [1993] 1 W.L.R. 1361 (C.A.). See Waddams, "Breach of Contract and the Concept of Wrongdoing" (2000), 12 Sup. Ct. L. Rev. (2d) 1.

[51a] Posner, *Economic Analysis of Law*, 5th ed. (New York, Aspen Law & Business Publishers, 1998), pp. 131-4. But this is not a persuasive argument against specific performance itself, because if the plaintiff has a right to specific performance, there is nothing inefficient in allowing the plaintiff to capture part of the benefits of breach. See Macneil, "Efficient Breach of Contract: Circles in the Sky", 68 Va. L. Rev. 947 (1982).

[52] [2002] 2 S.C.R. 601, 211 D.L.R. (4th) 385.

the English Court of Appeal in *Attorney-General v. Blake*,[52a] while recognizing that this was the general rule, suggested, *obiter*, that a restitutionary claim for profits might be available in cases of "skimped performance" and where a party profits by doing the very thing that the party had contracted not to do. This suggestion raises difficulties. Cases of "skimped performance" would include those discussed in an earlier chapter[52b] where the cost of performance to the defendant greatly exceeds the benefit of it to the plaintiff. If, as many cases have held, the plaintiff is usually sufficiently compensated in those cases by the smaller measure, it seems undesirable to allow this conclusion to be circumvented by giving restitution of the costs saved by the defendant. The second suggested category of doing "the very thing" that a party contracted not to do would, it is submitted, be very difficult to apply. It would not be desirable for the availability of restitution to depend on the precise wording of contracts: every case of breach is, in a sense, a case of doing something incompatible with performance of the contract. Partly for these reasons, the House of Lords rejected the tests proposed by the Court of Appeal but said that in an exceptional case the court could grant the discretionary remedy of an accounting of profit. The *Blake* case, involving unauthorized memoirs of a former secret service agent, was held to be a suitable case for such an award. The House of Lords, while careful not to lay down a rigid rule, suggested as "a useful general guide, although not exhaustive, whether the plaintiff had a legitimate interest in preventing the profit-making activity".[52c] This will usually be the kind of case in which the plaintiff would be entitled to an injunction and where the plaintiff could be said to have a proprietary right. In many such cases (though not in all), there will be a loss of opportunity to bargain.[52d]

9.210 If the contract is one that would have been specifically enforceable,[53] restitution will often be available. Thus, where the defendant agrees to sell land to the plaintiff, the defendant is bound to account for profits made from the land after the date fixed for completion,[54] and if the land is sold to a third party, for any profit made on that transaction.[55] The same principle has been applied to other contracts.[56] As appears from the discussion in Chapter 1, the effect of postponing the date for the assessment of damages is to deprive the

---

[52a] [1998] Ch. 439 (C.A), affd on other grounds [2001] 1 A.C. 268 (H.L.).

[52b] See 1.2310-1.2480, *supra*.

[52c] *Supra*, footnote 52a, at p. 285 (H.L.).

[52d] See 9.110, *supra*.

[53] See Sharpe, *Injunctions and Specific Performance*, looseleaf ed. (Toronto, Canada Law Book, 1999).

[54] *Ibid.*, at 11.350, and 1.1160, *supra*.

[55] *Lake v. Bayliss*, [1974] 1 W.L.R. 1073 (Ch.); *Webb v. Dipenta*, [1925] S.C.R. 565, [1925] 1 D.L.R. 216 (on theory of specific performance cy-pres). But see now *Semelhago v. Paramedevan*, [1996] 2 S.C.R. 415, 136 D.L.R. (4th) 1, holding that specific performance is not automatically available to a purchaser of land.

[56] *Wercholoz-Honel Systems Inc. v. Stelenco Inc.* (1989), 27 C.P.R. (3d) 86 at p. 88, citing this passage (Ont. H.C.J.), affd 33 C.P.R. (3d) 575 (C.A.).

defaulting vendor of the increase in value of the land between the date of the wrong and the date of judgment.[57] It was suggested in that context that such a rule of damage assessment is only appropriate where the plaintiff does have a right to specific performance. The plaintiff's entitlement to specific performance enables what is, in effect, a proprietary interest to be asserted.

9.220 Although, as has been said, there is no general principle requiring the defendant to account for profits derived from a breach of contract, the defendant can, in some circumstances, be required to restore the benefits conferred by the plaintiff. The typical case is where the plaintiff pays in advance for a performance that the defendant wholly fails to render. The plaintiff is entitled to recover the money.[58] The same principle has been extended to enable the plaintiff to recover the value of benefits other than money.[59] Though older cases had denied a remedy unless the contractual performance by the defendant had wholly failed,[60] more recent cases suggest that receipt of some benefit by the plaintiff is not always a bar.[61] Receipt of a substantial benefit, however, will often raise problems of valuation and where the plaintiff has an adequate remedy for breach of contract, the difficulty of valuing benefits received will justify the court in restricting the plaintiff to the contractual remedy.[62]

9.230 The basis for the plaintiff's claim in such cases is restitutionary. The plaintiff claims not compensation for breach of the contract but restitution of the benefits conferred, because it is unjust that the defendant should retain them. Courts have often emphasized the non-contractual basis of the plaintiff's claim.[63] However, the contract cannot, it is submitted, be wholly ignored. The plaintiff's restitutionary claim can be made out only if it is unjust for the defendant to retain the benefit, and it is unjust for it to be retained only where the benefit expected to be received by the plaintiff in exchange has substantially failed.

9.240 The plaintiff's restitutionary claim becomes significant in two cases: where it is difficult to prove what benefits would have been received by the

---

57 See 1.650-1.1110, *supra*.

58 *Giles v. Edwards* (1797), 7 T.R. 181, 101 E.R. 920; *Jay Trading Corp. v. Ifax Export & Import Ltd.*, [1954] 2 D.L.R. 110 (N.S.S.C.); *Rafuse Motors Ltd. v. Mardo Construction Ltd.* (1963), 41 D.L.R. (2d) 340 (N.S.S.C. in banco).

59 *Planche v. Colburn* (1831), 8 Bing. 14, 131 E.R. 305; *De Bernardy v. Harding* (1853), 8 Ex. 822, 155 E.R. 1586; *Lodder v. Slowey*, [1904] A.C. 442 (P.C.); *Allan v. Peters* (1876), 10 N.S.R. 365 (S.C. in banco); *Festing v. Hunt* (1890), 6 Man. R. 381 (Q.B.); *Alkok v. Grymek*, [1968] S.C.R. 452, 67 D.L.R. (2d) 718; *Gettle Bros. Construction Co. Ltd. v. Alwinsal Potash of Canada Ltd.* (1969), 5 D.L.R. (3d) 719 (Sask. C.A.), affd [1971] S.C.R. 320, 15 D.L.R. (3d) 128*n*; *Clermont v. Mid-West Steel Products Ltd.* (1965), 51 D.L.R. (2d) 340 (Sask. Q.B.).

60 *Hunt v. Silk* (1804), 5 East 449, 102 E.R. 1142.

61 *Erlanger v. New Sombrero Phosphate Co.* (1878), 3 App. Cas. 1218 (H.L.); *Rowland v. Divall*, [1923] 2 K.B. 500 (C.A.); *Patson v. Abalon Construction Ltd.* (1996), 110 Man. R. (2d) 2, 26 C.L.R. (2d) 155 (C.A.). See Goff and Jones, *The Law of Restitution*, 5th ed. (London, Sweet & Maxwell, 1998), pp. 527-30.

62 See *Brighton v. Auston* (1892), 19 O.A.R. 305.

63 *Deglman v. Guaranty Trust Co.*, [1954] S.C.R. 725, [1954] 3 D.L.R. 785.

performance of the contract and where the plaintiff has made a losing bargain, that is, where the plaintiff could prove the value of the benefits that would have been received by performance, but they are less than the value of the benefit conferred on the defendant. If, in the latter case, the plaintiff is entitled to restitution, the effect will be to put the plaintiff in a substantially better position than if the contract had been performed and to effect a forfeiture against the defendant of the benefit of the contract. This result can be justified only where the defendant's breach is substantial. Moreover, if the plaintiff has fully performed the agreement and the price of the plaintiff's performance has become payable as a debt, restitution is not permitted, for if the plaintiff can by litigation secure the agreed price, there is no unjust enrichment.[64]

9.250 In the California case of *Boomer v. Muir*,[65] the plaintiff, a building contractor, recovered a much larger sum in restitution for the value of services than would have been recovered in payment for them on full performance of the contract. The result is supported by the argument that a restitutionary claim is unrelated to the contract, but the result seems anomalous, for it means that a builder may recover more for part performance than would have been recovered for full performance. The existence of such a rule will encourage a builder, who realizes that a losing contract has been made, to lure the other party into what can be classified as a substantial breach. It may, indeed, be argued that the defendant can retain the benefit of the contract by avoiding such breach, but construction contracts often give rise to situations in which the occurrence of substantial breach turns on very fine points of interpretation of specifications or contractual terms, and it seems undesirable for very large differences in results to turn on such fine points. There is little English or Canadian authority on the question of the proper measure of restitutionary recovery in such circumstances, but it is submitted that the plaintiff could justifiably be limited to the appropriate proportion of the contract price and this is now the view of the American Law Institute.[65a] The reason for recovery is unjust enrichment. In considering the injustice of the enrichment, it is not improper, it is submitted, to take account of all the circumstances, including the fact that the defendant has lawfully made a profitable contract.[66] Admittedly, this approach allows the defendant

---

[64] *Morrison-Knudsen Co. Inc. v. British Columbia Hydro and Power Authority (No. 2)* (1978), 85 D.L.R. (3d) 186 (B.C.C.A.). See also *Brighton v. Auston, supra*, footnote 62. Older cases denied a restitutionary recovery where the plaintiff could assert rights under an unrescinded contract: *Weston v. Downes* (1778), 1 Dougl. 23, 99 E.R. 19; *Atkinson v. Bell* (1828), 8 B. & C. 277, 108 E.R. 1046; *Goodman v. Pocock* (1850), 15 Q.B. 576, 117 E.R. 577. There is, however, no general requirement for restitution that damages should be an inadequate remedy. See Palmer, *The Law of Restitution* (Boston, Little, Brown & Co., 1978), §4.7.

[65] 24 P. (2d) 570 (Cal. C.A., 1933); Palmer, *ibid.*, at §4.4. See also *Korycki v. Korycki*, [1937] 3 W.W.R. 419 (Sask. K.B.); *Lindsay v. Sutton*, [1947] O.W.N. 951 (H.C.J.), revd on other grounds [1948] O.W.N. 252 (C.A.).

[65a] American Law Institute, *Restatement of the Law: Restitution and Unjust Enrichment*, Tentative Draft No. 3 (2004), s. 38. See pp. 327-330, 333-4, and 338-41.

to secure a part of the anticipated profit despite a substantial breach by the defendant.[67] The alternative, however, amounts to exacting a forfeiture and seems inconsistent with the basic compensatory principles of damage assessment.

---

66 The full restitutionary measure is favoured by Maddaugh and McCamus: see Maddaugh and McCamus, *The Law of Restitution* (Aurora, Canada Law Book), looseleaf ed., 19:200. In *Kehoe v. Mayor of Borough of Rutherford*, 56 N.J.L. 221, 27 A. 912 (N.J.S.C., 1893), a proportional recovery only was allowed. See also *Noyes v. Pugin*, 2 Wash. 653, 27 P. 548 (S.C. 1891).

67 The point is made by Palmer, *op. cit.*, footnote 64, at §4.4. Goff and Jones, *op. cit.*, footnote 61, at pp. 467-8, favour denial of the restitutionary claim altogether.

CHAPTER 10

NOMINAL AND SYMBOLIC DAMAGES

1. Meaning of Nominal Damages

10.10 Nominal damages is a sum awarded where the plaintiff's legal right has been invaded, but no damage has been proved.[1] Lord Halsbury L.C. said in *The "Mediana"*:[1a]

> "Nominal damages" is a technical phrase which means that you have negatived anything like real damage, but that you are affirming by your nominal damages that there is an infraction of a legal right which, though it gives you no right to any real damages at all, yet gives you a right to the verdict or judgment because your legal right has been infringed.[2]

Nominal damages are awarded if the plaintiff establishes a breach of contract[3] or a tort of the kind that is said to be "actionable *per se*"[4] but fails to establish a loss caused by the wrong. In the case of tort not actionable *per se* as, for example, negligence, if the plaintiff fails to establish a loss, the action will be dismissed.[5] The practical significance of a judgment for nominal damages is that the plaintiff thereby establishes a legal right. The judgment has the effect of a declaration of legal rights and may deter future infringements or may enable the plaintiff to obtain an injunction to restrain a repetition of the wrong.[6] The obtaining of nominal damages will also, in

---

1 *Hill v. Kilbrei*, [2005] 11 W.W.R. 1 (Man. C.A.) at para. 27.

1a [1900] A.C. 113 (H.L.).

2 *Supra*, at p. 116. This statement (as adopted by *Mayne on Damages*) was approved in *Slone v. Margolian* (1957), 12 D.L.R. (2d) 507 (N.S.S.C. in banco).

3 See *Gibbons v. Westminster Bank, Ltd.*, [1939] 2 K.B. 882; *Sykes v. Midland Bank Executor & Trustee Co.*, [1971] 1 Q.B. 113 (C.A.); *McGee v. Clarke*, [1927] 1 W.W.R. 593 (B.C.C.A.); *State Vacuum Stores of Canada Ltd. v. Phillips*, [1954] 3 D.L.R. 621 (B.C.C.A.); *Marsh v. Royal Bank of Canada* (1922), 63 D.L.R. 659 (Sask. C.A.); *Caines v. Bank of Nova Scotia* (1978), 90 D.L.R. (3d) 271 (N.B.S.C. App. Div.). But nominal damages were refused in *Mid-Western News Agency Ltd. v. Vanpinxteren* (1975), 62 D.L.R. (3d) 555 (Sask. Q.B.), and *Serban v. Egolf* (1983), 43 B.C.L.R. 209 (S.C.).

4 See Street, *Principles of the Law of Damages* (London, Sweet & Maxwell, 1962), pp. 15-16, referring to the following torts as actionable *per se*: passing off, interference with voting rights, trespass, libel, detinue, interference with contract, obstruction of access to a highway, negligently slow execution on property by a sheriff, and improper refusal of accommodation. See also *Pfeifer v. Morrison* (1973), 42 D.L.R. (3d) 314 (B.C.S.C.), at pp. 315-16.

5 See Fleming, *The Law of Torts*, 9th ed. (Sydney, Law Book Co., 1998), p. 115.

6 An appeal will not be allowed solely for the purpose of enabling the plaintiff to recover nominal damages: *Wilson v. London Free Press Printing Co.* (1918), 45 D.L.R. 503, 44 O.L.R. 12 (S.C. App. Div.); *Simonds v. Chesley* (1891), 20 S.C.R. 174; *Scammell v. Clarke* (1894), 23 S.C.R. 142; *Day v. Horton* (1913), 14 D.L.R. 763 (Man. C.A.); *Milligan v. Jamieson* (1902), 4 O.L.R. 650 (Div. Ct.); *Alteman v. Ferguson* (1919), 47 D.L.R. 618 (Man. C.A.).

many cases, entitle a plaintiff to costs,[7] though in *Anglo-Cyprian Trade Agencies v. Paphos Wine Industries*,[8] Devlin J. said that the plaintiff who obtained only nominal damages would not always be regarded as the successful party for the purpose of costs. Further, a defendant can usually secure protection by making a small payment into court.[9] Street has suggested also that nominal damages might serve as a peg upon which to hang an award of exemplary damages.[10]

2. Amount of Nominal Damages

10.20 The usual amount of nominal damages awarded by English courts is £2,[11] but there have been variations.[12] Canadian courts have awarded varying figures. Early cases, including decisions of the Supreme Court of Canada and of the Privy Council, appear to have assumed that the proper amount was $1,[13] and this amount has been awarded in recent cases also.[14] On the other hand, many cases are to be found that have adopted different figures. These include 20¢,[15] $5,[16] $10,[17] $20,[18] $25,[19] $40,[20] $50,[21] $100,[22] $150,[22a] $200,[23] and $250.[24] Even larger sums have been referred to as nominal damages,[25] but in most such cases there is evidence that the court intended to give compensation for a loss that it found difficult to quantify.[26] Reliance was placed in two British Columbia cases[27] on a dictum of Lord Halsbury[28] to the effect that nominal damages are not the same thing as small damages, but it seems evident from the context that Lord Halsbury meant that compensatory

7 See *Beaumont v. Greathead* (1846), 2 C.B. 494 at p. 499, 135 E.R. 1039, "a mere peg on which to hang costs", *per* Maule J.; *Marsh v. Royal Bank of Canada, supra*, footnote 3, at p. 662; *Whitling v. Fleming* (1908), 16 O.L.R. 263 (H.C.J.); *Edwards v. Shore* (1956), 20 W.W.R. 240 (B.C.S.C.).

8 [1951] 1 All E.R. 873 (K.B.), followed in *Neville v. Page* (1977), 5 A.R. 8 (S.C.T.D.).

9 See *Dering v. Uris*, [1964] 2 Q.B. 669.

10 Street, *op. cit.*, footnote 4, p. 18. *Johnston Terminals & Storage Ltd. v. Miscellaneous Workers* (1975), 61 D.L.R. (3d) 741 (B.C.S.C.). But exemplary damages were awarded without an award of nominal damages in *Cash & Carry Cleaners Ltd. v. Delmas* (1973), 44 D.L.R. (3d) 315 (N.B.S.C. App. Div.).

11 *E.g., Sykes v. Midland Bank Executor & Trustee Co., supra*, footnote 3.

12 See *Steam Herring Fleet v. S. Richards & Co.* (1901), 17 T.L.R. 731 (one shilling); *Constantine v. Imperial Hotels, Ltd.*, [1944] K.B. 693 (five guineas); *Brandeis Goldschmidt & Co. Ltd. v. Western Transport Ltd.*, [1981] 3 W.L.R. 181 (C.A.) (five pounds).

13 *Kinkel v. Hyman*, [1939] S.C.R. 364, [1939] 4 D.L.R. 1; *Zurouvinski v. Duke*, [1924] 4 D.L.R. 326 (Sask. C.A.); *Brenner v. Consumers Metal Co.* (1917), 41 D.L.R. 339, 41 O.L.R. 534 (S.C. App. Div.); *McEachern v. Corey* (1916), 34 D.L.R. 165 (Alta. S.C. App. Div.); *Johnson v. Roche* (1914), 17 D.L.R. 74 (N.S.S.C.), vard 24 D.L.R. 305, 49 N.S.R. 12 (S.C. App. Div.), revd 53 S.C.R. 18, 29 D.L.R. 329; *Delbridge v. Pickersgill* (1912), 3 D.L.R. 786 (Sask. S.C.); *Lemon v. Grand Trunk Ry. Co.* (1914), 32 O.L.R. 37 (S.C. App. Div.); *Canadian Woodmen of the World v. Hooper*, [1935] 2 D.L.R. 802, [1935] O.W.N. 113 (C.A.); *United Shoe Machinery Co. v. Brunet*, [1909] A.C. 330 (P.C.); *Aicken v. Baxter*, [1929] 4 D.L.R. 327 (B.C.C.A.), *per* McPhillips J.A., at p. 333; *Whitling v. Fleming* (1908), 16 O.L.R. 263 (H.C.J.); *Publishers' Syndicate (Re)* (1904), 7 O.L.R. 223 (C.A.); *McLaren v. Jensen* (1906), 4 W.L.R. 162 (Yukon Terr. Full Court); *Lucas v. Hooper* (1920), 19 O.W.N. 208 (H.C.); *Walker v. Gallipau* (1920), 18 O.W.N. 422 (H.C.); *Fuller v. Thames Quarry Co.* (1921), 20 O.W.N. 374 (Div. Ct.); *Steen v. Wallace*, [1937] 3 W.W.R. 654 (Alta. S.C.); *French v. Paris*, [1928] 3 D.L.R. 555 (Sask. C.A.); *Forler v. Brenner* (1922), 21 O.W.N. 489 (S.C.).

damages might sometimes be small not that nominal damages should be

[14] *Cofrin v. Bicchieri* (1977), 3 B.C.L.R. 122 (S.C.); *Wood v. Williams* (1980), 40 N.S.R. (2d) 63 (S.C.T.D.); *Caines v. Bank of Nova Scotia* (1978), 90 D.L.R. (3d) 271 (N.B.S.C. App. Div.); *Leitch Gold Mines Ltd. v. Texas Gulf Sulphur Co. (Inc.)* (1968), 3 D.L.R. (3d) 161, [1969] 1 O.R. 469 (H.C.J.); *Burgoyne v. Murphy*, [1951] 2 D.L.R. 556 (N.B.S.C. App. Div.); *Zimmer v. Ringrose* (1978), 89 D.L.R. (3d) 646 (Alta. S.C.T.D.), vard 124 D.L.R. (3d) 215 (C.A.), leave to appeal to S.C.C. refused 37 N.S.R. 289*n*, 28 A.R. 92*n*; *Cobbold v. Time Canada Ltd.* (1980), 109 D.L.R. (3d) 611, 28 O.R. (2d) 326 (H.C.J.); *Edwards v. Shore* (1956), 20 W.W.R. 240 (B.C.S.C.); *Fisher v. Pemberton* (1969), 8 D.L.R. (3d) 521 (B.C.S.C.); *Canadian Credit Men's Trust Ass'n Ltd. v. Heinke* (1957), 11 D.L.R. (2d) 505 (B.C.S.C.); *Coffin v. MacLellan Lincoln Mercury Sales Ltd.* (1993), 123 N.S.R. (2d) 171 (S.C.); *Mason v. Westside Cemeteries Ltd.* (1996), 135 D.L.R. (4th) 361 (Ont. Ct. (Gen. Div.)); *B.M.P. Global Distribution Inc. v. Bank of Nova Scotia* (2007), 278 D.L.R. (4th) 501 (B.C.C.A.) at para. 51, citing this passage, leave to appeal to S.C.C. granted 283 D.L.R. (4th) vi and leave to appeal to S.C.C. granted 288 D.L.R. (4th) vi.

[15] *Melanson v. Wright* (1896), 40 N.S.R. 598*n*.

[16] *McCune v. Good* (1915), 23 D.L.R. 662, 34 O.L.R. 51 (S.C. App. Div.); *Strang v. Township of Arran* (1913), 12 D.L.R. 41, 28 O.L.R. 106 (S.C. App. Div.); *Stetz v. Stetz*, [1946] 2 D.L.R. 665 (Sask. C.A.); *Rowan v. Costello*, [1928] 3 D.L.R. 744 (Alta. Dist. Ct.); *Greenwood v. Rae* (1916), 30 D.L.R. 796, 36 O.L.R. 367 (S.C. App. Div.); *Hessey v. Quinn* (1910), 21 O.L.R. 519 (Div. Ct.); *Haggerty v. Latreille* (1913), 14 D.L.R. 532, 29 O.L.R. 300 (S.C. App. Div.); *Medalta Potteries Ltd. v. Medicine Hat*, [1931] 1 W.W.R. 217 (Alta. S.C.); *Barber v. Andrews* (1921), 20 O.W.N. 239 (H.C.); *Bos v. Brauer*, [1992] 5 W.W.R. 557, 3 Alta. L.R. (3d) 318 (C.A.).

[17] *Mines Ltd. v. Woodworth*, [1940] 4 D.L.R. 676 (B.C.S.C.), vard [1941] 4 D.L.R. 101 (C.A.), affd [1942] 1 D.L.R. 135 (S.C.C.); *O'Toole v. Walters* (1979), 96 D.L.R. (3d) 202 (N.S.S.C.T.D.); *Hodgkinson v. Martin*, [1929] 1 D.L.R. 367 (B.C.C.A.) (said to be equivalent to forty shillings); *Amicale Yarns Inc. v. Canadian Worsted Manufacturing Ltd.* (1968), 68 D.L.R. (2d) 131, [1968] 2 O.R. 59 (H.C.J.); *Hayden v. Rudd* (1921), 60 D.L.R. 483 (Alta. S.C.), affd 66 D.L.R. 618 (S.C. App. Div.); *Hart v. Johnston* (1916), 27 D.L.R. 450 (Sask. S.C. en banc); *Sommerfeldt v. Petrovitch*, [1949] 4 D.L.R. 825 (Sask. C.A.); *Wilson v. Rowswell*, [1970] S.C.R. 865, 11 D.L.R. (3d) 737 ($10 reversed on other grounds); *Wendt v. Roos* (1977), 5 A.R. 278 (Dist. Ct.); *Canadian Ironworkers Union No. 1 v. International Association of Bridge, Structural & Ornamental Ironworkers Union, Local 97* (1968), 63 W.W.R. 377 (B.C.S.C.), revd on other grounds 13 D.L.R. (3d) 559 (C.A.), affd 21 D.L.R. (3d) 469 (S.C.C.); *Bergman v. Bergman* (2004), 9 E.T.R. (3d) 6 (Alta. C.A.).

[18] *Chaytor v. London, New York & Paris Ass'n of Fashion Ltd.* (1961), 30 D.L.R. (2d) 527 (Nfld. S.C.); *Marshall v. Woodlands Rural Municipality*, [1948] 1 D.L.R. 351 (Man. C.A.).

[19] *Forrest v. Greaves*, [1923] 3 D.L.R. 816 (Sask. K.B.); *Knowles v. Goldt*, [1951] 1 D.L.R. 458 (Sask. C.A.); *Cousins v. Wilson*, [1994] 1 N.Z.L.R. 462 (H.C.).

[20] *Delta Construction Co. Ltd. v. Lidstone* (1979), 96 D.L.R. (3d) 457 (Nfld. S.C.T.D.).

[21] *Peerless Laundry & Cleaners Ltd. v. Neal*, [1953] 2 D.L.R. 494 (Man. C.A.); *McGee v. Clarke*, [1927] 1 W.W.R. 593 (B.C.C.A.).

[22] *MacKay v. Southam Co. Ltd.* (1955), 1 D.L.R. (2d) 1 (B.C.C.A.); *State Vacuum Stores of Canada Ltd. v. Phillips*, [1954] 3 D.L.R. 621 (B.C.C.A.); *Hudson's Bay Oil & Gas Co. Ltd. v. Dynamic Petroleums Ltd.* (1959), 28 W.W.R. 480*n* (Alta. S.C. App. Div.); *Johnston Terminals & Storage Ltd. v. Miscellaneous Workers* (1975), 61 D.L.R. (3d) 741 (B.C.S.C.); *Witwicki v. Yadlowski* (1978), 91 D.L.R. (3d) 340 (Alta. Dist. Ct.); *Slone v. Margolian* (1957), 12 D.L.R. (2d) 507 (N.S.S.C. in banco); *Fisher v. Knibbe*, [1992] 5 W.W.R. 385, 3 Alta. L.R. (3d) 97 (C.A.); *Aikmac Holdings Ltd. v. Loewen* (1993), 86 Man. R. (2d) 56 (Q.B.); *Marynowsky v. Stuartburn (District)*, [1994] 10 W.W.R. 602, 97 Man. R. (2d) 60 (C.A.); *Hudson's Bay Co. v. White* (1997), 32 C.C.L.T. (2d) 163 (Ont. Ct. (Gen. Div.)), vard 1 C.P.C. (5th) 333 (S.C.J. (Div. Ct.)); *Canadian Pacific Ltd. v. Lowe* (1998), 172 N.S.R. (2d) 89 (S.C.), affd 177 N.S.R. (2d) 330 (C.A.), leave to appeal to S.C.C. refused 178 D.L.R. (4th) 764 (C.A.), leave to appeal to S.C.C. refused 185 D.L.R. (4th) vii.

[22a] *Ouellette v. Fleck* (1995), 158 N.B.R. (2d) 141 (Q.B.).

[23] *Irving Pulp & Paper Ltd. v. McBrine* (1973), 9 N.B.R. (2d) 194 (Q.B.); *Frerotte v. Irwin* (1986), 51 Sask. R. 108 (Q.B.).

large. In one Manitoba case[29] nominal damages were awarded in English currency (one shilling), but this seems undesirable as comparison will often be required with money paid into court.

10.30 It is submitted that there is good reason for the courts to re-establish a conventional figure. This is particularly important where the defendant wishes to make a payment into court. If the defendant knows that the figure for nominal damages is, say, $1, the defendant can safely make a payment into court of that amount. It is in the public interest to discourage unnecessary litigation, and the rule governing payment into court is designed to further that interest. The defendant who concedes that the plaintiff's right has been infringed but asserts (as it turns out correctly) that there is no loss, should be entitled to know what amount to pay into court in anticipation of an award of nominal damages. In inflationary times some might argue that the amount should be perpetually increasing, but this argument ignores the nature of nominal damages, which is not to give compensation for anything that could

---

24 *Bowlay Logging Ltd. v. Domtar Ltd.* (1978), 87 D.L.R. (3d) 325 (B.C.S.C.), affd 135 D.L.R. (3d) 179 (C.A.).

25 *Gastebled v. Stuyck*, [1973] F.C. 1039 (T.D.), affd [1974] 1 F.C. 429 (C.A.) ($300 — but said by Walsh J., at p. 1043, to be "perhaps erroneously referred to as "nominal""); *Green v. Stanton* (1969), 6 D.L.R. (3d) 680 (B.C.C.A.) ($1,000); *Fread v. Chislett* (1981), 123 D.L.R. (3d) 181, 32 O.R. (2d) 733 (H.C.J.) ($1,000); *Eastwalsh Homes Ltd. v. Anatal Developments Ltd.* (1993), 100 D.L.R. (4th) 469, 12 O.R. (3d) 675 (C.A.), leave to appeal to S.C.C. refused 104 D.L.R. (4th) vii, 162 N.R. 399*n* ($1,000); *Messineo v. Beale* (1976), 71 D.L.R. (3d) 31, 13 O.R. (2d) 329 (H.C.J.), affd 86 D.L.R. (3d) 713, 20 O.R. (2d) 49 (C.A.) ($500); *Baran v. Wilensky* (1959), 20 D.L.R. (2d) 440 (Ont. H.C.J.) ($500); *Polischuk v. Hagarty* (1983), 149 D.L.R. (3d) 65, 42 O.R. (2d) 417 (H.C.J.), revd on other grounds 14 D.L.R. (4th) 446*n*, 49 O.R. (2d) 71*n* (C.A.) ($500); *Melanson v. Cochrane, Sargeant, Nicholson & Paterson* (1986), 68 N.B.R. (2d) 370 (C.A.) ($500); *Restauronics Services Ltd. v. Foster* (2004), 239 D.L.R. (4th) 98 (B.C.C.A.) ($500); *Western Oil Consultants Ltd. v. Bankeno Resources Ltd.*, [1995] 6 W.W.R. 475, 168 A.R. 81 (Q.B.) ($1,000); *Ireland v. Victoria Real Estate Board*, [1996] 1 W.W.R. 349, 12 B.C.L.R. (3d) 265, supplementary reasons [1996] 1 W.W.R. at p. 388, 12 B.C.L.R. (3d) at p. 304 (S.C.) ($5,000); *Hildebrandt v. W.F. Botkin Construction Ltd.*, [1998] 7 W.W.R. 418, 162 Sask. R. 92 (Q.B.) ($3,000); *Lajoie v. Kelly*, [1997] 3 W.W.R. 181, 116 Man. R. (2d) 221 (Q.B.) ($1,000); *Kelsie v. Canada (Attorney General)* (2003), 230 Nfld. & P.E.I.R. 255 (Nfld. & Lab. S.C.T.D.), affd 139 A.C.W.S. (3d) 597 (Nfld. & Lab. C.A.); *Arabian Muslim Assn. v. Canadian Islamic Centre* (2004), 246 D.L.R. (4th) 351 (Alta. Q.B.), affd 266 D.L.R. (4th) 536 (Alta. C.A.) ($1000); *True Blue Cattle Co. v. Toronto-Dominion Bank*, [2005] 2 W.W.R. 532 (Alta. Q.B.) ($1000); *Trew v. 313124 Saskatchewan Ltd.* (2005), 259 Sask. R. 155 (Q.B.) ($500); *RBC Dominion Securities Inc. v. Merrill Lynch Canada Inc.* (2004), 36 B.C.L.R. (4th) 138 (S.C.), vard 275 D.L.R. (4th) 385 (B.C.C.A.) ($1000).

26 In *Green v. Stanton, supra*, footnote 25, it seems from the context that substantial compensation was intended for a loss of business that could not be precisely proved. In *Fread v. Chislett, supra*, footnote 25, the context indicates a "conventional" award for loss of companionship. In *Messineo v. Beale, supra*, footnote 25, the sum was evidently intended to be set off against the fee owed to the negligent defendant solicitor. In *Baran v. Wilensky, supra*, footnote 25, the award was for misrepresentation of marital status inducing cohabitation and may have been intended to compensate intangible injuries. In *Hildebrandt v. W.F. Botkin Construction Ltd, supra*, the award was for loss of housekeeping capacity.

27 *McGee v. Clarke*, [1927] 1 W.W.R. 593 (B.C.C.A.); *State Vacuum Stores of Canada Ltd. v. Phillips*, [1954] 3 D.L.R. 621 (B.C.C.A.).

28 In *The "Mediana"* [1900] A.C. 113 (H.L.), at p. 116.

29 *Dipple v. Wylie* (1916), 30 D.L.R. 59 (Man. K.B.).

be bought with money but to mark symbolically the infringement of a right. Provided that the amount is not so low as to be confused with contemptuous damages, a small and fixed conventional sum seems appropriate. It is suggested that $1, which appears to be the figure having most authoritative support in Canadian cases, should be adhered to.[30]

3. Contemptuous Damages

10.40 Where the court wishes to express strong disapproval of the plaintiff, while finding a technical infringement of rights, contemptuous damages are awarded of the lowest current coin.[31] Commonly, such an award is made in defamation cases where the jury finds the words complained of technically untrue but wishes to indicate its view that "the action should never have been brought".[32] In *Wood v. Cox*[33] the plaintiff, a jockey, was alleged to have "pulled" a horse in a race; it was proved that though he had not pulled the horse in the race referred to, he had a reputation as one who often pulled horses. The jury awarded one farthing damages. In *Kelly v. Sherlock,*[34] the plaintiff was a quarrelsome clergyman who himself had made vituperative comments about the defendant and others. He was awarded damages of a

---

30 *Kinkel v. Hyman,* [1939] S.C.R. 364, [1939] 4 D.L.R. 1; *Zurouvinski v. Duke,* [1924] 4 D.L.R. 326 (Sask. C.A.); *Brenner v. Consumers Metal Co.* (1917), 41 D.L.R. 339, 41 O.L.R. 534 (S.C. App. Div.); *McEachern v. Corey* (1916), 34 D.L.R. 165 (Alta. S.C. App. Div.); *Johnson v. Roche* (1914), 17 D.L.R. 74 (N.S.S.C.), vard 24 D.L.R. 305, 49 N.S.R. 12 (S.C. App. Div.), revd 53 S.C.R. 18, 29 D.L.R. 329; *Delbridge v. Pickersgill* (1912), 3 D.L.R. 786 (Sask. S.C.); *Lemon v. Grand Trunk Ry. Co.* (1914), 32 O.L.R. 37 (S.C. App. Div.); *Canadian Woodmen of the World v. Hooper,* [1935] 2 D.L.R. 802, [1935] O.W.N. 113 (C.A.); *United Shoe Machinery Co. v. Brunet,* [1909] A.C. 330 (P.C.); *Aicken v. Baxter,* [1929] 4 D.L.R. 327 (B.C.C.A.), *per* McPhillips J.A., at p. 333; *Whitling v. Fleming* (1908), 16 O.L.R. 263 (H.C.J.); *Publishers' Syndicate (Re)* (1904), 7 O.L.R. 223 (C.A.); *McLaren v. Jensen* (1906), 4 W.L.R. 162 (Yukon Terr. Full Court); *Lucas v. Hooper* (1920), 19 O.W.N. 208 (H.C.); *Walker v. Gallipau* (1920), 18 O.W.N. 422 (H.C.); *Fuller v. Thames Quarry Co.* (1921), 20 O.W.N. 374 (Div. Ct.); *Steen v. Wallace,* [1937] 3 W.W.R. 654 (Alta. S.C.); *French v. Paris,* [1928] 3 D.L.R. 555 (Sask. C.A.); *Forler v. Brenner* (1922), 21 O.W.N. 489 (S.C.); *Cofrin v. Bicchieri* (1977), 3 B.C.L.R. 122 (S.C.); *Wood v. Williams* (1980), 40 N.S.R. (2d) 63 (S.C.T.D.); *Caines v. Bank of Nova Scotia* (1978), 90 D.L.R. (3d) 271 (N.B.S.C. App. Div.); *Leitch Gold Mines Ltd. v. Texas Gulf Sulphur Co. (Inc.)* (1968), 3 D.L.R. (3d) 161, [1969] 1 O.R. 469 (H.C.J.); *Burgoyne v. Murphy,* [1951] 2 D.L.R. 556 (N.B.S.C. App. Div.); *Zimmer v. Ringrose* (1978), 89 D.L.R. (3d) 646 (Alta. S.C.T.D.), vard 124 D.L.R. (3d) 215 (C.A.), leave to appeal to S.C.C. refused 37 N.S.R. 289*n*, 28 A.R. 92*n*; *Cobbold v. Time Canada Ltd.* (1980), 109 D.L.R. (3d) 611, 28 O.R. (2d) 326 (H.C.J.); *Edwards v. Shore* (1956), 20 W.W.R. 240 (B.C.S.C.); *Fisher v. Pemberton* (1969), 8 D.L.R. (3d) 521 (B.C.S.C.); *Canadian Credit Men's Trust Ass'n Ltd. v. Heinke* (1957), 11 D.L.R. (2d) 505 (B.C.S.C.); *Coffin v. MacLellan Lincoln Mercury Sales Ltd.* (1993), 123 N.S.R. (2d) 171 (S.C.); *Mason v. Westside Cemeteries Ltd.* (1996), 135 D.L.R. (4th) 361 (Ont. Ct. (Gen. Div.)). This passage was quoted with approval by Catliff J. in *Rusche v. Insurance Corp. of British Columbia* (1992), 4 C.P.C. (3d) 12 (B.C.S.C.), and by the Ontario Court of Appeal in *Place Concorde East Limited Partnership v. Shelter Corp. of Canada Ltd.* (2006), 270 D.L.R. (4th) 181 (Ont. C.A.) at para 78.

31 *Paletta v. Lethbridge Herald Co. (No. 2)* (1976), 4 Alta. L.R. (2d) 97 (S.C.T.D.), at p. 105 ("the lowest coin of the realm"); *Dennison v. Sanderson,* [1946] 4 D.L.R. 314, [1946] O.R. 601 (C.A.) (one cent verdict upheld).

32 *Paletta, supra.*

33 (1888), 4 T.L.R. 652 (Q.B.).

34 (1866), L.R. 1 Q.B. 686. See 4.190, *supra*.

farthing. In *Dering v. Uris*[35] the plaintiff, a physician, complained of an allegation that he had collaborated with the Nazis in a concentration camp. The jury evidently took the view that, though the defendant's statement was untrue, the plaintiff had collaborated to some degree. He was awarded damages of one halfpenny (the farthing having ceased to be legal tender). The Canadian equivalent would be an award of one cent.

4. Symbolic Damages

10.50 In a number of cases money awards have been made under the *Canadian Charter of Rights and Freedoms*,[36] and similar constitutional documents in other countries,[36a] to vindicate rights or to symbolize recognition of their infringement.[37] These cases exhibit some characteristics of compensatory damages, of nominal damages, and of exemplary damages, but they cannot be classified as purely compensatory, since proof of actual loss is not required, nor as nominal, because substantial sums have been awarded, nor as exemplary, since punishable conduct is not required. Though the *Canadian Charter of Rights and Freedoms* is the most common source of such awards, it is not the only one. Similar kinds of awards have been made in cases involving loss of autonomy in the medical context.[38] In a sexual assault case, where the court could not determine what loss had been caused by the assault, the court awarded $40,000 "nominal damages for the violation of personal autonomy and dignity inherent in the battery itself".[39] The use of the word "nominal" to describe an award of $40,000 is very unusual, and the award might be more readily classified as symbolic. This is an area in which awards, though comparatively few in number, have varied widely, and where there is no natural or rational limit to the sums that might plausibly be awarded. As in analogous areas of the law of damages, a conventional range of awards will be necessary if consistency, predictability and fairness between one plaintiff and another are to be maintained.

---

35 [1964] 2 Q.B. 669.

36 Section 24 ("such remedy as the court considers appropriate and just in the circumstances"). The question is fully discussed in Kent Roach, *Constitutional Remedies in Canada*, Canada Law Book, looseleaf ed. (Aurora, Canada Law Book), chapter 11. See especially paras. 11.740 and 11.759.

36a *Attorney General of Trinidad and Tobago v. Ramanoop*, [2006] 1 A.C. 328; *Merson v. Cartwright*, 2005 UKPC 38.

37 *Dulude v. Canada* (2000), 192 D.L.R. (4th) 714 (F.C.A.) ("moral damages" of $10,000); *Auton (Guardian ad litem of) v. British Columbia (Attorney General)* (2001), 197 D.L.R. (4th) 165 (B.C.S.C.), affd 220 D.L.R. (4th) 411 (B.C.C.A.) at para. 98 ("symbolic damages" of $20,000 to each petitioner), revd on other grounds [2004] 3 S.C.R. 657, 245 D.L.R. (4th) 1. See *Bevis v. Burns* (2006), 269 D.L.R. (4th) 696 (N.S.C.A.) at para. 64 ("enhanced general damage award could meaningfully affirm the Charter rights which have been violated"); *Hawley v. Bapoo* (2005), 76 O.R. (3d) 649 (S.C.J.), at paras. 205 and 206 ($2,500 awarded against each of two police officers for assault, to vindicate Charter rights, and to deter future misconduct).

38 See para. 14.730, *infra*.

39 *Olsen v. Olsen* (2006), 266 D.L.R. (4th) 209 (B.C.S.C.) at para. 65.

CHAPTER 11

PUNITIVE DAMAGES

1. Introduction

An exception exists to the general rule that damages are compensatory. This is the case of an award made for the purpose not of compensating the plaintiff but of punishing the defendant.[1] Such awards have been called exemplary, vindictive, penal, punitive, aggravated, and retributory, but the expressions in common modern use to describe damages going beyond compensatory are exemplary and punitive damages.[1a] "Exemplary" was preferred by the House of Lords in *Cassell & Co. Ltd. v. Broome,*[1b] but "punitive" is the more common word in modern Canadian usage. The words are used interchangeably in this chapter. The expression "aggravated damages", though it has sometimes been used interchangeably with punitive or exemplary damages,[3] has more frequently in recent times been contrasted with exemplary damages.[4] In this contrasting sense, aggravated damages describes an award that aims at compensation but takes full account of the intangible injuries, such as distress and humiliation, that may have been caused by the defendant's insulting behaviour. The expressions vindictive, penal and retributory have dropped out of common use.[4a] **11.10**

2. Theoretical Basis

The theoretical justification for an award of punitive damages has long been debated, for it appears anomalous for a civil court to impose what is in effect a fine[5] for conduct it finds to be worthy of punishment, and then to remit the fine, not to the State Treasury, but to an individual plaintiff who will, by definition, be over-compensated.[5a] The arguments in favour of exemplary damages are that deterrence, as well as compensation, is a legitimate aim of the civil law and that conduct worthy of punishment may **11.20**

[1] *Wallace v. United Grain Growers Ltd.*, [1997] 3 S.C.R. 701, 152 D.L.R. (4th) 1 at p. 28; *Health Care Developers Inc. v. Newfoundland* (1996), 136 D.L.R. (4th) 609 (Nfld. C.A.), at p. 641; *Kaddoura v. Hammoud* (1998), 168 D.L.R. (4th) 503 (Ont. Ct. (Gen. Div.)), at p. 506; *Schurko v. Tutkaluk* (1998), 125 Man. R. (2d) 290 (Q.B.), at p. 292; all citing this paragraph.

[1a] Held to be synonymous in *Bekkattla v. Saskatchewan* (2005), 274 Sask. R. 7 (Q.B.).

[1b] [1972] A.C. 1027 (H.L.).

[2] [Footnote deleted.]

[3] *Denison v. Fawcett* (1958), 12 D.L.R. (2d) 537, [1958] O.R. 312 (C.A.), appeal to S.C.C. withdrawn [1958] O.W.N. 468*n; Grenn v. Brampton Poultry Co. Ltd.* (1959), 18 D.L.R. (2d) 9 (Ont. C.A.); *S. v. Mundy* (1969), 9 D.L.R. (3d) 446, [1970] 1 O.R. 764 (Co. Ct.); *Bahner v. Marwest Hotel Co.* (1969), 6 D.L.R. (3d) 322 (B.C.S.C.), affd 12 D.L.R. (3d) 646 (C.A.).

often not fall within the scope of the criminal law, or may not be thought to justify prosecution, or if prosecuted, may be insufficiently punished. A reason given more commonly in earlier times than recently is that an award of exemplary damages suppresses the likelihood of duelling and private vengeance.[6]

11.30 Even if it is conceded that one of the effects of the civil law is deterrence, this concession does not necessarily justify exemplary damages. The award of compensatory damages has, in itself, a deterrent effect, and one can support this effect, without supporting an award expressly made for deterrent purposes.[7]

11.40 The main argument against exemplary damages is that punishment and the avoidance of private vengeance is the function of the criminal law. If the conduct in question falls outside the scope of the criminal law, that is because Parliament has chosen not to make it punishable, and in Canada, where the criminal law is reserved exclusively for Parliament, which has expressly

---

[4] *Rookes v. Barnard*, [1964] A.C. 1129 (H.L.), at p. 1230; *Golnik v. Geissinger* (1967), 64 D.L.R. (2d) 754 (B.C.S.C.); *Amos v. Vawter* (1969), 6 D.L.R. (3d) 234 (B.C.S.C.); *Loomis v. Rohan* (1974), 46 D.L.R. (3d) 423 (B.C.S.C.); *Johnston Terminals & Storage Ltd. v. Miscellaneous Workers* (1975), 61 D.L.R. (3d) 741 (B.C.S.C.); *Abboud v. Ayoub* (1994), 127 N.S.R. (2d) 52 (S.C.); *Dalsin v. T. Eaton Co. of Canada Ltd.* (1975), 63 D.L.R. (3d) 565 (Alta. Dist. Ct.); *Walker v. CFTO Ltd.* (1987), 37 D.L.R. (4th) 224, 59 O.R. (2d) 104 (C.A.); *C. (M.) v. M. (F.)* (1990), 74 D.L.R. (4th) 129 (Ont. Ct. (Gen. Div.)); *Makryllos v. George Laurens (NT) Ltd.* (1992), 111 F.L.R. 204 (N.T.S.C.); *Attorney-General v. Niania*, [1994] 3 N.Z.L.R. 107 (H.C.); *A. (C.) v. Critchley* (1998), 166 D.L.R. (4th) 475 (B.C.C.A.); *Lord (Litigation Guardian of) v. Downer* (1999), 179 D.L.R. (4th) 430 at p. 434 (Ont. C.A.), leave to appeal to S.C.C. refused 183 D.L.R. (4th) vii, citing this passage; *Laufer v. Bucklaschuk* (1999), 181 D.L.R. (4th) 83, [2000] 2 W.W.R. 462 at p. 499 (Man. C.A.), leave to appeal to S.C.C. refused 189 D.L.R. (4th) vii. The instance cited in *Merest v. Harvey* (1814), 5 Taunt. 442 at p. 444, 128 E.R. 761, *per* Heath J.: "I remember a case where a jury gave £500 damages for merely knocking a man's hat off; and the Court refused a new trial", might be explained as a case of aggravated damages. Damages for mental distress are not synonymous with aggravated damages: *Fidler v. Sun Life Assurance Co. of Canada*, [2006] 2 S.C.R. 3, 271 D.L.R. (4th) 1, at para. 53. It was held in *Ager v. Canjex Publishing Ltd.* (2005), 259 D.L.R. (4th) 727 (B.C.C.A.), that an award of aggravated damages requires a finding of actual malice.

[4a] *Vorvis v. Insurance Corp. of British Columbia*, [1989] 1 S.C.R. 1085, 58 D.L.R. (4th) 193 at pp. 201-2, citing this paragraph; *Dixon v. British Columbia Transit* (1995), 9 B.C.L.R. (3d) 108 at p. 126, 13 C.C.E.L. (2d) 272 (S.C.), citing this paragraph; *Noseworthy v. Riverside Pontiac-Buick Ltd.* (1998), 168 D.L.R. (4th) 629 (Ont. C.A.), at p. 632; *A. (C.) v. Critchley* (1998), 166 D.L.R. (4th) 475 (B.C.C.A.), at p. 508; *MacKinnon (Litigation Guardian of) v. Devine*, [2004] 7 W.W.R. 695 (Sask. Q.B.), at pp. 701-2, citing this paragraph.

[5] *Bains v. Indo-Canadian Times Inc.* (1995), 38 C.P.C. (3d) 53, 94 W.A.C. 90 (B.C.C.A.) (use of exemplary damages to be restrained). See *Cassell & Co. Ltd. v. Broome, supra*, footnote 1, at p. 1086, *per* Lord Reid: "In my view the word "fine' is an entirely accurate description of that part of any award which goes beyond anything justly due to the plaintiff and is purely punitive", but see p. 1082, *per* Lord Hailsham.

[5a] *Vorvis v. Insurance Corp. of British Columbia*, [1989] 1 S.C.R. 1085 at p. 1104, 58 D.L.R. (4th) 193 at p. 205, citing this paragraph.

[6] *Merest v. Harvey, supra*, footnote 4, cited in *Fleming v. Spracklin* (1921), 64 D.L.R. 382 at p. 393, 50 O.L.R. 289 at p. 301 (S.C. App. Div.).

[7] Thus Posner, in *Economic Analysis of Law*, 2nd ed. (Toronto, Little, Brown & Co., 1977), p. 143, described the purpose of negligence law as deterrence of uneconomic accidents, but added that the proper measure of the deterrence was the amount of the victim's loss.

abolished common law crimes,[8] there seems even greater reason than in other jurisdictions for the courts to refrain from creating new crimes in civil cases. The argument that public authorities may often be reluctant to prosecute for minor offences can be met by the right of private prosecution, expanded if this is thought to be in the public interest. The argument that the private prosecutor has insufficient financial incentive to prosecute could be met by allowing a successsful prosecutor to recover costs, again if this were thought to be in the public interest. Of course, the incentive would still not be equal to the prospect of recovering large punitive damages, but here the question arises whether it is in the public interest to give awards to private persons for punishing their fellow citizens, the penalties for common informers having been long ago abolished in most Commonwealth jurisdictions.

11.50 Another argument against exemplary damages is that the defendant is punished without the protection afforded by criminal procedure, particularly the burden of proof, the right not to give evidence, the right to jury trial on the facts, the right to sentencing by a judge, the right to appeal against sentence, and protection against double jeopardy, though against this may be set the consideration that the defendant in a civil case is not in so great a jeopardy as the accused in a criminal case. Lord Devlin in *Rookes v. Barnard* said: "I do not care for the idea that in matters criminal an aggrieved party should be given an option to inflict for his own benefit punishment by a method which denies to the offender the protection of the criminal law."[9]

11.60 Lord Reid summed up these objections in *Cassell & Co. Ltd. v. Broome:*

> I think that the objections to allowing juries to go beyond compensatory damages are overwhelming. To allow pure punishment in this way contravenes every principle which has been evolved for the protection of offenders. There is no definition of the offence except that the conduct punished must be oppressive, high-handed, malicious, wanton or its like — terms far too vague to be admitted to any criminal code worthy of the name. There is no limit to the punishment except that it must not be unreasonable. The punishment is not inflicted by a judge who has experience and at least tries not to be influenced by emotion: it is inflicted by a jury without experience of law or punishment and often swayed by considerations which every judge would put out of his mind. And there is no effective appeal against sentence. All that a reviewing court can do is to quash the jury's decision if it thinks the punishment awarded is more than any twelve reasonable men could award. The court cannot substitute its own award. The punishment must then be decided by another jury and if they too award heavy punishment the court is virtually powerless. It is no excuse to say that we need not waste sympathy on people who behave outrageously. Are we wasting sympathy on vicious criminals when we insist on proper legal safeguards for them? The right to give punitive damages in certain cases is so firmly embedded in our law that only Parliament can remove it. But I must say that I am surprised by the enthusiasm of Lord Devlin's critics in supporting this form of palm tree justice.[10]

8 *Criminal Code* (Can.), s. 9.
9 *Supra,* footnote 4, at p. 1230.
10 *Supra,* footnote 1b, at p. 1087.

11.70 A further objection to exemplary damages is that even if punishment of the defendant were acceptable, there is no reason why the "fine" levied should go into the plaintiff's pocket. It is often said that compensatory damages fail to give full compensation, and in the United States, where a successful party cannot recover full costs, it is very commonly argued in support of exemplary damages that they will compensate the plaintiff for the costs of litigation.[11] The answer to this objection is surely to expand the scope of compensatory damages or (in American jurisdictions) to alter the rules on costs.[12] In so far as the plaintiff suffers mental distress and humiliation for the defendant's wrong, the plaintiff can be compensated by aggravated damages without departure from the compensatory principle. In several fields of law there has, indeed, been an increase in the willingness of courts to award compensation for mental distress.[13] One writer has suggested that exemplary damages should in fact be paid to the State,[14] but this would amount to openly empowering the civil court to impose a fine in every case of tort and would exacerbate the problems referred to previously of imposing a criminal sanction in the course of civil proceedings. Another objection to awards of exemplary damages is that they create uncertainty, increasing the costs of litigation.[15]

11.80 Another kind of objection to exemplary damages is that they make little sense from an administrative law point of view. If the community desires to enact product safety standards, for example, the result can be achieved far more effectively by regulation than by sporadic awards of exemplary damages, which may have the effect of punishing what the legislature, in the public interest, intended to permit.

11.90 The House of Lords in *Rookes v. Barnard,*[16] though setting out "to remove an anomaly from the law",[17] did not abolish exemplary damages but announced that they were to be restricted (except for statutory authorization) to two categories. As has been pointed out, if the theoretical arguments against exemplary damages were so strong as to require such a restriction, one would have expected the House of Lords to abolish exemplary damages altogether.[18] But Lord Devlin retains the two categories (which may be

[11] McCormick, *Handbook on the Law of Damages* (St. Paul, West Publishing Co., 1935), p. 277. In Connecticut exemplary damages are restricted to the costs of litigation. See *Craney v. Donovan,* 92 Conn. 236, 102 A. 640 (S.C. of Errors, 1917). In *Becker v. Cleland's Estate* (1980), 30 N.B.R. (2d) 12 (Q.B.T.D.), vard 35 N.B.R. (2d) 542 (C.A.), and in *Urquhart v. J. Clark & Son Ltd.* (1975), 12 N.B.R. (2d) 400 (S.C. App. Div.), exemplary damages were explicitly equated with solicitor-and-client costs.

[12] Described by McCormick, *op. cit.*, footnote 11, as "one of the glaring defects in our system".

[13] See 3.1250-3.1480, *supra.*

[14] Hawley, "Punitive and Aggravated Damages in Canada", 18 Alta. L. Rev. 485 (1980), at p. 508.

[15] See Ellis, "Fairness and Efficiency in the Law of Punitive Damages", 56 So. Cal. L.R. 1 (1982).

[16] [1964] A.C. 1129 (H.L.).

[17] *Supra,* at p. 1221.

[18] Fridman, "Punitive Damages in Tort", 48 Can. Bar Rev. 373 (1970), at pp. 383-4.

summarized as abuse of power by government, and torts committed with intention to make a profit), with equanimity and even enthusiasm, saying: "there are certain categories of cases in which an award of exemplary damages can serve a useful purpose in vindicating the strength of the law and thus affording a practical justification for admitting into the civil law a principle which ought logically to belong to the criminal".[19] But this comment undercuts the whole case against exemplary damages, for if exemplary damages serve a useful purpose and vindicate the strength of the law in the two categories preserved by Lord Devlin, there seems no compelling reason to reject these advantages in other areas of the law also. Lord Reid in *Cassell & Co. Ltd. v. Broome,*[20] though he had concurred with Lord Devlin in *Rookes v. Barnard,* expressly dissociated himself from this comment, putting his support of the two categories on the basis of an anomaly so firmly embedded in the law that only parliament could remove it.[21] Supporters of exemplary damages can therefore justly point to the fact that even a court theoretically hostile to the principle felt the need to preserve the practice, but confined it within boundaries that are illogical and difficult to apply.

11.100 A second point that can justly be made in favour of exemplary damages is that, in several Canadian jurisdictions, legislation has expressly empowered the courts to award exemplary damages on introducing new statutory causes of action.[22] This certainly suggests that the legislature sees nothing anomalous in the concept, though it could always be argued that the express legislative introduction of the power in limited circumstances does not necessarily empower the courts to adopt such a power elsewhere. In *Vorvis v. Insurance Corp. of British Columbia,* the Supreme Court of Canada said that the discretion to award exemplary damages should be "most cautiously exercised"[22a] and their exceptional nature was emphasized in *Sylvan Lake Golf & Tennis Club Ltd. v. Performance Industries Ltd.*[22b]

3. The Law in England

11.110 The power to award exemplary damages in England was, as has been mentioned, restricted by *Rookes v. Barnard.* Apart from cases where exemplary damages were authorized by statute, Lord Devlin held that there were only two classes of cases in which exemplary damages were to be awarded. The first category he described as "oppressive, arbitrary or unconstitutional action by the servants of the government".[23] *Cassell & Co.*

---

19 *Rookes, supra,* footnote 16, at p. 1226.

20 [1972] A.C. 1027 (H.L.), at p. 1087.

21 *Supra,* at p. 1086.

22 The Business Practices Acts of several provinces, see 3.1410, *supra; Criminal Code* (Can.), s. 194.

22a [1989] 1 S.C.R. 1085 at p. 1104, 58 D.L.R. (4th) 193. See also *Bains v. Indo-Canadian Times Inc.* (1995), 38 C.P.C. (3d) 53, 94 W.A.C. 90 (B.C.C.A.); *Warrington v. Great-West Life Assurance Co.* (1996), 139 D.L.R. (4th) 18, [1996] 10 W.W.R. 691 (B.C.C.A.).

22b (2002), 209 D.L.R. (4th) 318 (S.C.C.), at pp. 343-4.

Ltd. v. Broome[24] made it clear that this was not to be restricted to government servants in a strict sense — the police and local authority agents would be included. But Lord Devlin made it clear that the category was not to be extended to oppressive action by private persons and organizations, however powerful.[25] The case itself involved a trade union.

11.120 The second category is potentially much wider:

> Cases in the second category are those in which the defendant's conduct has been calculated by him to make a profit for himself which may well exceed the compensation payable to the plaintiff ... It is a factor also that is taken into account in damages for libel; one man should not be allowed to sell another man's reputation for profit. Where a defendant with a cynical disregard for a plaintiff's rights has calculated that the money to be made out of his wrongdoing will probably exceed the damages at risk, it is necessary for the law to show that it cannot be broken with impunity. This category is not confined to moneymaking in the strict sense. It extends to cases in which the defendant is seeking to gain at the expense of the plaintiff some object — perhaps some property which he covets — which either he could not obtain at all or not obtain except at a price greater than he wants to put down. Exemplary damages can properly be awarded whenever it is necessary to teach a wrongdoer that tort does not pay.[26]

11.130 In *Cassell & Co. Ltd. v. Broome,*[27] it was held that to bring a case within this category it was not necessary to show that the defendant had made any sort of precise financial calculation. It was held to be sufficient that the defendant had deliberately published a book in the hope of a profit, knowing that the plaintiff complained of it and knowing that the book defamed the plaintiff or not caring whether it did or not. It is plain, also, that exemplary damages in this category will often greatly exceed any amount that the plaintiff might recover on a restitutionary basis. It is the defendant's calculation not the accuracy of it that lays the defendant open to an award. In *Cassell & Co. Ltd. v. Broome* itself, the defendant presumably made nothing out of the book, but an award of £25,000 was upheld.

11.140 In a subsequent English case, *Drane v. Evangelou,*[28] an award of exemplary damages was upheld against a landlord who resorted to trespass to remove a tenant unlawfully from possession of an apartment. The award of £1,000 might, in the opinion of two members of the court, have been supported as aggravated damages. However, all agreed that it came within Lord Devlin's second category and was supportable as exemplary damages. Again it was stressed that no explicit financial calculation is required. In the case itself the landlord had used the apartment to accommodate his wife's parents. The award would have been supportable if he had wanted the

---

23 *Rookes, supra,* footnote 16, at p. 1226.

24 *Supra,* footnote 20, at pp. 1077-8, *per* Lord Hailsham; pp. 1087-8, *per* Lord Reid.

25 *Rookes, supra,* at p. 1226.

26 *Rookes, supra,* at pp. 1226-7.

27 *Supra,* footnote 20, at pp. 1078-9, *per* Lord Hailsham, p. 1088, *per* Lord Reid.

28 [1978] 1 W.L.R. 455 (C.A.).

premises for his own use. Again it is clear that exemplary damages are not restricted to profit actually made by the defendant.

11.150 It might be argued that Lord Devlin's second category to some extent fills a gap in the law of restitution.[29] It has already been pointed out that exemplary damages are not restricted, as would be a restitutionary claim, to the actual benefit obtained by the wrongdoer. On the other hand, it should be noted that a restitutionary claim will lie even against an innocent wrongdoer, whereas exemplary damages can only be awarded to mark deliberate misconduct.[30] The category is, therefore, by no means an equivalent to a restitutionary claim.

11.160 In considering the extent of the restriction imposed on English law by *Rookes v. Barnard,* attention must be paid to Lord Devlin's comments on aggravated damages. He drew a sharp distinction between aggravated damages (that rested on a compensatory basis and took account of any distress caused to the plaintiff by the defendant's misconduct) and exemplary damages. But he recognized that in former times a sharp distinction had not been drawn, so that Lord Devlin felt able to support the result reached in almost all[31] the cases discussed, on the basis that, though the courts might have described the damages as exemplary or punitive, in reality they could be supported as compensatory. Lord Devlin indicated that he did not consider that he was making a drastic change in the law: "[This conclusion] will not, I think, make much difference to the substance of the law or rob the law of the strength which it ought to have. Aggravated damages in this type of case can do most, if not all, of the work that could be done by exemplary damages."[32]

11.170 In the field of defamation, one of the primary sources of exemplary damages, it seems that *Rookes v. Barnard* has had very little effect. *Cassell & Co. Ltd. v. Broome,* as mentioned above, held that an award of exemplary damages was appropriate when the defendant deliberately published the defamation in the hope of making a profit. But even where these factors are not present, a punitive element cannot be realistically excluded from general damages for defamation, because it is impossible to measure that amount that the plaintiff should recover on purely compensatory principles.[33]

11.180 Overall, then, it may be said that *Rookes v. Barnard* has had less of an effect on English law than was at first anticipated. This does not make the decision easier to defend or to accept in other jurisdictions because the larger the area in which exemplary damages can still be awarded, the more anomalous appear the restrictions imposed by *Rookes v. Barnard.* That it does impose restrictions cannot be doubted. Consequently, arbitrary or oppressive conduct by a powerful individual corporation or trade union is

[29] *McGregor on Damages,* 16th ed. (London, Sweet & Maxwell, 1997), §465; Lord Diplock in *Broome v. Cassell, supra,* footnote 20, at p. 1129.
[30] See 11.210, 11.220, *infra.*
[31] The only case expressly overruled was *Loudon v. Ryder,* [1953] 2 Q.B. 202 (C.A.).
[32] *Rookes v. Barnard,* [1964] A.C. 1129 (H.L.), at p. 1230.
[33] See 4.50-4.140, *supra.*

excluded from the purview of exemplary damages. So also is a wrong committed with no profit-making motive, for example, out of sheer spite. Lord Reid in *Cassell & Co. Ltd. v. Broome* freely admitted the illogicality of these restrictions.[34] He defended them only as a "second best" solution on the assumption that the total abolition of exemplary damages was impractical. This might be acceptable if the remaining categories were small and likely to diminish. But if it appears that there is no prospect of abolition but rather the movement is to extend the categories of cases in which exemplary damages can be awarded,[34a] the illogical restrictions become more difficult to accept.

4. The Law in Canada

11.190 In Commonwealth jurisdictions, where decisions of the House of Lords are not binding, *Rookes v. Barnard* received a cool reception. The High Court of Australia in *Uren v. John Fairfax & Sons Pty., Ltd.*[35] determined that it was not to be followed in Australia and this decision was affirmed by the Privy Council.[36] In *Fogg v. McKnight*,[37] the New Zealand Supreme Court indicated that it did not consider the case binding, though later cases have left the matter open.[38] In Canada some cases have referred to *Rookes v. Barnard* with approval,[39] but the weight of decisions is heavily against accepting the restrictions of the case as part of Canadian law.[40] Even some of the cases citing *Rookes v. Barnard* with approval have relied on Lord Devlin's statement that "exemplary damages can properly be awarded whenever it is necessary to teach a wrongdoer that tort does not pay" to support an award that does not apparently fit within the two categories.[41] In *McElroy v. Cowper-Smith*[42] Spence J., dissenting on another point, said: "in Canada the jurisdiction to award punitive damages in tort actions is not so limited as Lord Devlin outlined in *Rooke v. Barnard*".[43]

11.200 In *H.L. Weiss Forwarding Ltd. v. Omnus*[44] the court, by a majority,

[34] [1972] A.C. 1027 (H.L.), at p. 1088.

[34a] See *Kuddus v. Chief Constable of Leicestershire Constabulary*, [2002] 2 A.C. 122 (H.L.).

[35] (1966), 117 C.L.R. 118 (Aust. H.C.).

[36] *Australian Consolidated Press Ltd. v. Uren*, [1969] 1 A.C. 590 (P.C.).

[37] [1968] N.Z.L.R. 330 (S.C.).

[38] *News Media Ownership v. Finlay*, [1970] N.Z.L.R. 1089 (C.A.), at p. 1100.

[39] *MacDonald v. Hees* (1974), 46 D.L.R. (3d) 720 (N.S.S.C.T.D.); *Wasson v. California Standard Co.* (1964), 47 D.L.R. (2d) 71 (Alta. S.C. App. Div.); *Banks v. Campbell* (1973), 45 D.L.R. (3d) 603 (N.S.S.C.T.D.); *Schuster v. Martin* (1965), 50 D.L.R. (2d) 176 (B.C.S.C.).

[40] *Gouzenko v. Lefolii* (1967), 63 D.L.R. (2d) 217, [1967] 2 O.R. 262 (C.A.); vard 70 D.L.R. (2d) 337 (S.C.C.); *Fraser v. Wilson* (1969), 6 D.L.R. (3d) 531 (Man. Q.B.); *Eagle Motors (1958) Ltd. v. Makaoff* (1970), 17 D.L.R. (3d) 222 (B.C.C.A.); *Turnbull v. Calgary Power Ltd.* (1974), 51 D.L.R. (3d) 562 (Alta. S.C. App. Div.); *Paragon Properties Ltd. v. Magna Envestments Ltd.* (1972), 24 D.L.R. (3d) 156 (Alta. S.C. App. Div.); *Holowaty v. Ford Motor Credit Co. of Canada Ltd.*, [1974] 1 W.W.R. 225 (Alta. Dist. Ct.); *Walker v. CFTO Ltd.* (1987), 37 D.L.R. (4th) 224, 59 O.R. (2d) 104 (C.A.); *Norberg v. Wynrib*, [1992] 2 S.C.R. 226, 92 D.L.R. (4th) 449.

[41] See *Gebauer v. Bourassa* (1978), 11 A.R. 123 (Dist. Ct.).

[42] [1967] S.C.R. 425, 62 D.L.R. (2d) 65.

[43] *Supra*, at p. 432 S.C.R., p. 71 D.L.R.

allowed a plaintiff's appeal and took the unusual course of imposing exemplary damages that had been refused by both lower courts. The case might have been brought within Lord Devlin's second category, but neither the majority nor the minority referred to *Rookes v. Barnard.* It seems unlikely that the case can have been overlooked by the court. It seems a fair inference that, had it been thought authoritative, the case would have been cited by the dissenting judges against exemplary damages or by the majority for the purpose of justifying inclusion of the case within Lord Devlin's second category. In the light of this and of the many subsequent cases rejecting *Rookes v. Barnard,* it is clear that the restrictions laid down in *Rookes v. Barnard* are not part of Canadian law.[45]

5. Type of Conduct Required

11.210 The kind of conduct that attracts punitive damages has been described with a wide variety of colourful words and phrases. These include malicious, high-handed, arbitrary, oppressive, deliberate, vicious, brutal, grossly fraudulent, evil, outrageous, egregious, callous, disgraceful, wilful, wanton, in contumelious disregard of the plaintiff's rights, or in disregard of "ordinary standards of morality or decent conduct".[46] Lord Devlin said of such phrases: "these sorts of adjectives are used in the judgments by way of comment on the facts of a particular case. It would, on any view, be a mistake to suppose that any of them can be selected as definitive".[47] Where the defendant acts in good faith, exemplary damages have, with some exceptions,[48] been refused.[49]

---

44 [1976] 1 S.C.R. 776, 63 D.L.R. (3d) 654.

45 *Vorvis v. Insurance Corp. of British Columbia,* [1989] 1 S.C.R. 1085, 58 D.L.R. (4th) 193 at p. 206, citing this work; *Walker v. CFTO Ltd.* (1987), 37 D.L.R. (4th) 224 at p. 239, 59 O.R. (2d) 104 (C.A.), citing this paragraph.

46 *Paragon Properties Ltd. v. Magna Envestments Ltd.* (1972), 24 D.L.R. (3d) 156 at p. 167, [1972] 3 W.W.R. 106 at p. 117 (Alta. S.C. App. Div.). See *Denison v. Fawcett* (1958), 12 D.L.R. (2d) 537, [1958] O.R. 312 (C.A.), appeal to S.C.C. withdrawn [1958] O.W.N. 468*n*; *Lauscher v. Berryere* (1999), 172 D.L.R. (4th) 439 (Sask. C.A.). And see Fridman, "Punitive Damages in Tort", 48 Can. Bar Rev. 373 (1970), at p. 375. See also *Delta Hotels Ltd. v. Magrum* (1975), 59 D.L.R. (3d) 126 (B.C.S.C.); *Grenn v. Brampton Poultry Co.* (1959), 18 D.L.R. (2d) 9 (Ont. C.A.); *Fleming v. Spracklin* (1921), 64 D.L.R. 382 at p. 393, 50 O.L.R. 289 (S.C. App. Div.); *Fleck v. Stewart* (1992), 80 Alta. L.R. (2d) 334, 18 A.R. 345 (Q.B.). See *Dandurand v. Pier I Imports* (1986), 55 O.R. (2d) 329 (C.A.), at p. 331; *Heighington v. Ontario* (1987), 41 D.L.R. (4th) 208 at p. 225, 60 O.R. (2d) 641, supplementary reasons D.L.R. *loc. cit.* p. 222, O.R. *loc. cit.* p. 655 (H.C.J.), affd on other grounds 61 D.L.R. (4th) 190, 69 O.R. (2d) 484 (C.A.); *MacDonald Estate v. Martin* (1993), 89 Man. R. (2d) 161 at p. 212 (Q.B.), vard 95 Man. R. (2d) 123, 70 W.A.C. 123, *sub nom.* MacDonald Estate (Re) (C.A.); *Herman v. Graves,* [1998] 9 W.W.R. 542 (Alta. Q.B.), at p. 555; *Evans v. Newfoundland* (2001), 197 Nfld. & P.E.I.R. 44 (Nfld. C.A.), at para. 30; *Salamon v. Morrow* (2004), 259 Sask. R. 112 (Q.B.), at p. 116; all citing this passage.

47 *Rookes v. Barnard,* [1964] A.C. 1129 (H.L.), at p. 1229.

48 *Mayo v. Hefferton* (1972), 3 Nfld. & P.E.I.R. 236 (Nfld. S.C.); *Rowland's Transport Ltd. v. Nasby Sales & Services Ltd.* (1978), 16 A.R. 192 (S.C.T.D.); *Hayward v. F. W. Woolworth Co. Ltd.* (1979), 98 D.L.R. (3d) 345 (Nfld. S.C.T.D.); *Lister (Ronald Elwyn) Ltd. v. Dayton Tire Canada Ltd.* (1985), 52 O.R. (2d) 88 (C.A.). See also *Holden v. Chief Constable of Lancashire,* [1987] Q.B. 380 (C.A.); *R. v. LeBar,* [1989] 1 F.C. 603, 46 C.C.C. (3d) 103 (C.A.) (malice not required); *Prebushewski v. Dodge City Auto,* [2005] 1 S.C.R. 649, 253 D.L.R. (4th) 209 (malice not required under statutory provision).

In *Keays v. Honda Canada Inc.*, the Supreme Court of Canada said that "punitive damages are restricted to advertent wrongful acts that are so malicious and outrageous that they are deserving of punishment on their own".[49a] Generally, therefore, exemplary damages are not awarded for negligence[50] but where the defendant deliberately exposes the plaintiff to a risk without justification — which can be said to amount to recklessness — some courts have awarded exemplary damages.[51] In *Jackson v. Canadian Pacific Ry.*,[52] Beck J. said:

> In the cases of personal injuries occasioned by negligence, exemplary, vindictive, retributory, or punitive damages cannot be recovered unless there was such entire want of care as to raise a presumption that the

[49] *Atlantic Concrete Ltd. v. LeVatte Construction Co.* (1975), 62 D.L.R. (3d) 663 (N.S.S.C. App. Div.); *Berezowski v. Reimer*, [1927] 3 D.L.R. 232 (Sask. C.A.); *Zurouvinski v. Duke*, [1924] 4 D.L.R. 326 (Sask. C.A.); *Zamacois v. Douville*, [1944] Ex. C.R. 208, [1943] 2 D.L.R. 257; *Can-Alta Carriers Ltd. v. Ford Motor Credit Co. of Canada Ltd.* (1974), 49 D.L.R. (3d) 319 (Alta. S.C. App. Div.); *Phillips v. Soloway* (1956), 6 D.L.R. (2d) 570 (Man. Q.B.) (defendant insane); *Klein v. Jenoves*, [1932] 3 D.L.R. 571 at p. 582, [1932] O.R. 504 (C.A.); *Lundy v. Powell* (1922), 70 D.L.R. 659 (Sask. C.A.); *Bell v. Foley Bros.* (1917), 34 D.L.R. 391 (N.S.S.C. in banco); *Northern Agency Ltd. v. Army & Navy Department Store Ltd.*, [1939] 1 D.L.R. 44 (Alta. S.C. App. Div.); *Cullerton v. Miller* (1894), 26 O.R. 36 (H.C.), at pp. 45-6, *per* Rose, J.; *Dancey v. Grand Trunk Ry.* (1892), 19 O.A.R. 664, and see footnote 59, *infra; Allan v. Bushnell T.V. Co. Ltd.* (1969), 4 D.L.R. (3d) 212, [1969] 2 O.R. 6 (C.A.); *Brown v. Waterloo Regional Board of Com'rs of Police* (1982), 136 D.L.R. (3d) 49, 37 O.R. (2d) 277 (H.C.J.); *Rumsey v. The Queen* (1984), 12 D.L.R. (4th) 44, [1984] 5 W.W.R. 585 (F.C.T.D.); *Dandurand v. Pier I Imports, supra* , footnote 46; *Roynat Ltd. v. Northern Meat Packers* (1986), 29 D.L.R. (4th) 139 at p. 145, 71 N.B.R. (2d) 212 (C.A.), leave to appeal to S.C.C. refused 27 N.R. 158*n*, 78 N.B.R. (2d) 90*n*, citing this paragraph; *Warner v. Arsenault* (1982), 53 N.S.R. (2d) 146, 27 C.P.C. 200 (C.A.); *Bridges Bros. Ltd. v. Beth-Canada Mining Co.* (1983), 50 N.B.R. (2d) 42 (C.A.); *Tucker v. Gosse* (1987), 62 Nfld. & P.E.I.R. 116 (Nfld. C.A.); *Ross v. Acorn* (1986), 46 Sask. R. 69 (C.A.); *Cook v. Bowen Island Realty Ltd.*, [1998] 1 W.W.R. 647, 39 B.C.L.R. (3d) 12 (S.C.).

[49a] (2008), 294 D.L.R. (4th) 577 (S.C.C.), at para. 62.

[50] *Blacquiere's Estate v. Canadian Motor Sales Corp. Ltd.* (1975), 10 Nfld. & P.E.I.R. 178 (P.E.I.S.C.); *Cosgrove v. Canadian Northern Rys.*, [1923] 4 D.L.R. 818 (Alta. S.C. App. Div.), at p. 821; *Peters v. Diamond* (1963), 41 D.L.R. (2d) 311, [1964] 1 O.R. 139 (Co. Ct.); *Doyle v. Garden of the Gulf Security & Investigation Inc.* (1980), 25 Nfld. & P.E.I.R. 167 (P.E.I.S.C.); *Kaytor v. Lion's Driving Range Ltd.* (1962), 35 D.L.R. (2d) 426 (B.C.S.C.); *MacLeod v. Bridge Park Ltd.* (1979), 35 N.S.R. (2d) 169 (S.C.T.D.); *Thompson v. Zurich Insurance Co.* (1984), 7 D.L.R. (4th) 664, 45 O.R. (2d) 744 (H.C.J.); *B.P.I. Resources Ltd. v. Merrill Lynch Canada Inc.* (1986), 72 A.R. 6, 46 Alta. L.R. (2d) 321 (Q.B.), affd 95 A.R. 211, 67 Alta. L.R. (2d) 97 (C.A.); *Nichols v. Guiel* (1983), 145 D.L.R. (3d) 186, [1983] 4 W.W.R. 175 (B.C.S.C.); *Di Domenicantonio v. Stamper* (1988), 49 D.L.R. (4th) 342 (N.B.C.A.); *Canada Cement LaFarge Ltd. v. British Columbia Lightweight Aggregate Ltd.* (1981), 123 D.L.R. (3d) 66, [1981] 4 W.W.R. 385 (B.C.C.A.), revd on other grounds [1983] 1 S.C.R. 452, 145 D.L.R. (3d) 385; *Houle v. Calgary (City)* (1983), 44 A.R. 271, 26 Alta. L.R. (2d) 34 (Q.B.), vard 20 D.L.R. (4th) 15, 60 A.R. 366 (C.A.), leave to appeal to S.C.C. refused [1985] 2 S.C.R. vi, 62 N.R. 394*n*; *Nelson v. Welsh* (1985), 70 N.S.R. (2d) 422 (S.C.T.D.). See *Dhalla v. Jodrey* (1985), 16 D.L.R. (4th) 732, at p. 739 (C.A.), leave to appeal to S.C.C. refused [1985] 1 S.C.R. ix, citing this paragraph; *Ellison v. L.*, [1998] 1 N.Z.L.R. 416 (C.A.); *McBeth v. Boldt* (1998), 164 D.L.R. (4th) 247 (B.C.C.A.); *A. (C.) v. Critchley* (1998), 166 D.L.R. (4th) 475 (B.C.C.A.); *Welburn v. Westfair Foods Ltd.* (2000), 146 Man. R. (2d) 114 (Q.B.). But in *Van Oirschot v. Dow Chemical Canada Inc.* (1995), 174 A.R. 157, 31 Alta. L.R. (3d) 212 (C.A.), an award of exemplary damages was upheld in a products liability case, and in *McIntyre v. Grigg* (2006), 274 D.L.R. (4th) 28 (Ont. C.A.), for impaired driving.

defendant was conscious of the probable consequences of his carelessness and was indifferent, or worse, to the danger of the injury to other persons.[53]

11.220 In *Emblen v. Myers*[54] the defendant had damaged the plaintiff's premises by allowing his workmen, demolishing an adjoining building, to throw debris onto the plaintiff's property. Despite the plaintiff's remonstrance, the defendant told his workmen to "work anyhow", and it was suggested that the defendant's motive was to persuade the plaintiff to abandon the premises. The jury were directed that: "if they were of opinion that what was done by the defendant was done wilfully, with a high hand, for the purpose of trampling on the plaintiff and driving him out of possession of the stable, they might find exemplary damages".[55] The jury's verdict for £75 was upheld by the Exchequer Court. The facts might justify a finding of trespass, but the award would, it seems, have been upheld on the basis of negligence combined with the deliberate intention of trampling on the plaintiff's rights. Other cases have awarded exemplary damages where negligence is combined with high-handed conduct.[56]

6. Type of Legal Wrong

11.230 Punitive damages have been awarded in actions for most non-contractual wrongs, including cases of defamation,[57] assault,[58] battery,[58a] false imprisonment,[59] trespass,[60] nuisance,[61] interference with contract and other economic interests,[62] slander of title,[63] conversion and wrongful seizure of goods,[64] breach of copyright,[65] conspiracy,[66] abuse of legal process,[67] wrongful registration of a certificate of pending litigation,[67a] violation of constitutional rights,[68] wrongful sterilization,[68a] wrongful denial of a building permit,[69] invasion of privacy,[69a] abuse of state power,[69b] misfeasance in public office,[69c] fraud[70] and conspiracy to defraud.[71] There seems no reason

[51] See *MacDonald v. Sebastian* (1987), 43 D.L.R. (4th) 636, 81 N.S.R. (2d) 189 (S.C.T.D.); *Josefsberg v. Wilson* (1984), 45 C.P.C. 260 (Ont. H.C.J.); *McIntyre v. Atlantic Hardchrome Ltd.* (1991), 102 N.S.R. (2d) 1 (S.C.), revd 109 N.S.R. (2d) 309 (C.A.); *Petten v. E.Y.E. Marine Consultants* (1994), 120 Nfld. & P.E.I.R. 313 (Nfld. S.C.); *McLaren Transport Ltd. v. Somerville*, [1996] 3 N.Z.L.R. 424 (H.C.); *A v. Bottrill*, [2002] 3 W.L.R. 1406 (P.C.).

[52] (1915), 24 D.L.R. 380 (Alta. S.C. App. Div.), affd 52 S.C.R. 281, 27 D.L.R. 86.

[53] *Supra*, at p. 387. See also *Thompson v. Zurich Insurance Co., supra*, footnote 50, at pp. 673-4 D.L.R.

[54] (1860), 6 H. & N. 54, 158 E.R. 23, followed in *Whitehouse v. National Biscuit & Confectionery Co. Ltd.*, [1943] 2 D.L.R. 540 (Alta. S.C.); See *Westhaver v. Halifax & South Western Ry. Co.* (1913), 14 D.L.R. 633 (N.S.S.C. in banco) (persistent disregard of safety justifies assessment of damages "with a liberal hand").

[55] *Emblen v. Myers, supra*, footnote 52, at p. 56.

[56] *Robitaille v. Vancouver Hockey Club Ltd.* (1979), 19 B.C.L.R. 158 (S.C.), affd 124 D.L.R. (3d) 228 (B.C.C.A.), cited with approval by the Supreme Court of Canada in *Whiten v. Pilot Insurance Co.* (2002), 209 D.L.R. (4th) 257 (S.C.C.), at p. 287; *Westhaver v. Halifax & South Western Ry. Co., supra*, footnote 52; *MacLeod v. Bridge Park Ltd., supra*, footnote 49, at p. 178; *Vlchek v. Koshel* (1988), 52 D.L.R. (4th) 371, [1989] 1 W.W.R. 469 (B.C.S.C.); *Coloca v. B.P. Australia Ltd.*, [1992] 2 V.R. 441 (S.C. Vict.); *Trend Management Ltd. v. Borg* (1996), 40 N.S.W.L.R. 500 (C.A.).

[57] *Hill v. Church of Scientology of Toronto*, [1995] 2 S.C.R. 1130, 126 D.L.R. (4th) 129; *Barrick Gold Corp. v. Lopehandia* (2004), 239 D.L.R. (4th) 577 (Ont. C.A.).

to distinguish in this respect between deceit and conspiracy to defraud.

---

[58] *Fraser v. Wilson* (1969), 6 D.L.R. (3d) 531 (Man. Q.B.); *Basil v. Spratt* (1918), 45 D.L.R. 554, 44 O.L.R. 155 (S.C. App. Div.); *Guillet v. Charlebois*, [1935] 3 W.W.R. 438 (Sask. C.A.); *Sakowski v. Rusiecki* (1960), 67 Man. R. 256 (Q.B.); *Roundall v. Brodie* (1972), 7 N.B.R. (2d) 486 (S.C.Q.B.); *Karpow v. Shave*, [1975] 2 W.W.R. 159 (Alta. S.C.T.D.); *Kingsmith v. Denton* (1977), 3 A.R. 315 (S.C.T.D.); *Dodge v. Bridger* (1977), 4 C.C.L.T. 83 (Ont. H.C.J.), vard 6 C.C.L.T. 71 (C.A.); *Pettis v. McNeil* (1979), 32 N.S.R. (2d) 146 (S.C.T.D.); *Moore v. Slater* (1979), 101 D.L.R. (3d) 176 (B.C.S.C.); *Stinson v. Woodrow* (1982), 20 Sask. R. 265 (Q.B.) (assault); *Price v. Stoley* (1984), 59 A.R. 1, 34 Alta. L.R. (2d) 356 (Q.B.); *B. (A.) v. J. (I.)*, [1991] 5 W.W.R. 748, 119 A.R. 210 (Q.B.) ($50,000 for sexual assault over many years); *M. (K.) v. M. (H.)*, [1992] 3 S.C.R. 6, 96 D.L.R. (4th) 289; *Norberg v. Wynrib*, [1992] 2 S.C.R. 226, 92 D.L.R. (4th) 449 ; *Y. (S.) v. C. (F.G.)*, [1997] 1 W.W.R. 229, 26 B.C.L.R. (3d) 155 (C.A.); *Lawrence v. Lawrence*, [2001] 7 W.W.R. 315, *sub nom.* L. (R.L.) v. L. (R.) (B.C.C.A.).

[58a] *Gerula v. Flores* (1995), 126 D.L.R. (4th) 506, 83 O.A.C. 128 (C.A.); *H. v. R.*, [1996] 1 N.Z.L.R. 299 (H.C.).

[59] *Whitehouse v. Reimer* (1979), 107 D.L.R. (3d) 283 (Alta. Q.B.), revd on other grounds 116 D.L.R. (3d) 594 (C.A.); *Bahner v. Marwest Hotel Co.* (1969), 6 D.L.R. (3d) 322 (B.C.S.C.), affd 12 D.L.R. (3d) 646 (C.A.); *Hayward v. F.W. Woolworth Co. Ltd.* (1979), 98 D.L.R. (3d) 345 (Nfld. S.C.T.D.); *Hopper v. Clark* (1911), 10 E.L.R. 305 (N.B.S.C. en banc), at p. 319 (if wilful or grossly negligent misconduct); *Dalsin v. T. Eaton Co. of Canada Ltd.* (1975), 63 D.L.R. (3d) 565 (Alta. Dist. Ct.); *Lang v. Burch* (1982), 140 D.L.R. (3d) 325 (Sask. C.A.). Where the defendant acts in good faith but beyond her powers, aggravated damages may well be justified to compensate the plaintiff for humiliation and distress, even though exemplary damages are not appropriate. See *Dancey v. Grand Trunk Ry.*, (1892), 19 O.A.R. 664, where damages of $1,000 were reduced to $500.

[60] *Pollard v. Gibson*, [1924] 4 D.L.R. 354, 55 O.L.R. 424 (S.C. App. Div.); *Schwartz v. Heisler* (1921), 59 D.L.R. 640 (N.S.S.C. in banco); *Spencer v. Grant*, [1928] 1 D.L.R. 820 (Sask. C.A.); *Nantel v. Parisien* (1981), 18 C.C.L.T. 79 (Ont. H.C.J.); *Johnson v. British Columbia Hydro & Power Authority* (1981), 123 D.L.R. (3d) 340 (B.C.S.C.); *Unrau v. Barrowman* (1966), 59 D.L.R. (2d) 168 (Sask. Q.B.), vard December 29, 1967 (Sask. C.A.); *Cash & Carry Cleaners Ltd. v. Delmas* (1973), 44 D.L.R. (3d) 315 (N.B.S.C. App. Div.); *Wasson v. California Standard Co.* (1964), 47 D.L.R. (2d) 71 (Alta. S.C. App. Div.); *Townsview Properties Ltd. v. Sun Construction & Equipment Co. Ltd.* (1974), 56 D.L.R. (3d) 330, 7 O.R. (2d) 666 (C.A.); *Irving Pulp & Paper Ltd. v. McBrine* (1973), 9 N.B.R. (2d) 194 (Q.B.); *Starkman v. Delhi Court Ltd.* (1961), 28 D.L.R. (2d) 269, [1961] O.R. 467 (C.A.); *Fleming v. Spracklin* (1921), 64 D.L.R. 382, 50 O.L.R. 289 (S.C. App. Div.) (illegal search of yacht); *Lundy v. Powell* (1922), 70 D.L.R. 659 (Sask. C.A.), at p. 668, *per* Martin J.A.; *Spencer v. Grant*, [1928] 1 D.L.R. 820 (Sask. C.A.); *Holowaty v. Ford Motor Credit Co. of Canada Ltd.*, [1974] 1 W.W.R. 225 (Alta. Dist. Ct.); *Jeans v. Carl B. Potter Ltd.* (1977), 24 N.S.R. (2d) 106 (S.C. App. Div.); *Taylor v. Ginter* (1979), 108 D.L.R. (3d) 223 (B.C.S.C.); *Lester D. Collicutt Lumber & Building Supplies Ltd. v. Dorey* (1980), 42 N.S.R. (2d) 204 (S.C.T.D.); *McLachlan v. Canadian Imperial Bank of Commerce* (1984), 57 D.L.R. (4th) 687, [1989] 4 W.W.R. 341 (B.C.C.A.); *Kitchen v. Harbour Grace* (1983), 43 Nfld. & P.E.I.R. 146 (Nfld. C.A.); *Epstein v. Cressey Development Corp.* (1992), 89 D.L.R. (4th) 32, [1992] 3 W.W.R. 566 (B.C.C.A.). *Contra: Stewart v. Traders Trust Co.*, [1936] 4 D.L.R. 139 (Man. C.A.).

[61] *Culp v. Township of East York* (1957), 6 D.L.R. (2d) 417, [1956] O.R. 983 (H.C.J.), affd 9 D.L.R. (2d) 749, [1957] O.W.N. 515 (C.A.); *Nippa v. C.H. Lewis (Lucan) Ltd.* (1991), 82 D.L.R. (4th) 417, 7 C.E.L.R. (N.S.) 149 (Ont. Ct. (Gen. Div.)), stay denied 7 C.E.L.R. (N.S.) 163 (Ont. C.A.).

[62] *Gersham v. Manitoba Vegetable Producers' Marketing Board* (1976), 69 D.L.R. (3d) 114 (Man. C.A.); *Klein v. Jenoves*, [1932] 3 D.L.R. 571, [1932] O.R. 504 (C.A.); *Canadian Ironworkers Union No. 1 v. International Association of Bridge, Structural & Ornamental Ironworkers Union, Local 97* (1979), 45 D.L.R. (3d) 768*n* (B.C.C.A.); *H.L. Weiss Forwarding Ltd. v. Omnus*, [1976] 1 S.C.R. 776, 63 D.L.R. (3d) 654; *Royal Bank of Canada v. Wilton* (1995), 123 D.L.R. (4th) 266, [1995] 6 W.W.R. 285 (Alta. C.A.), leave to appeal to S.C.C. refused 126 D.L.R. (4th) vii, 195 N.R. 160*n*.

Exemplary damages have been awarded for refusal to obey an injunction[72] and for criminal manslaughter.[72a] Exemplary damages have, however, been

---

[63] *Captain Developments Ltd. v. Nu-West Group Ltd.* (1982), 136 D.L.R. (3d) 502, 37 O.R. (2d) 697 (H.C.J.), revd on other grounds 6 D.L.R. (4th) 179, 45 O.R. (2d) 213, leave to appeal to S.C.C. refused 55 N.R. 273*n*. See *Lundy v. Powell* (1921), 60 D.L.R. 607 (Sask. K.B.), vard 70 D.L.R. 659 (C.A.).

[64] *McKenzie v. Bank of Montreal* (1975), 55 D.L.R. (3d) 641, 7 O.R. (2d) 521 (H.C.J.), affd 70 D.L.R. (3d) 113, 12 O.R. (2d) 719 (C.A.); *Mandelin v. Stan Reynolds Auto Sales Ltd.* (1961), 31 D.L.R. (2d) 697 (Alta. S.C.); *Grenn v. Brampton Poultry Co.* (1959), 18 D.L.R. (2d) 9 (Ont. C.A.); *Ronald Elwyn Lister Ltd. v. Dunlop Canada Ltd.*, [1982] S.C.R. 726, 135 D.L.R. (3d) 1; *Steiman v. Steiman* (1981), 11 Man. R. (2d) 376, 18 C.C.L.T. 133 (Q.B.), vard 143 D.L.R. (3d) 396, 18 Man. R. (2d) 203 (C.A.); *Owen & Smith v. Reo Motors (Britain) Ltd.* (1934), 151 L.T. 274 (C.A.), approved in *Denison v. Fawcett* (1958), 12 D.L.R. (2d) 537, [1958] O.R. 312 (C.A.), appeal to S.C.C. withdrawn [1958] O.W.N. 468*n*, but explained in *Rookes v. Barnard*, [1964] A.C. 1129 (H.L.), as compensatory; *Holowaty v. Ford Motor Credit Co., supra*, footnote 60; *Connors v. Doak* (1978), 24 N.B.R. (2d) 85 (S.C. App. Div.); *MacKay v. Canada Steamship Lines Ltd.* (1926), 29 O.W.N. 334 (H.C.); *Griffiths v. Fordyce Motors Ltd.*, [1930] 4 D.L.R. 451 (B.C.C.A.); *Wilcox v. Hammond* (1977), 17 Nfld. & P.E.I.R. 316 (Nfld. Dist. Ct.); *Lister (Ronald Elwyn) Ltd. v. Dayton Tire Canada Ltd.* (1985), 52 O.R. (2d) 88 (C.A.); *Clunie Enterprises Ltd. v. Melfort Credit Union Ltd.* (1986), 49 Sask. R. 131, 60 C.B.R. (N.S.) 129 (Q.B.), affd 66 Sask. R. 112, 68 C.B.R. (N.S.) 220 (C.A.); *Eli v. Royal Bank of Canada* (1986), 24 D.L.R. (4th) 127, 68 B.C.L.R. 353 (S.C.); *Mining & Allied Supplies (Canada) Ltd. v. 2390869 Manitoba Ltd.* (1997), 118 Man. R. (2d) 136, 149 W.A.C. 136 (C.A.); *Gu v. Tai Foong International Ltd.* (2003), 168 O.A.C. 47 (C.A.). But some earlier cases are to the contrary: *Campbell v. Northern Crown Bank* (1914), 18 D.L.R. 187 (Man. C.A.); *Basted v. Grafton*, [1948] 1 W.W.R. 614 (B.C. Co. Ct.); *Ingre v. Maxwell* (1964), 44 D.L.R. (2d) 764 (B.C.S.C.). And see *Hutscal v. I.A.C. Ltd.* (1974), 48 D.L.R. (3d) 638 (Yukon Terr. C.A.), doubting whether exemplary damages can be awarded for conversion.

[65] *Williams v. Settle*, [1960] 1 W.L.R. 1072 (C.A.) (vindictive damages awarded under U.K. statute, explained in *Rookes v. Barnard, supra*, footnote 64, as compensatory); *Underwriters' Survey Bureau Ltd. v. Massie & Renwick Ltd.*, [1942] Ex. C.R. 1, [1942] 1 D.L.R. 434; *Hay v. Sloan* (1957), 12 D.L.R. (2d) 397, [1957] O.W.N. 445 (H.C.J.). See *Zamacois v. Douville*, [1944] Ex. C.R. 208, [1943] 2 D.L.R. 257; *Association des Compositeurs, Auteurs et Editeurs du Canada Ltée v. Keet Estates Inc.*, [1972] C.S. 315 (Que. S.C.); *Pro Arts, Inc. v. Campus Crafts Holdings Ltd.* (1980), 110 D.L.R. (3d) 366, 28 O.R. (2d) 422 (H.C.J.); *Profekta International Inc. v. Lee* (1997), 75 C.P.R. (3d) 369, 214 N.R. 309 (F.C.A.); *2703203 Manitoba Inc. v. Parks* (2007), 280 D.L.R. (4th) 653 (N.S.C.A.).

[66] *McKinnon v. F. W. Woolworth Co. Ltd.* (1968), 70 D.L.R. (2d) 280 (Alta. S.C. App. Div.); *Claiborne Industries v. National Bank of Canada* (1989), 59 D.L.R. (4th) 533, 69 O.R. (2d) 65 (C.A.); *Meehan v. Tremblett* (1996), 133 D.L.R. (4th) 738, 174 N.B.R. (2d) 360 (C.A.) (conspiracy to dismiss employees wrongfully); *Golden Capital Securities Ltd. v. Holmes* (2003), 22 B.C.L.R. (4th) 171 (S.C.).

[67] *Guilford Industries Ltd. v. Hankinson Management Services Ltd.* (1973), 40 D.L.R. (3d) 398 (B.C.S.C.); *Tedford v. Nitch* (1976), 13 O.R. (2d) 471 (Co. Ct.); *Flame Bar-B.-Q. Ltd. v. Hoar* (1979), 106 D.L.R. (3d) 438 (N.B.C.A.). See *White Hatter Limousine Service Ltd. v. Calgary (City)*, [1994] 1 W.W.R. 620, 13 Alta. L.R. (3d) 362 (Q.B.).

[67a] *Mellco Developments Ltd. v. Portage la Prairie (City)* (2002), 222 D.L.R. (4th) 67 (Man. C.A.).

[68] *Crossman v. The Queen*, [1984] 1 F.C. 681, 9 D.L.R. (3d) 588 (F.C.T.D.). See also Cooper-Stephenson, *Charter Damage Claims* (Toronto, Carswell, 1990), pp. 364-8.

[68a] *Muir v. Alberta* (1996), 132 D.L.R. (4th) 695, [1996] 4 W.W.R. 177 (Alta. Q.B.).

[69] *Barthropp v. District of West Vancouver* (1979), 17 B.C.L.R. 202 (S.C.).

[69a] *F. (J.M.) v. Chappell* (1998), 158 D.L.R. (4th) 430, [1998] 7 W.W.R. 57 (B.C.C.A.), leave to appeal to S.C.C. refused 162 D.L.R. (4th) vii, 231 N.R. 400*n*; *Hollinsworth v. BCTV* (1996), 34 C.C.L.T. (2d) 95 (B.C.S.C.), affd [1999] 6 W.W.R. 54 (C.A.); *Hiltz and Seamone Co. v. Nova Scotia (Attorney General)* (1998), 164 N.S.R. (2d) 161 (S.C.), vard 172 D.L.R. (4th) 488 (C.A.).

refused in enticement and related torts[72b] and in actions for wrongful death.[72c]

11.240 In *Fern Brand Waxes Ltd. v. Pearl,*[73] the Ontario Court of Appeal held that exemplary damages could not be awarded in a claim for damages for breach of fiduciary duty, because the action was equitable, not tortious. This conclusion has been criticized[74] persuasively, it is submitted, on the ground that the availability of exemplary damages should not be determined by classification of the wrong as a common law tort or as a breach of an equitable obligation. In later cases, exemplary damages have been awarded for breach of fiduciary duty[75] and for breach of trust.[75a]

11.250 Punitive damages are not normally awarded for breach of contract.[76] This rule is based on the assumption underlying much of contract law that a breach of contract, coupled with an offer to pay just compensation, does no harm to the plaintiff, is not morally wrong and may be desirable on the grounds of

69b *LaPointe v. Canada (Minister of Fisheries and Oceans)* (1992), 4 Admin. L.R. (2d) 298, supplementary reasons 4 Admin. L.R. (2d) at p. 319 (T.D.); *Hashemian v. Wilde*, [2007] 2 W.W.R. 52 (Sask. C.A.). See *Air Canada v. Ontario (Liquor Control Board)*, [1997] 2 S.C.R. 581, 148 D.L.R. (4th) 193 at p. 215.

69c *Sanders v. Snell* (1997), 143 A.L.R. 426 (F.C. (Full Ct.)); *Longley v. M.N.R.* (2000), 184 D.L.R. (4th) 590 (B.C.C.A.), leave to appeal to S.C.C. refused 193 D.L.R. (4th) vii; *Kuddus v. Chief Constable of Leicestershire Constabulary*, [2002] 2 A.C. 122 (H.L.); *Uni-Jet Industrial Pipe Ltd. v. Canada (Attorney General)* (2001), 198 D.L.R. (4th) 577 (Man. C.A.).

70 *Insurance Corp. of British Columbia and Sanghera (Re)*, [1991] 4 W.W.R. 714, 55 B.C.L.R. (2d) 125 (C.A.) ($15,000 exemplary damages for fraud); *Harland v. Fancsali* (1994), 121 D.L.R. (4th) 182, 21 O.R. (3d) 798 (Div. Ct.); *Durrani v. Augier* (2000), 190 D.L.R. (4th) 183 (Ont. S.C.J.); *Phillips v. 707739 Alberta Ltd.*, [2000] 6 W.W.R. 280 (Alta. Q.B.). But see *Carnahan v. McGregor* (1994), 149 N.B.R. (2d) 342 (C.A.).

71 *Denison v. Fawcett, supra,* footnote 64; see *Mafo v. Adams,* [1970] 1 Q.B. 548 (C.A.); *Cassell & Co. Ltd. v. Broome,* [1972] A.C. 1027 (H.L.), at pp. 1079-80, *per* Lord Hailsham (availability of exemplary damages for deceit not finally determined), and p. 1131, *per* Lord Diplock; *Max Sonnenberg Inc. v. Stewart, Smith (Canada) Ltd.*, [1987] 2 W.W.R. 75, 48 Alta. L.R. (2d) 367 (Q.B.). In *C.R.F. Holdings Ltd. v. Fundy Chemical Int'l Ltd.* (1980), 21 B.C.L.R. 345 (S.C.), vard [1982] 2 W.W.R. 385 (C.A.), leave to appeal to S.C.C. refused 42 N.R. 357*n*, 42 N.R. 358*n*, exemplary damages were refused for "ordinary commercial dishonesty".

72 *Lubrizol Corp. v. Imperial Oil Ltd.* (1992), 98 D.L.R. (4th) 1, 45 C.P.R. (3d) 449 (F.C.A.), leave to appeal to S.C.C. refused 104 D.L.R. (4th) vii, 50 C.P.R. (3d) v.

72a *Cyr v. Williams* (1995), 14 B.C.L.R. (3d) 289 (S.C.).

72b *Judge v. Smith* (1961), 30 D.L.R. (2d) 521 (B.C.S.C.); *Singh v. Basi* (1957), 26 W.W.R. 96 (B.C.C.A.); *Powell v. Billington* (1958), 27 W.W.R. 24 (B.C.S.C.); *Jestley v. Jestley* (1977), 4 B.C.L.R. 313 (S.C.); *Mowder v. Roy,* [1946] 2 D.L.R. 427, [1946] O.R. 154 (C.A.) (criminal conversation); *Stephen v. Stephen,* [1931] 2 D.L.R. 892 (Sask. C.A.); *Marangos v. Harold,* [1923] 4 D.L.R. 520, 52 O.L.R. 395 (S.C. App. Div.); *Hanselman v. Gezy* (1921), 61 D.L.R. 32 (Sask. C.A.).

72c *Lord (Litigation Guardian of) v. Downer* (1999), 179 D.L.R. (4th) 430 (Ont. C.A.), leave to appeal to S.C.C. refused 183 D.L.R. (4th) vii.

73 (1972), 29 D.L.R. (3d) 662, [1972] 3 O.R. 829 (C.A.). See also *Guertin v. Royal Bank of Canada* (1983), 1 D.L.R. (4th) 68, 43 O.R. (2d) 363 (H.C.J.), affd 12 D.L.R. (4th) 640*n*, 47 O.R. (2d) 799*n* (C.A.); *Worobel Estate v. Worobel* (1988), 67 O.R. (2d) 151, 31 E.T.R. 290 (H.C.J.). Exemplary damages were awarded in *Flame Bar-B.-Q. Ltd. v. Hoar* (1979), 106 D.L.R. (3d) 438 (N.B.C.A.), for misuse of confidential information by an accountant.

74 Vaver, "Civil Liability for Taking or Using Trade Secrets in Canada", 5 Can. Bus. L.J. 253 (1980-81), at p. 292.

efficiency.[77] A number of recent cases, however, have rejected any absolute rule against the award of punitive damages.[77a] Awards have been made against insurers,[78] against banks,[78a] against franchisors,[78b] utility companies[78c] and against the Crown[78d] for breach of the duty of good faith but in

[75] *G.E. Cox Ltd. v. Adams* (1979), 26 N.B.R. (2d) 49 and 628, [1979] I.L.R. 1-1107 (S.C. App. Div.); *MacDonald Estate v. Martin* (1993), 89 Man. R. (2d) 161 (Q.B.), vard 95 Man. R. (2d) 123, 70 W.A.C. 123 *sub nom.* MacDonald Estate (Re) (C.A.). See the judgment of McLachlin J. in *Norberg v. Wynrib*, [1992] 2 S.C.R. 226, 92 D.L.R. (4th) 449. See also *57134 Manitoba Ltd. v. Palmer* (1985), 65 B.C.L.R. 355, 30 B.L.R. 121 (S.C.), affd 37 B.C.L.R. (2d) 50, 44 B.L.R. 94 (C.A.); *Guay v. Societe Franco-Manitoban* (1981), 37 Man. R. (2d) 16 (Q.B.); *M. (K.) v. M. (H.)*, [1992] 3 S.C.R. 6, 96 D.L.R. (4th) 289; *J. (L.A.) v. J. (H.)* (1993), 102 D.L.R. (4th) 177, 13 O.R. (3d) 306 (Gen. Div.); *C. (S.L.) v. M. (M.J.)* (1996), 179 A.R. 200, 37 Alta. L.R. (3d) 90 (Q.B.); *Mustaji v. Tjin* (1996), 25 B.C.L.R. (3d) 220, 30 C.C.L.T. (2d) 53 (C.A.); *Jones v. Klassen* (2006), 55 Alta. L.R. (4th) 354 (Q.B.). But see *C. (P.) v. C. (R.)* (1994), 114 D.L.R. (4th) 151 (Ont. Ct. (Gen. Div.)); *Sweet Factory Inc. v. Hudson's Bay Co.* (1999), 86 C.P.R. (3d) 417 (Ont. Ct. (Gen. Div.)), citing this paragraph at p. 439; *Ward v. Manufacturers Life Insurance Co.* (2007), 288 D.L.R. (4th) 733 (Ont. C.A.). But see *West v. Eisner* (1999), 48 C.C.L.T. (2d) 274 (Ont. S.C.J.).

[75a] *692331 Ontario Ltd. v. Garay* (1997), 36 B.L.R. (2d) 231 (Ont. Ct. (Gen. Div.)).

[76] *A.-G. Nfld. v. Newfoundland Association of Public Employees* (1976), 74 D.L.R. (3d) 195 (Nfld. S.C.); *Guildford v. Anglo-French Steamship Co.* (1883), 9 S.C.R. 303; *Addis v. Gramophone Co.*, [1909] A.C. 488 (H.L.); *Toronto Hockey Club Ltd. v. Arena Gardens of Toronto, Ltd.*, [1926] 4 D.L.R. 1 (P.C.); *Burford v. Cosa Corp. of Canada Ltd.*, [1955] O.W.N. 8 (H.C.J.); *Perera v. Vandiyar*, [1953] 1 W.L.R. 672 (C.A.); *Turner v. Jatko* (1978), 93 D.L.R. (3d) 314 (B.C. Co. Ct.); *Harvey Foods Ltd. v. Reid* (1971), 18 D.L.R. (3d) 90 (N.B.S.C. App. Div.); *Cardinal Construction Ltd. v. The Queen in right of Ontario* (1981), 128 D.L.R. (3d) 662, 38 O.R. (2d) 161 (C.A.); *Greening Industries Ltd. v. Penny* (1965), 53 D.L.R. (2d) 643 (N.S.S.C.); *Alpine Resources Ltd. v. Bowtex Resources Ltd.* (1989), 96 A.R. 278, 66 Alta. L.R. (2d) 144 (Q.B.); *Fouillard Implement Exchange Ltd. v. Kello-Bilt Industries Ltd.*, [1986] 2 W.W.R. 93, 37 Man. R. (2d) 111 (C.A.); *Smith v. Lasko*, [1987] 5 W.W.R. 412, 47 Man. R. (2d) 199 (C.A.); *A.-G. Ontario v. Tiberius Productions Inc.* (1984), 8 D.L.R. 479, 46 O.R. (2d) 152 (H.C.J.); *Beaird v. Westinghouse Canada Inc.* (1999), 171 D.L.R. (4th) 279 (Ont. C.A.).

[77] See 9.200, *supra*; *Delphinium Ltée v. 512842 N.B. Inc.*, 2008 NBCA 56, at para. 51, citing this paragraph.

[77a] *Whiten v. Pilot Insurance Co.* (2002), 209 D.L.R. (4th) 257 (S.C.C.); *Royal Bank of Canada v. W. Got & Associates Electric Ltd.*, [1999] 3 S.C.R. 408, 178 D.L.R. (4th) 385; *Rowland's Transport Ltd. v. Nasby Sales & Services Ltd.* (1978), 16 A.R. 192 (S.C.T.D.); *Brown v. Waterloo Regional Board of Com'rs of Police* (1982), 136 D.L.R. (3d) 49, 37 O.R. (2d) 277 (H.C.J.), vard 150 D.L.R. (3d) 729, 43 O.R. (2d) 113 (C.A.); *Edwards v. Lawson Paper Converters Ltd.* (1984), 5 C.C.E.L. 99 (Ont. H.C.J.); *Centennial Centre of Science and Technology v. VS Services Ltd.* (1982), 40 O.R. (2d) 253, 31 C.P.C. 97 (H.C.J.); *Thompson v. Zurich Insurance Co.* (1984), 7 D.L.R. (4th) 664, 45 O.R. (2d) 744 (H.C.J.); *Fazzari v. Pellizzari* (1988), 28 O.A.C. 38 (Div. Ct.); *Perusse (Dale) Ltd. v. Cason* (1985), 6 C.P.C. (2d) 129 (Ont. H.C.J.); *Polish National Union of Canada Inc. v. Dopke* (2000), 38 R.P.R. (3d) 64 (Ont. S.C.J.). See discussion of *Vorvis v. Insurance Corp. of British Columbia*, [1989] 1 S.C.R. 1085, 58 D.L.R. (4th) 193, 11.270, *infra*.

[78] *Adams v. Confederation Life Insurance Co.*, [1994] 6 W.W.R. 662, 18 Alta. L.R. (3d) 324 (Q.B.); *Whiten v. Pilot Insurance Co.*, *supra*, footnote 77a; *Asselstine v. Manufacturers Life Insurance Co.* (2005), 254 D.L.R. (4th) 464 (B.C.C.A.). See *Jennett v. Federal Insurance Co.* (1976), 72 D.L.R. (3d) 20, 13 O.R. (2d) 617 (H.C.J.).

[78a] *Haggart Construction Ltd. v. Canadian Imperial Bank of Commerce*, [1998] 5 W.W.R. 586 (Q.B.), affd [1999] 11 W.W.R. 486, supplementary reasons [2000] 2 W.W.R. 722 (C.A.).

[78b] *Katotikidis v. Mr. Submarine Ltd.* (2002), 26 B.L.R. (3d) 140 (Ont. S.C.J.), supplementary reasons 29 B.L.R. (3d) 258 (Ont. S.C.J.).

[78c] *Princeton Light & Power Co. v. MacDonald* (2005), 254 D.L.R. (4th) 431 (B.C.C.A.).

702535 Ontario Inc. v. Lloyd's London, Non-Marine Underwriters[78e] the Ontario Court of Appeal emphasized that disputing a meritorious claim is not in itself bad faith and that "[i]n a general sense insurers and insureds have a common interest in ensuring that only meritorious claims are paid."[78f] This case was approved by the Supreme Court of Canada in *Fidler v. Sun Life Assurance Co. of Canada.*[78g]

11.255 In *Royal Bank of Canada v. W. Got & Associates Electric Ltd.*,[78h] a creditor had given insufficient notice of a demand for repayment of a debt and had moved with what the courts found to be undue haste to appoint a receiver, supporting its application by what was found to be a misleading affidavit. The trial judge had found the bank liable for conversion as well as for breach of contract and had awarded exemplary damages of $100,000. The Supreme Court of Canada found it unnecessary to deal with the claim in tort but upheld the award of exemplary damages on the basis of the breach of contract, while saying that "an award of exemplary damages in commercial disputes will remain an extraordinary remedy".[78i]

11.257 In *Whiten v. Pilot Insurance Co.*,[78j] the court, in restoring a $1 million jury award against an insurer, held that an award of punitive damages required "an independent actionable wrong"[78k] but found this requirement satisfied by the breach by the insurer of the obligation of good faith, which the court found to be "independent of and in addition to the breach of contractual duty to pay the loss".[78l] It is not clear to what other kinds of contract this reasoning would extend. Obligations of good faith have been particularly associated with insurance contracts. They have also been implied in other contracts for a variety of purposes having to do with the substantive obligations of the parties but it does not necessarily follow that all such contracts ought to attract punitive damages. There were features of the *Whiten* case not common to ordinary commercial contracts, notably a public, *quasi*-regulatory, interest in inducing insurers to investigate claims fairly and to meet their obligations, and the fact that the defendant's breach of contract involved not a simple failure to pay a debt but also an opprobrious and defamatory[78m] accusation of arson. Another feature of the *Whiten* case was that the insured had suffered exceptional personal hardship, including loss of

[78d] *Carrier Lumber Ltd. v. British Columbia* (1999), 47 B.L.R. (2d) 50 (B.C.S.C.).

[78e] (2000), 184 D.L.R. (4th) 687 (Ont. C.A.).

[78f] *Supra*, at p. 697; *Ferme Gerald Laplante & Fils Ltee. v. Grenville Patron Mutual Fire Insurance Co.* (2002), 217 D.L.R. (4th) 34 (Ont. C.A.).

[78g] [2006] 2 S.C.R. 3, 271 D.L.R. (4th) 1.

[78h] [1999] 3 S.C.R. 408, 178 D.L.R. (4th) 385.

[78i] *Supra*, at p. 395 (D.L.R.).

[78j] *Supra*, footnote 77a; *Khazzaka v. Commercial Union Assurance Co. of Canada* (2002), 162 O.A.C. 293 (C.A.); *Plester v. Wawanesa Mutual Insurance Co.* (2006), 269 D.L.R. (4th) 624 (Ont. C.A.); *Halligan v. Liberty Tax Service Inc.*, [2006] 8 W.W.R. 97 (Man. Q.B.).

[78k] *Supra*, at p. 291, following *Vorvis v. Insurance Corp. of British Columbia*, [1989] 1 S.C.R. 1085, 58 D.L.R. (4th) 257.

[78l] *Whiten v. Pilot Insurance Co.* (2002), 209 D.L.R. (4th) 257 (S.C.C.), at p. 290.

[78m] *Supra*, at p. 270.

her home and much mental distress pending resolution of the dispute. Aggravated damages were not claimed,[78n] and the court, while stressing that punitive damages were not compensatory, added that "there is a good deal of evidence of emotional stress and financial cost over and above the loss that would have been incurred had the claim been settled in good faith within a reasonable time".[78o] It is possible, therefore, that some members of the majority were partly influenced, in restoring the award, by compensatory considerations. Other factors suggesting that breaches of contract ought not always to attract punitive damages are the insistence in the *Whiten* case and in a companion case decided on the same day[78p] that punitive damages must serve a rational purpose, together with the statement by the unanimous court two months later in another case. The court stated: "Efficient breach [of contract] should not be discouraged by the courts. This lack of disapproval emphasizes that a court will usually award money damages for breach of contract equal to the value of the bargain to the plaintiff."[78q] In *Fidler v. Sun Life Assurance Co. of Canada*,[78r] the Supreme Court of Canada, reversing the British Columbia Court of Appeal, restored the finding of a trial judge that refusal by an insurer to pay disability insurance benefits, though erroneous and the result of a "rather zealous approach", did not manifest improper motive or bad faith. The court said that "ultimately each case revolves around its own facts".[78s]

11.260 Refusal of exemplary damages is, it is submitted, appropriate in most commercial cases.[79] Where, however, the plaintiff does have a personal interest in performance of the sort the court would protect by a decree of specific performance or by an injunction to restrain the breach, a case can be made for deterring interference with such interests. One such case might be a landlord's refusal to supply essential services to a tenant in order wrongfully to secure the tenant's eviction.[80] Another example might be a case where an employee had a specifically enforceable right to employment and the employer acted deliberately in order to defeat that right. A third kind of case might be deliberate breach of an obligation of confidentiality.[80a] Deliberate

[78n] *Supra*, at p. 294. Aggravated damages were awarded against an insurer (and punitive damages refused) in *Fowler v. Maritime Life Assurance Co.* (2002), 217 D.L.R. (4th) 473 (Nfld. & Lab. S.C.T.D.).

[78o] *Ibid.*

[78p] *Sylvan Lake Golf & Tennis Club Ltd. v. Performance Industries Ltd.* (2002), 209 D.L.R. (4th) 318 (S.C.C.), at p. 343.

[78q] *Bank of America Canada v. Mutual Trust Co.* [2002] 2 S.C.R. 601, 211 DLR (4th) 385, at p. 395; *Delphinium Ltée v. 512842 N.B. Inc.*, 2008 NBCA 56. See 3.1420, 9.200, *supra.*

[78r] [2006] 2 S.C.R. 3, 271 D.L.R. (4th) 1.

[78s] *Supra*, at para. 72. But whether conduct should be legally characterized as "bad faith" is not a pure question of fact.

[79] See *A.-G. Ontario v. Tiberius Productions Inc., supra*, footnote 76; *Hillspring Farms Ltd. v. Leland Walton & Sons Ltd.* (2007), 312 N.B.R. (2d) 109 (C.A.), at para. 11 ("Rarely does contract law seek to punish wrongdoers..."); *CivicLife.com Inc. v. Canada (Attorney General)* (2006), 215 O.A.C. 43 (C.A.), at para. 35 ("only . . . in the most exceptional circumstances and only for very harsh and outrageous conduct"); *Keays v. Honda Canada Inc.* (2008), 294 D.L.R. (4th) 577 (S.C.C.), at paras. 62 and 68.

misuse of the judicial process may emerge as another category, following the *Got* case, though it may be observed that, if it is desirable to reduce the availability to creditors of court-appointed receiverships, there must be more effective ways of doing this than occasional awards of exemplary damages against banks — amendment of the rules governing the appointment of receivers, for example. In such cases, the defendant will usually, though not necessarily, be guilty of a tort as well as a breach of contract and there is no doubt that exemplary damages can be given for the tort.[81] It is increasingly held that concurrent liability in contract and tort exists in many cases formerly treated as purely contractual.[82] This development will, it seems, have the effect of enlarging the scope of exemplary damages. Thus, if a professional person deliberately gives bad advice to a client, or breaks a confidence for the purpose of causing the client damage or embarrassment, or of making a profit, exemplary damages would seem to be quite appropriate.[83] Where a breach of contract is alleged to constitute a defamation, it has been held that the plaintiff must bring a separate action for defamation.[84] The question seems to be, at root, one of procedural convenience. There is no general objection to joining actions in contract and tort, provided the joinder is fair to the defendant. In such a case there would seem to be no objection to exemplary damages. It has been held in recent years that damages for breach of contract can include intangible matters such as mental distress caused by the breach and loss of mental satisfaction that would have accompanied performance.[85] The analogy with aggravated damages[86] and tort cases is obvious. Although in the leading case, *Jarvis v. Swans Tours Ltd.*,[87] the

---

80 See *Drane v. Evangelou*, [1978] 1 W.L.R. 455 (C.A.); *Parkes v. Howard Johnson Restaurants Ltd.* (1970), 74 W.W.R. 255 (B.C.S.C.); *Tefft v. Kooiman* (1978), 87 D.L.R. (3d) 740 (Man. Q.B.); *Ozmond v. Young* (1980), 109 D.L.R. (3d) 304, 28 O.R. (2d) 225 (Div. Ct.); *Nantel v. Parisien* (1981), 18 C.C.L.T. 79 (Ont. H.C.J.); *Shaw v. Pajelle Investments Ltd.* (1985), 11 O.A.C. 70 (Ont. Div. Ct.); *M.D. Sloan Consultants Ltd. v. Derrickson* (1991), 85 D.L.R. (4th) 449, 61 B.C.L.R. (2d) 370 (C.A.), leave to appeal to S.C.C. refused 90 D.L.R. (4th) viii, 140 N.R. 240*n*; *Chater v. Elia* (1998), 167 N.S.R. (2d) 166, 16 R.P.R. (3d) 187 (C.A.); *Cooper v. Fantasy Construction*, [2004] 4 W.W.R. 473 (Alta. Q.B.).

80a *RBC Dominion Securities Inc. v. Merrill Lynch Canada Inc.* (2004), 36 B.C.L.R. (4th) 138 (S.C.), vard 275 D.L.R. (4th) 385 (B.C.C.A.).

81 See *Denison v. Fawcett* (1958), 12 D.L.R. (2d) 537, [1958] O.R. 312 (C.A.), appeal to S.C.C. withdrawn [1958] O.W.N. 468*n; Grenn v. Brampton Poultry Co.* (1959), 18 D.L.R. (2d) 9 (Ont. C.A.); *Tsoukalas v. Domgroup Properties Ltd.* (1993), 33 R.P.R. (2d) 317 (Ont. Ct. (Gen. Div.)).

82 See Reiter, "Contracts, Torts, Relations and Reliance" in *Studies in Contract Law*, Reiter and Swan, eds. (Toronto, Butterworths, 1980), pp. 269-72.

83 See *Flame Bar-B.-Q. Ltd. v. Hoar* (1979), 106 D.L.R. (3d) 438 (N.B.C.A.) (accountant presenting petition in bankruptcy against client); *Guay v. Societe Franco-Manitoban, supra*, footnote 75; *IT/NET Ottawa Inc. v. Berthiaume* (2002), 29 B.L.R. (3d) 261 (Ont. S.C.J.), revd on other grounds 13 B.L.R. (4th) 15 (Ont. C.A.). See *Royal Bank of Canada v. Keung* (1985), 3 C.P.C. (2d) 22 (Ont. Dist. Ct.), at p. 27, citing this passage.

84 See 4.250-4.310, *supra*.

85 See 3.1310-3.1450, *supra*.

86 Aggravated damages were awarded in *Thompson v. Zurich Insurance Co.*, *supra*, footnote 77a, for failure by an insurer to make prompt payment.

court disavowed the intention of awarding exemplary damages,[88] it is not easy, in seeking to compensate such intangible losses, entirely to exclude punitive considerations.

11.270 Some cases have held that punitive damages may be available to employees wrongfully dismissed.[89] In *Vorvis v. Insurance Corp. of British Columbia,*[90] the majority of the Supreme Court of Canada, while refusing exemplary damages in the particular case, left open the possibility of exemplary damages for wrongful dismissal, and for breach of contract generally, in "very unusual cases"[90a] and, as interpreted in *Whiten v. Pilot Insurance Co.*, if there is "an independent actionable wrong".[91] Such a case might, perhaps, arise where an employee had a specifically enforceable right to employment and the employer acted with the intention of defeating the right.

7. Amount of Award

11.280 In *Rookes v. Barnard,*[92] Lord Devlin said the awards should be moderate and even suggested that it might be appropriate for the House of Lords to lay down a conventional limit as had been done in respect of damages for loss of expectation of life.[93] However, in *Cassell & Co. Ltd. v. Broome,*[94] the House of Lords approved a total award of £40,000 in a defamation case, of which £15,000 was said to be compensatory damages and £25,000 exemplary

---

87 [1973] Q.B. 233 (C.A.).

88 All the judges rested their conclusion on compensatory principles: see p. 238, *per* Lord Denning; p. 40, *per* Edmund Davies L.J.; p. 241, *per* Stephenson L.J.

89 *Brown v. Waterloo Regional Board of Com'rs of Police, supra,* footnote 77a; *Ribeiro v. Canadian Imperial Bank of Commerce* (1989), 67 O.R. 385, 24 C.C.E.L. 225 (H.C.J.), vard 13 O.R. (3d) 278, 44 C.C.E.L. 165 (C.A.), leave to appeal to S.C.C. refused 157 N.R. 400*n*, 65 O.A.C. 79*n* (damages increased); *Pilato v. Hamilton Place Convention Centre* (1984), 7 D.L.R. (4th) 342, 45 O.R. (2d) 652 (H.C.J.); *Perkins v. Brandon University*, [1985] 5 W.W.R. 740, 35 Man. R. (2d) 177 (C.A.); *Francis v. Canadian Imperial Bank of Commerce* (1994), 120 D.L.R. (4th) 393, 21 O.R. (3d) 75 (C.A.). But see *Brennan v. Henley Publishing Ltd.* (1997), 188 N.B.R. (2d) 338, 29 C.C.E.L. (2d) 180 (C.A.); *Wenarchuk v. Comstock Canada*, [1998] 2 W.W.R. 669, 160 Sask. R. 119 (Q.B.).

90 [1989] 1 S.C.R. 1085, 58 D.L.R. (4th) 193.

90a *Supra,* at p. 207 D.L.R.; *Royal Bank of Canada v. W. Got & Associates Electric Ltd.*, [1999] 3 S.C.R. 408, 178 D.L.R. (4th) 385. See also *Taylor v. Pilot Insurance Co.* (1990), 75 D.L.R. (4th) 370, [1991] I.L.R. 1-2677 (Ont. Ct. (Gen. Div.)) (exemplary damages only available for independently actionable wrong); *Conrad v. Household Financial Corp.* (1992), 115 N.S.R. (2d) 153 (S.C.), affd 118 N.S.R. (2d) 56, 45 C.C.E.L. 81 (C.A.). And see the 1993 *Law Reform Act* (N.B.), s. 3(1); *Bishop v. Carleton Co-operative Ltd.* (1996), 176 N.B.R. (2d) 206, 21 C.C.E.L. (2d) 1 (C.A.).

91 (2002), 209 D.L.R. (4th) 257 (S.C.C.). See 11.257, *supra*; *Marshall v. Watson Wyatt & Co.* (2001), 209 D.L.R. (4th) 411 (Ont. C.A.); *Sommerard v. I.B.M. Canada Ltd.* (2006), 265 D.L.R. (4th) 484 (Ont. C.A.) (independent actionable wrong must be specifically pleaded and proved); *Keays v. Honda Canada Inc.* (2008), 294 D.L.R. (4th) 577 (S.C.C.) (breach of human rights legislation not sufficient); *Schimp v. RCR Catering Ltd.* (2004), 236 D.L.R. (4th) 461 (N.S.C.A.) (exemplary damages refused).

92 [1964] A.C. 1129 (H.L.).

93 *Supra,* at pp. 1227-8. See *Thompson v. Commissioner of Police of the Metropolis,* [1998] Q.B. 498 (C.A.) (£50,000 "absolute maximum" for false imprionment by police).

94 [1972] A.C. 1027 (H.L.).

damages. In assessing the appropriate sum for punitive purposes, the total of compensatory and punitive damages is considered[95] and this is particularly necessary in a defamation case where compensatory damages consist of intangible elements.[96] Forty thousand pounds in 1970 cannot be described as a moderate sum and though the members of the House of Lords evidently considered that the award was higher than they would themselves have awarded, the majority refused to interfere. It should be noted that, on the evidence, the jury would have been justified in concluding that the defendants deliberately persisted in the publication of the book, knowing it to be defamatory, in the expectation that their profits would exceed the risk of liability. The House of Lords plainly felt that an award was justified of sufficient magnitude to change the calculus in the mind of a future publisher faced with a similar choice.

11.290 On this basis sums exceeding the defendant's probable profit will often be awarded, for the defendant may well calculate that the probability of being sued is small. In *Starkman v. Delhi Court Ltd.,*[97] a case of trespass to land, the Ontario Court of Appeal said, in upholding a total award of $5,000: "a nominal amount added to the actual damages ... would be but an invitation to contractors to violate property rights for what would amount to an insignificant licence fee".[98] In another case of trespass to land, *Townsview Properties Ltd. v. Sun Construction & Equipment Co. Ltd.,*[99] the Ontario Court of Appeal upheld an award of $5,000 in respect of general damages, including exemplary damages, in addition to certain items of proved compensatory damage. In the earlier case of *Carr-Harris v. Shachter,*[100] the judge awarded $5,000, specifically as exemplary damages. Other cases have emphasized that the amount of exemplary damages must be sufficient for its purpose, that is, to deter.[101] On the other hand, if the purpose of the award is restitutionary rather than deterrent, the proper measure will be the amount of the defendant's profit.[102]

11.300 In an Ontario defamation case, *Ross v. Lamport,*[103] the Court of Appeal,

---

[95] See 11.320-11.390, *infra.*

[96] See 4.50-4.140, *supra.*

[97] (1961), 28 D.L.R. (2d) 269, [1961] O.R. 467 (C.A.).

[98] *Supra,* at p. 274 D.L.R., p. 472 O.R.

[99] (1974), 56 D.L.R. (3d) 330, 7 O.R. (2d) 666 (C.A.).

[100] (1957), 6 D.L.R. (2d) 225, [1956] O.R. 994 (H.C.J.).

[101] *Fleming v. Spracklin* (1921), 64 D.L.R. 382, 50 O.L.R. 289 (S.C. App. Div.); *Holowaty v. Ford Motor Credit Co. of Canada Ltd.*, [1974] 1 W.W.R. 225 (Alta. Dist. Ct.), at p. 230; *Wasson v. California Standard Co.* (1964), 47 D.L.R. (2d) 71 (Alta. S.C. App. Div.). See *Basil v. Spratt* (1918), 45 D.L.R. 554, 44 O.L.R. 155 (S.C. App. Div.) ($24,000 jury verdict upheld); *Horseshoe Bay Retirement Society v. S.I.F. Development Corp.* (1990), 66 D.L.R. (4th) 42, 3 C.C.L.T. (2d) 75 (B.C.S.C.).

[102] *Austin v. Rescon Construction (1984) Ltd.* (1989), 57 D.L.R. (4th) 591, 36 B.C.L.R. (2d) 21 (C.A.); *Claiborne Industries Ltd. v. National Bank of Canada* (1989), 59 D.L.R. (4th) 533, 69 O.R. (2d) 65 (C.A.); *MacKnight v. MacCallum Building Supplies Ltd.* (1990), 109 N.B.R. (2d) 83, 31 C.P.R. (3d) 526 (Q.B.), revd 115 N.B.R. (2d) 168, 35 C.P.R. (3d) 393 (C.A.).

[103] [1955] 4 D.L.R. 826, [1955] O.R. 542 (C.A.), affd [1956] S.C.R. 366, 2 D.L.R. (2d) 225.

affirmed by the Supreme Court of Canada, set aside a verdict of $40,000. In the Supreme Court, Rand J. said:

> Although in such a matter damages are substantially what a jury thinks fit to find, whether as speculatively estimated actual damages, as so-called general damages, or as exemplary or punitive damages — the words simply define an area almost at large — yet the judgment upon these considerations must be proportionate to the situation in which they were uttered.[104]

Rand J. went on to point to the fact that the circumstances of the defamation were not so bad as they might have been, in that the defendant, who was the mayor of Toronto, had been acting as a public official intending to vindicate, though as Rand J. said "in a somewhat crude manner",[105] the action of a public body (the plaintiff had been denied a taxi-cab licence, and the words complained of implied that he intended to resell the licence at a profit). The case was remitted for a new trial on damages, and the second jury awarded $25,000. The case again came to the Ontario Court of Appeal, which upheld the verdict, pointing to aspects of the matter that could properly justify a large award, namely, that the defendant knew the facts alleged were untrue, yet persisted in a plea of justification at trial up to the moment of his counsel's closing speech, that the jury was entitled to consider the defamation an abuse of power by a public official and that the defendant had deliberately sought to have the statements published in newspapers with wide circulations.[106] In *Hill v. Church of Scientology of Toronto*,[106a] another libel case, an award of $800,000 exemplary damages was upheld in addition to $800,000 compensatory damages and in *Whiten v. Pilot Insurance Co.*[106b] a jury award of $1 million against an insurer was restored. The Supreme Court of Canada commented in both cases, and in a third case decided together with *Whiten*,[106c] that awards of punitive damages must "serve a rational purpose" and absence of rational purpose has been used as a reason to set aside awards.[106d] In England it has been held by the Court of Appeal that strict guidance is to be given to juries[106e] but Canadian courts have not, so far, laid down any similar rule.[106f] The US Supreme Court, in a decision of 2003, set aside an award of $145m against an insurer, the majority holding that it was excessive in relation to compensatory damages of $1m.[106g]

[104] *Supra*, at p. 376 S.C.R., p. 234 D.L.R.
[105] *Supra*, at p. 377 S.C.R., p. 234 D.L.R.
[106] *Ross v. Lamport* (1957), 9 D.L.R. (2d) 585, [1957] O.R. 402 (C.A.). See Chapter 4, "Loss of Reputation", *supra*.
[106a] [1995] 2 S.C.R. 1130, 126 D.L.R. (4th) 129.
[106b] (2002), 209 D.L.R. (4th) 257 (S.C.C.).
[106c] *Sylvan Lake Golf & Tennis Club Ltd. v. Performance Industries Ltd.* (2002), 209 D.L.R. (4th) 318 (S.C.C.).
[106d] *Colborne Capital Corp. v. 542775 Alberta Ltd.*, [1999] 8 W.W.R. 222 (Alta. C.A.). And see *Whiten v. Pilot Insurance Co.*, *supra*, footnote 106b, at p. 297.
[106e] *Thompson v. Commissioner of Police of the Metropolis*, [1998] Q.B. 498 (C.A.).
[106f] But see *Whiten v. Pilot Insurance Co.*, *supra*, footnote 106b, at p. 296, suggesting that they may do so in the future.
[106g] *State Farm Mutual Automobile Insurance Co. v. Campbell*, 123 S. Ct. 1513 (2003).

8. Means of the Defendant

11.310 Since the purpose of an award of punitive damages is punishment, the means of the defendant are relevant.[107] In *Cassell & Co. Ltd. v. Broome,*[108] for example, the fact that the corporate defendant was a large publishing company must have been an important factor in fixing upon the large sum of damages. Lord Devlin, in *Rookes v. Barnard,*[109] spoke of "the means of the parties"[110] but presumably the means of the plaintiff cannot be relevant to exemplary damages.

9. Relationship with Compensatory Damages

11.320 It has been held in some jurisdictions that a claim for punitive damages does not have to be specifically pleaded.[111] In *Starkman v. Delhi Court Ltd.,*[112] objection was made to an award of $5,000 for trespass to land on the ground that the statement of claim contained no demand for punitive damages. The plaintiff claimed to have "suffered damage in the amount of $5,000". McGillivray J.A., for the Ontario Court of Appeal, said:

> In the present case the award was of a lump sum of $5,000. In claims of this nature it is not the practice to allow a separate and distinct sum for punitive damages but such, when the circumstances justify it, may be taken into account in the overall assessment. As they are not to be assessed separately there is no compelling necessity that they should be specifically claimed.[113]

The decision of the Supreme Court of Canada in *H. L. Weiss Forwarding Ltd. v. Omnus*[114] appeared to confirm this approach. In *Cassell & Co. Ltd. v. Broome,*[115] Lord Hailsham, while upholding the decision of the Court of Appeal that the claim need not be specifically pleaded, said: "I propose to refer to the Rules Committee the question whether in the light of *Rookes v. Barnard* and the present decision the present practice should not be altered. There is much to be said for the view that a defendant against whom a claim of this kind is made ought not to be taken by surprise".[116] Following this

---

[107] *735619 Ontario Ltd. v. Stone* (1989), 36 C.P.C. (2d) 313 (Ont. H.C.J.); *Fung v. Lu* (1997), 9 C.P.C. (4th) 81 (B.C.S.C.).

[108] [1972] A.C. 1027 (H.L.).

[109] [1964] A.C. 1129 (H.L.).

[110] *Supra,* at p. 1228.

[111] *Cassell & Co. Ltd. v. Broome, supra,* footnote 108; *Doyle v. Garden of the Gulf Security & Investigation Inc.* (1980), 25 Nfld. & P.E.I.R. 167 (P.E.I.S.C.); *Paragon Properties Ltd. v. Magna Envestments Ltd.* (1972), 24 D.L.R. (3d) 156 (Alta. S.C. App. Div.); *Edwards v. Harris-Intertype (Canada) Ltd.* (1983), 40 O.R. (2d) 558 (H.C.J.), affd 9 D.L.R. (4th) 319, 46 O.R. (2d) 286 (C.A.); *Alwest Neon Signs Ltd. v. 464460 Alberta Ltd.* (1994), 58 C.P.R. (3d) 176, 24 Alta. L.R. (3d) 420 (Prov. Ct.).

[112] (1961), 28 D.L.R. (2d) 269, [1961] O.R. 467 (C.A.).

[113] *Supra,* at p. 274 D.L.R., p. 472 O.R.

[114] [1976] 1 S.C.R. 776, 63 D.L.R. (3d) 654, affg 5 C.P.R. (2d) 142 (Ont. H.C.J.). The trial judge, in refusing any award above compensatory damages, had said at p. 156: "It is argued that if intention to harm is found the damages should be increased." He made no reference to exemplary or punitive damages having been expressly claimed.

[115] *Supra,* footnote 108.

decision, the English Rules of Practice were amended to provide: "A claim for exemplary damages must be specifically pleaded together with the facts on which the party pleading relies". The reasons for the rule are given succinctly in the comment to the Supreme Court Practice: "the object of the rule is to give the defendant fair warning of what is going to be claimed with the relevant facts, and thus to prevent surprise at the trial, to avoid the need for any adjournment of the trial on this ground, and, at the same time, to extend the ambit of the discovery before trial".[117] In Saskatchewan also, a claim for exemplary damages must be expressly pleaded.[117a]

11.330 The question of pleadings is linked with the relationship between compensatory and punitive damages. If punitive damages are regarded as part of a single award there is, as the Ontario Court of Appeal said in *Starkman v. Delhi Court,* no compelling reason for separate pleadings. Every claim for damages can be taken to be a claim for exemplary damages if appropriate. On the other hand, if the award of exemplary damages is to be differentiated from the award of compensatory damages and if the facts that justify the two awards are different, there seems a strong argument for giving early notice to the defendant that such a claim will be made, for the defendant may well wish to call evidence of intentions and motives that would not be relevant unless exemplary damages were in issue. In *Whiten v. Pilot Insurance Co.*,[118] the Supreme Court of Canada held that a claim for punitive damages should be specifically pleaded and that the defendant was entitled to demand particulars of the claim.

11.340 Before *Rookes v. Barnard,* as mentioned earlier, the courts had often failed to distinguish between aggravated and punitive damages.[119] The thrust of *Rookes v. Barnard* was that many of the cases formerly described as exemplary damages could be justified on a compensatory basis as aggravated damages. Even though, as indicated above, the restrictive categories laid down in *Rookes v. Barnard* have not been accepted in Canada, the distinction between exemplary damages and compensatory damages developed in the case and in *Cassell & Co. Ltd. v. Broome*[120] has been adopted.[121] It is submitted that an analysis of the relationship between compensatory and exemplary damages requires such a distinction,[122] and that it can be expected to be accepted in Canada as part of the increasing attention paid by modern courts to reasoned analysis of damage awards.

11.350 In *Rookes v. Barnard,* Lord Devlin said:

> In a case in which exemplary damages are appropriate, a jury should be

[116] *Cassell & Co., supra,* at p. 1083.
[117] Supreme Court Practice 1982, pp. 307-8.
[117a] *Rieger v. Burgess,* [1988] 4 W.W.R. 577 (Sask. C.A.); *Lauscher v. Berryere* (1999), 172 D.L.R. (4th) 439 (Sask. C.A.).
[118] (2002), 209 D.L.R. (4th) 257 (S.C.C.), at pp. 292-3.
[119] See 11.10, *supra.*
[120] [1972] A.C. 1027 (H.L.).
[121] See 11.10, *supra.*

> directed that if, but only if, the sum which they have in mind to award as compensation (which may, of course, be a sum aggravated by the way in which the defendant has behaved to the plaintiff) is inadequate to punish him for his outrageous conduct, to mark their disapproval of such conduct and to deter him from repeating it, then it can award some larger sum. If a verdict given on such direction has to be reviewed upon appeal, the appellate court will first consider whether the award can be justified as compensation and if it can, there is nothing further to be said. If it cannot, the court must consider whether or not the punishment is, in all the circumstances, excessive.[123]

Lord Devlin went on to say that there was no objection to a jury being asked to give separate assessments, pointing out that the statute dealing with survival of actions, excluding exemplary damages, would require such a distinction to be made.[124]

11.360 In *Cassell & Co. Ltd. v. Broome,*[125] the jury were asked to make separate assessments of the compensatory and exemplary damages, which they did, at £15,000 and £25,000 respectively. All the law lords were concerned that this direction might have been misunderstood, because it did not indicate very plainly that the compensatory award was to be considered first, and only if it fell short of what was needed by way of exemplary considerations should the jury award *any* additional sum. By a majority of 4 to 3, the direction was held to be adequate, but Lord Hailsham stressed that it was barely adequate, and that the relationship between the two kinds of damages should be emphasized in future cases.[126] Lord Reid said:

> The only practical way to proceed is first to look at the case from the point of view of compensating the plaintiff. He must not only be compensated for proved actual loss but also for any injury to his feelings and for having had to suffer insults, indignities and the like. And where the defendant has behaved outrageously very full compensation may be proper for that. So the tribunal will fix in their minds what sum would be proper as compensatory damages. Then if it has been determined that the case is a proper one for punitive damages the tribunal must turn its attention to the defendant and ask itself whether the sum which it has already fixed as compensatory damages is or is not adequate to serve the second purpose of

[122] For example, where the defendant makes a wrongful arrest acting in good faith, aggravated damages may be appropriate, where exemplary damages are not. See *Whitehouse v. Reimer* (1979), 107 D.L.R. (3d) 283 (Alta. Q.B.), revd on other grounds 116 D.L.R. (3d) 594 (C.A.); *Bahner v. Marwest Hotel Co.* (1969), 6 D.L.R. (3d) 322 (B.C.S.C.), affd 12 D.L.R. (3d) 646 (C.A.); *Hayward v. F.W. Woolworth Co. Ltd.* (1979), 98 D.L.R. (3d) 345 (Nfld. S.C.T.D.); *Hopper v. Clark* (1911), 10 E.L.R. 305 (N.B.S.C. en banc), at p. 319 (if wilful or grossly negligent misconduct); *Dalsin v. T. Eaton Co. of Canada Ltd.* (1975), 63 D.L.R. (3d) 565 (Alta. Dist. Ct.); *Lang v. Burch* (1982), 140 D.L.R. (3d) 325 (Sask. C.A.). Where the defendant acts in good faith but beyond her powers, aggravated damages may well be justified to compensate the plaintiff for humiliation and distress, even though exemplary damages are not appropriate. See *Dancey v. Grand Trunk Ry.*, (1892), 19 O.A.R. 664, where damages of $1,000 were reduced to $500.

[123] *Rookes v. Barnard,* [1964] A.C. 1129 (H.L.), at p. 1228.

[124] *Supra.*

[125] *Cassell & Co., supra,* footnote 120.

[126] *Supra,* at p. 1062.

> punishment or deterrence. If they think that that sum is adequate for the second purpose as well as for the first they must not add anything to it. It is sufficient both as compensatory and as punitive damages. But if they think that sum is insufficient as a punishment then they must add to it enough to bring it up to a sum sufficient as punishment. The one thing which they must not do is to fix sums as compensatory and as punitive damages and add them together. They must realise that the compensatory damages are always part of the total punishment.[127]

The dissenting law lords were afraid that the jury had intended the sum of £25,000 to include the £15,000. Even Lord Hailsham, though upholding the direction, said: "the thought crossed my mind more than once during the hearing" that a double counting might have occurred.[128] The principle, agreed by all, was that the tribunal must consider the adequacy of the compensatory damages from a deterrent point of view before adding exemplary damages (if any).[128a] This is particularly necessary in defamation cases, where it is practically impossible to exclude punitive considerations from the assessment of compensatory damages.[128b] But, in principle, the approach is applicable elsewhere, especially where aggravated damages are awarded. This approach has been adopted in several Canadian cases[129] and in *Sylvan Lake Golf & Tennis Club Ltd. v. Performance Industries Ltd.* [129a] the Supreme Court of Canada set aside an award of punitive damages for fraud, explaining that "only in exceptional cases does [fraud] attract punitive damages",[129b] and that an award could only be justified if more punishment is rationally required than supplied by compensatory damages.[129c]

11.370 The amount of punitive damages is unrelated to the actual loss suffered by the plaintiff, and it has, indeed, been held that exemplary damages may be awarded where the plaintiff has suffered no loss at all.[130] It is, however,

[127] *Supra,* at p. 1089. See also *Hill v. Church of Scientology of Toronto,* [1995] 2 S.C.R. 1130, 126 D.L.R. (4th) 129 at p. 186; *Haas v. Davis* (1998), 37 O.R. (3d) 528 (Ont. Ct. (Gen. Div.)); *Herman v. Graves,* [1998] 9 W.W.R. 542 (Alta. Q.B.), at p. 562.

[128] *Supra,* at p. 1072.

[128a] The principle was applied and this passage cited in *C. (M.) v. M. (F.)* (1990), 74 D.L.R. (4th) 129, 46 C.P.C. (2d) 254 (Ont. Ct. (Gen. Div.)). See also *Epstein v. Cressey Development Corp.* (1992), 89 D.L.R. (4th) 32, [1992] 3 W.W.R. 566 (B.C.C.A.); *Huff v. Price* (1990), 76 D.L.R. (4th) 138, 51 B.C.L.R. (2d) 282 (C.A.), leave to appeal to S.C.C. refused 83 D.L.R. (4th) vii, 136 N.R. 409*n*; *Coughlan v. Westminer Canada Ltd.* (1994), 127 N.S.R. (2d) 241 (C.A.); *Canada Life Assurance Co. v. Stewart* (1994), 118 D.L.R (4th) 67, 132 N.S.R. (2d) 324 (C.A.); *Lubrizol Corp. v. Imperial Oil Ltd.,* [1996] 3 F.C. 40, 67 C.P.R. (3d) 1 (C.A.); *Keays v. Honda Canada Inc.* (2008), 294 D.L.R. (4th) 577 (S.C.C.), at paras. 69-70; *Hockley v. Riley* (2007), 287 D.L.R. (4th) 424 (Ont. C.A.).

[128b] See *Colour Your World Corp. v. Canadian Broadcasting Corp.* (1994), 17 O.R. (3d) 308 (Ont. Ct. (Gen. Div.)), at pp. 352-3.

[129] See *Walker v. CFTO Ltd.* (1987), 37 D.L.R. (4th) 224 at p. 241 (C.A.), and *C. (M.) v. M. (F.)* (1990), 74 D.L.R. (4th) 129 (Ont. Ct. (Gen. Div.)), at p. 135, citing this paragraph; *Bains v. Indo-Canadian Times Inc.* (1995), 38 C.P.C. (3d) 53, 94 W.A.C. 90 (B.C.C.A.); *Hodgson v. Canadian Newspapers Co.,* (2000), 189 D.L.R. (4th) 241 (Ont. C.A.), leave to appeal to S.C.C. refused 197 D.L.R. (4th) vii.

[129a] (2002), 209 D.L.R. (4th) 318 (S.C.C.).

[129b] *Supra,* at pp. 344-5.

[129c] *Supra,* at p. 344.

essential that the plaintiff has an independent cause of action against the defendant,[130a] or else a person entirely unaffected by the defendant's conduct could sue for exemplary damages. Lord Devlin said on this point: "the plaintiff cannot recover exemplary damages unless he is the victim of the punishable behaviour. The anomaly inherent in exemplary damages would become an absurdity if a plaintiff totally unaffected by some oppressive conduct which the jury wished to punish obtained a windfall in consequence."[131]

11.380 In *Guaranty Trust Co. of Canada v. Public Trustee*,[132] a corporation brought an action against the estate of one of its former officers, making several separate allegations of wrongdoing, some of which had caused no loss to the corporation. On a motion to strike out these allegations, the plaintiff argued that they were relevant to the issue of exemplary damages. Craig J. however, held that a claim for exemplary damages must be related to loss actually sustained by the plaintiff:

> The plaintiff does not allege in the statement of claim that it sustained any compensatory or real damages related to the sale of the shares [one of the allegations]; and no claim is made in the prayer for relief directed towards the sale of shares (unless it can be said that the claim for punitive damages is related), *i.e.*, it must be taken that the plaintiff did not suffer any real or compensatory loss or damages resulting from the alleged sale of shares; and not having suffered any such real or compensatory loss or damages it cannot be said that "loss or damages" is aggravated by this conduct of the defendants or that punitive or exemplary damages can be awarded to the plaintiff for conduct unrelated to the loss or damage actually sustained by the plaintiff. It seems to me that to decide otherwise would permit any and all allegations of outrageous conduct in cases where punitive damages are claimed; even though such conduct bears no relationship to the real or compensatory damages or the manner in which they were caused.[133]

11.390 The question is a difficult one, for once the connection between compensation and remedy is lost, as it is by the acceptance of the concept of punitive damages, there is no strictly logical reason why punitive damages should not be awarded whenever conduct comes to light which the court considers worthy of punishment. It is irrelevant from the point of view of the purposes of exemplary damages whether they happen to go into the pocket of

[130] *Johnston Terminals & Storage Ltd. v. Miscellaneous Workers* (1975), 61 D.L.R. (3d) 741 (B.C.S.C.) (nominal damages); *Cash & Carry Cleaners Ltd. v. Delmas* (1973), 44 D.L.R. (3d) 315 (N.B.S.C. App. Div.) (injunction only); *Cousins v. Wilson*, [1994] 1 N.Z.L.R. 462 (H.C.).

[130a] *Vorvis v. Insurance Corp. of British Columbia*, [1989] 1 S.C.R. 1085 at pp. 1105-6, 58 D.L.R. (4th) 193 at p. 206; *Ontex Resources Ltd. v. Metalore Resources Ltd.* (1993), 103 D.L.R. (4th) 158, 13 O.R. (3d) 229 (C.A.), leave to appeal to S.C.C. refused 107 D.L.R. (4th) vii, 69 O.A.C. 160*n*; *Graceffo v. Alitalia*, [1995] 2 W.W.R. 351 (Man. Q.B.); *Beaird v. Westinghouse Canada* (1999), 171 D.L.R. (4th) 279 (Ont. C.A.). See *Watkins v. Secretary of State for the Home Department*, [2006] 2 W.L.R. 807 (H.L.).

[131] *Rookes, supra*, footnote 123, at p. 1227.

[132] (1978), 87 D.L.R. (3d) 417, 20 O.R. (2d) 247 (H.C.J.).

[133] *Supra*, at pp. 421-2 D.L.R.

one plaintiff or another, but this would open the door to actions by informers who had no connection with the conduct complained of. It is submitted, therefore, that the courts are on sound ground in insisting that the punishable conduct must be wrongful vis-à-vis the plaintiff and that the plaintiff cannot attach a complaint of conduct that is not wrongful in this sense to an entirely unrelated cause of action.[133a] All exemplary damages constitute, by hypothesis, a windfall to the plaintiff, but, as Lord Diplock said in *Cassell & Co. Ltd. v. Broome,* the plaintiff "can only profit from the windfall if the wind was blowing his way".[134]

10. Multiple Defendants

11.400 As the purpose of exemplary damages is to punish and deter conduct of which the court disapproves, there cannot be any justification for making such an award against persons who have acted innocently. This principle raises difficulties where there are joint defendants. It is common in defamation cases, for example, for the plaintiff to sue the author, the printer, and the publisher. Generally, the printer will be innocent of any deliberate wrongdoing, but it is usual for a single judgment to be entered against joint tortfeasors. In *Cassell & Co. Ltd. v. Broome,* the House of Lords held that damages must not exceed the lowest sum that could properly be found against any of the defendants. Lord Reid said:

> Unless we are to abandon all pretence of justice, means must be found to prevent more being recovered by way of punitive damages from the least guilty than he ought to pay. We cannot rely on his being able to recover some contribution from the other. Suppose printer, author and publisher of a libel are all sued. The printer will probably be guiltless of any outrageous conduct but the others may deserve punishment beyond compensatory damages. If there has to be one judgment against all three, then it would be very wrong to allow any element of punitive damages at all to be included because very likely the printer would have to pay the whole and the others might not be worth suing for a contribution.[135]

11.410 The House of Lords assumed that a single judgment only could be given against joint tortfeasors. The authorities cited for this conclusion[136] appear to rest on the proposition that each of the joint tortfeasors is liable for the whole loss caused to the plaintiff, an argument that is, of course, not applicable to exemplary damages, which do not depend on the plaintiff's loss at all. In *Townsview Properties Ltd. v. Sun Construction & Equipment Co. Ltd.*[137] where a single judgment had been entered against a developer who had deliberately intended to trespass on the plaintiff's land, and a construction

[133a] *Fatimi Pty Ltd. v. Bryant,* [2004] NSWCA 140, at para. 78, citing this passage.

[134] [1972] A.C. 1027 (H.L.), at p. 1126.

[135] *Supra,* at p. 1090.

[136] *Supra,* at p. 1063. See *Basil v. Spratt* (1918), 45 D.L.R. 554 at p. 567, 44 O.L.R. 155, where the Court of Appeal expressly dissented from English authority.

[137] (1974), 56 D.L.R. (3d) 330, 7 O.R. (2d) 666 (C.A.). Separate judgments were also entered in *Gillett v. Nissen Volkswagen Ltd.* (1975), 58 D.L.R. (3d) 104 (Alta. S.C.T.D.); *Basil v. Spratt, supra,* footnote 136.

company which had carried out the trespass as an independent contractor acting in good faith, the Ontario Court of Appeal held that the trial judge had wrongly failed to consider the two defendants separately and that the award of exemplary damages was only justified against the developer. The Ontario Court of Appeal felt no difficulty in allowing the contractor's appeal and ordering that exemplary damages should be assessed against the developer only, and other Canadian cases support this approach.[138] This seems a better solution than that reached in *Cassell & Co. Ltd. v. Broome,* for if the plaintiff can recover only the damages that the least guilty defendant ought to pay, the plaintiff will, by perhaps inadvertently including an innocent defendant, lose the damages and excuse the guilty defendants from paying a substantial sum of money. A similar division may be appropriate in case of aggravated damages where only one of several defendants is responsible for the aggravating circumstances.[139]

11.420 The question of the liability of a principal or employer for exemplary damages awarded against an agent or employee has been little discussed by English or Canadian writers. As McCormick says, the question raises difficult problems of policy.[140] From the point of view of the considerations of justice, mentioned by Lord Reid, in respect of joint tortfeasors, there would seem to be no justification for punishing the principal for the agent's misconduct. Where the principal or employer is a corporation, there is another problem of policy, for the actual punishment will fall upon the shareholders who may be entirely innocent. This, however, is the case whenever punishment is imposed on a corporation. Canadian cases have regularly awarded exemplary damages against corporations for misconduct of employees.[141] In *H. L. Weiss Forwarding Ltd. v. Omnus,*[142] exemplary damages were awarded against several defendants one of which was a corporation, the Supreme Court of Canada making it clear that it was the conduct of the corporation that was considered worthy of punishment. No reference was made to the position of the individual defendants or to the question of whose action should be considered the actions of the corporation for these purposes. In the criminal law, it has been said in English cases that a corporation should only be punished for actions of a person who can be described as the *alter ego* or the "directing mind and will" of the corporation.[143] There is some support in Canadian criminal law for a slightly wider view,[144] but still it does not extend to every case in which a corporation would be civilly liable for acts of its

[138] *Vogel v. Canadian Broadcasting Corp.*, [1982] 3 W.W.R. 97 (B.C.S.C.); *Munro v. Toronto Sun* (1982), 39 O.R. (2d) 100 (H.C.J.).

[139] See *Cassell & Co. v. Broome, supra,* footnote 134, at p. 1063, *per* Lord Hailsham; p. 1131, *per* Lord Diplock.

[140] McCormick, *Handbook on the Law of Damages* (St. Paul, West Publishing Co., 1935), p. 282.

[141] *Dalsin v. T. Eaton Co. of Canada Ltd.* (1975), 63 D.L.R. (3d) 565 (Alta. Dist. Ct.).

[142] [1976] 1 S.C.R. 776, 63 D.L.R. (3d) 654.

[143] See Williams, *Criminal Law,* The General Part, 2nd ed. (London, Stevens & Sons Ltd., 1961), §§279-280.

employees. In principle, it would seem that an award of exemplary damages against a corporation can be justified only where the corporation can be held criminally responsible.[145] Otherwise, it cannot be said that the corporation itself has done anything that makes it worthy of punishment. But, in practice, exemplary damages have sometimes been awarded against corporations on the basis of the misconduct of employees whenever the same misconduct justifies holding the corporation liable for compensatory damages.[146] McCormick comments that this approach has the merit of workable simplicity, and that it may be supported on the theory that it creates an incentive for the employer to control employees' behaviour.[147] In *Peeters v. Canada*,[147a] an award of exemplary damages against the Crown was upheld in respect of an assault committed by prison employees. The Federal Court of Appeal conceded that the plaintiff must establish some degree of fault on the part of the Crown as employer, but held that lack of adequate training was sufficient for this purpose. It is submitted that this result cannot be justified on the general principles of exemplary damages. The effect is to punish the employer for what is, at worst, negligence. Later cases have declined to follow *Peeters* on this point.[147b]

11.425 The twin decisions of the Supreme Court of Canada in 1999 on vicarious liability[147c] also, it is suggested, point in the direction of excluding punitive

[144] See *R. v. J.J. Beamish Construction Co. Ltd.* (1966), 59 D.L.R. (2d) 6, [1966] 2 O.R. 867 (H.C.J.), affd 65 D.L.R. (2d) 260, [1968] 1 O.R. 5 (C.A.), appeal to S.C.C. refused D.L.R. *loc. cit.* p. 286*n*. But, on a related issue (establishment of a defence of due diligence), Dickson J., in *R. v. City of Sault Ste. Marie*, [1978] 2 S.C.R. 1299 at p. 1331, 85 D.L.R. (3d) 161 at p. 185, spoke of "those who are the directing mind and will of the corporation, whose acts are therefore in law the acts of the corporation itself".

[145] *B.P.I. Resources Ltd. v. Merrill Lynch Canada Inc.* (1986), 72 A.R. 6 at p. 43, 46 Alta. L.R. (2d) 321 (Q.B.), affd 95 A.R. 211, 67 Alta. L.R. (2d) 97 (C.A.); *Price v. Stoley* (1984), 59 A.R. 1, 34 Alta. L.R. (2d) 356 (Q.B.).

[146] See *Dalsin v. T. Eaton Co., supra*, footnote 141; *Boothman v. Canada*, [1993] 3 F.C. 381, 49 C.C.E.L. 109. And see *Asselstine v. Manufacturers Life Insurance Co.* (2005), 254 D.L.R. (4th) 464 (B.C.C.A.) (award against principal for misconduct of agent); *Rowlands v. Chief Constable of Merseyside Police*, [2007] 1 W.L.R. 1065 (C.A.). See also *New South Wales v. Ibbett*, [2006] HCA 57. But in *Robitaille v. Vancouver Hockey Club Ltd.* (1981), 124 D.L.R. (3d) 228 (B.C.C.A.), the status of the wrongdoing employees as "top management" was emphasized.

[147] McCormick, *op. cit.*, footnote 140, p. 285.

[147a] [1994] 1 F.C. 562, 108 D.L.R. (4th) 471 (C.A.); *R. (G.B.) v. Hollett* (1996), 139 D.L.R. (4th) 260, 154 N.S.R. (2d) 161 *sub nom.* Roose v. Hollett (C.A.), leave to appeal to S.C.C. refused 145 D.L.R. (4th) vii, 160 N.S.R. (2d) 80*n*. See also *Muir v. Alberta* (1996), 132 D.L.R. (4th) 695, [1996] 4 W.W.R. 177 (Alta. Q.B.); *G. (B.M.) v. Nova Scotia (Attorney General)* (2007), 288 D.L.R. (4th) 88 (C.A.), at para. 3 (exemplary damages refused).

[147b] *671122 Ontario Ltd. v. Sagaz Industries Canada Inc.* (2000), 183 D.L.R. (4th) 488 at p. 498 (Ont. C.A.), revd on other grounds [2001] 2 S.C.R. 983, 204 D.L.R. (4th) 542; *A. (M.) v. Canada (Attorney General)*, [2002] 5 W.W.R. 686 (Sask. Q.B.), at pp. 719-21, vard 224 D.L.R. (4th) 688 (Sask. C.A.), both citing this para. and the following para. In *Whiten v. Pilot Insurance Co.*, (2002), 209 D.L.R. (4th) 257 (S.C.C.), at p. 268, the court stressed that the misconduct was "not restricted to middle-level management but was made known to the directing minds of the respondent company". But see *Asselstine v. Manufacturers Life Insurance Co.* (2005), 254 D.L.R. (4th) 464 (B.C.C.A.).

[147c] *Bazley v. Curry*, [1999] 2 S.C.R. 534, 174 D.L.R. (4th) 45; *Jacobi v. Griffiths*, [1999] 2 S.C.R. 570, 174 D.L.R. (4th) 71.

damages. In those cases, it was held that an agency (charitable or non-charitable) may be liable for wrongs deliberately committed by agents or employees, despite the absence of any fault on the part of the agency. The reasoning of the court makes clear that the grounds for imposition of liability in these circumstances are compensation and internalization of costs: the agency is bound to insure the victim against loss because it is unjust that the victim should bear the loss himself or herself. Internalization of the costs of the enterprise is justified, but not punishment, for the agency has done no wrong, and it would be contrary to the public interest to deter charitable agencies from good works, provided that full compensation is made to victims.

11. Multiple Plaintiffs

11.430 Very little attention has been paid to problems of multiple claimants to punitive damages. The problem is unlikely to arise so long as punitive damages are restricted to intentional torts such as assault, defamation and trespass. But if exemplary damages are extended to cases of products liability, for example, such as deliberate neglect of a risk of injury by a manufacturer, difficult problems arise as to entitlement. In a well-known California case,[148] exemplary damages of $125 million were awarded to an individual plaintiff against an automobile manufacturer. The sum was reduced by the court to $3.5 million, but the jury apparently calculated the large sum on the basis of the total profit that the defendant expected to make by omitting a safety feature. No English or Canadian cases have awarded exemplary damages in such a situation, but it is not inconceivable that they might do so.[149] The case falls readily into Lord Devlin's second category in *Rookes v. Barnard.*[150] But no solution has been worked out as to entitlement. If $125 million is the total punishment that is proper, it cannot be right for every plaintiff to recover so much.[150a] On the other hand, it seems anomalous that the first to sue should recover all. The possibility would emerge, if that were the rule, of an unseemly rush to the court-house. Even a plaintiff whose injury was very minor would have an incentive to try for so rich a prize; perhaps even a plaintiff who had not suffered any personal injury at all could assert a cause of action (perhaps in some jurisdictions for breach of warranty), in order to attach a claim for exemplary damages. These considerations tend against the award of any exemplary damages in such cases.[150b] In *Riches v. News Group Newspapers Ltd.*,[151] it was held that the jury should be instructed, where there were multiple plaintiffs, to aggregate

148 *Grimshaw v. Ford Motor Co.*, 119 Cal. App. 3d 757, 174 Cal. Rptr. 348 (C.A., 1981).

149 See *Vlchek v. Koshel* (1988), 52 D.L.R. (4th) 371, [1989] 1 W.W.R. 469 (B.C.S.C.); *Van Oirschot v. Dow Chemical Canada Inc.* (1995), 174 A.R. 157, 31 Alta. L.R. (3d) 212 (C.A.).

150 See 11.120-11.180, *supra*.

150a This point was made in *State Farm Mutual Automobile Insurance Co. v. Campbell*, 123 S. Ct. 1513 (2003). See also *O'Neill v. MacDougall* (2006), 54 B.C.L.R. (4th) 142 (S.C.).

150b See *A.B. v. South West Water Services Ltd.*, [1993] Q.B. 507 (C.A.).

151 [1986] Q.B. 256 (C.A.).

the compensatory damages, and if that sum were insufficient as a penalty, to add a further sum and then to divide that further sum equally among the plaintiffs.

12. Survival of Actions

11.440 It might be thought that since a dead person cannot be punished by temporal courts, an action for exemplary damages would die with the defendant. Moreover, an award against the estate amounts to punishing the innocent beneficiaries. On the other hand, there seems no reason why the death of the plaintiff should affect an award, for it is not for the plaintiff's benefit that the power to award exemplary damages is supposed to exist. Yet the legal position in most Canadian jurisdictions is the reverse. Exemplary damages can be, and have been, awarded against the estate of a wrongdoer,[152] but statute provides that a claim for exemplary damages does not survive for the benefit of the claimant's estate.[153] The survival of a claim against the deceased defendant can, perhaps, be defended on the ground that the award may deter others. The thinking behind the provision that the claim does not survive to the claimant's estate appears to be that the estate should succeed to what represents the deceased person's property and that the deceased can only be said to have a property interest in a claim to compensatory damages that replaces something of value that has been lost, that is, remedies a depletion of the estate for which the defendant is responsible.[153a] But this line of thinking is really incompatible with the existence of exemplary damages at all, for it must be conceded, wherever exemplary damages are awarded to a living plaintiff, that they cannot be justified on a compensatory basis. So if enrichment of a living plaintiff is tolerable, presumably in the public interest, so also should be enrichment of an estate. On the other hand, if enrichment of the estate seems anomalous, that must lead the observer to question the whole basis of exemplary damages.[153b]

13. Conduct of the Plaintiff

11.450 The conduct of the plaintiff, in provoking an assault for example, is not, in general, relevant to the assessment of compensatory damages.[154] It has, however, an obvious relevance to exemplary damages, because just as in the criminal law, where provocation by the victim is always relevant to sentencing, provocation by the plaintiff will usually reduce the impropriety of the defendant's reaction, and so may reduce or extinguish the award of

---

152 *Flame Bar-B.-Q. Ltd. v. Hoar* (1979), 106 D.L.R. (3d) 438 (N.B.C.A.). However, in *Breitkreutz v. Public Trustee* (1978), 89 D.L.R. (3d) 442 (Alta. S.C.T.D.), an award of exemplary damages against an estate was refused.

153 See 12.150, *infra*.

153a A similar line of reasoning has led to the conclusion that a claim for exemplary damages does not pass to a trustee in bankruptcy: *Gano v. Alberta Motor Assn. Insurance Co.*, [1997] 6 W.W.R. 484, 202 A.R. 118 (Q.B.).

153b *Plester v. Wawanesa Mutual Insurance Co.* (2006), 269 D.L.R. (4th) 624 (Ont. C.A.), citing this paragraph.

154 See 15.30-15.60, *infra*.

exemplary damages.[155] In *BMO Nesbitt Burns Inc. v. Wellington West Capital Inc.*,[155a] it was held that the defendant was entitled to plead and prove that the plaintiff had engaged in similar conduct to that alleged against the defendant. It was permissible, in judging the egregiousness of the defendant's conduct, to consider whether or not the conduct objected to was widely accepted in the industry, and the plaintiff's practices were relevant to this question.

14. Conduct of the Defendant after the Wrong

11.460 In the criminal law, the defendant's conduct after the wrong is often relevant to sentence, and similarly, in a number of cases, the subsequent apology or remorse of the defendant has been taken into account to reduce or eliminate an award of punitive damages;[156] the failure to apologize has been taken into account to increase punitive damages.[157] In defamation cases, where the defendant persists in attempting to justify, this factor is commonly taken into account to increase damages.[158] In *Ross v. Lamport*[159] the defendant, after attempting to justify a libel throughout the trial, withdrew the libel in his counsel's closing speech. The Ontario Court of Appeal indicated both that the conduct of the defendant in justifying could be taken into account to support an award of punitive damages and that an apology that was obviously made simply in the hope of reducing damages was too late:

> Before the action was started, the defendant was given the opportunity ... to make some amends by retracting the statements and apologizing for having made them, but he refused to do so. Instead he persisted that they were true when they knew they were not and at the last minute, after the evidence was closed, he sought to have his counsel apologize during the course of the latter's address to the jury. An apology at that stage if it had been permitted, and it was not, could hardly be inspired by a sincere desire to make amends and could only be motivated by a desire to escape from, or minimize the penalty a jury might impose.[160]

15. Criminal Proceedings

11.470 Difficult problems arise in considering the relationship of punitive damages to criminal proceedings. Where the defendant has been convicted and sentenced before the civil trial, Canadian courts have generally held that

---

[155] *Reeves v. Pollard* (1977), 10 A.R. 349 (S.C.T.D.); *March v. Janes* (1991), 91 Nfld. & P.E.I.R. 307 (Nfld. S.C.). See also *Moase Produce Ltd. v. Royal Bank of Canada* (1987), 66 Nfld. & P.E.I.R. 196, 64 C.B.R. 191 (P.E.I.S.C.); and *Murano v. Bank of Montreal* (1998), 163 D.L.R. (4th) 21 (Ont. C.A.), at p. 54; and *Herman v. Graves*, [1998] 9 W.W.R. 542 (Alta. Q.B.), at p. 560; both citing this paragraph. See 15.30-15.60, *infra*.

[155a] (2005), 257 D.L.R. (4th) 122 (Ont. C.A.).

[156] *Karpow v. Shave*, [1975] 2 W.W.R. 159 (Alta. S.C.T.D.).

[157] *O'Connor v. City of Victoria* (1913), 11 D.L.R. 577 (B.C.S.C.) (tender of insultingly small sum); *Fleming v. Spracklin* (1920), 56 D.L.R. 518 at p. 521, 48 O.L.R. 533 (H.C.), affd 64 D.L.R. 382, 20 O.W.N. 152 (S.C. App. Div.).

[158] See 4.160, 4.180, *supra*.

[159] (1957), 9 D.L.R. (2d) 585, [1957] O.R. 402 (C.A.).

[160] *Supra*, at p. 589 D.L.R.

exemplary damages should not be awarded.[160a] In *Natonson v. Lexier,*[161] Taylor J. said: "The defendant was sentenced to a period of imprisonment, and having thus received punishment, the imposition of punitive damages for the benefit of the plaintiff would be a double punishment."[162] This principle has been widely followed,[163] though rejected in some cases.[164] Difficulties arise where the defendant, though convicted, has received a punishment considered lenient by the civil court or has received an absolute or conditional discharge. For the civil court to accept a criminal disposition as an absolute bar to exemplary damages seems anomalous; the defendant receives a financial benefit from a criminal conviction. On the other hand, for

[160a] See *R. (G.B.) v. Hollet* (1995), 143 N.S.R. (2d) 38 at p. 47 *sub nom.* Roose v. Hollet (S.C.), affd on this point 139 D.L.R. (4th) 260, 154 N.S.R. (2d) 161 (C.A.), leave to appeal to S.C.C. refused 145 D.L.R. (4th) vii, citing this passage; *H. (H.) v. Nataluk,* [2001] 5 W.W.R. 711 *sub nom.* Henderson v. Nataluk (Man. Q.B.); *F. (L.) v. F. (J.R.)* (2001), 9 C.P.C. (5th) 222 (Ont. C.A.).

[161] [1939] 3 W.W.R. 289 (Sask. K.B.).

[162] *Supra,* at p. 291.

[163] *Loomis v. Rohan* (1974), 46 D.L.R. (3d) 423 (B.C.S.C.); *Scott v. Fulton* (1978), 30 N.S.R. (2d) 267 (S.C.T.D.); *Fenwick v. Staples* (1977), 82 D.L.R. (3d) 145, 18 O.R. (2d) 128 (Co. Ct.); *Kirisits v. Morrell* (1965), 52 W.W.R. 123 (B.C.S.C.); *Schuster v. Martin* (1965), 50 D.L.R. (2d) 176 (B.C.S.C.); *Radovskis v. Tomm* (1957), 9 D.L.R. (2d) 751 (Man.Q.B.); *Amos v. Vawter* (1969), 6 D.L.R. (3d) 234 (B.C.S.C.); *Banks v. Campbell* (1973), 45 D.L.R. (3d) 603 (N.S.S.C.T.D.); *Chedrawe v. Chediac* (1980), 37 N.S.R. (2d) 285 (S.C.T.D.); *B.P.I. Resources Ltd. v. Merrill Lynch Canada Inc.* (1986), 72 A.R. 6, 46 Alta. L.R. (2d) 321 (Q.B.), affd 95 A.R. 211, 67 Alta. L.R. (2d) 97 (C.A.); *Gallant v. Fraser* (1985), 52 Nfld. & P.E.I.R. 164 (P.E.I.S.C.); *Hachey v. Hachey* (1987), 77 N.B.R. (2d) 293 (Q.B.); *Rioux v. Smith* (1983), 48 B.C.L.R. 126 (C.A.); *Caleval v. Miller* (1983), 26 Sask. R. 209 (Q.B.); *Canada Cement LaFarge Ltd. v. British Columbia Lightweight Aggregate Ltd.* (1981), 123 D.L.R. (3d) 66, [1981] 4 W.W.R. 385 (B.C.C.A.), revd on other grounds [1983] 1 S.C.R. 452, 145 D.L.R. (3d) 385; *Archer v. Brown,* [1985] Q.B. 401. See also *B. (P.) v. B.(W.)* (1992), 11 O.R. (3d) 161, supplementary reasons November 27, 1992 (Gen. Div.); *G.(E.D.) v. D.(S.)* (1993), 101 D.L.R. (4th) 101, 77 B.C.L.R. (2d) 106 (C.A.); *Taylor v. McGillivray* (1993), 110 D.L.R. (4th) 64, 143 N.B.R. (2d) 241 *sub nom.* T. (L.) v. McGillivray (Q.B.) (discipline by professional body); *C. (J.) v. Keats,* [1995] 8 W.W.R. 570, 133 Sask. R. 65 *sub nom.* C. (J.) v. K. (R.) (Q.B.); *McDonald v. Mombourquette* (1995), 145 N.S.R. (2d) 360, 28 C.C.L.T. (2d) 157 *sub nom.* M. (F.W.) v. Mombourquette (S.C.), revd on other grounds 152 N.S.R. (2d) 109 (C.A.), leave to appeal to S.C.C. refused 222 N.R. 80*n*, 164 N.S.R. (2d) 239*n*; *Weber v. Dufault* (1996), 147 Sask. R. 76 (Q.B.); *T. (C.) v. K. (S.)* (1997), 119 Man. R. (2d) 59, 13 C.P.C. (4th) 191 (Q.B.); *A. (C.) v. Critchley* (1997), 35 B.C.L.R. (3d) 234 *sub nom.* A. (C.) v. C. (J.W.), 36 C.C.L.T. (2d) 224 (S.C.), affd as to exemplary damages 166 D.L.R. (4th) 475, 60 B.C.L.R. (3d) 92 (C.A.); *K. (W.) v. Pornbacher,* [1998] 3 W.W.R. 149, 32 B.C.L.R. (3d) 360 (S.C.) (punitive damages refused for assault but allowed for compelling plaintiff to testify again at civil trial); *Gray v. Motor Accident Commission* (1998), 73 A.L.J.R. 45 (H.C.); *H. (C.) v. British Columbia* (2003), 16 B.C.L.R. (4th) 113 (B.C.S.C.), affd 242 D.L.R. (4th) 470 (B.C.C.A.); *John Doe v. O'Dell* (2003), 230 D.L.R. (4th) 383 (Ont. S.C.J.)

[164] *Pollard v. Gibson* (1986), 1 Y.R. 167 (S.C.); *Wittig v. Wittig* (1986), 53 Sask. R. 138 (Q.B.); *Canada v. Lukasik* (1985), 18 D.L.R. (4th) 245, 58 A.R. 313 (Q.B.). See *B. (A.) v. J. (I.),* [1991] 5 W.W.R. 748, 119 A.R. 210 (Q.B.); *P. (S.) v. K. (F.),* [1997] 3 W.W.R. 161, 150 Sask. R. 173 (Q.B.) (criminal charges applying to particular time period only); *G. (E.D.) v. D. (S.), supra,* at p. 108; *Roth v. Roth* (1991), 4 O.R. (3d) 740, 9 C.C.L.T. (2d) 141 (Gen. Div.); *Willington v. Marshall* (1994), 21 C.C.L.T. (2d) 198, 27 C.P.C. (3d) 34 (B.C.S.C.); *Joanisse v. Y. (D.)* (1995), 15 B.C.L.R. (3d) 224, 27 C.C.L.T. (2d) 278 (S.C.); *Donaghy (Litigation Gaurdian of) v. S. (A.)* (1998), 173 Sask. R. 87 *sub nom. Donaghy v. Schutte* (Q.B.); *McIntyre v. Grigg* (2006), 274 D.L.R. (4th) 28 (Ont. C.A.).

the civil court to add to the punishment seems a usurpation of the function of the criminal court.[164a] If the defendant has been acquitted, on the other hand, there seems to be no bar to an award of punitive damages.[165] Difficulties may arise here, in the provision of the *Criminal Code*, to the effect that a person who receives a discharge is deemed not to have been convicted. The problems are intractable and spring from the very nature of exemplary damages. It seems that the most rational solution is for the civil court to consider the extent of the criminal punishment and to reduce accordingly the exemplary damages that otherwise would have been appropriate.[165a] The objection that, by thus adding to punishment, the civil court usurps the function of the criminal court is, in effect, an objection to the whole concept of exemplary damages.[165b] Where the criminal conviction is for an offence that does not correspond exactly with the civil cause of action, though arising out of the same incident, the disposition of the criminal court should, it is submitted, be taken into account, if the punishment imposed upon the defendant is punishment for the same conduct as would be punished by exemplary damages.[166] The precise framing of the criminal charge or of the civil statement of claim ought not to affect the substance of the matter.

11.480 Where the civil action is tried before the criminal prosecution (though this is a rare case), there seems no bar to a full award of punitive damages.[167] The civil court cannot be sure that the prosecution will proceed, or that the defendant will be convicted, or that (unless there is a minimum sentence) the defendant will be severely punished. The sentencing judge in the criminal case will usually have discretion to take account of an earlier award of punitive damages in mitigation of punishment.

[164a] *Daniels v. Thompson*, [1998] 3 N.Z.L.R. 22 (C.A.).

[165] Exemplary damages were awarded in such circumstances in *Moore v. Slater* (1979), 101 D.L.R. (3d) 176 (B.C.S.C.). See *Banks v. Campbell, supra*, footnote 163, at p. 607, *per* Cowan C.J.T.D.; *Loedel v. Eckert* (1977), 3 C.C.L.T. 145 (B.C.S.C.). But see *Daniels v. Thompson, supra*, footnote 164a.

[165a] See *Herbert v. Misuga* (1994), 111 D.L.R. (4th) 193 at pp. 213-14, [1994] 3 W.W.R. 457 (Sask. C.A.), citing this passage; *T. (C.) v. K. (S.)* (1997), 119 Man. R. (2d) 59 at p. 62, 13 C.P.C. (4th) 191 (Q.B.), citing this passage; *Reese v. Falkowsky* (1996), 145 Sask. R. 66 (Q.B.).

[165b] *Herman v. Graves*, [1998] 9 W.W.R. 542 (Alta. Q.B.), at p. 557, citing this paragraph.

[166] See *Loedel v. Eckert, supra*, footnote 165; Hawley, "Punitive and Aggravated Damages in Canada", 18 Alta. L. Rev. 485 (1980), at p. 504.

[167] See *Allard v. Delorme* (1987), 47 Man. R. (2d) 119 (Q.B.).

CHAPTER 12

SURVIVAL ACTIONS

1. Introduction

12.10 At common law, actions in tort did not survive for the benefit of the estate of the injured person.[1] This position has now been reversed in all Canadian jurisdictions[2] but the provisions are not uniform, some being based on Ontario legislation of 1886[3] and others on a 1934 United Kingdom statute.[4] Indeed, no two Canadian jurisdictions have identical legislation.[5] The basic provision of each statute is that the estate shall succeed to the rights of the deceased person but there are variations in each jurisdiction that affect the assessment of damages.

2. Actions Excluded

12.20 The following actions are excluded altogether from the operation of the survival legislation in various Canadian jurisdictions: defamation[6] (B.C., Manitoba, Newfoundland and Labrador, Northwest Territories, Ontario, Saskatchewan), malicious prosecution[7] (Manitoba, Newfoundland), false imprisonment[8] (Manitoba, Newfoundland and Labrador), false arrest[9] (Manitoba, Newfoundland and Labrador), adultery[10] (Nova Scotia),

---

1 See *Walpole v. Canadian Northern Ry.*, [1923] A.C. 113 at p. 118, 70 D.L.R. 201 at p. 204 (P.C.), *per* Viscount Cave. Actions also died with the death of the wrongdoer. This rule is now reversed everywhere by statute and raises no particular problems of damages.

2 *Survival of Actions Act* (Alta.), s. 2; N.S., s. 2(1); P.E.I., s. 4(1); Nfld. & Lab., s. 2; N.B., s. 2(1); Sask., s. 3; Yukon, s. 2(1); *Estate Administration Act* (B.C.), s. 59; *Trustee Act* (Man.), s. 53(1); Ont., s. 38(1); Sask., s. 58(1) (repealed 1990-91, c. S-66.1, s. 13); *Trustee Act* (N.W.T.), s. 31. See *Ordon Estate v. Grail*, [1998] 3 S.C.R. 437, 166 D.L.R. (4th) 193 at p. 248.

3 *An Act respecting Trustees and Executors and the Administration of Estates*, s. 8 (rep. & sub. 1886, c. 16, s. 23).

4 *Law Reform (Miscellaneous Provisions) Act 1934*, s. 1.

5 See Bowker, "The Uniform Survival of Actions Act", 3 Alta. L. Rev. 197 (1964).

6 *Survival of Actions Act* (Nfld. & Lab.), s. 11(a); *Estate Administration Act* (B.C.), s. 59(1)(a); *Trustee Act* (Man.), s. 53(1); Ont., s. 38(1); Sask., s. 58(1) (repealed 1990-91, c. S-66.1, s. 13); *Trustee Act* (N.W.T.), s. 31.

7 *Survival of Actions Act* (Nfld. & Lab.), s. 11(b); *Trustee Act* (Man.), s. 53(1).

8 *Survival of Actions Act* (Nfld. & Lab.), s. 11(c); *Trustee Act* (Man.), s. 53(1).

9 *Survival of Actions Act* (Nfld. & Lab.), s. 11(d); *Trustee Act* (Man.), s. 53(1).

10 *Survival of Actions Act* (N.S.), s. 2(2)(a).

seduction[11] (Newfoundland and Labrador) and inducing one spouse to leave or remain apart from the other[12] (Newfoundland and Labrador, Nova Scotia).

12.30 It should be noted also that seven jurisdictions, including all that do not expressly exclude actions for defamation (Alberta, New Brunswick, Newfoundland and Labrador, Nova Scotia, Prince Edward Island, Saskatchewan, the Yukon), restrict recovery to actual pecuniary loss,[13] which will have the effect of excluding certain actions altogether.

3. Non-pecuniary Loss

12.50 Seven jurisdictions restrict recovery to actual pecuniary loss (Alberta, New Brunswick, Newfoundland, Nova Scotia, Prince Edward Island, Saskatchewan, the Yukon)[14] and the legislation in these jurisdictions (based on the Uniform Survival of Actions Act),[15] goes on to provide that "without restricting the generality of the foregoing"[16] certain heads of damages are specifically excluded. These will be mentioned in the following paragraphs.

12.60 Newfoundland and Nova Scotia require the actual pecuniary loss to be "to the estate"; the other jurisdictions speak of actual pecuniary loss "to the deceased or to the estate". It will be suggested subsequently, that there may be a distinction between the two expressions in respect of lost future earning capacity, which has been held to be an actual capital loss to an injured person, but which would, it seems, not be an actual pecuniary loss to the estate if the person died.[17]

12.70 In the discussion of personal injury claims in an earlier chapter,[18] it was shown that many recent decisions have allowed recovery by a living plaintiff of the value of services voluntarily rendered to the plaintiff between the date of injury and the trial, often on the basis that the damages will be paid over to the provider of the services. The basis of these decisions is that the injured person suffers an actual loss by incurring a need for the services. The loss is of a pecuniary nature and would, it is submitted, amount to an "actual pecuniary loss" to the deceased. Whether there is, in such a case, an actual pecuniary loss to the estate is a more difficult question. It would be difficult to argue that the estate is worse off

---

11 *Survival of Actions Act* (Nfld. & Lab.), s. 11(e).

12 *Survival of Actions Act* (Nfld. & Lab.), s. 11(f); N.S., s. 2(2)(b).

13 *Survival of Actions Act* (Alta.), s. 5 ("actual financial loss to the deceased or his estate"); N.B., s. 5(1) ("actual pecuniary loss to the deceased person or the estate"); Nfld. & Lab., s. 4 ("actual monetary loss to the estate"); N.S., s. 4 ("actual pecuniary loss to the estate"); P.E.I., s. 5 ("actual pecuniary loss to the deceased person or his estate"); Sask. s. 6(1); Yukon, s. 5(1) ("actual pecuniary loss to the deceased person or the estate").

14 See footnote 13, *supra*. See *James v. Rentz* (1986), 27 D.L.R. (4th) 724, 69 A.R. 198 (C.A.) (health services supplied before death).

15 See Bowker, "The Uniform Survival of Actions Act", 3 Alta. L.R. Rev. 197 (1964).

16 The wording in Nova Scotia differs slightly ("and in no case . . .").

17 See 6.760-6.1090, *supra* and 12.170-12.250, *infra*.

18 See 3.440-3.470, *supra*.

by reason of the defendant's wrong; the voluntary provision of services for the deceased appears to cause the estate no loss. This conclusion, though it seems to be required by the statutes in Newfoundland and Nova Scotia, is most unfortunate, for it will have the consequence of restoring (in the case of death of the injured person) the old and unsatisfactory position whereby the provider of services will recover only if it can be shown that the deceased had undertaken to pay for them.

12.80 The policy underlying the exclusion of non-pecuniary loss is evidently that the estate would be over-compensated if it recovered damages based on losses personal to the deceased. Bowker wrote:

> The basis of damages in tort is compensation. Survival of a cause of action for the benefit of the victim's estate should be to enable the estate to recover pecuniary losses but nothing more. The common law rule clearly worked a hardship where the wrongdoer negligently burned down the victim's barn or smashed his car and by chance the victim died of a heart attack before he could take action and obtain judgment. However, there are some items of damage that are in a different category. Like claims for adultery, seduction and enticement, they are peculiarly personal. Compensation for pain and suffering, disfigurement, and loss of expectation of life and heavy damages for defamation, false imprisonment and malicious prosecution are the main examples. To allow them to the victim's estate as one would allow them to the victim himself is to give to the estate a windfall.[19]

12.90 There is, however, another side to the argument. This is that the purpose of the survival legislation is not to compensate survivors for their own losses — that is the function of the *Fatal Accidents Act* — but to enable the estate to inherit the wealth represented by the deceased's own right of action. This, it is submitted, is no more a "windfall" to the estate than is any inheritance of wealth. If the deceased lives to obtain a judgment (even though it is not satisfied before death occurs), the estate will inherit the right to enforce it in full. It is anomalous that the plaintiff's death just before the trial[20] should have the effect of depriving the estate of wealth represented by a valuable cause of action.[21] This view

19 Bowker, *op. cit., supra,* footnote 15, at p. 199.

20 Where the plaintiff dies between trial and judgment, it has been held that the estate's rights are not prejudiced: *Hubert v. DeCamillis* (1963), 41 D.L.R. (2d) 495 (B.C.S.C.); *Turner v. London & South-Western Ry. Co.* (1874), L.R. 17 Eq. 561; *Gunn v. Harper* (1902), 3 O.L.R. 693 (C.A.); *Young v. Town of Gravenhurst* (1911), 24 O.L.R. 467 (C.A.); *Krujelis v. Esdale* (1971), 25 D.L.R. (3d) 557 (B.C.S.C.). See also *Wing Lee v. Lew,* [1925] A.C. 819, [1925] 3 D.L.R. 1009 (P.C.). The opposite view was taken, however, in *Eagles v. St. Peter* (1960), 26 D.L.R. (2d) 670 (N.S. Co. Ct.). See *Rayner v. Knickle* (1991), 88 Nfld. & P.E.I.R. 214, supplementary reasons 32 A.C.W.S. (3d) 702 (P.E.I.C.A.); *Harvey v. Harte* (1999), 176 Nfld. & P.E.I.R. 279 (Nfld. C.A.); *Monahan v. Nelson* (2000), 186 D.L.R. (4th) 193 (B.C.C.A.) (judgment backdated but death taken into account in assessment of damages).

21 See *Lankenau v. Dutton,* [1988] 6 W.W.R. 337, 27 B.C.L.R. (2d) 234 (S.C.), affd 26 A.C.W.S. (3d) 739 (C.A.).

was reflected in the Ontario case of *Bowler v. Blake*[22] where Garrow J. said, in a case where an injured person had died after considerable pain:

> . . . to hold that such an action cannot be revived in the name of the administrator of the deceased and that the injuries sustained and the pain suffered and the medical expense incurred are to be lost to the estate of the deceased, is, to my mind, to ignore entirely the very broad language of the . . . Trustee Act . . .
>
> It has been held that this statute was passed to prevent the wrongdoer escaping liability by reason of the death of the person injured, and not for the purpose of creating a new right of action . . . That being so, and the language of the section being as broad as it is, it appears to me that the personal representative of the deceased injured person is fully entitled to revive the action already brought and to recover all the damages down to the date of death which the deceased herself could have recovered had her action been brought to trial at that date. I can see no reason for excluding from the assessment of damages an allowance for the physical injury done to the plaintiff and the pain and suffering which she was obliged to undergo for several months.[23]

This view, it is submitted, is persuasive and the limitation of damages to pecuniary loss, in the jurisdictions mentioned, seems misplaced. The occurrence of the death should be taken into account, as a fact that is now known, to exclude recovery for loss that the deceased will not now suffer.[24] But otherwise, it is submitted, the estate should, so far as the legislation permits this result, recover what the deceased would have recovered if the latter had lived to continue the action.

4. Physical Disfigurement

12.100 Damages for physical disfigurement are specifically excluded in Alberta, British Columbia, New Brunswick, Newfoundland and Labrador, Prince Edward Island, Saskatchewan and the Yukon.[25]

---

22 [1930] 1 D.L.R. 683, 64 O.L.R. 499 (H.C.). See also *Major v. Bruer*, [1937] 4 D.L.R. 760, [1938] O.R. 1 (C.A.); *Riehl v. Condy*, [1939] 1 D.L.R. 601 (Man. C.A.).

23 *Bowler v. Blake, supra*, footnote 22, at pp. 686-7 D.L.R., pp. 503-4 O.L.R. See also *Hartman v. Fisette*, [1977] 1 S.C.R. 248, 66 D.L.R. (3d) 516; *Smoke v. Assiniboine*, [1987] 2 W.W.R. 217, 45 Man. R. (2d) 241 (Q.B.); *Woollard v. Coles* (1999), 132 Man. R. (2d) 271 (Q.B.); *Monahan v. Nelson, supra*, footnote 20. It was held in *Major v. Bruer, supra*, footnote 22, and *George Estate v. Harris* (2001), 204 D.L.R. (4th) 218 (Ont. S.C.J.), and assumed in *Lefebvre v. Dowdall* (1964), 46 D.L.R. (2d) 426 at p. 428, [1965] 1 O.R. 1 (H.C.J.), that an action for pain and suffering survives under the Ontario *Trustee Act*. See *Hicks v. Chief Constable of the South Yorkshire Police*, [1992] 2 All E.R. 65 (H.L.).

24 See 13.500-13.650, *infra; Pratt v. Beaman*, [1930] S.C.R. 284, [1930] 2 D.L.R. 868.

25 *Survival of Actions Act* (Alta.), s. 5; *Estate Administration Act*, B.C., s. 59(3)(a); N.B., s. 5(1); Nfld., s. 11(g); P.E.I., s. 5(d); Sask., s. 6(2)(d); Yukon, s. 5(1).

5. Loss of Amenities

12.110 Damages for loss of amenities are specifically excluded in Alberta, Prince Edward Island and Saskatchewan.[26] In *Child v. Stevenson*,[27] damages for loss of amenities were held to be excluded in British Columbia also as damages "for the death" of the deceased where death was caused by the injuries in question. In *Cromwell v. Dave Buck Ford Lease Ltd.*,[28] the British Columbia Supreme Court held that damages for loss of amenities occurring before death[29] fell within the exclusion of damages for pain and suffering and therefore excluded from the estate's action, even where the deceased's death was caused by an event unrelated to the defendant's wrong. Recovery for loss of amenities will also be excluded in the other four jurisdictions excluding non-pecuniary loss.[30] In the light of *Andrews v. Grand & Toy Alberta Ltd.* and the other cases decided at the same time,[31] where the Supreme Court of Canada held that damages for non-pecuniary losses were to be regarded as a solace to a seriously injured plaintiff, it may be doubted whether substantial damages should now be awarded for loss of amenities in case of early death.[32]

6. Damages for the Death

12.120 Damages for the death are excluded in British Columbia and Ontario if death results from such injuries.[33] The meaning of the phrase is not immediately apparent. It would seem that it has much the same scope as damages for loss of expectation of life with which it is coupled in both jurisdictions. In *Child v. Stevenson*,[34] the phrase was interpreted by the British Columbia Court of Appeal to include damages for loss of amenities of life. In *Balkos Estate v. Cook*,[35] the phrase was construed to cover loss of earning capacity.

7. Loss of Expectation of Life

12.130 Damages for loss of expectation of life are excluded in Alberta, Manitoba, New Brunswick, Nova Scotia, Prince Edward Island, Saskatchewan and the

---

26 *Survival of Actions Act* (Alta.), s. 5; P.E.I., s. 5(b); Sask., s. 6(2)(e).

27 (1973), 37 D.L.R. (3d) 429 (B.C.C.A.). A contrary earlier decision is *Krujelis v. Esdale* (1971), 25 D.L.R. (3d) 557 (B.C.S.C.). The same phrase occurs in the Ontario statute.

28 (1980), 109 D.L.R. (3d) 82 (B.C.S.C.). See also *Dalzell v. Viereck*, [1985] 3 W.W.R. 248 (B.C.S.C.).

29 On the question of lost amenities after the date of death, see 12.130, *infra*.

30 In *Rhodenizer v. Powell* (1960), 22 D.L.R. (2d) 563 (N.S.S.C.), it was held that exclusion of damages for loss of expectation of life and pain and suffering had the effect of excluding a claim for damages for "loss of prospective happiness".

31 See 3.510-3.700, *supra*.

32 In *Crosby v. O'Reilly*, [1975] 2 S.C.R. 381 at p. 386, 51 D.L.R. (3d) 555 at pp. 558-9, Laskin C.J.C. held that, in the context of a survival action, a claim for loss of amenities was duplicative of a claim for loss of expectation of life, which is expressly excluded in several provinces. See 12.130, *infra*.

33 *Estate Administration Act* (B.C.), s. 59(3); *Trustee Act* (Ont.), s. 38(1).

34 *Supra*, footnote 27.

35 (1991), 75 O.R. (2d) 593, 41 O.A.C. 151 (C.A.).

Yukon, and in British Columbia and Ontario "if death results from such injuries".[36] Since Newfoundland and Labrador excludes all non-pecuniary loss,[37] only one jurisdiction remains (the Northwest Territories) in which damages for loss of expectation of life are generally available against a wrongdoer who causes death. Damages for loss of expectation of life may, it seems, survive in Saskatchewan, British Columbia, and Ontario where the defendant shortens the plaintiff's life, but death is caused independently[38] of the tortfeasor. Substantial damages were held in *Rose v. Ford*[39] to survive to the estate under the head of loss of expectation of life, but in *Benham v. Gambling*[40] the House of Lords held that the award was to be restricted to a conventional figure.[41] In *Crosby v. O'Reilly*,[42] the Supreme Court of Canada, while agreeing that the award should be "conventional", rejected any fixed ceiling. The Manitoba Court of Appeal, following this and other decisions of the Supreme Court,[43]

36 *Survival of Actions Act* (Alta.), s. 5(2)(b); N.B., s. 5(1); N.S., s. 4(b); P.E.I., s. 5(b); Sask., s. 6(2)(a); Yukon, s. 5(1); *Estate Administration Act* (B.C.), s. 59(3); *Trustee Act* (Ont.), s. 38(1); Man., s. 53(1). In *Rhodenizer v. Powell, supra*, footnote 32, the phrase was held to include a claim for "loss of prospective happiness".

37 *Survival of Actions Act* (Nfld. & Lab.), s. 4. See *Anthony v. Fleming* (1962), 37 D.L.R. (2d) 93 (Nfld. S.C.).

38 *Love v. Bennett* (1979), 9 B.C.L.R. 397 (Co. Ct.); *Lankenau v. Dutton* (1991), 79 D.L.R. (4th) 705, [1991] 5 W.W.R. 71 (B.C.C.A.), leave to appeal to S.C.C. refused 83 D.L.R. (4th) vii, 136 N.R. 237*n*. A distinction is required according to whether or not the death is tortiously caused. See 13.550-13.650, *infra*. In *Cromwell v. Dave Buck Ford Lease Ltd.* (1980), 109 D.L.R. (3d) 82 (B.C.S.C.), where death was caused by a non-tortious accident, Taylor J. held that (as events now demonstrate) the defendant had not *in fact* caused a shortening of the plaintiff's life. However, if the event causing death is wrongful, it would seem that the first tortfeasor should be liable in full, on the principle of *Baker v. Willoughby*, [1970] A.C. 467 (H.L.).

39 [1937] A.C. 826 (H.L.).

40 [1941] A.C. 157 (H.L.).

41 £200 in 1941, increasing with inflation to £500 in 1968 (*Yorkshire Electricity Board v. Naylor*, [1968] A.C. 529 (H.L.)) and £1,250 by 1982 (see, *e.g.*, *White v. London Transport Executive*, [1982] 1 All E.R. 410 (Q.B.)). By the *Administration of Justice Act 1982* (U.K.), the action for loss of expectation of life is abolished, except in so far as it contributes to pain and suffering.

42 *Supra*, footnote 32 (reduction from $90,000 to $10,000 approved).

43 In *Anderson v. Chasney*, [1949] 4 D.L.R. 71 (Man. C.A.), affd [1950] 4 D.L.R. 223, followed in *Maltais v. C.P.R.*, [1950] 2 W.W.R. 145 (Alta. S.C.), *Benham v. Gambling, supra*, footnote 40, was rejected. Then in *Bechthold v. Osbaldeston*, [1953] 2 S.C.R. 177, [1953] 4 D.L.R. 783 and in *Northland Greyhound Lines Inc. v. Bryce*, [1956] S.C.R. 408, 3 D.L.R. (2d) 81, *Benham v. Gambling* was approved by the Supreme Court of Canada, though $7,500 was allowed in the former case and $2,500 in the latter. In *Gayhart v. Registrar of Motor Vehicles* (1956), 6 D.L.R. (2d) 474, the Manitoba Court of Appeal explained this discrepancy on the basis of the difference in ages of the deceased in the two cases. Differences in age are ignored in England. See *Yorkshire Electricity Board v. Naylor, supra*, footnote 41. However, in *Pollock v. Milbery* (1975), 65 D.L.R. (3d) 472 (Man. C.A.), O'Sullivan J.A. considered (though regretfully) that the law in Manitoba was that the award should vary with the age of the deceased, increasing to a maximum for persons in the prime of life: see pp. 484-5. *Crosby v. O'Reilly*, [1975] 2 S.C.R. 381 at p. 386, 51 D.L.R. (3d) 555 at p. 559, also suggests that account must be taken of individual circumstances affecting the deceased's prospects of happiness. In *Rodzinski v. Modern Dairies*, [1949] 4 D.L.R. 438 (Man. K.B.), damages in a personal injury case were reduced because the plaintiff led a life of crime and laziness.

held in *Pollock v. Milbery*[44] that although no legally fixed ceiling should be imposed, the principle remained that "only a very moderate sum" should be awarded. In that case the Court of Appeal reduced an award of $20,000 to $6,500. In the light of the Supreme Court of Canada's view in the 1978 "trilogy" that damages for loss of expectation of life are part of a solace to make life more endurable for a seriously injured plaintiff,[45] it can be forcefully argued that no damages should be awarded in respect of a period after the date of the death. The question is analogous to that of the unconscious plaintiff and as argued elsewhere in that context,[46] the logic of the "functional" approach adopted in the 1978 trilogy appears to exclude damages for future non-pecuniary loss. Expenses actually incurred between the date of the injury and the date of death that are attributable to the purchase of a solace for the injuries should, it is submitted, be recoverable in all jurisdictions as pre-trial pecuniary losses,[47] just as they would have been recoverable by the deceased had there been no death.

8. Pain and Suffering

12.140 Damages for pain and suffering are excluded in Alberta, British Columbia, New Brunswick, Nova Scotia, Prince Edward Island, Saskatchewan and the Yukon,[48] and presumably in Newfoundland, as non-pecuniary loss.[49] The Supreme Court of Canada held in *Andrews v. Grand & Toy Alberta Ltd.*[50] that in the case of a living plaintiff no distinction was to be drawn between the various heads of non-pecuniary loss. However, it appears that the wording of the survival statutes will compel a distinction to be drawn where the plaintiff has died. Thus, in Ontario, for example, damages for loss of expectation of life are excluded "if death results from such injuries"[51] but

---

[44] (1975), 65 D.L.R. (3d) 472 (Man. C.A.) ($6,500 for fixty-six year old). See also *Gallant v. Boklaschuk* (1978), 90 D.L.R. (3d) 370 (Man. Q.B.) ($7,500 for thirteen year old); *Kernested v. Desorcy*, [1978] 3 W.W.R. 623 (Man. Q.B.), affd [1979] 1 W.W.R. 512 (C.A.), leave to appeal to S.C.C. refused January 23, 1979 ($7,200 for twenty year old); *Fostey v. Moore's Taxi (1961) Ltd.*, [1973] 1 W.W.R. 673 (Man. Q.B.) ($8,500 for twenty-two year old); *Katz v. Little* (1963), 38 D.L.R. (2d) 515 (Man. Q.B.) ($4,000 for sixty-two year old); *Constable v. Ulan* (1969), 7 D.L.R. (3d) 377 (Alta. S.C. App. Div.) ($4,000 for sixty-seven year old); *Ralston v. Smoky Lake Municipal District* (1957), 8 D.L.R. (2d) 250 (Alta. S.C. App. Div.), affd 11 D.L.R. (2d) 673 (S.C.C.) ($3,500 for forty-seven year old); *Konowalchuk v. Korpasho*, [1955] 4 D.L.R. 404 (Man. C.A.) ($5,000 for twenty-six year old); *Weidl v. Karesa* (1956), 6 D.L.R. (2d) 183 (Man. Q.B.) ($2,500 for seven and one-half year old); *Lysack v. Anderson*, [1955] 4 D.L.R. 248 (Man. C.A.) (conventional sum of $5,000); *Kuzikowski v. Abell*, [1955] 2 D.L.R. 278 (Alta. S.C. App. Div.) ($5,500 for twenty-nine-year old).

[45] See 3.510-3.700, *supra*.

[46] See 3.660, 3.670, *supra*.

[47] See 3.410-3.490, *supra*.

[48] *Survival of Actions Act* (Alta.), s. 5; *Estate Administration Act* (B.C.), s. 59(3)(a); N.B., s. 5(1); N.S., s. 4(c); P.E.I., s. 5(c); Sask., s. 6(2)(c); Yukon, s. 7(1). But in *Monahan v. Nelson* (2000), 186 D.L.R. (4th) 193 (B.C.C.A.), where the plaintiff died after trial and before judgment, the judgment was backdated.

[49] See *Survival of Actions Act* (Nfld. & Lab.), s. 4.

[50] See 3.650, *supra*.

[51] *Trustee Act* (Ont.), s. 38(1).

damages for pain and suffering are not. Thus, damages for pain and suffering would appear to survive to the estate,[52] though the amount recoverable will be limited by the plaintiff's shortened life.

9. Punitive or Exemplary Damages

12.150 Six jurisdictions expressly exclude punitive or exemplary damages (Alberta, Manitoba, Newfoundland and Labrador, Nova Scotia, Prince Edward Island, the Yukon),[53] presumably on the principle that such damages do not represent actual pecuniary loss to the deceased and therefore the recovery would enrich the estate unjustly. However, as has been pointed out elsewhere,[54] there seems a strong case for the survival of punitive damages,[54a] the presumed purpose of which is to punish the defendant not compensate the plaintiff. The deceased's estate therefore is no more unjustly enriched by the award of punitive damages than is a living plaintiff. It would seem more logical to prevent recovery of punitive damages where the wrongdoer has died, but most of the survival statutes do not address this question[55] and the cases are divided.[56]

10. Breach of Promise of Marriage

12.160 Two jurisdictions (Newfoundland and Labrador, and Prince Edward Island) have specific provisions relating to the action of breach of promise of marriage restricting recovery in the case of Newfoundland to damages to the estate[57] and in the case of Prince Edward Island to "such damages as ... flow from the breach".[58]

---

[52] *Gukert v. Kuntz* (1970), 22 D.L.R. (3d) 458 (Sask. C.A.), affd [1971] S.C.R. vi, 23 D.L.R. (3d) 384*n*.

[53] *Survival of Actions Act* (Alta.), s. 5; Nfld. & Lab., s. 4(b); N.S., s. 4(a); P.E.I., s. 5(a); Yukon, s. 5(1); *Trustee Act* (Man.), s. 53(1) ("for a tort causing the death of a person"). In *Campbell v. Insurance Corp. of British Columbia* (1987), 49 D.L.R. (4th) 51, [1988] 3 W.W.R. 236 (B.C.C.A.), and *Allan Estate v. Co-operators Life Insurance Co.* (1997), 37 B.C.L.R. (3d) 45, 18 E.T.R. (2d) 146 (S.C.), affd [1999] 8 W.W.R. 328, 62 B.C.L.R. (3d) 329 (C.A.), the same conclusion was reached on interpretation. See also *Legal Services Board v. Dwyer*, [1996] 1 N.Z.L.R. 142 (C.A.). The New Brunswick Act expressly permits exemplary damages: s. 5(2); as does the Saskatchewan Act: s. 3(a).

[54] See 11.440, *supra*.

[54a] The New Brunswick Act has been amended to this effect: *Survival of Actions Act*, s. 5(2). See *George Estate v. Harris* (2001), 204 D.L.R. (4th) 218 (Ont. S.C.J.), at para. 37, citing this paragraph (claim not struck out); *Plester v. Wawanesa Mutual Insurance Co.* (2006), 269 D.L.R. (4th) 624 (Ont. C.A.), citing this paragraph.

[55] The Saskatchewan *Survival of Actions Act*, s. 3, does make this distinction, permitting exemplary damages where the plaintiff dies, but not where the defendant dies, except in a case where damages represent a gain to the wrongdoer.

[56] See 11.440, *supra*.

[57] *Survival of Actions Act* (Nfld. & Lab.), s. 4(c).

[58] *Survival of Actions Act* (P.E.I.), s. 5(e). The meaning of the phrase is not entirely clear, but it would seem to apply to such elements as aggravated damages for seduction of the plaintiff under promise of marriage.

11. Loss of Future Earning Capacity

12.170 It has been held both by the Supreme Court of Canada in *Andrews v. Grand & Toy Alberta Ltd.*[59] and by the House of Lords in *Pickett v. British Rail Engineering Ltd.*[60] and in *Gammell v. Wilson*[61] that an injured plaintiff whose life expectancy is shortened by the defendant's wrong is entitled to recover damages in respect of loss of earnings during the so-called "lost years" — the years during which the plaintiff would have been earning but during which the plaintiff is not now expected to live.[62] This holding gives rise to the possibility of the defendant being made to pay damages twice over, once to the plaintiff's estate and again to the claimants under the fatal accidents legislation. In most cases, the beneficiaries of the estate will be the same persons as the fatal accidents legislation claimants, in which case the benefits received or receivable from the estate would go to reduce the fatal accidents claim. However, if the estate were insolvent or if there were other beneficiaries of a will not susceptible to attack under dependant's relief legislation, the defendant might indeed have to pay twice over.[63] The House of Lords in the *Pickett* case indicated that this possibility would have to be dealt with when it arose, possibly with legislation,[64] but even if the problem were not soluble, the evil of compelling the defendant to pay twice seemed less than undercompensating the injured person's surviving dependants; this would have been the result in *Pickett* where the injured person had lived long enough to obtain a judgment, of excluding damages for the lost years from the claim, for the judgment was assumed to extinguish the claim by survivors under the fatal accidents legislation.[65]

12.180 Three solutions seem in principle to be available to solve the problem of double recovery. These are: (1) the claim in respect of "lost years" does not survive to the estate at all; (2) the claim survives but is to be reduced by the amount that the deceased would have spent on dependants had death not occurred; (3) the estate recovers in full but the *Fatal Accidents Act* claim is correspondingly reduced.

12.190 The first suggested solution, that the claim in respect of the "lost years" does not survive to the estate at all,[66] was rejected by the House of Lords in *Gammell v. Wilson*[67] where it was held that even in the case of immediate death the claim did survive to the estate under the English legislation. In Alberta, British Columbia and Saskatchewan the survival legislation expressly excludes damages in respect of expectancy of earnings subsequent

59 [1978] 2 S.C.R. 229, 83 D.L.R. (3d) 452.

60 [1980] A.C. 136 (H.L.).

61 [1982] A.C. 27 (H.L.).

62 See 3.910-3.930, *supra*.

63 See 6.760-6.1090, *supra*.

64 *Supra*, footnote 60, at p. 150.

65 See 6.810, *supra*.

66 This solution is favoured by Jolowicz: "Damages – Prospective Loss of Earnings – Reduced Expectation of Life", [1960] Camb. L.J. 160.

67 *Supra*, footnote 61.

to death.[68] Similar legislation has been enacted in Scotland[69] and in England.[70] This legislation seems to go too far, for it excludes a claim where there is no *Fatal Accident Act* claim as, for example, where the deceased is killed by a third person.[71]

12.200 In most Canadian jurisdictions the question is affected by the statutory provisions excluding various kinds of non-pecuniary losses. Damages for loss of earnings during the "lost years" were treated by the House of Lords in *Pickett* as a capital loss actually suffered by the deceased before death, and presumably this loss is in theory suffered equally by the deceased whether death occurs a year, a week, or a second after the defendant's wrong.[72] This view is consistent with the Supreme Court of Canada's treatment of loss of earnings in *The Queen in right of Ontario v. Jennings*[73] and in the 1978 trilogy[74] where the loss was also held to be of a capital nature. It was held by the Alberta courts[75] that such recovery was "actual pecuniary loss" to the deceased, but the statute was later amended to exclude such claims,[76]which have also been held to be excluded in several other jurisdictions.[77]

12.210 In favour of treating loss of expectation of earning capacity as part of loss of expectation of life is the consideration that the claim was so

68 *Survival of Actions Act* (Alta.), s. 5(2)(c); *Estate Administration Act* (B.C.), s. 59(3)(c); *Survival of Actions Act* (Sask.), s. 6(2)(b).

69 *Damages (Scotland) Act 1976.*

70 *Administration of Justice Act 1982.*

71 See 6.930, *supra*. The problem only arises where the death occurs wrongfully. See footnote 38, *supra*.

72 *Gammell v. Wilson*, [1982] A.C. 27 (H.L.); *Kandalla v. British European Airways Corp.*, [1981] Q.B. 158. In *Barr v. Miller*, [1938] 4 D.L.R. 278 (Man. K.B.), it was held that instant death does not prevent survival of a cause of action for the wrongful act causing the death. See also *Crosby v. O'Reilly*, [1975] 2 S.C.R. 381, 51 D.L.R. (3d) 555. The contrary suggestion in *Wilson v. Zeron*, [1941] 4 D.L.R. 510, [1941] O.W.N. 353 (H.C.J.), affd [1942] 2 D.L.R. 580, [1942] O.W.N. 195 (C.A.), appears not to have been followed by the High Court. The Court of Appeal, in affirming the judgment, left the question open. In Quebec law, no action survives in the case of instant death: *Driver v. Coca-Cola Ltd.*, [1961] S.C.R. 201, 27 D.L.R. (2d) 20; *Mack v. Air Canada*, [1976] 1 S.C.R. 144, 57 D.L.R. (3d) 572.

73 [1966] S.C.R. 532, 57 D.L.R. (2d) 644.

74 See 3.710, *supra*.

75 *Galand Estate v. Stewart*, [1993] 4 W.W.R. 205 (Alta. C.A.); *Duncan Estate v. Baddeley* (1997), 145 D.L.R. (4th) 708 (Alta. C.A.); *Brooks v. Stefura* (2000), 192 D.L.R. (4th) 40, (Alta. C.A.).

76 Note 68, *supra*.

77 *MacLean v. MacDonald* (2002), 211 D.L.R. (4th) 474 (N.S.C.A.); *Balkos Estate v. Cook* (1990), 41 O.A.C. 151 (C.A.); *MacKay Estate v. Smith* (2003), 232 D.L.R. (4th) 692 (P.E.I.C.A.); *Grennan Estate v. Alton* (2002), 290 W.A.C. 83 *sub nom. Grennan Estate v. Reddoch*, [2002] Y.J. No. 118 (QL) (Y.T.C.A.).

treated by the English Court of Appeal in *Oliver v. Ashman*.[78] It is true that *Oliver v. Ashman* was overruled in *Pickett v. British Rail Engineering Ltd.*,[79] but it was overruled on a question of whether a living plaintiff could recover in respect of the "lost years" not on the question of survival to the estate. Secondly, this construction could be supported by the consideration that the Canadian legislatures, in excluding survival of damages for loss of expectation of life while saving rights under fatal accident legislation, might have been presumed to intend to exclude double recovery by reducing the claim of the estate. It could be argued that it is in keeping with this policy to interpret the phrase "loss of expectation of life" so as to include the claim for the lost years. Against this it might be said that loss of expectation of life is hardly an apt phrase to describe damages for loss of earnings, held in *Pickett* and in *Jennings* to be a real capital loss actually suffered by the deceased, and that it is not to be assumed that the legislature, in divesting persons of civil rights, has intended more than it has plainly said.[80] Secondly, if the purpose of the exclusion is to avoid double recovery, one would expect it to have been limited to cases where the defendant is responsible for the death. Suppose a case where the defendant injures the plaintiff, destroying a lifetime earning capacity but not shortening lifespan. The next day the plaintiff is killed by a third party.[81] It would plainly be unjust to prevent survival of the action to the estate, for this would leave the plaintiff's dependants with no compensation at all, since there would be no action under the fatal accidents legislation against the defendant, and the second wrongdoer would not be liable for the loss of earning capacity.[82]

12.220 The second solution, that is, reduction of the estate's claim by the amount the deceased would have spent on dependants, appears in several Australian cases.[83] The objection to this solution is that, in the case of a living plaintiff, it is clear that the amount spent on dependants is not to be excluded — indeed the whole point of the *Pickett* case was to allow a living plaintiff to recover this amount (for the ultimate benefit of the dependants). It is not clear, therefore, why recovery by the estate should be calculated on a different principle on the application of legislation that says simply that the estate succeeds to the claims of the deceased. Again a distinction would be required according to whether or not the defendant

78 [1962] 2 Q.B. 210 (C.A.).

79 [1980] A.C. 136 (H.L.).

80 Although the basic provision of the survival statutes enlarges civil rights, the references to damages for loss of expectation of life take the form of subsequently enacted limitations.

81 A wrongful killing must be supposed, since otherwise the defendant could argue successfully that the wrong had not in fact caused a loss of earning capacity. See footnote 38, *supra*, and 13.500-13.650, *infra*.

82 See 6.930, *supra*.

83 *Skelton v. Collins* (1966), 115 C.L.R. 94 (Aust. H.C.); *Jackson v. Stothard*, [1973] 1 N.S.W.L.R. 292; *Gannon v. Gray*, [1973] Qd. R. 411.

was responsible for the death, for reduction of the estate's claim would only be justifiable where an action was available under fatal accidents legislation.[84]

12.230 The third possible solution to the problem of double recovery, that is, recovery in full by the estate and abatement of the *Fatal Accidents Act* claim, has been discussed in an earlier chapter,[85] where it was suggested that this offers the most satisfactory theoretical solution to the problem of the relationship between the two statutes.

12. Loss or Gain to the Estate

12.240 Seven jurisdictions provide that, where the defendant is responsible for the death, damages are to be calculated "without reference to any loss or gain to the estate as the result of the death" (Alberta, Manitoba, New Brunswick, Newfoundland and Labrador, Prince Edward Island, Saskatchewan and the Yukon).[86] This provision, modelled on the English legislation of 1934,[87] is somewhat obscure. The reference to "gain" appears to be intended to exclude such payments to the estate as life insurance, guaranteed annuity payments, and retirement pension contributions.[88] The reference to "loss" would appear to apply to such things as funeral expenses and the costs of administration of the estate, though it should be noted that funeral expenses are specifically allowed in all seven jurisdictions, and costs of administration up to $500 are allowed in Prince Edward Island.[89] In *Gammell v. Wilson*,[90] the House of Lords held that the provision did not prevent the survival of a right of action for loss of future earnings of a person killed immediately by the defendant's wrong.

13. Funeral Expenses

12.250 Funeral expenses, not being recoverable by the deceased before death, are not recoverable by the estate in the absence of express provision.[91] Express reference to funeral expenses is made in the seven jurisdictions discussed earlier[92] and, in addition to these, in British Columbia.[93] In all

---

84 See *Benham v. Gambling*, [1941] A.C. 157 (H.L.). And see footnote 81, *supra*.

85 See 6.760-6.1090, *supra*.

86 *Survival of Actions Act* (Alta.), s. 6; N.B., s. 6; Nfld. & Lab., s. 4(d); P.E.I., s. 6; Sask., s. 7(1); Yukon, s. 6(1); *Trustee Act* (Man.), s. 53(1).

87 *Law Reform (Miscellaneous Provisions) Act 1934*, s. 1(2)(c).

88 Examples given by Lord Wright in *Rose v. Ford*, [1937] A.C. 826 (H.L.), at p. 842.

89 See 12.260, *infra*.

90 [1982] A.C. 27 (H.L.).

91 *Earl v. Steinhauer* (1957), 7 D.L.R. (2d) 457 (Alta. S.C. App. Div.).

92 *Survival of Actions Act* (Alta.), s. 6; P.E.I., s. 6; Yukon, s. 6(1) ("reasonable expenses of the funeral and the disposal of the body"); N.B., s. 6 ("expenses of the funeral and the disposal of the body"); Nfld. & Lab., s. 4(d) ("funeral expenses"); Sask. s. 7(2) ("reasonable expenses of the funeral and disposal of the body"); *Trustee Act* (Man.), s. 53(1) ("funeral expenses").

93 *Estate Administration Act* (B.C.), s. 59(5), "reasonable expenses of the funeral and the disposal of the remains".

these jurisdictions, recovery is allowed only if the defendant is responsible for the death and the estate bears the cost or the liability. Fatal accident legislation in several jurisdictions also provides for recovery of funeral expenses by the statutory beneficiaries, and it has been held that double recovery is to be avoided.[94] The expenses must be reasonable in all the circumstances,[95] including the social status of the deceased[96] and the size of the estate.[97]

14. Costs of Administration

12.260 Costs of administration up to $500 are allowed in Prince Edward Island where the defendant is responsible for the death.[98]

94 See 6.430, *supra*.

95 *Hart v. Griffiths-Jones*, [1948] 2 All E.R. 729 (K.B.) (embalming allowed; monument disallowed); *Anthony v. Fleming* (1962), 37 D.L.R. (2d) 93 (Nfld. S.C.) (grave marker allowed); *Weidl v. Karesa* (1956), 6 D.L.R. (2d) 183 (Man. Q.B.) (gravedigging cost and burial plot allowed). See also 6.240, *supra*.

96 *Dowhy v. Lamontagne*, [1945] 2 D.L.R. 515 (Man. K.B.); *Crown Trust Co. (Cook Estate) v. Snowden* (1960), 31 W.W.R. 238 (Man. Q.B.).

97 *Crown Trust Co., supra*.

98 *Survival of Actions Act* (P.E.I.), s. 6(b).

PART III

LIMITING PRINCIPLES

CHAPTER 13

CERTAINTY

1. Proof of Loss

13.10 The general burden of proof lies upon the plaintiff to establish the case and to prove the loss for which compensation is claimed.[1] In many cases the loss claimed by the plaintiff depends on uncertainties; these are of two kinds: first, imperfect knowledge of facts that could theoretically be known and secondly, the uncertainty of attempting to estimate the position the plaintiff would have occupied in hypothetical circumstances, that is to say, supposing that the wrong complained of had not been done.[2]

13.20 American law has had considerable difficulty with this second type of uncertainty. The courts have used the requirement of certainty to inhibit or set aside what they consider to be excessive jury awards, with rigorous standards laid down in many cases. The consequence is that, where recovery is thought to be justified, the courts must strive to reconcile the results desired with prior restrictive holdings.[3]

[1] See *British Columbia v. Canadian Forest Products Ltd.*, [2004] 2 S.C.R. 74, 240 D.L.R. (4th) 1; *Reliable Leather Sportwear Ltd. v. Industrial Tanning Co. Ltd.*, [1955] 2 D.L.R. 284 (S.C.C.); *Bessette v. Sheehan* (1968), 2 D.L.R. (3d) 479 (B.C.C.A.); *Cotter v. General Petroleums Ltd.*, [1951] S.C.R. 154, [1950] 4 D.L.R. 609; *100 Main Street Ltd. v. W.B. Sullivan Ltd.* (1978), 88 D.L.R. (3d) 1, 20 O.R. (2d) 401 (C.A.); *Crayden's Pharmacy Ltd. v. Standard Paving Co.* (1973), 37 D.L.R. (3d) 167, [1973] 3 O.R. 435 (C.A.); *Bonham-Carter v. Hyde Park Hotel Ltd.* (1948) 64 T.L.R. 177 (K.B.), at p. 178, *per* Lord Goddard C.J.; *General Tyre & Rubber Co. v. Firestone Tyre & Rubber Co. Ltd.*, [1975] 1 W.L.R. 819 (H.L.), at p. 824, *per* Lord Wilberforce; *Mah Ming Yu v. Terminal Cartage Ltd.*, [1943] 2 D.L.R. 208 (B.C.C.A.); *Potts v. Miller* (1940), 64 C.L.R. 282 (Aust. H.C.), at p. 299, *per* Dixon J.; *Everatt v. Elgin Electric Ltd.* (1973), 38 D.L.R. (3d) 37, [1973] 3 O.R. 691 (H.C.J.); *Godfrey v. Good Rich Refining Co.*, [1940] 2 D.L.R. 164, [1940] O.R. 190 (C.A.); *Burthwick v. Lucas*, [1940] 4 D.L.R. 288 (Sask. C.A.); *Lastowski v. Zazula* (1954), 12 W.W.R. (N.S.) 53 (Sask. C.A.); *Gass v. Childs* (1959), 43 M.P.R. 87 (N.B.S.C. App. Div.); *Williams v. Stephenson* (1903), 33 S.C.R. 323; *Lengert v. Gladstone* (1970), 11 D.L.R. (3d) 726 (B.C.C.A.); *Municipal Spraying & Contracting Ltd. v. J. Harris & Sons Ltd.* (1979), 35 N.S.R. (2d) 237 (S.C.); *Merger Restaurants v. Lakeview Development of Canada Ltd.* (1991), 86 D.L.R. (4th) 379, [1992] 1 W.W.R. 667 (Man. C.A.), leave to appeal to S.C.C. refused 139 N.R. 400*n*, 78 Man. R. (2d) 239*n*; *Marynowsky v. Stuartburn (District)*, [1994] 10 W.W.R. 602, 97 Man. R. (2d) 60 (C.A.); *Dlot v. Choi*, [1996] 3 W.W.R. 533, 107 Man. R. (2d) 242 (C.A.); *Lowe v. Larue*, [2000] 4 W.W.R. 197 (Alta. C.A.); *Satara Farms Inc. v. Parrish & Heimbecker, Ltd.* (2006), 280 Sask. R. 44 (Q.B.), at para. 51, citing this paragraph; *2703203 Manitoba Inc. v. Parks* (2007), 280 D.L.R. (4th) 653 (N.S.C.A.), at para. 85, citing this passage.

[2] The distinction was made by Lord Diplock in *Mallett v. McMonagle*, [1970] A.C. 166 (H.L.). See passage cited at 13.330, *infra*.

[3] See McCormick, *Handbook on the Law of Damages* (St. Paul, West Publishing Co., 1935), pp. 97-126.

13.30 In Anglo-Canadian law, on the other hand, perhaps because of the decline in the use of the jury, the courts have consistently held that if the plaintiff establishes that a loss has probably been suffered, the difficulty of determining the amount of it can never excuse the wrongdoer from paying damages.[4] If the amount is difficult to estimate, the tribunal must simply do its best on the material available, though of course if the plaintiff has not adduced evidence that might have been expected to be adduced if the claim were sound, the omission will tell against the plaintiff.[4a] In *Ratcliffe v. Evans*,[5] Bowen L.J. said:

> As much certainty and particularity must be insisted on, both in pleading and proof of damage, as is reasonable, having regard to the circumstances and to the nature of the acts themselves by which the damage is done. To insist upon less would be to relax old and intelligible principles. To insist upon more would be the vainest pedantry.[6]

[4] *Haack v. Martin*, [1927] S.C.R. 413, [1927] 3 D.L.R. 19; *Sperry Rand Canada Ltd. v. Thomas Equipment Ltd.* (1982), 135 D.L.R. (3d) 197 (N.B.C.A.); *Wilson v. Rowswell*, [1970] S.C.R. 865 at p. 872, 11 D.L.R. (3d) 737 at p. 743, *per* Spence J.; *Chaplin v. Hicks*, [1911] 2 K.B. 786 (C.A.), at p. 792, *per* Vaughan Williams L.J.; *Biggin v. Permanite*, [1951] 1 K.B. 422 at p. 438, revd on other grounds [1951] 2 K.B. 314 (C.A.); *Talbot v. General Television Corp. Pty. Ltd.*, [1980] V.R. 224 (S.C.); *B.C. Lightweight Aggregate Ltd. v. Canada Cement Lafarge Ltd.* (1978), 93 D.L.R. (3d) 758 (B.C.S.C.); *Canadian Pacific Ltd. v. McCain Produce Co. Ltd.* (1980), 113 D.L.R. (3d) 584 (N.B.C.A.), affd [1981] 2 S.C.R. 219, 123 D.L.R. (3d) 764*n*; *Carson v. Willitts*, [1930] 4 D.L.R. 977 (Ont. S.C. App. Div.); *Kranz v. McCutcheon* (1920), 18 O.W.N. 395 (H.C.), affd 19 O.W.N. 161 (S.C. App. Div.); *Snell v. Miettienen*, [1931] 2 W.W.R. 209 (Sask. C.A.); *Frigidaire Corp. v. Steedman*, [1934] O.W.N. 139 (C.A.); *Messer v. J. Clark & Son Ltd.* (1961), 27 D.L.R. (2d) 766 (N.B.C.A.); *Toronto Transit Com'n v. Aqua Taxi Ltd.* (1956), 6 D.L.R. (2d) 721, [1957] O.W.N. 65 (H.C.J.); *City of Edmonton v. Hawrelak* (1972), 31 D.L.R. (3d) 498 (Alta. S.C. App. Div.), revd on other grounds [1976] 1 S.C.R. 387, 54 D.L.R. (3d) 45; *Whitehead v. R.B. Cameron Ltd.* (1967), 63 D.L.R. (2d) 180 (N.S.S.C. App. Div.); *Howe v. Teefy* (1927), 27 S.R. (N.S.W.) 301 (S.C.), at p. 306; *Capital Trust Corp. Ltd. v. Wilson*, [1937] 3 D.L.R. 178 at pp. 194-5, [1937] O.R. 769 (C.A.); *Cloverlawn Investments Ltd. v. MacPherson* (1975), 58 D.L.R. (3d) 212 (B.C.S.C.); *Henuset Bros. Ltd. v. Pancanadian Petroleum Ltd.* (1977), 82 D.L.R. (3d) 345 (Alta. S.C.T.D.); *McKinnon v. Acadian Lines Ltd.* (1977), 81 D.L.R. (3d) 480 (N.S.S.C. App. Div.); *Falkjar v. Buck* (1981), 36 N.B.R. (2d) 193 (C.A.); *Houweling Nurseries Ltd. v. Fisons Western Corp.* (1988), 49 D.L.R. (4th) 205, 37 B.C.L.R. (2d) 2 (C.A.), leave to appeal to S.C.C. refused 89 N.R. 398*n*; *Grosvenor Fine Furniture (1982) Ltd. v. Terrie's Plumbing & Heating Ltd.*, [1994] 1 W.W.R. 275, 113 Sask. R. 105 (C.A.), leave to appeal to S.C.C. refused 168 N.R. 400*n*; *Ticketnet Corp. v. Air Canada* (1997), 154 D.L.R. (4th) 271, 105 O.A.C. 87 (C.A.), leave to appeal to S.C.C. refused 161 D.L.R. (4th) vii; *Webster v. Ernst & Young* (2000), 184 D.L.R. (4th) 619 (B.C.C.A.), leave to appeal to S.C.C. refused 191 D.L.R. (4th) vi, second appeal (2003), 222 D.L.R. (4th) 193; *Decoste Manufacturing Ltd. v. A & B Roofing Ltd.* (2004), 223 N.S.R. (2d) 5 (S.C.), at pp. 36-7, citing this passage; *RBC Dominion Securities Inc. v. Merrill Lynch Canada Inc.* (2004), 36 B.C.L.R. (4th) 138 (S.C.), at p. 144, citing this passage, vard 275 D.L.R. (4th) 385 (B.C.C.A.); *G. (B.M.) v. Nova Scotia (Attorney General)* (2007), 288 D.L.R. (4th) 88 (C.A.), at para. 172, citing this passage.

[4a] *Acanthus Resources Ltd. v. Cunningham*, [1998] 5 W.W.R. 646 at p. 655, 213 A.R. 375 (Q.B.), citing this passage; *Martin v. Goldfarb* (1998), 163 D.L.R. (4th) 639 (Ont. C.A.); *Campeau v. Imperial Life Assurance Co. of Canada* (2005), 201 Man. R. (2d) 119 (C.A.); *0712914 B.C. Ltd. v. Aviva Insurance Co. of Canada* (2007), 69 B.C.L.R. (4th) 343 (S.C.), at para. 38, citing this passage (but losses must be credible).

[5] [1892] 2 Q.B. 524 (C.A.).

[6] *Supra*, at pp. 532-3.

In *Wood v. Grand Valley R. Co.*,[7] Davies J. said, referring to the English case of *Chaplin v. Hicks*:[8]

> It was clearly impossible under the facts of that case to estimate with anything approaching to mathematical accuracy the damages sustained by the plaintiffs, but it seems to me to be clearly laid down there by the learned Judges that such an impossibility cannot "relieve the wrongdoer of the necessity of paying damages for his breach of contract" and that on the other hand the tribunal to estimate them whether jury or Judge must under such circumstances do "the best it can" and its conclusion will not be set aside even if "the amount of the verdict is a matter of guess work".[9]

Although the majority of the court agreed to set aside the assessment of damages at trial in that case, this was, it seems, on the ground that the plaintiff had failed to put the trial court "in possession of information in his power". Anglin J. said: "The assessing tribunal is ... entitled to such assistance by proof of material relevant facts as the claimant may under the circumstances reasonably be expected to afford it."[10]

13.40 The case therefore stands for the same proposition as the passage cited from *Ratcliffe v. Evans*. The claimant must do as much by way of proof as can reasonably be expected in the circumstances but need not do more. Evidence of accountants, while admissible, and useful in many cases, cannot be conclusive. Assessment of damages is a task for the court not for accountants.[11]

13.50 In *Penvidic Contracting Co. v. International Nickel Co. of Canada*,[12] the Supreme Court of Canada held that a building contractor, having proved that the owner had wrongfully failed to facilitate its work, was entitled to damages based on an estimate of what it would reasonably have charged to perform the work knowing in advance of the adverse conditions. The Ontario Court of Appeal, which had disallowed an award so calculated, was reversed. The passage quoted previously from Davies J.'s judgment in *Wood v. Grand Valley R. Co.* was cited with approval, and the phrase "the amount of the verdict is a matter of guess-work"[13] was emphasized.

13.60 In personal injury cases, the cost of future care and future lost earnings are

---

7 (1915), 51 S.C.R. 283, 22 D.L.R. 614.

8 *Supra*, footnote 4.

9 *Supra*, footnote 7, at p. 289 S.C.R., p. 618 D.L.R. See *A.I.M. Steel Ltd. v. Gulf of Georgia Towing Co. Ltd.* (1964), 48 D.L.R. (2d) 549 (B.C.S.C.); *Millott Estate v. Reinhard*, [2002] 2 W.W.R. 678 (Alta. Q.B.), at pp. 748-9, citing this para.

10 *Supra*, footnote 7, at p. 301 S.C.R., p. 622 D.L.R. See also *Everatt v. Elgin Electric Ltd.*, *supra*, footnote 1; *Michelin Tires (Canada) Ltd. v. Bougeois* (1980), 32 N.B.R. (2d) 421 (Q.B.) (plaintiff must produce evidence available to it); *Martin v. Goldfarb* (1998), 163 D.L.R. (4th) 639 (Ont. C.A.), leave to appeal to S.C.C. refused 167 D.L.R. (4th) vii; *Ray Teese Pty. Ltd. v. Syntex Australia Ltd.*, [1998] 1 Qd. R. 104 (C.A.).

11 *Houweling Nurseries Ltd. v. Fisons Western Corp.* (1988), 49 D.L.R. (4th) 205 at p. 207, 37 B.C.L.R. (2d) 2 at p. 5 (C.A.), leave to appeal to S.C.C. refused 89 N.R. 398*n*.

12 [1976] 1 S.C.R. 267, 53 D.L.R. (3d) 748.

13 *Supra*, at p. 280 S.C.R., p. 757 D.L.R. See also *Toronto Hockey Club Ltd. v. Arena Gardens of Toronto Ltd.*, [1926] 4 D.L.R. 1 (P.C.); *Tai Hing Cotton Mill Ltd. v. Kamsing Knitting Factory*, [1979] A.C. 91 (P.C.).

always, by their nature, uncertain, especially in the case of young children. But this uncertainty does not inhibit the courts from awarding damages in respect of such claims.[14]

2. Onus of Proof

13.70 In *100 Main Street East Ltd. v. W.B. Sullivan Construction Ltd.*, the Ontario Court of Appeal said: "The basic principle is that the onus is on the plaintiff to prove its damages on a reasonable preponderance of credible evidence."[15] However, the practical effect of this burden is eased in several ways. The effect of placing the burden on one party or the other is not always what it seems at first sight. For example, to say that the onus of proof of damage rests on the plaintiff but that when the wrong is proved, it will be assumed that the plaintiff suffers some damage, amounts to much the same thing as saying that the onus, as to damage so assumed, rests on the defendant.

13.80 In several kinds of cases damages are said to be "at large", by which is meant that it will be presumed in the plaintiff's favour that there is a loss even though precise proof is lacking. Thus, in defamation cases, the plaintiff is commonly unable to prove loss of a single penny by reason of the defendant's wrong, but large awards of damages are common.[16] In *Ratcliffe v. Evans*,[17] a case of trade libel, the English Court of Appeal held that a verdict for £120 could be upheld even though there was no proof of particular losses. Bowen L.J. said:

> By the very fact that he has committed such a wrong, the defendant is prepared for the proof that some general damage may have been done ... If, indeed, over and above this general damage, further particular damage is under the circumstances to be relied on by the plaintiff, such particular damage must of course be alleged and shewn. But a loss of general custom, flowing directly and in the ordinary course of things from a libel, may be alleged and proved generally.[18]

Bowen L.J. in this formulation deliberately avoided the use of the term "special damages" which, as he pointed out, is used in several quite different ways and tends "to encourage confusion in thought".[19] He added:

> This case shews, what sound judgment itself dictates, that in an action for

---

14 See 3.710, *supra*.

15 (1978), 88 D.L.R. (3d) 1 at p. 22, 20 O.R. (2d) 401 (C.A.).

16 See 4.50-4.140, *supra*.

17 [1892] 2 Q.B. 524 (C.A.).

18 *Supra*, at p. 529. See also *Exchange Telegraph Co. v. Gregory*, [1896] 1 Q.B. 147 (C.A.); *Pratt v. British Medical Ass'n*, [1919] 1 K.B. 244; *Toronto Type Foundry Co. v. Publishers News Service, Ltd.*, [1920] 3 W.W.R. 339 (Sask. K.B.); *Western Canada Directories Ltd. v. Midwest Litho Ltd.* (1973), 37 D.L.R. (3d) 139 (Sask. C.A.); *Reliable Toy Co. Ltd. v. Collins*, [1950] 4 D.L.R. 499 at pp. 522-3, [1950] O.R. 360 (H.C.J.) (disclosure of trade secrets); *Vale v. International Longshoremen's & Warehousemen's Union Local 508*, [1979] 5 W.W.R. 231 (B.C.C.A.); *Alltrans Express Ltd. v. General Truck Drivers & Helpers Local Union No. 213*, [1982] 2 W.W.R. 533 (B.C.S.C.).

19 *Supra*, footnote 17, at p. 529.

falsehood producing damage to a man's trade, which in its very nature is intended or reasonably likely to produce, and which in the ordinary course of things does produce, a general loss of business, as distinct from the loss of this or that known customer, evidence of such general decline of business is admissible . . . To refuse . . . to admit such general evidence would be to misunderstand and warp the meaning of old expressions; to depart from, and not to follow, old rules; and, in addition to all this, would involve an absolute denial of justice and of redress for the very mischief which was intended to be committed.[20]

[*The next page is* 13-5]

[20] *Supra*, at pp. 533-4.

13.90 A similar presumption of damage is made in the case, analogous to trade libel, of failure by a banker to honour a customer's cheque. In *Wilson v. United Counties Bank*,[21] Lord Birkenhead said: "the refusal to meet the cheque ... is so obviously injurious to the credit of a trader that the latter can recover, without allegation of special damage, reasonable compensation for the injury done to his credit".[22]

13.100 Another way in which the burden upon the plaintiff is alleviated is by holding that, when a question of mitigation is in issue, it is for the defendant to prove that the plaintiff could have avoided the loss claimed. In *Red Deer College v. Michaels*,[23] the Supreme Court of Canada said, in a wrongful dismissal case:

> If it is the defendant's position that the plaintiff could reasonably have avoided some part of the loss claimed, it is for the defendant to carry the burden of that issue, subject to the defendant being content to allow the matter to be disposed of on the trial Judge's assessment of the plaintiff's evidence on avoidance consequences.[24]

13.110 It may thus become important to determine whether a legal rule does or does not rest on the principle of mitigation.[24a] A seller is entitled to recover the difference between the contract price and the market price, and this rule is often explained by saying that the seller must mitigate the loss by selling the goods on the market. But the onus of proof may vary according to whether or not the rule rests on mitigation. The question arose in *100 Main Street Ltd. v. W.B. Sullivan Construction Ltd.*,[25] an action for damages by a vendor of land. After the purchaser's default the vendor retained the land, which had declined sharply in value by the time of the trial. The trial judge had allowed the plaintiff to recover damages based on the full price, assuming in effect that the plaintiff's interest in the land was nil. The Ontario Court of Appeal held that this was wrong, because it was for the plaintiff to show that there was a difference between contract and market price at the time of the default, and it was not just for the defendant to have to pay the full price in the absence of showing what actual value the land had. Morden J.A. said:

---

21 [1920] A.C. 102 (H.L.).

22 *Supra*, at p. 112.

23 [1976] 2 S.C.R. 324, 57 D.L.R. (3d) 386; *Geest plc. v. Lansiquot*, [2002] 1 W.L.R. 311 (P.C.).

24 *Supra*, at p. 331 S.C.R., pp. 390-1 D.L.R. See also *Keneric Tractor Sales Ltd. v. Langille*, [1987] 2 S.C.R. 440, 43 D.L.R. (4th) 171 at p. 183; *Janiak v. Ippolito*, [1985] 1 S.C.R. 146, 16 D.L.R. (4th) 1 at p. 14; *Panarctic Oils v. Menasco Manufacturing Co.* (1983), 41 A.R. 451 (C.A.), at p. 471; *Western Canada Directories Ltd. v. Midwest Litho Ltd., supra*, footnote 18, at p. 141; *Petersen v. Bannon* (1993), 107 D.L.R. (4th) 616, 84 B.C.L.R. (2d) 350 (C.A.), leave to appeal to S.C.C. refused 112 D.L.R. (4th) viii, 176 N.R. 320*n* (defendant must plead mitigation); *Medlin v. State Government Insurance Commission* (1995), 182 C.L.R. 1 (Aust. H.C.); *Byron v. Larson*, [2005] 3 W.W.R. 337 (Alta. C.A.).

24a See *Lowe v. Jenkinson* (1994), 94 B.C.L.R. (2d) 147, 72 W.A.C. 203 (S.C.); *Dillon v. LeRoux*, [1994] 6 W.W.R. 280, 89 B.C.L.R. (2d) 376 (C.A.) (plaintiff must prove loss of earning capacity in personal injury case).

25 (1978), 88 D.L.R. (3d) 1, 20 O.R. (2d) 401 (C.A.).

> The basic principle is that the onus is on the plaintiff to prove its damages on a reasonable preponderance of credible evidence. Its damages are that sum of money which would put it in the same position as if the defendant had performed. The well-established method for determining this is to give the difference between the contract price and the market value. It is basic that the plaintiff cannot have the contract price and the land. Thus, I do not think that the plaintiff has proven its case by merely proving the contract price and then the defendant's breach, in the expectation that he will recover the full price unless the defendant proves that "the property could be sold to someone else without loss to the plaintiff" . . .
>
> As I have said, with respect to the issue of mitigation, the onus is on the defendant. However, the onus on the defendant to prove failure to mitigate does not relieve the plaintiff from proving an obvious element in the calculation of his damages. *McGregor on Damages* . . . puts the matter this way:
>
> > "The onus of proof on the issue of mitigation is on the defendant. If he fails to show that the plaintiff ought reasonably to have taken certain mitigating steps, then the normal measure will apply."
>
> Included in the "normal measure" is the difference between the contract price and the market price. Thus, I think that the proper course is for the plaintiff, in presenting its case, to adduce evidence of the contract price and of the market price or resale price upon which he relies in establishing the loss of bargain. The onus is then on the defendant to show, if he can, that if the plaintiff had taken certain reasonable mitigating steps the damages would be lower.[26]

13.120 A somewhat similar question arises where a seller, on the buyer's default, although reselling the particular goods at the contract price, claims the profits lost on one transaction.[27] If the defendant's argument is characterized as one based on mitigation, that is, that the seller has mitigated the loss by reselling, it might seem that the buyer would bear the onus of proving that the seller had fully mitigated the loss. But this would require the buyer to prove that the seller had inadequate stocks of identical goods to supply both customers and as the critical facts in such a dispute are peculiarly within the knowledge of the seller, it would seem that the seller could reasonably be expected to adduce the necessary evidence.[28] Alternatively, it might be said that, though the defendant bears the onus of proving mitigation, the onus is discharged by showing that the plaintiff

[*The next page is* 13-7]

26 *Supra*, at pp. 22-3 D.L.R. Against this is *Pankhurst v. Gairdner & Co. Ltd.* (1960), 25 D.L.R. (2d) 515 (Alta. S.C. App. Div.).

27 See 5.1380-15.1390, *supra*.

28 See *General Accident, Fire & Life Assurance Corp. v. Robertson*, [1909] A.C. 404 (H.L.), at p. 413.

has sold the goods at the contract price unless the plaintiff can show that, after all, there is a loss of profit. Where the *Sale of Goods Act* applies, it seems that the onus will be on the plaintiff to establish a loss of profits for, by what is said to be the *prima facie* measure of damages, the plaintiff will have suffered no loss.[29] The same conclusion seems desirable in cases such as sales of shares or rental of equipment or apartments where the Act does not apply.[30]

13.130 Conflicting statements have been made on the onus of proof of remoteness. If remoteness is regarded as akin to a question of factual causation, the tendency will be to place the onus on the plaintiff. Thus in *The "Paludina"*[31] Bankes L.J. said: "It seems to me that the plaintiff must always show, in a case in which he complains of damage resulting from negligence, that the negligence was the direct cause of the damage."[32] In the House of Lords, Lord Sumner said: "in order to succeed as to the fourth collision . . . the plaintiffs must prove that the *Paludina*'s negligence was the cause of it. The injury must have been caused directly, though not necessarily solely, by that negligence. If the *Paludina* merely created the occasion upon which this injury was inflicted, they fail."[33]

13.140 On the other hand if, as is common in modern discussions, a sharp distinction is drawn between factual causation and remoteness,[34] the tendency will be, while requiring the plaintiff to establish causation in fact, to see remoteness as a special excuse and consequently to require the defendant to establish it. In *The "Metagama"*[35] the House of Lords clearly took this approach. Viscount Haldane said:

> When a collision takes place by the fault of the defending ship in an action for damages the damage is recoverable if it is the natural and reasonable result of the negligent act, and it will assume this character if it can be shown to be such a consequence as in the ordinary course of things would flow from the situation which the offending ship had created. Further, what those in charge of the injured ship do to save it may be mistaken, but if they do whatever they do reasonably, although unsuccessfully, their mistaken judgment may be a natural consequence for which the offending ship is responsible, just as much as is any physical occurrence. Reasonable human conduct is part of the ordinary course of things, which extends to the reasonable conduct of those who have sustained the damage and who are seeking to save further loss . . . It follows that the burden lies on the negligent ship to show by clear evidence that the subsequent damage arose from negligence or great want of skill on the part of those on board the vessel damaged.[36]

---

29 *E.g.*, *Sale of Goods Act* (Ont.), s. 48(3).
30 See 5.1380, *supra*.
31 [1925] P. 40 (C.A.).
32 *Supra*, at p. 43.
33 [1927] A.C. 16 (H.L.), at pp. 25-6.
34 See 13.80-13.100, *infra*.
35 (1927), 29 Ll. L.R. 253.
36 *Supra*, at pp. 253-4.

13.150 In the Canadian case of *Dominion Natural Gas Co., Ltd. v. Collins*,[37] the Privy Council held that where the plaintiff had established the defendant's negligence (without which, on the facts, the damage complained of could not have occurred), it was for the defendants to show that "the true cause of the accident" was the act of a third party. In *Philco Radio Ltd. v. J. Spurling, Ltd.*,[38] dangerously inflammable material had been delivered by the defendant's negligence. It was held by the English Court of Appeal that the onus was on the defendant to show that the damage suffered by the plaintiff was caused by an intervening act.

13.160 It is submitted that these latter cases represent the sounder view; it is not unjust to hold the defendant liable for the damage the wrong in fact causes, with an excuse only if the application of the principle of remoteness is established. The *Philco Radio* case was one in which there were unknown facts: it was uncertain whether or not an employee of the plaintiff had deliberately set fire to the material. Where facts are unknown, the onus of proof is often important. But the same result could have been reached by resort to the more general rule of evidence that the onus of proving a fact lies on the party who asserts it.[39] Where, as is usual in remoteness cases, no question of fact is an issue, it may be doubted whether the allocation of the onus of proof is significant. Disputed questions of law cannot be resolved by resort to a rule designed to deal with uncertain facts.

3. Presumptions Operating against the Wrongdoer

13.170 Where a wrongdoer refuses to reveal facts within the wrongdoer's knowledge, the court will presume against the wrongdoer that the facts are adverse. In the old case of *Armory v. Delamirie*,[40] the defendant had wrongfully removed a jewel from its socket, returning only the empty socket to the plaintiff. Pratt C.J. directed the jury that: "unless the defendant did produce the jewel, and shew it not to be of the finest water, they should presume the strongest against him, and make the value of the best jewels the measure of their damages."[41]

13.180 The principle of *Armory v. Delamirie* has been invoked in cases where the defendant's wrongful conduct prevents anyone from knowing a

37 [1909] A.C. 640 (P.C.). See also *Papp v. Leclerc* (1977), 77 D.L.R. (3d) 536, 16 O.R. (2d) 158 (C.A.).

38 [1949] 2 All E.R. 882 (C.A.).

39 See, *e.g.*, *Robins v. National Trust Co.*, [1927] A.C. 515 at p. 520, [1927] 2 D.L.R. 97 at pp. 100-1 (P.C.).

40 (1722), 1 Strange 505, 93 E.R. 664, followed in *Mortimer v. Cradock* (1843), 12 L.J.C.P. 166; *Hammersmith & City Ry. Co. v. Brand* (1869), L.R. 4 H.L. 171 at p. 224; *Brandon Electric Light Co. v. City of Brandon* (1912), 1 D.L.R. 793 (Man. K.B.); *Lamb v. Kincaird* (1907), 38 S.C.R. 516; *Grenn v. Brampton Poultry Co.* (1958), 13 D.L.R. (2d) 279 (Ont. H.C.J.), vard 18 D.L.R. (2d) 9 (C.A.); *Calmont Leasing Ltd. v. Kredl*, [1993] 7 W.W.R. 428, 11 Alta. L.R. (3d) 232 (Q.B.), affd [1995] 8 W.W.R. 179, 165 A.R. 343 (C.A.); *Karteri v. Sugarman* (1999), 22 R.P.R. (3d) 38 (Ont. Ct. (Gen. Div.)).

41 *Armory v. Delamirie*, *supra*, footnote 40, at p. 505.

relevant fact. In *McGee v. Rosetown Electric Light & Power Co.*[42] the plaintiff, a well driller, was to drill to a maximum depth of 500 feet with payment at the rate of $2.50 per foot if water were found at or before that depth, and payment at $1.00 per foot if no water were found. The defendant wrongfully prevented the plaintiff from drilling. Brown J. pointed out that it was the defendant's fault that the evidence was not available to make the necessary calculation of what the plaintiff would have earned: "The defendants, by their action in refusing to carry out the contract, have placed the plaintiff in the position where he is deprived of the privilege of making the test."[43] He went on to hold that the most favourable possibility from the plaintiff's point of view should be assumed, that is, finding water at exactly 500 feet:

> As it was quite possible within the contemplation of the parties that the plaintiff would have sunk the well 500 feet, and at that depth secured the necessary flow of water, and as that is the possibility most favourable from the plaintiff's point of view, I am of opinion that damages should be assessed on that basis.[44]

13.190 In an earlier chapter, the problem was discussed of compensation for the loss of an opportunity to bargain.[45] The problem arises where the defendant, instead of bargaining with the plaintiff to purchase some interest in property belonging to the latter, simply takes it, but causes no diminution in market

42 [1918] 1 W.W.R. 552 (Sask. S.C.).

43 *Supra*, at p. 555.

44 *Supra*, at p. 556. See also *Rainbow Industrial Caterers Ltd. v. Canadian National Railway Co.*, [1991] 3 S.C.R. 3 at pp. 15-16, 84 D.L.R. (4th) 291; *Boon v. Bell*, [1932] 2 W.W.R. 304 (Sask. C.A.), at p. 311 (plaintiff entitled to "every reasonable presumption"); *General Tyre & Rubber Co. v. Firestone Tyre & Rubber Co. Ltd.*, [1975] 1 W.L.R. 819 (H.L.), at p. 824, *per* Lord Wilberforce ("the defendants being wrongdoers, damages should be liberally assessed"); *Banque Provinciale du Canada v. Gagnon*, [1981] 2 S.C.R. 98, 131 D.L.R. (3d) 174; *Wilson v. Northampton & Banbury Junction Ry. Co.* (1874), L.R. 9 Ch. 279 at p. 285 ("established maxim . . . that every reasonable presumption may be made"), followed in *Mortgage & Agreement Purchasing Co. v. Townsend* (1920), 56 D.L.R. 637 (Man. C.A.); *Morse v. Mac & Mac Cedar Co.*, [1918] 2 W.W.R. 205 (B.C.S.C.); *Land v. Canada Permanent Toronto General Trust Co.* (1964), 47 D.L.R. (2d) 448 (B.C.S.C.); *McNeil v. Fultz* (1906), 38 S.C.R. 198 (presumption that shares would have been sold at best price obtainable); *City of London Board of Education v. East Middlesex District High School Board*, [1967] S.C.R. 49, 59 D.L.R. (2d) 213 (on proof that defendant removed school records, onus of adducing evidence that this caused no loss shifts to defendant); *Mackenzie v. Township of West Flamborough* (1899), 26 O.A.R. 198; *Townsend v. Canadian Northern Ry. Co.* (1922), 65 D.L.R. 85 (Alta. S.C. App. Div.); *Brown v. Town of Morden* (1958), 12 D.L.R. (2d) 576 (Man. Q.B.); *Kelley v. Canadian Northern Ry. Co.*, [1950] 2 D.L.R. 760 (B.C.C.A.); *Lee v. Rural Municipality of Arthur* (1964), 46 D.L.R. (2d) 448 (Man. Q.B.), revd on other grounds 52 D.L.R. (2d) 263 (C.A.); *Kohler v. Thorold Natural Gas Co.* (1916), 52 S.C.R. 514, 27 D.L.R. 319; *Last Chance Mining Co. Ltd. v. American Boy Mining Co. Ltd.* (1904), 2 M.M.C. 150 (B.C.S.C.); *Sturrock v. Ancona Petroleum Ltd.* (1991), 111 A.R. 86, 75 Alta. L.R. (2d) 216 (Q.B.); *Blue Moon Logging Ltd. v. Finning Ltd.*, [1995] 9 W.W.R. 85, 8 B.C.L.R. (3d) 293 (S.C.); *Webster v. Ernst & Young* (2000), 184 D.L.R. (4th) 619 (B.C.C.A.), leave to appeal to S.C.C. refused 191 D.L.R. (4th) vi, second appeal (2003), 222 D.L.R. (4th) 193; *Gauthier v. Canada (Attorney General)* (2000), 185 D.L.R. (4th) 660 (N.B.C.A.).

45 See 9.70-9.130, *supra*.

value to the plaintiff's property. It was earlier argued that the defendant can justly be required to pay by way of compensation the highest amount that the defendant would rationally have paid for the right to act as the defendant has acted. It is the defendant's wrong that prevents the tribunal from knowing what bargain would have been struck and, it is suggested, no injustice is done to the defendant if it is presumed that the defendant would have paid the highest amount for the right that a rational person would have paid — that is, the amount of the net advantage to the defendant of the wrongful action.

13.200 Another instance of easing the plaintiff's burden has been developed by Canadian courts in cases of the supply of defective goods. It has been held that where goods are supplied that are wholly unfit for their purpose, the buyer is entitled to recover the full purchase price, with the onus on the supplier to establish what value, if any, is possessed by the defective goods. In *Massey Harris Co. Ltd. v. Skelding*,[46] the Supreme Court of Canada held that a buyer of farm machinery, having lost the right to rescind the contract and return the goods, was *prima facie* entitled to recover the full price. Duff C.J.C. said:

> There is some evidence that the tractor, although useless for the purposes for which it was purchased, had some merchantable value and the appellants [suppliers] contend that it was incumbent upon the respondent [buyer] to establish that value in order to determine the amount of damages to which he was entitled.
>
> We cannot accept this view. Having regard to the nature of the warranties and the complete failure of the tractor in respect of the fulfilment of the warranties, which evidence, accepted by the learned trial Judge, discloses, we think, that, *prima facie*, the loss incurred by the respondent amounted to the full purchase-price; and that the burden rested on the appellants to show that the damages so measured should be reduced by reason of the possession of the tractor of some merchantable value.[47]

The case was followed in *Ford Motor Co. v. Haley*[48] and in *Evanchuk Transport Ltd. v. Canadian Trailmobile Ltd.*[49] In the latter case it was admitted that the goods had a residual value of $12,194.10, and the plaintiff's recovery was reduced accordingly.

13.210 Some of the terminology used in these cases is confusing. First, it should be emphasized that the action is not a restitutionary action for the return of the price; such an action would require the plaintiff to restore benefits received under the contract or at least to restore their value. These are cases where the buyer is expressly held to have lost the right

46 [1934] S.C.R. 431, [1934] 3 D.L.R. 193.

47 *Supra*, at pp. 435-6 S.C.R., p. 194 D.L.R.

48 [1967] S.C.R. 437, 62 D.L.R. (2d) 329.

49 (1971), 21 D.L.R. (3d) 246 (Alta. S.C. App. Div.); also in *Wojakowski v. Pembina Dodge Chrysler Ltd.*, [1976] 5 W.W.R. 97 (Man. Q.B.); *Belanger v. Fournier Chrysler Dodge (1975) Ltée* (1979), 25 N.B.R. (2d) 673 (S.C. App. Div.).

to rescind; the action therefore is not for the return of the price but for damages measured by the difference between the value of the goods in fact and the value they would have had if they had answered to the warranty. This latter figure might well exceed the purchase price. Evidently, however, in the cases considered here, the court has assumed, as is not uncommon in sale cases,[50] that the purchase price is equal to the value the goods would have had if they had answered to the warranty. Very often this assumption is fully justified. The second point is that the difference between the values is to be measured at the time of the breach, that is the time of delivery of the defective goods.[51] The "residual value", that is the value at the date of the hearing, must therefore be taken to be relevant in so far as it establishes the actual value of the goods at the date of delivery. With these qualifications, it is submitted that the decisions are sound. A business supplier of goods will usually have better access to evidence of values than the buyer. If the goods are of no use for their purpose, it is not unreasonable to call upon the supplier to demonstrate what use they are. However, the discharge of the onus should not be made so difficult as to be impracticable, for often, as in the *Evanchuk* case, goods that are held to be unfit for their purpose may still have a substantial value, and it would be penal to allow the buyer to recover the full amount of the price and to retain valuable goods.

13.220 A presumption in favour of an innocent party also operated in *Wilson v. Rowswell*[52] where the defendant solicitor had negligently failed to obtain proper security for a loan made by his client. The borrower defaulted and had insufficient assets to satisfy the plaintiff's claim, but the debt was secured by an assignment of the borrower's remainder interest in an estate. This was a most unsatisfactory security, being conditional on the borrower surviving the life tenant, subject to the life tenant's power to encroach, and subject to two or possibly three prior assignments. However, the defendant argued that future events might prove this security to be adequate and therefore that the plaintiffs could not prove any loss until after the death of the life tenant. This argument succeeded at trial, and the plaintiff recovered only nominal damages. This left the plaintiff in a most unsatisfactory position, waiting for an indefinite period for a security which might well eventually prove valueless, perhaps after the limitation period for action against the defendant had expired.[53] The Ontario Court of Appeal and the Supreme Court of Canada, reversing the trial judge, held that the plaintiff was entitled to recover the full amount of the unpaid debt. In the Ontario Court of Appeal, McGillivray J.A. said: "The plaintiff having shown the

50 See 1.2550, *supra.*

51 *Sale of Goods Act* (Ont.), s. 51(3); Alta., s. 52; B.C., s. 56; Man., s. 54; N.B., s. 50; Nfld. & Lab., s. 54; N.W.T., s. 60; N.S., s. 54; P.E.I., s. 53; Sask., s. 52; Yukon, s. 50. See 1.650-1.1100, 1.2490-1.2510, *supra.*

52 [1970] S.C.R. 865, 11 D.L.R. (3d) 737.

53 *Supra*, at pp. 871-2, 875 S.C.R., pp. 742, 745 D.L.R.

variation in the securities from those he was entitled to anticipate the onus fell upon the defendant to prove affirmatively that no loss resulted to the plaintiff thereby."[54] Spence J. said for the Supreme Court of Canada: "With respect, I . . . view as absurd the proposition that the respondent Rowswell had in this case to wait until the termination of the life interest before he could prove any damages due to the solicitor's negligence."[55] This decision placing the onus upon the defendant to show what present value the security has, seems fully justified in the circumstances. No injustice is done to the defendant, who, on satisfaction of the judgment should, it is suggested, be subrogated to the plaintiff's interest in the security, a result effected in *Wilson v. Rowswell* by the plaintiff's undertaking to assign the security. Thus, if the security should prove adequate after all, the defendant will be entitled eventually to recoup the amount of the judgment.

13.230 Another instance of a presumption in favour of the plaintiff arose in *Heywood v. Wellers*[56] where the defendant solicitors had failed to take proper proceedings to protect the plaintiff against molestation. The defendants argued that even if they had taken proper proceedings, protection might not have been effective, but this argument was rejected in the absence of proof by the defendants:

> It was suggested that even if the solicitors had done their duty and taken the man to court he might still have molested her. But I do not think they can excuse themselves on that ground. After all, it was not put to the test: and it was their fault that it was not put to the test. If they had taken him to court as she wished — and as they ought to have done — it might well have been effective to stop him from molesting her any more. We should assume that it would have been effective to protect her, unless they prove that it would not.[57]

In cases of misrepresentation followed by a losing transaction, it is presumed in the plaintiff's favour that the representation induced the transaction. The Supreme Court of Canada said in *Baker v. Guaranty Savings and Loan Assn.*: "Where . . . an untrue representation has been made, the onus of shewing that it was not relied on rests upon the party who made it."[57a] In other cases too it has been held that when it is the defendant's own wrong that prevents proof of whether the wrong has caused a loss, it will be presumed against the defendant, unless the defendant proves the contrary, that the wrong did cause the loss. In

54 (1968), 1 D.L.R. (3d) 268 at p. 269, [1969] 1 O.R. 22 (C.A.).

55 [1970] S.C.R. 865 at p. 876, 11 D.L.R. (3d) 737 at p. 745.

56 [1976] 1 Q.B. 446 (C.A.).

57 *Supra*, at p. 459.

57a [1931] S.C.R. 199 at p. 208, [1931] 1 D.L.R. 968 at p. 976, *per* Lamont J. See also *Redgrave v. Hurd* (1881), 20 Ch. D. 1 (C.A.); *Sidhu Estate v. Bains*, [1996] 10 W.W.R. 590, 25 B.C.L.R. (3d) 41 (C.A.), leave to appeal to S.C.C. refused 209 N.R. 80*n*, 145 W.A.C. 240*n*.

Coldman v. Hill,[58] Scrutton L.J. said, referring to an unreported House of Lords case:

> The House of Lords held that the man who had, by breaking his contract, destroyed the possibility of any evidence on the subject, could not be heard to say that there was no evidence that his breach of contract caused the loss. It was his duty as bailee to prove that his breach of duty did not cause the loss, not the plaintiff's duty to show that it did. This appears to be merely an application of the principle omnia praesumuntur contra spoliatorem, under which a man who, having converted property, refuses to produce it that its exact value may be known, is liable for the greatest value that such article could have.[59]

13.240 In *Scottish Co-operative Wholesale Society Ltd. v. Meyer*[60] where it was again argued that performance of the defendant's duty would have been useless, Lord Denning said: "The answer is that no one knows whether it would have done any good ... And it does not come well from their [the defendants'] mouths to say it would have done no good, when they never put it to the test."[61]

13.250 The maxim *omnia praesumuntur contra spoliatorem* (all is presumed against a despoiler or wrongdoer), referred to by Scrutton L.J. in *Coldman v. Hill*, is certainly too wide as a general rule (if *spoliatorem* is taken to mean any wrongdoer) for it would amount to reversing the onus of proof of damage in all cases.[61a] However, the examples collected in the preceding paragraphs, and elsewhere in this work,[62] indicate that in cases where the nature of the wrong itself makes it difficult for the plaintiff to establish a loss or where the critical facts are peculiarly within the defendant's knowledge, the maxim, or its equivalent, will be invoked for the plaintiff's benefit.[62a] Though the onus of proof may rest in theory upon the plaintiff, the approach in practice of many courts has been to be "very indulgent and always bear in mind who was to blame".[63]

13.255 In the important case of *Snell v. Farrell*,[63a] the Supreme Court of Canada held that an inference of causation should be drawn in favour of the plaintiff in a medical negligence case. Even though the medical witness declined to say that the defendant's negligence had probably caused the plaintiff's loss,

58 [1919] 1 K.B. 443 (C.A.).

59 *Supra*, at p. 458, referring to *Morison v. Walton*. The passage was cited with approval in *Grenn v. Brampton Poultry Co.* (1958), 13 D.L.R. (2d) 279 (Ont. H.C.J.), vard 18 D.L.R. (2d) 9 (C.A.).

60 [1959] A.C. 324 (H.L.).

61 *Supra*, at p. 367.

61a *Ticketnet Corp. v. Air Canada* (1997), 154 D.L.R. (4th) 271 at p. 298, 105 O.A.C. 87 (C.A.), leave to appeal to S.C.C. refused 161 D.L.R. (4th) vii, citing this passage.

62 See 1.2220, 1.2400, 2.40, 3.1160, 5.230, 5.300, 5.1020, 5.1030, 5.1170, 5.1190, 5.1460, 9.70-9.130, *supra*.

62a *Ticketnet Corp. v. Air Canada*, *supra*, footnote 61a, at p. 298, citing this passage.

63 *Lodge Holes Colliery Co. v. Wednesbury Corp.*, [1908] A.C. 323 (H.L.), at p. 325. See also *Huff v. Price* (1990), 76 D.L.R. (4th) 138 at p. 173, 51 B.C.L.R. (2d) 282 (C.A.).

63a [1990] 2 S.C.R. 311, 72 D.L.R. (4th) 289.

the court held that the trier of fact could and should, have drawn an inference in the plaintiff's favour by "the application of common sense".[63b]

4. Evaluation of Chances

13.260 Another means by which the burden on the plaintiff to establish the case is eased is by the award of damages for the loss of a chance.

13.270 Where the defendant's wrongful conduct deprives the plaintiff of a chance of profit that is fifty per cent or less, it might be thought that the plaintiff has failed on the balance of probabilities to prove any loss at all. As likely as not, it could be said, the plaintiff has suffered no loss at all by the defendant's wrong and so should be entitled only to nominal damages. This line of reasoning however fails to give weight to the common sense view that in some contexts at least, chances of fifty per cent or less do have a real value. Suppose that the plaintiff holds a lottery ticket that gives a ten per cent chance of winning a prize of $1,000 and the defendant in breach of a legal duty destroys the ticket so that the plaintiff is deprived of the opportunity of participating in the draw. More probably than not the plaintiff would not have won even if the defendant had fulfilled the duty, and yet it would be odd to conclude that the plaintiff has lost nothing by the defendant's wrong. If the plaintiff can recover no damages for the loss of a ten per cent chance, the same reasoning would seem to deprive the plaintiff of damages also in the case of the loss of a fifty per cent chance.

13.280 In *Chaplin v. Hicks*,[64] the plaintiff was one of the fifty persons shortlisted for twelve positions. The defendant, in breach of conduct, failed to give the plaintiff an opportunity of being interviewed, and the twelve positions were filled from the other forty-nine persons. The plaintiff had less than a twenty-five per cent chance of success, but the English Court of Appeal held that she was entitled to proportionate damages for the loss of the chance. The case has frequently been followed and cited with approval in Canada.[65]

13.290 The principle has been applied in a number of cases against solicitors for negligence. In several cases[66] damages have been given against solicitors for negligent advice, due allowance being made for the chance that the loss claimed would have occurred after careful advice. In *Sykes v. Midland Bank*,[67] however, a plaintiff was held entitled only to nominal damages for a solicitor's negligent advice, because the plaintiff failed to establish on the balance of probabilities that the loss claimed would have been avoided if the solicitor's advice had been accurate. It is suggested below that this case is difficult to reconcile with the general principle. In *Prior v. McNab*,[68] a case where a solicitor had failed to issue a writ in time against the possibly negligent third party, Reid J. held that the question to be asked in such a case was whether the plaintiff had "a right of value, a chose in action of reality and

---

63b *Supra*, at p. 336 S.C.R., p. 306 D.L.R., applied in *Joyal v. Starreveld*, [1996] 4 W.W.R. 707, 180 A.R. 141 (Q.B.). See also *Fairchild v. Glenhaven Funeral Services Ltd.*, [2002] 3 W.L.R. 89 (H.L.).

64 [1911] 2 K.B. 786 (C.A.).

substance".[69] This question could well be answered in the affirmative even though the plaintiff had only a fifty per cent chance or less of success in the action against the third party. A cause of action with a fifty per cent chance of success has a definite "settlement value" which disappears when the limitation period expires.

13.300 Other recent cases have affirmed that a plaintiff can be compensated for a substantial[69a] possibility of loss even if less than fifty per cent.[70] In *Multi-Malls Inc. v. Tex-Mall Properties Ltd.*,[71] damages were awarded for a breach of contract that prevented the rezoning of the plaintiff's property as a shopping mall. The court found that even if there had been no breach of contract the chances of rezoning were only twenty per cent. Accordingly, the plaintiff recovered twenty per cent of the loss claimed.

---

65 *Toronto Hockey Club v. Arena Gardens of Toronto Ltd.*, [1925] 4 D.L.R. 546, 57 O.L.R. 610 (S.C. App. Div.), affd [1926] 4 D.L.R. 1 (P.C.); *Kinkel v. Hyman*, [1939] S.C.R. 364, [1939] 3 D.L.R. 1 (cited with approval but distinguished); *Hornak v. Paterson* (1967), 62 D.L.R. (2d) 289 (B.C.S.C.); *Hawrysh v. St. John's Sportsmen's Club* (1964), 46 D.L.R. (2d) 45 (Man. Q.B.); *McWhirter v. Governors of University of Alberta* (1977), 80 D.L.R. (3d) 609 (Alta. S.C.T.D.), revd on other grounds 103 D.L.R. (3d) 255 (C.A.), leave to appeal to S.C.C. refused D.L.R. *loc. cit.*; *A.I.M. Steel Ltd. v. Gulf of Georgia Towing Co. Ltd.* (1964), 48 D.L.R. (2d) 549 (B.C.S.C.); *Prozak v. Bell Telephone Co. of Canada* (1982), 37 O.R. (2d) 761 (H.C.J.), vard 10 D.L.R. (4th) 382, 46 O.R. (2d) 385 (C.A.); *The King v. Dominion Building Corp.*, [1935] S.C.R. 338, [1935] 4 D.L.R. 18; *Johnson v. Roche* (1915), 24 D.L.R. 305 (N.S.S.C. App. Div.), revd on other grounds 53 S.C.R. 18, 29 D.L.R. 329; *Broderick v. Forbes* (1912), 5 D.L.R. 508 (N.S.S.C.); *Hearndon v. Rondeau* (1984), 54 B.C.L.R. 145, 29 C.C.L.T. 149 (C.A.) (loss of chance of care); *Butt v. USWA, Loc. 5795* (1993), 106 Nfld. & P.E.I.R. 181 (Nfld. S.C.); *Northeast Marine Services Ltd. v. Atlantic Pilotage Authority*, [1995] 2 F.C. 132 at p. 172, 179 N.R. 17 (C.A.), citing this paragraph; *St. Thomas Subdividers Ltd. v. 639373 Ontario Ltd.* (1996), 2 R.P.R. (3d) 133, 91 O.A.C. 193 (C.A.).

66 *Hall v. Meyrick*, [1957] 2 Q.B. 455 (C.A.); *Otter v. Church, Adams, Tatham & Co.*, [1953] Ch. 280; *Kitchen v. Royal Air Force Association*, [1958] 1 W.L.R. 563 (C.A.); *Yeoman's Executrix v. Ferries*, [1967] S.L.T. 332 (Ct. of Sess.); *Yardley v. Coombes* (1963), 107 Sol. Jo. 575 (Q.B.), approved in *Wilson v. Rowswell*, [1970] S.C.R. 865, 11 D.L.R. (3d) 737; *McMorran's Cordova Bay Ltd. v. Harman & Co.* (1979), 106 D.L.R. (3d) 495 (B.C.C.A.); *Graybriar Industries Ltd. v. Davis & Co.* (1992), 72 B.C.L.R. (2d) 190, 34 W.A.C. 77 (C.A.); *Henderson v. Hagblom*, [2003] 7 W.W.R. 590 (Sask. C.A.). In *Page v. Solicitor* (1971), 20 D.L.R. (3d) 532 (N.B.S.C. App. Div.), affd [1972] S.C.R. vi *sub nom.* Pelletier v. Page, 29 D.L.R. (3d) 386*n*, the court determined that, if the writ had been issued in time, the third party would have been liable, and the plaintiff recovered from the solicitor to the limit of the third party's liability insurance policy, that being the probable limit of recovery against the third party. See *Charles v. Hugh, James, Jones and Jenkins*, [2000] 1 W.L.R. 1278 (C.A.) (evidence arising after date of notional trial).

67 [1971] 1 Q.B. 113 (C.A.).

68 (1976), 78 D.L.R. (3d) 319, 16 O.R. (2d) 380 (H.C.J.).

69 *Supra*, at p. 322 D.L.R., p. 384 O.R.

69a *Eastwalsh Homes Ltd. v. Anatal Developments Ltd.* (1993), 100 D.L.R. (4th) 469, 12 O.R. (3d) 675 (C.A.), leave to appeal to S.C.C. refused 104 D.L.R. (4th) vii, 162 N.R. 399*n* ("substantial" possibility only to be compensated). See also *Meyer v. Bright; Dalgliesh v. Green; Lento v. Castaldo* (1993), 110 D.L.R. (4th) 354, 15 O.R. (3d) 129 (C.A.), leave to appeal to S.C.C. refused 110 D.L.R. (4th) vii, 172 N.R. 160*n*; *Cairns v. Harris* (1994), 117 Nfld. & P.E.I.R. 216 (P.E.I.C.A.); *Franklin v. Aviscar Inc.*, [1997] 3 W.W.R. 521, 27 B.C.L.R. (3d) 181 (C.A.); *Fasken Campbell Godfrey v. Seven-Up Canada Inc.* (2000), 182 D.L.R. (4th) 315 (Ont. C.A.), leave to appeal to S.C.C. refused 189 D.L.R. (4th) vii (onus of proof of value of chance on plaintiff).

13.310 Another aspect of the matter is that if the plaintiff has a sixty per cent chance of success that is lost by the defendant's wrongful conduct, the plaintiff would seem to be over-compensated on recovery of one hundred per cent of the loss. So, in the case of a missed limitation period where the plaintiff had a sixty per cent chance of success against the original defendant, it can be said that if the solicitor had issued the writ in time the action would probably have succeeded. But it would seem that the solicitor would be liable for only sixty per cent of the damages that would have been recovered in the event of success or else the plaintiff is in a better position after the solicitor's negligence than before.[72] The clearest example of the application of these principles is in cases of personal injury and fatal accidents. As to all unknowable facts, past or future, the plaintiff is entitled to an award, even if the probability of the loss is less than fifty per cent. On the other hand, the plaintiff is only entitled to recover a proportion of the loss, even if the probability of loss is greater than fifty per cent.[73]

13.320 It would seem appropriate to apply the same method to all claims in which the plaintiff would be entitled to compensation for loss of a chance of less than fifty per cent. If the plaintiff enjoys the benefit of proportionate recovery

---

70 *Schrump v. Koot* (1977), 82 D.L.R. (3d) 553, 18 O.R. (2d) 337 (C.A.); *Conklin v. Smith*, [1978] 2 S.C.R. 1107, 88 D.L.R. (3d) 317; *Kovats v. Ogilvie* (1970), 17 D.L.R. (3d) 343 (B.C.C.A.); *Jones v. Griffiths*, [1969] 2 All E.R. 1015 (C.A.); *Davies v. Taylor*, [1974] A.C. 207 (H.L.); *Hawkins v. New Mendip Engineering Ltd.*, [1966] 1 W.L.R. 1341 (C.A.); *Yorke v. Campbell*, [1965-69] 3 N.S.R. 765 (S.C. App. Div.); *Hearndon v. Rondeau, supra*, footnote 65; *Allied Maples Group Ltd. v. Simmons & Simmons*, [1995] 1 W.L.R. 1602 (C.A.); *Moyer v. Bosshart* (1994), 7 B.C.L.R. (3d) 201, 71 W.A.C. 161 (C.A.); *Young v. Fletcher* (1995), 161 N.B.R. (2d) 116, 12 M.V.R. (3d) 147 (C.A.); *Norris v. Blake (by his Tutor Porter) (No. 2)* (1997), 41 N.S.W.L.R. 49 (C.A.); *Smith v. Knudsen* (2004), 247 D.L.R. (4th) 256 (B.C.C.A.). In *Corrie v. Gilbert*, [1965] S.C.R. 457 at p. 461, 52 D.L.R. (2d) 1 at p. 4, Ritchie J. said that "such matters as remain in the sphere of possibility" were to be disregarded, but this was in the context of affirming the principle that a plaintiff's pre-existing susceptibility is to be disregarded. *Corrie v. Gilbert* was specifically held in *Schrump v. Koot* and in *Kovats v. Ogilvie, supra*, not to preclude recovery for a loss of which the probability was less than 50%. The same conclusion is reached by Cooper-Stephenson, *Personal Injury Damages in Canada*, 2nd ed. (Toronto, Carswell, 1996), pp. 69-70. Dicta appear in a number of earlier cases to the effect that only "probable" not "possible" future injuries can be compensated. These appear inconsistent with the weight of modern authority. See *Wallace v. Wilson* (1962), 38 W.W.R. 511 (B.C.S.C.); *Turenne v. Chung* (1962), 36 D.L.R. (2d) 197 (Man. C.A.); *Robar v. Weagle*, [1955] 2 D.L.R. 541 (N.S.S.C. in banco); *Smith v. Transcontinental Coach Lines Ltd.*, [1942] 1 D.L.R. 499 (Sask. K.B.).

71 (1980), 108 D.L.R. (3d) 399, 28 O.R. (2d) 6 (H.C.J.), affd 128 D.L.R. (3d) 192*n*, 37 O.R. (2d) 133*n* (C.A.), leave to appeal to S.C.C. refused 41 N.R. 360*n*. See also *BEM Enterprises Ltd. v. Campeau Corp.* (1981), 32 B.C.L.R. 116 (C.A.) (80% recovery).

72 See *Kitchen v. Royal Air Force Association, supra*, footnote 66. In *Prior v. McNab, supra*, footnote 68, recovery against the third party seems to have been treated as a certainty.

73 *Ziehlke v. Amisk Drilling Co.* (1993), 110 D.L.R. (4th) 172, [1994] 2 W.W.R. 107 (Man. C.A.). The theory of proportionate recovery has been called the theory of "simple probability". See Note, "Damages Contingent upon Chance", 18 Rutgers L. Rev. 874 (1964); Cooper, "Assessing Possibilities in Damage Awards – The Loss of a Chance or the Chance of a Loss", 37 Sask. L. Rev. 193 (1972-73). Judicial usage, however, is not uniform. See *Duncan Estate v. Baddeley* (1997), 145 D.L.R. (4th) 708 at pp. 717-18, 196 A.R. 161 (C.A.), leave to appeal to S.C.C. refused 151 D.L.R. (4th) vii, 168 W.A.C. 397*n*.

when the loss could not be shown on the balance of probabilities, the plaintiff should incur the disadvantage of proportionate recovery where the loss can be shown to be more probable than not but substantially less than certain.

13.330 This approach was clearly adopted by Lord Diplock in a fatal accident case, *Mallett v. McMonagle*:[74]

> The role of the court in making an assessment of damages which depends upon its view as to what will be and what would have been is to be contrasted with its ordinary function in civil actions of determining what was. In determining what did happen in the past a court decides on the balance of probabilities. Anything that is more probable than not it treats as certain. But in assessing damages which depend upon its view as to what will happen in the future or would have happened in the future if something had not happened in the past, the court must make an estimate as to what are the chances that a particular thing will or would have happened and reflect those chances, whether they are more or less than even, in the amount of damages which it awards.[75]

13.340 In *Hampton & Sons Ltd. v. George*,[76] the defendant wrongfully deprived a real estate agent of the opportunity of earning a commission. It was held that the agent was entitled not to the full commission but to the value of the chance of earning it. The commission would have been £104; du Parcq L.J. awarded £80 damages.

13.350 The cases of missed limitation periods show that it is the practical value, rather than the strictly legal value of the loss, that is assessed. A right of action may be held by a tribunal to have had a settlement value, even though the same tribunal, if it had had to try the action, would have dismissed it.[77] An analogous case arose in *L.B. Martin Construction Ltd. v. Gaglardi*[78] where an insurance agent had failed to procure insurance for the plaintiff. Had the insurance been procured, the policy would have contained a clause that, on its probably correct construction, would have excluded the insurer's liability. It was held, however, that in view of the doubt on the matter a reputable insurer would probably have settled for half the loss and, accordingly, the broker was held liable for that amount.

13.360 As Lord Diplock pointed out,[79] past facts must be proven on the balance of probabilities and when so proven, are treated as if they were certain. If the

---

74 [1970] A.C. 166 (H.L.).

75 *Supra*, at p. 176, approved in *Athey v. Leonati*, [1996] 3 S.C.R. 458, 140 D.L.R. (4th) 235; *Smith v. Knudsen* (2004), 247 D.L.R. (4th) 256 (B.C.C.A.); *Smith v. Knudsen* (2007), 51 C.C.L.T. (3d) 220 (B.C.S.C.) (loss of a 50% chance to become the successful bidder on an ambulance contract). See also *York v. Johnston* (1997), 148 D.L.R. (4th) 225, [1997] 9 W.W.R. 739 (B.C.C.A.); *Thorpe v. Insurance Corp. of British Columbia* (1998), 45 B.C.L.R. (3d) 25, 169 W.A.C. 286 (C.A.); *Prince George (City) v. Rahn Bros. Logging Ltd.* (2002), 222 D.L.R. (4th) 608 (B.C.C.A.).

76 [1939] 3 All E.R. 627 (K.B.).

77 See *Yeoman's Executrix v. Ferries*, [1967] S.L.T. 332 (Ct. of Sess.).

78 (1978), 91 D.L.R. (3d) 393 (B.C.S.C.).

79 *Supra*, footnote 74. See *Hotson v. East Berkshire Area Health Authority*, [1987] A.C. 750 (H.L.); *Herskowits v. Group Health Corp. of Puget Sound*, 664 P.2d 474 (1983); *Falcon v. Memorial Hosp.*, 462 N.W.2d 44 (1990).

identity of a tortfeasor is in question and the plaintiff proves only that there is a forty per cent chance that it was the defendant, the action will be dismissed. If the plaintiff proves that the defendant probably was the tortfeasor, the action succeeds and the plaintiff recovers full damages even though the court may be only sixty per cent certain that the identity is proven. Past facts relevant to damage assessment have been similarly treated,[80] but both the Supreme Court of Canada and the High Court of Australia have suggested that past hypothetical events are to be treated in the same way as future events, that is, the plaintiff is entitled to compensation relative to the degree of probability that the defendant was responsible for the events.[80a] The implications are far-reaching and not necessarily beneficial to plaintiffs because a 60 per cent probability will only lead to 60 per cent damages, not 100 per cent as formerly was the case.[80b] Where purely economic interests are in issue, damages have often been given for loss of a chance. The result can often be justified by the consideration that the plaintiff can be said to have lost, in a recognizable sense, a valuable right by the defendant's wrong. Land with a twenty per cent chance of rezoning for lucrative use is more valuable than land with no chance of rezoning — loss of the chance is reflected in an actual decline in market value.[81] An action with a twenty per cent chance of success that is not statute-barred is more valuable than one that is statute-barred. A lottery ticket that gives the holder a twenty per cent chance of winning a prize is a thing of real value. In these cases, to adopt the words of Reid J. in *Prior v. McNab*,[82] the plaintiff has lost a "right of value" and a thing of "reality and substance"[83] and compensation is accordingly required. In the case of a physical injury, causing a forty per cent chance of epilepsy, it is again obvious that the plaintiff has suffered a real loss: health has suffered an actual present impairment.[84] The loss is not removed by contemplation of the fact that, more probably than not, epilepsy will never develop. Similar considerations apply to loss of earning capacity,[84a] whether

---

[80] *B.C. Electric Ry. Co. v. Clarke*, [1950] 3 D.L.R. 161 (S.C.C.).

[80a] *Janiak v. Ippolito*, [1985] 1 S.C.R. 146, 16 D.L.R. (4th) 1; *Malec v. J.C. Hutton Pty. Ltd.* (1990), 169 C.L.R. 638, 45 A.L.J.R. 316 (H.C.), approved in *Athey v. Leonati*, [1996] 3 S.C.R. 458, 140 D.L.R. (4th) 235; *York v. Johnston* (1997), 148 D.L.R. (4th) 225, [1997] 9 W.W.R. 739 (B.C.C.A.). See *Sellars v. Adelaide Petroleum N.L.* (1994), 179 C.L.R. 332 (Aust. H.C.), citing this paragraph; *Daniels v. Anderson* (1995), 37 N.S.W.L.R. 438 (C.A.).

[80b] See the remarks of Lord Bridge in *Hotson v. East Berkshire Area Health Authority*, [1987] A.C. 750 (H.L.), at p. 783. But see *Cabral v. Gupta*, [1993] 1 W.W.R. 648, 83 Man. R. (2d) 2 (C.A.) (full damages awarded).

[81] *Multi-Malls Inc. v. Tex-Mall Properties Ltd.*, *supra*, footnote 71; *Toronto Hockey Club v. Arena Gardens of Toronto Ltd.*, [1925] 4 D.L.R. 546, 57 O.L.R. 610 (S.C. App. Div.), affd [1926] 4 D.L.R. 1 (P.C.). But see now *Laferrière v. Lawson* (1991), 78 D.L.R. (4th) 609 (S.C.C.) (medical negligence (Quebec law)).

[82] (1976), 78 D.L.R. (3d) 319, 16 O.R. (2d) 380 (H.C.J.).

[83] *Supra*, at p. 322 D.L.R. Similar phrases were used in *Chaplin v. Hicks*, [1911] 2 K.B. 786 (C.A.), at pp. 793 and 797.

[84] *Albion v. Cochrane* (1969), 4 D.L.R. (3d) 667, [1969] 2 O.R. 184 (Co. Ct.) (loss of one kidney).

[84a] *Anderson v. James* (1992), 87 D.L.R. (4th) 419, 63 B.C.L.R. (2d) 176 (C.A.).

the claimant is the injured person or a dependent. In *Sykes v. Midland Bank*, referred to previously,[85] where the unknown and unknowable fact was

[*The next page is* 13-19]

[85] *Supra*, 13.290.

whether the plaintiff's conduct would have altered if the plaintiff had been properly advised, *Chaplin v. Hicks* was distinguished on the ground that it involved a chance "capable of valuation".[86] The distinction would be difficult to put into practice and seems inconsistent with earlier cases,[87] as well as with Lord Diplock's statement, quoted above, in *Mallett v. McMonagle*.[88] A person who enters into an unprofitable transaction after a misrepresentation is usually entitled to the benefit of a presumption that the misrepresentation induced the transaction.[88a] A client receiving misleading or incomplete information from an adviser is in much the same position.[88b] In light of the recognition by the Supreme Court of Canada that hypothetical questions are to be determined not on an all-or-nothing basis, but according to the degree of probability,[88c] the appropriate solution, it is suggested, lies in measurement of damages according to the degree of probability that the plaintiff would have made profitable use of the information or advice if it had been given.[88d]

13.365 When the House of Lords had to deal with the problem of loss of a less than even chance in a medical negligence case, it denied recovery on the ground that the plaintiff had failed to prove, on the balance of probabilities, that the defendant had caused a loss.[88e] A similar result was reached by the Supreme Court of Canada in a Quebec case.[88f] The argument for this result is that causation must be first proved (on a balance of probabilities), before any

[86] [1971] 1 Q.B. 113 at p. 129, *per* Salmon L.J.

[87] See *Hall v. Meyrick*, [1957] 2 Q.B. 455 (C.A.); *Otter v. Church, Adams, Tatham & Co.*, [1953] Ch. 280; *Kitchen v. Royal Air Force Association*, [1958] 1 W.L.R. 563 (C.A.); *Yeoman's Executrix v. Ferries*, [1967] S.L.T. 332 (Ct. of Sess.); *Yardley v. Coombes* (1963), 107 Sol. Jo. 575 (Q.B.), approved in *Wilson v. Rowswell*, [1970] S.C.R. 865, 11 D.L.R. (3d) 737; *McMorran's Cordova Bay Ltd. v. Harman & Co.* (1979), 106 D.L.R. (3d) 495 (B.C.C.A.); *Graybriar Industries Ltd. v. Davis & Co.* (1992), 72 B.C.L.R. (2d) 190, 34 W.A.C. 77 (C.A.).

[88] *Supra*, 13.330. The actual result in *Sykes* may be defensible on the basis that the chances that the plaintiff would have benefited by proper advice were so small as to be negligible.

[88a] See 13.230, *supra*.

[88b] In *Downs v. Chappell*, [1997] 1 W.L.R. 426 (C.A.), such a presumption operated, but in *Bristol and West Building Society v. Mothew*, [1998] Ch. 1 (C.A.), it was held that the plaintiff was still required to prove the amount of damage caused by the defendant's wrong.

[88c] *Janiak v. Ippolito*, [1985] 1 S.C.R. 146, 16 D.L.R. (4th) 1; *Malec v. J.C. Hutton Pty. Ltd.* (1990), 169 C.L.R. 638, 45 A.L.J.R. 316 (H.C.), approved in *Athey v. Leonati*, [1996] 3 S.C.R. 458, 140 D.L.R. (4th) 235; *York v. Johnston* (1997), 148 D.L.R. (4th) 225, 151 W.A.C. 181 (B.C.C.A.). See *Sellars v. Adelaide Petroleum N.L.* (1994), 179 C.L.R. 332 (Aust. H.C.); *Daniels v. Anderson* (1995), 37 N.S.W.L.R. 438 (C.A.); *Smith v. Knudsen* (2004), 247 D.L.R. (4th) 256 (B.C.C.A.).

[88d] *Decoste Manufacturing Ltd. v. A & B Roofing Ltd.*, [2004] N.S.J. No. 150 (Q.L.) (S.C.), at para. 191, citing this passage.

[88e] *Hotson v. East Berkshire Area Health Authority*, [1987] A.C. 750 (H.L.); *Gregg v. Scott*, [2005] 2 AC 176 (H.L.). But see *Barker v. Corus*, [2006] 2 W.L.R. 1027 (H.L.), where proportionate recovery was allowed against several defendants, none of whom could be proved individually to have caused the harm.

[88f] *Laferrière v. Lawson* (1991), 78 D.L.R. (4th) 609, [1991] 1 S.C.R. 541. In *Arndt v. Smith*, [1997] 2 S.C.R. 539 at para. 43, 148 D.L.R. (4th) 48, McLachlin J. suggested that "the principles discussed may be equally applicable in other provinces", and this was assumed by the Ontario Court of Appeal in *Cottrelle v. Gerrard* (2003), 233 D.L.R. (4th) 45 (Ont. C.A.) at para. 36.

question of quantification arises. The argument against it is cogently summarized in Professor Fleming's remark that "this construction hardly did justice to the argument that the defendant's negligence had destroyed the plaintiff's chance of a successful cure".[88g] Damages for loss of chance were awarded in *Rufo v. Hosking*.[88h]

13.370 There are some devices that enable a court to allow for uncertain future events without evaluating the chance of their occurrence. Subrogation may be regarded as such a device. Where the defendant is bound to indemnify the plaintiff against a loss but the plaintiff has a chance of reducing the loss by a possible action against a third party, the courts can avoid the necessity of evaluating the prospects of the latter action; the defendant, upon indemnifying the plaintiff, usually obtains an assignment of the plaintiff's rights against the third party.[89] Another device that has been used in occasional cases where it is uncertain whether or not the plaintiff will suffer a loss in future is to require the defendant to pay the amount of the loss into court to be paid out to the plaintiff if the loss materializes.[90] This device potentially raises many of the difficulties of periodic payments and will be appropriate, it is submitted, only when the uncertain event will be clearly resolved within a limited period of time.[90a]

5. Optional Performance

13.380 The fact that the chance of loss for which the plaintiff seeks compensation depends on the exercise of choice by a third party does not prevent the evaluation of the chance and the award of damages in respect of it.

13.390 Where however the option is one exercisable by the defendant, a different principle comes into play. Scrutton L.J., expressed it as follows in *Withers v. General Theatre Corp.*:[92]

> Now where a defendant has alternative ways of performing a contract at his option, there is a well settled rule as to how the damages for breach of such a contract are to be assessed ... A very common instance explaining how that works is this: A. undertakes to sell to B. 800 to 1200 tons of a

[88g] J.G. Fleming, "Probabilistic Causation in Tort Law: a Postscript", 70 Can. Bar Rev. 136 (1991), at p. 137. It does not seem a sufficient answer to Fleming's point to say that the plaintiff had, on balance of probabilities, no chance of a cure. If prompt treatment cures 25 of every 100 such injuries (the finding in *Hotson*), it is true to say that the plaintiff loses a chance by being deprived of treatment, being thereby placed in a class where there are no cures. See also A.H. Luntz, "Loss of Chance" in I. Freckleton and D. Mendelson, eds., *Causation in Law and Medicine* (Ashgate, Aldershot, 2002), p. 152.

[88h] (2004), 61 N.S.W.L.R. 678 (C.A.), in substance accepting Fleming's argument.

[89] Such an order was made in *Wilson v. Rowswell*, [1970] S.C.R. 865, 11 D.L.R. (3d) 737, though not described as subrogation. See also *Douglas v. Peacock*, [1924] 4 D.L.R. 1037 (S.C.C.); *Bailey v. Ornheim* (1962), 35 D.L.R. (2d) 402 (B.C.S.C.).

[90] *Cudney v. McKinney* (1925), 28 O.W.N. 416 (H.C.); *Norman v. Sobey's Stores Ltd.* (1992), 99 Nfld. & P.E.I.R. 95 (Nfld. S.C.). An analogous device was used in *Mason v. Freedman*, [1958] S.C.R. 483, 14 D.L.R. (2d) 529.

[90a] *Michaud v. PMM Assurance & Services Inc.* (2005), 256 D.L.R. (4th) 435 (N.B.C.A.) at para. 33, and at para. 18, citing paras. 13.260 to 13.370.

[91] [Text deleted.]

[92] [1933] 2 K.B. 536 (C.A.).

certain commodity; he does not supply B. with any commodity. On what basis are the damages to be fixed? They are fixed in this way. A. would perform his contract if he supplied 800 tons, and the damages must therefore be assessed on the basis that he has not supplied 800 tons, and not on the basis that he has not supplied 1200 tons, not on the basis that he has not supplied the average, 1000 tons, and not on the basis that he might reasonably be expected, whatever the contract was, to supply more than 800 tons. The damages are assessed . . . on the basis that the defendant will perform the contract in a way most beneficial to himself and not in the way that is most beneficial to the plaintiff.[93]

In *The "Mihalis Angelos"*[94] an analogous principle was applied to a case where a charterer wrongfully repudiated before performance was due. As it turned out, the owner could not possibly have had the vessel ready in time for loading, and if the charterer had not repudiated, it would have enjoyed an express option to cancel the contract on that ground. The owner had accepted the repudiation and claimed damages. The English Court of Appeal held that the measure of damages was the true value of the rights that had been lost and that these were worthless since the owner would not have been in a position to prevent the charterer from lawfully terminating the contract. Lord Denning M.R. said: **13.400**

. . . the damages must be measured by compensating the injured party for the loss he has suffered by reason of the renunciation. You must take into account all contingencies which might have reduced or extinguished the loss . . . It follows that if the defendant has under the contract an option which would reduce or extinguish the loss, it will be assumed that he would exercise it . . .

Seeing that the charterers would, beyond doubt, have cancelled, I am clearly of opinion that the shipowners suffered no loss: and would be entitled at most to nominal damages.[95]

In some cases of wrongful dismissal, compensation has been awarded for loss of benefits that the employee expected to receive which, though technically optional, in effect could not have been withheld from the plaintiff on an individual basis. The cases were discussed in an earlier chapter where it was suggested that they may be explained on the theory that the employee, **13.410**

93 *Supra*, at pp. 548-9. See also *Hamilton v. Open Window Bakery Ltd.*, [2004] 1 S.C.R. 303, 235 D.L.R. (4th) 193; *Cockburn v. Alexander* (1848), 6 C.B. 791, 136 E.R. 1459; *Lavarack v. Woods of Colchester Ltd.*, [1967] 1 Q.B. 278 (C.A.); *Re Thornett and Fehr & Yuills, Ltd.*, [1921] 1 K.B. 219; *Edwards v. Society of Graphical & Allied Trades*, [1971] Ch. 354 (C.A.), at p. 380; *Herman Log Sales Ltd. v. Whonnock Lumber Co. Ltd.* (1957), 21 W.W.R. 178 (B.C.S.C.); *Whitby v. Widen* (1922), 68 D.L.R. 206 (Sask. C.A.); *Deverill v. Burnell* (1873), L.R. 8 C.P. 475 at p. 481, *per* Borill C.J. In *Abrahams v. Herbert Reiach, Ltd.*, [1922] 1 K.B. 477 (C.A.), it was held that a reasonable print run was to be assumed in assessing damages against a defaulting publisher, apparently because the publisher's discretion had to be exercised (by the terms of the contract) reasonably. Similarly, in *Chaplin v. Hicks*, [1911] 2 K.B. 786 (C.A.), it must have been assumed that the defendant was under an implied obligation to act fairly in selecting among applicants for employment. Diplock L.J. so explained the case in *Lavarack v. Woods of Colchester Ltd.*, *supra*, at p. 295. See *Lion Nathan Ltd. v. CC Bottlers Ltd.*, [1996] 2 N.Z.L.R. 385, [1996] 1 W.L.R. 1438 (P.C.).

94 [1971] 1 Q.B. 164 (C.A.).

though not having a contractual right to the benefits as such, has a right to be treated fairly vis-á-vis fellow employees.[96] Thus, the defendant would not be entitled to argue that in the absence of the wrongful dismissal, the benefits in question could have lawfully been withheld from the plaintiff by the defendant. The defendant cannot sustain an argument that in the absence of the breach the benefit would have been withheld from all employees when the facts show that the benefits for all other employees have been continued.

6. Appellate Review

13.420 It has often been asserted that an appellate court will not set aside an assessment of damages simply because the court would itself have made a different assessment from the trial court. The leading Canadian case is *Nance v. B.C. Electric Ry.*[97] where Viscount Simon said:

> Whether the assessment of damages be by a judge or a jury, the appellate court is not justified in substituting a figure of its own for that awarded below simply because it would have awarded a different figure if it had tried the case at first instance. Even if the tribunal of first instance was a judge sitting alone, then, before the appellate court can properly intervene, it must be satisfied either that the judge, in assessing the damages, applied a wrong principle of law (as by taking into account some irrelevant factor or leaving out of account some relevant one); or, short of this, that the amount awarded is either so inordinately low or so inordinately high that it must be a wholly erroneous estimate of the damage . . . When on a proper direction the quantum is ascertained by a jury, the disparity between the figure at which they have arrived and any figure at which they could properly have arrived must, to justify correction by a court of appeal, be even wider than when the figure has been assessed by a judge sitting alone. The figure must be wholly "out of proportion".[98]

13.430 It is difficult to deduce precisely what this means in practice. In the *Nance* case itself the Privy Council did in fact reduce a jury award from $35,000 to $22,500.[99] This was in a fatal accident case in which pecuniary loss only is

[95] *Supra*, at pp. 196-7. In *E. & B. Mortgages Ltd. v. Skrivanos* (1980), 118 D.L.R. (3d) 139, 18 R.P.R. 215 (B.C.S.C.), however, it was held that a purchaser of land could not rely on a clause limiting liability, after his own anticipatory repudiation. This result appears to put the plaintiff in a better position than if there had been no anticipatory repudiation, and constitutes a trap for the defaulting purchaser who, having (legitimately, it is assumed) bargained for a limitation of liability, loses it by announcing intentions in advance. The vendor is sufficiently protected, it is submitted, by the vendor's right of specific enforcement. See Sharpe, *Injunctions and Specific Performance*, looseleaf ed. (Toronto, Canada Law Book, 1999), 8.100-8.220. In *Boon v. Bell*, [1932] 2 W.W.R. 304 (Sask. C.A.), it was held that the onus of proof was on the defendant to show that the plaintiff would not have performed his side of the contract in the absence of the defendant's breach. In *Braithwaite v. Foreign Hardwood Co.*, [1905] 2 K.B. 543 (C.A.), substantial damages were awarded against a buyer who repudiated, despite proof that the goods were defective, and could properly have been rejected on that ground. A similar result was reached in *Taylor v. Oakes, Roncoroni & Co.* (1922), 127 L.T. 267 (C.A.). It is submitted that the cases are wrongly decided. They are persuasively criticized by Dawson, "Waiver of Conditions Precedent on a Repudiation", 96 L.Q.R. 239 (1980).

[96] See 5.1230-5.1260, *supra*.

[97] [1951] A.C. 601, [1951] 3 D.L.R. 705 (P.C.).

awarded, and the Board had laid down fairly precise rules for calculating the loss. With the increasing tendency to reasoned analysis in damage assessments, there will be a greater readiness on the part of appellate courts to intervene, for where detailed reasons are given it will more often become plain that a wrong principle of law has been applied. In the personal injury field, the Supreme Court of Canada in the 1978 "trilogy" of personal injury cases, greatly increased the degree of reasoned explanation required of trial judges, one of the express reasons being to enable a dissatisfied party to challenge the assessment on appeal.[100] A quite small error in terms of percentage would, therefore, justify interference if it plainly sprang from an error of law.[101]

13.440 Jury findings have always been treated with greater respect than the findings of a judge.[102] Viscount Simon indicated, in the passage quoted earlier, particular reluctance to interfere with jury awards and similar reluctance has been expressed in many other cases, with suggestions that jury

98 *Supra*, at pp. 613-14 A.C., pp. 713-14 D.L.R. The passage was approved in *Andrews v. Grand & Toy Alberta Ltd.*, [1978] 2 S.C.R. 229 at p. 235, 83 D.L.R. (3d) 452 at p. 457; *Woelk v. Halvorson*, [1980] 2 S.C.R. 430, 114 D.L.R. (3d) 385; *Toneguzzo-Norvell (Guardian ad Litem of) v. Burnaby Hospital*, [1994] 1 S.C.R. 114, 110 D.L.R. (4th) 289; *Keen v. Stene* (1964), 44 D.L.R. (2d) 350 (B.C.C.A.); *Fagnan v. Ure*, [1958] S.C.R. 377, 13 D.L.R. (2d) 273. Similar formulations appear in *Municipal District of Smoky Lake v. Ralston* (1957), 11 D.L.R. (2d) 673 (S.C.C.); *Stein v. The Ship "Kathy K"*, [1976] S.C.R. 802, 62 D.L.R.(3d) 1 ("clearly wrong"); *Lai v. Gill*, [1980] 1 S.C.R. 431 ("wrong principle" or "wholly erroneous"); *Flint v. Lovell*, [1935] 1 K.B. 354 (C.A.) ("entirely erroneous"); *Alexandroff v. The Queen*, [1970] S.C.R. 753, 14 D.L.R. (3d) 66 ("entirely erroneous"); *Scott v. Glen* (1997), 44 B.C.L.R. (3d) 1, 154 W.A.C. 178 *sub nom.* Scott v. Abrahams (B.C.C.A.), leave to appeal to S.C.C. refused 227 N.R. 147*n* ("wholly erroneous"); *Reed v. Steele* (1997), 148 D.L.R. (4th) 695, 36 B.C.L.R. (3d) 90 (C.A.); *Yorke v. Campbell*, [1965-69] 3 N.S.R. 765 (S.C. App. Div.); *Larocque v. Lutz*, [1981] 5 W.W.R. 1 (B.C.C.A.); *Gehrmann v. Lavoie*, [1976] 2 S.C.R. 561, 59 D.L.R. (3d) 634; *Honan v. McLean*, [1953] 3 D.L.R. 193 (Sask. C.A.); *Pollard v. Chipperfield*, [1953] 1 D.L.R. 529 (Sask. C.A.); *Atkinson v. King* (1977), 21 N.S.R. (2d) 130 (S.C. App. Div.); *Swanson v. Mallow*, [1992] 2 W.W.R. 718, 97 Sask. R. 202 (C.A.); *Lang v. Porter* (1991), 57 B.C.L.R. (2d) 253, 7 W.A.C. 62 (C.A.); *Oleskiw v. Regina (City)* (1994), 125 Sask. R. 226, 81 W.A.C. 226 (C.A.); *Cairns v. Harris* (1994), 117 Nfld. & P.E.I.R. 216 (P.E.I. C.A.); *Mulholland (Guardian ad litem of) v. Riley* (1995), 12 B.C.L.R. (3d) 248, 104 W.A.C. 145 (C.A.); *Bruce v. Coliseum Management Ltd.* (1998), 165 D.L.R. (4th) 472 (B.C.C.A.).

99 In *Howes v. Crosby* (1984), 6 D.L.R. (4th) 698 at p. 709, 45 O.R. (2d) 449 (C.A.), the Ontario Court of Appeal said that a jury award would be set aside if too high or too low by fifty per cent. See now *Courts of Justice Act* (Ont.), s. 119. See also *Marky v. Arnold* (1995), 15 B.C.L.R. (3d) 294, 108 W.A.C. 209 (C.A.) (non-pecuniary award increased from $45,000 to $75,000).

100 See 3.300, *supra*.

101 *Cosgrove v. Canadian Northern Ry.*, [1923] 4 D.L.R. 818 (Alta. S.C. App. Div.); *Julian v. Northern & Central Gas Corp. Ltd.* (1980), 118 D.L.R. (3d) 458, 31 O.R. (2d) 388 (C.A.), leave to appeal to S.C.C. refused D.L.R. *loc. cit.*, O.R. *loc. cit.*; *Bunce v. Flick*, [1991] 5 W.W.R. 623, 93 Sask. R. 53 (C.A.), leave to appeal to S.C.C. refused 137 N.R. 395*n*; *Nanji v. Mercs* (1993), 7 Alta. L.R. (3d) 435, 135 A.R. 197 (C.A.), leave to appeal to S.C.C. refused March 17, 1994.

102 *Young v. Bella*, [2006] 1 S.C.R. 108, 261 D.L.R. (4th) 516; *Peterson v. McIntosh*, [1934] 1 D.L.R. 289 (S.C.C.); *Bateman v. County of Middlesex* (1912), 6 D.L.R. 533, 27 O.L.R. 122 (C.A.); *Rawson v. Kasman* (1956), 3 D.L.R. (2d) 376, [1956] O.W.N. 359 (C.A.); *Dilello v. Montgomery* (2005), 250 D.L.R. (4th) 83 (B.C.C.A.).

awards can only be set aside when perverse,[103] unconscionable,[104] shocking the conscience of the court,[104a] indicating gross error,[105] palpable and overriding error[105a] or improper motive,[106] wholly out of all proportion,[106a] manifestly unreasonable,[106b] or when such as no reasonable jury acting judicially could have reached.[107] But in *Stapley v. Hejslet*,[107a] it was said that deference to the jury must be balanced against the need for predictability.

13.450 Where an appeal is from an assessment of damages by a jury, the usual rule is that the appellate court has power only to order a new trial not to make its own assessment of damages except on consent.[108] It is understandable, in such circumstances, that the appellate court will be reluctant to disturb the verdict. However, with the development of more precise principles of damage assessment, it becomes easier to find misdirection or, in cases of a proper direction, to conclude that no jury could reasonably have reached a verdict that departs markedly from judicial estimate.[109]

13.460 One of the objectives of the Supreme Court of Canada in the 1978 trilogy of personal injury cases was to secure uniformity throughout Canada.[110] It is not yet apparent how this object will be achieved in the provinces where jury trial for personal injury action remains common.[111] It seems impossible to reconcile the requirement laid down by the Supreme Court of rational analysis, explanation, and uniformity of damages, with a system of assessment by a jury deprived of any guidance as to amount.[112] The solution

---

[103] *Ruetz v. Goetz*, [1955] O.W.N. 879 (C.A.), at p. 880; *Quillinan v. Stuart* (1917), 35 D.L.R. 35 at p. 41, 38 O.L.R. 623 (S.C. App. Div.); *Markey v. Sloat* (1912), 6 D.L.R. 827 (N.B.S.C. App. Div.).

[104] *McCullough v. Anderson* (1895), 27 O.R. 73*n* (H.C.J.), at p. 74. See *Rousseau v. Lynch & Fournier*, [1931] 4 D.L.R. 595 (N.B.S.C. App. Div.).

[104a] *Hill v. Church of Scientology of Toronto*, [1995] 2 S.C.R. 1130, 126 D.L.R. (4th) 129; *Darmanin v. Szczesny* (1970), 14 D.L.R. (3d) 48, [1970] 3 O.R. 724 (C.A.) (unduly low award).

[105] *Morin v. Ottawa Electric Ry.* (1909), 18 O.L.R. 209 (C.A.), at p. 214; *Markey v. Sloat, supra*, footnote 103.

[105a] *Young v. Bella*, [2006] 1 S.C.R. 108, 261 D.L.R. (4th) 516 at para. 64

[106] *Morin v. Ottawa Electric Ry., supra*, footnote 105; *Wright v. Toronto Ry.* (1910), 20 O.L.R. 498 (C.A.), at p. 500; *Markey v. Sloat, supra*, footnote 103.

[106a] *Foreman v. Foster* (2001), 196 DLR (4th) 11 (B.C.C.A.); *Boyd v. Harris* (2004), 237 D.L.R. (4th) 193 (B.C.C.A.); *Courdin v. Meyers* (2005), 250 D.L.R. (4th) 213 (B.C.C.A.).

[106b] *White v. Gait* (2004), 244 D.L.R. (4th) 347 (B.C.C.A.).

[107] *Praed v. Graham* (1889), 24 Q.B.D. 53 (C.A.), at p. 55; *Danley v. C.P.R.*, [1940] S.C.R. 290 at p. 297, [1940] 2 D.L.R. 145 at p. 151; *Sam v. C.P. Ltd.* (1975), 63 D.L.R. (3d) 294 (B.C.C.A.); *Peterson v. McIntosh*, [1934] 1 D.L.R. 289 (S.C.C.); *Canadian Pacific Ry. v. Jackson* (1915), 52 S.C.R. 281, 27 D.L.R. 86; *McNally v. City of Regina*, [1924] 2 D.L.R. 1211 (C.A.); *Cossette v. Dunn* (1890), 18 S.C.R. 222; *Quillinan v. Stuart* (1917), 35 D.L.R. 35, 38 O.L.R. 623 (S.C. App. Div.); *Hill v. Church of Scientology of Toronto* (1994), 114 D.L.R. (4th) 1, 18 O.R. (3d) 385 (C.A.); *Sharpe v. Abbott* (2007), 276 D.L.R. (4th) 80 (N.S.C.A.) ("out of all proportion"). See also *Carson v. John Fairfax & Sons Ltd.* (1993), 178 C.L.R. 44 (Aust. H.C.); *Wallace Construction Specialties Ltd. v. Manson Insulation Inc.* (1993), 106 D.L.R. (4th) 169, 51 C.P.R. (3d) 514 (Sask. C.A.), leave to appeal to S.C.C. refused 170 N.R. 78*n*, 125 Sask. R. 240*n*. A "nil" award for non-pecuniary loss was set aside in *Balla v. Insurance Corp. of British Columbia* (2001), 85 B.C.L.R. (3d) 70 (C.A.), rejecting the earlier decision in *Compas v. David* (1997), 144 W.A.C. 143 (B.C.C.A.).

[107a] (2006), 263 D.L.R. (4th) 19 (B.C.C.A.).

in personal injury and wrongful death cases, now adopted in Ontario, is to permit the trial judge to give guidance to the jury. The result is to reduce the

[108] *Sikora v. Asbestonos Corp. Ltd.*, [1975] 1 S.C.R. 115, 45 D.L.R. (3d) 715; *Morin v. Tardif* (1917), 45 N.B.R. 272 (S.C. App. Div.); *Watt v. Watt*, [1905] A.C. 115 (H.L.); *Keeley v. Evans* (1932), 41 O.W.N. 180 (C.A.); *Markle v. Boyce*, [1942] 3 D.L.R. 517 (Ont. C.A.); *Piper v. Hill*, [1923] 4 D.L.R. 1175, 53 O.L.R. 233 (S.C. App. Div.), to the contrary, was expressly disapproved in *Davey v. McManus Petroleum Ltd.*, [1949] 3 D.L.R. 715, [1949] O.R. 374 (C.A.), affd [1950] 1 D.L.R. 303 (S.C.C.). In *Lionel Barber & Co., Ltd. v. Deutsche Bank (Berlin) London Agency*, [1919] A.C. 304 (H.L.), it was held that the plaintiff could consent to forego a severable part of the award. In British Columbia express provision is made in the rules for assessment by the court of appeal. See *Collins v. B.C. Motor Transportation Ltd.*, [1952] 4 D.L.R. 439 (B.C.C.A.); *Robson v. Official Administrator, County of Cariboo-Prince George* (1979), 101 D.L.R. (3d) 306 (B.C.C.A.); *Vaillancourt v. Molnar Estate* (2002), 8 B.C.L.R. (4th) 260 (C.A.); In *Johnson v. Laing* (2004), 242 D.L.R. (4th) 48 (B.C.C.A.), reassessment of an unreasonably low award was ordered to be made by the trial judge. In personal injury cases in Ontario, the appellate court may substitute its own assessment: *Courts of Justice Act*, s. 119. For English law on this point, see *Thompson v. Commissioner of Police of the Metropolis*, [1998] Q.B. 498 (C.A.).

[109] See, *e.g.*, *Penticton v. LeBlanc*, [1981] 5 W.W.R. 317 (B.C.C.A.), leave to appeal to S.C.C. refused 40 N.R. 177*n* (jury award increased by court of appeal, though trial judge has no similar power); *Cory v. Marsh* (1993), 77 B.C.L.R. (2d) 248, 38 W.A.C. 118 (C.A.), leave to appeal to S.C.C. refused 157 N.R. 319*n*, 53 W.A.C. 238*n* (jury award reduced); *Gauld (Guardian ad Litem of) v. Jameson* (1994), 89 B.C.L.R. (2d) 79, 67 W.A.C. 285 (C.A.); *Baas v. Jellema* (1998), 158 D.L.R. (4th) 633, 48 B.C.L.R. (3d) 310 (C.A.), leave to appeal to S.C.C. refused 163 D.L.R. (4th) vii, 232 N.R. 199*n*; *Sharpe v. Abbott* (2007), 276 D.L.R. (4th) 80 (N.S.C.A.) (jury award reduced).

[110] See 3.550, *supra*. This seems to represent a modification of the court's earlier view that the quantum of damages is peculiarly a matter for the provincial court of last resort. See *Pratt v. Beaman*, [1930] S.C.R. 284 at p. 287, [1930] 2 D.L.R. 868 at p. 869; *Hanes v. Kennedy*, [1941] S.C.R. 384 at p. 387, [1941] 3 D.L.R. 397 at p. 399; *Widrig v. Strazer*, [1964] S.C.R. 376 at pp. 388-90, 44 D.L.R. (2d) 1 at pp. 11-12; *Lang v. Pollard*, [1957] S.C.R. 858 at p. 862, 11 D.L.R. (2d) 161 at p. 166; *Stein v. Lehnert*, [1963] S.C.R. 38, 36 D.L.R. (2d) 159; *Gorman v. Hertz Drive Yourself Stations of Ontario*, [1966] S.C.R. 13, 54 D.L.R. (2d) 133; *Dormuth v. Untereiner*, [1964] S.C.R. 122, 43 D.L.R. (2d) 135; *Stannard v. Kidner*, [1973] S.C.R. 493, 34 D.L.R. (3d) 650. In *Lai v. Gill*, [1980] 1 S.C.R. 431, the court summarily reversed a provincial court of appeal, holding that it had insufficient reason to modify the trial judgment.

[111] Ontario and British Columbia. See Watson, "Assisting the Jury in Assessing General Damages – *Gray v. Alanco Developments* Revisited", 48 Can. Bar Rev. 565 (1970), at p. 566 (footnote).

[112] See *Gray v. Alanco Developments Ltd.* (1967), 61 D.L.R. (2d) 652, [1967] 1 O.R. 597 (C.A.); *Force v. Gibbons, supra*, footnote 111; *Decorby v. Wascana Winter Club* (1980), 3 Sask. R. 96 (C.A.); *Watson, op. cit.*, footnote 111. *Gray v. Alanco* was expressly "reserved for future consideration" in *Byron v. Williams*, [1968] S.C.R. 314 at p. 321, 67 D.L.R. (2d) 111 at pp. 118-19. In *Crosby v. O'Reilly*, [1975] 2 S.C.R. 381, 51 D.L.R. (3d) 555, followed by the majority in *Foreman v. Foster* (2001), 196 D.L.R. (4th) 11 (B.C.C.A.), the Supreme Court of Canada approved of guidance to the jury but in *Brisson v. Brisson* (2002), 213 D.L.R. (4th) 428 (B.C.C.A.), the contrary view prevailed. There are conflicting Alberta decisions: *Nguyen v. Collette* (2002), 219 D.L.R. (4th) 135 (Q.B.) (guidance favoured); *contra Ginter v. Sidhu* (2003), 122 A.C.W.S. (3d) 241 (Q.B.); *Hollebeke v. Breeze* (2003), 12 Alta. L.R. (4th) 236 (Q.B.). See 3.550, *supra*. See also *Foster v. Prins* (1979), 104 D.L.R. (3d) 643 (B.C.S.C.); *Allan v. Bushnell T.V. Co. Ltd.* (1969), 4 D.L.R. (3d) 212, [1969] 2 O.R. 6 (C.A.); *Howes v. Crosby, supra*, footnote 99. See now *Courts of Justice Act* (Ont.), s. 119. In *Hill v. Church of Scientology of Toronto*, [1995] 2 S.C.R. 1130, 126 D.L.R. (4th) 129, the Supreme Court of Canada held that no guidance was to be given in a defamation case, but in *Whiten v. Pilot Insurance Co.*, [2002] 1 S.C.R. 595, 209 D.L.R. (4th) 257, it was suggested that in the future guidance might be appropriate in respect of punitive damages.

independence of the jury, but, as Professor Watson has argued, that is not in itself undesirable: "The history of trial by jury is one of development of devices for controlling the jury."[113]

13.470 Where damages are at large and are given for intangible losses, appellate courts are naturally reluctant to intervene, for where there are no guiding principles, it can rarely be said that the assessment is plainly erroneous.[114] In some areas, conventional limits have been imposed, as by the Supreme Court of Canada in respect of damages for intangible losses in personal injury cases.[115] The approach of the appellate courts to damages for defamation is illustrated by *Ross v. Lamport*.[116] On the first trial, the jury awarded $40,000, which was set aside by the Ontario Court of Appeal and the Supreme Court of Canada as excessive. A new trial was ordered at which a second jury brought in a verdict of $25,000. The matter came to the Ontario Court of Appeal[117] for a second time and the verdict was upheld. Roach J.A. quoted Scrutton L.J. in *Youssoupoff v. Metro-Goldwyn-Mayer Pictures Ltd.*:[118] "The Court cannot go on sending the case back to the jury until at last they get a verdict with which the Judges agree." Roach J.A. added: "If the Court were to continue sending a case back to a jury until there was a verdict with which the Judges agree, then why have a jury in the first place."[119] In *Bray v. Ford*[120] Lord Herschell said:

> . . . in the case of an action for libel, not only have the parties a right to trial by jury, but the assessment of damages is peculiarly within the province of that tribunal. The damages cannot be measured by any standard known to the law; they must be determined by a consideration of all the circumstances of the case, viewed in the light of the law applicable to them. The latitude is very wide. It would often be impossible to say that the verdict was a wrong one, whether the damages were assessed at £500 or £1000.[121]

13.480 In *Cassell & Co., Ltd. v. Broome*,[122] the jury had awarded £40,000 including £25,000 exemplary damages in a defamation case. All members of the House of Lords considered the award to be high but the majority declined to interfere. Lord Hailsham said:

> It may very well be that, on the whole, judges, and the legal profession in general, would be less generous than juries in the award of damages for defamation. But I know of no principle of reason which would entitle judges, whether of appeal or at first instance, to consider that their own

[113] Watson, *op. cit.*, footnote 111, at p. 574. See also *Thompson v. Commissioner of Police of the Metropolis supra*, footnote 108.

[114] *Telegram Printing Co. v. Knott* (1917), 3 W.W.R. 335 (S.C.C.), at p. 341 (assessment of damages in libel "does not depend on any definite legal rule").

[115] See 3.510-3.700, *supra*.

[116] [1956] S.C.R. 366, 2 D.L.R. (2d) 225.

[117] (1957), 9 D.L.R. (2d) 585, [1957] O.R. 402 (C.A.).

[118] (1934), 50 T.L.R. 581 at p. 585.

[119] (1957), 9 D.L.R. (2d) 585 at p. 588, [1957] O.R. 402.

[120] [1896] A.C. 44 (H.L.).

[121] *Supra*, at pp. 52-3.

[122] [1972] A.C. 1027 (H.L.).

> sense of the proprieties is more reasonable than that of a jury, or which would entitle them to arrogate to themselves a constitutional status in this matter which Parliament has deliberately withheld from them, for aught we know, on the very ground that juries can be expected to be more generous on such matters than judges.[123]

Lord Reid had greater difficulty:

> I think [the £25,000 sum] was much too large, but that is not the test . . . I find it impossible to say that no jury of reasonable men, inexperienced but doing their best with virtually no guidance, could reach the sum of £25,000.[124]

Lord Kilbrandon, too, felt difficulties:

> The aspect of the case which has given me the greatest difficulty is the question whether the total amount of the damages awarded is so excessive that the verdict cannot stand. That it is excessive I do not doubt, but that is not a sufficient reason for the award to be set aside . . . When one looks at a jury's award in such a case one has to ask, whether it could have been made by sensible people acting reasonably, or whether it must have been arrived at capriciously, unconscionably or irrationally. On that test I think the present award must stand.[125]

The Supreme Court of Canada took a similar approach in upholding large jury awards in *Hill v. Church of Scientology of Toronto*,[125a] and in *Whiten v. Pilot Insurance Co.*[125b]

7. Events Occurring after the Wrong

13.490 Compensation is paid for a wrong done, and the task of the tribunal in assessing damages is to determine what sum of money represents fair compensation for that wrong. Where damage to property is in issue, the general rule is that damages "crystallize" at the date of the wrong or shortly afterwards.[126] In that case, the principal award will not vary according to events occurring between the date of the wrong and the date of the trial, and delay will be compensated by interest.[127] A similar approach has been taken to a claim for damages for wrongful dismissal where the employer became bankrupt shortly after the dismissal.[127a] But in *Golden Strait Corp. v. Nippon Yusen Kubishka Kaisha*,[127b] an event occurring after breach of a charterparty was taken into account to reduce the charterer's liability.

13.500 One area in which the general rule of early crystallization does not apply is the field of personal injury compensation, where all events right up to the date of assessment are taken into account. Thus, changes in the plaintiff's

[123] *Supra*, at p. 1066.
[124] *Supra*, at pp. 1090-91.
[125] *Supra*, at p. 1135.
[125a] [1995] 2 S.C.R. 1130, 126 D.L.R. (4th) 129.
[125b] [2002] 1 S.C.R. 595, 209 D.L.R. (4th) 257.
[126] See 1.650-1.1110, *supra*.
[127] See 7.330-7.1000, *supra*.
[127a] *Noble v. Principal Consultants Ltd. (Trustee of)* (2000), 187 D.L.R. (4th) 80 (Alta. C.A.).
[127b] [2007] 2 W.L.R. 691. See *Findlay v. Howard* (1919), 58 S.C.R. 516, 47 D.L.R. 441.

medical condition, increases in the cost of medical services, and increases in rates of remuneration occurring between the injury and the trial are all relevant.[128] In fatal accident cases, events that may reduce recovery, such as remarriage of the claimant,[129] are also relevant if they occur at any time before the assessment.

13.510 It is provided by Rules of Court in many jurisdictions that damages in respect of any continuing cause of action shall be assessed down to the time of assessment. The effect of the rule was explained in *Hole v. Chard Union*[130] as follows:

> What is a continuing cause of action? Speaking accurately, there is no such thing; but what is called a continuing cause of action is a cause of action which arises from the repetition of acts or omissions of the same kind as that for which the action was brought ... The cause of action complained of and existing in the present case [a continuing nuisance] appears to me precisely the kind of mischief at which [the rule] was aimed, its object being to prevent the necessity of bringing repeated actions in respect of expected nuisances of the same kind.[131]

Damage anticipated in the future from a repetition of the wrong must generally be claimed in a separate action[132] but the power to grant damages in lieu of an injunction enables the court, in effect, to compensate for future infringements of the plaintiff's right on a once and for all basis.[133]

13.520 Again, it has been held that, on breach of a contract to give support for life, the plaintiff can sue on breach for all damages once and for all.[134]

13.530 It has been held in some cases[135] that compensation cannot be awarded, where land has been damaged, for probable future consequential injury to the land flowing from the past damage. But if future consequential injury is probable, the present value of the land will be diminished, and there seems no reason, in principle, why the plaintiff should not recover compensation for

---

128 *Parsons Estate v. Guymer* (1993), 101 D.L.R. (4th) 279, 12 O.R. (3d) 743 (C.A.). See 3.340-3.500, *supra*. And see *Pratt v. Beaman*, [1930] S.C.R. 284, [1930] 2 D.L.R. 868. However, in *Krujelis v. Esdale* (1917), 25 D.L.R. (3d) 557 (B.C.S.C.), an event occurring between trial and judgment (death of plaintiff) was not taken into account. See also 12.90, *supra*. See *Rose v. Mitton* (1994), 111 D.L.R. (4th) 217 at p. 220 (N.S.C.A.), leave to appeal to S.C.C. refused September 1, 1994, citing this passage.

129 See 6.520-6.650, *supra*.

130 [1894] 1 Ch. 293 (C.A.).

131 *Supra*, at pp. 295-6. The passage was quoted and approved in *Toronto General Trusts Corp. v. Roman* (1962), 37 D.L.R. (2d) 16, [1963] 1 O.R. 312 (C.A.), affd [1963] S.C.R. vi, 41 D.L.R. (2d) 290*n*. See also *Hoffman v. McCloy* (1917), 33 D.L.R. 526, 38 O.L.R. 446 (S.C. App. Div.); *Aikman v. Mills & Co.*, [1934] 4 D.L.R. 264, [1934] O.R. 597 (H.C.J.); *McIntosh v. Parent*, [1924] 4 D.L.R. 420, 55 O.L.R. 552 (S.C. App. Div.); *East Middlesex District High School Board v. London Board of Education* (1965), 49 D.L.R. (2d) 586, [1965] 2 O.R. 51 (C.A.), affd 59 D.L.R. (2d) 213 (S.C.C.); *Paramuschuk v. Town of Meadow Lake* (1964), 47 D.L.R. (2d) 427 (Sask. C.A.).

132 See *Toronto General Trusts Corp. v. Roman, supra*, footnote 131; *East Middlesex District High School Board v. London Board of Education, supra*, footnote 131.

133 *Marcic v. Thames Water Utilities Ltd. (No. 2)*, [2002] Q.B. 929 (C.A.), revd on other grounds [2003] 3 W.L.R. 1603 (H.L.). See Sharpe, *Injunctions and Specific Performance*, 2nd ed. (Toronto, Canada Law Book, 1992), 4.40.

this loss. One difficulty is that if the cause of action arises at the time of the initial damage, the limitation period starts to run, and the cause of action may therefore be statute barred before the later injury occurs. When the initial damage was undetected, this seems a harsh result, and the courts have avoided it in some cases by holding that the cause of action in respect of the later injury only arises when the injury occurs.[136] This is a question of substantive law and of the policy of the statute of limitations. A writer on the law of damages can sympathize with the desire to preserve the cause of action in such cases but may quarrel with the inferred corollary that no action lies at the earlier point of time: it ought to be possible to preserve the position of the plaintiff who does not know of the damage to the land, without denying to another plaintiff, who does know, the right to sue for all the damage, including prospective damage, that can be shown to have been caused by the wrong.

13.540 Another difficulty is that, if the owner of land recovers its full diminution in value, it would be unjust to permit a subsequent owner of the land to recover further damages. The point was made by Moss C.J.O. in *Wigle v. Township of Gosfield South*:[137]

> A contrary view [to that denying a cause of action for the full diminution in value] would involve the possibility of a purchaser who acquired the property at a reduced price afterwards recovering for the future apprehended damage from persons who had already been charged for it by an allowance against them for depreciation in selling value.[138]

A similar problem arises where a landowner recovers damages in lieu of an injunction in respect of a continuing nuisance and subsequently disposes of the land. Again, it ought to be possible to devise a means of protecting the defendant, for example by putting the subsequent owner on notice by registration, without adopting a rule that denies compensation, on ordinary principles, for the full loss caused by a wrong.[139]

---

[134] *Zdan v. Hruden (No. 2)* (1912), 4 D.L.R. 255 (Man. C.A.). An "appropriate discount for accelerated payment" should be made: *Moschi v. Lep Air Services Ltd.*, [1973] A.C. 331 (H.L.), at p. 358. In *Hatton v. Provincial Ins. Co.* (1858), 7 U.C.C.P. 555, and *Melanson v. Dominion of Canada General Ins. Co.*, [1934] 2 D.L.R. 459 (N.B.S.C. App. Div.), it was held that a repudiation of an obligation under an insurance contract gave rise to no cause of action until the obligation to pay accrued, and there is American authority to the same effect, forcefully criticized by Corbin. See *Corbin on Contracts*, vol. 4 (St. Paul, West Publishing Co., 1951), §§962-968. See also Carter, "The Breach of Unilateral Contracts", 11 Anglo Am. L. Rev. 167 (1982), at pp. 180-1 and 300, criticizing the *Melanson* case.

[135] *Morrison v. Com'rs of Dewdney* (1922), 65 D.L.R. 409 (B.C.C.A.); *Wigle v. Township of Gosfield South* (1912), 2 D.L.R. 619, 25 O.L.R. 646 (C.A.), following *Rust v. Victoria Graving Dock Co.* (1887), 36 Ch. D. 113 (C.A.); *West Leigh Colliery Co., Ltd. v. Tunnicliffe & Hampson Ltd.*, [1908] A.C. 27 (H.L.); *Darley Main Colliery Co. v. Mitchell* (1886), 11 App. Cas. 127 (H.L.). The rule was approved in *Redland Bricks Ltd. v. Morris*, [1970] A.C. 652 (H.L.), at p. 654.

[136] See *Backhouse v. Bonomi* (1861), 9 H.L.C. 503, 11 E.R. 825, and the discussion in *Anns v. Merton London Borough Council*, [1978] A.C. 728 (H.L.), at pp. 769-71.

[137] *Supra*, footnote 135.

[138] (1912), 2 D.L.R. 619 (C.A.), at p. 628.

13.550 The prevailing rule is that a tribunal should not speculate when it knows and should make use of all available information up to the time of assessment.[140] The approach of the courts to adjustments for future contingencies almost requires this result. If an award is reduced because of a chance that some event will occur, it would be highly anomalous for the court to ignore evidence that such an event has actually occurred. The clearest example is death of the plaintiff from natural causes before trial.[140a] The action survives to the estate but the recovery for loss of earning capacity and for the costs of medical treatment will be limited to the period for which (as is now known) the plaintiff lived to incur those losses.[141] The same applies to a case where the plaintiff is permanently disabled by illness after the date of the wrong. Recovery for lost earning capacity will be limited to the period preceding the disabling illness. In *Jobling v. Associated Dairies Ltd.*[142] Lord Russell explained the chain of reasoning as follows:

> . . . it is well established that in assessing compensation for damage caused to a plaintiff by a tortfeasor among other considerations is the consequent loss or reduction in earning capacity in the working life of the plaintiff. It is also well established that it is appropriate, in arriving at an estimated figure under that head, that some allowance or discount should be made for the ordinary vicissitudes of life. It is also well established that if by the time of trial facts emerge which make known a vicissitude of life as applicable to the plaintiff, that knowledge should replace that which would have been only an estimate: where there is knowledge estimation has no part.
>
> One of these vicissitudes is that a plaintiff might thereafter succumb to a disease (unconnected with the tort) which would abbreviate the plaintiff's working life. Commonly the discount for such a possibility might well be small: but it is not to be ignored. If before trial the plaintiff does so succumb, in my opinion the evidence of its abbreviating effect must take the place of estimate, and reduce the amount of compensation for the tortious damage under that head.[143]

13.560 The same reasoning was applied and the same conclusion reached by the

---

[139] See *Jaggard v. Sawyer*, [1995] 1 W.L.R. 269 (C.A.), at pp. 280-81. It might be argued that the original owner will be able to sell the land at a price that reflects the right of the purchaser to recover damages in her own right, but the prospect of litigation will not be attractive to purchasers and, besides, there is, on general principles, merit in a once-and-for-all settlement of disputes involving damage to property.

[140] *Corrie v. Gilbert*, [1965] S.C.R. 457 at p. 461, 52 D.L.R. (2d) 1 at p. 4, *per* Ritchie J.; *Penner v. Mitchell* (1978), 89 D.L.R. (3d) 343 (Alta. S.C. App. Div.); *Carslogie S.S. Co. Ltd. v. Royal Norwegian Government*, [1952] A.C. 292 (H.L.); *Williamson v. John I. Thornycroft & Co., Ltd.*, [1940] 2 K.B. 658 (C.A.), approved in *Fleming v. Markovich*, [1942] 4 D.L.R. 287 (Ont. C.A.); *Smith v. Shade*, [1996] 6 W.W.R. 52, 18 B.C.L.R. (3d) 141 (C.A.). The cases on loss of use of property are discussed at 1.2010, 1.2020, *supra*. Where the award is based on the value of property, however, the full value is awarded without regard to subsequent events. See 1.1360-1.1430, *supra*.

[140a] *Monahan v. Nelson* (2000), 186 D.L.R. (4th) 193 (B.C.C.A.) (after trial but before judgment).

[141] See 12.90, *supra*.

[142] [1982] A.C. 794 (H.L.). In *Fanjoy v. Keller*, [1974] S.C.R. 315, 38 D.L.R. (3d) 81, damages were refused in respect of a period of disability caused by a coronary after the accident.

[143] *Jobling v. Associated Dairies Ltd., supra*, footnote 142, at pp. 809-10.

Alberta Appellate Division in *Penner v. Mitchell.*[144] The court said: "any event that would otherwise be assessed as a future contingency is a relevant factor for assessing damages, if it occurs before trial,"[145] quoting a statement of Scrutton L.J.: "In the Courts of common law two things are perfectly clear. The first thing clear is that when damages which would otherwise be prospective come to be assessed, facts which have actually happened may be taken into account".[146]

13.570 The Alberta Appellate Division pointed out in *Penner v. Mitchell* that a different approach is required where the subsequent event is wrongful. In a case where successive wrongs cause the same loss, the courts have been compelled to disregard events occurring after the date of the wrong. The problem arises, for example, where the defendant has disabled the plaintiff by injuring the plaintiff's foot. Subsequently another person, acting independently, tortiously causes the amputation of the plaintiff's leg. On a strict application of causation principles it would seem that the defendant should not be liable for the disability, for it is now known that the injury would have been suffered in any event by the action of the second wrongdoer. But the second wrongdoer could not be liable for the disability either, because the second wrongdoer can assert that the injured person was already disabled. In order to avoid the anomaly of leaving the plaintiff without compensation from either wrongdoer, it has been held by the Alberta Appellate Division in *Stene v. Evans*[147] and subsequently by the House of Lords in *Baker v. Willoughby*[148] that in such circumstances damages are to be assessed against the defendant as though the assessment had taken place the day before the second injury.

13.580 In *Jobling v. Associated Dairies,*[149] discussed previously, the plaintiff suffered a disabling injury for which the defendant was responsible. Subsequently, a pre-existing disease developed to a stage that would in any event have incapacitated him. The House of Lords held, distinguishing *Baker v. Willoughby*, that the subsequent incapacity was to be taken into account to reduce the damages payable by the defendant. This decision, like the decision

---

[144] *Supra*, footnote 140.

[145] *Penner v. Mitchell* (1978), 89 D.L.R. (3d) 343 (Alta. S.C. App. Div.), at p. 350; *Smith v. Shade*, *supra*, footnote 140.

[146] *The "Kingsway"*, [1918] P. 344 (C.A.), at p. 362.

[147] (1958), 14 D.L.R. (2d) 73 (Alta. S.C. App. Div.), followed in *Long v. Thiessen* (1968), 65 W.W.R. 577 (B.C.C.A.), and *Hicks v. Cooper* (1973), 41 D.L.R. (3d) 454, 1 O.R. (2d) 221 (C.A.); *Chapman v. Cameron* (1991), 116 N.B.R. (2d) 301 (Q.B.). See *Berns v. Campbell* (1974), 59 D.L.R. (3d) 44, 8 O.R. (2d) 680 (H.C.J.) (three successive accidents); *Dominquez v. Risling* (1995), 127 Sask. R. 241 (Q.B.) (three successive accidents); *Kozak v. Funk*, [1998] 5 W.W.R. 232, 158 Sask. R. 283 (C.A.) (apportionment); *Bourque v. Wells* (1990), 69 D.L.R. (4th) 121 , 106 N.B.R. (2d) 1 (Q.B.), vard 87 D.L.R. (4th) 574 (C.A.) (apportionment between wrongdoers); *Paine v. Donovan* (1994), 118 Nfld. & P.E.I.R. 91 (P.E.I.S.C.) (three successive incidents, apportionment among wrongdoers); *Beam v. Pittman* (1997), 147 Nfld. & P.E.I.R. 166 (Nfld. C.A.).

[148] [1970] A.C. 467 (H.L.). Lord Pearson relied expressly on *Long v. Thiessen*, *supra*, footnote 147.

[149] *Supra*, footnote 142.

of the Alberta Appellate Division in *Penner v. Mitchell*, seems sound, for otherwise the defendant would be made to pay for a disability that the plaintiff would certainly have suffered even if the wrong had not been done. The result is that the plaintiff has no legal redress, but this result (unlike the case of consecutive tortfeasors) seems acceptable, because the plaintiff would not, in any case, have had a legal redress for disability caused by disease. It is universal practice to reduce personal injury awards for anticipated contingencies that may have reduced earning capacity in any event. As suggested earlier, it seems logically impossible to continue that practice while ignoring such an event when it is actually known to have occurred.

13.590 The results in *Baker v. Willoughby* and *Jobling v. Associated Dairies*, therefore, both seem to be correct. But there seems to be a logical difficulty in reconciling the cases. *Baker v. Willoughby* was not directly attacked in argument in *Jobling v. Associated Dairies*, so the House of Lords did not feel it necessary to decide whether or not it was correct on its own facts. But several of the law lords indicated doubts about the correctness of the earlier decision. Lord Edmund-Davies was critical of *Baker v. Willoughby*, considering apparently that it had rested on the fear that the second wrongdoer might be a "man of straw"[150] and unable to satisfy any judgment against him. Lord Edmund-Davies went on to point out that the Criminal Injuries Compensation Board might make compensation instead. Lord Wilberforce made the same point.[151] But this is to underestimate the force of the argument in favour of the result reached in *Baker v. Willoughby*. The second wrongdoer would not have been liable at all for the disability in question because the second wrongdoer would be entitled to assert that the victim was already disabled before the wrong for which the second wrongdoer was responsible. The possibility of insolvency and the existence of the Criminal Injuries Compensation Board have nothing to do with this argument. However wealthy the second wrongdoer, the second wrongdoer simply would not be liable for this loss. And it would follow that the Criminal Injuries Compensation Board would not be liable for it either.

13.600 Professor Glanville Williams discussed this question in an article in 1961[152] and drew the conclusion that cases of a supervening tortious event had to be distinguished, on policy grounds, from cases of non-tortious events. He gives several examples. One is of murder. If D1 stabs and kills B and later D2, intending murder, stabs the corpse,[153] D1 must be liable (*e.g.*, for damages to the estate) in full, because there is no known principle on which D2 can be held liable when D2's act has caused no harm. But if, instead of being stabbed by D2, B's corpse had been blown up by an accidental explosion that would certainly have killed B if D1 had not done so, D1 should

[150] *Supra*, footnote 142, at p. 807.

[151] *Supra*, at p. 803.

[152] "Causation in the Law", [1961] Camb. L.J. 63, at p. 76.

[153] Though it may be pointed out that stabbing a corpse is not tortious. It is, however, an act that would have been tortious had it achieved its object.

not be liable for more than nominal damages because (as it has turned out) D1 has caused no loss.[154] As Professor Williams also pointed out, whether the third party (D2) "is or is not judgment proof does not affect the issue".[155]

13.610 Professor Williams' distinction was expressly accepted by the Alberta Appellate Division in *Penner v. Mitchell* and it is submitted that his analysis is persuasive. Another persuasive argument in favour of this result is that the first wrongdoer deprives the plaintiff of the opportunity of obtaining damages from the second wrongdoer.[156] It is submitted, therefore, that *Baker v. Willoughby* and *Jobling v. Associated Dairies* are both correctly decided and that the doubts cast in *Jobling v. Associated Dairies* upon the result reached in *Baker v. Willoughby* are unjustified, though the reasoning in the earlier case is, in its reliance on the "judgment proof" status of the second wrongdoer, open to criticism. In *Sunrise Co. v. The "Lake Winnipeg"*,[156a] a ship collision case, the majority of the Supreme Court of Canada said that a defendant responsible for the first incident remained liable whether or not the subsequent incident was tortious. It is not easy, however, to suppose that the court intended to overrule all the cases holding that a defendant is not liable if it turns out that the defendant's conduct causes no loss, particularly as the court approved one such case.[156b] Clarification will therefore be required in a future case.

13.620 In the case of an appeal, several years may have elapsed between the date of the wrong and the assessment by the appellate court. Important changes may have occurred after the trial, and these can only be taken into account by the introduction of new evidence. In *Lim Poh Choo v. Camden & Islington Area Health Authority*,[157] new evidence was admitted by the Court of Appeal and by the House of Lords in such a case. Lord Scarman described the proceedings as follows:

> The trial judge, giving judgment on December 7, 1977, assessed damages upon the basis of the facts as they were at that date. When the case reached the Court of Appeal in June 1978 Dr. Lim's [the plaintiff's] mother, who had been caring for her in Penang, had suffered a deterioration in her health, which made it very probable that in the near future Dr. Lim would have to be transferred to a nursing home in England. The Court of Appeal, therefore, granted leave to admit fresh evidence, and on July 7, 1978, gave judgment on the new basis. When the case reached your Lordships' House in March 1979, the transfer had taken place and an entirely new assessment of the cost of future care was needed, if justice was to be done. The House, in its turn, allowed fresh evidence to be called so that the cost of future care could be assessed upon the new factual basis which had developed since

[154] See *Dillon v. Twin State Gas & Electric Co.*, 163 A. 111 (S.C.N.H. 1932).

[155] *Supra*, footnote 152, at p. 78.

[156] Rosenthal, "The Effect of Subsequent Pre-assessment Wrongs on Damages for Personal Injury", 41 U.T.L.J. (1990).

[156a] [1991] 1 S.C.R. 3, 77 D.L.R. (4th) 701.

[156b] *Carslogie S.S. Co. Ltd. v. Royal Norwegian Government*, [1952] A.C. 292 (H.L.). See Waddams, "Causation in Canada and Australia", 1 Tort L. Rev. 75 (1993).

[157] [1980] A.C. 174 (H.L.).

trial and after the hearing in the Court of Appeal. The device of granting the parties leave to adduce fresh evidence at the appellate stages of litigation can, as in the present case, mitigate the injustices of a lump sum system by enabling the appellate courts to bring the award into line with what has happened since trial. But it is an unsatisfactory makeshift, and of dubious value in any case where the new facts are themselves in issue.[158]

13.630 It seems to be established that if an appeal is properly before the court on any ground, relevant evidence of all events occurring between trial and appeal may be heard and assessed.[159] In *Jenkins v. Richard Thomas & Baldwins Ltd.*,[160] damages had been assessed on the expectation that the plaintiff would be able to do a particular job; it turned out later that he was not able to do it and consequently earned less than had been anticipated. The English Court of Appeal gave leave to introduce fresh evidence and increased the award of damages. This raises obvious difficulties about the finality of assessments, and the court stressed that the general rule was that an assessment of damage was final. Lord Denning M.R. described it as "an unusual case" and spoke of "the very special circumstances of this case".[161] Salmon L.J. said: "Save in exceptional circumstances, the rule is that for better or for worse the assessment at the trial is once and for all". He added that the rule was "very rarely departed from" and that the present case was "quite exceptional".[162]

13.640 In *Dormuth v. Untereiner*,[163] the Supreme Court of Canada refused to admit evidence of remarriage in a fatal accident case on the grounds that the remarriage could have been discovered with reasonable diligence before the appeal to the Saskatchewan Court of Appeal and that proof of remarriage in itself was not "practically conclusive" of any issue in the case. In *Mercer v. Sijan*,[164] also a case of remarriage in a fatal accident claim, *Dormuth v. Untereiner* was distinguished by the Ontario Court of Appeal. In the *Mercer* case the remarriage (occurring as it did after the trial) could not have been discovered before trial, and proof was offered that the claimant's spouse was earning substantially more than had the deceased, a fact which the Ontario Court of Appeal considered "conclusive" of an issue, namely, the extent of the claimant's loss.

---

158 *Supra*, at p. 183.

159 *Mulholland v. Mitchell*, [1971] A.C. 666 (H.L.); *McCann v. Sheppard*, [1973] 1 W.L.R. 540 (C.A.); *Murphy v. Stone-Wallwork (Charlton) Ltd.*, [1969] 1 W.L.R. 1023 (H.L.); *Curwen v. James*, [1963] 1 W.L.R. 748 (C.A.); *Perry v. Sidney Phillips & Son*, [1982] 1 W.L.R. 1297 (C.A.). Leave to introduce new evidence to show that an unconscious plaintiff might regain consciousness was given in *Knutson v. Farr* (1984), 12 D.L.R. (4th) 658, [1984] 5 W.W.R. 315 (C.A.), leave to appeal to S.C.C. refused 58 N.R. 78*n*.

160 [1966] 1 W.L.R. 476 (C.A.).

161 *Supra*, at pp. 477, 479.

162 *Supra*, at p. 480.

163 [1964] S.C.R. 122, 43 D.L.R. (2d) 135.

164 (1976), 72 D.L.R. (3d) 464, 14 O.R. (2d) 12 (C.A.). See also *Cory v. Marsh* (1993), 77 B.C.L.R. (2d) 248, 38 W.A.C. 118 (C.A.), leave to appeal to S.C.C. refused 157 N.R. 319*n*, 53 W.A.C. 238*n*; *Sparge v. Greatorex* (1992), 59 S.A.S.R. 1 (S.C.) (death of plaintiff after trial).

13.650 The position seems to be that fresh evidence will be allowed at the appellate level when an event has occurred after trial that is not likely to require weighing of evidence[165] and which, if known at the trial, would certainly have made a measurable difference in the assessment of damages. The *Jenkins* case was one in which the appeal seems to have been made out of time, but in *Murphy v. Stone-Wallwork (Charlton) Ltd.*[166] the House of Lords indicated that it was only in "very special and exceptional cases indeed"[167] that leave to appeal out of time should be given. Such a rule is necessary, for otherwise an assessment of damages would never be final. A strong argument can be made against admitting any evidence of events after trial that were contemplated as contingencies when the assessment was made, for the possibility of the occurrence of the event will have already been taken into account.[167a] If a future loss may be great or small and the plaintiff accordingly recovers a moderate award, it seems unfair to reopen the assessment if events afterwards show that the loss has turned out to be small; in many cases there will be no corresponding opportunity to reopen the assessment if the loss turns out to be larger than anticipated.[168]

165 *Mercer v. Sijan, supra*, footnote 164 (evidence must be "wholly credible"); *Cory v. Marsh*, *supra*. In *Gard v. Slobodian*, [1951] 4 D.L.R. 512, the Manitoba Court of Appeal in refusing leave to introduce new medical evidence, stressed that evidence subject to rebuttal and evaluation could not be considered "conclusive". See also *Workmen's Compensation Board v. McCarthy* (1981), 37 N.B.R. (2d) 185 (Q.B.). Leave to introduce new medical evidence was given in *Hudson v. Burnett* (1973), 6 N.B.R. (2d) 741 (S.C. App. Div.).

166 *Supra*, footnote 159.

167 *Supra*, at p. 1031 (*per* Lord Upjohn). This aspect of the case was approved in *Mulholland v. Mitchell, supra*, footnote 159, and referred to in *Mercer v. Sijan, supra*, footnote 164. An exceptional case for granting leave to appeal out of time would be one where one of the parties had deceived the court. See also p. 1026 (Lord Pearce), p. 1030 (Lord Upjohn), p. 1034 (Lord Pearson).

167a See *Leenstra v. Miller*, [1994] 3 W.W.R. 751, 87 B.C.L.R. (2d) 255 (C.A.).

168 See *Dunn v. Gibson* (1912), 8 D.L.R. 297, 23 O.R. 356 (Ont. C.A.), where an award of damages for seduction was upheld although it was based on the probable cost of caring for a child who, as it turned out, died within a few days of birth. The court said that the jury must have taken account, in its award, of the contingency of early death. But against this are the cases cited in footnote 164, *supra*.

CHAPTER 14

REMOTENESS

1. Introduction

The arrangement of this book has the consequence that questions of remoteness have already been discussed in the context of claims for specific kinds of loss.[1] The present chapter is concerned with the general scope of remoteness as a limitation on the basic principle of compensatory damages. **14.10**

2. Contracts

(1) The rule in *Hadley v. Baxendale*

The general rule of contract damages is that the plaintiff is entitled to be put in as good a position as would have been occupied if the contract had been performed,[2] but a strict application of this principle would impose liability for any consequences of breach, however remote. Willes J. gave the following striking example: **14.20**

> Cases of this kind have always been found to be very difficult to deal with, beginning with a case said to have been decided about two centuries and a half ago, where a man going to be married to an heiress, his horse having cast a shoe on the journey, employed a blacksmith to replace it, who did the work so unskilfully that the horse was lamed, and, the rider not arriving in time, the lady married another; and the blacksmith was held liable for the loss of the marriage.[3]

Willes J. went on to call the imposition of liability an "absurdity."[4] It is of interest to note that Willes J. had been counsel for the successful defendant in the leading case of *Hadley v. Baxendale*.[5]

Until the mid-19th century there was little law on the point, for the jury had an almost unfettered discretion in assessing damages. In 1854 in *Hadley v. Baxendale*, the Court of Exchequer Chamber attempted to lay down a governing principle, the effect of which was to increase the control by judges over jury awards.[6] The principle adopted by the court was directly influenced by French and American writings.[7] Alderson B. expressed the rule as follows: **14.30**

---

1 See 1.120, 1.1250, 1.2150-1.2180, 7.430, 7.440, *supra*.

2 See 5.20, *supra*.

3 *British Columbia and Vancouver's Island Spar, Lumber & Saw-Mill Co. Ltd. v. Nettleship* (1868), L.R. 3 C.P. 499 at p. 508.

4 *Supra*.

5 (1854), 9 Ex. 341, 156 E.R. 145, followed by the Supreme Court of Canada in *Brown & Root Ltd. v. Chimo Shipping Ltd.*, [1967] S.C.R. 642, 63 D.L.R. (2d) 1. See p. 648 S.C.R., p. 6 D.L.R.

> Now we think the proper rule in such a case as the present is this: — Where two parties have made a contract which one of them has broken, the damages which the other party ought to receive in respect of such breach of contract should be such as may fairly and reasonably be considered either arising naturally, i.e., according to the usual course of things, from such breach of contract itself, or such as may reasonably be supposed to have been in the contemplation of both parties, at the time they made the contract, as the probable result of the breach of it. Now, if the special circumstances under which the contract was actually made were communicated by the plaintiffs to the defendants, and thus known to both parties, the damages resulting from the breach of such a contract, which they would reasonably contemplate, would be the amount of injury which would ordinarily follow from a breach of contract under these special circumstances so known and communicated. But, on the other hand, if these special circumstances were wholly unknown to the party breaking the contract, he, at the most, could only be supposed to have had in his contemplation the amount of injury which would arise generally, and in the great multitude of cases not affected by any special circumstances, from such a breach of contract. For, had the special circumstances been known, the parties might have specially provided for the breach of contract by special terms as to the damages in that case; and of this advantage it would be very unjust to deprive them.[8]

14.40 The facts of the case were that Baxendale, a common carrier, had delayed in delivering a broken mill shaft sent by Hadley to the makers to serve as a pattern for a new one. As applied to the facts of the case, Alderson B.'s rule resulted in the setting aside of the jury award of £25 in respect of profits lost by Hadley while his mill was stopped. The rule in *Hadley v. Baxendale* has often been applied by Canadian courts, both as an inclusive[9] and an exclusive[10] test of liability.

14.50 The apparent simplicity of the rule in *Hadley v. Baxendale* is deceptive, and some of the difficulties in store are revealed by an examination of the case itself. On the first key question of what events do arise "naturally and in the usual course of things" Alderson B. said: "But it is obvious that, in the great multitude of cases of millers sending off broken shafts to third persons by a carrier under ordinary circumstances, such consequences would not, in all probability, have occurred."[11] This sentence has a very odd appearance.

---

6 *Hadley v. Baxendale* is discussed in its historical context by Washington, "Damages in Contract at Common Law", 47 L.Q.R. 345 (1931), 48 L.Q.R. 90 (1932), at pp. 97-108; Danzig, "Hadley v. Baxendale: A Study in the Industrialization of the Law," 4 J. of Leg. Studies 249 (1975); Horwitz, "The Historical Foundations of Modern Contract Law", 87 Harv. L. Rev. 917 (1974), at pp. 923-5.

7 Sedgwick's discussion of Domat's view and a passage from a decision of Story J. were heavily relied on in argument. See *Hadley v. Baxendale, supra*, footnote 5, at pp. 350-1. In *British Columbia Saw-Mill Co. v. Nettleship, supra*, footnote 3, at p. 508, Willes J. cites Pothier.

8 *Hadley v. Baxendale, supra*, footnote 5, at pp. 354-5.

9 *General Securities Ltd. v. Don Ingram Ltd.*, [1940] S.C.R. 670, [1940] 3 D.L.R. 641 (collapse of business caused by failure to advance money); *Eaton v. The Queen*, [1972] F.C. 185, 31 D.L.R. (3d) 723 (T.D.), affd 42 D.L.R. (3d) 319*n* (C.A.); *Burrard Drydock Co. Ltd. v. Canadian Union Line Ltd.*, [1954] S.C.R. 307, [1954] 3 D.L.R. 561 (liability to a third party for defective workmanship).

There is a peculiarity in the use of the phrase "great multitude" to describe so specific a class of cases as of "millers sending off broken shafts to third persons by a carrier"; the addition of the words "under ordinary circumstances" makes the reader wonder what kind of extraordinary circumstances Alderson B. had in mind. Furthermore, it becomes clear that there is no evidence and can be no evidence of what in fact usually happens in such cases. The result depends merely on Alderson B.'s judgment of what "in all probability" would occur.

14.60 The second key question is the kind of notice required to be given to the defendant of the probability of loss in order to bring home liability. On this point, there is a puzzling discrepancy between the facts stated in the reporter's statement, where it is said that the "plaintiffs' servant told the [defendants'] clerk that the mill was stopped, and that the shaft must be sent immediately",[12] and the facts apparently assumed by Alderson B. who says "the only circumstances here communicated by the plaintiffs to the defendants at the time the contract was made, were, that the article to be carried was the broken shaft of a mill, and that the plaintiffs were the millers of that mill",[13] and that the "special circumstances were here never communicated by the plaintiffs to the defendants".[14] Various explanations have been attempted of this discrepancy,[15] of which the simplest and perhaps the most convincing is that the reporter's statement is wrong.[16] But the confusion on the point gives warning of future difficulties.

14.70 As early as 1860 Wilde, B., said:

> For my own part I think that, although an excellent attempt was made in *Hadley v. Baxendale* to lay down a rule on the subject, it will be found that the rule is not capable of meeting all cases; and when the matter comes to be

10 *Steinacker v. Squire* (1913), 19 D.L.R. 434, 30 O.L.R. 149 (S.C. App. Div.); *Corbin v. Thompson* (1907), 39 S.C.R. 575 (loss of profit caused by defective goods); *Andre Knight Ltd. v. Presement* (1967), 63 D.L.R. (2d) 314, [1967] 2 O.R. 289 (C.A.) (loss of credit rating caused by defendant's failure to pay promptly); *Brown & Root Ltd. v. Chimo Shipping Ltd., supra*, footnote 5 (damage to derrick caused by lifting overweight cargo); *Stevenson v. Montreal Telegraph Co.* (1858), 16 U.C.Q.B. 530 (market loss caused by delayed telegram); *Kinghorne v. Montreal Telegraph Co.* (1859), 18 U.C.Q.B. 60 (loss of contract caused by failure to deliver telegram); *Scott Maritimes Pulp Ltd. v. B.F. Goodrich Canada Ltd.* (1977), 72 D.L.R. (3d) 680 (N.S.S.C. App. Div.) (loss of profits caused by attempt to use damaged goods); *Walton v. Ferguson* (1914), 19 D.L.R. 816 (Alta. S.C.) (crop loss from unavailability of engine); *Vancouver Machinery Co. v. Vancouver Timber & Trading Co.* (1914), 18 D.L.R. 491 (B.C.C.A.) (loss of profits from non-delivery of goods).

11 *Hadley v. Baxendale* (1854), 9 Ex. 341 at p. 356, 156 E.R. 145.

12 *Supra*, at p. 344.

13 *Supra*, at p. 355.

14 *Supra*, at p. 356.

15 McCormick, *Handbook on the Law of Damages* (St. Paul, West Publishing Co., 1935), p. 573, accepts the reporter's statement, but assumes that Alderson B. found the information communicated to have been insufficient. Another possibility is that the court considered that notice to the clerk was insufficient to bind the defendant. See Danzig, *loc. cit.*, footnote 6, at pp. 262-3.

16 See *Victoria Laundry (Windsor) Ltd. v. Newman Industries Ltd.*, [1949] 2 K.B. 528 (C.A.), at p. 537, *per* Asquith L.J. ("the headnote is definitely misleading").

further considered, it will probably turn out that there is no such thing as a rule, as to the legal measure of damages applicable in all cases.[17]

14.80 In 1949 Lord du Parcq alluded to the wisdom of this forecast,[18] and it cannot be said that the events since 1949 have falsified it. In *Kienzle v. Stringer*,[19] Zuber J.A. said:

> The governing term is reasonable and what is reasonably foreseen or reasonably contemplated is a matter to be determined by a Court. These terms necessarily include more policy than fact as Courts attempt to find some fair measure of compensation to be paid to those who suffer damages by those who cause them.

(2) One rule or two?

14.90 The proper division of Alderson B.'s rule, or rules, has been the subject of disagreement. A division into three rules was made by Mayne. These were: (1) damages naturally arising are recoverable; (2) damages not naturally arising are not recoverable unless special circumstances are communicated; and (3) where special circumstances are communicated such damages are recoverable.[20] Later it became common to speak of two rules. Asquith L.J. explained the twofold division as follows:

> For this purpose, knowledge "possessed" is of two kinds; one imputed, the other actual. Everyone, as a reasonable person, is taken to know the "ordinary course of things" and consequently what loss is liable to result from a breach of contract in that ordinary course. This is the subject matter of the "first rule" in *Hadley v. Baxendale*. But to this knowledge, which a contract-breaker is assumed to possess whether he actually possesses it or not, there may have to be added in a particular case knowledge which he actually possesses, of special circumstances outside the "ordinary course of things," of such a kind that a breach in those special circumstances would be liable to cause more loss. Such a case attracts the operation of the "second rule" so as to make additional loss also recoverable.[21]

14.100 The distinction between the two rules, however, is not clear-cut. The defendant always knows something about the plaintiff's affairs, and there is no reliable guide as to whether such knowledge should be described as notice

[17] *Gee v. Lancashire & Yorkshire Ry. Co.* (1860), 6 H. & N. 211 at p. 221, 158 E.R. 87. See the similar comments of Pollock C.B. in *Wilson v. Newport Dock Co.* (1866), L.R. 1 Ex. 177 at pp. 180-81, and of Walsh J. in *Price v. International Harvester Co.* (1915), 23 D.L.R. 266 (Alta. S.C.), at p. 269.

[18] *Monarch Steamship Co. v. Karlshamns Oljefabriker (A/B)*, [1949] A.C. 196 (H.L.), at pp. 232-3.

[19] (1981), 130 D.L.R. (3d) 272 at p. 277, 35 O.R. (2d) 85 (C.A.), leave to appeal to S.C.C. refused D.L.R. *loc. cit.*, 38 O.R. (2d) 159*n*.

[20] *Mayne's Treatise on Damages*, 10th ed. by F. Gahan (London, Sweet & Maxwell, 1927), p. 11. See *Simon v. Pawsons & Leafs, Ltd.* (1932), 38 Com. Cas. 151 (C.A.), at pp. 162, 165; *Simmons & McBride Ltd. v. Kirkpatrick*, [1945] 4 D.L.R. 134 (B.C.S.C.), at p. 137. In *Mayne's Treatise on Damages*, 11th ed. by W. G. Earengey (London, Sweet & Maxwell, 1946), a twofold division was adopted "to conform with modern practice".

[21] *Victoria Laundry (Windsor) Ltd. v. Newman Industries Ltd., supra*, footnote 16, at p. 539.

of special circumstances. When liability is imposed, for example, on the supplier of a boiler for loss of profits suffered by a laundry, the result can be explained either as an operation of the first rule (anyone would expect lack of a boiler to cause such a loss) or of the second rule (the defendant having notice of the special circumstances, *i.e.*, that the plaintiff was a launderer and required the boiler for use). It has often been suggested, therefore, that in truth there is only one rule, namely, that the defendant is liable for such losses as, in all the circumstances, ought reasonably to have been contemplated. Lord Upjohn in *Koufos v. C. Czarnikow Ltd. (Heron II)*[22] said: "for my part I care not whether it is regarded as stating two rules or two branches of one rule, though I prefer the latter".[23]

(3) Intention of the parties

14.110 A pervasive problem in applying the rule in *Hadley v. Baxendale* is the relevance of the parties' intention. The theory of contractual liability is often said to rest on intention — at least, as objectively determined.[24] But contracting parties generally contemplate the performance not the breach of their agreement.[25] Liability may then be said to rest on the "presumed" intention of the parties, but as soon as such language is used it becomes evident that a legal fiction is in operation. Parties will be presumed to have intended that which the court decides is just.[26]

14.120 In *Victoria Laundry (Windsor) Ltd. v. Newman Industries Ltd.*[27] Asquith L.J. said this about the parties' intention:

> In order to make the contract-breaker liable under either rule it is not necessary that he should actually have asked himself what loss is liable to result from a breach. As has often been pointed out, parties at the time of contracting contemplate not the breach of the contract, but its performance. It suffices that, if he had considered the question, he would as a reasonable man have concluded that the loss in question was liable to result.[28]

This view has been universally followed, but the theory that liability rests on

---

22 [1969] 1 A.C. 350 (H.L.).

23 *Supra*, at p. 421. See also *Scyrup v. Economy Tractor Parts Ltd.* (1963), 40 D.L.R. (2d) 1026 (Man. C.A.), at p. 1033, *per* Freedman J.A., quoting with approval *Mayne & McGregor on Damages*, 12th ed. (London, Sweet & Maxwell, 1961), p. 127: "the modern restatement of the rule as a totality is a salutary trend".

24 The topic is discussed in Waddams, *The Law of Contracts*, 5th ed. (Toronto, Canada Law Book, 2005), ch. 3.

25 *Hydraulic Engineering Co. Ltd. v. McHaffie, Goslett, & Co.* (1878), 4 Q.B.D. 670 (C.A.), at p. 674, *per* Bramwell L.J.; *Victoria Laundry (Windsor) Ltd. v. Newman Industries Ltd.*, [1949] 2 K.B. 528 (C.A.) (see passage quoted at 14.120, *infra*).

26 "And the spokesman of the fair and reasonable man, who represents after all no more than the anthropomorphic conception of justice, is and must be the court itself", *per* Lord Radcliffe in *Davis Contractors Ltd. v. Fareham Urban District Council*, [1956] A.C. 696 (H.L.), at p. 728. See Fuller and Perdue, "The Reliance Interest in Contract Damages", 46 Yale L.J. 52 (1936), at p. 85.

27 [1949] 2 K.B. 528 (C.A.).

28 *Supra*, at p. 540.

presumed intention has had important consequences, as the following paragraphs will show.

14.130 A number of cases denying liability have suggested that it is not enough for the plaintiff to give notice of the probability of loss; the plaintiff must give notice in such a way that the defendant can be assumed to assent to possible liability. Willes J. said in *British Columbia and Vancouver's Island Spar, Lumber & Saw-Mill Co. Ltd. v. Nettleship*:[29]

> The mere fact of knowledge cannot increase the liability. The knowledge must be brought home to the party sought to be charged, under such circumstances that he must know that the person he contracts with reasonably believes that he accepts the contract with the special condition attached to it ... Knowledge on the part of the carrier is only important if it forms part of the contract.[30]

14.140 In *Horne v. Midland Ry. Co.*,[31] Blackburn J. favoured the view (though finding it unnecessary to decide) that: "in order that the notice may have any effect, it must be given under such circumstances, as that an actual contract arises on the part of the defendant to bear the exceptional loss".[32] In the lower court, Keating J. said: "There must, if it be sought to charge the carrier with consequences so onerous, be distinct evidence that he had notice of the facts and assented to accept the contract upon those terms."[33]

14.150 This really amounts to denying liability in all cases in which notice is found to be necessary, because an "actual contract" to indemnify can never be found unless the defendant is an insurer. Blackburn J. himself recognized this, for he said that he knew of no case in which the giving of notice had ever been held to enable the plaintiff to recover exceptional damages.[34] The "second contract" theory is in effect simply a device to justify the disallowance of damages where the court has determined that they are too remote. In *Horne v. Midland Ry. Co.*, Kelly C.B. laid stress on the position of the defendant as a common carrier. If it had no discretion to decline the contract, it could hardly be said that acceptance of the goods amounted to an assent to any exceptional liability.[35]

14.160 Another device for limiting the liability of the contract breaker is also illustrated by *Horne v. Midland Ry. Co.* In that case the plaintiffs were shoe manufacturers, shipping a consignment of shoes which they were bound to supply to a customer by a certain date. Notice was given to the railway that the plaintiffs were under contract to deliver the shoes by this date and that

---

29 (1868), L.R. 3 C.P. 499.
30 *Supra*, at p. 509.
31 (1873), L.R. 8 C.P. 131 (Ex. Ch.).
32 *Supra*, at p. 141. See also *per* Martin B., at p. 140.
33 *Horne v. Midland Ry. Co.* (1872), L.R. 7 C.P. 583 at p. 592.
34 *Horne, supra*, footnote 31, at p. 141.
35 *Horne, supra*, footnote 31, at p. 137. In *Rivers v. George White & Sons Co.* (1919), 46 D.L.R. 145 (Sask. C.A.), Haultain C.J.S. said: "It may be observed that this theory of a kind of second contract to pay damages has been mainly developed in actions against carriers, on the ground that a common carrier has no discretion to decline a contract."

unless they were so delivered, they would be "thrown upon the plaintiff's hands". This notice was held to be not sufficiently specific to warn the defendant railway that exceptional loss would occur if the shoes were not delivered on time. Some other cases, too, have held a notice of special circumstances to be inadequate because it did not specify the circumstances with sufficient precision.[36] Since the detail of information is infinitely variable, it is always open to the court to hold that the communication in a particular case is insufficient.

14.170 Despite the use of these devices, it has often been held that the defendant's actual knowledge[37] is relevant to liability, and liability has been imposed without a requirement of any "second contract". Lord Upjohn said in *Koufos v. C. Czarnikow Ltd. (Heron II)*:[38] "If parties enter into the contract with knowledge of some special circumstances, and it is reasonable to infer a particular loss as a result of those circumstances that is something which both must contemplate as a result of a breach. It is quite unnecessary that it should be a term of the contract."[39]

14.180 The perceived need of courts to resort to the "second contract" device shows, however, that the rule in *Hadley v. Baxendale* has been thought to be too generous to the plaintiff in some cases. Willes J. gave the following example in *British Columbia and Vancouver's Island Spar, Lumber & Saw-Mill Co. Ltd. v. Nettleship*:[40]

> Take the case of a barrister on his way to practise at the Calcutta bar, where he may have a large number of briefs awaiting him: through the default of the Peninsular & Oriental Company he is detained in Egypt or in the Suez boat, and consequently sustains great loss; is the company to be responsible for that, because they happened to know the purpose for which the traveller was going?[41]

An equivalent modern hypothetical case is of a business person who suffers a large loss because a cab-driver fails to take the person to a meeting on time. Even with notice of the customer's purpose, most would consider it odd to hold the cab-driver liable. Communication of the plaintiff's probable loss is therefore not always sufficient to warrant the defendant's liability for it. It is suggested below that insurance considerations may play a part.[42] McCormick pointed out that the implied agreement theory is a flexible one for "seldom is there anything in the situation more definite or mandatory than the judge's sense of justice to tell him to find the presence or absence of this silent promise to assume the risk".[43] McCormick added that the flexibility served a

---

36 *Munroe Equipment Sales Ltd. v. Canadian Forest Products Ltd.* (1961), 29 D.L.R. (2d) 730 (Man. C.A.); *Simon v. Pawsons & Leafs, Ltd.* (1932), 38 Com. Cas. 151 (C.A.).

37 An oral notice is sufficient, even if the contract is in writing: *Hydraulic Engineering Co. Ltd. v. McHaffie, Goslett & Co.* (1878), 4 Q.B.D. 670 (C.A.).

38 [1969] 1 A.C. 350 (H.L.).

39 *Supra*, at p. 422.

40 (1868), L.R. 3 C.P. 499.

41 *Supra*, at p. 510, quoted and applied in *Simon v. Pawsons & Leafs, Ltd.*, *supra*, footnote 36.

42 See 14.330-14.350, *infra*.

useful purpose: "The recurrent cropping up of the idea in the opinions of the courts indicates that some of the judges have found the conception useful in giving expression to their sense of the justice of the situation. If so, this serves as its justification."[44]

14.190 From time to time reference is made to the contract price. There are many cases, particularly those involving personal injuries caused by defective goods, when liability has been imposed for sums quite disproportionate to the contract price.[45] However, some cases denying liability have suggested that the price may be a relevant factor. McLean J. said in *Kinghorne v. Montreal Telegraph Co.*,[46] in denying liability for loss caused by non-delivery of a telegram: "It ought not to be expected that so great facilities are to be afforded for so small a remuneration, and at a risk which might bring ruin upon any company if obliged to indemnify for every possible loss."[47]

14.200 In *Munroe Equipment Sales Ltd. v. Canadian Forest Products Ltd.*,[48] Miller C.J.M. said, in denying liability for loss caused by the inability of the lessor of a defective tractor to remove pulpwood:

> In my opinion it is unreasonable to expect that such a burden of responsibility for damages as now claimed by the [lessee] should be assumed from the rental of a second-hand unit. Surely no reasonable person could contemplate, under the circumstances of the renting of this machine, that the lessor of one second-hand tractor was underwriting and virtually insuring the removal of all this pulpwood from the bush.[49]

It will be seen from this quotation that the references to price are linked with the second contract theory. If we were really looking for an express undertaking to indemnify, we would expect the defendant to charge a premium commensurate with the risk. The breach of warranty cases show that there is no rule that price must be commensurate with liability. The Supreme Court of Canada has upheld the imposition of liability on a delivery service for lost profits caused by late delivery of a tender.[50] The references to price in the cases mentioned might therefore be dismissed as erroneous. This seems too simple however. Like the second contract theory, the theory that price and liability must be commensurate is a device for restricting liability, and the perceived need for such a device indicates that the rule as announced in *Hadley v. Baxendale* is incomplete. In *Transfield Shipping Inc. v. Mercator Shipping Inc.*,[50a] the House of Lords held that the charterer of a

---

[43] McCormick, *Handbook on the Law of Damages* (St. Paul, West Publishing Co., 1935).
[44] McCormick, *op. cit.*, at p. 580.
[45] See footnote 90, *infra*.
[46] (1859), 18 U.C.Q.B. 60.
[47] *Supra*, at p. 73.
[48] (1961), 29 D.L.R. (2d) 730 (Man. C.A.).
[49] *Supra*, at p. 740.
[50] *Cornwall Gravel Co. Ltd. v. Purolator Courier Ltd.*, [1980] 2 S.C.R. 118, 120 D.L.R. (3d) 575*n*, distinguished in *B.D.C. Ltd. v. Hofstrand Farms Ltd.*, [1986] 1 S.C.R. 228, 26 D.L.R. (4th) 1, where the courier did not know the nature of the document.
[50a] [2008] UKHL 48.

ship was not liable for loss, caused by late redelivery of the ship, of an exceptionally profitable follow-on contract. Though the loss of a follow-on contract was readily foreseeable in general terms, it was held not to be the type of loss for which the charterer could be taken to have assumed responsibility.[50b]

14.210 Another question influenced by the theoretical basis of contractual liability is that of the time at which notice must be given. If the basis of liability is the parties' presumed agreement, notice given subsequently cannnot affect the scope of liability. This view is generally accepted as correct.[51] It has been occasionally suggested that in case of deliberate breach, a notice of exceptional loss given after the date of contract should serve to enlarge liability,[52] but there are difficulties with the suggestion. Apart from the difficulty of the theoretical basis of liability, referred to earlier, there is the problem of ascertaining what is meant by "deliberate" breach and of whether it is desirable to make this an important factor in contractual liability. Often a breach of contract is "deliberate" in the sense that the defendant chooses it as the lesser of several evils, for example, to avoid bankruptcy or because business is discontinued, in circumstances where most persons would say that there was no moral fault. Further, if the defendant's liability could be enlarged by notice given after the contract, the defendant would be deprived of the opportunity of refusing to contract or of charging a higher price, of which advantage, as Alderson B. said in *Hadley v. Baxendale* itself, it would be very unjust to deprive the defendant.[53]

14.220 However, where the breach of contract constitutes a tort, there seems no escape from the position that the question of remoteness in tort will be determined on the basis of the defendant's knowledge at the time of the tortious act.[54] This would apply whether the wrong was deliberate or negligent, and with the increasing tendency of courts to find concurrent tortious and contractual liability,[55] the possibility of an action in tort will often enable knowledge acquired after the date of the contract to be made relevant. This is not necessarily an undesirable result. If the plaintiff's case is solely contractual, the contract is the only source of obligation, and in assessing the scope of the obligation, it is quite rational to exclude subsequent events. On the other hand, an action in tort is based on the defendant's duty

---

[50b] This was the view of Lords Hoffmann and Hope, with whose opinions Lord Walker agreed. Lord Rodger and Baroness Hale (with whom Lord Walker also agreed) avoided the language of assumption of responsibility.

[51] See *Victoria Laundry (Windsor) Ltd. v. Newman Industries Ltd.*, [1949] 2 K.B. 528 (C.A.), at p. 539, *per* Asquith L.J.

[52] *Gee v. Lancashire & Yorkshire Ry. Co.* (1860), 6 H. & N. 211 at p. 218, 158 E.R. 87, *per* Bramwell B.; *Corbin on Contracts* (St. Paul, West Publishing Co., 1964), §1008; McCormick, *op. cit.*, footnote 43, at p. 581.

[53] See footnote 8, *supra*.

[54] See *Amell v. Maloney*, [1929] 4 D.L.R. 514 at pp. 517-18, 64 O.L.R. 285 (S.C. App. Div.), *per* Masten J.A.

[55] See Reiter, "Contracts, Torts, Relations and Reliance" in Reiter and Swan, *Studies in Contract Law* (Toronto, Butterworths, 1980), p. 235, at pp. 270-1.

not to cause harm by acting in disregard of the plaintiff's interest. It is perfectly rational, in assessing the scope of this duty, to consider the defendant's knowledge at the time of the wrongful action. If the defendant knows (or ought to know) then that the act will cause great harm, the defendant can justly be held responsible for it. Swinton has written:

> Absent express allocation of risk in the contract, why should a defendant who has harmed an individual by breaking his contract escape liability because such an injury was not foreseeable at the time of entering the contract, when he could be liable in tort to a bystander injured by the same conduct which constitutes the breach of contract?[56]

This point was made in the context of liability for personal injuries,[57] but is persuasive, it is submitted, whenever an act constituting a breach of contract can also justifiably be regarded as a tort.

(4) Degree of probability

14.230 In *Victoria Laundry (Windsor) Ltd. v. Newman Industries Ltd.*,[58] Asquith L.J. said:

> Nor, finally, to make a particular loss recoverable, need it be proved that upon a given state of knowledge the defendant could, as a reasonable man, foresee that a breach must necessarily result in that loss. It is enough if he could foresee it was likely so to result. It is indeed enough, ... if the loss (or some factor without which it would not have occurred) is a "serious possibility" or a "real danger". For short, we have used the word "liable" to result. Possibly the colloquialism "on the cards" indicates the shade of meaning with some approach to accuracy.[59]

14.240 It is ironic that Asquith L.J. thought the expression "on the cards" to approach accuracy, for in *Heron II*[60] where the law lords devoted many hundreds of words to this question, all agreed that the expression "on the cards" was unhelpful as being obscure or, alternatively, as indicating too remote a degree of probability.[61] A variety of other expressions used to describe uncertain events was discussed, including the following: serious possibility, real danger, foreseeable, liable to happen, not unlikely, quite likely. The first four of the above were vigorously repudiated by Lord Reid as indicating a degree of probability too remote. He considered that all would

---

[56] Swinton, "Foreseeability: Where Should the Award of Contract Damages Cease" in Reiter & Swan, *op. cit.*, footnote 55, at pp. 60 and 87.

[57] In *H. Parsons (Livestock) Ltd. v. Uttley Ingham & Co. Ltd.*, [1978] Q.B. 791 (C.A.), at p. 803, Lord Denning favoured a distinction between physical injury and economic loss, with foreseeability "at the time of the breach" the test for the former. The majority of the court, however, rejected the distinction.

[58] *Supra*, footnote 51.

[59] *Supra*, at p. 540.

[60] *Koufos v. C. Czarnikow Ltd. (Heron II)*, [1969] 1 A.C. 350 (H.L.).

[61] *Supra*, at p. 390 (Lord Reid), p. 399 (Lord Morris), p. 415 (Lord Pearce), p. 425 (Lord Upjohn). See also *Aruna Mills Ltd. v. Dhanrajmal Gobindram*, [1968] 1 Q.B. 655 (C.A.), at p. 668, *per* Donaldson J.

have resulted in liability in *Hadley v. Baxendale* itself. He gave the example of a deck of cards saying that the probability of drawing a particular card (about .02) was too remote, whereas the probability of drawing one of a named suit (.25) was not too remote.[62] The other law lords, however, were willing to accept the phrases "serious possibility", "real danger" and "liable to result".[63] Lord Pearce doubted whether mathematical considerations were even helpful. He gave the following example:

> A thing may be a natural (or even an obvious) result even though the odds are against it. Suppose a contractor was employed to repair the ceiling of one of the Law Courts and did it so negligently that it collapsed on the heads of those in court. I should be inclined to think that any tribunal (including the learned baron [Alderson] himself) would have found as a fact that the damage arose "naturally, i.e., according to the usual course of things." Yet if one takes into account the nights, weekends, and vacations, when the ceiling might have collapsed, the odds against it collapsing on top of anybody's head are nearly ten to one. I do not believe that this aspect of the matter was fully considered and worked out in the judgment. He was thinking of causation and type of consequence rather than of odds. The language of the judgment in the *Victoria Laundry* case was a justifiable and valuable clarification of the principles which *Hadley v. Baxendale* was intending to express. Even if it went further than that, it was in my opinion right.[64]

14.250 The law lords' long semantic discussion[65] was rather remote from the actual decision in *Heron II* itself. The question was whether a shipowner was liable to the charterer for loss caused by a nine-day delay. The ship was carrying a cargo of sugar to Basrah in Iraq and during the relevant nine-day period the market fell, which fall was caused partly by the arrival of another ship carrying a cargo of sugar from elsewhere. All five law lords agreed that the owner was liable for the loss caused by this drop in market. It is ironic that Lord Reid's anxiety, reflected in his rejection of foreseeability and other expressions, to protect the contract-breaker from extensive liability was not reflected in a decision favourable to the defendant in the particular case. Lord Reid said that the owner knew the cargo was being carried to a market. It was an "even chance" whether the market would go up or down.[66] Accordingly, the probability (.5) of a drop was well within the range of risks fairly to be imposed on contract-breakers.

14.260 It becomes apparent that sophisticated mathematical analysis is misplaced, for the result of cases will depend entirely on how the event is formulated that the defendant is supposed to have contemplated.[66a] Lord Reid's formulation

---

62 *Koufos, supra*, footnote 60, at p. 390.

63 *Koufos, supra*, at p. 399 (Lord Morris), p. 410 (Lord Hodson), p. 415 (Lord Pearce), p. 425 (Lord Upjohn).

64 *Koufos, supra*, at pp. 416-17.

65 Lord Denning confessed in *H. Parsons (Livestock) Ltd. v. Uttley Ingham & Co. Ltd., supra*, footnote 57, at p. 802: "I soon begin to get out of my depth. I cannot swim in this sea of semantic exercises – to say nothing of the different degrees of probability".

66 *Koufos, supra*, footnote 60, at p. 382.

(would the owner contemplate that a market price might decline?) of course leads to liability, and would do so even if the drop in the market were extraordinarily large and due to some quite unpredictable factor.[67] On the other hand, if the loss-causing event is described in narrower terms (the arrival of another ship at Basrah during the nine-day period carrying 8,000 tons of Formosan sugar), the defendant would need to be an expert on sugar markets and shipping schedules[68] in order to predict the loss.

14.270 The same point appears in *H. Parsons (Livestock) Ltd. v. Uttley Ingham & Co. Ltd.*[69] where the plaintiff's pigs developed an intestinal disease from eating nuts that became mouldy as a result of the inadequate ventilation of a feed container supplied by the defendant. Apparently this particular disease could not have been predicted by experts, but liability was imposed on the basis that the damage to the health of the animals was a natural consequence of feeding them food stored in an unfit container: "The assumption is of the parties asking themselves not what is likely to happen if the nuts are mouldy but what is likely to happen to the pigs if the hopper is unfit for storing nuts suitable to be fed to them."[70] By making the question to be contemplated more general, the liability of the defendant is enlarged. Indeed, the less a person knows about pigs the more likely he is to foresee the loss. An expert would have been astonished at the outcome, but on Scarman's L.J.'s assumption, as he said: "no more than common sense was needed for them to appreciate that food affected by bad storage conditions might well cause illness in the pigs fed upon it".[71]

(5) Damage of same type as that contemplated

14.280 The *Parsons* case also held that if damage is contemplated and is within the requisite degree of probability, the defendant will be liable even if it is more extensive than anticipated. Scarman L.J. adopted a passage from *McGregor on Damages* as follows: "in contract as in tort, it should suffice that, if physical injury or damage is within the contemplation of the parties, recovery is not to be limited because the degree of physical injury or damage could not have been anticipated".[72] Scarman L.J. then added:

> ... it would be absurd to regulate damages in such cases upon the necessity of supposing the parties had a prophetic foresight as to the exact nature of the injury that does in fact arise.
>
> . . . . .

[66a] See *Jackson v. Royal Bank of Scotland*, [2005] 2 All E.R. 71 (H.L.), at para. 46.

[67] *Koufos, supra*. But Lord Morris, at p. 394 and Lord Pearce, at p. 417 commented that the fall in price was not caused by any unusual or unpredictable factor.

[68] *Koufos, supra*, at p. 394, Lord Morris thought it relevant to note that the other ship arrived "on schedule". Contrast the approach of the House of Lords to a similar question in *Transfield Shipping Inc. v. Mercator Shipping Inc.*, [2008] UKHL 48.

[69] [1978] Q.B. 791.

[70] *Supra*, at p. 812.

[71] *Supra*, at p. 813.

[72] *Supra*, at p. 813, quoting *McGregor on Damages*, 13th ed. (London, Sweet & Maxwell, 1972), pp. 131-2.

> It does not matter . . . if they thought that the chance of physical injury, loss of profit, loss of market, or other loss as the case may be, was slight, or that the odds were against it, provided they contemplated as a serious possibility the type of consequence, not necessarily the specific consequence, that ensued upon breach.[73]

14.290 Another example of a similar principle, impliedly referred to by Scarman L.J. in the passage just quoted, is the rule that a defaulting seller or buyer is liable for the difference between the contract and market price however large this turns out to be, and however unpredictable the price change. In *Asamera Oil Corp. Ltd. v. Sea Oil & General Corp.*,[74] the Supreme Court of Canada endorsed this principle: "Once a foreseeable or contemplated consequence occurs, in this case the loss of opportunity to sell the shares, all of the damages of that kind are recoverable in assessing the quantum of damages on proper principles."[75]

(6) Type of contract

14.300 The rule in *Hadley v. Baxendale* is said to apply to all contracts, but it seems plain that in practice different kinds of contracts are treated differently. There have been persistent suggestions that a carrier is to be treated more leniently than a seller of goods. In *British Columbia and Vancouver's Island Spar, Lumber & Saw-Mill Co. Ltd. v. Nettleship*,[76] Bovill C.J. said: "It is to be observed that the defendant is a carrier, and not a manufacturer of goods supplied for a particular purpose."[77] In *Canada Foundry Co. Ltd. v. Edmonton Portland Cement Co. Ltd.*,[78] Stuart J. said: "There are indeed numbers of cases in which loss of profits has been awarded for breach of contract ... In actions against carriers the Courts have perhaps hesitated more than they have in actions against manufacturers and builders."[79] In *Victoria Laundry Ltd. v. Newman Industries Ltd.*,[80] Asquith L.J. expressed the view that the same principle applied in all cases but he conceded that its application varied from one type of case to another:

> The authorities on recovery of loss of profits as a head of damage are not easy to reconcile. At one end of the scale stand cases where there has been non-delivery or delayed delivery of what is on the face of it obviously a

[73] *Parsons, supra*, footnote 69, at p. 813. See also *Great Lakes S.S. Co. v. Maple Leaf Milling Co.*, [1923] 3 D.L.R. 308, 54 O.L.R. 174 (C.A.), revd [1924] 4 D.L.R. 1101 (P.C.); *Vacwell Engineering Co. Ltd. v. B.D.H. Chemicals Ltd.*, [1971] 1 Q.B. 88; *Houweling Nurseries Ltd. v. Fisons Western Corp.* (1988), 49 D.L.R. (4th) 205, 37 B.C.L.R. (2d) 2 (C.A.), leave to appeal to S.C.C. refused 89 N.R. 398*n*.

[74] [1979] 1 S.C.R. 633, 89 D.L.R. (3d) 1.

[75] *Supra*, at p. 655 S.C.R., p. 16 D.L.R., *per* Estey, J., referring to *Wroth v. Tyler*, [1974] Ch. 30. See 14.530-14.550, *supra*. And see *Hodgkinson v. Simms* (1994), 117 D.L.R. (4th) 161 (S.C.C.), at p. 209-10, citing this paragraph.

[76] (1868), L.R. 3 C.P. 499.

[77] *Supra*, at p. 505.

[78] (1916), 32 D.L.R. 114 (Alta. S.C. App. Div.), affd 43 D.L.R. 583 (P.C.).

[79] *Supra*, at p. 126.

[80] [1949] 2 K.B. 528.

> profit-earning chattel; for instance, a merchant or passenger ship: ... or some essential part of such a ship, for instance, a propeller, ... or engine ... In such cases loss of profit has rarely been refused. A second and intermediate class of case in which loss of profit has often been awarded is where ordinary mercantile goods have been sold to a merchant with knowledge by the vendor that the purchaser wanted them for resale; at all events, where there was no market in which the purchaser could buy similar goods against the contract on the seller's default . . . At the other end of the scale are cases where the defendant is not a vendor of the goods, but a carrier ... In such cases the courts have been slow to allow loss of profit as an item of damage. This was not, it would seem, because a different principle applies in such cases, but because the application of the same principle leads to different results. A carrier commonly knows less than a seller about the purposes for which the buyer or consignee needs the goods, or about other "special circumstances" which may cause exceptional loss if due delivery is withheld.[81]

In *Heron II*[82] Lord Upjohn said:

> . . . it must be remembered when dealing with the case of a carrier of goods by land, sea or air, he is not carrying on the same trade as the consignor of the goods and his knowledge of the practices and exigencies of the other's trade may be limited and less than between buyer and seller of goods who probably know far more about one another's business.[83]

It is impossible, however, to lay down any firm rule. Some cases have excused carriers[84] and senders of messages,[85] but many cases, including *Heron II* itself, have imposed liability on carriers for extensive losses.[86]

[81] *Supra*, at pp. 536-7.

[82] *Koufos v. C. Czarnikow Ltd. (Heron II)*, [1969] 1 A.C. 350 (H.L.).

[83] *Supra*, at p. 424.

[84] *Hadley v. Baxendale* (1854), 9 Ex. 341, 156 E.R. 145; *Horne v. Midland Ry. Co.* (1872), L.R. 7 C.P. 583, affd L.R. 8 C.P. 131 (Exch.); *British Columbia and Vancouver's Island Spar, Lumber, & Saw-Mill Co. Ltd. v. Nettleship, supra*, footnote 76; *Scott Maritimes Pulp Ltd. v. B. F. Goodrich Canada Ltd.* (1977), 72 D.L.R. (3d) 680 (N.S.S.C. App. Div.); *Thode Construction Ltd. v. Ross Bros. Cartage Ltd.* (1959), 20 D.L.R. (2d) 227 (Sask. C.A.); *Great Western Ry. Co. v. Redmayne* (1866), L.R. 1 C.P. 329; *Lengert Machinery Sales Ltd. v. Kordyban Transport Ltd.* (1968), 67 W.W.R. 386 (B.C.C.A.). See *B.D.C. Ltd. v. Hofstrand Farms Ltd.*, [1986] 1 S.C.R. 228, 26 D.L.R. (4th) 1.

[85] *Stevenson v. Montreal Telegraph Co.* (1858), 16 U.C.Q.B. 530; *Kinghorne v. Montreal Telegraph Co.* (1859), 18 U.C.Q.B. 60.

[86] *Simpson v. London & North Western Ry. Co.* (1876), 1 Q.B.D. 274; *Cornwall Gravel Co. Ltd. v. Purolator Courier Ltd.* (1979), 115 D.L.R. (3d) 511*n*, 28 O.R. (2d) 704*n* (C.A.), affd [1980] S.C.R. 118, 120 D.L.R. (3d) 575*n*; *Jameson v. Midland Ry. Co.* (1884), 50 L.T.R. 426 (Q.B. Div.); *Canadian Pacific Ltd. v. McCain Produce Co.* (1980), 113 D.L.R. (3d) 584 (C.A.), affd [1981] 2 S.C.R. 219, 123 D.L.R. (3d) 764*n; Cathcart Inspection Services Ltd. v. Purolator Courier Ltd.* (1981), 128 D.L.R. (3d) 227, 34 O.R. (2d) 187 (H.C.J.), affd 139 D.L.R. (3d) 371, 39 O.R. (2d) 656 (C.A.). See *Gee v. Buster's Auto Towing Service*, [1955] 5 D.L.R. 491 (B.C.C.A.) (truck damaged by frost after defendant's failure to tow it to garage). Damages have been awarded for illness caused by ejection of passengers at the wrong place: *Toronto Ry. Co. v. Grinsted* (1895), 24 S.C.R. 570; *Mizenchuk v. Thompson*, [1948] 1 D.L.R. 136 (Man. C.A.); *Hobbs v. London & South Western Ry. Co.* (1875), L.R. 10 Q.B. 111, holding such damage to be too remote, was doubted by the English Court of Appeal in *McMahon v. Field* (1881), 7 Q.B.D. 591 (C.A.), and by the Supreme Court of Canada in the *Grinsted* case, *supra*.

14.310 It may be suggested that in the case of a contract out of the defendant's normal line of business, the court will lean in the defendant's favour. In *Munroe Equipment v. Canadian Forest Products Ltd.*[87] where extensive losses were claimed on the breakdown of a rented tractor, Miller C.J.M. said: "It seems to me that the [claimant] company was seeking — and urgently seeking — a tractor, and was glad to obtain this rebuilt tractor. The [claimant] not the [supplier] was the originator of the contract in issue."[88] The suggestion appears to be that if, by way of a special favour to the plaintiff, the defendant makes a special effort to fulfil the latter's requirements, a more lenient standard will be applied than in the case of a defendant supplying in the normal course of business.[89] The distinction may, it is submitted, be justified by considerations of contractual exclusion of liability. One supplying goods or services in the ordinary course of business will certainly have considered the possibility of excluding liability. If the supplier chooses not to do so, it is not unreasonable to impose liability for the natural consequences of the breach. On the other hand, a unique transaction outside the supplier's normal course of business might not alert the supplier to the importance of contractual exclusion of liability, and, particularly where the transaction is entered into by way of a favour to the plaintiff, it seems unjust to impose upon the defendant a liability that would probably have been excluded if the defendant had thought of the question.

14.320 In breach of warranty actions, sellers of goods have been held liable for extensive damages including personal injury,[90] property damage,[91] and economic loss,[92] the rule in *Hadley v. Baxendale*, curiously enough, acting to assist rather than to suppress extension of liability. It may be suggested that the same principles are at work here as in other branches of products liability, that is, the allocation of the risk of loss to the business supplier of defective goods is seen to be desirable, particularly in the case of personal injuries. In some cases, however, economic losses have been held to be too remote.[93] In

[87] (1961), 29 D.L.R. (2d) 730 (Man. C.A.).

[88] *Supra*, at p. 739.

[89] This may explain the different result reached by the same court in *Scyrup v. Economy Tractor Parts Ltd.* (1963), 40 D.L.R. (2d) 1026 (Man. C.A.).

[90] *Wren v. Holt*, [1903] 1 K.B. 610 (C.A.); *Preist v. Last*, [1903] 2 K.B. 148 (C.A.); *Grant v. Australian Knitting Mills*, [1936] A.C. 85 (P.C.); *Wilson v. Rickett Cockerell & Co. Ltd.*, [1954] 1 Q.B. 598 (C.A.); *Godley v. Perry*, [1960] 1 All E.R. 36 (Q.B.); *Buckley v. Lever Bros.*, [1953] 4 D.L.R. 16, [1953] O.R. 704 (H.C.J.); *McMorran v. Dominion Stores Ltd.* (1977), 74 D.L.R. (3d) 186, 14 O.R. (2d) 559 (H.C.J.); *Sigurdson v. Hillcrest Service Ltd.* (1977), 73 D.L.R. (3d) 132 (Sask. Q.B.); *Gorman v. Ear Hearing Services Ltd.* (1969), 8 D.L.R. (3d) 765 (P.E.I.S.C.); *Negro v. Pietro's Bread Co.*, [1933] 1 D.L.R. 490, [1933] O.R. 112 (C.A.); *Coote v. Hudson's Bay Co.* (1977), 6 A.R. 59 (Dist. Ct.).

[91] *Brown v. Edgington* (1841), 2 Man. & G. 279, 133 E.R. 751; *Randall v. Raper* (1858), El. Bl. & El. 84, 120 E.R. 438; *Smith v. Green* (1875), 1 C.P.D. 92; *Randall v. Newson* (1877), 2 Q.B.D. 102 (C.A.); *Harbutt's "Plasticine" Ltd. v. Wayne Tank & Pump Co. Ltd.*, [1970] 1 Q.B. 447 (C.A.); *Canadian Building Materials Ltd. v. W.R. Meadows of Canada Ltd.* (1968), 66 D.L.R. (2d) 674, [1968] 1 O.R. 469 (H.C.J.); *Farmer v. Canada Packers Ltd.* (1956), 6 D.L.R. (2d) 63, [1956] O.R. 657 (H.C.J.); *H. Parsons (Livestock) Ltd. v. Uttley Ingham & Co. Ltd.*, [1978] Q.B. 791 (C.A.); *McKay v. Davey* (1913), 12 D.L.R. 458, 28 O.L.R. 322 (S.C. App. Div.).

actions against sellers for failure to deliver, general loss of profits has been allowed,[94] while loss based on unusual factors has been excluded.[95]

14.325 In *Fidler v. Sun Life Assurance Co. of Canada*,[95a] the Supreme Court of Canada held that damages for mental distress caused by breach of contract were recoverable, subject to the rule in *Hadley v. Baxendale*. This suggests that such damages would be very common, since some degree of vexation is almost always to be expected on breach of contract. But the court added that "in normal commercial contracts" damages for mental distress would not

---

[92] *British American Paint Co. v. Fogh* (1915), 24 D.L.R. 61 (B.C.C.A.); *Chapin v. Matthews* (1915), 24 D.L.R. 457 (Alta. S.C. App. Div.); *Wood v. Anderson* (1915), 21 D.L.R. 247, 33 O.L.R. 143 (S.C. App. Div.); *Rivers v. George White & Sons Co.* (1919), 46 D.L.R. 145 (Sask. C.A.); *Lakelse Dairy Products Ltd. v. General Dairy Machinery & Supply Ltd.* (1970), 10 D.L.R. (3d) 277 (B.C.S.C.); *Bezanson v. Kaintz* (1967), 61 D.L.R. (2d) 410 (N.S.S.C.); *New Hamburg Manufacturing Co. v. Webb* (1911), 23 O.L.R. 44 (Div. Ct.); *Uhle v. Kroeker*, [1928] 1 D.L.R. 97 (Man. C.A.); *Hammond & Co. v. Bussey* (1887), 20 Q.B.D. 79 (C.A.); *Kasler v. Slavouski*, [1928] 1 K.B. 78; *Cointat v. Myham & Son*, [1913] 2 K.B. 220, revd on other grounds 30 T.L.R. 282 (H.L.); *Mowbray v. Merryweather*, [1895] 2 Q.B. 640 (C.A.); *Alabastine Co. v. Canada Producer & Gas Engine Co.* (1914), 17 D.L.R. 813, 30 O.L.R. 394 (S.C. App. Div.); *R. W. Heron Paving Ltd. v. Dilworth Equipment Ltd.* (1963), 36 D.L.R. (2d) 462, [1963] 1 O.R. 201 (H.C.J.); *Feed-Rite Mills (1962) Ltd. v. East-West Packers (1969) Ltd.* (1975), 65 D.L.R. (3d) 175 (Man. Q.B.), affd 66 D.L.R. (3d) 768*n* (C.A.); *Amphenol Canada Ltd. v. City Cablevision Ltd.* (1974), 9 N.B.R. (2d) 444 (Q.B.); *Canlin Ltd. v. Thiokol Fibres Canada Ltd.* (1983), 142 D.L.R. (3d) 450, 40 O.R. (2d) 687 (C.A.); *Tower Equipment Rental Ltd. v. Joint Venture Equipment Sales* (1975), 60 D.L.R. (3d) 621, 9 O.R. (2d) 453 (H.C.J.); *Scyrup v. Economy Tractor Parts Ltd., supra*, footnote 89; *Stephenson v. Sanitaris Ltd.* (1913), 16 D.L.R. 695, 30 O.L.R. 60 (S.C. App. Div.) (fine imposed on plaintiff allowed but no fine imposed on sub-buyer from plaintiff); *Crispin & Co. v. Evans, Coleman & Evans, Ltd.* (1922), 68 D.L.R. 623 (B.C.S.C.), affd [1923] 3 D.L.R. 1190 (C.A.) (cost of defending action by third party); *GKN Centrax Gears Ltd. v. Matbro Ltd.*, [1976] 2 Lloyd's Rep. 555; *Hoggard v. McLennan, McFeely & Prior Ltd.*, [1953] 4 D.L.R. 794 (B.C.S.C.), affd [1954] 2 D.L.R. 516 (C.A.); *Canso Chemicals Ltd. v. Canadian Westinghouse Co. Ltd.* (1974), 54 D.L.R. (3d) 517 (N.S.S.C. App. Div.); *Dow Chemical of Canada Ltd. v. R.V. Industries Ltd.* (1979), 18 A.R. 461 (S.C.T.D.); *Maughan v. International Harvester Co. of Canada Ltd.* (1980), 112 D.L.R. (3d) 243 (N.S.C.A.); *Carlstadt Development Co. v. Alberta Pacific Elevator Co.* (1912), 7 D.L.R. 200 (Alta. S.C.) (breach of warranty of quality of seed); *Premium Grain & Seed Ltd. v. Finora Canada Ltd.*, [2000] 2 W.W.R. 506 (Sask. Q.B.).

[93] *Corbin v. Thompson* (1907), 39 S.C.R. 575; *Hamilton Gear & Machine Co. v. Lewis Bros. Ltd.*, [1924] 3 D.L.R. 367, 54 O.L.R. at p. 586 (H.C.J.), affd D.L.R. *loc. cit.*, O.L.R. *loc. cit.* p. 585 (S.C. App. Div.); *Munroe Equipment Sales Ltd. v. Canadian Forest Products Ltd.* (1961), 29 D.L.R. (2d) 730 (Man. C.A.); *Freedman v. French* (1921), 64 D.L.R. 494, 50 O.L.R. 432 (S.C. App. Div.) (damages paid by plaintiff to sub-buyer); *Bostock & Co., Ltd. v. Nicholson & Sons, Ltd.*, [1904] 1 K.B. 725; *Price v. International Harvester Co.* (1915), 23 D.L.R. 266 (Alta. S.C.) (loss of crop due to defective machinery).

[94] *Victoria Laundry (Windsor) Ltd. v. Newman Industries Ltd.*, [1949] 2 K.B. 528 (C.A.); *Leonard & Son v. Kremer* (1912), 7 D.L.R. 244 (Alta. S.C. App. Div.), vard 48 S.C.R. 518, 11 D.L.R. 491; *Brown v. Hope* (1912), 2 D.L.R. 615 (C.A.); *Union Carbide Canada Ltd. v. Scott-Foster Ltd.* (1965), 53 D.L.R. (2d) 407 (B.C.C.A.); *Canada Foundry Co. v. Edmonton Portland Cement Co.* (1918), 43 D.L.R. 583 (P.C.).

[95] *Victoria Laundry (Windsor) Ltd. v. Newman Industries Ltd., supra*, footnote 94; *Brown v. Hope, supra*, footnote 94; *Simmons & McBride Ltd. v. Kirkpatrick*, [1945] 4 D.L.R. 134 (B.C.S.C.). In *Fougere v. Talbot* (1973), 12 N.S.R. (2d) 676 (S.C.T.D.), first damage to a heating system resulting from failure to deliver oil was held to be recoverable. On damages for loss of use of property, see also 1.1830-1.2300, *supra*.

[95a] [2006] 2 S.C.R. 3, 271 D.L.R. (4th) 1.

ordinarily be within the reasonable contemplation of the parties: "It is not unusual that a breach of contract will leave the wronged party feeling frustrated or angry. The law does not award damages for such incidental frustration." However, the court continued: "The matter is otherwise . . . when the parties enter into a contract, an object of which is to secure a particular psychological benefit."[95b]. It would seem therefore that the type of contract will be significant in determining claims for mental distress. In normal commercial contracts such damages are excluded, but in contracts to secure a particular psychological benefit they are admitted. The boundaries of these categories are not entirely clear, and some contracts fall into neither category.[95c] In the later case of *Mustapha v. Culligan of Canada Ltd.*,[95d] the Supreme Court of Canada held that damages for mental distress caused by seeing a dead fly in a bottle of drinking water were not within the reasonable contemplation of the parties.

(7) Insurance considerations

14.330 Insurance considerations cannot be excluded from a full assessment of the rule in *Hadley v. Baxendale.* Where a business loss is in issue, like the stoppage of the mill in *Hadley v. Baxendale* itself, there is much to be said for a rule that the plaintiff should bear the risk of loss. Many businesses have interruption insurance covering interruption caused by factors other than breach of contract. A rational miller might well agree to carry business interruption insurance and to pay Baxendale for carriage services only. If Baxendale is liable, the latter will add, as a cost of doing business, the predicted[96] liablity and it is not clear that it is in the interest of the users of Baxendale's services in the long run to pay indirect liability insurance premiums in addition to purchasing Baxendale's services and, in many cases, carrying their own first party insurance. Similar considerations lie behind government approved limitations of liability of carriers and others offering services to the public,[97] and behind agreed exclusions of contractual liability. The point was made in the latter context by Lord Diplock in *Photo Production Ltd. v. Securicor Transport Ltd.*:[98] "it is generally more economical for the person by whom the loss will be directly sustained to [insure against it] rather than that it should be covered by the other party by liability insurance".[99]

14.340 *Hadley v. Baxendale* has sometimes been explained as an implied

[95b] *Supra*, at para. 45.

[95c] See *Kelly v. Aliant Telecom/Island Tel* (2008), 273 Nfld. & P.E.I.R. 177 (P.E.I.S.C.) (damages awarded for interruption of telephone service); *Doucette v. Eastern Regional Integrated Health Authority* (2007), 271 Nfld. & P.E.I.R. 39 (Nfld. & Lab. S.C.T.D.), at para. 42.

[95d] (2008), 293 D.L.R. (4th) 29 (S.C.C.).

[96] Predicted either by the carrier or by a liability insurer.

[97] See *B. G. Linton Construction Ltd. v. C.N.R. Co.*, [1975] 2 S.C.R. 678, 49 D.L.R. (3d) 548.

[98] [1980] A.C. 827 (H.L.).

[99] *Supra*, at p. 851.

standard form contract that the parties would, presumably, have made if they had had the time and resources to deal in their agreement with every contingency.[100] On this approach, it is plain that a rational person in the plaintiff's position would not have stipulated for the defendant's liability in every case, for the price paid by the plaintiff will reflect the full expected cost of performance to the defendant. If the defendant is required, by the contract, to indemnify the plaintiff against a risk, an appropriate premium will be charged. Usually property insurance and business interruption insurance can be arranged more cheaply by the proprietor directly, because a rational insurer will require information about the value of the property or businesses and the precautions likely to be taken against loss by the plaintiff. A plaintiff who wishes to purchase services, for example, for carriage of goods, may well find it cheaper to take out insurance against loss than to pay the carrier an indirect insurance premium in addition to the net price of the services.

14.350 In the case of personal injuries caused by defective goods, insurance considerations, it is suggested, cut the other way, for there is a strong tendency in law, most apparent in tort law, to spread the cost of personal injuries.[101] The imposition of liability for personal injuries caused by breach of warranty is in harmony with this tendency.[102] In the case of physical injuries, liability insurance has proved a reasonably efficient expedient for spending losses, in the absence of a general accident compensation scheme. These considerations, however, suggest that caution is desirable in extending compensation to mental distress, for third party liability insurance is unlikely to prove an efficient method of insuring against such risks.[103]

(8) Control of remoteness by express agreement

14.360 In *Robophone Facilities Ltd. v. Blank*,[104] the question arose whether an agreement for payment of a specific sum representing the plaintiff's actual loss was enforceable where, in the absence of the agreement, the plaintiff's loss would have been held to be too remote. The English Court of Appeal held the agreement enforceable. The case has been criticized on the ground that the parties should not be permitted to exclude the rule of remoteness or to control judicial remedies.[105] However, the case seems rightly decided, for there is nothing inherently unfair in the parties agreeing to pay the promisee's actual loss. If the promisee explains how the loss will arise, the explanation might well be notice of special circumstances within the rule of *Hadley v. Baxendale* itself. Even if no detailed explanation is given, however, it would

---

[100] See Barton, "The Economic Basis of Damages for Breach of Contract", 1 J.Leg.Stud. 277 (1972).

[101] See, *e.g.*, Fleming, *The Law of Torts*, 9th ed. (Sydney, Law Book Co., 1998), pp. 11-13.

[102] See 14.320, *supra*.

[103] See 3.1310-3.1420, *supra*.

[104] [1966] 1 W.L.R. 1428 (C.A.).

[105] See Law Commission, Working Paper No. 61, *Penalty Clauses and Forfeiture of Monies Paid* (London, H.M.S.O., 1975), p. 32.

seem that an agreement to pay a specific sum that turns out to represent the plaintiff's actual loss should be enforceable, subject to a rule of unconscionability to prevent a party from taking advantage of oppression or unfair surprise.[106]

14.370 An agreement simply to pay the plaintiff's "actual loss" with no figure specified or to exclude the rule in *Hadley v. Baxendale* creates more difficulties. Here the court would often be justified in interpreting the agreement to exclude very unexpected losses or, if the significance of the clause were not brought home to the defendant or if it were imposed upon the defendant by abuse of unequal bargaining power, the clause might be struck down for reasons of mistake or unconscionability. It is submitted that, in principle, the matter is one for the parties' agreement, subject to the doctrines of contract law just mentioned. There seems no sufficient reason why an express agreement that passes these tests should not be enforced, just as are other contractual arrangements. In *Robophone Facilities Ltd. v. Blank* Diplock L.J. said:

> If the contract contained an express undertaking by the defendant to be responsible for all actual loss to the plaintiff occasioned by the defendant's breach, whatever that loss might turn out to be, it would not affect the defendant's liability for the loss actually sustained by the plaintiff that the defendant did not know of the special circumstances which were likely to cause any enhancement of the plaintiff's loss.[107]

(9) Intervening acts

14.380 The intervening act of a third party may excuse the contract breaker if unforeseeable,[108] but will not do so if the act can be reasonably anticipated as a likely consequence of the breach. Thus in *London Joint Stock Bank v. Macmillan*,[109] a customer was held liable to a bank for drawing a cheque in such a way as to facilitate forgery. In *De La Bere v. Pearson*,[110] a newspaper was held liable for fraud of a person whom it carelessly recommended to the plaintiff as a reliable stockbroker. There can be no doubt that a person who contracted to supply a night-watchman would be liable for a burglary that would have been prevented if the contract had been performed. As crime becomes more common, contracts designed to protect persons against crime will also become more common, and damage from criminal activity will be more readily in the parties' contemplation as liable to result from the breach.

14.390 *Weld-Blundell v. Stephens*[111] is sometimes cited against this view. There, an accountant, in breach of duty, allowed a confidential letter written by the plaintiff that was defamatory of third persons to fall into the hands of an

[106] See 8.280-8.300, *supra*.
[107] *Supra*, footnote 104, at p. 1448.
[108] See *Brown & Root Ltd. v. Chimo Shipping Ltd.*, [1967] S.C.R. 642, 63 D.L.R. (2d) 1.
[109] [1918] A.C. 777 (H.L.).
[110] [1908] 1 K.B. 280 (C.A.).
[111] [1920] A.C. 956 (H.L.).

unauthorized person who revealed it to the persons defamed. The accountant was held not to be liable for the damages and costs that the plaintiff was compelled to pay to the persons he had defamed. Although one of the grounds of decision is said to be that the loss was not a natural consequence of the defendant's negligence and this appears in the headnote as the only ground of decision, it is plain that the court was strongly influenced in reaching its conclusion by the fact that it was the plaintiff's own wrong that caused his loss.[112] There can, it is submitted, be little doubt that the decision would have been otherwise if the defendant had carelessly allowed a trade secret to fall into the hands of a person who then revealed it to the plaintiff's competitor.

(10) Conclusion

14.400 The rule in *Hadley v. Baxendale* has generally been defended by economists as efficient.[113] It saves transaction costs in that it represents the usual agreement that most parties would make if they negotiated on the question. It saves the plaintiff the cost of explaining the obvious consequences of breach, of which the defendant knows just as much. It creates an incentive upon the plaintiff to reveal facts peculiarly within the plaintiff's knowledge that will cause the cost of breach to be greater than the defendant would have expected. The defendant, knowing of these peculiar facts, can act accordingly by making a rational allocation of resources to reduce the probability of breach, by refusing to contract, by raising the price, or by excluding liability. This is, in substance, the very point made by Alderson B. in *Hadley v. Baxendale* itself: "had the special circumstances been known, the parties might have specially provided for the breach of contract by special terms as to the damages in that case; and of this advantage it would be very unjust to deprive them".[114] These arguments suggest that the rule is not too generous to the defendant. It might be suggested that the rule is too generous to the plaintiff in ever allowing consequential damages. It might be argued that since business suppliers and carriers commonly exclude any liability for consequential damages a complete exclusion represents the most "efficient" rule. However, against this it may be argued that the defendant is adequately protected by the power to exclude liability by agreement: a

[112] *Supra*, footnote 111. See p. 976, *per* Lord Dunedin; p. 981, *per* Lord Sumner; p. 998, *per* Lord Wrenbury.

[113] See Posner, *Economic Analysis of Law*, 5th ed. (New York, Aspen Law & Business Publishers, 1998), pp. 140-41; Barton, "The Economic Basis of Damages for Breach of Contract", 1 J.Leg.Stud. 277 (1972), at pp. 295-6. Perloff, "Breach of Contract and the Foreseeability Doctrine of Hadley v. Baxendale", 10 J.Leg.Stud. 39 (1981). But, as Swinton points out ("Foreseeability: Where Should the Award of Contract Damages Cease" in Reiter and Swan, *Studies in Contract Law* (Toronto, Butterworths, 1980), at p. 66), the economic theory of efficient breach – that both parties jointly are better off upon breach with full compensation (see 9.200, *supra*) – might well suggest that compensation should be made for *all* the actual losses of the innocent party, for it is only on receipt of such compensation that it can justly be said that the innocent party is no worse off by the breach.

[114] *Hadley v. Baxendale* (1854), 9 Ex. 341 at p. 356, 156 E.R. 145.

supplier or carrier who gives an assurance of performance without excluding liability has no legitimate complaint if liability is imposed for some consequential losses. It follows from this argument, however, that an exclusion of liability is not in itself objectionable and that the courts should endeavour to give effect to such clauses on ordinary principles of construction and enforcement of contracts.[115]

14.410 The foregoing discussion has shown that the formulation in *Hadley v. Baxendale* is incomplete as a guide to decisions in all cases but not, it is submitted, that it is basically unsound. It can be expected that, in the light of the considerations discussed here, further glosses and explanations of the rule will develop. It seems unlikely, however, that the rule itself will be displaced, for none better has been proposed.

3. Torts

(1) Introduction

14.420 In the law of contracts, the question of remoteness is always considered to be a remedial question. In torts, on the other hand, it is impossible to draw a clear dividing line between questions of liability and damages. This is because the test of foreseeability is used in the law of negligence to determine not only the extent of damages payable by the defendant but whether there is a sufficient legal nexus between plaintiff and defendant in the first place, whereas the legal nexus in a contract case is determined by the existence of the contract itself. A test of reasonable foresight is used in negligence cases to determine whether the defendant owed a duty, whether there was a breach of the duty, and whether the damage claimed is too remote.[116] As Denning L.J. said in *Roe v. Minister of Health*,[117] the questions of liability and damages cannot be kept separate: "you will find that the three questions, duty, causation, and remoteness, run continually into one another. It seems to be that they are simply three different ways of looking at one and the same problem".[118]

14.430 If the defendant negligently drives into a fence, ejecting staples into the field beyond, which are eaten by cattle causing the animals' death,[119] the question of liability for the destruction of the cattle will appear as one of damages if the cattle and the fence are owned by the same person, but as one of liability if they are separately owned. It might seem tempting to say, therefore, that whenever the defendant is liable for some loss and the question is as to liability for some other loss, the issue is one of damages. However, in

[115] It has been held that effect is to be given to the parties' true intentions: *Photo Production Ltd. v. Securicor Transport Ltd.*, [1980] A.C. 827 (H.L.); *Beaufort Realties (1964) Inc. v. Chomedy Aluminum Co. Ltd.*, [1980] 2 S.C.R. 718, 116 D.L.R. (3d) 193; *Hunter Engineering Co. v. Syncrude Canada Ltd.*, [1989] 1 S.C.R. 426, 57 D.L.R. (4th) 321.

[116] See Fleming, *The Law of Torts*, 9th ed. (Sydney, Law Book Co., 1998), p. 115.

[117] [1954] 2 Q.B. 66 (C.A.).

[118] *Supra*, at p. 85.

[119] *Falkenham v. Zwicker* (1978), 93 D.L.R. (3d) 289 (N.S.S.C.T.D.).

many such cases the question of liability for the other loss is one that raises issues more naturally discussed in a book on tort law than in one on damages, for example, the question of negligent liability for purely economic losses. It does not seem satisfactory to treat this as a question of liability when economic loss occurs alone, but as a question of damages when some physical loss, perhaps unconnected, is also suffered by the person claiming in respect of the economic loss. It must be admitted that it is impossible to draw a strictly logical line. The approach adopted here is to examine the law of remoteness in so far as it corresponds to the rule in *Hadley v. Baxendale*, referring to such parts of substantive tort law as seem necessary for that purpose. Other questions of substantive tort law and causation are left to the writers in those fields.

(2) Proximate cause

14.440 The rule of remoteness in tort law is usually expressed as a rule that the defendant's conduct must be the "proximate cause" of the loss claimed.[120] The phrase contains two notions, that the loss must actually be caused by the conduct and that a legal test of proximity must be satisfied. The first part (cause in fact) is not so simple as it might seem, for cases have held defendants responsible for loss in circumstances where the loss would or might have occurred even without the defendant's wrongful conduct.[121] These cases indicate that more than knowledge of facts is needed to determine the question of "cause in fact".[122]

14.450 The second question, the legal test of proximity, is not concerned with actual cause. It is assumed that, but for the defendant's wrong, the

[*The next page is* 14-23]

[120] From the maxim *proxima non remota causa in lege spectatur*.

[121] See *Cook v. Lewis*, [1951] S.C.R. 830, [1952] 1 D.L.R. 1; *Baker v. Willoughby*, [1970] A.C. 467 (H.L.).

[122] See Fleming, *op. cit.*, footnote 116, at pp. 219-32, and 13.250-13.255 and 13.365, *supra*. And see *March v. E.& M.H. Stramare Pty. Ltd.* (1991), 171 C.L.R. 506 (Aust. H.C.).

plaintiff's loss would not have occurred, yet a legal limit is put upon the defendant's liability. As Andrews J. said in *Palsgraf v. Long Island Ry. Co.:*[123] "what we . . . mean by the word 'proximate' is that, because of convenience, of public policy, of a rough sense of justice, the law arbitrarily declines to trace a series of events beyond a certain point. That is not logic. It is practical politics".[124]

14.460 Just as in the law of contracts the example of the rider's marriage lost by the blacksmith's default[125] illustrates that there must be limits to legal responsibility, so also in the law of torts the principle of proximity exercises a similar function.[126] In both branches of the law the rules are so flexible that it is very difficult to predict the results of borderline cases.

(3) Law or fact

14.470 In *Barnard v. Carnegie*,[127] Masten J.A. said: "The question of remoteness [of damages] is a question of fact upon the circumstances of each case . . . and the question must be submitted to the jury."[128] In *Fraser v. Algoma Central & Hudson Bay Ry. Co.*,[129] Garrow J.A. said, similarly: "Proximate cause is a question of fact, and therefore for the jury . . . subject of course to this, that the Court must first say whether there is any evidence from which the jury acting reasonably could draw the necessary inference."[130] More recent cases have suggested that the question is one of law. In *Duwyn v. Kaprielian*,[131] Morden J.A. said, for the majority of the Ontario Court of Appeal: "Obviously, although the facts of the case are crucial, [foreseeability] is not a question of fact alone."[132] Morden J.A. also quoted and described as "undebatable" Professor Goodhart's view that when: "a judge states that he finds that, having regard to certain established facts, no reasonable man could have foreseen a particular result, then this is a statement of opinion rather than a statement of pure fact".[133] Morden J.A. also approved Professor Goodhart's comment that: "It is particularly by those cases in which [appellate courts] differ from [the trial judges'] view concerning reasonable foresight that the law of negligence has been in large part constructed."[134]

---

123 162 N.E. 99 (N.Y.C.A., 1928).

124 *Supra*, at p. 103.

125 See 14.20, *supra*.

126 See *B.D.C. Ltd. v. Hofstrand Farms Ltd.*, [1986] 1 S.C.R. 228, 26 D.L.R. (4th) 1.

127 (1924), 26 O.W.N. 264 (S.C. App. Div.).

128 *Supra*, at pp. 265-6.

129 (1904), 3 O.W.R. 104 (C.A.).

130 *Supra*, at p. 105. The proviso allows considerable judicial powers of control.

131 (1978), 94 D.L.R. (3d) 424, 22 O.R. (2d) 736 (C.A.).

132 *Supra*, at p. 436 D.L.R. Remoteness was held to be a question of law in *Humphries v. Pictou County Power Board*, [1931] 2 D.L.R. 571 (N.S.S.C. in banco).

133 Goodhart, "Emotional Shock and the Unimaginative Taxicab Driver", 69 L.Q.R. 347 (1953), at p. 351.

134 *Ibid*. See also *Overseas Tankship (U.K.) Ltd. v. Miller Steamship Co. Pty. ("Wagon Mound No. 2")*, [1967] 1 A.C. 617 (P.C.), at p. 641 (foreseeability not a "primary finding of fact but an inference from the other findings"), and *Kienzle v. Stringer* (1981),

14.480 It is submitted that these views are sound. To state that loss proved in fact to have been caused by the defendant's wrong is or is not too remote is to state a legal conclusion not any empirically verifiable fact. The earlier dicta, asserting that remoteness and "proximate cause" are questions of fact, belong to an era where the distinction between cause in fact and remoteness was blurred. It is clearly established that remoteness in contract cases is a question of law.[135] It would be undesirable to have a distinction between contract and tort on this question. Moreover, to deny to appellate courts the power to review questions of remoteness would be contrary to the tendency, expressly approved by the Supreme Court of Canada in personal injury cases, towards rational analysis and uniformity on matters of damages.[136]

(4) Foreseeability

14.490 In *Re Polemis*[137] where a plank carelessly dropped into the hold of a ship struck a spark that ignited gasoline vapour and destroyed the ship, it was held that the negligent defendant was liable for all direct loss caused by his tort even though the loss was an unforeseeable consequence of his conduct. However, in the *Wagon Mound*,[138] an Australian appeal to the Privy Council, it was held that foreseeability was to be adopted as the controlling test to govern the extent of liability as well as the existence of it. The latter decision has been followed in Britain[139] and in Canada,[140] and problems of remoteness are now dealt with in the framework of foreseeability. The Privy Council evidently considered that the adoption of the test of foreseeability made an important change in the direction of simplicity and justice. The board thought that a test of foreseeability would be simpler to apply than the complex and artificial doctrines of causation that were necessary to determine whether an injury was direct, and they thought it obviously unjust to hold a defendant liable for consequences that could not have been foreseen. Forty years later, however, it seems doubtful whether the test of foreseeability is any simpler to apply than the test it replaced, and the justice of excusing a defendant for the direct (but

---

130 D.L.R. (3d) 272, 35 O.R. (2d) 85 (C.A.), leave to appeal to S.C.C. refused D.L.R. *loc. cit.*, 38 O.R. (2d) 159*n* (a question of policy to be determined by the court).

135 In *H. Parsons (Livestock) Ltd. v. Uttley Ingham & Co. Ltd.*, [1978] Q.B. 791 (C.A.), at p. 801, Lord Denning M.R. said: "Remoteness of damage is beyond doubt a question of law." In *Hadley v. Baxendale* (1854), 9 Ex. 341, 15 E.R. 145, it was said that the judge ought to have withdrawn the question from the jury.

136 See 3.300-3.330, *supra*.

137 [1921] 3 K.B. 560 (C.A.).

138 *Overseas Tankship (U.K.) Ltd. v. Morts Dock & Engineering Co. Ltd. ("Wagon Mound")*, [1961] A.C. 388 (P.C.).

139 *Hughes v. Lord Advocate*, [1963] A.C. 837 (H.L.).

140 *R. v. Côté*, [1976] 1 S.C.R. 595, 51 D.L.R. (3d) 244; *School Division of Assiniboine South No. 3 v. Hoffer* (1971), 21 D.L.R. (3d) 608 (Man. C.A.), affd [1973] S.C.R. vi, 40 D.L.R. (3d) 480*n*; *Price v. Milawski* (1977), 82 D.L.R. (3d) 130, 18 O.R. (2d) 113 (C.A.).

unforeseeable) consequences of the negligent conduct is, in any case, far from self-evident.[141] This last point is illustrated by an examination of actual applications of the *Wagon Mound* principle. As will be seen from the following paragraphs, the courts have considered that justice requires the imposition of liability on defendants in many cases where it might have been supposed that the *Wagon Mound* principle would afford an excuse. In consequence the change in the law effected by the *Wagon Mound* has proved to be much less drastic than was first supposed.[142]

(5) Pre-disposition of the plaintiff to suffer damage

14.500 It had been established long before the *Wagon Mound* that a tortfeasor had to take the victim as found, and if the victim was unusually susceptible to loss "so much the worse for the tortfeasor, who has got to be answerable for the damage he has caused".[143] The first English case to consider the *Wagon Mound* held that the Privy Council could not have intended to affect this principle at least in cases of personal injury.[144] In *Smith v. Leech Brain & Co. Ltd.*,[145] the defendant was held liable for cancer developing from a minor burn due to a latent susceptibility of the plaintiff's. Although the cancer was unforeseeable, the defendant was held liable. This principle has been accepted by Canadian courts.[146] Mental distress ensuing on physical injury to the plaintiff has been similarly compensated.[147] An unusual instance arose in *Olson v. Lange*, where it was suggested that if the plaintiff should be imprisoned on account of an earlier offence so as to interfere with proper medical treatment of injuries caused by the defendant's wrong, the latter would be liable for the aggravated injury.[148]

14.510 In *Allan v. New Mount Sinai Hospital*,[149] it was held that a physician who had used a procedure against the express wishes of a patient was liable in battery for unexpected consequences. Linden J. said: "In battery . . . any and

---

141 See *Winfield and Jolowicz on Tort*, 16th ed. by M.V.H. Rogers (London, Sweet & Maxwell, 2002), pp. 231-35.

142 See *MacInnes v. Inverness County* (1995), 141 N.S.R. (2d) 212 at pp. 227-8, 29 M.P.L.R. (2d) 69 (C.A.), citing this passage. And see Smith, "The Limits of Tort Liability in Canada: Remoteness, Foreseeability and Proximate Cause" in Linden, *Studies in Canadian Tort Law* (Toronto, Butterworths, 1968), c. 5, p. 88, at pp. 97 and 102.

143 *Clippens Oil Co., Ltd. v. Edinburgh and District Water Trustees*, [1907] A.C. 291 (H.L.), at p. 303, *per* Lord Collins. Causation must be proved: see, *e.g.*, *Mackie v. Wolfe* (1996), 184 A.R. 339, 41 Alta. L.R. (3d) 28 (C.A.).

144 The principle was not extended to a case of economic loss in *Gold v. DeHaviland Aircraft Canada Ltd.*, [1983] 6 W.W.R. 229, 25 C.C.L.T. 180 (B.C.S.C.).

145 [1962] 2 Q.B. 405.

146 *Corrie v. Gilbert*, [1965] S.C.R. 457, 52 D.L.R. (2d) 1; *Athey v. Leonati*, [1996] 3 S.C.R. 458, 140 D.L.R. (4th) 235; *Bishop v. Arts & Letters Club of Toronto* (1978), 83 D.L.R. (3d) 107, 18 O.R. (2d) 471 (H.C.J.); *Floyd v. Bowers* (1978), 89 D.L.R. (3d) 559, 21 O.R. (2d) 204 (H.C.J.), vard 106 D.L.R. (3d) 702, 27 O.R. (2d) 487 (C.A.); *Winteringham v. Rae* (1966), 55 D.L.R. (2d) 108, [1966] 1 O.R. 727 (H.C.J.); *Thompson v. Toorenburgh* (1973), 50 D.L.R. (3d) 717 (B.C.C.A.), leave to appeal to S.C.C. refused [1973] S.C.R. vii; *Marconato v. Franklin*, [1974] 6 W.W.R. 676 (B.C.S.C.); *Alderson v. Callaghan* (1998), 40 O.R. (3d) 136 (C.A.).

all damage is recoverable, if it results from the wrongful act, whether it is foreseeable or not. The limitation devices of foresight and remoteness are not applicable to intentional torts, as they are in negligence law."[150] It seems doubtful whether remoteness can be excluded in relation to all intentional torts except where the consequences themselves are intended.[151] It has been argued in an earlier chapter that damages for conversion are limited by principles of remoteness.[152] In relation to personal injuries, however, as has been shown, the defendant is liable for unexpected consequences, even in negligence, by the application of the "thin skull" rule. The defendant in *Allan v. New Mount Sinai Hospital* was, on the facts, not negligent. But if he had been liable in negligence, for example, because no reasonable physician would have conducted such an operation at all, he would, it seems, equally have been liable for the full damage.

14.520 It may be said, therefore, in respect of personal injuries that the rule in *Re Polemis* survives virtually intact. If the defendant is responsible for some injury, the defendant will be liable for all injuries that can be attributed to the plaintiff's pre-existing condition. It is doubtful, however, whether this principle extends beyond personal injuries,[153] for the effect of applying the principle to property damage would be to reinstate *Re Polemis* altogether. The *Polemis* might be described as a "thin skull" ship. It is submitted that the distinction is justified. The human body is so delicate an organism and the parts of it are so

[*The next page is* 14-26.1]

147 *Yoshikawa v. Yu*, [1996] 8 W.W.R. 239, 21 B.C.L.R. (3d) 318 (C.A.); *Kovach v. Smith*, [1972] 4 W.W.R. 677 (B.C.S.C.); *Malcolm v. Broadhurst*, [1970] 3 All E.R. 508 (Q.B.); *Duwyn v. Kaprielian* (1978), 94 D.L.R. (3d) 424, 22 O.R. (2d) 736 (C.A.); *Nauffts v. Langan* (1976), 16 N.S.R. (2d) 10 (S.C.T.D.); *Elloway v. Boomars* (1968), 69 D.L.R. (2d) 605 (B.C.S.C.); *Negro v. Pietro's Bread Co.*, [1933] 1 D.L.R. 490, [1933] O.R. 112 (C.A.) (same principle applicable in contract and tort); *Lockyer v. Bennett* (1996), 138 Nfld. & P.E.I.R. 236 (Nfld. S.C.); *Reid v. Joy* (1997), 146 Nfld. & P.E.I.R. 281 (Nfld. S.C.); *Brown's Valve Service Pty Ltd. v. Christina*, [1997] 1 V.R. 536 (Aust. C.A.) (compensation for psychological problems aggravated by back injury); *Gindis v. Brisbourne* (1997), 39 B.C.L.R. (3d) 64, 47 C.C.L.I. (2d) 63, supplementary reasons 75 A.C.W.S. (3d) 271 (S.C), revd on other grounds 183 D.L.R. (4th) 431 (B.C.C.A.), leave to appeal to S.C.C. refused 194 D.L.R. (4th) vii ("eggshell personality"). In *Page v. Smith*, [1996] 1 A.C. 55 (H.L.), damages were awarded for *unforeseeable mental distress* even where no other personal injury had occurred. But in *Enge v. Trerise* (1960), 26 D.L.R. (2d) 529 (B.C.C.A.), schizophrenia consequent on the infliction of a scar was held to be too remote. See also *Buteikis v. Adams*, [1994] 7 W.W.R. 119, 90 B.C.L.R. (2d) 213 (S.C.). And see Linden, *Canadian Tort Law*, 5th ed. (Toronto, Butterworths, 1993), pp. 374-8.

148 (1958), 13 D.L.R. (2d) 46 (Man. C.A.).

149 (1980), 109 D.L.R. (3d) 634, 28 O.R. (2d) 356 (H.C.J.), revd on other grounds 125 D.L.R. (3d) 276*n*, 33 O.R. (2d) 603*n* (C.A.).

150 *Supra*, at p. 643 D.L.R.

151 See *Quinn v. Leathem*, [1901] A.C. 495 (H.L.); *Jones v. Fabbi* (1973), 37 D.L.R. (3d) 27 and 49 D.L.R. (3d) 316 (B.C.S.C.).

152 See 1.1270-1.1290, *supra*. But see *Lister (Ronald Elwyn) Ltd. v. Dayton Tire Canada Ltd.* (1985), 52 O.R. (2d) 88 (C.A.).

153 But see *Macaulay v. Winslow* (1973), 13 N.S.R. (2d) 614 (S.C.).

interdependent that one who wrongfully injures a part can be justly held liable for injury to other parts or to the whole.

[*The next page is* 14–27]

(6) Damage of same type as could be foreseen

14.530 It has often been said in cases applying the *Wagon Mound* that the defendant need not foresee the exact way in which the damage will occur. Dickson J. said in *R. v. Côté*[154] the defendant need not foresee the "precise concatenation of events". He added: "it is enough to fix liability if one can foresee in a general way the class or character of injury which occurred".[155] The operation of the principle of remoteness is made to depend therefore on the very malleable concept of "class or character". If the class of damage is widely defined, the liability of the defendant will be enlarged accordingly. In *Hughes v. Lord Advocate*,[156] the House of Lords held that a defendant who could have foreseen that the plaintiff might be burnt by a kerosene lamp was liable for injury caused by an explosion occurring when the lamp overturned, though the explosion could not have been foreseen. The flexibility of this line of thinking is illustrated by *Heeney v. Best*[157] where the defendant knocked out a power cable and was held liable for the death of the plaintiff's chickens which died because of the failure of an electrically powered oxygen supply. The court said that one can foresee "that damage will ensue to property in some form or other".[158]

14.540 On the other hand the operation of the principle is not predictable. In *Doughty v. Turner Manufacturing Co.*,[159] the defendant was excused from liability for injury caused by an explosion due to a chemical change occurring when a lid fell into a vat of chemicals. It was held that injury by splashing would have been foreseeable but that injury by explosion was of a different type. In *Harsim Construction v. Olsen*,[160] an electrician was held not liable for extensive fire damage occurring on the failure of a circuit-breaker, though it was admitted that he foresaw that his conduct was liable to cause a flash and some damage to the circuit-breaker.

14.550 A related principle, which also has been taken to survive the *Wagon Mound*, is the rule that, if the defendant is liable for damage to a particular interest, it is no defence that it proves much more costly than would have been anticipated.[161] Commonly cited examples include the

---

154 [1976] 1 S.C.R. 595, 51 D.L.R. (3d) 244.

155 *Supra*, at p. 604 S.C.R., p. 252 D.L.R. Dickson J. had expressed the same view in *School Division of Assiniboine South No. 3 v. Hoffer* (1971), 21 D.L.R. (3d) 608 at p. 613 (Man. C.A.), affd [1973] S.C.R. vi, 40 D.L.R. (3d) 480*n*; *Abbott v. Kasza*, [1975] 3 W.W.R. 163 (Alta. S.C.), vard 71 D.L.R. (3d) 581, (S.C. App. Div.), leave to appeal to S.C.C. refused 1 A.R. 99*n*.

156 [1963] A.C. 837 (H.L.).

157 (1978), 94 D.L.R. (3d) 451, 23 O.R. (2d) 19 (H.C.J.), vard 108 D.L.R. (3d) 366, 28 O.R. (2d) 71 (C.A.).

158 *Supra*, at p. 455 D.L.R., *per* Stark J.

159 [1964] 1 Q.B. 518 (C.A.).

160 (1972), 29 D.L.R. (3d) 121 (Alta. S.C.).

161 See 14.280, 14.290, *supra*. In *Horne v. Midland Ry. Co.* (1873), L.R. 8 C.P. 131 (Ex. Ch.), at p. 140,, Blackburn J. said: "if a man contracts to carry a chattel and loses it, he must pay the value, though he may discover that it was more valuable than he supposed".

shabby person knocked down in the street who turns out to be a high income earner and the cheap looking ornament that turns out to be a valuable vase.[162] In these cases it can be said that the damage is foreseeable: it is only the cost of making it good that is unexpectedly high.

(7) The meaning of foreseeability

14.560 Another factor that limits the effect of the *Wagon Mound* is a very expansive interpretation given by subsequent courts to the concept of foreseeability. Curiously enough, the leading case arose out of the same facts as the original *Wagon Mound* and is commonly referred to by the same name.[163] The issue in both cases was the liability of the defendant, who had unlawfully discharged oil into a harbour, for damage caused by fire when the floating oil ignited. In the first *Wagon Mound*, it was accepted that damage by fouling harbour installations was foreseeable but that damage by fire was not. In the second case, on different evidence, the Privy Council held that, after all, fire, though very improbable, could be foreseen as a possibility, and that this was enough to justify liability. It appears that the court here has given a wider meaning to foreseeability as a test for remoteness of damage than is generally considered appropriate for initial determination of liability.[164] The effect is to go a considerable way towards restoring *Re Polemis*, for direct damage is almost always foreseeable as *possible*. It may be observed too that if the meaning of foreseeability is to vary in this way the attractions of a single simple test for both liability and remoteness diminish substantially.

(8) Reduction of damages for pre-existing condition

14.570 Although a defendant is liable for losses caused by the plaintiff's pre-existing condition, it has been held in several cases that damages are to be reduced if it can be shown that the plaintiff would probably have

---

162 See *The "Arpad"* [1934] P. 189 (C.A.), at pp. 202-3, *per* Scrutton L.J. dissenting. See 14.290, *supra*. Although Scrutton L.J. was dissenting, the passage is often cited as representing modern law. See *McGregor on Damages*, 16th ed. (London, Sweet & Maxwell, 1997), §211; Fleming, *The Law of Torts*, 9th ed. (Sydney, Law Book Co., 1998), pp. 235-6. In *Parallel Productions Ltd. v. Goss Contracting Ltd.* (1968), 69 D.L.R. (2d) 609 (B.C.S.C.), the defendant was held liable for damaging a bridge and attached machinery, even though he was unaware of the presence of the latter. See also *Municipal Spraying & Contracting Ltd. v. J. Harris & Sons Ltd.* (1979), 35 N.S.R. (2d) 237 (S.C.) (slight collision causing unpredictably large loss); *Macaulay v. Winslow* (1973), 13 N.S.R. (2d) 614 (S.C.).

163 *Overseas Tankship (U.K.) Ltd. v. Miller Steamship Co. Pty. (The "Wagon Mound" No. 2)*, [1967] 1 A.C. 617 (P.C.).

164 See Fleming, *op. cit.*, footnote 162, at pp. 115-16.

suffered a similar loss in the absence of the defendant's tort. This has sometimes been called the "crumbling skull" doctrine (described by the Supreme Court of Canada as an "awkward label"), the concept being that a wrongdoer is liable for losses attributable to a "thin skull" but not to those attributable to a skull already disintegrating before the accident.[164a] Thus, in *Cutler v. Vauxhall Motors*[165] where the defendant caused the plaintiff an injury necessitating an immediate operation, damages were reduced because the operation would in any event have become necessary within a few years. In the well-known case of *Dillon v. Twin State Gas & Electric Co.*,[166] the plaintiff was electrocuted by the defendant's wires against which he fell after losing his balance on a bridge. The defendant was held liable, but damages were reduced because of the probability that the plaintiff would have in any case been killed or seriously injured by the fall. If the plaintiff's pre-accident life expectancy was short, damages will be correspondingly reduced.[167]

14.580 The same principle was applied in *Smith v. Maximovitch*[168] where the defendant caused the loss of eight of the plaintiff's teeth. The condition of the teeth before the accident was so poor that the remaining teeth had to be removed to permit the installation of dentures. The defendant was held liable for the loss of all the teeth, but the damages were less than they would have been if the plaintiff's teeth had been initially healthy. The court said:

> The damages for the loss of the teeth are to be measured by the value of his teeth to the plaintiff at the time of their loss. It seems obvious to me that if a man with a useless withered arm had to have it amputated as the result of another person's negligence, he would not be entitled to be compensated in the amount which would be appropriate had he lost a normal and healthy arm. In the case at bar the plaintiff did not lose sound and healthy teeth, but, instead, poor, neglected and diseased teeth, some of which should have been extracted even if there had never been an accident. The condition and possible "life expectancy" of the plaintiff's teeth must be taken into consideration in determining the value of the teeth to the plaintiff at the time of their loss, and a fair and reasonable discount made for their condition in arriving at their value. This, of course, results in the plaintiff receiving less than he would have received had the teeth been sound and healthy, but he will still receive fair compensation for the teeth having regard to their condition.[169]

The Supreme Court of Canada accepted this view in *Athey v. Leonati*, though the findings of fact were not thought sufficient to apply it to the particular case. Major J. said that the "general rule" was "that the plaintiff

---

[164a] *Athey v. Leonati*, [1996] 3 S.C.R. 458, 140 D.L.R. (4th) 235; *B. (K.L.) v. British Columbia*, [2003] 2 S.C.R. 403, 230 D.L.R. (4th) 513, at para. 60.

[165] [1971] 1 Q.B. 418, distinguished in *Enge v. Piers* (1973), 41 D.L.R. (3d) 623 (B.C.C.A.), where the plaintiff could have chosen the time for correction of his pre-existing disability so as not to interfere with his earning capacity. See also *Bates v. Fraser* (1963), 38 D.L.R. (2d) 30, [1963] 1 O.R. 539 (H.C.J.).

[166] 163 A. 111 (S.C.N.H., 1932).

[167] *Windrim v. Wood* (1974), 54 D.L.R. (3d) 667, 7 O.R. (2d) 211 (H.C.J.).

[168] (1968), 68 D.L.R. (2d) 244 (Sask. Q.B.).

must be returned to the position he would have been in, with all of its attendant risks and shortcomings, and not a better position".[170] Uncertainty on the question should, it would seem, be assessed according to the degree of probability (not on an all-or-nothing basis).[170a] The proper measure would seem to be reached by calculating, first, what damages a healthy plaintiff would have recovered, and then deducting the damages that would be payable by a hypothetical wrongdoer, supposing one to have been responsible for the diminution of the plaintiff's health to the level at which the defendant found it at the time of the injury.[171]

(9) New intervening acts

14.590 A commonly recurring problem in the law of remoteness is the effect on liability of voluntary acts after the time of the defendant's wrong. Where the plaintiff contributes to the loss, recovery has been allowed in cases where the courts consider that the subsequent injury can be fairly attributed to the defendant. Thus, in *Wieland v. Cyril Lord Carpets, Ltd.*,[172] Eveleigh J. said: "It can be said that it is foreseeable that one injury may affect a person's ability to cope with the vicissitudes of life and thereby be a cause of another injury."[173] On the other hand, by the principle of mitigation the plaintiff will

---

[169] *Supra*, at p. 247, *per* Disbery J. See also *Sund v. Hogg*, [1974] 5 W.W.R. 395 (Man. C.A.); *Barnaby v. O'Leary* (1956), 5 D.L.R. (2d) 41 (N.S.S.C.); *Finch v. Herzberger*, [1993] 4 W.W.R. 178, 107 Sask. R. 230 (Q.B.). In *Corrie v. Gilbert*, [1965] S.C.R. 457, 52 D.L.R. (2d) 1, the Supreme Court of Canada held improper a reduction of damages effected by the British Columbia Court of Appeal, saying that the court should not have taken into account the probability of the plaintiff's suffering a similar injury in the absence of the defendant's wrong. It seems, however, that the Supreme Court intended to affirm the "thin skull" rule, not to exclude altogether the plaintiff's pre-accident state of health; *Malone v. Chard* (1982), 34 B.C.L.R. 332 (S.C.) (damages for amputated leg reduced on account of formerly arthritic knee); *McKinney v. Roote*, [1929] 2 D.L.R. 604 (Alta. S.C.) (injury accelerating pre-existing disease), affd [1929] 4 D.L.R. 138 (S.C. App. Div.), affd [1930] S.C.R. 337, [1930] 2 D.L.R. 984; *Terris v. Crossman* (1995), 129 Nfld. & P.E.I.R. 181 (P.E.I.S.C.), affd 139 Nfld. & P.E.I.R. 87 (C.A.), leave to appeal to S.C.C. refused 206 N.R. 160*n*, 148 Nfld. & P.E.I.R. 360*n*; *Koukounakis v. Stainrod* (1995), 23 O.R. (3d) 299 at p. 306, 12 M.V.R. (3d) 78 (C.A.); *Woods v. Hubley* (1995), 130 D.L.R. (4th) 119, 146 N.S.R. (2d) 97 (C.A.), leave to appeal to S.C.C. refused 136 D.L.R. (4th) vii, 204 N.R. 79*n*; *Maligmat v. Ross* (1995), 10 B.C.L.R. (3d) 318 (S.C.); *Butler v. Caboway Development Ltd.* (1995), 136 Nfld. & P.E.I.R. 176 (Nfld. C.A.); *Harrison v. Brassard* (1994), 127 Sask. R. 147 (Q.B.), affd 144 Sask. R. 61, 124 W.A.C. 61 (C.A.); *Jeworski v. Nguyen*, [1996] 10 W.W.R. 563, 148 Sask. R. 45 (C.A.), leave to appeal to S.C.C. refused 212 N.R. 400*n*, 158 Sask. R. 240*n*; *Malloch v. Moenke* (1996), 20 B.C.L.R. (3d) 359, 117 W.A.C. 307 (C.A.); *Cameron v. Royal Insurance Co. of Canada* (1996), 174 N.B.R. (2d) 266 (Q.B.); *York v. Johnston* (1997), 148 D.L.R. (4th) 225, [1997] 9 W.W.R. 739 (B.C.C.A.); *Edgar v. Freedman*, [1998] 4 W.W.R. 473, 40 B.C.L.R. (3d) 87 (C.A.); *Madge v. Meyer*, [2000] 5 W.W.R. 38 (Alta. Q.B.), affd [2001] 7 W.W.R. 635 (C.A.); *Rhine* v. *Millan*, [2000] 7 W.W.R. 136 (Alta. Q.B.); *Zacharias v. Leys* (2005), 36 C.C.L.T. (3d) 93 (B.C.C.A.).

[170] *Athey v. Leonati*, [1996] 3 S.C.R. 458 at pp. 473-4, 140 D.L.R. (4th) 235 at p. 244.

[170a] *Malec v. J.C. Hutton Pty. Ltd.* (1990), 45 A.L.J.R. 316 (H.C.), was expressly approved in *Athey v. Leonati, supra*. See *Banga v. Takhar* (2003), 22 B.C.L.R. (4th) 372 (S.C.); *A. (T.W.N.) v. Clarke* (2003), 235 D.L.R. (4th) 13 (B.C.C.A.); *M. (E.R.) v. Clarke*, [2004] 3 W.W.R. 11 (B.C.C.A.), 13.360, *supra*. In *Lyne v. McClarty*, [2003] 5 W.W.R. 598 (Man. C.A.) the burden of proof was held to be on the defendant.

not be able to recover for damage that could, by reasonable action, have been avoided.[174] Where the plaintiff's carelessness contributes to a subsequent loss, apportionment is a third possible solution.[175]

14.600 Where the intervening act is that of a child, liability has in many cases remained on the original wrongdoer, the courts taking a wide view of the foreseeability of the propensity of children to mischief.[176] Again, where the defendant creates an emergency, the defendant is generally held liable for the damage caused by the conduct of persons acting to deal with the emergency.[177]

14.610 Where a third party's negligence intervenes, some cases have held the defendant liable on the ground that negligence of others is foreseeable.[178] In other cases, as, for example, where a physician mistreats the plaintiff after an injury, to a degree constituting actionable negligence, it has been held that

171 In *Baker v. Willoughby*, [1970] A.C. 467 (H.L.), at p. 493, Lord Reid said that the general rule, that a wrongdoer must take the plaintiff (or the plaintiff's property) as found, may work to the wrongdoer's advantage. The second of two wrongdoers would only have to pay the *additional* loss caused. The same conclusion must follow if the first of the two injuries is due to non-culpable causes. See 13.550-13.650, *supra*. See *Phillips v. Gallagher's Estate* (1980), 28 N.B.R. (2d) 559 (Q.B.); *Pryor v. Bains* (1986), 69 B.C.L.R. 395 (C.A.); *Bennett v. Mitchell* (1988), 32 B.C.L.R. (2d) 92 (C.A.); *Wenden v. Trikha* (1992), 116 A.R. 81, 1 Alta. L.R. (3d) 283 (Q.B.); *Hooiveld v. Van Biert*, [1994] 4 W.W.R. 143, 87 B.C.L.R. (2d) 160 (C.A.); *Tailleur (Next friend of) v. Grande Prairie General and Auxiliary Hospital and Nursing Home District #14* (1996), 180 A.R. 389, 38 Alta. L.R. (3d) 112 (Q.B.); *Landry v. Doucette* (1997), 194 N.B.R. (2d) 69 (C.A.) (damages reduced by 50% for pre-existing condition); *Mills v. Moberg* (1996), 27 B.C.L.R. (3d) 277, 34 C.C.L.T. (2d) 103 (S.C.); *Kozak v. Funk*, [1998] 5 W.W.R. 232, 158 Sask. R. 283 (C.A.); *Premack v. McGovern* (1997), 45 B.C.L.R. (3d) 181, 155 W.A.C. 232 (C.A.); *Reeves v. Arsenault* (1998), 168 Nfld. & P.E.I.R. 251 (P.E.I.C.A.). See *Blackwater v. Plint*, [2005] 3 S.C.R. 3, 258 D.L.R. (4th) 275.

172 [1969] 3 All E.R. 1006 (Q.B.).

173 *Supra*, at p. 1010. See also *Block v. Martin*, [1951] 4 D.L.R. 121 (Alta. S.C.); *Saccardo v. City of Hamilton* (1970), 18 D.L.R. (3d) 271, [1971] 2 O.R. 479 (H.C.J.); *Burrard Drydock Co. Ltd. v. Canadian Union Line Ltd.*, [1954] S.C.R. 307, [1954] 3 D.L.R. 561; *Urzi v. Board of Education for Borough of North York* (1980), 116 D.L.R. (3d) 687, 30 O.R. (2d) 300 (H.C.J.), affd 127 D.L.R. (3d) 768*n* (C.A.); *Boss v. Robert Simpson Eastern Ltd.* (1968), 2 D.L.R. (3d) 114 (N.S.S.C.); *Wardleworth v. Green* (1995), 66 S.A.S.R. 421 (S.C.) But see *Carpenter (Litigation Guardian of) v. Beck* (1997), 145 D.L.R. (4th) 574, [1997] 10 W.W.R. 294 (Man. C.A.) (cost of legal representation at inquest following accident too remote).

174 See *McKew v. Holland & Hannen & Cubitts (Scotland), Ltd.*, [1969] 3 All E.R. 1621 (H.L.); *Priestly v. Gilbert* (1972), 28 D.L.R. (3d) 553, [1972] 3 O.R. 501 (H.C.J.), affd 40 D.L.R. (3d) 349, 1 O.R. (2d) 365 (C.A.); *The King v. Hochelaga Shipping Co.*, [1940] S.C.R. 153, [1940] 1 D.L.R. 369; *Dudek v. Li*, [2000] 6 W.W.R. 209 (B.C.C.A.) (liability continues for loss caused by first accident).

175 *Sayers v. Harlow Urban District Council*, [1958] 1 W.L.R. 623 (C.A.); *The "Calliope"*, [1970] P. 172. This approach is persuasively advocated by Cooper-Stephenson, *Personal Injury Damages in Canada*, 2nd ed. (Toronto, Carswell, 1996), pp. 900-902.

176 See Fleming, *The Law of Torts*, 9th ed. (Sydney, Law Book Co., 1998), p. 249; *Haynes v. Harwood*, [1935] 1 K.B. 146 (C.A.).

177 Fleming, *ibid.*, at pp. 247-8.

178 *Martin v. McNamara Construction Co. Ltd.*, [1955] 3 D.L.R. 51, [1955] O.R. 523 (C.A.); *Duwyn v. Kaprielian* (1978), 94 D.L.R. (3d) 424, 22 O.R. (2d) 736 (C.A.); *Van Wynsberghe v. Knockaert*, [1954] 4 D.L.R. 510 (Man. Q.B.). See *Benjamin v. Mosher*, [1953] 1 D.L.R. 826 (N.S.S.C.) (onus of proof on defendant).

only the physician is liable, and the original wrongdoer is excused,[179] unless the defendant's wrong has actually contributed to the physician's error.[180] As Fleming has suggested,[181] this seems unduly restrictive, and applying the test formulated in the *Wagon Mound (No. 2)* it can certainly be foreseen as possible that a patient will be negligently treated.[182] In *Yepremian v. Scarborough General Hospital*,[183] a physician who failed to diagnose the plaintiff's diabetic condition was excused on the ground that a second physician (a specialist) subsequently made the same error. The court held that it was not foreseeable that a specialist would make such an error. In this context, as in others, the result will often depend on the formulation of what risk it is that the defendant was supposed to have foreseen. If one asked whether a physician failing to diagnose diabetes could reasonably foresee that damage would ensue, the answer would surely be that the physician could. No consequence is more probable and natural than that a failure to diagnose diabetes will lead to injury or death. It is only when the defendant is supposed to have foreseen a subsequent examination by a specialist that it could be said that the defendant would not expect damage to ensue. Unless the physician had reason to expect such an examination, it is submitted that the physician should be liable to the plaintiff. This would not, however, preclude a claim for contribution from the subsequent wrongdoer.

14.620 Where the intervening conduct is deliberate, the original wrongdoer has often been excused,[184] but liability has been imposed where the wrongful act is a failure to guard against the very risk that materializes, as where a person who left a house unlocked was held liable for a burglary.[185] As crime becomes more common, and therefore more to be expected, it can be anticipated that the liability of the original wrongdoer will be enlarged.

14.630 Some cases have imposed liability under fatal accident legislation for death caused by suicide of a person injured by the defendant,[186] but other cases have denied liability in such circumstances.[187] In *Swami v. Lo*,[188] the

179 *Mercer v. Gray*, [1941] 3 D.L.R. 564, [1941] O.R. 127 (C.A.); *David v. Toronto Transit Com'n* (1976), 77 D.L.R. (3d) 717, 16 O.R. (2d) 248 (H.C.J.); *Brown v. Parker* (1980), 33 N.B.R. (2d) 10 (Q.B.T.D.); *Lee v. O'Farrell* (1988), 30 B.C.L.R. (2d) 130 (S.C.). See *Walls v. MacRae* (1981), 36 N.B.R. (2d) 1 (Q.B.T.D.). Non-actionable medical error, however, was stated to be within the risks attributable to the wrongdoer: *Mercer v. Gray, supra*, at p. 567 D.L.R. See *Papp v. Leclerc* (1977), 77 D.L.R. (3d) 536, 16 O.R. (2d) 158 (C.A.); *Watson v. Grant* (1970), 72 W.W.R. 665 (B.C.S.C.); *Thompson v. Toorenburgh* (1973), 50 D.L.R. (3d) 717 (B.C.C.A.), leave to appeal to S.C.C. refused [1973] S.C.R. vii; *Block v. Martin*, [1951] 4 D.L.R. 121 (Alta. S.C.); *McMartin v. Tucek* (1962), 40 W.W.R. 195 (Alta. S.C.). In *Katzman v. Yaeck* (1982), 136 D.L.R. (3d) 536, 37 O.R. (2d) 500 (C.A.), the Ontario Court of Appeal said that the question was still open. In *Bradford v. Kanellos*, [1974] 1 S.C.R. 409, 40 D.L.R. (3d) 578, the intervening negligence of a bystander who caused panic by raising a false alarm, was held to excuse the original wrongdoer.

180 *Price v. Milawski* (1977), 82 D.L.R. (3d) 130, 18 O.R. (2d) 113 (C.A.).

181 Fleming, *op. cit.*, footnote 176, at p. 221, followed by Haines J. in *Kolesar v. Jeffries* (1974), 59 D.L.R. (3d) 367 at p. 369, 9 O.R. (2d) 41 (H.C.J.), affd 68 D.L.R. (3d) 198, 12 O.R. (2d) 142 (C.A.), affd [1978] 1 S.C.R. 491, 77 D.L.R. (3d) 161 *sub nom.* Joseph Brant Memorial Hospital v. Koziol.

182 See 14.560, *supra*.

183 (1980), 110 D.L.R. (3d) 513, 28 O.R. (2d) 494 (C.A.).

defendant had caused a fracture of the deceased's hip and subsequently the deceased shot himself. The defendant was held not to be responsible for the death, the court remarking, however, that "[h]ad this accident resulted in an injury to the head, which then led to a mental disturbance that culminated in suicide, the plaintiff's argument may have been more persuasive."[189] There are difficulties with this distinction, for severe injuries to parts of the body other than the head can cause mental disturbance and head injuries may be minor.[189a] It would seem that the defendant should be liable where the injuries are sufficiently severe for suicide to be, in medical experience, a not uncommon occurrence. Where the injury causes the plaintiff to engage in conduct that attracts criminal or analogous sanctions, the question arises whether the defendant is liable for the consequences. In *Coulter (Guardian ad Litem of) v. Ball*,[189b] the British Columbia Court of Appeal suggested that damages could be awarded for conduct that the plaintiff could not control, "but not for criminal conduct that he has the volition to avoid".

4. Distinction between Contract and Tort

14.640 Much discussion has been addressed to the question of whether the tests of remoteness differ in tort and contract. It has been asserted on various occasions that the tests are in substance the same,[190] that tortious liability is wider,[191] and that contractual liability is wider.[192] Contradictions of this kind

[184] *Antell v. Simons*, [1976] 6 W.W.R. 202 (B.C.S.C.); *Duce v. Rourke* (1951), 1 W.W.R. (N.S.) 305 (Alta. S.C.); *Cobb v. Great Western Ry.*, [1894] A.C. 419 (H.L.); *Lamb v. London Borough of Camden*, [1981] 2 All E.R. 408 (C.A.); *Lauritzen v. Barstead* (1965), 53 D.L.R. (2d) 267 (Alta. S.C.) (wife deserting injured plaintiff); *Meah v. McCreamer*, [1986] 1 All E.R. 943 (Q.B.); *Hewson v. City of Red Deer* (1977), 146 D.L.R. (3d) 32 (Alta. S.C.); *Pritchard v. J.H. Cobden Ltd.*, [1987] 2 W.L.R. 627 (C.A.) (marriage breakdown). *Contra: Patten v. Silberschein*, [1936] 3 W.W.R. 169 (B.C.S.C.); *Neilson v. Atlantic Rentals Ltd.* (1973), 8 N.B.R. (2d) at p. 605 (Q.B.), affd *loc. cit.* p. 594 (S.C. App. Div.); *Shortt v. Lawrence* (1980), 43 N.S.R. (2d) 361 (S.C.T.D.) (theft of tools from car); *Ward v. Cannock Chase District Council*, [1986] Ch. 546 (vandalism to unoccupied house).

[185] *Stansbie v. Troman*, [1948] 2 K.B. 48 (C.A.); *Win Gat v. Johnson* (1908), 9 W.L.R. 293 (Sask. Full Court); *Home Office v. Dorset Yacht Co. Ltd.*, [1970] A.C. 1004 (H.L.); *Coopers & Lybrand Ltd. v. Sterling Circuits Inc.* (1988), 47 D.L.R. (4th) 614 (B.C.S.C.).

[186] *Pigney v. Pointer's Transport Services Ltd.*, [1957] 1 W.L.R. 1121; *Gray v. Coltic* (1981), 124 D.L.R. (3d) 641, 33 O.R. (2d) 356 (C.A.), affd [1983] 2 S.C.R. 2, 1 D.L.R. (4th) 187; *Corr v. I.B.C. Vehicles*, 2008 UKHL 13; *Hayes v. Green* (1983), 30 Sask. R. 166 (Q.B.); *Costello v. Blakeson*, [1992] 2 W.W.R. 562, 74 B.C.L.R. (2d) 3, supplementary reasons 37 A.C.W.S. (3d) 253 (S.C.).

[187] *Swami v. Lo* (1979), 105 D.L.R. (3d) 451 (B.C.S.C.); *Wright Estate v. Davidson* (1992), 88 D.L.R. (4th) 698, [1992] 3 W.W.R. 611 (B.C.C.A.), leave to appeal refused 147 N.R. 394*n*, 48 W.A.C. 160*n*.

[188] *Supra*.

[189] *Supra*, at p. 454.

[189a] *Wright Estate v. Davidson*, *supra*, footnote 187.

[189b] [2005] 9 W.W.R. 14 (B.C.C.A.) at para. 90.

[190] *Morrison v. Pere Marquette Ry. Co.* (1912), 27 O.L.R. 551 (Div. Ct.), affd 12 D.L.R. 344, 28 O.L.R. 319 (S.C. App. Div.); *Haynes v. Harwood*, [1935] 1 K.B. 146 (C.A.), at p. 156, *per* Greer L.J.; *Canlin Ltd. v. Thiokol Fibres Canada Ltd.* (1983), 142 D.L.R. (3d) 450, 42 O.R. (2d) 687 (C.A.); *BG Checo International Ltd. v. British Columbia Hydro and Power Authority*, [1993] 1 S.C.R. 12 at p. 42, 99 D.L.R. (4th) 577 at p. 594 .

[191] *Koufos v. C. Czarnikow Ltd. ("Heron II")*, [1969] 1 A.C. 350 (H.L.).

often turn out to be semantic only. If sufficiently wide words are chosen, a single formula will serve as the basic test for contractual and tortious damages (the object of both is to put the party complaining in the position that would have been occupied if the wrong had not been done). It is only when refinements are introduced as, for example, by reference to the position that the plaintiff would have occupied if the contract had been fulfilled, that a difference appears. It is questionable, however, whether this can be usefully described as a difference between contract and tort. The basic rule of contract damages might justifiably be said not to be different from that governing damages in tort, but to be an application of the same rule in the light of all the circumstances of the case including the existence of an enforceable contract. Little purpose is served by a debate on whether there is one rule with two branches, or two rules.

14.650 Similar considerations apply, it is suggested, to the question of remoteness. The search for perfect compensation in awarding damages for legal wrongs is universally restricted by refusal to award compensation for very unexpected losses. Such a restriction applies to tortious and contractual liability. It is true that its operation varies from case to case, and the circumstance that liability springs from the breach of an enforceable contract between the parties is certainly relevant. But there are differences also between one tort and another and between one kind of contract and another, and it is not clear that there is any advantage in a search for two distinct rules applicable exclusively to tort on the one hand and to contract on the other, especially in the light of the weakening distinction between the two branches of legal liability.[193] There may be a more significant difference between conversion and negligence than between negligence and breach of a contract to render professional services.

14.660 In *The "Arpad"*[194] Scrutton L.J. said that damages in tort were wider than in contract:

> It is often said that the measure of damages in contract and tort is the same; I do not think this is strictly accurate. The second branch of the rule in *Hadley v. Baxendale* requires, in the case of breach of contract, where the damages are alleged to flow from the existence of another special contract which is affected by the breach of the first contract, that that consequence may be supposed to be in the contemplation of both parties ... In the cases of claims in tort, damages are constantly given for consequences of which the defendant had no notice. You negligently run down a shabby-looking man in the street, and he turns out to be a millionaire ... You have to pay the actual loss ...[195]

[192] See *The "Argentino"* (1888), 13 P.D. 191 (C.A.), at p. 201, *per* Bowen L.J.; *Cobb v. Great Western Ry Co.*, [1893] 1 Q.B. 459 (C.A.), at p. 464, *per* Bowen L.J., affd [1894] A.C. 419 (H.L.); *Weld-Blundell v. Stephens*, [1920] A.C. 956 (H.L.), at p. 979, *per* Lord Sumner; *The "Edison"* [1932] P. 52 (C.A.), at p. 61, *per* Scrutton L.J., and p. 68, *per* Greer L.J.; *The "Arpad"* [1934] P. 189 (C.A.), at p. 216, *per* Greer L.J.

[193] See Reiter, "Contracts, Torts, Relations and Reliance" in Reiter and Swan, *Studies in Contract Law* (Toronto, Butterworths, 1980), p. 235, at pp. 270-1.

[194] *Supra*, footnote 192.

[195] *Supra*, footnote 192, at pp. 201-2.

Though Scrutton L.J. was dissenting in the *Arpad*, this last proposition was not doubted by the majority and is commonly referred to in modern cases as sound law.[196]

14.670 At the time the *Arpad* was decided, *Re Polemis*[197] was the leading case establishing the proposition that a tortfeasor was liable for all direct damage caused by the wrongful act, even if unforeseeable. In the *Wagon Mound* it was held that *Re Polemis* was wrongly decided and that a tortfeasor was only to be liable for foreseeable damage.[198]

14.680 Subsequent cases, however, have, as suggested above, indicated that the actual impact of the *Wagon Mound* has been much less than was at first supposed. One of the important restrictions on the scope of the *Wagon Mound* principle is that if damage of the same type is foreseeable as actually occurs, the tortfeasor is liable for the loss, even though the manner in which it occurred was unforeseeable.[199] The decision of the English Court of Appeal in the *Parsons* case, also discussed earlier,[200] shows that this principle is not confined to torts but extends to breaches of contract also. There the supplier of a defective pig-feed container was held liable for damage caused to the pigs by eating mouldy food even though the manner in which the loss occurred could not have been foreseen.

14.690 After the decision in the first *Wagon Mound*,[201] it was widely thought that the test of remoteness in contract and tort was the same. Lord Reid vigorously repudiated this idea in the *Heron II*,[202] on the ground that the test of foreseeability in tort was much wider than the appropriate test of remoteness in contract. In his opinion quite a remote chance is "foreseeable" (he gives the example of a random choice of a particular card from a shuffled deck and of *Hadley v. Baxendale* itself, where he says that the stoppage of the mill was plainly foreseeable), but such remote possibilities ought not, in his opinion, to impose liability on contract breakers. Lord Reid said "a great many extremely unlikely results are reasonably foreseeable".[203]

14.700 The other law lords in the *Heron II*, however, were much more restrained in their criticism of the use of "foreseeability" in the context of contractual liability. Lord Morris described the *Victoria Laundry* case (in which the test was set out in terms of foreseeability) as "a most valuable analysis".[204] Lord Pearce said "the expressions used in the *Victoria Laundry* case were right" (with the exception of "on the cards").[205] As indicated above, he also doubted the propriety of reducing all questions of remoteness to terms of numerical

[196] See footnote 162, *supra.*
[197] [1921] 3 K.B. 560 (C.A.).
[198] See 14.490, *supra.*
[199] See 14.530-14.550, *supra.*
[200] See 14.280, *supra.*
[201] [1961] A.C. 388 (H.L.).
[202] *Koufos v. C. Czarnikow ("Heron II")*, [1969] 1 A.C. 350 (H.L.).
[203] *Supra*, at p. 389.
[204] *Supra*, at p. 399.
[205] *Supra*, at p. 415.

probability.[206] Lord Hodson agreed with Lord Reid that the measure of damages differed as between tort and contract, but seemed to regard this not as a rule depending on the classification of the action but as a statement simply of the usual position in most cases. He said: "the approach in tort will ... *normally* be different simply because the relationship of the parties is different".[207] This seems to suggest that if the relationship of the parties did not differ, neither would the measure of damages. Lord Upjohn, though agreeing that it was preferable to avoid the word in contract cases, indicated that foreseeability had often been used in such cases with appropriate results and he said: "as a matter of language there will in many cases be no great difference between foreseeing the possibility of an event happening and contemplating the possibility of that event happening".[208] In the *Parsons*[209] case Scarman L.J. said:

> It may be that the necessary reconciliation is to be found, notwithstanding the strictures of Lord Reid ... in holding that the difference between "reasonably foreseeable" (the test in tort) and "reasonably contemplated" (the test in contract) is semantic, not substantial. Certainly, Asquith L.J. in *Victoria Laundry (Windsor) Ltd. v. Newman Industries Ltd.* ... and Lord Pearce in *C. Czarnikow Ltd. v. Koufos* ... thought so; and I confess I think so too.[210]

14.710 It is ironic that after all the discussion of the restricted liability of the contract breaker as compared with the tortfeasor, the actual result in *Heron II* was to widen the liability for breach of contract beyond what it was formerly thought to be. It would appear, therefore, that, though the tests in contract and in tort are framed in different language, both tests are so flexible that it is very difficult to predict differences in results in actual cases on the basis of which test is applied. In *Kienzle v. Stringer*,[211] Zuber J.A. said "It is, I think, apparent that neither of these tests [in contract and tort] is a measure of precision and I number myself among those who are unable to see any real difference between them."[212]

14.720 In support of the view that liability may be wider in contract than in tort it has often been remarked that contractual liability may be extended by the communication of knowledge of special circumstances.[213] Some cases have suggested that where special circumstances are communicated, liability depends on an implied undertaking to bear the risk of the exceptional loss.[214] Such an implied undertaking will generally be difficult to discover in tort

[206] See 14.240, *supra*.
[207] *Koufos, supra*, footnote 202, at p. 411 [emphasis added].
[208] *Koufos, supra*, at pp. 422-3.
[209] *H. Parsons (Livestock) Ltd. v. Uttley Ingham & Co. Ltd.*, [1978] Q.B. 791 (C.A.).
[210] *Supra*, at p. 807.
[211] (1981), 130 D.L.R. (3d) 272, 35 O.R. (2d) 85 (C.A.), leave to appeal to S.C.C. refused D.L.R. *loc. cit.*, 38 O.R. (2d) 159*n*.
[212] *Supra*, at p. 276 D.L.R., p. 89 O.R. See *MacInnes v. Inverness County* (1995), 141 N.S.R. (2d) 212 at p. 226, 29 M.P.L.R. (2d) 69 (C.A.), citing this paragraph.
[213] See *McGregor on Damages*, 16th ed. (London, Sweet & Maxwell, 1997), §817.
[214] See 14.130-14.150, *supra*.

cases. However, as was suggested above, it is doubtful whether a genuine implied undertaking to be liable for damages can be discerned even in contract cases.[215] Moreover, the knowledge of the defendant may in some tort cases be relevant to the scope of the liability. An obvious example is that of a physician whose conduct and liability will be judged in the light of what the physician knows about the patient's condition. In *Asamera Oil Corp. Ltd. v. Sea Oil & General Corp.*,[216] the Supreme Court of Canada indicated that it favoured a single rule for contractual and tortious liability, but a rule flexible enough to take into account the voluntary element in contractual relationships. Estey J. said:

> We therefore approach the matter of the proper appraisal of the damages assessable in the peculiar circumstances of this case on the following basis: that the same principles of remoteness will apply to the claims made whether they sound in tort or contract subject only to special knowledge, understanding or relationship of the contracting parties or to any terms express or implied of the contractual arrangement relating to damages recoverable on breach.[217]

This view seems particularly desirable in light of the many recent cases holding that causes of action may be stated alternatively as contractual or tortious.[218] It would be most inconvenient in such cases for the measure of damages to vary according to the name chosen for the action. What Greer L.J. said in 1934 has even more force today: "In my judgment, where the wrong complained of may be stated either in tort or in contract, the same rules as to damages must be applied."[219]

5. Breach of Fiduciary Duty

14.725 In *Canson Enterprises Ltd. v. Boughton & Co.*,[219a] the Supreme Court of Canada discussed the liability of a solicitor for breach of fiduciary duty. In consequence of the solicitor's breach of duty the plaintiff purchased land and subsequently suffered loss from the construction of a defective building on the land. The solicitor was held not to be liable for this loss, with the majority of the court accepting the applicability of principles of remoteness.[219b] A claim for compensation implies a causal link between the defendant's wrong

---

215 *Ibid.*

216 [1979] 1 S.C.R. 633, 89 D.L.R. (3d) 1.

217 *Supra*, at p. 673 S.C.R., p. 30 D.L.R., quoted in *B.D.C. Ltd. v. Hofstrand Farms Ltd.*, [1986] 1 S.C.R. 228, 26 D.L.R. (4th) 1.

218 See Reiter, "Contracts, Torts, Relations and Reliance" in Reiter and Swan, *Studies in Contract Law* (Toronto, Butterworths, 1980).

219 *The "Arpad"* [1934] P. 189 (C.A.), at p. 219.

219a [1991] 3 S.C.R. 534, 85 D.L.R. (4th) 129, distinguished in *Hodgkinson v. Simms*, [1994] 3 S.C.R. 377, 117 D.L.R. (4th) 161. See also *Schwartz v. Longview Motel and Saloon Corp.* (1994), 18 Alta. L.R. (3d) 358, 152 A.R. 241 (Q.B.); *Reid v. Graybriar Industries Ltd.*, [2006] 10 W.W.R. 271 (Alta. Q.B.).

219b *Supra*, footnote 219a, S.C.R. *loc. cit.* pp. 580-81, D.L.R. *loc. cit.* p. 148, *per* La Forest J., and S.C.R. *loc. cit.* p. 590, D.L.R. *loc. cit.* p. 165, *per* Stevenson J. See also *Wynne v. William M. Mercer Ltd.* (1995), 131 D.L.R. (4th) 256, [1996] 4 W.W.R. 418 (B.C.C.A.) (mitigation).

and the loss in respect of which compensation is claimed.[219c] Similarly, double compensation is excluded.[219d] Different considerations apply to a restitutionary action, where recovery is based not on compensation of the plaintiff's loss but on avoidance of unjust enrichment.[219e]

6. Public Policy[219f]

14.730 Occasional cases have refused damages on grounds of public policy. An example is *Doiron v. Orr*[220] where the plaintiff claimed damages against a physician for failing to sterilize her effectively. She claimed the cost of bringing up the child who was conceived as a result. The judge, following an earlier unreported case,[221] held that such a claim was against public policy, describing it as "just simply grotesque".[222] It does not follow from *Doiron v. Orr* that the trauma caused by an abortion would not be compensable.[224] In *McFarlane v. Tayside Health Board*,[224a] a case of a failed vasectomy, damages were allowed in respect of the physical effects of pregnancy and birth but disallowed on general policy grounds for the costs of bringing up the child. This conclusion, however, was rejected in Australia[224b] and was subsequently modified in England in *Rees v. Darlington Memorial Hospital NHS Trust*[224c] where a substantial but conventional award (£15,000) was held to be appropriate. Such an award might be supported on the ground that it is compensation not for the financial loss of bringing up the child, but for

---

[219c] See *Canson Enterprises Ltd. v. Boughton & Co., supra*, footnote 219a, at pp. 160-63, *per* McLachlin J., followed on this point in *Target Holdings Ltd. v. Redferns*, [1995] 3 All E.R. 785 (H.L.), and *Swindle v. Harrison*, [1997] 4 All E.R. 705 (C.A.). *Hodkinson v. Simms, supra*, footnote 219a, however, casts some doubt on the question of causation.

[219d] *Gaudet v. Barrett* (1998), 170 N.S.R. (2d) 201 at p. 217, *sub nom.* Barrett v. Reynolds (C.A.), leave to appeal to S.C.C. refused 239 N.R. 199*n*.

[219e] See *Atlanta Industrial Sales Ltd. v. Emerald Management & Realty Ltd.*, [2006] 10 W.W.R. 515 (Alta. Q.B.).

[219f] See also 3.395, *supra*.

[220] (1978), 86 D.L.R. (3d) 719, 20 O.R. (2d) 71 (H.C.J.).

[221] *Colp v. Ringrose* (unreported, October 6, 1976, Alta. S.C.T.D.), *per* Lieberman J.).

[222] *Doiron v. Orr, supra*, footnote 220, at p. 723 D.L.R., p. 74 O.R.; *Kealey v. Berezowski* (1996), 136 D.L.R. (4th) 708, 30 O.R. (3d) 37 (Gen. Div.). See P.R. Glazebrook, Note, [1992] Camb. L.J. 226. But see *Emeh v. Kensington and Chelsea and Westminster Area Health Authority*, [1985] Q.B. 1012 (C.A.); *Thake v. Maurice*, [1986] Q.B. 644 (C.A.); *Fredette v. Wiebe* (1986), 29 D.L.R. (4th) 534 (B.C.S.C.); *Cherry (Guardian ad Litem of) v. Borsman* (1990), 75 D.L.R. (4th) 668, supplementary reasons *loc. cit.* p. 720 (B.C.S.C.), vard 94 D.L.R. (4th) 487, 70 B.C.L.R. 273 (C.A.), leave to appeal to S.C.C. refused 99 D.L.R. (4th) vii, 52 N.R. 240*n*; *Allen v. Bloomsbury Health Authority*, [1993] 1 All E.R. 651 (Q.B.); *Walkin v. South Manchester Health Authority*, [1995] 4 All E.R. 132 (C.A.); *S. (G.R.M.) v. M. (T.)* (1994), 113 D.L.R. (4th) 443, [1994] 7 W.W.R. 482 (B.C.S.C.); *Bovingdon (Litigation Guardian of) v. Hergott* (2008), 290 D.L.R. (4th) 126 (Ont. C.A.).

[223] [Footnote deleted.]

[224] See *Zimmer v. Ringrose* (1978), 89 D.L.R. (3d) 646 (S.C.T.D.), vard 124 D.L.R. (3d) 215 (C.A.), leave to appeal to S.C.C. refused 37 N.R. 289*n*.

[224a] [2000] 2 A.C. 59 (H.L. (Sc.)).

[224b] *Cattanach v. Melchior* (2003) 215 C.L.R. 1 (Aust. H.C.). In *Harriton v. Stephens*, [2006] H.C.A. 15, and *Waller v. James; Waller v. Hoolahan*, [2006] H.C.A. 16, the Australian High Court held that no action could be brought by the child.

[224c] [2004] 1 A.C. 309 (H.L.).

the loss of autonomy inflicted on the plaintiff by the defendant's negligence. In *Bevilacqua v. Altenkirk*[224d] a British Columbia Court held that damages in the case of a failed vasectomy were "essentially non-pecuniary in nature," awarding a sum of $30,000 to the mother and $20,000 to the father. The result is not dissimilar to that reached in *Rees*, though based on somewhat different grounds.[224e] Where the child is born with disabilities some cases have allowed recovery of the extra cost attributable to the disability.[224f]

14.740 Another instance of denial of recovery on policy grounds is *Weld-Blundell v. Stephens*,[225] where the defendant in breach of duty allowed to be revealed a confidential letter written by the plaintiff containing a libel on a third party. As a result of the revelation, the plaintiff was successfully sued for defamation. The House of Lords held that the defendant was not liable for this loss, first, because it was too remote, but secondly because it was the plaintiff's own tort that made him liable to the third parties; the two grounds are linked. The gist of the decision is that the defendant's revelation of the letter had simply enabled the third parties to vindicate their legal right. Lord Sumner said it was as though the plaintiffs had been in unlawful possession of another's property and the defendant had betrayed to the owner the secret of its whereabouts.[226] Lord Wrenbury went so far as to say that the plaintiff had suffered no damage at all, for "a man is not damnified by being compelled to satisfy his legal obligation".[227] Similar considerations would, it is submitted, apply to a case where negligent disclosure of a document led to a criminal conviction, and presumably also to a case of trespass leading to the discovery of incriminating evidence.

[224d] (2004), 242 D.L.R. (4th) 338 (B.C.S.C.). A very similar conclusion was reached almost contemporaneously in *Roe v. Dabbs*, [2004] 10 W.W.R. 478 (B.C.S.C.).

[224e] Groberman J dismissed a "purely conventional" award but accepted that the award he made was "arbitrary . . . to some degree".

[224f] *Parkinson v. St James and Seacroft University Hospital NHS Trust*, [2002] Q.B. 266 (C.A.); *Jones (Guardian ad litem of) v. Rostvig* (2003), 17 C.C.L.T. (3d) 253 (B.C.S.C.). The status of *Parkinson* is in some doubt in England after *Rees*.

[225] [1920] A.C. 956 (H.L.).

[226] *Supra*, at p. 981.

[227] *Supra*, at p. 998.

CHAPTER 15

MITIGATION

1. Introduction

Mitigation is used in several different senses in the law of damages. Its basic meaning is reduction of loss, and in some contexts it is used simply to refer to a factor that reduces the loss, for example, the plaintiff's pre-existing bad reputation which reduces the loss caused by defamation.[1] The principal meaning of the word in the law of damages, however, is to refer to conduct of the plaintiff that might have diminished or to events that have in fact diminished the loss complained of. It is in that sense that the word is used in this chapter. **15.10**

2. Contributory Negligence

At common law, contributory negligence by the plaintiff constituted a complete bar to an action at tort.[2] So applied, the doctrine of contributory negligence was a matter of substantive law and not of damages. In every Canadian jurisdiction, there is now legislation replacing the common law rule with a rule that damages should be apportioned between the parties.[3] In the light of this legislation, a case can be made that contributory negligence should now be regarded as part of the law of damages. However, the applicability of the apportionment legislation is not usually considered until after the initial assessment of damages. Questions concerning the interpretation of the apportionment legislation may be considered, therefore, to be separable from questions governing the initial assessment of appropriate money compensation for the loss, and a full discussion of the statutes goes far beyond the area normally considered as damages. The topic is related to questions of causation rather than of compensation. Accordingly no such discussion is included in this book. **15.20**

3. Provocation in Intentional Torts

Where the plaintiff is responsible for provoking an assault by the defendant or a trespass to the plaintiff's property, it is universally accepted that the plaintiff's conduct is relevant to the assessment of exemplary damages.[4] Plainly provocation is a relevant factor in assessing whether the **15.30**

1 See 4.200, *supra*.
2 See Fleming, *The Law of Torts*, 9th ed. (Sydney, Law Book Co., 1998), p. 303; Linden, *Canadian Tort Law*, 5th ed. (Toronto, Butterworths, 1993), p. 525.
3 Linden, *ibid.*, at pp. 461-7.
4 See 11.210, 11.220, *supra*.

defendant's conduct is worthy of punishment. It may be relevant also to any assessment of aggravated damages, for one who provokes an assault can less reasonably complain of insult or humiliation.[5]

15.40 A division of judicial opinion has appeared on the question of ordinary compensatory damages. In *Lane v. Holloway*[6] the English Court of Appeal held, following an earlier decision of the Australian High Court,[7] that provocation could never reduce compensatory damages. Lord Denning said: "The defendant has done a civil wrong and should pay compensation for the physical damage done by it. Provocation by the plaintiff can properly be used to take away any element of aggravation. But not to reduce the real damages."[8] Salmon L.J. said: "I cannot see how logically or on any principle of law the fact that the plaintiff has behaved rather badly and is a cantankerous old man can be even material when considering what is the proper compensation for the physical injury which he has suffered."[9] However, nine years later, in *Murphy v. Culhane*,[10] the English Court of Appeal reached the opposite conclusion, distinguishing *Lane v. Holloway* as a case "where the conduct of the injured man was trivial — and the conduct of the defendant was savage — entirely out of proportion to the occasion".[11]

15.50 Canadian authority is divided. In a number of cases account has been taken of the plaintiff's conduct in assessing damages for assault,[12] but the majority of the Manitoba Court of Appeal in *Check v. Andrews Hotel Co. Ltd.*[13] followed *Lane v. Holloway*, as did the Ontario Court of Appeal in *Shaw v. Gorter*.[14] This position was reaffirmed by the Ontario Court of Appeal after *Murphy v. Culhane* in *Landry v. Patterson*[15] where MacKinnon A.C.J.O. said that *Murphy* had so distinguished *Lane* as to make it "virtually

---

5 In *Lane v. Holloway*, [1968] 1 Q.B. 379 (C.A.), at p. 387, Lord Denning said that provocation could remove "any element of aggravation".

6 *Supra*, footnote 5.

7 *Fontin v. Katapodis* (1962), 108 C.L.R. 177.

8 *Lane v. Holloway, supra*, footnote 5, at p. 387.

9 *Lane v. Holloway, supra*, at p. 390.

10 [1976] 3 All E.R. 533 (C.A.).

11 *Supra*, at p. 535.

12 *Veinot v. Veinot* (1976), 22 N.S.R. (2d) 77 (S.C.T.D.), affd 81 D.L.R. (3d) 549 (S.C. App. Div.); *Collins v. Keenan* (1914), 18 D.L.R. 795 (P.E.I.S.C.); *Hartlen v. Chaddock* (1957), 11 D.L.R. (2d) 705 (N.S.S.C.); *Griggs v. Southside Hotel Ltd.*, [1946] 4 D.L.R. 73, [1947] O.R. (H.C.J.), affd [1947] 4 D.L.R. 49, O.R. *loc. cit.* p. 680 (C.A.); *Miska v. Sivec* (1959), 18 D.L.R. (2d) 363, [1959] O.R. 144 (C.A.); *Rouleau v. Rex Drive-In Theatre (1972) Ltd.* (1980), 16 C.C.L.T. 218 (B.C. Co. Ct.); *Curry v. Curry* (1977), 21 N.S.R. (2d) 454 (S.C. App. Div.); *Agar v. Canning* (1965), 54 W.W.R. 302 (Man. Q.B.), affd 55 W.W.R. 384 (C.A.); *Short v. Lewis* (1833), 3 U.C.Q.B. (O.S.) 385; *Holt v. Verbruggen* (1981), 20 C.C.L.T. 29 (B.C.S.C.); *Cottreau v. Rodgerson* (1965), 53 D.L.R. (2d) 549 (N.S.S.C.); *Cachay v. Nemeth* (1972), 28 D.L.R. (3d) 603 (Sask. Q.B.); *Durharme v. Dahms* (1980), 25 A.R. 291 (Q.B.), revd 31 A.R. 179*n sub nom. Ducharme v. Dahms* (C.A.) (but greater amount awarded as exemplary damages); *Hurley v. Moore* (1993), 107 D.L.R. (4th) 664, 12 Nfld. & P.E.I.R. 40 (Nfld. C.A.); *Bruce v. Coliseum Management Ltd.* (1998), 165 D.L.R. (4th) 472 (B.C.C.A.); *Kuehn v. Hougen* (1997), 74 A.C.W.S. (3d) 395 (Alta. C.A.). See *Green v. Costello*, [1961] N.Z.L.R. 1010; *Wilson v. Bobbie* (2006), 263 D.L.R. (4th) 332 (Alta. Q.B.); *Wilson v. Bobbie* (2006), 394 A.R. 118 (Q.B.).

13 (1974), 56 D.L.R. (3d) 364 (Man. C.A.).

meaningless" and so as to "for most intents and purposes, reverse it".[16] MacKinnon A.C.J.O. while holding himself bound by *Shaw v. Gorter* to follow *Lane v. Holloway*, nevertheless added: "There is much to be said for the argument that, if the injured party in large part brought the injuries upon himself by his provocative behaviour, then that behaviour should be considered when general damages are being assessed ... It may be that the time has come for the Court of final resort in this country to resolve the issue".[17]

15.60 A consideration of the merits of the question is therefore important. It must be assumed, in discussing provocation, that the provocation is not of such a nature as actually to justify the defendant's conduct, for then the defendant would not be liable at all. On the question of liability for loss actually caused by an unjustified assault, it is submitted that compensatory damages ought not to be reduced. No question of punishment is in issue and there seems no reason why the defendant should not pay for the actual loss caused. It seems misleading to speak of the plaintiff causing the injuries or "bringing them upon himself" for, by hypothesis, the defendant's attack is wrongful and it is that wrongful conduct that is the direct cause of the injuries complained of.[18] To deprive the plaintiff of full compensation is, it is submitted, to effect a forfeiture by taking away, on account of conduct of which the court disapproves, compensation to which the plaintiff would otherwise be entitled.[19]

4. Plaintiff's Conduct after the Wrong

(1) The basis of the rule of mitigation

15.70 A plaintiff is not entitled to recover compensation for loss that could, by taking reasonable action, have been avoided.[20] This rule rests partly on the principle of causation: losses that could reasonably have been avoided are caused by the plaintiff's inaction rather than by the defendant's wrong and partly on a policy of avoiding economic waste. As McCormick points out, the causation explanation is not entirely satisfactory, standing alone, because "it

---

[14] (1977), 77 D.L.R. (3d) 50, 16 O.R. (2d) 19 (C.A.). See also *Reeves v. Pollard* (1977), 10 A.R. 349 (S.C.T.D.); *Long v. Gardner* (1983), 144 D.L.R. (3d) 73 (Ont. H.C.J.); *Simpson v. Geswein*, [1995] 6 W.W.R. 233, 103 Man. R. (2d) 69 (Q.B.) (provocation only relevant to reduce punitive damages); *Wilson v. Bobbie* (2006), 263 D.L.R. (4th) 332 (Alta. Q.B.) at para. 39, doubting *Kuehn v. Hougen, supra*, at footnote 12.

[15] (1978), 93 D.L.R. (3d) 345, 22 O.R. (2d) 335 (C.A.).

[16] *Supra*, at p. 349 D.L.R.

[17] *Supra*, at p. 350 D.L.R.

[18] The case is different from one where the plaintiff directly contributes to the injury, as for example, by not wearing a seat-belt in an automobile.

[19] Such considerations are relevant to compensation for criminal injuries but only by express statutory provision. See e.g., *Compensation for Victims of Crime Act* (Ont.), s. 17(1).

[20] The most commonly quoted statement is that of Viscount Haldane in *British Westinghouse Electric & Manufacturing Co., Ltd. v. Underground Electric Rys. Co. of London, Ltd.*, [1912] A.C. 673 (H.L.). See *Jones v. Fabbi* (1973), 37 D.L.R. (3d) 27 and 49 D.L.R. (3d) 316 at p. 317 (B.C.S.C.) (inducing breach of contract); *Wynne v. William M. Mercer Ltd.* (1995), 131 D.L.R. (4th) 256, [1996] 4 W.W.R. 418 (B.C.C.A.) (breach of fiduciary duty).

is obvious that the defendant's wrongdoing *is* an active and substantial factor in producing the plaintiff's loss" but the plaintiff cannot recover compensation if the loss could reasonably have been avoided.[21] For that reason, McCormick considers it more realistic to recognize that the rule rests on reasons of social and economic policy, as he puts it, "to protect and conserve the economic welfare and prosperity of the whole community".[22] This however, standing alone, is equally difficult to accept as a complete explanation, because many typical cases, such as the plaintiff's failure to buy in a rising market, involve no waste of community resources yet the defendant is held not to be liable for a loss that could have been avoided. A further basis for the rule, it is suggested, is that it tends to reduce the total cost of breach to the plaintiff and defendant jointly. Another explanation is that it is unfair to the defendant that the defendant should be compelled to compensate the plaintiff for a loss that the latter could reasonably have avoided. The plaintiff can be wasteful, but it is unfair that the plaintiff should be wasteful at the defendant's expense. In the words of a Saskatchewan judge, the plaintiff has no "privilege to sit with his arms folded, as it were, and incur all the damage possible".[23]

15.80 This last point is supported by the case of *Darbishire v. Warran*,[24] discussed in an earlier chapter,[25] where the plaintiff had effected uneconomic repairs to a car damaged by the defendant. It was held by the English Court of Appeal that the defendant was not liable for more than the diminution in market value of the car caused by the damage. It is doubtful that any waste of community resources was involved in the plaintiff's conduct: he employed the services of others, for which he paid sufficient money to satisfy those persons, to effect the repairs, and it may be assumed the money expended upon the repairs represented to the plaintiff a fair price for their value to him. Pearson L.J. said: "he is fully entitled to be as extravagant as he pleases but not at the expense of the defendant."[26] Again, in *Asamera Oil Corp. v. Sea Oil & General Corp.*[27] the Supreme Court of Canada held that an owner of shares wrongfully retained by a baillee was bound to mitigate his loss by buying replacement shares on a rising market. But no waste of community resources was involved in the plaintiff's failing to buy substitute shares.

15.90 The leading case on mitigation is generally taken to be *British Westinghouse Electric & Manufacturing Co., Ltd. v. Underground Electric Rys. Co. of London Ltd.*[28] where Viscount Haldane said:

[21] McCormick, *Handbook on the Law of Damages* (St. Paul, Minn., West Publishing Co., 1935), p. 128.
[22] *Supra*, at p. 127.
[23] *Howell v. Armour & Co.* (1913), 9 D.L.R. 125 (Sask. S.C.), at p. 128, *per* Brown J.
[24] [1963] 1 W.L.R. 1067 (C.A.).
[25] See 1.2430 - 1.2550, *supra*.
[26] *Supra*, footnote 24, at p. 1075.
[27] [1979] 1 S.C.R. 633, 89 D.L.R. (3d) 1.
[28] [1912] A.C. 673 (H.L.).

> The fundamental basis [of damage assessment] is thus compensation for pecuniary loss naturally flowing from the breach; but this first principle is qualified by a second, which imposes on a plaintiff the duty of taking all reasonable steps to mitigate the loss of consequent on the breach, and debars him from claiming any part of the damage which is due to his neglect to take such steps.[29]

Viscount Haldane speaks of a "duty" to mitigate, and this is a convenient expression used in various contexts by the present writer. However, it is not strictly speaking accurate, as no question can arise of an enforceable obligation owed to the defendant. The point is again illustrated by *Darbishire v. Warran*, where Pearson L.J. said:

> For the purposes of the present case it is important to appreciate the true nature of the so-called "duty to mitigate the loss" or "duty to minimise the damage". The plaintiff is not under any actual obligation to adopt the cheaper method: if he wishes to adopt the more expensive method, he is at liberty to do so and by doing so he commits no wrong against the defendant or anyone else. The true meaning is that the plaintiff is not entitled to charge the defendant by way of damages with any greater sum than that which he reasonably needs to expend for the purpose of making good the loss.[30]

(2) Relationship with other rules of damage assessment

15.100 Very often rules of damage assessment discussed in earlier chapters incorporate and give effect to the principle of mitigation. Often, established rules can be explained by reference to mitigation, as for example the basic rules of assessment of damages in sale cases, whereby the buyer is entitled to recover the difference between the contract price and the market value.[31] This rule can be explained as resting on the basis that the buyer has a duty to mitigate the loss by purchasing substitute goods in the market on the seller's default. It has been submitted in an earlier chapter, however, that it is not entirely accurate to rest the rule on the principle of mitigation, for it can rarely be said that a buyer who fails to purchase a substitute, or fails to anticipate a rise in market prices, acts unreasonably. For this reason, it has been submitted that the sounder basis for the rule of damage assessment in sale cases is that convenience is served by a crystallization of the buyer's entitlement at an early stage.[32]

15.110 Mitigation principles are also closely related to remoteness. Thus, in *Wingold Construction Co. Ltd. v. Kramp*[33] the Supreme Court of Canada

[29] *Supra*, at p. 689.

[30] *Darbishire, supra*, footnote 24, at p. 1075. This paragraph was cited in *Duchene v. Venoit* (1989), 90 N.S.R. (2d) 74 at p. 75, 2 R.P.R. (2d) 157 (S.C.).

[31] See 1.1480 - 1.1540, *supra*.

[32] See 1.780, *supra*.

[33] [1960] S.C.R. 556, 23 D.L.R. (2d) 350. See also *The King v. Hochelaga Shipping Co.*, [1940] S.C.R. 153, [1940] 1 D.L.R. 369; *Scott Maritimes Pulp Ltd. v. B.F. Goodrich Canada Ltd.* (1977), 72 D.L.R. (3d) 680 (N.S.S.C. App. Div.).

rejected a buyer's claim for loss caused by his knowingly using defective goods, holding first that the loss resulted from failure to mitigate, and also that the loss did not arise "directly and naturally". Indeed the principle of mitigation could be subsumed by that of remoteness, for it could be said that the defendant will always contemplate that the plaintiff will act reasonably to minimize loss. But little would be gained by such a formulation since the basic principle of mitigation does not depend on the defendant's actual knowledge, contemplation, or foresight, and it is clearer, therefore, to treat mitigation as a separate rule.

15.120 Other considerations favour treating remoteness and mitigation as separate reasons for limiting recovery. One is the rule that even where the plaintiff acts reasonably in the particular circumstances, the plaintiff will not recover if the circumstances were so unexpected as to make the loss claimed too remote. In *The Borag*,[34] as the result of the defendant's wrongful arrest of a ship, the plaintiff had to provide a bank guarantee to secure her release. By reason of the plaintiff's poor credit position, it had to pay interest to its bank on the full amount of the principal sum guaranteed — a procedure that Lord Denning called "unheard of". On an arbitration the umpire held this claim to be too remote. Mustill J. reversed this result on the ground that remoteness was "the wrong legal category". Looked at from the point of view of mitigation he considered that the expenditure was recoverable.[35] The English Court of Appeal restored the decision of the umpire. Lord Denning M.R. said:

> It seems to me, as a matter of common sense and common law, that expenditure made to obtain the release of a vessel from arrest should be regarded as an item of damages, and not as mitigation. It is the natural way of dealing with it.
>
> . . . . .
>
> They are entitled to all the reasonable expenditure which they incurred as a result of the wrongful arrest and getting the ship released: but not "unheard-of" overdraft interest of this kind.[36]

15.130 Another illustration is *Simpson v. Grove Tomkins & Co.*,[37] where the defendant solicitor, in breach of his duty to the plaintiff, failed to secure a binding contract for the purchase of land. The vendor sold the land to another person from whom the plaintiff then bought it at an extravagant price. The trial judge considered that the plaintiff was "entitled to go to any length to purchase the property" and awarded damages based on the actual price paid. The English Court of Appeal held that the plaintiff was restricted to damages measured by the difference between the originally agreed price and the market value of the land. The court held the extravagant price to be too

---

[34] *Compania Financiera "Soleada" S.A. v. Hamoor Tanker Corp. Inc. (The Borag)*, [1981] 1 W.L.R. 274 (C.A.).

[35] *Compania Financiera "Soleada" S.A. v. Hamoor Tanker Corp. Inc. (The Borag)*, [1980] 1 Lloyd's Rep. 111 (Q.B.), at pp. 125-6, umpire's decision restd [1981] 1 W.L.R. 274 (C.A.).

[36] *The Borag, supra*, footnote 34, at pp. 281-2.

[37] The Times, May 17, 1982, noted 132 New Law J. 807.

remote, even though from the plaintiff's point of view the expenditure might be considered reasonable: "The question was whether the purchase of the identical property by the plaintiff, if the original agreement to purchase fell through, ought reasonably to have been foreseen by the defendant. The answer is no, even if it was reasonable for the plaintiff to pay the price that he did".[38] It is submitted that these decisions are right. In almost all remoteness cases the plaintiff can claim to have acted reasonably in the particular circumstances, and if this were sufficient to ensure recovery, the law of remoteness would be overturned.

(3) The meaning of avoidable loss

15.140 The plaintiff is barred from recovering in respect of loss that could have been avoided by acting reasonably. What is reasonable has been called a question of fact depending on the particular circumstances of the case.[39] However, as with remoteness, a finding that the plaintiff ought to have mitigated is not a simple question of fact because it involves a legal conclusion.[40] In case of doubt, the plaintiff will usually receive the benefit, because it does not lie in the mouth of the defendant to be over-critical of good faith attempts by the plaintiff to avoid difficulty caused by the defendant's wrong.[41] In *Banco de Portugal v. Waterlow & Sons, Ltd.*,[42] Lord Macmillan said:

> Where the sufferer from a breach of contract finds himself in consequence of that breach placed in a position of embarrassment the measures which he may be driven to adopt in order to extricate himself ought not to be weighed in nice scales at the instance of the party whose breach of contract has occasioned the difficulty. It is often easy after an emergency has passed to criticize the steps which have been taken to meet it, but such criticism does not come well from those who have themselves created the emergency. The law is satisfied if the party placed in a difficult situation by reason of the breach of a duty owed to him has acted reasonably in the adoption of remedial measures, and he will not be held disentitled to recover the cost of such measures merely because the party in breach can suggest that other measures less burdensome to him might have been taken.[43]

The defendant is not entitled to complain of a failure to mitigate that is

---

38 *Ibid.* However, in *White v. Carson* (1975), 13 N.B.R. (2d) 357 (Q.B.), on similar facts the higher price was held to be recoverable.

39 *McAuley v. London Transport Executive*, [1958] 2 Lloyd's Rep. 500 (C.A.); *Benjamin v. Mosher*, [1953] 1 D.L.R. 826 (N.S.S.C.); *Payzu, Ltd. v. Saunders*, [1919] 2 K.B. 581 at p. 588, *per* Bankes L.J., and p. 589, *per* Scrutton L.J.

40 *2438667 Manitoba Ltd. v. Husky Oil Ltd.*, [2007] 9 W.W.R. 642 (Man. C.A.), at para. 53, citing this passage. See 14.470, *supra*.

41 The burden of proof is on the defendant. See 13.100, *supra*.

42 [1932] A.C. 452 (H.L.).

43 *Supra*, at p. 506, followed in *Inland Feeders Ltd. v. Virdi* (1981), 18 C.C.L.T. 72 (B.C.S.C.), and *Panarctic Oils v. Menasco Manufacturing Co.* (1983), 41 A.R. 451 (C.A.), at p. 470. See also *The "Metagama"* (1927), 29 Lloyd's Rep. 253.

caused by the defendant's own fault.[44] The plaintiff may take account of aesthetic considerations in repairing damaged property.[44a]

15.150 The fact that the expenditure of time or money is required to avoid a larger loss will not excuse the plaintiff from making the expenditure if the expenditure is reasonably small and the chances of avoiding the greater loss favourable.[45] On the other hand, the plaintiff is not bound to embark on a speculative venture for the defendant's benefit.[45a] In *Pilkington v. Wood*,[46] Harman J. said: "the so-called duty to mitigate does not go so far as to oblige the injured party, even under an indemnity, to embark on a complicated and difficult piece of ligitation against a third party."[47]

15.160 That there is a limit to the expenditure of time and energy required is indicated by *Lesters Leather & Skin Co., Ltd. v. Home & Overseas Buyers Brokers, Ltd.*[48] where Lord Goddard C.J. said that disappointed buyers of goods were not "bound to go hunting the globe"[49] in search of a substitute. In other cases it has been said that the plaintiff need not "nurse the interests"[50] of the wrongdoer or undertake to "become [his] banker".[51] The plaintiff is not bound to give up rights against third parties if more would thereby be lost in the long run than would be gained in the short run. If a tenant under a long lease, or under a lease that carried security of tenure, were wrongfully excluded from occupation by a stranger it would not be reasonable to expect the tenant to stop paying rent to the landlord and to give up the lease, especially in the case of a residential tenancy.[52] The saving of rent in the

---

44 *Smith v. Tamblyn (Alta.) Ltd.* (1979), 23 A.R. 53 (S.C.T.D.) (failure of employer to provide employment records); *Smeed v. Foord* (1859), 28 L.J.Q.B. 178, followed in *Walker v. Sharpe* (1921), 56 D.L.R. 668 (Sask. C.A.) (equally divided) (defaulting seller giving constant assurances of ultimate delivery); *Copperview Haven Ltd. v. Waverley Park Estates Ltd.*, [1984] 4 W.W.R. 673, 55 B.C.L.R. 230 (C.A.).

44a *University of Regina v. Pettick* (1987), 77 D.L.R. (4th) 615, 90 Sask. R. 241 (C.A.). See also 1.2430, *supra*.

45 This is illustrated by many cases, *e.g.*, *Asamera Oil Corp. Ltd. v. Sea Oil & General Corp.*, [1979] 1 S.C.R. 633, 89 D.L.R. (3d) 1, where purchase of substitute shares on a rising market was required. On expenditure of time, see *Falkenham v. Zwicker* (1978), 93 D.L.R. (3d) 289 (N.S.S.C.T.D.), where damages were reduced because of the plaintiff's failure to search long enough for fence staples that were liable to harm his cattle. Other illustrations are repairs to property and medical treatment of injuries.

45a *Mundell v. Wesbild Holdings Ltd.* (2007), 63 C.L.R. (3d) 230 (B.C.S.C.), at para. 40, citing this passage.

46 [1953] Ch. 770.

47 *Supra*, at p. 777, followed in *Bailey v. Ornheim* (1962), 35 D.L.R. (2d) 402 (B.C.S.C.); *Bank of Montreal v. MacInnis* (1987), 83 N.B.R. (2d) 342, 47 R.P.R. 188 (C.A.); *Gallop v. Abdoulah*, [2006] 12 W.W.R. 474 (Sask. Q.B.), at para. 24, appeal allowed in part [2008] 5 W.W.R. 231 (Sask. C.A.), at para. 39, citing this passage. See *Finance America Realty v. Block* (1979), 37 N.S.R. (2d) 370 (S.C.T.D.), vard 38 N.S.R. (2d) 374 (S.C. App. Div.) (mortgagee not bound to develop land to reduce loss caused by faulty appraisal). See also *Cade Pty. Ltd. v. Thomson Simmons* (1998), 71 S.A.S.R. 571 (S.C. (Full Ct.)).

48 (1948), 64 T.L.R. 569 (C.A.). See *MacDougall v. Edmunds* (1987), 80 N.S.R. (2d) 161 (S.C.), vard 83 N.S.R. (2d) 147, 30 C.C.L.I. 23 (C.A.) (employee not bound to relocate).

49 (1948), 64 T.L.R. 569 (C.A.).

50 *Harlow & Jones, Ltd. v. Panex (Int'l) Ltd.*, [1967] 2 Lloyd's Rep. 509 (Q.B.), at p. 530.

51 *Caine v. Schultz*, [1927] 1 W.W.R. 600 (B.C.C.A.), at p. 602, *per* McPhillips J.A.

short term would often in such cases be outweighed by the loss of the value of the lease.

15.170 A related situation is one where the plaintiff can save money in the short run, but only at the cost of jeopardizing reputation. If the latter course is likely to be more costly in the long run, the plaintiff will not be obliged to pursue it. This principle is illustrated by *James Finlay & Co. v. N. V. Kwik Hoo Tong Handel Maatschappij*[53] where the defendants had shipped goods late, but the plaintiff could have forced them upon reluctant sub-buyers by taking advantage (contrary to commercial practice) of its strict legal rights (the date shown in the documents, though in fact erroneous, was deemed by the terms of the bill of lading to be conclusive). The English Court of Appeal held that the plaintiff was not bound to act so as to jeopardize its reputation. Scrutton L.J. said that the course of conduct urged by the defendant "would not be in the ordinary course of business, would violate the standard of morality which should attach to an English firm of standing, and would in fact ruin their credit in India."[54]

15.180 Another illustration is provided by *Banco de Portugal v. Waterlow & Sons, Ltd.*,[55] where the defendant was a printer of bank notes for the plaintiff, an issuing bank. The defendant, in breach of contract, delivered a quantity of bank notes to an unauthorized person, and the plaintiff cancelled the issue, refunding the value of the notes to applicants who appeared to be *bona fide* holders. It was held that the plaintiff had acted reasonably, for an issuing bank cannot afford to dishonour its own currency. Any short-term saving by such a course would be outweighed by the damage caused by loss of confidence in the currency. As in the *Finlay* case, the principle is that in judging the reasonableness of the plaintiff's conduct a long view can be taken, and the plaintiff will not be bound to take a short-term gain at the cost of jeopardizing an important long-term interest.[55a]

15.190 In some cases, the question has arisen of the effect of an offer made by the defaulting party. In *Payzu, Ltd. v. Saunders*,[56] it was held that a commercial buyer of silk was bound to accept the defendant's offer, despite the fact that the defendant had wrongfully refused to honour the terms of the contract as to

---

52 See *Elliott Steam Tug Co. v. Shipping Controller*, [1922] 1 K.B. 127 (C.A.), at p. 141, *per* Scrutton L.J.

53 [1929] 1 K.B. 400 (C.A.). See also *Kuzych v. Stewart*, [1944] 4 D.L.R. 775 (B.C.S.C.); *Kuzych v. White*, [1949] 4 D.L.R. 662 (B.C.S.C.), affd [1950] 4 D.L.R. 187 (C.A.), revd [1951] A.C. 585, [1951] 3 D.L.R. 641 (P.C.) (expelled union member not bound to take non-union employment); *Joseph v. National Magazine*, [1959] Ch. 14 (author entitled to forbid alterations to article). The *Finlay* case was distinguished in *Canso Chemicals Ltd. v. Canadian Westinghouse Co. Ltd.* (1974), 54 D.L.R. (3d) 517 (N.S.S.C. App. Div.), where the customers of the plaintiff were closely associated companies.

54 *James Finlay & Co., supra*, footnote 53, at p. 410. See also *London and South of England Building Society v. Stone*, [1983] 1 W.L.R. 1242 (C.A.).

55 [1932] A.C. 452 (H.L.). See also *Moore v. DER, Ltd.*, [1971] 1 W.L.R. 1476 (C.A.) (dentist entitled to hire replacement car, rather than buy a used car).

55a See *Rau v. Rau*, [1993] 1 W.W.R. 701, 106 Sask. R. 47 (Q.B.).

56 *Payzu, Ltd. v. Saunders*, [1919] 2 K.B. 581.

credit, casting doubt, indeed, on the plaintiff's reliability. It was held that the plaintiff was, nevertheless, bound to accept the defendant's offer. McCardie J. said: "I feel no inclination to allow in a mercantile dispute an unhappy indulgence in far-fetched resentment or an undue sensitiveness to slights or unfortunately worded letters. Business often gives rise to certain asperities."[57] In the Court of Appeal, Scrutton L.J. said: "in commercial contracts it is generally reasonable to accept an offer from the party in default. However, it is always a question of fact."[58] In cases of personal service contracts, the Court of Appeal indicated that the result might be different. Bankes L.J. gave this example:

> If [the plaintiff] had been rendering personal services and had been dismissed after being accused in the presence of others of being a thief, and if after that his employer had offered to take him back into his service, most persons would think he was justified in refusing the offer, and that it would be unreasonable to ask him in this way to mitigate the damages in an action of wrongful dismissal. But that is not to state a principle of law, but a conclusion of fact to be arrived at on a consideration of all the circumstances of the case.[59]

15.200 In cases where the plaintiff has been wrongfully dismissed, it has frequently been held that the plaintiff need not accept what amounts to an offer of demotion from the defaulting employer. Often in such cases the plaintiff in accepting the offer would suffer the humiliation of a loss of status,[60] or be compelled to work with fellow employees with whom there had been quarrels,[61] or would have to abandon a legal right to complain of the employer's wrongful act.[62] Even if, eventually, the plaintiff has to accept a loss of status, it will generally be reasonable, before being driven to that conclusion, to attempt to find other employment of equal status with the

57 *Supra*, at p. 586.

58 *Supra*, at p. 589. In *Canadian Sander Manufacturing Co. v. Canadian General Electric Co. Ltd.* (1921), 64 D.L.R. 214, 50 O.L.R. 186 (S.C. App. Div.), where there was no offer of immediate delivery and the defendant had failed to supply any goods, *Payzu, Ltd. v. Saunders* was distinguished. See also *Western Alberta Family Dental Centre Management Ltd. v. Spurr* (1992), 133 A.R. 36 (Q.B.); *Union Industries Inc. v. Beckett Packaging Ltd.* (1993), 48 C.P.R. (3d) 523, 9 B.L.R. (2d) 39 (Ont. Ct. (Gen. Div.)).

59 *Payzu, Ltd. v. Saunders, supra,* footnote 56, at pp. 588-9; *Cox v. Robertson* (1999), 181 D.L.R. (4th) 214 (B.C.C.A.). In *Damery v. Matchless Inc.* (1996), 151 N.S.R. (2d) 321, 22 C.C.E.L. (2d) 272 (S.C.), rejection of an offer of reinstatement was held to be unreasonable. See also *Gordon v. Gabriel Dumont Institute of Native Studies and Applied Research, Inc.* (1996), 145 Sask. R. 111, 21 C.C.E.L. (2d) 145 (Q.B.).

60 *Yetton v. Eastwoods Froy*, [1967] 1 W.L.R. 104 (Q.B.); *Robertson v. Wing* (1978), 95 D.L.R. (3d) 424 (B.C.S.C.), affd 119 D.L.R. (3d) 17 (C.A.); *Allison v. Amoco Production Co.* (1975), 58 D.L.R. (3d) 233 (Alta. S.C.T.D.); *O'Grady v. Ins. Corp. of British Columbia* (1975), 63 D.L.R. (3d) 370 (B.C.S.C.); *Thiessen v. Leduc*, [1975] 4 W.W.R. 387 (Alta. S.C.); *Washer v. British Columbia Toll Highways & Bridges Authority* (1965), 53 D.L.R. (2d) 620 (B.C.C.A.); *Herrschaft v. Vancouver Community College* (1978), 91 D.L.R. (3d) 328 (B.C.S.C.).

61 *Shindler v. Northern Raincoat Co.*, [1960] 1 W.L.R. 1038; *Vanderleest v. Regina (City)* (1992), 91 D.L.R. (4th) 538, [1992] 4 W.W.R. 1 (Sask. Q.B.); *Anderson v. Tecsult Eduplus Inc.* (1999), 179 N.S.R. (2d) 284 (S.C.); *Walerius* v. *McDiarmid Lumber Ltd.* (2000), 143 Man. R. (2d) 90 (Q.B.), affd 191 D.L.R. (4th) 742 (C.A.).

former position.[62a] There is no rigid rule, however, applicable to employment contracts and in some cases the employee's failure to accept a demotion has been held to be a failure to mitigate damages.[63] In *Brace v. Calder*,[64] the dissolution of a partnership involved technical dismissal of the plaintiff, but the remaining partners offered to continue the plaintiff's employment. It was held that the plaintiff ought to have accepted the offer in mitigation of damages. A similar result was reached by the Supreme Court of Canada in *Evans v. Teamsters Local Union No. 31*.[64a] Before any question of damages or mitigation arises, it must be established that the employer is in substantial breach of contract so as to justify termination by the employee. In *Longman v. Federal Business Development Bank*,[65] it was held by the British Columbia Supreme Court that a minor diminution in status did not amount to a substantial breach at all. It has been held that the plaintiff is not required to relocate to another area where there may be greater employment opportunities.[65a]

15.210 One of the limitations on the principle of *Payzu, Ltd. v. Saunders* is that a plaintiff is not bound to accept an offer from the defaulting party if acceptance involves abandoning rights against the defendant.[66] Suppose the defendant agrees to supply goods for $10, the market price at the time of due delivery is $12, and the defendant offers to supply the goods for $11 if the

---

[62] *Shindler v. Northern Raincoat Co., supra*, footnote 61; *Washer v. British Columbia Toll Highways & Bridges Authority* (1965), 53 D.L.R. (2d) 620 (B.C.C.A.). See *Peterson v. Electro Sonic Inc.* (2000), 96 A.C.W.S. (3d) 621 at para. 58, supplementary reasons 98 A.C.W.S. (3d) 198 (Ont. S.C.J.), citing this passage. In *Campbell v. MacMillan Bloedel Ltd.*, [1978] 2 W.W.R. 686 (B.C.S.C.), it was held that the mere fact of accepting a demotion did not amount to an abandonment of rights. See also *Foremost Foods Ltd. v. UFCW, Local 2000* (1989), 62 D.L.R. (4th) 201, 40 B.C.L.R. (2d) 64 (C.A.); *Schumacher v. Toronto-Dominion Bank* (1997), 147 D.L.R. (4th) 128, 29 C.C.E.L. (2d) 96, supplementary reasons 153 D.L.R. (4th) 187 (Ont. Ct. (Gen. Div.)), affd 173 D.L.R. (4th) 577, 44 C.C.E.L. (2d) 48 (C.A.), leave to appeal to S.C.C. refused 180 D.L.R. (4th) vi; *Constantinoff v. Racine* (2000), 191 Sask. R. 60 (Q.B.), at p. 66.

[62a] *Farquhar v. Butler Brothers Supplies Ltd.*, [1988] 3 W.W.R. 347, 23 B.C.L.R. (2d) 89 (C.A.); *Farmer v. Foxridge Homes Ltd.* (1992), 6 Alta. L.R. (3d) 150, 134 A.R. 55 (Q.B.), vard 18 Alta. L.R. (3d) 182, 149 A.R. 139 (C.A.).

[63] *Mifsud v. MacMillan Bathurst Inc.* (1989), 63 D.L.R. (4th) 714, 70 O.R. (2d) 701 (C.A.), leave to appeal to S.C.C. refused 68 D.L.R. (4th) vii, 113 N.R. 400*n*, and see *Lesiuk v. British Columbia Forest Products Ltd.* (1986), 33 D.L.R. (4th) 1 at p. 11, 8 B.C.L.R. (2d) 297 (C.A.); *Johnson v. Moncton Chrysler Dodge (1980) Ltd.* (1991), 114 N.B.R. (2d) 192 (C.A.).

[64] [1895] 2 Q.B. 253 (C.A.). A similar result was reached in *Lloy v. Billman* (1906), 1 E.L.R. 351 (N.S.S.C.), where an employer offered to reinstate an employee after what was held to amount to a wrongful dismissal. No dissatisfaction with the employee's work, or personal hostility was involved.

[64a] (2008), 292 D.L.R. (4th) 577 (S.C.C.).

[65] (1982), 131 D.L.R. (3d) 533 (B.C.S.C.). And see *Cayen v. Woodwards Stores Ltd.* (1993), 100 D.L.R. (4th) 294, [1993] 4 W.W.R. 11 (B.C.C.A.). See also 5.1200, 5.1210, *supra*.

[65a] *Wall v. McGrath* (1996), 139 Nfld. & P.E.I.R. 208 (Nfld. S.C.).

[66] See footnote 62, *supra*. But in *Westland Investment Corp. v. Carswell Collins Ltd.* (1996), 179 A.R. 272, 26 C.L.R. (2d) 186 (Q.B.), it was held that it might be reasonable for a plaintiff to pay a demand under protest and dispute it later. See also *A.B.D. (Metals & Waste), Ltd. v. Anglo Chemical & Ore Co. Ltd.*, [1955] 2 Lloyd's Rep. 456 (Q.B.); *Houndsditch Warehouse Co., Ltd. v. Waltex, Ltd.*, [1944] K.B. 579.

plaintiff will agree to a binding modification of the original contract. In these circumstances, it is submitted, the plaintiff would be justified in refusing the defendant's offer and the latter would be liable for damages of $2. It is not reasonable to expect the plaintiff to abandon contractual rights, and a defendant who demands such an abandonment cannot complain of the plaintiff's refusal. If the rule were otherwise the defendant could, in effect, deprive the plaintiff of contractual rights.[67] The result might be otherwise, however, if the defendant offered to supply the goods at $11 without prejudice to the plaintiff's rights to claim damages of $1.[68] In these circumstances the plaintiff would still be better off than buying in the market for $12 and suing the defendant for $2.

15.220 The principle that a plaintiff is not obliged to abandon rights against the defendant is illustrated by *Heaven & Kesterton Ltd. v. Establishment François Albiac & Cie*,[69] where the buyer rejected a shipment of timber that was substandard. The seller offered to make a price allowance if the buyer would accept the goods, but the buyer refused the offer. The arbitrator held that the buyer should have mitigated its loss by accepting the seller's offer, but Devlin J. reversed this decision and held the buyer entitled to damages on the basis that the rejection was justified. If the rule were otherwise, as Devlin J. pointed out, the buyer would be, in effect, deprived of its right to reject:

> What, in effect, the arbitrator is saying is: "From a business point of view" — if I may put it that way — "you could very well have taken up these goods and suffered no business disadvantage, providing you were given an allowance of £1 per standard for the defects in quality." Of course, that is tantamount to depriving a buyer of his right to reject altogether, and saying that, notwithstanding that he is properly rejecting, he is to be put in precisely the same position as if he had taken up the goods, and as if his only remedy was to be compensated for the damage on the basis of defective quality.[70]

On the other hand, if the goods had been of contract quality, but rejected only because of late shipment or defects in documents, the position would have been different:

> If goods are rejected in a c.i.f. contract for some reason that has nothing to do with quality — the shipment date was wrong, or documents were not in order, or something of that sort, so that the goods are properly rejected — and then the buyer goes out into the market to buy goods of the contract quality, it is open to the seller to go to him and say: "Well, then, I tender you these goods. These goods are of the contract quality. You are looking for goods of the contract quality. You rightly rejected them upon a basis

[67] See *Canadian Flexible Skate Co. Ltd. v. Monarch Brass Mfg. Co. Ltd.*, [1925] 2 D.L.R. 387 at p. 391, 56 O.L.R. 362 (S.C. App. Div.), *per* Hodgins J.A. That case involved also a "wholly unwarranted" demand for an immediate cash advance.

[68] *R. G. McLean Ltd. v. Canadian Vickers Ltd.* (1970), 15 D.L.R. (3d) 15 at pp. 18 and 23, [1971] 1 O.R. 207 (C.A.), where Arnup J.A. stressed that the defendant's offer was not conditional on abandonment of rights by the plaintiff.

[69] [1956] 2 Lloyd's Rep. 316 (Q.B.).

[70] *Supra*, at p. 321.

that had nothing to do with their quality. If you are looking, therefore, for goods to make good your loss, here they are, and I can supply cheaper than you would be able to buy them at the market rate outside." If the seller does that, that is a matter which must be taken into

[*The next page is* 15-13]

> consideration in arriving at what is the proper sum of damages to award to the buyer. It may or may not be conclusive, but it has to be taken into consideration in answering the question of whether or not the buyer has acted reasonably, as it is his duty to do, in mitigating damage.[71]

15.230 The distinction, it is suggested, lies in the fact that in the case of late delivery Devlin J. assumes that the buyer is not required to give up any right; the buyer can accept the seller's offer and retain all the former rights to damages caused by the delay. On the other hand, in the case of defective quality, the buyer can only accept the seller's offer by giving up the contractual right to have conforming goods.[72]

15.240 Another illustration is to be found in the case of *Strutt v. Whitnell*[73] where the vendor of a house, in breach of contract by reason of inability to give vacant possession, offered to repurchase the land at the contract price. The plaintiff refused the offer and asserted a right to take the land and to recover damages representing the loss of value caused by the fact that a tenant was in occupation. The English Court of Appeal held that he was entitled to do so. It is submitted that the case is correctly decided, for otherwise the plaintiff would be deprived of his right to ownership of the land. As MacKenna J. put it: "the seller cannot compel him to forgo his right to substantial damages as the price of retaining what has become his own property".[74] The situation is the opposite of that in the *Heaven & Kesterton* case: there the plaintiff could only accept the defendant's offer by giving up its right to reject; in *Strutt v. Whitnell*, the plaintiff could only accept the defendant's offer by giving up his right to ownership of the land. In both cases it was unreasonable to expect the plaintiff to give up those rights.

15.250 A somewhat similar problem arose in *Ideal Phonograph Co. v. Shapiro*[75] where by the terms of a lease the lessor undertook to install an elevator, failing which the lessee could install it and charge the cost to the lessor not exceeding $350. The lessor defaulted, and the cost of installation exceeded $350. It was held that the lessee had a contractual right to the installation and was not bound to mitigate the loss by installing the elevator for this would have the consequence of precluding the lessee from recovering the cost in

---

[71] *Supra.*

[72] It may be argued, however, that the "perfect tender" rule in sales law is too generous to the buyer. In some cases, specific performance with an abatement of price is available to a defaulting seller. See Sharpe, *Injunctions and Specific Performance*, looseleaf ed. (Toronto, Canada Law Book, 1999), 11.90-11.190.

[73] [1975] 1 W.L.R. 870 (C.A.).

[74] *Supra*, at p. 874. See also *Costello v. Calgary (City)* (1997), 152 D.L.R. (4th) 453, [1998] 1 W.W.R. 222 (Alta. C.A.), leave to appeal to S.C.C. refused 154 D.L.R. (4th) ix, 227 N.R. 149*n*. The analogy is with specific performance with an abatement of price: see Sharpe, *op. cit.*, footnote 72, 11.20-11.80. But it will be otherwise where specific performance is not available or where the plaintiff has no legitimate interest in retaining ownership, as in the case of commercial goods: see *R. G. McLean Ltd. v. Canadian Vickers Ltd., supra*, footnote 68, at p. 24 D.L.R.

[75] (1920), 58 D.L.R. 302, 48 O.L.R. 618 (S.C. App. Div.).

excess of $350, that is, in effect, of relieving the lessor of part of the lessor's obligation, an effect that the court considered unreasonable.

15.260 In personal injury cases, the plaintiff is obliged to submit to reasonable medical treatment[76] and to seek and follow medical advice where appropriate.[77] The test of reasonable conduct implies an element of objectivity. The plaintiff cannot refuse treatment for reasons of personal idiosyncracy.[78] Often, however, a reasonable person might decide either way on a question of treatment, and in such a case recovery will not be reduced.[79]

15.270 Where the plaintiff's pre-accident psychological condition prevents the plaintiff from making a rational choice, it has been argued that, on the principle that the defendant takes the plaintiff as found, damages should not

---

[76] See, *e.g.*, *Janiak v. Ippolito*, [1985] 1 S.C.R. 146, 16 D.L.R. (4th) 1; *Marcroft v. Scruttons, Ltd.*, [1954] 1 Lloyd's Rep. 395 (C.A.); *McAuley v. London Transport Executive*, [1957] 2 Lloyd's Rep. 500 (C.A.); *Cunningham v. Harrison*, [1973] Q.B. 942 (C.A.); *Mitchell v. Day* (1981), 44 N.S.R. (2d) 541 (S.C.); *Cheevers v. Van Norden* (1980), 42 N.S.R. (2d) 337 (S.C.T.D.); *Rogers v. Levy* (1980), 39 N.S.R. (2d) 310 (S.C.T.D.); *Carr v. Cashin* (1980), 36 N.S.R. (2d) 104 (S.C.T.D.); *Dominey v. Sangster* (1980), 38 N.S.R. (2d) 403 (S.C.T.D.); *Selvanayagam v. University of the West Indies*, [1983] 1 W.L.R. 585 (P.C.); *Koscik v. Baier* (1987), 46 Man. R. (2d) 64 (Q.B.); *Knoblauch v. Biwer Estate; Biwer v. Sopatyk; Besteman v. Biwer*, [1992] 5 W.W.R. 725, 104 Sask. R. 31 (Q.B.); *Gray v. Gill* (1993), 18 C.C.L.T. (2d) 120 (B.C.S.C.); *Williamson v. Guitard* (1993), 134 N.B.R. (2d) 305 (Q.B.); *Boothman v. Canada*, [1993] 3 F.C. 381, 49 C.C.E.L. 109 (T.D.); *Woods v. Hubley* (1995), 130 D.L.R. (4th) 119, 146 N.S.R. (2d) 97 (C.A.), leave to appeal to S.C.C. refused 136 D.L.R. (4th) vii; *De Meyer v. National Trust Co.* (1995), 104 Man. R. (2d) 170 (Q.B.); *White v. Slawter* (1996), 149 N.S.R. (2d) 321 (C.A.), leave to appeal to S.C.C. refused 208 N.R. 78*n*, 161 N.S.R. (2d) 80*n*. In *Andrews v. Grand & Toy Alberta Ltd.*, [1978] 2 S.C.R. 229 at p. 240, 83 D.L.R. (3d) 452 at p. 461, Dickson J. said: "I do not believe that the doctrine of mitigation of damages which might be applicable, for example, in an action for conversion of goods, has any place in a personal injury claim." But later, at p. 242 S.C.R., p. 462 D.L.R., he said "there is no duty to mitigate, in the sense of being forced to accept less than real loss. There is a duty to be reasonable." The context indicates that Dickson J. did not intend to exclude altogether the duty of mitigation in personal injury cases. His point is that an injured plaintiff should not be forced to accept less than an adequate level of care. In *Elloway v. Boomars* (1968), 69 D.L.R. (2d) 605 (B.C.S.C.), and *Montgomery v. Murphy* (1982), 136 D.L.R. (3d) 525, 37 O.R. (2d) 631 (H.C.J.), where failure to mitigate was caused by a mental state itself induced by the injury, damages were not reduced. See also *Labonte v. Sowers* (1994), 24 Alta. L.R. (3d) 53, 158 A.R. 350 (Q.B.); *Laframboise v. Billet* (1994), 25 Alta. L.R. (3d) 416, 160 A.R. 25 (Q.B.).

[77] *Brain v. Mador* (1985), 9 O.A.C. 87, 32 C.C.L.T 157 (C.A.), leave to appeal to S.C.C. refused 64 N.R. 240*n*, 13 O.A.C. 79*n*. See *Clark v. Canada*, [1994] 3 F.C. 323, 3 C.C.E.L. (2d) 172 (T.D.); *Hanna v. M.D. Realty Canada Inc.*, [1996] 10 W.W.R. 37, 24 B.C.L.R. (3d) 185 (S.C.); ; *Reeves v. Arsenault* (1998), 168 Nfld. & P.E.I.R. 251 (P.E.I.C.A.), leave to appeal to S.C.C. refused 256 N.R. 193*n*; *Daum v. Schroeder* (1997), 152 Sask. R. 161, 140 W.A.C. 161 (C.A.). See also *Cochrane v. O'Brien* (2000), 190 Nfld. & P.E.I.R. 8 (Nfld. S.C.); *Greenwood v. Dietz* (2005), 261 Sask. R. 25 (Q.B.), at para. 43.

[78] *Cunningham v. Harrison, supra*, footnote 76; *McAuley v. London Transport Executive*, [1958] 2 Lloyd's Rep. 500 (C.A.).

[79] *Engel v. Salyn*, [1993] 1 S.C.R. 306, 99 D.L.R. (4th) 401 (reasonableness a question of fact); *Steele v. Robert George Ltd.*, [1942] A.C. 497 (H.L.); *Richardson v. Redpath, Brown & Co.*, [1944] A.C. 62 (H.L.); *Savage v. T. Wallis, Ltd.*, [1966] 1 Lloyd's Rep. 357 (C.A.); *Sandhu v. Kuntz*, [1996] 6 W.W.R. 75, 18 B.C.L.R. (3d) 167 (C.A.). See *McAuley v. London Transport Executive, supra*, at p. 505; *Jaillet v. Allain* (1995), 165 N.B.R. (2d) 161 (Q.B.). See also *Byron v. Larson*, [2005] 3 W.W.R. 337 (Alta. C.A.); *Pfob v. Bakalik*, [2005] 1 W.W.R. 407 (Alta. C.A.).

be reduced.[80] The acceptance of this argument would require a distinction, difficult to maintain in practice, between a psychological deficiency and a simple predisposition to be unreasonable, and would go far towards abolishing the requirement of mitigation in this field.

15.280 If religious beliefs prevent the plaintiff from following recommended treatment, it would seem that recovery should not be diminished, unless perhaps the religion has so few adherents as to amount to an idiosyncracy. In a criminal case, *R. v. Blaue*,[81] it was held that an accused was responsible for the death of a woman whose life could have been saved by a blood transfusion that she refused on religious grounds. It would seem that an action under the *Fatal Accidents Act* by the woman's relatives should succeed, for the test is the same as in the criminal law (or, at any rate, not more generous to the defendant) that is, whether the death is caused by the defendant's wrongful act. In the case where the woman survives but with injuries that might have been alleviated by a blood transfusion, it might be argued that by refusing an operation that would offend deeply held religious beliefs she mitigates a possibly larger non-pecuniary loss.[82]

(4) Expense incurred in attempt to mitigate

15.290 Often the plaintiff incurs expenses in attempting to mitigate loss. If the mitigation is successful and a larger loss is avoided by expenditure of a lesser sum, the plaintiff is entitled to recover the lesser sum. The plaintiff will in such a case have reduced the loss (to the amount of the lesser sum) but will not have avoided all loss.[83] It follows that if the plaintiff incurs expense in a reasonable but unsuccessful attempt to mitigate, the defendant will be liable for the expense even though, in the result, liability is greater than it would have been if the plaintiff had done nothing.[83a] Thus, the cost of the plaintiff's reasonable medical care is recoverable from the person responsible for an injury even if the care proves ineffective.[84] In *Wilson v. United Counties Bank*,[85] Lord Atkinson said: "If one man inflicts an injury upon another the resort by the sufferer to reasonable expedients for the bona fide purpose of counteracting, curing or lessening the evil effects of the injury done to him,

80 *Tomizza v. Fraser* (1990), 71 O.R. (2d) 705 (argument rejected on the facts); *Frawley v. Asselstine* (1990), 70 D.L.R. (4th) 536, 73 O.R. (2d) 525 (H.C.J.). See *Turczinski v. Dupont Heating & Air Conditioning Ltd.* (2004), 246 D.L.R. (4th) 95 (Ont. C.A.), leave to appeal to S.C.C. refused 252 D.L.R. (4th) vi (contract distinguished from tort).

81 [1975] 1 W.L.R. 1411 (C.A.).

82 See 15.320, *infra*.

83 See *McCain Produce Ltd. v. Christy Crops Ltd.* (1977), 33 N.S.R. (2d) 546 (S.C.).

83a *Granville Savings and Mortgage Corp. v. Campbell*, [1993] 4 S.C.R. 279, 108 D.L.R. (4th) 383; *Christianson v. North Hill News Inc.* (1993), 106 D.L.R. (4th) 747, 13 Alta. L.R. (3d) 78 (C.A.); *P.G. Restaurant Ltd. v. British Columbia (Northern Interior Regional Health Board)*, [2004] 4 W.W.R. 287 (B.C.S.C.), citing this passage, revd on other grounds 38 B.C.L.R. (4th) 77 (C.A.).

84 This is assumed in many personal injury cases. See also *Gardner v. The King*, [1933] N.Z.L.R. 730 (S.C.) (veterinary surgeon's bills).

85 [1920] A.C. 102 (H.L.).

does not necessarily absolve the wrongdoer, even though the sufferer's efforts should, in the result, undesignedly aggravate the result of injury."[86]

15.300 The application of this principle is illustrated by *Farish v. National Trust Co. Ltd.*[87] where the defendant trust company had misadvised the plaintiff. In an effort (ultimately unsuccessful) to alleviate the adverse tax consequences of the defendant's erroneous advice, the plaintiff incurred accounting expenses. Bouck J. held that these were allowable in addition to the principal loss: "Because it was reasonable for the plaintiff to attempt to mitigate his damages in this way, I am satisfied that they were reasonable and therefore foreseeable and must be paid by the defendants."[88]

15.305 There must, however, be a close link between the defendant's wrong and the expenses. If the plaintiff embarks on a radically different venture from that originally contemplated, the defendant will not be liable for losses. In such a case, the Ontario Court of Apppeal said: "These damages are not in mitigation of loss but in aggravation. There is no authority for the proposition that the injur[ing] party must pay the innocent party the cost of putting his property to a completely different use."[88a]

15.310 McCormick has suggested, citing conflicting American cases, that the plaintiff ought to be entitled to recover "the value of his own personal time and services expended in prudent efforts to reduce the loss resulting from the defendant's wrongdoing."[89] If the plaintiff actually foregoes an opportunity of earning in order to reduce the loss, recovery seems in principle no different from the recovery regularly allowed in personal injury cases for earnings lost by the injured person or by others in caring for the person. More difficulty arises in a case where the plaintiff does not forego earnings. In such a case, the plaintiff has, in effect, foregone leisure time in order to mitigate the loss. If the plaintiff had employed another person to perform the mitigating service, the plaintiff could presumably have recovered the expense. It would seem that, in principle, up to the same amount should be recovered if the

---

86 *Supra*, at p. 125.

87 (1974), 54 D.L.R. (3d) 426 (B.C.S.C.). See also *Lloyds & Scottish Finance Ltd. v. Modern Cars & Caravans (Kingston) Ltd.*, [1966] 1 Q.B. 764; *Rooney v. Reed Ltd.* (1978), 88 D.L.R. (3d) 414, 20 O.R. (2d) 665 (H.C.J.); *Hawboldt Industries Ltd. v. Sanborn's Motor Express Ltd.* (1979), 36 N.S.R. (2d) 1 (S.C.T.D.); *McMorran's Cordova Bay Ltd. v. Harman & Co.* (1979), 106 D.L.R. (3d) 495 (B.C.C.A.); *Gillman v. Saan Stores Ltd.* (1992), 6 Alta. L.R. (3d) 7, 132 A.R. 144 (Q.B.); *Graceffo v. Alitalia*, [1995] 2 W.W.R. 351, 99 Man. R. (2d) 81 (Q.B.). In *Blomquist v. Tymchorak* (1912), 6 D.L.R. 337 (Man. K.B.), affd 10 D.L.R. 822 (C.A.), the plaintiff recovered for expenses incurred in urging the defendant to perform.

88 *Farish, supra*, footnote 87, at p. 441.

88a *Ossory Canada Inc. v. Wendy's Restaurants of Canada Inc.* (1998), 36 O.R. (3d) 483 at p. 502, 105 O.A.C. 321 (C.A.). See also *Walker v. Copp Clark Publishing Co.* (1962), 33 D.L.R. (2d) 338, [1962] O.R. 622 (H.C.J.); *Baumgartner v. Remus* (1997), 116 Man. R. (2d) 274 (Q.B.).

89 McCormick, *Handbook on the Law of Damages* (St. Paul, Minn., West Publishing Co., 1935), at p. 155, referring to *Mitchell v. Burch*, 36 Ind. 529 (1871); *St. Louis & San Francisco Ry. Co. v. Sharp*, 27 Kan. 134 (S.C., 1882), in favour of recovery and *Spencer v. Murphy*, 6 Colo. A. 453, 41 P. 841 (C.A., 1895), against recovery.

plaintiff performs the service. If the plaintiff's own time is less valuable than that of the person that might have been employed, the value of the plaintiff's

[*The next page is* 15-17]

time will be the limit of recovery. If more valuable, the cost of paying the other person will be the limit of recovery, for that would be the less costly course to pursue.

15.320 The enlargement of liability leads, incidentally, to a wider view of what is reasonable mitigation. If the law recognizes that a loss caused by mental distress is recoverable, it might follow that expenses reasonably incurred to alleviate the distress are also recoverable. Thus, a person deprived, in breach of contract, of promised vacation facilities, might be justified in purchasing a substitute at greater cost so long as the excess cost did not exceed a reasonable estimate of the damages recoverable for mental distress and disappointment on the failure to procure the substitute.[90]

(5) Plaintiff's impecuniosity

15.330 In *Liesbosch Dredger v. S. S. Edison*,[91] the House of Lords held that a plaintiff, whose dredger had negligently been put out of use by the defendant, could not recover losses caused by his own lack of funds where this compelled him to hire rather than to buy a replacement dredger. The reason given by Lord Wright for the decision was that the loss caused by the plaintiff's impecuniosity was too remote a consequence of the defendant's wrong for liability to be imposed. Lord Wright said that "the appellants' actual loss in so far as it was due to their own impecuniosity arose from that impecuniosity as a separate and concurrent cause, extraneous to and distinct in character from the tort; the impecuniosity was not traceable to the respondents' acts, and in my opinion was outside the legal purview of the consequences of these acts."[92] It is unclear whether Lord Wright was here laying down a rule of law that loss caused by the plaintiff's impecuniosity is never compensable, or whether the decision is to be explained as holding the loss in the particular case to be too remote. Lord Wright himself said, in *Monarch S.S. Co. Ltd. v. Karlshamns Oljefabriker (A/B)*,[93] that the result depended on reasonable contemplation as to damages and that there was no difference in this respect between contract and tort.[93a]

15.340 Street[94] points out that Lord Wright distinguished, without disapproving, an earlier House of Lords case holding that in respect of impecuniosity, the tortfeasor takes the victim as the victim is.[95] Lord Collins had there said: "in my opinion the wrong-doer must take his victim talem qualem, and if the position of the latter is aggravated because he is without the means of mitigating it, so much the worse for the wrong-doer, who has got to be

90 See 3.1310 - 3.1420, *supra*.
91 [1933] A.C. 449 (H.L.).
92 *Supra*, at p. 460.
93 [1949] A.C. 196 (H.L.), at pp. 223-4.
93a See *Alcoa Minerals of Jamaica Inc. v. Broderick*, [2002] 1 A.C. 371 (P.C.), citing this paragraph.
94 Street, *Principles of the Law of Damages* (London, Sweet & Maxwell, 1962), p. 41.
95 *Clippens Oil Co., Ltd. v. Edinburgh and District Water Trustees*, [1907] A.C. 291 (H.L.).

answerable for the consequences flowing from his tortious act."[96] It may be regarded as doubtful, therefore, whether the *Liesbosch* case can be taken as laying down any universal rule that damages caused by the plaintiff's impecuniosity are always irrecoverable.[97] The *Liesbosch* case was overruled on this point as a matter of English law in 2003[97a] but the Canadian position is not quite certain since many Canadian cases have cited the *Liesbosch* case with approval.[98]

15.350 A number of cases, English and Canadian, had held, before 2003, that damages may be recoverable in respect of loss caused by impecuniosity, provided that the loss meets the ordinary test of remoteness, that is, in a contract case, the test laid down by *Hadley v. Baxendale*.[99] In *Trans Trust S.P.R.L. v. Danubian Trading Co. Ltd.*,[100] Denning L.J. said: "It was ... said that the damages were the result of the impecuniosity of the sellers and that it was a rule of law that such damages are too remote. I do not think there is any such rule. In the case of a breach of contract, it depends on whether the damages were reasonably foreseeable or not. In the present case they clearly were."[101]

15.360 The same view was taken by the Supreme Court of Canada in *General Securities Ltd. v. Don Ingram Ltd.*[102] where consequential damages were awarded for breach of a promise to lend money. The defendant's knowledge

96 *Supra*, at pp. 303-4, applied in *Kolan v. Solicitor* (1969), 7 D.L.R. (3d) 481, [1970] 1 O.R. 41 (H.C.J.), affd 11 D.L.R. (3d) 672, [1970] 2 O.R. 686 (C.A.).

97 *Duchene v. Venoit* (1989), 90 N.S.R. (2d) 74 at p. 75, 2 R.P.R. (2d) 157 (S.C.), citing this passage; *Amar Cloth House Ltd. v. La Van & Co.*, [1997] 6 W.W.R. 382 at p. 392, 33 B.C.L.R. (3d) 312 (S.C.), citing this passage.

97a *Lagden v. O'Connor*, [2004] 1 All E.R. 277 (H.L.).

98 *Stilling v. Clarke Simpkins Ltd.* (1951), 2 W.W.R. (N.S.) 302 (B.C.S.C.); *Bischoff v. Sams* (1965), 50 D.L.R. (2d) 179 (Alta. S.C.); *The King v. C.P.R.*, [1947] S.C.R. 185, [1947] 2 D.L.R. 1; *Stewart v. Industrial Acceptance Corp. Ltd.*, [1949] 3 D.L.R. 42 (B.C.S.C.); *Smith v. McConnell Bros.* (1954), 11 W.W.R. (N.S.) 600 (Man. Q.B.); *Western Processing & Cold Storage Ltd. v. Hamilton Construction Co. Ltd.* (1964), 47 W.W.R. 150 (Man. Q.B.), vard 51 D.L.R. (2d) 245 (C.A.); *Dawson v. Helicopter Exploration Co. Ltd.* (1958), 12 D.L.R. (2d) 1 (S.C.C.), at p. 11; *Alberta Caterers Ltd. v. R. Volkan (Alta.) Ltd.* (1977), 81 D.L.R. (3d) 672 (Alta. S.C.T.D.); *Abbeyview Enterprises Ltd. v. Corp. of District of Matsqui* (1980), 22 B.C.L.R. 113 (S.C.), at p. 138; *Chiasson v. Tremblay* (1976), 12 N.B.R. (2d) 590 (S.C. App. Div.), at p. 595; *Davies v. Safeco Ins. Co. of America* (1982), 137 D.L.R. (3d) 66 (B.C.S.C), at pp. 66-7 (though the decision was in favour of recovery). In *Re 140 Developments Ltd. v. Steveston Meat & Frozen Food Lockers (1973) Ltd.* (1975), 59 D.L.R. (3d) 470 (B.C.S.C.), impecuniosity was disregarded, but expressly on the ground of unforeseeability. See also *Jones v. Fabbi* (1973), 37 D.L.R. (3d) 27 and 49 D.L.R. (3d) 316 (B.C.S.C.). In *Andre Knight Ltd. v. Presement* (1967), 63 D.L.R. (2d) 314, [1967] 2 O.R. 289 (C.A.), recovery was also disallowed as too remote, but not on grounds of impecuniosity. See p. 317 D.L.R.

99 (1854), 9 Ex. 341, 156 E.R. 145. See *Compania Financiera "Soleada" S.A. v. Hamoor Tanker Corp. Inc. (The Borag)*, [1981] 1 W.L.R. 274 (C.A.), for a case where the loss was held to be too remote.

100 [1952] 2 Q.B. 297 (C.A.).

101 *Supra*, at p. 306. See also *Martindale v. Duncan*, [1973] 1 W.L.R. 574 (C.A.); *Muhammad Issa El Sheikh Ahmad v. Ali*, [1947] A.C. 415 (P.C.); *Beaman v. Tully*, [1927] 4 D.L.R. 143 (Sask. C.A.); *Marriott v. Carson's Construction Ltd.* (1983), 146 D.L.R. (3d) 126 (N.S.S.C.T.D.); *T. Rose Construction Ltd. v. Omex International, Inc.* (1994), 122 Nfld. & P.E.I.R. 280 (Nfld. S.C.).

of the likely consequences of breach was stressed. In *Perry v. Sidney Phillips & Son*[103] in the English Court of Appeal, Lord Denning said that Lord Wright's statement in *The Liesbosch* "must be restricted to the facts of *The Liesbosch.* It is not of general application".[104] Kerr L.J. said that the principle of *The Liesbosch* "no longer applies in its full rigour",[105] explaining the result as based on lack of foreseeability.

15.370 Two more recent decisions of the Ontario Court of Appeal have cast some doubt on the position in Ontario. In *R. G. McLean Ltd. v. Canadian Vickers Ltd.*,[106] damages against the supplier of a defective colour printing machine were reduced on the principle that the plaintiff should have mitigated its loss by accepting an offer to refund the purchase price and buying a new machine. Arnup J.A. said: "The frailties (if any) of the plaintiff's credit, or its inability to purchase a new press from available assets, cannot be set up to destroy the effect of the defendant's offer."[107] In *Freedhoff v. Pomalift Industries Ltd.*[108] where the defendant had supplied a defective ski-tow, the plaintiff was held entitled to recover loss of profits but not further loss caused by his resulting insolvency. The court said of the loss claimed: "It does not meet the test of foreseeability."[109]

15.380 It would seem that these cases do not lay down a universal rule that damage caused by impecuniosity is irrecoverable. Such a rule would be incompatible with the decision of the Supreme Court of Canada in *General Securities Ltd. v. Don Ingram Ltd.* Rather, it would seem, the cases are simply to be regarded as decisions, depending on their own facts, to the effect that the loss claimed was, in those cases, too remote. This conclusion is supported by *Kienzle v. Stringer*,[110] when Zuber J.A. expressly left the

---

102 [1940] S.C.R. 670, [1940] 3 D.L.R. 641, following the earlier English cases of *Prehn v. Royal Bank of Liverpool* (1870), L.R. 5 Ex. 92, and *Manchester and Oldham Bank Ltd. v. W. A. Cook & Co.* (1883), 49 L.T. 674 (Q.B.). The *Don Ingram* case was followed in *Pelletier v. Pe Ben Industries Co. Ltd.*, [1976] 6 W.W.R. 640 (B.C.S.C.) (wrongful dismissal), and in *Prince Rupert Sawmills Ltd. v. M.C. Logging Ltd.* (1967), 65 D.L.R. (2d) 300 (B.C.C.A.). See also *Davies v. Safeco Ins. Co. of America* (1982), 137 D.L.R. (3d) 66 (B.C.S.C.) (liability insurer held liable for costs imposed upon the insured by the execution of the judgment against the insured by a third party); *Smith v. Richardson* (1977), 23 N.S.R. (2d) 407 (S.C.T.D.); *Trans-Canada Forest Products Ltd. v. Heaps, Waterous Ltd.*, [1952] 1 D.L.R. 827 (B.C.S.C.), revd [1953] 3 D.L.R. 672 (C.A.), restd [1954] S.C.R. 240, [1954] 2 D.L.R. 545, leave to appeal to P.C. refused July 14, 1954 (loss of credit, and consequently of business, caused by fire); *Jarvis v. Hall* (1912), 8 D.L.R. 412, 23 O.W.R. 282 (Div. Ct.) (loss of income caused by wrongful seizure of goods).

103 [1982] 1 W.L.R. 1297 (C.A.).

104 *Supra*, at p. 1302.

105 *Supra*, at p. 1307. The same view was taken in *Archer v. Brown*, [1985] Q.B. 401, and in *Alcoa Minerals of Jamaica Inc. v. Broderick*, [2002] 1 A.C. 371 (P.C.).

106 (1970), 15 D.L.R. (3d) 15, [1971] 1 O.R. 207 (C.A.).

107 *Supra*, at p. 24 D.L.R.

108 (1971), 19 D.L.R. (3d) 153, [1971] 2 O.R. 773 (C.A.).

109 *Supra*, at p. 158 D.L.R.

110 (1981), 130 D.L.R. (3d) 272, 35 O.R. (2d) 85 (C.A.), leave to appeal to S.C.C. refused D.L.R. *loc. cit.*, 38 O.R. (2d) 159*n*.

question open, and has been adopted by the Saskatchewan and British Columbia Courts.[111]

15.390 Another comment to be made on *McLean* and *Freedhoff* is that, in both cases, disclaimer clauses plainly designed to exclude consequential damages had been struck down by the courts. In both cases the plaintiffs were business buyers, and it is not clear that the disclaimer clauses were in any respect improper or unconscionable. It may well be, therefore, that a limitation on damages appeared to the court to be a technique of giving partial effect to the disclaimer clauses in order that, as was said in a similar context, "The wind . . . be tempered to the shorn lamb."[112]

(6) Anticipatory breach

15.400 Where a party announces in advance an intention not to perform a contractual obligation, the innocent party may sue immediately for damages or may await the date of promised performance and sue then. It the innocent party sues immediately or otherwise accepts the repudiation, the plaintiff is bound to mitigate the loss,[113] a result often expressed by holding that damages crystallize at that time.[114] Problems have arisen, however, where the innocent party asserts a right to ignore the repudiation and thereby incurs loss that could reasonably have been avoided.[115] In some cases the innocent party seeks to perform against the wishes of the repudiating party, and to be entitled to the contractually agreed compensation.

15.410 It will be seen that, strictly speaking, this last case is not a damages question at all, for if the innocent party is entitled to succeed in such a claim it is because that party has, by the terms of the contract, become entitled to the agreed compensation, which, if in money form, will be recoverable as a debt not as damages. Nevertheless, the problem is intimately connected with mitigation of damages and is usually considered with it. The question in such cases is whether by the terms of the contract as properly construed, the plaintiff is entitled to earn the agreed compensation by rendering performance against the wishes of the defendant. Rarely will the terms of the contract deal expressly with the point. Generally, therefore, the question, though in reality one of substantive contract law, falls to be determined by general considerations of justice of the same kind as affect the assessment of damages. It is true to say that if the defendant is liable on the contract (for

---

[111] *Kozak v. Gruza* (1989), 63 D.L.R. (4th) 129 at p. 135, 80 Sask. R. 197 (C.A.), citing this paragraph; *Mundell v. Wesbild Holdings Ltd.* (2007), 63 C.L.R. (3d) 230 (B.C.S.C.). See also *Hillspring Farms Ltd. v. Leland Walton & Sons Ltd.* (2007), 312 N.B.R. (2d) 109 (C.A.), at para. 25.

[112] *Per* Lord Denning M.R. in *Harbutt's "Plasticine" Ltd. v. Wayne Tank & Pump Co. Ltd.*, [1970] 1 Q.B. 447 (C.A.), at p. 468.

[113] See *Frost v. Knight* (1872), L.R. 7 Ex. 111 (Chambers); *Foley v. McIlwee* (1916), 27 D.L.R. 196 (P.C.).

[114] See 1.780, 1.560-1.1630, 5.1420, *supra*.

[115] Other aspects of this problem are discussed at 1.1560 - 1.1630, 5.1080, 5.1090, 5.1420, *supra*.

example to pay a debt), no duty to mitigate arises, but the very question at issue in these cases is whether the defendant is, by the terms of the contract, liable.

15.420 It was early established that an anticipatory repudiation amounted to a present breach of contract excusing the innocent party from the duty to render performance and giving rise to an immediate right to damages.[116] The innocent party, however, was entitled to await the date fixed for performance and sue for damages then. This view was adopted because it was thought anomalous that the repudiating party should be able by wrongful conduct to compel the innocent party to accept an alteration in contractual rights. So it was said that the innocent party had an election whether or not to accept the repudiation. An unaccepted repudiation was said by one judge to be "a thing writ in water".[117]

15.430 In a Scottish case, *White & Carter (Councils) Ltd. v. McGregor*,[118] the defender agreed to advertise on the pursuer's refuse containers for a three-year period, but cancelled the agreement almost immediately.

[*The next page is* 15-21]

116 *Hochster v. De La Tour* (1853), 2 El. & Bl. 678, 118 E.R. 922.
117 *Howard v. Pickford Tool Co. Ltd.*, [1951] 1 K.B. 417 (C.A.), at p. 421, *per* Asquith L.J.
118 [1962] A.C. 413 (H.L.).

The pursuer refused to accept the cancellation, prepared and displayed the advertisements, and raised an action for the contract price due under the agreement. It was held by a majority of the House of Lords that the action succeeded. Lord Reid said that, however unreasonable the pursuer's conduct appeared to be, there was an absolute right to ignore an anticipatory repudiation, to await an actual breach, and then to sue for whatever rights the contract afforded.[119] A duty to mitigate did not, in his view, arise.

15.440 The case has been much criticized,[120] and in *Finelli v. Dee*[121] the Ontario Court of Appeal, distinguishing *White & Carter v. McGregor*, expressed the view that if it were necessary to decide the question, the case would not be followed in Ontario. The facts in *Finelli v. Dee* were that the plaintiff sought to cancel an agreement whereby he would pave the defendant's driveway. While the defendant was absent, the plaintiff, in spite of the cancellation, came on the defendant's land and paved the drive. Laskin J.A. found that there had been a cancellation of the contract agreed to by the plaintiff. In any event, he said that *White & Carter v. McGregor* could be distinguished by the fact that there no co-operation from the defender was required in carrying out the contract, whereas in *Finelli v. Dee* entry on the defendant's land was required, presumably in Laskin J.A.'s view, to be treated as a trespass after the defendant's revocation of permission.

15.450 In *Hounslow London Borough Council v. Twickenham Garden Developments Ltd.*[122] where a building owner had, in breach of contract, sought to exclude the contractor from the site, the question was raised of whether or not such conduct would amount to a trespass. Megarry J. held, after a discussion of *White & Carter v. McGregor*, that the contractor had no "right" to continue the work in the face of the owner's repudiation. However, he refused to grant an injunction to restrain the contractor from continuing the work, on the ground that "equity will not assist a man to break his contract".[123] It is submitted that these conclusions are barely consistent, for if the contractor has no right to continue, the owner is entitled to exclude the contractor. It is not satisfactory to say that the owner can do this by force, while refusing to extend to the owner the aid of the court. On the other hand, if the owner cannot obtain an injunction to exclude the contractor, it must be doubted whether the contractor is

119 This is difficult to reconcile, however, with the requirement of substantial and legitimate interest. See 15.480, *infra*.

120 See Goodhart, "Measure of Damages When a Contract is Repudiated", Note, 78 L.Q. Rev. 263 (1962).

121 (1968), 67 D.L.R. (2d) 393, [1968] 1 O.R. 676 (C.A.). In *Consolidated Plate Glass Co. v. McKinnon Dash Co.* (1917), 40 D.L.R. 47, 41 O.L.R. 188 (H.C.J.), Middleton J. commented that it would be "absolutely suicidal" for the plaintiff to prepare unwanted goods after the buyer's repudiation. See p. 48 D.L.R.

122 [1971] Ch. 233.

123 *Supra*, at p. 248.

properly described as a "trespasser". It is submitted that an injunction should be available to the owner unless the case is one in which the interest of the contractor in actual performance is so strong that the court would consider the contract a proper one for specific enforcement.[124] In the early American case of *Clark v. Marsiglia*,[125] it was held that a person employed to clean a picture had no right to continue with the work in the face of the owner's instruction (albeit in breach of contract) to stop the work. An even clearer case would be that of a patient who agreed to undergo a surgical operation. If the patient withdrew consent (even in breach of contract) before the operation, manifestly the surgeon could not lawfully continue with the operation. In such a case surely the law would restrain the surgeon, if called upon to do so, even if it were thereby assisting in a breach of contract.

15.460 The appropriate reconciliation of the various legal principles would seem to be that, where work is to be done on the defendant's property, the plaintiff has a contractual licence to perform the work, but that the defendant can effectively put an end to the licence (though the defendant will be liable for damages if in breach of contract), unless the plaintiff has such a special interest in actual performance that damages would be an inadequate remedy, in which case the court would award a decree of specific performance to the plaintiff or an injunction to restrain the defendant from interfering with the contract. In that case, the licence is irrevocable, the plaintiff is not a trespasser, and no injunction will be awarded to the defendant to eject the plaintiff.

15.470 An early British Columbia case indicates that the wider implications of *White & Carter v. McGregor* have never been accepted. In *Sells v. Thomson*,[126] a buyer had cancelled an order for books, but the seller proceeded to ignore the cancellation, packed and sent the books, and sued for the agreed price. The British Columbia Court of Appeal held that he was not entitled to recover the price. Macdonald C.J.A. said:

> The defendants cabled to the plaintiffs cancelling the order for a balance of 13 volumes which had not been sent out. Counsel for the plaintiffs admitted that no appropriation of these had been made prior to the receipt of the cablegram. The plaintiffs nevertheless thereafter appropriated 13 volumes to this contract, and the defendants having refused to accept the books action was brought for the price as upon a contract for goods sold and delivered. I have therefore to ask myself whether or not the implied assent of the defendants, to the future appropriation of goods, to the contract, was withdrawn or destroyed by the notification

[124] See Sharpe, *Injunctions and Specific Performance*, looseleaf ed. (Toronto, Canada Law Book, 1999), 7.360-7.400.

[125] 1 Denio (N.Y.) 317, 43 Am. Dec. 670 (1845). A similar illustration was given by Megarry J. in *Hounslow London Borough Council v. Twickenham Garden Developments Ltd., supra*, footnote 122, at p. 253.

[126] (1914), 17 D.L.R. 737 (B.C.C.A.).

> that they would not accept the goods; in other words, whether or not the plaintiffs, after receipt of that notification, could proceed to convert the executory agreement into an executed one by setting the goods apart as applicable to the contract and thus pass the property in them to the defendants against their will. I have not been able to find any direct authority upon this point. I am, however, of opinion that the implied assent to an appropriation of the goods was withdrawn by the notice, and that the plaintiffs could not thereafter without the defendant's assent convert the executory contract into an executed one.[127]

15.480 Lord Reid, in his speech in *White & Carter v. McGregor*, included a puzzling reference to the "substantial and legitimate interest" in actual performance of the innocent party. He said:

> If I may revert to the example which I gave of a company engaging an expert to prepare an elaborate report and then repudiating before anything was done, it might be that the company could show that the expert had no substantial or legitimate interest in carrying out the work rather than accepting damages: I would think that the de minimis principle would apply in determining whether his interest was substantial, and that he might have a legitimate interest other than an immediate financial interest. But if the expert had no such interest then that might be regarded as a proper case for the exercise of the general equitable jurisdiction of the court. But that is not this case. Here the respondent did not set out to prove that the appellants had no legitimate interest in completing the contract and claiming the contract price rather than claiming damages; there is nothing in the findings of fact to support such a case, and it seems improbable that any such case could have been proved.[128]

15.490 The reference is puzzling because it is by no means clear how Lord Reid applied his principle to the facts of the case before him. He was seeking to deal with a hypothetical case of an expert being employed to prepare an elaborate report followed by wrongful cancellation by the expert's employer. Lord Reid appears to concede that the expert ought not to be allowed to carry out the preparation of the report in the face of the repudiation and then to sue for the full agreed price. But it is not clear on what principle the case is to be distinguished from the actual case decided. If the hypothetical expert had no substantial or legitimate interest in actual performance, one would have thought that White & Carter Ltd. would have had still less of an interest. The context of the latter's case was purely commercial. It is difficult to see why damages would not fully compensate the pursuer for the lost advertising. If a difference is to be made between the real and the hypothetical case in this respect, one would expect it to be the other way around. That is, one could conceive of circumstances in which an expert's reputation might depend on actual performance of some project with which the

---

127 *Supra*, at p. 738.

128 *Supra*, footnote 118, at p. 431.

expert's name had been linked. It is very hard to see any similar interest that an owner of refuse containers could have in exhibiting the name of a particular advertiser.

15.500 Lord Reid attempted to meet this argument by saying that the defendant had not "set out to prove" the absence of a legitimate interest. But, with respect, it seems unsatisfactory to say that the respondent did not "set out to prove that the appellant had no legitimate interest" when, though the exact phraseology in Lord Reid's speech may not have been used, the whole gist and tenor of the argument was precisely that it was most unreasonable for the pursuer to behave as it did. To rest the conclusion on the absence of a specific finding of fact again seems odd. The courts below had both decided against the pursuer, and though the trial judge presumably did not say "I find as a fact that the pursuer had no legitimate interest" the tenor of his judgment (dismissing the action) can surely be reasonably taken to have implied such a finding.

15.510 The actual result in *White & Carter v. McGregor* may, however, be defensible. Criticisms of the case generally assume that the pursuer could have reduced its loss by finding another advertiser and that the loss was actually exacerbated by the preparation and exhibition of unwanted advertisements. But a full knowledge of the facts might reveal that no other advertisers were available. It is stated by various judges that the pursuer proceeded to "prepare" advertising plates[129] but no details are given of what was involved, and it seems altogether possible that the advertisements had already been prepared and were already in place on the refuse containers (the contract being a simple renewal of a former agreement to come into effect immediately on the expiry of the old).[130] In that case the pursuer would not have acted at all unreasonably in leaving the advertisements in place and suing for the agreed price.

15.520 In so far as *White & Carter v. McGregor* lays down a wider principle, it has been disapproved not only, as mentioned above, by the Ontario Court of Appeal but also by the English Court of Appeal. In *Attica Sea Carriers Corp. v. Ferrostaal Poseidon Bulk Reederei G.m.b.H.*,[131] the owner of a ship refused to accept redelivery of it in a damaged state, asserting that the charterer was bound to repair it and that until it did so, the hire continued to accrue under the charterparty. As the repairs to the ship were, in the circumstances, uneconomic, this put the charterer in an impossible position. As Lord Denning, M.R., said: "Either the charterers pay the charter hire for years to come, whilst the vessel lies idle and useless for want of repairs. Or the charterers must do

---

129 See *White & Carter (Councils) Ltd. v. McGregor*, [1962] A.C. 413 (H.L.), at p. 415 and p. 426.

130 *Supra*, at pp. 414-15, [1960] S.C. 277.

131 [1976] 1 Lloyd's Rep. 250 (C.A.).

repairs which cost twice as much as the ship would be worth when repaired".[132]

15.530 The owner argued that *White & Carter v. McGregor* entitled it to ignore the (allegedly wrongful) attempt to redeliver the ship and to sue on the contract for the accruing hire as a debt. Lord Denning said, of *White & Carter v. McGregor*:

> The decision has been criticized in a leading textbook ... It is said to give a "grotesque" result. Even though it was a Scots case, it would appear that the House of Lords, as at present constituted, would expect us to follow it in any case that is precisely on all fours with it. But I would not follow it otherwise. It has no application whatever in a case where the plaintiff ought, in all reason, to accept the repudiation and sue for damages — provided that damages would provide an adequate remedy for any loss suffered by him.[133]

Orr L.J. distinguished *White & Carter v. McGregor* as follows:

> The present case differs from that case in that here it cannot be said that the owners could fulfil the contract without any co-operation from the charterers and also because in this case the charterers have set out to prove that the owners have no legitimate interest in claiming the charter hire rather than claiming damages, and the passages above quoted strongly suggest to me that if either or both of these factors had been present in *White & Carter v. McGregor* Lord Reid might well have agreed with [the dissenting law lords] as to the outcome of the appeal, with the result that there would have been a majority in favour of dismissing it.[134]

15.540 So interpreted, *White & Carter v. McGregor* will not apply to a case where the plaintiff, in the view of the court, can be shown to have acted unreasonably in seeking to establish a contractual debt rather than claiming damages. In other words, it will only apply where damages are an inadequate compensation.

15.550 Another point may be made here. As was said at the outset of this section, *White & Carter v. McGregor* is not, technically, a case of damages, but of substantive contract law. One may readily agree with Lord Reid's statement that the law does not require a person to exercise rights reasonably but the point at issue was whether, on the true construction of the contract, the pursuer had the right to act as he did. The actual decision can stand for no more than that the pursuer, under the particular contract involved in the case, did have the right so to act. But each case requiring the interpretation of a contract must depend on all the circumstances surrounding the particular contract. It may be suggested that it will rarely be appropriate, in such cases, to hold as a matter of construction that the plaintiff is entitled to act so as to exacerbate the loss. This is not because the plaintiff is required to exercise

---

132 *Supra*, at p. 255.

133 *Supra*.

134 *Supra*, at p. 256. But see *Gator Shipping Corp. v. Trans-Asiatic Oil Ltd. S.A. (The "Odenfeld")*, [1978] 2 Lloyd's Rep. 357 (Q.B.), at p. 374, where Kerr J. said that the fetter on the innocent party's election would only be applied in "extreme cases".

rights reasonably, but because, in determining what the rights in fact are, it will be assumed that the parties intended to set reasonable limits upon them.

15.560 This question is closely related to the question of the right of a vendor of land to specific performance[135] or the right of a lessor to sue for the rent in respect of premises abandoned by the lessee. In effect, where such a remedy is sought, the vendor or lessor seeks to ignore a wrongful repudiation by the purchaser or tenant; the action is analogous to an action for the amount of the price as a debt.[136] An action for an agreed sum raises, strictly speaking, a question not of remedies but of substantive law. It depends on the construction of the contract whether or not the sum has become absolutely due and payable as a debt. But where the contract does not expressly deal with the matter, its interpretation will depend on what the parties can reasonably be supposed to have intended. In a case where the plaintiff can more conveniently take steps to mitigate the loss, it will often be appropriate to construe the agreement as requiring the plaintiff to restrict the claim to damages. As in the *Attica Sea Carriers* case, it can be said that this is "a case where the plaintiff ought in all reason to accept the repudiation and sue for damages — provided that damages would provide an adequate remedy for any loss suffered by him". The present law, it seems, entitles the vendor or lessor to recover the price or rent. On the repudiation by a tenant of a lease, the Supreme Court of Canada said:

> The developed case law has recognized three mutually exclusive courses that a landlord may take where a tenant is in fundamental breach of the lease or has repudiated it entirely ... He may do nothing to alter the relationship of landlord and tenant, but simply insist on performance of the terms and sue for rent or damages on the footing that the lease remains in force.[137]

15.570 However, it is submitted that, as the conclusion rests simply on the construction of the particular lease, it need not govern every case and that it does not require a court to hold that a landlord may act unreasonably in refraining from reletting the abandoned premises. Legislation provides in several provinces that, in respect of residential tenancies, reasonable steps must be taken to minimize losses.[138]

---

[135] See Sharpe, *Injunctions and Specific Performance*, looseleaf ed. (Toronto, Canada Law Book, 1999), 8.100-8.220.

[136] See *McTavish v. Langer*, [1933] 4 D.L.R. 609 (S.C.C.).

[137] *Highway Properties Ltd. v. Kelly, Douglas & Co. Ltd.*, [1971] S.C.R. 562 at p. 570, 17 D.L.R. (3d) 710 at p. 716. But see *Ansdell v. Crowther* (1984), 11 D.L.R. (4th) 614, 55 B.C.L.R. 216 (C.A.) (vendor of land obliged to mitigate loss).

[138] *Residential Tenancies Act* (Ont.), s. 16. See also *Residential Tenancies Act* (N.S.), s. 9(1), stat. con. 6; *Residential Tenancies Act* (N.W.T.), s. 5. See *Transco Mills Ltd. v. Percan Enterprises Ltd.* (1993), 100 D.L.R. (4th) 359, 76 B.C.L.R. (2d) 129 , supplementary reasons D.L.R. *loc. cit.* p. 375, R.P.R. *loc. cit.* p. 250 (C.A.).

[139] [Text deleted.]

15.580 An important case on mitigation of damages reached the Supreme Court of Canada in 1978. In *Asamera Oil Corp. Ltd. v. Sea Oil & General Corp.*,[140] an action was brought for failure, in breach of contract, to return shares that had been lent. The value of the shares at the date of contract breach was twenty-nine cents. They subsequently rose to a value of over $45, dropping by the date of trial to about $21. The choice of date of valuation of the shares for purposes of damage calculation made a difference of millions of dollars. The Supreme Court of Canada held that the plaintiff was bound to purchase substitute shares within a reasonable time of the breach of contract, but then used a fairly generous measure of what was a reasonable time allowing, in the circumstances of the case, six years. One of the issues was whether the obtaining of an injunction by the plaintiff had the effect of removing the plaintiff's duty to mitigate his loss by buying substitute shares. The court discussed the relationship between specific remedies and damages and made reference to *White & Carter v. McGregor*.

15.590 Estey J., having concluded that the mere issue of a specific order in the particular circumstances did not excuse the plaintiff from mitigating, added:

> It is, of course, an eminently reasonable position to take if, as Lord Reid suggests in *White and Carter (Councils) Ltd. v. McGregor*, in the case of anticipatory breach, there is substantial and legitimate interest in looking to performance of a contractual obligation. So a plaintiff who has agreed to purchase a particular piece of real estate, or a block of shares which represent control of a company, or has entered into performance of his own obligations and where to discontinue performance might aggravate his losses, might well have sustained the position that the issuance of a writ for specific performance would hold in abeyance the obligation to avoid or reduce losses by acquisition of replacement property. Yet, even in these cases, the action for performance must be instituted and carried on with due diligence. This is but another application of the ordinary rule of mitigation which insists that the injured party act reasonably in all of the circumstances. Where those circumstances reveal a substantial and legitimate interest in seeking performance as opposed to damages, then a plaintiff will be able to justify his inaction and on failing in his plea for specific performance might then recover losses which in other circumstances might be classified as avoidable and thus unrecoverable; but such is not the case here.[141]

15.600 This approach offers a useful means of protecting the plaintiff's legitimate interests while preventing the plaintiff from running up damages at the defendant's expense. Where, but only where, a plaintiff

---

140 [1979] 1 S.C.R. 633, 89 D.L.R. (3d) 1. See also *Hongkong Bank of Canada v. Richardson Greenshields of Canada Ltd.* (1990), 72 D.L.R. (4th) 161, [1990] 6 W.W.R. 1 (B.C.C.A.).

141 *Supra*, at pp. 668-9 S.C.R., p. 26 D.L.R. See also *Domowicz v. Orsa Investments Ltd.* (1994), 20 O.R. (3d) 722 (Gen. Div.), var'd 40 O.R. (4th) 256 (C.A.).

has such a substantial and legitimate interest in actual performance as a court will recognize as justifying a claim for specific enforcement, is the plaintiff entitled to insist on actual performance and to reject the possibility of the purchase of substitute performance or of its monetary equivalent. Thus, the words of Lord Reid's speech are approved by the Supreme Court of Canada, but the implication that a plaintiff can act unreasonably in the face of an anticipatory repudiation is rejected.

15.610 Another point arising out of the *Asamera* case is that often the plaintiff cannot be expected to act immediately on receipt of the defendant's repudiation. Often it will be reasonable to spend some time in urging the defendant to perform;[142] in the *Asamera* case the defendant's conduct justified the plaintiff in waiting for six years before purchasing substitute shares.

15.620 It is submitted, therefore, that the preferable rule is that, on an anticipatory repudiation, the innocent party cannot recover any loss that could reasonably have been avoided, and that this rule is supported by the weight of Canadian authority. Where there is a case for specific performance the plaintiff will not act unreasonably in insisting on actual performance. The cases of anticipatory repudiation by sellers of goods were discussed in an earlier chapter.[143] It was there suggested that it will often be reasonable for a buyer to wait, for unless there is a readily available futures market in the goods, the buyer will not be able to acquire an exact substitute on the seller's repudiation. It would not generally be reasonable to expect the buyer to buy substitute goods at spot prices and store them until the date when they were needed. These cases are not inconsistent, it is submitted, with a rule that the buyer must act reasonably on receipt of the repudiation; they decide that, in some circumstances, the buyer does act reasonably by waiting. That there is no universal rule entitling the buyer to wait is illustrated by *Campbell v. Mahler*,[144] where buyers who had refrained from purchasing substitute goods were restricted to nominal damages (the market price at the time of the repudiation being below the contract price). Falconbridge C.J.K.B. said: "When they found that defendants would not carry out the contract, they ought then to have gone into the market and done the best they could with a similar contract".[145] The reference to "similar contract" seems to imply that a substitute contract for future delivery could have been found, and on this basis, it is submitted that the case is rightly decided.

15.630 In employment cases there are conflicting dicta on the effect of a unilateral repudiation. Megarry V.-C. said in 1979 that "the authorities

---

142 See also *Schrider v. Lang Bay Lumber Co. Ltd.* (1961), 34 W.W.R. 319 (B.C.C.A.), esp. at p. 320.

143 See 1.1560 - 1.1630, *supra*.

144 (1918), 43 O.L.R. 395 (H.C.), affd 47 D.L.R. 722, 45 O.L.R. 44 (S.C. App. Div.).

145 *Supra*, at p. 399.

on the point are in a far from satisfactory state"[146] and in 1980 Shaw L.J. described it as a "vexed area of the common law".[147] The difficulty is that the resolution of different legal problems has been made to turn on the same question. In *Thomas Marshall (Exports) Limited v. Guinle*,[148] the employer sought to enforce obligations of confidentiality against a defaulting employee. It was held that the employee could not, by the employee's own wrongful repudiation, put an end to the obligations. Where the employer repudiates by purporting to dismiss the employee unlawfully, it was said in one case that "the employment is effectively terminated, albeit in breach of contract".[149] This appears to be the prevailing view also in Canada.[150] In *Gunton v. Richmond-upon-Thames London Borough Council*,[151] where an employer had dismissed an employee by improper procedures, all three members of the English Court of Appeal agreed that the employee could not remain idle and sue for wages, because the employee could not render the services necessary to earn them without the employer's co-operation.[152] The majority of the court, however, refused to hold that the contract of employment was necessarily terminated by the employer's unilateral act, pointing out that an employee might have legitimate reasons for asserting the continuation of the employment contract.[153] It is submitted that the conclusion suggested above should be applied to employment contracts, unless statute compels a contrary result,[154] that is, upon a unilateral repudiation by the employer, the employee is bound to act reasonably to mitigate damages, but that the employee will not be held to act unreasonably if the employee had a

---

146 *Thomas Marshall (Exports Ltd.) v. Guinle*, [1979] Ch. 227 at p. 239.

147 *Gunton v. Richmond-upon-Thames London Borough Council*, [1981] Ch. 448 (C.A.), at p. 459.

148 *Supra*, footnote 146.

149 *Vine v. National Dock Labour Board*, [1957] A.C. 488 (H.L.), at p. 500, *per* Viscount Kilmuir L.C.

150 See 5.1080, 5.1090, *supra*. But see *Smart v. South Saskatchewan Hospital Centre* (1989), 60 D.L.R. (4th) 8, [1989] 5 W.W.R. 289 (Sask. C.A.).

151 *Supra*, footnote 147.

152 See *Gunton, supra, per* Shaw L.J., at p. 460; Buckley L.J., at p. 468; Brightman L.J., at p. 474.

153 See *Gunton, supra, per* Buckley L.J., at p. 469, Brightman L.J., at p. 475.

154 See *Emms v. The Queen*, [1979] 2 S.C.R. 1148 at pp. 1164-5, 102 D.L.R. (3d) 193 at pp. 203-4, *per* Pigeon J. In several cases involving teachers it has been held that a dismissal not authorized by the statute is void, and the contract continues in full force: *Mahoney v. Newcastle Board of School Trustees* (1966), 61 D.L.R. (2d) 77 (N.B.S.C. App. Div.); *Knight v. Board of Yorkton School Unit No. 36* (1972), 34 D.L.R. (3d) 592 (Sask. C.A.); *Wheaton v. Flin Flon School Division No. 46* (1981), 131 D.L.R. (3d) 393 (Man. Q.B.) (salary held to continue, but substitute earnings deducted). In *Re Nicholson and Haldimand-Norfolk Regional Board of Commissioners of Police* (1981), 117 D.L.R. (3d) 604, 31 O.R. (2d) 195 (C.A.), leave to appeal to S.C.C. refused D.L.R. *loc. cit.*, O.R. *loc. cit.*, it was held that a police constable, invalidly dismissed, though entitled to back pay, was bound to bring actual earnings into account. In *Crease v. Metropolitan Toronto Board of Police Com'rs* (1982), 139 D.L.R. (3d) 238, 39 O.R. (2d) 89 (H.C.J.), affd 143 D.L.R. (3d) 575*n* (C.A.), this principle was extended by requiring a deduction of earnings that could reasonably have been acquired.

legitimate interest in asserting a continuing employment relationship, as would be the case if the employee had a right to specific performance[155] or if important collateral benefits depended on the continuation of the relationship. Such cases will be rare.

15.640 The Ontario Law Reform Commission recommended the inclusion of quite detailed provisions in the Sale of Goods Bill,[156] including a provision that: "the repudiating party is not liable in any event for loss or damage that the aggrieved party should have foreseen and could have mitigated or avoided without undue risk, expense or prejudice." The wording of this provision is not entirely apt to deal with the situation discussed in this section, because the plaintiff does not claim compensation for "loss or damage"; the claim is for a debt. However, the intent of the clause would appear to be in harmony with what has been proposed here, that is, in the absence of a clear contrary intent, the contract should be interpreted to preclude the plaintiff from suing on a debt in circumstances where the plaintiff "ought in all reasons to accept repudiation and sue for damages".

15.650 Where the plaintiff does act on the defendant's repudiation, the latter cannot be permitted unilaterally to reinstate the contract and tender a performance that the plaintiff might no longer expect or require. The Ontario Law Reform Commission dealt with this matter by proposing the following clause:

> 8.11(1) The repudiating party may retract his repudiation at any time before his next performance is due unless the aggrieved party has since the repudiation cancelled the contract, or materially changed his position or otherwise indicated that he considers the repudiation final.
>
> (2) Retraction may be by any method that clearly indicates to the aggrieved party that the repudiating party intends to perform, but must include any assurance justifiably demanded under section 8.9.
>
> (3) Retraction reinstates the repudiating party's rights under the contract but the aggrieved party is not liable, and is entitled to be compensated for any delay occasioned by the repudiation.

In an uncodified area of contract law the court would hold, it is submitted, that a repudiating party would be estopped from retracting the repudiation when the other party had changed position in reliance on the repudiation.

(7) Valuation of chance of avoiding loss

15.660 In some cases the plaintiff unreasonably refrains from a course of action that if pursued would have given the plaintiff a chance, but not a certainty, of avoiding the loss claimed. The question then arises as to

---

155 See Sharpe, *Injunctions and Specific Performance*, looseleaf ed. (Toronto, Canada Law Book, 1999), 7.590-7.630.

156 Ontario Law Reform Commission, *Report on Sale of Goods* (Ministry of Attorney-General, 1979), cl. 8.10(4).

how to value the chance. The problem occurred in *Janiak v. Ippolito*[157] where the plaintiff, having suffered disabling injuries, refused to undergo an operation that would have had a 70% chance of restoring his earning capacity. The Supreme Court of Canada held that the plaintiff was entitled to damages assessed on the same basis as though assessment had taken place in the expectation that the plaintiff would undergo the operation. In that case, the plaintiff would have been entitled to compensation for the chance of loss, and it was held that it would be punitive to deprive him, because of his refusal to undergo the operation, of the right to recover the same amount. It is submitted that the decision is sound. Compensation for contingencies that are less than probable is well established in the law of personal injuries and elsewhere.[158] Consequently it seems appropriate to compensate the plaintiff for the 30% chance of loss, for his refusal to undergo the operation does not reduce his actual loss. He might still change his mind, undergo the operation, but find it, after all, unsuccessful. With a 30% chance of such an outcome, the plaintiff is in the position of suffering a real present loss that can, it is submitted, only be measured as the court decided.

5. Avoided Loss

15.670 The proposition that the plaintiff cannot recover compensation for loss avoided has the appearance of a truism. If the plaintiff has avoided the loss then none is suffered, so the proposition asserts no more than that the plaintiff cannot recover compensation for a loss that has not been suffered. But, like many apparently simple statements, this proposition conceals a very difficult problem.

15.680 After the defendant's wrong, the plaintiff continues to engage in the ordinary transactions of business; some of these will turn out to be profitable. The difficulty is to determine when such profits should be taken into account for the benefit of the wrongdoer. The problem is akin to some of the intractable problems of legal causation. After the wrong has been done the plaintiff finds a state of affairs that includes the alteration caused by the wrong. In that altered state of affairs, the plaintiff enters into a profitable transaction which could not have been entered into in exactly the same form if events had been unaltered by the defendant's wrong. In one sense it can be said that all such profits are attributable to the wrong, for in the absence of the wrong they would not have been made. But this rule would plainly be too generous to the defendant. In another sense it might be said that all such profits are due to the plaintiff's enterprise, not to the defendant's wrong, but this would be too generous to the plaintiff, for where a profit is very closely linked

157 [1985] 1 S.C.R. 146, 16 D.L.R. (4th) 1. See also *Emery v. Butters* (1982), 36 O.R. (2d) 328 (Co. Ct.).

158 See 13.260 - 13.370, *supra*.

with the defendant's wrong, common sense requires the conclusion that the effect of the profit is to reduce the loss caused by the wrong.[159]

15.690 Problems of this nature arise throughout the law of damages and are inherent in the most basic principles governing damage assessment. They have accordingly already been discussed in various contexts in earlier chapters.[160] The discussion here is concerned with attempts that have been made to lay down general tests.

15.700 It is very common for the courts to speak of gains made by the plaintiff as "collateral"[161] or as *"res inter alios acta"*.[162] These phrases indicate the court's conclusion that the particular gain is not to be taken into account for the defendant's benefit, but they provide very little guidance to one seeking to determine what gains are to be so classified. In many cases the argument turns on whether the plaintiff suffers an actual loss by the defendant's wrong or whether the effect of subsequent events is to prevent any loss from arising.[163] Again, it is clear what conclusion is indicated by saying that the plaintiff suffers no actual loss. It is less clear that the phrase gives useful guidance in the difficult cases.

15.710 The leading case is generally taken to be *British Westinghouse Electric & Manufacturing Co., Ltd. v. Underground Electric Rys. Co. of London, Ltd.*,[164] where the defendant had, in breach of warranty, delivered defective machinery. The plaintiff replaced the machinery with machines of a superior design that were more efficient than the defendant's machines would have been even if they had answered to the warranty. It was held that the increased profitability of the new machines was to be taken into account with the consequence (so profitable were the new machines by comparison with those of the old design) that the plaintiff recovered only nominal damages.

15.720 In the Canadian Privy Council case of *Erie County Natural Gas & Fuel Co. v. Carroll*,[165] the plaintiff acquired gas leases to secure a supply

159 See *Pagnan & Fratelli v. Corbisa Industrial Agropacuaria*, [1970] 1 W.L.R. 1306 (C.A.) ("contrary to justice common sense and authority" to allow recovery of "fictitious loss"); *Trizec Equities Ltd. v. Ellis-Don Management Services Ltd.*, [1999] 5 W.W.R. 1 at pp. 231-2 (Q.B.), affd [2000] 2 W.W.R. 371 (C.A.), citing this paragraph. Damages were not reduced in *Hussey v. Eels*, [1990] Q.B. 227 (C.A.), at p. 241; or *1874000 Nova Scotia Ltd. v. Adams* (1997), 146 D.L.R. (4th) 466 at p. 487, 159 N.S.R. (2d) 260 (C.A.), citing this paragraph; *Nesi Energy Marketing Canada Ltd. (Trustee of) v. NGL Supply (Gas) Co.* (2000), 201 D.L.R. (4th) 419 (Alta. C.A.).

160 See 1.30, 1.40, 1.1460, 1.2570, 1.2580, 5.1480 - 5.1510, *supra*.

161 *Royal Bank of Canada v. Clark* (1978), 88 D.L.R. (3d) 76 (N.B.S.C. App. Div.), affd [1980] 1 S.C.R. 177*n*, 105 D.L.R. (3d) 85*n*; *Girling v. Crown Cork & Seal Canada Inc.*, [1994] 7 W.W.R. 525, 92 B.C.L.R. (2d) 181 (S.C.), affd 127 D.L.R. (4th) 448, [1995] 9 W.W.R. 743 (C.A.).

162 See *Joyner v. Weeks*, [1891] 2 Q.B. 31 (C.A.).

163 See footnote 160, *supra*.

164 [1912] A.C. 673 (H.L.). See also *Redpath Industries Ltd. v. The "Cisco"*, [1994] 2 F.C. 279, 110 D.L.R. (4th) 583 (C.A.), leave to appeal to S.C.C. refused 116 D.L.R. (4th) vii, 179 N.R. 319*n*.

165 [1911] A.C. 105 (P.C.).

of gas in substitution for a supply wrongfully held by the defendant. Ultimately the plaintiff disposed of these leases at a profit. It was held that

[*The next page is* 15–33]

he was bound to bring the profit into account. Otherwise the plaintiff would make "a profit by the defendants' breach of their obligation of about $128,965.22, a somewhat grotesque result."[166] A Supreme Court of Canada case where, again, a profit made by the plaintiff was taken into account is *Cockburn v. Trusts & Guarantee Co.*,[167] where the plaintiff lost his employment on the liquidation of the company that employed him. He attended the liquidation sale and bought goods, which he resold at a profit. It was held that the plaintiff's claim for damages for wrongful dismissal was to be reduced by the profit he made on the sale.

15.730 It is clear that these principles apply in tort as well as contract.[168] It is always assumed that if the plaintiff recovers part of the loss from one tortfeasor, damages against another tortfeasor liable for the same loss are reduced.[169]

15.740 On the other hand, there are many cases where the plaintiff has been held entitled to recover damages from the defendant in respect of a loss despite an offsetting transaction that might appear to reduce or remove the loss. Many such cases have been discussed in earlier chapters. Thus, a buyer of defective goods is entitled to damages for breach of warranty even though the goods are resold to a sub-buyer who pays the full price.[170] A seller is entitled to damages representing the difference between contract price and market price, even though the goods or shares are resold at above the contract price.[171] A buyer is entitled to the difference between the contract price and the market price even though the goods are resold at a lower price and the buyer will not be liable to the sub-buyer.[172] In many cases these rules can be supported on grounds of convenience, for an inquiry into exactly what position the plaintiff would have occupied if the wrong had not been done often proves impractical. In *Neste Canada Inc. v. Allianz Insurance Co. of Canada*,[172a] it was held that a business interruption insurer was not entitled to reduce its liability because the insured took advantage of the interruption to perform cleaning and maintenance work at its plant.

15.750 The "lost volume" problem is another instance. Where a buyer of goods fails to accept delivery and the plaintiff resells at the same price, it appears, at

[166] *Supra*, at p. 115, *per* Lord Atkinson.
[167] (1917), 55 S.C.R. 264, 37 D.L.R. 701. See 5.1220, *supra*.
[168] *Bellingham v. Dhillon*, [1973] Q.B. 304.
[169] *Burn v. Morris* (1834), 2 Cr. & M. 579, 149 E.R. 891; *Nowell v. B.C. Electric Ry. Co.*, [1929] 4 D.L.R. 280 (B.C.S.C.), revd [1930] 1 D.L.R. 491 (C.A.). See *Hawboldt Industries Ltd. v. Sanborn's Motor Express Ltd.* (1979), 36 N.S.R. (2d) 1 (S.C.T.D.).
[170] See 1.2570, 1.2580, *supra*. And see *Hussey v. Eels*, [1990] 2 Q.B. 227 (C.A.); *Gardner v. Marsh & Parsons*, [1997] 1 W.L.R. 469 (C.A.) (repair by landlord of defective building); *Needler Financial Services Ltd. v. Taber*, [2002] 3 All E.R. 501 (Ch. Div.). On the other hand, in *Redpath Industries Ltd. v. The "Cisco"*, [1994] 2 F.C. 279, 110 D.L.R. (4th) 583 (C.A.), leave to appeal to S.C.C. refused 116 D.L.R. (4th) vii, 179 N.R. 319*n*, the owner of sugar damaged by the defendant's fault was bound to take account of the greater than market value the sugar had in the plaintiff's hands.
[171] See 5.1480 -5.1510, *supra*.
[172] See 1.1380 - 1.1400, *supra*.
[172a] (2008), 291 D.L.R. (4th) 279 (Alta. C.A.), following cases of ship collisions.

first sight, that the loss is made good. But the seller will suffer a loss of profit if there was a surplus of goods, for the seller can justifiably assert that one sale has been lost.[173] A similar conclusion was reached by the Supreme Court of Canada in *APECO of Canada, Ltd. v. Windmill Place*,[174] where the lessor of space in a building, on the lessee's repudiation, rented the same space to another tenant. The Supreme Court of Canada quoted from Viscount Haldane's speech in *British Westinghouse*: "The subsequent transaction, if to be taken into account, must be one arising out of the consequences of the breach and in the ordinary course of business."[175] The Supreme Court of Canada held that the rent from the second transaction need not be taken into account, describing it as: "an independent transaction which in no way arose out of the consequences of the breach by the appellant".[176]

15.760 Though this passage does not make it obvious why the case differs from *British Westinghouse*, it is suggested that the distinction and the result are sound. In *APECO*, the plaintiff would probably have rented other space to the second tenant (the building was still half vacant) even if the defendant had fulfilled its contract and occupied the premises itself, so the plaintiff would have had two tenants instead of one. On the other hand, in *British Westinghouse*, the plaintiff was not a dealer in machinery. It could use only one set of machinery at a time, and consequently could not have profited from purchasing the new machines without scrapping the old — a step that it would have found profitable even if the defendant had fulfilled the contract.

15.770 A similar distinction was made by McCormick in relation to a contract to sell advertising space:

> When the advertiser fails to take space contracted for in a newspaper, magazine, street car, or the like, the question arises, has the advertiser been assigned certain particular space by the contract? If not, has the publisher or person letting the advertising only a limited amount of such space available so that, when the particular advertiser cancels, the other party's opportunity to sell advertising is thereby increased? If either of these questions is answered "Yes", then the space freed by the advertiser's breach must be relet if it can be by reasonable efforts, and the advertiser must be

[173] See 5.1380 - 5.1400, *supra*.

[174] [1978] 2 S.C.R. 385, 82 D.L.R. (3d) 1. See *West Edmonton Mall Ltd. v. McDonald's Restaurants of Canada Ltd.*, [1996] 3 W.W.R. 191, 178 A.R. 127 (C.A.).

[175] *British Westinghouse*, [1912] A.C. 673 (H.L.) at p. 690, applied in *Porter & Sons v. Muir Bros. Dry Dock Co.*, [1929] 2 D.L.R. 561, 63 O.L.R. 437 (S.C. App. Div.), where the plaintiff's profit, on raising for the insurer a scow sunk by the defendant, was not taken into account to reduce the damages payable for the sinking.

[176] *APECO, supra*, footnote 174, at p. 389 S.C.R., p. 3 D.L.R., distinguished in *Toronto Housing Co. Ltd. v. Postal Promotions Ltd.* (1981), 128 D.L.R. (3d) 51, 34 O.R. (2d) 518 (H.C.J.), affd 140 D.L.R. (3d) 117, 39 O.R. (2d) 627 (C.A.), and in *Parks West Mall Ltd. v. Jennet*, [1996] 4 W.W.R. 87, 178 A.R. 45, supplementary reasons 181 A.R. 239, 38 Alta. L.R. (3d) 423 (C.A.), leave to appeal to S.C.C. refused 193 A.R. 179*n*, 135 W.A.C. 179*n*. In *Acadia University v. Sutcliffe* (1978), 30 N.S.R. (2d) 423 (S.C. App. Div.), where the plaintiff, on the defendant's default, filled his room with another occupant, damages were reduced, but as the new occupant moved from a double room, only by the difference between double and single rates.

given credit for the proceeds which have been or could have been thus realized when damages against him are assessed. On the other hand,

[*The next page is* 15-35]

> if, as is usually the case, the advertiser merely contracts to use a certain amount of space generally, and the publisher or advertising agency can expand the space available indefinitely to meet the demands of other customers, then the advertiser's default has resulted in no benefit to the seller of space, and no credit for similar space sold to others should be allowed.[177]

15.780 The same point arises in service contracts. If the plaintiff has promised to devote services exclusively to the defendant, as in the ordinary full-time employment contract, the plaintiff must give credit in an action against the employer for wrongful dismissal for earnings from other sources.[178] On the other hand, if the contract is for part-time work or for services that the plaintiff could have performed vicariously, earnings from other sources will not normally be taken into account, because it will generally be the case that the plaintiff could have earned them in addition to earning the profit on the defendant's contract. If, but only if, it is shown that the plaintiff is working to full capacity, credit should be given to the defendant for the extraneous earnings.

15.790 In *Karas v. Rowlett*[179] the distinction was put as follows by Rand J.:

> It is settled ... that the performance in mitigation and that provided or contemplated under the original contract must be mutually exclusive, and the mitigation, in that sense, a substitute for the other. Stated from another point of view, by the default or wrong there is released a capacity to work or to earn. That capacity becomes an asset in the hands of the injured party, and he is held to a reasonable employment of it in the course of events flowing from the breach.[180]

The Supreme Court of Canada refused to reduce the damages for loss of a lease of a business by business profits derived from other sources, on the ground that the latter were not incompatible with the earning of profits under the lost lease.

15.800 These considerations suggest what seems to be a test often applied, that is, whether the plaintiff could, even in the absence of the wrong, have made the disputed profit.[180a] If so, it is treated as collateral. If not, it goes to reduce the plaintiff's loss. A profitable purchase of shares or goods would usually be treated as collateral because usually it could have been made even if the wrong had not been done.[180b] But the result in *Cockburn v. Trust &*

177 McCormick, *Handbook on the Law of Damages* (St. Paul, Minn., West Publishing Co., 1935), at p. 151.

178 *Cemco Electrical Manufacturing Co. Ltd. v. Van Snellenberg*, [1947] S.C.R. 121, [1946] 4 D.L.R. 305; *PCL Construction Management Inc. v. Holmes*, [1995] 3 W.W.R. 502, 157 A.R. 306 (C.A.). See 5.1190, 5.1200, *supra*.

179 [1944] S.C.R. 1, [1944] 1 D.L.R. 241.

180 *Supra*, at p. 8 S.C.R., pp. 252-3 D.L.R. See also *Ed Learn Ford Sales Ltd. v. Giovannone* (1990), 74 D.L.R. (4th) 761 (Ont. Ct. (Gen. Div.)); *Brewer Bros. v. Canada (Attorney General)* (1991), 80 D.L.R. (4th) 321, [1992] 1 F.C. 25 (F.C.A.).

180a *British Columbia v. Canadian Forest Products Ltd.*, [2004] 2 S.C.R. 74 at p. 125, 240 D.L.R. (4th) 1, citing this passage; *Dawson v. Helicopter Exploration Co. Ltd.* (1958), 12 D.L.R. (2d) 1 (S.C.C.), at p. 10.

Guarantee Co.[181] may be defended on the basis that the opportunity to buy at the company's liquidation sale would never have arisen but for the wrong complained of (that is the plaintiff's dismissal caused by the liquidation). In the *Erie County*[182] case the plaintiffs were users of natural gas who required a supply to operate their limestone kiln. The profitable purchase of the gas lease in question was made solely to secure the supply. Lord Atkinson expressly said: "They did not require the gas, and did not use it, for any purpose other than to supply their plant."[183] The assumption is that the plaintiffs could not, in the absence of the defendant's breach, have made the profit in question, and on that assumption, it is submitted that the case is rightly decided. In *Pagnan & Fratelli v. Corbisa Industrial Agropacuaria Limitada*,[184] the buyer of goods rejected them as damaged but subsequently bought the same goods at a reduced price. It was held that the profit on the second purchase was to be brought into account. The court described the loss claimed as "fictitious",[185] saying that it was contrary to justice, common sense, and authority[186] to allow it. Again the case is one where the particular profit could not possibly have been made if the contract had been performed: it was the breach itself that created the opportunity of profit. Similarly, tax savings flowing from a transaction wrongfully induced by the defendant are taken into account in calculating the plaintiff's loss.[186a]

15.805 When an employee remains unemployed for a period of time after a wrongful dismissal but then obtains other employment at a higher rate of pay, the question arises of how to treat the excess pay earned during the period of reasonable notice. Some cases have held that it should be brought into account;[186b] others have come to the opposite conclusion.[186c] The question is a difficult one. On the one hand, it may be argued that if the excess earnings are left out of account the employee will be better off than if the wrong had not been done. On the other hand, it may be argued that if due notice had been given the employee would in practice have been free to take up the new

180b See *1874000 Nova Scotia Ltd. v. Adams* (1997), 146 D.L.R. (4th) 466 at p. 487, 159 N.S.R. (2d) 260 (C.A).

181 (1917), 55 S.C.R. 264, 37 D.L.R. 701. See also *Dipple v. Wylie* (1916), 30 D.L.R. 59 (Man. K.B.) (damages for defective and delayed threshing of grain reduced by profit realized on account of rise in market prices).

182 [1911] A.C. 105 (P.C.).

183 *Supra*, at p. 112.

184 [1970] 1 W.L.R. 1306 (C.A.).

185 *Supra*, at p. 1314.

186 *Supra*, at p. 1316.

186a *Jacks v. Davis* (1980), 112 D.L.R. (3d) 223, [1980] 6 W.W.R. 11 (B.C.S.C.), affd [1983] 1 W.W.R. 327, 141 D.L.R. (3d) 355 (C.A.); *Hodgkinson v. Simms*, [1994] 3 S.C.R. 377 at p. 440, 117 D.L.R. (4th) 161 at p. 199; *Toronto-Dominion Bank v. Leigh Instruments Ltd. (Trustee of)* (1997), 33 O.R. (3d) 696 (Ont. Ct. (Gen. Div.)).

186b *Bremner v. Trend Housewares Ltd.* (1985), 51 O.R. (2d) 101 (H.C.J.); *Ross v. Philips Electronics Ltd.* (1986), 69 A.R. 178 (Q.B.).

186c *Winsor v. Stephenville (Town)* (1976), 12 Nfld. & P.E.I.R. 302 (Nfld. S.C.); *McOnie v. River Pub Ltd.* (1987), 79 N.S.R. (2d) 379 (S.C.); *LeBlanc v. Eurodata Support Services Inc.* (1998), 164 D.L.R. (4th) 763 (N.B.C.A.).

position as soon as it became available: employees under notice usually expect and are expected to leave as soon as they find alternative employment. On balance, therefore, it seems that the excess should not be brought into account.

15.810 In *Nadreph Ltd. v. Willmett & Co.*,[187] the defendant solicitor by giving negligent advice caused the plaintiff's tenant to vacate certain premises as a result of which the plaintiff was compelled to compensate the tenant. It was held that the solicitor's liability was to be reduced by the benefit to the plaintiff of being able to relet, at a higher rent, the vacated premises. The test was said to be whether the benefit "can be said to relate sufficiently closely to a particular head of damage as to be appropriate to be set off against that head of damage".[188] Again, the plaintiff could not have had the higher rent if the defendant had not caused the vacancy. Where the defendant's default causes a loss of business but creates an opportunity for business that would not otherwise have been available to the plaintiff, the plaintiff is only entitled to recover the net loss of business. In *Hill & Sons v. Edwin Showell & Sons Ltd.*[189] where such a case arose, Viscount Haldane said:

> [The plaintiff] can therefore *prima facie* claim what would have been his profit. But he is none the less bound by another principle which imposes on him the duty of taking all reasonable steps to mitigate the loss to himself consequent on the breach. Moreover, if, in the course of his business, he has taken action which has actually arisen out of the situation in which his machinery was rendered free by reason of the breach, and by taking on new contracts occasioned by this situation has diminished his loss, he must give credit for the diminution, even though he may have gone somewhat out of his way to make fresh efforts because of the position in which he found himself with unemployed machinery.[190]

It is submitted that this line of reasoning is sound and is to be preferred to an earlier case in which, on the defendant's preventing the plaintiff from carrying passengers on one ship, the plaintiff carried them on another, but the profits made by the alternative arrangement were not brought into account.[191]

15.820 In *Royal Bank of Canada v. Clark*,[192] the defendant solicitor negligently advanced the plaintiff bank's money without security. The borrower failed to repay the advance, but part of the advance was used to repay an earlier loan. It was held that the repayment was a collateral benefit and not taken into account, though it was also described as a "windfall"[193] to the bank. It is submitted that the case is rightly decided, for the bank was entitled to have its earlier loan repaid and might have done so even if the defendant had obtained proper security for the subsequent loan.

187 [1978] 1 All E.R. 746 (Ch.).
188 *Supra*, at p. 753.
189 (1918), 87 L.J.K.B. 1106 (H.L.).
190 *Supra*, at p. 1108. See also *Andros Springs (Owners) v. World Beauty (Owners) (The World Beauty)*, [1970] P. 144 (C.A.).
191 *Jebsen v. East & West India Dock Co.* (1875), L.R. 10 C.P. 300.
192 (1978), 88 D.L.R. (3d) 76 (S.C. App. Div.), affd [1980] 1 S.C.R. 177*n*, 105 D.L.R. (3d) 85*n*.
193 *Supra*, at p. 82.

15.830 *Oshawa Group Ltd. v. Great American Ins. Co.*[194] was an action on a fidelity insurance bond for loss caused by the fraudulent receipt of bribes by a purchasing agent. The defendant argued that the plaintiff had suffered no loss in that its resale prices reflected the actual cost of the goods purchased by its agent. This argument was rejected by the Ontario Court of Appeal, rightly, it is submitted. In a free market, the price charged for goods reflects market prices. Had the fraud not been committed the plaintiff would have obtained its goods more cheaply and could have sold the same quantity at the prices actually charged making a larger profit on the same quantity or (if it thought it profitable to do so) could have reduced the price and sold a larger quantity. If the defendant's argument, sometimes framed in terms of a defence of "passing on",[194a] were sound, many enterprises would be incapable of suffering losses. The defence of passing on was rejected by the Supreme Court of Canada in *Kingstreet Investments Ltd. v. New Brunswick (Department of Finance)*.[194b] It is suggested that the key factor is that the plaintiff in the *Oshawa Group* case could have charged the prices actually charged, in addition to retaining the benefit of the cheaper goods that it would have obtained from its suppliers in the absence of the fraud.

15.840 Support is also given to this approach by *Dawson v. Helicopter Exploration Co. Ltd.*,[195] where the plaintiff, on breach of the defendant's contract to employ his services to point out mineral deposit showings, was held not to be bound to bring into account a profit derived from his staking his own claim in the same area. The lower court in coming to the opposite conclusion had relied on *Cockburn v. Trusts & Guarantee Co.*,[196] being of the view that the profit could not have been acquired if there had been no breach. The Supreme Court of Canada reversed the decision but accepted the test. Rand J. said: "The rule, in such a case, governing mitigation is not in dispute. If the interest acquired by the damaged person is something he could not have been able to obtain if the contract had been carried out, it must be brought into account; if it could have been acquired consistently with his performance of the contract, it is not available as mitigation."[197]

15.850 In *Male v. Hopmans*,[198] the defendant physician was held liable for hearing loss caused by a drug administered to cure an infection of the knee. The Ontario Court of Appeal, reversing the decision of the trial judge, held that damages for the loss of hearing were not to be reduced by an allowance

---

[194] (1982), 132 D.L.R. (3d) 453, 36 O.R. (2d) 424 (C.A.), leave to appeal to S.C.C. refused 43 N.R. 267*n*.

[194a] *Law Society of Upper Canada v. Ernst & Young* (2002), 213 D.L.R. (4th) 167 (Ont. S.C.J.), revd on other grounds 227 D.L.R. (4th) 577 (Ont. C.A.), leave to appeal to S.C.C. refused 236 D.L.R. (4th) viii. See *British Columbia v. Canadian Forest Products Ltd.*, [2004] 2 S.C.R. 74, 240 D.L.R. (4th) 1, at p. 126 S.C.R. (Binnie J.) and pp. 162-72 S.C.R. (LeBel J., dissenting).

[194b] [2007] 1 S.C.R. 3, 276 D.L.R. (4th) 342.

[195] (1958), 12 D.L.R. (2d) 1 (S.C.C.).

[196] (1917), 55 S.C.R. 264, 37 D.L.R. 701.

[197] *Dawson, supra*, footnote 195, at p. 10.

[198] (1967), 64 D.L.R. (2d) 105, [1967] 2 O.R. 457 (C.A.).

for the improvement to the knee. The court said that the point was a "troublesome" one but that a reduction would be proper only if the defendant proved that the benefit to the knee was a direct result of the deafness. It is submitted that this decision is sound: in the absence of the defendant's wrong the plaintiff might have had both an improved knee and his hearing.

15.860 Other considerations must explain the approach of the courts to gifts and welfare, and to insurance benefits. Many of the cases involve personal injuries and have been discussed in an earlier chapter,[199] but the question can arise also in cases of commercial loss[199a] and of wrongful dismissal. In *Jack Cewe Ltd. v. Jorgenson*,[200] the question in issue was whether, in an action for wrongful dismissal, the defendant should be credited with unemployment insurance benefits received by the plaintiff. It was held that such benefits were not to be taken into account, on the ground that the wrongdoing employer ought not to benefit from unemployment insurance. The argument for the employer is that the plaintiff could not, in the absence of the wrong, have received the benefits and will consequently be over-compensated on receipt of damages representing full salary in addition to the benefits. If the plaintiff had found alternative employment, it is plain that earnings would have been brought into account. It seems anomalous that when paid for doing nothing (a greater benefit it would seem), the plaintiff should not equally be bound to account. An ideal solution would seem to be to hold that the employee, though entitled to recover full salary from the wrongdoing employer, would then be bound to account for the benefits and the statute now provides for this result.[201] In a number of cases, it has been held that private insurance benefits are not deductible.[201a] On the other hand, workers' compensation benefits have been held to be deductible.[201b]

[199] See 3.1490 - 3.1810, *supra*.

[199a] *Bristol and West Building Society v. May May & Merrimans*, [1998] 1 W.L.R. 336 (Ch.); *Arab Bank v. John D. Wood Commercial*, [2000] 1 W.L.R. 857 (C.A.) (insurance benefits not taken into account).

[200] [1980] 1 S.C.R. 812, 111 D.L.R. (3d) 577. Similar conclusions were reached in *Sublett v. Facit-Addo Canada Ltd.* (1977), 79 D.L.R. (3d) 286, 16 O.R. (2d) 791 (H.C.J.) (defendant required to pay Unemployment Insurance Commission), and *Zachoda v. Stelco Steel Co. of Canada* (1980), 111 D.L.R. (3d) 308 (Alta. Q.B.). In England, unemployment benefits are deductible but only to the extent of the net benefit received, taking account of any limit on the period of eligibility: *Westwood v. Secretary of State for Employment*, [1985] A.C. 20 (H.L.).

[201] *Employment Insurance Act*, s. 45.

[201a] *Edwards v. Royal Alexandra Hospitals* (1994), 154 A.R. 226, 19 Alta. L.R. (3d) 277 (Q.B.); *Emery v. Royal Oak Mines Inc.* (1995), 24 O.R. (3d) 302, 11 C.C.E.L. (2d) 149 (Gen. Div.); *Datardina v. Royal Trust Corp. of Canada*, [1995] 6 W.W.R. 531, 6 B.C.L.R. (3d) 1 (C.A.); *Girling v. Crown Cork & Seal Canada Inc.* (1995), 127 D.L.R. (4th) 448, [1995] 9 W.W.R. 743 (B.C.C.A.); *Wawro v. Westfair Foods Ltd.* (1996), 148 Sask. R. 221, 23 C.C.E.L. (2d) 247 (C.A.). It was held in *Sylvester v. British Columbia*, [1997] 2 S.C.R. 315, 146 D.L.R. (4th) 207, and *Kingsberry v. Minto Developments Inc.* (1999), 41 C.C.E.L. (2d) 265 (Ont. Ct. (Gen. Div.), that benefits paid under employment contract were to be deducted, but the opposite conclusion was reached in *Sills v. Children's Aid Society of the City of Belleville and the County of Hastings and the City of Trenton* (2001), 198 D.L.R. (4th) 485 (Ont. C.A.), and *McNamara v. Alexander Centre Industries Ltd.* (2001), 199 D.L.R. (4th) 717 (Ont. C.A.), leave to appeal to S.C.C. refused 204 D.L.R. (4th) vi.

15.870 The case for excluding welfare benefits, like that for excluding gifts made to the plaintiff by third parties, may be supported on the basis of "crystallization" of the loss. The defendant causes a loss at the time of the wrong and the plaintiff is entitled to be compensated for it whatever happens afterwards. As Wright J. put it, in another context, in *Joyner v. Weeks*:[202] "a cause of action vested in the plaintiff against the defendant, and this could not be taken away or affected by the subsequent res inter alios acta".[203]

15.880 If the plaintiff makes arrangements to secure a subsequent indemnity by accepting a gift from a third party, it is well established that this does not detract from the existence of the loss at the time of its occurrence.[204] The same principle, it is submitted, applies to indemnity paid by prior arrangement. If a person who had insured against loss were unable to recover from the wrongdoer, anomalous distinctions would appear. One who burns a building causes a loss whether the building is insured or not. The loss does not disappear because, by prior arrangement, an insurer has agreed to share the loss or to indemnify the owner. If the owner could not recover, justice would require the wrongdoer to be liable to the insurer for the economic loss suffered by the latter. In the case of co-insurance and re-insurance, complex proceedings would be required. The present law, whereby the owner recovers in full from the wrongdoer in a single action and the insurer's rights to subrogation are determined as between insurer and insured, is a convenient way of achieving the appropriate result. If the insurer has not contracted for the right of subrogation, it might appear that the plaintiff is over-compensated, but that will be because of the terms of the insurance contract, for the benefit of which the plaintiff will have paid in full by premiums. In the case of social welfare benefits, if the plaintiff is over-compensated, this is because of the generosity of the welfare legislation, to the benefits of which the plaintiff is entitled by social insurance, or by the statute itself if, on its proper construction, there is no right of subrogation. The remedy, if this is thought to be an evil, is to amend the legislation not to reduce the wrongdoer's liability.

6. Money Obtained from Defendant after the Wrong

15.890 Where the plaintiff obtains an order against the defendant requiring

---

[201b] *Salmi v. Greyfriar Developments Ltd.* (1985), 17 D.L.R. (4th) 186 (Alta. C.A.); *White v. F.W. Woolworth Co.* (1996), 139 Nfld. & P.E.I.R. 324 (Nfld. C.A.), leave to appeal to S.C.C. refused 222 N.R. 80*n*; *Dowsley Estate v. Viceroy Fluid Power International Inc.* (1997), 34 O.R. (3d) 57 (C.A.); *Antonacci v. Great Atlantic & Pacific Co. of Canada, Ltd.* (2000), 181 D.L.R. (4th) 577 (Ont. C.A.).

[202] [1891] 2 Q.B. 31 (C.A.).

[203] *Supra*, at p. 34.

[204] See 3.1550 - 3.1580, 6.510, *supra*. See *A.-G. Nfld. v. Newfoundland Association of Public Employees* (1976), 74 D.L.R. (3d) 195 (Nfld. S.C.); *Arab Bank v. John D. Wood Commercial, supra*, footnote 199a. See also *Saskatchewan v. Mountain Pacific Transport Ltd.*, [1994] 8 W.W.R. 153 at p. 171, 121 Sask. R. 241 at p. 256 (Q.B.), citing this paragraph. But see *Pitawanakat v. Canada (Attorney General)*, [1994] 3 F.C. 298, 21 C.H.R.R. D/355 (T.D.) (bursary deducted).

restitution of a benefit obtained from the wrong, the amount so obtained must be brought into account to reduce the plaintiff's loss. In *Mahesan S/O Thambiah v. Malaysian Government Offices' Co-operative Housing Society Ltd.*[205] the defendant, an agent whose task it was to arrange for a purchase of land by his principal, accepted a bribe of $122,000 from the vendor and arranged a sale at an overvalue of $443,000. The principal claimed to be entitled to recover the total of the two sums from the agent, but the Privy Council held that it must elect between them. The reason given by the Board was that: "damages are limited to the actual loss sustained; and if the principal has recovered the bribe from the bribed agent the actual loss he has sustained in consequence of entering into the contract is reduced by that amount."[206] This reasoning, it is submitted, is sound, and would presumably apply also to a case where the defendant had been compelled by a criminal court to make restitution. The plaintiff, on receipt of the restitution, has the loss partly made good. Against this, it might be argued that a criminal restitution order is intended to punish the defendant as well as to compensate the victim, but if it, in fact, has the effect of compensating the victim, there can be no justification, it is submitted, for a civil court to close its eyes to that effect. The defendant does not reap any undeserved benefit by this line of reasoning. The criminal court can be taken to know that a restitution order will reduce the defendant's civil liability and to have taken this into account in fixing the appropriate penalty.

15.900 It may be argued against the *Mahesan* case that since restitution of the bribe could have been obtained by the principal in the absence of any loss, restitution should always be additional to compensation.[207] But, it is submitted that the conclusion does not follow. It is possible to support recovery of the bribe as a minimum, on restitutionary principles, where the amount of the bribe exceeds the plaintiff's loss, without favouring the recovery of the bribe in addition to full compensation.

15.910 Where the defendant pays money on account of the plaintiff's claim, the payment is deducted from the plaintiff's damages. Not all payments, however, will be treated as payments on account. In *Jerome v. Anderson*,[208] the plaintiff sued for wrongful dismissal and defamation. The action proceeded, pursuant to an interlocutory order, as one for defamation only. The trial judge deducted from the damages a sum paid by the defendants to the plaintiff after his dismissal. The Supreme Court of Canada held that the deduction was improper, because the amount was "not paid on account of the plaintiff's claim for damages for libel, but either *ex gratia* or on account of

[205] [1979] A.C. 374 (P.C.); *Borough of Salford v. Lever*, [1891] 1 Q.B. 168 (C.A.), was overruled. In *A.-G. N.S. v. Christian* (1974), 49 D.L.R. (3d) 742 (S.C. App. Div.), double recovery of a bribe was disallowed.

[206] *Mahesan S/O Thambiah, supra*, footnote 205, at p. 381, *per* Lord Diplock.

[207] See Tettenborn, "Bribery, Corruption and Restitution – The Strange Case of Mr. Mahesan", 95 L.Q.R. 68 (1979).

[208] [1964] S.C.R. 291, 44 D.L.R. (2d) 516. See also *McKay v. Camco, Inc.* (1986), 24 D.L.R. (4th) 90, 53 O.R. (2d) 257 (C.A.).

his claim for damages for wrongful dismissal which ... was excluded as a head of damage in this action".[209]

[209] *Supra*, at p. 309 S.C.R., p. 533 D.L.R. See 3.460 and 6.510, *supra*.

INDEX

[References are to paragraph numbers]

PROPERTY